The EPL Book

The Practical Guide To Employment Practices Liability And Insurance

Second Edition

The EPL Book

The Practical Guide To Employment Practices Liability And Insurance

Second Edition

Gary W. Griffin, ARM
Andrew Kaplan
Rachel McKinney
Beth A. Schroeder
Leonard Surdyk

Griffin Communications, Inc.

The EPL Book, Policy Express and PolicyAnalysis Plus are
Copyright 1999 by Griffin Communications, Inc. All rights reserved.

Includes copyrighted material of Insurance Services Office, Inc. with its permission.
Copyright, Insurance Services Office, Inc.

It is a violation of federal copyright law to reproduce any part of this publication. This means you are not allowed to photocopy, fax, scan or duplicate by any means the contents of this publication for any purpose. Reproduction of all or part of this publication may be made only with the express written permission of the publisher.

Published by:
Griffin Communications, Inc.
1420 Bristol Street North, Suite 220
Newport Beach, CA 92660
949/752-1058
http://www.griffincom.com

Gary W. Griffin, ARM, Author
Andrew Kaplan, Author
Rachel McKinney, Author
Beth Schroeder, Author
Leonard Surdyk, Author

Gary W. Griffin, ARM, Senior Editor
C.C. Griffin, CPCU, Editor
Marcus Covas, Assistant Editor
Alan Schreibman, ARM, Research Editor
Diana Wolverton, Graphic Designer

This publication is based in part on policy forms, endorsements and other information obtained from insurers and other sources prior to publication. Griffin Communications, Inc. and the co-authors make no warranty as to the completeness or accuracy of such material nor of this or any other analysis or comparison derived therefrom.

Specific EPL insurance policy form citations contained in *The EPL Book* are used to illustrate and support text discussion only. Such references are illustrative in nature and are neither an endorsement for nor criticism of any particular policy form. In some instances policy forms cited in *The EPL Book* may no longer be in use and may be superceded by later editions. Neither *The EPL Book* nor any other reference is a substitute for the reader's own analysis, due diligence and careful reading of the policy form(s) in question.

Griffin Communications, Inc. is an independent publisher of insurance and risk management references and periodicals. It is not owned by, nor does it own any interest in any insurance company, agent, broker, claim administrator, law firm or other entity whose services may be the subject of this or any other analysis. Griffin Communications, Inc. does not sell insurance nor does it receive any form of compensation other than revenues from its publications.

Nothing contained in this book is a recommendation by the authors or publisher of coverage or an endorsement of any particular policy form, policy wording, agent, broker, insurance company or other service provider.

ISBN 0-941360-14-8
Library of Congress Cataloging in Publication No. 95-77963

Contents

Page

PART I
Understanding Employment Practices Liability

1 History And Status Of Employment Practices Liability 1
    Discrimination In Employment 2
        Federal Law 3
            Title VII Of The 1964 Civil Rights Act 3
            Civil Rights Act Of 1866 7
            Equal Pay Act Of 1963 7
            Age Discrimination In Employment Act Of 1967 8
            Americans With Disabilities Act Of 1990 10
            Family And Medical Leave Act 11
            Uniformed Services Employment And Reemployment Rights Act
            Of 1994 12
            Immigration Reform And Control Act Of 1986 13
            National Labor Relations Act 14
            Conclusion 15
        State Law 15
    Third-Party Liability 19
        State And Local Laws 19
    Sexual Harassment 21
        The Legal Basis For Sexual Harassment Actions 22
        The Definition Of *Sexual Harassment* 22
        Recognizing Sexual Harassment 23
            Hypothetical 1—The Company Affair 23
            Hypothetical 2—The Demanding Boss 25
            Hypothetical 3—Employees and the Coffee Room 27
        Assessment Of Liability 28
        Potential Damages 28
    Wrongful Discharge 29
        The "Employment-At-Will" Doctrine 29
        Theories Of Wrongful Discharge 31
            Discharge In Violation Of Public Policy 31
            Breach Of An Express Or Implied Contract 33
            Breach Of The Implied Covenant Of Good Faith And Fair Dealing 34

		Page
	Summary	34
	Other State Common-Law And Quasi Contract Claims	35

2 Frequency And Economic Impact Of Wrongful Employment Practices Charges ... 37

- EEOC Charge Data ... 37
  - Frequency Of Wrongful Employment Practices Charges (All Statutes Combined) ... 38
  - Economic Impact Of Wrongful Employment Practices (All Statutes Combined) ... 39
  - Frequency And Economic Impact Of Claims Under Title VII ... 40
    - Frequency Of Alleged Title VII Violations Filed With EEOC ... 40
    - Title VII Claims By Issue (1994) ... 41
    - Economic Impact ... 41
  - Frequency And Economic Impact Of Claims Under ADA ... 42
    - Frequency Of Alleged ADA Violations ... 42
    - Total ADA Claims By Issue ... 43
    - Economic Impact ... 44
  - Frequency And Economic Impact Of Claims Under ADEA ... 45
    - Frequency Of Alleged Violations ... 45
    - Total ADEA Claims By Issue ... 45
    - Economic Impact ... 46
  - Frequency And Economic Impact Of Claims Under The EPA ... 47
    - Frequency Of Alleged Violations ... 47
    - Total EPA Claims By Issue ... 47
    - Economic Impact ... 48
  - EEOC Litigation Data ... 49
    - Direct Suits Filed By EEOC—All Statutes Combined ... 49
    - Monetary Benefits Secured Through EEOC Litigation— All Statutes Combined ... 50
    - EEOC Suits Filed—By Statute ... 51
    - Monetary Benefits Obtained Through EEOC Litigation— By Statute ... 52
- Jury Verdict EPL Litigation Award Data ... 52
  - Distribution Of Verdict Amounts ... 54
  - Verdict Midpoint (Median) Amounts ... 54
  - Punitive Damage Awards ... 55
  - Litigation Activity By State ... 56
- Employment Practices National Survey ... 57
- Employment Litigation Survey ... 59
  - Who's Being Sued And By Whom? ... 60
  - Legitimacy Of Lawsuits ... 60
  - Litigation Costs ... 61
  - Lawsuits Experienced In The Past Five Years ... 62
- Summary ... 62
- Conclusion ... 63

PART II
Developing A Risk Management Strategy

3 Understanding Risk Management 67
    The Risk-Management Process 68
        Who Does It? 68
        Risk Identification 69
        Loss Prevention And Reduction 70
            Written Procedures 70
            Training 70
        Risk Retention 71
            Amount Of Risk Retention 72
        Insurance 72
        Conclusion 73

4 Employment Practices Liability Loss Prevention 75
    Written Procedures 75
        Interviewing, Pre-Employment Screening And Testing 76
            Interview Dos And Don'ts 76
            The Employment Application 78
            Reference And Background Checks 78
            Drug And Alcohol Testing 79
            Job Offers 80
            Job Descriptions 80
        Employee Handbooks 81
            Employer Excuses For Not Having A Handbook 83
            The Outdated Employee Handbook 84
            Design And Implementation Of Employee Handbooks 85
    Sexual Harassment And Employee Awareness Training 88
        The Scope Of Sexual Harassment Claims 88
        Non-Fraternization Policies 89
        Harassment Policies And Communication 89
        Diversity Management 90
            Defining A New Field 90
            The Audience Is Listening 91
            The Potential Downside Of Diversity Management 91
            Buyer Beware 92
            Conclusion 93
    Preventing Wrongful Discharge Suits 94
        Specify The Rules 94
        Be Candid With Employees 95
        Employee Discipline 95
        Consider The Options 96
        Discharge 96
        Post-Termination References 97
    Settlement Agreements And Release Of Claims 97
    Arbitration And Mediation 98
        Advantages Of Arbitration 98

		Page
	Disadvantages Of Arbitration	99
	EEOC Position On Mandatory Binding Arbitration Provisions	100
	Limitations Of Mandated Arbitration As Articulated By EEOC	101
	Drafting An Arbitration Agreement	103
	Mediation	104
	Other Considerations	104
	Arbitration And EPL Insurance	105

5 Handling Employment Practices Claims: Intervention And Investigation 107

- Investigation 108
  - Pre-Litigation Investigation 108
  - Conducting An Investigation 109
  - Post-Litigation Investigation 110
  - Investigation Files 110
- Initial Response Within 30 Days 110
  - Responding To Verbal Complaints 110
  - Responding To Written Complaints 111
  - Responding To Administrative Complaints 112
  - Responding To Lawsuits 112
  - Corrective Action 113
- Discipline 113
- Insurance Company And Defense Issues 114
  - Selection Of Defense Counsel 115
- The Role Of Mediation In Resolving Claims 116
- Conclusion 117

6 Insurance Coverage For Employment Practices 119

- Commercial General Liability 119
  - Personal Injury And Bodily Injury Requirements 120
  - The Occurrence Requirement 121
- Expected-Or-Intended-Injury Exclusion 123
- Employers Liability Exclusion 123
- EPL Exclusion Endorsement 124
- Public Policy Prohibitions 125
- Inability Of Occurrence-Based Policies To Change With The Insurance Market 125
- Workers' Compensation And Employers Liability Insurance ... 126
  - A Recent Exception 127
    - The New Jersey Supreme Court's Decision 128
    - Conclusion 129
- Not-For-Profit Organization Liability Insurance 129
- Directors And Officers Insurance 129
- Specialized EPL Insurance 131
- Insurability Of Employment Practices Liability (EPL) Claims . 132
  - Support For The Willful-Act Rule 132
  - Subsequent Opposing Decisions 132

		Page
	What It All Means	133
	Conclusion	134

PART III
Understanding Employment Practices Liability Insurance

7 Underwriting And Application Considerations 137
    Underwriting Criteria 138
        Type Of Organization 138
        Employer Size 139
        Loss History 139
        Past And Future Turnover 140
        Employment Documentation 140
        Composition Of Workforce (EEO-1) And Hiring Practices 141
        Pay Distribution 141
        State Issues 141
        Financial Statements 141
    EPL Insurance Application Considerations 142
        Warranties 144
        Material Misrepresentations And Coverage Implications 145
        Severability And Non-Imputation Provisions 146
        Tips For Completing The Application 147
            Read The Application 147
            Read The Policy 148
            Reporting Changes 148
            Maintenance Of Scheduled Insurance 148
            Confidentiality 149
            Provide Complete Information 149
            Claim Information 150
            Reporting Information Not The Subject Of Inquiry 151
            Involving Your Broker 151
            Peer Review 152
            Summary 152

8 EPL Insurance Policy Format 153
    Understanding Claims-Made Coverage Features 153
        What Constitutes A Claim? 154
        Claim-Reporting Requirements To The Insurer 155
        Potential Claim 156
        Retroactive Dates—Time Limitations Regarding When Wrongful Acts
        Or Employment Practices Take Place 157
        Extended-Reporting-Period (ERP) Provisions 160
        Under What Circumstances Is The ERP Available? 161
        For What Period Of Time Is The ERP Effective And At What Cost? .. 162
        When And How Are ERPs Activated? 162
        Special Considerations 163
    Insuring Agreement 164
        Coverage Grant 164

	Page
Third-Party Liability Coverage	165
"Pay On Behalf" Versus "Indemnify" Coverage	166
Stand-Alone Versus Combined-Coverage Format	167
Scope of Coverage	168
Limit of Liability	168
Cost	168
Conclusion	169
Who Is Insured	169
Business Entity	169
Directors And Officers	170
Supervisors And Managers	170
Other Employees	171
Independent Contractors	172
Acquisitions	173
Limits, Deductible And Coinsurance	173
Policy Limits	173
Deductibles	174
Self-Insured Retentions	175
Deductible Reduction Clauses	176
Coinsurance	177

9   Defense And Settlement Provisions ... 179

Duty To Defend	179
Choice Of Counsel In Non-Duty-To-Defend Policies	181
Consent To Settlement	181
Allocation, Advancement And Timing Of Defense Expense Payments	183
Right Of Association And Right To Assume Defense	185

10   Exclusions ... 187

General Rules	187
Bodily Injury And Personal Injury Exclusions	189
Assault And Battery	191
Breach Of Employment Contract	192
Consequential Loss	194
Failure To Provide Benefits	195
Property Damage	196
Retaliatory Action And Violation Of Public Policy Exclusions	197
Exclusions Directed To Various Federal And State Laws	199
Exclusions For Non-Monetary Relief	201
Exclusion For ADA-Accommodation Expenses	202
Fines, Penalties And Punitive Damages	203
Exclusions For Front Or Back Pay	207
Exclusion For Liquidated Damages Under ADEA	208
Exclusions For Arbitration Under Collective Bargaining Agreements	208
Exclusion For Claims Arising From Financial Impairment	209
Exclusions For Plant Or Facility Closings	210
Downsizing/Reorganization	211
Mergers And Acquisitions/Change Of Control	212

		Page
	Intentional Acts	213
	Other Insurance/Other Indemnification	214
	Criminal Acts/Proceedings	215
	Retroactive Date And Prior Knowledge Exclusions	218
	Prior And Pending Litigation Exclusion	219
	Class-Action-Suit Exclusion	220

11 Definitions 221
Claim 221
    Oral Complaint Or Notice 222
    Written Notice To Management 222
    Filing Of A Complaint With State Agency/EEOC 222
    Lawsuit 223
    Policy Definitions Of *Claim* 223
    Requirement That Damages Are Alleged 223
    Other Demands 224
    Arbitration 224
    Administrative Proceedings 225
    Policies Without A Definition Of *Claim* 226
    Potential-Claim Reporting Considerations 226
    Conclusion 227
Discrimination 228
Sexual Harassment 232
    Workplace Torts 233
Wrongful Termination 235

12 Conditions 237
Acquisitions/Change Of Control 237
Arbitration 239
Coverage Territory 241
Other Insurance 242
Severability And Non-Imputation Of Liability 245
    Severability 245
    Non-Imputation Of Liability 246

13 The EPL Insurance Market 249
Evolution Of EPL Insurance 249
Effect Of Employers' Buying Habits 250
Market Profile 250
Pricing 253
Coverage 253
Conclusion 254

14 ISO's Employment-Related Practices Liability Policy 255
Who Is Insured 256
Insuring Agreement 256
Defense 257
Exclusions 258

	Page
Criminal, Fraudulent Or Malicious Acts	258
Violation Of Laws Applicable To Employers	259
Strikes And Lockouts	259
Sexual Harassment	260
Employment Termination Or Relocation Due To Business Decisions	260
Intentional Injury	261
Retaliatory Actions	261
Endorsements	262
Conclusion	262

PART IV
Policy Comparison Worksheets

15 Policy Comparison Worksheets 265

	Page
Specimen Policy Comparison Worksheet	266
Policy Forms	266
Can't Find What You Need?	266
Internet Services	267
Index To Policy Comparison Worksheets	269
Sample Template	271
Admiral Insurance Company	275
Agricultural Excess & Surplus Insurance Company (AESIC)	279
American Equity Insurance Company	283
American International Specialty Lines Insurance Company	287
Associated Electric & Gas Insurance Services, Limited (AEGIS)	291
Chubb Group	295
Chubb Group	299
Chubb Group	303
Chubb Group	307
CNA Reinsurance Company (NAS Insurance Services, Inc.)	311
Colonia (AUSCO)	315
Connecticut Indemnity Company (Professional Risk Facilities, Inc.)	319
Connecticut Specialty Insurance Company (Professional Risk Facilities, Inc.)	323
Employers Reinsurance Corporation	327
Evanston Insurance Company (Shand Morahan)	331
Executive Risk Specialty Insurance Company	335
Executive Risk Specialty Insurance Company	339
Executive Risk Specialty Insurance Company	343
Executive Risk Specialty Insurance Company	347
Fireman's Fund Insurance Company	351
Fireman's Fund Insurance Company	355
Fireman's Fund Insurance Company	359
Fireman's Fund Insurance Company	363
First Specialty Insurance Corporation (Employers Reinsurance Group)	367
Genesis Indemnity Insurance Company	371

	Page
Genesis Insurance Company	375
Great American Insurance Companies	379
Great American Insurance Companies	383
Gulf Insurance Group (Rockwood Programs, Inc.)	387
Hartford Insurance Companies	391
Insurance Services Office (ISO)	395
Legion Insurance Companies	399
Lexington Insurance Company	403
Lexington Insurance Company	407
London Market (American Technology Excess & Surplus Insurance Services)	411
London Market (CNA Re/St. Paul Re)	415
London Market (NAS Insurance Services, Inc.)	419
London Market (NAS Insurance Services, Inc.)	423
London Market (NAS Insurance Services, Inc.)	427
London Market (NAS Insurance Services, Inc.)	431
London Market (U.S. Risk Underwriters, Inc.)	435
National Union Fire Insurance Co. (American International Companies)	439
Northland Insurance Companies	443
Pacific Insurance Company, Ltd. (First State Management Group, Inc.)	447
Philadelphia Indemnity Insurance Company	451
Philadelphia Insurance Companies	455
Reliance Insurance Company of Illinois (Reliance National Risk Specialists)	459
Reliance Insurance Company of Illinois (Reliance National Risk Specialists)	463
Reliance National	467
Steadfast Insurance Company	471
Steadfast Insurance Company	475
Swett & Crawford (CNA Reinsurance Co., Limited or Lloyd's of London)	479
Travelers Property Casualty (G. J. Sullivan Company)	483
United Educators Risk Retention Group, Inc.	487
United States Fidelity & Guaranty Company	491
United States Liability Insurance Group	495
X.L. Insurance Company, Ltd.	499
Zurich American Insurance Company	503
Zurich Insurance Company	507
Zurich Insurance Company	511
About The Authors	599
Index	603

Appendices

		Page
A	Specimen EPL Form	515
B	ISO's Employment-Related Practices Liability Coverage Form (EP 00 01 04 98)	531
C	Index of Insurers	549
D	Quick Checklist of Desirable EPLI Policy Features	555
E	EPL Insurance Exclusions Usage	557
F	EPL Insurance Capacity—Maximum Per-Claim Limit Of Liability	559
G	EEOC District Offices	563
H	State Agencies Regulating Employment Practices	567
I	Questions And Answers About Sexual Harassment	571
J	Facts About The Americans With Disabilities Act	575
K	Facts About Disability-Related Tax Provisions	577
L	Other Labor- And Employment-Related Agencies	581
M	EEOC Task Force	585
N	EPL Policy Comparison Worksheet Request Form	595

Exhibits

1	State Employment Discrimination Laws	16
2	Typical Allocation Of Risk Management Duties	69
3	Possible Employee Handbook Provisions	82
4	Insurability Of Punitive Damages	204
5	Legally Protected Classes	229

Charts

1	Total Charges Filed (All Statutes)	39
2	Total Monetary Benefits Obtained Through EEOC Enforcement (All Statutes Combined)	39
3	Total Charge Receipts (Title VII)	40
4	Most Frequent Charges Filed With EEOC (Title VII) By Issue (1994)	41
5	Monetary Benefits Obtained Through EEOC Enforcement (Title VII)	42
6	Total Charge Receipts (ADA)	42
7	Most Frequent Charges Filed With EEOC (ADA) By Issue (1994)	44
8	Monetary Benefits Obtained Through EEOC Enforcement (ADA)	44
9	Total Charge Receipts (ADEA)	45
10	Most Frequent Charges Filed With EEOC (ADEA) By Issue (1994)	46
11	Monetary Benefits Obtained Through EEOC Enforcement (ADEA)	46
12	Total Charge Receipts (EPA)	47
13	Most Frequent Charges Filed With EEOC (EPA) By Issue (1994)	48
14	Monetary Benefits Obtained Through EEOC Enforcement (EPA)	48
15	Direct Suits Filed By EEOC (All Statutes Combined)	50
16	Monetary Benefits Secured Through EEOC Litigation (All Statutes Combined)	51
17	Largest Total Number Of EPL Verdicts In Excess Of $300,000	57

		Page
18	Largest Dollar Value Of EPL Verdicts In Excess Of $300,000	57
19	Percent Of Respondents Expressing Very Or Moderate Degree Of Concern	58
20	Percent Of Claims By Type Of Discrimination, Harassment Or Other Illegal Employment Practice	59
21	If Your Organization Has Been Sued, Has It Been By A	60
22	Policy Limits Distribution—1997	251
23	Policy Limits Distribution—1998	251

Tables

1	Charges By Basis Of Discrimination (Title VII)	40
2	Impairments Most Cited (ADA) (7/26/92–6/30/96)	43
3	Violations Most Cited (ADA) (7/26/92–6/30/96)	43
4	EEOC Suits Filed, By Statute	51
5	Monetary Benefits Obtained Through EEOC Litigation, By Statute	52
6	Distribution of Verdicts—Wrongful Employment Practices (Average for Period 1987–1994)	54
7	Verdict Midpoint (Median) Amounts—Employment Practices Litigation (Average for Period 1987–1994)	55
8	Midpoint (Median) Punitive Damage Awards—Employment Practices Litigation (Average for Period 1987–1994)	55
9	Litigation Activity Related To EPL Claims, By State	56
10	Degree Of Concern	58
11	Agree Or Disagree: "The Majority Of Employment-Related Litigated Cases Are Legitimate Claims"	61
12	Litigation Costs For Employment-Related Matters	61
13	EPL Insurance Capacity	252

PART I

Understanding Employment Practices Liability

1 History And Status Of Employment Practices Liability

Today, every business faces not only the traditional challenges of competition and rapidly changing technology, but also a relatively new category of potential adversary—its own workforce. Not-for-profit corporations and public entities, in addition to public and private businesses, are experiencing an explosion of employment-related claims based on:

- Discrimination
- Sexual harassment
- Wrongful discharge litigation
- Wage and hour disputes
- Allegations of negligent hiring, retention and supervision
- Failure to provide benefits
- Alleged violations of federal and state leave-of-absence laws

While the employment relationship is of ancient origin, few laws governing employment existed in the United States until well into the nineteenth century. One of the earliest employment laws was the Civil Rights Act of 1866, enacted following the Civil War to prohibit employment discrimination based on race. But even as laws governing the employment relationship were evolving, the unwritten law of the land for many years continued to be that the employer owed little, if any, duty to its employees. Enforcement of early laws governing employment was sporadic at best, and prior to the development of workers' compensation laws, employees who were injured on the job had little practical recourse. The idea that an employee would expect some form of legal protection was, for much of the workforce, unthinkable.

Passage of the Civil Rights Act of 1964 signaled a dramatic change in attitudes about the employment relationship, and laws governing the employment relationship have been vigorously enforced ever since. Today, relations between employer and employee are governed by a complex and constantly changing body of laws and regulations.

Whether a reaction to the inadequacies of past employment laws, a heightened general awareness of employee and civil rights, or other factors, such as "a new and potent wave of feminism,"[1] both public and private organizations are being challenged on a broad range of wrongful employment practices. Even the President of the United States is not immune from attack.

The following discussions are a review of some of the federal and state laws that have been codified. These laws reflect society's desire to eliminate discrimination and other wrongful employment practices from the workplace and to guarantee the fair treatment of all employees.

Discrimination In Employment

Many employers believe that the vast majority of employment laws limit an employer's ability to run its business and to manage its employees. But no law, either federal or state, prohibits an employer from deciding which employees to hire, promote, transfer, demote, discipline or terminate, provided that such decisions are based on legitimate business factors that are not "discriminatory" in nature. What equal employment laws do prohibit are employment decisions based upon the characteristics, traits or situations of employees that the law defines as "protected classes" or categories. Federal, state and local anti-discrimination laws make it illegal for an employer to make employment decisions based upon a person's protected status.

Among the earliest federal employment law to be vigorously enforced was Title VII of the 1964 Civil Rights Act (Title VII),[2] which established a limited number of protected classes. Over the years, however, Title VII has been amended and additional federal laws have been adopted, as well. State and local laws have added even more protected classes. The result has been an overall expansion of the original protected classes. Title VII expressly provides that it does not "preempt" such laws. To the extent that state or local legislation gives employees and applicants greater protection against discrimination than Title VII, employees have the benefit of both. Employees and applicants for employment have the choice of bringing a discrimination claim under applicable federal, state or local law.

The classes now protected under federal law include race, color, religion, sex (including sexual harassment and pregnancy), national origin, ancestry, citizenship, age (40 years of age and over), mental and physical disability, and veteran status. Although state and local laws vary, among the classes protected by these laws are marital status, various medical conditions (such as cancer and sickle cell anemia), sexual orientation, political activity, employees who serve on juries and those who suffer work-related injuries.

---

[1] Anita Hill. Quoted from the Women's Conference on Feminism, NY, April 25, 1992.
[2] 42 U.S.C. §§ 2000, *et seq.*

The following discussion covers the principal federal laws that prohibit employment discrimination.

Federal Law

Title VII Of The 1964 Civil Rights Act

The most wide-ranging federal anti-discrimination statute is Title VII of the 1964 Civil Rights Act. With some limited exceptions,[3] Title VII applies to state and local governments and all employers doing business in the United States, Puerto Rico and the Virgin Islands that are engaged in any "industry affecting commerce." In order to be subject to Title VII, employers must employ or have employed 15 or more persons for each working day in 20 or more calendar weeks in the current or preceding calendar year.[4] Because nearly all businesses are deemed to affect commerce,[5] almost any employer located within the United States that has the requisite number of employees is governed by Title VII.

Title VII prohibits discrimination based on an employee's or job applicant's race, color, religion, sex or national origin.[6] The Pregnancy Discrimination Act of 1978 amended Title VII to clarify that sex discrimination includes discrimination on the basis of pregnancy, childbirth and related medical conditions.[7] Title VII makes it unlawful for an employer to use any of the protected classes as a basis for employment-related decisions, including:

---

[3] Title VII applies to both state and local governmental bodies, but not to federal employees. Tax-exempt bona fide membership clubs and Native American tribes also are exempted from Title VII coverage. Title VII does not prohibit discrimination based on religion by religious corporations and associations.

[4] Title VII has been held to apply to domestically incorporated subsidiaries of foreign companies doing business in the United States. Foreign companies with 15 or more employees involved in recruiting or other employment-related activities within the United States are covered by Title VII, even if they do not have any employees permanently working in this country.

[5] The United States Constitution provides that Congress has the power to enact legislation regulating commerce between the states. In a line of decisions arising from constitutional challenges to President Roosevelt's 1930's New Deal legislation, the Supreme Court greatly expanded the scope of the term *industry affecting commerce,* going so far as to hold that any business that used the instrumentalities of interstate commerce, such as the United States mail or the telephone, "affected commerce."

[6] Presidential Executive Order 11246 makes it unlawful for any federal contractor or subcontractor with a contract in excess of $10,000 to discriminate against an employee on the basis of race, color, religion, sex or national origin. In addition, contractors and subcontractors that have 50 or more employees and a federal government contract or subcontract of at least $50,000, and banks receiving deposits of any type of federal funds, must develop a written affirmative-action plan. Such a plan must analyze the race and sex of the employer's work force, analyze the race and sex of the available labor pool, determine whether the employer is underutilizing minority or women employees in any job categories, and establish goals and timetables to overcome any such underutilization.

Employees and applicants who claim discrimination in violation of Executive Order 11246 have no private right of action. They cannot bring a lawsuit nor attempt to recover damages. However, the Office of Federal Contract Compliance (OFCC) may seek a variety of sanctions against a non-compliant employer. These include cancellation, suspension or termination of government contracts and disqualification from future contracts.

[7] Federal courts have uniformly held that discrimination on the basis of sex does not apply to sexual-orientation discrimination, nor does it apply to discrimination against transsexuals or transvestites. However, a number of states have prohibited discrimination on the basis of sexual orientation, and in February 1995, San Francisco enacted a local ordinance protecting transsexuals and transvestites against employment discrimination.

1. Failing or refusing to hire an applicant for employment

2. Discharging or otherwise disciplining an employee

3. Determining an employee's compensation, including fringe benefits or other terms, conditions or privileges of employment

4. Classifying an employee in a way that would tend to deprive him or her of an employment opportunity or otherwise adversely affect employment status

Title VII also bans discrimination against an employee who has opposed an employment practice that is unlawful under Title VII or who has filed a charge of discrimination or participated in any proceeding under Title VII. For example, it is unlawful for an employer to discharge a male employee because he has complained to his supervisor about gender discrimination against a female employee. Similarly, an employer cannot demote a white supervisor who is a witness in court on behalf of a black employee who claims racial discrimination by the employer.

Under Title VII, an employer is absolutely liable for any act of discrimination by a managing agent, such as an officer, director or a supervisor,[8] even if the employer had no actual knowledge of the discrimination. The employer also may be liable for the discriminatory acts of non-supervisory employees, but only if the employer knew or reasonably should have known of the unlawful conduct and then failed to take steps to stop it.

Title VII defines *employer* not only as a "person engaged in an industry affecting commerce," but "any agent of such person." Based upon this definition, many courts have held that Title VII subjects individuals, including managing agents, supervisors and rank and file employees, to personal liability for engaging in unlawful employment discrimination. However, some recent cases have suggested that only the entity or person who was the actual employer, not individuals, can be held liable for Title VII violations. Until and unless the United States Supreme Court resolves this issue, the question will be determined by the decisions of the federal circuit court in which an employer is sued. As noted above, the federal circuit courts are divided as to whether individuals face liability under Title VII.

The federal administrative agency that enforces Title VII is the Equal Employment Opportunity Commission (EEOC). The EEOC has offices in every major US city. An

---

[8] In general, a "supervisor" is someone who has the discretion to hire, fire, discipline, promote, demote, transfer, layoff or recall employees, or who can effectively recommend such actions. An employee who can resolve employee grievances or disputes, or who uses discretion in the assignment of work to employees also may be a supervisor. For the purposes of Title VII and other federal and state anti-discrimination laws, it is necessary to distinguish between supervisors and "lead people." A lead person may be the senior person on an assembly line who routinely directs the work of other employees and answers their work-related questions. Unlike supervisors, lead people have no real authority over hiring, firing or other employment-related decisions, and an employer is not absolutely liable for discrimination by a lead person.

employee who believes that he or she has suffered employment discrimination based on race, color, religion, sex or national origin must file a charge of discrimination with the EEOC in order to set in motion the enforcement mechanisms of Title VII. The charge must be filed with the EEOC within 180 days of the last alleged wrongful act committed by the employer.[9]

Upon receipt of a charge of discrimination, the EEOC will conduct an investigation for the purpose of determining whether there is reasonable cause to conclude that the allegations of the charge are true.[10] If reasonable cause is found to exist, the EEOC will attempt to convince the employer and the employee to "conciliate" their dispute. A successful conciliation occurs when the employer and employee voluntarily agree to a mutually satisfactory settlement of the matter. Absent conciliation, the EEOC may file a suit in federal district court on behalf of the employee. However, because of limited governmental resources, an EEOC suit rarely occurs except in class-action cases. More often the EEOC issues a "right-to-sue" letter to the employee, advising him or her that a private lawsuit may be filed.[11,12] Such a suit must be filed within 90 days of the issuance of the right-to-sue letter, or it will be barred by the statute of limitations under Title VII.

The 1991 Civil Rights Act amended Title VII to guarantee that an employee bringing a discrimination claim will have the right to trial by jury.[13] Following trial, if an employer is found to have engaged in a prohibited discrimination, the employer can be required to do any combination of the following:

1. Hire the applicant to the position originally unlawfully denied

2. Reinstate an employee who was unlawfully discharged

3. Pay back wages and other benefits lost by an employee or applicant as a result of the employer's unlawful employment practices

4. Pay the costs and attorneys' fees of the prevailing employee

5. Pay compensatory damages, including damages for emotional injuries

---

[9] If the state in which the employment practice occurred has its own laws prohibiting discrimination of the type complained of, the charge of discrimination must be filed with the EEOC within 300 days of the alleged violation or within 30 days from receipt of notice that the state anti-discrimination agency has terminated its proceedings, whichever is later. A state having such anti-discrimination laws is known as a "deferral state."

[10] As of January 1, 1995, the EEOC had a backlog of 96,000 pending cases. As a result, completion of the investigation, including an employer's written response to the charge of discrimination, records review and possible on-site interviews of witnesses, may take a year or more to complete.

[11] Even if the EEOC concludes that the charge of discrimination is without merit, a right-to-sue letter will be issued and the employee may elect to file a lawsuit in federal district court.

[12] An employee who wishes to avoid the investigative process altogether may file a charge of discrimination with the EEOC and immediately request that the agency close its case file and issue a right-to-sue letter. The EEOC will do so on the basis that the employee has elected court action. In such a circumstance, the right-to-sue letter may be issued just a few weeks after the discrimination charge was originally filed.

[13] The 1991 Civil Rights Act also extended the right to a jury trial to claims brought under the Americans with Disabilities Act, which is discussed below.

6. Pay any medical costs incurred by the employee who has suffered emotional distress

7. Pay punitive damages, if it is determined that the employer acted willfully or with a conscious disregard of the individual's rights[14]

Recent Supreme Court Rulings

On June 26, 1998, the United States Supreme Court issued two important decisions. In both *Faragher v. City of Boca Raton*, 66 U.S.L.W. 4634 (1998) and *Burlington Industries, Inc. v. Ellerth*, 66 U.S.L.W. 4634 (1998), the Supreme Court held that employers are vicariously liable to employees who have been subjected to sexual harassment by their immediate supervisor or another employee of higher authority.

What The Supreme Court Decided

In essence, the Supreme Court confirmed that under Title VII of the 1964 Civil Rights Act, employers are absolutely responsible for sexual harassment of employees by their managers or supervisors, even if a company's senior management and owners have no knowledge of the supervisor's conduct. However, in both opinions, the Court held that an employer which has implemented certain measures (such as a detailed and well publicized sexual harassment policy, education of employees and supervisors about such harassment, a system for employees to report alleged sexual harassment, and a program of effective employer investigation and response to sexual harassment complaints) may establish a defense which could defeat this otherwise automatic liability.

What The Supreme Court Did Not Decide

Most news reports have failed to point out that the Supreme Court's decision only applies to cases of sexual harassment brought under Title VII. The decisions have no direct impact on cases brought under state laws, which prohibit discrimination and harassment such as the California Fair Employment and Housing Act (FEHA). In states such as California, employers must comply with both Title VII and FEHA, and while these two statutes are similar, they are not identical. While California courts enforcing FEHA often look to decisions under Title VII for guidance, state courts are not bound by the Supreme Court's interpretation of Title VII in interpreting state law. This is particularly significant since in states like California (because of a longer statute of limitations and fewer restrictions on the amount of damages available to employees), the vast majority of sexual harassment cases are brought under state rather than federal law.

---

[14] The Civil Rights Act of 1991 set a $500,000 maximum on punitive damages awarded under Title VII. However, the size of punitive damage awards are unlimited under some state anti-discrimination statutes.

Importance Of Supreme Court Decisions

While states like California are not required to follow federal precedent when enforcing FEHA, state judges may look to Title VII cases and, in particular, the Supreme Court for direction. Often what starts out as federal law is subsequently adopted and applied by the state courts. Until such adoption, juries may still question an employer that did not use the well-publicized, employer-provided means of complaining about and remedying alleged sexual harassment. Even if proactive steps do not currently immunize an employer from liability for sexual harassment under state law, such steps may well eliminate the possibility of punitive damages in these cases.

The Supreme Court's decision in these cases signals an increased likelihood that an organization may be held vicariously liable for sexual harassment committed by supervisors and managers. No longer is the burden on the plaintiff to prove some responsibility on the part of the employer. The burden is on the employer to prove an affirmative defense.

Civil Rights Act Of 1866

The Civil Rights Act of 1866,[15] also known as Section 1981, prohibits certain types of employment discrimination based upon a person's race. Enacted immediately after the Civil War to protect the rights of recently freed slaves and other African-Americans, Section 1981 provides that "all persons within the jurisdiction of the United States shall have the same right...to make and enforce contracts...and to the full and equal benefit of all laws and proceedings for the security of persons and property as is enjoyed by white citizens...."

Section 1981 overlaps the race discrimination provisions of Title VII,[16] with, however, some significant differences between the two. For example, Section 1981 is applicable to all employers, regardless of the number of persons they employ. An employee who alleges discrimination need not exhaust any administrative remedies before bringing a lawsuit under Section 1981. The statute of limitations for a Section 1981 claim, which is governed by the law of the state in which the action is brought, is usually much longer than the Title VII statute of limitations. But unlike Title VII, Section 1981 is limited to claims of *intentional* discrimination.

Equal Pay Act Of 1963

The Equal Pay Act of 1963[17] is an amendment to the basic federal wage and hour law, the Fair Labor Standards Act (FLSA), and only applies to employers covered by the FLSA.

---

[15] 42 U.S.C. § 1981.

[16] Section 1981 is limited to claims of discrimination by non-whites. However, a white employee can bring a Section 1981 action if he or she is retaliated against for protesting racial discrimination against a non-white employee.

[17] 29 U.S.C. § 206(d).

The FLSA, and thus the Equal Pay Act, governs any employer that has gross annual sales of $500,000 or more and that has two or more employees engaged in interstate commerce, in the production of goods for interstate commerce, or in the handling or selling of goods moved in or produced for interstate commerce. Like the FLSA, the Equal Pay Act also applies to governmental entities.[18]

The Equal Pay Act requires that an employer cannot pay employees of one sex lower wages than employees of the opposite sex for equal work.[19] The Equal Pay Act does permit pay differentials based on factors other than sex, such as a seniority or merit.

Like Title VII, the Equal Pay Act is enforced by the EEOC. In general, the same enforcement mechanisms applicable to Title VII apply to Equal Pay Act claims. Under the Equal Pay Act, however, an employee has two years (three years if the employer's violation was willful) to bring a lawsuit.

An employer that has been found to have violated the Equal Pay Act may be ordered to pay actual damages in an amount that will meet its equal pay obligations, an amount equal to these actual damages as "liquidated damages" and the attorneys' fees and court costs of the prevailing employee. An employer also may be prosecuted criminally and fined up to $10,000 for a willful violation of the Equal Pay Act.

Age Discrimination In Employment Act Of 1967

The Age Discrimination in Employment Act of 1967 (ADEA)[20] prohibits discrimination against any employee or applicant who is 40 years of age or older[21] by any employer engaged in "an industry affecting commerce" that employs, or has employed, 20 or more employees for each working day in each of 20 or more calendar weeks in the current or preceding year.[22, 23] Like Title VII, the ADEA also applies to state and local public-sector employers.

---

[18] Although it is a part of the FLSA, the Equal Pay Act does not exempt "white collar" employees, such as outside sales personnel, professionals, executives and administrative employees, like the FLSA does.

[19] The requirements of the Equal Pay Act must be distinguished from the concept of "comparable worth." The theory underlying comparable worth is that jobs that are "equal in value" should be equally compensated, even if the jobs are not "equal in content." Except in those rare cases where it has been found that the wages of a protected class of employees, i.e., women, were set lower than those of men as the result of intentional discrimination in violation of Title VII, comparable worth lawsuits have been rejected by the courts. The decisions in these cases have concluded that a Title VII violation does not occur where employees of different sexes receive different compensation for work of differing skills that may be of equal value to the employer but which does not command an equal price in the labor market.

[20] 29 U.S.C. §§ 621, *et seq*.

[21] In most states, statutes relating to age discrimination have the same threshold age, 40 years, as does federal law. In a few states, however, discrimination against younger employees is prohibited, e.g., Minnesota and New York both prohibit discrimination against any employee who is at least 18 years old. In some states, such as Louisiana, Missouri and Nebraska, the restrictions against age discrimination only apply until an employee reaches age 70.

[22] In 1984, Congress amended the ADEA to extend its protections to American citizens employed abroad by American companies or by employers controlled by American companies. However, an employer has a defense to a charge of unlawful age discrimination under the ADEA where compliance with the ADEA would require the employer to violate the laws of the country in which the employee works.

The ADEA protects covered employees against employment decisions based on age, including mandatory retirement. There are, however, four major exceptions to the prohibition on mandatory retirement: (1) executive employees,[24] (2) law enforcement officers, (3) fire fighters and (4) tenured faculty at institutions of higher learning.[25]

The ADEA also contains specific exemptions to its prohibition against age discrimination where age is a bona fide occupational qualification (BFOQ) reasonably necessary to the operation of the employer's business,[26] the employer's action is in observance of a bona fide seniority system, or the employer's action is in observance of a bona fide employee benefit plan. These exceptions and exemptions have been narrowly construed by the courts.

The ADEA makes unlawful the same employment practices as does Title VII. In addition, an employer commits unlawful discrimination under the ADEA if it:

1. Places an employment notice, posting or advertisement indicating a preference, limitation or specification based on age; or

2. Reduces the wage rate of an employee in order to comply with other requirements under the ADEA, for example, to purchase mechanical devices to assist a physically disabled employee.

In addition to enforcing Title VII, the EEOC enforces the ADEA. The same provisions and rules that govern the filing and handling of claims with the EEOC under Title VII also apply to ADEA cases.

If an employer is found to have engaged in an unlawful employment practice under the ADEA, the employer can be required to do one or more of the following, depending on the situation:

1. Hire an applicant for employment who was unlawfully denied a job

2. Reinstate an employee who was unlawfully discharged

---

[23] In addition to the ADEA, the Age Discrimination Employment Act of 1975 prohibits age discrimination by any employer that receives federal financial assistance. The prohibition against age discrimination under this law is not restricted to any particular age range.
Presidential Executive Order 11141 prohibits age discrimination by federal contractors and subcontractors.

[24] Applies if the executive employee is at least 65, has been employed as an executive for at least two years prior to retirement, and is entitled to an immediate nonforfeitable retirement benefit of at least $44,000 per year.

[25] An institution of higher education may have a mandatory retirement age of 70 for tenured faculty members.

[26] In order to establish a BFOQ defense, an employer must prove that (1) the age limit is reasonably necessary to the essence of the business, and (2) either all or substantially all of the persons excluded from the job involved are actually disqualified, or some of the persons excluded possess a disqualifying trait that cannot be determined except by reference to age. If the employer asserts a BFOQ defense as a matter of "public safety," the employer also must prove that the challenged employment practice does result in improved safety and that there is no acceptable alternative that would achieve the same result with a less discriminatory impact.
Applying these standards, several courts have upheld a mandatory retirement age for both test pilots and commercial pilots.

3. Pay back wages and other benefits lost by an employee or applicant as a result of the employer's unlawful employment practices[27]

4. Pay "liquidated damages"[28] if the employer's conduct is deemed to be willful

5. Pay "front pay"[29] until the employee reaches age 70

6. Pay the costs and attorneys' fees of the prevailing employee or applicant

Americans With Disabilities Act Of 1990

The Americans with Disabilities Act of 1990 (ADA) prohibits covered employers from discriminating against any qualified employee with a physical or mental disability.[30] The ADA applies to all employers that have 15 or more employees and are engaged in an industry affecting commerce.[31] In determining whether an employee is qualified for a particular position, the employer must evaluate whether the employee, with or without "reasonable accommodation," can perform the "essential functions" of the position.[32]

The ADA covers an employer's hiring procedures, job training, promotions, discharges and compensation practices.

---

[27] An employee bringing an ADEA claim is limited to receiving two years of back pay unless the employer's conduct is found to be willful, in which case liability may extend for three years.

[28] Liquidated damages is an amount equal to the amount of back wages actually awarded to the employee. Thus liquidated damages are often referred to as "double damages."

[29] In some cases, the judge or jury hearing an age-discrimination case might conclude that it is highly unlikely, if not impossible, that the complaining employee will ever find another job. For example, a 61-year-old engineer who is unlawfully laid off by an aerospace company because of his age would find it extremely difficult to get another position. In such a circumstance, the employee might be awarded the pay that he will lose from the time his case is heard until he is 70. This is "front pay."

[30] In addition to the ADA, the Rehabilitation Act of 1973 prohibits covered employers from discriminating against qualified individuals with physical or mental handicaps.

Section 503 of the Rehabilitation Act applies to any employer or subcontractor that has a contract in excess of $2,500 with the federal government. Such an employer must adopt an affirmative-action program intended to qualify and advance handicapped individuals in employment. If the employer has at least 50 employees, it must maintain a written affirmative-action plan similar to that which is required for women and minorities under Executive Order 11246. However, goals and timetables are not required as part of a Rehabilitation Act affirmative-action plan. A majority of courts have held that an employee or applicant who believes that they have been discriminated against in violation of Section 503 may not bring an individual lawsuit against an employer. However, as under Executive Order 11246, the offending employer may face cancellation, suspension or termination of its government contracts and disbarment from future contracts.

Section 504 of the Rehabilitation Act applies to employers that, although not federal contractors, receive "federal financial assistance." Such assistance includes the receipt of Medicare or Medicaid funds. Section 504 does not create an affirmative-action obligation on the part of a covered employer; however, the employer must make a reasonable accommodation to the known physical or mental handicap of an employee. In distinction to Section 503, Section 504 does allow for an individual lawsuit against an employer that violates its obligations.

[31] The ADA does not apply to the employees of the United States government, to tax-exempt bona fide membership clubs or to employees of Indian tribes. A partial exemption to the ADA allows religious organizations to give preference to members of a particular religion to perform work connected with their activities. Religious organizations also may require employees and applicants to conform to the organization's religious beliefs.

[32] Determination of what constitutes the essential functions of a job, and whether or not accommodation is reasonable, is fact-based, and consideration of the many criteria that go into such a determination is beyond the scope of this work.

The ADA is enforced by the EEOC, and the same provisions and rules that govern the filing and processing of claims under Title VII apply to ADA cases.

Family And Medical Leave Act

The Family and Medical Leave Act of 1993 (FMLA)[33] was adopted in order to ensure that employees have the opportunity to take leaves of absence to meet their own medical needs, for the birth or adoption of a child, or to care for a parent, child or sibling with a serious health condition. To be eligible for an FMLA leave, an employee must have been employed by a covered employer for at least one year. The employee also must have worked at least 1,250 hours in the preceding 12-month period. FMLA applies to any employer engaged "in commerce or in any industry or activity affecting commerce," provided that the employer employs 50 or more employees within a 75-mile radius of the employee seeking leave, for each working day in each of 20 or more calendar work weeks in the current or preceding year. An employee may take up to 12 weeks of FMLA leave in any 12-month period.

FMLA is enforced by the United States Department of Labor. An employee claiming to have suffered discrimination because he or she exercised or attempted to exercise FMLA rights may file a charge with the Labor Department. The charge must be filed within two years of the alleged discrimination (three years if the employer's actions were willful). Upon receipt, the charge will be investigated. If the Labor Department determines that the charge has merit, it will try to get the parties to conciliate the matter.

In addition to filing an administrative charge with the Labor Department, an employee may choose to file a lawsuit directly against the employer in a court of law. The Labor Department also may elect to file a complaint against the employer. If the Labor Department does file suit, the right of the employee to bring his or her own action is terminated, and the Secretary of Labor will represent the employee in litigation.

If an employer is found to have violated FMLA, it can be required to do any or all of the following:

1. Pay back wages, benefits or other compensation lost by an employee on account of the employer's unlawful conduct

2. If no wages or benefits have been lost by the employee, pay any actual monetary loss suffered by the employee as a result of the violation (for example, the cost of providing care to a seriously ill child for up to 12 weeks, in an amount not to exceed 12 weeks of wages)

3. Pay liquidated damages in an amount equal to the actual damages paid

---

[33] 29 U.S.C. § 2601, *et seq.*

4. Hire, reinstate or promote an employee

5. Pay costs and attorneys' fees

Uniformed Services Employment And Reemployment Rights Act Of 1994

The Uniformed Services Employment and Reemployment Rights Act of 1994 (Uniformed Services Act) provides employment protections to persons who serve in the United States Armed Forces or have obligations as a member of a reserve unit. The Uniformed Services Act applies to all employers, regardless of their size.

Under the Uniformed Services Act, an employee who leaves a position to enter the Armed Forces[34] is entitled to reinstatement by the employer provided that the employee is honorably discharged from military service, applies for reemployment within 90 days after discharge and is still qualified to perform the duties of the position. An eligible employee must be reinstated to his or her former job or to a position with like seniority, status and pay.[35, 36] The employer may not discharge a reinstated employee without cause within one year following reemployment.

The Uniformed Services Act also prohibits an employer from refusing to hire, retain or promote any person because of his or her obligation as a member of a reserve component of the Armed Forces.

Finally, the Uniformed Services Act requires that any employer with a federal contract in excess of $10,000 undertake affirmative action to employ and advance qualified disabled veterans. If the employer has 50 or more employees and a contract of at least $50,000, it must develop a written affirmative-action program.

Those portions of the Uniformed Services Act that guarantee the reemployment rights of veterans and the rights of reservists are enforced by the Office of Veterans Reemployment Rights of the Department of Labor. If this agency cannot resolve a charge of discrimination, the claim is referred to the United States Attorney, who may file an action on behalf of the employee. The Veterans' Employment Service of the Department of Labor administers the affirmative-action provisions of the Uniformed Services Act.

---

[34] The provisions of the Uniformed Services Act not only include an employee's service in the Army, Navy, Air Force or Marine Corps, but in the Reserves, the United States Health Service or the Coast Guard.

[35] An employer's obligations are slightly different where the employee has been hospitalized following military discharge or where the employee is not qualified to perform the duties of his or her former position. An employer has a duty to reasonably accommodate service-related disabilities and to provide necessary training for returning employees.

[36] An employer need not reinstate an employee when business circumstances have so changed that it is impossible or unreasonable to reinstate the employee. This exception, however, is narrowly applied.

Immigration Reform And Control Act Of 1986

The Immigration Reform and Control Act of 1986 (IRCA)[37] was enacted for the purpose of "effectively controlling unauthorized immigration to the United States." IRCA prohibits the employment of undocumented aliens and requires that an employer verify that any employee hired after November 7, 1986 is legally employable in this country. In an effort to prevent discrimination against "foreign appearing" or "foreign speaking" individuals in the guise of compliance with IRCA, the law prohibits employment discrimination based upon an individual's citizenship or national origin, so long as the individual legally is able to work in this country. This prohibition includes an employer's recruiting, hiring, discharging and referral practices.

Because an employer with 15 or more employees is covered by Title VII's ban on discrimination on the basis of national origin, such an employer, although subject to the IRCA provisions against citizenship discrimination, is not covered by the national origin discrimination provisions of IRCA. This means that if an employer has between four and 15 employees, it is exempt from Title VII coverage, but is covered by both IRCA's citizenship and national-origin-discrimination prohibitions. Employers with fewer than four employees are exempt from all of IRCA's discrimination provisions.[38]

IRCA only protects United States citizens and nationals, permanent resident aliens, aliens lawfully admitted for temporary residence, refugees and newly legalized aliens who have filed a notice of intent to become citizens. IRCA does not prohibit discrimination against undocumented aliens.

Despite IRCA's general rule against employment discrimination based on citizenship, an employer may select a United States citizen or national over an alien where the two individuals are equally qualified. As a practical matter, however, almost never are two people "equally" qualified for a job. An employer also may discriminate on the basis of citizenship in those few jobs where such discrimination is required in order to comply with law, a government contract or a decision of the Attorney General. For example, there may be a job where a security clearance is required and only US citizens are eligible for such a clearance.

IRCA is enforced by the Special Counsel of the United States Department of Justice. An employee or job applicant who believes that he or she has been discriminated against may file a claim with the Justice Department. Such a charge must be filed within 180 days of the alleged discrimination. Upon receipt of a charge, the Justice Department will investigate. If the Justice Department concludes that the charge has merit, it will attempt to conciliate the matter. Failing a conciliation, the Justice Department will prosecute on

---

[37] 8 U.S.C. § 1324 (a) and (b).

[38] All employers, including those with fewer than four employees, are prohibited from employing undocumented aliens. Every employer, regardless of size, is required to verify a new employee's identity and eligibility to work in the United States at the time of hire.

behalf of the employee or applicant. Employer sanctions for violations of IRCA include hiring or rehiring the individual who was the subject of the unlawful discrimination, back pay and the possible payment of fines.

National Labor Relations Act

Unlike the anti-discrimination laws discussed above, the National Labor Relations Act (NLRA)[39] does not protect employees on the basis of unchangeable characteristics such as race, national origin or age. Rather, the NLRA prohibits discrimination against employees because they engage in certain types of "protected activity."

The NLRA was enacted to guarantee employees the right of self-organization and selection of representatives for the purpose of collectively negotiating the terms and conditions of their employment. Under the NLRA, employees have the right to form, join or assist unions; to bargain collectively through representatives of their choice; and to engage in other concerted activities for the purpose of collective bargaining and mutual support.

The NLRA applies to almost all employers engaged in an industry affecting commerce.[40] Employers covered by the NLRA are prohibited from interfering with, restraining or coercing employees in the exercise of their statutory rights. Such prohibited activities may include, but are not limited to, termination, demotion and reductions in wages or benefits.

The NLRA is enforced by the General Counsel of the National Labor Relations Board (NLRB). Like the EEOC, the NLRB has offices in every major city across the country. Each of these regional offices is headed by a regional director who supervises a staff of attorneys and field investigators.

An employee who claims that he or she suffered employer discrimination prohibited by the NLRA must file a charge with the NLRB within six months of the alleged discrimination. Upon receipt of an unfair labor practice charge, the Regional Office of the National Labor Relations Board conducts an investigation. The purpose of the investigation is to determine if there is "reasonable cause" to believe that a violation of the NLRA has occurred. Such investigations usually are completed within 45 days of the filing of an unfair labor practice charge. If reasonable cause is found to exist, the Regional Director issues a complaint and a hearing is held before an administrative law judge. An attorney from the regional office represents the General Counsel of the National Labor Relations Board at this hearing. While a private attorney may represent the employee at

---

[39] 29 U.S.C. §§ 151 *et seq*.

[40] The NLRA does not govern federal and state governmental agencies except for the Post Office. It does not cover railroads or airlines, which are subject to the Railway Labor Act. The NLRA does not apply to agricultural workers, although some states, like California, have enacted parallel legislation that covers these workers. Finally, certain small employers are exempted from coverage under the NLRA, i.e., retail businesses with sales volume under $500,000 and non-retail businesses that purchase or sell less than $50,000 in interstate commerce.

the hearing, the responsibility for presenting the case against the employer rests with the General Counsel.

The decision of the administrative law judge is appealable to the five-member NLRB, which usually delegates its role to a three-member panel. Decisions of the NLRB are not self-enforcing. If an employer is found to have unlawfully discriminated against an employee for engaging in protected activity and chooses not to abide by the Board's decision, the NLRB must go to a United States Court of Appeals and seek enforcement of its order.

Where an employer is found to have engaged in prohibited discrimination, it can be required to do any or all of the following:

1. Reinstate an employee who was unlawfully discharged
2. Promote or transfer an employee who was unlawfully demoted or transferred
3. Pay back wages and other benefits lost by an employee as a result of the employer's unlawful employment practices
4. Post a notice to all employees acknowledging its unlawful conduct and agreeing to refrain from such conduct in the future

Conclusion

The discussion in this section has focused on the primary federal anti-discrimination laws. There are, however, other federal anti-discrimination laws that can hold employers responsible for wrongful employment conduct. Among these are the Consumer Credit Protection Act,[41] the Railway Labor Act (RLA)[42] and the Employee Retirement Income Security Act (ERISA).[43]

State Law

The 1960s saw Congressional enactment of Title VII of the 1964 Civil Rights Act, prohibiting employment discrimination based upon race, color, national origin, religion or sex; the Equal Pay Act, requiring employers to equally pay men and women for equal

---

[41] The Consumer Credit Protection Act, 15 U.S.C. § 1674, prohibits the discharge of an employee on the ground that his or her earnings have been subjected to garnishment for a single indebtedness.

[42] The Railway Labor Act, 45 U.S.C. §§ 151, *et seq.*, serves much the same purpose as the National Labor Relations Act, but its application is restricted to the railroad and airline industries. The RLA provides a comprehensive framework for the resolution of grievances and disputes in covered industries.

[43] ERISA is a comprehensive body of law regulating employer-funded pension and benefit plans. ERISA prohibits discrimination against an employee on any basis related to such plans and preempts state laws, regulations and rules that relate to employee benefit plans (29 U.S.C. § 1144).

work; and the Age Discrimination in Employment Act, barring discrimination on the basis of age.

During this same ten-year period, a number of states also adopted so-called *fair employment practices laws*. Indeed, some state statutes had even preceded the federal laws. Now, some 30 years later, most states have fair employment laws that parallel the protections accorded to employees under federal law. More than 40 states also prohibit discrimination against employees who have handicaps or disabilities. Still others have added provisions barring discrimination because of an employee's marital status, sexual orientation and a myriad of other factors not addressed by federal laws.

The following exhibit of state employment discrimination laws provides an overview of many of the classes of employees protected against employment discrimination under the fair-employment-practices laws of the various states.

Exhibit 1
State Employment Discrimination Laws

	Race/Color	National Origin/Ancestry	Religion	Sex	Marital Status	Sexual Orientation	Age	Disability	Arrest Record	Jury Duty	Witness Appearance	Off-Duty Conduct	Political Activity	Whistle Blower	Unemployment Compensation Testimony	Workers' Compensation Claims
Alabama		●	●					●[2]		●		●				
Alaska	●	●	●	●[1]	●		●	●		●		●[2]				
Arizona	●	●	●	●			Ⓕ	●		●						
Arkansas	●[2]	●	●	●			Ⓒ[2]	●		●					●	●
California	●	●	●	●[3]	●	●	Ⓕ	●	●	●	●		●	●	●	●
Colorado	●	●	●	●[4]			Ⓒ	●	●	●		●				
Connecticut	●	●	●	●[3]	●	●	●	●		●	●	●		●		
Delaware	●	●	●	●	●		Ⓒ	●		●						
District of Columbia	●	●	●	●[3]	●	●	Ⓐ	●		●		●	●			●
Florida	●	●	●	●	●	●[2]	●	●		●	●			●		●
Georgia	●[2]	●[2]	●[2]	●			Ⓒ	●		●	●					
Hawaii	●	●	●	●[3]	●	●	●	●	●	●	●			●		●
Idaho	●	●	●	●			Ⓕ	●		●						
Illinois	●	●	●	●[4]	●		Ⓕ	●	●	●		●		●		●
Indiana	●	●	●	●			Ⓑ	●			●	●				
Iowa	●	●	●	●[1]			Ⓓ	●		●				●		
Kansas	●	●	●	●			Ⓓ	●		●			●[2]			
Kentucky	●	●	●	●[1]			Ⓕ	●		●		●	●[2]			●
Louisiana	●	●	●	●[1]			●	●		●	●		●	●		●
Maine	●	●	●	●[3]			●	●		●			●[2]	●		
Maryland	●	●	●	●[3]	●		●	●		●	●		●[2]			●
Massachusetts	●	●	●	●[3]	●	●	Ⓖ	●	●	●						●
Michigan	●	●	●	●[3]	●		●	●	●	●	●			●		●
Minnesota	●	●	●	●[3]	●	●	Ⓔ	●		●	●	●		●		
Mississippi	●[2]	●[2]	●[2]	●			●[2]	●[2]				●	●			
Missouri	●	●	●	●[3]			Ⓒ	●				●				●
Montana	●	●	●	●[3]	●		●	●				●	●[2]			

	Race/Color	National Origin/Ancestry	Religion	Sex	Marital Status	Sexual Orientation	Age	Disability	Arrest Record	Jury Duty	Witness Appearance	Off-Duty Conduct	Political Activity	Whistle Blower	Unemployment Compensation Testimony	Workers' Compensation Claims
Nebraska	●	●	●	●³	●		Ⓕ	●		●			●	●		
Nevada	●	●	●	●³			Ⓕ	●		●	●	●	●			
New Hampshire	●	●	●	●³	●		●	●		●		●		●		
New Jersey	●	●	●	●³	●	●	●	●						●		●
New Mexico	●	●	●	●³	●	●	●	●		●		●	●²			●
New York	●	●	●	●³	●	●²	Ⓓ	●	●	●	●	●	●²	●		●
North Carolina	●	●	●	●³			Ⓕ	●		●		●	●	●	●	●
North Dakota	●	●	●	●³	●		Ⓕ	●		●		●	●	●		
Ohio	●	●	●	●³			Ⓒ	●		●				●		●
Oklahoma	●	●	●	●			Ⓕ	●	●	●		●	●²			●
Oregon	●	●	●	●³	●	●²	Ⓓ	●		●		●	●	●	●	●
Pennsylvania	●	●	●	●³		●²	Ⓕ	●		●	●					
Rhode Island	●	●	●	●³		●	Ⓒ	●	●	●			●	●		
South Carolina	●	●	●	●³			Ⓕ	●		●		●	●			●
South Dakota	●²	●	●	●³	●		Ⓕ	●		●			●	●²		
Tennessee	●	●	●	●¹			Ⓕ	●		●		●	●	●		
Texas	●	●	●	●³			Ⓕ	●		●	●					●
Utah	●	●	●	●¹			Ⓕ	●		●			●²	●		
Vermont	●	●	●	●⁴		●	Ⓓ	●		●	●		●²			
Virginia	●	●	●	●³	●		●	●	●	●		●	●²			●
Washington	●	●	●	●³	●		Ⓕ	●		●						
West Virginia	●	●	●	●³			Ⓕ	●		●		●	●²			●
Wisconsin	●	●	●	●³	●	●	Ⓕ	●	●	●	●	●	●²			●
Wyoming	●	●	●	●			Ⓒ	●		●	●					

KEY TO SYMBOLS
[1]Includes provisions prohibiting pregnancy discrimination
[2]Prohibition applies only to public employees
[3]Includes provisions prohibiting pregnancy discrimination and sexual harassment
[4]Includes provision prohibiting sexual harassment

Ⓐ 18 to 65
Ⓑ 40 to 69
Ⓒ 40 to 70
Ⓓ 18 and over
Ⓔ 25 and over
Ⓕ 40 and over
Ⓖ over 50

It should be noted that such laws are in a constant state of change, however, and Exhibit 1 is not intended as a complete catalogue of the anti-discrimination protections that may apply to an employee in any given state.[44]

Further, while two states may each prohibit discrimination on a particular basis (such as against an employee because of his or her political activities), the extent of the protection afforded, the process for the employee to make a claim and the possible remedies available against the employer may widely vary.

---

[44] Examples of less common forms of employment discrimination laws include the following: Minnesota's ban on discrimination against employees who refuse to make charitable contributions; New Mexico's prohibition of discrimination against employees whose wages are garnished; and provisions found in Indiana, Maryland, Nevada, Oregon, Texas and Washington against employment discrimination on account of an employee's volunteer activities.

For example, several states have recently adopted statutes that prohibit discrimination against employees based on their off-duty conduct. Most of these statutes prohibit employers from discriminating against employees for engaging in certain types of lawful activity, such as smoking tobacco products or drinking alcohol outside of the workplace during non-working hours.[45] New York goes further, prohibiting employers from refusing to hire, employ or discharge an employee or applicant for employment because of that person's lawful political activities off premises during non-working hours; and an individual's legal recreational activities, including sports, games, hobbies, exercise, reading or watching television or movies.[46] Two other states, Colorado[47] and North Dakota,[48] have broad statutes that prohibit an employer from discriminating against employees who participate in lawful activities while off duty and off the employer's property. However, these statutes are not as specific as the New York law.

Yet another example of the wide divergence found among the fair-employment-practices laws of the various states is in the protection from discrimination based on a person's sexual orientation. A number of states prohibit discrimination on this basis.[49,50] In the last few years, however, both state legislators and voters have taken action to curtail the protections accorded to homosexual employees. In both Oregon and Colorado, steps have been taken to exclude sexual orientation from protected-class status. In 1988, Oregon voters adopted a provision whereby "no state official shall forbid the taking of any personnel action against any state employee based on the sexual orientation of such employee."[51] In 1992, the Colorado electorate voted for an amendment to that state's constitution providing that neither the state nor any municipality "shall enact, adopt or enforce any statute, regulation, ordinance or policy whereby homosexual, lesbian or bisexual orientation, conduct, practices or relationships shall constitute or otherwise be the basis of or entitle any person or class of persons to have or claim any minority status quota preferences, protected status or claim of discrimination."[52] Although approved by the voters, both of these statutes have been subjected to constitutional challenge and were declared unconstitutional by their respective state supreme courts.[53] Despite these

---

[45] States that have such statutes include Illinois, Minnesota, Missouri, Nevada, North Carolina, Wisconsin and Wyoming.

[46] NY Lab. Law § 201-d.

[47] Colo. Rev. Stat. §§ 24-34-401 *et seq.*

[48] N.D. Cent. Code §§ 14-02.4-03 *et seq.*

[49] The states prohibiting discrimination on the basis of sexual orientation include California, Connecticut, Hawaii, Massachusetts, Minnesota, New Jersey, New Mexico, Vermont and Wisconsin.

[50] In excess of 50 municipalities also prohibit employment discrimination based on sexual orientation. These municipalities range from Pittsburgh, Pennsylvania to West Hollywood, California; from Key West, Florida to Watertown, New York.

[51] Or. Rev. Stat. § 236.380.

[52] Colo. Const. art. II, § 30b.

[53] *Merrick v. Board of Higher Education*, 116 Or. App. 258, 841 P. 2d 646 (1992) and *Evans v. Romer*, No. CV 7223 (Colo. Dist. Ct. (Dec. 14, 1993) (unpublished), aff'd 63 U.S.L.W. 2219 (Oct. 11, 1994).

setbacks, a group of Oregonians has continued their efforts to enact constitutional provisions banning the extension of protected-class status to homosexuals.[54]

Third-Party Liability

Third-party liability for discrimination, sexual harassment and sexual misconduct (in states like California) can exist when such claims are made by customers, patients, clients, vendors, or other non-employees.

The primary statutory basis for third-party discrimination is found in the 1964 Civil Rights legislation. The public protection section Title II states that "All persons shall be entitled to the full and equal enjoyment of the goods, services, facilities, privileges, advantages, and accommodations of any place of public accommodation, as defined in this section, without discrimination or segregation on the ground of race, color, religion, or national origin." The protected places are "Establishments affecting interstate commerce or supported in their activities by State action as places of public accommodation; lodgings; premises; gasoline stations; places of exhibition or entertainment; other covered establishments." While the establishments covered are primarily hotels, restaurants, theaters and sports arenas, an action under the Civil Rights legislation was brought recently against a car rental company for racial discrimination in the rental of cars.

In addition to the 1964 Civil Rights Act, the other major source of third-party exposure is from the American Disabilities Act of 1990, which governs access and accommodation for the disabled.

State And Local Laws

Some states and cities also have laws prohibiting discrimination, sexual harassment or sexual misconduct. In California, for example, the Unruh Civil Rights Act (Section 51 of the Civil Code) states that:

> *All persons within the jurisdiction of this state are free and equal, and no matter what their sex, race, color, religion, ancestry, national origin or disability are entitled to the full and equal accommodations, advantages, facilities, privileges, or services in all business establishments of every kind whatsoever.*
>
> *This section shall not be construed to confer any right or privilege on a person which is conditioned or limited by law or which is applicable alike to persons of every sex, color, race, religion, ancestry, national origin, or disability…A violation of the right of*

---

[54] There also have been several local efforts to roll back anti-discrimination provisions protecting homosexuals. Both Riverside, California and Cincinnati, Ohio have been involved in litigation arising from these efforts.

any individual under the Americans with Disabilities Act of 1990 (Public Law 101-336) shall also constitute a violation of this section.

A further expansion of the Unruh Act occurred in 1997 when California legislators passed Civil Code 51.9 whereby they declared, "...that sexual harassment occurs not only in the workplace, but in relationships between providers of professional services and their clients." The law states that:

- a) *A person is liable in a cause of action for sexual harassment when the plaintiff proves all of the following elements:*
  1) *There is a business, service, or professional relationship between the plaintiff and defendant. Such a relationship may exist between a plaintiff and a person, including but not limited to, any of the following persons:*
     - A) *Physician, psychotherapist, or dentist...*
     - B) *Attorney, holder of a master's degree in social work, real estate agent, real estate appraiser, accountant, banker, trust officer, financial planner, loan officer, collection services, building contractor, or escrow loan officer,*
     - C) *Executor, trustee or administrator,*
     - D) *Landlord or property manager,*
     - E) *Teacher,*
     - F) *A relationship that is substantially similar to any of the above.*
  2) *The defendant has made sexual advances, solicitations, sexual requests, or demands for sexual compliance by the plaintiff that were unwelcome and persistent or severs, continuing after a request by the plaintiff to stop.*
  3) *There is an inability by the plaintiff to easily terminate the relationship without tangible hardship.*
  4) *The plaintiff has suffered or will suffer economic loss or disadvantage or personal injury as a result of the conduct described in paragraph (2).*

In addition, California has adopted a unique provision prohibiting sexual harassment where there is a business, service, or professional relationship between the complaining individual and the service provider. This statute applies to such service providers as doctors, dentists, psychotherapists, attorneys, real estate agents, bankers, and teachers.[55]

It should be noted that under federal (and sometimes state and local) public housing laws, licensed real estate brokers who are required to show, sell, rent and lease property

---

[55] Cal. Civil Code Sec. 51.9.

must do so without regard to a client's race, color, religion, age, sex, disability or national origin.

Sexual Harassment

A watershed year for sexual harassment claims was 1991. Not only was the Civil Rights Act of 1991 passed, but Anita Hill testified before the United States Senate and a national television audience that she had been subjected to ongoing sexual harassment by then-Supreme Court-nominee Clarence Thomas. Employment attorneys, the EEOC, the OFCC and state anti-discrimination agencies all report that the number of sexual harassment claims has dramatically risen since 1991. Surveys reported in newspapers such as the *Los Angeles Times* disclose that from one-third to one-half of women polled claim to have encountered some form of sexual harassment in the workplace. Therefore, it is not surprising that employers in every industry nationwide are facing both sexual harassment complaints and lawsuits.

While most of the attention and publicity during the last few years has been focused on *sexual* harassment, particularly since the Thomas/Hill hearings in 1991, harassment on the basis of any protected class status may be in violation of federal and/or state law. In some situations, the prohibitions against harassment are significantly broader in coverage than are other anti-discrimination statutes. In California, for example, the anti-discrimination provisions of the Fair Employment and Housing Act only apply to employers with five or more employees, while that state's anti-harassment laws apply to all employers that regularly employ even a single individual.[56]

However, in order to be actionable under federal or state anti-discrimination statutes, harassment must be predicated upon protected class status. When a supervisor allegedly treats an employee poorly or unfairly, and 'harasses' the employee merely because he or she does not like the employee and without regard to such class status, the employee may have a tort claim for the infliction of emotional distress or a workers' compensation claim for job related stress, but the employee does not have a viable claim for harassment under either federal or state civil rights statutes.

---

[56] Cal. Gov. Code Sec. 12940(h).

The Legal Basis For Sexual Harassment Actions

Title VII and many state anti-discrimination laws prohibit harassment based on an employee's sex or gender.[57] While most people who read or hear about sexual harassment immediately think about a man harassing a woman, a woman can unlawfully sexually harass a man, a man can sexually harass another man and a woman can sexually harass another woman.

Although Title VII's sexual harassment proscriptions only apply to employers with 15 or more employees, legislation was introduced during the 1994 Congressional session to extend these rules to smaller employers. With the Republican sweep of the 1994 and 1996 elections, the likelihood of such a bill passing the Congress has been substantially lessened. Many states, however, already have sexual harassment laws that apply to employers with just a few employees. California's sexual harassment laws, for example, govern employers with only one employee, even though that state's other anti-discrimination provisions require five or more employees. As with other aspects of anti-discrimination laws, if an employer has a sufficient number of employees, it may be governed by both federal and state laws.

The Definition Of *Sexual Harassment*

There are two types of sexual harassment. One type is "quid pro quo" harassment, where sexual favors are demanded in order for an employee to obtain work benefits or to avoid unfavorable treatment in the workplace. By definition, quid pro quo harassment exists where the employee is subject to unwelcome sexual advances or conduct, the conduct has a sexual component to it and the employee's reaction or required conduct affects the terms and conditions of employment. While quid pro quo harassment is what most often comes to mind when people think of sexual harassment, it is not the most common type of sexual harassment.

The second, and most common, type of sexual harassment involves allegations of a "hostile environment." Since the mid-1980s, the courts have been flooded with hostile environment claims. In 1985, the United States Supreme Court, in *Vinson v. Meritor Savings Bank*, held that an employee could bring a claim of hostile environment even if the harassment lead solely to non-economic damages.

According to the *Vinson* court, hostile environment sexual harassment is "conduct which has the purpose or effect of substantially interfering with an individual's work

---

[57] Although not specifically addressed by either federal or most state anti-discrimination laws, workplace harassment can be based upon impermissible factors such as race, national origin, religion or age. Indeed, the EEOC's published harassment guidelines are expressly applicable to both sex and national origin. In 1994, the EEOC proposed rules for harassment based on religion, only to withdraw them when Congress threatened to cut the agency's funding. Nevertheless, there has been litigation alleging other non-traditional forms of harassment, and more are to be expected over the next few years.

performance or creating an intimidating, hostile or offensive work environment." In other words, an unlawful hostile environment exists when a reasonable person would conclude that harassment in the workplace is so severe or pervasive that it alters the terms and conditions of an employee's employment and creates an abusive working environment. Some federal courts have found that if the alleged victim of hostile environment sexual harassment is a woman, the question that must be decided is whether a "reasonable woman" would have been offended by the conduct or language complained of. Most psychologists agree that what would offend a "reasonable woman" may be very different from what would offend a "reasonable man."

In hostile environment cases, the harassment need not be, and often is not, physical. Sexual harassment may be caused by jokes, comments or pictures. In many instances, the alleged harasser may not even be interacting with the complaining employee. Many hostile work environment cases are brought by employees who have simply overheard other consenting employees exchanging comments that the complaining employee finds offensive.

It should also be noted that an employer's liability is not necessarily restricted to sexual harassment carried out by its own managers, supervisors and employees. An employer may also be held liable for third party sexual harassment of one of its employees by a customer, vendor, supplier or other visitor to the employer's premises, provided that the employer knew or reasonably should have known of the offending conduct.

Recognizing Sexual Harassment

Although the legal definition of sexual harassment is fairly concise, actually relating such a definition to the workplace can prove difficult. The following hypothetical examples help to illustrate some of these difficulties.

Hypothetical 1 — The Company Affair

Ms. George was employed at Crowell Manufacturing, a large manufacturer of incandescent fixtures. During her probationary period at Crowell, the Production Manager, Mr. Thomas, assisted Ms. George in a manner she regarded as "fatherly."

As time passed, a relationship developed between Ms. George and Mr. Thomas. Mr. Thomas helped Ms. George to finance her apartment, they began to see each other socially and eventually they began a sexual relationship. Over the course of the next two years, Ms. George and Mr. Thomas had intercourse 40 or 50 times, in various locations, including the production office at Crowell Manufacturing.

Ms. George never complained of potentially offensive conduct to her own supervisor at Crowell or to the general manager who supervised Mr. Thomas. However, upon leaving Crowell, she filed a lawsuit for sexual harassment.

ISSUES TO CONSIDER

- *If a supervisor asks a subordinate out on a date one time, is it sexual harassment? Two times? Ten? Fifty?*

  There is no absolute cut-off as to how many times a supervisor may ask a subordinate out before such actions rise to the level of sexual harassment. Sexual harassment exists when a reasonable individual of the complainant's sex and sexual orientation would be offended by the conduct or language complained of. Such a standard may clearly be open to substantial debate and second guessing if the requested date results in subsequent litigation.

- *Can there be sexual harassment where the relationship between a supervisor and a rank-and-file employee is consensual? Was the relationship between Mr. Thomas and Ms. George consensual? Did Ms. George feel pressured into the relationship because of Mr. George's position in the company?*

  There is no actionable sexual harassment where there is a truly consensual relationship between a supervisor and a rank-and-file employee. However, there is not always a bright line between a relationship that is consensual and one that isn't. Even though a supervisor has no direct authority over a rank-and-file employee, the employee may still claim that he or she felt pressured because of the supervisor's senior position in the employer's organization, and a jury may well accept such a claim.

- *Does it matter that Ms. George did not complain of sexual harassment before leaving Crowell? To whom could she have complained? Did Crowell have a sexual harassment policy? Was it in writing?*

  There is no legal requirement that an employee make an internal claim of sexual harassment before filing either an administrative charge or a lawsuit. However, if an employee does not make such an internal claim it may be evidence that the claimed harassment didn't really occur and that the claim is only an after the fact attempt by the employee to "hold up" the employer for some sort of payoff.

  On the other hand, the hypothetical does not disclose whether the employer had an established sexual harassment policy, let alone whether the policy had been reduced to writing. Certainly, there is nothing to show that the employee had been advised of how she was to make the employer aware of a claim of sexual harassment. If an employer is to make use of the absence of any pre-separation complaint of harassment, it is imperative that the employer adopt and disseminate a written policy to all of its employees informing them, at a minimum, of the employer's strong opposition to harassment, the mechanism for making an internal claim of harassment, and guaranteeing employees that they will not be subject to retaliation as the result of making such a claim.

Hypothetical 2 — The Demanding Boss

Mr. Carney was employed as a staff secretary at the Shamrock Company. From time to time over a two-year period, Ms. Scott, the executive for whom Mr. Carney worked, would put her arm around Mr. Carney's shoulder. Toward the end of this period, Ms. Scott told Mr. Carney that she found him to be very attractive and invited him to engage in a sexual relationship even though he was happily married. Mr. Carney thought that Ms. Scott was joking and just laughed the matter off. However, a few weeks later, Ms. Scott told Mr. Carney that if he did not have an affair with her, he would be fired. Less than two days later, Mr. Carney was discharged by Shamrock.

During his exit interview, Mr. Carney complained to Shamrock's vice president of human resources, Mr. Wright, that he had been fired because of his refusal to submit to Ms. Scott's sexual demands. Mr. Wright immediately spoke with Ms. Scott, who unequivocally denied Mr. Carney's claim.

ISSUES TO CONSIDER

> *Can a man be sexually harassed by a woman? A woman harassed by a woman? A man by a man? A supervisor by a subordinate? An employee by a customer, supplier or vendor?*

During its October, 1997 term, the United States Supreme Court heard oral argument on the question of whether a man who claimed to have been harassed by other men could bring a claim under Title VII of the 1964 Civil Rights Act. As of this writing, the Court had not yet rendered its opinion in this matter. However, the Equal Employment Opportunity Commission vigorously supported the position of the complaining employee. In any event, many state courts have expressly held that various state anti-discrimination laws apply to protect employees against same sex harassment.

It is equally clear that state laws prohibit the sexual harassment of a man by a woman. Thus, in a case that gained substantial national publicity, renowned plaintiff's attorney Gloria Allred won a $1,000,000 jury verdict on behalf of a male employee who claimed to have been harassed by his female supervisor.

Finally, an employer can also be held responsible for an employee's harassment by one of the employer's customers, suppliers or vendors, but only where the employer knew, or reasonably should have known, of the harassment.

▸ *Did Shamrock meet its obligation to thoroughly investigate Mr. Carney's claim of sexual harassment when Ms. Scott was interviewed? Why was Mr. Carney fired? What does his personnel file reflect? What did other employees in the department see or hear? Have any other employees ever made sexual harassment claims against Ms. Scott?*

Once an employer becomes aware of a sexual harassment complaint, it has an obligation to thoroughly and objectively investigate the matter. In this case, however, the employer's investigation was less than thorough. First, the employer never questioned the manager as to why she terminated her subordinate, nor was the employee's personnel file examined to see if the proffered reason for termination was adequately supported in the record, or conversely if the personnel file belied the termination rationale. Nor did the employer ask the complaining employee if there were any witnesses to the alleged harassment, and then interview these witnesses. Finally, the employer neither questioned other employees working in the same general area as the complaining party, asking them what they might have seen or overheard, nor did they attempt to question former subordinates of the charged manager to see what relevant information they might be able to offer about her past conduct.

▸ *If Shamrock believes Mr. Carney's claim, should he be reinstated? In what job? What should be done with Ms. Scott?*

When an employer learns that an employee has been the subject of harassment or discrimination, one of the first things that the employer should do is ask the employee what sort of resolution he or she seeks. In many cases, all that the employee wants is an apology and an end to the offending conduct. At the other extreme, the employee may want to leave the employer's employment, but with some settlement monies in hand. Thus, whether the complaining employee should be reinstated depends, in large part, on whether he wants to be reinstated. If he does, he may want to be reinstated to the same job that he had before (he may like the environment in which he works, the people surrounding him, and even find his manager to be a good mentor) or to another comparable position elsewhere in the company. Of course, if he does go back to work with the same manager, she must be counseled that any repeat of the offending conduct will result in her immediate termination. The complaining party should be urged to come forward to senior management if there are any further problems. Management should periodically follow up with the employee to make certain that there are no such problems.

Hypothetical 3—Employees and the Coffee Room

XYZ Manufacturing is a medium-sized manufacturing company employing 63 people. All but four of XYZ's employees are men, and most of them are young and single. The XYZ plant is located in a semi-rural area in the upper Midwest. Because employees are given only 30 minutes for a meal break, meals must be eaten in XYZ's coffee room.

Ms. White, XYZ's 56-year-old receptionist, regularly eats her lunch in the coffee room at the same time as three men who work in the shipping department. These employees are nothing but respectful when talking directly to Ms. White. However, almost every Monday, when the three shipping employees get together for lunch, they talk among themselves about their dates of the previous weekend. They spend each Friday's meal period discussing their social plans for the coming weekend.

ISSUES TO CONSIDER

- *Are the discussions sexual harassment? Were they directed to Ms. White? Does it matter?*

  An employee may bring a claim of sexual harassment based on conduct that was not directed at the employee. Thus, comments and jokes between two willingly participating employees which are overheard by another employee may give rise to a claim of harassment. Similarly, pictures and other graphics posted in the workplace may support a claim of sexual harassment even if they were not intended to be seen by the complaining employee.

- *Does XYZ have knowledge of the nature of the discussions? Should the company have had knowledge? What if a supervisor was involved?*

  An employer is absolutely liable for sexual harassment (or any form of discrimination) engaged in by one of its managers or supervisors. However, in order for an employer to be held responsible for sexual harassment by rank and file employees, as opposed to supervisors and managers, the employer has to either actually know or reasonably know of the offending conduct. Here, it is likely, given the configuration of the employer's facility, that at some time or another a manager or supervisor walked through the coffee room and overheard the employee's while they were discussing their social plans and exploits.

- *Can an employer limit the types of things discussed by employees on their own time? What about freedom of speech?*

  Contrary to the belief of most Americans, there simply is no such thing as free speech in the work place, unless the work place happens to be the government. Private employers simply are not governed by the First Amendment guarantees of free speech. On the contrary, not only is an employer not obligated to allow employees to engage in any sort of conversation they want, but an employer has an affirmative obligation to prevent employees from discussing matters that might constitute harassment or discrimination.

All three of the foregoing hypotheticals have the potential to create a liability exposure to the employer. As demonstrated by these hypotheticals, workplace sexual harassment can arise in a variety of contexts and can be difficult to recognize by the untrained eye.

Assessment Of Liability

As with any other type of employment-related discrimination, an employer is absolutely liable under Title VII as well as under most state anti-discrimination laws for quid pro quo sexual harassment by a managing agent of the employer. Managing agents can include officers, directors and supervisors. The employer may be liable even when there is no actual knowledge of such harassment by the employer. The Supreme Court has rejected the contention that an employer is strictly liable for hostile environment harassment by non-managing agent employees of which it had no knowledge. However, if the employer knew or reasonably should have known of the unlawful conduct of any non-managing agent employees, then the employer could be liable for those acts of harassment.

Not only can an employer be liable for sexual harassment by its employees (both supervisors and non-supervisors), it can even be liable for harassment committed by a third party, such as a customer or vendor. According to sexual harassment guidelines issued by the EEOC and upheld by several courts, if the employer knew or should have known about third-party harassment of employees and failed to take corrective measures, the employer is liable. Such corrective measures might very well require the employer to go so far as to stop doing business with the third-party harasser.

Potential Damages

As noted above, under Title VII an employer can be held liable for the same types of damages arising out of sexual harassment as from any other form of discrimination. This includes damages for emotional distress and punitive damages, which are statutorily limited.[58] However, punitive-damage awards are not limited under some state sexual harassment laws. In one recent case, a California jury awarded over $7 million in damages to a legal secretary who claimed that she had been sexually harassed by an attorney while working for Baker & McKenzie, the largest law firm in the world. Fully $6.9 million of this award was for punitive damages. The parties subsequently agreed to a

---

[58] As amended in 1991, the maximum amount of damages is dependent upon the size of an employer: 15–100 employes, $50,000; 101–200 employees, $100,000; 201–500 employees, $200,000; and 501 or more employees, $300,000.

settlement in excess of $3 million and agreed not to file appeals. As a result of the size of this and other state court verdicts, employees often choose to bring their claims of sexual harassment in state, rather than federal, court.

Wrongful Discharge

The most significant employment law development of the last two decades has been in the area of "wrongful discharge."[59] In most states, this body of law has placed limits on the previously unrestricted right of an employer to discharge "at-will" an employee. While the precise parameters of wrongful discharge claims vary from state to state and are undergoing continual statutory and judicial development and refinement, it is apparent that an employer that discharges an employee is no longer free from the possibility of legal challenge.

The "Employment-At-Will" Doctrine

For the past century, employment relationships in this country generally have been subject to the "employment at-will" doctrine. Under this principle, the employer and the employee are free to terminate the employment relationship at any time, for any reason, with or without prior notice.[60]

The employment at-will doctrine finds its roots in English laws governing the relationships between employers and employees. Early English "common law"[61] generally provided for some sort of job security for workers. The English courts felt that because of the economic realities of the times, employees were dependent on their employers for many of the basic necessities of life. As a result, employees were given protections against discharge in the absence of the employer having a good cause or reason to do so. Prior to and during the eighteenth century, the English courts developed a presumption that unless an employment agreement contained a provision to the contrary, there was an implied one-year employment term, and employment could only be terminated earlier for good cause.

---

[59] Courts in various jurisdictions interchangeably use the terms *wrongful discharge, wrongful termination, unlawful discharge, unfair termination* and *unfair dismissal,* among others.

[60] There are several long-standing exceptions to employment at-will. The first of these is for company executives, entertainers, athletes and other highly compensated employees who have sufficient individual bargaining power to obtain written employment contracts. These contracts usually are for a fixed term and permit early termination only in case of specified forms of misconduct or non-performance. Almost all collective-bargaining agreements negotiated by unions provide that covered employees can only be discharged for good cause. Finally, federal and state employees covered by civil service laws cannot be discharged without good cause, and only after a hearing, and subject to court review.

While these exceptions encompass substantial numbers of employees, non-union, private-sector employers account for over 60 percent of the American workforce. For these approximately 70 million employees, there has been no general protection from the at-will doctrine.

[61] Common law is that body of law developed by judicial interpretation and not contained in legislative enactments.

This presumption changed with the coming of the nineteenth century and the Industrial Revolution. The English courts began to emphasize the freedom of the employer and the employee to negotiate the terms of their relationship. The length of the relationship and the circumstances under which it could be terminated were among these terms. As a practical matter, however, the bargaining power of employers and employees was substantially unequal, and employers were able to obtain almost unlimited rights to sever the employment relationship.

Borrowing liberally from English law, the employment at-will doctrine was first articulated in an American legal treatise in 1877.[62] Under this rule, "a general or indefinite hiring is prima facie a hiring at-will." While the presumption of at-will employment was rebuttable, the employee had the burden of establishing that his or her employment was for an agreed-upon term or was subject to termination only for good cause. The employment at-will rule was adopted by the vast majority of American states, either by statute or by case law.

During the last 50 years, however, there has been an ever-increasing political, social and intellectual movement against at-will employment.

Labor arbitrators, called upon to interpret and apply collective bargaining agreements, have written tens of thousands of published arbitration awards analyzing the right of an employer to discharge an employee. Almost universally, these arbitrators found an express-contract provision requiring good cause for discharge or they implied such a requirement into the contract. The general considerations that evolved from these cases include the following: (1) Was the employee guilty of misconduct or poor performance? (2) Did the employer follow proper procedures in handling the employee's discipline and discharge? and (3) Was discharge too severe a penalty for the employee's offense? In applying these considerations, the employer has the burden of persuasion.

Since the end of the Second World War, there has been an accelerated decline in loyalty between employer and employee. For millions of Americans, the workplace has become the primary source of individual identity and a prime social unit. As a result, discharge has come to be viewed as the "capital punishment of the industrial world" and employees are no longer willing to defer to the unilateral decisions of their employer to discharge or demote.

The Civil Rights Act of 1964 was another catalyst in the demise of the at-will employment doctrine. Although Title VII only prohibited certain specified forms of employment discrimination, employers had to articulate reasonable, fair bases for their actions as part of their defense to claims of discrimination. As a result, employers, employees and government regulators became sensitized to the concept of fairness in the employment relationship.

---

[62] H. Wood, *A Treatise on the Law of Master and Servant*, § 134 (1st Ed. 1877).

By the late 1960s the United States had become a highly litigious society. Citizens and their attorneys, often working on a contingency-fee basis, were willing to take on the government and other established institutions in the courtroom. Employees became more and more aware of their rights and their power. This trend was compounded by the civil disobedience movements of that decade, when employees began to question the orders of managers and supervisors that they felt were illegal, unsafe or wrong. Both the Vietnam War and Watergate further eroded the confidence of the general citizenry in their government and of employees in their employers.

In the late 1970s and early 1980s, the at-will doctrine began to collapse. Court after court held that there were remedies for non-union, non-governmental employees who were discharged without good cause. During the last 20 years, courts have developed a wide array of exceptions to the at-will rule.[63] These developments all have contributed to the ever-increasing number of wrongful discharge claims.

Theories Of Wrongful Discharge

The legal bases for wrongful discharge claims can generally be grouped into three major categories:

1. Violation of public policy

2. Breach of an express or implied contract to discharge only for good cause

3. Breach of an implied covenant of good faith and fair dealing

Discharge In Violation Of Public Policy

Over two-thirds of all states now recognize an exception to at-will employment when an employee's discharge violates public policy. The employer's liability grows out of the duty legally imposed on all employers to implement the public policies of the state. Such liability is independent of any agreement, express or implied, between an employer and an employee. Therefore, the employer cannot avoid liability for a wrongful discharge that is in violation of public policy by the simple expedient of including at-will language in its employee handbook, employment documentation or employment contracts. Similarly, while length of an employee's service is a factor looked at by many courts in implied contract cases, it has no bearing on a public policy claim that is not based upon contract. Even probationary employees can bring a claim of discharge in violation of public policy.

---

[63] When an employee brings a claim of wrongful discharge without good cause, he or she often makes associated claims as well. Among these are claims for promissory estoppel, intentional or negligent infliction of emotional distress, interference with contractual relations or prospective economic advantage, defamation, invasion of privacy, fraud, negligent misrepresentation, false imprisonment, negligent hiring, negligent supervision and loss of consortium.

In some states, public policy can form the basis for a wrongful discharge lawsuit only if the policy is set forth in a statute or regulation.[64] In other states, public policy also can be established by court decision.[65] In those states that follow the latter rule, there tend to be a greater number of wrongful discharge claims. This tendency develops because the courts are free to recognize a broader range of public policies than the state legislatures may have enacted. Most courts, however, are hesitant to recognize a public policy unless there has been prior legislative or judicial action.[66]

Whatever the source of public policy, the exception to at-will employment usually is limited to those cases where "clearly defined" or "firmly established" public policies are affected by the employer's discharge of an employee. The exception does not apply if the interests of the employer and the employee are entirely private in nature and not a matter of public concern.[67] An employee can pursue a wrongful discharge claim only if his or her discharge affects a public right.

While the type of conduct that might constitute such a violation differs from state to state, public policy claims may arise when an employer discharges an employee for (1) refusing to participate in illegal activity, (2) performing a public obligation, (3) exercising a legal right, (4) reporting employer wrongdoing or (5) performing an act that public policy encourages or refusing to perform an act that public policy condemns.

The most strongly established claim of discharge in violation of public policy involves the termination of an employee who refuses to commit an unlawful act.[68] An employee is protected from having to decide between keeping his or her job and complying with the law. Examples of this type of claim are employees who allege that they have been discharged for refusing to violate health and safety laws, commit perjury or violate antitrust laws. An employee can make such a claim even in the absence of an explicit statute proscribing discharge on such grounds.

A second public policy exception protects employees against discharge for performing lawful acts. The lawful act may involve the performance of a legal duty, such as responding to a subpoena,[69] or may consist of the exercise of a legal right such as refusing to undergo a drug-and-alcohol screening where the law protects such refusal. In some situations, such as when an employee files a workers' compensation claim or complains about an unsafe condition in the workplace, the discharge of an employee may be

---

[64] New York—*Kovalesky v AMC Associated Merchandizing Corp.*, 551 F.Supp. 544 (S.D.N.Y. 1982); Texas—*Sabine Pilot Service, Inc. v. Hauk*, 687 S.W.2d 733 (1983).

[65] Illinois—*Palmateer v. International Harvester Co.*, 85 Ill.2d 124 (1981); New Jersey—*Pierce v. Ortho Pharmaceutical Corp.*, 84 N.J. 58 (1980).

[66] California—*Foley v. Interactive Data Corp.*, 47 Cal.3d 654 (1988).

[67] Pennsylvania—*Marsh v. Boyle*, 366 Pa. Super. 1 (1987); Maine—*Larrabee v. Penobscot Frozen Foods, Inc.*, 486 A.2d 97 (1984).

[68] California—*Tameny v. Atlantic Richfield Co.*, 164 Cal. Rptr. 839 (1980); Indiana—*McClanahan v. Remington Freight Lines, Inc.*, 517 N.E.2d 390 (1988); Massachusetts—*DeRose v. Putnam Management Co.*, 398 Mass. 205 (1986).

[69] Idaho—*Jackson v. Minidoka Irrigation District*, 98 Idaho 330 (1977); Oregon—*Nees v. Hocks*, 272 Or. 210 (1975).

expressly prohibited by state statute.[70] Other states have permitted this type of public policy claim without any such express statutory provision.[71]

Yet another type of public policy claim involves employee "whistle blowers." These cases usually involve an employee who is discharged for disclosure of some form of unlawful conduct by his or her employer. Even those states that recognize this exception are divided as to whether the disclosure must be made to public authorities or whether the disclosure can be made within the employer's own organization. There also are questions as to whether an employee who makes a false accusation is protected from discharge or whether an employee has to exhaust the employer's internal complaint procedure before going public.

Only a few states that recognize a public policy exception to the at-will doctrine have extended it to whistle blowers.[72] Many states, however, have adopted laws that address particular issues, such as employment discrimination and workers' compensation. These laws usually ban retaliation for either the filing of a claim or testifying in a case brought by another employee. In a few states, broad protection against whistle blowers has received legislative recognition.

Breach Of An Express Or Implied Contract

An employer and an employee are free to enter into an express written or oral contract governing the terms and conditions of their relationship. Such a contract may specify the duration of the employment and the circumstances under which the employment relationship may be terminated. A contract can provide that the employee may be discharged only for good cause or only for specifically listed reasons.

Even in the absence of an express written or oral employment contract, at-will employment may be supplanted by an implied-in-fact contract requiring good cause for discharge. Such an implied contract may be based upon the "totality of circumstances" of employment. These circumstances can include the length of the employment relationship, commendations and promotions received by the employee, a lack of criticism of the employee's work, written employer policies, employer practices and industry-wide practices relating to the discipline and discharge of employees.[73]

Of course, there are wide variations in state laws relating to the formation and enforcement of contracts. The kinds of evidence that can be used to prove the existence of an employment contract, the types of conduct that constitute breach of such a

---

[70] California—Labor Code § 6310.

[71] West Virginia—*Cordle v. General Hugh Mercer Corp.*, 325 S.E.2d 111 (1984).

[72] Connecticut—*Sheets v. Teddy's Frosted Foods, Inc.*, 179 Conn. 471 (1980); Kansas—*Palmer v. Brown*, 752 P.2d 685 (1988); Michigan—*Watasek v. Michigan Department of Mental Health*, 372 N.W.2d 617 (1985)

[73] California—*Pugh v. See's Candies, Inc.*, 116 Cal.App.3d 311 (1981).

contract, the defenses available to an employer faced with such a claim and the possible remedies also vary from state to state.

Breach Of The Implied Covenant Of Good Faith And Fair Dealing

Of the three exceptions to the at-will employment rule, the one that has resulted in the most divergence among the various states is the implied covenant exception. In some states, violation of the implied covenant of good faith and fair dealing can result in an employer's liability for breaching the employment contract. In a lesser number of states, an employee also may recover tort damages, including damages for emotional distress and punitive damages. Some states refuse to recognize a claim for breach of the implied covenant, reasoning that it is inconsistent with the absolute freedom of an employer to discharge an at-will employee. To date, most states have not addressed this issue and less than 15 have expressly recognized an action based upon breach of the implied covenant.

Most states that do apply an implied covenant of good faith and fair dealing to employment relationships have not construed the covenant to require good cause for termination. The implied covenant, in and of itself, does not convert an at-will relationship to one that only can be terminated for good cause.[74] In these states, the implied covenant is nothing more than an additional theory available to an employee who is challenging his or her discharge on the basis that it violated an express or implied contract.

While "good faith" is not susceptible to a simple definition, the covenant serves to prevent an employer from engaging in any unjustified conduct that would deny the employee the reasonably expected benefits of the employment contract.

Summary

Wrongful discharge is a developing body of law, differing substantially in its particulars from state to state. While this section of *The EPL Book* has addressed some of the principle trends and issues involved in this area, it is not intended to serve as a guide to the law in any given jurisdiction. For a comprehensive understanding of wrongful discharge issues in a particular state, employers or other interested persons should consult with a knowledgeable labor law practitioner in that state.

---

[74] Arizona—*Wagenseller v. Scottsdale Memorial Hospital*, 147 Ariz. 370 (1985); Connecticut—*Magnam v. Anaconda Industries, Inc.*, 193 Conn. 558 (1984).

Other State Common-Law And Quasi Contract Claims

In light of today's increasingly litigious environment, it is not unusual to find a variety of common-law tort, quasi contract, or other state law claims attached to a complaint alleging discrimination, sexual harassment or wrongful discharge. Once again, these claims vary widely from state to state, and it is well beyond the scope of this work to attempt to review, define or even to classify them.

An employer should be aware that an employee may bring a claim for, among other things, assault, battery, false imprisonment, slander, libel, defamation, fraud, negligent misrepresentation, conversion, promissory estoppel, interference with contractual relations or interference with prospective business advantage.

In some states, some or all of these claims have been codified. In other jurisdictions, only portions of these claims can be found in statute. Not all states recognize all of the above causes of action. In other states, employees may bring suit against their employer based on all of the theories mentioned above.

2 Frequency And Economic Impact Of Wrongful Employment Practices Charges

In addition to understanding the laws governing unfair or wrongful employment, employers and others should attempt to quantify the potential for loss in failing to comply with state common law and various wrongful employment practices statutes. Reviewing compiled data on the frequency of wrongful employment practices claims and their economic impact as well as the results of national surveys of employer concerns can help quantify this exposure.

This section of *The EPL Book* contains charts, tables and discussions of compiled data as well as the findings of national surveys that illustrate the historic frequency and economic impact of claims filed under the principal federal anti-discrimination statutes. Information is provided from the following sources:

- EEOC charge data

- Jury verdict EPL litigation award data

- Employment Practices National Survey

- 1997 Employment Litigation Survey

EEOC Charge Data[1]

Employees who feel they have been discriminated against by their employer may file charges with the Equal Employment Opportunity Commission (EEOC) directly, or with

---

[1] Information on the number of charges received by the EEOC and the monetary benefits obtained through EEOC enforcement of the above statutes, as well as the frequency of lawsuits filed by the EEOC and the economic benefits obtained for employees through EEOC litigation, is provided. The data presented does not reflect all wrongful employment practices claims and litigation activity for several reasons: Data published by the EEOC includes statistics from some, but not all FEPAs, Not all employment-discrimination disputes result in the filing of charges with the EEOC or a FEPA, Not all wrongful employment practices litigation involves the EEOC or FEPA. Many lawsuits are filed directly against an employer by an employee. These direct suits, as well as suits filed by FEPAs, are not included in the EEOC litigation data presented. The amount of economic benefits obtained for employees does not include pre-suit settlements, the results of arbitration o other dispute resolution proceedings, or legal expenses.

state or local Fair Employment Practices Agencies (FEPAs). FEPAs may attempt to resolve claims directly, or they may seek EEOC assistance in achieving resolution. The EEOC reviews all charges filed with or referred to that office that attempts to resolve the dispute without formal litigation. If the decision is made to file suit against the employer, the EEOC can initiate the suit or intervene in a suit filed by a state FEPA. Both the EEOC and FEPAs may file suits on behalf of a class or group of employees or on behalf of an individual employee.

The following tables and charts illustrate the number of wrongful employment practices charges received by the EEOC and the dollar amount of benefits obtained for employees through EEOC enforcement of various anti-discrimination statutes[2]. The number of charges received includes claims that ultimately result in private civil litigation. The dollar amount of benefits obtained is limited to cases that did not involve private civil litigation and therefore dramatically understate the amounts recovered, because a large percentage of EEOC filings result in private litigation. Information regarding the frequency and economic impact of EEOC litigation is presented in the subsection captioned "EEOC Litigation Data" beginning on page 48.

The data used in preparing the tables and charts included in this section was obtained from numerous EEOC studies and reports. Some of the data includes charges in which only the EEOC is involved. In other instances, the data includes charges filed with Fair Employment Practices Agencies (FEPAs). Also, the percentages shown in the tables and charts may total more or less than 100% due to rounding, claims containing multiple allegations or alleged violations of more than one statute.

Frequency Of Wrongful Employment Practices Charges (All Statutes Combined)

Chart 1 illustrates the number of wrongful employment practices charges received by the EEOC during the period 1986 through 1997. The number of charge filings increased steadily from a low of 59,411 in 1989 and reached a peak of over 90,000 in 1994. Since that time, the number of charges filed declined in 1995 and 1996, but increased in 1997. This reduction in filings since 1994 may be due to increased use of arbitration, mediation or other methods of dispute resolution. The EEOC has not published an explanation for the increase in filings in 1997.

Because the EEOC began enforcement of the ADA in July 1992, the number of filings shown for the years prior to 1992 do not include charges under this statute.

---

[2] These statutes include Title VII of the Civil Rights Act of 1964 (Title VII), the Americans with Disabilities Act (ADA) of 1990, The Equal Pay Act (EPA) of 1963 and the Age Discrimination in Employment Act (ADEA) of 1967 (as amended). Overall claim statistics are shown, as well as statistics regarding claims filed under each statute.

Chart 1

**Total Charges Filed
(All Statutes)**

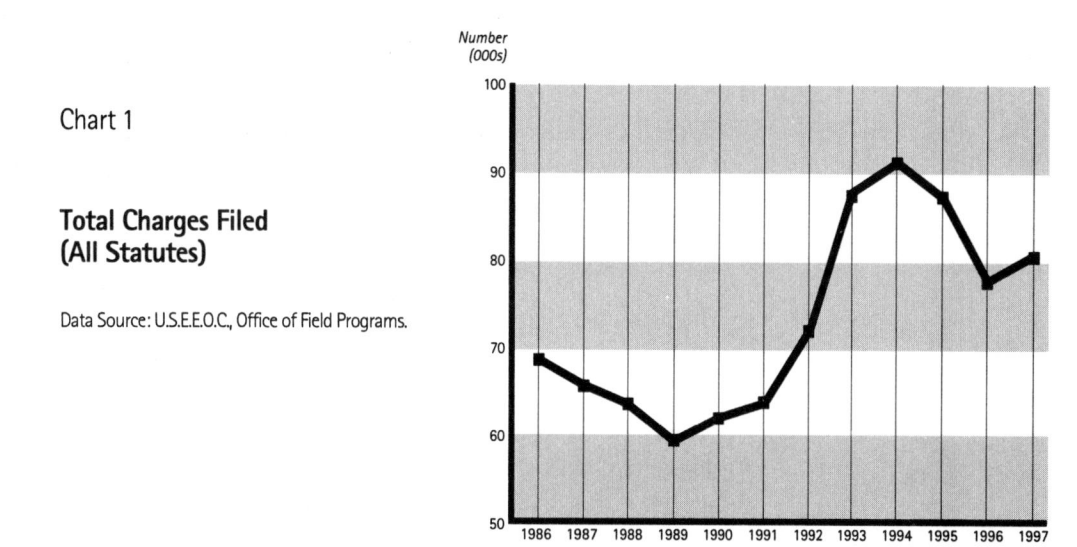

Data Source: U.S.E.E.O.C., Office of Field Programs.

Economic Impact Of Wrongful Employment Practices
(All Statutes Combined)

Chart 2 depicts the monetary benefits obtained by claimants as a result of EEOC enforcement activity during the period 1986 through 1997. These benefits include back pay, compensatory damages and medical expenses. During this 11-year period, the dollar amount of benefits obtained has increased steadily from a low of $48 million in 1987 to over $176 million in 1997. Benefits during the years 1992 through 1997 include those obtained as respects claims involving the ADA.

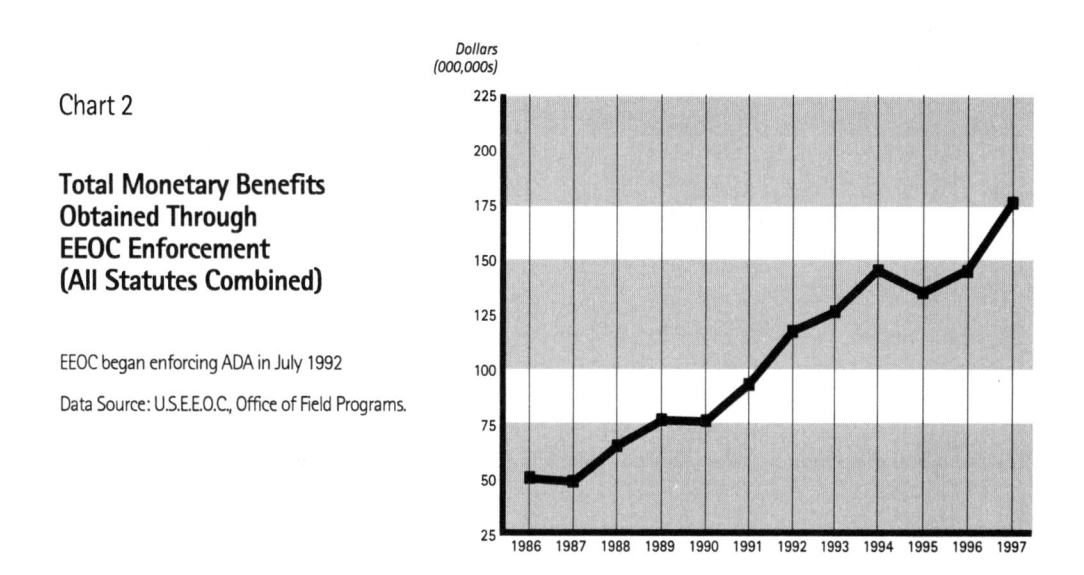

Chart 2

**Total Monetary Benefits
Obtained Through
EEOC Enforcement
(All Statutes Combined)**

EEOC began enforcing ADA in July 1992

Data Source: U.S.E.E.O.C., Office of Field Programs.

Frequency And Economic Impact Of Claims Under Title VII

Frequency Of Alleged Title VII Violations Filed With EEOC

Chart 3 reflects the total number of charges received each year by the EEOC during the period 1990 through 1997 that allege Title VII violations.

Chart 3

Total Charge Receipts (Title VII)

Data Source: U.S.E.E.O.C., Office of Research, Information & Planning.

Receipts include all charges filed under Title VII, as well as those filed concurrently under ADA, ADEA and EPA.

Number of Charges Filed

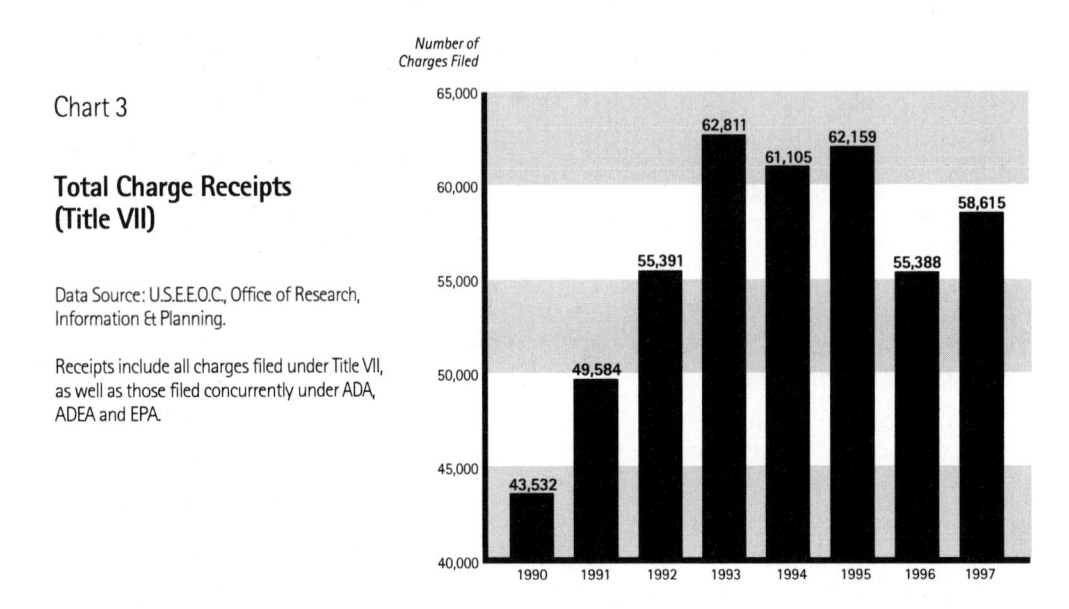

Year	Charges
1990	43,532
1991	49,584
1992	55,391
1993	62,811
1994	61,105
1995	62,159
1996	55,388
1997	58,615

Table 1 lists the most frequent bases of discrimination alleged in claims filed with the EEOC during 1995, the most recent year for which this information is available. Discrimination based on race was the most frequent charge (37%), followed closely by discrimination based on sex (33%). Discrimination based on religion (2%) was the least frequent charge.

Table 1
Charges By Basis Of Discrimination (Title VII)(1995)

Data Source: EEOC 1995 Annual Report.

Category	Number	% of Total
Race	30,047	37%
Sex	26,214	33%
Retaliation	15,377	19%
National Origin	7,047	9%
Religion	1,586	2%

THE EPL BOOK

Title VII Claims By Issue **(1994)**

Chart 4 shows the most frequently alleged categories of discrimination (issues) in claims filed under Title VII during 1994, the most recent year for which this information is available. An average of 28% of all claims filed during this year contain allegations of wrongful discharge.

Chart 4

Most Frequent Charges Filed With EEOC (Title VII) By Issue (1994)

Many claims contain multiple charges/issues.
Data Source: E.E.O.C. 1994 Annual Report.

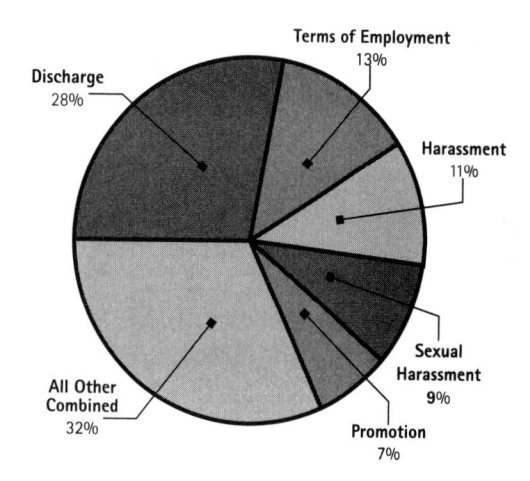

- Discharge 28%
- Terms of Employment 13%
- Harassment 11%
- Sexual Harassment 9%
- Promotion 7%
- All Other Combined 32%

Economic Impact

Chart 5 reflects the total monetary benefits obtained as a result of EEOC enforcement of Title VII during the period 1990 through 1997. The amounts shown do not include monetary benefits obtained through EEOC litigation. The chart includes the number of persons benefited and the average benefit received by each person. Although the number of persons who benefited each year has declined since 1992, the average benefit received per person has increased. The EEOC has not published a specific explanation for this trend. However, the increase in average benefit received may be due to the availability of compensatory and punitive damages as provided for in the Civil Rights Act of 1991. Data regarding the number of persons benefiting and the average benefit received is not available for 1997.

Chart 5

Monetary Benefits Obtained Through EEOC Enforcement (Title VII)

Data Source: U.S.E.E.O.C., Office of Program Operations.

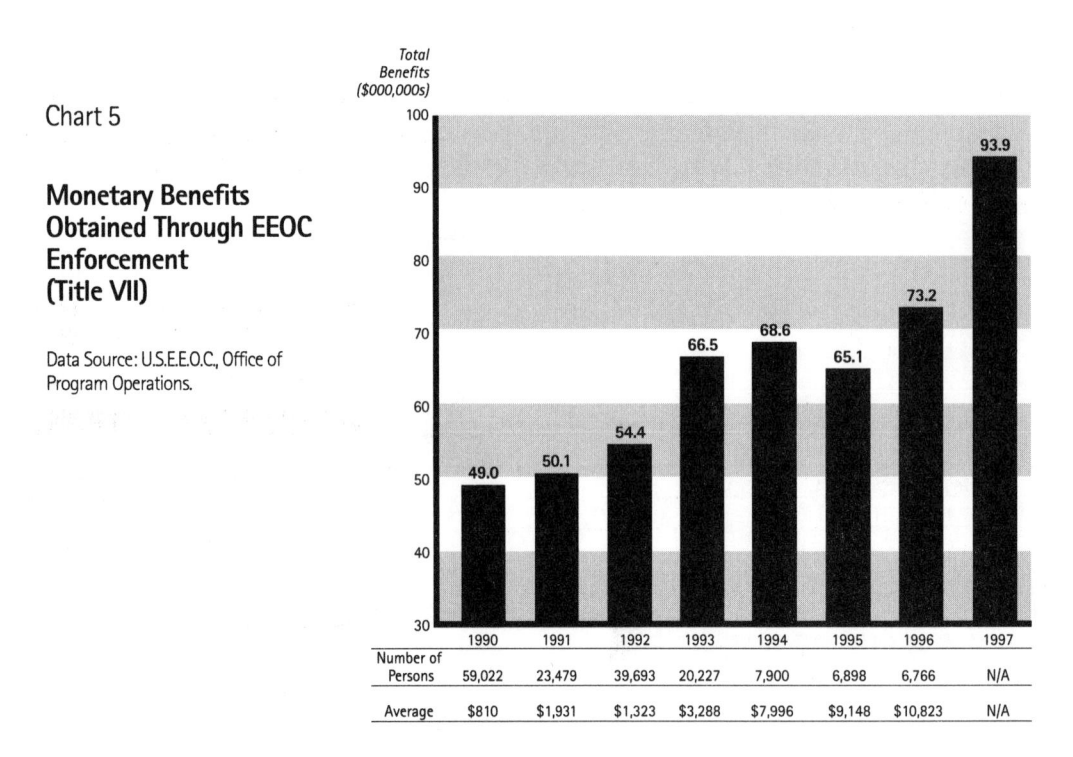

Total Benefits ($000,000s)

Year	1990	1991	1992	1993	1994	1995	1996	1997
Total Benefits	49.0	50.1	54.4	66.5	68.6	65.1	73.2	93.9
Number of Persons	59,022	23,479	39,693	20,227	7,900	6,898	6,766	N/A
Average	$810	$1,931	$1,323	$3,288	$7,996	$9,148	$10,823	N/A

Frequency And Economic Impact Of Claims Under ADA

Frequency Of Alleged ADA Violations

Chart 6 shows the number of claims received by the EEOC during the period 1992 through 1997 that allege ADA violations. The ADA became effective July 26, 1992, and the EEOC began enforcement of this statute on that date. The number of charges filed has remained relatively steady since 1994.

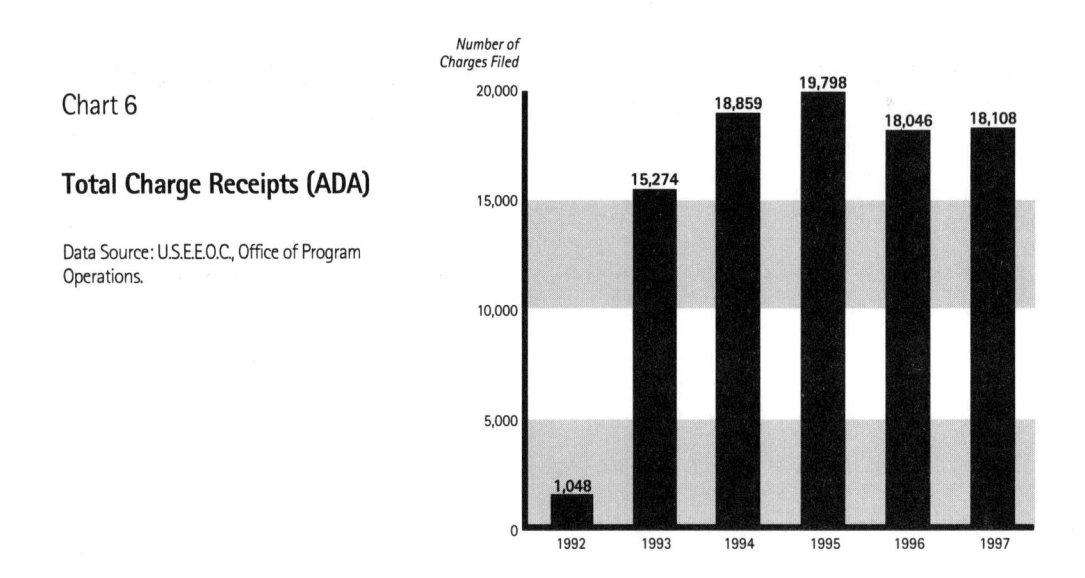

Chart 6

Total Charge Receipts (ADA)

Data Source: U.S.E.E.O.C., Office of Program Operations.

Number of Charges Filed

Year	1992	1993	1994	1995	1996	1997
Charges	1,048	15,274	18,859	19,798	18,046	18,108

By Impairment

Table 2 lists the physical and mental impairments most frequently cited in charges alleging ADA violations during the period July 26, 1992, through September 30, 1997. Eighteen percent of all claims alleged discrimination based on impairment of the back. Only 4% of claims cite heart-related disability.

Table 2
Impairments Most Cited (ADA)
(7/26/92–9/30/97)

Data Source: EEOC Office of Program Operations.

Impairment	Number of Claims	% of Total*
Back	15,942	18%
Emotional/Psychiatric	12,018	13%
Neurological	9,994	11%
Extremities	8,490	9%
Heart	3,675	4%
All Other	18,729	21%

*Many claims contain multiple allegations.

By Violation

Table 3 shows that more than half of all ADA violations cited during the period July 26, 1992, through September 30, 1997 involved unlawful discharge. Failure to provide reasonable accommodations for disabled persons represented almost 30% of all ADA claims.

Table 3
Violations Most Cited (ADA)
(7/26/92–9/30/97)

Data Source: EEOC Office of Program Operations.

Violation	Number of Claims	% of Total*
Discharge	47,510	52%
Failure to Accommodate	26,302	29%
Harassment	11,404	13%
Hiring	8,532	9%
Discipline	7,299	8%
All Other	19,352	21%

*Many claims contain multiple allegations.

Total ADA Claims By Issue

Chart 7 shows the percentage of alleged ADA violations by issue during 1994, the most recent year for which this information is available. While some claims allege more than one category of discriminatory act, one-third of all claims contained allegations of wrongful discharge.

Chart 7

Most Frequent Charges Filed With EEOC (ADA) By Issue (1994)

Data Source: E.E.O.C. 1994 Annual Report.

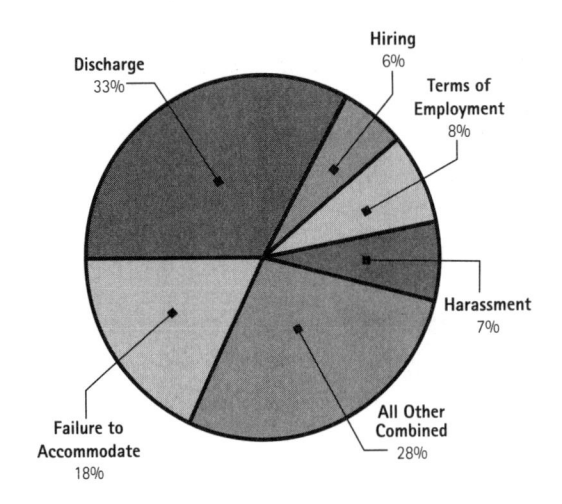

- Discharge 33%
- Hiring 6%
- Terms of Employment 8%
- Harassment 7%
- All Other Combined 28%
- Failure to Accommodate 18%

Economic Impact

Chart 8 reflects the total monetary benefits obtained as a result of EEOC enforcement of ADA during the period 1992 through 1997. Also included is the number of persons benefited and the average benefit received by each person. The average benefit almost doubled from 1993 to 1994 and has remained relatively constant since that time.

Chart 8

Monetary Benefits Obtained Through EEOC Enforcement (ADA)

Data Source: U.S.E.E.O.C., Office of Program Operations.

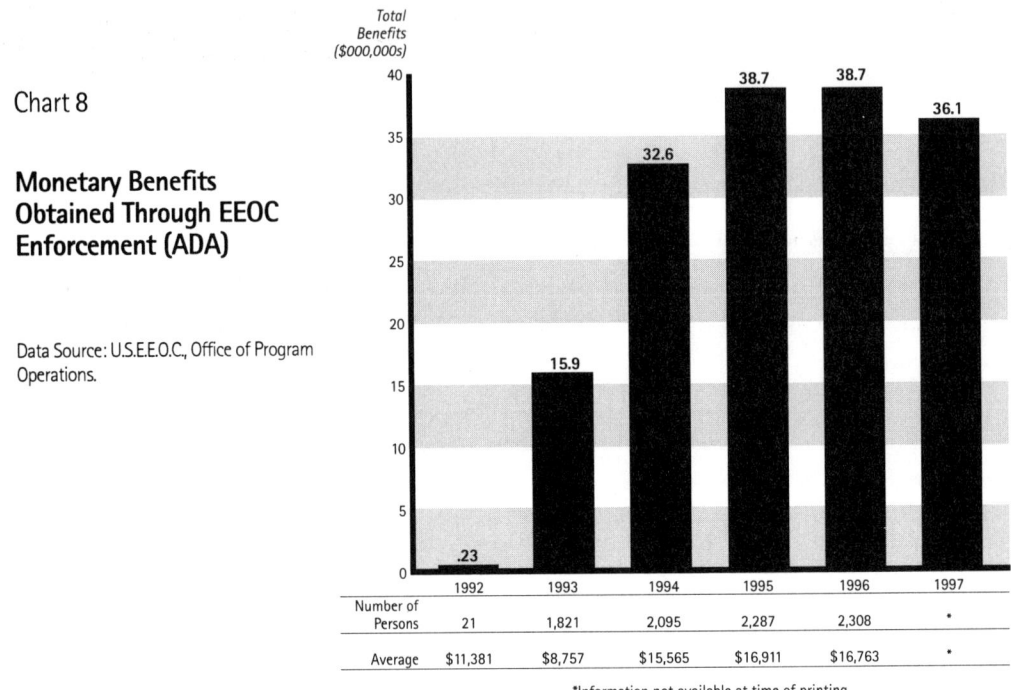

Total Benefits ($000,000s)

Year	Total Benefits	Number of Persons	Average
1992	.23	21	$11,381
1993	15.9	1,821	$8,757
1994	32.6	2,095	$15,565
1995	38.7	2,287	$16,911
1996	38.7	2,308	$16,763
1997	36.1	*	*

*Information not available at time of printing.

Frequency And Economic Impact Of Claims Under ADEA

Frequency Of Alleged Violations

Chart 9 reflects the number of claims received by the EEOC from 1990 through 1997 that allege ADEA violations. The frequency of claim filings reached a peak in 1993, but has declined since that time and remained constant in 1996 and 1997. The EEOC has not published a specific explanation for the high number of claims filed from 1992 through 1994, nor for the reduction in filings since 1994. However, employee awareness of ADEA requirements as a result of media attention is considered a possible factor contributing to the high filing rates.

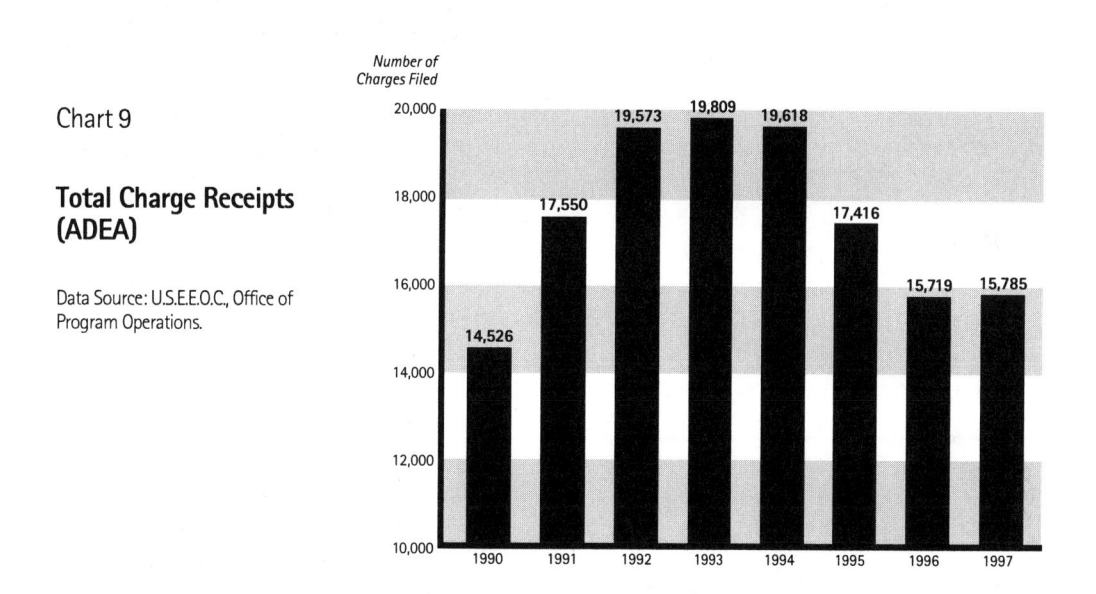

Chart 9

Total Charge Receipts (ADEA)

Data Source: U.S.E.E.O.C., Office of Program Operations.

Year	Number of Charges Filed
1990	14,526
1991	17,550
1992	19,573
1993	19,809
1994	19,618
1995	17,416
1996	15,719
1997	15,785

Total ADEA Claims By Issue

Chart 10 shows the percentage of alleged ADEA violations by category (issue) during 1994, the most recent year for which information is available. While many claims allege more than one category of discriminatory act, 34% of all claims contained allegations of wrongful discharge.

Chart 10

Most Frequent Charges Filed With EEOC (ADEA) By Issue (1994)

Data Source: E.E.O.C. 1994 Annual Report.

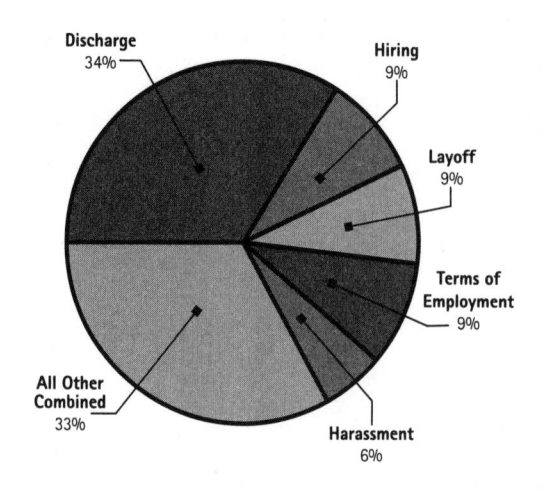

- Discharge 34%
- Hiring 9%
- Layoff 9%
- Terms of Employment 9%
- Harassment 6%
- All Other Combined 33%

Economic Impact

Chart 11 reflects the total monetary benefits obtained through EEOC enforcement of ADEA during the period 1990 through 1996. Also included is the number of persons benefited and the average benefit received by each person. The number of persons who benefited financially has decreased each year during the period. However, the average benefit has risen to a high of over $18,000 in 1996. Total benefits obtained reached a peak of $57 million in 1992. The large recovery amount shown for 1992 may be the result of an extraordinary number of claims filed during this period.

Chart 11

Monetary Benefits Obtained Through EEOC Enforcement (ADEA)

Data Source: U.S.E.E.O.C., Office of Program Operations.

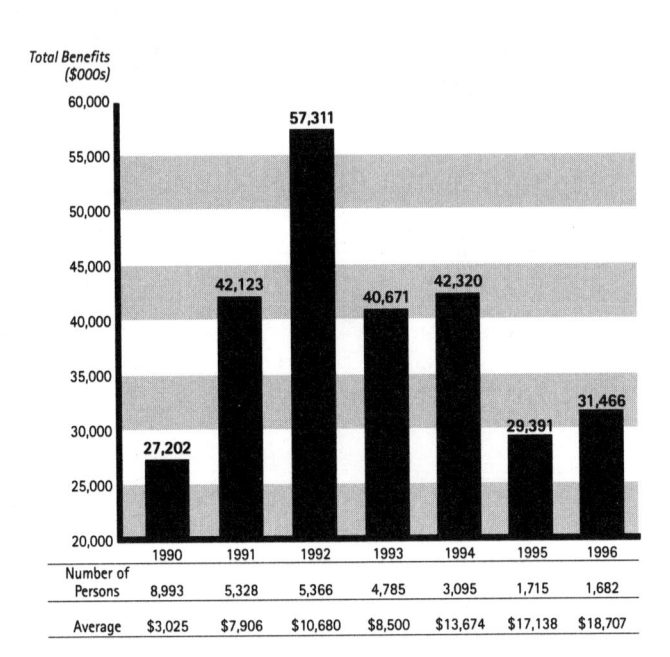

Year	Total Benefits ($000s)	Number of Persons	Average
1990	27,202	8,993	$3,025
1991	42,123	5,328	$7,906
1992	57,311	5,366	$10,680
1993	40,671	4,785	$8,500
1994	42,320	3,095	$13,674
1995	29,391	1,715	$17,138
1996	31,466	1,682	$18,707

Frequency And Economic Impact Of Claims Under The EPA

Frequency Of Alleged Violations

Chart 12 reflects the number of claims received by the EEOC during the period 1990 through 1997 that allege Equal-Pay-Act violations. The frequency of charge filings alleging EPA violations has remained relatively constant over the eight-year period.

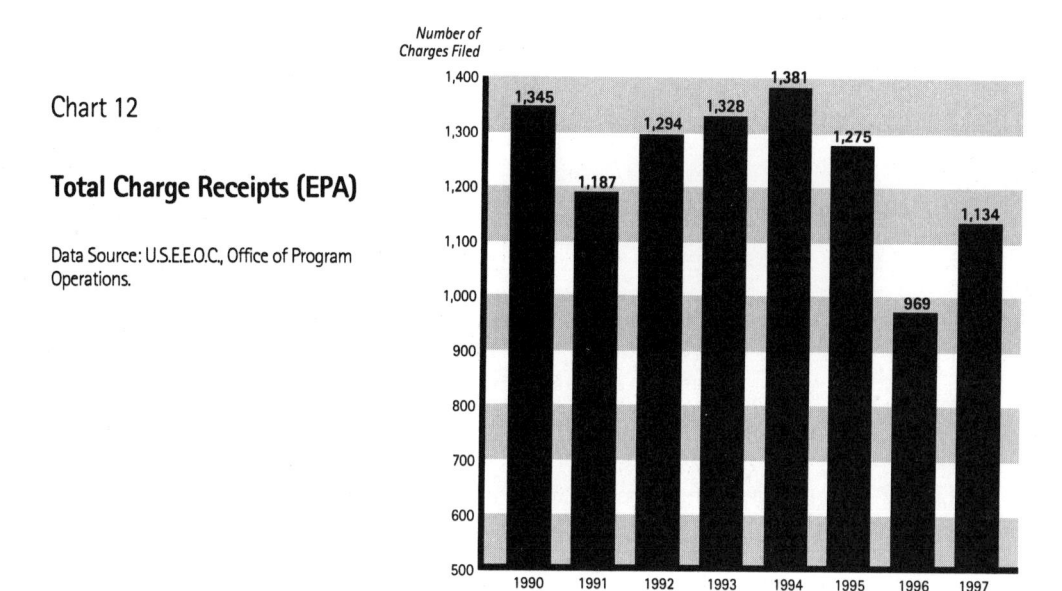

Chart 12

Total Charge Receipts (EPA)

Data Source: U.S.E.E.O.C., Office of Program Operations.

Year	Number of Charges Filed
1990	1,345
1991	1,187
1992	1,294
1993	1,328
1994	1,381
1995	1,275
1996	969
1997	1,134

Total EPA Claims By Issue

Chart 13 shows the percentage of alleged EPA violations by category (issue) during 1994, the most recent year for which information is available. While many claims allege more than one category of discriminatory act, 43% of all claims contained allegations of wage discrimination. Thirteen percent of claims contained allegations of wrongful discharge.

Chart 13

Most Frequent Charges Filed With EEOC (EPA) By Issue (1994)

Data Source: E.E.O.C. 1994 Annual Report.

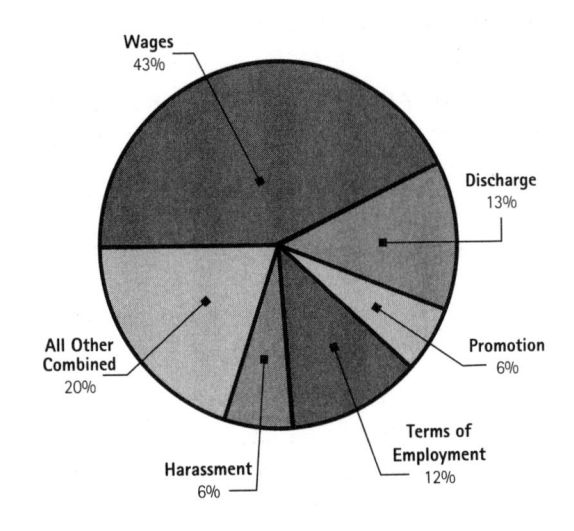

- Wages 43%
- Discharge 13%
- Promotion 6%
- Terms of Employment 12%
- Harassment 6%
- All Other Combined 20%

Economic Impact

Chart 14 reflects the total monetary benefits obtained as a result of EEOC enforcement of the EPA from 1991 through 1997. Also included is the number of persons benefited and the average benefit received by each person. The average benefit jumped dramatically after 1992 and has remained relatively constant since that year, despite the total number of persons benefiting from EEOC enforcement activities declining since 1993.

Chart 14

Monetary Benefits Obtained Through EEOC Enforcement (EPA)

Data Source: U.S.E.E.O.C., Office of Program Operations.

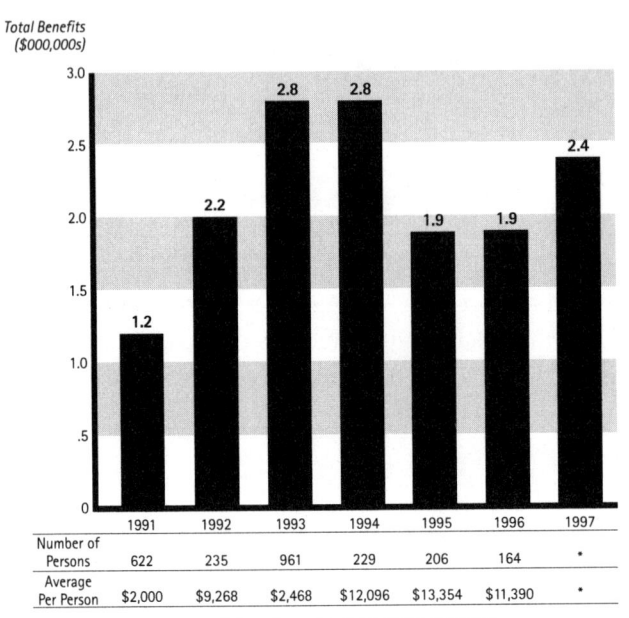

Total Benefits ($000,000s)

	1991	1992	1993	1994	1995	1996	1997
Total Benefits	1.2	2.2	2.8	2.8	1.9	1.9	2.4
Number of Persons	622	235	961	229	206	164	*
Average Per Person	$2,000	$9,268	$2,468	$12,096	$13,354	$11,390	*

*Information not available at time of printing.

EEOC Litigation Data

The following tables and charts illustrate the frequency of EEOC lawsuits filed and the monetary benefits obtained through EEOC litigation. Only a small percentage of wrongful employment practices claims result in litigation. Also, since the EEOC is not involved in all wrongful employment practices litigation, the data presented reflects only a portion of all suits involving wrongful employment practices.

The data regarding EEOC litigation activity as presented below is subject to the following qualifications:

1. EEOC litigation activity is representative of only a small portion of all employment practices litigation activity. Many lawsuits are filed under various state and local statutes. In addition, claims are often resolved through mediation, arbitration or other dispute resolution techniques.

2. Lawsuits initiated by FEPAs may not be referred to the EEOC for assistance in prosecution.

3. Many wrongful employment practices suits allege violations of more than one statute. Accordingly, there is some overlap in the presented statistics when the frequency and results of litigation is illustrated by statute.

4. The EEOC did not begin enforcing the ADA until July 1992. Accordingly, 1993 is the first full year in which the agency enforced (and filed lawsuits) under this statute.

Direct Suits Filed By EEOC—All Statutes Combined

Chart 15 reflects the number of direct suits and interventions filed by the EEOC from 1985 through the first quarter of fiscal year 1998. Data for 1998 is preliminary. For the year 1993 only, the number of suits filed includes pre-suit settlements.

Several factors may account for the reduction in the number of lawsuits filed after 1990. These factors include a decrease in EEOC funding and staffing, an increase in direct suits filed by FEPAs, increased employer awareness and compliance with wrongful employment statutes and an increased use of negotiation, arbitration, mediation or other alternative-dispute-resolution methods. The EEOC has not published an explanation for the dramatic reduction in lawsuits filed during 1996.

Chart 15

**Direct Suits Filed By EEOC
(All Statutes Combined)**

1992–1997 includes suits filed under ADA.

Data Source: E.E.O.C. Litigation Statistics.

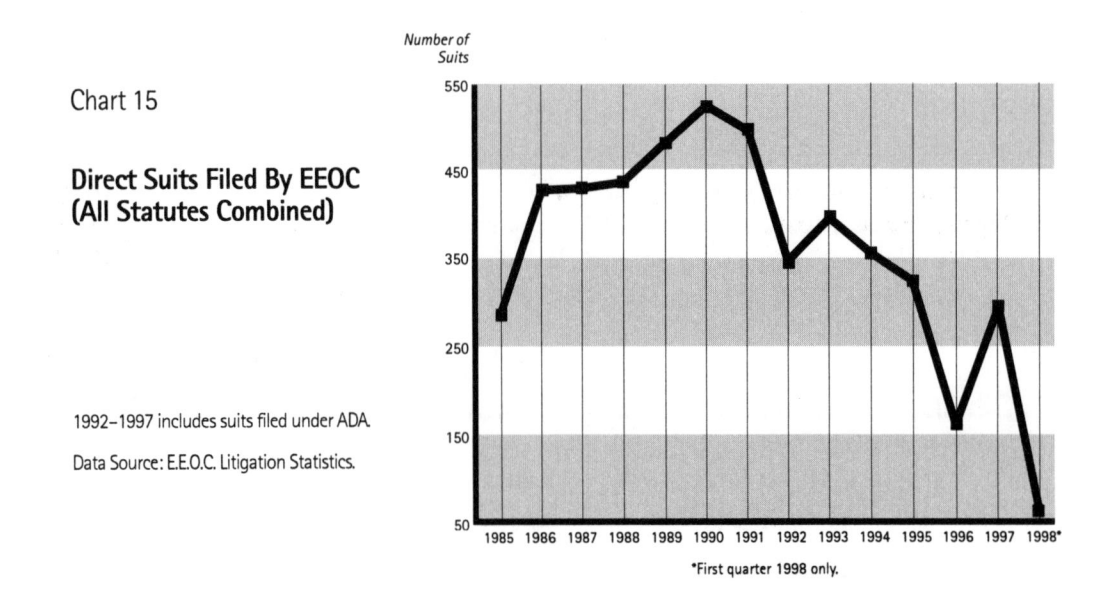

*First quarter 1998 only.

Monetary Benefits Secured Through EEOC Litigation — All Statutes Combined

Chart 16 reflects the monetary benefits obtained as a result of direct suits and interventions filed by the EEOC from 1985 through the first quarter of fiscal year 1998 (1998 data is preliminary). Monetary benefits include wage loss, compensatory damages and, in some cases, punitive damages assessed against an employer. The large amounts obtained in 1991 and 1992 were primarily the result of two cases in which extraordinarily high multi-million dollar verdicts were rendered. The EEOC has not yet published an explanation for the large amount of benefits obtained in 1997.

Chart 16

Monetary Benefits Secured Through EEOC Litigation (All Statutes Combined)

1992–1998 includes suits filed under ADA.

Data Source: E.E.O.C., Office of General Counsel.

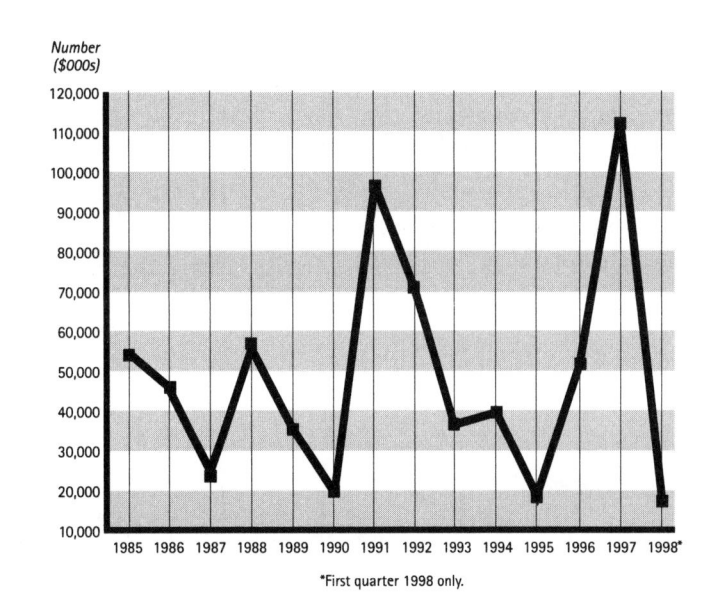

*First quarter 1998 only.

EEOC Suits Filed—By Statute

Table 4 lists the number and percentage of total suits filed by the EEOC (by statute) from 1991 through the first quarter of fiscal year 1998 (1998 data is preliminary). During this seven and a quarter-year period, more than 59% of all suits filed by the EEOC involved alleged Title VII violations and 18% or more involved ADEA violations. Since 1995, more than 20% of all suits filed by the EEOC involved ADA violations.

Table 4
EEOC Suits Filed, By Statute

Data Source: U.S.E.E.O.C., Office of General Counsel.

Statute	1991	1992	1993	1994	1995	1996	1997	1998
Title VII	352	242	260	247	186	105	173	40
(% of Total)	(71%)	(70%)	(65%)	(66%)	(59%)	(65%)	(59%)	(66%)
ADA*	N/A	0	3	35	75	36	76	12
(% of Total)		(0%)	(1%)	(9%)	(24%)	(22%)	(26%)	(20%)
ADEA	102	84	115	75	37	12	35	7
(% of Total)	(21%)	(24%)	(29%)	(20%)	(18%)	(8%)	(11%)	(12%)
EPA	6	2	2	0	1	2	0	0
(% of Total)	(1%)	(1%)	(1%)	(0%)	(neg.)	(4%)	(0%)	(0%)
Other	35	19	18	16	15	6	11	2
(% of Total)	(7%)	(6%)	(5%)	(4%)	(5%)	(4%)	(4%)	(3%)

* EEOC began enforcing ADA in 1992.
"Other" includes charges filed under more than one statute.
Totals more or less than 100% due to rounding and filing of suits under other statutes

Monetary Benefits Obtained Through EEOC Litigation—By Statute

The amount of monetary benefits and the percentage of total benefits obtained (by statute) as a result of EEOC litigation from 1991 through the first quarter of fiscal year 1998 is listed in Table 5 (1998 data is preliminary). In 1992, 1993 and the first quarter of fiscal year 1998, more than 70% of awarded benefits involved litigation under ADEA. However, in 1991, 1994 and 1997, more than 75% of awarded benefits resulted from litigation involving Title VII.

Table 5
Monetary Benefits Obtained Through EEOC Litigation, By Statute
Data Source: U.S.E.E.O.C., Office of General Counsel.

(DOLLAR AMOUNTS IN 000s)

Statute	1991	1992	1993	1994	1995	1996	1997	1998
Title VII	$81,500	$14,700	$7,100	$23,300	$9,000	$19,550	$93,400	$3,100
(% of Total)	(84%)	(21%)	(19%)	(79%)	(48%)	(38%)	(83%)	(17%)
ADA*	N/A	$0	$200	$400	$1,400	$2,400	$900	$600
(% of Total)		(0%)	(1%)	(1%)	(7%)	(5%)	(1%)	(3%)
ADEA	$13,800	$55,500	$26,600	$5,200	$8,000	$10,500	$17,200	$14,600
(% of Total)	(14%)	(78%)	(73%)	(18%)	(42%)	(20%)	(15%)	(78%)
EPA	$100	$200	$100	$46	$200	$0	$66	$0
(% of Total)	(neg.)	(neg.)	(neg.)	(neg.)	(1%)	(0%)	(neg)	(0%)
Other	$1,100	$700	$2,500	$397	$300	$18,800	$300	$300
(% of Total)	(1%)	(1%)	(1%)	(1%)	(2%)	(37%)	(neg)	(2%)

* EEOC began enforcing ADA in 1992.
Includes investigations, pre-suit settlements.
"Other" includes charges filed under more than one statute.

Jury Verdict EPL Litigation Award Data

The following chart and tables illustrate litigation activity as respects all litigated wrongful employment practice claims that resulted in a jury verdict, including litigation involving the EEOC. The information used in preparing this data was obtained from a sampling of employment discrimination jury verdicts for plaintiffs nationwide from 1987 through 1994. Information also was obtained from a sampling of jury verdicts for plaintiffs in cases specifically involving wrongful termination from 1988 through 1995 (1995 data is preliminary).

While the compensatory portion of awards include damages for physical pain and suffering and medical expenses, the largest component of the verdict awards was compensation for emotional distress and wage loss. Not included in the data are arbitration awards, settlements and the results of appeals.

The wrongful employment practice categories shown in the following tables and charts are defined as follows:

Discrimination—A denial of equal treatment because of an employee's race, sex, age, physical or mental disability, marital status, sexual orientation, weight or pregnancy. Allegations may include unequal pay or responsibilities, unfair performance reviews, lack of pay raises, verbal harassment, physical intimidation and unfair disciplinary measures. This category also includes the provision of inferior equipment, assignment to less favorable workshifts or sales territories, denial of opportunity to work overtime, work sabotage or failure to provide an accommodating workplace for disabled persons.

Sexual Harassment—Unwanted sexual advances, forced sexual contact, obscene or offensive remarks, lewd behavior or indecent exposure. This category also includes unfair treatment by the employer or a co-worker in retaliation for failure to submit to sexual advances.

Demoted/Not Promoted—Employee was demoted or not promoted because of unfair employer policies or standards. The precipitating cause of the employer's unfair actions was the employee's resistance to sexual advances, the filing of a discrimination or sexual harassment complaint, exercise of First Amendment rights, complaints regarding working conditions, illegal or criminal activities on the part of the employer or the filing of a workers' compensation claim by the employee.

Wrongful Termination With Discrimination—Discharge of the employee based on age, race, sex, disability (actual or perceived) or pregnancy.

Wrongful Termination With Sexual Harassment—The employee was discharged because he or she failed to remain silent following sexual harassment or because of a reported instance of sexual harassment.

Wrongful Termination With No Discrimination—The employee was discharged following complaints of intolerable working conditions, as retaliation for filing a workers' compensation claim, the reporting of unethical or criminal activities on the part of the employer, or the employee's attempt to exercise First Amendment rights. This category also includes allegations that the employer terminated the employee to avoid having to pay retirement or pension benefits.

Constructive Discharge—Employee felt compelled to resign because of intolerable working conditions. This category includes charges that the employer intentionally created such an environment to force the resignation.

Refusal Of Employment—Plaintiff was qualified for the job, but was prevented from applying for the job or was refused the job because the employer discriminated against him or her. This category does not include allegations of failure to promote.

Distribution Of Verdict Amounts

Table 6 lists the distribution of compensatory verdicts, by percentage, within specified dollar ranges. All cases involved emotional injuries resulting from various wrongful employment practices.

Table 6
Distribution of Verdicts—Wrongful Employment Practices
(Average for Period 1987–1994)

Data Source: Jury Verdict Research Reports,* "Basic Injury Values for Claims of Emotional Distress Resulting From a Hostile Work Environment" and "Basic Injury Values For Claims of Emotional Distress Resulting From Wrongful Termination, Constructive Discharge or Refusal of Employment"

	To $49,999	$50,000–$99,999	$100,000–$249,999	$250,000–$499,999	$500,000–$1,000,000	Over $1,000,000
Discrimination	24%	16%	22%	16%	11%	11%
Sexual Harassment	34%	32%	12%	15%	5%	2%
Demoted/Not Promoted	23%	23%	27%	10%	10%	7%
Wrongful Termination						
w/ Discrimination	21%	19%	20%	24%	11%	5%
w/ Sexual Harassment	48%	3%	22%	13%	4%	10%
w/ No Discrimination	35%	13%	21%	14%	9%	8%
Constructive Discharge						
w/ Discrimination or Sexual Harassment	34%	13%	27%	20%	3%	3%
w/ No Discrimination	36%	22%	N/A	N/A	N/A	N/A
Refusal To Employ for Discriminatory Reasons	53%	15%	24%	N/A	N/A	N/A

N/A = Data regarding the percentage of verdicts within this dollar range not available.
*Jury Verdict Research, An LRP Publications Company, 747 Dresher Road, P.O. Box 980, Horsham, PA 19044-0980. Copyright 1995. All rights reserved.

Verdict Midpoint (Median) Amounts

The average midpoint (median) of verdict amounts in wrongful employment practices cases during the period 1987 through 1994 is listed in Table 7. Individual verdict amounts may be higher or lower than this amount. Median awards are considered to be the most representative of the average award for a specific injury. As shown, the highest median awards were in the category of wrongful termination with discrimination.

Table 7
Verdict Midpoint (Median) Amounts—Employment Practices Litigation
(Average for Period 1987–1994)

Data Source: Jury Verdict Research Reports,* "Basic Injury Values for Claims of Emotional Distress Resulting From a Hostile Work Environment" and "Basic Injury Values For Claims of Emotional Distress Resulting From Wrongful Termination, Constructive Discharge or Refusal of Employment"

Category		Verdict Midpoint
Discrimination		$150,000
Sexual Harassment		67,500
Demoted/Not Promoted		97,557
Wrongful Termination	w/ Discrimination	168,800
	w/ Sexual Harassment	60,000
	w/ No Discrimination	102,000
Constructive Discharge	w/ Discrimination or Sexual Harassment	100,000
	w/ No Discrimination	72,316
Refusal To Employ for Discriminatory Reasons		47,476

*Jury Verdict Research, An LRP Publications Company, 747 Dresher Road, P.O. Box 980, Horsham, PA 19044-0980. Copyright 1995. All rights reserved.

Punitive Damage Awards

Table 8 lists the percentage of awards in which punitive damages were included to punish the employer for wrongful employment practices or as an incentive to avoid such practices in the future. Also included is the midpoint amount of punitive damages awarded by category of wrongful practice during the period 1987 through 1994. The midpoint, or median, amount is the middle-award value among awards listed in ascending order.

Table 8
Midpoint (Median) Punitive Damage Awards—Employment Practices Litigation
(Average for Period 1987–1994)

Data Sources: Jury Verdict Research Reports,* "Basic Injury Values for Claims of Emotional Distress Resulting From a Hostile Work Environment" and "Basic Injury Values For Claims of Emotional Distress Resulting From Wrongful Termination, Constructive Discharge or Refusal of Employment"

Category		% of Awards	Midpoint
Discrimination		43%	$160,000
Sexual Harassment		27%	83,500
Demoted/Not Promoted		32%	175,000
Wrongful Termination		24%	150,000
	w/ Discrimination	20%	197,875
	w/ Sexual Harassment	29%	125,000
	w/ No Discrimination	26%	150,000
Constructive Discharge		14%	350,000
	w/ Discrimination or Sexual Harassment	10%	501,000
	w/ No Discrimination	21%	350,000
Refusal To Employ for Discrimination Reasons		15%	17,500

*Jury Verdict Research, An LRP Publications Company, 747 Dresher Road, P.O. Box 980, Horsham, PA 19044-0980. Copyright 1995. All rights reserved.

Litigation Activity By State

Table 9 and Charts 17 and 18 below illustrate litigation activity related to all employment practices liability claims, by state, during the period 1993 through 1997. Shown on the chart are the total amount of jury verdicts in excess of $300,000[3]. The number of verdicts shown for 1997 may be less than for prior years because the data for 1997 is preliminary. The majority of verdicts in excess of $300,000 occurred in California, Texas, Michigan and Florida.

Table 9
Litigation Activity Related To EPL Claims, By State
Data Source: LEXIS Verdict Library

State	1993 #	1993 Amount	1994 #	1994 Amount	1995 #	1995 Amount	1996 #	1996 Amount	1997 #	1997 Amount
California	18	$222,943,992	40	$135,146,287	39	$40,805,284	40	$55,224,342	18	$20,403,278
Texas	4	6,201,545	7	8,725,565	7	8,877,861	8	38,310,572	3	16,445,300
Michigan	7	5,326,382	6	4,077,124	3	5,189,000	4	2,505,000	3	11,699,237
Florida	2	1,600,001	1	6,128,308	1	501,500	4	10,188,700	3	13,719,978
New Jersey	0	0	2	15,375,300	0	0	2	2,748,784	1	704,800
New York	1	703,250	2	767,206	0	0	2	7,558,310	2	6,975,000
Massachusetts	1	950,000	3	6,885,000	2	1,426,000	2	1,707,477	1	1,275,000
Ohio	4	9,333,309	1	315,372	1	490,000	1	950,000	3	2,052,959
Pennsylvania	1	550,000	2	1,477,874	3	4,114,000	3	5,313,364	0	0
Washington	2	945,547	2	2,037,285	1	1,177,469	4	3,517,224	0	0
Illinois	1	572,000	3	1,891,625	2	1,175,467	2	3,269,789	0	0
Missouri	0	0	1	600,000	2	975,000	3	5,351,368	0	0
Georgia	4	2,542,044	1	465,000	1	420,159	1	360,000	1	1,800,000
Alabama	1	330,000	1	1,000,000	1	1,250,000	2	3,658,000	0	0
Kansas	1	491,504	0	0	0	0	1	736,575	2	2,350,000
Connecticut	0	0	0	0	2	668,221	3	1,207,213	0	0
South Dakota	0	0	0	0	1	1,861,275	0	0	0	0
Washington, DC	0	0	1	500,000	0	0	2	1,443,816	0	0
Oklahoma	0	0	1	372,034	2	1,650,657	1	375,000	0	0
Maine	0	0	1	400,000	2	1,305,000	1	610,000	1	375,000
Arizona	0	0	0	0	1	1,470,000	1	500,000	0	0
Nebraska	0	0	0	0	1	1,482,315	0	0	0	0
North Carolina	1	1,300,000	0	0	0	0	0	0	0	0
Virginia	0	0	1	350,000	2	716,534	0	0	0	0
Iowa	2	1,012,009	0	0	0	0	0	0	0	0
Alaska	0	0	0	0	1	687,000	0	0	0	0
Vermont	0	0	2	840,000	0	0	0	0	0	0
Maryland	1	352,400	0	0	0	0	0	0	0	0
Mississippi	0	0	0	0	0	0	1	550,000	0	0
Montana	0	0	0	0	0	0	1	312,802	0	0
Total	51	$255,153,983	78	$187,353,980	75	$76,242,742	89	$146,398,336	38	$77,800,552

---

[3] (verdicts for lesser amounts are not included in Table 9)

Chart 17

Largest Total Number of EPL Verdicts in Excess of $300,000

Top 10 States (1990–1997)

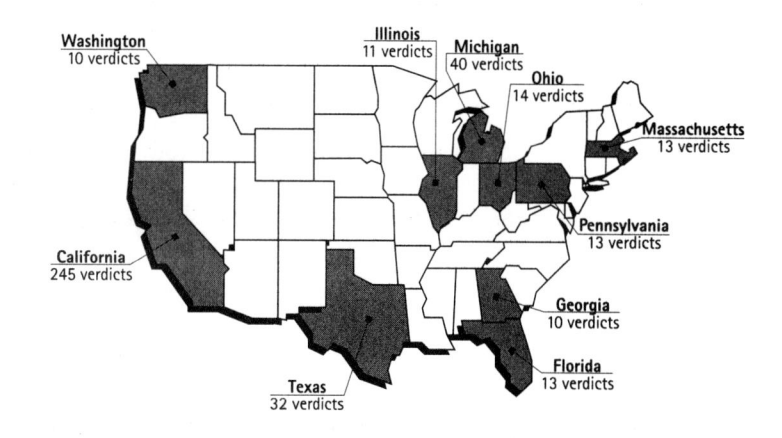

- Washington: 10 verdicts
- Illinois: 11 verdicts
- Michigan: 40 verdicts
- Ohio: 14 verdicts
- Massachusetts: 13 verdicts
- Pennsylvania: 13 verdicts
- California: 245 verdicts
- Georgia: 10 verdicts
- Florida: 13 verdicts
- Texas: 32 verdicts

Chart 18

Largest Dollar Value of EPL Verdicts in Excess of $300,000

Top 10 States (1990–1997)

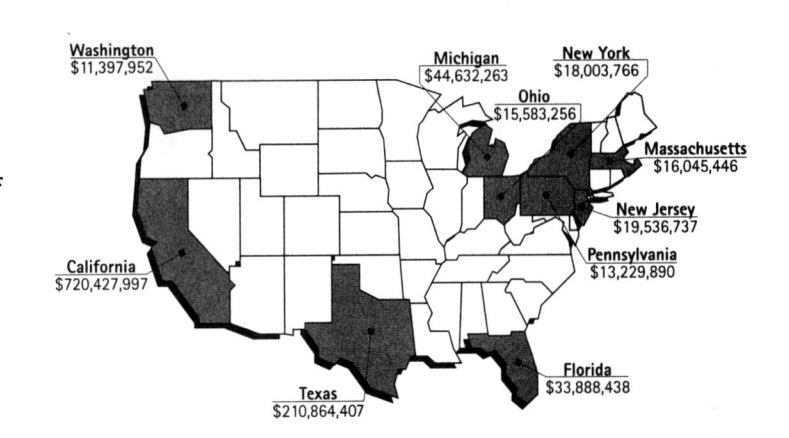

- Washington: $11,397,952
- Michigan: $44,632,263
- New York: $18,003,766
- Ohio: $15,583,256
- Massachusetts: $16,045,446
- New Jersey: $19,536,737
- Pennsylvania: $13,229,890
- California: $720,427,997
- Florida: $33,888,438
- Texas: $210,864,407

Employment Practices National Survey

A national survey of publicly owned companies, privately held firms and public entities was conducted by Sedgwick Financial Risk Specialists to establish a clearer picture of the employment concerns and practices of American employers.

Responses to the survey were furnished principally by financial officers, human resources managers and risk managers. Preliminary results depict some distinct patterns and activities in employment practices. A partial result of the survey is presented below.

Wrongful termination topped the list of exposures that respondents were most concerned about, with religious discrimination at the bottom. Approximately 93% of the respondents identified wrongful termination as a very strong or a moderate concern. This was followed closely by a 89% response for exposures from sexual harassment. Workplace harassment was third on the list; it concerned 79% of the respondents. The Americans with Disabilities Act ranked fourth with a 71% response, followed by exposures arising out of the Family and Medical Leave Act, 66%, and age discrimination placed sixth with 65% of the respondents rating that exposure as of high or moderate concern. The same six exposures led the list in the category of "very concerned."

Chart 19

Percent Of Respondents Expressing Very Or Moderate Degree Of Concern

Data Source: Sedgwick (4/7/98).

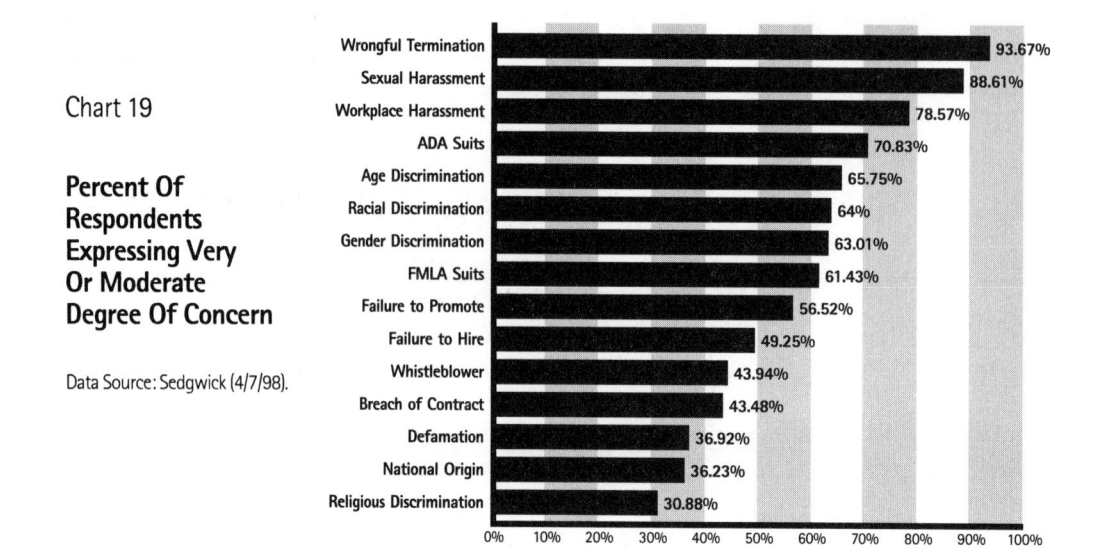

Category	Percentage
Wrongful Termination	93.67%
Sexual Harassment	88.61%
Workplace Harassment	78.57%
ADA Suits	70.83%
Age Discrimination	65.75%
Racial Discrimination	64%
Gender Discrimination	63.01%
FMLA Suits	61.43%
Failure to Promote	56.52%
Failure to Hire	49.25%
Whistleblower	43.94%
Breach of Contract	43.48%
Defamation	36.92%
National Origin	36.23%
Religious Discrimination	30.88%

Table 10
Degree Of Concern

Data Source: Sedgwick (4/7/98)

Category	Very	Moderate	Not Concerned
Wrongful Termination	35.44%	58.23%	6.33%
Sexual Harassment	36.71%	21.90%	11.39%
Workplace Harassment	27.14%	51.43%	21.43%
ADA Suits	19.44%	51.39%	29.17%
FMLA Suits	18.57%	42.86%	38.57%
Age Discrimination	17.81%	47.95%	34.25%
Gender Discrimination	13.70%	49.32%	36.99%
Racial Discrimination	14.67%	49.33%	36.00%
Failure to Promote	10.14%	46.38%	43.48%
Failure to Hire	7.46%	41.79%	50.75%
Retaliation/Whistleblower	15.15%	28.79%	56.06%
Breach of Contract	11.59%	31.88%	56.52%
Defamation	9.23%	27.69%	63.08%
National Origin Discrimination	7.25%	28.99%	63.77%
Religious Discrimination	5.88%	25.00%	69.12%

Fifty-six percent of the companies responding to the Sedgwick survey experienced at least one employment practices claim. Age discrimination, which ranked sixth among 15 employment-related exposures, led the list of claims filed against these same employers. One-fourth of all charges made specified age discrimination; some claims contained multiple charges. Gender discrimination accounted for 17% of the employment-related charges, although it ranked seventh in the list of exposure concerns. The number-one ranked concern, wrongful termination, took third place with almost 14% of the charges. ADA claims, with 2.5% of the charges, ranked ninth in the category, far below the level of concern expressed for this exposure. The fifth-ranking concern, FMLA, placed last in the number of charges filed, zero. Failure to hire and failure to promote accounted for less than 2% of the charges filed; they ranked much higher in the list of exposures of concern, with approximately 46% and 53%, respectively.

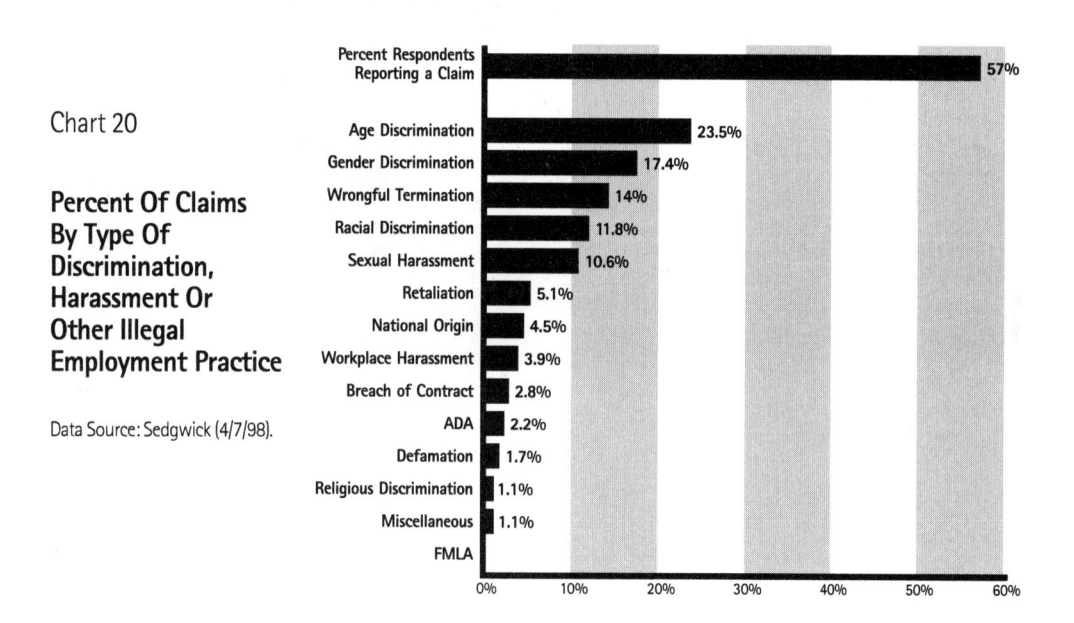

Chart 20

Percent Of Claims By Type Of Discrimination, Harassment Or Other Illegal Employment Practice

Data Source: Sedgwick (4/7/98).

Category	Percent
Percent Respondents Reporting a Claim	57%
Age Discrimination	23.5%
Gender Discrimination	17.4%
Wrongful Termination	14%
Racial Discrimination	11.8%
Sexual Harassment	10.6%
Retaliation	5.1%
National Origin	4.5%
Workplace Harassment	3.9%
Breach of Contract	2.8%
ADA	2.2%
Defamation	1.7%
Religious Discrimination	1.1%
Miscellaneous	1.1%
FMLA	

Employment Litigation Survey

The Society for Human Resource Management[4] (SHRM), and Jackson Lewis[5] conducted the 1997 *Employment Litigation Survey* to determine some of the trends involving lawsuits against employers, and what employers do to prevent employment-related litigation. The survey, produced in conjunction with the SHRM Foundation[6] was mailed to 4,900 randomly selected SHRM members in March 1997. The following results are based on the responses of 616 human resource professionals.

---

[4] The Society for Human Resource Management (SHRM) is a leading voice of the human resource profession. SHRM provides its membership with education and information services, conferences and seminars, government and media representation, on-line services and publications. The Society is a founding member and Secretariat of the World Federation of Personnel Management Associations (WFPMA) which links human resource associations from around the globe.

[5] Jackson Lewis has represented management exclusively in all aspects of employment, labor and benefits law since 1958. Jackson Lewis is one of the largest law firms in the country, with offices nationwide, concentrating in all aspects of workplace law and human resources management issues.

[6] The SHRM Foundation is a non-profit organization established in 1966 to fund and support applied research, publications, scholarships and educational programs to help HR professionals and their employers prepare for the future. The Foundation's goal is to continuously improve standards of practice and performance for the HR profession and to help HR leaders stay current with the latest developments and trends.

Who's Being Sued And By Whom?

Over half (57%) of the organizations responding to the survey indicated that they had been named as defendants in at least one employment-related lawsuit during the past five years. Nearly all respondents (93%) said their organizations were sued by former employees, and over one-third (37%) reported being sued by current employees.[7] Ten percent of organizations who have been sued in the past five years were sued by unsuccessful candidates for employment, and five percent were sued by prospective employees (Chart 21).

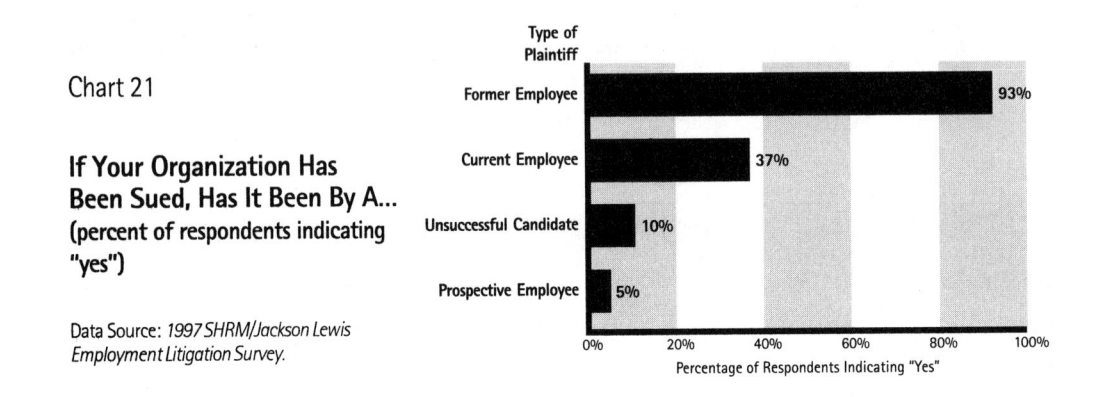

Chart 21

If Your Organization Has Been Sued, Has It Been By A...
(percent of respondents indicating "yes")

Data Source: *1997 SHRM/Jackson Lewis Employment Litigation Survey.*

Type of Plaintiff	Percentage
Former Employee	93%
Current Employee	37%
Unsuccessful Candidate	10%
Prospective Employee	5%

Respondents were asked if any individuals at their organizations have been named in employment-related lawsuits recently. Seven out of 10 (70%) respondents said "no". Twenty-three percent of respondents, however, said individuals at their organizations have been sued personally, and the individuals named as defendants tended to be high-level employees. Of the respondents who said individuals have been personally named in lawsuits, 35% said the individuals held the titles of manager or director, and 17% said presidents or CEOs were named in employment-related lawsuits. In addition, 16% of respondents said human resource directors or managers were named in the suits, and a similar percentage named vice presidents or senior vice presidents.

Legitimacy Of Lawsuits

When asked if they agreed with the statement "The majority of employment-related litigation cases today are legitimate claims," 74% of respondents either disagreed or strongly disagreed (Table 11). Six percent of respondents agreed with the statement, while 18% were undecided. Respondents from larger organizations and from organizations that had been named recently in an employment-related suit were most likely to disagree with the statement.

---

[7] Respondents' organizations may have been sued more than once by various parties.

Table 11
Agree or Disagree: "The Majority of Employment-Related Litigation Cases are Legitimate Claims"

Data Source: *1997 SHRM/Jackson Lewis Employment Litigation Survey.*

	Percent of All Respondents
Strongly agree	**
Agree	6
Undecided	18
Disagree	52
Strongly disagree	22
No answer	1

** less than one percent
Note: Column may not total 100% due to rounding.

Litigation Costs

Attorney fees, damages, court fees, settlement costs, and other litigation costs associated with employment-related matters increased during the past five years, according to a large share of survey respondents (Table 12). Four out of 10 respondents said litigation costs for employment-related matters have increased either substantially (21%) or slightly (21%), particularly at larger organizations. Respondents from organizations with more than 250 employees (51%) were more likely to report increased litigation costs than were respondents from smaller organizations (31%). Also, respondents who said their organizations have been named in employment-related lawsuits were more likely to report increased litigation costs than those from organizations that have not been sued.

Table 12
Litigation Costs for Employment-Related Matters

Data Source: *1997 SHRM/Jackson Lewis Employment Litigation Survey.*

	Percent of All Respondents
Increased substantially	21
Increased slightly	21
Stayed about the same	31
Decreased slightly	3
Decreased substantially	4
Don't know	14
No answer	6

Three out of 10 respondents (31%) said their organizations' litigation costs have remained stable in the past five years, while approximately one out of 10 respondents said litigation costs associated with employment-related matters have either decreased substantially (4%) or decreased slightly (3%).

Lawsuits Experienced In The Past Five Years

In the final section of the questionnaire, respondents were asked to give detailed accounts of the employment-related lawsuits their organizations had experienced in the past five years. Approximately half of the survey participants responded. The other half were unable to provide the information either for legal reasons or because they did not have access to the information. The following information is based on 611 lawsuits described by respondents. While that number is too small to draw definitive conclusions about employment-related lawsuits in general, the responses do offer some interesting anecdotal insights.

Of all the suits mentioned by respondents, nearly half involved a discrimination claim of some sort.[8] Race or national origin discrimination accounted for 15% of claims, age discrimination was mentioned in 14% of the claims, and 11% of the claims involved sexual discrimination or equal pay. In addition, 2% of the lawsuits involved religious discrimination. The remainder were unspecified discrimination claims.

Aside from discrimination claims, a third of the lawsuits mentioned involved wrongful termination (33%), and 12% alleged sexual harassment. Approximately one out of 20 lawsuits included claims related to an NLRB or FMLA charge (6%), workers' compensation or wrongful death (6%), or wrongful retaliation (5%).

Most employment-related lawsuits (80%) mentioned by survey respondents were filed by former employees. Lawsuits were filed by current employees in one out of seven (14%) suits, and 3% of the suits were brought by unsuccessful candidates for employment.

More than a third (35%) of the 611 lawsuits mentioned were resolved by reaching a settlement or private agreement, and a quarter of them (25%) are still pending. Approximately one out of 10 lawsuits either went to trial (12%) or were dismissed (9%).

Summary

The frequency of wrongful employment practices charges filed with the EEOC (including referrals from state and local Fair Employment Practices Agencies) has been increasing since 1990. One factor contributing to this increase has been the Americans with Disabilities Act, which the EEOC began enforcing in July 1992. As for charges filed with the EEOC, those citing racial and sex discrimination in violation of Title VII are the most prevalent. Claims alleging violations of the ADA most frequently cite wrongful discharge and back impairments as the disability most discriminated against. The largest category of claims under the ADEA also involves wrongful discharge, while claims

---

[a]Lawsuits may have involved more than one claim.

alleging EPA violations most often involve wage-discrimination issues. The economic impact of benefits obtained by the EEOC as respects charges of wrongful employment practices has similarly been increasing since 1990.

The number of lawsuits filed annually on behalf of employees against employers by the EEOC increased from 1984 to 1990, but has decreased since that time. This decrease may be attributable to several factors, such as a decrease in EEOC funding, increased employer compliance with wrongful employment practices statutes, use of various alternative-dispute resolution and a general heightened awareness by employers of potential liability.

As a result of EEOC litigation, the monetary benefits obtained in all statutes combined fluctuated dramatically during the period 1984 to 1994. This fluctuation is the result of extraordinarily high verdicts rendered in 1991 and 1992. Aside from these verdicts, the total amount of benefits obtained has steadily decreased since 1991. Most suits filed from 1989 to 1993 involve actions under Title VII, with suits filed under the EPA representing the lowest number. However, the largest awards were obtained in cases alleging ADEA violations.

Approximately 10% of all awards in cases involving discrimination or wrongful termination with discrimination are in excess of $1 million. Also, the highest midpoint verdict is found in cases involving wrongful termination with discrimination. Punitive damages are awarded in at least 10% of wrongful employment practices cases, including almost half of cases involving employment discrimination.

According to employer surveys[9] 57% of respondents said their organizations have been named as defendants in at least one employment-related lawsuit in the past five years. In addition, nearly one fourth of respondents said individuals at their organizations had been sued personally in recent years for employment-related matters. Although individuals and entire organizations can help protect themselves against employment-related litigation by purchasing specialized EPL insurance approximately half (47%) of survey respondents do not have such coverage

Conclusion

As illustrated, real or alleged wrongful employment practices and their resulting claims can present significant financial risk to employers. That risk can only be partially quantified by the data presented in this section and should be viewed solely as a partial indicator of the risk posed by real or perceived wrongful employment practices. Other factors can significantly affect both the likelihood and severity of employment-related loss. These additional factors can include:

---

[9] SHRM/Jackson Lewis, 1997.

1. The specific laws that may apply to the employers particular jurisdiction or operations
2. The size and geographic location of the employer's operations
3. The existence or absence of personnel trained in human resource management
4. The employer's effectiveness at preventing claims through implementation of formal employment rules and procedures
5. The employer's effectiveness at investigating and treating employment-related complaints and disputes in a timely manner
6. The use of alternative-dispute-resolution techniques
7. The capriciousness with which juries can react when employment disputes are concluded by verdict
8. The potential for punitive damages
9. The extent to which insurance coverage is available

In addition, the cost to successfully defend employment disputes can be enormous. Even so-called nuisance suits can cost $25,000 or more just to defend, and very large verdicts and settlements in excess of $100 million are not unheard of. Also, many employers have been hurt by numerous smaller claims that individually may be absorbed but in the aggregate can pose a severe financial burden.

PART II

Developing A Risk Management Strategy

3 Understanding Risk Management

The term *risk management* has been defined as:

- ▸ An approach of management concerned with the preservation of the assets and earning power of a business against risks of accidental loss[1]

- ▸ A process that includes the four functions of planning, organizing, leading and controlling the activities of the organization in order to minimize the adverse effects of accidental losses on that organization at reasonable cost[2]

There have been great efforts in recent years to formalize and refine the theory and methodology of risk management. Unfortunately, attempts at implementing such processes have sometimes resulted in lackluster or poor results. One reason, articulated over 20 years ago, is that:

> *Top management sometimes wishes it could put Risk Management in its place, but as yet, top management doesn't know which place to put it.*[3]

Because risks of loss arising out of an organization's employment practices are so varied, it is often difficult for one department or one person to thoroughly understand and address the entire exposure. For example, although human resources personnel are primarily responsible for the implementation of employment policies and procedures, they do not normally make the decision to retain or insure losses. Also, because employment is highly regulated and subject to frequent changes in law, the organization's legal counsel may become closely involved in employment issues. With the development of specialized insurance products covering liability arising out of wrongful employment practices, the organization's risk manager may have the responsibility and authority to decide whether insurance should be purchased.

---

[1] J.M. Rosenberg, Ph.D., *Dictionary Of Business And Management*. (John Wiley & Sons, 1988).

[2] G.L. Head and Stephen Horn, *Essentials Of Risk Management*, Volume I, Insurance Institute Of America (1991).

[3] R.A. Muckleston, *Risk Management For The Smaller Company*, The Association Of Insurance And Risk Managers In Industry And Commerce (AIRMIC) (1977).

While many organizations are aware of the potential benefits risk management can provide, attempts to formally manage the EPL exposure often suffer from a lack of understanding of the basic concepts of risk management or from improper implementation of those concepts. The fragmentation of responsibilities and lack of centralized management of the EPL exposure also can complicate the coordinated management of risk.

Because specific chapters of *The EPL Book* have been devoted to EPL risk identification (Chapters 1 and 2), loss prevention (Chapter 4), loss control (Chapter 5) and insurance (Chapters 7 through 12), this chapter is limited to a brief description of the risk-management process in general and how such processes can be applied to the treatment of risk arising out of an organization's employment policies, practices and procedures.

The Risk-Management Process

The goals of managing the EPL exposure are to reduce or control the cost of risk and to protect the corporation against catastrophic loss. The cost of EPL risk can be viewed as the total of all costs incurred in the management of the EPL exposure, including:

- Incurred losses
- Claims-adjusting costs
- Loss-prevention and awareness-training costs
- Insurance premiums
- Administrative and overhead costs

The generally accepted sequence of risk management activities is to:

1. Identify and measure the risk of loss.
2. Eliminate the risk of loss or reduce it through loss-prevention and loss-control techniques.
3. Assume without insurance some or all of the EPL exposure as a budgeted cost.
4. As a last resort, insure potential EPL losses that cannot otherwise be treated in the above fashion.

Who Does It?

Although one department or one person may sometimes oversee or have executive responsibility for all risk-management functions, such centralization is not always believed to be desirable or practical by senior management. In a large organization, there may be a separate risk-management department, which itself may be a part of a finance, legal or administrative department. In smaller organizations, the president or other executive officer may carry out the functions of risk manager. But even in large organizations, there may be confusion over who or which departments are responsible for which risk-management functions.

Applying the risk-management process to the employment exposure usually necessitates assigning responsibility for each element to one or more functional departments. This allocation of responsibility is important because no single person or department normally has the needed skills or knowledge to carry out all of the risk-management functions. Such assignment of responsibility may vary by type and size of organization, and while there is no single best breakdown, a common allocation of duties is illustrated in the following exhibit.

Exhibit 2
Typical Allocation of Risk Management Duties

	Finance	Human Resources (HR)	Legal	Risk Management
Risk Identification		●	●	●
Loss Control		●	●	●
Retention	●			●
Insurance	●			●

In general, insurance has been so heavily relied upon as a risk-management tool, and its cost so visible, that other aspects of risk management sometimes receive inadequate attention. In regards to employment practices liability, insurance only recently has become available or needed as a risk-transfer option. Previously, organizations were forced to rely solely on prevention and loss-control techniques for treating the EPL risk. But because the frequency and severity of EPL claims is rising, the importance of a coordinated risk-management approach, including the consideration of specialized EPL insurance, should not be overlooked.

Risk Identification

Risks must be identified before they can be treated properly. Although this may sound obvious, risk identification is not always easy to put into practice. Risk identification is needed to determine the types of losses that are significant and to assign an approximate value to their potential magnitude. This practice will suggest the limits of insurance needed and also will indicate whether the risk can be handled without insurance.

A thorough understanding of the laws governing the employment relationship, along with an analysis of the organization's own employment practices, policies and procedures, is a necessary starting point in the risk-identification process. Studying compiled data from government and private sources also can help identify claim trends for specific wrongful employment practices.[4] Input from the HR, financial, legal and risk management departments should be solicited in order to help arrive at a reasonable estimation of the organization's overall exposure to EPL loss. Such input is necessary because no single department is likely to have sufficient knowledge of all the areas of exposure.

Loss Prevention And Reduction

Human-resource professionals have known for years that effective communication to all employees of the employer's rules, policies and procedures, as well as an early intervention in employment disputes or complaints, can limit both the frequency and severity of employment-related claims. Chapters 4 and 5 provide a more thorough discussion of these critical elements, but because of their importance, a brief description is provided here.

Written Procedures

Many employment-related claims arise out of ignorance. This problem may be the result of poor communication of the employer's policies and procedures, inconsistent hiring, discharge, discipline and anti-discrimination practices, or the employer may simply not know what the law requires. Employees or job applicants who have a dispute or complaint regarding their employment should always have clear written procedures available for the purpose of resolving problems quickly.

Without an internal means of resolving problems, many employees will seek assistance from an attorney. Also, once a claim or allegation is made that may result in a formal charge, it is imperative to have investigation and intervention procedures in place to help avoid further escalation and mitigate damages or fines. Many employees who complain of wrongdoing may only want the offending behavior or practice to cease. Money damages may not initially be requested or demanded.

Training

Employees need to be thoroughly trained in the corporation's policies, rules and procedures. The contents of employee handbooks must be clearly and periodically communicated to the firm's employees or it is likely that any potential benefit of using the handbook will be lost.

Aside from periodic, formal reinforcement of the company's policies, training focused on the identification and prevention of sexual harassment (one of the more pervasive of

---

[4] See Chapter 2, "Frequency And Economic Impact Of Wrongful Employment Practices Charges."

employment problems) also can be an effective prevention tool. Managers and employees who have been trained and made aware of the kinds of behavior that might be construed as harassment have a better chance of avoiding such behavior. In many instances the harasser is simply unaware that their behavior is offensive to others.

To give further support to the employer's commitment to a non-discriminatory and harassment-free workplace, pre- and post-training testing can be used to document employee education and training. Testing verifies that employees understand the corporate rules and laws forbidding sexual harassment. Ideally, both supervisors and employees will be more inclined to detect and prevent such behavior before it becomes a problem.

Risk Retention[5]

Most organizations retain risk as a cost of doing business unless there is some specific reason or requirement to do otherwise. In the past, little consideration was given to retaining losses that might arise out of EPL claims. This lack of thought stemmed from the fact that the risk was often unrecognized or considered by employers and others to be so small that it was of little consequence. Now, however, the EPL exposure is better recognized and understood. Now with the option to insure against loss arising out of employment practices, a more thorough analysis is warranted to determine how much and under what conditions EPL loss should be retained.

One reason for retaining risk is that there is a charge for insurance (the principal means of risk transfer). The insurer must charge an amount of premium in excess of what it pays in losses to at least cover overhead. Because of this, insurance will usually cost much more than retention. Risk retention for EPL claims has the following benefits:

- It reduces or eliminates the cost of risk transfer, including insurer overhead, producer's commission and state and federal taxes
- It focuses attention on and promotes the prevention and control of loss
- It allows more flexibility in claims administration by giving the employer the opportunity to control important decisions regarding claims management or settlement

A possible disadvantage of risk retention is that there may be greater variation of costs from year to year. However, past insurance market conditions have demonstrated that even insured programs are subject to unplanned, substantial fluctuations in cost.

---

[5] Although there are many terms used to describe self-insurance and risk retention, retention is little more than the acceptance of loss by deductibles, self insured retention or non-insurance.

Another approach to understanding retention is to examine the meaning of risk itself. In a word, risk is uncertainty. Those losses that occur with predictable regularity should not even be considered risks, but instead are reasonably predictable costs of operation that should be paid as they occur.

Amount Of Risk Retention

A general rule of thumb is that all predictable losses should be retained. It may be desirable, however, to retain loss at an even higher level. In order to establish what amount of retention is acceptable, it usually is necessary to examine annual revenues, which are a measure of an entity's loss-absorbing capacity. When a sudden expense occurs, it is normally possible to shift expenditures, defer projects or readjust finances to accommodate the need. The degree of flexibility within an organization's budget to make such accommodations is one measure of a tolerable loss level.

Perhaps the most common method of selecting a retention amount is to have premium quotations provided at different retention levels. A decision usually can be made on an intuitive weighing of dollars saved versus expected losses assumed, but such an approach also can be misleading. A fixed premium credit does not measure all the advantages of risk retention. For example, the employer may not have to give control of claims management and loss adjustment to an insurer for those claims within its retention layer. Also, the premium reduction gained by retaining risk may be small in relation to the possible assumed loss where the occurrence of loss is infrequent. Premium savings may appear insignificant, but usually the insured has no way to calculate the actual frequency of claims and thus may reject a premium reduction that is small but beneficial in the long run.

Whatever risk-retention level is chosen, it should be selected by the chief financial officer after consideration of how unbudgeted losses will impact the organization's present and future financial condition.

Insurance

Loss prevention and control techniques (like those mentioned above and more fully described in Chapters 4 and 5) should be part of any overall employment policy, but they cannot completely protect an organization from the risk of serious financial loss. Any claim or incident can lead to litigation. And once in litigation, even nuisance suits can cost $25,000 or more to resolve. Defense of more serious claims can cost many multiples of this figure. While many large organizations may find it economically feasible to self insure much or even all of their EPL exposure, smaller or thinly capitalized firms may be severely impacted by even a single claim. Even some larger firms might find it difficult to absorb the cost of multiple suits or a large class-action suit.

Numerous insurers now provide a specialized form of insurance specifically designed to protect against loss incurred in litigating and settling wrongful employment practices-liability claims. The generic name for this coverage is employment practices liability (EPL) insurance.

For many employers unable to absorb the risk of loss from an employment practices claim, EPL insurance may be an attractive alternative. In recent years there has been increased availability of products specifically designed to insure against employment practices claims. The number of insurers offering such coverage has increased dramatically since the middle 1980s, when specialized EPL insurance was first introduced. In addition, there are now very high limits available, making it possible to buy excess EPL coverage above a relatively large retention.

When evaluating EPL insurance, the most important points to consider are scope of coverage, adequacy of limits and an understanding of who controls the claims-handling process—the insured or the insurer. Because the insurance is relatively new and there is much variation in the degree of protection offered, employers must be cautious in their evaluation of such policies. Seemingly minor differences in policy wording can drastically affect coverage. One of the benefits of purchasing insurance is that it reduces the uncertainty of loss. But because of the wide variation in EPL insurance policy forms, knowing what you actually are buying can be difficult unless you know what to look for.

Conclusion

Some employers view recent developments in employment law with fear, and ignore problems that can arise by taking a passive position. But viewed in a more positive light, the EPL exposure, once recognized and measured, usually can be dealt with in an effective manner.

While EPL insurance may be effective at reducing the uncertainty of loss, it is not a substitute for sound employment policies, practices and procedures. Most EPL insurance underwriters require that the insured has at least rudimentary prevention and post-incident investigation plans in place. Failure to have such plans may result in insurers refusing to offer EPL coverage at any price. When preventive measures are firmly established, insurance can play an effective role in protecting against catastrophic loss.

4 Employment Practices Liability Loss Prevention

Although the frequency of employment-related claims has increased dramatically in recent years, one encouraging aspect is that both frequency and severity of loss can be controlled through various prevention techniques, including but not limited to:

- Developing and implementing concise, written employment policies and procedures
- Sexual harassment, employee-awareness and diversity management training
- Specific policy and procedure to avoid wrongful discharge suits
- Settlement agreements and claim releases
- Alternative-dispute resolution: Arbitration and mediation

The goal of each of these techniques is to prevent employees from bringing a formal claim of wrongdoing or lawsuit against the employer in the first place. But even when a claim of wrongdoing is not prevented by such measures, the existence of sound employment policies and procedures can be important evidence of the employer's commitment to its workforce. Such evidence may help absolve the employer of any wrongdoing or help to mitigate damages or punitive awards when a claim is found to be meritorious.

Written Procedures

In today's increasingly regulated business environment, it is more important than ever that employers have clear, well-considered, comprehensive written strategies for the prevention of employment practices liability claims. It is equally important to document the implementation of such procedures through training and education programs.

Interviewing, Pre-Employment Screening And Testing

A sound strategy to avoid employment-related claims should begin even before an employer hires an employee. Federal labor laws and the labor laws of many states place strict limitations on the pre-employment inquiries that a prospective employer may make of a job applicant. Within these parameters, however, there is much that an employer can do to protect itself against possible employment practices claims.

Interview Dos And Don'ts

Anyone who conducts an employment interview should use a written interview guide. Such a guide should contain a detailed script for conducting the interview, including all of the questions that are needed to enable the interviewer to obtain a complete and accurate overview of the applicant's skills and experience. An interview guide assures that applicants are handled in such a way as to make comparisons between applicants both valid and reliable. Remember, however, that an interview guide is just that, a guide. Effective interviewing obviously requires flexibility. Interview questions need not be asked in the order shown in the guide, and some may even be omitted as an interview progresses. Digression from the interview guide, both in order to retain spontaneity and to pursue particular inquiries about a given applicant, are always appropriate.

A structured interview should cover the following basic areas:

- Background information about the applicant
- Questions about job related behavior (for example, the applicant is asked to describe what decisions and/or actions he or she has made in situations similar to those that will be encountered on the job being interviewed for)
- Follow-up questions (such as questions concerning information that may be missing from the application form)
- Questions about the applicant's education history
- Questions relating to specialized training and skills
- Questions about intangible factors such as the applicant's goals and attitudes
- A description of the job being interviewed
- A description of the next step in the interview/hiring process

Questions asked in an interview should be open-ended in order to elicit descriptive responses rather than a simple "yes" or "no" answer. For example, rather than asking the applicant if he or she is currently a production supervisor, a better question is to ask the applicant to "tell me about your job as a production supervisor," and then let the applicant talk. The interviewer should use silence, neutral comments such as "I see," "yes," and "uh huh," to encourage the applicant to keep speaking. This will often result in details of experience and behavior that might not otherwise come out in an interview.

In judging an applicant's experience, the real question for the interviewer is to determine just how relevant that experience is to the employer's needs. Before an interview begins, the employer should determine what the job requires. The interviewer should look for the applicant who has met similar requirements in the past. The strongest consideration should be given to the applicant who has met these requirements with success.

Of course, all of the above is subject to the constraints of federal, state and local civil rights laws.

An employer should not ask a job applicant any question, whether in an interview or on an employment application, that when answered might limit the applicant's employment opportunities because of some precluded criteria such as race, age or sex. An employer's questions should not require an applicant to identify himself or herself as a member of a protected category, nor should it result in the disproportionate screening out of members of a protected group.

For example, an employer should not ask an applicant for her "maiden name," although the applicant can be asked if she has ever used another name. While an applicant can be asked "If hired, can you show proof of age?" or "Are you over 18 years of age?", an employer should not ask an applicant's "age," "birthdate," "dates of attendance or completion of elementary or high school," or any other question that tends to identify applicants over a certain age. An applicant can be asked for the date of graduation from college or technical school, as such graduation dates are not necessarily indicative of the applicant's age.

An employer should not ask an applicant if he or she is a US citizen or where he or she was born. However, the employer can and should ask "Can you, after employment, submit verification of your legal right to work in the United States?" If the use of a language other than English is relevant to the job being applied for, an employer can ask if the applicant reads, speaks or writes that language. The employer should not ask about the applicant's nationality or ancestry.

While an employer should not ask about an applicant's general medical condition, state of health or prior workers' compensation injuries or claims, the employer may advise the applicant that a job offer may be made contingent on the passing of a pre-employment physical. The applicant may also be given a written job description setting forth the essential functions of the job for which he or she is applying. Such a job description should include the physical requirements of the job.

Although an employer should not ask about an applicant's religion, religious holidays observed or whether the applicant's religion prevents the applicant from working holidays or weekends, the application may include a statement of the regular days, hours or shifts to be worked.

The Employment Application

An employer's application form should notify applicants that any material misrepresentation or omission will be grounds for refusal to hire them. It also should be made clear to applicants that even if they are hired, any later discovered misrepresentations or omissions on their application may result in discharge.

The application should require complete disclosure of the applicant's educational and work history. A request for references should also be included on the application. Overstated or falsified job applications are an endemic problem for employers. Before an offer of employment is made, the employer should independently confirm the information provided by the applicant. It is particularly important that the employer question the applicant about any time gaps in his or her educational or work history. References should be called and background information sought before an offer of employment is extended. An employer that fails to carefully review an employment application and check references might subsequently be the target of a claim if it becomes necessary to terminate the employment relationship at a later date.

The employment application also should include a clear, concise statement that employment is "at-will." *At-will* means that the employment relationship may be terminated at any time, by either the employer or the employee, without notice and for any reason that is not otherwise illegal. Many courts have held that an "at-will" statement contained in the application protects an employer against claims of wrongful termination or termination without good cause in breach of an implied contract of employment. An "at-will" statement does not, however, prevent an employee from claiming discriminatory discharge in violation of Title VII, the ADEA, the ADA or some other federal or state anti-discrimination statute.

Reference And Background Checks

Obtaining References. Recent surveys suggest that anywhere between 25 and 35 percent of job applicants lie, misrepresent and/or omit material information from their employment applications. These misrepresentations and omissions may relate to an applicant's educational qualifications, work experience, or other relevant matters. Therefore, it is important that an employer check an applicant's references in order to confirm at least basic information about the dates of employment and positions held, attendance and performance at various schools.

Of course, personal references will usually present a favorable picture of the applicant, but they should be followed through anyway. Many applicants will list as references the most important people that they know. These people are often particularly frank and objective.

When attempting to elicit meaningful information from a personal reference, it may be helpful to ask about some weakness in the applicant that the employer has already independently discovered. Normally, this will result in either a confirmation or a detailed denial.

If a reference does raise concerns about an applicant who has been tentatively chosen for employment, the employer should not automatically disqualify the applicant. If the unfavorable information is inconsistent with the information gathered from other reference checks, it may suggest a biased or mistaken reference. At minimum, another interview should be scheduled with the applicant so that the negative information can be explored.

Giving References. References given by an employer can result in claims of defamation, intentional or negligent infliction of emotional distress, discrimination or blacklisting. To protect against such a possibility, an employer should designate one or two individuals within its organization who are authorized to give out references. No one else, regardless of their position, should give out a reference. The designated individuals should limit their responses to "job neutral" information, such as employee name, classification held and dates of employment. If the current or former employee for whom the reference is sought has given written consent, the employer might also disclose the employee's current or final rate of pay.

Background Checks. As a supplement to reference checks, background checks are a useful way to ferret out applicants who have misrepresented or omitted pertinent information from their employment applications and interview responses. For well under $50.00 per applicant, commercial background check companies can supply an employer with detailed information about an applicant's educational and employment history. Depending on the state and locale of the employer, a background check company may be able to supply additional information about an applicant's conviction and arrest record, workers' compensation claim history, litigation experience, and credit history.

Drug And Alcohol Testing

An employer may elect to have applicants undergo drug and alcohol testing (if the applicant is applying for a job as a driver which is covered by regulations of the Department of Transportation, a pre-employment drug screen is required). This type of testing often is an effective technique for screening out potential employees who may prove problematic if hired. Drug and alcohol tests may be done in conjunction with a pre-employment physical or they may be required by employers that do not make use of such physical examinations. In either case, the drug and alcohol test should only be administered by a medical facility using state-of-the-art equipment, such as a gas chromatographer. If the applicant does not pass the drug and alcohol test, a sufficient sample should be maintained so that a second, confirming test can be performed.

Some states, however, restrict or prohibit such testing altogether, and under the federal Americans with Disabilities Act such testing can only be conducted after a conditional offer of employment has been extended. The test then must be uniformly given to all persons who are hired for a particular position. An employer that implements a drug and alcohol testing program in violation of law, or which implements a poorly designed program, runs the risk of a claim of unlawful discrimination by an applicant who is denied employment because he or she refused to take the test or did not pass it. In some states an employer's demand that an applicant take such a test may be a violation of statutorily protected privacy rights, giving rise to yet another possible claim against the employer.

Job Offers

In order to avoid misunderstanding and potential claims, all job offers to applicants should be clear and unambiguous. Job offers should address (1) compensation and benefits, (2) relocation requirements and benefits, if any, (3) working hours, (4) travel requirements, (5) starting date, (6) deadline for accepting the offer, and (7) any special job requirements. Job offers are normally based on certain conditions, such as passing a physical examination and/or drug and alcohol test, receipt and verification of references and academic degrees, and proof of citizenship or legal ability to work in this country. While most job offers are made orally, some employers may choose to confirm them in writing, particularly for senior employees.

Job Descriptions

An employer should develop written job descriptions for every position in the organization's work force. Job descriptions should set forth the educational, experiential and physical requirements of each position. The essential functions of each job should be clearly defined. In addition, job descriptions should delineate each employee's supervisory and reporting roles.

How Are Job Descriptions Used? A properly written job description can serve as the basis for screening and hiring the right employee for a position. At the same time, a job description can protect an employer against claims of discrimination in the hiring process. During the interview, an applicant can be given a copy of the job description for the position they are applying for. The applicant then can be asked if they are able to perform with or without reasonable accommodation each of the essential functions listed. An employer is not required to hire an applicant who cannot perform the essential functions.

Additionally, job descriptions can and should form the basis for an employer's evaluation of an employee's performance, and determinations of pay adjustments, promotions, lateral transfers, discipline and discharge.

Benefits Of Job Descriptions Under The Law. The ADA prohibits discrimination against an employee who has a physical or mental disability, but is able to perform the "essential functions" of a job with or without reasonable accommodations. Job descriptions setting forth the essential functions of a job are given substantial weight by courts and administrative agencies adjudicating claims of unlawful discrimination, especially when the job descriptions are prepared prior to a claim of discrimination.

In the workers' compensation context, the use of job descriptions is imperative if an employee's treating and evaluating doctors are to determine if the employee can return to regular or modified duty. Job descriptions also function as guidelines to decide if the employee is eligible for costly vocational-rehabilitation services.

Employers with 50 or more employees, who are statutorily required by federal law to grant employees family and medical care leave, must restore an employee to the same or similar position held prior to the leave. An employer and its chosen medical professionals can use a carefully crafted job description to judge the employee's ability to perform the job.

Employee Handbooks

After an applicant has been hired, the employee needs to be made aware of what the employer expects of the employee and what the employee can expect from the employer as a part of the employment relationship. This information often is best provided by clearly stating the employer's policies, rules and procedures in an employee handbook or manual.

The possible topics to include in an employee handbook can be extensive, ranging from non-discrimination and hours of operation to sick leave and at-will employment. While the actual content of a handbook will depend upon the nature and size of the employer's operation, a listing of some of the policies that an employer might consider for inclusion is illustrated in Exhibit 3 on page 82. An employee handbook also is an indispensable resource for orienting and training new employees. A handbook can serve as a readily available guide for personnel administration and can be used to instruct supervisors and managers who themselves may be unclear about the employer's policies, or who may otherwise commit unintentional violations of law.

For an employer, particularly one with a small or medium-sized workforce, effectively managing employees is an increasingly complicated and time-consuming task. Employers often find themselves without consistent or cohesive policies on a multitude of subjects, including proper hiring procedures, discipline rules and termination techniques. Subsequently, the employer is forced to resort to managing its employees on an ad hoc basis. This situation arises for employers that are not large enough to employ an experienced personnel administrator.

Problems associated with the lack of formal and comprehensive policies and procedures on matters such as leaves of absence, absenteeism and sick leave often lie dormant for long periods of time. Unfortunately, when such problems do surface, they often come in the form of a charge of discrimination, the denial of pregnancy or family-care leave, an administrative investigation, or a lawsuit alleging wrongful termination in breach of an implied contract of employment.

Frequently, the employer does not recognize the need for an employee handbook until it is too late. With carefully drafted and legally reviewed provisions in an employee handbook that clearly discuss issues such as non-discrimination, leaves of absence and equal employment, the likelihood of disputes and litigation are greatly reduced. At minimum, a well-written employee handbook can significantly reduce the time, energy and money that employers may be required to expend in the defense of judicial and administrative claims by their employees. For example, the EEOC will give great deference to properly written and implemented equal employment and non-harassment policies.

Exhibit 3
Possible Employee Handbook Provisions

Employers have the option of including in their handbooks any number of provisions. Such provisions can include, but are not limited to, the following:

Introductory And General Information Policies

Introductory Statement	Non-Harassment Policy	Employment Of Relatives
Company History	Employee-Relations Policy	Immigration Law Compliance
Equal Employment Opportunity Statement	Non-Fraternization	

Employment Classifications

Employment Categories	Job Descriptions

Orientation, Transfer And Promotion Policies

Physical Examinations	Reference Checks	Transfer And Promotion Policies
Pre-Employment Drug And Alcohol Screening	Orientation Policies	

Payroll, Scheduling And Overtime Practices

Hours Of Operation And Work Schedules	Time Card Policies	Access To Personnel Files
Meal And Break Periods	Payroll Deductions	Compensatory Time-Off
Overtime Policies	Paydays	
	Wage Garnishment Policies	

Benefits (Both Discretionary And Legislated)

Sick Leave	Group Insurance	Unemployment Insurance
Vacation	Workers' Compensation Benefits	Social Security
Holidays	State Disability Insurance	Tuition Reimbursement

Leave Of Absence Policies

Medical Leave	Personal Leave	Jury Duty
Pregnancy Leave	Drug And Alcohol	Witness Duty
Workers' Compensation Leave	Rehabilitation Leave	Voting Time
Family Care Leave	Bereavement Leave	School Visitation

Performance And Discipline Policies

At-Will Employment Statement	Conflict Of Interest Statement	Return Of Company Property
Performance Evaluations	No-Solicitation Rules	Employee References
Attendance	Open Door Policy	Drug Testing Policy
Employee Conduct And Work Rules	Arbitration	Right To Inspect Property On Premises
Discipline	No Smoking Policy	Security
Dress And Grooming Standards	Telephone Use	Moonlighting
Uniforms	Permission To Leave Premises	Outplacement Services
Confidentiality And Non-Disclosure	Housekeeping	Contagious Diseases Policy
	Safety	
	Exit Interviews And Final Pay	

Also, many federal and state labor laws, including FMLA and various state anti-discrimination statutes, now require that employees receive written notification of their statutory rights relating to employment. An employee handbook can help employers comply with these legislative mandates, while at the same time provide employees with a balanced and understandable explanation of their rights and benefits.

Employer Excuses For Not Having A Handbook

Despite the benefits that can be derived from a well-written employee handbook, many employers resist or do not bother to use them. Some employers fear that an employee handbook will reduce their flexibility when problems arise with their employees. Unquestionably, a poorly drafted handbook can limit the flexibility that an employer needs to effectively operate in today's fast-moving and ever-changing business environment. However, a carefully drafted employee handbook can preserve, and even increase, employer flexibility by clearly informing employees that the employer retains the right to modify, amend, reduce or restructure compensation, benefits, job assignments and operations.

Employers may hesitate to adopt an employee handbook because they fear that the handbook will be viewed as an "employment contract." In many states, however, there is a legal presumption of "at-will" employment. This means that the employer or the employee can terminate the employment relationship at any time, for any lawful reason, with or without giving prior notice. Despite this presumption, courts increasingly find that the employment relationship is contractual, whether or not such a contract has been formalized in writing. Courts usually will consider a variety of factors when looking at how contractual relationships are established. These factors include unwritten employer policies and practices, and verbal assurances of long-term or permanent employment.

Employers that believe that they can avoid the contractual nature of an employment relationship, simply by foregoing written terms of employment, may instead find themselves confronting a discharged employee who claims that the termination breached the provisions of an implied contract of employment. The risk of such claims can be reduced by including express "at-will" provisions as part of an employee handbook. Many federal and state courts have ruled that a properly written at-will provision in an employee handbook can negate an employee's claim that the employer was required to have good cause for termination.

Some employers are concerned that their employees will not accept an employee handbook, and that employees will react negatively to the implementation of written policies. Such objections do not stem from the handbook itself; rather it is a matter of how the handbook is implemented. Employers that take adequate time to explain the purpose of a handbook generally find that employees appreciate having the company's policies and procedures communicated in writing. Sometimes when an employer creates a handbook, pre-existing, company-provided benefits are revealed for employees to take advantage of.

The most common excuse for not implementing an employee handbook is that the employer is too small. However, small employers often become the targets of employee claims because of unwritten, inconsistently applied and misunderstood employment practices. Regardless of the employer's size, all employees benefit from a clear explanation of what they can expect to receive and what is expected of them in return. Clear communication results in fewer employee claims.

The Outdated Employee Handbook

The only consistent and reliable aspect of personnel laws and regulations is that they are in a constant state of flux. Federal and state legislatures frequently enact new legislation and amend existing statutes. Courts continuously reinterpret the meaning of established labor laws. As a result, an employee handbook not regularly reviewed for legal compliance will likely contain unintended violations of the law or ambiguous provisions that could be construed and used against an employer. Any handbook that is older than a year is likely outdated. Even an employer that had its handbook originally prepared by an attorney should continue to have it regularly reviewed by a professional who understands labor relations in the states in which the employer operates. Handbooks borrowed from other employers or approved by counsel in other states may contain obsolete, inapplicable or even illegal provisions.

Design And Implementation Of Employee Handbooks

While there is no single best approach to the design, implementation and updating of an employee handbook, the following elements can form the basis of the employer's formal policies and procedures.

1. Clear and understandable
2. Comprehensive and all-inclusive
3. Internally consistent and non-discriminatory
4. Reflective of actual employer policies
5. Prepared or reviewed by a knowledgeable labor law professional
6. Distributed to all existing and new employees
7. Translated or explained in employees' native language
8. Acknowledged by employees in writing
9. Implemented and followed
10. Regularly reviewed and updated

The Handbook Should Be Clear And Understandable. Even the most comprehensive handbook will not be effective unless it can be understood by all employees. An employee handbook must be written in a language and style that employees will understand. A handbook is neither a college text nor a legal brief. Rules, policies and procedures should be presented simply and in a clear and concise manner. The use of long sentences, buzzwords and complex or technical terms should be avoided. Some of the most popular word-processing programs include a function that will automatically analyze and adjust the level and complexity of written text. Such programs can be a helpful tool. If the handbook is written to the lowest common denominator, the chances of having it understood by all employees will be greatly increased.

Before the handbook is finalized, an employer should give a discussion draft to its managers and supervisors for review. If managers and supervisors cannot understand the handbook, neither will the employees. Such a peer review has the added benefit of making managers and supervisors feel that they are a part of the handbook-development process. It also serves to help familiarize and reinforce their own understanding of the employer's policies. A well-trained management team that is prepared to answer employee questions can be an effective way to continue educating employees on the personnel policies and procedures.

The Handbook Should Be Non-Discriminatory. Because one of the primary purposes of an employee handbook is to help the employer avoid claims made by its employees, it is absolutely essential for the handbook to be written in non-discriminatory language. Gender-specific references such as "he" or "she" should be avoided. The handbook should use terms like "he/she," "the employee" or a plural word like "they."

The employer's policies and rules also should be written to anticipate and avoid unintended discrimination. For example, many employers include a "non-fraternization" policy in their handbooks. Such policies prohibit romantic relationships between co-workers. Non-fraternization policies often require that the two employees who are romantically involved either end their relationship or no longer work together. If the employees choose not to end their relationship, many employers require that one of the employees be transferred. Termination may be required if this proves impossible. An employer's first inclination often is to transfer or terminate the employee with the "lowest" job classification. While this may appear to be a non-discriminatory approach, the net effect can be the transfer or termination of the female employee if the employer has more women in "lower" job classifications than men. To avoid such unintended discrimination, the non-fraternization policy should instead state that the employee with the least seniority will be terminated.

An Employee Handbook Should Be Reflective Of Actual Employer Policies. Many employers prepare their employee handbooks using "one-size-fits-all" formats purchased from a trade association, chamber of commerce or other provider. Other employers copy their handbooks from those of competitors or other businesses. Sometimes an employer simply takes a photocopied, preprinted or computer-generated handbook and puts its own name and logo on the cover without making any changes. Unfortunately these "instant" handbooks seldom reflect the employer's actual employment policies, and may in fact contain provisions that by law or practice are totally inapplicable to the employer's operations, or even illegal.

Before adopting any handbook, particularly a handbook prepared by someone outside of the employer's organization or copied from another source, it should be carefully reviewed to verify that it accurately describes the employer's policies and benefits as they truly exist. An employer should be aware that a handbook implements rules that both the employer and the employees must abide by. An employer should not set rules that it is not willing to live with.

An Employee Handbook Should Be Prepared Or Reviewed By A Knowledgeable Labor Law Professional. With the proliferation of federal, state and local labor laws and regulations, which cover issues that range from sexual harassment to workers' compensation, many employers find it impossible to keep up with the constant changes. Even human resource professionals can be frustrated when they attempt to make sense of labor laws that contradict each other.

To avoid this frustration, an employer (particularly a small or medium-sized employer that does not have a full-time, in-house human resource professional) should have its employee handbook prepared and periodically reviewed by a knowledgeable labor law attorney or consultant. An employer should not ask its corporate or business lawyer for help in this area. While a corporate or business lawyer may be the right person to consult with on the purchase of a building or lease of equipment, he or she may not have sufficient knowledge of labor law. Expertise is important.

The Employee Handbook Should Be Distributed To All Existing And New Employees. A copy of the employee handbook should be distributed to all existing employees and given to all new hires as a part of a formal orientation process. An employer may wish to meet with its employees in order to explain important provisions, answer questions about a newly adopted handbook, or discuss changes to existing policy. The employer might even consider using an outside labor professional or trainer during these meetings to explain why certain handbook provisions are necessary and what effect they will have.

Employees should be urged to read the handbook and ask their supervisors about anything they do not understand. They also should be asked to sign a written acknowledgment that they have received, read and understand the handbook. This acknowledgment should be kept as part of the employee's personnel file as proof that the handbook was issued. If an employee later brings a wrongful discharge lawsuit, a claim of discrimination or harassment, or a wage-and-hour claim, the employee's signed acknowledgment can be used as proof that the employee was fully informed of and bound by the provisions of the employer's handbook. A signed acknowledgement can be a vital part of an employer's defense against such a claim.

The Employee Handbook Should Be Translated Or Explained In The Employees' Native Languages. While it is important that the employee handbook be written in plain English, with today's multilingual work force, this may not be enough. Some employers have high percentages of non-English-speaking employees. Communicating the rules of employment to these workers presents special problems.

Translating the handbook into the employees' native languages is one solution, but this can be expensive. Although there is translation software available that will automatically convert text into a foreign language, accuracy usually is less than 100%. While these may be sufficient for personal travel and correspondence uses, such programs may not be reliable enough for business documents like an employee handbook.

An alternative to complete translation is to explain the highlights of the handbook orally through the use of a translator. In either case, care must be taken to assure that the specifics of the employee handbook are not lost through the translation process.

The Employer Should Follow The Employee Handbook. It might seem unnecessary to say, but the employer also must follow the provisions of its employee handbook. Too often, employers that adopt handbooks do not follow their own rules.

Therefore, it is important that an employer carefully consider the employee policies and benefits that it adopts. An employer should not promise employees more than it intends to deliver, and it must deliver what it promises. A failure to follow its own employee handbook may result in a lawsuit for breach of contract, or worse, a finding of discrimination.

The Employee Handbook Should Be Regularly Reviewed And Updated. Even the most carefully prepared and reviewed employee handbook will require updating over time. An employer's policies change, new labor laws are passed and old labor laws frequently are amended. The courts constantly interpret and reinterpret the meaning of labor laws and regulations. This underscores the need for handbooks to be regularly reviewed and updated.

Periodic updating can be streamlined if some thought is given to the handbook when it is first designed. Is the handbook produced in a bound volume that must be completely reprinted each time changes are made, or is it in a three-ring binder format that facilitates updating? Is each individual policy, rule or procedure printed on a separate page so that a single policy can be rewritten, deleted or added without requiring the whole handbook to be redone? Is each page of the handbook dated so that original and update pages can be kept separate from each other? A little pre-planning can help an employer avoid problems when it comes time to update the handbook.

Sexual Harassment And Employee Awareness Training

Most employers will benefit by changing the way they think about sexual harassment and the way that their employees interact with one another. What used to be considered safe, consensual conduct often can be misconstrued and should be avoided entirely.

The Scope Of Sexual Harassment Claims

Items as innocuous as birthday cards, Christmas gifts or even supportive "hugs" can be taken out of context and used against employers. In such an environment, employers should counsel their employees to avoid sexual jokes or comments altogether. Countless cases involve employees who laughed at a joke and seemingly participated in the fun, only to later contend they simply felt too embarrassed to complain. The fact that an employee merely laughed at a joke, comment or gesture does not insulate the employer from liability or bar the employee from later bringing a claim.

One of the most common complaints of sexual harassment involves the consensual relationship between employees. Often, a spurned lover later claims that he or she was pressured into granting sexual favors for the sake of keeping the job or advancing in the business. Other employees claim that when they have attempted to break off the relationship, the co-worker refused to listen and continued to pressure the employee at work. Either scenario makes for the need to sort through the stories by way of messy, expensive and often embarrassing depositions and written discovery in litigation. An employer's claim that the relationship was consensual will not make a lawsuit go away. It usually is left to a jury to decide whether the relationship was truly consensual. Some juries have decided that where a relationship involves a supervisor and a subordinate, an implied threat is inherent in the relationship.

Non-Fraternization Policies

Because of the increased exposure arising from sexual relationships among employees, many businesses are implementing non-fraternization policies by prohibiting sexual relationships between co-workers, especially in employee/supervisor relations. However, before implementing such a policy, employers should consult with expert counsel in their state, as some states prohibit employment policies that affect employees' activities outside the workplace.

Harassment Policies And Communication

The key to controlling sexual harassment in the workplace is communication. Employers must adopt strong and clear policies prohibiting such conduct and make their employees aware of these policies. At a minimum, a sexual harassment policy should describe and give examples of the various types of conduct that might be deemed as harassment. The policy also should make clear that the employer will not permit or condone sexual harassment in the workplace and that any such harassment will result in severe discipline, up to and including termination. A sexual harassment policy should tell employees to inform within management of any claimed harassment. More than one person should be designated in the event that the designated person is the harasser. The policy should affirm that the employer will fully investigate any charge of harassment and will take all appropriate actions if harassment is found to have occurred. The policy also should state that steps will be taken to ensure that an employee is not retaliated against for reporting an incident. Some states, such as California, actually dictate the specific requisites of a sexual harassment policy and require that the policy be disseminated in writing to all employees.

Managers and supervisors should be trained to handle all harassment claims and issues with care. If employees feel that they can go to their employer for help, they are less likely to make a claim with an administrative agency or to find an attorney who is more eager to help them.

Diversity Management

As the frequency and severity of harassment and discrimination claims continue to rise in the U.S., more companies and public agencies are attempting to reduce their exposure to such risks by investing in workplace diversity and awareness programs. However, without careful planning and a critical evaluation of the effectiveness of such programs, the risk of claims may not be reduced. Poorly executed programs may even increase the potential for claims.

Because media scrutiny increasingly focuses on high-profile sexual harassment and discrimination cases, such as those involving Texaco or Mitsubishi, some corporations are actively pursuing diversity management programs, betting that such initiatives can improve worker morale, improve productivity and ultimately reduce their exposure to potential lawsuits and claims. Other companies are implementing diversity programs simply for their perceived public relations value. However, critics of diversity management warn that companies may need to temper their enthusiasm and take a critical look at diversity initiatives that promise to manage or mitigate the risks of sexual harassment and racial discrimination.

Defining A New Field

Diversity management refers to any number of initiatives or training programs that attempt to alleviate purported problems associated with the development of an increasingly diverse workforce. Diversity management programs can be composed of classes on race and gender awareness, affirmative-action initiatives, multi-cultural marketing programs or long-range corporate restructuring featuring diversity as an organizing principle. However, a common approach to diversity management is the implementation of training that seeks to improve interpersonal communication among employees and increase sensitivity to the issues of race and gender in the workplace.[1]

Diversity management advocates argue that one of the keys to reducing racial discrimination and sexual harassment in the workplace is to increase education and awareness about the multi-racial, multi-ethnic, multi-gendered, multi-sexual and multi-generational nature of today's workforce. Many experts believe that as the American workforce becomes increasingly diverse, both employers and employees need develop the social tools and training necessary to facilitate communication, cooperation and productivity across cultural lines. Moreover, some advocates argue that corporate culture itself needs to undergo a drastic makeover to fully utilize the talents of its workforce and eliminate the potential for various forms of discrimination and harassment.

---

[1] A complete discussion of the various types of programs that can be placed under the rubric of diversity management is beyond the scope of this book. We are primarily interested in diversity training as a tool to prevent or reduce the potential for racial discrimination and sexual harassment.

The Audience Is Listening

Diversity consultants have found a receptive audience in corporate America. Looking for ways to bolster their public image while fending off potential lawsuits, many companies turn to diversity consultants for a "quick-fix" to what may be complex problems. Recent reports indicate that over one-third of the nation's 500 largest industrial companies already have some form of workplace diversity program in place, while a third more are planning to implement them.[2] The field of diversity management consulting has grown rapidly over the past few years and is now a billion-dollar industry. Many of the country's largest corporations, including General Motors, Xerox, Motorola, Proctor and Gamble, and Coca-Cola, have invested in diversity management programs.[3]

While many companies are voluntarily establishing diversity management programs, others have been forced to implement them. Take, for example, the case of Mitsubishi Corporation, which was boycotted for eight months after several women made allegations that they were sexually harassed. Mitsubishi responded with what executive vice president Kohei Ikuta called "one of the most comprehensive sexual harassment training programs in the automotive industry." The company also said that it would increase the number of minority-owned dealerships from 10 to 15 percent in five years and offer "company-assisted funding" to do it.[4] In another case, after Circuit City Stores, Inc. lost a racial discrimination suit, the judge in the case ordered the company to appoint a "director of diversity" and employ an outside consultant to handle any diversity issues that may arise within the company.

Sometimes companies jump on the diversity management bandwagon simply to bolster their public image. In an age where public perception of companies is just as important as the products they sell, many corporations are hoping that the mere presence of diversity programs will ingratiate them with consumers.

The Potential Downside Of Diversity Management

The diversity management movement, however, is not without its critics. Many outspoken critics of diversity management argue that the movement is largely a veiled affirmative-action initiative that may actually worsen already strained workplace relations by emphasizing the differences between employees, resulting in a lack of cohesiveness.

Critics argue that many diversity programs go beyond education and awareness training and adversely affect employment and promotion policies by advocating changes in the ways companies judge employee performance. Dinesh D'Souza, a scholar at the

---

[2] Douglas A. Blackmon. "Familiar Refrain." *The Wall Street Journal,* March 11, 1997.
[3] Dinesh D'Souza. "The Perils of Managing Diversity." *Chief Executive,* December 1996.
[4] Rayner Pike. "Mitsubishi Boycott Called Off as Company Promises Reform." *Orange County Register,* January 16, 1997.

American Enterprise Institute, argues that many diversity management programs attempt to do away with essential merit standards, which may "sacrifice performance and productivity at the altar of social and cultural diversity." D'Souza argues for a more "pragmatic" approach to the question of diversity in the workplace that does not involve changing the way in which worker performance is judged; different standards of performance drawn along racial or gender lines may only exacerbate tensions among workers.[5]

Buyer Beware

One of the major problems in attempting to evaluate the merits and shortcomings of diversity management is the lack of reliable research on its effect on the occurrence of sexual harassment and racial discrimination in the workplace. Organizations should approach the question of managing diversity with caution. Keep the following points in mind when considering the implementation of diversity management programs:

- There exists little empirical evidence to suggest that diversity management programs reduce or contain sexual harassment or racial discrimination claims or lawsuits. While some forms of diversity training may lead to an increased awareness of issues surrounding race and gender in the workplace, it does not necessarily follow that such training will actually lead to behavioral changes in individuals.

- If companies are hoping diversity programs will increase productivity and profits, they should be aware that there is no empirical evidence that diversity management programs enhance either. On the contrary, there is some evidence to suggest that extremely heterogeneous groups may become less productive, owing largely to the inability to develop consensus and cohesiveness. The optimal level of diversity for any organization depends on its size, industry, public image and productivity.

- Diversity management as a discipline is relatively new. As such, the theory, orientation and methodologies used in the field are varied and undergoing constant development and refinement. Companies need to have a clear conception of what they hope to accomplish and be secure that the techniques and programs being used will achieve that goal.

- Beware of consultants who provide "cookie-cutter" approaches. One of the nation's largest consulting firms was recently criticized for delivering almost identical reports and recommendations to several different companies after

---

[5] D'Souza, op. cit.

promising to develop custom workplace diversity programs tailored to each company.[6]

- Sometimes bad management is worse than no management. Diversity management programs can actually backfire if not implemented properly. One California grocery store chain, for example, recently found itself on the losing end of a discrimination case in which incriminating evidence came directly from company-sponsored diversity training sessions. In those sessions, managers were asked to discuss racial and sexual stereotypes. After a discrimination suit was filed by several employees, notes taken during those sessions were admitted as evidence. Companies need to make sure that diversity training is conducted by qualified individuals who know as much about employment practices liability as they do about multi-cultural awareness.

Conclusion

Any potential diversity management program should be reviewed carefully before implementation. Such a review should focus on the following areas:

- Objective—Companies need to clearly define the objective or goal of any diversity initiative. The objective may be clearly defined by the underlying motivation for pursuing diversity management; bolstering current anti-harassment and anti-discrimination efforts, diversifying the workforce, or raising public image are all possible objectives and all require individually tailored programs.

- Scope—Companies need to determine whether the program can be administered "in-house" or whether outside assistance will be needed. A program that only calls for the communication and reinforcement of existing company policies on discrimination and harassment likely can be implemented internally, whereas a long-term workforce diversification program may require outside assistance.

- Effectiveness—Diversity management, like any other management technique, should be judged on its effectiveness in fulfilling its objective. If the goal is to increase employee productivity, seek evidence that such programs will work as advertised.

In light of the litigious atmosphere that pervades American society, especially where racial discrimination and sexual harassment are concerned, companies need to consider all potential methods that can reduce their exposures; diversity management may be an

---

[6] Blackmon, op.cit.

important part of such programs. Diversity management should not, however, be viewed as a "quick fix" or "silver bullet" to the potentially catastrophic problems of racial discrimination and sexual harassment in the workplace.

Preventing Wrongful Discharge Suits

Specify The Rules

As noted above, an employer should take care not to promise employees more than it can or is willing to deliver. For example, an employer should not talk about "permanent" or "lifetime employment" when it does not really mean that it will keep the employee forever, regardless of circumstances. Close attention should be paid to employee handbooks, employment applications and other employment documentation that may suggest that an employee's employment is permanent or that discharge will occur only for "good cause." Employers should avoid discipline policies that provide for termination only when an employee violates a specifically identified rule. Such a policy might be interpreted to mean that an employee cannot be terminated for any other reason, even something as serious as theft. Similarly, an employer should avoid creating a progressive discipline process that restricts the employer's ability to terminate an employee without taking every step in the process. It should be noted, however, that some employers, such as governmental bodies receiving federal funds, are required to afford certain classes of employees' due process rights prior to a demotion or termination. These employers, therefore, have limitations on their actions to terminate employees without following specified procedures.

An employer should consider expressly defining its employee-discharge policy as "at-will." This can be accomplished by including a clear "at-will" employment statement as part of the employment application completed by prospective employees, or by having newly hired and existing employees sign an at-will employment agreement. However, since such a disclaimer may have a negative impact on employee morale, some employers prefer to adopt detailed rules advising employees of what conduct will result in discharge. On the other hand, such a list of rules may inadvertently omit some appropriate grounds for discharge. Each approach has its advantages and disadvantages, but in either case, the employer must take care that employees clearly understand the rules.

Many employers require a newly hired employee to serve a probationary period. Such a requirement is thought to give the employee a trial period during which the employer is free to discharge the employee for little or no reason. But many courts have found an implication that discharge may be made only for good cause when the employee successfully completes the probationary period. Also keep in mind that an employee discharged during a probationary period still can make a claim for unlawful discrimination. Employers should consider avoiding any reference to a probationary period. Use of the term *trial period* may help, but to avoid any misunderstanding of the intent of a trial period, the employer may choose to discontinue the practice of a formal probationary period and instead informally observe a new employee's performance and document deficiencies as needed. A waiting period still may be required for benefit eligibility, but without the negative implication that arises from a formal probationary period.

Be Candid With Employees

An employer should give employees regular, periodic written evaluations of their work performance. Unfortunately, many employers that evaluate employees seek to avoid the sometimes difficult task of informing an employee of less-than-adequate performance. The resulting inflated evaluation can be used against the employer at a later date. For example, an employee discharged because he or she did not get along with co-workers might point out that such a problem was never mentioned in any performance evaluations, and in fact he or she was always rated above average in their peer interactions. Where this occurs, a jury might be persuaded that the reason given by the employer for the discharge was actually a subterfuge, and that the discharge was based on unlawful discrimination. Therefore, it is important that evaluations accurately and candidly reflect the employee's performance as compared with the employer's standards and expectations.

If an employee's performance is so poor that he or she is in danger of discharge, the evaluation should specify the areas of needed improvement, give a specific time frame within which the employee is to improve, and put the employee on notice as to the consequences of non-improvement.

Employees should be provided with a copy of their performance evaluation. They also should be given an opportunity to make comments. The employee should be asked to sign the evaluation form. If the employee chooses not to exercise this right, the employer should have that fact witnessed and documented. The employer should keep the signed evaluation, along with other employment documents, such as employment applications, warning notices and termination reports, in readily identifiable and confidential employee personnel files. The most comprehensive employment documentation in the world is meaningless unless the employer can find it when needed.

Employee Discipline

Except in cases such as theft, intoxication at work or gross misconduct, progressive discipline should precede discharge. In other words, an employee ought to be given one or more warnings or some other type of discipline, such as a suspension, demotion or transfer prior to discharge.

In the case of employee evaluation, a disciplinary notice should be honest and direct. The employee should be informed as to the reason for the warning or discipline, accorded a specific period within which to meet the employer's standards of performance and advised as to the consequences of non-performance. The employee, after having an opportunity to comment upon and sign the warning notice, should be given a copy, with the original being retained in the employee's personnel file.

Consider The Options

Discharge is not the only possible solution to the problem of an employee who performs unsatisfactorily or violates employer rules and policies. If the employee has a long record of good service but has recently been promoted to a job that is beyond his or her ability, an employer might consider demotion, possibly by return to a job in which the employee adequately performed. If the employee's problem arises from a personality conflict with peers, counseling might be considered. Other alternatives might consist of a referral to an employee-assistance program, a disciplinary suspension without pay or the granting of outplacement assistance or other benefits in exchange for a written release of claims against the employer.

Discharge

In those situations where it becomes necessary for an employer to discharge an employee, the reasons for the discharge should be documented in writing. Care must be taken when stating the reasons for discharge. In any subsequent administrative or judicial proceedings, an employer may not be able to rely upon grounds other than those originally presented to the employee to support the discharge, even if there were other reasons. Additionally, care should be taken to avoid any implication that discharge was based on an illegal reason. For example, if an employer discharges a woman because of her inability to fulfill the aspects of their job that require travel, the employer may be exposed to a claim of sex discrimination if she is unable to travel because of child care.

The discharge interview is not an appropriate time for the employer to try to avoid hurting an employee's feelings by being less than absolutely candid. This is not to say that the final meeting between the employer and the employee should degenerate into a name-calling session. On the contrary, the discharge interview should be handled as tactfully as possible, since in some states the manner and method of an employee's discharge may actually be the basis for a lawsuit. Therefore, the employer should have two representatives at the discharge meeting: one who conducts the meeting and one to witness the event. Both employer representatives should prepare a file memo immediately after the meeting, detailing what happened and what was said. These memos should be put into the employee's personnel file in case of any subsequent administrative or judicial claim. The discharge meeting should be conducted behind closed doors, to avoid involving the entire company. While other employees ought to be informed of the discharge, it is usually best that they not be given detailed explanations. To avoid claims of defamation, such matters should be left between the employer and the employee. The discharged employee should be allowed to collect his or her personal belongings and leave the employer's premises without being humiliated.

Post-Termination References

Often, an employer will be approached by a discharged employee or their prospective employer for a reference. The employer may feel some obligation to give a positive reference to help the employee get a new position. Such a reference, however, may undermine the reason given for discharge and may be used against the employer in case of subsequent litigation. On the other hand, a negative reference, even if truthful, may provide fuel for a discharged and already disgruntled ex-employee to bring a claim against the former employer for defamation, blacklisting or discrimination. To avoid this possibility, an employer should give a "neutral" job reference that includes only length of service, final position held and rate-of-pay at termination.

Settlement Agreements And Release Of Claims

If an employer is in the process of discharging an employee and believes that the employee may respond with some sort of administrative or judicial claim, the employer may consider the use of a settlement agreement and release of claims. Under such an agreement, the employee may receive severance pay, outplacement assistance or an extension of benefits that he or she would not otherwise legally be entitled to. In return, the employee waives all claims relating to his or her discharge, or any other aspect of the employment. Thus, the employer is protected from post-employment litigation.

However, there are some restrictions on the use of such settlement agreements. For example, an employee cannot give up an age-discrimination claim under the federal Age Discrimination in Employment Act unless he or she has been given 21 days to consider the waiver. Even then, the employee has a seven-day period to cancel the settlement agreement. Similarly, some states restrict the types of claims (such as workers' compensation and unemployment) that employees can waive. Employers also should be aware that employees sometimes claim that they were in a position of duress at the time of signing a release or waiver, and therefore such release or waiver is ineffective. The employer should therefore take care to avoid placing undue pressure on an employee to sign a release or waiver agreement.

Arbitration And Mediation

In an effort to control the cost of litigation, employers increasingly are turning to arbitration agreements and mediation to resolve employment-related disputes. While arbitration and mediation generally are effective loss-control tools, some employers favor these alternative-dispute-resolution procedures while others do not. Depending on how the arbitration or mediation agreements are structured, there may be a debate whether such agreements are just and fair for both the employer and the employee.

An increasing number of employers are requiring as a *condition* of employment that applicants and employees give up their right to pursue employment discrimination claims in court and agree to resolve disputes through *binding* arbitration. These agreements may be presented in the form of an employment contract or be included in an employee handbook or elsewhere. Some employers have even included such agreements in employment applications.

The use of such agreements is not limited to particular industries, but can be found in various sectors of the workforce, including, for example, the securities industry, retail, restaurant and hotel chains, health care, broadcasting, and security services. Some individuals subject to mandatory arbitration agreements have challenged the enforceability of these agreements by bringing employment discrimination actions in the courts. The EEOC, while mindful of case law enforcing specific mandatory arbitration agreements,[7] nonetheless, believes that such agreements are inconsistent with the civil rights laws.

Advantages Of Arbitration

Some of the arguments used to support the use of mandatory arbitration to resolve employment disputes cite reduced legal fees, avoidance of large, emotionally based jury awards, less adverse publicity (because arbitration awards usually are sealed) and less administrative time spent by management assisting in the defense of a claim. Arbitration also can foster positive employee/employer relations because both parties are able to resolve disputes faster and in a less formal and less adversarial environment than traditional litigation.

Those employers favoring arbitration of employment disputes often point to the fact that Congress and the US Supreme Court clearly prefer arbitration over formal litigation. For example, the Civil Rights Act of 1991 and the Age Discrimination in Employment Act (ADEA) both contain wording that expressly encourages the use of arbitration to resolve discrimination claims.

---

[7] In particular, the Supreme Court's decision in *Gilmer v. Interstate/Johnson Lane Corp.*, 500 U.S. 33 (1991).2

Disadvantages Of Arbitration

Some aspects of arbitration can be disadvantageous. Although arbitration may be the fastest way to resolve an employment dispute, a binding arbitration decision generally cannot be appealed, and the losing party may be required to accept an incorrect and possibly unjust decision by the arbitrator. Also, the lack of formality in the arbitration process often allows the arbitrator to ignore the traditional rules of evidence or other legal constraints, and this may make it difficult or impossible for each party to discover the other's position in advance of the hearing. However, at least one federal court of appeals recently held that the parties to an arbitration agreement can mutually agree to expand judicial review of an arbitration award beyond the limits imposed by either federal or state statute.[8] If the employee presents a complex set of issues or possesses numerous important documents, the employer may be hampered in its defense by the very informality that drew it to arbitration in the first place. Concerns are sometimes expressed that arbitrators tend to "split the difference," while courts are more inclined to rule directly on the merits of each party's case.

Those who oppose the mandatory and binding arbitration of employment disputes also maintain that employees are unjustly deprived of due process, have fewer and less beneficial remedies available, and will prevail less often than in a court of law. These critics feel that requiring a worker to sign an arbitration agreement as a condition of employment is unfair because, in effect, the employee has no other choice but to sign such an agreement.

The Equal Employment Opportunity Commission has openly opposed mandatory arbitration of discrimination claims when the requirement to do so is made a condition of new or continuing employment.[9] Even the American Arbitration Association has adopted policies that encourage (but do not require) employers to offer voluntary, rather than mandatory, arbitration to the workforce.

When deciding whether or not to implement an arbitration agreement to new and/or current employees, employers should consider several factors. Requiring new hires to sign a mandatory arbitration agreement as a condition of employment can be risky for the employer. There is the possibility that a legal challenge will be made by the employee on the grounds that because the prospective employee had no alternative, the agreement to waive the right to litigation was not voluntary. Some courts hold that such an agreement *is* voluntary because the individual could always choose to work elsewhere. Other courts point to the economic realities of the situation and hold that there often is no choice of alternate employment.

---

[8] *Lapine Technology Corporation v. Kyocera Corporation,* (9th Cir., 1997). In this case, the parties agreed that the arbitrator's award could be reviewed by the court for errors of fact or law. This heightened judicial scrutiny went well beyond the limitations of the Federal Arbitration Act which permit a court to vacate or modify an arbitration award only if the award is "completely irrational," exhibits a "manifest disregard of the law," or otherwise falls within one of the grounds set forth in 9 U.S.C. Secs. 10 or 11).

[9] Refer to EEOC discussion on page 100.

Many experts agree that an employer usually cannot require a current employee to sign any contract regarding the employment relationship without some additional form of consideration being given. Such consideration might include a beneficial change in employment status, a raise or bonus, or something else of value to the employee. Some employers have satisfied the consideration requirement by offering a "for-cause" employment relationship to those employees who agree to arbitrate disputes, while retaining an "at-will" relationship with those employees who choose not to sign such an agreement. In most instances where these alternatives have been implemented, the majority of workers opted in favor of the arbitration agreement.

EEOC Position[10] On Mandatory Binding Arbitration Provisions

On record, the EEOC strongly supports voluntary alternative-dispute-resolution programs that resolve employment discrimination disputes in a fair and credible manner. This position is based on the recognition that while even the best arbitral systems do not afford the benefits of the judicial system, well-designed ADR programs (including binding arbitration) can offer in particular cases other valuable benefits to civil rights claimants, such as significant savings in time and expense.

Moreover, the EEOC recognizes that the judicial system itself has drawbacks. Accordingly, an individual may decide in a particular case to forego the judicial forum and resolve the case through arbitration. This is consistent with civil rights enforcement as long as the individual's decision is made *freely* after a dispute has arisen.

The EEOC believes however that the use of unilaterally imposed agreements mandating binding arbitration of employment discrimination disputes as a *condition* of employment harms both the individual civil rights, and the public's interest in eradicating discrimination.

EEOC believes that those whom the law seeks to regulate should not be permitted to exempt themselves from federal enforcement of civil rights laws. Nor should they be permitted to deprive civil rights claimants of the choice to vindicate their statutory rights in the courts—an avenue of redress determined by Congress to be essential to enforcement.

Although the EEOC has challenged (by litigation, amicus curiae[11] participation, or EEOCer charge) particular mandatory arbitration agreements with provisions that flagrantly eviscerate core rights and remedies available under the civil rights laws, employers continue to require such agreements as a condition of employment.

---

[10] Coordination and Guidance Programs, Office of Legal Counsel.
[11] *Amicus Curiae*—Friendly intervention of counsel to remind court of legal matters which has escaped its notice. (*Black's Law Dictionary*).

Limitations Of Mandated Arbitration As Articulated By EEOC

Mandatory arbitration has inherent limitations and problems that cannot be cured by any improvement in existing arbitration systems.

- **The Arbitral Process Is Private In Nature And Allows For Little Public Accountability**

    The nature of the arbitral process allows—by design—for minimal, if any, public accountability of arbitrators or arbitral decision-making. Unlike counterparts in the judiciary, the arbitrator only answers to the private parties of the dispute, and not to the public at large.

    Also, because such decisions are private, there is little, if any, public accountability, even for employers found to have violated the law. This lack of public disclosure prevents assessment of whether practices of individual employers or particular industries are in need of reform.

- **Arbitration, By Its Nature, Does Not Allow For The Development Of The Law**

    Because of the limited judicial review of arbitrated decisions, arbitration affords no opportunity to build upon the law through precedent.

    There is also virtually no opportunity for meaningful scrutiny of arbitrated decision-making. This leaves higher courts and Congress unable to act to correct errors in statutory interpretation.

- **Arbitration Limits Claimants' Rights**

    Arbitration systems, regardless of how fair they may be, limit the rights of injured individuals in important ways. Civil rights litigants often have the choice to have their case heard by a jury of peers, while, by definition, the arbitral forum juries are unavailable. Discovery is significantly limited compared with that available in court and permitted under the Federal Rules of Civil Procedure. In addition, arbitration systems are not suitable for resolving class or pattern or practice claims of discrimination.

    In fact, arbitration systems may protect systemic discriminators by adjudicating claims one at a time, in isolation, without reference to a broader (and more accurate) view of an employer's conduct.

▸ Mandatory Arbitration Systems Include Structural Biases Against Discrimination Plaintiffs

The employer is a party to arbitration in all disputes with its employees. In contrast, the employee is a "one-shot player" in his or her own dispute with the employer. As a result, the employee is generally less capable of making an informed selection of arbitrators than the employer, who can keep better track of an arbitrator's record. In addition, results are possibly influenced by the fact that the employer, not the employee, is a potential source of future business for the arbitrator. A recent study of nonunion employment law disputes found that the more frequent an employer uses arbitration, the better the employer fares.

Very few, if any, employees insist on the mandatory arbitration of future statutory employment disputes as a condition of accepting a job offer. The very suggestion seems far-fetched.

Rather, employers impose these agreements because they are in their best interest, and they are made possible by the employer's superior bargaining power. Thus, it is not surprising that many employer-mandated arbitration systems fall far short of basic concepts of fairness.

▸ Mandatory Arbitration Agreements Adversely Affect The EEOC's Ability To Enforce The Civil Rights Laws

The trend to impose mandatory arbitration agreements as a condition of employment also poses a significant threat to the EEOC's statutory responsibility to enforce the federal employment discrimination laws. Effective enforcement by the EEOC depends in large part on the initiative of individuals to report instances of discrimination to the EEOC. Although employers may not lawfully deprive individuals of their statutory right to file employment discrimination charges with the EEOC or otherwise interfere with individuals' protected participation in investigations or proceedings under these laws, employees who are bound by mandatory arbitration agreements may be unaware that they nonetheless may file an EEOC charge.

Moreover, individuals are likely to be discouraged from coming to the EEOC when they know they will be unable to litigate their claims in court. These chilling effects on charge filing undermine the EEOC's enforcement efforts by decreasing channels of information, limiting the agency's awareness of potential violations of law, and impeding its ability to investigate possible unlawful actions.

Drafting An Arbitration Agreement

Employers that choose to encourage arbitration as a means of resolving employment disputes should make sure that the procedures are both fair and impartial from the standpoint of the employee. Employers should make sure their arbitration agreement contains the following elements:

- A complete, clear and understandable description of the types of disputes and claims covered by the agreement.

- A statement that both parties agree that arbitration is to be the exclusive remedy for employment disputes.

- A comprehensive description of the procedures included in the arbitration process, such as discovery of documents, depositions, expert witness participation and right to counsel.

- The remedies available to the employee under the arbitration agreement, such as general damages, job reinstatement, etc. These remedies should closely mirror the remedies that otherwise would have been available to the employee if the dispute were resolved through litigation.

- The procedure for selecting an unbiased arbitrator.

- A requirement that the arbitrator follow the law governing the underlying dispute, and that the parties be permitted to communicate to the arbitrator, orally or in writing, their respective legal and factual positions.

- A requirement that the arbitrator issue a "reasoned" opinion, in writing, with findings of fact and conclusions of law, within a specified period of time after the hearing.

- An applicable statute of limitations.[12]

- A provision for the payment of the arbitrator, court reporter (if any), and other related costs. Based on recent judicial pronouncements, such a provision may give the arbitrator the authority to require either party to pay the fee for the other party's representation during the arbitration proceeding, if this is otherwise permitted under federal or state law (such as is the case for a prevailing party under many federal and state civil rights statutes).

---

[12] There is disagreement among the courts as to whether the statute of limitations set forth in an arbitration agreement may be shorter than the statute of limitations provided for under applicable federal or state law.

Mediation

There are some employment disputes that are best resolved by methods other than arbitration or litigation. One such alternative method is mediation. Mediation is a dispute resolution technique that focuses on achieving a "win-win" result for both parties. Disputes involving current employees who are expected to remain employed after the issues have been resolved often are suited for mediation. When mediation procedures are implemented early in the dispute, litigation is less likely because the parties are not yet intractable or emotionally invested in the outcome.

Unlike arbitration and litigation, mediation essentially is a settlement process. Each party conveys its respective position to the other and agrees to work together toward a resolution of the issue(s). An appointed neutral third-party mediator hears each party's version of the dispute privately, then conveys each party's perspective of the dispute to the other party (if the mediator has been authorized to share the information). In this manner, both parties are allowed to vent their feelings in a safe and confidential environment without the immediate presence of the other party. The end result of mediation often is a negotiated settlement, which permits both parties to maintain a future relationship with little or no rancor.

Unlike arbitration, mediation also can take place after litigation has commenced, provided that both parties are prepared to focus on resolution of the issues rather than winning their case. When a current, prospective or former employee brings suit against the employer, mediation is strategically sound at any one of several stages of the litigation process.

The first stage is during the period prior to when the employer is required to file a formal response to the lawsuit. Mediation at this stage usually results in substantial cost savings to the employer and much less stress to the plaintiff. Another opportunity for mediation is shortly after most of the discovery has been completed. By this time, the parties have become more realistic about the cost and value of their respective positions. Lastly, it is not uncommon for one of the parties to suggest mediation immediately prior to the filing of a dispositive motion, such as a motion for summary judgment, in a last-ditch effort to resolve the dispute.

Other Considerations

While many employment-related disputes will continue to be resolved through formal litigation, arbitration and mediation appear to be the dispute-resolution models most likely to predominate in the future. If approached with a focus on fairness, an arbitrated or mediated resolution of employment problems often results in a less acrimonious and more productive workplace for all concerned. However, employers should give careful consideration to the benefits and possible pitfalls of arbitration and mediation before deciding if these procedures are right for the company. Employers also should consult with qualified counsel experienced in employment-related matters prior to developing and implementing any employment agreement that requires arbitration or mediation of employment disputes.

Arbitration And EPL Insurance

It is important to note that not all EPL insurance policies provide coverage for disputes settled by arbitration or mediation. The definition of *claim* in some policies specifically includes arbitration proceedings. In these policies, the insured's deductible may be reduced if arbitration or mediation successfully resolves the dispute prior to litigation. However, in other policies, coverage for arbitration proceedings is specifically precluded. A few EPL insurance policies exclude coverage for damages and costs associated with arbitration only in certain situations, such as disputes related to collective bargaining agreements or employee handbooks. Accordingly, an employer that has adopted mandatory mediation or arbitration should check to ensure that any EPL coverage that is purchased covers mediation and arbitration.

5 Handling Employment Practices Claims: Intervention And Investigation

Human-resource professionals and others have known for many years that expedient handling of employment-related disputes, complaints and claims is essential in order to reduce the consequences and ultimate cost of alleged or actual wrongful employment practices. Effective claim handling can be achieved by the employer whether acting alone, in conjunction with legal counsel or with an insurance company representative. Some employers have personnel trained and experienced in investigation techniques, but many employers do not. For employers without such resources, the early assignment of counsel can avert costly mistakes and the mishandling of employee disputes and grievances. Although there are costs attendant to the retention of counsel, they may be far less than the costs incurred when assistance is not sought. The potential damage that can be caused by making a wrong decision or conducting a flawed investigation can be enormous.

For the small to mid-sized employer, the handling of an employment practices claim can mean the difference between having a business and being out of business. For large employers, the handling of employment practices claims, especially class action claims or individual claims with substantial punitive damage exposure, can mean the difference between a profitable year and an unprofitable year. Employment practices claims can also lead to the embarrassing removal of senior corporate officers and can ruin the reputation and image of an entire company.

For employment practices liability insurers, the handling of employment practices claims is perhaps the single most important issue they face. Because D&O and CGL insurers are not immune from employment liability claims, they too can be substantially affected by the manner in which such claims are handled or mishandled.

It is not uncommon for claims that initially appear to be non-serious to result in expensive settlements or judgments when mishandled.[1] This chapter discusses four critical components of the claims handling process. These components are (1) investigation (2) initial response to an employment claim within 30 days, (3) insurance company and defense issues, and (4) the role of alternative-dispute resolution.

Investigation

The purpose of a wrongful employment practices investigation is to determine the facts surrounding an employee's allegations of wrongful employment conduct, or the employer's awareness or suspicion that it might not be in compliance with relevant employment laws. Investigations should be thorough. Care should be taken to avoid making any snap judgment of whether any wrongdoing has occurred. Avoiding such judgments is important because the employer may decide to take corrective or disciplinary measures in instances where no illegal activity has taken place. For example, instances have occurred where the employer was alleged to have harassed employees by using derogatory names in connection with their weight. While most employers avoid such conduct, it is not against any federal or state laws to behave in such a fashion.

Also, in order to establish liability on the part of the employer regarding charges of sexual harassment, it may be necessary for the employee to show that the employer failed to investigate his or her complaints promptly, failed to take corrective measures or failed to properly respond. While there are no definitive guidelines from the courts or regulatory agencies as to what constitutes a prompt and thorough good-faith investigation by the employer, the following investigative procedures may be effective.

Pre-Litigation Investigation

Because many employee complaints can be resolved without litigation, employers should be alert to opportunities to resolve potential problems before litigation is initiated. Too often employers undertake a cursory investigation, reach a conclusion that no wrongful behavior or practice has taken place and brace themselves for litigation. This is an unfortunate practice because in many instances the employee only wants the

---

[1] Probably the most publicized example is the case of *Weeks v. Baker & McKenzie*. One can understand how the initial allegations in the *Weeks v. Baker & McKenzie* case could be viewed as non-serious. The claimant in the case, Virginia Weeks, was a recent hire having been employed as a secretary for only several weeks before her complaint of sexual harassment against a partner in the law firm. The complaint was that a partner had placed candy in the claimant's blouse pocket. After the incident, the claimant was transferred to work for other lawyers with the firm. The incident was short in duration and did not involve any sexual relations. Because there were no economic damages and some remedial measures taken, it is easy to see how such an incident might have been considered non-serious. However, the result of a jury trial was a verdict in excess of $7 million against the employer.

offending behavior to stop and does not initially intend to seek the recovery of damages. Also, the offending behavior may be perfectly legal, though inappropriate.

Conducting An Investigation

Once the employer is aware of potential improper conduct, it is important for management to move swiftly and purposefully in its investigation of the alleged or suspected incident. A well-documented account of the investigation, reflecting that it was prompt and impartial, may be sufficient to disprove certain allegations of employment misconduct.

The investigation should be conducted by one person. This helps keep findings and information regarding the investigation confidential. Keep in mind that while the person responsible for investigating employee complaints does not need to have specialized investigative skills or a background in law enforcement, some specialized training in the investigation of employment-related allegations is desirable. The investigator should have good interpersonal skills and should be perceived as neutral by both parties. Many in-house human resource personnel have been successfully trained in employment dispute investigation techniques.

When meeting with an employee who has complained of sexual harassment or other wrongful employment practice, the employer should try to obtain as many facts about the alleged wrongful practice as possible. Obtaining the information may entail asking the employee:

- To describe in his or her own words exactly what happened or the nature of the complaint or request

- To describe the number of times the offensive behavior has occurred

- To describe the entire sequence of events that occurred prior to or led up to the offensive conduct

- Whether he or she in any way consented to the offensive behavior or wrongful employment practice

- The nature of the employee's relationship to the accuser

- The names of any witnesses to the offensive behavior or practice

Post-Litigation Investigation

Where the employer's first knowledge of a potential wrongful employment practice is the filing of a lawsuit, investigation findings are still useful in helping to reduce or prevent the assessment of punitive damages. Pre-litigation and post-litigation investigative techniques are the same. Post-litigation investigation is, however, somewhat more difficult than pre-litigation investigation because an adversarial relationship already has developed between the employee and the employer. Additionally, once the employee has filed a lawsuit, the employer may be unable to interview the employee until a deposition takes place.

Investigation Files

Proper and detailed documentation regarding the conduct and findings of an investigation are critical. Often it is the party who best documents their position that prevails in court, arbitration, etc. Employers should keep all information related to each wrongful employment practices investigation in a separate file and in a place where such information is not readily accessible to employees. Failure to make any investigation once a complaint of prohibited harassment or discrimination has been made is a substantial factor in deciding whether punitive damages are appropriate.

Initial Response Within 30 Days

The most critical period in claims handling is the first 30 days after a complaint, dispute or claim is made. It is during this period that the employer has the best opportunity to complete its investigation and (1) reach a non-monetary resolution, (2) reach a favorable cash settlement, or (3) reduce the potential damage exposure of the claim if the claim cannot be resolved.

Responding To Verbal Complaints

Many EPL claims, which eventually end up in an actual lawsuit, start out as a simple verbal complaint by an employee to either management or the human resources director. This is true of single plaintiff lawsuits as well as multiple plaintiff lawsuits and class actions, which can involve thousands of similarly situated employees. Often at this level, the employee has not retained a lawyer. The absence of a plaintiff's lawyer makes it much easier to obtain an inexpensive resolution of a claim. Consider the following:

> ▸ A sexual harassment claim against a California bank was resolved without a monetary payment because the investigation was completed promptly and

professionally. Appropriate action was taken and the claimant was kept advised of the progress of the investigation and was satisfied with the result.

- A sexual harassment claim against a California County Club was settled at a favorable level before the claimant hired a lawyer. In that case, the investigation revealed that in all likelihood the alleged sexual harassment took place and the claimant had suffered economic damage as well as having a valid case of emotional distress.

If a verbal complaint is ignored, mishandled or allowed to fester, a lawsuit is the usual result. This is unfortunate because many verbal complaints can be handled by an experienced human resources person without the intervention or assistance of an attorney. However, if the employer senses that the complaint is not wholly resolved to the satisfaction of the complaining party or is unsure of the steps to take in resolving a complaint, it is usually best to consult with experienced counsel.

Alternatively, some EPL insurance policies can be triggered by a verbal complaint. Employers with such policies can give notice of the verbal complaint to their insurer and in many instances an experienced claims representative can help guide the employer through the process or appoint qualified counsel to do so.

Responding To Written Complaints

Employees can also make a complaint in writing, either alone or with the assistance of a plaintiff's attorney. As a general rule, all written complaints should be responded to in writing. Also, as a general rule, letters written by a plaintiff's attorney should be responded to by an attorney with adequate experience in employment law matters. Responses by non-attorneys or attorneys inexperienced in employment law could result in the unintentional creation of damaging evidence against the employer. The following is an example of how the wrong response to a complaint created damaging evidence:

An employee complains in a letter that she was wrongfully terminated because of her sex. The employer refutes the allegation by stating in writing that she was terminated because the employer was concerned that the employee's bad back created a workplace hazard to the employer, as well as co-workers. Such a response letter might be introduced as evidence at trial supporting the argument that the employer discriminated on the basis of a physical disability and failed to make a reasonable accommodation, thereby violating requirements of The Americans With Disabilities Act.

Persons untrained in the complex maze of employer obligations to their employees might easily overlook the hazard in making a response like the one in the above example. For this reason, it is best for an attorney to respond to all written complaints, even if an employee who has not yet retained counsel makes the complaint.

Responding To Administrative Complaints

The next level of an employee complaint is a written complaint filed with the EEOC or a similar state agency. This is commonly referred to as an administrative complaint. An employee can file an administrative complaint without the assistance of counsel and many employees who file administrative complaints have not retained an attorney.

Likewise, an employer may respond to an administrative complaint without the assistance of an attorney. However, it is generally not advisable to do so without the assistance of an experienced attorney. In addition to investigating complaints, administrative agencies frequently become involved in an effort to settle the employee complaint. In this regard, it is standard procedure for some administrative agencies to invite the complaining employee and the employer to participate in a non-binding, voluntary mediation at the very outset of an administrative complaint.

If both the employee and employer attend the mediation without being represented by counsel, the employer can be at a significant disadvantage. This occurs because the mediator will often act as an advocate for the employee and may pressure the employer to pay a significant sum to settle. A frequent negotiating tactic employed by agency mediators is to threaten the employer by advising them that if a settlement is not reached that day, the administrative agency will immediately commence an exhaustive investigation of the employer's employment practices. For these reasons, it is wise for employers that are called before an administrative agency to be represented by employment counsel.

Responding To Lawsuits

The final level of claim is an actual lawsuit filed in state or federal court. For obvious reasons, experienced counsel is always required at this point. But even when the first notice of a claim is the filing of a lawsuit, the first 30 days of a claim can still represent the most advantageous opportunity to settle. During the first 30 days, the plaintiff's lawyer has not yet invested a substantial amount of time in the case. Since most plaintiffs' lawyers work on a contingency fee basis, they have an economic incentive to settle early and maximize their fee in relation to the number of hours spent on a case.

In addition to being economically attractive, a settlement within the first 30 days saves defense expenses, avoids potential negative publicity, and avoids business interruption by obviating the need to devote resources to help defend the claim. Moreover, under the right circumstances an early settlement can actually lessen the potential that other employees find out that a settlement payment was made. Some employers believe that if other employees find out about a settlement that such knowledge increases the probability that other employees will bring similar claims.

Unfortunately, the window of opportunity to resolve a claim in the first 30 days is wasted because most employers and insurers have not fully ascertained all of the relevant facts in order to make an informed settlement evaluation. But 30 days is a sufficient period to ascertain enough information about the case to begin settlement dialogue.

Corrective Action

Once an investigation has been completed, the employer may conclude that some form of corrective action may be warranted. Prior to taking corrective action, however, the employer should check with counsel to make sure the desired action is appropriate and lawful.

There are many types of corrective actions available to employers to help mitigate the employee's damages and to avoid the imposition of punitive damages. Corrective action may include:

- Offering a severance package to an employee who has resigned
- Rehiring a wrongfully terminated employee
- Transferring, demoting or terminating the person who committed the wrongful act
- Disciplinary procedures against the wrongdoer
- Reassignment of either the complaining party or the alleged wrongdoer

Discipline

An important element of any intervention program begins with the policies and procedures designed to eliminate inappropriate or unsatisfactory work performance or conduct. The emphasis of any discipline program should be to resolve problems and to restore workplace harmony and productivity.

While disciplinary action can result in termination of the offending employee, many employers prefer less drastic methods of correcting wrongful employment practices. Other methods may include verbal or written warnings, suspension, demotion or the transfer of an employee to another position.

The purpose of giving warnings is to make it clear to the offender that certain actions will not be tolerated and that unless changes in behavior are made, the employee may be terminated. Disciplinary warnings should not be construed as a form of punishment. Instead, they should be clear, concise warnings that state the corrective measures the employee must make in order to remain employed.

Termination should not be the first step in the disciplinary process unless the act committed by the employee was egregious (such as embezzlement, assault and battery of a co-worker, etc.). Discipline usually is most effective when imposed in progressively severe stages. For example, many employers will give an employee one or two verbal warnings prior to issuing a written warning that is retained in the employee's personnel file. After a specified number of written warnings, the employee may be demoted or terminated. Such a program of progressive discipline gives the employee ample time to correct undesirable conduct and is viewed favorably by the courts and regulatory agencies.

Insurance Company And Defense Issues

If the employer has purchased EPL insurance, or where other insurance may provide coverage for wrongful employment practices, it is usually beneficial for the insured to be able to trigger coverage as early as possible. While the early triggering of coverage sometimes means the insurer is obligated to immediately begin some form of investigation, an individual insurer's response (once a claim or incident is reported) can vary. Some insurers appoint counsel as soon as notice of a claim or incident is received. Very aggressive insurers may appoint counsel to investigate reported incidents that have only a remote potential for escalating into a formal claim or suit.

Some insurers, however, only conduct a cursory investigation of incidents and will not engage legal counsel until a formal claim or suit has been filed. Such a conservative approach may only encourage a disgruntled employee to file a lawsuit. Once the employee files suit against the employer, the opportunity to have prevented litigation is lost.

Early investigation by the insurer not only offers the employer the best chance of avoiding litigation, but also sends an important message to employees that wrongful employment practice complaints are taken seriously. Knowing how the insurer will respond to reported incidents or claims is important, and the conduct of the insurer should reflect the insured's own philosophies as respects proactive intervention. The best method of determining the insurer's approach to intervention is to candidly discuss such issues with your broker or, preferably, the insurer prior to the placement of coverage. The claim-reporting provisions in insurance policies often are a good indicator of how the insurer will respond to claim or incident reports. Some policies contain strict, early reporting requirements so that the insurer can begin investigation and take appropriate action as early as possible. But make sure the reporting provisions are not overly burdensome. Complicated or elaborate reporting requirements may be difficult to comply with in a timely manner. Failure to report wrongful employment practice claims or incidents in a timely manner may result in an attempt by the insurer to deny coverage.

Selection Of Defense Counsel

Once an employer determines that outside counsel is required to defend an employee claim, or if an insurance company will be providing a defense, the selection of that counsel is an important component in the ultimate cost of the claim. The wrong defense lawyer can significantly increase the amount of defense expenses incurred. Choosing the wrong defense counsel or having the wrong defense counsel appointed by an insurer is a critical mistake in the handling of an employment practices claim. Defense counsel can vary significantly based on a number of factors. Some of these factors include (1) whether the defense lawyer is an employment practice specialist; (2) whether the defense lawyer is disposed to exploring early settlement; (3) whether the defense lawyer takes a "scorched earth" approach to the defense whereby no point, no matter how small, is conceded without extensive litigation; and (4) the hourly rate charged by defense counsel.

Many EPL insurers have a network of defense lawyers located throughout the country who have been pre-screened and who can be assigned on short notice. In many instances these firms:

- Specialize in employment law

- Are not adverse to exploring early settlement where appropriate

- Take a reasonable, cost-effective approach to litigation

- Agree to a reasonable hourly rate in return for a steady stream of work

When defense expenses are kept to a reasonable level, the likelihood that the entire case can be settled for a reasonable amount is increased. This occurs because virtually all plaintiffs' lawyers involved in employment practices cases work on a contingency fee basis. If the defense lawyer incurs large legal fees, and causes the plaintiff's lawyer to incur comparably large legal fees, the plaintiff's lawyer will be more likely to settle for a small amount because the plaintiff's lawyer will not get paid sufficiently for the time put into the case. On the other hand, if the plaintiff's lawyer has not been forced by an aggressive defense to invest a substantial amount of time and money in a case, it becomes more economically viable for the plaintiff's lawyer to advise his or her client to settle for a smaller amount should the facts of the case warrant such a settlement.

Also in many sexual harassment and discrimination cases, a prevailing plaintiff is entitled to an award of plaintiff's attorney fees. Accordingly, the more aggressive (and expensive) the defense, the higher the potential plaintiff's fee award is. If such a case is settled, that settlement is likely to be higher, given the potentially higher plaintiff's fee award. If the same case was to be tried and the plaintiff prevails, the judgment will likely be higher as well. Because of these reasons, selection of the right defense counsel is critical to the ultimate cost of an employment practices claim.

Insurers, including EPL insurers, are major purchasers of legal services. Accordingly, EPL insurers tend to have a vast amount of experience in selecting and negotiating rates with attorneys. Employers that purchase EPL insurance often gain the benefit of the insurer's experience in defense counsel, as well as the insurer's superior negotiating position in terms of keeping hourly rates and overall defense expenses reasonable.

The Role Of Mediation In Resolving Claims

A common mistake in the claims handling process is that employers (and many times insurers) fail to take advantage of alternative-dispute-resolution opportunities.[2] One of the most effective claim mitigation techniques is arbitration. Unfortunately, many employers avoid using arbitration for a variety of reasons. For example, some employers feel that a binding arbitration clause in an employment handbook creates a contractual right for employees that would not otherwise exist. Other employers believe that arbitration clauses encourage employees to make claims or that arbitration agreements are unenforceable. Perhaps the most significant obstacle to adopting binding arbitration agreements is that many employers believe that the implementation of such mandated policy would be unpopular with the employees and would damage company morale.

Another effective claims handling tool, one that is often underutilized, is non-binding mediation. Non-binding mediation is a settlement process, which can help reduce or avoid the expense and agony of litigation for all parties.[3] Unfortunately, non-binding mediation done incorrectly can result in the overpayment of an employment practices claim.

For an *uninsured* claim, the success of mediation is highly dependent on the abilities of the defense lawyer representing the employer. It is critical for the defense lawyer representing the insurer to have substantial experience in employment practices claims. Such experience is necessary in order to accurately assess the settlement values of the case. An improper assessment of the settlement value of the case usually results in too much money being paid or the failure to achieve a settlement at all. The defense lawyer must have the ability to be both a strong advocate of the employer's position, while at the

---

[2] See Chapter 4 for additional discussion of alternative-dispute-resolution methods.
[3] Mediation can also be effective in reaching a settlement even after litigation has started.

same time have the ability to compromise and meaningfully participate in the negotiation process. If defense counsel cannot be both an advocate and negotiator at the same time, the mediation will likely fail to produce a settlement (the defense lawyer was too much of an advocate) or will produce a settlement which is too high (the defense lawyer was too much of a negotiator).

For *insured* EPL claims, many employment practice insurers have found that skillfully conducted mediation, whereby the insurer is represented by separate counsel who is representing only the interests of the insurer, can substantially reduce the ultimate loss in employment practices claims. Where a claim is insured, the employer may have little or no economic incentive to help negotiate for the lowest possible settlement. In such instances, if the insurer is represented by counsel only concerned with the insured's interest, then the insurer will be at a severe disadvantage. Because the mediation process is only concerned with results, the mediator is focused primarily on achieving a settlement, not on the cost of the settlement. If the employer and the defense counsel have no economic interest in achieving the lowest possible settlement, then the insurer, who is either not represented in person at the mediation conference, or who is not represented by qualified counsel, is it at a substantial disadvantage.

When an insurer's counsel is present, the insurer's representative can focus on being the negotiator and the defense lawyer can focus solely on being an advocate for the employer.

Conclusion

Once the employer is aware of an incident that has the potential for a wrongful employment practices claim, it should immediately take some predetermined course of action. Having an established plan of action can help streamline the investigation process and help the employer resolve any employment-related dispute or complaint quickly and at minimum cost. However, many employers have no established procedure in place for dealing with such disputes or complaints. Too often, nothing is done when an incident comes to management's attention. Even when the employer takes action, that action is frequently inappropriate or illegal. Inappropriate action or inaction often only exacerbates an already tenuous situation. It also can result in substantial expense being incurred if the employee brings suit against the employer or files a complaint with the EEOC or similar state agency.

Employment-related problems that are not quickly investigated and resolved often result in lawsuits costing $25,000 to several hundred thousand dollars or more just to defend. If an employer and/or employment practice insurers can identify and respond to employment claims early, select the right defense counsel and take advantage of alternative-dispute resolution, the claims handling process is more likely to be less traumatic and result in a lower overall cost.

6 Insurance Coverage For Employment Practices[1]

Prior to the introduction of specialized EPL insurance policies, many employers faced with claims alleging wrongful employment practices sought coverage under one or more of their standard business-insurance policies.

Insurers sometimes paid claims based on wrongful employment practices, but such payment often occurred only after protracted coverage litigation. This is because employment-related claims (especially those of the severity and frequency that began to appear in the early 1990s due to the creation of new laws governing the employment relationship) were never really contemplated by underwriters and factored into the underwriting process. Since few standard policies contained outright EPL exclusions that specifically precluded coverage for employment-related claims, underwriters relied on the meaning and intent of other terms, conditions and exclusions in attempts to avoid paying employment-related claims. Today, many standard business insurance policies either explicitly exclude employment-related claims, or contain endorsements which are intended to cover certain types of employment-related claims. However, because there still are many standard business policies which do not specifically address employment-related claims, it is worthwhile to examine what coverage may exist under such policies.

The following discussions are a review of basic business-insurance policies and how such policies limit coverage for employment-related liability claims.

Commercial General Liability

Recent editions of the Insurance Service Office (ISO) Commercial General Liability (CGL) policy and some non-ISO policies provide coverage for the following:

---

[1] Specific EPL insurance policy form citations contained in *The EPL Book* are used to illustrate and support text discussion only. Such references are illustrative in nature and are neither an endorsement for nor criticism of any particular policy form. In some instances, policy forms cited in *The EPL Book* may no longer be in use and may be superceded by later editions. Neither *The EPL Book* nor any other reference is a substitute for the reader's own analysis, due diligence and careful reading of the policy form(s) in question.

- Bodily injury and property damage liability (coverage part A)
- Personal and advertising injury liability (coverage part B)
- Medical payments (coverage part C)
- Supplementary payments applicable to coverage parts A and B

As respects liability arising out of employment practices, much attention has been focused by plaintiffs on the bodily injury and personal injury coverage components of the CGL policy. Although the ISO-CGL policy does not contain specific EPL exclusions, it does contain certain conditions and provisions that may preclude coverage for many employment-related claims. These provisions include:

- The meaning of *personal injury* and *bodily injury*
- The definition of *occurrence*
- The exclusion of bodily injury that is expected or intended from the standpoint of the insured
- The exclusion of employment-related liability as respects bodily injury claims

In addition to these provisions, specific EPL exclusions are frequently endorsed to the basic policy form. Also, some jurisdictions may have public policy prohibitions against insuring against the kinds of intentional conduct alleged in some EPL claims.

Personal Injury And Bodily Injury Requirements

Relatively few employment practices lawsuits involve allegations of bodily injury, although such allegations sometimes arise in sexual harassment cases. Far more common in employment practice lawsuits are allegations of emotional distress or mental anguish, especially in cases involving sexual harassment, discrimination or wrongful termination. In some jurisdictions, courts have ruled that emotional distress and mental anguish are in fact forms of bodily injury for purposes of triggering coverage under the ISO-CGL policy. Case law conflicts on this issue, however, and some courts have ruled that emotional distress and mental anguish *do not* constitute bodily injury for purposes of triggering coverage under a general liability policy.

Even when courts determine that emotional distress and mental anguish are bodily injury, the insured must still satisfy the accident requirement incorporated into the definition of *occurrence*. Because claims of emotional distress and mental anguish can range from sexual assault with an intent to cause bodily injury to the termination of an employment relationship for ostensibly legitimate business purposes, the ability to satisfy the CGL accident requirement usually depends on the specific facts of the case.

The ISO-CGL policy also provides coverage for personal injury and advertising injury arising out of specific offenses. Under the ISO-CGL policy, *personal injury* means injury, other than bodily injury, arising out of one or more of the following offenses:[2]

- False arrest, detention or imprisonment
- Malicious prosecution
- The wrongful eviction from, wrongful entry into or invasion of the right of private occupancy of a room, dwelling or premises that a person occupies by or on behalf of its owner, landlord or lessor
- Oral or written publication of material that violates a person's right of privacy

The term *advertising injury* is defined to mean injury arising out of one or more of the following:

- Oral or written publication that slanders or libels a person or organization or disparages a person's or organization's goods, products or services
- Oral or written publication of material that violates a person's right of privacy
- Misappropriation of advertising ideas or style of doing business
- Infringement of copyright, title or slogan

Although the CGL personal injury and advertising injury coverage parts are not subject to the accident requirement or to the employers liability or intentional acts exclusions as found under coverage part A, its coverage is specific to only those offenses listed.

The Occurrence Requirement[3]

Even if a claim meets the definition of bodily injury, the bodily injury must be caused by an "occurrence." Under the ISO-CGL policy, *occurrence* is defined to mean:

> ...an accident, including continuous or repeated exposure to substantially the same general harmful conditions.
>
> ISO Commercial General Liability Coverage Form
> CG 00 01 07 98

In sexual harassment cases, the accident requirement in the definition of *occurrence* often is a difficult precondition of coverage for the insured to satisfy. Because the definition of *occurrence* connotes an unintentional event and because sexual harassment

---

[2] Prior to 1988 discrimination was a covered offense.
[3] See also on page 163., Special Considerations.

is often considered to be an intentional tort, many courts have held that the act of sexual harassment does not constitute an occurrence.

However, depending upon the particular state law applied, coverage *may* be available under a general liability policy for bodily injury or emotional distress allegations brought under a sexual harassment claim. For example, some courts have held that although the harasser may have intentionally committed the act of sexual harassment, no harm was intended to result from the act. Therefore, the occurrence or accident requirement is satisfied.

A common type of sexual harassment claim involves what is termed a "hostile work environment." A hostile work environment may be created, for instance, by the displaying of sexually explicit material in the workplace. Although the person displaying the sexually explicit material may clearly have intended to display such material he or she may not have intended to offend or harm anyone. For example, a person displaying such materials may have done so as a joke or may have thought that no one else would notice the materials. If a hostile work environment claim is brought under these circumstances, a court may rule that the injury was unintended and therefore accidental. Accordingly, if a claimant suffered emotional distress from viewing the sexually explicit material, coverage may be found to exist under the CGL policy.

Similarly, if an employee suffers emotional distress because he or she was terminated, it is not uncommon for an employee to bring a wrongful termination claim and allege emotional distress. If the employment termination was not carried out vindictively, it often is the case that the employer did not intend to cause emotional distress to the employee by the intentional act of terminating the employment relationship. As in the hostile work environment example discussed above, some courts have ruled that if the employer did not intend to cause emotional distress and if there are no other policy terms that would preclude coverage, the claim for emotional distress is covered under the CGL policy.

As a general rule, the occurrence requirement is more easily satisfied in an employment termination case than in a case of sexual assault and battery. However, some courts have ruled that an employment termination is an intended act and not an occurrence, while other courts have ruled that sexual harassment allegations constitute an occurrence because the alleged harasser did not intend to cause injury.

Even in EPL claims where the insurer may be required or chooses to provide a defense to the insured, the insurer would only be required to pay that portion of a judgment or settlement attributable to the claims for bodily injury, emotional distress or mental anguish.

Expected-Or-Intended-Injury Exclusion

Bodily injury that is expected or intended from the standpoint of the insured is specifically excluded by the following exclusion.[4]

> This insurance does not apply to:
>
> **a. Expected or Intended Injury**
>
> "Bodily injury" or "property damage" expected or intended from the standpoint of the insured...
>
> ISO Commercial General Liability Coverage Form
CG 00 01 07 98

The exclusion clarifies that deliberate or intentional bodily injury is not covered. It should be noted that most specialized EPL insurance policies and other policies that may cover EPL claims generally also contain a variation of this exclusion.

Employers Liability Exclusion

The ISO-CGL policy also contains the following exclusion for bodily injury arising out of the employment relationship.

> This insurance does not apply to:
>
> **e. Employer's Liability**
>
> "Bodily injury" to:
>
> **(1)** An "employee" of the insured arising out of and in the course of:
>
>   **(a)** Employment by the insured; or
>
>   **(b)** Performing duties related to the conduct of the insured's business; or
>
> **(2)** The spouse, child, parent, brother or sister of that "employee" as a consequence of paragraph **(1)** above.
>
> This exclusion applies:
>
> **(1)** Whether the insured may be liable as an employer or in any other capacity; and
>
> **(2)** To any obligation to share damages with or repay someone else who must pay damages because of the injury.
>
> This exclusion does not apply to liability assumed by the insured under an "insured contract".
>
> ISO Commercial General Liability Coverage Form
CG 00 01 07 98

---

[4] This exclusion does not apply to bodily injury resulting from the use of reasonable force to protect persons or property.

The primary purpose of this exclusion is to avoid any overlapping of coverage with workers' compensation and employers liability coverage, but it has been used successfully to restrict or preclude coverage for EPL claims as well.

EPL Exclusion Endorsement

Even though the ISO-CGL policy may exclude many kinds of employment-related claims, plaintiffs have extracted coverage with enough success that the ISO moved in 1988 to incorporate an employment practices liability exclusion into coverage A of the basic CGL policy form. In the face of much opposition from risk management, insurance agents and broker groups, ISO relented and, instead, published the exclusion as an optional endorsement. The current version of this endorsement, number CG 21 47 10 93, has been described as an extension on the employers liability exclusion and specifically restricts coverage for EPL claims under coverage parts A and B by adding two important provisions shown below.

A. The following exclusion is added to paragraph 2., Exclusions of COVERAGE A – BODILY INJURY AND PROPERTY DAMAGE LIABILITY (Section I – Coverages):

This insurance does not apply to:

"Bodily injury" to:

(1) A person arising out of any:

  (a) Refusal to employ that person;

  (b) Termination of that person's employment; or

  (c) Employment-related practices, policies, acts or omissions, such as coercion, demotion, evaluation, reassignment, discipline, defamation, harassment, humiliation or discrimination directed at that person; or

(2) The spouse, child, parent, brother or sister of that person as a consequence of "bodily injury" to that person at whom any of the employment-related practices described in paragraphs **(a)**, **(b)**, or **(c)** above is directed.

This exclusion applies:

(1) Whether the insured may be liable as an employer or in any other capacity; and

(2) To any obligation to share damages with or repay someone else who must pay damages because of the injury.

B. The following exclusion is added to paragraph 2., Exclusion of COVERAGE B – PERSONAL AND ADVERTISING INJURY LIABILITY (Section I – Coverages):

This insurance does not apply to:

"Personal injury" to:

(1) A person arising out of any:

  (a) Refusal to employ that person;

> **(b)** Termination of that person's employment; or
>
> **(c)** Employment-related practices, policies, acts or omissions, such as coercion, demotion, evaluation, reassignment, discipline, defamation, harassment, humiliation or discrimination directed at that person; or
>
> **(2)** The spouse, child, parent, brother or sister of that person as a consequence of "personal injury" to that person at whom any of the employment-related practices described in paragraphs (a), (b), or (c) above is directed.
>
> This exclusion applies:
>
> **(1)** Whether the insured may be liable as an employer or in any other capacity; and
>
> **(2)** To any obligation to share damages with or repay someone else who must pay damages because of the injury.
>
> ISO Commercial General Liability Coverage Form
CG 21 47 10 93

The ISO and similar EPL exclusions appear to have been effective in their intended purpose to preclude coverage under the CGL policy for claims based on wrongful employment practices.

Public Policy Prohibitions

Because of exclusions, other policy language that may act to preclude coverage for EPL claims and restrictive optional endorsements (such as CG 21 47 10 93) that are widely applied, the prospects for obtaining coverage for EPL claims under the ISO-CGL policy are limited at best. Coverage may be further restricted because many states have statutes or case law precluding the insuring against liability arising out of some kinds of intentional conduct. The extent to which public policy prohibitions apply to employment-related offenses, such as wrongful termination, sexual harassment and some forms of discrimination, remains unsettled in many jurisdictions. But many courts may be more willing to broadly enforce these public policy restrictions when coverage is sought under CGL policies, which were not specifically designed to provide coverage for employment-related claims.

Inability Of Occurrence-Based Policies To Change With The Insurance Market

As discussed above, CGL policies which do not contain employment practices claim exclusions, may in some circumstances provide some coverage for employment-related claims. Also, as discussed above, some CGL insurers have added endorsements to their policies which cover certain employment-related claims. Accordingly, some employers may believe that they are adequately insured under their CGL policies for employment-related claims. However, even if there is an endorsement adding broad EPL coverage, if the endorsement is on an occurrence basis, then the employer may be substantially limiting its ability to have the broadest EPL coverage available in the market.

The stand-alone EPL insurance market is a dynamic, intensely competitive market. It is not uncommon for EPL insurers to improve their policies on a yearly basis. Since the vast majority, if not all, stand-alone EPL insurance policies are written on a claims-made basis, if the policy is enhanced, the employer receives the full benefit of that enhancement on all claims made after the inception of the enhanced policy. However, if coverage is written on an occurrence basis, when coverage is enhanced due to market competition, the employer does not receive the full benefit of the improved coverage for all claims made after the inception date. Under occurrence-based policies, the coverage that applies is the coverage in force on the date of the occurrence. Therefore, if an employment-related claim is made after the inception date of an enhanced policy, the enhanced coverage might not apply at all or apply only in part if the occurrence, or any part thereof, which gave rise to the claim happened in a previous policy year.

Workers' Compensation And Employers Liability Insurance

Workers' compensation policies cover an employer's obligation to pay certain statutory benefits to employees who suffer work-related bodily injury or disease. These benefits vary from state to state, but generally include medical benefits, disability payments, rehabilitation expenses, etc. Also, if an insured is successful in triggering coverage for an employment practices bodily injury claim under a workers' compensation policy, as a general rule there exists a duty of the insurer to defend the insured.

However, some of the same problems of coverage that exist under general liability policies also exist with respect to workers' compensation policies. The injury as respects coverage under workers' compensation insurance must be for "bodily injury" and must be "by accident." There is no provision under a workers' compensation policy for the insurer to pay damages that are not the result of bodily injury or disease.

Recent decisions in California and in other states have clearly limited the scope of workers' compensation insurance under coverage part 1 to the extent of the state's statutorily mandated level for some employment-related liability claims. Although some coverage may exist for EPL claims under the employers liability coverage part 2 of the workers' compensation policy, most insurers now add broad EPL exclusions that effectively eviscerate any coverage that may have existed. Such exclusions specifically exclude injury arising out of termination of employment, coercion, demotion reassignment, discipline, defamation, harassment, discrimination, etc. The courts have generally upheld such exclusions and neither impose a duty to defend nor an obligation to indemnify the insured.

In the past year, a few workers' compensation insurers have added endorsements to their policies providing coverage for employment-related claims. The premium charged for such endorsements may be tied to the employer's payroll in a similar fashion as the workers' compensation premium.

A Recent Exception

The New Jersey Supreme Court recently affirmed a decision of the Appellate Division of the Superior Court of New Jersey that found an employer vicariously liable for "hostile work environment sexual harassment"[5] covered under a workers' compensation and employers liability insurance policy.

The plaintiff in the case, an employee of Personalized Audio Visual, Inc. (PAV), filed suit against her employer and PAV's president, Dennis Smith (Smith), alleging several causes of action, including a claim of "hostile work environment sexual harassment" brought under New Jersey's Law Against Discrimination ("LAD"). The case was based on the plaintiff's allegations that Smith hired her as an office manager in January 1991, and subsequently sexually harassed her until she resigned in February of that same year. In an amended complaint she alleged that PAV and Smith were liable under various negligence theories, including Smith's negligence in inflicting emotional distress and PAV's negligence in failing to train or supervise Smith.

PAV and Smith submitted claims to United States Fidelity & Guaranty Company ("USFG") seeking coverage under one of PAV's insurance policies, including their workers' compensation and employers liability insurance policy. Because USFG denied coverage, PAV and Smith instituted a third-party action seeking a declaratory judgment.

Before the declaratory judgment action was decided, the trial court tried the plaintiff's action against Smith and PAV. Following that trial, the jury returned an $80,000 verdict in favor of the plaintiff. Among other findings, the jury determined that Smith and PAV were liable for hostile work environment sexual harassment. The trial court then awarded the plaintiff $80,000 in compensatory damages and entered a judgment against PAV and Smith for almost $182,000, which included the compensatory damage award, counsel fees under LAD, and prejudgment interest and disbursements. On appeal, the Appellate Division found that USFG was obligated to defend and indemnify PAV under the employers liability coverage section of PAV's workers' compensation policy. The court based its decision on the fact that a policy exclusion for harassment was not applicable to sexual harassment claims when liability was imposed vicariously, as opposed to directly. USFG appealed the Appellate Division's ruling to the Supreme Court.

---

[5] *Schmidt v. Smith*, 1998 WESTLAW 329267 (N.J. June 15, 1998).

The New Jersey Supreme Court's Decision

The Supreme Court began its decision by reviewing New Jersey's workers' compensation law. It found that all employers are required to carry workers' compensation insurance and that such insurance must afford coverage for claims adjudicated in both New Jersey's workers' compensation court and for work-related injuries asserted in a common civil law court.[6] Citing an earlier decision,[7] the court stated:

> *The terms of a policy issued pursuant to [New Jersey's workers' compensation law] cannot conflict with the statutory mandate that there be coverage provided for all occupational injuries. Employers [sic] liability coverage...is traditionally written in conjunction with workers' compensation and is intended to serve as a `gap filler' providing protection to the employer in those situations where the employee has a right to bring a tort action despite provisions of the workers' compensation statute.*

The court then focused on the language of one of the policy's employers liability exclusions, which provided that the insurance did not cover:

> 7. Damages arising out of coercion, demotion, evaluation, reassignment, discipline, defamation, harassment, humiliation, discrimination against or termination of any employee, or any personnel practices, policies, acts or omissions.

While the court concluded that PAV was indeed liable for damages "arising out of" harassment and that the above exclusion seemed to preclude coverage, it also found that an employer would "reasonably expect" coverage for the types of injuries[8] alleged by the plaintiff. Because New Jersey workers' compensation law required PAV to obtain coverage to pay any obligation arising out of bodily injury to an employee, and despite what the policy actually stated, the court reasoned that PAV contracted with USFG to provide coverage of bodily injuries falling inside or outside of the workers' compensation laws. The Supreme Court further limited the effect of the exclusion by stating that the exclusion:

> *...disclaims coverage for a class of discomforts that one typically would not associate with bodily injury—criticism, demotion, evaluation, and defamation, for example—and that one typically would not expect to be covered by a scheme designed to insure that employees' bodily injuries be compensated. The*

---

[6] Citing *N.J. Stat. Ann.* § 34:15—72, *Schmidt*, 1998 WESTLAW 329267 at *1. Although Section 34:15—72 requires employers to "make sufficient provision for the complete payment of any obligation which he may incur to an injured employee," it does not expressly require that every employer do so through workers' compensation insurance.

[7] Id., citing *Producers Dairy Delivery Co. v. Sentry Ins. Co.*, 718 P.2d 920, 927 (Cal. 1986).

[8] The plaintiff alleged that she had suffered "emotional injuries accompanied by physical manifestations" as a result of the hostile work environment sexual harassment. See *supra* note 5.

exclusion is valid as long as the liability arising from those discomforts is not related to bodily injury.

However, PAV's liability was primarily related to the personal injuries that the plaintiff suffered as a result of Smith's conduct, and the alleged personal injuries fell within the definition of "bodily injuries" adhered to by New Jersey courts. Therefore, the court concluded that the employment practices exclusion violated public policy underlying the workers' compensation scheme and was void.

Conclusion

The Supreme Court decision focused on the "reasonable expectations" of the insured and public policy considerations underlying New Jersey's workers' compensation law. Based on the decision, it does not appear possible to exclude "hostile work environment sexual harassment" claims under a workers' compensation policy in New Jersey, at least when such suits include allegations that the harassment led to "bodily injury" of the employee.[9]

Because of the added loss exposure created by this decision, insurers may begin to reconsider the adequacy of their rates for workers' compensation insurance sold in New Jersey. Although it is difficult to estimate exactly how other jurisdictions will receive the decision, in a previous case the Iowa Supreme Court rejected the argument that employers liability coverage extends to sexual discrimination claims.[10]

Not-For-Profit Organization Liability Insurance

It should be noted that special policies designed for not-for-profit organizations have routinely provided or could be endorsed to provide coverage for EPL claims. These policies have been available for many years and can include entity coverage as well as an affirmative duty to defend. But such policies are not standardized, and the extent of EPL coverage can vary dramatically. Although not-for-profit EPL issues are not specifically addressed by *The EPL Book*, readers will find many of the book's discussions applicable regardless of the form of legal entity under consideration.

Directors And Officers Insurance

Directors and officers liability policies (D&O policies) usually provide coverage only when a director or officer is named as a defendant. Many employment practice lawsuits are brought only against the employer or against the employer and other individuals,

---

[9] New Jersey case law defines "bodily injury" to include "emotional injuries accompanied by physical manifestations." *Voorhees v. Preferred Mut. Ins. Co.*, 128 N.J. 165, 179 (1992). 1-2.

[10] *Ottumwa Housing Auth. v. State Farm and Cas. Co.*, 495 N.W.2d 723 (Iowa 1993).

such as supervisors, who usually are not insureds under the policy. Under such a policy, there would be no coverage unless an insured director or officer is a defendant.

But even in those employment practices lawsuits that do name a director or officer as a defendant, the coverage available is often inadequate. This occurs because there usually is no coverage for the corporation's own liability unless the policy has been specially endorsed.[11] The corporation usually is covered only to the extent it indemnifies its directors or officers for loss incurred by the directors and officers. Therefore, only the losses of the directors or officers potentially are covered under most D&O policies. The corporation's own liability as the employing entity is not normally covered.

Although some not-for-profit D&O policies provide a duty to defend, most D&O policies do not provide an affirmative duty by the insurer to defend the insured. Because of this, the insurer usually is obligated to pay only for defense expenses of the directors and officers, and not those of the corporation or any other persons, such as employees or supervisors, who are not insureds under the policy.

In addition, most D&O policies contain one or more exclusions that apply, in part, to employment practices lawsuits. Such exclusions include those relating to claims for bodily injury, emotional distress, mental anguish, defamation, libel, slander, invasion of privacy, false arrest, etc. Allegations such as these frequently are included in employment practices lawsuits. Accordingly, where such exclusions apply, the D&O insurer may not be obligated to pay defense expenses incurred in defending against such allegations nor would it have to pay for any portion of a settlement or judgment attributable to such excluded allegations.

In recent years, some D&O policies have been endorsed to provide EPL coverage. These endorsements typically extend the coverage under the D&O policy for those claims that involve allegations of discrimination, sexual harassment or wrongful termination. These coverage extensions frequently involve deleting the exclusion for bodily injury and emotional distress and broadening the definition of *directors* and *officers* to include all employees as insured persons. As well, such endorsements often provide that the insured-versus-insured exclusion would not apply to an EPL claim. Some EPL endorsements on D&O policies extend the coverage even further by providing coverage to the corporation for its direct liability for employment-related claims.

While EPL endorsements broaden the coverage available under a D&O policy, such endorsements often do not provide a duty to defend, and often the coverage for employment-related claims is subject to a substantial deductible. Accordingly, some insureds may find that the costs of defending employment practices claims are not

---

[11] Some D&O insurance policies may be endorsed to provide coverage for direct suits brought against the organization. Coverage, however, is often limited to certain types of suits, such as those alleging securities-related issues. Some not-for-profit D&O policies or policies issued to privately owned for-profit companies may also provide coverage for direct actions brought against the organization.

covered because they fall within the deductible amount. Even when the costs of defense are in excess of the deductible, the insured may find that the insurer requires an allocation of defense costs between covered and uncovered allegations because of the absence of a duty to defend. Moreover, for corporations retaining significant deductibles or retentions, the entire expense of defending, settling or paying a judgment in an employment practices claim may fall within the retention.

Another potential disadvantage of an EPL endorsement in a D&O policy is that the limit of liability normally available to protect a director's or officer's personal assets may be reduced or exhausted by the payment of an employment practices claim that did not involve any of the directors and officers. Most EPL endorsements do not provide for a separate limit of liability in addition to the limit available under the D&O policy. Therefore, directors or officers of a corporation may not be willing to remain as directors or officers because they fear their personal assets will be at risk if the D&O limit is reduced or exhausted by payment of an employment practices claim involving the wrongful conduct of an employee of the corporation. This problem can be an especially serious concern for a director who may receive little compensation for serving as a director and who has little or no control or involvement in the conduct or supervision of an employee of the corporation.

Specialized EPL Insurance

Because of the rapidly increasing frequency and severity of employment practices claims in recent years, and in response to the shortcomings in standard liability policies, the insurance industry developed the EPL insurance product. The importance and impact of EPL insurance does not begin and end with providing a limit of liability to pay losses. EPL insurance also serves a critical function in loss control and prevention.

Unlike liability insurance, D&O or workers' compensation insurance, which were not designed to address employment practices liability, EPL insurance was specifically designed for the sole purpose of addressing employment practices liability. Therefore, EPL insurers are keenly aware of the challenges facing employers by the complex and changing environment of employment law. More importantly, many EPL insurers offer critical guidance to employers to help them comply with employment laws and to reduce their exposure to employment practices claims. For example, many EPL insurers will not issue a policy unless an employer has an up-to-date employment handbook that complies with all applicable laws. Employers that have deficient policies and procedures often can receive assistance and guidance from their insurers or consultants on how to improve these important policies and procedures.

Insurability Of Employment Practices Liability (EPL) Claims

One of the peculiarities of employment practices claims is that many of the actions which precipitate such claims are considered by law to be intentional in nature. Public policy considerations in numerous states provide that insurers are not liable for loss when that loss is caused by the willful actions of the insured. For example, in California such public policy is articulated in Section 533 of the California Insurance Code, which reads in part:

> *An insurer is not liable for a loss caused by the wilful act of the insured; but he is not exonerated by the negligence of the insured, or of the insured's agents or others.*

Such laws raise interesting questions for employers considering the purchase of insurance against liability arising out of willful employment-related practices.

Support For The Willful-Act Rule

In *Coit Drapery Cleaners Inc. v. Sequoia Insurance Company,* California's First District Court of Appeals held in 1993 that Insurance Code section 533 barred the attempt to shift liability for the employer's intentional sexual harassment and employment-related torts (claims of wrongful discharge, infliction of emotional distress, battery and sexual assault) to an insurer. The case involved a sexual harassment claim brought against the president of the company who allegedly had made graphic and lewd propositions to his assistant. The assistant was later terminated for refusing to submit to the president's propositions. Because the president's actions were so egregious, the Court's decision based on public policy was not itself surprising.

However, the opinion of the *Coit* Court went far beyond the facts presented in the case and suggested that all sexual harassment claims involve intentional acts. As such, these acts are precluded from insurance coverage by the willful act provisions of Section 533 in California, and possibly by similar provisions in other jurisdictions. In the absence of conflicting decisions in other cases, the *Coit* court's decision might be cited by other courts to challenge the enforceability of insurance policies designed to cover discrimination, sexual harassment, wrongful termination and other employment-related torts.

Subsequent Opposing Decisions

Fortunately for employers that are considering purchase of EPL insurance coverage, the *Coit* decision has been substantially repudiated and circumscribed by subsequent judicial decisions. In *Kleis v. Superior Court,* a convalescent hospital's workers' compensation and general liability insurance carriers both argued that coverage for alleged sexual harassment was precluded because of the *Coit* willful-act rule. However, the Appeals Court disagreed, noting that several significant factual differences existed between the *Coit* and *Kleis* cases. First, the coverage litigation in *Coit* occurred after the underlying sexual harassment matter had been settled. Second, the parties in that case had an opportunity to fully litigate the nature of the wrongful actions of the alleged harasser. Third, negligent supervision was not an issue in *Coit,* whereas negligent supervision (clearly a covered act) was alleged in the *Kleis* case.

The *Kleis* court also noted that a claim of sexual misconduct may result in a potential defense of consent or mistaken belief in the right to engage in the conduct. Such a defense could negate any allegation of intent to sexually harass or discriminate. The mere fact that a claim of sexual harassment is filed, does not preclude a court from finding that no such harassment took place.

Another subsequent case provides further support for the insurability of employment practices claims. In *Melugin v. Zurich Canada,* the same appellate district that ruled on the *Coit* case held that, notwithstanding Insurance Code Section 533, a commercial general liability policy that provided coverage for sexual discrimination obligated the insurer to at least *defend* sexual discrimination claims that did not include allegations of intentional misconduct. The court reasoned that in the *Coit* case, the insurer had not specifically granted coverage for discrimination claims and then sought to disavow such coverage. The court then noted that there could be some acts that constitute sexual discrimination in the workplace, but which involve only unintentional, negligent conduct.

Significantly, the *Melugin* court also found that even if Section 533 barred coverage to a manager for his own intentional discriminatory acts, the employer company might still be covered in regards to its own strict liability for the manager's actions. Further, the court held the ruling in the *Coit* case to apply only to those cases where an insurer actually proves an employer condoned a manager or supervisor's intentional acts of discrimination or harassment.

What It All Means

The courts' decisions in the *Kleis* and *Melugin* cases establish that employers may limit, if not completely nullify, the *Coit* willful-act rule. However, some courts continue to find the *Coit* rule applicable. Two weeks after the *Melugin* decision, in *Michaelian v. State Compensation,* the Fifth District Court of Appeals used Section 533 as a basis for finding no insurance coverage under an employer's general liability policy for a manager who allegedly committed sexual harassment. The *Michaelian* court is, however, currently reconsidering that decision.

While the decisions in the *Coit* and *Michaelian* cases have arguably created some doubt regarding the applicability of coverage provided by EPL insurance policies, the decisions in the *Kleis* and *Melugin* cases appear to be better reasoned and to have greater statutory support. These latter decisions should make both insurers and insureds more confident about the protection afforded by EPL insurance policies for claims of unintentional discrimination and sexual harassment.

Conclusion

Although insurance policy coverage interpretation is complex, based not only on case law but on the specific and individual facts surrounding a claim, the following generalizations normally apply:

- Standard business policies of the type described in this section likely contain terms and conditions that limit or exclude coverage for many types of employment-related claims.

- Insurers often endorse these same policies to specifically exclude a wide variety of employment-related claims.

Although some policies (such as many package policies for not-for-profit organizations) do sometimes contain broad coverage for a wide variety of employment-related claims, most standard insurance policies are not designed nor intended to do so.

PART III

Understanding
Employment Practices Liability Insurance

7 Underwriting And Application Considerations[1]

Most insurers writing employment practices liability (EPL) insurance consider a variety of factors in determining whether to offer EPL insurance to a particular employer and at what price. Some factors often considered include the following:

- Type of business or organization
- Size of business (number of employees)
- Loss history
- Employment termination and turnover rates
- Employment policies, procedures and documentation
- Composition of workforce
- State issues
- Pay distributions
- Financial condition

The relative importance of each factor can vary between individual underwriters. In addition to the factors mentioned above, further criteria may be relied upon in the underwriting process. Some insurers engage the services of third-party employment law firms to evaluate the prospective insured's employment policies and procedures. In some instances, the review may involve a personal visit to the employer's place of business for the purpose of interviewing key personnel and verifying documentation and other procedures.

---

[1] Specific EPL insurance policy form citations contained in *The EPL Book* are used to illustrate and support text discussion only. Such references are illustrative in nature and are neither an endorsement for nor criticism of any particular policy form. In some instances, policy forms cited in *The EPL Book* may no longer be in use and may be superceded by later editions. Neither *The EPL Book* nor any other reference is a substitute for the reader's own analysis, due diligence and careful reading of the policy form(s) in question.

Underwriting Criteria

The following discussion is presented as an *aid* (i.e., not a guide or standard) to employers and brokers in understanding and gaining insight into the application and underwriting process.

Type Of Organization

Most insurers focus on or specialize in providing EPL insurance coverage to certain classes of businesses or organizations. An insurer's target market may be well defined so that it only provides coverage to a specific business segment, such as to restaurants or manufacturers, or the target class may be broad, encompassing all commercial businesses. But even those insurers that appear anxious to write all classes of business likely exclude at least some classes of legal entities or types of operations. Difficult or hard-to-place operations that are frequently excluded include governmental entities, operations subject to high turnover, seasonal employers and businesses composed primarily of highly paid professionals.

Some insurers consider governmental entities more likely to experience EPL claims than commercial organizations. Government workers often are perceived by insurers as having an expectation of lifetime employment and, therefore, less willing to accept adverse employment decisions than employees in the private sector. Furthermore, government entities receiving federal funding owe due-process protections to certain classes of their employees, which can be cumbersome and difficult to properly administer. The failure to administer proper due-process procedures can result in costly litigation and added exposure. Also, given the resistance or prohibition in some instances against the purchase of insurance products by governmental entities, some EPL insurers believe this class of business is unlikely to yield a profit.

Businesses that experience or that may be subject to high turnover or whose employment relationships are seasonal in nature are considered poor risks by many insurers. These businesses may include growers or packing operations, seasonal retail operations, and manufacturers whose staffing needs fluctuate with short-term contracts. Employers with high turnover rates or employment relationships that are short-term often are prone to wrongful termination and other wrongful employment practice claims once employment ends.

Some EPL insurers will avoid or prohibit the placement of EPL coverage on businesses that primarily are composed of highly paid professionals, such as law firms, accounting practices and medical offices. Because some damages associated with wrongful employment practices are based upon an employee's rate of pay, such businesses may represent an unacceptable severity exposure in the eyes of the insurer.

When seeking EPL coverage, it is advisable to identify those insurers most interested in providing coverage to similar organizations. By doing so, the insured is more likely to receive a competitive quotation. Insurers also may be more likely to understand the nuances and needs of the employer and provide the type of coverage features most needed. While many agents and brokers now have departments specializing in EPL coverage and are able to identify the most suitable markets, do not overlook industry associations and purchasing groups that may be able to provide special coverage enhancements and features not readily available to others.

Employer Size

For most EPL insurers, "employer size" usually refers to the number of persons in the employment of the organization seeking coverage. Some insurers avoid or will refuse to insure employers with few employees for fear that their employment practices are too primitive or inadequate to be effective. These insurers seek insureds with sophisticated human resources departments with experience in a wide range of employment-management issues, including the handling and resolution of employment-related disputes.

Other insurers specialize in providing coverage to smaller employers on the theory that the closer proximity between owners and employees engenders good will, so that employees are more willing to resolve disputes and less likely to complain of technical violations of the law. Some insurers avoid larger organizations. They believe that the management hierarchy typical of large organizations creates an employment environment in which employees tend to be aggressive in asserting their rights. Whether the insurer's target market is the large or small employer, most insurers have developed rates based in large part on the number of employees as the basic exposure unit.

Loss History

A basic element in the underwriting of EPL insurance is an examination of past claims and losses. Although past claims and losses are no guarantee of future experience, they usually are relied upon heavily by the underwriter. Frequent claims or poor loss history usually are viewed as an indication that problems exist. As a minimum, the underwriter may require a greater premium to offset the real or perceived risk represented by the loss experience. Alternately, the underwriter may choose not to offer coverage at any reasonable price.

When reporting claim and loss history to insurers, be sure to carefully distinguish between EEOC or state-agency charges and litigated cases. Underwriters usually want to know the nature of the allegations involved for each EEOC or state-agency charge, including the dates of occurrence and whether the insured incurred any legal costs or made any settlements. With respect to litigated cases, all of the foregoing information usually must be reported, as well as estimated future defense costs, if any. In addition, the applicant must accurately report the dollar amount of all adverse judgments and settlements.

While poor claim and loss history cannot be erased, most underwriters recognize that remedial actions taken by the employer can prevent similar claims from reoccurring. Be sure to advise underwriters of all steps taken or new policies implemented that will likely result in a turnaround in your loss picture.

Past And Future Turnover

Every time an employer terminates an employee, there is the potential for the terminated employee to allege that he or she was terminated in violation of one or more state, federal or local employment laws. The hiring process also may itself create the potential for unlawful failure-to-hire claims.

Many underwriters use past turnover rates as a means of estimating future turnover. The underwriter also may ask the insured to estimate its future turnover. Such information can be helpful in gauging the potential for wrongful termination or failure-to-hire claims during future policy periods.

Many insurers establish turnover standards that, when exceeded, result in a declination of coverage or substantial rate increase. When turnover for a particular risk has been unusually high during a prior period but is not expected to continue, the remedial actions taken or other reasons for improved turnover should be explained.

Employment Documentation

Employment policies, procedures and documentation usually are closely scrutinized by underwriters for many reasons. For example, some wrongful termination claims can be prevented simply by informing employees in the employment manual or other document that employment is "at will" and that neither the employment manual nor other employment documentation is a contract that extends the length of employment or confers any other right regarding employment. In addition, well-communicated sexual harassment policies coupled with effective grievance procedures can make it more difficult for employers to be held vicariously liable for sexual harassment committed by other employees. Finally, underwriters need to know whether employers are keeping adequate and complete records that may be relevant in the future defense of alleged wrongdoing. These records include, but are not limited to, applications, employment evaluations and disciplinary warnings. Deficiencies in documentation procedures usually result in a declination or rate debit.

Composition Of Workforce (EEO-1) And Hiring Practices

Because plaintiffs frequently attack the testing procedures for disparate treatment[2] on women and minorities, underwriters often want to know the composition of an employer's workforce. Federal law requires all federal contractors and employers with more than 100 employees to file a Composition of Workforce (EEO-1) report. The EEO-1 document, when completed, identifies the workforce by gender and ethnicity in terms of managerial, professional, clerical and other worker categories.

Pay Distribution

There usually is a large difference between what highly skilled professionals and unskilled laborers are paid within the same organization. This difference and the makeup of skilled to unskilled workers can affect the potential catastrophic measures of loss faced by an organization. Businesses that are composed of professionals with higher-than-average remuneration may be subjected to liability for higher-than-average damages.

State Issues

The locations of an employer's operations can impact the exposure to employment-related claims and thus affect the availability and pricing of coverage. For instance, some states prohibit discrimination against smokers, sexual orientation or otherwise protect certain groups not covered by federal laws. Punitive damages for violations of employment laws may be uncapped in some states, and state laws governing the insurability of punitive damages is subject to much variation. States with liberal employment laws may be viewed negatively by some insurers who may choose not to offer coverage in those jurisdictions. Additionally, some states have a historical pattern of higher jury awards in employment cases than other states.

Financial Statements

Financial statements provide information regarding two important areas. First, financial statements can be used to verify payroll information since such costs usually are separately identified in the income statement. Second, financial reports can help establish an organization's financial well-being and viability as an ongoing concern. Organizations that are in poor financial condition may be more susceptible to layoffs and downsizing, which often spawn wrongful termination claims. Recently, some EPL

---

[2] Differential treatment of employees or applicants on the basis of their race, color, religion, sex, national origin, handicap or veteran status.

insurers in an effort to streamline the application process have dropped the requirement for an employer to provide financial information.

The decision by an underwriter to offer EPL insurance to an employer is based almost exclusively on documentary evidence provided by the insured. Although this also is true of most other lines of insurance, what is unique to EPL insurance is the fact that the documentary information fails to measure subjective elements of the employment relationship. These elements include the intentions and attitudes of many different people within the organization and are reflected in employee morale and corporate culture. Yet it is business's morale and corporate culture that can create an environment prone to EPL claims.

EPL Insurance Application Considerations

EPL insurance, like most other commercial insurance, is underwritten based on information provided by the insured in the application for insurance.[3] In many instances, the application attaches to and forms an integral part of the policy form. This is important because EPL insurance applications can contain conditions, warranties or reporting requirements some insureds normally might expect to be found only within the policy form. For this reason, important coverage elements or restrictions may go unnoticed unless careful scrutiny is given to the application.

EPL applications can be tedious for the insured to complete, requiring much detailed information and the attachment of numerous employment policies and documents.[4] Insureds may be required to complete an "initial" application if they are seeking coverage for the first time, seeking to replace expired or cancelled coverage, or seeking to change insurers. These initial applications sometimes are referred to as *long-form* applications because of the detailed information requested. Long-form applications normally seek information in the following areas:

- General or background information
- Financial statements and reports
- Description of the specific limits and deductibles sought
- Questions regarding ownership
- Information regarding subsidiary operations
- Information about who will be insured under the policy

---

[3] See Appendix for specimen application form.
[4] Some insurers may release an initial indication of EPL insurance terms and pricing based on limited information.

- Disclosure of anticipated changes in the corporation's operations involving merger, acquisition or divestiture
- Specific information regarding
  - Prior employment practice insurance
  - Description of employment contracts
  - Human resource office description
  - Employee handbook
  - Employee job descriptions
  - Employment applications
  - Supervisor manuals
  - Grievance or alternative-dispute-resolution procedures
  - New employee orientation procedures
  - Employee performance evaluation procedures
  - Termination and exit-interview procedures
  - Employment-related claim-handling procedures
  - EEO and sexual harassment policy statements
  - Affirmative-action plans

The specific information requested can vary greatly, depending on the individual insurer and specific class of business under consideration. Certain organizations, such as restaurants and not-for-profit associations, may require the completion of specialized applications. Most applications also contain statements regarding warranty and imputation of the information provided and require the signatures of the president, CEO, human resources or other department head.

Insureds renewing coverage with the same insurer may be required to complete a renewal application, sometimes referred to as a *short-form* application. As a general rule, short-form renewal applications often omit the requirement of the insured to provide claim information and soften or eliminate some or all warranty provisions. The term *short form*, though, can be misleading, as many insurers require the completion of renewal applications that can be every bit as detailed as the initial application and can include a requirement to rewarrant existing information already on file with the insurer.

Whether for a first-time submission or renewal of existing coverage, completion of the application should not be undertaken casually. Insurance brokers or agents experienced in placing EPL insurance can provide valuable assistance to the insured in this area. While such assistance usually does not mean that the agent or broker will actually complete the application on behalf of the insured, the experienced agent or broker can help guide the insured and help assemble and produce a coherent and well-organized proposal. All questions should be answered truthfully and completely, but the following areas should be given special attention.

Warranties

EPL insurance policy forms and applications for coverage often contain important conditions and warranties that sometimes are overlooked. These conditions and warranties can act as guarantees by the insureds that the information in the application is complete and correct. Misrepresentations that materially affect underwriting can result in specific claims being precluded from coverage or in total rescission of the policy. Warranty provisions may be found both in the application and in the policy form.

One of the greatest concerns is that misrepresentations by the completer of the application may void coverage for all insureds, including those insureds who were unaware that a misrepresentation was made.

Particularly troublesome problems also can arise when the application contains detailed questions about the existence or knowledge of claims or of situations that might give rise to a future claim under the policy. The following are representative of how such questions may be worded.

1. Has any claim been made, or is any now pending, against the Organization, or any person proposed for this insurance in the capacity of either Director, Officer, Trustee or Employee? (If Yes, give details.)

2. Is any person proposed for this insurance cognizant of any fact, circumstance or situation which said person has reason to suppose might afford valid ground for any future claim against said person and/or the Organization? (If Yes, give details.)

   If such facts, circumstances or situations exist, any claim or action arising therefrom is excluded from the proposed coverage.

Notice that question 1 asks whether claims have been made or are pending against those persons proposed for insurance. In most EPL insurance policies the word *claim* is a defined term having special meaning and usually is identified by bold or other obvious type style to signify its special meaning. When used in the application, the word *claim* may not be so identified and may have a meaning different than that defined in the policy. Care should be taken to ensure the term *claim* is understood. The undefined term *claim* may be broader than a narrowly defined term *claim* as used in the policy. Unnoticed, such nuances may result in an inaccurate answer to the question.

Question 2 in the above example asks the applicants whether they are cognizant of any fact, circumstance or situation that might give rise to a future claim. While knowledge of certain facts, circumstances or situations might be easily identifiable as having the potential of materializing into a claim, other facts, circumstances or situations might go unnoticed or appear so innocuous that the insured might not expect a claim to develop. It is possible that an insured could have knowledge of certain actions but, because there may be no reason to suspect a claim, might answer the question in good faith that no such circumstances were known.

The question goes on to state that if such facts, circumstances or situations "exist," resultant claims would be excluded. Use of the word *exist* might be interpreted to mean that because information or involvement existed, a claim could be denied even though the insured had no reason to suspect a claim to materialize. Warranty provisions like those contained in question 2 act as broad exclusions for claims based on prior acts of which the insured had knowledge or possibly which the insured should have suspected would give rise to future claims.

Great care should be taken in answering these types of questions. It may be wise to provide a conditional answer when responding to some questions. A simple yes or no response might not fully or correctly answer the question and could restrict coverage if it is later interpreted to be a breach of warranty. The completer of the application might consider describing how the answer was verified. Were the appropriate corporate officers, supervisors or human resource personnel polled and asked to review the application? Responses by the application completer also might include the qualification that to the best of his or her knowledge and having polled the prospective insureds, he or she does not know of any circumstances reasonably likely to give rise to a claim.

It also may be difficult or impossible for the completer to verify the sometimes voluminous amount of information required by the application. Even where a procedure is in place for key officials to review the application, it may be difficult for any one person, particularly someone new, to verify the accuracy of all entries to the application. There probably are many insureds who are unaware that the validity of their individual insurance protection hinges on the truthful and complete execution of the application.

Material Misrepresentations And Coverage Implications

Most insurers consider the insured's responses to questions in the application to be material representations or material facts. Some applications also contain statements that all documents and attachments are material to the insurer's acceptance of the risk and agreement to provide coverage.

The exact impact of such statements and the meaning of the word *material* is not always well understood by insureds. In matters of insurance, a material fact often is considered to be information that would increase the risk to the insurer and influence the underwriter's decision on whether to offer coverage. Material facts also are those that could affect the premium or scope of coverage offered.

While some insurers may state that all information requested in the application is material, it is likely that some information is more material than other information, or that misrepresentations could be made that would not be material at all. The overstatement of financial records that reflect net worth of $100 million versus $99 million may be insignificant, but the failure to report adverse claims history may have a great influence on the insurer's decision to provide coverage. The degree to which misrepresentations are deemed to be material can have varying effects on whether or not coverage would be available under the policy. Without specific language to the contrary, misrepresentation made in the application may cause the insurer to attempt to

- Deny coverage for specific types of claims
- Deny coverage for specific insureds
- Rescind the policy

While the first two actions certainly are undesirable, the policy could presumably continue for future claims not otherwise affected by the misrepresentation. Rescission, on the other hand, means that the policy would be voided and claims treated as if the contract had never been made.

Severability And Non-Imputation Provisions

In an effort to overcome some of the problems certain application questions can pose, some insurers include in their policies or applications (or both) a severability clause regarding statements made in or in connection with the application. Sometimes referred to as *non-imputation provisions,* these clauses typically provide that the omissions, misrepresentations and warranties made by one insured shall not be imputed to another insured for the purpose of determining the insured's right of recovery under the policy. While such clauses can vary in the degree of protection provided, they usually are preferable to policy forms or applications that do not contain such provisions. An example of a non-imputation provision is illustrated in the following example:

> In issuing this policy, the company has relied on the declarations and statements which are contained in the application and which are deemed to be incorporated in this policy, provided, however, that except for material circumstances known to the person who subscribed the application, any misstatement or omission in such application in respect of a specified WRONGFUL ACT by a particular INSURED or his cognizance of any manner which he has reason to suppose might afford grounds for a future CLAIM against him shall not be imputed to any other INSURED for the purpose of determining the availability of coverage under this policy.
>
> Coregis Non-Profit Organization Liability Insurance
> CFM 93.1.0494
> (8/93)

The lack of such wording can have serious consequences for innocent insureds. Not all policy forms or applications contain such provisions. Even policies that do include some type of severability clause may not protect all insureds under all situations.

Because the accurate and honest completion of the application has important implications on coverage, care must be taken to ensure that the scope of the application's questions and severability provisions are fully understood. Look for language in severability clauses that protects innocent insureds in all situations.

Tips For Completing The Application

Although the main purpose of the application is to inform the underwriter, it often includes important conditions in addition to those already discussed. Completing an application for insurance coverage is an important task that often does not get proper attention. While sometimes tedious, lack of attention to detail when completing the application can result in a bad quote or no quote at all. As previously discussed, an even worse result can be that once submitted and a policy issued, the insurer may attempt to deny coverage for a claim because the information on the application was not complete or accurate. The following are general guidelines that can help in preparing the application.

Read The Application

Always be sure to allocate adequate time to fully review the application. Some risk managers or others who must complete the application mistakenly assume that all EPL insurance applications are the same and dash them out with little thought or preparation. In many respects, certain policy forms and applications may appear very similar or identical to one another. But even applications that are similar can have important differences in the scope of the questions asked.

Some applications may be quite detailed and lengthy, requiring information that might not be readily at hand. Before filling out the application, give it a quick read to identify the information that will require additional time to obtain or that could be compiled by others. Also, be alert to unclear or ambiguous questions, and seek clarification from your broker or the insurer (who should respond in writing) as to their meaning.

Insurers may go beyond the basic application form and require the insured to provide additional information. When additional information is requested by the insurer, applicants should make sure that the request is in writing and that they fully understand exactly what is needed. Obtaining written documentation helps avoid disputes surfacing later about what was requested.

The application also may provide the insured with pertinent information regarding important or unusual policy features, such as claims-made or defense provisions. While these features normally are fully described in the policy form, their inclusion in the application may make it difficult for an insured to claim it was unaware or unfamiliar with these important and often restrictive features.

Read The Policy

Although it may not always be possible, it usually is a good idea to read through the policy form before completing the application. Even a cursory reading may identify deficiencies or provisions that make the proposed coverage inappropriate or unsuitable, regardless of the price. Also, having the policy form close at hand makes referring to any defined terms or other provisions for clarification much easier. If a prior reading is impractical, request a summary of the policy features and provisions from the agent or broker.

If the application attaches to and forms a part of the policy, as is often the case, consider attaching the specimen policy form and any contemplated endorsements to the application when submitting it to the underwriter. This helps avoid disagreements over what coverage actually was bound, should a different or more restrictive policy inadvertently get issued.

Reporting Changes

Some applications may contain explicit requirements that the insured must report if any information in the application changes between the time the application is executed and the time coverage is effected.

EPL applications sometimes are submitted to underwriters well in advance of the proposed inception date, it is possible that at least some information may have changed by the time the policy takes effect. It is important to advise the underwriter of any changes that have occurred in order to comply with the specific reporting provisions. These reporting provisions vary. Some policies may impose strict requirements that such changes be reported "immediately" or "in writing." Other policies may soften the requirement by requiring only that "material" or "significant" changes be reported. But what is material or significant may not be universally agreed upon and may pose difficulties.

Maintenance Of Scheduled Insurance

Although rare, some applications may contain provisions that require the insured to maintain a specific schedule of insurance during the proposed policy period. Such provisions can impose an onerous burden on the insured to report changes in its insurance program. Also, changes in market conditions may cause certain coverages or limits of coverage to be unavailable. For these reasons, such clauses should be avoided or the requirement to maintain scheduled insurance should be removed from the application.

Confidentiality

Some of the information requested in the application may be sensitive or proprietary. In some instances, questions requiring disclosure of proposed or pending merger or acquisition activity or other sensitive matters, including those dealing with claim settlement, may present problems. The insureds may be bound by confidentiality or non-disclosure agreements that prevent them from releasing such information. Because of this, the response to the insurer's inquiry may require careful drafting. An acceptable response normally can be developed that will meet the insurer's needs for underwriting information while keeping the insured within bounds of legal and contractual confidentiality requirements. Some applications contain a statement of confidentiality by the insurer, which at least in part addresses concerns many applicants may have that the information will be used by the insurer internally for underwriting purposes only. If this statement does not appear on the application, ask for it, as most insurers should be willing to provide such a written statement upon request.

Be aware, however, that the person or persons completing the application may not be privy to information that is being requested. This possibility underscores the importance that those persons signing the application are completely informed or briefed as to the questions being asked and answers disclosed. Having the president or CEO "rubber stamp" an application can have a catastrophic effect should relevant information be inadvertently omitted or a question answered incorrectly.

Provide Complete Information

The application process may require negotiation between the applicant and the underwriter. The applicant is seeking the best coverage at the best price, and the underwriter is looking for an acceptable risk. Therefore, it is in the applicant's best interest to work *with* the underwriter to provide whatever information may be needed. For best results, consider applying the following tips to your application process.

- Unless the applicant has legible handwriting, make sure all responses are typed. Even the best penmanship may make the application appear unprofessional.

- Submit the application well in advance of the policy renewal or inception date. Sixty to ninety days may be adequate; a month or less often is not. The underwriter likely has a stack of new and renewal applications on his or her desk, each just as urgent and important as the next. The application will do no good, no matter how well prepared, if it is shunted aside and not quoted because the underwriter is not given enough time.

- Avoid leaving questions blank. Underwriters hate this. If the question is not pertinent, state that it is not and give a brief explanation. Do not use terms such as "N/A," the meaning of which is not universally recognized.

- Avoid answering questions with "see attached." If the underwriter requests payroll for the last three years, broken down by year and classification, applicants should not just attach an accounting journal and expect the underwriter to extract the information. Providing backup data on your own summaries and compilations is acceptable, but do not ask the underwriter to do your job for you.

A thorough, concise, neatly arranged application package allows the underwriter to perform a review quickly and increases the likelihood that your application will be given a fair evaluation. Some brokers are masters at submitting clear, concise applications within their detailed proposal packages. For example, one broker we know delivers all proposals to the underwriter bound in a distinctive cover. Because the broker has a reputation for submitting complete underwriting information and the packages are easily identifiable, the broker claims that his proposals are given preferential treatment. We cannot confirm such statements, but one underwriter we spoke with said she has a preponderance of ragged, dog-eared and handwritten applications at the bottom of her in basket.

Claim Information

Few would argue against the insurer's right to have access to claim details, but what is a "claim"? As discussed earlier, problems can arise when applications contain questions about past claims that have been made or about the insured's knowledge or awareness of circumstances that might give rise to a future claim under the policy. These questions sometimes are so sweeping that they become difficult or impossible to answer with certainty. Because such answers often are policy warranties, they have been the source of numerous coverage disputes.

One way to respond to broadly worded questions is to provide a conditional answer. The completer of the application might consider restating the question to articulate the applicant's perception of the question and to describe how the answer was arrived at. Responses by the application completer also might include the qualification that to the best of his or her knowledge and having polled key managers and executives (but not every employee), he or she is not aware of any circumstances likely to give rise to a claim.

When in doubt, talk to your broker, legal counsel or consultant who has experience in such matters. Some applications are so onerous regarding potential claim and claim-awareness warranty provisions that it may be necessary to negotiate amendments to both the policy form and application before coverage reasonably can be considered.

Reporting Information Not The Subject Of Inquiry

In addition to providing the underwriter with everything requested, it may be prudent to alert the underwriter to information that is not specifically referenced in the application. This could include information that will give the underwriter a more favorable view of the applicant's account. For example, beneficial information might include the existence of specialized worker training or state-of-the-art loss-prevention measures. If the insured has had a poor loss history in certain areas but has initiated remedial measures, this too should be brought to the underwriter's attention.

There may exist some information that could negatively influence the underwriter's evaluation of the applicant's account but which, for reasons of uncertainty or a desire for full disclosure, the applicant may wish to divulge. Such a situation might arise where the insured is considering a change in the nature of its operations. For example, not all insurers write all exposures. Declaring an anticipated change will help a company discover whether an insurer is willing to write the anticipated exposure and at what cost. Knowing such information beforehand can help avoid the difficulty of finding coverage on short notice later on.

But unless requested, applicants generally should limit their responses to conform with the questions asked. When in doubt, applicants should talk with their broker, consultant or legal counsel about whether and how to best present such addendum material.

Involving Your Broker

Years ago, it was not uncommon for the agent or broker to place some kinds of insurance over the phone. The broker conveyed only a bare minimum of information to the underwriter, and only later would the application follow. Applications often were done entirely by the broker. Frequently they were submitted to and accepted by insurers without the insured's signature attesting to the application's accuracy. Such practices are now rare or non-existent.

What is the broker's role in the application process today? The answer is that it varies. Some brokers will compile information, loss runs and schedules, draft out the application and then sit down with the insured to fill in the remaining gaps and confirm that the information as stated is accurate and complete. Other brokers simply give the insured an application and have them complete it with little or no input or assistance. There are risk managers comfortable with both approaches. Some broker involvement is valuable, however, if only to help guide the insured in assembling and producing a coherent and well-organized package for the underwriter's review.

Although most brokers are willing to help with the application when asked to do so, it is important that the broker is knowledgeable in employment practices liability and coverage issues.

Peer Review

Even in smaller organizations, it is not uncommon for someone other than the person required to sign the application to actually complete the form. Unfortunately, the person completing the application may not have sufficient knowledge of all of the organization's affairs or be privy to information that is being requested. In one instance, for example, a risk manager omitted important information from the application concerning previously reported claims, complaints or occurrences. Unbeknown to the risk manager, other department managers had been handling certain employment disputes that should have been reported to the insurer as claims.

To avoid such a breakdown, risk managers or other persons responsible for completing the application can establish a peer-review panel to look over and give comment on questions posed by the application. Such a panel might include top management designees from each department or subsidiary, corporate or outside counsel, or a consultant. Going through such an exercise helps ensure that claims or other important information is reported properly.

Summary

Applications can be fraught with hidden hazards, but giving complete and accurate information helps eliminate the possibility of future problems. Following the procedures outlined above can help avoid common mistakes and oversights, but do not overlook your broker, lawyer or outside consultant as sources of guidance and assistance. The availability of coverage may hinge on how well the application is completed. Always give the application the same degree of review and scrutiny that would be given to analyzing the insurance contract itself. Both are legal documents and should be treated as such.

8 EPL Insurance Policy Format[1]

Understanding Claims-Made Coverage Features

Nearly all policies that provide EPL coverage do so on a claims-made basis. The obligation of an insurer to pay for a claim and related expenses under a claims-made policy usually is triggered when a claim is first made against the insured during the policy period or extended reporting period and on or after any retroactive date. Claims-made policies contrast with the more common occurrence-basis general liability and umbrella policies, which are triggered by the loss occurrence or by the injury, even though a claim may not be made against the insured until months or years after the policy expires. A graphic example of the key difference between these two types of policies is shown below.

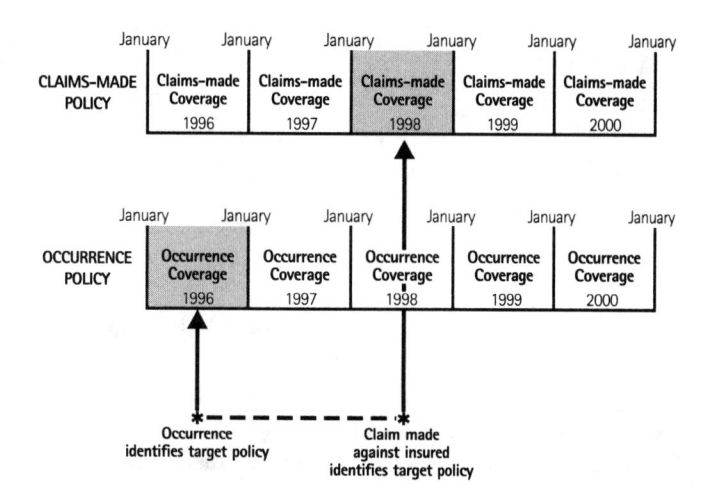

---

[1] Specific EPL insurance policy form citations contained in *The EPL Book* are used to illustrate and support text discussion only. Such references are illustrative in nature and are neither an endorsement for nor criticism of any particular policy form. In some instances, policy forms cited in *The EPL Book* may no longer be in use and may be superceded by later editions. Neither *The EPL Book* nor any other reference is a substitute for the reader's own analysis, due diligence and careful reading of the policy form(s) in question.

The mechanics of claims-made EPL insurance policy forms often are not as simple as depicted in the above example. Definitions, claim provisions and other reporting requirements are integral factors in defining the scope of the policy's claims-made features. As such, they demand careful review.

The term *trigger*, which is used frequently in discussions of claims-made coverages, refers to the events or circumstances that activate the policy's coverage. The act of triggering a policy does not establish coverage for a specific claim. A claim may not be covered for any number of reasons even though a proper trigger was effected.

To determine the policy's trigger requirements, it is necessary to locate and identify the following claims-made features and requirements within the policy form being reviewed. These elements combined constitute the policy trigger.

1. What constitutes a claim and when is a claim made?

2. What are the requirements in reporting the claim to the insurer?

3. What are the time limitations regarding when the wrongful employment practice is deemed to take place?

The policy provisions that answer these questions sometimes are not easy to identify. For example, they may be found in the most unexpected parts of the policy. In some cases there may be nothing in the policy to answer the question. For example, most insurers define *claim*, but some policies may not define *claim* at all.

What Constitutes A Claim?[2]

A good place to start in evaluating the important elements of any claims-made policy is by examining the definition of *claim*. Many EPL insurance policies provide a specific definition, but some may not. An example of a policy definition of *claim* is given below.

> **Claim** means:
>
> (1) any written demand received by the **Insured** which seeks monetary relief from the Insured for a **Wrongful Act**;
>
> (2) any civil proceeding or lawsuit received by the **Insured**, whether through service or otherwise, which seeks monetary relief from the **Insured** for a **Wrongful Act** and which has been filed within the Policy Territory set forth in Section VII.;
>
> (3) any investigative order or notice of charge received by the **Insured** relative to an administrative or regulatory proceeding initiated before the Equal

---

[2] See the *Definitions* section (pp. 221–236) for a more detailed discussion of the meaning of *claim* under an EPL insurance policy.

Employment Opportunity Commission or a similar state agency, which names the **Insured** for a **Wrongful Act** and which has been filed within the Policy Territory set forth in Section VII.; and

(4) any written notice received by the **Insured** of an arbitration, mediation or other form of alternative dispute resolution proceeding which seeks monetary relief from the **Insured** for a **Wrongful Act** and which has been commenced within the Policy Territory set forth in Section VII.;

however, **Claim** shall not include any organized labor or grievance proceeding or arbitration subject to a collective bargaining agreement.

Pacific Insurance Company
PL-364
5/98

Although EPL insurance policies vary widely in definitions of *claim*, the absence of a definition of *claim* is not necessarily a negative feature. Some policies that do not define *claim* may provide more liberal coverage than policies that restrictively define *claim*.

Claim-Reporting Requirements To The Insurer

EPL insurance policy claim-reporting requirements establish when and how claims made against the insured must be reported to the insurer. Often the policy requires that the claim be reported to the insurer during the policy period or within a specified number of days after the claim is made or the policy period ends. Sometimes language in the insuring agreement includes such requirements, but most policies provide an elaborate description elsewhere in the policy under headings such as *Notice of Claims, Notice, Claim Reporting*, etc. Some examples are given below.

> **NOTICE REQUIRED DURING THE POLICY PERIOD**
>
> ...the term "claims first made" shall mean that the Insured has received notice of legal process, including notice of a complaint being filed with the Equal Employment Opportunity Commission or any state or local civil or human rights agency, or that a demand for money or services has been made against the Insured, or that the Insured has become aware of a proceeding, event or development which could in the future result in the institution of a claim against the Insured. In the event of any such proceeding, event or development, notice must be given to the Corporation during the policy period;...
>
> First Specialty Insurance Corporation
FSIC-1491A (01/96)
>
> **NOTICE REQUIRED WITHIN A SPECIFIED TIME**
>
> 1. **Duties in the event of a "claim", or potential "claim" or "suit".**
>
>   a. You must see to it that we or our authorized representative are notified as soon as possible, but not more than thirty (30) days after a "claim" is made. Notice shall include:...
>
> Legion Insurance Company
ERP-1
7/98

NOTICE REQUIRED AS SOON AS PRACTICABLE

The **Insureds** shall, as a condition precedent to exercising their rights under this coverage section, give to the Company written notice as soon as practicable of any **Claim** made against any of them for a **Wrongful Act.**

Chubb Group
14-02-0953 (Rev. 8/96)

Compliance with provisions that require reporting either during the policy period, some limited time after the claim is made, or some specified period after policy expiration, may be difficult or impossible to meet when claims are made against the insured at or near the end of the policy period. Even under the most favorable circumstances, it may take a number of days to advise the insurer of a claim made against the insured. The corporate risk manager or other executive responsible for reporting claims may not be available to respond, or the specific procedures and requirements of claim reporting may not be fully understood by the person who actually first receives the claim. Policy forms that do not impose a time limitation upon the insurer and require only that the claim be reported as soon as "practicable" are preferable for some insureds. Other insureds may find a benefit in complying with short-notice requirements so as to take advantage of an insurer's claims-handling expertise at the earliest possible point in a claim. Such early intervention can result in the favorable resolution of claims that otherwise might result in litigation of costly settlement later on.

Potential Claim[3]

Although it has been nearly a decade since the widespread introduction of claims-made policy forms, questions over how such policies are triggered by the reporting of *potential claims* still are the source of much confusion and dispute.

For example, negligent acts or other events may take place during a claims-made policy period, but because such events or occurrences do not always constitute a claim as defined in the policy, the reporting of such events may not always trigger coverage.

Fortunately, most claims-made policies contain provisions that allow the insured to trigger the policy by reporting circumstances that ultimately may give rise to a claim but which technically may not constitute a claim. These provisions are referred to as *discovery, notice of potential claim* or *awareness* provisions.

It should be noted, however, that there can be much variation in how discovery provisions are worded. Some discovery provisions are very liberal, giving the insured much latitude in the reporting of potential claims. But some reporting provisions can be quite rigid, requiring the insured to report information in great detail, such as the identity

---

[3] See the *Definitions* section (pp. 221–236) for further discussion of the meaning of *claim* and *potential claim* under an EPL insurance policy.

of each potential claimant, the precise nature of the claim, a description of damages and the amount expected out of such damages.

Overly restrictive notice requirements can severely impair the insured's ability to trigger the policy as respects claims that may be made in the future. Even when the insured believes a claim is inevitable, unless the specific notice provisions can be met, the policy will not be triggered. Policies that have limited specificity requirements or provisions that require the insured only to describe the general circumstances afford the insured greater control in triggering coverage. But with such control comes the requirement that the insured be ever vigilant in reporting all circumstances that might result in a claim.

Claims-made reporting requirements imposed on the insured either for actual or potential claims—including provisions that require written notice or special mailing requirements—often have been strictly upheld by the courts.

Retroactive Dates—Time Limitations Regarding When Wrongful Acts Or Employment Practices Take Place

Many policy forms contain no reference to when the wrongful employment practice or insured event must take place. When issued without language to the contrary, the policy is said to provide full prior acts coverage, regardless of the time lag between the wrongful employment practice and the claim being made against the insured.

Although increasingly rare, some EPL insurance policies may contain or be endorsed with language that is sometimes referred to as a *retroactive date limitation*. Such provisions preclude coverage for claims arising from wrongful acts occurring prior to the stipulated retroactive date. Examples of where these provisions may be found are given below.

Generally there are three ways insurers may apply retroactive dates.

1. **The insurer may impose a retroactive date that is the same as the policy inception date.**

This restriction normally occurs when the insured organization is a newly formed entity, when no previous coverage existed, or when a change in the insurer is made. Underwriters are reluctant to provide coverage for wrongful acts that may have occurred in a prior period, especially if no prior insurance was in force. The risk is that the insurer may inadvertently assume the exposure for an unknown number of wrongful acts that may develop into future claims.

The following chart illustrates a claims-made policy in which the insurer has imposed a retroactive date that is the same as the policy inception date. There is no coverage for claims made during the policy period that are based on wrongful acts that occurred prior to the retroactive date. This period is represented by the shaded area.

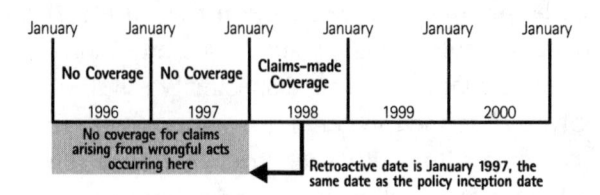

A potential problem with all claims-made policies occurs when each successive renewal policy imposes a retroactive date that is the same as the renewal date. This condition is known as *advancement of the retroactive date*. When this condition occurs, the policy provides coverage only for claims made and based on wrongful acts occurring during the current policy period. An example is given below.

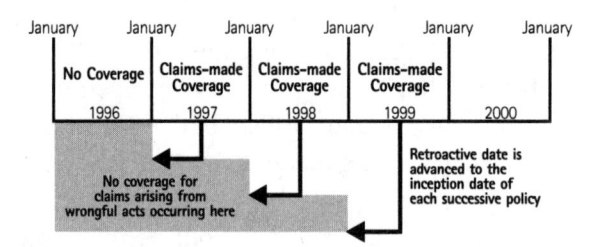

Retroactive date advancement normally occurs only when a policy has been cancelled, when the insurer declines to renew or when the insured changes insurers. New insurers often are unwilling to provide coverage for claims based on unknown wrongful acts committed in prior periods. Another instance when a retroactive date advancement might occur is when the insurer discovers that the insured has not fully disclosed information considered material to its underwriting decision. Such material could include information about past circumstances that the insurer feels may develop into a future claim and, as a condition of renewal, the insurer advances the retroactive date. As a practical matter, however, insurers can advance the retroactive date on any renewal. There usually is no guarantee that a specific retroactive date will be maintained.

2. **The insurer may impose retroactive dates that are the same as the expiring policy (policy provides "prior acts" coverage).**

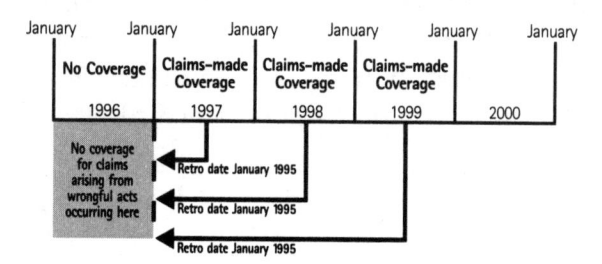

The above example depicts successive policies maintaining the original retroactive date of the previous policy. While none of the policies will cover claims based on wrongful acts occurring in the shaded area of the above illustration, subsequent wrongful acts would be covered in the policy period in which the claim was brought against the insured. Successive policy renewals maintaining the expiring policy's retroactive date are said to provide prior acts coverage.

3. **The insurer may choose to impose no retroactive date or provide provisions stating that all prior wrongful acts are covered (policy provides "full prior acts" coverage).**

Because this arrangement imposes the lightest restriction on the insured, it is the most desirable.

As the following chart illustrates, there is no restriction in the year 2000 policy as to when the wrongful act must take place, only that a claim based on the wrongful act be made against the insured during the policy period. Full prior acts coverage is extremely desirable. It is an improvement over any policy containing a specified retroactive date limitation. Competing insurers sometimes offer full prior acts coverage as an enticement for insureds to switch insurers.

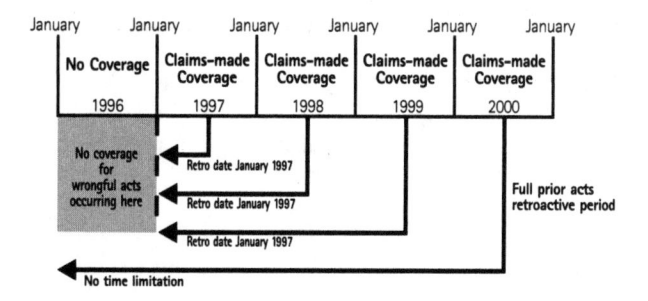

EPL INSURANCE POLICY FORMAT

The extent to which prior acts coverage may be provided also can be effected by how the insured events or wrongful employment practices are defined. For example, although an EPL insurance policy may require the insured event to have occurred after a specified retroactive date, some insurers may define *insured event* or *wrongful employment practice* to mean the "knowledge by management" of those events or practices. It may be possible under some policies that an actual wrongful employment practice occurred prior to the retroactive date but was not known by management until after the retroactive date. In such instances, the policy may indeed provide prior acts coverage.

Extended-Reporting-Period (ERP) Provisions

Most EPL insurance policy forms contain provisions allowing the insureds to extend the policy's coverage to include claims first made after the policy expiration or cancellation for wrongful acts occurring on or after the policy's retroactive date and before the policy's expiration or cancellation. Such provisions are especially desirable in the event of policy cancellation or non-renewal, or when a renewal policy contains a retroactive date later than the retroactive date of the expired policy. The following language is representative of ERP provisions.

> If the Insurer shall cancel or refuse to renew this policy the Insureds shall have the right, upon payment of the additional premium of twenty percent (20%) of the three year prepaid premium hereunder, to an extension of the cover granted by this policy in respect of a claim or claims which are made against the Insureds, during the period of twelve (12) calendar months after the date of such cancellation or non-renewal, but only with respect to any **Wrongful Act** committed before the date of such cancellation or non-renewal.

The following illustration depicts an insured that exercised its policy's 12-month ERP when the policy was not renewed for the 1999 policy term.

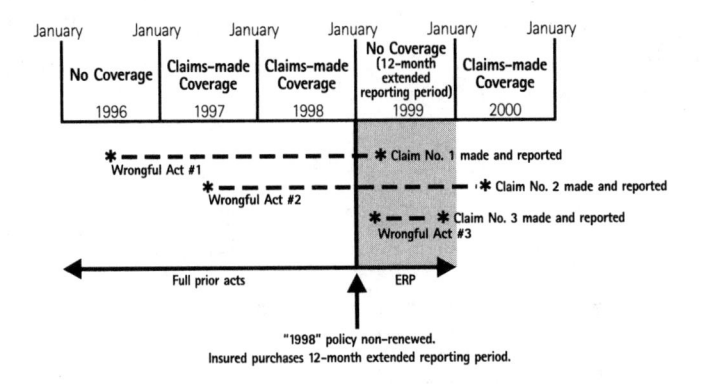

January 1996	January 1997	January 1998	January 1999	January	January 2000
No Coverage	Claims-made Coverage	Claims-made Coverage	No Coverage (12-month extended reporting period)		Claims-made Coverage

* — — — — — — — — — — — * Claim No. 1 made and reported
  Wrongful Act #1
         * — — — — — — — — — * Claim No. 2 made and reported
           Wrongful Act #2
                    * — — * Claim No. 3 made and reported
                    Wrongful Act #3

←——————— Full prior acts ———————|——— ERP ———→

"1998" policy non-renewed.
Insured purchases 12-month extended reporting period.

This claim scenario would result in the following:

Claim No. 1   Because the claim was made against the insured within the extended reporting period with subsequent reporting to the insurer, these actions would trigger the 1998 policy for potential coverage.

Claim No. 2   Because the claim was not brought against the insured until 2000 (after the ERP has expired), the claim would not trigger the 1998 policy. The claim would trigger the year 2000 policy unless a retroactive date was imposed. There is no 1999 policy.

Claim No. 3   Most ERP language provides coverage only for claims based on wrongful acts occurring prior to the policy expiration date. Claims based on wrongful acts taking place during the extended reporting period usually are not covered. In this example, the claim was made and reported to the insurer during the extended reporting period; however, the wrongful act occurred after the policy expiration date and would be precluded from coverage under the 1998 policy and the 1999 ERP.

ERPs are desirable because they give insureds some protection if coverage is cancelled or not renewed by the insurer. ERP language varies among insurers. The value of an ERP depends on a number of factors, including:

1. Under what circumstances is the ERP available?
2. For what time period does the ERP apply and at what cost?
3. When and how is the ERP activated?

Under What Circumstances Is The ERP Available?

Most policies allow the ERP to be purchased only when cancellation or non-renewal is initiated by the insurer.

Policies with such provisions sometimes are referred to as having a *one-way* tail. A *two-way* tail is a policy provision that also would allow the insured to cancel the policy and still be able to trigger the ERP. The two-way tail is rare in EPL insurance policies, but some insurers provide flexibility when renewal terms are more restrictive than those of the expiring policy.

It may be argued that when an insurer offers to renew, but only with overly restrictive terms, conditions, exclusions or a substantial increase in premium, the result is virtually the same as a non-renewal or cancellation by the insurer. If this occurs, the insured might try to enforce the ERP by using the argument that the insurer effectively has refused to renew. However, many policies contain language effectively eliminating such an argument.

> The offer of renewal terms and conditions different from those in effect prior to renewal shall not constitute refusal to renew.
>
> Chubb Group
> 14-02-0953 (Ed. Rev. 8/96)

Most policy forms contain language that precludes the insured from exercising the ERP when the policy has been cancelled for non-payment of premium. The ERP also may not be available when the policy has been terminated under change-of-control provisions, which can apply to situations such as mergers and acquisitions for which the insurer reserves the right to cancel or terminate the policy due to a material change in exposure.

For What Period Of Time Is The ERP Effective And At What Cost?

Most policies clearly define both the period of the ERP and the additional cost. Most ERPs provide for extended reporting periods of between three and twelve months. Some insurers provide reporting periods of up to five or six years, but ERPs exceeding twelve months are exceptional. The premium required to exercise the ERP option usually is a percentage or multiple of the annual or three-year premium. This additional premium percentage is normally found within the policy's discovery clause, but also may appear in the declarations page.

Not all insurers fully describe the ERP in the policy form. Certain features, such as the period of discovery and additional premium, may be specifically negotiated and may appear on the policy declarations page or in an endorsement. All aspects of the ERP should be fully disclosed and evaluated prior to policy inception. If the ERP is not satisfactorily in place at policy inception, the insured may have little ability to negotiate suitable terms during the policy period.

When And How Are ERPs Activated?

The ERP typically is available upon the payment of the total additional premium within a specified number of days after the policy expiration or cancellation date. This length of time is referred to as the *election period*. The most common election period is ten days, but a few insurers allow 30 or 60 days. The following is an example of language describing how the ERP is activated.

> The **Named Insured's** right to purchase the Extended Reporting Period must be exercised by written notice postmarked not later than thirty (30) days after the cancellation or expiration date in the event of non-renewal of this policy AND MUST INCLUDE PAYMENT OF THE PREMIUM FOR THE EXTENDED

> REPORTING PERIOD. Failure to pay the premium at the time of exercise of this option will render the option void and unenforceable. As the commencement of the Extended Reporting period, the entire premium shall be deemed fully earned and non-refundable.
>
> Steadfast Insurance Company
STF-PL-D-100-B CW
(4/97)

Notice that the above language requires the insured to notify the insurer in writing that the discovery period is desired. Failure to elect coverage under the ERP within the election period and in the fashion described terminates the insurer's obligation to provide such coverage.

Special Considerations

When comparing claims-made coverage with occurrence-based coverage,[4] it is necessary to consider the ramifications of moving from one form of policy to the other and to be aware of the possible gaps in coverage that can occur due to the differences in how coverage under each type of policy is triggered.

When moving from an occurrence policy to a claims-made policy, few problems occur, except for the insured's need to be aware of the inherent differences between claims-made and occurrence-basis coverage. Inversely, moving from a claims-made policy to an occurrence policy can result in a coverage gap. When the insured has changed from claims-made coverage to occurrence coverage, a gap may exist for occurrences taking place during the period of claims-made coverage but which are not reported until later when occurrence coverage is in force. The claims-made policy in force when the incident giving rise to the claim occurred would exclude the claim if it is not brought within the period of coverage or within some ERP. If the claim is made after the expiration of the claims-made policy or after an applicable ERP, then the claim likely would not be covered under the claims-made or succeeding occurrence policy.

There are two ways to avoid such gaps. The preferred method is to endorse the new occurrence policy to recognize and accept claims resulting from occurrences that took place in prior years irrespective of when the claim is reported. An alternate and somewhat less-effective method is for the claims-made policy to contain an ERP that allows the insured to report claims for some period of time after expiration of the policy. But unless a very long or indefinite ERP is obtained, there still is the potential for a gap in coverage due to the difference between policy triggers. Also, unless such a provision has been negotiated at the time coverage is placed, obtaining such a provision later may be difficult or impossible.

---

[4] See also page 121, the occurrence requirement under CGL insurance policies.

Because other factors such as the definition of *claim* and the specific claim and incident reporting provisions of each policy also can affect the potential for a coverage gap, great care must be taken when evaluating the practical impact of changing to a policy form with a different coverage trigger.

Insuring Agreement

EPL insurance policy insuring agreements typically contain three types of provisions. These provisions are whether the insurer will "pay on behalf of" or "indemnify" the insured for covered loss, the coverage grant and the defense provisions. In some EPL insurance policies, the defense provisions are contained in a separate *Defense Provisions* section of the policy.

Coverage Grant

The insuring agreement in some EPL insurance policies contains a list of specific wrongful employment practices for which coverage is granted under the policy. The wrongful practices listed may include acts such as discrimination, sexual harassment and wrongful discharge or termination. In other policies, however, the insuring agreement does not contain a list of specifically covered acts. Rather, these policies contain a more generic reference to "wrongful employment practices," "wrongful torts," etc.

The following illustrates both approaches:

> **INSURED OFFENSES LISTED INDIVIDUALLY**
>
> **What We Will Pay.** We will pay damages which the **insured** is legally required to pay as a result of **sexual harassment, discrimination,** or **wrongful discharge** that arise out of a **wrongful employment practice.**
>
> Fireman's Fund Insurance Company
7006-10-96

> **COMBINED REFERENCE**
>
> The Insurer will pay on behalf of the **Insureds Loss** which the **Insureds** shall become legally obligated to pay as a result of a **Claim** first made during the **Policy Period** or **Discovery Period,** if applicable, against the **Insureds** for a **Wrongful Act** which takes place during or prior to the **Policy Period;...**
>
> Reliance Insurance Company of Illinois
GL 00 R424 00 0498

Regardless of how the insuring agreement is worded, it is necessary to review the policy definitions of the covered acts to determine the full scope of coverage granted by the insurer.

Third-Party Liability Coverage

As discussed in Chapter 1, third-party liability for discrimination, sexual harassment and, in California, sexual misconduct, can exist when such claims are made by customers, patients, clients, vendors or other non-employees.

Although there have been few claims brought against employers based on third-party discrimination or sexual harassment, the potential for loss can be substantial and should not be ignored. Sensing a potentially important coverage feature that either is not addressed or is specifically excluded under many EPL insurance policies, some insurers now offer third-party liability coverage as part of or as an amendment to their standard EPL insurance policy. The following are examples of insurance policy clauses granting third-party liability coverage:

> We will pay Loss amounts that the Insured is legally obligated to pay to (1) your client, customer or patient; or (2) your former client, former customer or former patient; or (3) any other person(s); because of an Insured Event to which this policy applies. However, the amount we will pay is limited as described in the COVERAGE LIMITS, SELF-INSURED RETENTION AND CO-PAYMENT sections.
>
> London Market
EPL (11/97A Broad)
11/97

> With respect to any customer(s), client(s) or any other individual or group of individuals, other than an Employee or applicant for employment with the Company or an Outside Entity, Employment Practices Violation shall mean only any actual or alleged discrimination, sexual harassment or violation of an individual's civil rights relating to such discrimination or sexual harassment, whether direct, indirect, intentional or unintentional.
>
> National Union
67976
6/97

> The Underwriters agree to pay Loss on behalf of the Insured(s) on account of a Claim by a Third Party Claimant because of a Third Party Insured Event to which this policy applies. Subject to the terms, conditions and exclusions, this policy applies if (1) the Third Party Insured Event takes place within the Coverage Territory, and (2) the Claim is first made against the Insured during the Policy Period or any extension thereof. Insured Event where used in this policy applies also to Third Party Insured Event unless insuring agreement A2 has been deleted by endorsement. Coverage for Claims by Third Party Claimants is not available for (a) class actions; (b) assault and battery; or (c) bodily injury.
>
> Swett & Crawford
EPLX-987
7/1/98

When evaluating such grants of coverage, pay particular attention to who is considered a third-party claimant. In each of the above examples, a third-party claimant is described broadly to include non-employees who bring a claim or allege some specified wrongful practice or act. Some EPL insurance policies may limit who a third-party claimant can be by defining a third-party claimant only as a customer, client or other specified claimant. Such a definition would limit the effectiveness of the coverage grant and should be avoided.

Another feature that requires careful examination is the types of liability the third-party coverage applies to. Each of the examples given above takes a different approach. In the first example, coverage is for amounts the insured is legally obligated to pay because of an "Insured Event." The term *insured event* is defined elsewhere in the policy. Untangling what is truly covered can be frustrating for insureds and insurance professionals alike.

Because of the paucity of third-party claims and the fact that such coverage is new, there is little precedence in how insurers will actually respond in handling such claims. Where third-party coverage is desired or provided, it is best to confirm with the insurer the limitations that third-party coverage is subject to beyond coverage provided for employee claimants.

"Pay On Behalf" Versus "Indemnify" Coverage

Most EPL insurance policies and many D&O policies that provide EPL coverage promise to "pay on behalf" of the insured that loss which the insured becomes legally obligated to pay as damages. A typically worded "pay-on-behalf" provision is shown below.

> The Company shall pay on behalf of the **Insureds** all **Loss** for which the **Insured** becomes legally obligated to pay on account of any **Claim** first made against the **Insured** during the **Policy Period** or, if exercised, during the Extended Reporting Period, for a **Wrongful Act** committed, attempted, or allegedly committed or attempted, by an **Insured** before or during the **Policy Period.**
>
> Chubb Group
14-02-0953 (Rev. 8/96)

Other EPL insurance policies promise to "indemnify" or reimburse the insured for covered loss only after the loss has been incurred. A portion of a typical "indemnify" provision in an EPL insuring agreement is shown below.

> Subject to all the terms and conditions of this Policy, the Insurer shall indemnify any **Insured** for **Loss Amounts** that such **Insured** is legally obligated to pay because of a **Claim**...
>
> X.L. Insurance Co., Ltd.
EPLI-005
(7/98)

Indemnity wording such as that shown immediately above implies that the insured must first pay the loss and then be reimbursed by the insurer. The obvious disadvantage to this approach is that the insured may have to front the sometimes substantial loss payment and then wait some indeterminate amount of time to be reimbursed by the insurer. Even where there is no finding of liability or judgment against the insured, employment practices liability cases can be quite protracted and cost several hundred thousand dollars just to defend.

Other EPL insurance policy insuring agreements promise to "pay the loss." However, the difference between policies that promise to "pay on behalf" and those that promise to "pay the loss" is not clear. The term *pay the loss* does not indicate *when* the loss will be paid. In that regard, the term may be ambiguous when compared to policies that promise to "pay on behalf" of the insured.

As a practical matter, most stand-alone EPL insurance policies contain an affirmative duty to provide the insured with a defense. So whether a policy pays on behalf, pays the loss or indemnifies the insured, ongoing defense expenses are not affected where a duty to defend exists. Because of the broad nature of an insurer's duty to defend, where such duty has been made a condition of the policy, the insurer likely will pay defense expenses for claims where coverage may be questionable and as those expenses are incurred.

Problems may arise, however, where there is no affirmative duty to defend and where the policy is unclear as to when loss or expenses will be paid. Because defense can drag on for months or years before liability is established or a settlement is reached, insureds could suffer a severe financial burden without prompt payment of ongoing legal expenses. Where the timing of loss and expense payments are a concern, the insured should seek pay-on-behalf coverage together with a duty to defend.

Stand-Alone Versus Combined-Coverage Format

Insurance coverage for employment practices liability is widely available as a stand-alone, unitary contract. In recent years, however, such coverage has also evolved as an endorsement or additional coverage component to other kinds of insurance. Coverage for the EPL exposure can now be purchased in conjunction with D&O, general, umbrella, workers' compensation and a wide range of professional and other liability insurance policies.

Because of the increased availability of employment practices liability insurance coverage under other than a stand-alone format, employers considering purchasing EPL insurance must also decide which format, if any, is preferable. The analysis for such a decision is usually based on the following three factors:

- Scope of coverage provided
- Limit of liability
- Cost

Scope of Coverage

Because the majority of EPL insurance over the last decade has been written on a stand-alone basis, most of the latest developments, including improvements in coverage, have also first appeared in stand-alone policies. As a general rule, stand-alone policies are believed to provide the broadest terms and conditions currently available in the insurance marketplace. Early policies that added EPL coverage, such as D&O policies, often were deficient from a coverage standpoint. For example, in nearly all EPL claims the entity (employer) is named as a defendant. Most D&O policies, however, do not automatically cover the entity. Tacking on EPL coverage without correcting this deficiency created a major coverage gap. While many policies that add EPL coverage have corrected such deficiencies, care must be taken to ensure that the EPL coverage meshes with the terms and conditions of the host policy. Also, some endorsements adding EPL coverage only provide coverage for harassment and wrongful termination if such acts are discrimination-related. This coverage is clearly more restrictive than that provided by most stand-alone EPL insurance policies.

Whenever EPL coverage is added by endorsement, the wording of both the endorsement and the policy should be carefully compared to make sure the resulting coverage is as intended.

Limit of Liability

Stand-alone EPL insurance, by definition, provides coverage that is specifically tailored to the EPL exposure. Because such policies cover only the EPL exposure, the limit of liability is available solely to pay EPL-related claims and defense expense. The limit of liability is not shared with other coverage as is common when EPL coverage is added to or incorporated within so-called combination policies.

For example, a combination D&O/EPL insurance policy may be written with a single coverage limit applicable to both the D&O and EPL coverages. Payment or defense under either one of the coverage parts could reduce or deplete the limits available to pay subsequent claims under the other coverage.

In response to concern over the sharing of limits, some insurers who write EPL insurance in a combined format may offer a separate limit of liability for the EPL coverage component. This separation of limits may assuage any concerns an employer may have about dilution of limits under a combined policy.

Cost

One of the primary advantages of purchasing EPL coverage under a combined policy is that the cost may be less than comparable coverage purchased under a stand-alone policy. In recent years the cost of stand-alone coverage has plummeted, in part due to the increased competition from new insurers entering the EPL marketplace. While such reductions may have blurred the cost distinction between stand-alone and combined policies, some employers are hesitant to buy an "extra" policy, preferring instead to add EPL coverage under an existing policy. Many employers find this "one-stop shopping" both attractive and cost-effective.

Conclusion

Although the perception is that stand-alone EPL coverage is generally broader and more expensive than combination policies, there is little empirical evidence to support this notion. In addition, there is no clear-cut answer as to which is the preferred method. Only through a careful analysis of cost, coverage and limits will the employer be able to determine which approach is best.

Who Is Insured

The interests insured under an EPL insurance policy can include the following:

- The entity or entities
- The directors and officers, if the entity is a corporation
- Supervisors and managers
- Other employees (including part-time or temporary workers)
- Acquisitions

Business Entity

The insured business entity can include an individual if that person is sole owner of a proprietorship, a for-profit or not-for-profit corporation, a public entity, a partnership or a joint venture, or an association. Most stand-alone EPL insurance policies do not specifically enumerate the various types of entities covered but simply identify the name of the insured entity on the policy declarations page.

The inclusion of the entity as a named insured is a valuable coverage feature because the employment relationship generally is considered to exist between the employee and the employing entity. The entity also may have special relationships with certain classes of employees and others that make inclusion of the entity as an insured a crucial element of coverage. The corporation may have statutory and/or contractual obligations to indemnify its directors and officers or others for a broad range of liability. Also, many laws can hold the corporation responsible for the actions of the corporation's supervisors and managers even in instances where the corporation was unaware of the supervisor or manager's wrongful behavior. Also, as a practical matter, many EPL suits usually name the entity as a primary co-defendant. While most stand-alone EPL insurance policies provide direct coverage for the employing entity, other methods of insuring against employment practices liability, such as under a directors and officers insurance policy, may not always cover the corporate entity for claims made directly against it.

Directors And Officers

A corporation's directors and officers are fiduciaries of the corporation, having duties of utmost good faith, fair dealing and loyalty to conduct their affairs for the betterment of the corporation. While directors and officers often are removed from day-to-day management of the corporation and insulated from personal contact with much of the work force, they can be just as susceptible to allegations of wrongful employment conduct or decisionmaking.

Much of the loss that may be incurred by directors or officers because of their wrongful acts, including wrongful employment practices, may be subject to indemnification from the corporation. State laws and corporate charters often dictate the level of indemnification available. But such indemnification usually is quite broad, offering the directors and officers impunity from their actions, except in the most egregious of cases.

It is unclear whether EPL insurance policies that do not include directors and officers as insureds would cover the corporation's indemnity obligations as part of the definition of *loss* in all cases. For this reason, it is prudent to make sure directors and officers are included as insureds under the policy, thereby avoiding any argument over coverage. Doing so also can ensure that coverage is available in instances where the corporation may be financially unable to provide indemnification. But check policies carefully; some policies may exclude coverage when the corporation is bankrupt or otherwise insolvent.

If the corporation is a limited liability company, it will probably be necessary to endorse any EPL insurance policy to provide that the board of managers of the limited liability company are insureds.

Supervisors And Managers

Supervisors and managers, like directors and officers, act for and on behalf of the employing entity. Stated differently, the corporation can act only through its managers and others who are given authority to act on behalf of and manage the corporation. In the context of employment-related responsibilities, the supervisory and managerial roles usually have authority and responsibility to hire, fire, conduct reviews and promote or demote. For this reason, it is important that supervisors and managers also be insureds under the EPL insurance policy. While the corporation may not have indemnity obligations to this class of employee, many state laws will hold the corporation responsible for the actions of supervisors and managers. Under federal law, employers are liable for any sexual harassment committed by a manager or supervisor. Part of a manager's or supervisor's duties in carrying out the goals of the corporation usually requires them to interact with and maintain close contact with the corporation's other employees. Because of this, supervisors and managers frequently are charged with committing a wrongful employment practice and end up named in an employment-related suit along with the corporation.

Other Employees

Depending on the specific jurisdiction, the corporation may have no duty to indemnify employees for expenses incurred in defending an EPL suit, nor be legally responsible for the wrongful actions of a rogue employee. There may, however, be instances where it is prudent for the employer to ally itself with an accused employee and to undertake a defense or otherwise provide for a defense of the employee. Individually, few employees have sufficient assets to pay the legal expenses and large awards usually sought by plaintiffs. Because of this lack of funds, innocent employees often are named in EPL suits solely as a means of leveraging the employer and its insurer into a settlement. But failure to provide a defense may place pressure on the employee to cut a deal with the plaintiff as a means of getting dismissed from the suit in return for giving testimony favorable to the plaintiff.

Most EPL insurance policies include employees as insureds under their basic policy forms. Although usually there is little additional expense in waging a united defense, automatically including employees as insureds under the EPL insurance policy should not be done without first considering some of the arguments against such a practice.

One such argument is that the offending employee may not be innocent of alleged wrongful conduct. Under such a scenario, the employer may wish to distance itself from the offending party. Where the employee is an insured, he or she is likely entitled to the same coverage benefits as is the employer, and in most instances this means that the insurer owes the employee a defense. It is easy to visualize the many conflicts of interest that might arise between the insured parties and the insurer under such a scenario.

Two additional aspects of employment law—those involving punitive damages and sexual harassment—also can prove troublesome. While the legality of insuring against punitive damages is governed by varying state law, there appears to be an increasing pressure on insurers to provide such coverage. And indeed, more and more insurers now offer this coverage where there is no legal restriction against doing so. When punitive damages potentially are covered under an EPL insurance policy, it should be realized that there are instances where such damages might be assessed against an individual employee and not against the employer. By insuring employees under the EPL insurance policy, the employer might be picking up the punitive damage exposure of the employee vis-à-vis its EPL insurance policy that otherwise would not exist.

As respects sexual harassment, if after becoming aware of harassing behavior by non-supervisory employees, the corporation takes prompt corrective measures, it may avoid the imposition of liability altogether, while the harasser may be required to pay substantial damages. Here, too, by insuring the employee, the employer has picked up the liability exposure under its insurance policy which reduces or exhausts the amount of insurance otherwise available to cover the employer's exposure in other employment practices claims.

By including employees as insureds under the EPL insurance policy, there exists a contractual right of the employee to the proceeds and benefits of the policy. Even in the absence of the corporation filing a claim with its insurer, the employee may be able to seek his or her own coverage, even when doing so might be against the wishes of the corporation.

Because most insurers automatically include employees as insureds, there may be some justifiable reluctance in not wishing to restrict coverage that otherwise is available. However, the fact that an EPL insurance policy does not automatically cover employees should not necessarily be considered a negative feature. In all instances, coverage should be selected only after a careful reading of the proposed policy. Consultation with a knowledgeable broker, attorney or consultant, taking into consideration the insured's own claims-handling philosophy is also recommended.

Also, if employees are to be insured under the policy, determine whether a distinction is made between full-time, part-time and temporary workers. Some policies may exclude part-time and temporary employees.

Independent Contractors

By definition, independent contractors are not employees. They are not on an employer's payroll, they do not receive benefits such as health or life insurance, and the employer does not pay employment taxes on behalf of an independent contractor. However, some independent contractors act very much like employees. For example, they may only work for one company, they may have a permanent office at the one company they work for and they may even supervise employees of the company. In such cases, the independent contractor may allege that they were effectively an employee for purposes of bringing an employment-related claim. In these instances, an employer will probably want such a claim to be covered under its EPL insurance policy. However, since many EPL insurance policies limit coverage to claims brought by employees or applicants for employment, there may not be coverage. Some EPL insurers will agree to cover suits brought by independent contractors who allege that they were employees.

Additionally, independent contractors who supervise employees of a company may become defendants in an employment-related claim brought by the employee. In these instances, an employer may wish to afford coverage to the independent contractor under the employer's EPL insurance policy. Many EPL insurance policies would not cover the independent contractor because an independent contractor is not an insured. However, some EPL insurers are willing to cover independent contractors who are dedicated agents of an employer and who are sued in an employment-related claim.

Acquisitions

Most EPL insurance policies contain provisions for extending coverage to newly acquired or formed entities or subsidiaries, including the named insureds of those entities when the original named insureds' ownership is 50% or greater. Coverage for newly formed or acquired operations can either be automatic or subject to prior approval of the underwriter. Often when coverage is automatic, it is only for a limited period of time, usually 30 to 90 days.

Where an automatic coverage period exists, underwriters usually must be notified and given the opportunity to underwrite the new exposure. Most policies do not guarantee that coverage for a newly acquired or formed entity will extend beyond the automatic coverage period. Even where newly acquired or formed entities are automatically covered, underwriters normally reserve the right to charge an additional premium.

Where no automatic coverage provisions exist, care must be exercised to make sure coverage can be secured prior to the new business entity being created or acquired. Unless some agreement at policy inception is made regarding the pricing parameters for newly formed entities, the insurer is free to charge any amount it sees fit. In some instances, the additional premium may be prohibitive and the insured may be forced to forego coverage for the new organization. One solution would be to secure agreement with the insurer that newly formed or acquired entities meeting specific guidelines would be subject to predetermined acceptance and rating.

Limits, Deductible And Coinsurance

Policy Limits

EPL insurance policies can provide either a single limit of liability that covers defense expenses only, separate aggregate limits for defense and indemnity, or a single aggregate limit for defense and indemnity combined. Most stand-alone EPL insurance policies are subject to a single policy aggregate limit of liability covering defense and indemnity. When EPL insurance first became available, it was difficult to purchase more than $5 million in limits. Today, however, it is possible for some insureds to purchase limits as high as $100 million. Also, it may be possible to purchase excess EPL coverage to provide even higher levels of protection.

Most EPL insurance policies clearly state that costs and expenses associated with defense of claims are included within, and are not in addition to, the overall aggregate limit of liability. Coverage for such defense usually would apply in the same fashion as indemnity for liability, subject to the applicable deductible and any coinsurance provisions. Some insurers may offer a sublimit of $50,000 or more for first-dollar defense costs that are not subject to a deductible until the sublimit is exhausted.

In all instances, the aggregate limit of liability is the maximum the insurer will pay for all claims combined during the life of the policy.

Deductibles

Most EPL insurance policies contain a deductible, or what is sometimes referred to in the policy as a *retention clause*. Such clauses provide that the insured will absorb some specific amount of loss. For example, typical deductibles generally apply to both indemnity and defense and can range from the first $2,500 to $250,000 or more of loss.

In most instances, the deductible applies to each claim or interrelated claim and does not serve to reduce the stated limit of liability. In some instances, however, the deductible *does* serve to reduce the stated limit of liability. The application of both approaches can be seen in the following examples.

Example 1

Deductible	$100,000 Non-Limit-Reducing	$100,000 Limit-Reducing
Policy Limit	$1,000,000	$1,000,000
Total Loss	500,000	500,000
Insurer Pays	400,000	400,000
Insured Pays	100,000	100,000

Example 2

Deductible	$100,000 Non-Limit-Reducing	$100,000 Limit-Reducing
Policy Limit	$1,000,000	$1,000,000
Total Loss	1,100,000	1,100,000
Insurer Pays	1,000,000	900,000
Insured Pays	100,000	200,000

It is important to carefully read and understand how deductible or retention clauses apply in order to avoid an unanticipated assumption of loss.

In most instances, the deductible or retention amount will apply to each claim made under the policy. Some policies, however, apply the deductible on the basis of each wrongful employment practice or insured event. For example, it is common for a single wrongful employment practice to result in multiple claims. Where the EPL insurance policy stipulates a per-claim deductible, the insured might be subject to an inordinate and unanticipated burden created by the financial responsibility to absorb multiple deductibles.

In order to avoid the burden such "per-claim" deductible provisions can pose, many EPL insurance policies contain specific provisions that prevent more than one deductible applying to a claim or claims arising out of a single or related wrongful employment practice. These provisions sometimes are referred to as *anti-stacking-deductible provisions.*

While less common, deductibles that apply on a per wrongful practice basis can pose similar problems. For example, it is common for many employment-related claims to include multiple allegations of wrongdoing. Under the per wrongful practice deductible approach, a separate deductible might apply for each separate alleged wrongful practice. Here, too, anti-stacking provisions can be used to limit the number of deductibles that will be applied to the loss adjustment.

If an EPL insurance policy contains unfavorable deductible provisions like those discussed above or if it is unclear how the deductible applies, it is best to have the policy endorsed to clarify the insurer's intent or to provide specific anti-stacking-deductible provisions.

Self-Insured Retentions

Some EPL insurance policies contain a self-insured retention (SIR). An SIR is similar to a deductible in that it is a retention of loss by the insured for the purpose of reducing the cost of insurance. The practical differences of an SIR compared with a deductible is that claims within the SIR normally are controlled by and paid for by the insured. Only after covered claims exceed the SIR amount does the insurance apply. SIR amounts usually range from $250,000 to $1,000,000 or more. They are best suited for sophisticated insureds wishing to exert the maximum control over the claims-handling process while retaining the protection provided by insurance.

It should be noted, however, that there often is much variation in how retention amounts actually apply and the distinction between a deductible, retention or SIR may be vague. Also, the meaning of such terms is not be universal and insurers sometimes use these terms interchangeably. Relying solely on policy captions may lead to confusion or misunderstanding. For these reasons, a careful reading of the policy is mandatory to understand the actual impact of such clauses.

Deductible Reduction Clauses

In addition to the normal deductible wording, some EPL insurance policies contain special retention clauses that act to reduce or eliminate the deductible in exchange for the insured taking certain actions or following certain procedures regarding claim settlement. The following is an example of a deductible-reducing provision:

> **SECTION VI – SPECIAL RETENTION PROVISIONS**
>
> The **RETENTION** indicated in the Declarations will be decreased by fifty percent (50%) (i.e., a $5,000 **RETENTION** will be $2,500) if one or both of the following conditions are met:
>
> 1. **Wrongful Termination or Demotion Condition.** For any "Inappropriate Employment Conduct" "claim" or "suit" alleging wrongful termination or wrongful demotion of an employee if prior to the termination or demotion of that employee you have consulted with and materially complied with the advice of our appointed attorney. This Provision does not apply unless the contact with our appointed attorney is made at least 24 hours prior to the termination or demotion, and the attorney has had a reasonable length of time to respond to the information provided. To determine the name of our appointed attorney, contact American Technology Excess & Surplus Insurance Services (Telephone 1-800-611-7345).
>
> 2. **Mediation of Claims Condition.** If a "claim" is fully and finally resolved to the satisfaction of all parties, including us, through "mediation," provided that such "mediation" is initiated and concluded and/or abandoned before and not subsequent to commencement of any litigation or arbitration. In the event such "mediation" does not fully and finally resolve the "claim," there shall be no reduction of the **RETENTION** obligation, and all "loss" expenses incurred in the "mediation" shall be included in the total "loss" expenses for the "claim."
>
> Legion Insurance Group
ERP-1
7/98

One of the purposes of such clauses is to encourage the insured to follow the advice of counsel before terminating or demoting an employee. In the provisions cited above, the insured must consult with appointed counsel prior to terminating or demoting an employee and to comply with any recommendations relating to such termination or demotion. The retention amount may also be reduced if a claim is resolved through mediation and does not involve litigation.

Keep in mind that such clauses normally require strict compliance and it is possible that recommendations made by appointed counsel may be contradictory or in conflict with current policy and procedure. But because there is limited downside to such provisions, they are widely considered to be beneficial in controlling overall claim costs.

Coinsurance

In addition to deductible or retention provisions, some EPL insurance policies contain coinsurance provisions that require the insured to bear a percentage of the loss that is in excess of the deductible or retention amount. Policies that contain coinsurance provisions may set the percentage between 5% and 20%. Some insurers have the coinsurance percentage preprinted in the form; others stipulate the applicable percentage on the declarations page or elsewhere in the policy at the time of issuance. Insurers may be willing to reduce or eliminate the coinsurance requirement for an additional premium. Many EPL insurance policy forms do not require a coinsurance retention.

Some insurers believe that a coinsurance provision causes the policyholder to have a greater vested interest in the defense and settlement of a claim, and the provision helps in achieving the lowest cost resolution of a claim.

9 Defense And Settlement Provisions[1]

Defense expenses associated with employment-related claims can exceed several hundred thousand dollars, and defense expenditures in excess of a million dollars are not uncommon. For many insureds, coverage for defense expenses can be one of the most important coverage features. Yet it is an area where important variations in policy wording exist.

Duty To Defend

Defense coverage under liability insurance policies is a purely contractual obligation. In the absence of an affirmative promise by the insurer to defend the insured, no such duty is assumed to exist. Most stand-alone EPL insurance policies contain an affirmative statement by the insurer that they will defend the insured. EPL coverage endorsed to or contained within other policies, such as some D&O policies, may not contain such a duty. An example of an affirmative duty to defend in an EPL insurance policy is:

> The Underwriter will have the right and duty to defend any covered **Claim** even if the allegations thereof are groundless, false, or fraudulent; provided, that the Underwriter's obligation to defend is subject to the applicable coinsurance, retention and Limit of Liability provisions as set forth in CONDITION (E) below.
>
> Executive Risk Specialty Insurance Company
> B22170 (2/97)

For many insureds, an affirmative duty by the insurer to defend the insured is a very desirable feature. One of the key reasons is that the duty to defend generally is considered to be broader than the duty to pay indemnity. This means that where a duty to defend exists, the insurer may be required to defend the insured at the time a claim is reported to the insurer even if the claim contains allegations that are only potentially within the scope of coverage. An insurer may have a duty to defend the insured even if

---

[1] Specific EPL insurance policy form citations contained in *The EPL Book* are used to illustrate and support text discussion only. Such references are illustrative in nature and are neither an endorsement for nor criticism of any particular policy form. In some instances, policy forms cited in *The EPL Book* may no longer be in use and may be superceded by later editions. Neither *The EPL Book* nor any other reference is a substitute for the reader's own analysis, due diligence and careful reading of the policy form(s) in question.

indemnity is ultimately excluded by the policy. Often when a suit is brought against an insured or a claim is made for damages, the claim or suit will contain numerous allegations. Some allegations may lie within the policy's coverage grant and not be precluded by exclusions within the policy. However, some allegations may be outside the scope of coverage. Other allegations may be specifically excluded. However, if any allegation in a complaint is potentially covered, the insurer is usually obligated to defend the entire complaint.

Not all EPL insurance policies contain an affirmative duty to defend. Other policies, such as D&O policies, that provide or have been endorsed to provide EPL coverage often do not contain a duty to defend. When the policy does not contain a duty to defend, this fact usually will be clearly stated in the policy, as illustrated in the following example:

> The **Insured** retains the responsibility to defend any **Claim.** The Insurer has no duty to provide a defense to any **Claim.**
>
> X.L. Insurance Company Limited
> EPLI-005
> (7/98)

While an affirmative duty to defend is a highly desirable feature for most employers, there are situations when an insured may not think such a duty is desirable. Many employers carry high self-insured retentions as part of their overall risk-financing approach. Such self-insured retentions can be $250,000, $500,000 or even $1,000,000 or more. In such cases, the insured usually wishes to exercise control over claims. Because of the insured's desire to control claim and defense costs, a duty to defend and the insurer's contractual right to select counsel may not be a desirable feature for all insureds.

A relatively new development in EPL insurance has been the introduction of policies that contain provisions that give the insured flexibility in how defense is handled. The following defense clause states clearly that there is no duty by the insurer to defend the insured but gives the insured the option of tendering a claim to the insurer if it so chooses:

> Notwithstanding the foregoing, the Insureds shall have the right to tender the defense of the Claim to the Insurer, which right shall be exercised in writing by the Named Entity on behalf of all Insureds to the Insurer pursuant to the notice provisions of Clause 7 of this policy. This right shall terminate if not exercised within 30 days of the date the Claim is first made against an Insured, pursuant to Clause 7 of the policy.
>
> National Union Fire Insurance Company
> 67548 (4/97)

In order for the insurer to assume defense of a claim, the insured must give notice to the insurer in writing and within 30 days of when claim has been made against the insured. While such clauses give a certain degree of flexibility in how defense is handled, insureds should keep in mind that unless policy-reporting requirements are complied with, the policy will respond without an affirmative duty to provide defense. Great care should be exercised by insureds to ensure that they understand the procedures and requirements for activating optional defense coverages under such policies and to understand whether such optional defense coverage is limited in any way.

Choice Of Counsel In Non-Duty-To-Defend Policies

In policies containing an affirmative duty to defend, the insurer normally has the right and discretion to appoint defense counsel. Under non-duty-to-defend policies, it often is presumed that the insured has absolute control over defense issues. This assumption is often incorrect because many policies that do not contain a duty to defend still retain at least some control over the selection of defense counsel. A common approach is to give the insured control of counsel selection, subject to the insurer's consent or approval of such selection. This provision can be seen in the following example.

> The Company shall have the right and be given the opportunity to approve in advance counsel selected by an Insured to defend any Claim, such approval not to be unreasonably withheld or delayed, and to require the Insured to revoke such counsel's appointment. Defense Costs incurred prior to the Company's approval of defense counsel shall not be counted toward fulfillment of the Insureds' retention obligations, nor shall the Company be liable for such Defense Costs, without the written consent of the Company. The Company shall have the right and shall be given the opportunity to have counsel of its choice associated in the defense of the Claim at its own expense. The Company reserves the right at any time to take over control of the defense of the Claim.
>
> Philadelphia Insurance Company
PI-ES-1560 (12/96)

At least one insurer, under a defense-cost-reimbursement policy, leaves the entire selection and control of defense counsel with the insured. Defense coverage is provided on a strict indemnification basis with no duty of the insurer to provide a defense nor to pay any damages or judgments. This approach provides the insured the greatest flexibility and control over litigation management, but with broad coverage limitations.

Consent To Settlement

Most EPL insurance policies contain provisions granting the insurer significant control over the settlement of claims. Under early EPL insurance policies, decisions regarding whether to settle and at what cost were often at the sole discretion of the insurer. An example of such a provision is illustrated below:

> We have the right to investigate and settle up to the applicable Limits of Insurance any claim in the manner and to the extent we, in our sole discretion, deem proper. Upon receipt by us of notice of circumstances which are likely to give rise to a Claim, we also have the right (but not the duty) to investigate and make such a settlement even before a Claim is made.
>
> Lexington Insurance Company
LEX-CM-EPLIT(ED.06/95)
LX0557

The above provision gives the insurer sole authority to settle claims even when such settlement might be against the wishes of the insured. Insureds accused of wrongful conduct, especially alleged sexual impropriety, often do not want to settle such claims, believing instead that only an adjudication will fully absolve them of wrongdoing. Some policies recognize this concern and contain provisions requiring the insurer to obtain the insured's consent before a settlement can be made. An example of such a provision is:

> We have the right to investigate and with the consent of the Insured which is a subject of Claim (which consent shall not be unreasonably withheld), settle any Claim up to the Limit of Liability. Upon receipt by us of notice of an Insured Event which is likely to give rise to a Claim, we also have the right (but not the duty) to investigate and make such a settlement even before a Claim is made.
>
> Steadfast Insurance Company
STF-PL-D-100-B
(4/97)

It also is common for the insurer to have the right to recommend settlement. But refusal by the insured to settle may limit the insured's recovery to the amount recommended by the insurer. Such provisions are sometimes referred to as *hammer* clauses. An example of a hammer clause is shown below:

> **Consent to Settle.** We will not settle any Loss without your consent. If you refuse to consent to any settlement recommended by us or our representatives and you elect to contest or continue any legal proceedings, then our liability shall not exceed the amount for which the Loss could have been settled including Defense Costs incurred with our consent, up to the date of such refusal.
>
> American Technology Excess and Surplus Insurance Services (AmTech)
AmTech Form ERP-1 (11/96)

Because of the volatile and often emotionally charged nature of employment practices liability claims, innocent insureds may feel that a settlement, rather than adjudication by the court, will not fully vindicate them of the alleged wrongdoing. Insureds argue that consent and hammer clauses like the examples above make it difficult to litigate because loss costs in excess of a suggested settlement amount will be borne by the insured. Insurers argue that without such clauses, they may be subjected to loss far in excess of what a claim might otherwise be settled for without seeking an adjudication.

As a practical matter, problems regarding whether to settle a claim or to litigate may be lessened by the insured and insurer agreeing on experienced counsel prior to policy inception. When both the insured and insurer have trust in defense counsel, they are more likely to concur with counsel's recommendations regarding settlement or trial.

Allocation, Advancement And Timing Of Defense Expense Payments

Because many EPL insurance policies contain an affirmative duty by the insurer to defend the insured, payment and timing of defense costs normally are not problematic. Defense counsel is retained by the insurer, and expenses for defense services usually are paid directly by the insurer as they are incurred. Any loss amounts within the deductible or co-payment provisions are either paid by the insurer and then collected from the insured, or billed directly to the insured by defense counsel.

However, as previously discussed, not all EPL insurance policies contain a duty to defend. Some policies endorsed to cover EPL claims, such as most D&O policies, also do not contain an affirmative duty to defend. Accordingly, in the absence of a promise by the insurer to reimburse the insured contemporaneously as expenses are incurred, the insured may be required to fund an expensive defense and obtain reimbursement only at the conclusion of the case. Having to wait potentially long periods of time for reimbursement of expenses might place an inordinate strain on the financial well-being of some organizations.

Another potential problem of policies that do not contain an affirmative duty to defend is the allocation-of-loss provision. In the context of EPL insurance and other kinds of insurance that do not provide a duty to defend, the word *allocation* often is used to describe the apportionment of a claim between covered and uncovered elements of loss.

When the duty to defend exists, the insurer normally is obligated to defend the insured against all counts alleged, even if some of them clearly are excluded by the policy or otherwise fall outside the scope of coverage. Where there is no duty to defend, the insurer usually is only obligated to pay loss and expense arising out of acts covered by the policy. Where this occurs, the insurer likely will attempt to make an allocation or determination of what elements of loss are covered. This process is depicted in the following illustration.

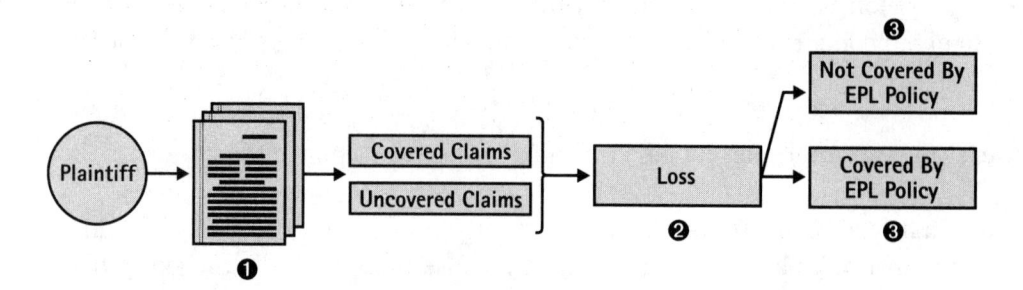

❶ Plaintiff files complaint alleging covered and uncovered counts.
❷ Loss including defense costs incurred by defendants.
❸ The insurer may attempt to apportion loss between covered and uncovered elements.

The result of an allocation is that some portion of loss may not be recoverable by the insured. Allocation between insured and uninsured parties has been the subject of substantial litigation in D&O policies. Disputes involving allocation between insured and uninsured parties often are avoided by inclusion of the employer as an insured under the policy. But such action does not eliminate the potential that an allocation will be made or attempted by the insurer as respects other covered and uncovered elements of loss. For example, some claims based on sexual harassment contain allegations of bodily injury, but bodily injury is sometimes excluded under EPL insurance policies. If some amount of the settlement or judgment is based on the bodily injury portion of the claim, then the insurer may attempt to allocate or treat that element of loss as non-covered.

It also should be noted that an insurer may attempt an allocation of defense expenses even under a duty-to-defend policy. Even though the insurer may be required to defend potentially uncovered claim elements, the insurer may attempt to allocate defense expenses for clearly uncovered items if such an allocation is possible. Some recent case law suggests that an insurer with a duty to defend may allocate defense costs if it can conclusively prove that a cause of action potentially is not covered. While this kind of allocation is possible, to date it has rarely been done.

Because employment-related litigation often is complex, it can take months or even years to resolve. In a non-duty-to-defend-policy where defense costs are reimbursed at the conclusion of the case, the insured may suffer a financial burden by funding the defense. This delay may be acceptable for larger, well-financed organizations, but small, thinly capitalized businesses might not have the financial resources to weather such a battle.

To relieve the insured of the financial burden of funding a defense, some non-duty-to-defend insurers provide for advancement of defense expenses. Examples of such provisions are shown below:

> The Insurer shall advance on behalf of the **Insureds Claims Expenses** which the **Insureds** have incurred in connection with **Claims** made against them, prior to the final disposition of such **Claims,** provided always that to the extent it is established that any such **Claims Expenses** are not covered under this Policy, the **Insureds,** as appropriate, agree to repay to the Insurer such non-covered **Claims Expenses.**
>
> Reliance Insurance Company of Illinois
GL 00 R424 00 0498

> When the Insurer has not assumed the defense of a Claim pursuant to Clause 8, the Insurer shall advance nevertheless, at the written request of the Insured, Defense Costs prior to the final disposition of a Claim. Such advanced payments by the Insurer shall be repaid to the Insurer by the Insureds or the Company, severally according to their respective interests, in the event and to the extent that the Insureds or the Company shall not be entitled under the terms and conditions of this policy to payment of such loss.
>
> National Union Fire Insurance Company
67548 (4/97)

It should be noted, however, that some advancement provisions may fall short of an affirmative promise to advance expenses. This can occur if the decision to advance expenses remains at the discretion of the insurer. EPL insurance policies that do not contain an affirmative duty to defend should contain clearly worded advancement provisions to help avoid the possible burden of awaiting the conclusion of a suit before collecting defense and other expenses from the insurer.

Right Of Association And Right To Assume Defense

In policies that do not contain an affirmative duty to defend, the insurer usually has the right to associate with the defense of the insured.

Some EPL insurance policies that do not contain an affirmative duty to defend may contain provisions that give the insurer the right to assume and take control of the defense at its own discretion.

Policies that contain such provisions should be carefully considered. If the insured makes an informed decision to purchase an EPL insurance policy or other policy without a duty to defend, it often is doing so at least in part because the insured wishes to maintain maximum control over defense issues and strategies. This control usually includes counsel selection. When control of defense issues is important, the insured should avoid policies that contain provisions giving the insurer the right to assume control of defense.

Some EPL insurance policies specify that if the insurer assumes the defense, then defense costs incurred by the insurer will be included within the policy limit of liability. But some policies that allow the insurer to take over defense do not state whether those expenses are within or in addition to the policy limit of liability. Silence on this issue can give rise to coverage disputes and possible litigation.

As with all policy provisions, if questions or ambiguities over intent or meaning exist, always seek clarification in writing from the broker or insurer.

Most EPL insurance policies containing an affirmative duty to defend provide the following benefits for the insured:

- May provide defense coverage, even in instances where elements of a claim are not covered or where it is indeterminable whether coverage exists

- Help avoid litigation as respects disputes regarding the timing of defense expenses payments

- Provide expert intervention early on when it is most effective[2]

In exchange for the insurer's obligation to defend, the insured typically relinquishes control over selection of defense counsel and settlement decisions. While many insureds will benefit from the insurer's affirmative duty to defend, there may be instances when the insured is better served by a policy that does not contain an affirmative duty to defend, as discussed previously.

---

[2] It should be noted that insurance company involvement is largely a function of when the policy is triggered. This, in turn, usually is determined by (1) the employer's timely reporting of the claim, (2) the definition of what actually constitutes a claim under the policy, (3) the specific claim-reporting provisions and (4) the insurance company's claim handling philosophy regarding aggressive intervention and investigation.

10 Exclusions[1]

An exclusion is any policy provision that eliminates or restricts coverage for certain types of claims or losses. All EPL insurance policies contain exclusions. Most exclusions are found in a separate section of the policy entitled *Exclusions*. However, exclusionary language or other language restricting or limiting coverage can be found in any section of the policy. Exclusions also are frequently added by endorsement, and they may even appear in the policy application.

Because exclusions limit coverage, it is essential that all exclusions be understood. Too often exclusions are given only a cursory reading and the full meaning of the exclusion is missed or glossed over. Some exclusions are considered to be standard and are commonly included in most EPL insurance policies. Other exclusions can be specially drafted for a particular insured for the purpose of excluding a risk that the insurer is unwilling or unable to accept. These specially drafted exclusions usually are contained in an endorsement to the policy. In order to understand the relative coverage benefits and limitations under a given policy, it is necessary to know the purpose and effect of all exclusions.

General Rules

Most exclusions begin with a prefatory or introductory phrase that can affect the scope of the exclusion. When articulating an exclusion, one approach of underwriters is to simply state that the policy does not apply to claims "for" the specifically enumerated item being excluded.

Another approach is to not only refer to that which is specifically excluded but also to exclude any other claims that might arise out of or in consequence of the excluded item. The following is an example of this approach:

---

[1] Specific EPL insurance policy form citations contained in *The EPL Book* are used to illustrate and support text discussion only. Such references are illustrative in nature and are neither an endorsement for nor criticism of any particular policy form. In some instances, policy forms cited in *The EPL Book* may no longer be in use and may be superceded by later editions. Neither *The EPL Book* nor any other reference is a substitute for the reader's own analysis, due diligence and careful reading of the policy form(s) in question.

> The Company shall not be liable to make payment for **Loss** or **Defense Costs** in connection with any **Claim** made against any **Insured** arising out of, directly or indirectly resulting from or in consequence of, or in any way involving...
>
> USLI Companies
EPL (2/94)

The effect of the introductory language contained in the above example is to broaden the exclusion so that it applies not only to the specifically excluded item, but conceivably to claims that may only be loosely attributable to the excluded item. Because such prefatory language can further reduce or eliminate coverage, care should be taken to avoid such modifying clauses if possible.

It also is important to note that while some policies take the approach of stating the introductory language and then have it apply on a blanket basis to all exclusions, other EPL insurance policies state the introductory language individually for each exclusion. Where the introductory language is stated within the individual exclusions, that language may vary between individual exclusions. It is also possible that some exclusions will be subject to narrow prefatory wording, while other exclusions within the same policy are subject to the broad prefatory wording. Consider the following:

> **BROAD INTRODUCTORY LANGUAGE**
>
> The Company shall not be liable to make payment for Loss in connection with any Claim made against any Insured based upon or arising out of any actual or alleged bodily injury, sickness, disease or death of any person...
>
> **LIMITED INTRODUCTORY LANGUAGE**
>
> The Underwriters shall not be liable to indemnify the **INSURED** for **LOSS**, including **CLAIMS EXPENSES**, as a result of any claim or claims made against the **INSURED**...For bodily injury, sickness, loss of consortium, disease or death of any person, or for damage to, or destruction of any tangible property including loss of use thereof...

Broad introductory wording in the first example likely would exclude not only the actual bodily injury contemplated by the exclusion, but also any other damages in connection with a claim based upon or arising out of the bodily injury. For example, if a plaintiff suffered an assault and battery as part of a pattern of sexual harassment and also suffered lost wages due to the same act of sexual harassment, the broadly worded exclusion might act to exclude damages for the assault and battery as well as for lost wages. On the other hand, the narrower exclusion would probably not exclude the lost wages resulting from the sexual harassment.

The following discussion provides a brief but concise overview of many exclusions found in EPL insurance policy forms. While the list of exclusions discussed is extensive, it is not exhaustive. Also, not all exclusions discussed will appear in all policy forms. Readers also are cautioned that many exclusions are added by endorsement, and the number of possible exclusionary endorsements often are limited only by the underwriter's ingenuity and imagination.

Bodily Injury And Personal Injury Exclusions

Although coverage for bodily injury and personal injury liability is provided under most general liability policies, coverage for employment-related claims usually is either limited or totally excluded.

While some EPL insurance policies exclude liability arising out of or attributable to bodily injury or personal injury, some do not. Many insurance professionals and risk managers associate the terms *bodily injury* and *personal injury* in the context of standardized general liability policies similar to those developed by the Insurance Services Office. Recent editions of ISO-CGL policies define the terms *bodily injury* and *personal injury* as follows:

> "Bodily injury" means bodily injury, sickness or disease sustained by a person, including death resulting from any of these at any time.
>
> "Personal and advertising injury" means injury, other than "bodily injury", arising out of one or more of the following offenses:
>   a. False arrest, detention or imprisonment;
>   b. Malicious prosecution;
>   c. The wrongful eviction from, wrongful entry into, or invasion of the right of private occupancy of a room or dwelling or premises that a person occupies by or on behalf of its owner, landlord or lessor;
>   d. Oral or written publication of material that slanders or libels a person or organization or disparages a person's or organization's goods, products or services;
>   e. Oral or written publication of material that violates a person's right of privacy;
>   f. The use of another's advertising idea in your "advertisement"; or
>   g. Infringing upon another's copyright, trade dress or slogan in your "advertisement."
>
> ISO Commercial General Liability Coverage Form
CG 00 01 07 98

While the above definitions of bodily injury and personal injury are typical in general liability policies, bodily injury and personal injury may be defined differently under an EPL insurance policy. Sometimes bodily injury or personal injury may not be defined and it may be unclear to the insured exactly what such undefined terms mean. For example, the undefined term *personal injury* might include loss of consortium, emotional distress, mental anguish, humiliation and invasion of privacy. When such undefined terms are used in exclusions, the effect can be very limiting.

Employees asserting employment claims often allege that as a result of harassment or other wrongful employment practices, they suffered damages that can include all of the types of bodily injury and personal injury described in the above example. Therefore, in examining an EPL insurance policy, it is important to bear in mind the scope and effect of any bodily injury or personal injury exclusion contained in the policy.

The following are examples of bodily injury and/or personal injury exclusions contained in EPL insurance policies:

> **BODILY INJURY ONLY**
>
> For bodily injury, sickness, loss of consortium, disease or death of any person, or for damage to, or destruction of any tangible property including loss of use thereof.
>
> London Market
U.S. Risk Underwriters, Inc.
DISC3/98/CO

> **BODILY INJURY AND PERSONAL INJURY OFFENSE COMBINED**
>
> ...for any actual or alleged bodily injury, mental anguish, emotional distress, libel, slander or defamation, sickness, loss of consortium, disease or death of any person, or any actual or alleged damage to or destruction of any tangible property including the loss of use thereof...
>
> Philadelphia Insurance Company
PI-ES-1560
12/96

> **BODILY INJURY WITH EXCEPTION FOR LIMITED PERSONAL INJURIES**
>
> ...arising out of any actual or alleged bodily injury to, or sickness, loss of consortium, disease or death of, any person, or damage to or destruction of property, including the loss of use thereof; provided, that this EXCLUSION (D) does not apply to **Claims** for emotional distress, mental anguish or humiliation actually or allegedly resulting from **an Employment Practices Wrongful Act**...
>
> Executive Risk Specialty Insurance Company
B22170
2/97

The first example does not state whether claims of mental anguish or emotional distress are excluded. Some courts have held that the undefined term *bodily injury* includes claims of mental anguish or emotional distress. However, other courts have held that an exclusion for bodily injury does not exclude claims of emotional distress or mental anguish.

The second example excludes not only bodily injury, but also specifically excludes personal injury such as mental anguish, libel, slander, defamation, humiliation and emotional distress. Such personal injury—especially mental anguish, libel, slander and defamation—often are alleged in many wrongful employment practice suits. From an insurer's standpoint, this wording alleviates the concern that a court might conclude that a bodily injury exclusion does not exclude emotional distress and mental anguish.

The third example has important exceptions to the exclusion, which include emotional distress, mental anguish and humiliation. From an insured's standpoint, these exceptions alleviate the risk that a court might find that emotional distress and mental anguish claims are within the scope of bodily injury and therefore excluded. However, it should be noted that the exclusion does not name other types of personal injury allegations frequently brought in wrongful termination suits, such as defamation, libel, slander and invasion of privacy.

As a general rule and absent policy language specifically excluding defamation, libel, slander and invasion of privacy, a bodily injury exclusion likely would not preclude coverage for these kinds of claims. But claims for defamation, libel, slander and invasion of privacy may or may not be covered in the insuring clauses of the policy.

As noted above, employment-related claims can allege acts of bodily injury or personal injury. For example, sexual harassment claims often contain allegations of physical contact, mental anguish, humiliation or emotional distress. Personal injury also can be alleged in discrimination and wrongful termination claims. For example, a woman terminated for poor job performance may complain that her former employer defamed her by communicating the prior poor job performance to prospective employers.

Because of this, it is desirable from an insured's standpoint to purchase policies that do not contain bodily injury or personal injury exclusions. Where it is impossible to completely eliminate such exclusions, insureds should look for exclusions that make exceptions for certain types of personal injury such as mental anguish, humiliation, emotional distress, libel, slander, defamation, invasion of privacy and false imprisonment.

Where bodily injury or personal injury claims are excluded and where those terms are undefined, the insured may be able to endorse or clarify the policy regarding the meaning of those terms. By clarifying the meaning, an overly restrictive interpretation of those terms can be avoided.

Assault And Battery

Assault means the threat of unwelcome physical contact. *Battery* is an unwelcome touching. Assault and battery allegations can be made either in a civil or a criminal context. When assault and battery charges are brought as part of a civil lawsuit, the aggrieved plaintiff may be able to recover compensatory and, in some cases, punitive damages. If the alleged assault and battery is reported to the appropriate governmental officials, such as the local police, and these officials feel the charges warrant prosecution, criminal proceedings can result. Such proceedings usually are quite expensive to defend and can result in the imposition of criminal fines payable to the state or even in jail sentences.

Some EPL insurance policies contain exclusions for assault and battery. Such exclusions may be incorporated into a bodily injury or personal injury exclusion or they may appear independently as a separate exclusion.

A broadly worded bodily injury exclusion can serve to exclude assault and battery allegations in both a civil and a criminal context. Also, some EPL insurance policies contain exclusions for criminal proceedings. An exclusion of criminal proceedings, however, probably would not act to exclude coverage for civil allegations of assault and battery. The civil allegations would not be excluded because criminal proceeding exclusions typically do not exclude the cause of action for assault and battery, but rather only a criminal complaint. Therefore, a civil complaint for assault and battery likely would fall outside the scope of a criminal proceedings exclusion.

Assault and battery exclusions are important in the EPL context because charges of sexual harassment can contain allegations of assault and battery. Therefore, insureds should carefully examine any existing or proposed EPL insurance policies to determine whether or not assault and battery allegations in connection with employment practice allegations would be covered.

It should be noted that determining whether coverage exists under an EPL insurance policy for any given claim scenario is often a complex issue. Even if an EPL insurance policy does not contain an assault and battery exclusion, assault and battery allegations should not automatically be presumed to be covered.

For example, if an assault and battery claim does not arise from a wrongful employment practice as defined in the EPL insurance policy, it would not be covered. Therefore, if an employee commits an assault and battery on a customer, that situation is not covered because there is not an underlying claim for harassment, discrimination or wrongful termination made by an employee.

EPL insurance policies only cover allegations that include one of the wrongful employment practice perils identified within the particular policy. The claimant also must normally be an employee, a former employee or an applicant for employment. Insureds also must consider whether public policy or an intentional act exclusion would preclude coverage for assault and battery claims.

Breach Of Employment Contract

Most EPL insurance policies exclude liability arising out of the insured's breach of an employment contract with its employees. Some breach-of-contract exclusions apply to any express contracts, whether oral or written. Other EPL insurance policies may exclude all breaches of employment contract whether they are express or implied, and some EPL insurance policies are silent on the issue.

An express employment contract is similar to other types of commercial contracts in that it sets forth the rights and obligations of each party to the contract.

Most express employment contracts are written contracts. Express employment contracts ordinarily attempt to set forth some or all of the agreements and conditions of employment. Such agreements or conditions may or may not include specifying the duration of employment, specific compensation to be paid and the provisions and conditions governing termination of the contract. For example, a written employment contract may provide for a five-year term at $100,000 per year and also provide that the contract may only be terminated for good cause, such as inadequate job performance. If such a contract were terminated without cause after three years, the employee may have a claim for the remaining two years, or $200,000.

Many EPL insurance policies exclude any obligation of the insured under an express contract. Accordingly, in the above example, there would be no coverage for the $200,000 compensation claim. Exclusions relating to contracts often are incorporated into the definition of *wrongful termination* but are sometimes made part of the definition of *loss* or *damages*. The example below is of an express employment contract exclusion found in a policy definition of the term *loss*.

> Loss means damages, judgment (including prejudgment and post-judgment interest awarded against an Insured on that part of any judgment paid by us) settlements, Punitive Damages, statutory attorney fees, front pay, back pay and Defense Costs. However, Loss does not include...(7) amounts determined to be owing under an express contract of employment or an express obligation to make payments in the event of the termination of employment
>
> CNA Reinsurance (NAS Insurance Services)
> C/NA/S
> 12/97

In the absence of an express employment contract, the employment relationship is sometimes thought of by employers as being an at-will relationship. An at-will relationship means that either the employer or the employee may terminate the employment relationship at any time and for any reason. In some states, an at-will employment relationship can be modified by provisions contained in an employer's handbook or by statements made by the employer that imply that an employee may be terminated only for cause.[2] Where the laws governing at-will employment recognize implied employment contracts and an employee is terminated without cause, that employee may then be able to successfully bring suit against the employer for breach of an implied contract.

Some policies do not exclude breach of contract, which is a beneficial feature. The breach-of-express-contract exclusions have the effect of limiting coverage for claims by

---

[2] See *The "Employment-At-Will" Doctrine* section, pp. 29–31.

the most highly paid employees of an employer because these highly paid individuals usually are the ones most likely to be subject to employment contracts.

It should be noted that some EPL insurance policies that contain contractual liability exclusions may actually offer some protection for claims based on express contracts. The following contractual liability exclusion makes an exception for claims where liability does not arise under such express contract.

> The Insurer shall not be liable to make any payment for Loss in connection with a Claim made against an Insured...alleging, arising out of, based upon or attributable to any actual or alleged contractual liability of the Company or any other Insured under any express employment contract or agreement; provided, however, that this exclusion shall not apply to the extent any liability does not arise under such express contract or agreement;
>
> National Union Fire Insurance Co.
> 67548 (4/97)

This exception presumably would not preclude coverage for defense costs where no liability was found to exist under an alleged employment or other contract.

Consequential Loss

In employment law, *consequential loss* generally refers to the loss suffered by an employee's family members or domestic partner because of or in consequence of injury to the employee arising out of one or more wrongful employment practices. Typical claims by family members or a domestic partner include loss of consortium, loss of economic support and mental anguish.

Many EPL insurance policies contain some form of exclusion for consequential loss. The purpose of the consequential loss exclusion is to limit coverage to claims brought only by employees or applicants for employment. The exclusion limits the class of plaintiffs who can assert a claim under the policy. The following is an example of such an exclusion:

> The Insuring Agreements and all other provisions of this Policy shall not apply to:...Any claim made by any claimant's domestic partner, spouse, child, parent, brother or sister as a consequence of the actual or alleged Wrongful Employment Practice...
>
> American Equity Insurance Company
> 11197
> 11/97

The purpose of such exclusions is simply to exclude claims brought by anyone other than the employee, former employee or applicant for employment. This serves to exclude any possible third-party claims from relatives of the employee.

It should be noted that some EPL insurance policies include the word *consequential* as a modifier or part of a prefatory statement to any number of exclusions. When the word *consequential* is used in this fashion, the effect is to broaden the particular exclusion in much the same way phrases like *arising out of, directly or indirectly* and *any way involving* broaden an exclusion.[3] While use of the word *consequential* in the context of an exclusion may possibly have the effect of excluding family members and relatives as covered plaintiffs, it should not be confused with a "consequential loss exclusion" that specifically limits the policy as described above.

Failure To Provide Benefits

Most EPL insurance policies contain an exclusion of any liability arising out of providing or failing to provide employee benefits. It is important to understand the effect of such exclusions because wrongful termination claims often seek to recover damages based on the value of lost medical and other benefits. These benefits can include the following:

Disability—Insurance benefits including income-continuation benefits if an employee is disabled.

ERISA—Benefits, primarily pension benefits, protected by the federal government through ERISA regulations.

Unemployment—Continued income from the state for a specified time following a layoff.

COBRA—A federal plan that requires employers to provide terminated employees (or their dependents) the opportunity to continue certain medical benefits for a specified time after termination.

Retirement—Pension benefits that are due the employee or may have been earned by the employee if they had not been wrongfully terminated.

Social Security—Federal retirement benefits funded by contributions from both the employee and the employer.

Workers' Compensation—State laws that provide medical expenses and income to employees that are injured as a result of their employment activities.

Health Benefits—Life, medical or dental insurance benefits that employers routinely provide to employees.

---

[3] See *Exclusions* chapter, *General Rules*, pages 187–189.

When an employer provides employment benefits either voluntarily or as required by state or federal law, the terminated employee may be able to collect the value of such benefits under one or more theories of recovery in a wrongful employment practice lawsuit. Most EPL insurance policies exclude claims for such benefits because they are exposures that the underwriters do not wish to cover.

The exclusion of employer-provided benefits may appear as a separate exclusion or be incorporated into the policy definition of *loss,* as shown below:

> Loss means damages, settlements and Defense Costs; but shall not include: any insurance plan benefits, including but not limited to benefits payable pursuant to either the Comprehensive Omnibus Budget Reconciliation Act (COBRA) or the Employees Retirement Income Security Act (ERISA) and any similar federal, state or local law, and any amendments thereto and any rules or regulations promulgated thereunder, that the claimant may have been entitled to as an employee or former employee of the Named Insured.
>
> Colonia (AUSCO)
> EPL 6000 (3/95)

Coverage for employee benefits liability usually can be added to the employer's general liability policy. Such endorsements are non-standardized, but generally are designed to protect employers against liability arising out of errors or omissions related to the administration of employee benefit plans. The kinds of errors and omissions contemplated by such endorsements include those relating to enrollment, recordkeeping and interpretation or description of benefits. Employee benefits liability coverage also can be purchased on a stand-alone basis.

It also should be noted that fiduciary liability, such as that imposed under ERISA and COBRA, normally is not covered by EPL insurance policies. In some instances, however, specific fiduciary liability coverage sections may be included in or added to D&O policies that also provide EPL coverage.

Some EPL insurers have limited the exclusion for employer-provided benefits. For example, if a former employee brings suit for wrongful termination and receives a jury award for compensatory damages which consists in part of the value of lost employer-provided benefits (such as health, dental and life insurance), the EPL insurance policy may then provide coverage based on the value of the lost benefits.

Property Damage

Damage to or loss of use of tangible and intangible property is excluded in some EPL insurance policies. Where property damage is excluded, such exclusion often is made part of a combined bodily injury and property damage liability exclusion. The exclusion of property damage also may appear as an independent exclusion or may be incorporated into the definition of *damages* as illustrated in the following examples:

SPECIFIC EXCLUSION

The Company shall not be liable for Loss on account of any Claim made against any Insured:...for bodily injury (except mental anguish), sickness, disease or death of any person or damage to or destruction of any tangible property including loss of use thereof...

Chubb Group
14-02-0953 (Rev. 8/96)

INCLUDED IN DEFINITION OF DAMAGES

"Damages" means monetary compensation for a Claimant's economic or non-economic loss that is directly related to a **Claim,** but does not include loss of use, injury to or destruction of tangible or intangible business or personal property or medical expenses for physical injury to a person's body.

Evanston Insurance Company
EIC 3071-1 9/97

Although allegations of property damage usually are not associated with employment-related disputes or claims, it is possible that property damage claims may arise. For example, a terminated employee may claim that the loss of income suffered as a result of the wrongful termination prevented the employee from being able to complete construction of a home that was subsequently damaged by weather because it was not completed. Although the likelihood and potential for a severe property damage loss in connection with a wrongful employment practices suit may be remote, the existence of an exclusion does present a limitation, and from the insured's standpoint, should be avoided if possible. Alternatively, if the exclusion cannot be avoided, a narrower exclusion is preferable.

In the two citations above, the first exclusion applies to tangible property, such as houses and cars, whereas the second exclusion applies to intangible property, such as intellectual property, as well as tangible property. Because the first exclusion is narrower in the types of property damage excluded, it is preferable from an insured's standpoint.

Retaliatory Action And Violation Of Public Policy Exclusions

Background.[4] The California Supreme Court has stated that a public policy claim must be based on the violation of a fundamental public policy that exists for the benefit of the public at large and not simply a private individual. Due to the fact that damages for emotional distress and punitive damages may be available for such claims, it is not surprising that terminated employees frequently allege public policy violations.

In 1994 the California Supreme Court set forth a three-part test for wrongful termination in violation of public policy. The employee's termination must violate a public policy that is:

---

[4] See also *Discharge in Violation of Public Policy* discussion on pages 31–33 for more detailed analysis.

1. fundamental,
2. beneficial to the public, and
3. embodied in a statute or constitutional provision.

Even though an employer may hire all of its employees on an at-will basis, it is nonetheless against the law to fire an employee for assisting in upholding fundamental public policy as set forth by statute or constitution.

Another illustration of a public policy violation is when an employee is terminated or discriminated against for "whistle blowing." *Whistle blowing* is the term given to the act of an employee reporting its employer to governmental or regulatory authorities for the employer's violation of a statute that benefits the general public. One of the largest single awards in a wrongful termination suit was $124 million to the former CFO of a corporation. The CFO became aware that his company was violating the law and blew the whistle on his employer by reporting the violation to the proper regulatory authority. The CFO's employer ultimately fired him for disloyalty, but the courts found that the employee owed a higher loyalty to the public. Therefore, when the employer terminated him, it committed a public policy violation.

Similar to a discharge in violation of public policy, employees sometimes are discharged in retaliation for asserting their lawful rights. For example, the law prohibits the termination of an employee for filing a lawful workers' compensation claim.

The Exclusions. Some EPL insurance policies exclude claims based on retaliatory actions or actions that are against public policy. An example is as follows:

> Any liability arising out of:
>
> a. Retaliatory action by an insured against an employee who declines to perform an act that would require a violation of a mandate of public policy as reflected in legislation, administrative rules, regulations or decisions, judicial decisions, and professional codes of ethics;
>
> b. Retaliatory action by an insured against a claimant for filing a complaint or claim, giving testimony, or otherwise participating in proceedings related to a wrongful employment act; or
>
> c. Retaliatory action by an insured against an employee who engages in or threatens to engage in whistleblower activities…
>
> American International Specialty Lines Insurance Company
64198 (12/95)

Exclusions like the one above can eliminate coverage for some of the most serious charges that an employee can level against his or her employer. Given the highly emotional charged nature of claims of retaliatory discharge or of discharge in violation of public policy, these claims also frequently result in substantial jury verdicts and/or settlements.

Because allegations of retaliatory acts and violations of public policy pose a substantial employment practices liability exposure, a policy that excludes claims based on such actions can leave the policyholder with an extensive gap in coverage. Therefore, it is important for a risk manager or policyholder to know whether an EPL insurance policy contains exclusions for retaliatory discharge, whistle blowing or public policy violations. An EPL insurance policy containing such exclusions offers substantially less coverage than an EPL insurance policy without such exclusions.

Exclusions Directed To Various Federal And State Laws

Many EPL insurance policies exclude claims brought under various federal or state laws that could apply to employers. Such exclusions often apply to specific laws such as the Occupational Safety and Health Act of 1970 (OSHA), pollution laws, the Racketeer Influenced Corruption Act (RICO), securities laws and the Workers' Adjustment and Retraining Notification Act (WARN Act). Individual laws are singled out for exclusion because underwriters want to make it clear that these exposures are not covered, even if they probably would never appear in allegations of wrongful employment practices.

The following are examples of exclusions applying to specific laws:

OSHA[5]

This policy does not apply to:...Any obligation of any insured under...The Occupational Safety and Health Act,...This Exclusion applies to any similar rules, regulations or provisions of any federal, state or local statutory law or common law.

Hartford Insurance Companies
HC 00 55 03 96

POLLUTION LAWS

The Company shall not be liable for Loss on account of any Claim made against any insured:...based upon, arising from, or in consequence of **Pollution.** However, this exclusion shall not apply to any **Claim** for wrongful dismissal, discharge or termination of employment of any claimant in retaliation for such claimant's actual or alleged (i) refusal to violate any federal, state or local statutory law or common law regarding **Pollution** or (ii) disclosure regarding any actual or alleged **Pollution** by any **Insured Organization**;...

Chubb Group
14-02-0953 (Rev. 8/96)

---

[5] Under OSHA, employers can be subject to fines if a dangerous or unhealthy work environment exists. Employees usually would not be able to sue their employer for damages from an OSHA violation because their damages would be an injury and workers' compensation would be the sole remedy in most states. Also, the employer would be penalized by a fine, and fines usually are excluded from all EPL insurance policies.

RICO[6]

The Underwriters shall not be liable to indemnify the **INSURED** for **LOSS,** including **CLAIMS EXPENSES,** as a result of any claim or claims made against the **INSURED:**...arising out of allegations of violation of the Racketeer Influenced and Corrupt Organizations Act, or any rules or regulations issued pursuant to said statute.

U. S. Risk Underwriters, Inc.
DISC3/98/CO

SECURITIES LAWS

The Company shall not be liable for Loss on account of any Claim made against any Insured:...based upon, arising from, or in consequence of (i) any actual or alleged violation of any federal, state or common law relating to securities, or (ii) any actual or alleged purchase, sale or distribution of or offer, representation or agreement relating to securities. However, this exclusion shall not apply to any **Claim** for any retaliatory treatment of any claimant for (i) such claimant's actual or alleged refusal to violate any such securities laws or (ii) any actual or threatened disclosure by such claimant of any actual or alleged violation of such securities laws; or...

Chubb Group
14-02-0953 (Rev. 8/96)

WARN ACT[7]

The Underwriter shall not be liable for **Loss** on account of any **Claim** made against any **Insured:**...for an actual or alleged violation of the responsibilities, obligations or duties imposed by...(v) the Worker Adjustment and Retraining Notification Act,...provided this exclusion shall not apply to any **Claim** for any actual or alleged retaliatory treatment of the claimant by the **Insured** on account of the claimant's exercise of rights pursuant to any such statute, law, rule or regulation...

Zurich American Insurance Company
STF-EPL-101-A CW (3/98)

With respect to such exclusions, the introductory wording can dramatically affect their scope and practical impact. If an exclusion contains broad prefatory wording such as *based upon, arising out of,* or *directly or indirectly resulting from,* then the exclusion might apply to a claim by an employee that they were wrongfully terminated for reporting an OSHA, pollution or securities-law violation. These claims are known as *whistle blowing* claims. Some insurers, however, will specifically grant varying degrees of coverage for whistle-blowing claims by making exceptions to such exclusions. This can be seen in the above example of pollution and securities claim exclusions. While the insurer clearly excludes claims based on or arising out of pollution and securities actions, exceptions are made for certain employment- and retaliation-related claims. Also, if the prefatory wording is not broad, then the exclusion is likely to have only a negligible impact on the

---

[6] RICO provides for civil and criminal penalties to a business enterprise that engages in a pattern and practice of racketeering activity.

[7] WARN is a federal law that, among other provisions, mandates a minimum of 60 days' notice by employers to employees before closing a plant or facility. Violation of the law can result in fines being levied against the employer and employees may bring suit for back wages.

coverage available under an EPL insurance policy. This is because OSHA, pollution, RICO, securities and other such claims typically do not arise out of an employment decision or as a result of discrimination or harassment. WARN Act exclusions are an exception because claims *could* be brought as a result of an employment decision. Underwriters who exclude WARN Act claims often do so because they feel the employer should be able to comply with the notice provisions of the law. If the employer does not comply, most underwriters will not agree to cover the exposure.

EPL insurance policies may contain many separate exclusions pertaining to various state and federal laws, and although the existence of such exclusions is not in itself a negative feature, care should be taken to ensure that such exclusions are not made overly broad by the existence of onerous prefatory language.

Exclusions For Non-Monetary Relief

In employment litigation, the usual relief sought by a plaintiff is for money damages, but sometimes a plaintiff will seek non-monetary relief, such as an injunction. In the context of employment litigation, an injunction might be sought to prohibit an employer from taking certain actions, such as removing an employee from his or her office, reducing the job duties of an employee or requiring an employer to rehire a discharged employee. Non-monetary relief also might include demands that the employer modify the workplace to accommodate workers with covered disabilities under the Americans With Disabilities Act of 1990. Some EPL insurance policies exclude claims for non-monetary relief. An example of a non-monetary relief exclusion is the following:

> The Insurer shall not be liable to make any payment for **Loss** in connection with any **Claim** made against the **Insureds:**...based upon, arising from, or in any way related to any request for injunctive relief, declaratory relief, disgorgement, job reinstatement, or any other equitable remedy, provided that this exclusion shall not apply to **Claims Expenses.**
>
> Reliance Insurance Company of Illinois
> GL 00 R424 00 0498

An exclusion like the one above can be problematic if the EPL insurance policy does not contain an affirmative duty of the insurer to defend the insured. A duty-to-defend obligation usually will require the insurer to defend all covered and uncovered allegations even if only one allegation is covered. Therefore, if a lawsuit seeks both monetary and injunctive relief, the insurer usually will be required to defend the claim for injunctive relief. However, if there is no duty to defend, as may occur in the above example[8], it may be necessary to negotiate an allocation between covered (money damages) and uncovered (injunction) components of the loss. When an allocation occurs, the result usually is that the insured is able to recover only some percentage of the total

---

[8] Unless otherwise provided by written endorsement, this EPL insurance policy does not include an affirmative duty to defend the insured. The insured, at its option, may tender to the insurer defense of a claim.

loss amount. Allocation disputes can drive the claims process into low gear, forcing a wedge between the insured and insurer at a time when both should be concentrating on claim resolution with the claimant.

For these reasons, policies that contain provisions requiring a loss allocation should be carefully evaluated, and the process of allocation and any limitations on loss recovery should be fully understood.

Another example of policy wording that excludes non-monetary remedies is the following:

> Fines, Multiplied Damages, Or Non-monetary Relief. We do not cover:
> - fines, taxes, penalties, or liquidated damages;
> - the multiplied portion of any damage award that is subject to a multiplier;
> - non-monetary relief; or
> - any other uninsurable amounts.
>
> Fireman's Fund Insurance Company
> 7006-1-98

The EPL insurance policy containing the above exclusion does contain an affirmative duty to defend. Accordingly, as previously noted, if a lawsuit brings claims for money damages and claims for injunctive relief or other non-monetary relief, the duty to defend will probably extend to all claims. However, if the lawsuit did not bring any claim for money damages, there may be no coverage or duty to defend whatsoever.

Exclusion For ADA-Accommodation Expenses

The Americans With Disabilities Act of 1990, as amended in 1992, requires that an employer provide "reasonable accommodation" to employees and others with covered disabilities. Such reasonable accommodations can include physical modification of the employer's workplace in order to enable a disabled person to perform their requisite job functions. Most EPL insurance policies explicitly exclude such accommodation expenses. The following is an example of a typical ADA-accommodation exclusion:

> This insurance does not apply to **claims:**…for any damages, costs, or expenses incurred by an Insured in making physical changes, modifications, alterations or improvements as part of an accommodation or improvement of accessibility pursuant to the Americans with Disabilities Act of 1990, including any amendments thereto, the Rehabilitation Act of 1973, including any amendments thereto, or any similar federal, state, or local law or regulation;…
>
> General Star Indemnity Company
> UMEPLI (2/29/97)

It is important to note that exclusions like the one above do not eliminate coverage for damages suffered by an employee because of disability discrimination. Rather, such exclusions are intended to apply only to the costs to modify a building or property to accommodate handicapped persons.

Fines, Penalties And Punitive Damages

In addition to compensatory damages for such things as back pay, front pay, emotional distress, etc., a plaintiff in an employment lawsuit may be entitled to recover fines, penalties and/or punitive damages depending upon applicable state or federal law. For example, many states allow for the recovery of punitive damages for malicious, intentional or grossly negligent conduct.

Also, under state law, fines and penalties are recoverable for certain conduct such as firing an employee in retaliation for his or her filing of a workers' compensation claim. Further, federal statutes such as the Americans with Disabilities Act provide for the recovery of punitive damages up to certain caps based on the size of the employer.

The amount of any fine or penalty usually is a prescribed amount set by statute. On the other hand, punitive damages awardable under state law typically are not limited and juries have discretion to award any amount that they deem appropriate.

The insurability of punitive damages is governed by state law. Some states view insuring punitive damages to be against public policy, and in those instances punitive damages are uninsurable. In many states, however, punitive damages *are* insurable. Historically, many EPL insurance policies excluded fines, penalties and punitive damages.

A typical punitive damages exclusion reads as follows:

> Punitive Damages. This policy does not cover any liability arising out of any fines, penalties, punitive damages, exemplary damages or any additional damages resulting from the multiplication of compensatory damages.
>
> Swett & Crawford
> EPLX-96

In a typical EPL insurance policy with a duty to defend, the insurer usually will have an obligation to defend the punitive damage claim. If the claim results in a trial and punitive damages are awarded by the court, an EPL insurance policy with a punitive damages exclusion will not cover the punitive component of any judgment.

Effect Of Punitive Damages On Settlement. A large number of employment-related claims seeking compensatory and punitive damages are settled before trial. In a settlement, the plaintiff's lawyer normally will factor in the potential value of the punitive damage claim in determining an acceptable overall settlement for a claim.

If the potential compensatory damages in an employment lawsuit are small and the proposed settlement is large, or if the proposed settlement simply exceeds the potential compensatory award, the insurer usually will argue that some portion of the settlement is attributable to the claim for punitive damages. In such a situation, it is not uncommon for the insured to be asked to contribute to a settlement. However, when the potential compensatory damages are larger than the settlement amount, it is more difficult for an insurer to attempt to allocate a portion of the settlement to the punitive damage claim. In this situation, an insured may be reluctant to contribute to a settlement even when that settlement nullifies a potential punitive damage exposure that is not insured.

These exclusions of punitive damages are highly disadvantageous for employers for several reasons. First, employers may be liable for the intentional acts of their agents and thus can be liable to pay punitive damages even when the entity itself does not act intentionally in any collective sense. In most states, insureds may insure their exposures for vicariously assessed punitive damages. It is rarely the case that an employer (as an entity) acts intentionally; therefore, the punitive exposure almost always is a vicarious one. An exception would be if the board of directors passed a board resolution not to hire members of some particular protected class, a highly unusual prospect.

Second, particularly in those cases where intentional conduct is the primary focus of the law, such as in the ADEA, ADA, "quid pro quo" sexual harassment cases and intentional racial discrimination cases under the civil rights statutes, cases that defendants lose at trial very commonly result in multiple, liquidated or punitive damages. And when they are assessed, these exemplary damages often are a significant multiple of any compensatory damages awarded.

Recently, EPL insurers have begun to offer coverage for punitive damages. At first, insurers offered coverage for punitive damages on a limited basis. The amount available to cover punitive damages was frequently only a small percentage of the total limit of liability under the EPL insurance policy, and coverage for punitive damages was available only in those cases where punitive damages were insurable. See Exhibit 4.

Exhibit 4
Insurability Of Punitive Damages

Data Source: Copyright 1998 American Re-Insurance Company, Reprinted with Permission from American Re-Insurance Company.

	Insurable	Insurable if Vicarious	Duty to Defend
Alabama	Yes	Yes	Yes
Alaska	Yes (if governmental entity). Probably Yes (if nongovernmental entity or individual).	Probably Yes	Yes
Arizona	Yes	Yes	Yes
Arkansas	Yes (not for intentional acts)	Yes	Yes
California	No (except for those punitive damages imposed in other states for grossly negligent conduct)	Yes	Yes

	Insurable	Insurable if Vicarious	Duty to Defend
Colorado	No	Undecided	
Connecticut	No (Coverage for punitive damages is not barred if they are considered an element of compensatory damages—they cannot exceed plaintiff's litigation expenses less taxable costs.)	Yes (If pursuant to statute)	Yes
Delaware	Yes (Unless specifically excluded by the policy)	Yes	Yes
District of Columbia	Undecided (Not for intentional acts)	Yes	Yes
Florida	No	Yes	Yes
Georgia	Yes	Yes	Yes
Hawaii	Yes (If specifically included in policy)	Yes (If specifically included in policy)	Yes
Idaho	Yes (Unless specifically excluded)	Yes	Yes
Illinois	No	Yes	
Indiana	No	Yes	
Iowa	Yes (Unless specifically excluded)	Yes	Yes
Kansas	No	Yes	
Kentucky	Undecided	Yes (Not for intentional conduct)	Yes
Louisiana	Yes (Only if statute expressly authorizes the imposition of a penalty)	Yes	Yes
Maine	No	Probably Yes	
Maryland	Yes	Yes	Yes
Massachusetts	Yes only if statutory as not recognized at common law	Undecided	
Michigan	Not recognized at common law	Not applicable	Yes
Minnesota	No (Except for governing body of a municipality)	Undecided (Except for governing body of a municipality)	
Mississippi	Yes (not for uninsured motorist coverage)	Yes	Yes
Missouri	Undecided (But Yes where insured is governmental entity)	Yes	Yes
Montana	Yes (Must be expressly included in contract)	Yes (Must be expressly included in contract)	Yes
Nebraska	Not recognized at common law		
Nevada	Probably No	Undecided	
New Hampshire	Yes	Yes	Yes
New Jersey	No	Yes	
New Mexico	Yes	Yes	Yes
New York	No	Probably No	Yes
North Carolina	Yes, unless specifically excluded. (Not for intentional acts.)	Yes	Yes
North Dakota	Yes (If expressly included in policy; insurer may seek indemnity from insured)	Undecided	
Ohio	No	No	
Oklahoma	No	Yes	Yes
Oregon	Yes (Not for intentional acts)	Yes	Yes
Pennsylvania	No	Yes	
Puerto Rico	Not recognized		
Rhode Island	No	Undecided	

EXCLUSIONS

	Insurable	Insurable if Vicarious	Duty to Defend
South Carolina	Yes	Yes	Yes
South Dakota	No	Undecided	
Tennessee	Yes (Not for intentional acts)	Yes	Yes
Texas	Yes	Yes	Yes
Utah	No	Undecided	
Vermont	Yes	Yes	Yes
Virgin Islands	No (Unless specifically covered under policy)	No (Unless specifically covered under policy)	
Virginia	Yes (Not for intentional acts)	Not recognized	Yes
Washington	Not recognized unless provided by statute		
West Virginia	Yes (Not for intentional acts)	Yes	Yes
Wisconsin	Yes	Yes	Yes
Wyoming	Yes	Yes	Yes

However, it is now common for EPL insurance policies to offer coverage for punitive damages in amounts up to the full limit of liability.

Coverage for punitive damages may be incorporated into the basic policy form or added by the attachment of an endorsement. The following examples illustrate both approaches:

BY ENDORSEMENT

In consideration of the premium charged, it is hereby understood and agreed that definition (I), "Loss", is amended as follows:

1. "(2) punitive or exemplary damages; 93) the multiplied portion of multiplied damages," is deleted in its entirety;

2. the following paragraph is added to the end thereof:

   Notwithstanding the foregoing, Loss shall specifically include (subject to the policy's other terms, conditions and exclusions, including but not limited to exclusions relating to personal profit or advantage, deliberate fraud or criminal acts), punitive, exemplary and multiple damages (including the multiple or liquidated damages awards under the Age Discrimination in Employment Act and the Equal Pay Act).

   National Union Fire Insurance Co.
   67549 (4/98)

INCLUDED IN DEFINITION OF LOSS

Loss means (1) damages, including, but not limited to, **Punitive Damages,**...

Swett & Crawford
EPLS-987
7/1/98

It is also common for an EPL insurer to agree to pay a punitive damage award if the law of any potentially applicable jurisdiction allows for the insurability of punitive damages. This type of provision is commonly referred to as a "most favorable venue" clause.

A typical most favorable venue clause will provide that the insurer will pay a punitive award if the jurisdiction where (1) the insured is located or incorporated, (2) the insurer is located or incorporated, (3) the wrongful act giving rise to the punitive award happened, or (4) the lawsuit is pending; allows for the insurability of punitive damages. Other EPL insurance policies provide that punitive damages will be covered regardless of whether the punitive damages are insurable or uninsurable. Insureds should be aware that both the most favorable venue clause and clauses covering punitive damages regardless of insurability may potentially raise regulatory issues for insurers and tax issues for insureds.

Exclusions For Front Or Back Pay

Front pay, sometimes called *future pay,* is the amount of wages that would have been earned by employees up to their retirement age (usually 65) had they not been wrongfully terminated or forced to leave their job due to discrimination, harassment or other wrongful employment practice.

Front pay is an element of damages that a jury may award after a trial for future damages of the claimant. For example, if a 30-year-old claimant is unemployed at the time the trial ends, the jury may award damages based on the difference between what the claimant would have earned for the next 35 years if the claimant were employed with the former employer, minus what the jury determines the claimant is likely to earn over the next 35 years. If the jury determines (based on evidence offered at trial) that the claimant is essentially unemployable, the damages can be substantial. *Back pay* is the amount of wages that an employee has actually lost at the time of the trial as a result of the claimant's unemployment.

The following is an example of an exclusion that eliminates coverage for the payment of back pay:

> Unpaid or withheld wages, overtime, vacation or leave pay, back benefits, or any similar types of damages or restitution, even if designated as compensatory or liquidated damages.

London Market
U.S. Risk Underwriters, Inc.
DISC3/98/CO

A variation of the exclusion that applies only to front pay is as follows:

> The Company shall not be liable for that part of **Loss,** other than **Defense Costs:**...which constitutes front pay, future damages or other future economic relief or the equivalent thereof, if the **Insured Organization** is ordered, pursuant to a judgment or other final adjudication, but fails to reinstate the claimant as an employee;...

Chubb Group
14-02-0953 (Rev. 8/96)

This exclusion would not exclude front pay unless the employer had an option to reinstate the employee, but failed to do so, resulting in the imposition of front pay damages.

As front pay and back pay damages often make up a large percentage of the total damages awarded in employment cases, and sometimes the only element of damages awarded, an exclusion for front pay and back pay is a serious limitation of coverage.

Exclusion For Liquidated Damages Under ADEA

The Age Discrimination in Employment Act of 1967 (ADEA) provides that if an employee protected by the Act is terminated because of age, he or she is entitled to double the amount of back pay lost as a result of the termination. The ADEA applies to employees who are 40 and over.

An example of an exclusion for liquidated damages under the ADEA found within the definition of *loss* is as follows:

> **"Loss"** means any damages (including back pay awards, front pay awards, compensatory damages and punitive damages if insurable under the law pursuant to which this policy is construed), pre-judgment interest, post-judgment interest, and settlements which an **Insured** is legally obligated to pay as a result of a **Claim;** provided, that **Loss** does not include: (1) civil or criminal fines, sanctions, liquidated damages,...
>
> Executive Risk Specialty Insurance Company
B22167
2/97

Until recently, most EPL insurance underwriters excluded liquidated damages under ADEA because they are "multiplied damages" and are similar to fines and penalties. Currently, however, some underwriters specifically include coverage for liquidated damages. Such a specific grant of coverage can be seen in the following definition of *loss*:

> "Loss Amounts" shall not include:...multiplied portions of multiplied damages, other than liquidated damages awarded under the Age Discrimination in Employment Act of 1967 (as amended) or the Equal Pay Act (29 U.S.C. 206 (d));...
>
> Steadfast Insurance Company
STF-PL-100-B CW (4/97)

Exclusions For Arbitration Under Collective Bargaining Agreements

Many EPL insurance policies exclude coverage for amounts awarded pursuant to an arbitration proceeding under a collective bargaining agreement. An example of such an exclusion contained within the definition of *claim* is as follows:

> Claim shall not include labor or grievance arbitration subject to a collective bargaining agreement.
>
> American Equity Insurance Co.
11197
11/97

The exclusion in the definition of *claim* of labor or grievance arbitration subject to a collective bargaining agreement may exclude both defense expenses as well as any actual damages and obviates the need for any exclusionary language in other sections of the policy.

Some policies exclude arbitration hearings pursuant to an employment handbook or other employment policies and procedures, as well as collective bargaining agreements. The following example illustrates some of the language used in these types of exclusions:

> ...**claim** does not include a labor or grievance arbitration under a collective bargaining agreement, employment handbook or other employment policies or procedures.
>
> Fireman's Fund Insurance Company
7006-10-96
10/96

If an employer provides for the arbitration of employment-related disputes in its employee handbook or in other employment policies or procedures, the employer should determine whether any EPL insurance policy it may purchase contains an exclusion such as the one above. If the EPL insurance policy does contain such an exclusion, a substantial gap in coverage may exist because any arbitration awards or expenses incurred in the arbitration would be excluded.

Exclusion For Claims Arising From Financial Impairment

When experiencing financial difficulties, businesses often will attempt to reduce operating costs, which usually means the elimination of jobs (layoffs). But when jobs are eliminated or layoffs occur, the potential for wrongful employment-related claims is heightened. Some insurers are unwilling to cover this heightened exposure and exclude claims arising out of financial impairment. Examples of such exclusions include the following:

> ### Termination Of Employment Related To Possible Insolvency
> Termination of employment when or after you file for or are placed in bankruptcy, receivership, liquidation, or court ordered reorganization.
>
> Hartford Insurance Companies
HC 00 55 03 96
3/96

> ...for any **Employment Termination** when or after the **Named Insured** 1) files or is placed in bankruptcy, receivership, liquidation, conservatorship or reorganization, 2) closes one or more plants or places of business operation, or 3) merges with or is acquired by any other business entity;...
>
> Colonia (AUSCO)
EPL 6000 (3/95)

When evaluating any financial impairment exclusion, it is necessary to identify both the scope of financial impairment and the specific employment practices that are affected by the exclusion. In the above examples, the exclusions only apply to termination of employment and not to other claims that might arise out of financial impairment, such as a suit charging discrimination as a consequence of a demotion or change in pay structure that resulted from financial impairment.

Careful attention should be given to the types of impairment contemplated by any financial impairment exclusion. In prior years it was common for EPL insurance policies to contain financial impairment exclusions that were quite broad, encompassing a wide range of financial difficulties, including bankruptcy, receivership, liquidation, reorganization and even "financial inability to pay." Today, many EPL insurance policies do not contain financial impairment exclusions. Those EPL insurance policies that do contain such exclusions are usually limited to termination claims arising out of bankruptcy, receivership or other governmentally regulated takeovers.

But because alleging a wide range of employment practices can arise out of even a limited definition of *financial impairment*, the broadest EPL insurance policies are those that do not contain such exclusions.

Exclusions For Plant Or Facility Closings

Some EPL insurance policies exclude coverage for claims that result from plant or facility closings. The following is an example:

> This policy does not apply to any Claim for any Employment Termination when or after the Named Insured...closes one or more plants or places of business operation.
>
> Colonia (AUSCO)
EPL 6000 (3/95)

The exclusion is particularly broad because it applies regardless of the number of employees involved in a plant or facility closing. Conceivably a claim resulting from the closure of a one-person office could be excluded from coverage. Also, purely fortuitous events such as fire or other natural disaster might force the employer to close a plant or place of business.

The following is another example of a plant/facility closing exclusion. It is similar to the example above with the notable exception that it applies only to terminations occurring within 60 days and involving more than 20% of the total number of employees. While this exclusion is not as sweeping as in the first example, it represents a limitation in coverage that most EPL insurance policies do not contain.

> This certificate does not cover any "loss" which arises out of any reorganization, downsizing operations or closure of one or more plants or places of business operations resulting in the termination, within any sixty (60) day period, of more than twenty percent (20%) of the total number of your "employees".
>
> London Market
> American Technology Excess and Surplus Insurance Services
> AmTech Form ERP-1
> 11/96

Downsizing/Reorganization

Downsizing and reorganization exclusions are similar to exclusions for plant or facilities closings in that they exclude claims arising out of layoffs or terminations. Insurers use these exclusions because they do not wish to cover the heightened exposure to employee suits associated with layoffs or downsizing. Unlike plant and facility closing exclusions, though, they do not require a plant or facility to close. Examples of downsizing/reorganization exclusions include the following:

> Any liability arising out of a **wrongful act** which takes place after you reorganize, downsize operations, or close one or more plants or places of business operations resulting in the termination within a sixth (60) day period of more than 20% of **your employees** at any plant or place of business operation;...
>
> American International Specialty Lines Insurance Company
> 64198 (12/95)
> 12/95

> Any Wrongful Employment Practice, failure to grant tenure, negligent evaluation, deprivation of a career opportunity, or wrongful discipline which occurs when or after the Insured reorganizes, downsizes or closes one or more plants or places of business resulting in the termination, within any sixth (60) day period, of 50 employees or more than twenty percent (20%) of the total number of employees, whichever is less;...
>
> American Equity Insurance Company
> 11197
> 11/97

Downsizing exclusions are generally characterized by the fact that they only apply to claims or liability arising within a specified period after downsizing and involving more than a specified number or percentage of employees. Both the time period and percentage and number of employees involved can vary.

For any business in a challenging and quickly changing economic climate, a downsizing exclusion could result in a substantial gap in coverage. A large number of layoffs, for example, particularly involving employees in a protected class, such as employees 40 years or age or older, can result in multiple claims or even a class-action lawsuit. If uninsured, such claims can have a material, negative impact on a company, especially a company already suffering from adverse economic pressures.

For these reasons, downsizing exclusions, either contained within the EPL insurance policies or added by endorsement, should be avoided. Where such exclusions exist in EPL insurance policies, those with the shortest time limitation and largest percentage of affected employees are generally the least broad.

Mergers And Acquisitions/Change Of Control

When a business acquires another entity or is itself acquired, the process of merging the two business entities often results in layoffs that may bring employment-termination litigation. Accordingly, some insurers have adopted exclusions to eliminate the increased exposure of a merger, acquisition or other change of control. Examples include the following:

> This policy does not apply to any Claim arising directly or indirectly from any Employment Termination where such Employment Termination occurs when or after the Insured...merges with or is acquired by any other business entity.
>
> Colonia (AUSCO)
EPL 6000 (3/95)

> ..."Injury" arising out of termination of employment, job relocation or reassignment, if the action is taken because:...You have merged with or been acquired by another business entity;...
>
> Insurance Services Office, Inc.
EP 00 01 04 98
4/98

These exclusions would extend to all mergers or acquisitions of any size. Although no longer common, some EPL insurance policies may contain change-of-control provisions or endorsements that terminate all coverage under the policy if control of the company changes. An example of such a provision is seen in the following exclusion:

> In the event 51% or more of the controlling interest of any insured is changed during this policy, then this policy shall automatically terminate upon the completion of such change in control. From that point forward, only claims which had been made prior to the change in control shall continue to be covered and serviced by us.
>
> Lexington Insurance Company
LEX-CM-EPLIT
9/97

Intentional Acts

Employment practices liability litigation differs from other types of litigation because the plaintiff typically will allege intentional wrongdoing as opposed to or in addition to allegations of negligence. Discrimination and harassment are "intentional torts" and most terminations from employment are the result of intentional conduct. This poses interesting insurance coverage issues because most EPL insurance policies exclude intentional conduct. Moreover, some states have laws that prohibit insurance coverage for intentional wrongdoing. For example, California Insurance Code Section 533 states, "An Insurer is not liable for a loss caused by the willful act of the insured; but he is not exonerated by the negligence of the insured, or of the insured's agents or others." Such laws are premised on the perception that public policy considerations dictate that an intentional wrongdoer pay a personal price for his or her intended actions.

Most intentional act exclusions focus on the intent of causing damage rather than on intent to commit the act. This is illustrated in the following examples:

> As respects coverage of any individual **Insured** who, at the time any act was committed, undertook any act giving rise to a **Claim** with the intention of causing harm to any person; however, we will afford the defense to which such individual **Insured** would otherwise be entitled until such time as the individual **Insured** is judicially determined to have intentionally caused the alleged resulting harm; and…
>
> X. L. Insurance Company, Ltd.
EPLI-005
7/98

> The **Insurer** shall not be liable to make any payment for **Loss** in connection with any **Claim** made against the **Insureds:**…based upon, arising out of, directly or indirectly resulting from, in a consequence of, or in any way involving in face willfully or intentionally committed **Wrongful Acts,** except to the extent that liability is imposed vicariously for the willfully or intentionally committed **Wrongful Acts** of other **Insureds;**…
>
> United States Fidelity & Guaranty Company
FID 600
(11/95)

Regardless of whether an intentional act exclusion is found in the EPL insurance policy or whether a state statute or public policy prohibits insurance for intentional acts, the issue of coverage usually first arises when a lawsuit is filed alleging intentional wrongdoing. As noted above, most EPL lawsuits contain one or more allegations of intentional conduct. However, just because intentional wrongdoing is pleaded in a lawsuit does not mean the conduct actually occurred or the intent to cause harm or injury actually existed. No current statistics are available, but it is probably fair to state that over 90% of all employment practices lawsuits are settled before trial. Further, in those cases that are tried and appealed, most cases are settled before the appeal is finalized. Therefore, in the vast majority of cases, there will not be a final adjudication of intentional conduct. Without a final adjudication of intentional wrongdoing, a policyholder and/or insurer might take the position that neither state law nor the policy exclusions prevent the payment of loss in order to settle the claim.

On the other hand, if the EPL insurance policy exclusion does not require a final adjudication of intentional wrongdoing, the insurer may be able to argue that it has the right to deny coverage if the intentional conduct can be proved in a separate proceeding. Accordingly, the reputation of the insurer for either paying claims or denying claims can be very important consideration for the policyholder.

Other Insurance/Other Indemnification

All EPL insurance policies and most other policies exclude coverage for loss that is insured under another insurance policy. One purpose for an other insurance exclusion is to ensure that only one payment is made for a single loss and to prevent the insured from collecting more than the actual loss sustained. Other insurance exclusions are frequently found in the *Exclusions* section, but they also may be found in the *Conditions* section of the policy.[9]

The following are representative examples of other insurance provisions:

> Other insurance. If other valid and collectable insurance is available to the Insured covering a Loss also covered by this policy, other than insurance that is specifically stated to be in excess of this policy, the insurance afforded by this policy shall be in excess of and shall not contribute with such other insurance. Nothing herein shall be construed to make this policy subject to the terms, conditions and limitations of any other insurance. Notwithstanding the foregoing this policy shall assume control of the defense and seek contribution directly from such other insurance.
>
> Swett & Crawford
> EPLX-987
> 7/98

> Section XIII. Other Insurance. If, but for the insurance afforded by this policy, the insured would have other insurance against a loss otherwise covered hereby, the insurance afforded by this policy shall be excess over such other insurance.
>
> Employers Reinsurance Corporation
> ERC 1491A Dec (1995)

> Other Insurance: This insurance shall be in excess of the amount of the Self-Insureds Retention, Insured's Co-Insurance Obligation and of any other insurance available to the Insured whether the other insurance is stated to be primary, pro rata, contributory, excess, contingent or otherwise, unless the other insurance is written only as specific excess insurance over the Limits of Liability provided by this policy.
>
> Evanston Insurance Company
> EIC 3071-1 9/97

---

[9] See *Other Insurance* section, pp. 242–245.

In a similar vein, some insurers may attempt to exclude coverage if the claim also is reported under another policy issued by the same insurer. Such exclusions become important, for example, if an insurer issues both D&O coverage and EPL coverage to the same insured. The insurer does not want coverage that may be available under a D&O policy to apply in addition to the same coverage provided under the EPL insurance policy. For example, if a $2,000,000 wrongful employment practices claim is brought against an employer, one or more officers and the EPL insurance policy has a coverage limit of $1,000,000 and the D&O policy has a coverage limit of $1,000,000, the insurer may not want to have the full $2,000,000 in coverage limits available.

Amounts for which the insured is indemnified by another insurer or "indemnifying organization" also may be excluded:

> No benefits shall be payable under Section I or Section II of this Certificate for: DAMAGES if the DAMAGES arise out of a CLAIM or occurrence or lawsuit for which indemnity is owed by another insurer or another indemnifying organization, which is or may be obligated to reimburse, indemnify or pay on behalf of the ASSURED for any or all of its liability in the matter, under the terms of a liability insurance policy or contract or other type of indemnification agreement or arrangement.
>
> NAS Insurance Services, Inc.
Form AIF 1653/95A
2/97

> ...Loss does not include (i) any amount not indemnified by the Insured Organization for which the Insured is absolved from payment by reason of any covenant, agreement or court order...
>
> Chubb Group
14-02-0953 (Rev. 8/96)

This last exclusion applies to the same type of situations as the first two exclusions but is broader because it is not limited to only other insurance. This last exclusion applies regardless of whether the source of payment is other insurance or payment from any other source.

Criminal Acts/Proceedings

Insurance is not meant to cover criminal behavior, and in many states laws have been passed to prohibit the insuring of criminal behavior and proceedings. Most EPL insurance policies have intentional acts or willful violation of the law exclusions that often apply to criminal behavior. There is an issue, however, of whether an intentional act exclusion will exclude unproven allegations of criminal behavior or if the exclusion will apply only if the allegations are proven true.

Many EPL insurance policies expressly exclude criminal acts or proceedings. An example of an exclusion for criminal acts is as follows:

> No benefits shall be payable under Section I or Section II of this Certificate for: Any criminal act of the ASSURED. Criminal act shall be defined as a violation of a criminal statute which can result in incarceration in a penal institution.
>
> NAS Insurance Services, Inc.
Form AIF 1653/95A
2/97

Under this exclusion, it may be unclear as to whether there is coverage for an unproven allegation of a criminal act. Accordingly, the same issue that exists with an intentional acts exclusion can exist with this criminal acts exclusion.

An example of an exclusion for criminal proceedings is as follows:

> This Policy does not apply to any Claim or portion thereof made against the Insured:...arising out of any criminal proceedings...
>
> Evanston Insurance Company
EIC 3071 9/97

Most criminal proceedings exclusions make it clear that there is no coverage for a criminal proceeding whether the allegations are proved to be true or not. An exclusion of criminal proceedings that applies regardless of whether the allegations are proved true usually is broader and more onerous than a criminal acts exclusion that applies only if such allegations are proven true.

However, an exclusion solely for criminal proceedings in an EPL insurance policy that does not contain an intentional acts exclusion could be narrower than a criminal acts exclusion. A criminal act of assault and battery could be the subject of a civil lawsuit alleging wrongful employment practices. But a typical criminal proceeding exclusion would not exclude a civil claim for assault and battery.

In a non-duty-to-defend EPL insurance policy, a criminal acts exclusion can be even more restrictive.

The combination of a criminal acts exclusion in a non-duty-to-defend policy means that an unproved civil allegation of assault and battery, or other criminal conduct, would be completely outside the scope of coverage if the allegation is ultimately proved to be true. Under a duty-to-defend policy, however, an unproved civil allegation of assault and battery would probably trigger the insurer's duty to defend the insured. Once triggered, the duty to defend would not cease until the allegation was proved to be true in a final adjudication. This could mean the insurer must defend through an appeal.

Criminal proceedings also can be excluded in an EPL insurance policy by the definition of *claimant*. Some older EPL insurance policies limited coverage only to claims brought by a specific group of claimants. This group of claimants usually did not include a government prosecutor in a criminal action. For example, a definition of *claimant* read as follows:

> Whenever used in this policy...**Claimant** means an **Employee,** an applicant for employment with the **Named Insured,** or an individual or entity, including the Equal Employment Opportunity Commission or other similar state agency, acting on behalf of such **Employee** or applicant.
>
> Reliance Insurance Company of Illinois
GL 00 1005 02 (08/96)

Employee was further defined as:

> Whenever used in this policy...**Employee** means an individual other than an independent contractor whose labor service was, is, or shall become employed, engaged and directed by the **Named Insured,** including part-time, seasonal, and temporary employees, as well as supervisory and managerial employees. The status of an individual as an **Employee** shall be determined as of the date of the alleged **Wrongful Employment Practice.**
>
> Reliance Insurance Company of Illinois
GL 00 1005 02 (08/96)

The above definitions excluded coverage for criminal charges brought by a prosecutor because the prosecutor did not fall in the "claimant" category.

Additionally, most EPL insurance policies exclude claims that are uninsurable under applicable law. An example of such an exclusion is:

> Loss shall mean money paid as damages or settlement and Defense Costs. However, Loss shall not include...matters which are deemed uninsurable under the law to which this policy shall be construed...
>
> Philadelphia Insurance Company
PI-ES-1560
12/96

Criminal conduct can be excluded in states that have laws prohibiting insurance for intentional and/or criminal acts.

Determining whether coverage exists under an EPL insurance policy for unproven allegations of criminal conduct is a complex issue because many different provisions in an EPL insurance policy must be reviewed. Even after such review, it may still be unclear as to whether coverage would apply. If an insured has questions regarding coverage for allegations of criminal conduct, it is best to seek clarification from the insurer or experienced insurance professional or coverage counsel.

There are some policies, however, that do include coverage for criminal proceedings. The following are two examples of how such coverage is specifically granted:

> "Claim" means: (1) a written demand for monetary or non-monetary relief (including any request to toll or waive any statute of limitations), or (2) a civil, criminal, administrative or arbitration proceeding for monetary or non-monetary relief which is commenced by: (i) service of a complaint or similar proceeding; or (ii) return of an indictment (in the case of a criminal proceeding); or (iii) receipt or filing of a notice of charges...
>
> National Union Fire Insurance Company
Forms 67976 (6/97) (non-admitted) and 67548 (4/97) (admitted)

> Optional Defense of Criminal Claims. At the request of the Named Insured, Underwriters shall have the option, but not the duty, to defend any criminal proceedings brought against any Insured. Should Underwriters in their sole discretion exercise the option to defend any criminal proceeding, any Defense Costs incurred therein shall reduce and may exhaust the Coverage Limits. The exercise of the option to defend any criminal proceeding shall not serve to render Underwriters liable for any other Loss incurred in connection with any criminal proceedings, and Underwriters shall retain the right to withdraw from the defense upon giving 30 days notice. Whether or not Underwriters exercise the option to defend criminal proceedings, Underwriters shall defend, subject to the policy's terms and conditions, any civil proceedings brought against an Insured which alleges the same or similar Insured Events as a criminal proceeding.
>
> Swett & Crawford
EPLX-987
7/1/98

Note that in the second example the insurer makes criminal defense optional in that both the insurer and the named insured must agree to the defense of such matters.

Retroactive Date And Prior Knowledge Exclusions

As previously mentioned, most EPL insurance policies currently available are issued without a retroactive date limitation. However, it is possible that some EPL insurance policies may include or be endorsed so that they contain such a limitation.[10] Such provisions are important to identify because they preclude coverage for claims based on wrongful acts or employment practices occurring prior to the inception date of the policy or other specified date. In general, a retroactive date exclusion is broader than a prior knowledge exclusion because the retroactive date exclusion bars all claims arising from incidents occurring prior to a policy inception or other specified date, regardless of whether the insured had reason to believe a claim was likely to occur because of such incidents. On the other hand, a prior knowledge exclusion excludes coverage only for incidents occurring prior to policy inception if the insured had a reasonable basis for anticipating a claim.

A retroactive date limitation and a prior knowledge exclusion can be seen in the following examples:

---

[10] For a more complete discussion of retroactive date limitation, see pages 157–160.

RETROACTIVE DATE LIMITATION

We will pay those sums that the insured becomes legally obligated to pay as damages because of a "wrongful employment practice" provided always that:...Such "wrongful employment practice" or series of related wrongful employment practices first took place after the retroactive date, if any, shown in Items 3. of the Declarations and before the end of the policy period; and...

Northland Insurance Companies
S1110-EP (6/97)

PRIOR KNOWLEDGE EXCLUSION

Any facts or circumstances known to the Insured prior to the inception of the Policy Period which facts or circumstances would cause a reasonable person to believe that a Claim alleging a Wrongful Employment Practice might be made;...

American Equity Insurance Company
11197 (11/97)

Unlike a retroactive date limitation, the above prior knowledge exclusion focuses on whether a management or supervisory employee had knowledge of incidents or circumstances prior to the inception date. As noted above, the retroactive date exclusion applies regardless of whether management or supervisory personnel were aware of the incidents or circumstances.

When an insured is first contemplating the purchase of EPL coverage, or when an insured is changing insurers, it is important to carefully examine whether or not prior acts coverage is being offered and, if it is, under what circumstances, so that a potential gap in coverage can be recognized and avoided. Care should be taken to check the policy application, which can also contain prior knowledge limitations.

Prior And Pending Litigation Exclusion

Similar to a retroactive date or prior knowledge exclusion, which excludes claims arising from incidents occurring before the policy inception date, a prior and pending litigation exclusion excludes claims made after policy inception that arise from litigation that was pending before the policy inception date. For example, if prior to policy inception a claimant filed a lawsuit alleging the employer had a practice of terminating employees when they reached age 55, and then after the policy inception a different claimant alleged they were terminated pursuant to the same practice, the prior and pending litigation exclusion could exclude coverage for the claim made after the policy inception. An example of this exclusion is:

> This Policy does not apply to any **Claim**:...arising directly or indirectly from any **Wrongful Employment Practice** or any fact, circumstance or situation which has been the subject of any notice given prior to the effective date of this Policy under any prior policy, or any other **Wrongful Employment Practice** whenever occurring, which, together with a **Wrongful Employment Practice** which has been the subject of such notice, would constitute **Interrelated Wrongful Employment Practices**...
>
> Colonia (AUSCO)
> EPL 6000 (3/95)

An EPL insurer usually discovers the existence of prior litigation through the application process. If in the application process an insurer learns of prior litigation, the insurer may not want to cover similar or related litigation that may arise in the future. If the insurer does not wish to cover potential litigation that is related to the current litigation, the insurer frequently will endorse a prior and pending litigation exclusion to the policy if such limitation is not already part of the policy.

Class-Action-Suit Exclusion

Class-action suits are suits by a representative plaintiff who sues on his own behalf and on behalf of all people similarly situated. For example, if a company terminates 1,000 employees over age 40, a terminated employee can file a class action on behalf of all 1,000 employees terminated. If liability is proved, the damages awardable are calculated by measuring the damages of all the class members. Accordingly, class actions can present a very significant liability.

Because class-action suits can be expensive, complex and often protracted, they represent a significant exposure. Although seldom, if ever, found in modern EPL insurance policies, the existence of such an exclusion would create a substantial gap in coverage.

11 Definitions[1]

Most EPL insurance policy forms contain a section titled *Definitions,* in which words with special meaning are defined. When specifically defined words or phrases are used in the policy form, they normally appear in boldface type. They also may appear in italics, within quotation marks, in capital letters, underlined or in another prominent type style.

Regardless of how defined words, terms or phrases appear in the policy, they have special meaning and should be carefully reviewed because the policy defined word may differ considerably from its everyday or normal legal meaning.

Some insurers define only a few key words, while others give special meaning to a long list. The following discussions give a brief review of some of the key defined words that appear in nearly all EPL insurance policies. While these definitions help form the cornerstones of coverage, all defined terms must be read in conjunction with other policy provisions and conditions to determine the relative strengths or weaknesses of a given EPL insurance policy.

Claim

The definition of *claim* is important because it usually is one of the triggers in an EPL insurance policy. Unless the insured can report a claim that fits the specific definition within its EPL insurance policy, the insurer may not be required to deliver the benefits of the insurance contract. Those benefits normally begin with the insurer's duty to defend the insured. Most EPL insurance policies define the term *claim* and contain specific provisions on how a claim is to be reported to the insurer. Yet some EPL insurance policies, and some other types of policies such as directors and officers liability insurance policies that have been endorsed to provide EPL coverage, do not define the term *claim.*

---

[1] Specific EPL insurance policy form citations contained in *The EPL Book* are used to illustrate and support text discussion only. Such references are illustrative in nature and are neither an endorsement for nor criticism of any particular policy form. In some instances, policy forms cited in *The EPL Book* may no longer be in use and may be superceded by later editions. Neither *The EPL Book* nor any other reference is a substitute for the reader's own analysis, due diligence and careful reading of the policy form(s) in question.

To evaluate the comparative strengths or weaknesses of a particular definition of *claim* or *claim-reporting provision,* it is helpful to review how claims in general are communicated to the employer as compared to what actually constitutes a claim under an EPL insurance policy.

Employers typically receive notice of an employment practices problem in one of four ways:

- An oral notice to management by the claimant (s)
- A written notice to management by the claimant (s) or claimant's attorney
- A letter received by the employer from a State Agency/EEOC
- A lawsuit served on the employer

Oral Complaint Or Notice

Under ideal circumstances, the relationship between an employee and the employer will foster open dialog and candor. Where such an atmosphere has the support of top management, the employees are more likely to notify management orally of possible problems. This gives management the opportunity to find out about complaints or disagreements early on before more serious problems, such as a lawsuit or complaint to a regulatory authority, occur.

Written Notice To Management

Notice to management of alleged wrongdoing may be contained in a letter, memo or other written documentation directly from the employee. Often, however, such notice is in the form of a demand letter from the employee's attorney alleging one or more wrongful employment practices and often asking for specific remedies.

Unfortunately, by the time a written demand letter has been received, the employee is likely to have retained counsel. The parties often are in an adversarial posture, making the potential for an early and inexpensive resolution more difficult. This sense of conflict often is heightened when the demand letter makes a substantial monetary demand to settle the claims asserted in the letter.

Filing Of A Complaint With State Agency/EEOC

Both federal and state laws prohibit wrongful employment practices involving harassment and discrimination. The Equal Employment Opportunity Commission (EEOC) is the federal agency responsible for enforcing federal employment law. These federal employment laws include Title VII of The Civil Rights Act and its amendments, the Age Discrimination in Employment Act (ADEA) (for persons over 40), the American Disability Act (ADA), the Immigration Reform & Control Act (granting citizenship protected-class status) and one of the most recently enacted federal employment laws, the Family & Medical Leave Act (FMLA).

A prerequisite to bringing a complaint in a federal court for violation of federal discrimination and harassment laws is the filing of an administrative complaint with the EEOC. Most states have similar requirements for claims brought under state discrimination or harassment statutes.

Lawsuit

Where a claimant is not required by law to exhaust administrative remedies, an employer's first notice of alleged wrongful conduct often comes in the form of a lawsuit. Unfortunately once a lawsuit is filed, the employer and claimant are in an adversarial posture. The probability of a swift resolution is often low. Additionally, once a lawsuit is filed, defense expenses can mount rapidly.

Policy Definitions Of *Claim*

Ideally, for many organizations, the insured should be able to give notice to the insurer and trigger the EPL insurance policy's involvement when the insured receives an oral notice of alleged wrongdoing or otherwise has some suspicion that problems are brewing. Whether coverage under an EPL insurance policy can be triggered by the reporting to the insurer of an oral notice received from a claimant, by a written notice, regulatory agency notification or by the receipt of a lawsuit, usually depends on how the policy specifically defines the term *claim*.

Among EPL insurance policies that do define *claim*, the definition varies. Sometimes the definition of *claim* is overly restrictive. Often the only clue that a policy contains an overly restrictive definition of *claim* is subtle and its importance can go unnoticed. The discussion below focuses on some of the issues that can arise from the definition of *claim*.

Requirement That Damages Are Alleged

Most EPL insurance policy definitions of *claim* require that a written demand or notice be received by the insured in which damages are alleged that result from covered acts. These covered acts may include discrimination, sexual harassment, wrongful termination and other common law violations as specifically defined in the policy. Some policy definitions of *claim* include "oral demands or notices." Such definitions would likely broaden the scope of claim to include oral threats that an employee or covered person intends to take some action against the employer. Such wording gives the insured the ability to trigger coverage early, before a formal suit is brought. However, an oral notice of wrongful employment practices not accompanied by a demand for damages would not trigger an EPL insurance policy where the definition of *claim* required that damages be alleged.

Other Demands

Some EPL insurance policy definitions of *claim* do not specifically require that a demand for damages be made, or they may be unclear as to whether a demand for damages must be made in order to trigger the policy.

The defense provisions, however, sometimes reveal that the insurer will undertake a defense only of "any claim against an insured that seeks damages." It is unclear whether, and to what extent, an insurer would have any obligation to investigate a claim or to make a determination of coverage where the definition of *claim* was met, but where there were no demands for damages. To avoid misunderstanding, the insurer should be queried as to what actions, if any, it would take under such circumstances. The policy should then be clarified through endorsement.

Other EPL insurance policies clearly state that a claim is made when the insured receives an oral complaint by the claimant for an employment-related wrongful act and that the duty to defend and investigate is triggered regardless of whether damages are alleged. This is the broadest trigger of coverage available.

Arbitration

Nearly 90% of businesses with more than 100 employees have used some form of alternative-dispute-resolution technique to resolve discrimination and other employment-related complaints. About 10% of those cases are arbitrated. Arbitration may be individually agreed to under an employment contract, or made part of a collective bargaining agreement, or an arbitration provision may be contained in the employee handbook.

EPL insurance policies vary as to whether arbitration is considered a claim. Many policies exclude the type of arbitration mandated by a collective bargaining agreement by inserting the following language into the definition of *claim*:

> **Claim** shall not include a labor or grievance arbitration or other proceeding subject to a collective bargaining agreement.
>
> Philadelphia Insurance Companies
PI-ES-1560 [12/96]

More restrictive definitions of *claim* exclude all forms of labor or grievance arbitration:

> But **claim** does not include a labor or grievance arbitration under a collective bargaining agreement, employment handbook or other employment policies or procedures.
>
> Fireman's Fund Insurance Company
7006-1-98

An insured that has an arbitration provision in its handbook or in employment contracts should be aware that not all EPL insurance policies cover such arbitration.

Administrative Proceedings

Problems can occur regarding how the definition of *claim* addresses administrative proceedings, which are common in employment-related disputes. Administrative proceedings usually involve an employee or prospective employee filing a complaint with the Federal Equal Employment Opportunity Commission (EEOC) or similar state authority. Broad definitions of *claim* specifically include charges filed with such bodies. Other policy definitions of *claim* may include administrative proceedings, but only those "in which the insured may be subjected to a binding adjudication of liability." This provision, which is included in some policy definitions of *claim*, could provide insurers the opportunity to deny or (more likely) to delay coverage until the time an actual suit has been brought.

The EEOC and many state administrative authorities only have conciliatory powers and must "refer" any charges to a court of law in order to effect a binding adjudication of liability. When this is the case, it may be argued that it is the court, and not the agency, that has the power to adjudicate. As such, a mere charge made to an agency that lacks the power to adjudicate liability or which is in an investigation phase may not constitute a claim under some policies. Some insurers might take the position that the policy cannot be triggered by an administrative proceeding that involves only investigation. Therefore, any attorney fees or costs incurred in responding to such an investigation may not be covered under the policy. Once a suit alleging covered damages has been filed, whether directly by a claimant or by the administrative agency, the requirements for a claim likely will be met.

Policies Without A Definition Of *Claim*

As noted above, some policies do not have a definition of *claim*. Where a policy does not define *claim*, a court interpreting that policy may look to applicable state law for a definition. In some jurisdictions, *claim* may be definable as a demand for money or services. Accordingly, the act of filing a charge with an administrative agency such as the EEOC, which does not award damages, may not constitute a claim within the common-law meaning of the term. Many state agencies responsible for enforcing anti-discrimination statutes have powers and authority similar to those of the EEOC. Therefore, filing a charge with those agencies may not constitute a claim under a policy where the term *claim* has not been defined to include administrative proceedings.

While any policy provision that is ambiguous likely will be interpreted by a court of law in favor of the insured, in most instances insureds benefit from a clearly drafted policy that affords an understanding by all parties of the meaning of *claim*.

Potential-Claim Reporting Considerations

While the definition of *claim* can have far-reaching consequences in determining whether an event triggers the policy, it also is necessary to evaluate the policy's provisions in relation to circumstances or incidents that do not meet the technical definition of *claim*, but which may give rise to a claim in the future. For example, an oral threat by one or more employees to sue the employer over damages suffered due to discrimination might not trigger the policy if the definition of *claim* requires written demand or notice. If such an incident occurs immediately before an EPL insurance policy is about to expire, the insured is potentially uninsured if a claim is made later.

From an insured's perspective, it is desirable for an EPL insurance policy to provide a mechanism whereby an insured can trigger coverage for an incident that may result in a claim. Although most EPL insurance policies address this issue, there can be much variation in how such provisions are worded and in the resulting degree of protection provided. In most policies that contain such notice or incident reporting provisions, the insured is required to provide the insurer with specific details regarding the circumstances. The policy may require the insured to identify specific events and persons likely to give rise to a claim, the specific potential injury or damages, the likely claimants and other pertinent information. If these provisions are not complied with, then no coverage would be available for a claim made later.

The wording of such provisions can vary. As a general rule, the insured should avoid notice provisions that are overly burdensome or that require the insured to provide reams of detailed information. The most favorable notice condition will require the insured to simply state reasons a given incident may develop into a claim. Overly restrictive notice requirements may exclude or restrict coverage for claims that may be made in the future. Even when the insured believes a claim is inevitable, unless the specific notice provisions can be met, the policy will not be triggered. Policies that have limited specificity requirements or provisions requiring the insured only to describe the general circumstances afford the insured greater control in triggering coverage.

Not all policies contain notice provisions. This is not always a bad feature, however, because the definition of *claim* might be broad enough to obviate the need for such a provision. The operative word here is *might*, and policies that rely on a broad definition of *claim* to preclude the need for an awareness provision warrant a close look.

Policies containing a restrictive definition of *claim* and an ineffective, or lack of a potential-claim reporting provision should be avoided. The insured may be unable to trigger the current policy for possible resulting claims in such a policy. This inability to trigger the policy may pose no problem if the facts are sufficient to support a claim within the current policy period or even during a later policy period with the same insurer. But problems are likely if a claim arising from a previous incident develops under a policy period where another insurer is covering the risk.

Most applications for coverage require the insureds to warrant that they are unaware of any circumstances likely to give rise to a claim. If the insureds respond that there are no known circumstances and a claim does develop, the insurer may have grounds for denying coverage on the basis that the insured has breached a policy warranty. If the insured responds that incidents have occurred that may result in a claim, the claim resulting from those events will likely be specifically excluded by the insurer.

Conclusion

If a policy strictly defines *claim* to include only a lawsuit or a written demand for damages, the insured may lose the opportunity to avoid litigation. Remember, an employee who complains of sexual harassment or discrimination may only wish the offending behavior to stop and may not necessarily expect compensation for alleged damages. It is at this stage that appropriate damage control by a savvy human resources professional or guidance by defense counsel often can halt escalation of the claim. A claimant's threat to sue, if not reported to the insurer because it does not meet the definition of *claim*, can rapidly result in a substantial loss. Even frivolous nuisance suits can cost tens of thousands of dollars when allowed to fester.

Although there may seem to be much similarity between policy forms regarding the definition of *claim*, subtle differences can have a great impact on when and by what events coverage is triggered. Always weigh the definition of *claim* in balance with the policy's awareness or potential-claim reporting provisions. The lack of a definition of *claim* or an awareness provision is not a bad feature in itself, but should trigger a very close look for a potential coverage gap.

Since it may be possible to prevent a suit from ever being filed or to control the severity of loss through an early intervention, look for definitions of *claim* that allow you to report occurrences at the earliest possible time. We have been told by some insurers that they include very broad definitions of *claim* in their policies and encourage early claim and incident reporting in order to start investigations at the earliest possible time. By waiting to begin investigating a claim until after a suit has been filed, many insurers will lose the opportunity to avoid litigation and to close a claim with minimum expense. Be aware, however, that broad definitions of *claim* require the insured to be ever vigilant in their reporting of occurrences to the insurer.

EPL insurance coverage is in its infancy, and like D&O and other specialty coverages, certain features may be improved simply by asking the underwriter to modify the form.

Discrimination

The word *discrimination* in its normal and common usage usually is quite broad and can encompass a variety of meanings. Some common definitions of *discrimination* include the following:

> Unfair treatment or denial of normal privileges to persons because of their race, age, sex, nationality or religion. A failure to treat all persons equally where no reasonable distinction can be found between those favored and those not favored.
>
> Black's Law Dictionary (West Publishing Company 1995)

> **a :** The act, practice, or an instance of discriminating categorically rather than individually **b :** prejudiced or prejudicial outlook, action, or treatment <racial ~>
>
> Webster's Dictionary (Houghton Mifflin Co.)

> The word "discriminate" may be defined as treating one differently from another.
> Term "discriminate" means distinction in treatment of individuals based upon impermissible or irrelevant factors such as race, color, creed, or sex.
> The word "discriminate" means "to make a difference or distinction."
>
> Words and Phrases (West Publishing Company 1995)

The definition of discrimination as used in an EPL insurance policy is often more restrictive than those definitions given above. Consider the following specimen definition.

> ┌─ *Discriminating Acts*
> Discrimination means termination of an employment relationship or a demotion or a failure or refusal to hire or promote any individual because of race, color, religion, age, sex, disability, pregnancy or national origin.
> └─ *Protected Classes*

Discriminating Acts	■ *Termination of Employment Relationship* ■ *Demotion* ■ *Failure or Refusal to Hire or Promote*
Protected Classes	■ *Race* ■ *Sex* ■ *Color* ■ *Disability* ■ *Religion* ■ *Pregnancy* ■ *Age* ■ *National Origin*

Note that it is composed of two distinct parts. The first part lists those employment actions taken by the employer that negatively impact an employee. The second part of the definition consists of the classifications that are protected by federal, state or local law.

While the definition may appear broad, it is limited to only those employment practices and protected classes enumerated in the definition. One of the problems with this approach is that the definition may not adequately contemplate every conceivable wrongful practice or protected class that may exist. By comparing the protected classes contained in the above definition with the following list of classes protected by federal and some state laws, the potential inadequacy in coverage is evident with this approach.

Exhibit 5
Legally Protected Classes

Federal Protected Classes

Title VI:
Race
Color
Religion
Sex
National Origin
Pregnancy

ADEA:
Persons Over 40

ADA:
Actual or perceived disabilities
AIDS

Immigration Reform & Control Act:
Citizenship

Family & Medical Leave Act:
Failure to grant leave

Some States' Protected Classes	

Fair Employment & Housing Act:
  Race
  Color
  Religious Creed
  Sex
  National Origin
  Pregnancy
  Ancestry
  Sexual Orientation
  Physical or Mental Disability
  Medical Condition (cancers)
  Age
	Discrimination based on filing a work-related injury claim

Even though a narrow definition of *discrimination* may be acceptable to some insureds, an uninsured exposure might exist when new laws are passed or new protected classes are created. In such an instance, the insured would need to be alert to such developments and request that the definition be modified to address the new exposure. Even if the insured is able to make such a request, there is no guarantee that the insurer would modify the policy.

A better approach is to seek policies in which the definition of *discrimination* contemplates or anticipates the very broad nature of wrongful acts that might be alleged and that the list of protected classes may be subject to change. Some insurers add partial or broad omnibus wording that can expand the scope of employment action to include acts not specifically listed and expand the protected classes to include classes not specifically listed.

OMNIBUS WORDING FOR PROTECTED CLASSES

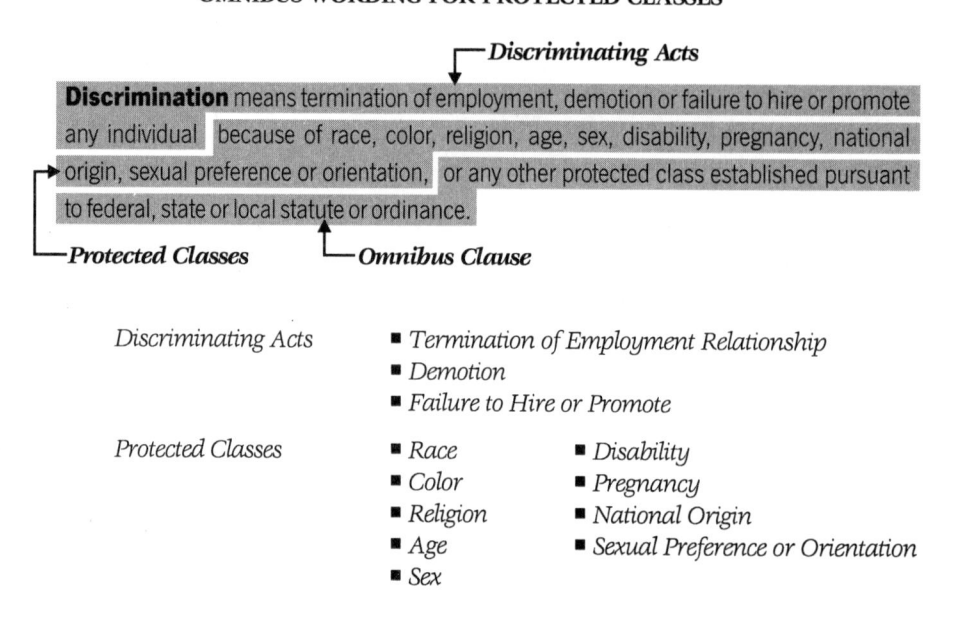

Discrimination means termination of employment, demotion or failure to hire or promote any individual [*Protected Classes:*] because of race, color, religion, age, sex, disability, pregnancy, national origin, sexual preference or orientation, [*Omnibus Clause:*] or any other protected class established pursuant to federal, state or local statute or ordinance.

— *Discriminating Acts* (termination of employment, demotion, failure to hire or promote)

Discriminating Acts
- *Termination of Employment Relationship*
- *Demotion*
- *Failure to Hire or Promote*

Protected Classes
- *Race*
- *Color*
- *Religion*
- *Age*
- *Sex*
- *Disability*
- *Pregnancy*
- *National Origin*
- *Sexual Preference or Orientation*

THE EPL BOOK

Omnibus Clause
- Expands discrimination basis to include any other protected classes
- Established pursuant to
  - Federal
  - State
  - Local

  Statute or ordinance

BROAD OMNIBUS WORDING

Discrimination means termination of the employment relationship, a demotion or failure or refusal to hire or promote or denial or an employment benefit [*Omnibus Wording — Discriminating Acts:*] or the taking of any adverse or differential employment action because of race, color, religion, age, sex, disability, pregnancy or national origin, [*Omnibus Wording — Protected Classes:*] or any other basis prohibited by federal, state or local law.

Discriminating Acts
- Termination of The Employment Relationship
- A Demotion
- Failure or Refusal to Hire or Promote
- Denial of an Employment Benefit

Protected Classes
- Race
- Color
- Religion
- Age
- Sex
- Disability
- Pregnancy
- National Origin

Broad Omnibus Clause
- Expands discriminating acts to include the taking of any adverse or differential employment action
- Expands discrimination basis to include any other protected classes

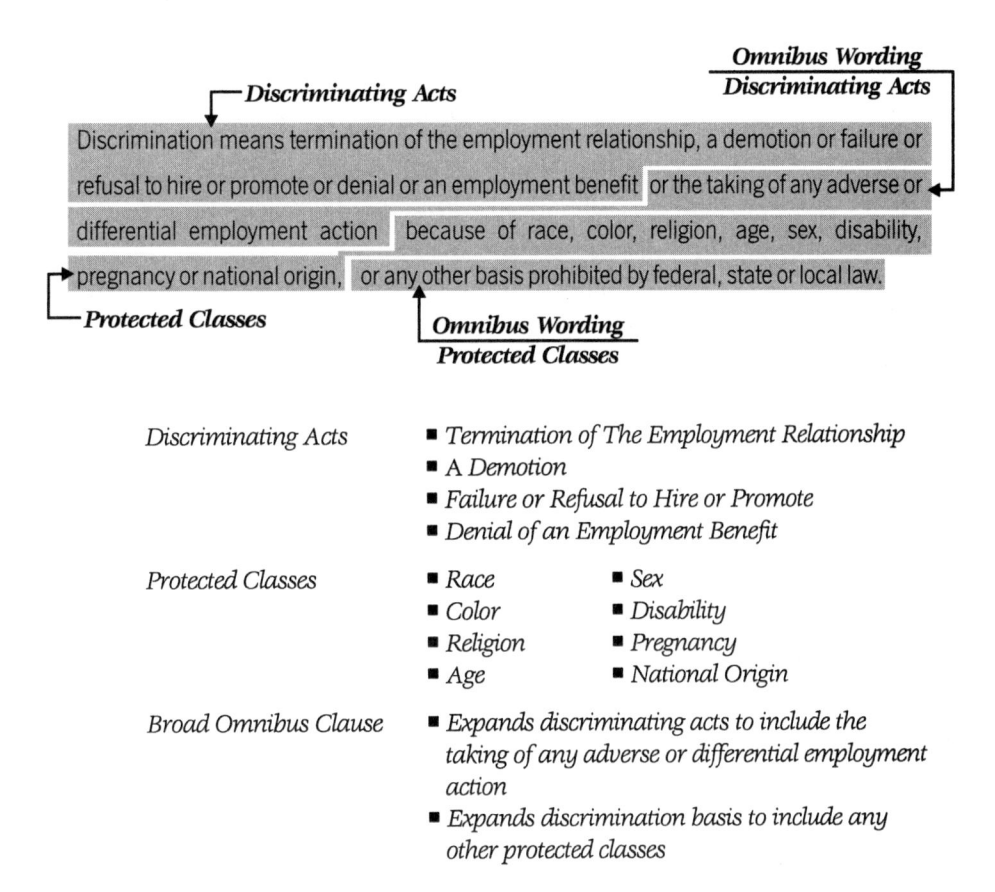

The problem with definitions that do not include broad omnibus wording is that (1) all possible employment actions are not covered, and (2) all possible protected classes are not covered. For example, a claim for wrongful termination on account of marital status discrimination would not be covered under the first definition shown above because marital status is not a protected class in the definition.

Accordingly, it is important for a policyholder to make sure that all possible employment actions and all possible protected classes are included in the definition. One way to find out if the coverage is broad is to look for the omnibus wording in a policy form.

Sexual Harassment

As discussed previously in this book, there are two types of sexual harassment in the workplace that are prohibited under federal law: quid pro quo harassment and hostile environment harassment.

Quid Pro Quo Harassment is where sexual favors are demanded in order for an employee to obtain work benefits or to avoid unfavorable treatment.

Hostile Environment Sexual Harassment involves conduct that interferes with an individual's work performance.

Federal law prohibits unwelcome sexual advances, requests for sexual favors and other verbal or physical conduct of a sexual nature when the following quid pro quo or hostile environment tests are met:

Quid pro quo:

- Submission to such conduct is made either explicitly or implicitly a term or condition of an individual's employment
- Submission to or rejection of such conduct by an individual is used as the basis for employment decisions affecting such individual

Hostile environment:

- Such conduct has the purpose or effect of unreasonably interfering with an individual's work performance or creating an intimidating, hostile or offensive working environment

Most EPL insurance policies mirror the federal definition of *sexual harassment*. An example of a policy definition is:

> Sexual harassment, including unwelcome sexual advances, requests for sexual favors, or other verbal or physical conduct of a sexual nature that (1) is made an explicit or implicit term or condition of employment; or (2) is used as the basis for employment decisions; or (3) creates a work environment that is intimidating, hostile or offensive;...
>
> Northland Insurance Company
> S1110-EP (6/97)

Recently the definition of *sexual harassment* in many EPL insurance policies has been expanded to include both sexual and non-sexual harassment. Non-sexual harassment is often referred to as *workplace harassment*. An example of an expanded definition of *harassment* is as follows:

Harassment means unwelcome sexual or non-sexual advances, requests for sexual or non-sexual favors or other verbal or physical conduct of a sexual or non-sexual nature that (1) explicitly or implicitly are made a condition of employment, (2) are used as a basis for employment decisions, or (3) create a work environment that interferes with performance. **Harassment** includes allegations of assault and battery, but only if they are related to a charge of sexual harassment.

Swett & Crawford
EPLX-987
7/1/98

"Harassment", includes Sexual "Harassment", which is defined as unwelcome sexual advances, requests for sexual favors, or other verbal, visual or physical conduct of a sexual nature when (1) submission to such conduct is made either explicitly or implicitly a term and condition of an "Employee's" employment; or (2) submission to or rejection of such conduct by an "Employee" is used as the basis for employment decisions affecting such an individual; or (3) such conduct has the purpose or effect of unreasonably interfering with an "Employee's" work performance or creating an intimidating, hostile, or offensive work environment.

Steadfast
STF-PL-100-B CW (4/97)

These broader definitions of *harassment* recognize that sex is only one of the classes protected by law and that harassment can also take the form of racial taunting, teasing, or even physical assault and battery based upon membership in a protected class.

Workplace Torts

In addition to allegations of discrimination, sexual harassment or wrongful termination, employment practice claims can include a wide range of other employment or workplace torts. These can include, but would not be limited to, the following:

- Defamation
- Libel
- Slander
- Humiliation
- Retaliation
- Wrongful discipline
- Negligent or wrongful evaluation
- Negligent hiring
- Negligent supervision
- Fraud

- Emotional distress
- Misrepresentation
- Interference with contract
- False imprisonment

Early EPL insurance policies were often silent regarding whether such affiliated claims were covered under the policy. Other EPL insurance policies contained exclusions for such claims. Today, outright exclusions for workplace torts in connection with a covered employment practice are rare. Many EPL insurance policies will define the scope of coverage for workplace torts within the definition of one or more of the covered wrongful practices. For example, the following definition of *wrongful employment decision* encompasses a wide range of workplace torts the insurer agrees to cover:

Wrongful Employment Decision means:

(1) termination, actual or constructive, of an employment relationship in any manner which is against the law and wrongful;

(2) allegations of wrongful demotion, retaliation, misrepresentation, promissory estoppel and, intentional interference with contract, which arise from an employment decision to employ, terminate, evaluate, discipline, promote or demote;

(3) defamation, infliction of emotional distress or mental anguish, humiliation, false imprisonment, invasion of privacy and other personal injury allegations which arise from the employing, terminating, evaluating, disciplining, promoting or demoting of an Employee;

(4) allegations of breach of an implied employment contract, breach of the covenant of good faith and fair dealing in the employment contract;

(5) employmen* terminations, disciplinary actions, demotion other employment decisions which violate public policy or the Family Medical Leave Act or similar state law;

(6) violations of the Uniformed Services Employment and Reemployment Rights Act;

(7) allegations of breach of an Employee' federal, state or local civil rights including but not limited to any violation of the Civil Rights Act of 1886 or 42 U.S.C. Section 1983;

(8) allegations of retaliation against Employees including but not limited to retaliation for filing claims under the Federal False Claims Act, retaliation in connection with whistle blowing, retaliation for union activities or in connection with strikes or lockouts;

(9) allegations of wrongful deprivation of career opportunity or failure to grant tenure.

Swett & Crawford
EPLX-987
7/1/98

When evaluating the extent of coverage for workplace torts, it may be necessary to look at each covered employment practice definition separately. The best definitions include broad descriptions of what is covered and are not limited to only a specific list of offenses.

If you are in doubt as to whether or to what extent coverage for common law torts is provided by the EPL insurance policy in question, it may be necessary to seek clarification or confirmation from the insurance broker or insurer. Such clarification is best done in writing.

Wrongful Termination

The definition of *wrongful termination* varies greatly between currently available EPL insurance policy forms. The variations in the definition of *wrongful termination* can be significant and should be a critical concern to policyholders. Wrongful termination claims consist of a wide variety of state common law and statutory causes of action. Wrongful termination claims can include allegations of promissory estoppel,[2] breach of contract, breach of implied contract, intentional interference with contract,[3] breach of the covenant of good faith and fair dealing, violation of whistle blowing statutes, defamation, infliction of emotional distress, fraud, misrepresentations or invasion of privacy, and others.

None of these allegations in a wrongful termination claim require a showing of discrimination or sexual harassment. Accordingly, a policyholder should carefully examine the definition of *wrongful termination* to determine which, if any, of the allegations that can comprise a wrongful termination claim are potentially covered under the EPL insurance policy. It also is important to note that most definitions of *wrongful termination* exclude coverage for damages from a breach of an express or written employment contract.

It also is important that the definition of *wrongful termination* be broad enough to cover constructive termination and demotions. Many former employees file charges of wrongful termination even if they appear to have quit voluntarily. A typical constructive-termination allegation is that the atmosphere of the workplace was so intolerable that the employee could not stay on the job. Also, employees who are still employed may file

---

[2] Promissory estoppel is a cause of action which usually arises when an employee relocates from one city to another based upon the promise of a job. If the promise of a job is broken, the employee can file a lawsuit for promissory estoppel, alleging detrimental reliance on the promise of a job. In such a cause of action, the employee can recover damages for moving expenses and lost wages if the employee left one job for the promise of a new job.

[3] Intentional interference with contract is a common law tort cause of action that applies to employment contracts whether written or unwritten. If a person intentionally, without legal justification, attempts to convince an employer to either terminate an employment relationship or demote an employee, that person faces potential liability. The classic example of intentional interference with contract is when a person manufactures a false charge of sexual harassment in order to cause an employer to terminate the accused employee. That was the situation in the Miller Brewing case where a male supervisor won a judgment against a female subordinate for falsely accusing the supervisor of sexual harassment so that the subordinate could be promoted to the supervisor's position.

claims of wrongful demotion. Policy definitions limited solely to wrongful termination would not cover wrongful demotion claims.

Examples of the definitions of *wrongful termination* include the following:

> **Wrongful Termination** means (1) violation of **your** employee's rights, other than rights based on an express, written, or oral agreement of employment, when terminating an employment relationship; or (2) failure to exercise duty and care on the part of the employer when terminating an employment relationship.
>
> American International Specialty Lines Insurance Company
> AISL 64198 (12/95)

This definition is silent on coverage for employment-related torts such as defamation, infliction of emotional distress, misrepresentation or invasion of privacy. It also does not appear to cover allegations of constructive termination or demotion.

Another definition is:

> The Term **"WRONGFUL ACT OF TERMINATION"** shall mean termination of an employment relationship in a manner which is against the law and wrongful or in breach of an implied agreement to continue employment. Wrongful termination shall not include damages determined to be owing under an express contract of employment or an express obligation to make payments in the event of the termination of employment.
>
> London Market (U.S. Risk Underwriters, Inc.)
> DISC3/98/CO
> 3/98

This definition also is silent regarding employment-related torts and appears not to include constructive-termination allegations or allegations of wrongful demotion.

It should be noted that sometimes *wrongful termination* is not separately defined but is contained in a definition of *wrongful employment act or practice.*

When this occurs, the extent of coverage for employment-related torts must be assessed as part of that larger definition.

12 Conditions[1]

Policy conditions are provisions of the policy that may alter or qualify the scope or application of coverage or provide for certain undertakings on the part of the insured or insurer. Although an EPL insurance policy may promise to pay for specific types of loss, such promise generally is subject to one or more specified provisions or a requirement that the insured fulfill certain duties.

EPL insurance policies often contain numerous conditions in a specific *Conditions* section of the policy, but conditional language also may be found elsewhere in the policy form, such as in the policy insuring agreement or the *Exclusions* section. The number and scope of policy conditions varies, but most EPL insurance policies contain the same types of conditions that appear in other types of liability policies. A few EPL insurance policy conditions that have not been discussed in previous chapters, however, are worthy of special comment and appear in the following discussion.

Acquisitions/Change Of Control

Most EPL insurance policy forms contain provisions stating how coverage is intended to apply in the event one of the following situations occurs during the policy period:

- The insured acquires or forms a new organization

- The insured merges or consolidates with another organization and remains the controlling entity (i.e., the insured survives)

- The insured is acquired by or merges with another entity and the other organization becomes the controlling entity (i.e., the insured does not survive)

---

[1] Specific EPL insurance policy form citations contained in *The EPL Book* are used to illustrate and support text discussion only. Such references are illustrative in nature and are neither an endorsement for nor criticism of any particular policy form. In some instances, policy forms cited in *The EPL Book* may no longer be in use and may be superceded by later editions. Neither *The EPL Book* nor any other reference is a substitute for the reader's own analysis, due diligence and careful reading of the policy form(s) in question.

- The insured creates or dissolves a subsidiary company

Provisions that address such changes in operations usually are found in the *Conditions* or *Who Is Insured* section of the policy, but they also may be found within the *Definitions* or *Exclusions* section.

Policy conditions regarding changes in exposure can vary. For instance, some EPL insurance policies may treat each of the above exposures individually and contain specific wording that will apply to that particular change. Other policies may treat changes more generally and have one provision that applies regardless of the nature of the change.

Under either approach, insurers generally will apply one or more of the following provisions to changes in exposure caused by an acquisition or a change in control of the organization.

- *Limited automatic coverage.* Coverage automatically is granted for the new entity following an acquisition or merger, but only for a specified time period (usually 30 to 90 days). After the stated period, the "new" exposure presented by the acquisition or merger must be evaluated by the insurer, who may then decide to continue or terminate coverage. A few EPL insurance policies provide automatic coverage only for newly acquired or merged entities that meet predetermined criteria. For example, a newly acquired entity may be extended full coverage under the existing policy if less than a specified percentage of the insured's assets was involved in the transaction or if the new entity has less than a specified number of employees.

- *Conditional coverage.* Coverage for newly acquired or formed organizations is provided only when certain conditions are met. Such conditions may include one or more of the following: the insured (1) retains at least a 50% ownership interest in the new entity, (2) notifies the insurer within some specified time period (30 days is common) prior to the acquisition, merger or creation of a subsidiary, (3) gives the underwriter all relevant information about the new entity and (4) agrees to accept any new terms and conditions imposed by the insurer. If the insured fulfills these requirements, the insurer may then issue an endorsement confirming coverage for the new entity.

- As respects newly created or acquired subsidiaries, most EPL insurers usually will grant coverage if the insured informs the insurer of the new subsidiary in writing within a specified time period either before or after the creation or purchase. If a subsidiary is sold or dissolved, most EPL insurance policies will provide coverage only for acts that occurred prior to the sale or dissolution, although some EPL insurers *may* agree to continue coverage if the insurer is informed of the sale.

> *Coverage terminates.* Coverage terminates as of the effective date of any change of control. Coverage for the original insured may continue, but usually only in regard to acts that occurred prior to the change of control.

Even though insureds may not contemplate an acquisition, merger or other change of corporate or other organizational structure, such changes may occur suddenly or unexpectedly to the person responsible for insurance. Policy provisions pertaining to any change in the insured's operations should therefore be reviewed carefully to avoid coverage problems if and when changes do take place. When no automatic coverage provisions exist, care must be exercised to determine whether coverage is needed for the new entity and to make sure coverage can be secured prior to the new business entity being created or acquired.

When evaluating acquisition and change-of-control provisions, look for an automatic coverage feature of sufficient length. If the insured must notify the insurer of changes, avoid those that require an "immediate" notice to the insurer. Such a requirement can cause problems should changes in the insured's operation become effective before the insured's insurance department, risk manager or other responsible person becomes aware of such change or is able to provide the required notice in a timely manner.

Arbitration

Many EPL insurance policies require the arbitration of any coverage disputes between the insurer and the insured. Whether such requirements are part of the basic policy form or attached as an endorsement, such seemingly innocuous clauses sometimes can contain onerous language.

Arbitration ordinarily involves a voluntary proceeding undertaken by parties who want a dispute resolved on the merits of the case by an impartial decisionmaker of their choosing. In many cases, the parties agree in advance to accept the arbitrator's decision as final and binding. Proponents say that arbitration often is less costly than litigation, much faster and reduces court congestion. When an arbitration provision is contained in an EPL insurance policy, it loses its voluntary nature.

An example of a typical mandatory and binding arbitration clause in an EPL insurance policy is shown below.

> Any dispute, including but not limited to claims sounding in contract or tort, between the **Insureds** and the Company arising in connection with or relating to this coverage section shall be submitted to binding arbitration.
>
> Chubb Group
14-02-0953 (Rev. 8/96)

EPL insurance policy arbitration conditions typically contain one or more of the following provisions:

> *Whether the results of the arbitration are to be binding and/or final.* In some policies, there is no requirement that the arbitration be either mandatory or binding.

> *The forum in which the arbitration is to be conducted.* Many EPL insurance policies require submission of disputes to the American Arbitration Association and may state that the arbitration will be conducted under the Commercial Rules of Arbitration. Some policies also contain provisions that all or part of the arbitration will be conducted under the laws or rules of the jurisdiction in which the arbitration is held. Such laws may not be beneficial to the insured's position or interpretation of coverage, and it may be difficult for many insureds to determine the actual impact of such binding requirements.

> *The location where the arbitration must be held* (*situs* requirement). Some arbitration provisions state that arbitration proceedings are to be conducted in New York, London or even Bermuda. Such requirements can present logistical problems for some insureds. The cost of participating in an arbitration proceeding held in a foreign country, for example, might dissuade some insureds from even pursuing the dispute.

> *A description of how the arbitration is to be conducted.* Some policies set forth the method to be used for selecting or replacing arbitrators, their necessary qualifications and the time frame in which the arbitrator's decision must be rendered.

Arbitration provisions often favor the insurer. This is because arbitrators typically are not required to follow the traditional rule that ambiguities in policy language are to be construed in favor of the insured. Also, the arbitrators may choose to ignore the doctrine of the insured's reasonable expectation of coverage, which has been adopted by many courts to protect purchasers with limited knowledge of insurance. When the doctrine is applied, the insured is often able to recover loss—even though the policy technically excludes coverage—if the insured's expectations of coverage are found by the court to be objectively reasonable.

In some EPL insurance policies, arbitration is mandated only in disputes involving more than a stated minimum amount (usually $5,000). Disputes involving less than this minimum amount are to be subject to small claims court procedure unless the insured chooses to have such dispute resolved through arbitration instead.

Some insurers soften the effect of mandatory and binding arbitration clauses by giving the insured some flexibility and choice regarding the dispute-resolution process. Such choice and control is illustrated in the following example:

> The Insurer and Insureds agree that there shall be two choices of ADR: (1) non-binding mediation administered by the American Arbitration Association, in which the Insurer and Insureds shall try in good faith to settle the dispute by mediation under or in accordance with its then-prevailing Commercial Mediation Rules; or (2) arbitration submitted to the American Arbitration Association under or in accordance with its then-prevailing commercial arbitration rules, in which the arbitration panel shall be composed of three disinterested individuals. In either mediation or arbitration, the mediator(s) or arbitrators shall have knowledge of the legal, corporate management, or insurance issues relevant to the matters in dispute.
>
> National Union Insurance Company
67548 (4/97)

In the above example, the insured or the insurer may elect either binding arbitration or non-binding mediation as the dispute-resolution process. Under this arrangement, the insured has the right to reject the insured's choice prior to commencement. If mediation is chosen as the dispute-resolution method and no resolution is reached, the insured or the insurer may still bring a judicial proceeding, but only after a specified period of time after conclusion of the mediation.

Whether or not an arbitration clause is present, the insurer and insured still could agree to submit any coverage disputes to arbitration, and some insurers may provide mandatory-arbitration language through endorsement upon request by the insured.

Coverage Territory

The territory in which EPL insurance policy coverage applies varies by insurer. In some policy forms, the coverage territory is described in the *Conditions* section of the policy. In other forms, the coverage-territory provision is found in the *Definitions* section, within the insuring agreement, or in a separate *Coverage Territory* section of the policy. A few EPL insurance policies do not contain any reference to the coverage territory.

There are three basic variations in the geographic scope of EPL coverage. These variations are described below.

- *Worldwide coverage.* This is the broadest scope of coverage and may be provided by insurers in one of two ways. The policy may state specifically that coverage applies anywhere in the world, or the policy may be silent as respects the coverage territory. When there is no stated territorial limitation, coverage may be presumed to be worldwide. However, to avoid any misunderstanding, insureds may want to seek clarification of the coverage territory from the insurer.

- *Limited worldwide coverage.* Coverage is worldwide, but claims and/or suits must be brought within a specified and limited geographic area. The area typically includes the United States, its territories or possessions, and Canada. In a few EPL insurance policies, Puerto Rico also is included.

A limited worldwide-coverage provision can present a problem for some insureds. Employees working for US companies outside the policy-coverage territory may make a claim or file suit in the country in which they are working. In such a situation, the insured's EPL insurance policy may not provide coverage for the claim or suit. Fortunately, such instances appear to be rare.

- *Limited geographical coverage.* Some EPL insurance policies provide coverage for claims arising from incidents that *occur* only within a specified geographical area. The geographical area usually consists of the United States and its territories or possessions, although Puerto Rico and/or Canada also may be included. Sometimes there is no requirement as respects where a claim or suit must be filed for coverage to apply, but some policies specifically state that the claim or suit also must be filed within the coverage territory.

Because the EPL coverage-territory provisions vary, insureds need to be aware of any limitations or restrictions that apply as respects both policy coverage and where claims or suits must be filed. This is especially important for insureds that maintain operations that are outside the coverage territory or that occasionally or regularly require employees to travel outside the coverage territory on company business. Worldwide coverage always is preferred, even if the insured does not have an identified worldwide exposure.

Other Insurance

Most EPL insurance policies contain an "other insurance" condition that explains how other available insurance affects loss adjustment. Other insurance conditions are generally intended to limit an insurer's liability where other coverage covering the same loss can be established. Other insurance provisions generally can be classified into one of three categories: excess, pro rata and escape/non-liability clauses.

Excess other insurance provisions, which are the most common, state that coverage applies in excess of any other insurance available to pay for the loss. Insurance specifically purchased to be excess of the EPL insurance policy, however, usually is not subject to the provision. A typical other insurance provision is shown below.

> If other valid and collectable insurance is available to the insured covering a Loss also covered by this policy, other than insurance that is specifically stated to be in excess of this policy, the insurance afforded by this policy shall be in excess of and shall not contribute with such other insurance. Nothing herein shall be construed to make this policy subject to the terms, conditions and limitations of other insurance.
>
> American Technology Excess and Surplus Insurance Services (AmTech)
AMTECH/RD (09/95)

Some EPL other insurance provisions reaffirm that coverage only applies excess of any amounts payable by the insured under a required self-insured retention and/or coinsurance obligation. An example is shown below.

> This insurance shall be in excess of the amount of the **Self-Insured Retention, Insured's Co-Insurance Obligation** and of any other insurance available to the Insured whether the other insurance is stated to be primary, pro rata, contributory, excess, contingent or otherwise, unless the other insurance is written only as specific excess insurance over the Limits of Liability provided by this Policy.
>
> Evanston Insurance Company
EIC 3071-1 9/97

Policy forms that do not include specific reference to an insured's self-insured retention in the other insurance condition may, however, do so within the insuring agreement or *Limit of Liability* section of the policy. Also, the wording of some EPL other insurance clauses states that coverage applies on an excess basis only if another insurer has a duty to defend the claim. Otherwise, coverage applies on a primary basis.

Pro rata other insurance conditions apportion the amount of coverage for a loss between insurers in the same ratio as each insurer's policy limits bear to the total policy limits of all available insurance. Pro rata other insurance provisions are rare in EPL insurance policies.

Escape/non-liability clauses, like excess clauses, are intended to relieve the insurer of any obligation to pay if there is other insurance available to pay for the loss. However, where the limits of the policy with the escape clause are greater than the limits of other available insurance, the coverage provided by the policy with the escape clause is excess of the other insurance, but only to the extent of policy limits. The use of escape clauses in EPL insurance policies is rare, possibly due to the onerous language and the courts' dim view of such clauses. The following wording is an example of an escape/non-liability other insurance provision.

> If all or part of any covered CLAIM for ACTUAL DAMAGES is covered by any other insurance, whether on a primary, excess, umbrella, contingent or other basis, then this insurance shall not apply and no coverage shall be afforded under this insurance; except, when the limits of this policy are greater than the limits of all other insurance, then this policy shall provide excess insurance up to an amount sufficient to give the INSURED, as respects the amount of insurance afforded by this policy, a total limit of insurance equal to the limit of insurance

provided herein. In no event shall this policy be construed to contribute more than on an excess basis. This shall not apply to coverage under an excess policy which specifically is written to be in excess of this policy and which specifically refers to this policy as an underlying policy.

TIG Insurance Group
22955
Ed. 5/95

Some insurers write both EPL insurance policies and other policies (such as directors & officers liability) that could provide coverage for EPL claims. In such cases, the EPL insurance policy may include an other insurance condition that specifically applies when more than one policy issued by the same company provides coverage for the loss. Such clauses are intended to prevent the pyramiding of coverage limits under both policies by limiting coverage to the policy with the higher limit of liability. Such a clause is shown below.

> If this policy and any other policy issued to you by us or any of our affiliated companies apply to the same **claim**:
>
> - The limits that apply to that **claim** shall not exceed the highest applicable limit available under any one policy that applies; and
>
> - The total limits applicable to all such **claims** made during the **policy period** shall not exceed the highest applicable total or aggregate limit available
>
> But this does not apply to any policy issued specifically to apply as excess insurance over this policy.

Fireman's Fund Insurance Company
7006-10-96

Such clauses should be read carefully because there have been instances in older EPL insurance policies where the other-insurance provision is worded such that the policy with the lower limit of liability would apply. Obviously such a provision would be unfavorable from the insured's standpoint.

Some EPL insurance policies contain wording designed to clarify the insurer's coverage intent where multiple policies and conflicting other insurance provisions are involved in the same insurance program. An example of such wording is shown below.

> If other valid and collectible insurance is available to the Insured for a Loss we cover under this policy, our obligations are limited as follows:
>
> 1. <u>Primary Insurance</u>. This insurance is primary except when 2. below applies. If this insurance is primary, our obligations are not affected unless any of the other insurance is also primary. Then, we will share with all that other insurance by the method described in 3. below.
>
> 2. <u>Excess Insurance</u>. This insurance is excess over any of the other insurance, whether primary, excess, contingent or on any other basis, that is effective prior to the beginning of the **policy period** shown in the Declarations of this insurance and applies on other than a claims-made basis if the other insurance has a policy term which continues after the Retroactive Date shown in the Declarations of this insurance.

> When this insurance is excess, we will have no duty to defend any **claim** that any other insurer has a duty to defend. If no other insurer defends, we will undertake to do so, but we will be entitled to the **insured's** rights against all those other insurers. When this insurance is excess over other insurance, we will pay only our share of the amount of the Loss, if any, that exceeds the sum of:
>
> - The total amount that all such other insurance would pay for the Loss in the absence of this insurance; and
>
> - The total of all deductible and self-insured amounts under all that other insurance.
>
> We will share the remaining Loss, if any, with any other insurance that is not described in this Excess Insurance provision and was not bought specifically to apply in excess of the Limits shown in the Declarations.
>
> 3. <u>Method of Sharing</u>. If all of the other insurance permits contribution by equal shares, we will follow this method also. Under this approach, each insurer contributes equal amounts until it has paid its applicable limit of insurance or none of the loss remains, whichever comes first. If any of the other insurance does not permit contribution by equal shares, we will contribute by limits. Under this method, each insurer's share is based on the ratio of its applicable limit of insurance to the total applicable limits of insurance of all insurers.
>
> Fireman's Fund Insurance Company
7006-10-96

When more than one policy may provide coverage for a loss, potential problems with conflicting other insurance conditions can occur. These potential problems might be avoided if the insured requests endorsements to specifically state which coverage is primary and which is to be excess. When the other insurance provisions of the policies conflict (i.e., one policy contains a "pro rata" clause and another policy contains an "excess" clause), each policy should be modified by endorsement to clarify which applies first.

Severability And Non-Imputation Of Liability

Many EPL insurance policy forms contain severability and non-imputation-of-liability provisions. These provisions prevent policy coverage from being restricted or voided if one insured does something that would otherwise limit or void coverage for other insureds. While severability and non-imputation-of-liability provisions are similar in nature, they differ as respects the circumstances in which they are applied.

Severability

A severability provision may appear as a separate policy condition or may be included within the wording of a "representations" condition. The provision applies with respect to information provided in the coverage application. Severability conditions usually provide that any misrepresentations, omissions or warranties made by one person shall not be imputed to any other person for the purpose of determining the insured's right of recovery under the policy. A typical severability provision is shown below.

> Except for material facts or circumstances known to the person or persons signing the Application, no statement in the Application or knowledge or information possessed by any **Insured** shall be imputed to any other **Insured** for the purpose of determining the availability of coverage.
>
> Philadelphia Insurance Company
PI-DF-1
9/95

Some severability provisions specifically state that if the person completing the application is aware of the falsity of any statements made, coverage may be voided for *all* insureds under the policy. An example is shown below.

> **Representations; Severability:**
>
> The **Insureds** represent that the particulars and statements contained in the **Application** are true, accurate and complete, and agree that this Policy is issued in reliance on the truth of that representation, and that such particulars and statements, which are deemed to be incorporated into and to constitute a part of this Policy, are the basis of this Policy. No knowledge or information possessed by any **Insured** will be imputed to any other **Insured,** except for material facts or information known to the person or persons who signed the **Application.** In the event of any material untruth, misrepresentation or omission in connection with any of the particulars or statements in the **Application,** this Policy will be void with respect to any **Insured** who knew of such untruth, misrepresentation or omission or to whom such knowledge is imputed.
>
> Executive Risk Specialty Insurance Company
B24775
8/97

Whenever a policy does not contain a severability provision, even an unintentional misrepresentation made by the insured may result in a limiting or voiding of policy coverage. For this reason, policies containing severability provisions are beneficial even if the provision does not protect all insureds in all situations.

Non-Imputation Of Liability

In contrast with severability clauses, non-imputation-of-liability provisions usually are contained within the *Exclusions* section of the policy and apply as respects wrongful acts intentionally committed by the insured. Such provisions typically state that liability for such wrongful acts committed by one insured will not be imputed to (and will therefore not affect coverage for) other insureds. Two examples of non-imputation-of-liability clauses are shown below.

With respect to the Exclusions in subsections 5 and 6 of this coverage section, no fact pertaining to or knowledge possessed by any **Insured** shall be imputed to any other **Insured** to determine if coverage is available.

Chubb Group
Form 14-02-0953 (Rev. 8/96)

Exclusions H and I are several as respects each Insured. With respect to the application of these Exclusions, no act committed by any **Insured** shall be imputed to any other **Insured.**

X.L. Insurance Co., Ltd.
EPLI-005 (7/98)

Non-imputation-of-liability provisions also may be found at the beginning or end of the *Exclusions* section of the policy and can apply to several or all of the exclusions.

13 The EPL Insurance Market

Information regarding the current state of the EPL insurance marketplace was gathered from the following sources:

- Insurance company survey responses to *EPL Book* surveys collected in 1997 and 1998
- Insurance company interviews
- Broker interviews
- Interviews with wholesalers
- Interviews with employers
- Other published data

Evolution Of EPL Insurance

Underwriters at Lloyds were probably the first to market a low-limit, defense-only EPL insurance product as early as the mid-1980s, well before other insurers were even aware that a potential market for such a product existed.

In early 1992, Reliance National, Lexington Insurance Company and New Hampshire Insurance Company (American International Group) introduced domestic EPL insurance products. While limited in scope when compared to modern policies, the introduction of a stand-alone EPL insurance product by a major U.S. insurer garnered much attention and speculation about the future of such products. Shortly after the introduction of these early EPL insurance policies, the Chubb Group and others introduced their own EPL insurance products. Since that time, a steady stream of insurers have entered and left the marketplace.

In April 1998, the Insurance Services Office introduced a standardized EPL insurance product it hoped would gain widespread acceptance among smaller insurers. While its new EPL insurance form was the first new product it had introduced in nearly 20 years, the scope of coverage paled in comparison to existing EPL insurance. While the ISO policy has not yet achieved what its drafters had hoped for, ISO's foray into the EPL arena signaled that EPL insurance had achieved a certain legitimacy that had eluded it in prior years among some buyers.

Effect Of Employers' Buying Habits

The potential for catastrophic loss from employment-related litigation has become widely recognized by business, industry, and non-profit and public sector entities. This awareness level fostered over the past several years appears to have motivated a larger number of employers to purchase coverage for employment practices liability. This is in contrast to previous years, when insurers and brokers reported a large number of insurers inquiring about EPL insurance and soliciting price quotations but who did not buy. Many insurers and brokers reported receiving orders on between 10–20% of all proposals. This compares to reports of 5–10% in 1996, when we conducted an informal telephone poll.

Although brokers and insurers both report increased interest in EPL insurance by employers, the percentage of employers actually purchasing EPL insurance remains relatively low when compared with general liability or other standard forms of business insurance. A 1997 survey of employers conducted by The Society for Human Resource Management (SHRM) and Jackson Lewis revealed that 22% of respondents reported purchasing EPL insurance.[1] Insurers and brokers alike described the EPL insurance market as having huge potential for growth.

Market Profile

The *EPL Book* began surveying EPL insurers in 1996. At that time, we identified 23 insurers who were actively writing EPL insurance, primarily in the form of a stand-alone product. Because some insurers offer more than one policy form, the total number of policies reviewed at that time was 30. In 1998, the number of insurers[2] responding to our survey rose to 39, with 60 separate policy forms submitted and evaluated. The actual number of insurers writing EPL insurance is likely higher than our surveys indicate. We estimate that the total number of insurers covering liability arising out of employment practices through stand-alone, D&O, general liability, umbrella, professional liability, and association and other specialty programs probably exceeds 60. Because many insurers offer more than one policy form, the number of different policy forms may well exceed 80.

---

[1] The actual percentage may be higher, however, as 30% indicated that they did not know whether the organization purchased such insurance.

[2] Multiple insurers within the same insurance group counted as one insurer.

It is interesting to note the composition of the total capacity as measured by available limits per policy. Charts 22 and 23 below show the distribution of policy limits by number of insurers for survey years 1997 and 1998. In addition to a substantial increase in the number of insurers actively competing in the marketplace, a similar increase in available capacity has been observed.

Chart 22

Policy Limits Distribution—1997

Data Source: *The EPL Book* Insurance Market Survey

Mean = $11.3 million
Median = $5 million
Mode = $1 million & $5 million

Individual Policy Limits ($000,000)	Number of EPL Insurance Policies
0.5	1
1	7
2	3
3	1
5	7
10	4
25	6
100	1

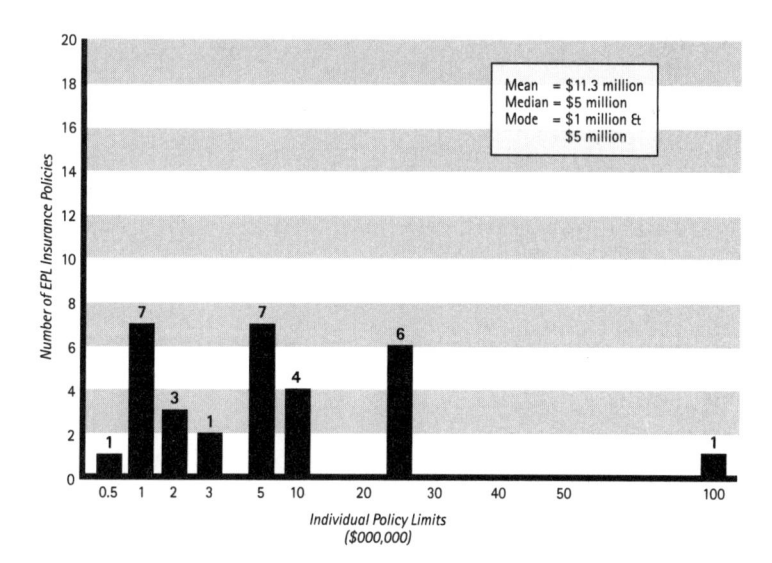

Chart 23

Policy Limits Distribution—1998

Data Source: *The EPL Book* Insurance Market Survey

Mean = $17.8 million
Median = $5 million
Mode = $5 million

Individual Policy Limits ($000,000)	Number of EPL Insurance Policies
0.5	1
1	4
2	4
5	19
10	9
15	2
20	1
25	8
35	1
50	7
100	2

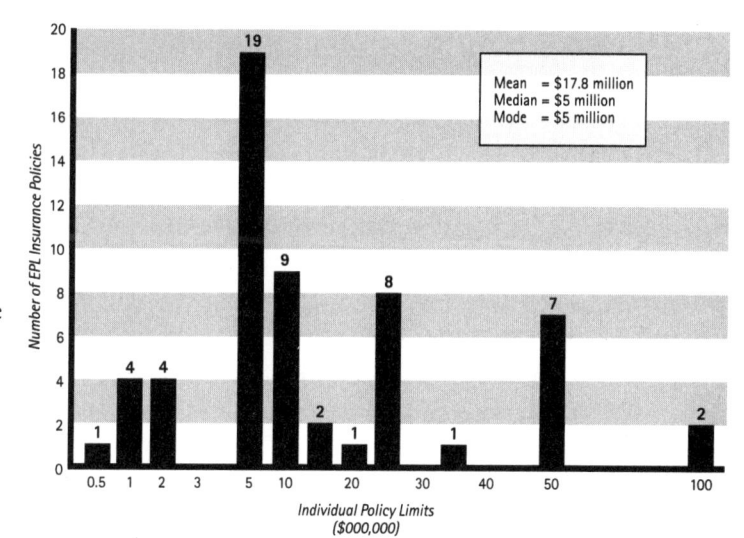

Table 13 below summarizes total market capacity, mean,[3] median,[4] mode[5] and range of maximum available per policy limits for 1997 and 1998. In addition, information regarding the number of insurers writing EPL insurance, as well as the number of different policy forms available, is provided.

In calculating limit capacity figures, we used the highest per-claim limit for each individual policy.[6] We separately calculated total aggregate capacity based on each insurer's maximum individual policy limit. For example, if an insurer offers three different EPL products with limits of $5, $10, and $15 million, we used only the highest figure in our second calculation. The purpose of the second calculation method was to give consideration to the fact that some insurers who offer multiple policy forms may draw capacity from a common source. In such instances, counting individual policy limits separately would tend to inflate the total-capacity figures.

Table 13
EPL Insurance Capacity

Data Source: *The EPL Book* 1997 and 1998 surveys

	1997 ($000,000)	1998 ($000,000)	% change
Number of Insurers	23	39	70
Number of Policy Forms	30	60	100
Total Per-Policy Capacity	340.5	1,032.5	203
Total Per-Insurer Capacity	293.5	715.5	144
Mean Policy Limit	11.3	17.8	58
Median Policy Limit	5	5	no change
Mode Policy Limit	bimodal at 1 & 5	5	N/A
Range	95.5	95.5	no change

*Calculated using maximum policy limit only for insurer offering multiple policy forms.

While our survey response data was not exhaustive, it should provide readers with a relative indication of market condition between the two survey periods. From the compiled data, we observe that:

- The number of insurers identified by us as writing EPL insurance, and who responded to our survey, increased from 23 in 1997 to 39 in 1998.

- The number of different EPL insurance policy forms increased by 100%, to 60 separate policy forms.

---

[3] **Mean**—Statistical measure of central tendency.

[4] **Median**—A statistical average indicating central tendency where one-half of the items being averaged fall below and on-half fall above the midpoint.

[5] **Mode**—A statistical measure of common tendency or average that identifies the value of the variable giving the greatest height on a graph of the frequency distribution.

[6] See Appendix M.

- Depending on measurement techniques, the total capacity has increased between 140% to 200% in one survey period.
- Total EPL capacity, as measured by our survey responses, stands at between $715 million to just over $1 billion.
- The median policy limit of $5 million has not changed.

Charts 22 and 23 indicate that much of the increase in capacity is due to the addition of a second insurer offering single policy limits of $100 million and seven insurers offering limits of $50 million.

Pricing

In a word, pricing remains extremely competitive, with overall prices reported by some insurers dropping 10-20% per year over the past two years. Reasons include the following:

- Continued soft global insurance market
- Increased capacity
- Relative increase in supply versus demand

Some insurers expect prices to begin to flatten out beginning in 1999, but perhaps with slight increases for some insureds. If prices do rise, insureds with operations in high/difficult litigation states such as California, Texas, Michigan and others will likely be impacted most. Some insurers may refuse to write in these states. Insurers also are likely to focus more attention on public entities, professional entities, the entertainment industries, and others with historically poor loss ratios and to increase rates accordingly. As more data that is historic is collected and gathered, insurers will be better equipped to actuarially underwrite the EPL exposure based on geographic location and industry.

While the outlook may be grim for some insureds, even those in high-risk industries or geographic locations may still realize price decreases or at least stability. The essential factor will be how well these insureds manage the employment exposure using proven risk management techniques.

Coverage

Between the time of our first market survey (published in 1997) and now, many older EPL insurance policy forms have been replaced with new versions. Other policies that have not been replaced are being modified by endorsement to eliminate or limit the scope of certain exclusions.[7] In both instances, most current policy forms provide broader coverage than they did just a year ago. Most notable in new policy forms is the lack of exclusions. Downsizing, class action, punitive damage, breach of contract and other exclusions are seen far less often today.

Changes in the scope of coverage are not only limited to a reduction in the number and breadth of exclusion. Coverage is now being specifically granted for exposures such as third-party liability and punitive damages.

While there has been an increase in the availability of coverage for employment practices liability vis-à-vis the addition of such coverage to D&O, umbrella, general liability and other policies, the market for stand-alone products is reported to be strong.

Conclusion

After many years of limited interest, EPL insurance appears poised for acceptance by a growing number of employers as a viable and necessary business insurance policy. While prices have been in free-fall for the past two years, many insurers predict stability at least for the short term as markets seek a reasonable balance with the status quo of broad coverage.

Many sources we spoke with acknowledged that any major changes in pricing and coverage would likely reflect greater reliance on historical loss and other actuarial data as insurers become better able to determine the adequacy of their underwriting and pricing.

---

[7] See Appendix L for an exhibit showing the percentage of policy forms containing various exclusions.

14 ISO's Employment-Related Practices Liability Policy

ISO publicly stated that the new Employment Related Practices Liability (ERPL) form[1] is designed to provide a benchmark for the insurance industry and to secure economies of scale that will benefit insurers and their customers.[2]

For many insurers eager to compete in the EPL insurance market, a major obstacle has been how to design and price a policy when the full extent of the risk is difficult to ascertain.

This limitation meant that until recently, only the largest or most adventurous insurers have written EPL insurance coverage. The trick has been to offer a product that is broad enough to cover the kinds of exposures that organizations are concerned about and be competitive from a price standpoint, yet still allow the insurer to make a profit.

By using its vast technical and statistical resources, ISO seeks to offer insurers a standardized insurance policy including advisory projections of average future claim payments and loss-adjustment expenses. Many insurers not willing or able to design coverage and develop loss costs on their own are now able to compete in the burgeoning EPL insurance market by taking advantage of ISO's services.

The new ISO-ERPL program provides coverage that is triggered by a claim first made during the policy period. The ERPL form is designed to be written as a stand-alone policy or made part of ISO's Commercial Package Policy. The Employment Related Practices Liability Policy provides base limits of $100,000 with options to increase the limits to $10,000,000. Below is a review of the most important coverage elements of the new ISO form.

---

[1] See specimen policy form in Appendix B.
[2] *The ISO Solution.* Volume 7, Issue 3, Fall 1997.

Who Is Insured

Under the ISO-ERPL, the following may be insured under the policy when so designated in the declarations:

- A limited liability company, including its members and managers

- A partnership or joint venture, including partners and members

- Organizations other than a partnership, joint venture or limited liability company including executive officers, when such positions are created by charter, by-law or other governing documents, and directors

In addition, employees who hold managerial or supervisory positions and those leased or temporarily employed are insured. Keep in mind that non-supervisory or non-managerial employees are not automatically insured, and no person or organization is an insured with respect to any current or past partnership or joint venture not shown as the named insured in the declarations.

Endorsements are available to extend coverage to all employees (EP 01 02 04 98), designated persons or organizations (EP 20 01 04 98) and newly acquired organizations (EP 01 01 04 98).

Insuring Agreement

The insuring agreement promises to pay those sums the insured becomes legally obligated to pay because of damages resulting from an injury to which the policy applies. Although the word *damages* is not defined, there is wording within the insuring agreement stating that there is no obligation to pay civil or criminal fines nor to provide services or perform acts not specifically described in the policy. Because the policy also contains a broad Americans With Disabilities Act exclusion, equitable relief[3] as respects that Act would not be covered. *Injury* is defined as an injury to a person arising out of:

- Refusal to employ, termination, failure to promote, negative evaluation, reassignment, discipline, defamation or humiliation when based on discrimination directed at that person

- Coercing that person to commit an unlawful act within the scope of employment

---

[3] **Equitable relief**—Relief sought in a court with equity powers as, for example, in the case of one seeking an injunction or specific performance instead of money damages. (*Black's Law Dictionary*, 6th Edition, 1991.)

- Work-related sexual harassment

- Other work-related verbal, physical, mental or emotional abuse based on any protected class or characteristic established by any federal, state law or local statutes, rules or regulations.

The covered items contained in the definition of *injury* are used in place of the terms *wrongful termination, discrimination, sexual harassment* and *wrongful employment torts* frequently used in other EPL insurance policies. Keep in mind, though, that such terms have no standardized meaning and it is necessary to carefully review how such terms are defined in order to determine the actual scope of coverage.

It also should be noted that the coverage grant under the ISO policy for refusal to employ, termination, failure to promote, negative evaluation, reassignment, discipline, defamation and humiliation applies only when such claims are based on discrimination. This requirement severely limits coverage as wrongful termination claims can be based upon a wide variety of common law and statutory causes of action. These can include allegations of breach of implied contract, breach of the covenant of good faith and fair dealing, violation of whistle blowing statutes, defamation, infliction of emotional distress, fraud, misrepresentations or invasion of privacy or constructive discharge, none of which may require a showing of discrimination.

Note, too, that the coverage grant extends to other work-related verbal, physical, mental or emotional abuse based on any protected class or characteristic. This grant is an important extension; however, employees may bring a host of alleged employment-related torts not specifically identified in the insuring agreement. When torts such as negligent hiring, promotion, retention, invasion of privacy or others are not specifically mentioned in the policy, it may be unclear how such claims will be treated.

Defense

The policy promises to defend the insured against any suit seeking damages because of those injuries described by the insuring agreement. This promise to defend means that the insurer normally has the right to choose counsel and control defense procedure and strategy. Defense expenses[4] are included within the limit of liability. *Suit* means a civil proceeding in which damages from a covered injury are alleged. Suit can include, but is not limited to, certain arbitration proceedings, alternate-dispute-resolution proceedings and any administrative proceeding or hearing.

---

[4] Includes reasonable expenses incurred by the insured at the request of underwriters, including up to $250.00 per day actual loss of earnings for time off of work.

The insurer may also settle claims, subject to the insured's consent to do so. Failure of the insured to consent to a settlement limits the insurer's liability to an amount no greater than the proposed settlement.

There is no duty to defend the insured against any suit seeking damages because of an injury not covered by the policy. Policy conditions also stipulate that if the insured is permitted by the insurer or by court order to retain separate defense counsel, then an allocation between covered and non-covered defense expenses *may* be made.

Exclusions

The ISO-ERPL policy form contains 10 exclusions. A few of the exclusions (ADA, contractual liability and workers' compensation and similar laws) appear to be similar or identical to those found in many other EPL insurance policies, while others warrant comment.

Criminal, Fraudulent Or Malicious Acts

The ISO criminal acts exclusion reads as follows:

> This insurance does not apply to:
>
> 1 An Insured's liability arising out of criminal, fraudulent or malicious acts or omissions by that Insured, or arising out of that insured's knowing acquiescence or failure to act, or instruction, direction, or approval given to another concerning such acts or omissions.
>
> Insurance Services Office, Inc.
Employment-Related Practices Liability
EP 00 01 04 98

The exclusion appears only to exclude coverage for the liability of that individual insured committing fraudulent or criminal acts or liability of any other insured who fails to act, such as in the instance of a supervisor being aware of wrongful conduct but failing to stop it. It should be noted, however, that the exclusion might be the basis for excluding punitive damages; as such, damages are often only awarded when the insured's conduct is found to be malicious, fraudulent or willful.

The exclusion does not affect the insurer's duty to defend prior to determining through the appropriate legal process that the insured is responsible for such fraudulent, criminal or malicious acts.

Violation Of Laws Applicable To Employers

The ISO violation of laws exclusion reads as follows:

> A violation of your responsibilities or duties required by any other federal, state or local statutes, rules or regulations, and any rules or regulations promulgated therefor or amendments thereto, except for the following: Title VII of the Civil Rights Act of 1964 and amendments thereto, the Age Discrimination in Employment Act, the Equal Pay Act, the Pregnancy Discrimination Act of 1978, the Immigration Reform Control Act of 1986 and the Family and Medical Leave Act of 1993 or any other similar state or local statutes, rules or regulations to the extent that they prescribe responsibilities or duties concerning the same acts or omissions.
>
> Insurance Services Office, Inc.
Employment-Related Practices Liability
EP 00 01 04 98

The problem with listing what is excepted from an exclusion is that the list may not completely address all the laws for which the insured may be found liable. Furthermore, such approach may not contemplate changes in the law or entirely new laws coming into effect. These concerns are partially assuaged by the inclusion of a qualifying statement that makes an exception for "any other similar state or local statutes, rules or regulations to the extent that they prescribe responsibilities or duties concerning the same acts or omissions." Although the qualifying statement lessens the impact of the exclusion, the statement may be open to differing interpretations. Narrowly construed, it might broaden the exclusion to the detriment of the insured, as respects laws not specifically listed, new laws, or changes to existing laws.

Strikes And Lockouts

The ISO strikes and lockouts exclusion reads as follows:

> "Injury" to any striking or locked-out "employee", or to an "employee" who has been temporarily or permanently replaced due to any labor dispute.
>
> Insurance Services Office, Inc.
Employment-Related Practices Liability
EP 00 01 04 98

While many EPL insurance policies contain a strike and lockout exclusion, the ISO exclusion encompasses claims based upon injury not only to striking or locked-out employees, but also to employees who have been temporarily or permanently replaced due to any labor dispute. The phrase *any labor dispute* could conceivably encompasses any kind of dispute in which an employee was fired and replaced. Such an interpretation could severely limit coverage. While such a broad interpretation may not be intended by ISO, the current wording is nonetheless ambiguous. Insureds should seek clarification as to the intent of this exclusion, preferably in writing, from the issuing insurer.

Sexual Harassment

The ISO sexual harassment exclusion reads as follows:

> Liability of that insured who commits a "sexual harassment" offense.
>
> This exclusion does not affect our duty to defend that insured prior to determining, through the appropriate legal processes, that that insured has committed a "sexual harassment" offense, other than an assault or battery.
>
> Insurance Services Office, Inc.
Employment-Related Practices Liability
EP 00 01 04 98

This exclusion specifically precludes coverage for liability of that insured committing sexual harassment and does not appear intended to exclude any liability that the organization may have because of sexual harassment. The exclusion presumably also applies to instances where sexual harassment exists simply out of ignorance by that insured committing the sexual harassment offense. The exclusion goes on to state that the insured has a duty to defend that insured "prior to determining, through the appropriate legal processes, that the insured has committed a sexual harassment offense other than assault and battery."

Employment Termination Or Relocation Due To Business Decisions

The ISO employment termination exclusion reads as follows:

> "Injury" arising out of termination of employment, job relocation or reassignment, if the action is taken because:
>
> a. You have filed for bankruptcy protection, or you are placed in receivership or liquidation;
>
> b. You have merged with or been acquired by another business entity;
>
> c. You have closed an operation or a business location; or
>
> d. Your business location is partly closed or the size of an operation must be reduced because of fire or other disasters beyond your control.
>
> Insurance Services Office, Inc.
Employment-Related Practices Liability
EP 00 01 04 98

Keep in mind that not all EPL insurance policies exclude claims based on downsizing or reductions in force, and even those EPL insurance policies that do exclude such claims do so only if such reductions in force exceed a certain percentage of the workforce within a specified period of time. The ISO exclusion applies to any claims arising out of the above actions, regardless of the number of persons affected or time period involved.

Intentional Injury

The ISO intentional injury exclusion reads as follows:

> Liability of that insured who commits an act of intentional "discrimination" or coercion.
>
> This exclusion does not affect our duty to defend that insured prior to determining, through the appropriate legal processes, whether than insured committed such act.
>
> Insurance Services Office, Inc.
Employment-Related Practices Liability
EP 00 01 04 98

Liability of that insured who commits an act of intentional discrimination is excluded. In addition, intentional coercion is also excluded, thereby limiting the coverage for coercion found in the definition of injury. The insured has a duty to defend the insured prior to determining whether that insured committed such acts.

Retaliatory Actions

The ISO retaliatory actions exclusion reads as follows:

> Liability arising out of an insured's retaliatory action against a person because the person has:
>
> a. Declined to perform an illegal or unethical act;
>
> b. Filed a complaint with a governmental authority or a "suit" against you or any other insured in which damages are claimed;
>
> c. Testified against you or any other insured at a legal proceeding; or
>
> d. Notified a proper authority of any aspect of your business operation which is illegal.
>
> Insurance Services Office, Inc.
Employment-Related Practices Liability
EP 00 01 04 98

This exclusion eliminates coverage for some of the most serious charges that an employee can level against his or her employer. Given the emotional nature of claims of retaliatory discharge or of discharge in violation of public policy, these claims also frequently result in substantial jury verdicts and/or settlements.

Keep in mind, however, that the definition of *injury* as used in the insuring agreement provides coverage for "coercing that person to commit an unlawful act or omission within that person's scope of employment" providing some limited coverage not affected by this exclusion.

It should also be noted that as respects the reference to unethical acts, the employee, employer and underwriter might all have different notions of what represents unethical behavior.

Endorsements

In addition to the coverage features outlined above, a number of optional endorsements will make it possible to add the following:

- Extended three-year claim reporting period

- Coverage extension to all employees

- 90-day automatic acquisition clause

- Coverage for persons or organizations who have financial control over the insured's employment-related practices

Conclusion

Many current non-ISO forms offer coverage features that go well beyond those available under the new ISO form and endorsements we reviewed. Nevertheless, the ISO-ERPL policy provides many important coverage features for those insureds not requiring or able to purchase state-of-the-art coverage.

ISO's position has been and continues to be that the policy wording speaks for itself. But because we found some of the language to be ambiguous, it is recommended that those ambiguities be clarified with the issuing insurer, preferably in writing. The unfortunate reality for many small or medium-sized insureds, however, is that such requests are often ignored.

While ISO's venture into this new line of coverage may benefit insureds by allowing a greater variety of insurers to compete for both existing and new EPL business, we expect that most insurers currently offering EPL insurance will continue to do so using non-ISO policy forms.

PART IV

Policy Comparison Worksheets

15 Policy Comparison Worksheets

This section of *The EPL Book* contains completed worksheets that compare some of the coverages provided by many currently available EPL insurance policies. These EPL insurance policy comparison worksheets are designed to provide a quick, at-a-glance evaluation of key policy features. The information provided is based on a review of the various policy forms and survey information received from insurers or their representatives. Each worksheet contains the policy form number, edition date and the name of the person or organization to contact for more information regarding the coverage provided by that insurer.

The worksheet entries are grouped to generally correspond to the discussion contained in Part 3, "Understanding Employment Practices Liability Insurance." However, some worksheet entries may not be specifically discussed in the text. Also, because of the wide variation in policy forms, not every coverage element of every form is included on the comparison worksheets. Unusual or infrequently used terms, definitions, conditions and exclusions may not be identified by the worksheets.

Each worksheet uses coded symbols to indicate whether a policy form contains a particular provision. The key to these symbols is located on the first page of each comparison worksheet. A "●" symbol is used to indicate that the policy substantially contains the coverage feature. A dash (—) indicates the policy does not contain or directly address that particular coverage feature. Other symbols are used to indicate an inability to determine policy wording as respects the coverage feature or to indicate that the feature only applies in certain situations or circumstances.

Each comparison worksheet contains more than 200 line entries relating to the application, coverage format, definitions, exclusions, conditions, extended reporting periods and other policy features and provisions. However, insurers sometimes use more than one form or modify their policy forms by attaching mandatory or optional endorsements that restrict or broaden coverage. Because the underwriter's use of policy forms and endorsements varies in response to the specific risk characteristics of the insured, our comparison is limited to the basic policy form and any mandatory endorsements provided to us by the insurer.

The information contained in this chapter is intended to be educational and to illustrate the many variations in EPL insurance policy forms. The worksheets are intended to help the reader conduct his or her own evaluation of policy coverage. They are not our coverage recommendations, nor do we endorse the use of any particular insurer or policy form.

Every effort has been made to include information felt to be pertinent to most insureds. But because the exposures and needs of insureds varies, readers are reminded that no reference work is a substitute for a thorough and independent review of the application, basic policy form and mandatory or optional endorsements. ***Always read the policy***.

Specimen Policy Comparison Worksheet

For readers wishing to conduct their own analysis, we have included a blank policy comparison worksheet to aid you in completing your own review. For a less detailed review, see our Quick Checklist Of Desirable Policy Features located in Appendix D.

Policy Forms

A specimen policy form is included in Appendix A as an example of the content and structure of EPL insurance coverage. Readers are cautioned that there is a wide variety of policy forms currently available and these forms are subject to frequent revision without prior notice. The most current information regarding policy forms and endorsements is best obtained directly from the insurers. We have provided an index of insurers currently writing EPL in Appendix C. This index includes contact information that was current as of the edition date of this publication. For more information or inquiries or comments regarding policy form information you may fax your request or comment to *The EPL Book* Editor at 949/955-1929.

Can't Find What You Need?

While we attempted to base the information contained in the worksheets on the latest versions of the various EPL insurance policies, the forms are constantly being revised and updated. If you do not find a summary comparison worksheet in the latest edition of *The EPL Book* that you need, we can help. Simply complete an EPL Policy Comparison Worksheet Request Form (Appendix N) and send it to us. One of our technical editors will complete a review of the policy form using our standard summary comparison worksheets and fax it back to you.

Internet Services

For the latest information on EPL liability and insurance, including Policy Comparison Worksheet forms and reprint request forms, visit our *Policy Express—EPL Policy Archive* area located on the world wide web at www.griffincom.com.[1]

---

[1] Available to paid subscribers beginning first quarter 1999. Password and user ID required.

Index To Policy Comparison Worksheets

Insurer	Policy Form Number [Date]	Page
Sample Template	—	271
Admiral Insurance Company	EPL 4000 [10/97]	275
Agricultural Excess & Surplus Insurance Company (AESIC)	D 5717-19 [6/93]	279
American Equity Insurance Company	11197 [11/97]	283
American International Specialty Lines Insurance Company	64198 (12/95) [12/95]	287
Associated Electric & Gas Insurance Services, Limited (AEGIS)	8262 (1/98) [1/98]	291
Chubb Group	14-02-0953 [8/96]	295
Chubb Group	14-02-1968 [5-96]	299
Chubb Group	14-02-2009 [5-96]	303
Chubb Group	17-02-1345 [3-97]	307
CNA Reinsurance Company (NAS Insurance Services, Inc.)	C/NA/S [12/97]	311
Colonia (AUSCO)	EPL 6000 (3/95) [3/95]	315
Connecticut Indemnity Company (Professional Risk Facilities, Inc.)	40609-0 [2/94]	319
Connecticut Specialty Insurance Company (Professional Risk Facilities, Inc.)	OL 001-0 [4/98]	323
Employers Reinsurance Corporation	ERC 1491A [1995]	327
Evanston Insurance Company (Shand Morahan)	EIC 3071-1 9/97 [9/97]	331
Executive Risk Specialty Insurance Company	B22130 [1/96]	335
Executive Risk Specialty Insurance Company	B22167 [2/97]	339
Executive Risk Specialty Insurance Company	B22170 [2/97]	343
Executive Risk Specialty Insurance Company	B24775 [8/97]	347
Fireman's Fund Insurance Company	5240-12-94 [12/94]	351
Fireman's Fund Insurance Company	5241-6-96 [6/96]	355
Fireman's Fund Insurance Company	7006-10-96 [10/96]	359
Fireman's Fund Insurance Company	7006-1-98 [1/98]	363
First Specialty Insurance Corporation (Employers Reinsurance Group)	FSIC-1491A [01/96]	367
Genesis Indemnity Insurance Company	GIIC-8001 [06/97]	371
Genesis Insurance Company	Frontline 8000 [6/97]	375
Great American Insurance Companies	D.710-35 [11/85]	379
Great American Insurance Companies	D.9100 [6/97]	383
Gulf Insurance Group (Rockwood Programs, Inc.)	RP 8002g [11/97]	387
Hartford Insurance Companies	HC 00 55 03 96 [3/96]	391
Insurance Services Office (ISO)	EP 00 01 04 98 [04 98]	395
Legion Insurance Companies	ERP-1 [7/98]	399
Lexington Insurance Company	65200 [12/95]	403
Lexington Insurance Company	LEX-CM-EPLIT [9/97]	407
London Market (American Technology Excess & Surplus Insurance Services)	AmTech Form ERP-1 [11/96]	411
London Market (CNA Re/St. Paul Re)	EPL (11/97A Broad) [11/97]	415
London Market (NAS Insurance Services, Inc.)	AIF 835/95 [2/97]	419
London Market (NAS Insurance Services, Inc.)	AIF 1653/95A [2/97]	423
London Market (NAS Insurance Services, Inc.)	AIF 2314 [4/98]	427
London Market (NAS Insurance Services, Inc.)	CBPLI98 [4/98]	431
London Market (U.S. Risk Underwriters, Inc.)	DISC3/98/CO [3/98]	435

Insurer	Policy Form Number [Date]	Page
National Union Fire Insurance Co. (American International Companies)	67548 [4/97]	439
Northland Insurance Companies	S1110-EP [6/97]	443
Pacific Insurance Company, Ltd. (First State Management Group, Inc.)	PL-364 [5/98]	447
Philadelphia Indemnity Insurance Company	PI-DF-1 [9/95]	451
Philadelphia Insurance Companies	PI-ES-1560 [12/96]	455
Reliance Insurance Company of Illinois (Reliance National Risk Specialists)	GL 00 R424 00 0498 [4/98]	459
Reliance Insurance Company of Illinois (Reliance National Risk Specialists)	GL 00 R430 00 0498 [4/98]	463
Reliance National	DO 00 R324 00 0696 [0696]	467
Steadfast Insurance Company	STF-PL-100-B CW [4/97]	471
Steadfast Insurance Company	U-DO-457-A (CW) [4/97]	475
Swett & Crawford (CNA Reinsurance Co., Limited or Lloyd's of London)	EPLX-987 [7/1/98]	479
Travelers Property Casualty (G. J. Sullivan Company)	DHN 1001 [4/98]	483
United Educators Risk Retention Group, Inc.	ELL [February 1997]	487
United States Fidelity & Guaranty Company	FID 600 [11/95]	491
United States Liability Insurance Group	EPLJ [1/98]	495
X.L. Insurance Company, Ltd.	EPLI-005 [7/98]	499
Zurich American Insurance Company	STF-EPL-101-A [3/98]	503
Zurich Insurance Company	U-DO-111-A (CW) [2/97]	507
Zurich Insurance Company	U-DO-457-A (CW) [4/97]	511

Policy Comparison Worksheet

Sample Template

Policy Form No.:
Edition Date:

Contact:

Risks Considered:
Limits Available:
Minimum Retention:

KEY TO SYMBOLS
● = Specifically contains queried provision of feature
○ = Unable to determine
— = Silent

	Comparison Query	Comment	Policy Reference
	1 APPLICATION		
1	ATTACHES TO AND FORMS A PART OF THE POLICY		
2	CONTAINS WARRANTY STATEMENTS		
3	CONTAINS SEVERABILITY PROVISIONS		
	2 POLICY TYPE		
4	UNITARY STAND ALONE POLICY		
	ENDORSEMENT OR PART OF		
5	DIRECTORS AND OFFICERS POLICY		
6	PACKAGE POLICY		
7	UMBRELLA POLICY		
8	ERRORS AND OMISSIONS POLICY		
9	OTHER		
10	CLAIMS-MADE		
11	OCCURRENCE		
	3 WHO IS INSURED		
12	BUSINESS ENTITY		
13	AUTOMATIC COVERAGE FOR SUBSIDIARIES		
14	DIRECTORS & OFFICERS		
15	EMPLOYEES		
16	PART-TIME		
17	SEASONAL		
18	TEMPORARY		
19	SUPERVISORS & MANAGERS		
20	FORMER EMPLOYEES		
21	VOLUNTEERS		
22	INDEPENDENT CONTRACTORS		
23	EXCLUDED		
24	SILENT		
25	SHAREHOLDERS		
	4 LIMIT OF LIABILITY		
26	AGGREGATE		
27	INCLUDES PUNITIVE DAMAGES WHERE NOT UNINSURABLE		
28	DEFENSE COSTS INCLUDED WITHIN LIMIT OF LIABILITY		
29	DEFENSE COSTS PAID IN ADDITION TO LIMIT OF LIABILITY		
	5 DEDUCTIBLE		
30	APPLIES TO EACH INDIVIDUAL CLAIM		
31	APPLIES TO EACH OCCURRENCE OR WRONGFUL PRACTICE		
32	INCLUDES ALL CLAIMS FROM ONE ACT		
33	SUBJECT TO ANNUAL AGGREGATE		
34	CO-PAYMENT APPLIES		
35	LIMIT OF LIABILITY NOT REDUCED		
36	INCLUDES DEFENSE COSTS		
37	REDUCED UNDER SPECIFIED CIRCUMSTANCES (SEE POLICY)		

	Comparison Query	Comment	Policy Reference
	6 WHAT IS A CLAIM		
38	**ORAL COMPLAINT TO INSURED**		
39	**WRITTEN COMPLAINT TO INSURED**		
40	**COMPLAINT MUST CONTAIN A DEMAND FOR DAMAGES**		
41	**COMPLAINT FILED WITH EEOC**		
42	OR SIMILAR STATE AUTHORITY		
43	AGENCY MUST HAVE POWER TO ADJUDICATE		
44	**ADMINISTRATIVE PROCEEDING**		
45	**ARBITRATION PROCEEDING**		
46	**ANY INCIDENT REPORTED TO INSURER**		
47	**SUIT**		
48	**CLAIM DOES NOT INCLUDE ARBITRATION SUBJECT TO**		
49	COLLECTIVE BARGAINING AGREEMENT		
50	EMPLOYEE POLICY OR MANUAL		
51	**CLAIM NOT DEFINED**		
	7 CLAIM REPORTING PROVISIONS TO INSURER		
52	**IMMEDIATELY**		
53	**AS SOON AS POSSIBLE**		
54	**AS SOON AS PRACTICABLE**		
55	**WITHIN POLICY PERIOD**		
56	**WITHIN X DAYS OF EXPIRATION**		
57	**WITHIN X DAYS**		
	8 EXTENDED REPORTING FEATURES		
58	**ELECTION PERIOD (DAYS)**		
59	**ADDITIONAL PREMIUM (% OF ANNUAL PREMIUM)**		
60	**ADDITIONAL REPORTING PERIOD (MONTHS)**		
61	**NO REINSTATEMENT OF LIMITS**		
	9 POTENTIAL CLAIM REPORTING PROVISIONS		
62	**NONE (SEE ALSO "CLAIM" ABOVE)**		
63	**INCIDENTS LIKELY TO RESULT IN A CLAIM**		
	10 DEFENSE PROVISIONS		
64	**AFFIRMATIVE DUTY TO DEFEND**		
65	**NO AFFIRMATIVE DUTY TO DEFEND**		
66	AFFIRMATIVE ADVANCEMENT PROVISIONS		
67	INSURED MUST RETURN ADVANCED AMOUNTS IF NOT COVERED		
68	**INSURED/INSURER CHOOSES COUNSEL**		
69	**INSURED/INSURER APPROVES COUNSEL**		
70	**INSURED/INSURER CONSULTED IN COUNSEL SELECTION**		
	11 SETTLEMENT PROVISIONS		
71	**HAMMER CLAUSE**		
72	**CONSULTATION PROVISION**		
73	**CONSENT PROVISION**		
	12 ALLOCATION OF LOSS PROVISIONS		
74	**STIPULATED PROVISIONS**		
	13 COVERAGES		
75	**DISCRIMINATION**		
76	SPECIFIC ENUMERATED ACTIVITIES		
77	*PLUS BROAD OMNIBUS WORDING*		
78	SPECIFIC ENUMERATED CLASSES		
79	*PLUS BROAD OMNIBUS WORDING*		
80	AGAINST THIRD PARTIES		
81	DISCRIMINATION NOT DEFINED		
82	**SEXUAL HARASSMENT**		
83	HOSTILE ENVIRONMENT		
84	QUID-PRO-QUO		
85	SEXUAL HARASSMENT NOT DEFINED		
86	**WRONGFUL TERMINATION**		
87	BREACH OF IMPLIED CONTRACT		
88	BREACH OF EXPRESS CONTRACT		
89	VIOLATION OF PUBLIC POLICY		
90	VIOLATION OF GOOD FAITH & FAIR DEALING		
91	OBLIGATIONS TO MAKE PAYMENTS		
92	CONSTRUCTIVE DISCHARGE		
93	WRONGFUL TERMINATION NOT DEFINED		
94	**OTHER EMPLOYMENT VIOLATIONS/OFFENSES**		
95	WRONGFUL HIRING		
96	WRONGFUL PROMOTION/DEMOTION		
97	WRONGFUL EVALUATION/DISCIPLINE		

#	Comparison Query	Comment	Policy Reference
98	FAMILY AND MEDICAL LEAVE ACT		
99	DEFAMATION		
100	MISREPRESENTATION		
101	RETALIATION		
102	MENTAL ANGUISH		
103	INVASION OF PRIVACY		
104	HUMILIATION		
105	EMOTIONAL DISTRESS		
106	OTHER PERSONAL INJURY OFFENSES		
107	POLICY SILENT		
	14 EXCLUSIONS		
108	**ADA ACCOMMODATION EXPENSES**		
109	**ASSAULT & BATTERY**		
110	**BACK PAY**		
111	**BODILY INJURY**		
112	BODILY INJURY		
113	DEATH		
114	DISEASE		
115	SICKNESS		
116	**BREACH OF EMPLOYMENT CONTRACT**		
117	EXPRESS CONTRACT		
118	*WRITTEN CONTRACT*		
119	*ORAL CONTRACT*		
120	IMPLIED CONTRACT		
121	**CLASS ACTION LAWSUITS**		
122	**CONSEQUENTIAL LOSS**		
123	APPLIES TO BODILY INJURY		
124	APPLIES TO INSURED EVENT		
125	BROTHER/SISTER		
126	CHILD		
127	DOMESTIC PARTNER		
128	PARENT		
129	SPOUSE		
130	**COST OF ARBITRATION HEARINGS SUBJECT TO**		
131	EMPLOYMENT HANDBOOK		
132	LABOR GRIEVANCE		
133	OTHER EMPLOYMENT POLICY OR PROCEDURE		
134	**COVERAGE ELSEWHERE**		
135	OTHER AVAILABLE INSURANCE		
136	OTHER INDEMNIFICATION		
137	SHARING PROVISION		
138	**FAILURE TO EXERCISE CARE WHEN TERMINATING**		
139	**FINES/PENALTIES**		
140	CIVIL		
141	CRIMINAL		
142	EXEMPLARY DAMAGES		
143	PUNITIVE DAMAGES		
144	MULTIPLIED DAMAGES		
145	**FRONT PAY**		
146	EXCLUSION APPLIES ONLY IF EMPLOYER HAD OPPORTUNITY TO REINSTATE EMPLOYEE BUT DID NOT DO SO		
147	**INTENTIONAL ACTS**		
148	CRIMINAL ACTS		
149	CRIMINAL PROCEEDING		
150	DISHONEST PURPOSE		
151	FRAUDULENT ACTS		
152	FRAUDULENT CLAIMS		
153	INTENTIONAL VIOLATIONS OF LAW		
154	WILLFUL FAILURE TO COMPLY WITH LAW		
155	MALICIOUS PURPOSE		
156	**LIABILITY OF OTHERS**		
157	**LIQUIDATED DAMAGES**		
158	**LOSS ARISING OUT OF CHANGES IN OPERATIONS**		
159	ACQUISITION		
160	CHANGE IN CONTROL		
161	DOWNSIZING OR REDUCTION IN FORCE		
162	*% OF WORKFORCE*		
163	*WITHIN X DAYS*		

	Comparison Query	Comment	Policy Reference
164	FINANCIAL IMPAIRMENT		
165	*BANKRUPTCY*		
166	*INSOLVENCY*		
167	*LIQUIDATION*		
168	*RECEIVERSHIP*		
169	FINANCIAL INABILITY TO PAY		
170	MERGER		
171	PLANT OR FACILITY CLOSING		
172	REORGANIZATION		
173	TEMPORARY SHUTDOWN		
174	**MATTERS DEEMED UNINSURABLE**		
175	**NON-MONETARY RELIEF**		
176	DECLATORY RELIEF		
177	DISGORGEMENT		
178	INJUNCTIVE RELIEF		
179	JOB REINSTATEMENT		
180	NON-MONETARY DAMAGES/RELIEF		
181	OTHER EQUITABLE REMEDIES		
182	**OBLIGATION TO PROVIDE BENEFITS**		
183	COBRA		
184	DISABILITY		
185	ERISA		
186	SOCIAL SECURITY		
187	OTHER RETIREMENT BENEFITS		
188	UNEMPLOYMENT		
189	WORKERS' COMPENSATION		
190	**PERSONAL INJURY OFFENSES**		
191	DEFAMATION		
192	EMOTIONAL DISTRESS/UPSET		
193	HUMILIATION		
194	LIBEL		
195	MENTAL ANGUISH		
196	PERSONAL INJURY		
197	SLANDER		
198	**PRIOR ACTS**		
199	PRIOR ACTS		
200	PRIOR KNOWLEDGE		
201	PRIOR/PENDING LITIGATION		
	PROPERTY DAMAGE		
202	INTANGIBLE PROPERTY		
203	LOSS OF USE		
204	TANGIBLE PROPERTY		
205	**RETALIATORY ACTIONS OF EMPLOYER**		
206	FOR FAILING TO PERFORM ACTS AGAINST PUBLIC POLICY		
207	FOR FILING A COMPLAINT OR BENEFIT CLAIM		
208	**STRIKES/LOCKOUTS**		
209	**VIOLATION OF LAWS**		
210	ANY LAW		
211	FMLA		
212	OSHA		
213	POLLUTION LAWS		
214	RICO		
215	SEC		
216	WARN		

15 CONDITIONS

	Comparison Query	Comment	Policy Reference
218	**ARBITRATION**		
219	MANDATORY		
220	BINDING		
221	CHOICE OF LAW PROVISION		
222	SITUS		
223	**TERRITORY**		
224	LIMITED		
225	WORLDWIDE		
226	**NEWLY FORMED/ACQUIRED ENTITIES**		
227	AUTOMATIC COVERAGE (X DAYS)		
228	NOTIFY INSURER WITHIN X DAYS		

Policy Comparison Worksheet

Admiral Insurance Company

Policy Form No.: EPL 4000
Edition Date: 10/97

Risks Considered: General accounts not subject to state or federal regulation
Limits Available: $5,000,000
Minimum Retention: $5,000

Contact: Derek M. Lucas
Monitor Liability Managers, Inc.
2850 W. Golf Road, Suite 800
Rolling Meadows, IL 60008
847/806-6590
847/806-6282 (fax)
dlucas@monitorgroup.com

KEY TO SYMBOLS
● = Specifically contains queried provision of feature
○ = Unable to determine
— = Silent

#	Comparison Query	Symbol	Comment	Policy Reference
	1 APPLICATION			
1	ATTACHES TO AND FORMS A PART OF THE POLICY	●		VIII.B., page 6
2	CONTAINS WARRANTY STATEMENTS	—		
3	CONTAINS SEVERABILITY PROVISIONS	●	Non-imputation	VIII.B., page 6
	2 POLICY TYPE			
4	UNITARY STAND ALONE POLICY	●		
	ENDORSEMENT OR PART OF	—		
5	DIRECTORS AND OFFICERS POLICY	—		
6	PACKAGE POLICY	—		
7	UMBRELLA POLICY	—		
8	ERRORS AND OMISSIONS POLICY	—		
9	OTHER	—		
10	CLAIMS-MADE	●		
11	OCCURRENCE	—		
	3 WHO IS INSURED			
12	BUSINESS ENTITY	●		III.F., page 2
13	AUTOMATIC COVERAGE FOR SUBSIDIARIES	●		III.F., page 2
14	DIRECTORS & OFFICERS	●		III.E., page 2
15	EMPLOYEES	●		III.E., page 2
16	PART-TIME	●	See also III.D., page 1	III.E., page 2
17	SEASONAL	●	See also III.D., page 1	III.E., page 2
18	TEMPORARY	●	See also III.D., page 1	III.E., page 2
19	SUPERVISORS & MANAGERS	●	As employees	III.E., page 2
20	FORMER EMPLOYEES	●		III.D., page 1
21	VOLUNTEERS	—		
22	INDEPENDENT CONTRACTORS	—		
23	EXCLUDED	●		III.D., page 1
24	SILENT	—		
25	SHAREHOLDERS	—		
	4 LIMIT OF LIABILITY			
26	AGGREGATE	●		V.A., page 4
27	INCLUDES PUNITIVE DAMAGES WHERE NOT UNINSURABLE	●	$1MM limit per claim	III.H. following 7., page 2
28	DEFENSE COSTS INCLUDED WITHIN LIMIT OF LIABILITY	●	See also III.H., page 2	V.B., page 4
29	DEFENSE COSTS PAID IN ADDITION TO LIMIT OF LIABILITY	—		
	5 DEDUCTIBLE			
30	APPLIES TO EACH INDIVIDUAL CLAIM	●		V.D., page 4
31	APPLIES TO EACH OCCURRENCE OR WRONGFUL PRACTICE	—		
32	INCLUDES ALL CLAIMS FROM ONE ACT	●		VII.C., page 5
33	SUBJECT TO ANNUAL AGGREGATE	—		
34	CO-PAYMENT APPLIES	—		
35	LIMIT OF LIABILITY NOT REDUCED	—		
36	INCLUDES DEFENSE COSTS	●	See also III.H., page 2	V.C., page 4
37	REDUCED UNDER SPECIFIED CIRCUMSTANCES (SEE POLICY)	—		

ADMIRAL INSURANCE COMPANY EPL 4000 [10/97]

#	Comparison Query		Comment	Policy Reference
	6 WHAT IS A CLAIM			
38	ORAL COMPLAINT TO INSURED	—		
39	WRITTEN COMPLAINT TO INSURED	●		III.A.1., page 1
40	COMPLAINT MUST CONTAIN A DEMAND FOR DAMAGES	●	Monetary or non-monetary relief	III.A.1., page 1
41	COMPLAINT FILED WITH EEOC	—		
42	OR SIMILAR STATE AUTHORITY	—		
43	AGENCY MUST HAVE POWER TO ADJUDICATE	—		
44	ADMINISTRATIVE PROCEEDING	●		III.A.2., page 1
45	ARBITRATION PROCEEDING	●		III.A.2., page 1
46	ANY INCIDENT REPORTED TO INSURER	—		
47	SUIT	●		III.A.2., page 1
48	CLAIM DOES NOT INCLUDE ARBITRATION SUBJECT TO	●		III.A.2., page 1
49	COLLECTIVE BARGAINING AGREEMENT	●		III.A.2., page 1
50	EMPLOYEE POLICY OR MANUAL	—		
51	CLAIM NOT DEFINED	—		
	7 CLAIM REPORTING PROVISIONS TO INSURER			
52	IMMEDIATELY	—		
53	AS SOON AS POSSIBLE	—		
54	AS SOON AS PRACTICABLE	●		VII.A.1. & 2., page 5
55	WITHIN POLICY PERIOD	—		
56	WITHIN X DAYS OF EXPIRATION	—		
57	WITHIN X DAYS	15/90	Lawsuits/claims	VII.A.1. & 2., page 5
	8 EXTENDED REPORTING FEATURES			
58	ELECTION PERIOD (DAYS)	30		II.A., page 1
59	ADDITIONAL PREMIUM (% OF ANNUAL PREMIUM)	200		II.A., page 1
60	ADDITIONAL REPORTING PERIOD (MONTHS)	36		II.A., page 1
61	NO REINSTATEMENT OF LIMITS	●		V.A., page 4
	9 POTENTIAL CLAIM REPORTING PROVISIONS			
62	NONE (SEE ALSO "CLAIM" ABOVE)	—		
63	INCIDENTS LIKELY TO RESULT IN A CLAIM	●		VII.B., page 5
	10 DEFENSE PROVISIONS			
64	AFFIRMATIVE DUTY TO DEFEND	●		VI.B., page 4
65	NO AFFIRMATIVE DUTY TO DEFEND	—		
66	AFFIRMATIVE ADVANCEMENT PROVISIONS	—		
67	INSURED MUST RETURN ADVANCED AMOUNTS IF NOT COVERED	—		
68	INSURED/INSURER CHOOSES COUNSEL	—		
69	INSURED/INSURER APPROVES COUNSEL	—		
70	INSURED/INSURER CONSULTED IN COUNSEL SELECTION	—		
	11 SETTLEMENT PROVISIONS			
71	HAMMER CLAUSE	●		VI.D., page 5
72	CONSULTATION PROVISION	—		
73	CONSENT PROVISION	●	Two-way	VI.A., page 4 and VI.D., page 5
	12 ALLOCATION OF LOSS PROVISIONS			
74	STIPULATED PROVISIONS	—		
	13 COVERAGES			
75	DISCRIMINATION	●	As wrongful employment act	III.N.1., page 3
76	SPECIFIC ENUMERATED ACTIVITIES	●		III.N.1., page 3
77	*PLUS BROAD OMNIBUS WORDING*	●		III.N.1., page 3
78	SPECIFIC ENUMERATED CLASSES	●		III.N.1., page 3
79	*PLUS BROAD OMNIBUS WORDING*	●		III.N.1., page 3
80	AGAINST THIRD PARTIES	—		
81	DISCRIMINATION NOT DEFINED	—		
82	**SEXUAL HARASSMENT**	●		III.N.2., page 3
83	HOSTILE ENVIRONMENT	●		III.N.2., page 3
84	QUID-PRO-QUO	●		III.N.2., page 3
85	SEXUAL HARASSMENT NOT DEFINED	—		
86	**WRONGFUL TERMINATION**	●		III.N.3., page 3
87	BREACH OF IMPLIED CONTRACT	●		III.N.3., page 3
88	BREACH OF EXPRESS CONTRACT	—		
89	VIOLATION OF PUBLIC POLICY	—		
90	VIOLATION OF GOOD FAITH & FAIR DEALING	—		
91	OBLIGATIONS TO MAKE PAYMENTS	—		
92	CONSTRUCTIVE DISCHARGE	●		III.N.3., page 3
93	WRONGFUL TERMINATION NOT DEFINED	●		III.N.3., page 3
94	**OTHER EMPLOYMENT VIOLATIONS/OFFENSES**	●		III.N.3., page 3
95	WRONGFUL HIRING	●		III.N.3., page 3
96	WRONGFUL PROMOTION/DEMOTION	●		III.N.3., page 3
97	WRONGFUL EVALUATION/DISCIPLINE	●	Wrongful evaluation	III.N.3., page 3

ADMIRAL INSURANCE COMPANY EPL 4000 [10/97]

#	Comparison Query	Comment		Policy Reference
98	FAMILY AND MEDICAL LEAVE ACT	—		
99	DEFAMATION	●		III.N.3., page 3
100	MISREPRESENTATION	●		III.N.3., page 3
101	RETALIATION	●		III.N.3., page 3
102	MENTAL ANGUISH	—		
103	INVASION OF PRIVACY	●		III.N.3., page 3
104	HUMILIATION	●		III.N.3., page 3
105	EMOTIONAL DISTRESS	●		III.N.3., page 3
106	OTHER PERSONAL INJURY OFFENSES	—		
107	POLICY SILENT	—		
	14 EXCLUSIONS			
108	**ADA ACCOMMODATION EXPENSES**	●		III.H.3., page 2
109	**ASSAULT & BATTERY**	●		IV.A., page 3
110	**BACK PAY**	—		
111	**BODILY INJURY**	●		IV.A., page 3
112	BODILY INJURY	●		IV.A., page 3
113	DEATH	●		IV.A., page 3
114	DISEASE	●		IV.A., page 3
115	SICKNESS	●		IV.A., page 3
116	**BREACH OF EMPLOYMENT CONTRACT**	—		
117	EXPRESS CONTRACT	—		
118	*WRITTEN CONTRACT*	—		
119	*ORAL CONTRACT*	—		
120	IMPLIED CONTRACT	—		
121	**CLASS ACTION LAWSUITS**	—		
122	**CONSEQUENTIAL LOSS**	—		
123	APPLIES TO BODILY INJURY	—		
124	APPLIES TO INSURED EVENT	—		
125	BROTHER/SISTER	—		
126	CHILD	—		
127	DOMESTIC PARTNER	—		
128	PARENT	—		
129	SPOUSE	—		
130	**COST OF ARBITRATION HEARINGS SUBJECT TO**	—		
131	EMPLOYMENT HANDBOOK	—		
132	LABOR GRIEVANCE	—		
133	OTHER EMPLOYMENT POLICY OR PROCEDURE	—		
134	**COVERAGE ELSEWHERE**	●		VI.E., page 3
135	OTHER AVAILABLE INSURANCE	●		VI.E., page 3
136	OTHER INDEMNIFICATION	—		
137	SHARING PROVISION	—		
138	**FAILURE TO EXERCISE CARE WHEN TERMINATING**	—		
139	**FINES/PENALTIES**	●		III.H.1., page 2
140	CIVIL	●		III.H.1., page 2
141	CRIMINAL	●		III.H.1., page 2
142	EXEMPLARY DAMAGES	●	> $1MM per claim	III.H., following 7., page 2
143	PUNITIVE DAMAGES	●	> $1MM per claim	III.H., following 7., page 2
144	MULTIPLIED DAMAGES	●	> $1MM per claim	III.H., following 7., page 2
145	**FRONT PAY**	—		
146	EXCLUSION APPLIES ONLY IF EMPLOYER HAD OPPORTUNITY TO REINSTATE EMPLOYEE BUT DID NOT DO SO	—		
147	**INTENTIONAL ACTS**	—		
148	CRIMINAL ACTS	—		
149	CRIMINAL PROCEEDING	—		
150	DISHONEST PURPOSE	—		
151	FRAUDULENT ACTS	—		
152	FRAUDULENT CLAIMS	—		
153	INTENTIONAL VIOLATIONS OF LAW	—		
154	WILLFUL FAILURE TO COMPLY WITH LAW	—		
155	MALICIOUS PURPOSE	—		
156	**LIABILITY OF OTHERS**	●		IV.D., page 3
157	**LIQUIDATED DAMAGES**	—		
158	**LOSS ARISING OUT OF CHANGES IN OPERATIONS**	—		
159	ACQUISITION	—		
160	CHANGE IN CONTROL	—		
161	DOWNSIZING OR REDUCTION IN FORCE	—		
162	*% OF WORKFORCE*	—		
163	*WITHIN X DAYS*	—		

ADMIRAL INSURANCE COMPANY EPL 4000 [10/97]

#	Comparison Query		Comment	Policy Reference
164	**FINANCIAL IMPAIRMENT**	—		
165	*BANKRUPTCY*	—		
166	*INSOLVENCY*	—		
167	*LIQUIDATION*	—		
168	*RECEIVERSHIP*	—		
169	FINANCIAL INABILITY TO PAY	—		
170	MERGER	—		
171	PLANT OR FACILITY CLOSING	—		
172	REORGANIZATION	—		
173	TEMPORARY SHUTDOWN	—		
174	**MATTERS DEEMED UNINSURABLE**	●		III.H.7., page 2
175	**NON-MONETARY RELIEF**	—		
176	DECLATORY RELIEF	—		
177	DISGORGEMENT	—		
178	INJUNCTIVE RELIEF	—		
179	JOB REINSTATEMENT	—		
180	NON-MONETARY DAMAGES/RELIEF	—		
181	OTHER EQUITABLE REMEDIES	—		
182	**OBLIGATION TO PROVIDE BENEFITS**	—		
183	COBRA	●	Retaliation exception	IV.J., page 4
184	DISABILITY	●	Retaliation exception	III.H.2., page 2 and IV.K., page 4
185	ERISA	●		IV.B., page 3
186	SOCIAL SECURITY	●	Retaliation exception	IV.K., page 4
187	OTHER RETIREMENT BENEFITS	—		
188	UNEMPLOYMENT	●	Retaliation exception	IV.K., page 4
189	WORKERS' COMPENSATION	●	Retaliation exception	IV.K., page 4
190	**PERSONAL INJURY OFFENSES**	—		
191	DEFAMATION	●	Unless a wrongful employment act	IV.A., page 3
192	EMOTIONAL DISTRESS/UPSET	●	Unless a wrongful employment act	IV.A., page 3
193	HUMILIATION	●	Unless a wrongful employment act	IV.A., page 3
194	LIBEL	—		
195	MENTAL ANGUISH	●	Unless a wrongful employment act	IV.A., page 3
196	PERSONAL INJURY	—		
197	SLANDER	—		
198	**PRIOR ACTS**	—		
199	PRIOR ACTS	—		
200	PRIOR KNOWLEDGE	—		
201	PRIOR/PENDING LITIGATION	●	Prior to continuity date	IV.G.1., page 4
202	**PROPERTY DAMAGE**	—		
203	INTANGIBLE PROPERTY	—		
204	LOSS OF USE	—		
205	TANGIBLE PROPERTY	—		
206	**RETALIATORY ACTIONS OF EMPLOYER**	—		
207	FOR FAILING TO PERFORM ACTS AGAINST PUBLIC POLICY	—		
208	FOR FILING A COMPLAINT OR BENEFIT CLAIM	—		
209	**STRIKES/LOCKOUTS**	●		IV.I., page 4
210	**VIOLATION OF LAWS**	—		
211	ANY LAW	—		
212	FMLA	—		
213	OSHA	●	Retaliation exception	IV.J., page 4
214	POLLUTION LAWS	—		
215	RICO	—		
216	SEC	—		
217	WARN	●	Retaliation exception	IV.J., page 4

15 CONDITIONS

#			Comment	Policy Reference
218	**ARBITRATION**	—		
219	MANDATORY	—		
220	BINDING	—		
221	CHOICE OF LAW PROVISION	—		
222	SITUS	—		
223	**TERRITORY**	●		VIII.I., page 7
224	LIMITED	—		
225	WORLDWIDE	●		VIII.I., page 7
226	**NEWLY FORMED/ACQUIRED ENTITIES**	●		III.M.3., page 3
227	AUTOMATIC COVERAGE (X DAYS)	90	> 25% company assets involved	III.M.3., page 3
228	NOTIFY INSURER WITHIN X DAYS	90	> 25% company assets involved	III.M.3., page 3

ADMIRAL INSURANCE COMPANY EPL 4000 [10/97]

Policy Comparison Worksheet

Agricultural Excess & Surplus Insurance Company
(AESIC)

Policy Form No.: D 5717-19
Edition Date: 6/93

Risks Considered: Hard-to-place companies
Limits Available: $5,000,000
Minimum Retention: $35,000

Contact: Tom Siebers
1515 Woodfield Road, Suite 850
Schaumberg, IL 60130
847/330-6750
847/330-6890 (fax)
gaiceld@megsinet.net

KEY TO SYMBOLS
● = Specifically contains queried provision of feature
○ = Unable to determine
— = Silent

#	Comparison Query		Comment	Policy Reference
	1 APPLICATION			
1	ATTACHES TO AND FORMS A PART OF THE POLICY	●		Policy, Preamble, page 1
2	CONTAINS WARRANTY STATEMENTS	—		
3	CONTAINS SEVERABILITY PROVISIONS	●		
	2 POLICY TYPE			
4	UNITARY STAND ALONE POLICY	—		
	ENDORSEMENT OR PART OF	—		
5	DIRECTORS AND OFFICERS POLICY	●	Policy form D.5100 (2/90)	
6	PACKAGE POLICY	—		
7	UMBRELLA POLICY	—		
8	ERRORS AND OMISSIONS POLICY	—		
9	OTHER	—		
10	CLAIMS-MADE	●		
11	OCCURRENCE	—		
	3 WHO IS INSURED			
12	BUSINESS ENTITY	●	See also Policy I.B., page 2	Policy III.A., page 2
13	AUTOMATIC COVERAGE FOR SUBSIDIARIES	●		Policy III.A., page 2
14	DIRECTORS & OFFICERS	●		Policy I.A., page 2
15	EMPLOYEES	●	If entitled to indemnification	Endorsement, (1)., page 1
16	PART-TIME	—		
17	SEASONAL	—		
18	TEMPORARY	—		
19	SUPERVISORS & MANAGERS	—		
20	FORMER EMPLOYEES	—		
21	VOLUNTEERS	—		
22	INDEPENDENT CONTRACTORS	—		
23	EXCLUDED	—		
24	SILENT	●		
25	SHAREHOLDERS	—		
	4 LIMIT OF LIABILITY			
26	AGGREGATE	●		Policy V.E., page 3
27	INCLUDES PUNITIVE DAMAGES WHERE NOT UNINSURABLE	—		
28	DEFENSE COSTS INCLUDED WITHIN LIMIT OF LIABILITY	●	See also Policy V.D., page 3	Policy III.E., page 2
29	DEFENSE COSTS PAID IN ADDITION TO LIMIT OF LIABILITY	—		
	5 DEDUCTIBLE			
30	APPLIES TO EACH INDIVIDUAL CLAIM	●		Policy V.B., page 3
31	APPLIES TO EACH OCCURRENCE OR WRONGFUL PRACTICE	—		
32	INCLUDES ALL CLAIMS FROM ONE ACT	●		Policy V.B., page 3
33	SUBJECT TO ANNUAL AGGREGATE	—		
34	CO-PAYMENT APPLIES	—		
35	LIMIT OF LIABILITY NOT REDUCED	—		
36	INCLUDES DEFENSE COSTS	●		Policy V.E., page 3
37	REDUCED UNDER SPECIFIED CIRCUMSTANCES (SEE POLICY)	—		

AGRICULTURAL EXCESS & SURPLUS INSURANCE COMPANY (AESIC) D 5717-19 [6/93]

#	Comparison Query	Comment	Policy Reference
6	**WHAT IS A CLAIM**		
38	ORAL COMPLAINT TO INSURED	—	
39	WRITTEN COMPLAINT TO INSURED	—	
40	COMPLAINT MUST CONTAIN A DEMAND FOR DAMAGES	—	
41	COMPLAINT FILED WITH EEOC	●	Endorsement (2)(2), page 1
42	OR SIMILAR STATE AUTHORITY	●	Endorsement (2)(2), page 1
43	AGENCY MUST HAVE POWER TO ADJUDICATE	—	
44	ADMINISTRATIVE PROCEEDING	●	Endorsement (2)(1), page 1
45	ARBITRATION PROCEEDING	●	Endorsement (2)(1), page 1
46	ANY INCIDENT REPORTED TO INSURER	—	
47	SUIT	●	Endorsement (2)(1), page 1
48	CLAIM DOES NOT INCLUDE ARBITRATION SUBJECT TO	—	
49	COLLECTIVE BARGAINING AGREEMENT	—	
50	EMPLOYEE POLICY OR MANUAL	—	
51	CLAIM NOT DEFINED	—	
7	**CLAIM REPORTING PROVISIONS TO INSURER**		
52	IMMEDIATELY	—	
53	AS SOON AS POSSIBLE	—	
54	AS SOON AS PRACTICABLE	●	Policy VII.A., page 4
55	WITHIN POLICY PERIOD	—	
56	WITHIN X DAYS OF EXPIRATION	—	
57	WITHIN X DAYS	90	Policy VII.A., page 4
8	**EXTENDED REPORTING FEATURES**		
58	ELECTION PERIOD (DAYS)	10	Policy II.C., page 2
59	ADDITIONAL PREMIUM (% OF ANNUAL PREMIUM)	50%	Policy II.A., page 2
60	ADDITIONAL REPORTING PERIOD (MONTHS)	3	Policy II.A., page 2
61	NO REINSTATEMENT OF LIMITS	●	Policy II.D., page 2
9	**POTENTIAL CLAIM REPORTING PROVISIONS**		
62	NONE (SEE ALSO "CLAIM" ABOVE)	—	
63	INCIDENTS LIKELY TO RESULT IN A CLAIM	●	Policy VII.B., page 4
10	**DEFENSE PROVISIONS**		
64	AFFIRMATIVE DUTY TO DEFEND	—	
65	NO AFFIRMATIVE DUTY TO DEFEND	●	Policy VI.B., page 2
66	AFFIRMATIVE ADVANCEMENT PROVISIONS	● Conditional	Policy VI.D., page 2
67	INSURED MUST RETURN ADVANCED AMOUNTS IF NOT COVERED	●	Policy VI.D., page 2
68	INSURED/INSURER CHOOSES COUNSEL	●	Policy VI.B., page 2
69	INSURED/INSURER APPROVES COUNSEL	● Mutually agreed	Policy VI.B., page 2
70	INSURED/INSURER CONSULTED IN COUNSEL SELECTION	● Insurer	Policy VI.B., page 2
11	**SETTLEMENT PROVISIONS**		
71	HAMMER CLAUSE	—	
72	CONSULTATION PROVISION	—	
73	CONSENT PROVISION	● Insurer must consent	Policy VI.A., page 3
12	**ALLOCATION OF LOSS PROVISIONS**		
74	STIPULATED PROVISIONS	—	
13	**COVERAGES**		
75	DISCRIMINATION	●	Endorsement, page 1
76	SPECIFIC ENUMERATED ACTIVITIES	—	
77	PLUS BROAD OMNIBUS WORDING	—	
78	SPECIFIC ENUMERATED CLASSES	—	
79	PLUS BROAD OMNIBUS WORDING	—	
80	AGAINST THIRD PARTIES	—	
81	DISCRIMINATION NOT DEFINED	●	
82	SEXUAL HARASSMENT	●	Endorsement, page 1
83	HOSTILE ENVIRONMENT	●	Endorsement, page 1
84	QUID-PRO-QUO	●	Endorsement, page 1
85	SEXUAL HARASSMENT NOT DEFINED	●	
86	WRONGFUL TERMINATION	●	Endorsement, page 1
87	BREACH OF IMPLIED CONTRACT	—	
88	BREACH OF EXPRESS CONTRACT	—	
89	VIOLATION OF PUBLIC POLICY	—	
90	VIOLATION OF GOOD FAITH & FAIR DEALING	—	
91	OBLIGATIONS TO MAKE PAYMENTS	—	
92	CONSTRUCTIVE DISCHARGE	●	Endorsement, page 1
93	WRONGFUL TERMINATION NOT DEFINED	●	
94	OTHER EMPLOYMENT VIOLATIONS/OFFENSES	●	Endorsement, page 1
95	WRONGFUL HIRING	●	Endorsement, page 1
96	WRONGFUL PROMOTION/DEMOTION	●	Endorsement, page 1
97	WRONGFUL EVALUATION/DISCIPLINE	●	Endorsement, page 1

AGRICULTURAL EXCESS & SURPLUS INSURANCE COMPANY (AESIC) D 5717-19 [6/93]

#	Comparison Query	Comment	Policy Reference
98	FAMILY AND MEDICAL LEAVE ACT	—	
99	DEFAMATION	—	
100	MISREPRESENTATION	●	Endorsement, page 1
101	RETALIATION	—	
102	MENTAL ANGUISH	—	
103	INVASION OF PRIVACY	—	
104	HUMILIATION	—	
105	EMOTIONAL DISTRESS	—	
106	OTHER PERSONAL INJURY OFFENSES	—	
107	POLICY SILENT	—	

14 EXCLUSIONS

#	Comparison Query	Comment	Policy Reference
108	**ADA ACCOMMODATION EXPENSES**	—	
109	**ASSAULT & BATTERY**	●	Endorsement (3), page 1
110	**BACK PAY**	—	
111	**BODILY INJURY**	●	Endorsement (3), page 1
112	BODILY INJURY	●	Endorsement (3), page 1
113	DEATH	●	Endorsement (3), page 1
114	DISEASE	●	Endorsement (3), page 1
115	SICKNESS	●	Endorsement (3), page 1
116	**BREACH OF EMPLOYMENT CONTRACT**	—	
117	EXPRESS CONTRACT	—	
118	*WRITTEN CONTRACT*	—	
119	*ORAL CONTRACT*	—	
120	IMPLIED CONTRACT	—	
121	**CLASS ACTION LAWSUITS**	—	
122	**CONSEQUENTIAL LOSS**	—	
123	APPLIES TO BODILY INJURY	—	
124	APPLIES TO INSURED EVENT	—	
125	BROTHER/SISTER	—	
126	CHILD	—	
127	DOMESTIC PARTNER	—	
128	PARENT	—	
129	SPOUSE	—	
130	**COST OF ARBITRATION HEARINGS SUBJECT TO**	—	
131	EMPLOYMENT HANDBOOK	—	
132	LABOR GRIEVANCE	—	
133	OTHER EMPLOYMENT POLICY OR PROCEDURE	—	
134	**COVERAGE ELSEWHERE**	●	Policy IV.E., page 3
135	OTHER AVAILABLE INSURANCE	●	Policy IV.E., page 3
136	OTHER INDEMNIFICATION	—	
137	SHARING PROVISION	—	
138	**FAILURE TO EXERCISE CARE WHEN TERMINATING**	—	
139	**FINES/PENALTIES**	●	Policy, III.E., page 2
140	CIVIL	●	Policy, III.E., page 2
141	CRIMINAL	●	Policy, III.E., page 2
142	EXEMPLARY DAMAGES	●	Policy, III.E., page 2
143	PUNITIVE DAMAGES	●	Policy, III.E., page 2
144	MULTIPLIED DAMAGES	●	Policy, III.E., page 2
145	**FRONT PAY**	—	
146	EXCLUSION APPLIES ONLY IF EMPLOYER HAD OPPORTUNITY TO REINSTATE EMPLOYEE BUT DID NOT DO SO	—	
147	**INTENTIONAL ACTS**	●	Policy, IV.D., page 3
148	CRIMINAL ACTS	●	If established in fact	Policy, IV.D., page 3
149	CRIMINAL PROCEEDING	—	
150	DISHONEST PURPOSE	●	If established in fact	Policy, IV.D., page 3
151	FRAUDULENT ACTS	●	If established in fact	Policy, IV.D., page 3
152	FRAUDULENT CLAIMS	—	
153	INTENTIONAL VIOLATIONS OF LAW	—	
154	WILLFUL FAILURE TO COMPLY WITH LAW	—	
155	MALICIOUS PURPOSE	—	
156	**LIABILITY OF OTHERS**	—	
157	**LIQUIDATED DAMAGES**	—	
158	**LOSS ARISING OUT OF CHANGES IN OPERATIONS**	—	
159	ACQUISITION	—	
160	CHANGE IN CONTROL	—	
161	DOWNSIZING OR REDUCTION IN FORCE	—	
162	*% OF WORKFORCE*	—	
163	*WITHIN X DAYS*	—	

AGRICULTURAL EXCESS & SURPLUS INSURANCE COMPANY (AESIC) D 5717-19 [6/93]

#	Comparison Query	Comment	Policy Reference
164	FINANCIAL IMPAIRMENT	—	
165	BANKRUPTCY	—	
166	INSOLVENCY	—	
167	LIQUIDATION	—	
168	RECEIVERSHIP	—	
169	FINANCIAL INABILITY TO PAY	—	
170	MERGER	—	
171	PLANT OR FACILITY CLOSING	—	
172	REORGANIZATION	—	
173	TEMPORARY SHUTDOWN	—	
174	**MATTERS DEEMED UNINSURABLE**	●	Policy III.E., page 2
175	**NON-MONETARY RELIEF**	—	
176	DECLATORY RELIEF	—	
177	DISGORGEMENT	—	
178	INJUNCTIVE RELIEF	—	
179	JOB REINSTATEMENT	—	
180	NON-MONETARY DAMAGES/RELIEF	—	
181	OTHER EQUITABLE REMEDIES	—	
182	**OBLIGATION TO PROVIDE BENEFITS**	—	
183	COBRA	—	
184	DISABILITY	—	
185	ERISA	●	Policy III.H., page 3
186	SOCIAL SECURITY	—	
187	OTHER RETIREMENT BENEFITS	—	
188	UNEMPLOYMENT	—	
189	WORKERS' COMPENSATION	—	
190	**PERSONAL INJURY OFFENSES**	—	
191	DEFAMATION	—	
192	EMOTIONAL DISTRESS/UPSET	—	
193	HUMILIATION	—	
194	LIBEL	—	
195	MENTAL ANGUISH	—	
196	PERSONAL INJURY	—	
197	SLANDER	—	
198	**PRIOR ACTS**	—	
199	PRIOR ACTS	—	
200	PRIOR KNOWLEDGE	—	
201	PRIOR/PENDING LITIGATION	—	
202	**PROPERTY DAMAGE**	●	Endorsement (3)., page 1
203	INTANGIBLE PROPERTY	—	
204	LOSS OF USE	●	Endorsement (3)., page 1
205	TANGIBLE PROPERTY	●	Endorsement (3)., page 1
206	**RETALIATORY ACTIONS OF EMPLOYER**	—	
207	FOR FAILING TO PERFORM ACTS AGAINST PUBLIC POLICY	—	
208	FOR FILING A COMPLAINT OR BENEFIT CLAIM	—	
209	**STRIKES/LOCKOUTS**	—	
210	**VIOLATION OF LAWS**	—	
211	ANY LAW	—	
212	FMLA	—	
213	OSHA	—	
214	POLLUTION LAWS	●	Policy III.J., page 3
215	RICO	—	
216	SEC	—	
217	WARN	—	

15 CONDITIONS

#	Comparison Query	Comment	Policy Reference
218	**ARBITRATION**	—	
219	MANDATORY	—	
220	BINDING	—	
221	CHOICE OF LAW PROVISION	—	
222	SITUS	—	
223	**TERRITORY**	—	
224	LIMITED	—	
225	WORLDWIDE	—	
226	**NEWLY FORMED/ACQUIRED ENTITIES**	●	Policy III.C., page 2
227	AUTOMATIC COVERAGE (X DAYS)	●	Subsidiaries—no time limit	Policy III.C., page 2
228	NOTIFY INSURER WITHIN X DAYS	90	Subsidiaries—no time limit	Policy III.C., page 2

AGRICULTURAL EXCESS & SURPLUS INSURANCE COMPANY (AESIC) D 5717-19 [6/93]

Policy Comparison Worksheet

American Equity Insurance Company

Policy Form No.: 11197
Edition Date: 11/97

Risks Considered: All except leasing companies
Limits Available: $2,000,000
Minimum Retention: $2,500

Contact: Ram Chandarana
Professional Underwriters Agency, Inc.
2907 Butterfield Road, Suite 320
Oak Brook, IL 60523
630/575-8111
630/575-0033 (fax)
www.puainc.comm

KEY TO SYMBOLS
● = Specifically contains queried provision of feature
○ = Unable to determine
— = Silent

#	Comparison Query		Comment	Policy Reference
	1 APPLICATION			
1	ATTACHES TO AND FORMS A PART OF THE POLICY	●		Preamble, page 1
2	CONTAINS WARRANTY STATEMENTS	—		
3	CONTAINS SEVERABILITY PROVISIONS	—		
	2 POLICY TYPE			
4	UNITARY STAND ALONE POLICY	●		
	ENDORSEMENT OR PART OF			
5	DIRECTORS AND OFFICERS POLICY	—		
6	PACKAGE POLICY	—		
7	UMBRELLA POLICY	—		
8	ERRORS AND OMISSIONS POLICY	—		
9	OTHER	—		
10	CLAIMS-MADE	●		
11	OCCURRENCE	—		
	3 WHO IS INSURED			
12	BUSINESS ENTITY	●		III.3., page 1
13	AUTOMATIC COVERAGE FOR SUBSIDIARIES	●		III.3., page 1
14	DIRECTORS & OFFICERS	●		III.3., page 1
15	EMPLOYEES	●		III.5., page 1
16	PART-TIME	●		III.5., page 1
17	SEASONAL	●		III.5., page 1
18	TEMPORARY	—		
19	SUPERVISORS & MANAGERS	—		
20	FORMER EMPLOYEES	●		III.5., page 1
21	VOLUNTEERS	—		
22	INDEPENDENT CONTRACTORS	—		
23	EXCLUDED	—		
24	SILENT	●		
25	SHAREHOLDERS	●		III.3., page 1
	4 LIMIT OF LIABILITY			
26	AGGREGATE	●		IV., page 2
27	INCLUDES PUNITIVE DAMAGES WHERE NOT UNINSURABLE	—	Limited coverage available by endorsement	
28	DEFENSE COSTS INCLUDED WITHIN LIMIT OF LIABILITY	●		IV., page 2
29	DEFENSE COSTS PAID IN ADDITION TO LIMIT OF LIABILITY	—		
	5 DEDUCTIBLE			
30	APPLIES TO EACH INDIVIDUAL CLAIM	●		V., page 2
31	APPLIES TO EACH OCCURRENCE OR WRONGFUL PRACTICE	●		IV., page 2
32	INCLUDES ALL CLAIMS FROM ONE ACT	●		IV., page 2
33	SUBJECT TO ANNUAL AGGREGATE	—		
34	CO-PAYMENT APPLIES	—		
35	LIMIT OF LIABILITY NOT REDUCED	—		
36	INCLUDES DEFENSE COSTS	●		Declarations page
37	REDUCED UNDER SPECIFIED CIRCUMSTANCES (SEE POLICY)	—		

AMERICAN EQUITY INSURANCE COMPANY 11197 [11/97]

#	Comparison Query	Comment	Policy Reference
6	**WHAT IS A CLAIM**		
38	ORAL COMPLAINT TO INSURED	—	
39	WRITTEN COMPLAINT TO INSURED	●	III.B., page 1
40	COMPLAINT MUST CONTAIN A DEMAND FOR DAMAGES	—	
41	COMPLAINT FILED WITH EEOC	●	III.B., page 1
42	OR SIMILAR STATE AUTHORITY	●	III.B., page 1
43	AGENCY MUST HAVE POWER TO ADJUDICATE	—	
44	ADMINISTRATIVE PROCEEDING	●	III.B., page 1
45	ARBITRATION PROCEEDING		
46	ANY INCIDENT REPORTED TO INSURER		
47	SUIT	●	III.B., page 1
48	CLAIM DOES NOT INCLUDE ARBITRATION SUBJECT TO	●	III.B., page 1
49	COLLECTIVE BARGAINING AGREEMENT	●	III.B., page 1
50	EMPLOYEE POLICY OR MANUAL	—	
51	CLAIM NOT DEFINED	—	
7	**CLAIM REPORTING PROVISIONS TO INSURER**		
52	IMMEDIATELY	—	
53	AS SOON AS POSSIBLE	—	
54	AS SOON AS PRACTICABLE	●	Conditions I.(a)., page 3
55	WITHIN POLICY PERIOD	—	
56	WITHIN X DAYS OF EXPIRATION	—	
57	WITHIN X DAYS	—	
8	**EXTENDED REPORTING FEATURES**		
58	ELECTION PERIOD (DAYS)	10	VIII., page 3
59	ADDITIONAL PREMIUM (% OF ANNUAL PREMIUM)	100	VIII., pages 2–3
60	ADDITIONAL REPORTING PERIOD (MONTHS)	12	VIII., pages 2–3
61	NO REINSTATEMENT OF LIMITS	—	
9	**POTENTIAL CLAIM REPORTING PROVISIONS**		
62	NONE (SEE ALSO "CLAIM" ABOVE)	—	
63	INCIDENTS LIKELY TO RESULT IN A CLAIM	●	VI., page 2
10	**DEFENSE PROVISIONS**		
64	AFFIRMATIVE DUTY TO DEFEND	●	VII.A., page 2
65	NO AFFIRMATIVE DUTY TO DEFEND	—	
66	AFFIRMATIVE ADVANCEMENT PROVISIONS	—	
67	INSURED MUST RETURN ADVANCED AMOUNTS IF NOT COVERED	—	
68	INSURED/INSURER CHOOSES COUNSEL	● Insurer	VII.B., page 2
69	INSURED/INSURER APPROVES COUNSEL	—	
70	INSURED/INSURER CONSULTED IN COUNSEL SELECTION	—	
11	**SETTLEMENT PROVISIONS**		
71	HAMMER CLAUSE	●	VII.D., page 2
72	CONSULTATION PROVISION	—	
73	CONSENT PROVISION	● Two-way	VII.D. & E., page 2
12	**ALLOCATION OF LOSS PROVISIONS**		
74	STIPULATED PROVISIONS	—	
13	**COVERAGES**		
75	DISCRIMINATION	● Wrongful employment practice	III.F.2., page 2
76	SPECIFIC ENUMERATED ACTIVITIES	●	III.F.2.(i)., page 2
77	PLUS BROAD OMNIBUS WORDING	—	
78	SPECIFIC ENUMERATED CLASSES	●	III.F.2.(i)., page 2
79	PLUS BROAD OMNIBUS WORDING	—	
80	AGAINST THIRD PARTIES	—	
81	DISCRIMINATION NOT DEFINED	—	
82	SEXUAL HARASSMENT	● Wrongful employment practice	III.F.3., page 2
83	HOSTILE ENVIRONMENT	●	III.F.3.(i).(a)., (b)., & (c)., page 2
84	QUID-PRO-QUO	●	III.F.3.(i).(a)., (b)., & (c)., page 2
85	SEXUAL HARASSMENT NOT DEFINED	—	
86	WRONGFUL TERMINATION	● Wrongful employment practice	III.F.1., page 2
87	BREACH OF IMPLIED CONTRACT	—	
88	BREACH OF EXPRESS CONTRACT	—	
89	VIOLATION OF PUBLIC POLICY	—	
90	VIOLATION OF GOOD FAITH & FAIR DEALING	—	
91	OBLIGATIONS TO MAKE PAYMENTS	—	
92	CONSTRUCTIVE DISCHARGE	●	III.F.1.(i)., page 2
93	WRONGFUL TERMINATION NOT DEFINED	—	
94	OTHER EMPLOYMENT VIOLATIONS/OFFENSES	●	
95	WRONGFUL HIRING	—	
96	WRONGFUL PROMOTION/DEMOTION	—	
97	WRONGFUL EVALUATION/DISCIPLINE	●	III.F.4. & 7., page 2

AMERICAN EQUITY INSURANCE COMPANY 11197 [11/97]

	Comparison Query		Comment	Policy Reference
98	FAMILY AND MEDICAL LEAVE ACT	—		
99	DEFAMATION	●		III.F.8., page 2
100	MISREPRESENTATION	—		
101	RETALIATION	●		III.F.10., page 2
102	MENTAL ANGUISH	●		III.B., page 1
103	INVASION OF PRIVACY	—		
104	HUMILIATION	●		III.B., page 1
105	EMOTIONAL DISTRESS	●		III.B., page 1
106	OTHER PERSONAL INJURY OFFENSES	—		
107	POLICY SILENT	—		
14 EXCLUSIONS				
108	**ADA ACCOMMODATION EXPENSES**	●		III.D., page 1
109	**ASSAULT & BATTERY**	—		
110	**BACK PAY**	—		
111	**BODILY INJURY**	●	Exceptions apply	Exclusions C., page 3
112	BODILY INJURY	●	Exceptions apply	Exclusions C., page 3
113	DEATH	●	Exceptions apply	Exclusions C., page 3
114	DISEASE	●	Exceptions apply	Exclusions C., page 3
115	SICKNESS	●	Exceptions apply	Exclusions C., page 3
116	**BREACH OF EMPLOYMENT CONTRACT**	●		III.D., page 1
117	EXPRESS CONTRACT	●	Exception applies	III.D., page 1
118	WRITTEN CONTRACT	—		
119	ORAL CONTRACT	—		
120	IMPLIED CONTRACT	●		Exclusions L., page 3
121	**CLASS ACTION LAWSUITS**	—		
122	**CONSEQUENTIAL LOSS**	●	Loss of consortium	Exclusions C., page 3
123	APPLIES TO BODILY INJURY	—		
124	APPLIES TO INSURED EVENT	—		
125	BROTHER/SISTER	●		Exclusions J., page 3
126	CHILD	●		Exclusions J., page 3
127	DOMESTIC PARTNER	●		Exclusions J., page 3
128	PARENT	●		Exclusions J., page 3
129	SPOUSE	●		Exclusions J., page 3
130	**COST OF ARBITRATION HEARINGS SUBJECT TO**	●		III.D., page 1
131	EMPLOYMENT HANDBOOK	—		
132	LABOR GRIEVANCE	●		III.D., page 1
133	OTHER EMPLOYMENT POLICY OR PROCEDURE	—		
134	**COVERAGE ELSEWHERE**	●		II.(b)., page 1
135	OTHER AVAILABLE INSURANCE	●	See also Conditions VI., pages 3–4	II.(b)., page 1
136	OTHER INDEMNIFICATION	—		
137	SHARING PROVISION	—		
138	**FAILURE TO EXERCISE CARE WHEN TERMINATING**	—		
139	**FINES/PENALTIES**	●		III.D., page 1
140	CIVIL	●		III.D., page 1
141	CRIMINAL	●		III.D., page 1
142	EXEMPLARY DAMAGES	●		III.D., page 1
143	PUNITIVE DAMAGES	●		III.D., page 1
144	MULTIPLIED DAMAGES	●		III.D., page 1
145	**FRONT PAY**	—		
146	EXCLUSION APPLIES ONLY IF EMPLOYER HAD OPPORTUNITY TO REINSTATE EMPLOYEE BUT DID NOT DO SO	—		
147	**INTENTIONAL ACTS**	●		Exclusioons A., page 3
148	CRIMINAL ACTS	●	If established in fact—severability applies	Exclusioons A., page 3
149	CRIMINAL PROCEEDING	—		
150	DISHONEST PURPOSE	●	If established in fact—severability applies	Exclusioons A., page 3
151	FRAUDULENT ACTS	●	If established in fact—severability applies	Exclusioons A., page 3
152	FRAUDULENT CLAIMS	●		Conditions, IX., page 4
153	INTENTIONAL VIOLATIONS OF LAW	—		
154	WILLFUL FAILURE TO COMPLY WITH LAW	—		
155	MALICIOUS PURPOSE	●	If established in fact—severability applies	Conditions, IX., page 4
156	**LIABILITY OF OTHERS**	●		Exclusions B., page 3
157	**LIQUIDATED DAMAGES**	—		
158	**LOSS ARISING OUT OF CHANGES IN OPERATIONS**	●		Exclusions G., page 3
159	ACQUISITION	—		
160	CHANGE IN CONTROL	—		
161	DOWNSIZING OR REDUCTION IN FORCE	●	Coverage available by endorsement	Exclusions G., page 3
162	% OF WORKFORCE	20	Coverage available by endorsement	Exclusions G., page 3
163	WITHIN X DAYS	60	Coverage available by endorsement	Exclusions G., page 3

AMERICAN EQUITY INSURANCE COMPANY 11197 [11/97]

#	Comparison Query		Comment	Policy Reference
164	FINANCIAL IMPAIRMENT	—		
165	*BANKRUPTCY*	—		
166	*INSOLVENCY*	—		
167	*LIQUIDATION*	—		
168	*RECEIVERSHIP*	—		
169	FINANCIAL INABILITY TO PAY	—		
170	MERGER	—		
171	PLANT OR FACILITY CLOSING	●	Coverage available by endorsement	Exclusions G., page 3
172	REORGANIZATION	—		
173	TEMPORARY SHUTDOWN	—		
174	**MATTERS DEEMED UNINSURABLE**	●		III.D., page 1
175	**NON-MONETARY RELIEF**	●		Exclusions K., page 3
176	DECLATORY RELIEF	●	Exceptions apply	Exclusions K., page 3
177	DISGORGEMENT	●	Exceptions apply	Exclusions K., page 3
178	INJUNCTIVE RELIEF	—		
179	JOB REINSTATEMENT	—		
180	NON-MONETARY DAMAGES/RELIEF	●	Exceptions apply	Exclusions K., page 3
181	OTHER EQUITABLE REMEDIES	●	Exceptions apply	Exclusions K., page 3
182	**OBLIGATION TO PROVIDE BENEFITS**	—		
183	COBRA	●		III.D., page 1
184	DISABILITY	—		
185	ERISA	●	See also Exclusions E.(i)., page 3	III.D., page 1
186	SOCIAL SECURITY	—		
187	OTHER RETIREMENT BENEFITS	—		
188	UNEMPLOYMENT	—		
189	WORKERS' COMPENSATION	●	Retaliation exception	Exclusions F., page 3
190	**PERSONAL INJURY OFFENSES**	—		
191	DEFAMATION	—		
192	EMOTIONAL DISTRESS/UPSET	—		
193	HUMILIATION	—		
194	LIBEL	—		
195	MENTAL ANGUISH	—		
196	PERSONAL INJURY	—		
197	SLANDER	—		
198	**PRIOR ACTS**	—		
199	PRIOR ACTS	—		
200	PRIOR KNOWLEDGE	●	See also Exclusions I., page 3	II.(b)., page 1
201	PRIOR/PENDING LITIGATION	—		
202	**PROPERTY DAMAGE**	●		Exclusion D., page 3
203	INTANGIBLE PROPERTY	●		Exclusion D., page 3
204	LOSS OF USE	●		Exclusion D., page 3
205	TANGIBLE PROPERTY	●		Exclusion D., page 3
206	**RETALIATORY ACTIONS OF EMPLOYER**	—		
207	FOR FAILING TO PERFORM ACTS AGAINST PUBLIC POLICY	—		
208	FOR FILING A COMPLAINT OR BENEFIT CLAIM	—		
209	**STRIKES/LOCKOUTS**	●		Exclusions M., page 3
210	**VIOLATION OF LAWS**	—		
211	ANY LAW	—		
212	FMLA	—		
213	OSHA	—		
214	POLLUTION LAWS	—		
215	RICO	—		
216	SEC	—		
217	WARN	●		Exclusions E.(iii)., page 3
	15 CONDITIONS			
218	**ARBITRATION**	—		
219	MANDATORY	—		
220	BINDING	—		
221	CHOICE OF LAW PROVISION	—		
222	SITUS	—		
223	**TERRITORY**	●		I., page 1
224	LIMITED	—		
225	WORLDWIDE	●		I., page 1
226	**NEWLY FORMED/ACQUIRED ENTITIES**	●		III.6., page 1
227	AUTOMATIC COVERAGE (X DAYS)	30		III.6., page 1
228	NOTIFY INSURER WITHIN X DAYS	30		III.6., page 1

AMERICAN EQUITY INSURANCE COMPANY 11197 [11/97]

Policy Comparison Worksheet

American International Specialty Lines Insurance Company

Policy Form No.: 64198 (12/95)
Edition Date: 12/95

Risks Considered: All but temporary help agencies and employee leasing
Limits Available: $5,000,000/$5,000,000
Minimum Retention: $2,500

Contact: Morefar Marketing, Inc.
501 Carr Road, Suite 101
Wilmington, DE 19809
302/761-5600
302/761-5659 (fax)

KEY TO SYMBOLS
● = Specifically contains queried provision of feature
○ = Unable to determine
— = Silent

#	Comparison Query	Comment		Policy Reference
	1 APPLICATION			
1	ATTACHES TO AND FORMS A PART OF THE POLICY	●		Preamble, page 1
2	CONTAINS WARRANTY STATEMENTS	—		
3	CONTAINS SEVERABILITY PROVISIONS	—		
	2 POLICY TYPE			
4	UNITARY STAND ALONE POLICY	●		
	ENDORSEMENT OR PART OF	—		
5	DIRECTORS AND OFFICERS POLICY	—		
6	PACKAGE POLICY	—		
7	UMBRELLA POLICY	—		
8	ERRORS AND OMISSIONS POLICY	—		
9	OTHER	—		
10	CLAIMS-MADE	●		
11	OCCURRENCE	—		
	3 WHO IS INSURED			
12	BUSINESS ENTITY	●		II.B., page 3
13	AUTOMATIC COVERAGE FOR SUBSIDIARIES	—		
14	DIRECTORS & OFFICERS	●		II.B., page 4
15	EMPLOYEES	●		II.E., page 4
16	PART-TIME	●		VIII.D., page 9
17	SEASONAL	●		VIII.D., page 9
18	TEMPORARY	●		VIII.D., page 9
19	SUPERVISORS & MANAGERS	●		VIII.D., page 9
20	FORMER EMPLOYEES	●	If employee at time of wrongful act	II.E., page 4
21	VOLUNTEERS	—		
22	INDEPENDENT CONTRACTORS	●		VIII.D., page 9
23	EXCLUDED	●		VIII.D., page 9
24	SILENT	—		
25	SHAREHOLDERS	●		I.B., page 3
	4 LIMIT OF LIABILITY			
26	AGGREGATE	●		III.B., page 4
27	INCLUDES PUNITIVE DAMAGES WHERE NOT UNINSURABLE	—		
28	DEFENSE COSTS INCLUDED WITHIN LIMIT OF LIABILITY	●		VIII.E., page 9
29	DEFENSE COSTS PAID IN ADDITION TO LIMIT OF LIABILITY	—		
	5 DEDUCTIBLE			
30	APPLIES TO EACH INDIVIDUAL CLAIM	—		
31	APPLIES TO EACH OCCURRENCE OR WRONGFUL PRACTICE	●		V., page 4
32	INCLUDES ALL CLAIMS FROM ONE ACT	●		V., page 4
33	SUBJECT TO ANNUAL AGGREGATE	—		
34	CO-PAYMENT APPLIES	●		IV., page 4
35	LIMIT OF LIABILITY NOT REDUCED	—		
36	INCLUDES DEFENSE COSTS	●		V., page 4
37	REDUCED UNDER SPECIFIED CIRCUMSTANCES (SEE POLICY)	—		

#	Comparison Query	Comment		Policy Reference
	6 WHAT IS A CLAIM			
38	ORAL COMPLAINT TO INSURED	●		VI.F.1., page 5
39	WRITTEN COMPLAINT TO INSURED	●	See also I.A.1.b.(i), page 2	VIII.B., page 9
40	COMPLAINT MUST CONTAIN A DEMAND FOR DAMAGES	●		VIII.B., page 9
41	COMPLAINT FILED WITH EEOC	—		
42	OR SIMILAR STATE AUTHORITY	—		
43	AGENCY MUST HAVE POWER TO ADJUDICATE	—		
44	ADMINISTRATIVE PROCEEDING	●		VIII.J., page 9
45	ARBITRATION PROCEEDING	●		
46	ANY INCIDENT REPORTED TO INSURER	●		I.A.1.b.(i), page 1
47	SUIT	●	See also VIII.J., page 9	I.A.2.a., page 1
48	CLAIM DOES NOT INCLUDE ARBITRATION SUBJECT TO	●		VIII.J., page 9
49	COLLECTIVE BARGAINING AGREEMENT	●		VIII.J., page 9
50	EMPLOYEE POLICY OR MANUAL	—		
51	CLAIM NOT DEFINED	—		
	7 CLAIM REPORTING PROVISIONS TO INSURER			
52	IMMEDIATELY	—		
53	AS SOON AS POSSIBLE	—		
54	AS SOON AS PRACTICABLE	●		VI.F.2.b., page 5
55	WITHIN POLICY PERIOD	●		VI.F.1., page 5
56	WITHIN X DAYS OF EXPIRATION	60		VI.H.1., page 6
57	WITHIN X DAYS	—		
	8 EXTENDED REPORTING FEATURES			
58	ELECTION PERIOD (DAYS)	60		VI.I.3., page 6
59	ADDITIONAL PREMIUM (% OF ANNUAL PREMIUM)	○	Specified by underwriter	VI.I.1., page 6
60	ADDITIONAL REPORTING PERIOD (MONTHS)	36		VI.I.1., page 6
61	NO REINSTATEMENT OF LIMITS	—		
	9 POTENTIAL CLAIM REPORTING PROVISIONS			
62	NONE (SEE ALSO "CLAIM" ABOVE)	—		
63	INCIDENTS LIKELY TO RESULT IN A CLAIM	●		VI.F.1., page 5
	10 DEFENSE PROVISIONS			
64	AFFIRMATIVE DUTY TO DEFEND	●		I.A.2.a., page 1
65	NO AFFIRMATIVE DUTY TO DEFEND	—		
66	AFFIRMATIVE ADVANCEMENT PROVISIONS	—		
67	INSURED MUST RETURN ADVANCED AMOUNTS IF NOT COVERED	—		
68	INSURED/INSURER CHOOSES COUNSEL	●	Insurer	I.A.2.a., page 1
69	INSURED/INSURER APPROVES COUNSEL	—		
70	INSURED/INSURER CONSULTED IN COUNSEL SELECTION	—		
	11 SETTLEMENT PROVISIONS			
71	HAMMER CLAUSE	—		
72	CONSULTATION PROVISION	—		
73	CONSENT PROVISION	—		
	12 ALLOCATION OF LOSS PROVISIONS			
74	STIPULATED PROVISIONS	—		
	13 COVERAGES			
75	DISCRIMINATION	●	As wrongful employment act	I.A.1.a., page 1
76	SPECIFIC ENUMERATED ACTIVITIES	●		VIII.C., page 9
77	*PLUS BROAD OMNIBUS WORDING*	○		VIII.C., page 9
78	SPECIFIC ENUMERATED CLASSES	●		VIII.C., page 9
79	*PLUS BROAD OMNIBUS WORDING*	—		
80	AGAINST THIRD PARTIES	—		
81	DISCRIMINATION NOT DEFINED			
82	SEXUAL HARASSMENT	●	As wrongful employment act	I.A.1.a., page 1
83	HOSTILE ENVIRONMENT	●		VIII.I., page 9
84	QUID-PRO-QUO	●		VIII.I., page 9
85	SEXUAL HARASSMENT NOT DEFINED			
86	WRONGFUL TERMINATION	●	As wrongful employment act	I.A.1.a., page 1
87	BREACH OF IMPLIED CONTRACT	—		
88	BREACH OF EXPRESS CONTRACT	—		
89	VIOLATION OF PUBLIC POLICY	—		
90	VIOLATION OF GOOD FAITH & FAIR DEALING	—		
91	OBLIGATIONS TO MAKE PAYMENTS	—		
92	CONSTRUCTIVE DISCHARGE	—		
93	WRONGFUL TERMINATION NOT DEFINED	—		
94	OTHER EMPLOYMENT VIOLATIONS/OFFENSES	●		VIII.C., page 9
95	WRONGFUL HIRING	●	If discrimination	VIII.C., page 9
96	WRONGFUL PROMOTION/DEMOTION	●	If discrimination	VIII.C., page 9
97	WRONGFUL EVALUATION/DISCIPLINE	—		

#	Comparison Query		Comment	Policy Reference
98	FAMILY AND MEDICAL LEAVE ACT	—		
99	DEFAMATION	—		
100	MISREPRESENTATION	—		
101	RETALIATION	—		
102	MENTAL ANGUISH	—		
103	INVASION OF PRIVACY	—		
104	HUMILIATION	—		
105	EMOTIONAL DISTRESS	—		
106	OTHER PERSONAL INJURY OFFENSES	—		
107	POLICY SILENT	—		
14 EXCLUSIONS				
108	**ADA ACCOMMODATION EXPENSES**	●		I.B.10., page 2
109	**ASSAULT & BATTERY**	●		I.B.18, page 3
110	**BACK PAY**	—		
111	**BODILY INJURY**	●		I.B.2., page 2
112	BODILY INJURY	●	Physical injury	VIII.A., page 9
113	DEATH	●		VIII.A., page 9
114	DISEASE	●		VIII.A., page 9
115	SICKNESS	●		VIII.A., page 9
116	**BREACH OF EMPLOYMENT CONTRACT**	●		VIII.N., pages 9–10
117	EXPRESS CONTRACT	●		VIII.N., pages 9–10
118	WRITTEN CONTRACT	●		VIII.N., pages 9–10
119	ORAL CONTRACT	●		VIII.N., pages 9–10
120	IMPLIED CONTRACT	—		
121	**CLASS ACTION LAWSUITS**	—		
122	**CONSEQUENTIAL LOSS**	●		I.B.15., page 3
123	APPLIES TO BODILY INJURY	—		
124	APPLIES TO INSURED EVENT	—		
125	BROTHER/SISTER	●		I.B.15., page 3
126	CHILD	●		I.B.15., page 3
127	DOMESTIC PARTNER	●		I.B.15., page 3
128	PARENT	●		I.B.15., page 3
129	SPOUSE	●		I.B.15., page 3
130	**COST OF ARBITRATION HEARINGS SUBJECT TO**	●	Civil/administrative proceeding	VIII.J., page 9
131	EMPLOYMENT HANDBOOK	—		
132	LABOR GRIEVANCE	●		VIII.J., page 9
133	OTHER EMPLOYMENT POLICY OR PROCEDURE	—		
134	**COVERAGE ELSEWHERE**	●		VI.L., page 7
135	OTHER AVAILABLE INSURANCE	—		
136	OTHER INDEMNIFICATION	—		
137	SHARING PROVISION	●		VI.L., page 7
138	**FAILURE TO EXERCISE CARE WHEN TERMINATING**	●		VII.N., page 10
139	**FINES/PENALTIES**	●		I.B.20., page 3
140	CIVIL	—		
141	CRIMINAL	—		
142	EXEMPLARY DAMAGES	●		I.B.20., page 3
143	PUNITIVE DAMAGES	●		I.B.20., page 3
144	MULTIPLIED DAMAGES	●		I.B.20., page 3
145	**FRONT PAY**	—		
146	EXCLUSION APPLIES ONLY IF EMPLOYER HAD OPPORTUNITY TO REINSTATE EMPLOYEE BUT DID NOT DO SO	—		
147	**INTENTIONAL ACTS**	—		
148	CRIMINAL ACTS	●		I.B.17., page 3
149	CRIMINAL PROCEEDING	—		
150	DISHONEST PURPOSE	●		I.B.17., page 3
151	FRAUDULENT ACTS	●		I.B.17., page 3
152	FRAUDULENT CLAIMS	—		
153	INTENTIONAL VIOLATIONS OF LAW	—		
154	WILLFUL FAILURE TO COMPLY WITH LAW	●		I.B.4., page 2
155	MALICIOUS PURPOSE	●		I.B.17., page 3
156	**LIABILITY OF OTHERS**	●		I.B.5., page 2
157	**LIQUIDATED DAMAGES**	—		
158	**LOSS ARISING OUT OF CHANGES IN OPERATIONS**	—		
159	ACQUISITION	—		
160	CHANGE IN CONTROL	—		
161	DOWNSIZING OR REDUCTION IN FORCE	●		I.B.16., page 3
162	% OF WORKFORCE	20		I.B.16., page 3
163	WITHIN X DAYS	60		I.B.16., page 3

AMERICAN INTERNATIONAL SPECIALTY LINES INSURANCE COMPANY 64198 (12/95) [12/95]

#	Comparison Query	Comment	Policy Reference
164	FINANCIAL IMPAIRMENT	—	
165	BANKRUPTCY	—	
166	INSOLVENCY	—	
167	LIQUIDATION	—	
168	RECEIVERSHIP	—	
169	FINANCIAL INABILITY TO PAY	—	
170	MERGER	—	
171	PLANT OR FACILITY CLOSING	●	I.B.16., page 3
172	REORGANIZATION	●	
173	TEMPORARY SHUTDOWN	—	
174	**MATTERS DEEMED UNINSURABLE**	●	I.B.21., page 3
175	**NON-MONETARY RELIEF**	●	I.B.19., page 3
176	DECLATORY RELIEF	●	I.B.19., page 3
177	DISGORGEMENT	●	I.B.19., page 3
178	INJUNCTIVE RELIEF	●	I.B.19., page 3
179	JOB REINSTATEMENT	●	I.B.19., page 3
180	NON-MONETARY DAMAGES/RELIEF	●	I.B.19., page 3
181	OTHER EQUITABLE REMEDIES	●	I.B.19., page 3
182	**OBLIGATION TO PROVIDE BENEFITS**	—	
183	COBRA	●	I.B.0., page 2
184	DISABILITY	●	I.B.3., page 2
185	ERISA	●	I.B.6., page 2
186	SOCIAL SECURITY	●	I.B.12., page 2
187	OTHER RETIREMENT BENEFITS	—	
188	UNEMPLOYMENT	●	I.B.3., page 2
189	WORKERS' COMPENSATION	●	I.B.3., page 2
190	**PERSONAL INJURY OFFENSES**	—	
191	DEFAMATION	—	
192	EMOTIONAL DISTRESS/UPSET	—	
193	HUMILIATION	—	
194	LIBEL	—	
195	MENTAL ANGUISH	—	
196	PERSONAL INJURY	—	
197	SLANDER	—	
198	**PRIOR ACTS**	●	I.A.1.a., page 1
199	PRIOR ACTS	●	I.A.1.a., page 1
200	PRIOR KNOWLEDGE	●	I.B.22., page 3
201	PRIOR/PENDING LITIGATION	—	
202	**PROPERTY DAMAGE**	●	I.B.1., page 2
203	INTANGIBLE PROPERTY	—	
204	LOSS OF USE	●	VIII.G., page 9
205	TANGIBLE PROPERTY	●	VIII.G., page 9
206	**RETALIATORY ACTIONS OF EMPLOYER**	●	I.B.13., page 3
207	FOR FAILING TO PERFORM ACTS AGAINST PUBLIC POLICY	●	I.B.13., page 3
208	FOR FILING A COMPLAINT OR BENEFIT CLAIM	●	I.B.13., page 3
209	**STRIKES/LOCKOUTS**	●	I.B.14., page 3
210	**VIOLATION OF LAWS**	—	
211	ANY LAW	—	
212	FMLA	—	
213	OSHA	●	I.B.11., page 2
214	POLLUTION LAWS	—	
215	RICO	—	
216	SEC	—	
217	WARN	●	I.B.7., page 2
	15 CONDITIONS		
218	**ARBITRATION**	●	VI.A., page 4
219	MANDATORY	●	VI.A., page 4
220	BINDING	●	VI.A., page 4
221	CHOICE OF LAW PROVISION	—	
222	SITUS	●	New York	VI.A., page 4
223	**TERRITORY**	●	VI.E., page 5
224	LIMITED	●	VI.E., page 5
225	WORLDWIDE	—	
226	**NEWLY FORMED/ACQUIRED ENTITIES**	●	II.D., page 4
227	AUTOMATIC COVERAGE (X DAYS)	●	I.D., page 4
228	NOTIFY INSURER WITHIN X DAYS	—	

AMERICAN INTERNATIONAL SPECIALTY LINES INSURANCE COMPANY 64198 (12/95) [12/95]

Policy Comparison Worksheet

Associated Electric & Gas Insurance Services, Limited
(AEGIS)

Policy Form No.: 8262 (1/98)
Edition Date: 1/98

Risks Considered: Utilities, energy and telecommunications
Limits Available: $35,000,000
Minimum Retention: $1,000,000

Contact: Sandra A. Johnson
Vice President, Underwriting
Associated Electric & Gas Insurance Services, Limited
10 Exchange Place
Jersey City, NJ 07302
201/521-4658
201/521-4642 (fax)
johnsos%aegis@mcimail.com

KEY TO SYMBOLS
● = Specifically contains queried provision of feature
○ = Unable to determine
— = Silent

#	Comparison Query		Comment	Policy Reference
	1 APPLICATION			
1	ATTACHES TO AND FORMS A PART OF THE POLICY	—		
2	CONTAINS WARRANTY STATEMENTS	—		
3	CONTAINS SEVERABILITY PROVISIONS	—		
	2 POLICY TYPE			
4	UNITARY STAND ALONE POLICY	—		
	ENDORSEMENT OR PART OF	—		
5	DIRECTORS AND OFFICERS POLICY	—		
6	PACKAGE POLICY	—		
7	UMBRELLA POLICY	●		
8	ERRORS AND OMISSIONS POLICY	—		
9	OTHER	—		
10	CLAIMS-MADE	●		
11	OCCURRENCE	—		
	3 WHO IS INSURED			
12	BUSINESS ENTITY	○	See policy	
13	AUTOMATIC COVERAGE FOR SUBSIDIARIES	○	See policy	
14	DIRECTORS & OFFICERS	○	See policy	
15	EMPLOYEES	○	See policy	
16	PART-TIME	○	See policy	
17	SEASONAL	○	See policy	
18	TEMPORARY	○	See policy	
19	SUPERVISORS & MANAGERS	○	See policy	
20	FORMER EMPLOYEES	○	See policy	
21	VOLUNTEERS	○	See policy	
22	INDEPENDENT CONTRACTORS	○	See policy	
23	EXCLUDED	○	See policy	
24	SILENT	○	See policy	
25	SHAREHOLDERS	○	See policy	
	4 LIMIT OF LIABILITY			
26	AGGREGATE	●		(H), page 4
27	INCLUDES PUNITIVE DAMAGES WHERE NOT UNINSURABLE	○	See policy	
28	DEFENSE COSTS INCLUDED WITHIN LIMIT OF LIABILITY	○	See policy	
29	DEFENSE COSTS PAID IN ADDITION TO LIMIT OF LIABILITY	○	See policy	
	5 DEDUCTIBLE			
30	APPLIES TO EACH INDIVIDUAL CLAIM	●		
31	APPLIES TO EACH OCCURRENCE OR WRONGFUL PRACTICE	—		
32	INCLUDES ALL CLAIMS FROM ONE ACT	—		
33	SUBJECT TO ANNUAL AGGREGATE	—		
34	CO-PAYMENT APPLIES	●	Specified by underwriter — see Item 3 of Supplemental Declarations page	(I), page 4
35	LIMIT OF LIABILITY NOT REDUCED	—		
36	INCLUDES DEFENSE COSTS	○	See policy	
37	REDUCED UNDER SPECIFIED CIRCUMSTANCES (SEE POLICY)	○	See policy	

#	Comparison Query		Comment	Policy Reference
	6 WHAT IS A CLAIM			
38	ORAL COMPLAINT TO INSURED	○	See policy	
39	WRITTEN COMPLAINT TO INSURED	○	See policy	
40	COMPLAINT MUST CONTAIN A DEMAND FOR DAMAGES	○	See policy	
41	COMPLAINT FILED WITH EEOC	—		
42	OR SIMILAR STATE AUTHORITY	—		
43	AGENCY MUST HAVE POWER TO ADJUDICATE	—		
44	ADMINISTRATIVE PROCEEDING	○	See policy	
45	ARBITRATION PROCEEDING	○	See policy	
46	ANY INCIDENT REPORTED TO INSURER	○	See policy	
47	SUIT	○	See policy	
48	CLAIM DOES NOT INCLUDE ARBITRATION SUBJECT TO	—		
49	COLLECTIVE BARGAINING AGREEMENT	—		
50	EMPLOYEE POLICY OR MANUAL	—		
51	CLAIM NOT DEFINED	○	See policy	
	7 CLAIM REPORTING PROVISIONS TO INSURER			
52	IMMEDIATELY	○	See policy	
53	AS SOON AS POSSIBLE	○	See policy	
54	AS SOON AS PRACTICABLE	○	See policy	
55	WITHIN POLICY PERIOD	○	See policy	
56	WITHIN X DAYS OF EXPIRATION	○	See policy	
57	WITHIN X DAYS	○	See policy	
	8 EXTENDED REPORTING FEATURES			
58	ELECTION PERIOD (DAYS)	○	See policy	
59	ADDITIONAL PREMIUM (% OF ANNUAL PREMIUM)	○	See policy	
60	ADDITIONAL REPORTING PERIOD (MONTHS)	○	See policy	
61	NO REINSTATEMENT OF LIMITS	○	See policy	
	9 POTENTIAL CLAIM REPORTING PROVISIONS			
62	NONE (SEE ALSO "CLAIM" ABOVE)	○	See policy	
63	INCIDENTS LIKELY TO RESULT IN A CLAIM	○	See policy	
	10 DEFENSE PROVISIONS			
64	AFFIRMATIVE DUTY TO DEFEND	○	See policy	
65	NO AFFIRMATIVE DUTY TO DEFEND	○	See policy	
66	AFFIRMATIVE ADVANCEMENT PROVISIONS	○	See policy	
67	INSURED MUST RETURN ADVANCED AMOUNTS IF NOT COVERED	○	See policy	
68	INSURED/INSURER CHOOSES COUNSEL	○	See policy	
69	INSURED/INSURER APPROVES COUNSEL	○	See policy	
70	INSURED/INSURER CONSULTED IN COUNSEL SELECTION	○	See policy	
	11 SETTLEMENT PROVISIONS			
71	HAMMER CLAUSE	○	See policy	
72	CONSULTATION PROVISION	○	See policy	
73	CONSENT PROVISION	○	See policy	
	12 ALLOCATION OF LOSS PROVISIONS			
74	STIPULATED PROVISIONS	○		
	13 COVERAGES			
75	DISCRIMINATION	●	As "Wrongful Employment Practice"	(B)(1)(a), page 1
76	SPECIFIC ENUMERATED ACTIVITIES	●		(B)(2)(a),(b),(c) and (d), page 2
77	PLUS BROAD OMNIBUS WORDING	●		(B)(2) following (d), page 2
78	SPECIFIC ENUMERATED CLASSES	●		(B)(2) following (d), page 2
79	PLUS BROAD OMNIBUS WORDING	●		(B)(2) following (d), page 2
80	AGAINST THIRD PARTIES	—		
81	DISCRIMINATION NOT DEFINED	—		
82	SEXUAL HARASSMENT	●	As "Wrongful Employment Practice"	(B)(1)(b), page 1
83	HOSTILE ENVIRONMENT	●		(B)(3)(d), page 2
84	QUID-PRO-QUO	●		(B)(3)(a)&(b), page 2
85	SEXUAL HARASSMENT NOT DEFINED	—		
86	WRONGFUL TERMINATION	●	As "Wrongful Employment Practice"	(B)(1)(c), page 1
87	BREACH OF IMPLIED CONTRACT	●		(B)(4), page 2
88	BREACH OF EXPRESS CONTRACT	—		
89	VIOLATION OF PUBLIC POLICY	—		
90	VIOLATION OF GOOD FAITH & FAIR DEALING	—		
91	OBLIGATIONS TO MAKE PAYMENTS	—		
92	CONSTRUCTIVE DISCHARGE	●		(B)(4), page 2
93	WRONGFUL TERMINATION NOT DEFINED	—		
94	OTHER EMPLOYMENT VIOLATIONS/OFFENSES	—		
95	WRONGFUL HIRING	●	See also (B)(4), page 2	(B)(2)(a), page 2
96	WRONGFUL PROMOTION/DEMOTION	●	See also (B)(4), page 2	(B)(1)(c), page 1 & (B)2(b), page 2 & (B)(2)(c), page 2
97	WRONGFUL EVALUATION/DISCIPLINE	—		

ASSOCIATED ELECTRIC & GAS INSURANCE SERVICES, LIMITED 8262 (1/98) [1/98]

	Comparison Query		*Comment*	*Policy Reference*
98	FAMILY AND MEDICAL LEAVE ACT	—		
99	DEFAMATION	—		
100	MISREPRESENTATION	—		
101	RETALIATION	●		(B)(2) following (d), page 2
102	MENTAL ANGUISH	●		(A), page 1
103	INVASION OF PRIVACY	—		
104	HUMILIATION	—		
105	EMOTIONAL DISTRESS	●	Emotional upset	(A), page 1
106	OTHER PERSONAL INJURY OFFENSES	—		
107	POLICY SILENT	—		
	14 EXCLUSIONS			
108	**ADA ACCOMMODATION EXPENSES**	—		
109	**ASSAULT & BATTERY**	—		
110	**BACK PAY**	—		
111	**BODILY INJURY**			
112	BODILY INJURY	—		
113	DEATH	—		
114	DISEASE	—		
115	SICKNESS	—		
116	**BREACH OF EMPLOYMENT CONTRACT**	●		(C)(9), page 3
117	EXPRESS CONTRACT	●		(C)(9), page 3
118	*WRITTEN CONTRACT*	—		
119	*ORAL CONTRACT*	—		
120	IMPLIED CONTRACT	—		
121	**CLASS ACTION LAWSUITS**	—		
122	**CONSEQUENTIAL LOSS**	—		
123	APPLIES TO BODILY INJURY	—		
124	APPLIES TO INSURED EVENT	—		
125	BROTHER/SISTER	—		
126	CHILD	—		
127	DOMESTIC PARTNER	—		
128	PARENT	—		
129	SPOUSE	—		
130	**COST OF ARBITRATION HEARINGS SUBJECT TO**	—		
131	EMPLOYMENT HANDBOOK	—		
132	LABOR GRIEVANCE	—		
133	OTHER EMPLOYMENT POLICY OR PROCEDURE	—		
134	**COVERAGE ELSEWHERE**			
135	OTHER AVAILABLE INSURANCE	○	See policy	
136	OTHER INDEMNIFICATION	○	See policy	
137	SHARING PROVISION	○	See policy	
138	**FAILURE TO EXERCISE CARE WHEN TERMINATING**	—		
139	**FINES/PENALTIES**	○	See policy	
140	CIVIL	○	See policy	
141	CRIMINAL	○	See policy	
142	EXEMPLARY DAMAGES	○	See policy	
143	PUNITIVE DAMAGES	○	See policy	
144	MULTIPLIED DAMAGES	○	See policy	
145	**FRONT PAY**	●		(C)(8), page 3
146	EXCLUSION APPLIES ONLY IF EMPLOYER HAD OPPORTUNITY TO REINSTATE EMPLOYEE BUT DID NOT DO SO	●		(C)(8), page 3
147	**INTENTIONAL ACTS**	●	If established—defense provided	(C)(7), page 3
148	CRIMINAL ACTS	●	If established—defense provided	(C)(7), page 3
149	CRIMINAL PROCEEDING	—		
150	DISHONEST PURPOSE	●	If established—defense provided	(C)(7), page 3
151	FRAUDULENT ACTS	—		
152	FRAUDULENT CLAIMS	—		
153	INTENTIONAL VIOLATIONS OF LAW	—		
154	WILLFUL FAILURE TO COMPLY WITH LAW	—		
155	MALICIOUS PURPOSE	●	If established—defense provided	(C)(7), page 3
156	**LIABILITY OF OTHERS**	●	If established—defense provided	(C)(10), page 3
157	**LIQUIDATED DAMAGES**	—		
158	**LOSS ARISING OUT OF CHANGES IN OPERATIONS**	○	See policy	
159	ACQUISITION	○	See policy	
160	CHANGE IN CONTROL	○	See policy	
161	DOWNSIZING OR REDUCTION IN FORCE	○	See policy	
162	*% OF WORKFORCE*	○	See policy	
163	*WITHIN X DAYS*	○	See policy	

ASSOCIATED ELECTRIC & GAS INSURANCE SERVICES, LIMITED 8262 (1/98) [1/98]

#	Comparison Query	Comment		Policy Reference
164	FINANCIAL IMPAIRMENT	○	See policy	
165	BANKRUPTCY	○	See policy	
166	INSOLVENCY	○	See policy	
167	LIQUIDATION	○	See policy	
168	RECEIVERSHIP	○	See policy	
169	FINANCIAL INABILITY TO PAY	○	See policy	
170	MERGER	○	See policy	
171	PLANT OR FACILITY CLOSING	○	See policy	
172	REORGANIZATION	○	See policy	
173	TEMPORARY SHUTDOWN	○	See policy	
174	**MATTERS DEEMED UNINSURABLE**	○	See policy	
175	**NON-MONETARY RELIEF**	—		
176	DECLATORY RELIEF	—		
177	DISGORGEMENT	—		
178	INJUNCTIVE RELIEF	—		
179	JOB REINSTATEMENT	●		(C)(8), page 3
180	NON-MONETARY DAMAGES/RELIEF	●		(C)(4), page 3
181	OTHER EQUITABLE REMEDIES	—		
182	**OBLIGATION TO PROVIDE BENEFITS**	—		
183	COBRA	●	Retaliation exception	(C)(2), page 2
184	DISABILITY	—		
185	ERISA	●	Retaliation exception	(C)(2), page 2
186	SOCIAL SECURITY	—		
187	OTHER RETIREMENT BENEFITS	—		
188	UNEMPLOYMENT	●	Retaliation exception	(C)(3), page 3
189	WORKERS' COMPENSATION	●	Retaliation exception	(C)(3), page 3
190	**PERSONAL INJURY OFFENSES**	—		
191	DEFAMATION	—		
192	EMOTIONAL DISTRESS/UPSET	—		
193	HUMILIATION	—		
194	LIBEL	—		
195	MENTAL ANGUISH	—		
196	PERSONAL INJURY	—		
197	SLANDER	—		
198	**PRIOR ACTS**	—		
199	PRIOR ACTS	—		
200	PRIOR KNOWLEDGE	●	As respects wrongful termination	(C)(5), page 3
201	PRIOR/PENDING LITIGATION	●	As respects wrongful termination	(C)(6), page 3
202	**PROPERTY DAMAGE**	—		
203	INTANGIBLE PROPERTY	—		
204	LOSS OF USE	—		
205	TANGIBLE PROPERTY	—		
206	**RETALIATORY ACTIONS OF EMPLOYER**	—		
207	FOR FAILING TO PERFORM ACTS AGAINST PUBLIC POLICY	—		
208	FOR FILING A COMPLAINT OR BENEFIT CLAIM	—		
209	**STRIKES/LOCKOUTS**	—		
210	**VIOLATION OF LAWS**	—		
211	ANY LAW	—		
212	FMLA	—		
213	OSHA	●	Retaliation exception	(C)(2), pages 2–3
214	POLLUTION LAWS	—		
215	RICO	—		
216	SEC	—		
217	WARN	●	Retaliation exception	(C)(2), page 2
	15 CONDITIONS			
218	**ARBITRATION**	○	See policy	
219	MANDATORY	○	See policy	
220	BINDING	○	See policy	
221	CHOICE OF LAW PROVISION	○	See policy	
222	SITUS	○	See policy	
223	**TERRITORY**	—		
224	LIMITED	○	See policy	
225	WORLDWIDE	○	See policy	
226	**NEWLY FORMED/ACQUIRED ENTITIES**	—		
227	AUTOMATIC COVERAGE (X DAYS)	○	See policy	
228	NOTIFY INSURER WITHIN X DAYS	○	See policy	

ASSOCIATED ELECTRIC & GAS INSURANCE SERVICES, LIMITED 8262 (1/98) [1/98]

Policy Comparison Worksheet

Chubb Group

Policy Form No.: 14-02-0953
Edition Date: 8/96

Risks Considered: General accounts
Limits Available: $50 million
Minimum Retention: $10,000

Contact: Michael J. Maloney
Chubb & Son, Inc.
15 Mountain View Road
Warren, NJ 07059
908/903-3494
908/903-3591 (fax)

KEY TO SYMBOLS
● = Specifically contains queried provision of feature
○ = Unable to determine
— = Silent

#	Comparison Query		Comment	Policy Reference
	1 APPLICATION			
1	ATTACHES TO AND FORMS A PART OF THE POLICY	●		Representations and Severability, 15., page 7
2	CONTAINS WARRANTY STATEMENTS	—		
3	CONTAINS SEVERABILITY PROVISIONS	●	Exception applies	Representations and Severability, 15., page 7
	2 POLICY TYPE			
4	UNITARY STAND ALONE POLICY	●		
	ENDORSEMENT OR PART OF	—		
5	DIRECTORS AND OFFICERS POLICY	—		
6	PACKAGE POLICY	—		
7	UMBRELLA POLICY	—		
8	ERRORS AND OMISSIONS POLICY	—		
9	OTHER	—		
10	CLAIMS-MADE	●		
11	OCCURRENCE	—		
	3 WHO IS INSURED			
12	BUSINESS ENTITY	●	As "insured organization"	Definitions, 16., Insured, page 7
13	AUTOMATIC COVERAGE FOR SUBSIDIARIES	—		
14	DIRECTORS & OFFICERS	○	If designated on Declarations	Definitions, 16., Insured Persons, page 7
15	EMPLOYEES	○	If designated on Declarations	Definitions, 16., Insured Persons, page 7
16	PART-TIME	○	If designated on Declarations	Definitions, 16., Insured Persons, page 7
17	SEASONAL	○	If designated on Declarations	Definitions, 16., Insured Persons, page 7
18	TEMPORARY	○	If designated on Declarations	Definitions, 16., Insured Persons, page 7
19	SUPERVISORS & MANAGERS	○	If designated on Declarations	Definitions, 16., Insured Persons, page 7
20	FORMER EMPLOYEES	○	If designated on Declarations	Definitions, 16., Insured Persons, page 7
21	VOLUNTEERS	○	If designated on Declarations	Definitions, 16., Insured Persons, page 7
22	INDEPENDENT CONTRACTORS	●	Only if considered employees under law	Definitions, 16., Insured Persons, page 7
23	EXCLUDED	○	If designated on Declarations	Definitions, 16., Insured Persons, page 7
24	SILENT	○	If designated on Declarations	Definitions, 16., Insured Persons, page 7
25	SHAREHOLDERS	—		
	4 LIMIT OF LIABILITY			
26	AGGREGATE	●		Limit of Liability, 8., page 4
27	INCLUDES PUNITIVE DAMAGES WHERE NOT UNINSURABLE	—		
28	DEFENSE COSTS INCLUDED WITHIN LIMIT OF LIABILITY	●		Defense Provisions 3., page 2
29	DEFENSE COSTS PAID IN ADDITION TO LIMIT OF LIABILITY	—		
	5 DEDUCTIBLE			
30	APPLIES TO EACH INDIVIDUAL CLAIM	●		Limit of Liability, 8., page 4
31	APPLIES TO EACH OCCURRENCE OR WRONGFUL PRACTICE	●		Limit of Liability, 8., page 4
32	INCLUDES ALL CLAIMS FROM ONE ACT	●		Limit of Liability, 8., page 4
33	SUBJECT TO ANNUAL AGGREGATE	—		
34	CO-PAYMENT APPLIES	●		Limit of Liability, 8., page 5
35	LIMIT OF LIABILITY NOT REDUCED	—		
36	INCLUDES DEFENSE COSTS	●		Declarations, Item 2
37	REDUCED UNDER SPECIFIED CIRCUMSTANCES (SEE POLICY)	—		

CHUBB GROUP 14-02-0953 [8/96]

#	Comparison Query	Comment		Policy Reference
	6 WHAT IS A CLAIM			
38	ORAL COMPLAINT TO INSURED	—		
39	WRITTEN COMPLAINT TO INSURED	●		Definitions, 16., Claim, page 7
40	COMPLAINT MUST CONTAIN A DEMAND FOR DAMAGES	●		Definitions, 16., Claim, page 7
41	COMPLAINT FILED WITH EEOC	—		
42	OR SIMILAR STATE AUTHORITY			
43	AGENCY MUST HAVE POWER TO ADJUDICATE			
44	ADMINISTRATIVE PROCEEDING	●	Administrative or regulatory	Definitions, 16., Claim, page 7
45	ARBITRATION PROCEEDING	●		Definitions, 16., Claim, page 7
46	ANY INCIDENT REPORTED TO INSURER	—		
47	SUIT	●		Definitions, 16., Claim, page 7
48	CLAIM DOES NOT INCLUDE ARBITRATION SUBJECT TO	—		
49	COLLECTIVE BARGAINING AGREEMENT	—		
50	EMPLOYEE POLICY OR MANUAL	—		
51	CLAIM NOT DEFINED	—		
	7 CLAIM REPORTING PROVISIONS TO INSURER			
52	IMMEDIATELY	—		
53	AS SOON AS POSSIBLE	—		
54	AS SOON AS PRACTICABLE	●		Reporting and Notice, 9., page 5
55	WITHIN POLICY PERIOD	—		
56	WITHIN X DAYS OF EXPIRATION	—		
57	WITHIN X DAYS	—		
	8 EXTENDED REPORTING FEATURES			
58	ELECTION PERIOD (DAYS)	30		Extended Reporting Period, 4., page 2
59	ADDITIONAL PREMIUM (% OF ANNUAL PREMIUM)	○	Specified by underwriter—see item 7(A) of Declarations	Extended Reporting Period, 4., page 2
60	ADDITIONAL REPORTING PERIOD (MONTHS)	○	Specified by underwriter— see item 7(B) of Declarations	Extended Reporting Period, 4., page 2
61	NO REINSTATEMENT OF LIMITS	—		
	9 POTENTIAL CLAIM REPORTING PROVISIONS			
62	NONE (SEE ALSO "CLAIM" ABOVE)	—		
63	INCIDENTS LIKELY TO RESULT IN A CLAIM	—		
	10 DEFENSE PROVISIONS			
64	AFFIRMATIVE DUTY TO DEFEND	●		Defense Provisions, 3., page 2
65	NO AFFIRMATIVE DUTY TO DEFEND	—		
66	AFFIRMATIVE ADVANCEMENT PROVISIONS	—		
67	INSURED MUST RETURN ADVANCED AMOUNTS IF NOT COVERED	—		
68	INSURED/INSURER CHOOSES COUNSEL	—		
69	INSURED/INSURER APPROVES COUNSEL	—		
70	INSURED/INSURER CONSULTED IN COUNSEL SELECTION	—		
	11 SETTLEMENT PROVISIONS			
71	HAMMER CLAUSE	—		
72	CONSULTATION PROVISION	—		
73	CONSENT PROVISION	●	Insurer must consent	Defense Provisions, 3., page 2
	12 ALLOCATION OF LOSS PROVISIONS			
74	STIPULATED PROVISIONS	●	Best efforts	Arbitration and Allocation, 10., page 5
	13 COVERAGES			
75	DISCRIMINATION	●		Definitions, 16., Claim, page 7
76	SPECIFIC ENUMERATED ACTIVITIES	—		
77	*PLUS BROAD OMNIBUS WORDING*	—		
78	SPECIFIC ENUMERATED CLASSES	—		
79	*PLUS BROAD OMNIBUS WORDING*	—		
80	AGAINST THIRD PARTIES	—		
81	DISCRIMINATION NOT DEFINED	●		Definitions, 16., Claim, page 7
82	SEXUAL HARASSMENT	●		Definitions, 16., Claim, page 7
83	HOSTILE ENVIRONMENT	—		
84	QUID-PRO-QUO	—		
85	SEXUAL HARASSMENT NOT DEFINED	●		Definitions, 16., Claim, page 7
86	WRONGFUL TERMINATION	●		Definitions, 16., Claim, page 7
87	BREACH OF IMPLIED CONTRACT	○		Definitions, 16., Claim, page 7
88	BREACH OF EXPRESS CONTRACT	○		Definitions, 16., Claim, page 7
89	VIOLATION OF PUBLIC POLICY	—		
90	VIOLATION OF GOOD FAITH & FAIR DEALING	—		
91	OBLIGATIONS TO MAKE PAYMENTS	—		
92	CONSTRUCTIVE DISCHARGE	—		
93	WRONGFUL TERMINATION NOT DEFINED	—		
94	OTHER EMPLOYMENT VIOLATIONS/OFFENSES	—		
95	WRONGFUL HIRING	●		Definitions, 16., Claim, page 7
96	WRONGFUL PROMOTION/DEMOTION	●		Definitions, 16., Claim, page 7
97	WRONGFUL EVALUATION/DISCIPLINE	●		Definitions, 16., Claim, page 7

#	Comparison Query	Comment	Policy Reference
98	FAMILY AND MEDICAL LEAVE ACT	—	
99	DEFAMATION	●	Definitions, 16., Claim, page 7
100	MISREPRESENTATION	●	Definitions, 16., Claim, page 7
101	RETALIATION	—	
102	MENTAL ANGUISH	—	
103	INVASION OF PRIVACY	●	Definitions, 16., Claim, page 7
104	HUMILIATION	—	
105	EMOTIONAL DISTRESS	●	Definitions, 16., Claim, page 7
106	OTHER PERSONAL INJURY OFFENSES	●	Definitions, 16., Claim, page 7
107	POLICY SILENT	—	
	14 EXCLUSIONS		
108	**ADA ACCOMMODATION EXPENSES**	●	Exclusions, 6.(c), page 4
109	**ASSAULT & BATTERY**	—	
110	**BACK PAY**	—	
111	**BODILY INJURY**	●	Mental anguish exception	Exclusions, 5.(d), page 3
112	BODILY INJURY	●		Exclusions, 5.(d), page 3
113	DEATH	●		Exclusions, 5.(d), page 3
114	DISEASE	●		Exclusions, 5.(d), page 3
115	SICKNESS	●		Exclusions, 5.(d), page 3
116	**BREACH OF EMPLOYMENT CONTRACT**	—	
117	EXPRESS CONTRACT	—	
118	*WRITTEN CONTRACT*	—	
119	*ORAL CONTRACT*	—	
120	IMPLIED CONTRACT	—	
121	**CLASS ACTION LAWSUITS**	—	
122	**CONSEQUENTIAL LOSS**	—	
123	APPLIES TO BODILY INJURY	—	
124	APPLIES TO INSURED EVENT	—	
125	BROTHER/SISTER	—	
126	CHILD	—	
127	DOMESTIC PARTNER	—	
128	PARENT	—	
129	SPOUSE	—	
130	**COST OF ARBITRATION HEARINGS SUBJECT TO**	—	
131	EMPLOYMENT HANDBOOK	—	
132	LABOR GRIEVANCE	—	
133	OTHER EMPLOYMENT POLICY OR PROCEDURE	—	
134	**COVERAGE ELSEWHERE**	—	
135	OTHER AVAILABLE INSURANCE	●	As respects Chubb policies	Exclusions, 5.(a), page 3
136	OTHER INDEMNIFICATION	—	
137	SHARING PROVISION	—	
138	**FAILURE TO EXERCISE CARE WHEN TERMINATING**	—	
139	**FINES/PENALTIES**	●		Definitions, 16., Loss, page 8
140	CIVIL	—	
141	CRIMINAL	—	
142	EXEMPLARY DAMAGES	—	
143	PUNITIVE DAMAGES	—	
144	MULTIPLIED DAMAGES	●		Definitions, 16., Loss, page 8
145	**FRONT PAY**	●		Exclusions, 6.(b), page 4
146	EXCLUSION APPLIES ONLY IF EMPLOYER HAD OPPORTUNITY TO REINSTATE EMPLOYEE BUT DID NOT DO SO	●		Exclusions, 6.(b), page 4
147	**INTENTIONAL ACTS**	—	
148	CRIMINAL ACTS	—	
149	CRIMINAL PROCEEDING	—	
150	DISHONEST PURPOSE	—	
151	FRAUDULENT ACTS	●	If established through adjudication	Exclusions, 5.(f), page 3
152	FRAUDULENT CLAIMS	—	
153	INTENTIONAL VIOLATIONS OF LAW	—	
154	WILLFUL FAILURE TO COMPLY WITH LAW	—	
155	MALICIOUS PURPOSE	—	
156	**LIABILITY OF OTHERS**	●		Exclusions, 5.(i), page 4
157	**LIQUIDATED DAMAGES**	—	
158	**LOSS ARISING OUT OF CHANGES IN OPERATIONS**	—	
159	ACQUISITION	—	
160	CHANGE IN CONTROL	—	
161	DOWNSIZING OR REDUCTION IN FORCE	—	
162	*% OF WORKFORCE*	—	
163	*WITHIN X DAYS*	—	

CHUBB GROUP 14-02-0953 [8/96]

	Comparison Query	Comment	Policy Reference
164	**FINANCIAL IMPAIRMENT**	—	
165	*BANKRUPTCY*	—	
166	*INSOLVENCY*	—	
167	*LIQUIDATION*	—	
168	*RECEIVERSHIP*	—	
169	FINANCIAL INABILITY TO PAY	—	
170	MERGER	—	
171	PLANT OR FACILITY CLOSING	—	
172	REORGANIZATION	—	
173	TEMPORARY SHUTDOWN	—	
174	**MATTERS DEEMED UNINSURABLE**	●	Definitions, 16., Loss, page 8
175	**NON-MONETARY RELIEF**	—	
176	DECLATORY RELIEF	—	
177	DISGORGEMENT	—	
178	INJUNCTIVE RELIEF	●	Exclusions, 6.(d)., page 4
179	JOB REINSTATEMENT	—	
180	NON-MONETARY DAMAGES/RELIEF	●	Exclusions, 6.(d)., page 4
181	OTHER EQUITABLE REMEDIES	—	
182	**OBLIGATION TO PROVIDE BENEFITS**	—	
183	COBRA	●	Exclusions, 5.(c)., page 3
184	DISABILITY	●	Retaliation exception	Exclusions, 5.(g)., page 3
185	ERISA	●	Exclusions, 5.(c)., page 3
186	SOCIAL SECURITY	●	Retaliation exception	Exclusions, 5.(g)., page 3
187	OTHER RETIREMENT BENEFITS	—	
188	UNEMPLOYMENT	●	Retaliation exception	Exclusions, 5.(g)., page 3
189	WORKERS' COMPENSATION	●	Retaliation exception	Exclusions, 5.(g)., page 3
190	**PERSONAL INJURY OFFENSES**	—	
191	DEFAMATION	—	
192	EMOTIONAL DISTRESS/UPSET	—	
193	HUMILIATION	—	
194	LIBEL	—	
195	MENTAL ANGUISH	—	
196	PERSONAL INJURY	—	
197	SLANDER	—	
198	**PRIOR ACTS**	—	
199	PRIOR ACTS	—	
200	PRIOR KNOWLEDGE	—	
201	PRIOR/PENDING LITIGATION	●	Exclusions, 5.(b)., page 3
202	**PROPERTY DAMAGE**	●	Exclusions, 5.(d)., page 3
203	INTANGIBLE PROPERTY	—	
204	LOSS OF USE	●	Exclusions, 5.(d)., page 3
205	TANGIBLE PROPERTY	●	Exclusions, 5.(d)., page 3
206	**RETALIATORY ACTIONS OF EMPLOYER**	—	
207	FOR FAILING TO PERFORM ACTS AGAINST PUBLIC POLICY	—	
208	FOR FILING A COMPLAINT OR BENEFIT CLAIM	—	
209	**STRIKES/LOCKOUTS**	—	
210	**VIOLATION OF LAWS**	—	
211	ANY LAW	—	
212	FMLA	—	
213	OSHA	●	Retaliation exception	Exclusions, 5.(c)., page 3
214	POLLUTION LAWS	●	Retaliation exception	Exclusions, 5.(e)., page 3
215	RICO	—	
216	SEC	—	
217	WARN	●	Exclusions, 5.(c)., page 3

15 CONDITIONS

218	**ARBITRATION**	●	Arbitration and Allocation, 10., page 5
219	MANDATORY	●	Arbitration and Allocation, 10., page 5
220	BINDING	●	Arbitration and Allocation, 10., page 5
221	CHOICE OF LAW PROVISION	—	
222	SITUS	—	
223	**TERRITORY**	—	
224	LIMITED	—	
225	WORLDWIDE	—	
226	**NEWLY FORMED/ACQUIRED ENTITIES**	—	
227	AUTOMATIC COVERAGE (X DAYS)	●	If < 10% assets involved—no time limit specified	Changes in Exposure, 12., page 6
228	NOTIFY INSURER WITHIN X DAYS	●	If > 10% assets involved—no time limit specified	Changes in Exposure, 12., page 6

CHUBB GROUP 14-02-0953 [8/96]

Policy Comparison Worksheet

Chubb Group

Policy Form No.: 14-02-1968
Edition Date: 5-96

Risks Considered: General accounts
Limits Available: $10,000,000
Minimum Retention: $10,000

Contact: John A. Kuhn
Chubb Group
15 Mountain View Road
Warren, NJ 07059
908/903-2726
908/903-3591 (fax)

KEY TO SYMBOLS
● = Specifically contains queried provision of feature
○ = Unable to determine
— = Silent

#	Comparison Query		Comment	Policy Reference
	1 APPLICATION			
1	ATTACHES TO AND FORMS A PART OF THE POLICY	●		Representations & Severability, 27., page 12
2	CONTAINS WARRANTY STATEMENTS	●		
3	CONTAINS SEVERABILITY PROVISIONS			
	2 POLICY TYPE			
4	UNITARY STAND ALONE POLICY	●		
	ENDORSEMENT OR PART OF	—		
5	DIRECTORS AND OFFICERS POLICY	—		
6	PACKAGE POLICY	—		
7	UMBRELLA POLICY	—		
8	ERRORS AND OMISSIONS POLICY	—		
9	OTHER	—		
10	CLAIMS-MADE	●		
11	OCCURRENCE	—		
	3 WHO IS INSURED			
12	BUSINESS ENTITY	●		Definitions, 18. Insured, page 15
13	AUTOMATIC COVERAGE FOR SUBSIDIARIES	—		
14	DIRECTORS & OFFICERS	●		Definitions, 18. Insured Person, page 15
15	EMPLOYEES	●		Definitions, 18. Insured Person, page 15
16	PART-TIME	—		
17	SEASONAL	—		
18	TEMPORARY	—		
19	SUPERVISORS & MANAGERS	—		
20	FORMER EMPLOYEES	●		Definitions, 18. Insured Person, page 15
21	VOLUNTEERS	—		
22	INDEPENDENT CONTRACTORS	—		
23	EXCLUDED	—		
24	SILENT	—		
25	SHAREHOLDERS	—		
	4 LIMIT OF LIABILITY			
26	AGGREGATE	●		Limit of Liability, 15., page 8
27	INCLUDES PUNITIVE DAMAGES WHERE NOT UNINSURABLE	—		
28	DEFENSE COSTS INCLUDED WITHIN LIMIT OF LIABILITY	●		Defense & Settlement, 16., page 9
29	DEFENSE COSTS PAID IN ADDITION TO LIMIT OF LIABILITY	—		
	5 DEDUCTIBLE			
30	APPLIES TO EACH INDIVIDUAL CLAIM	—		
31	APPLIES TO EACH OCCURRENCE OR WRONGFUL PRACTICE	●		Limit of Liability, 15., page 8
32	INCLUDES ALL CLAIMS FROM ONE ACT	●		Limit of Liability, 15., page 8
33	SUBJECT TO ANNUAL AGGREGATE	—		
34	CO-PAYMENT APPLIES	—		
35	LIMIT OF LIABILITY NOT REDUCED	—		
36	INCLUDES DEFENSE COSTS	●		Limit of Liability, 15., page 8
37	REDUCED UNDER SPECIFIED CIRCUMSTANCES (SEE POLICY)	—		

#	Comparison Query	Comment	Policy Reference
	6 WHAT IS A CLAIM		
38	ORAL COMPLAINT TO INSURED	—	
39	WRITTEN COMPLAINT TO INSURED	●	Definitions, 38., Employment Claim, (a), page 14
40	COMPLAINT MUST CONTAIN A DEMAND FOR DAMAGES	●	Definitions, 38., Employment Claim, (a), page 14
41	COMPLAINT FILED WITH EEOC	—	
42	OR SIMILAR STATE AUTHORITY	—	
43	AGENCY MUST HAVE POWER TO ADJUDICATE	—	
44	ADMINISTRATIVE PROCEEDING	●	Definitions, 38., Employment Claim, (d), page 15
45	ARBITRATION PROCEEDING	●	Definitions, 38., Employment Claim, (c), page 15
46	ANY INCIDENT REPORTED TO INSURER	—	
47	SUIT	●	Civil proceeding	Definitions, 38., Employment Claim, (b), page 15
48	CLAIM DOES NOT INCLUDE ARBITRATION SUBJECT TO	—	
49	COLLECTIVE BARGAINING AGREEMENT	—	
50	EMPLOYEE POLICY OR MANUAL	—	
51	CLAIM NOT DEFINED		
	7 CLAIM REPORTING PROVISIONS TO INSURER		
52	IMMEDIATELY	—	
53	AS SOON AS POSSIBLE	—	
54	AS SOON AS PRACTICABLE	●	Reporting & Notice, 29., page 12
55	WITHIN POLICY PERIOD	—	
56	WITHIN X DAYS OF EXPIRATION	—	
57	WITHIN X DAYS	—	
	8 EXTENDED REPORTING FEATURES		
58	ELECTION PERIOD (DAYS)	30	Extended Reporting Period, 7., page 4
59	ADDITIONAL PREMIUM (% OF ANNUAL PREMIUM)	75	Extended Reporting Period, 7., page 4
60	ADDITIONAL REPORTING PERIOD (MONTHS)	12	Extended Reporting Period, 7., page 4
61	NO REINSTATEMENT OF LIMITS	●	Limit of Liability, 15., page 9
	9 POTENTIAL CLAIM REPORTING PROVISIONS		
62	NONE (SEE ALSO "CLAIM" ABOVE)	●	
63	INCIDENTS LIKELY TO RESULT IN A CLAIM	—	
	10 DEFENSE PROVISIONS		
64	AFFIRMATIVE DUTY TO DEFEND	●	Defense & Settlement, 16., page 9
65	NO AFFIRMATIVE DUTY TO DEFEND	—	
66	AFFIRMATIVE ADVANCEMENT PROVISIONS	—	
67	INSURED MUST RETURN ADVANCED AMOUNTS IF NOT COVERED	—	
68	INSURED/INSURER CHOOSES COUNSEL	—	
69	INSURED/INSURER APPROVES COUNSEL	—	
70	INSURED/INSURER CONSULTED IN COUNSEL SELECTION	—	
	11 SETTLEMENT PROVISIONS		
71	HAMMER CLAUSE	●	Defense & Settlement, 16., page 9
72	CONSULTATION PROVISION	—	
73	CONSENT PROVISION	●	Two-way	Defense & Settlement, 16., page 9
	12 ALLOCATION OF LOSS PROVISIONS		
74	STIPULATED PROVISIONS	●	Re: Insuring clauses	Allocation, 17., pages 9–10
	13 COVERAGES		
75	DISCRIMINATION	●	Definitions, 38., Employment Claim, page 15
76	SPECIFIC ENUMERATED ACTIVITIES	—	
77	PLUS BROAD OMNIBUS WORDING	—	
78	SPECIFIC ENUMERATED CLASSES	—	
79	PLUS BROAD OMNIBUS WORDING	—	
80	AGAINST THIRD PARTIES	—	
81	DISCRIMINATION NOT DEFINED	●	
82	SEXUAL HARASSMENT	●	Definitions, 38., Employment Claim, page 15
83	HOSTILE ENVIRONMENT	—	
84	QUID-PRO-QUO	—	
85	SEXUAL HARASSMENT NOT DEFINED	●	
86	WRONGFUL TERMINATION	●	Definitions, 38., Employment Claim, page 15
87	BREACH OF IMPLIED CONTRACT	—	
88	BREACH OF EXPRESS CONTRACT	●	Written or oral	Definitions, 38., Employment Claim, page 15
89	VIOLATION OF PUBLIC POLICY	—	
90	VIOLATION OF GOOD FAITH & FAIR DEALING	—	
91	OBLIGATIONS TO MAKE PAYMENTS	—	
92	CONSTRUCTIVE DISCHARGE	—	
93	WRONGFUL TERMINATION NOT DEFINED	●	
94	OTHER EMPLOYMENT VIOLATIONS/OFFENSES	●	Definitions, 38., Employment Claim, page 15
95	WRONGFUL HIRING	●	Definitions, 38., Employment Claim, page 15
96	WRONGFUL PROMOTION/DEMOTION	●	Definitions, 38., Employment Claim, page 15
97	WRONGFUL EVALUATION/DISCIPLINE	●	Definitions, 38., Employment Claim, page 15

	Comparison Query	Comment	Policy Reference
98	FAMILY AND MEDICAL LEAVE ACT	—	
99	DEFAMATION	●	Definitions, 38., Employment Claim, page 15
100	MISREPRESENTATION	●	Definitions, 38., Employment Claim, page 15
101	RETALIATION	—	
102	MENTAL ANGUISH	—	
103	INVASION OF PRIVACY	●	Definitions, 38., Employment Claim, page 15
104	HUMILIATION	—	
105	EMOTIONAL DISTRESS	●	Definitions, 38., Employment Claim, page 15
106	OTHER PERSONAL INJURY OFFENSES	●	Definitions, 38., Employment Claim, page 15
107	POLICY SILENT	—	

14 EXCLUSIONS

	Comparison Query	Comment	Policy Reference
108	**ADA ACCOMMODATION EXPENSES**	●	Exclusions, 10.(c)., page 6
109	**ASSAULT & BATTERY**	—	
110	**BACK PAY**	—	
111	**BODILY INJURY**	●	Exclusions, 9.(a)., page 5
112	BODILY INJURY	●	Exclusions, 9.(a)., page 5
113	DEATH	●	Exclusions, 9.(a)., page 5
114	DISEASE	●	Exclusions, 9.(a)., page 5
115	SICKNESS	●	Exclusions, 9.(a)., page 5
116	**BREACH OF EMPLOYMENT CONTRACT**	—	
117	EXPRESS CONTRACT	—	
118	WRITTEN CONTRACT	—	
119	ORAL CONTRACT	—	
120	IMPLIED CONTRACT	—	
121	**CLASS ACTION LAWSUITS**	—	
122	**CONSEQUENTIAL LOSS**	—	
123	APPLIES TO BODILY INJURY	—	
124	APPLIES TO INSURED EVENT	—	
125	BROTHER/SISTER	—	
126	CHILD	—	
127	DOMESTIC PARTNER	—	
128	PARENT	—	
129	SPOUSE	—	
130	**COST OF ARBITRATION HEARINGS SUBJECT TO**	—	
131	EMPLOYMENT HANDBOOK	—	
132	LABOR GRIEVANCE	—	
133	OTHER EMPLOYMENT POLICY OR PROCEDURE	—	
134	**COVERAGE ELSEWHERE**	●	Other Insurance, 19., page 10
135	OTHER AVAILABLE INSURANCE	●	Other Insurance, 19., page 10
136	OTHER INDEMNIFICATION	—	
137	SHARING PROVISION	—	
138	**FAILURE TO EXERCISE CARE WHEN TERMINATING**	—	
139	**FINES/PENALTIES**	●	Definitions, 38., Loss, page 16
140	CIVIL	—	
141	CRIMINAL	—	
142	EXEMPLARY DAMAGES	—	
143	PUNITIVE DAMAGES	—	
144	MULTIPLIED DAMAGES	●	Definitions, 38., Loss, page 16
145	**FRONT PAY**	●	Pays defense costs	Exclusions, 10.(b)., page 6
146	EXCLUSION APPLIES ONLY IF EMPLOYER HAD OPPORTUNITY TO REINSTATE EMPLOYEE BUT DID NOT DO SO	●	Pays defense costs	Exclusions, 10.(b)., page 6
147	**INTENTIONAL ACTS**	●	Exclusions, 9.(b)., page 5
148	CRIMINAL ACTS	—	
149	CRIMINAL PROCEEDING	—	
150	DISHONEST PURPOSE	—	
151	FRAUDULENT ACTS	●	Exclusions 9.(b)., page 5
152	FRAUDULENT CLAIMS	—	
153	INTENTIONAL VIOLATIONS OF LAW	●	Exclusions 9.(b)., page 5
154	WILLFUL FAILURE TO COMPLY WITH LAW	—	
155	MALICIOUS PURPOSE	—	
156	**LIABILITY OF OTHERS**	●	Exclusions 9.(f)., page 5
157	**LIQUIDATED DAMAGES**	—	
158	**LOSS ARISING OUT OF CHANGES IN OPERATIONS**	—	
159	ACQUISITION	—	
160	CHANGE IN CONTROL	—	
161	DOWNSIZING OR REDUCTION IN FORCE	—	
162	% OF WORKFORCE	—	
163	WITHIN X DAYS	—	

CHUBB GROUP 14-02-1968 [5/96]

	Comparison Query	Comment	Policy Reference
164	FINANCIAL IMPAIRMENT	—	
165	BANKRUPTCY	—	
166	INSOLVENCY	—	
167	LIQUIDATION	—	
168	RECEIVERSHIP	—	
169	FINANCIAL INABILITY TO PAY	—	
170	MERGER	—	
171	PLANT OR FACILITY CLOSING	—	
172	REORGANIZATION	—	
173	TEMPORARY SHUTDOWN	—	
174	**MATTERS DEEMED UNINSURABLE**	●	Definitions, 38., Loss, page 16
175	**NON-MONETARY RELIEF**	—	
176	DECLATORY RELIEF	—	
177	DISGORGEMENT	—	
178	INJUNCTIVE RELIEF	—	
179	JOB REINSTATEMENT	—	
180	NON-MONETARY DAMAGES/RELIEF	—	
181	OTHER EQUITABLE REMEDIES	—	
182	**OBLIGATION TO PROVIDE BENEFITS**		
183	COBRA	●	Exclusions, 9.(g)., page 6
184	DISABILITY	●	Exclusions, 9.(d)., page 5
185	ERISA	●	Exclusions, 9.(g)., page 6
186	SOCIAL SECURITY	●	Exclusions, 9.(d)., page 5
187	OTHER RETIREMENT BENEFITS	—	
188	UNEMPLOYMENT	●	Exclusions, 9.(d)., page 5
189	WORKERS' COMPENSATION	●	Exclusions, 9.(d)., page 5
190	**PERSONAL INJURY OFFENSES**	—	
191	DEFAMATION	—	
192	EMOTIONAL DISTRESS/UPSET	—	
193	HUMILIATION	—	
194	LIBEL	—	
195	MENTAL ANGUISH	—	
196	PERSONAL INJURY	—	
197	SLANDER	—	
198	**PRIOR ACTS**	—	
199	PRIOR ACTS	—	
200	PRIOR KNOWLEDGE	●	See also application	Exclusions, 8.(a)., page 4
201	PRIOR/PENDING LITIGATION	●	Exclusions, 8.(c)., page 5
202	**PROPERTY DAMAGE**	●	Exclusions, 9.(a)., page 5
203	INTANGIBLE PROPERTY	—	
204	LOSS OF USE	●	Exclusions, 9.(a)., page 5
205	TANGIBLE PROPERTY	●	Exclusions, 9.(a)., page 5
206	**RETALIATORY ACTIONS OF EMPLOYER**	—	
207	FOR FAILING TO PERFORM ACTS AGAINST PUBLIC POLICY	—	
208	FOR FILING A COMPLAINT OR BENEFIT CLAIM	—	
209	**STRIKES/LOCKOUTS**	—	
210	**VIOLATION OF LAWS**	—	
211	ANY LAW	●	Exclusions, 9.(g)., page 6
212	FMLA	—	
213	OSHA	●	Exception applies	Exclusions, 9.(g)., page 6
214	POLLUTION LAWS	—	
215	RICO	—	
216	SEC	—	
217	WARN	●	Exclusions, 9.(g)., page 6

15 CONDITIONS

218	**ARBITRATION**	●	Coverage Arbitration, 18., page 10
219	MANDATORY	●	Coverage Arbitration, 18., page 10
220	BINDING	●	Coverage Arbitration, 18., page 10
221	CHOICE OF LAW PROVISION	—	
222	SITUS	—	
223	**TERRITORY**	●	Territory, 28., page 12
224	LIMITED	—	
225	WORLDWIDE	●	Territory, 28., page 12
226	**NEWLY FORMED/ACQUIRED ENTITIES**	—	
227	AUTOMATIC COVERAGE (X DAYS)	—	
228	NOTIFY INSURER WITHIN X DAYS	●	As soon as practicable	Changes In Exposure, 21., page 10

CHUBB GROUP   14-02-1968 [5/96]

Policy Comparison Worksheet

Chubb Group

Policy Form No.: 14-02-2009
Edition Date: 5-96

Risks Considered: Nonprofit organizations
Limits Available: $50,000,000
Minimum Retention: None

Contact: A. Quentin Orza
Product Manager
Chubb Group
15 Mountain View Road
Warren, NJ 07059
908/903-2726
908/903-3591 (fax)

KEY TO SYMBOLS
● = Specifically contains queried provision of feature
○ = Unable to determine
— = Silent

#	Comparison Query	Symbol	Comment	Policy Reference
	1 APPLICATION			
1	ATTACHES TO AND FORMS A PART OF THE POLICY	●		Changes in Exposure, 27., page 12
2	CONTAINS WARRANTY STATEMENTS	●	If no prior coverage	Changes in Exposure, 27., page 12
3	CONTAINS SEVERABILITY PROVISIONS	●		Changes in Exposure, 27., page 12
	2 POLICY TYPE			
4	UNITARY STAND ALONE POLICY	●		
	ENDORSEMENT OR PART OF	—		
5	DIRECTORS AND OFFICERS POLICY	—		
6	PACKAGE POLICY	—		
7	UMBRELLA POLICY	—		
8	ERRORS AND OMISSIONS POLICY	—		
9	OTHER	—		
10	CLAIMS-MADE	●		
11	OCCURRENCE	—		
	3 WHO IS INSURED			
12	BUSINESS ENTITY	●		Definitions, 22., Insured, page 9
13	AUTOMATIC COVERAGE FOR SUBSIDIARIES	—		
14	DIRECTORS & OFFICERS	●		Definitions, 22., Insured Person, page 9
15	EMPLOYEES	●		Definitions, 22., Insured Person, page 9
16	PART-TIME	—		
17	SEASONAL	—		
18	TEMPORARY	—		
19	SUPERVISORS & MANAGERS	—		
20	FORMER EMPLOYEES	—		
21	VOLUNTEERS	●		Definitions, 22., Insured Person, page 9
22	INDEPENDENT CONTRACTORS	—		
23	EXCLUDED	—		
24	SILENT	—		
25	SHAREHOLDERS	—		
	4 LIMIT OF LIABILITY			
26	AGGREGATE	●		Limit of Liability, 6., page 5
27	INCLUDES PUNITIVE DAMAGES WHERE NOT UNINSURABLE	—		
28	DEFENSE COSTS INCLUDED WITHIN LIMIT OF LIABILITY	●		Defense & Settlement, 8., page 6
29	DEFENSE COSTS PAID IN ADDITION TO LIMIT OF LIABILITY	—		
	5 DEDUCTIBLE			
30	APPLIES TO EACH INDIVIDUAL CLAIM	—		
31	APPLIES TO EACH OCCURRENCE OR WRONGFUL PRACTICE	●	Indemnifiable loss only	Limit of Liability, 6., page 5
32	INCLUDES ALL CLAIMS FROM ONE ACT	●	Indemnifiable loss only	Limit of Liability, 6., page 5
33	SUBJECT TO ANNUAL AGGREGATE	—		
34	CO-PAYMENT APPLIES	—		
35	LIMIT OF LIABILITY NOT REDUCED	—		
36	INCLUDES DEFENSE COSTS	●	Indemnifiable loss only	Limit of Liability, 6., page 5
37	REDUCED UNDER SPECIFIED CIRCUMSTANCES (SEE POLICY)	—		

	Comparison Query	Comment	Policy Reference
	6 WHAT IS A CLAIM		
38	ORAL COMPLAINT TO INSURED	—	
39	WRITTEN COMPLAINT TO INSURED	●	Definitions, 22., Claim, page 9
40	COMPLAINT MUST CONTAIN A DEMAND FOR DAMAGES	●	Definitions, 22., Claim, page 9
41	COMPLAINT FILED WITH EEOC	—	
42	OR SIMILAR STATE AUTHORITY	—	
43	AGENCY MUST HAVE POWER TO ADJUDICATE	—	
44	ADMINISTRATIVE PROCEEDING	●	Definitions, 22., Claim, page 9
45	ARBITRATION PROCEEDING	—	
46	ANY INCIDENT REPORTED TO INSURER	—	
47	SUIT	●	Civil proceeding	Definitions, 22., Claim, page 9
48	CLAIM DOES NOT INCLUDE ARBITRATION SUBJECT TO	—	
49	COLLECTIVE BARGAINING AGREEMENT	—	
50	EMPLOYEE POLICY OR MANUAL	—	
51	CLAIM NOT DEFINED	—	
	7 CLAIM REPORTING PROVISIONS TO INSURER		
52	IMMEDIATELY	—	
53	AS SOON AS POSSIBLE	—	
54	AS SOON AS PRACTICABLE	●	Reporting & Notice, 7., page 6
55	WITHIN POLICY PERIOD	—	
56	WITHIN X DAYS OF EXPIRATION	—	
57	WITHIN X DAYS	—	
	8 EXTENDED REPORTING FEATURES		
58	ELECTION PERIOD (DAYS)	30	Insuring Clause 3., page 3
59	ADDITIONAL PREMIUM (% OF ANNUAL PREMIUM)	○	Specified by underwriter—see Item 5(A) of Declarations	Insuring Clause 3., page 3
60	ADDITIONAL REPORTING PERIOD (MONTHS)	○	Specified by underwriter—see Item 5(B) of Declarations	Insuring Clause 3., page 3
61	NO REINSTATEMENT OF LIMITS	●	Limit of Liability, 6., page 5
	9 POTENTIAL CLAIM REPORTING PROVISIONS		
62	NONE (SEE ALSO "CLAIM" ABOVE)	—	
63	INCIDENTS LIKELY TO RESULT IN A CLAIM	●	Reporting & Notice, 7., page 6
	10 DEFENSE PROVISIONS		
64	AFFIRMATIVE DUTY TO DEFEND	●	Defense & Settlement, 8., page 6
65	NO AFFIRMATIVE DUTY TO DEFEND	—	
66	AFFIRMATIVE ADVANCEMENT PROVISIONS	—	
67	INSURED MUST RETURN ADVANCED AMOUNTS IF NOT COVERED	—	
68	INSURED/INSURER CHOOSES COUNSEL	—	
69	INSURED/INSURER APPROVES COUNSEL	—	
70	INSURED/INSURER CONSULTED IN COUNSEL SELECTION	—	
	11 SETTLEMENT PROVISIONS		
71	HAMMER CLAUSE	●	Defense & Settlement, 8., page 6
72	CONSULTATION PROVISION	—	
73	CONSENT PROVISION	●	Two-way	Defense & Settlement, 8., page 6
	12 ALLOCATION OF LOSS PROVISIONS		
74	STIPULATED PROVISIONS	●	Re: Deductible provisions	Limit of Liability, 6., page 5
	13 COVERAGES		
75	DISCRIMINATION	●	Definitions, 22., Employment Practices, page 9
76	SPECIFIC ENUMERATED ACTIVITIES	—	
77	PLUS BROAD OMNIBUS WORDING	—	
78	SPECIFIC ENUMERATED CLASSES	—	
79	PLUS BROAD OMNIBUS WORDING	—	
80	AGAINST THIRD PARTIES	—	
81	DISCRIMINATION NOT DEFINED	●	
82	SEXUAL HARASSMENT	●	Definitions, 22., Employment Practices, page 9
83	HOSTILE ENVIRONMENT	—	
84	QUID-PRO-QUO	—	
85	SEXUAL HARASSMENT NOT DEFINED	●	
86	WRONGFUL TERMINATION	●	Definitions, 22., Employment Practices, page 9
87	BREACH OF IMPLIED CONTRACT	—	
88	BREACH OF EXPRESS CONTRACT	●	Written or oral	Definitions, 22., Employment Practices, page 9
89	VIOLATION OF PUBLIC POLICY	—	
90	VIOLATION OF GOOD FAITH & FAIR DEALING	—	
91	OBLIGATIONS TO MAKE PAYMENTS	—	
92	CONSTRUCTIVE DISCHARGE	○	Definitions, 22., Employment Practices, page 9
93	WRONGFUL TERMINATION NOT DEFINED	●	Definitions, 22., Employment Practices, page 9
94	OTHER EMPLOYMENT VIOLATIONS/OFFENSES	●	Definitions, 22., Employment Practices, page 9
95	WRONGFUL HIRING	●	Definitions, 22., Employment Practices, page 9
96	WRONGFUL PROMOTION/DEMOTION	●	Definitions, 22., Employment Practices, page 9
97	WRONGFUL EVALUATION/DISCIPLINE	●	Definitions, 22., Employment Practices, page 9

CHUBB GROUP 14-02-2009 [5-96]

#	Comparison Query	Comment	Policy Reference
98	FAMILY AND MEDICAL LEAVE ACT	—	
99	DEFAMATION	●	Definitions, 22., Personal Injury, page 10
100	MISREPRESENTATION	●	Definitions, 22., Employment Practices, page 9
101	RETALIATION	—	
102	MENTAL ANGUISH	—	
103	INVASION OF PRIVACY	●	Definitions, 22., Personal Injury, page 10
104	HUMILIATION	—	
105	EMOTIONAL DISTRESS	●	Definitions, 22., Employment Practices, page 9
106	OTHER PERSONAL INJURY OFFENSES	●	Definitions, 22., Personal Injury, page 10
107	POLICY SILENT	—	
	14 EXCLUSIONS		
108	**ADA ACCOMMODATION EXPENSES**	—	
109	**ASSAULT & BATTERY**	—	
110	**BACK PAY**	—	
111	**BODILY INJURY**	●	Exclusions, 4.2.(a)., page 4
112	BODILY INJURY	●	Exclusions, 4.2.(a)., page 4
113	DEATH	●	Exclusions, 4.2.(a)., page 4
114	DISEASE	●	Exclusions, 4.2.(a)., page 4
115	SICKNESS	●	Exclusions, 4.2.(a)., page 4
116	**BREACH OF EMPLOYMENT CONTRACT**	—	
117	EXPRESS CONTRACT	—	
118	WRITTEN CONTRACT	—	
119	ORAL CONTRACT	—	
120	IMPLIED CONTRACT	—	
121	**CLASS ACTION LAWSUITS**	—	
122	**CONSEQUENTIAL LOSS**	—	
123	APPLIES TO BODILY INJURY	—	
124	APPLIES TO INSURED EVENT	—	
125	BROTHER/SISTER	—	
126	CHILD	—	
127	DOMESTIC PARTNER	—	
128	PARENT	—	
129	SPOUSE	—	
130	**COST OF ARBITRATION HEARINGS SUBJECT TO**	—	
131	EMPLOYMENT HANDBOOK	—	
132	LABOR GRIEVANCE	—	
133	OTHER EMPLOYMENT POLICY OR PROCEDURE	—	
134	**COVERAGE ELSEWHERE**	●	Other Insurance, 9., page 7
135	OTHER AVAILABLE INSURANCE	●	Other Insurance, 9., page 7
136	OTHER INDEMNIFICATION	—	
137	SHARING PROVISION	—	
138	**FAILURE TO EXERCISE CARE WHEN TERMINATING**	—	
139	**FINES/PENALTIES**	●	Definitions, 22., Loss, page 10
140	CIVIL	—	
141	CRIMINAL	—	
142	EXEMPLARY DAMAGES	●	Definitions, 22., Loss, page 10
143	PUNITIVE DAMAGES	●	Definitions, 22., Loss, page 10
144	MULTIPLIED DAMAGES	●	Definitions, 22., Loss, page 10
145	**FRONT PAY**	—	
146	EXCLUSION APPLIES ONLY IF EMPLOYER HAD OPPORTUNITY TO REINSTATE EMPLOYEE BUT DID NOT DO SO	—	
147	**INTENTIONAL ACTS**	—	
148	CRIMINAL ACTS	—	
149	CRIMINAL PROCEEDING	—	
150	DISHONEST PURPOSE	—	
151	FRAUDULENT ACTS	●	Exclusions, 4.1.(c)., page 4
152	FRAUDULENT CLAIMS	—	
153	INTENTIONAL VIOLATIONS OF LAW	—	
154	WILLFUL FAILURE TO COMPLY WITH LAW	●	Exclusions, 4.1.(c)., page 4
155	MALICIOUS PURPOSE	—	
156	**LIABILITY OF OTHERS**	●	Exclusions, 4.2.(c)., page 4
157	**LIQUIDATED DAMAGES**	—	
158	**LOSS ARISING OUT OF CHANGES IN OPERATIONS**	—	
159	ACQUISITION	—	
160	CHANGE IN CONTROL	—	
161	DOWNSIZING OR REDUCTION IN FORCE	—	
162	% OF WORKFORCE	—	
163	WITHIN X DAYS	—	

CHUBB GROUP 14-02-2009 [5-96]

#	Comparison Query	Comment		Policy Reference
164	FINANCIAL IMPAIRMENT	–		
165	*BANKRUPTCY*	–		
166	*INSOLVENCY*	–		
167	*LIQUIDATION*	–		
168	*RECEIVERSHIP*	–		
169	FINANCIAL INABILITY TO PAY	–		
170	MERGER	–		
171	PLANT OR FACILITY CLOSING	–		
172	REORGANIZATION	–		
173	TEMPORARY SHUTDOWN	–		
174	**MATTERS DEEMED UNINSURABLE**	●		Definitions, 22., Loss, page 10
175	**NON-MONETARY RELIEF**	–		
176	DECLATORY RELIEF	–		
177	DISGORGEMENT	–		
178	INJUNCTIVE RELIEF	–		
179	JOB REINSTATEMENT	–		
180	NON-MONETARY DAMAGES/RELIEF	–		
181	OTHER EQUITABLE REMEDIES	–		
182	**OBLIGATION TO PROVIDE BENEFITS**	–		
183	COBRA	●		Exclusions, 4.2.(b)., page 4
184	DISABILITY	–		
185	ERISA	●		Exclusions, 4.2.(b)., page 4
186	SOCIAL SECURITY	–		
187	OTHER RETIREMENT BENEFITS	–		
188	UNEMPLOYMENT	–		
189	WORKERS' COMPENSATION	–		
190	**PERSONAL INJURY OFFENSES**	–		
191	DEFAMATION	–		
192	EMOTIONAL DISTRESS/UPSET	–		
193	HUMILIATION	–		
194	LIBEL	–		
195	MENTAL ANGUISH	–		
196	PERSONAL INJURY	–		
197	SLANDER	–		
198	**PRIOR ACTS**	–		
199	PRIOR ACTS	–		
200	PRIOR KNOWLEDGE	●		Exclusions, 4.1.(a)., page 3
201	PRIOR/PENDING LITIGATION	●		Exclusions, 4.1.(b)., page 4
202	**PROPERTY DAMAGE**	●		Exclusions, 4.2.(a)., page 4
203	INTANGIBLE PROPERTY	–		
204	LOSS OF USE	●		Exclusions, 4.2.(a)., page 4
205	TANGIBLE PROPERTY	●		Exclusions, 4.2.(a)., page 4
206	**RETALIATORY ACTIONS OF EMPLOYER**	–		
207	FOR FAILING TO PERFORM ACTS AGAINST PUBLIC POLICY	–		
208	FOR FILING A COMPLAINT OR BENEFIT CLAIM	–		
209	**STRIKES/LOCKOUTS**	–		
210	**VIOLATION OF LAWS**	–		
211	ANY LAW	●		Exclusions, 4.2.(b)., page 4
212	FMLA	–		
213	OSHA	●	Exception applies	Exclusions, 4.2.(b)., page 4
214	POLLUTION LAWS	–		
215	RICO	–		
216	SEC	–		
217	WARN	●		Exclusions, 4.2.(b)., page 4

15 CONDITIONS

#	Comparison Query	Comment		Policy Reference
218	**ARBITRATION**	–		
219	MANDATORY	–		
220	BINDING	–		
221	CHOICE OF LAW PROVISION	–		
222	SITUS	–		
223	**TERRITORY**	●		Territory, 13., page 8
224	LIMITED	–		
225	WORLDWIDE	●		Territory, 13., page 8
226	**NEWLY FORMED/ACQUIRED ENTITIES**	●		Changes in Exposure, 10., page 7
227	AUTOMATIC COVERAGE (X DAYS)	○	Time limit not specified	Changes in Exposure, 10., page 7
228	NOTIFY INSURER WITHIN X DAYS	–		

Policy Comparison Worksheet

Chubb Group

Policy Form No.: 17-02-1345
Edition Date: 3-97

Risks Considered: Financial institutions
Limits Available: $25,000,000
Minimum Retention: $50,000

Contact: Evan Rosenberg
Chubb Group of Insurance Companies
15 Mountain View Road
Warren, NJ 07059
908/903-3396
908/903-3246 (fax)
erosenberg@chubb.com

KEY TO SYMBOLS
● = Specifically contains queried provision of feature
○ = Unable to determine
— = Silent

#	Comparison Query	Symbol	Comment	Policy Reference
	1 APPLICATION			
1	ATTACHES TO AND FORMS A PART OF THE POLICY	●		15., page 7
2	CONTAINS WARRANTY STATEMENTS	●		
3	CONTAINS SEVERABILITY PROVISIONS	●		15., page 7
	2 POLICY TYPE			
4	UNITARY STAND ALONE POLICY	●		
	ENDORSEMENT OR PART OF	—		
5	DIRECTORS AND OFFICERS POLICY	—		
6	PACKAGE POLICY	—		
7	UMBRELLA POLICY	—		
8	ERRORS AND OMISSIONS POLICY	—		
9	OTHER	—		
10	CLAIMS-MADE	●		
11	OCCURRENCE	—		
	3 WHO IS INSURED			
12	BUSINESS ENTITY	●		Claim, Insureds, page 10
13	AUTOMATIC COVERAGE FOR SUBSIDIARIES	—		
14	DIRECTORS & OFFICERS	—		
15	EMPLOYEES	—		
16	PART-TIME	—		
17	SEASONAL	—		
18	TEMPORARY	—		
19	SUPERVISORS & MANAGERS	—		
20	FORMER EMPLOYEES	—		
21	VOLUNTEERS	—		
22	INDEPENDENT CONTRACTORS	—		
23	EXCLUDED	—		
24	SILENT	—		
25	SHAREHOLDERS	—		
	4 LIMIT OF LIABILITY			
26	AGGREGATE	●		6., page 4
27	INCLUDES PUNITIVE DAMAGES WHERE NOT UNINSURABLE	—		
28	DEFENSE COSTS INCLUDED WITHIN LIMIT OF LIABILITY	●		7., page 5
29	DEFENSE COSTS PAID IN ADDITION TO LIMIT OF LIABILITY	—		
	5 DEDUCTIBLE			
30	APPLIES TO EACH INDIVIDUAL CLAIM	—		
31	APPLIES TO EACH OCCURRENCE OR WRONGFUL PRACTICE	●		6., page 4
32	INCLUDES ALL CLAIMS FROM ONE ACT	●		6., page 4
33	SUBJECT TO ANNUAL AGGREGATE	—		
34	CO-PAYMENT APPLIES	●	Specified by underwriter—see Item 3 of Declarations	6., page 4
35	LIMIT OF LIABILITY NOT REDUCED	—		
36	INCLUDES DEFENSE COSTS	●		Declarations
37	REDUCED UNDER SPECIFIED CIRCUMSTANCES (SEE POLICY)	—		

CHUBB GROUP 17-02-1345 [3-97]

#	Comparison Query	Comment	Policy Reference
	6 WHAT IS A CLAIM		
38	ORAL COMPLAINT TO INSURED	—	
39	WRITTEN COMPLAINT TO INSURED	●	25., Claim, a., page 9
40	COMPLAINT MUST CONTAIN A DEMAND FOR DAMAGES	●	25., Claim, a., page 9
41	COMPLAINT FILED WITH EEOC	—	
42	OR SIMILAR STATE AUTHORITY	—	
43	AGENCY MUST HAVE POWER TO ADJUDICATE	—	
44	ADMINISTRATIVE PROCEEDING	●	25., Claim, d., page 9
45	ARBITRATION PROCEEDING	●	25., Claim, c., page 9
46	ANY INCIDENT REPORTED TO INSURER	—	
47	SUIT	●	Civil proceeding	25. Claim, b., page 9
48	CLAIM DOES NOT INCLUDE ARBITRATION SUBJECT TO	—	
49	COLLECTIVE BARGAINING AGREEMENT	—	
50	EMPLOYEE POLICY OR MANUAL	—	
51	CLAIM NOT DEFINED	—	
	7 CLAIM REPORTING PROVISIONS TO INSURER		
52	IMMEDIATELY	—	
53	AS SOON AS POSSIBLE	—	
54	AS SOON AS PRACTICABLE	●	8., page 5
55	WITHIN POLICY PERIOD	—	
56	WITHIN X DAYS OF EXPIRATION	—	
57	WITHIN X DAYS	—	
	8 EXTENDED REPORTING FEATURES		
58	ELECTION PERIOD (DAYS)	30	2., page 2
59	ADDITIONAL PREMIUM (% OF ANNUAL PREMIUM)	○	Specified by underwriter—see Item 8.(A) of Declarations	2., page 2
60	ADDITIONAL REPORTING PERIOD (MONTHS)	○	Specified by underwriter—see Item 8.(B) of Declarations	2., page 2
61	NO REINSTATEMENT OF LIMITS	—	
	9 POTENTIAL CLAIM REPORTING PROVISIONS		
62	NONE (SEE ALSO "CLAIM" ABOVE)	●	
63	INCIDENTS LIKELY TO RESULT IN A CLAIM	—	
	10 DEFENSE PROVISIONS		
64	AFFIRMATIVE DUTY TO DEFEND	●	7., page 5
65	NO AFFIRMATIVE DUTY TO DEFEND	—	
66	AFFIRMATIVE ADVANCEMENT PROVISIONS	—	
67	INSURED MUST RETURN ADVANCED AMOUNTS IF NOT COVERED	—	
68	INSURED/INSURER CHOOSES COUNSEL	●	Coverage modifiable by endorsement	
69	INSURED/INSURER APPROVES COUNSEL	—	
70	INSURED/INSURER CONSULTED IN COUNSEL SELECTION	—	
	11 SETTLEMENT PROVISIONS		
71	HAMMER CLAUSE	●	16., page 7
72	CONSULTATION PROVISION	—	
73	CONSENT PROVISION	●	Two-way	7., page 5 and 16., page 7
	12 ALLOCATION OF LOSS PROVISIONS		
74	STIPULATED PROVISIONS	●	Best efforts	24., page 9
	13 COVERAGES		
75	DISCRIMINATION	●	25., Claim, page 9
76	SPECIFIC ENUMERATED ACTIVITIES	—	
77	*PLUS BROAD OMNIBUS WORDING*	—	
78	SPECIFIC ENUMERATED CLASSES	—	
79	*PLUS BROAD OMNIBUS WORDING*	—	
80	AGAINST THIRD PARTIES	—	
81	DISCRIMINATION NOT DEFINED	●	
82	SEXUAL HARASSMENT	●	25., Claim, page 9
83	HOSTILE ENVIRONMENT	—	
84	QUID-PRO-QUO	—	
85	SEXUAL HARASSMENT NOT DEFINED	●	
86	WRONGFUL TERMINATION	●	25., Claim, page 9
87	BREACH OF IMPLIED CONTRACT	○	25., Claim, page 9
88	BREACH OF EXPRESS CONTRACT	●	25., Claim, page 9
89	VIOLATION OF PUBLIC POLICY	—	
90	VIOLATION OF GOOD FAITH & FAIR DEALING	—	
91	OBLIGATIONS TO MAKE PAYMENTS	—	
92	CONSTRUCTIVE DISCHARGE	—	
93	WRONGFUL TERMINATION NOT DEFINED	●	
94	OTHER EMPLOYMENT VIOLATIONS/OFFENSES	●	25., Claim, page 9
95	WRONGFUL HIRING	—	
96	WRONGFUL PROMOTION/DEMOTION	●	25., Claim, page 9
97	WRONGFUL EVALUATION/DISCIPLINE	●	25., Claim, page 9

CHUBB GROUP 17-02-1345 [3-97]

	Comparison Query	Comment		Policy Reference
98	FAMILY AND MEDICAL LEAVE ACT	—		
99	DEFAMATION	●		25., Claim, following d., page 9
100	MISREPRESENTATION	●		25., Claim, following d., page 9
101	RETALIATION	—		
102	MENTAL ANGUISH	—		
103	INVASION OF PRIVACY	●		25., Claim, following d., page 9
104	HUMILIATION	—		
105	EMOTIONAL DISTRESS	●		25., Claim, following d., page 9
106	OTHER PERSONAL INJURY OFFENSES	—		
107	POLICY SILENT	—		
	14 EXCLUSIONS			
108	**ADA ACCOMMODATION EXPENSES**	●		4.c., page 4
109	**ASSAULT & BATTERY**	—		
110	**BACK PAY**	—		
111	**BODILY INJURY**	●		3.d., page 3
112	BODILY INJURY	●		3.d., page 3
113	DEATH	●		3.d., page 3
114	DISEASE	●		3.d., page 3
115	SICKNESS	●		3.d., page 3
116	**BREACH OF EMPLOYMENT CONTRACT**	—		
117	EXPRESS CONTRACT	—		
118	*WRITTEN CONTRACT*	—		
119	*ORAL CONTRACT*	—		
120	IMPLIED CONTRACT	—		
121	**CLASS ACTION LAWSUITS**	—		
122	**CONSEQUENTIAL LOSS**	—		
123	APPLIES TO BODILY INJURY	—		
124	APPLIES TO INSURED EVENT	—		
125	BROTHER/SISTER	—		
126	CHILD	—		
127	DOMESTIC PARTNER	—		
128	PARENT	—		
129	SPOUSE	—		
130	**COST OF ARBITRATION HEARINGS SUBJECT TO**	—		
131	EMPLOYMENT HANDBOOK	—		
132	LABOR GRIEVANCE	—		
133	OTHER EMPLOYMENT POLICY OR PROCEDURE	—		
134	**COVERAGE ELSEWHERE**	●		11.a., page 6
135	OTHER AVAILABLE INSURANCE	●	If written by another insurer	11.a., page 6
136	OTHER INDEMNIFICATION	—		
137	SHARING PROVISION	—		
138	**FAILURE TO EXERCISE CARE WHEN TERMINATING**	—		
139	**FINES/PENALTIES**	—		
140	CIVIL	—		
141	CRIMINAL	—		
142	EXEMPLARY DAMAGES	—		
143	PUNITIVE DAMAGES	●		Loss, page 10
144	MULTIPLIED DAMAGES	●		Loss, page 10
145	**FRONT PAY**	●	Defense costs covered	4.b., page 4
146	EXCLUSION APPLIES ONLY IF EMPLOYER HAD OPPORTUNITY TO REINSTATE EMPLOYEE BUT DID NOT DO SO	●	Defense costs covered	4.b., page 4
147	**INTENTIONAL ACTS**	—		
148	CRIMINAL ACTS	—		
149	CRIMINAL PROCEEDING	—		
150	DISHONEST PURPOSE	—		
151	FRAUDULENT ACTS	●	If established in fact	3.f., page 3
152	FRAUDULENT CLAIMS	—		
153	INTENTIONAL VIOLATIONS OF LAW	—		
154	WILLFUL FAILURE TO COMPLY WITH LAW	—		
155	MALICIOUS PURPOSE	—		
156	**LIABILITY OF OTHERS**	●		3.i., page 3
157	**LIQUIDATED DAMAGES**	—		
158	**LOSS ARISING OUT OF CHANGES IN OPERATIONS**	—		
159	ACQUISITION	—		
160	CHANGE IN CONTROL	—		
161	DOWNSIZING OR REDUCTION IN FORCE	—		
162	*% OF WORKFORCE*	—		
163	*WITHIN X DAYS*	—		

#	Comparison Query	Comment		Policy Reference
164	**FINANCIAL IMPAIRMENT**	—		
165	*BANKRUPTCY*	—		
166	*INSOLVENCY*	—		
167	*LIQUIDATION*	—		
168	*RECEIVERSHIP*	—		
169	FINANCIAL INABILITY TO PAY	—		
170	MERGER	—		
171	PLANT OR FACILITY CLOSING	—		
172	REORGANIZATION	—		
173	TEMPORARY SHUTDOWN	—		
174	**MATTERS DEEMED UNINSURABLE**	●		Loss, page 10
175	**NON-MONETARY RELIEF**	●		4.d., page 4
176	DECLATORY RELIEF	—		
177	DISGORGEMENT	—		
178	INJUNCTIVE RELIEF	●		4.d., page 4
179	JOB REINSTATEMENT	—		
180	NON-MONETARY DAMAGES/RELIEF	●		4.d., page 4
181	OTHER EQUITABLE REMEDIES	—		
182	**OBLIGATION TO PROVIDE BENEFITS**	—		
183	COBRA	●		3.c., page 3
184	DISABILITY	●	Retaliation exception	3.g., page 3
185	ERISA	●		3.c., page 3
186	SOCIAL SECURITY	●	Retaliation exception	3.g., page 3
187	OTHER RETIREMENT BENEFITS	—		
188	UNEMPLOYMENT	●	Retaliation exception	3.g., page 3
189	WORKERS' COMPENSATION	●	Retaliation exception	3.g., page 3
190	**PERSONAL INJURY OFFENSES**	—		
191	DEFAMATION	—		
192	EMOTIONAL DISTRESS/UPSET	—		
193	HUMILIATION	—		
194	LIBEL	—		
195	MENTAL ANGUISH	—		
196	PERSONAL INJURY	—		
197	SLANDER	—		
198	**PRIOR ACTS**	—		
199	PRIOR ACTS	—		
200	PRIOR KNOWLEDGE	○	Prior notice	3.a., page 2
201	PRIOR/PENDING LITIGATION	○		3.b., page 2
202	**PROPERTY DAMAGE**	—		
203	INTANGIBLE PROPERTY	—		
204	LOSS OF USE	—		
205	TANGIBLE PROPERTY	—		
206	**RETALIATORY ACTIONS OF EMPLOYER**	—		
207	FOR FAILING TO PERFORM ACTS AGAINST PUBLIC POLICY	—		
208	FOR FILING A COMPLAINT OR BENEFIT CLAIM	—		
209	**STRIKES/LOCKOUTS**	—		
210	**VIOLATION OF LAWS**	—		
211	ANY LAW	—		
212	FMLA	—		
213	OSHA	●	Retaliation exception	3.c., page 3
214	POLLUTION LAWS	●		3.e., page 3
215	RICO	—		
216	SEC	○	Retaliation exception	3.h., page 3
217	WARN	●		3.c., page 3
	15 CONDITIONS			
218	**ARBITRATION**	—		
219	MANDATORY	—		
220	BINDING	—		
221	CHOICE OF LAW PROVISION	—		
222	SITUS	—		
223	**TERRITORY**	●		23., page 10
224	LIMITED	—		
225	WORLDWIDE	●		23., page 10
226	**NEWLY FORMED/ACQUIRED ENTITIES**	●		12., page 6
227	AUTOMATIC COVERAGE (X DAYS)	●	<10% company assets involved	12., page 6
228	NOTIFY INSURER WITHIN X DAYS	●	>10% company assets involved (no time limit specified)	12., page 6

CHUBB GROUP 17-02-1345 [3-97]

Policy Comparison Worksheet

CNA Reinsurance Company
(NAS Insurance Services, Inc.)

Policy Form No.: C/NA/S
Edition Date: 12/97

Risks Considered: Law firms, entertainment
Limits Available: Up to $5 million
Minimum Retention: $5,000

Contact: Richard J. Robin, Vice President
NAS Insurance Services, Inc.
16333 Ventura Boulevard, #500
Encino, CA 91436
818/382-2030
818/382-2040 (fax)
general@nasinsurance.com

KEY TO SYMBOLS
● = Specifically contains queried provision of feature
○ = Unable to determine
— = Silent

#	Comparison Query	Symbol	Comment	Policy Reference
	1 APPLICATION			
1	ATTACHES TO AND FORMS A PART OF THE POLICY	●		Declarations page
2	CONTAINS WARRANTY STATEMENTS	●		Application, page 4
3	CONTAINS SEVERABILITY PROVISIONS	—		
	2 POLICY TYPE			
4	UNITARY STAND ALONE POLICY	●		
	ENDORSEMENT OR PART OF	—		
5	DIRECTORS AND OFFICERS POLICY	—		
6	PACKAGE POLICY	—		
7	UMBRELLA POLICY	—		
8	ERRORS AND OMISSIONS POLICY	—		
9	OTHER	—		
10	CLAIMS-MADE	●		
11	OCCURRENCE	—		
	3 WHO IS INSURED			
12	BUSINESS ENTITY	●		II.A.2., page 1
13	AUTOMATIC COVERAGE FOR SUBSIDIARIES	—		
14	DIRECTORS & OFFICERS	—		
15	EMPLOYEES	●		II.A.5., page 2
16	PART-TIME	—		
17	SEASONAL	—		
18	TEMPORARY	—		
19	SUPERVISORS & MANAGERS	—		
20	FORMER EMPLOYEES	—		
21	VOLUNTEERS	—		
22	INDEPENDENT CONTRACTORS	—		
23	EXCLUDED	—		
24	SILENT	—		
25	SHAREHOLDERS	●		II.A.2., page 1
	4 LIMIT OF LIABILITY			
26	AGGREGATE	●		VI.B., page 4
27	INCLUDES PUNITIVE DAMAGES WHERE NOT UNINSURABLE	●		II.E., page 2
28	DEFENSE COSTS INCLUDED WITHIN LIMIT OF LIABILITY	●		II.E., page 2
29	DEFENSE COSTS PAID IN ADDITION TO LIMIT OF LIABILITY	—		
	5 DEDUCTIBLE			
30	APPLIES TO EACH INDIVIDUAL CLAIM	●		VII., page 4
31	APPLIES TO EACH OCCURRENCE OR WRONGFUL PRACTICE	—		
32	INCLUDES ALL CLAIMS FROM ONE ACT	●		VII., page 4
33	SUBJECT TO ANNUAL AGGREGATE	—		
34	CO-PAYMENT APPLIES	●	Specified by underwriter—See Item 6 of Declarations	VIII., page 4
35	LIMIT OF LIABILITY NOT REDUCED	●		VII., page 4
36	INCLUDES DEFENSE COSTS	●	See also II.E., page 2	VII., page 4
37	REDUCED UNDER SPECIFIED CIRCUMSTANCES (SEE POLICY)	●		VII.A. and B., page 4

#	Comparison Query	Comment	Policy Reference
6	**WHAT IS A CLAIM**		
38	ORAL COMPLAINT TO INSURED	○ Notice received by Insured	II.G., page 2
39	WRITTEN COMPLAINT TO INSURED	●	II.G., page 2
40	COMPLAINT MUST CONTAIN A DEMAND FOR DAMAGES	●	II.G., page 2
41	COMPLAINT FILED WITH EEOC	—	
42	OR SIMILAR STATE AUTHORITY	—	
43	AGENCY MUST HAVE POWER TO ADJUDICATE	—	
44	ADMINISTRATIVE PROCEEDING	●	II.G., page 2
45	ARBITRATION PROCEEDING	●	II.G., page 2
46	ANY INCIDENT REPORTED TO INSURER	—	
47	SUIT	●	II.G., page 2
48	CLAIM DOES NOT INCLUDE ARBITRATION SUBJECT TO	●	II.G., page 2
49	COLLECTIVE BARGAINING AGREEMENT	●	II.G., page 2
50	EMPLOYEE POLICY OR MANUAL	—	
51	CLAIM NOT DEFINED	—	
7	**CLAIM REPORTING PROVISIONS TO INSURER**		
52	IMMEDIATELY	—	
53	AS SOON AS POSSIBLE	—	
54	AS SOON AS PRACTICABLE	—	
55	WITHIN POLICY PERIOD		
56	WITHIN X DAYS OF EXPIRATION	—	
57	WITHIN X DAYS	30	IX.A.1)., page 5
8	**EXTENDED REPORTING FEATURES**		
58	ELECTION PERIOD (DAYS)	30	IV.4., page 4
59	ADDITIONAL PREMIUM (% OF ANNUAL PREMIUM)	100/145/165	IV.4.A., B. and C., page 4
60	ADDITIONAL REPORTING PERIOD (MONTHS)	12/24/36	IV.4.A., B. and C., page 4
61	NO REINSTATEMENT OF LIMITS	●	IV.5., page 4
9	**POTENTIAL CLAIM REPORTING PROVISIONS**		
62	NONE (SEE ALSO "CLAIM" ABOVE)	—	
63	INCIDENTS LIKELY TO RESULT IN A CLAIM	●	IX.A.4)., page 5
10	**DEFENSE PROVISIONS**		
64	AFFIRMATIVE DUTY TO DEFEND	●	I.3., page 1
65	NO AFFIRMATIVE DUTY TO DEFEND	—	
66	AFFIRMATIVE ADVANCEMENT PROVISIONS		
67	INSURED MUST RETURN ADVANCED AMOUNTS IF NOT COVERED	—	
68	INSURED/INSURER CHOOSES COUNSEL	—	
69	INSURED/INSURER APPROVES COUNSEL	—	
70	INSURED/INSURER CONSULTED IN COUNSEL SELECTION	—	
11	**SETTLEMENT PROVISIONS**		
71	HAMMER CLAUSE	●	I.6., page 1
72	CONSULTATION PROVISION	—	
73	CONSENT PROVISION	● Insured must consent	I.6., page 1
12	**ALLOCATION OF LOSS PROVISIONS**		
74	STIPULATED PROVISIONS	—	
13	**COVERAGES**		
75	DISCRIMINATION	●	Preamble, page 1
76	SPECIFIC ENUMERATED ACTIVITIES	●	II.I., page 2
77	*PLUS BROAD OMNIBUS WORDING*	●	II.I., page 2
78	SPECIFIC ENUMERATED CLASSES	●	II.I., page 2
79	*PLUS BROAD OMNIBUS WORDING*	●	II.I., page 2
80	AGAINST THIRD PARTIES	—	
81	DISCRIMINATION NOT DEFINED	—	
82	SEXUAL HARASSMENT	●	Preamble, page 1
83	HOSTILE ENVIRONMENT	●	II.J., page 2
84	QUID-PRO-QUO	●	II.J., page 2
85	SEXUAL HARASSMENT NOT DEFINED	●	II.J., page 2
86	WRONGFUL TERMINATION	● As inappropriate employment conduct	Preamble, page 1
87	BREACH OF IMPLIED CONTRACT	●	II.K.1., page 3
88	BREACH OF EXPRESS CONTRACT	—	
89	VIOLATION OF PUBLIC POLICY		
90	VIOLATION OF GOOD FAITH & FAIR DEALING	—	
91	OBLIGATIONS TO MAKE PAYMENTS	—	
92	CONSTRUCTIVE DISCHARGE	●	II.K.1., page 3
93	WRONGFUL TERMINATION NOT DEFINED	—	
94	OTHER EMPLOYMENT VIOLATIONS/OFFENSES	—	
95	WRONGFUL HIRING	—	
96	WRONGFUL PROMOTION/DEMOTION	●	II.K.2., page 3
97	WRONGFUL EVALUATION/DISCIPLINE	●	II.K.2., page 3

CNA REINSURANCE COMPANY (NAS INSURANCE SERVICES, INC.) C/NA/S [12/97]

#	Comparison Query	Comment	Policy Reference
98	FAMILY AND MEDICAL LEAVE ACT	—	
99	DEFAMATION	●	II.K.3., page 3
100	MISREPRESENTATION	●	II.K.3., page 3
101	RETALIATION	●	II.K.7., page 4
102	MENTAL ANGUISH	●	II.K.4., page 3
103	INVASION OF PRIVACY	●	II.K.6., page 3
104	HUMILIATION	—	
105	EMOTIONAL DISTRESS	●	II.K.4., page 3
106	OTHER PERSONAL INJURY OFFENSES	●	II.K.4., 5., 6., and 7., page 3
107	POLICY SILENT	—	
	14 EXCLUSIONS		
108	**ADA ACCOMMODATION EXPENSES**	●	II.E.(6)., page 2
109	**ASSAULT & BATTERY**	—	
110	**BACK PAY**	—	
111	**BODILY INJURY**	—	
112	BODILY INJURY	—	
113	DEATH	—	
114	DISEASE	—	
115	SICKNESS	—	
116	**BREACH OF EMPLOYMENT CONTRACT**	●	II.E.(7)., page 2
117	EXPRESS CONTRACT	●	
118	*WRITTEN CONTRACT*	—	
119	*ORAL CONTRACT*	—	
120	IMPLIED CONTRACT	—	
121	**CLASS ACTION LAWSUITS**	—	
122	**CONSEQUENTIAL LOSS**	●	II.5., page 3
123	APPLIES TO BODILY INJURY	—	
124	APPLIES TO INSURED EVENT	●	II.5., page 3
125	BROTHER/SISTER	●	II.5., page 3
126	CHILD	●	II.5., page 3
127	DOMESTIC PARTNER	●	II.5., page 3
128	PARENT	●	II.5., page 3
129	SPOUSE	●	II.5., page 3
130	**COST OF ARBITRATION HEARINGS SUBJECT TO**	—	
131	EMPLOYMENT HANDBOOK	—	
132	LABOR GRIEVANCE	—	
133	OTHER EMPLOYMENT POLICY OR PROCEDURE	—	
134	**COVERAGE ELSEWHERE**	—	
135	OTHER AVAILABLE INSURANCE	—	
136	OTHER INDEMNIFICATION	—	
137	SHARING PROVISION	●	IX.E., page 5
138	**FAILURE TO EXERCISE CARE WHEN TERMINATING**	—	
139	**FINES/PENALTIES**	●	II.E.(1)., page 2
140	CIVIL	●	II.E.(1)., page 2
141	CRIMINAL	●	II.E.(1)., page 2
142	EXEMPLARY DAMAGES	—	
143	PUNITIVE DAMAGES	—	
144	MULTIPLIED DAMAGES	—	
145	**FRONT PAY**	—	
146	EXCLUSION APPLIES ONLY IF EMPLOYER HAD OPPORTUNITY TO REINSTATE EMPLOYEE BUT DID NOT DO SO	—	
147	**INTENTIONAL ACTS**	—	
148	CRIMINAL ACTS	—	
149	CRIMINAL PROCEEDING	—	
150	DISHONEST PURPOSE	—	
151	FRAUDULENT ACTS	—	
152	FRAUDULENT CLAIMS	●	IX.L., page 6
153	INTENTIONAL VIOLATIONS OF LAW	—	
154	WILLFUL FAILURE TO COMPLY WITH LAW	—	
155	MALICIOUS PURPOSE	—	
156	**LIABILITY OF OTHERS**	●	III.2., page 3
157	**LIQUIDATED DAMAGES**	●	If finding of wilfulness	II.E.(4)., page 2
158	**LOSS ARISING OUT OF CHANGES IN OPERATIONS**	—	
159	ACQUISITION	—	
160	CHANGE IN CONTROL	—	
161	DOWNSIZING OR REDUCTION IN FORCE	—	
162	*% OF WORKFORCE*	—	
163	*WITHIN X DAYS*	—	

#	Comparison Query		Comment	Policy Reference
164	FINANCIAL IMPAIRMENT	—		
165	*BANKRUPTCY*	—		
166	*INSOLVENCY*	—		
167	*LIQUIDATION*	—		
168	*RECEIVERSHIP*	—		
169	FINANCIAL INABILITY TO PAY	—		
170	MERGER	—		
171	PLANT OR FACILITY CLOSING	—		
172	REORGANIZATION	—		
173	TEMPORARY SHUTDOWN	—		
174	**MATTERS DEEMED UNINSURABLE**	●		II.E.(2)., page 2
175	**NON-MONETARY RELIEF**	—		
176	DECLATORY RELIEF	—		
177	DISGORGEMENT	—		
178	INJUNCTIVE RELIEF	—		
179	JOB REINSTATEMENT	—		
180	NON-MONETARY DAMAGES/RELIEF	●		II.E.(3)., page 2
181	OTHER EQUITABLE REMEDIES	—		
182	**OBLIGATION TO PROVIDE BENEFITS**	—		
183	COBRA	—		
184	DISABILITY	●	Exceptions apply	III.1., page 3
185	ERISA	●		III.3., page 3
186	SOCIAL SECURITY	—		
187	OTHER RETIREMENT BENEFITS	—		
188	UNEMPLOYMENT	●	Exceptions apply	III.1., page 3
189	WORKERS' COMPENSATION	●	Exceptions apply	III.1., page 3
190	**PERSONAL INJURY OFFENSES**	—		
191	DEFAMATION	—		
192	EMOTIONAL DISTRESS/UPSET	—		
193	HUMILIATION	—		
194	LIBEL	—		
195	MENTAL ANGUISH	—		
196	PERSONAL INJURY	—		
197	SLANDER	—		
198	**PRIOR ACTS**	—		
199	PRIOR ACTS	●		IV.1., page 3
200	PRIOR KNOWLEDGE	●		I.2.c., page 1
201	PRIOR/PENDING LITIGATION	—		
202	**PROPERTY DAMAGE**	—		
203	INTANGIBLE PROPERTY	—		
204	LOSS OF USE	—		
205	TANGIBLE PROPERTY	—		
206	**RETALIATORY ACTIONS OF EMPLOYER**	—		
207	FOR FAILING TO PERFORM ACTS AGAINST PUBLIC POLICY	—		
208	FOR FILING A COMPLAINT OR BENEFIT CLAIM	—		
209	**STRIKES/LOCKOUTS**	●		III.4., page 3
210	**VIOLATION OF LAWS**	—		
211	ANY LAW	—		
212	FMLA	—		
213	OSHA	—		
214	POLLUTION LAWS	—		
215	RICO	—		
216	SEC	—		
217	WARN	●		III.6., page 3

15 CONDITIONS

#	Comparison Query		Comment	Policy Reference
218	**ARBITRATION**	—		
219	MANDATORY	—		
220	BINDING	—		
221	CHOICE OF LAW PROVISION	—		
222	SITUS	—		
223	**TERRITORY**	—		
224	LIMITED	—		
225	WORLDWIDE	●		V., page 4
226	**NEWLY FORMED/ACQUIRED ENTITIES**	●		II.A.4., page 1
227	AUTOMATIC COVERAGE (X DAYS)	30		II.A.4., page 1
228	NOTIFY INSURER WITHIN X DAYS	—		

CNA REINSURANCE COMPANY (NAS INSURANCE SERVICES, INC.) C/NA/S [12/97]

Policy Comparison Worksheet

Colonia (AUSCO)

Policy Form No.: EPL 6000 (3/95)
Edition Date: 3/95

Contact: Available through excess and surplus lines brokers only

Risks Considered: All except municipalities and government entities
Limits Available: $100,000 to $1,000,000
Minimum Retention: $1,000

KEY TO SYMBOLS
● = Specifically contains queried provision of feature
○ = Unable to determine
— = Silent

#	Comparison Query		Comment	Policy Reference
	1 APPLICATION			
1	ATTACHES TO AND FORMS A PART OF THE POLICY	●	See also II.A.(1)., page 1	VII.A., page 5
2	CONTAINS WARRANTY STATEMENTS	○		VII.A., page 5
3	CONTAINS SEVERABILITY PROVISIONS	●		VII.A., page 5
	2 POLICY TYPE			
4	UNITARY STAND ALONE POLICY	●		
	ENDORSEMENT OR PART OF	—		
5	DIRECTORS AND OFFICERS POLICY	—		
6	PACKAGE POLICY	—		
7	UMBRELLA POLICY	—		
8	ERRORS AND OMISSIONS POLICY	—		
9	OTHER	—		
10	CLAIMS-MADE	●		
11	OCCURRENCE	—		
	3 WHO IS INSURED			
12	BUSINESS ENTITY	●		II.G., page 2
13	AUTOMATIC COVERAGE FOR SUBSIDIARIES	○		III.I.(a). (b). & (c)., page 4
14	DIRECTORS & OFFICERS	●		II.F.(1)., page 1
15	EMPLOYEES	●		II.F.(2)., page 2
16	PART-TIME	●		II.F.(2)., page 2
17	SEASONAL	●		II.F.(2)., page 2
18	TEMPORARY	●		II.F.(2)., page 2
19	SUPERVISORS & MANAGERS	—		
20	FORMER EMPLOYEES	—		
21	VOLUNTEERS	—		
22	INDEPENDENT CONTRACTORS	—		
23	EXCLUDED	●		II.F.(2)., page 2
24	SILENT	—		
25	SHAREHOLDERS	—		
	4 LIMIT OF LIABILITY			
26	AGGREGATE	●		IV.B., page 4
27	INCLUDES PUNITIVE DAMAGES WHERE NOT UNINSURABLE	—		
28	DEFENSE COSTS INCLUDED WITHIN LIMIT OF LIABILITY	●	See also IV.D., page 4	Declarations page
29	DEFENSE COSTS PAID IN ADDITION TO LIMIT OF LIABILITY	—		
	5 DEDUCTIBLE			
30	APPLIES TO EACH INDIVIDUAL CLAIM	●		IV.C., page 4
31	APPLIES TO EACH OCCURRENCE OR WRONGFUL PRACTICE			
32	INCLUDES ALL CLAIMS FROM ONE ACT	●		VII.B., page 5
33	SUBJECT TO ANNUAL AGGREGATE	—		
34	CO-PAYMENT APPLIES	—		
35	LIMIT OF LIABILITY NOT REDUCED			
36	INCLUDES DEFENSE COSTS	●	See also IV.C., page 4	Declarations page
37	REDUCED UNDER SPECIFIED CIRCUMSTANCES (SEE POLICY)	—		

#	Comparison Query	Comment	Policy Reference
	6 WHAT IS A CLAIM		
38	ORAL COMPLAINT TO INSURED	—	
39	WRITTEN COMPLAINT TO INSURED	●	II.B.(1)., page 1
40	COMPLAINT MUST CONTAIN A DEMAND FOR DAMAGES	—	
41	COMPLAINT FILED WITH EEOC	—	
42	OR SIMILAR STATE AUTHORITY	—	
43	AGENCY MUST HAVE POWER TO ADJUDICATE	—	
44	ADMINISTRATIVE PROCEEDING	●	II.B.(2)., page 1
45	ARBITRATION PROCEEDING	●	II.B.(2)., page 1
46	ANY INCIDENT REPORTED TO INSURER	●	VI.B., page 5
47	SUIT	●	II.B.(2)., page 1
48	CLAIM DOES NOT INCLUDE ARBITRATION SUBJECT TO	●	II.B.(2)., page 1
49	COLLECTIVE BARGAINING AGREEMENT	●	II.B.(2)., page 1
50	EMPLOYEE POLICY OR MANUAL	—	
51	CLAIM NOT DEFINED	—	
	7 CLAIM REPORTING PROVISIONS TO INSURER		
52	IMMEDIATELY	—	
53	AS SOON AS POSSIBLE	—	
54	AS SOON AS PRACTICABLE	●	VI.A., page 5
55	WITHIN POLICY PERIOD	●	I.A., page 1
56	WITHIN X DAYS OF EXPIRATION	—	
57	WITHIN X DAYS	—	
	8 EXTENDED REPORTING FEATURES		
58	ELECTION PERIOD (DAYS)	10	VIII.C., page 6
59	ADDITIONAL PREMIUM (% OF ANNUAL PREMIUM)	50	VIII.A., page 6
60	ADDITIONAL REPORTING PERIOD (MONTHS)	12	VIII.A., page 6
61	NO REINSTATEMENT OF LIMITS	●	VIII.E., page 6
	9 POTENTIAL CLAIM REPORTING PROVISIONS		
62	NONE (SEE ALSO "CLAIM" ABOVE)	—	
63	INCIDENTS LIKELY TO RESULT IN A CLAIM	●	VI.B., page 5
	10 DEFENSE PROVISIONS		
64	AFFIRMATIVE DUTY TO DEFEND	●	I.B., page 1
65	NO AFFIRMATIVE DUTY TO DEFEND	●	
66	AFFIRMATIVE ADVANCEMENT PROVISIONS	—	
67	INSURED MUST RETURN ADVANCED AMOUNTS IF NOT COVERED	—	
68	INSURED/INSURER CHOOSES COUNSEL	● Insurer	II.C., page 1
69	INSURED/INSURER APPROVES COUNSEL	—	
70	INSURED/INSURER CONSULTED IN COUNSEL SELECTION	—	
	11 SETTLEMENT PROVISIONS		
71	HAMMER CLAUSE	●	V.A., page 4
72	CONSULTATION PROVISION	—	
73	CONSENT PROVISION	● Two-way	V.A. and B., page 4
	12 ALLOCATION OF LOSS PROVISIONS		
74	STIPULATED PROVISIONS	—	
	13 COVERAGES		
75	DISCRIMINATION	● As wrongful employment practice	II.N.(2)., page 3
76	SPECIFIC ENUMERATED ACTIVITIES	●	II.D., page 1
77	PLUS BROAD OMNIBUS WORDING	—	
78	SPECIFIC ENUMERATED CLASSES	●	II.D., page 1
79	PLUS BROAD OMNIBUS WORDING	●	II.D., page 1
80	AGAINST THIRD PARTIES	—	
81	DISCRIMINATION NOT DEFINED	—	
82	SEXUAL HARASSMENT	● As wrongful employment practice	II.N.(3)., page 3
83	HOSTILE ENVIRONMENT	●	II.M., page 2
84	QUID-PRO-QUO	●	II.M., page 2
85	SEXUAL HARASSMENT NOT DEFINED	—	
86	WRONGFUL TERMINATION	● As wrongful employment practice	II.N.(1)., page 3
87	BREACH OF IMPLIED CONTRACT	—	
88	BREACH OF EXPRESS CONTRACT	—	
89	VIOLATION OF PUBLIC POLICY	—	
90	VIOLATION OF GOOD FAITH & FAIR DEALING	—	
91	OBLIGATIONS TO MAKE PAYMENTS	—	
92	CONSTRUCTIVE DISCHARGE	●	II.E., page 1
93	WRONGFUL TERMINATION NOT DEFINED	—	
94	OTHER EMPLOYMENT VIOLATIONS/OFFENSES	●	II.D., page 1
95	WRONGFUL HIRING	● If discrimination	II.D., page 1
96	WRONGFUL PROMOTION/DEMOTION	● If discrimination	II.D., page 1
97	WRONGFUL EVALUATION/DISCIPLINE	—	

COLONIA (AUSCO) EPL 6000 (3/95) [3/95]

	Comparison Query	Comment	Policy Reference
98	FAMILY AND MEDICAL LEAVE ACT	●	II.D., page 2
99	DEFAMATION	●	II.N., page 3
100	MISREPRESENTATION	—	
101	RETALIATION	—	
102	MENTAL ANGUISH	●	II.N., page 3
103	INVASION OF PRIVACY	—	
104	HUMILIATION		
105	EMOTIONAL DISTRESS	●	II.N., page 3
106	OTHER PERSONAL INJURY OFFENSES	●	II.N., page 3
107	POLICY SILENT	—	

14 EXCLUSIONS

	Comparison Query	Comment	Policy Reference
108	**ADA ACCOMMODATION EXPENSES**	●	II.J.(5)., page 2
109	**ASSAULT & BATTERY**	—	
110	**BACK PAY**	●	II.(J).(2)., page 2
111	**BODILY INJURY**	●	III.C., page 3
112	BODILY INJURY	●	III.C., page 3
113	DEATH	●	III.C., page 3
114	DISEASE	●	III.C., page 3
115	SICKNESS	●	
116	**BREACH OF EMPLOYMENT CONTRACT**	—	
117	EXPRESS CONTRACT	—	
118	WRITTEN CONTRACT	—	
119	ORAL CONTRACT	—	
120	IMPLIED CONTRACT	—	
121	**CLASS ACTION LAWSUITS**	—	
122	**CONSEQUENTIAL LOSS**	—	
123	APPLIES TO BODILY INJURY	—	
124	APPLIES TO INSURED EVENT	—	
125	BROTHER/SISTER	—	
126	CHILD	—	
127	DOMESTIC PARTNER	—	
128	PARENT	—	
129	SPOUSE	—	
130	**COST OF ARBITRATION HEARINGS SUBJECT TO**	—	
131	EMPLOYMENT HANDBOOK	—	
132	LABOR GRIEVANCE	—	
133	OTHER EMPLOYMENT POLICY OR PROCEDURE	—	
134	**COVERAGE ELSEWHERE**	●	III.H., page 3
135	OTHER AVAILABLE INSURANCE	●	III.H., page 3
136	OTHER INDEMNIFICATION	—	
137	SHARING PROVISION	—	
138	**FAILURE TO EXERCISE CARE WHEN TERMINATING**	—	
139	**FINES/PENALTIES**	●	II.J.(1)., page 2
140	CIVIL	●	II.J.(1)., page 2
141	CRIMINAL	●	II.J.(1)., page 2
142	EXEMPLARY DAMAGES	●	II.J.(2)., page 2
143	PUNITIVE DAMAGES	●	II.J.(2)., page 2
144	MULTIPLIED DAMAGES	●	II.J.(2)., page 2
145	**FRONT PAY**	—	
146	EXCLUSION APPLIES ONLY IF EMPLOYER HAD OPPORTUNITY TO REINSTATE EMPLOYEE BUT DID NOT DO SO	—	
147	**INTENTIONAL ACTS**	● If established in fact	III.A., page 3
148	CRIMINAL ACTS	● If established in fact	III.A., page 3
149	CRIMINAL PROCEEDING	—	
150	DISHONEST PURPOSE	● If established in fact	III.A., page 3
151	FRAUDULENT ACTS	● If established in fact	III.A., page 3
152	FRAUDULENT CLAIMS	—	
153	INTENTIONAL VIOLATIONS OF LAW	● If established in fact	III.A., page 3
154	WILLFUL FAILURE TO COMPLY WITH LAW	—	
155	MALICIOUS PURPOSE	● If established in fact	III.A., page 3
156	**LIABILITY OF OTHERS**	●	III.B., page 3
157	**LIQUIDATED DAMAGES**	—	
158	**LOSS ARISING OUT OF CHANGES IN OPERATIONS**	—	
159	ACQUISITION	●	III.G., page 3
160	CHANGE IN CONTROL		
161	DOWNSIZING OR REDUCTION IN FORCE		
162	% OF WORKFORCE	—	
163	WITHIN X DAYS	—	

COLONIA (AUSCO) EPL 6000 (3/95) [3/95]

#	Comparison Query	Comment		Policy Reference
164	FINANCIAL IMPAIRMENT	●		III.G., page 3
165	BANKRUPTCY	●		III.G., page 3
166	INSOLVENCY	—		
167	LIQUIDATION	●		III.G., page 3
168	RECEIVERSHIP	●		III.G., page 3
169	FINANCIAL INABILITY TO PAY	—		
170	MERGER	●		III.G., page 3
171	PLANT OR FACILITY CLOSING	●		III.G., page 3
172	REORGANIZATION	●		III.G., page 3
173	TEMPORARY SHUTDOWN	—		
174	**MATTERS DEEMED UNINSURABLE**	●		II.J.(6)., page 2
175	**NON-MONETARY RELIEF**	—		
176	DECLATORY RELIEF	—		
177	DISGORGEMENT	—		
178	INJUNCTIVE RELIEF	—		
179	JOB REINSTATEMENT	—		
180	NON-MONETARY DAMAGES/RELIEF	—		
181	OTHER EQUITABLE REMEDIES	—		
182	**OBLIGATION TO PROVIDE BENEFITS**	—		
183	COBRA	●		II.J.(4)., page 2
184	DISABILITY	●		III.F., page 3
185	ERISA	●		II.J.(4)., page 2
186	SOCIAL SECURITY	●		III.F., page 3
187	OTHER RETIREMENT BENEFITS	—		
188	UNEMPLOYMENT	●		III.F., page 3
189	WORKERS' COMPENSATION	●		III.F., page 3
190	**PERSONAL INJURY OFFENSES**	—		
191	DEFAMATION	—		
192	EMOTIONAL DISTRESS/UPSET	—		
193	HUMILIATION	—		
194	LIBEL	—		
195	MENTAL ANGUISH	—		
196	PERSONAL INJURY	—		
197	SLANDER	—		
198	**PRIOR ACTS**	—		
199	PRIOR ACTS	—		
200	PRIOR KNOWLEDGE	—		
201	PRIOR/PENDING LITIGATION	●	Subject of any notice	III.D., page 3
202	**PROPERTY DAMAGE**	●		III.C., page 3
203	INTANGIBLE PROPERTY	—		
204	LOSS OF USE	●		III.C., page 3
205	TANGIBLE PROPERTY	●		III.C., page 3
206	**RETALIATORY ACTIONS OF EMPLOYER**	—		
207	FOR FAILING TO PERFORM ACTS AGAINST PUBLIC POLICY	—		
208	FOR FILING A COMPLAINT OR BENEFIT CLAIM	—		
209	**STRIKES/LOCKOUTS**	●		III.E., page 3
210	**VIOLATION OF LAWS**	—		
211	ANY LAW	—		
212	FMLA	—		
213	OSHA	●		III.F., page 3
214	POLLUTION LAWS	—		
215	RICO	—		
216	SEC	—		
217	WARN	—		
	15 CONDITIONS			
218	**ARBITRATION**	—		
219	MANDATORY	—		
220	BINDING	—		
221	CHOICE OF LAW PROVISION	—		
222	SITUS	—		
223	**TERRITORY**	—		
224	LIMITED	—		
225	WORLDWIDE	—		
226	**NEWLY FORMED/ACQUIRED ENTITIES**	—		
227	AUTOMATIC COVERAGE (X DAYS)	—		
228	NOTIFY INSURER WITHIN X DAYS	—		

COLONIA (AUSCO) EPL 6000 (3/95) [3/95]

Policy Comparison Worksheet

Connecticut Indemnity Company
(Professional Risk Facilities, Inc.)

Policy Form No.: 40609-0
Edition Date: 2/94

Risks Considered: Public/Hard-to-place companies
Limits Available: $5,000,000
Minimum Retention: $15,000

Contact: Joseph S. Gravier, Jr.
Professional Risk Facilities, Inc.
300 Old Country Road
Mineola, NY 11501-4192
516/747-6060
516/747-6074 (fax)
prf@i-2000.com

KEY TO SYMBOLS
● = Specifically contains queried provision of feature
○ = Unable to determine
— = Silent

#	Comparison Query	Symbol	Comment	Policy Reference
	1 APPLICATION			
1	ATTACHES TO AND FORMS A PART OF THE POLICY	●		Policy, Preamble, page 3
2	CONTAINS WARRANTY STATEMENTS	—		
3	CONTAINS SEVERABILITY PROVISIONS	—		
	2 POLICY TYPE			
4	UNITARY STAND ALONE POLICY	—		
	ENDORSEMENT OR PART OF	—		
5	DIRECTORS AND OFFICERS POLICY	●	Policy form 40275-OJKT (7/93)	
6	PACKAGE POLICY	—		
7	UMBRELLA POLICY	—		
8	ERRORS AND OMISSIONS POLICY	—		
9	OTHER	—		
10	CLAIMS-MADE	●		
11	OCCURRENCE	—		
	3 WHO IS INSURED			
12	BUSINESS ENTITY	●	Indemnification only	Policy II.E., page 4
13	AUTOMATIC COVERAGE FOR SUBSIDIARIES	●	Indemnification only	Policy II.F., page 4
14	DIRECTORS & OFFICERS	●		Endorsement A.(2).(i)., page 1
15	EMPLOYEES	●		Endorsement A.(2).(ii)., page 2
16	PART-TIME	—		
17	SEASONAL	—		
18	TEMPORARY	—		
19	SUPERVISORS & MANAGERS	●		Endorsement A.(2).(ii)., page 2
20	FORMER EMPLOYEES	●		Endorsement A.(2)., page 2
21	VOLUNTEERS	—		
22	INDEPENDENT CONTRACTORS	—		
23	EXCLUDED	—		
24	SILENT	●		
25	SHAREHOLDERS	—		
	4 LIMIT OF LIABILITY			
26	AGGREGATE	●		Policy IV.B.1., page 6
27	INCLUDES PUNITIVE DAMAGES WHERE NOT UNINSURABLE	—		
28	DEFENSE COSTS INCLUDED WITHIN LIMIT OF LIABILITY	●		Policy IV.B.4., page 6
29	DEFENSE COSTS PAID IN ADDITION TO LIMIT OF LIABILITY	—		
	5 DEDUCTIBLE			
30	APPLIES TO EACH INDIVIDUAL CLAIM	●		Policy IV.B.2., page 6
31	APPLIES TO EACH OCCURRENCE OR WRONGFUL PRACTICE	●		Policy IV.B.2., page 6
32	INCLUDES ALL CLAIMS FROM ONE ACT	●		Policy IV.B.2., page 6
33	SUBJECT TO ANNUAL AGGREGATE	—		
34	CO-PAYMENT APPLIES	●	Specified by underwriter—see Declarations	Policy IV.B.1., page 6
35	LIMIT OF LIABILITY NOT REDUCED	—		
36	INCLUDES DEFENSE COSTS	●	See also Policy II.G., page 4	Policy IV.B.1., page 6
37	REDUCED UNDER SPECIFIED CIRCUMSTANCES (SEE POLICY)	—		

CONNECTICUT INDEMNITY COMPANY (PROFESSIONAL RISK FACILITIES, INC.) 40609-0 [2/94]

Comparison Query	Comment	Policy Reference
6 WHAT IS A CLAIM		
38 ORAL COMPLAINT TO INSURED	—	
39 WRITTEN COMPLAINT TO INSURED	—	
40 COMPLAINT MUST CONTAIN A DEMAND FOR DAMAGES	●	Endorsement A.(1)., page 1
41 COMPLAINT FILED WITH EEOC	●	Endorsement A.(1)., page 1
42 OR SIMILAR STATE AUTHORITY	●	Endorsement A.(1)., page 1
43 AGENCY MUST HAVE POWER TO ADJUDICATE	—	
44 ADMINISTRATIVE PROCEEDING	●	Endorsement A.(1)., page 1
45 ARBITRATION PROCEEDING	—	
46 ANY INCIDENT REPORTED TO INSURER	—	
47 SUIT	●	Judicial proceeding	Endorsement A.(1)., page 1
48 CLAIM DOES NOT INCLUDE ARBITRATION SUBJECT TO	—	
49 COLLECTIVE BARGAINING AGREEMENT	—	
50 EMPLOYEE POLICY OR MANUAL	—	
51 CLAIM NOT DEFINED	—	
7 CLAIM REPORTING PROVISIONS TO INSURER		
52 IMMEDIATELY	—	
53 AS SOON AS POSSIBLE	—	
54 AS SOON AS PRACTICABLE	●	Policy IV.D.1., page 7
55 WITHIN POLICY PERIOD	—	
56 WITHIN X DAYS OF EXPIRATION	—	
57 WITHIN X DAYS	60	Policy IV.D.1., page 7
8 EXTENDED REPORTING FEATURES		
58 ELECTION PERIOD (DAYS)	10	Policy III.B.2., page 4
59 ADDITIONAL PREMIUM (% OF ANNUAL PREMIUM)	○	Specified by underwriter—see Item 8 of Declarations	Policy III.B.2., page 4
60 ADDITIONAL REPORTING PERIOD (MONTHS)	○	Specified by underwriter—see Item 9 of Declarations	Policy III.B.2., page 4
61 NO REINSTATEMENT OF LIMITS	—	
9 POTENTIAL CLAIM REPORTING PROVISIONS		
62 NONE (SEE ALSO "CLAIM" ABOVE)	—	
63 INCIDENTS LIKELY TO RESULT IN A CLAIM	●	Policy IV.D.2., page 7
10 DEFENSE PROVISIONS		
64 AFFIRMATIVE DUTY TO DEFEND	—	
65 NO AFFIRMATIVE DUTY TO DEFEND	●	Policy IV.C.2., page 6
66 AFFIRMATIVE ADVANCEMENT PROVISIONS	●	Policy IV.C.3., page 6
67 INSURED MUST RETURN ADVANCED AMOUNTS IF NOT COVERED	●	Policy IV.C.3., pages 6–7
68 INSURED/INSURER CHOOSES COUNSEL	—	
69 INSURED/INSURER APPROVES COUNSEL	—	
70 INSURED/INSURER CONSULTED IN COUNSEL SELECTION	—	
11 SETTLEMENT PROVISIONS		
71 HAMMER CLAUSE	—	
72 CONSULTATION PROVISION	—	
73 CONSENT PROVISION	●	Policy IV.C.2., page 6
12 ALLOCATION OF LOSS PROVISIONS		
74 STIPULATED PROVISIONS	—	
13 COVERAGES		
75 DISCRIMINATION	●	Endorsement A.(4).(i)., page 2
76 SPECIFIC ENUMERATED ACTIVITIES	●	Endorsement A.(4).(i)., page 2
77 *PLUS BROAD OMNIBUS WORDING*	—	
78 SPECIFIC ENUMERATED CLASSES	●	Endorsement A.(4).(i)., page 2
79 *PLUS BROAD OMNIBUS WORDING*	●	Endorsement A.(4).(i)., page 2
80 AGAINST THIRD PARTIES	—	
81 DISCRIMINATION NOT DEFINED	●	
82 SEXUAL HARASSMENT	●	Endorsement A.(4).(ii)., page 2
83 HOSTILE ENVIRONMENT	●	Endorsement A.(4).(ii)., page 2
84 QUID-PRO-QUO	●	Endorsement A.(4).(ii)., page 2
85 SEXUAL HARASSMENT NOT DEFINED	●	
86 WRONGFUL TERMINATION	●	Endorsement A.(4).(i)., page 2
87 BREACH OF IMPLIED CONTRACT	—	
88 BREACH OF EXPRESS CONTRACT	—	
89 VIOLATION OF PUBLIC POLICY	—	
90 VIOLATION OF GOOD FAITH & FAIR DEALING	—	
91 OBLIGATIONS TO MAKE PAYMENTS	—	
92 CONSTRUCTIVE DISCHARGE	●	Endorsement A.(4).(i)., page 2
93 WRONGFUL TERMINATION NOT DEFINED	●	
94 OTHER EMPLOYMENT VIOLATIONS/OFFENSES	●	Endorsement A.(4).(i)., page 2
95 WRONGFUL HIRING	●	Endorsement A.(4).(i)., page 2
96 WRONGFUL PROMOTION/DEMOTION	●	Endorsement A.(4).(i)., page 2
97 WRONGFUL EVALUATION/DISCIPLINE	●	Endorsement A.(4).(i)., page 2

CONNECTICUT INDEMNITY COMPANY (PROFESSIONAL RISK FACILITIES, INC.) 40609-0 [2/94]

	Comparison Query		Comment	Policy Reference
98	FAMILY AND MEDICAL LEAVE ACT	—		
99	DEFAMATION	—		
100	MISREPRESENTATION	●		Endorsement A.(4).(i)., page 2
101	RETALIATION	—		
102	MENTAL ANGUISH	—		
103	INVASION OF PRIVACY	—		
104	HUMILIATION	—		
105	EMOTIONAL DISTRESS	—		
106	OTHER PERSONAL INJURY OFFENSES	—		
107	POLICY SILENT	—		
14	**EXCLUSIONS**			
108	ADA ACCOMMODATION EXPENSES	—		
109	**ASSAULT & BATTERY**	●		Endorsement B.(1)., page 2
110	**BACK PAY**	—		
111	**BODILY INJURY**	●		Endorsement B.(1)., page 2
112	BODILY INJURY	●		Endorsement B.(1)., page 2
113	DEATH	●		Endorsement B.(1)., page 2
114	DISEASE	●		Endorsement B.(1)., page 2
115	SICKNESS	●		Endorsement B.(1)., page 2
116	**BREACH OF EMPLOYMENT CONTRACT**	—		
117	EXPRESS CONTRACT	—		
118	WRITTEN CONTRACT	—		
119	ORAL CONTRACT	—		
120	IMPLIED CONTRACT	—		
121	**CLASS ACTION LAWSUITS**	—		
122	**CONSEQUENTIAL LOSS**	●		Policy IV.A.4., page 4
123	APPLIES TO BODILY INJURY	●	Loss of consortium	Policy IV.A.4., page 4
124	APPLIES TO INSURED EVENT	—		
125	BROTHER/SISTER	—		
126	CHILD	—		
127	DOMESTIC PARTNER	—		
128	PARENT	—		
129	SPOUSE	—		
130	**COST OF ARBITRATION HEARINGS SUBJECT TO**	—		
131	EMPLOYMENT HANDBOOK	—		
132	LABOR GRIEVANCE	—		
133	OTHER EMPLOYMENT POLICY OR PROCEDURE	—		
134	**COVERAGE ELSEWHERE**	●		Policy IV.A.13., page 5
135	OTHER AVAILABLE INSURANCE	●		Policy IV.A.13., page 5
136	OTHER INDEMNIFICATION	—		
137	SHARING PROVISION	—		
138	**FAILURE TO EXERCISE CARE WHEN TERMINATING**	—		
139	**FINES/PENALTIES**	●		Policy II.G., page 4
140	CIVIL	●		Policy II.G., page 4
141	CRIMINAL	●		Policy II.G., page 4
142	EXEMPLARY DAMAGES	●		Policy II.G., page 4
143	PUNITIVE DAMAGES	●		Policy II.G., page 4
144	MULTIPLIED DAMAGES	●		Policy II.G., page 4
145	**FRONT PAY**	—		
146	EXCLUSION APPLIES ONLY IF EMPLOYER HAD OPPORTUNITY TO REINSTATE EMPLOYEE BUT DID NOT DO SO	—		
147	**INTENTIONAL ACTS**	●		Policy IV.A.1., page 5
148	CRIMINAL ACTS	●	If established	Policy IV.A.1., page 5
149	CRIMINAL PROCEEDING	—		
150	DISHONEST PURPOSE	●	If established	Policy IV.A.1., page 5
151	FRAUDULENT ACTS	●	If established	Policy IV.A.1., page 5
152	FRAUDULENT CLAIMS	—		
153	INTENTIONAL VIOLATIONS OF LAW	—		
154	WILLFUL FAILURE TO COMPLY WITH LAW	—		
155	MALICIOUS PURPOSE	—		
156	**LIABILITY OF OTHERS**	—		
157	**LIQUIDATED DAMAGES**	—		
158	**LOSS ARISING OUT OF CHANGES IN OPERATIONS**	—		
159	ACQUISITION	—		
160	CHANGE IN CONTROL	—		
161	DOWNSIZING OR REDUCTION IN FORCE	—		
162	% OF WORKFORCE	—		
163	WITHIN X DAYS	—		

CONNECTICUT INDEMNITY COMPANY (PROFESSIONAL RISK FACILITIES, INC.) 40609-0 [2/94]

	Comparison Query	Comment		Policy Reference
164	FINANCIAL IMPAIRMENT	—		
165	BANKRUPTCY	—		
166	INSOLVENCY	—		
167	LIQUIDATION	—		
168	RECEIVERSHIP	—		
169	FINANCIAL INABILITY TO PAY	—		
170	MERGER	—		
171	PLANT OR FACILITY CLOSING	—		
172	REORGANIZATION	—		
173	TEMPORARY SHUTDOWN	—		
174	**MATTERS DEEMED UNINSURABLE**	—		
175	**NON-MONETARY RELIEF**	—		
176	DECLATORY RELIEF	—		
177	DISGORGEMENT	—		
178	INJUNCTIVE RELIEF	—		
179	JOB REINSTATEMENT	—		
180	NON-MONETARY DAMAGES/RELIEF	—		
181	OTHER EQUITABLE REMEDIES	—		
182	**OBLIGATION TO PROVIDE BENEFITS**	—		
183	COBRA	—		
184	DISABILITY	—		
185	ERISA	●		Policy IV.A.7., page 5
186	SOCIAL SECURITY	—		
187	OTHER RETIREMENT BENEFITS	—		
188	UNEMPLOYMENT	—		
189	WORKERS' COMPENSATION	—		
190	**PERSONAL INJURY OFFENSES**	—		
191	DEFAMATION	—		
192	EMOTIONAL DISTRESS/UPSET	—		
193	HUMILIATION	—		
194	LIBEL	—		
195	MENTAL ANGUISH	—		
196	PERSONAL INJURY	—		
197	SLANDER	—		
198	**PRIOR ACTS**	●		Endorsement C.(1)., page 3
199	PRIOR ACTS	●	Prior to retroactive date	Endorsement C.(1)., page 3
200	PRIOR KNOWLEDGE	●		Endorsement C.(2)., page 3
201	PRIOR/PENDING LITIGATION	●		Endorsement C.(1)., page 3
202	**PROPERTY DAMAGE**	●		Endorsement B.(1)., page 2
203	INTANGIBLE PROPERTY	—		
204	LOSS OF USE	●		Endorsement B.(1)., page 2
205	TANGIBLE PROPERTY	●		Endorsement B.(1)., page 2
206	**RETALIATORY ACTIONS OF EMPLOYER**	—		
207	FOR FAILING TO PERFORM ACTS AGAINST PUBLIC POLICY	—		
208	FOR FILING A COMPLAINT OR BENEFIT CLAIM	—		
209	**STRIKES/LOCKOUTS**	—		
210	**VIOLATION OF LAWS**	—		
211	ANY LAW	—		
212	FMLA	—		
213	OSHA	—		
214	POLLUTION LAWS	●		Policy IV.A.6., page 5
215	RICO	—		
216	SEC	—		
217	WARN	—		

15 CONDITIONS

	Comparison Query	Comment		Policy Reference
218	**ARBITRATION**	—		
219	MANDATORY	—		
220	BINDING	—		
221	CHOICE OF LAW PROVISION	—		
222	SITUS	—		
223	**TERRITORY**	—		
224	LIMITED	—		
225	WORLDWIDE	—		
226	**NEWLY FORMED/ACQUIRED ENTITIES**	●		Policy IV.E.1., page 7
227	AUTOMATIC COVERAGE (X DAYS)	●	Subsidiaries	Policy IV.E.1., page 7
228	NOTIFY INSURER WITHIN X DAYS	90	Subsidiaries	Policy IV.E.1., page 7

CONNECTICUT INDEMNITY COMPANY (PROFESSIONAL RISK FACILITIES, INC.) 40609-0 [2/94]

Policy Comparison Worksheet

Connecticut Specialty Insurance Company
(Professional Risk Facilities, Inc.)

Policy Form No.: OL 001-0
Edition Date: 4/98

Risks Considered: General accounts
Limits Available: $5,000,000
Minimum Retention: $25,000

Contact: Joseph S. Gravier, Jr.
Professional Risk Facilities, Inc.
300 Old Country Road
Mineola, NY 11501-4192
516/747-6060
516/747-6074 (fax)
prf@i-2000.com

KEY TO SYMBOLS
● = Specifically contains queried provision of feature
○ = Unable to determine
— = Silent

#	Comparison Query		Comment	Policy Reference
	1 APPLICATION			
1	ATTACHES TO AND FORMS A PART OF THE POLICY	●	See also II.A., page 2	XI.A., page 21
2	CONTAINS WARRANTY STATEMENTS	—		
3	CONTAINS SEVERABILITY PROVISIONS	●		XI.C., page 21
	2 POLICY TYPE			
4	UNITARY STAND ALONE POLICY	—		
	ENDORSEMENT OR PART OF	—		
5	DIRECTORS AND OFFICERS POLICY	●	Combination form	
6	PACKAGE POLICY	—		
7	UMBRELLA POLICY	—		
8	ERRORS AND OMISSIONS POLICY	—		
9	OTHER	—		
10	CLAIMS-MADE	●		
11	OCCURRENCE	—		
	3 WHO IS INSURED			
12	BUSINESS ENTITY	●		II.J., page 5
13	AUTOMATIC COVERAGE FOR SUBSIDIARIES	●		II.K., page 5
14	DIRECTORS & OFFICERS	●		II.E., page 2
15	EMPLOYEES	●		II.E.3., page 3
16	PART-TIME	●		II.G.1., page 3
17	SEASONAL	●		II.G.1., page 3
18	TEMPORARY	●		II.G.1., page 3
19	SUPERVISORS & MANAGERS	●		II.G.1., page 3
20	FORMER EMPLOYEES	●		II.G.1., page 3
21	VOLUNTEERS	—		
22	INDEPENDENT CONTRACTORS	●	Coverage available by endorsement	II.G.3., page 3
23	EXCLUDED	—		
24	SILENT	—		
25	SHAREHOLDERS	—		
	4 LIMIT OF LIABILITY			
26	AGGREGATE	●		V.A., page 14
27	INCLUDES PUNITIVE DAMAGES WHERE NOT UNINSURABLE	●	Limitation applies	II.M., page 5
28	DEFENSE COSTS INCLUDED WITHIN LIMIT OF LIABILITY	●		V.E., page 15
29	DEFENSE COSTS PAID IN ADDITION TO LIMIT OF LIABILITY	—		
	5 DEDUCTIBLE			
30	APPLIES TO EACH INDIVIDUAL CLAIM	●		V.C., page 14
31	APPLIES TO EACH OCCURRENCE OR WRONGFUL PRACTICE			
32	INCLUDES ALL CLAIMS FROM ONE ACT	●		V.C., page 14
33	SUBJECT TO ANNUAL AGGREGATE	—		
34	CO-PAYMENT APPLIES	○	Per Item 8 of Declarations	V.B., page 14
35	LIMIT OF LIABILITY NOT REDUCED	—		
36	INCLUDES DEFENSE COSTS	●		
37	REDUCED UNDER SPECIFIED CIRCUMSTANCES (SEE POLICY)	—		V.E., page 15

CONNECTICUT SPECIALTY INSURANCE COMPANY OL 001-0 [4/98]

#	Comparison Query	Comment	Policy Reference
	6 WHAT IS A CLAIM		
38	ORAL COMPLAINT TO INSURED	—	
39	WRITTEN COMPLAINT TO INSURED	●	II.C., page 2
40	COMPLAINT MUST CONTAIN A DEMAND FOR DAMAGES	—	
41	COMPLAINT FILED WITH EEOC	—	
42	OR SIMILAR STATE AUTHORITY	—	
43	AGENCY MUST HAVE POWER TO ADJUDICATE	—	
44	ADMINISTRATIVE PROCEEDING	—	
45	ARBITRATION PROCEEDING	—	
46	ANY INCIDENT REPORTED TO INSURER	—	
47	SUIT	—	
48	CLAIM DOES NOT INCLUDE ARBITRATION SUBJECT TO	—	
49	COLLECTIVE BARGAINING AGREEMENT	—	
50	EMPLOYEE POLICY OR MANUAL	—	
51	CLAIM NOT DEFINED	—	
	7 CLAIM REPORTING PROVISIONS TO INSURER		
52	IMMEDIATELY	—	
53	AS SOON AS POSSIBLE	—	
54	AS SOON AS PRACTICABLE	●	IX.A., page 18
55	WITHIN POLICY PERIOD	—	
56	WITHIN X DAYS OF EXPIRATION	30	IX.A., page 18
57	WITHIN X DAYS	—	
	8 EXTENDED REPORTING FEATURES		
58	ELECTION PERIOD (DAYS)	30	III.D.2., page 9
59	ADDITIONAL PREMIUM (% OF ANNUAL PREMIUM)	○	Per Item (7a) of Declarations	III.D.1., page 9
60	ADDITIONAL REPORTING PERIOD (MONTHS)	○	Per Item (7b) of Declarations	III.D.1., page 9
61	NO REINSTATEMENT OF LIMITS	●	Coverage available by endorsement	III.D.4., page 9
	9 POTENTIAL CLAIM REPORTING PROVISIONS		
62	NONE (SEE ALSO "CLAIM" ABOVE)	—	
63	INCIDENTS LIKELY TO RESULT IN A CLAIM	●	IX.B., page 19
	10 DEFENSE PROVISIONS		
64	AFFIRMATIVE DUTY TO DEFEND	—	Coverage available by endorsement	
65	NO AFFIRMATIVE DUTY TO DEFEND	●	VII.A., page 15
66	AFFIRMATIVE ADVANCEMENT PROVISIONS	●	Covered loss only	VIII.C., page 17
67	INSURED MUST RETURN ADVANCED AMOUNTS IF NOT COVERED	●	VIII.D., page 17
68	INSURED/INSURER CHOOSES COUNSEL	—	
69	INSURED/INSURER APPROVES COUNSEL	—	
70	INSURED/INSURER CONSULTED IN COUNSEL SELECTION	—	
	11 SETTLEMENT PROVISIONS		
71	HAMMER CLAUSE	—	
72	CONSULTATION PROVISION	—	
73	CONSENT PROVISION	●	Insurer must consent	VII.B., page 15
	12 ALLOCATION OF LOSS PROVISIONS		
74	STIPULATED PROVISIONS	—	
	13 COVERAGES		
75	DISCRIMINATION	●	II.H.3., page 4
76	SPECIFIC ENUMERATED ACTIVITIES	—	
77	PLUS BROAD OMNIBUS WORDING	—	
78	SPECIFIC ENUMERATED CLASSES	●	II.H.3., page 4
79	PLUS BROAD OMNIBUS WORDING	●	II.H.3., page 4
80	AGAINST THIRD PARTIES	●	II.H. following 12., page 4
81	DISCRIMINATION NOT DEFINED	●	
82	SEXUAL HARASSMENT	●	II.H.2., page 3
83	HOSTILE ENVIRONMENT	●	II.H.2., page 3
84	QUID-PRO-QUO	●	II.H.2., page 3
85	SEXUAL HARASSMENT NOT DEFINED	●	
86	WRONGFUL TERMINATION	●	II.H.1., page 3
87	BREACH OF IMPLIED CONTRACT	●	II.H.1., page 3
88	BREACH OF EXPRESS CONTRACT	—	
89	VIOLATION OF PUBLIC POLICY	—	
90	VIOLATION OF GOOD FAITH & FAIR DEALING		
91	OBLIGATIONS TO MAKE PAYMENTS		
92	CONSTRUCTIVE DISCHARGE	●	II.H.1., page 3
93	WRONGFUL TERMINATION NOT DEFINED	●	
94	OTHER EMPLOYMENT VIOLATIONS/OFFENSES	●	II.H.7., page 4
95	WRONGFUL HIRING	●	II.H.7., page 4
96	WRONGFUL PROMOTION/DEMOTION	●	II.H.7., page 4
97	WRONGFUL EVALUATION/DISCIPLINE	●	See also II.H.9., page 4	II.H.8., page 4

CONNECTICUT SPECIALTY INSURANCE COMPANY OL 001-0 [4/98]

#	Comparison Query	Comment	Policy Reference
98	FAMILY AND MEDICAL LEAVE ACT	—	
99	DEFAMATION	●	II.H.6., page 4
100	MISREPRESENTATION	●	II.H.5., page 4
101	RETALIATION	●	II.H.4., page 4
102	MENTAL ANGUISH	—	
103	INVASION OF PRIVACY	●	II.H.4., page 4
104	HUMILIATION	●	II.H.6., page 4
105	EMOTIONAL DISTRESS	—	
106	OTHER PERSONAL INJURY OFFENSES	●	II.H.6., page 4
107	POLICY SILENT	—	
	14 EXCLUSIONS		
108	**ADA ACCOMMODATION EXPENSES**	—	
109	**ASSAULT & BATTERY**	●	IV.A.7., page 11
110	**BACK PAY**	—	
111	**BODILY INJURY**	●	IV.A.7., page 11
112	BODILY INJURY	●	IV.A.7., page 11
113	DEATH	●	IV.A.7., page 11
114	DISEASE	●	IV.A.7., page 11
115	SICKNESS	●	IV.A.7., page 11
116	**BREACH OF EMPLOYMENT CONTRACT**	●	IV.B., page 13
117	EXPRESS CONTRACT	●	Exception applies	IV.B., page 13
118	*WRITTEN CONTRACT*	●	Exception applies	IV.B., page 13
119	*ORAL CONTRACT*	●	Exception applies	IV.B., page 13
120	IMPLIED CONTRACT	—	
121	**CLASS ACTION LAWSUITS**	—	
122	**CONSEQUENTIAL LOSS**	—	
123	APPLIES TO BODILY INJURY	—	
124	APPLIES TO INSURED EVENT	—	
125	BROTHER/SISTER	—	
126	CHILD	—	
127	DOMESTIC PARTNER	—	
128	PARENT	—	
129	SPOUSE	—	
130	**COST OF ARBITRATION HEARINGS SUBJECT TO**	—	
131	EMPLOYMENT HANDBOOK	—	
132	LABOR GRIEVANCE	—	
133	OTHER EMPLOYMENT POLICY OR PROCEDURE	—	
134	**COVERAGE ELSEWHERE**	●	IV.A.13., page 12
135	OTHER AVAILABLE INSURANCE	●	IV.A.13., page 12
136	OTHER INDEMNIFICATION	—	
137	SHARING PROVISION	—	
138	**FAILURE TO EXERCISE CARE WHEN TERMINATING**	—	
139	**FINES/PENALTIES**	●	II.M., page 6
140	CIVIL	●	II.M., page 6
141	CRIMINAL	●	II.M., page 6
142	EXEMPLARY DAMAGES	—	
143	PUNITIVE DAMAGES	—	
144	MULTIPLIED DAMAGES	●	II.M., page 6
145	**FRONT PAY**	—	
146	EXCLUSION APPLIES ONLY IF EMPLOYER HAD OPPORTUNITY TO REINSTATE EMPLOYEE BUT DID NOT DO SO	—	
147	**INTENTIONAL ACTS**	●	IV.A.1., page 10
148	CRIMINAL ACTS	●	If established—non-imputation	IV.A.1., page 10
149	CRIMINAL PROCEEDING	—	
150	DISHONEST PURPOSE	●	If established—non-imputation	IV.A.1., page 10
151	FRAUDULENT ACTS	●	If established—non-imputation	IV.A.1., page 10
152	FRAUDULENT CLAIMS	—	
153	INTENTIONAL VIOLATIONS OF LAW	●	If established—non-imputation	IV.A.1., page 10
154	WILLFUL FAILURE TO COMPLY WITH LAW	—	
155	MALICIOUS PURPOSE	—	
156	**LIABILITY OF OTHERS**	—	
157	**LIQUIDATED DAMAGES**	—	
158	**LOSS ARISING OUT OF CHANGES IN OPERATIONS**	—	
159	ACQUISITION	—	
160	CHANGE IN CONTROL	—	
161	DOWNSIZING OR REDUCTION IN FORCE	—	
162	*% OF WORKFORCE*	—	
163	*WITHIN X DAYS*	—	

CONNECTICUT SPECIALTY INSURANCE COMPANY OL 001-0 [4/98]

#	Comparison Query		Comment	Policy Reference
164	FINANCIAL IMPAIRMENT	—		
165	BANKRUPTCY	—		
166	INSOLVENCY	—		
167	LIQUIDATION	—		
168	RECEIVERSHIP	—		
169	FINANCIAL INABILITY TO PAY	—		
170	MERGER	—		
171	PLANT OR FACILITY CLOSING	—		
172	REORGANIZATION	—		
173	TEMPORARY SHUTDOWN	—		
174	**MATTERS DEEMED UNINSURABLE**	●		II.M., page 6
175	**NON-MONETARY RELIEF**	●		IV.C.2.a., page 14
176	DECLATORY RELIEF	—		
177	DISGORGEMENT	—		
178	INJUNCTIVE RELIEF	—		
179	JOB REINSTATEMENT	—		
180	NON-MONETARY DAMAGES/RELIEF	●	Defense cost exception	IV.C.2.a., page 14
181	OTHER EQUITABLE REMEDIES	—		
182	**OBLIGATION TO PROVIDE BENEFITS**	—		
183	COBRA	●	Retaliation exception	IV.C.1., page 13
184	DISABILITY	●	Retaliation exception	IV.C.1., page 13
185	ERISA	●	See also IV.C.1., page 13	IV.A.9., page 11
186	SOCIAL SECURITY	●	See also IV.C.1., page 13	IV.C.1., page 13
187	OTHER RETIREMENT BENEFITS	—		
188	UNEMPLOYMENT	●	See also IV.C.1., page 13	IV.C.1., page 13
189	WORKERS' COMPENSATION	●	See also IV.C.1., page 13	IV.C.1., page 13
190	**PERSONAL INJURY OFFENSES**	—		
191	DEFAMATION	—		
192	EMOTIONAL DISTRESS/UPSET	—		
193	HUMILIATION	—		
194	LIBEL	—		
195	MENTAL ANGUISH	—		
196	PERSONAL INJURY	—		
197	SLANDER	—		
198	**PRIOR ACTS**	—		
199	PRIOR ACTS	—		
200	PRIOR KNOWLEDGE	●		IV.A.5., page 11
201	PRIOR/PENDING LITIGATION	●		IV.A.10., page 12
202	**PROPERTY DAMAGE**	●		IV.A.7., page 11
203	INTANGIBLE PROPERTY	—		
204	LOSS OF USE	●		IV.A.7., page 11
205	TANGIBLE PROPERTY	●		IV.A.7., page 11
206	**RETALIATORY ACTIONS OF EMPLOYER**	—		
207	FOR FAILING TO PERFORM ACTS AGAINST PUBLIC POLICY	—		
208	FOR FILING A COMPLAINT OR BENEFIT CLAIM	—		
209	**STRIKES/LOCKOUTS**	—		
210	**VIOLATION OF LAWS**	—		
211	ANY LAW	—		
212	FMLA	—		
213	OSHA	●	Retaliation exception	IV.C.1., page 13
214	POLLUTION LAWS	●		IV.A.8., page 11
215	RICO	—		
216	SEC	—		
217	WARN	●	Retaliation exception	IV.C.1., page 13
	15 CONDITIONS			
218	**ARBITRATION**	—		
219	MANDATORY	—		
220	BINDING	—		
221	CHOICE OF LAW PROVISION	—		
222	SITUS	—		
223	**TERRITORY**	●		XII.D., page 23
224	LIMITED	—		
225	WORLDWIDE	●		XII.D., page 23
226	**NEWLY FORMED/ACQUIRED ENTITIES**	●		X.A., page 19
227	AUTOMATIC COVERAGE (X DAYS)	●	<25% company assets involved	X.A., page 19
228	NOTIFY INSURER WITHIN X DAYS	90	>25% company assets involved	X.A., page 19

CONNECTICUT SPECIALTY INSURANCE COMPANY OL 001-0 [4/98]

Policy Comparison Worksheet

Employers Reinsurance Corporation

Policy Form No.: ERC 1491A
Edition Date: 1995

Risks Considered: Mercantile, light manufacturers, office (non-profit)
Limits Available: $100,000–$5,000,000
Minimum Retention: $5,000

Contact: Betty Weeks/ERC Specialty
Employers Reinsurance Corporation
5200 Metcalf
Overland Park, KS 66201
913/676-5327
913/676-5359 (fax)
betty.weeks@ercgroup.com

KEY TO SYMBOLS
● = Specifically contains queried provision of feature
○ = Unable to determine
— = Silent

#	Comparison Query		Comment	Policy Reference
	1 APPLICATION			
1	ATTACHES TO AND FORMS A PART OF THE POLICY	●		XVIII., page 8
2	CONTAINS WARRANTY STATEMENTS	—		
3	CONTAINS SEVERABILITY PROVISIONS	—		
	2 POLICY TYPE			
4	UNITARY STAND ALONE POLICY	●		
	ENDORSEMENT OR PART OF	—		
5	DIRECTORS AND OFFICERS POLICY	—		
6	PACKAGE POLICY	—		
7	UMBRELLA POLICY	—		
8	ERRORS AND OMISSIONS POLICY	—		
9	OTHER	—		
10	CLAIMS-MADE	●		
11	OCCURRENCE	—		
	3 WHO IS INSURED			
12	BUSINESS ENTITY	●		V., page 3
13	AUTOMATIC COVERAGE FOR SUBSIDIARIES	—		
14	DIRECTORS & OFFICERS	●		V., page 3
15	EMPLOYEES	●		V., page 3
16	PART-TIME	—		
17	SEASONAL	—		
18	TEMPORARY	—		
19	SUPERVISORS & MANAGERS	—		
20	FORMER EMPLOYEES	—		
21	VOLUNTEERS	—		
22	INDEPENDENT CONTRACTORS	—		
23	EXCLUDED	—		
24	SILENT	●		
25	SHAREHOLDERS	●		V., page 3
	4 LIMIT OF LIABILITY			
26	AGGREGATE	●		IV., page 2
27	INCLUDES PUNITIVE DAMAGES WHERE NOT UNINSURABLE	—		
28	DEFENSE COSTS INCLUDED WITHIN LIMIT OF LIABILITY	●		IV., page 3
29	DEFENSE COSTS PAID IN ADDITION TO LIMIT OF LIABILITY	—		
	5 DEDUCTIBLE			
30	APPLIES TO EACH INDIVIDUAL CLAIM	●		IV., page 3
31	APPLIES TO EACH OCCURRENCE OR WRONGFUL PRACTICE	—		
32	INCLUDES ALL CLAIMS FROM ONE ACT	●		IV., page 3
33	SUBJECT TO ANNUAL AGGREGATE	—		
34	CO-PAYMENT APPLIES	—		
35	LIMIT OF LIABILITY NOT REDUCED	—		
36	INCLUDES DEFENSE COSTS	●		IV., page 3
37	REDUCED UNDER SPECIFIED CIRCUMSTANCES (SEE POLICY)	—		

#	Comparison Query	Comment		Policy Reference
6	**WHAT IS A CLAIM**			
38	ORAL COMPLAINT TO INSURED	—		
39	WRITTEN COMPLAINT TO INSURED	●		V.(C)., page 3
40	COMPLAINT MUST CONTAIN A DEMAND FOR DAMAGES	○		V.(C)., page 3
41	COMPLAINT FILED WITH EEOC	●		V.(C)., page 3
42	OR SIMILAR STATE AUTHORITY	●		V.(C)., page 3
43	AGENCY MUST HAVE POWER TO ADJUDICATE	—		
44	ADMINISTRATIVE PROCEEDING	—		
45	ARBITRATION PROCEEDING	—		
46	ANY INCIDENT REPORTED TO INSURER	—		
47	SUIT	—		
48	CLAIM DOES NOT INCLUDE ARBITRATION SUBJECT TO	—		
49	COLLECTIVE BARGAINING AGREEMENT	—		
50	EMPLOYEE POLICY OR MANUAL	—		
51	CLAIM NOT DEFINED	●		
7	**CLAIM REPORTING PROVISIONS TO INSURER**			
52	IMMEDIATELY	—		
53	AS SOON AS POSSIBLE	—		
54	AS SOON AS PRACTICABLE	—		
55	WITHIN POLICY PERIOD	●		V.(C)., page 3
56	WITHIN X DAYS OF EXPIRATION	—		
57	WITHIN X DAYS	—		
8	**EXTENDED REPORTING FEATURES**			
58	ELECTION PERIOD (DAYS)	60		VIII., page 5
59	ADDITIONAL PREMIUM (% OF ANNUAL PREMIUM)	100		VIII., page 5
60	ADDITIONAL REPORTING PERIOD (MONTHS)	12		VIII., page 5
61	NO REINSTATEMENT OF LIMITS	—		
9	**POTENTIAL CLAIM REPORTING PROVISIONS**			
62	NONE (SEE ALSO "CLAIM" ABOVE)	—		
63	INCIDENTS LIKELY TO RESULT IN A CLAIM	●		X.(b)., page 6
10	**DEFENSE PROVISIONS**			
64	AFFIRMATIVE DUTY TO DEFEND	●		II., page 1
65	NO AFFIRMATIVE DUTY TO DEFEND	—		
66	AFFIRMATIVE ADVANCEMENT PROVISIONS	—		
67	INSURED MUST RETURN ADVANCED AMOUNTS IF NOT COVERED	—		
68	INSURED/INSURER CHOOSES COUNSEL	—		
69	INSURED/INSURER APPROVES COUNSEL	—		
70	INSURED/INSURER CONSULTED IN COUNSEL SELECTION	—		
11	**SETTLEMENT PROVISIONS**			
71	HAMMER CLAUSE	●		II., page 1
72	CONSULTATION PROVISION	—		
73	CONSENT PROVISION	●		II., page 1
12	**ALLOCATION OF LOSS PROVISIONS**			
74	STIPULATED PROVISIONS	—		
13	**COVERAGES**			
75	DISCRIMINATION	●	See also V.(d)., page 3	I., page 1
76	SPECIFIC ENUMERATED ACTIVITIES	—		
77	PLUS BROAD OMNIBUS WORDING	●	Act of insured	V.(e)., page 4
78	SPECIFIC ENUMERATED CLASSES	●		V.(e)., page 4
79	PLUS BROAD OMNIBUS WORDING	—		
80	AGAINST THIRD PARTIES	—	Coverage available by endorsement	
81	DISCRIMINATION NOT DEFINED	—		
82	SEXUAL HARASSMENT	●		V.(d)., page 3
83	HOSTILE ENVIRONMENT	—		
84	QUID-PRO-QUO	—		
85	SEXUAL HARASSMENT NOT DEFINED	●		
86	WRONGFUL TERMINATION	●		V.(d)., page 3
87	BREACH OF IMPLIED CONTRACT	○		V.(d)., page 3
88	BREACH OF EXPRESS CONTRACT	○		V.(d)., page 3
89	VIOLATION OF PUBLIC POLICY	—		
90	VIOLATION OF GOOD FAITH & FAIR DEALING	—		
91	OBLIGATIONS TO MAKE PAYMENTS	—		
92	CONSTRUCTIVE DISCHARGE	—		
93	WRONGFUL TERMINATION NOT DEFINED	●		
94	OTHER EMPLOYMENT VIOLATIONS/OFFENSES	●		I., page 1
95	WRONGFUL HIRING	●		V.(d)., page 3
96	WRONGFUL PROMOTION/DEMOTION	●		V.(d)., page 3
97	WRONGFUL EVALUATION/DISCIPLINE	●		V.(d)., page 3

EMPLOYERS REINSURANCE CORPORATION ERC 1491A [1995]

#	Comparison Query	Comment	Policy Reference
98	FAMILY AND MEDICAL LEAVE ACT	—	
99	DEFAMATION	●	V.(d)., page 4
100	MISREPRESENTATION	●	V.(d)., page 3
101	RETALIATION	●	V.(d)., page 4
102	MENTAL ANGUISH	—	
103	INVASION OF PRIVACY	●	V.(d)., page 4
104	HUMILIATION	—	
105	EMOTIONAL DISTRESS	●	V.(d)., page 4
106	OTHER PERSONAL INJURY OFFENSES	●	V.(d)., pages 3, 4
107	POLICY SILENT	—	
	14 EXCLUSIONS		
108	**ADA ACCOMMODATION EXPENSES**	●	VI.(j)., page 5
109	**ASSAULT & BATTERY**	●	VI.(g)., page 4
110	**BACK PAY**	—	
111	**BODILY INJURY**	●	VI.(b)., page 4
112	BODILY INJURY	●	VI.(b)., page 4
113	DEATH	●	VI.(b)., page 4
114	DISEASE	●	VI.(b)., page 4
115	SICKNESS	●	VI.(b)., page 4
116	**BREACH OF EMPLOYMENT CONTRACT**	—	
117	EXPRESS CONTRACT	—	
118	*WRITTEN CONTRACT*	—	
119	*ORAL CONTRACT*	—	
120	IMPLIED CONTRACT	—	
121	**CLASS ACTION LAWSUITS**	—	
122	**CONSEQUENTIAL LOSS**	—	
123	APPLIES TO BODILY INJURY	—	
124	APPLIES TO INSURED EVENT	—	
125	BROTHER/SISTER	—	
126	CHILD	—	
127	DOMESTIC PARTNER	—	
128	PARENT	—	
129	SPOUSE	—	
130	**COST OF ARBITRATION HEARINGS SUBJECT TO**	—	
131	EMPLOYMENT HANDBOOK	—	
132	LABOR GRIEVANCE	—	
133	OTHER EMPLOYMENT POLICY OR PROCEDURE	—	
134	**COVERAGE ELSEWHERE**	●	XII., page 6
135	OTHER AVAILABLE INSURANCE	●	XII., page 6
136	OTHER INDEMNIFICATION	—	
137	SHARING PROVISION	—	
138	**FAILURE TO EXERCISE CARE WHEN TERMINATING**	—	
139	**FINES/PENALTIES**	●	VI.(e)., page 4
140	CIVIL	—	
141	CRIMINAL	—	
142	EXEMPLARY DAMAGES	●	VI.(e)., page 4
143	PUNITIVE DAMAGES	●	VI.(e)., page 4
144	MULTIPLIED DAMAGES	●	VI.(e)., page 4
145	**FRONT PAY**	—	
146	EXCLUSION APPLIES ONLY IF EMPLOYER HAD OPPORTUNITY TO REINSTATE EMPLOYEE BUT DID NOT DO SO	—	
147	**INTENTIONAL ACTS**	●	VI.(a)., page 4
148	CRIMINAL ACTS	●	VI.(a)., page 4
149	CRIMINAL PROCEEDING	—	
150	DISHONEST PURPOSE	●	VI.(a)., page 4
151	FRAUDULENT ACTS	●	VI.(a)., page 4
152	FRAUDULENT CLAIMS	—	
153	INTENTIONAL VIOLATIONS OF LAW	—	
154	WILLFUL FAILURE TO COMPLY WITH LAW	—	
155	MALICIOUS PURPOSE	●	IV.(a)., page 4
156	**LIABILITY OF OTHERS**	●	VI.(d)., page 4
157	**LIQUIDATED DAMAGES**	—	
158	**LOSS ARISING OUT OF CHANGES IN OPERATIONS**	—	
159	ACQUISITION	—	
160	CHANGE IN CONTROL	—	
161	DOWNSIZING OR REDUCTION IN FORCE	—	
162	*% OF WORKFORCE*	—	
163	*WITHIN X DAYS*	—	

#	Comparison Query		Comment	Policy Reference
164	**FINANCIAL IMPAIRMENT**	—		
165	*BANKRUPTCY*	—		
166	*INSOLVENCY*	—		
167	*LIQUIDATION*	—		
168	*RECEIVERSHIP*	—		
169	FINANCIAL INABILITY TO PAY	—		
170	MERGER	—		
171	PLANT OR FACILITY CLOSING	—		
172	REORGANIZATION	—		
173	TEMPORARY SHUTDOWN	—		
174	**MATTERS DEEMED UNINSURABLE**	—		
175	**NON-MONETARY RELIEF**	—		
176	DECLATORY RELIEF	—		
177	DISGORGEMENT	—		
178	INJUNCTIVE RELIEF	—		
179	JOB REINSTATEMENT	—		
180	NON-MONETARY DAMAGES/RELIEF	—		
181	OTHER EQUITABLE REMEDIES	—		
182	**OBLIGATION TO PROVIDE BENEFITS**	●		VI.(i)., page 4
183	COBRA	●		VI.(i)., page 4
184	DISABILITY	●		VI.(i)., page 4
185	ERISA	●		VI.(h)., page 4
186	SOCIAL SECURITY	●		VI.(i)., page 4
187	OTHER RETIREMENT BENEFITS	●		VI.(f)., page 4
188	UNEMPLOYMENT	●		VI.(i)., page 4
189	WORKERS' COMPENSATION	●		VI.(i)., page 4
190	**PERSONAL INJURY OFFENSES**	●		VI.(b)., page 4
191	DEFAMATION	—		
192	EMOTIONAL DISTRESS/UPSET	●	If result of wrongful employment practice	VI.(b)., page 4
193	HUMILIATION	●	If result of wrongful employment practice	VI.(b)., page 4
194	LIBEL	—		
195	MENTAL ANGUISH	●	If result of wrongful employment practice	VI.(b)., page 4
196	PERSONAL INJURY	—		
197	SLANDER			
198	**PRIOR ACTS**	●	If claim filed before inception	VI.(k)., page 5
199	PRIOR ACTS	—		
200	PRIOR KNOWLEDGE	—		
201	PRIOR/PENDING LITIGATION	—		
202	**PROPERTY DAMAGE**	●		VI.(c)., page 4
203	INTANGIBLE PROPERTY	●	Any property	VI.(c)., page 4
204	LOSS OF USE	●		VI.(c)., page 4
205	TANGIBLE PROPERTY	●	Any property	VI.(c)., page 4
206	**RETALIATORY ACTIONS OF EMPLOYER**	—		
207	FOR FAILING TO PERFORM ACTS AGAINST PUBLIC POLICY	—		
208	FOR FILING A COMPLAINT OR BENEFIT CLAIM	—		
209	**STRIKES/LOCKOUTS**	—		
210	**VIOLATION OF LAWS**	●		VI.(i)., page 4
211	ANY LAW	—		
212	FMLA	—		
213	OSHA	—		
214	POLLUTION LAWS	—		
215	RICO	●		VI.(i)., page 4
216	SEC	—		
217	WARN	●		VI.(i)., page 4

15 CONDITIONS

#	Comparison Query		Comment	Policy Reference
218	**ARBITRATION**	—		
219	MANDATORY	—		
220	BINDING	—		
221	CHOICE OF LAW PROVISION	—		
222	SITUS	—		
223	**TERRITORY**	—		
224	LIMITED	—		
225	WORLDWIDE	—		
226	**NEWLY FORMED/ACQUIRED ENTITIES**	●	Must notify insurer	XI., page 6
227	AUTOMATIC COVERAGE (X DAYS)	—		
228	NOTIFY INSURER WITHIN X DAYS	—		

EMPLOYERS REINSURANCE CORPORATION ERC 1491A [1995]

Policy Comparison Worksheet

Evanston Insurance Company
(Shand Morahan)

Policy Form No.: EIC 3071-1 9/97
Edition Date: 9/97

Risks Considered: All except public entities and municipalities
Limits Available: $5,000,000
Minimum Retention: $2,500

Contact: Gerard Albanese
Evanston Insurance Company
1007 Church Street
Evanston, IL 60091
847/866-0874
847/866-0717 (fax)
albanese@markelcorp.com

KEY TO SYMBOLS
● = Specifically contains queried provision of feature
○ = Unable to determine
— = Silent

#	Comparison Query		Comment	Policy Reference
	1 APPLICATION			
1	ATTACHES TO AND FORMS A PART OF THE POLICY	●		VIII.3.(a)., page 7
2	CONTAINS WARRANTY STATEMENTS	●		
3	CONTAINS SEVERABILITY PROVISIONS	—		
	2 POLICY TYPE			
4	UNITARY STAND ALONE POLICY	●		
	ENDORSEMENT OR PART OF	—		
5	DIRECTORS AND OFFICERS POLICY	—		
6	PACKAGE POLICY	—		
7	UMBRELLA POLICY	—		
8	ERRORS AND OMISSIONS POLICY	—		
9	OTHER	—		
10	CLAIMS-MADE	●		
11	OCCURRENCE	—		
	3 WHO IS INSURED			
12	BUSINESS ENTITY	●		III.3., page 3
13	AUTOMATIC COVERAGE FOR SUBSIDIARIES	—		
14	DIRECTORS & OFFICERS	●		III.3., page 3
15	EMPLOYEES	●	At insured's request	III.3., page 3
16	PART-TIME	—		
17	SEASONAL	—		
18	TEMPORARY	—		
19	SUPERVISORS & MANAGERS	—		
20	FORMER EMPLOYEES	●	At insured's request	III.3., page 3
21	VOLUNTEERS	—		
22	INDEPENDENT CONTRACTORS	—		
23	EXCLUDED	—		
24	SILENT	●		
25	SHAREHOLDERS	●		III.3., page 3
	4 LIMIT OF LIABILITY			
26	AGGREGATE	●		VI.2., page 6
27	INCLUDES PUNITIVE DAMAGES WHERE NOT UNINSURABLE	○		IV.8., page 5
28	DEFENSE COSTS INCLUDED WITHIN LIMIT OF LIABILITY	●	See also III.2.(a)., page 3	VI.2., page 6
29	DEFENSE COSTS PAID IN ADDITION TO LIMIT OF LIABILITY	—		
	5 DEDUCTIBLE			
30	APPLIES TO EACH INDIVIDUAL CLAIM	●	Self-Insured Retention	VI.3., page 6
31	APPLIES TO EACH OCCURRENCE OR WRONGFUL PRACTICE	—		
32	INCLUDES ALL CLAIMS FROM ONE ACT	—		
33	SUBJECT TO ANNUAL AGGREGATE	—		
34	CO-PAYMENT APPLIES	●	Specified by underwriter—see Item 6 of Declarations	I.4., page 2
35	LIMIT OF LIABILITY NOT REDUCED	—		
36	INCLUDES DEFENSE COSTS	●		I.6., page 2
37	REDUCED UNDER SPECIFIED CIRCUMSTANCES (SEE POLICY)	—		

#	Comparison Query		Comment	Policy Reference
	6 WHAT IS A CLAIM			
38	ORAL COMPLAINT TO INSURED	—		
39	WRITTEN COMPLAINT TO INSURED	●		I.1., page 2
40	COMPLAINT MUST CONTAIN A DEMAND FOR DAMAGES	●	Or other relief	I.1., page 2
41	COMPLAINT FILED WITH EEOC	—		
42	OR SIMILAR STATE AUTHORITY	—		
43	AGENCY MUST HAVE POWER TO ADJUDICATE	—		
44	ADMINISTRATIVE PROCEEDING	—		
45	ARBITRATION PROCEEDING	—		
46	ANY INCIDENT REPORTED TO INSURER	—		
47	SUIT	●		I.1., page 2
48	CLAIM DOES NOT INCLUDE ARBITRATION SUBJECT TO	—		
49	COLLECTIVE BARGAINING AGREEMENT	—		
50	EMPLOYEE POLICY OR MANUAL	—		
51	CLAIM NOT DEFINED	—		
	7 CLAIM REPORTING PROVISIONS TO INSURER			
52	IMMEDIATELY	●		VII.1., page 6
53	AS SOON AS POSSIBLE	—		
54	AS SOON AS PRACTICABLE	—		
55	WITHIN POLICY PERIOD	—		
56	WITHIN X DAYS OF EXPIRATION	60		VII.1., page 6
57	WITHIN X DAYS	—		
	8 EXTENDED REPORTING FEATURES			
58	ELECTION PERIOD (DAYS)	10		III.3.(d), page 5
59	ADDITIONAL PREMIUM (% OF ANNUAL PREMIUM)	150		III.3.(d), page 5
60	ADDITIONAL REPORTING PERIOD (MONTHS)	36		III.3., page 4
61	NO REINSTATEMENT OF LIMITS	●		III.3.(f), page 4
	9 POTENTIAL CLAIM REPORTING PROVISIONS			
62	NONE (SEE ALSO "CLAIM" ABOVE)	●		
63	INCIDENTS LIKELY TO RESULT IN A CLAIM	—		
	10 DEFENSE PROVISIONS			
64	AFFIRMATIVE DUTY TO DEFEND	●		III.2., page 3
65	NO AFFIRMATIVE DUTY TO DEFEND	—		
66	AFFIRMATIVE ADVANCEMENT PROVISIONS	—		
67	INSURED MUST RETURN ADVANCED AMOUNTS IF NOT COVERED	—		
68	INSURED/INSURER CHOOSES COUNSEL	●	Insurer-Exception applies	III.2.(b), page 3
69	INSURED/INSURER APPROVES COUNSEL	—		
70	INSURED/INSURER CONSULTED IN COUNSEL SELECTION	—		
	11 SETTLEMENT PROVISIONS			
71	HAMMER CLAUSE	●		III.2.(e), page 4
72	CONSULTATION PROVISION	—		
73	CONSENT PROVISION	●		III.2.(e), page 4
	12 ALLOCATION OF LOSS PROVISIONS			
74	STIPULATED PROVISIONS	—		
	13 COVERAGES			
75	DISCRIMINATION	●	As Wrongful Employment Practice	I.7., page 2
76	SPECIFIC ENUMERATED ACTIVITIES	—		
77	PLUS BROAD OMNIBUS WORDING	—		
78	SPECIFIC ENUMERATED CLASSES	—		
79	PLUS BROAD OMNIBUS WORDING	—		
80	AGAINST THIRD PARTIES	—		
81	DISCRIMINATION NOT DEFINED	●		
82	SEXUAL HARASSMENT	—		
83	HOSTILE ENVIRONMENT	—		
84	QUID-PRO-QUO	—		
85	SEXUAL HARASSMENT NOT DEFINED	—		
86	WRONGFUL TERMINATION	●	As Wrongful Employment Practice	I.7., page 2
87	BREACH OF IMPLIED CONTRACT	—		
88	BREACH OF EXPRESS CONTRACT	—		
89	VIOLATION OF PUBLIC POLICY	—		
90	VIOLATION OF GOOD FAITH & FAIR DEALING	—		
91	OBLIGATIONS TO MAKE PAYMENTS	—		
92	CONSTRUCTIVE DISCHARGE	●	As Wrongful Employment Practice	
93	WRONGFUL TERMINATION NOT DEFINED	●		
94	OTHER EMPLOYMENT VIOLATIONS/OFFENSES	—		
95	WRONGFUL HIRING	—		
96	WRONGFUL PROMOTION/DEMOTION	—		
97	WRONGFUL EVALUATION/DISCIPLINE	—		

EVANSTON INSURANCE COMPANY (SHAND MORAHAN) EIC 3071-1 9/97 [9/97]

#	Comparison Query		Comment	Policy Reference
98	FAMILY AND MEDICAL LEAVE ACT	●		I.7., page 2
99	DEFAMATION	—		
100	MISREPRESENTATION	—		
101	RETALIATION	—		
102	MENTAL ANGUISH	—		
103	INVASION OF PRIVACY	—		
104	HUMILIATION	—		
105	EMOTIONAL DISTRESS	—		
106	OTHER PERSONAL INJURY OFFENSES	—		
107	POLICY SILENT	●		

14 EXCLUSIONS

#	Comparison Query		Comment	Policy Reference
108	**ADA ACCOMMODATION EXPENSES**	—		
109	**ASSAULT & BATTERY**	—		
110	**BACK PAY**	—		
111	**BODILY INJURY**	●		I.3., page 2
112	BODILY INJURY	—		
113	DEATH	—		
114	DISEASE	—		
115	SICKNESS	—		
116	**BREACH OF EMPLOYMENT CONTRACT**	●		IV.10., page 6
117	EXPRESS CONTRACT	●		IV.10., page 6
118	*WRITTEN CONTRACT*	—		
119	*ORAL CONTRACT*	—		
120	IMPLIED CONTRACT	—		
121	**CLASS ACTION LAWSUITS**	—		
122	**CONSEQUENTIAL LOSS**	—		
123	APPLIES TO BODILY INJURY	—		
124	APPLIES TO INSURED EVENT	—		
125	BROTHER/SISTER	—		
126	CHILD	—		
127	DOMESTIC PARTNER	—		
128	PARENT	—		
129	SPOUSE	—		
130	**COST OF ARBITRATION HEARINGS SUBJECT TO**	—		
131	EMPLOYMENT HANDBOOK	—		
132	LABOR GRIEVANCE	—		
133	OTHER EMPLOYMENT POLICY OR PROCEDURE	—		
134	**COVERAGE ELSEWHERE**	●		VIII.6., page 8
135	OTHER AVAILABLE INSURANCE	●		VIII.6., page 8
136	OTHER INDEMNIFICATION	—		
137	SHARING PROVISION	—		
138	**FAILURE TO EXERCISE CARE WHEN TERMINATING**	—		
139	**FINES/PENALTIES**	●	Specified circumstances	IV.8., page 5
140	CIVIL	●	Specified circumstances	IV.8., page 5
141	CRIMINAL	●	Specified circumstances	IV.8., page 5
142	EXEMPLARY DAMAGES	—		
143	PUNITIVE DAMAGES	●	Specified circumstances	IV.8., page 5
144	MULTIPLIED DAMAGES	—		
145	**FRONT PAY**	—		
146	EXCLUSION APPLIES ONLY IF EMPLOYER HAD OPPORTUNITY TO REINSTATE EMPLOYEE BUT DID NOT DO SO	—		
147	**INTENTIONAL ACTS**	●		IV.1., page 5
148	CRIMINAL ACTS	—		
149	CRIMINAL PROCEEDING	●		IV.7., page 5
150	DISHONEST PURPOSE	—		
151	FRAUDULENT ACTS	—		
152	FRAUDULENT CLAIMS	●	Voids policy	VII.5., page 7
153	INTENTIONAL VIOLATIONS OF LAW	●		IV.1., page 5
154	WILLFUL FAILURE TO COMPLY WITH LAW	●		IV.1., page 5
155	MALICIOUS PURPOSE	●		IV.1., page 5
156	**LIABILITY OF OTHERS**	●	Exception applies	IV.2., page 5
157	**LIQUIDATED DAMAGES**	—		
158	**LOSS ARISING OUT OF CHANGES IN OPERATIONS**	—		
159	ACQUISITION	—		
160	CHANGE IN CONTROL	—		
161	DOWNSIZING OR REDUCTION IN FORCE	—		
162	*% OF WORKFORCE*	—		
163	*WITHIN X DAYS*	—		

EVANSTON INSURANCE COMPANY (SHAND MORAHAN) EIC 3071-1 9/97 [9/97]

#	Comparison Query		Comment	Policy Reference
164	FINANCIAL IMPAIRMENT	—		
165	BANKRUPTCY	—		
166	INSOLVENCY	—		
167	LIQUIDATION	—		
168	RECEIVERSHIP	—		
169	FINANCIAL INABILITY TO PAY	—		
170	MERGER	—		
171	PLANT OR FACILITY CLOSING	—		
172	REORGANIZATION	—		
173	TEMPORARY SHUTDOWN	—		
174	**MATTERS DEEMED UNINSURABLE**	—		
175	**NON-MONETARY RELIEF**	—		
176	DECLATORY RELIEF	—		
177	DISGORGEMENT	—		
178	INJUNCTIVE RELIEF	—		
179	JOB REINSTATEMENT	—		
180	NON-MONETARY DAMAGES/RELIEF	—		
181	OTHER EQUITABLE REMEDIES	—		
182	**OBLIGATION TO PROVIDE BENEFITS**			
183	COBRA	—		
184	DISABILITY	●	Retaliation exception	IV.3., page 5
185	ERISA	●		IV.6., page 5
186	SOCIAL SECURITY	—		
187	OTHER RETIREMENT BENEFITS	—		
188	UNEMPLOYMENT	●	Retaliation exception	IV.3., page 5
189	WORKERS' COMPENSATION	●	Retaliation exception	IV.3., page 5
190	**PERSONAL INJURY OFFENSES**	—		
191	DEFAMATION	—		
192	EMOTIONAL DISTRESS/UPSET	—		
193	HUMILIATION	—		
194	LIBEL	—		
195	MENTAL ANGUISH	—		
196	PERSONAL INJURY	—		
197	SLANDER	—		
198	**PRIOR ACTS**	●		I.7., page 2
199	PRIOR ACTS	●		I.7., page 2
200	PRIOR KNOWLEDGE	—		
201	PRIOR/PENDING LITIGATION	—		
202	**PROPERTY DAMAGE**	●		I.3., page 2
203	INTANGIBLE PROPERTY	●		I.3., page 2
204	LOSS OF USE	●		I.3., page 2
205	TANGIBLE PROPERTY	●		I.3., page 2
206	**RETALIATORY ACTIONS OF EMPLOYER**	—		
207	FOR FAILING TO PERFORM ACTS AGAINST PUBLIC POLICY	—		
208	FOR FILING A COMPLAINT OR BENEFIT CLAIM	—		
209	**STRIKES/LOCKOUTS**	—		
210	**VIOLATION OF LAWS**			
211	ANY LAW	—		
212	FMLA	—		
213	OSHA	—		
214	POLLUTION LAWS	—		
215	RICO	—		
216	SEC	—		
217	WARN	●		IV.5., page 5
	15 CONDITIONS			
218	**ARBITRATION**	—		
219	MANDATORY	—		
220	BINDING	—		
221	CHOICE OF LAW PROVISION	—		
222	SITUS	—		
223	**TERRITORY**			
224	LIMITED	●		V., page 6
225	WORLDWIDE	—		
226	**NEWLY FORMED/ACQUIRED ENTITIES**	●		II.4., page 3
227	AUTOMATIC COVERAGE (X DAYS)	60		II.4., page 3
228	NOTIFY INSURER WITHIN X DAYS	—		

EVANSTON INSURANCE COMPANY (SHAND MORAHAN) EIC 3071-1 9/97 [9/97]

Policy Comparison Worksheet

Executive Risk Specialty Insurance Company

Policy Form No.: B22130
Edition Date: 1/96

Risks Considered:
Limits Available: $10 million
Minimum Retention: $2,500

Contact: Executive Risk Communications
82 Hopmeadow Street
Simsbury, CT 06070-7683
800/432-8168
860/408-2288 (fax)
info@execrisk.com

KEY TO SYMBOLS
● = Specifically contains queried provision of feature
○ = Unable to determine
— = Silent

#	Comparison Query		Comment	Policy Reference
	1 APPLICATION			
1	ATTACHES TO AND FORMS A PART OF THE POLICY	●		II (A), page 2
2	CONTAINS WARRANTY STATEMENTS	—		
3	CONTAINS SEVERABILITY PROVISIONS	—		
	2 POLICY TYPE			
4	UNITARY STAND ALONE POLICY	—		
	ENDORSEMENT OR PART OF	—		
5	DIRECTORS AND OFFICERS POLICY	●		
6	PACKAGE POLICY	—		
7	UMBRELLA POLICY	—		
8	ERRORS AND OMISSIONS POLICY	—		
9	OTHER	—		
10	CLAIMS-MADE	●		
11	OCCURRENCE	—		
	3 WHO IS INSURED			
12	BUSINESS ENTITY	●		II (F), page 2
13	AUTOMATIC COVERAGE FOR SUBSIDIARIES	●		II (C), page 2
14	DIRECTORS & OFFICERS	●		II (G)(1), page 2
15	EMPLOYEES	●		II (G)(2), page 2
16	PART-TIME	—		
17	SEASONAL	—		
18	TEMPORARY	—		
19	SUPERVISORS & MANAGERS	—		
20	FORMER EMPLOYEES	●		II (G)(2), page 2
21	VOLUNTEERS	—		
22	INDEPENDENT CONTRACTORS	—		
23	EXCLUDED	—		
24	SILENT	—		
25	SHAREHOLDERS	—		
	4 LIMIT OF LIABILITY			
26	AGGREGATE	●		IV (A)(1), page 6
27	INCLUDES PUNITIVE DAMAGES WHERE NOT UNINSURABLE	●	Limited coverage	III (C), page 4
28	DEFENSE COSTS INCLUDED WITHIN LIMIT OF LIABILITY	●		IV (A)(2), page 6
29	DEFENSE COSTS PAID IN ADDITION TO LIMIT OF LIABILITY	—		
	5 DEDUCTIBLE			
30	APPLIES TO EACH INDIVIDUAL CLAIM	○		IV (B)(1) and (4), page 7
31	APPLIES TO EACH OCCURRENCE OR WRONGFUL PRACTICE	—		
32	INCLUDES ALL CLAIMS FROM ONE ACT	●		IV (G)(4), page 9
33	SUBJECT TO ANNUAL AGGREGATE	—		
34	CO-PAYMENT APPLIES	—		
35	LIMIT OF LIABILITY NOT REDUCED	—		
36	INCLUDES DEFENSE COSTS	●		IV (B)(1), page 7
37	REDUCED UNDER SPECIFIED CIRCUMSTANCES (SEE POLICY)	—		

EXECUTIVE RISK SPECIALTY INSURANCE COMPANY B22130 [1/96]

#	Comparison Query	Comment	Policy Reference
	6 WHAT IS A CLAIM		
38	ORAL COMPLAINT TO INSURED	—	
39	WRITTEN COMPLAINT TO INSURED	●	II (B), page 2
40	COMPLAINT MUST CONTAIN A DEMAND FOR DAMAGES	—	
41	COMPLAINT FILED WITH EEOC	—	
42	OR SIMILAR STATE AUTHORITY	—	
43	AGENCY MUST HAVE POWER TO ADJUDICATE	—	
44	ADMINISTRATIVE PROCEEDING	—	
45	ARBITRATION PROCEEDING	—	
46	ANY INCIDENT REPORTED TO INSURER	—	
47	SUIT	—	
48	CLAIM DOES NOT INCLUDE ARBITRATION SUBJECT TO	—	
49	COLLECTIVE BARGAINING AGREEMENT	—	
50	EMPLOYEE POLICY OR MANUAL	—	
51	CLAIM NOT DEFINED	—	
	7 CLAIM REPORTING PROVISIONS TO INSURER		
52	IMMEDIATELY	—	
53	AS SOON AS POSSIBLE	—	
54	AS SOON AS PRACTICABLE	●	IV (G)(1), page 9
55	WITHIN POLICY PERIOD	—	
56	WITHIN X DAYS OF EXPIRATION	—	
57	WITHIN X DAYS	—	
	8 EXTENDED REPORTING FEATURES		
58	ELECTION PERIOD (DAYS)	30	IV (F), pages 8–9
59	ADDITIONAL PREMIUM (% OF ANNUAL PREMIUM)	○	Specified by underwriter—see Item 7 of Declarations	IV (F), pages 8–9
60	ADDITIONAL REPORTING PERIOD (MONTHS)	○	
61	NO REINSTATEMENT OF LIMITS	—	
	9 POTENTIAL CLAIM REPORTING PROVISIONS		
62	NONE (SEE ALSO "CLAIM" ABOVE)	—	
63	INCIDENTS LIKELY TO RESULT IN A CLAIM	●	IV (G)(2), page 9
	10 DEFENSE PROVISIONS		
64	AFFIRMATIVE DUTY TO DEFEND	●	I (C), page 1
65	NO AFFIRMATIVE DUTY TO DEFEND	—	
66	AFFIRMATIVE ADVANCEMENT PROVISIONS	—	
67	INSURED MUST RETURN ADVANCED AMOUNTS IF NOT COVERED	—	
68	INSURED/INSURER CHOOSES COUNSEL	—	
69	INSURED/INSURER APPROVES COUNSEL	—	
70	INSURED/INSURER CONSULTED IN COUNSEL SELECTION	—	
	11 SETTLEMENT PROVISIONS		
71	HAMMER CLAUSE	●	IV (C)(1)(b), page 8
72	CONSULTATION PROVISION	—	
73	CONSENT PROVISION	●	Two-way	IV (C)(1), page 7
	12 ALLOCATION OF LOSS PROVISIONS		
74	STIPULATED PROVISIONS	—	
	13 COVERAGES		
75	DISCRIMINATION	●	As employment practices wrongful act.	II (E)(2), page 2
76	SPECIFIC ENUMERATED ACTIVITIES	—	
77	*PLUS BROAD OMNIBUS WORDING*	—	
78	SPECIFIC ENUMERATED CLASSES	—	
79	*PLUS BROAD OMNIBUS WORDING*	—	
80	AGAINST THIRD PARTIES	—	
81	DISCRIMINATION NOT DEFINED	●	
82	SEXUAL HARASSMENT	●	As employment practices wrongful act	II (E)(2), page 2
83	HOSTILE ENVIRONMENT	—	
84	QUID-PRO-QUO	—	
85	SEXUAL HARASSMENT NOT DEFINED	●	
86	WRONGFUL TERMINATION	●	As employment practices wrongful act	II (E)(1), page 2
87	BREACH OF IMPLIED CONTRACT	—	
88	BREACH OF EXPRESS CONTRACT	—	
89	VIOLATION OF PUBLIC POLICY	—	
90	VIOLATION OF GOOD FAITH & FAIR DEALING	—	
91	OBLIGATIONS TO MAKE PAYMENTS	—	
92	CONSTRUCTIVE DISCHARGE	—	
93	WRONGFUL TERMINATION NOT DEFINED	●	
94	OTHER EMPLOYMENT VIOLATIONS/OFFENSES	—	
95	WRONGFUL HIRING	●	II (E)(1), page 2
96	WRONGFUL PROMOTION/DEMOTION	●	II (E)(1), page 2
97	WRONGFUL EVALUATION/DISCIPLINE	—	

EXECUTIVE RISK SPECIALTY INSURANCE COMPANY B22130 [1/96]

	Comparison Query		Comment	Policy Reference
98	FAMILY AND MEDICAL LEAVE ACT	—		
99	DEFAMATION	●		III (D)(1), page 5
100	MISREPRESENTATION	—		
101	RETALIATION	●	As employment practices wrongful act	II (E)(3), page 2
102	MENTAL ANGUISH	●		III (D)(1), page 5
103	INVASION OF PRIVACY	—		
104	HUMILIATION	—		
105	EMOTIONAL DISTRESS	●		III (D)(1), page 5
106	OTHER PERSONAL INJURY OFFENSES	●		III (D)(1), page 5
107	POLICY SILENT	—		
14 EXCLUSIONS				
108	**ADA ACCOMMODATION EXPENSES**	—		
109	**ASSAULT & BATTERY**	●		III (D)(1), page 5
110	**BACK PAY**	—		
111	**BODILY INJURY**	●	Exception applies	III (D)(1), page 5
112	BODILY INJURY	●	Exception applies	III (D)(1), page 5
113	DEATH	●	Exception applies	III (D)(1), page 5
114	DISEASE	●	Exception applies	III (D)(1), page 5
115	SICKNESS	●	Exception applies	III (D)(1), page 5
116	**BREACH OF EMPLOYMENT CONTRACT**	●		III (B), page 4
117	EXPRESS CONTRACT	—		
118	WRITTEN CONTRACT	●		III (B), page 4
119	ORAL CONTRACT	—		
120	IMPLIED CONTRACT	—		
121	**CLASS ACTION LAWSUITS**	—		
122	**CONSEQUENTIAL LOSS**	—		
123	APPLIES TO BODILY INJURY	●	Loss of consortium	III (D)(1), page 5
124	APPLIES TO INSURED EVENT	—		
125	BROTHER/SISTER	—		
126	CHILD	—		
127	DOMESTIC PARTNER	—		
128	PARENT	—		
129	SPOUSE	—		
130	**COST OF ARBITRATION HEARINGS SUBJECT TO**	—		
131	EMPLOYMENT HANDBOOK	—		
132	LABOR GRIEVANCE	—		
133	OTHER EMPLOYMENT POLICY OR PROCEDURE	—		
134	**COVERAGE ELSEWHERE**	●		IV (D), page 8
135	OTHER AVAILABLE INSURANCE	●		IV (D), page 8
136	OTHER INDEMNIFICATION	●		IV (D), page 8
137	SHARING PROVISION	—		
138	**FAILURE TO EXERCISE CARE WHEN TERMINATING**	—		
139	**FINES/PENALTIES**	●		III (C), page 4
140	CIVIL	—		
141	CRIMINAL	—		
142	EXEMPLARY DAMAGES	●	Exception applies	III (C), page 4
143	PUNITIVE DAMAGES	●	Exception applies	III (C), page 4
144	MULTIPLIED DAMAGES	●	Exception applies	III (C), page 4
145	**FRONT PAY**	—		
146	EXCLUSION APPLIES ONLY IF EMPLOYER HAD OPPORTUNITY TO REINSTATE EMPLOYEE BUT DID NOT DO SO	—		
147	**INTENTIONAL ACTS**	●		III (A)(1), page 4
148	CRIMINAL ACTS	—		
149	CRIMINAL PROCEEDING	—		
150	DISHONEST PURPOSE	●		III (A)(1), page 4
151	FRAUDULENT ACTS	●		III (A)(1), page 4
152	FRAUDULENT CLAIMS	—		
153	INTENTIONAL VIOLATIONS OF LAW	●		III (A)(2), page 4
154	WILLFUL FAILURE TO COMPLY WITH LAW	●		III (A)(2), page 4
155	MALICIOUS PURPOSE	—		
156	**LIABILITY OF OTHERS**	●		III (H), page 6
157	**LIQUIDATED DAMAGES**	—		
158	**LOSS ARISING OUT OF CHANGES IN OPERATIONS**	—		
159	ACQUISITION	—		
160	CHANGE IN CONTROL	—		
161	DOWNSIZING OR REDUCTION IN FORCE	—		
162	% OF WORKFORCE	—		
163	WITHIN X DAYS	—		

#	Comparison Query		Comment	Policy Reference
164	**FINANCIAL IMPAIRMENT**	—		
165	*BANKRUPTCY*	—		
166	*INSOLVENCY*	—		
167	*LIQUIDATION*	—		
168	*RECEIVERSHIP*	—		
169	FINANCIAL INABILITY TO PAY	—		
170	MERGER	—		
171	PLANT OR FACILITY CLOSING	—		
172	REORGANIZATION	—		
173	TEMPORARY SHUTDOWN	—		
174	**MATTERS DEEMED UNINSURABLE**	●		III (C), page 4
175	**NON-MONETARY RELIEF**	—		
176	DECLATORY RELIEF	—		
177	DISGORGEMENT	—		
178	INJUNCTIVE RELIEF	—		
179	JOB REINSTATEMENT	—		
180	NON-MONETARY DAMAGES/RELIEF	●		III (A)(2), page 4
181	OTHER EQUITABLE REMEDIES	—		
182	**OBLIGATION TO PROVIDE BENEFITS**			
183	COBRA	●		III (A)(3), page 4
184	DISABILITY	●		III (A)(3), page 4
185	ERISA	●		III (F), page 6
186	SOCIAL SECURITY	●		III (A)(3), page 4
187	OTHER RETIREMENT BENEFITS	—		
188	UNEMPLOYMENT	●		III (A)(3), page 4
189	WORKERS' COMPENSATION	●		III (A)(3), page 4
190	**PERSONAL INJURY OFFENSES**			
191	DEFAMATION	—		
192	EMOTIONAL DISTRESS/UPSET	—		
193	HUMILIATION	—		
194	LIBEL	—		
195	MENTAL ANGUISH	—		
196	PERSONAL INJURY	—		
197	SLANDER	—		
198	**PRIOR ACTS**	—		
199	PRIOR ACTS	—		
200	PRIOR KNOWLEDGE	—		
201	PRIOR/PENDING LITIGATION	●		III (D)(4), page 5
202	**PROPERTY DAMAGE**	●		III (D)(1), page 5
203	INTANGIBLE PROPERTY	—		
204	LOSS OF USE	●		III (D)(1), page 5
205	TANGIBLE PROPERTY	●		III (D)(1), page 5
206	**RETALIATORY ACTIONS OF EMPLOYER**	—		
207	FOR FAILING TO PERFORM ACTS AGAINST PUBLIC POLICY	—		
208	FOR FILING A COMPLAINT OR BENEFIT CLAIM	—		
209	**STRIKES/LOCKOUTS**	—		
210	**VIOLATION OF LAWS**	—		
211	ANY LAW	—		
212	FMLA	—		
213	OSHA	●		III (A)(3), page 4
214	POLLUTION LAWS	●		III (D)(2), page 5
215	RICO	—		
216	SEC	—		
217	WARN	●		III (A)(3), page 4
	15 CONDITIONS			
218	**ARBITRATION**	—		
219	MANDATORY	—		
220	BINDING	—		
221	CHOICE OF LAW PROVISION	—		
222	SITUS	—		
223	**TERRITORY**	—		
224	LIMITED	—		
225	WORLDWIDE	—		
226	**NEWLY FORMED/ACQUIRED ENTITIES**	●		IV (H), page 10
227	AUTOMATIC COVERAGE (X DAYS)	—		
228	NOTIFY INSURER WITHIN X DAYS	○	No time limit specified—>25% company assets involved	IV (H), page 10

EXECUTIVE RISK SPECIALTY INSURANCE COMPANY B22130 [1/96]

Policy Comparison Worksheet

Executive Risk Specialty Insurance Company

Policy Form No.: B22167
Edition Date: 2/97

Risks Considered: Law firms
Limits Available: $40 million
Minimum Retention: $10,000

Contact: Executive Risk Communications
82 Hopmeadow Street
Simsbury, CT 06070-7683
800/432-8168
860/408-2288 (fax)
info@execrisk.com

KEY TO SYMBOLS
● = Specifically contains queried provision of feature
○ = Unable to determine
— = Silent

#	Comparison Query		Comment	Policy Reference
	1 APPLICATION			
1	ATTACHES TO AND FORMS A PART OF THE POLICY	●	See also V.(J)., page 12	II.(A)., page 1
2	CONTAINS WARRANTY STATEMENTS	—		
3	CONTAINS SEVERABILITY PROVISIONS	●		IV.(J).(1). & (2)., page 12
	2 POLICY TYPE			
4	UNITARY STAND ALONE POLICY	●		
	ENDORSEMENT OR PART OF	—		
5	DIRECTORS AND OFFICERS POLICY	—		
6	PACKAGE POLICY	—		
7	UMBRELLA POLICY	—		
8	ERRORS AND OMISSIONS POLICY	—		
9	OTHER	—		
10	CLAIMS-MADE	●		
11	OCCURRENCE	—		
	3 WHO IS INSURED			
12	BUSINESS ENTITY	●		II.(I), page 3
13	AUTOMATIC COVERAGE FOR SUBSIDIARIES	—		
14	DIRECTORS & OFFICERS	●	See also II.(I).(1)., page 3	II.(E)., page 2
15	EMPLOYEES	●		II.(I).(2)., page 2
16	PART-TIME	●		II.(E)., page 2
17	SEASONAL	●		II.(E)., page 2
18	TEMPORARY	●		II.(E)., page 2
19	SUPERVISORS & MANAGERS	●		II.(E)., page 2
20	FORMER EMPLOYEES	—		
21	VOLUNTEERS	—		
22	INDEPENDENT CONTRACTORS	—		
23	EXCLUDED	●		II.(E)., page 2
24	SILENT	—		
25	SHAREHOLDERS	●	See also II.(I).(1)., page 3	II.(E)., page 2
	4 LIMIT OF LIABILITY			
26	AGGREGATE	●		V.(E).(2)., page 10
27	INCLUDES PUNITIVE DAMAGES WHERE NOT UNINSURABLE	●		II.(J)., page 3
28	DEFENSE COSTS INCLUDED WITHIN LIMIT OF LIABILITY	●		IV.(E).(3)., page 10
29	DEFENSE COSTS PAID IN ADDITION TO LIMIT OF LIABILITY	—		
	5 DEDUCTIBLE			
30	APPLIES TO EACH INDIVIDUAL CLAIM	●		V.(E).(1)., page 10
31	APPLIES TO EACH OCCURRENCE OR WRONGFUL PRACTICE	—		
32	INCLUDES ALL CLAIMS FROM ONE ACT	●	See also V.(E).(1)., page 10	V.(C).(2)., page 9
33	SUBJECT TO ANNUAL AGGREGATE	—		
34	CO-PAYMENT APPLIES	●		V.(E).(4)., page 10
35	LIMIT OF LIABILITY NOT REDUCED	—		
36	INCLUDES DEFENSE COSTS	●		V.(E).(1)., page 10
37	REDUCED UNDER SPECIFIED CIRCUMSTANCES (SEE POLICY)	—		

Comparison Query	Comment	Policy Reference
6 WHAT IS A CLAIM		
38 ORAL COMPLAINT TO INSURED	—	
39 WRITTEN COMPLAINT TO INSURED	●	II.(B).(1)., page 1
40 COMPLAINT MUST CONTAIN A DEMAND FOR DAMAGES	—	
41 COMPLAINT FILED WITH EEOC	●	II.(B).(1)., pages 1–2
42 OR SIMILAR STATE AUTHORITY	●	II.(B).(1)., pages 1–2
43 AGENCY MUST HAVE POWER TO ADJUDICATE	—	
44 ADMINISTRATIVE PROCEEDING	●	II.(B).(2)., page 2
45 ARBITRATION PROCEEDING	—	
46 ANY INCIDENT REPORTED TO INSURER	—	
47 SUIT	●	II.(B).(2)., page 2
48 CLAIM DOES NOT INCLUDE ARBITRATION SUBJECT TO	●	II.(B). following (3)., page 2
49 COLLECTIVE BARGAINING AGREEMENT	●	II.(B). following (3)., page 2
50 EMPLOYEE POLICY OR MANUAL	—	
51 CLAIM NOT DEFINED	—	
7 CLAIM REPORTING PROVISIONS TO INSURER		
52 IMMEDIATELY	—	
53 AS SOON AS POSSIBLE	—	
54 AS SOON AS PRACTICABLE	●	V.(B).(1)., page 8
55 WITHIN POLICY PERIOD	—	
56 WITHIN X DAYS OF EXPIRATION	—	
57 WITHIN X DAYS	60	V.(B).(1)., page 8
8 EXTENDED REPORTING FEATURES		
58 ELECTION PERIOD (DAYS)	30	IV.(A).(1)., page 6
59 ADDITIONAL PREMIUM (% OF ANNUAL PREMIUM)	○ Specified by underwriter—see Item 8 of Declarations	IV.(A).(1)., page 6
60 ADDITIONAL REPORTING PERIOD (MONTHS)	24	IV.(A).(1)., page 6
61 NO REINSTATEMENT OF LIMITS	●	IV.(A).(2)., page 7
9 POTENTIAL CLAIM REPORTING PROVISIONS		
62 NONE (SEE ALSO "CLAIM" ABOVE)	—	
63 INCIDENTS LIKELY TO RESULT IN A CLAIM	●	V.(B).(2).(a) & (b), page 8
10 DEFENSE PROVISIONS		
64 AFFIRMATIVE DUTY TO DEFEND	—	
65 NO AFFIRMATIVE DUTY TO DEFEND	●	V.(D).(1)., page 9
66 AFFIRMATIVE ADVANCEMENT PROVISIONS	●	V.(D).(2)., page 9
67 INSURED MUST RETURN ADVANCED AMOUNTS IF NOT COVERED	●	V.(D).(2)., page 9
68 INSURED/INSURER CHOOSES COUNSEL	● Insured chooses	V.(D).(1)., page 9
69 INSURED/INSURER APPROVES COUNSEL	—	
70 INSURED/INSURER CONSULTED IN COUNSEL SELECTION	—	
11 SETTLEMENT PROVISIONS		
71 HAMMER CLAUSE	●	V.(D).(3)., page 9
72 CONSULTATION PROVISION	—	
73 CONSENT PROVISION	● Two-way	V.(D).(3)., page 9
12 ALLOCATION OF LOSS PROVISIONS		
74 STIPULATED PROVISIONS		
13 COVERAGES		
75 DISCRIMINATION	● As employment practices wrongful act	II.(F).(2)., page 2
76 SPECIFIC ENUMERATED ACTIVITIES	●	II.(D)., page 2
77 PLUS BROAD OMNIBUS WORDING	●	II.(D)., page 2
78 SPECIFIC ENUMERATED CLASSES	●	II.(D)., page 2
79 PLUS BROAD OMNIBUS WORDING	●	II.(D)., page 2
80 AGAINST THIRD PARTIES	—	
81 DISCRIMINATION NOT DEFINED	—	
82 SEXUAL HARASSMENT	● As employment practices wrongful act	II.(F).(3)., page 2
83 HOSTILE ENVIRONMENT	●	II.(H)., page 3
84 QUID-PRO-QUO	●	
85 SEXUAL HARASSMENT NOT DEFINED	—	
86 WRONGFUL TERMINATION	● As employment practices wrongful act	II.(F).(1)., page 2
87 BREACH OF IMPLIED CONTRACT	●	II.(Q)., page 4
88 BREACH OF EXPRESS CONTRACT		
89 VIOLATION OF PUBLIC POLICY	●	II.(Q)., page 4
90 VIOLATION OF GOOD FAITH & FAIR DEALING	—	
91 OBLIGATIONS TO MAKE PAYMENTS	—	
92 CONSTRUCTIVE DISCHARGE	●	II.(Q)., page 4
93 WRONGFUL TERMINATION NOT DEFINED	—	
94 OTHER EMPLOYMENT VIOLATIONS/OFFENSES	—	
95 WRONGFUL HIRING	—	
96 WRONGFUL PROMOTION/DEMOTION	●	II.(Q)., page 4
97 WRONGFUL EVALUATION/DISCIPLINE	● As workplace tort	II.(P)., page 4

EXECUTIVE RISK SPECIALTY INSURANCE COMPANY B22167 [2/97]

#	Comparison Query		Comment	Policy Reference
98	FAMILY AND MEDICAL LEAVE ACT	—		
99	DEFAMATION	—		
100	MISREPRESENTATION	●	As workplace tort	II.(P)., page 4
101	RETALIATION	●	As employment practices wrongful act	II.(F).(4)., page 2
102	MENTAL ANGUISH	●		III.(D)., page 5
103	INVASION OF PRIVACY	—		
104	HUMILIATION	●		III.(D)., page 5
105	EMOTIONAL DISTRESS	●		III.(D)., page 5
106	OTHER PERSONAL INJURY OFFENSES	—		
107	POLICY SILENT	—		
	14 EXCLUSIONS			
108	**ADA ACCOMMODATION EXPENSES**	●		II.(J).(2)., page 3
109	**ASSAULT & BATTERY**	—		
110	**BACK PAY**	—		
111	**BODILY INJURY**	●	Exceptions apply	III.(D)., page 5
112	BODILY INJURY	●	Exceptions apply	III.(D)., page 5
113	DEATH	●	Exceptions apply	III.(D)., page 5
114	DISEASE	●	Exceptions apply	III.(D)., page 5
115	SICKNESS	●	Exceptions apply	III.(D)., page 5
116	**BREACH OF EMPLOYMENT CONTRACT**	●		II.(J).(4)., page 4
117	EXPRESS CONTRACT	●		II.(J).(4)., page 4
118	*WRITTEN CONTRACT*	●		II.(J).(4)., page 4
119	*ORAL CONTRACT*	—		
120	IMPLIED CONTRACT	—		
121	**CLASS ACTION LAWSUITS**	—		
122	**CONSEQUENTIAL LOSS**	—		
123	APPLIES TO BODILY INJURY	●	Loss of consortium	III.(D)., page 5
124	APPLIES TO INSURED EVENT	—		
125	BROTHER/SISTER	—		
126	CHILD	—		
127	DOMESTIC PARTNER	—		
128	PARENT	—		
129	SPOUSE	—		
130	**COST OF ARBITRATION HEARINGS SUBJECT TO**	●		II.(J).(6)., page 4
131	EMPLOYMENT HANDBOOK	—		
132	LABOR GRIEVANCE	●		II.(J).(6)., page 4
133	OTHER EMPLOYMENT POLICY OR PROCEDURE	—		
134	**COVERAGE ELSEWHERE**	—		
135	OTHER AVAILABLE INSURANCE	—		
136	OTHER INDEMNIFICATION	—		
137	SHARING PROVISION	—		
138	**FAILURE TO EXERCISE CARE WHEN TERMINATING**	—		
139	**FINES/PENALTIES**	●		II.(J).(1)., page 3
140	CIVIL	●		II.(J).(1)., page 3
141	CRIMINAL	●		II.(J).(1)., page 3
142	EXEMPLARY DAMAGES	—		
143	PUNITIVE DAMAGES	—		
144	MULTIPLIED DAMAGES	●	Exception applies	II.(J).(1)., page 3
145	**FRONT PAY**	—		
146	EXCLUSION APPLIES ONLY IF EMPLOYER HAD OPPORTUNITY TO REINSTATE EMPLOYEE BUT DID NOT DO SO	—		
147	**INTENTIONAL ACTS**	—		
148	CRIMINAL ACTS	—		
149	CRIMINAL PROCEEDING	—		
150	DISHONEST PURPOSE	—		
151	FRAUDULENT ACTS	—		
152	FRAUDULENT CLAIMS	—		
153	INTENTIONAL VIOLATIONS OF LAW	—		
154	WILLFUL FAILURE TO COMPLY WITH LAW	—		
155	MALICIOUS PURPOSE	—		
156	**LIABILITY OF OTHERS**	●		III.(G)., page 6
157	**LIQUIDATED DAMAGES**	●		II.(J).(1)., page 3
158	**LOSS ARISING OUT OF CHANGES IN OPERATIONS**	—		
159	ACQUISITION	—		
160	CHANGE IN CONTROL	—		
161	DOWNSIZING OR REDUCTION IN FORCE	—		
162	*% OF WORKFORCE*	—		
163	*WITHIN X DAYS*	—		

	Comparison Query		Comment	Policy Reference
164	FINANCIAL IMPAIRMENT	—		
165	BANKRUPTCY	—		
166	INSOLVENCY	—		
167	LIQUIDATION	—		
168	RECEIVERSHIP	—		
169	FINANCIAL INABILITY TO PAY	—		
170	MERGER	—		
171	PLANT OR FACILITY CLOSING	—		
172	REORGANIZATION	—		
173	TEMPORARY SHUTDOWN	—		
174	**MATTERS DEEMED UNINSURABLE**	●		II.(J).(1)., page 3
175	**NON-MONETARY RELIEF**	—		
176	DECLATORY RELIEF			
177	DISGORGEMENT			
178	INJUNCTIVE RELIEF	●	Defense cost exception	II.(J).(3)., page 4
179	JOB REINSTATEMENT	—		
180	NON-MONETARY DAMAGES/RELIEF	●	Defense cost exception	II.(J).(3)., pages 3–4
181	OTHER EQUITABLE REMEDIES			
182	**OBLIGATION TO PROVIDE BENEFITS**	—		
183	COBRA	●		III.(C)., page 5
184	DISABILITY			
185	ERISA	●		III.(A)., page 5
186	SOCIAL SECURITY	●		III.(C)., page 5
187	OTHER RETIREMENT BENEFITS	—		
188	UNEMPLOYMENT	●		III.(C)., page 5
189	WORKERS' COMPENSATION	●		III.(C)., page 5
190	**PERSONAL INJURY OFFENSES**	—		
191	DEFAMATION			
192	EMOTIONAL DISTRESS/UPSET			
193	HUMILIATION			
194	LIBEL	—		
195	MENTAL ANGUISH			
196	PERSONAL INJURY			
197	SLANDER			
198	**PRIOR ACTS**	●		I., page 1
199	PRIOR ACTS	—		
200	PRIOR KNOWLEDGE	●	Exception applies	III.(F)., page 5
201	PRIOR/PENDING LITIGATION			
202	**PROPERTY DAMAGE**	●		III.(D)., page 5
203	INTANGIBLE PROPERTY			
204	LOSS OF USE	●		III.(D)., page 5
205	TANGIBLE PROPERTY	—		
206	**RETALIATORY ACTIONS OF EMPLOYER**	—		
207	FOR FAILING TO PERFORM ACTS AGAINST PUBLIC POLICY	—		
208	FOR FILING A COMPLAINT OR BENEFIT CLAIM	—		
209	**STRIKES/LOCKOUTS**	●		III.(H)., page 6
210	**VIOLATION OF LAWS**	—		
211	ANY LAW	—		
212	FMLA			
213	OSHA			
214	POLLUTION LAWS			
215	RICO			
216	SEC	—		
217	WARN	●		III.(B)., page 5

15 CONDITIONS

218	**ARBITRATION**	●		V.(K)., page 13
219	MANDATORY	●		V.(K)., page 13
220	BINDING	●		V.(K)., page 13
221	CHOICE OF LAW PROVISION	—		
222	SITUS	●	New York, NY	V.(K)., page 13
223	**TERRITORY**	●		V.(A)., page 7
224	LIMITED	—		
225	WORLDWIDE	●		V.(A)., page 7
226	**NEWLY FORMED/ACQUIRED ENTITIES**	—		
227	AUTOMATIC COVERAGE (X DAYS)	—		
228	NOTIFY INSURER WITHIN X DAYS	—		

EXECUTIVE RISK SPECIALTY INSURANCE COMPANY B22167 [2/97]

Policy Comparison Worksheet

Executive Risk Specialty Insurance Company

Policy Form No.: B22170
Edition Date: 2/97

Risks Considered: Mid-large companies, financial institutions
Limits Available: $25,000,000
Minimum Retention: none

Contact: Heather Anderson
Executive Risk Communications
82 Hopmeadow Street
Simsbury, CT 06070-7683
800/432-8168
860/408-2288 (fax)
info@execrisk.com

KEY TO SYMBOLS
● = Specifically contains queried provision of feature
○ = Unable to determine
— = Silent

#	Comparison Query		Comment	Policy Reference
	1 APPLICATION			
1	ATTACHES TO AND FORMS A PART OF THE POLICY	●	See also II.(A)., page 1	Application, page 4
2	CONTAINS WARRANTY STATEMENTS	—		
3	CONTAINS SEVERABILITY PROVISIONS	●		V.(I).(1). & (2)., page 13
	2 POLICY TYPE			
4	UNITARY STAND ALONE POLICY	●		
	ENDORSEMENT OR PART OF	—		
5	DIRECTORS AND OFFICERS POLICY	—		
6	PACKAGE POLICY	—		
7	UMBRELLA POLICY	—		
8	ERRORS AND OMISSIONS POLICY	—		
9	OTHER	—		
10	CLAIMS-MADE	●		
11	OCCURRENCE	—		
	3 WHO IS INSURED			
12	BUSINESS ENTITY	●		II.(H).(2)., page 3
13	AUTOMATIC COVERAGE FOR SUBSIDIARIES	●	If named	II.(H).(2)., page 3
14	DIRECTORS & OFFICERS	●		II.(H).(2)., page 3
15	EMPLOYEES	●		II.(H).(4)., page 3
16	PART-TIME	●		II.(E)., page 2
17	SEASONAL	●		II.(E)., page 2
18	TEMPORARY	●		II.(E)., page 2
19	SUPERVISORS & MANAGERS	●		II.(E)., page 2
20	FORMER EMPLOYEES	—		
21	VOLUNTEERS	—		
22	INDEPENDENT CONTRACTORS	—		
23	EXCLUDED	●		II.(E)., page 2
24	SILENT	—		
25	SHAREHOLDERS	—		
	4 LIMIT OF LIABILITY			
26	AGGREGATE	●		V.(E).(2)., page 11
27	INCLUDES PUNITIVE DAMAGES WHERE NOT UNINSURABLE	●		II.(I)., page 4
28	DEFENSE COSTS INCLUDED WITHIN LIMIT OF LIABILITY	●	See also V.(E).(3)., page 11	V.(E).(1)., page 4
29	DEFENSE COSTS PAID IN ADDITION TO LIMIT OF LIABILITY	—		
	5 DEDUCTIBLE			
30	APPLIES TO EACH INDIVIDUAL CLAIM	●		V.(E).(4)., page 11
31	APPLIES TO EACH OCCURRENCE OR WRONGFUL PRACTICE	—		
32	INCLUDES ALL CLAIMS FROM ONE ACT	●		V.(C).(2)., page 10
33	SUBJECT TO ANNUAL AGGREGATE	—		
34	CO-PAYMENT APPLIES	●		V.(E).(4)., pages 11–12
35	LIMIT OF LIABILITY NOT REDUCED	—		
36	INCLUDES DEFENSE COSTS	●		V.(E).(1)., page 11
37	REDUCED UNDER SPECIFIED CIRCUMSTANCES (SEE POLICY)	—		

EXECUTIVE RISK SPECIALTY INSURANCE COMPANY B22170 [2/97]

#	Comparison Query	Comment	Policy Reference
6	**WHAT IS A CLAIM**		
38	ORAL COMPLAINT TO INSURED	—	
39	WRITTEN COMPLAINT TO INSURED	●	II.(B).(1)., page 1
40	COMPLAINT MUST CONTAIN A DEMAND FOR DAMAGES	—	
41	COMPLAINT FILED WITH EEOC	●	II.(B).(1)., pages 1–2
42	OR SIMILAR STATE AUTHORITY	●	II.(B).(1)., pages 1–2
43	AGENCY MUST HAVE POWER TO ADJUDICATE	—	
44	ADMINISTRATIVE PROCEEDING	●	II.(B).(2)., page 2
45	ARBITRATION PROCEEDING	—	
46	ANY INCIDENT REPORTED TO INSURER	—	
47	SUIT	●	II.(B).(2)., page 2
48	CLAIM DOES NOT INCLUDE ARBITRATION SUBJECT TO	●	II.(B). following (2)., page 2
49	COLLECTIVE BARGAINING AGREEMENT	●	II.(B). following (2)., page 2
50	EMPLOYEE POLICY OR MANUAL	—	
51	CLAIM NOT DEFINED	—	
7	**CLAIM REPORTING PROVISIONS TO INSURER**		
52	IMMEDIATELY	—	
53	AS SOON AS POSSIBLE	—	
54	AS SOON AS PRACTICABLE	●	V.(B).(1)., page 9
55	WITHIN POLICY PERIOD	—	
56	WITHIN X DAYS OF EXPIRATION	—	
57	WITHIN X DAYS	60	V.(B).(1)., page 9
8	**EXTENDED REPORTING FEATURES**		
58	ELECTION PERIOD (DAYS)	30	IV.(A).(1)., page 7
59	ADDITIONAL PREMIUM (% OF ANNUAL PREMIUM)	○	Specified by underwriter—See Item 8 of Declarations	IV.(A).(1)., page 7
60	ADDITIONAL REPORTING PERIOD (MONTHS)	24	IV.(A).(1)., page 7
61	NO REINSTATEMENT OF LIMITS	●	IV.(A).(2)., page 7
9	**POTENTIAL CLAIM REPORTING PROVISIONS**		
62	NONE (SEE ALSO "CLAIM" ABOVE)	—	
63	INCIDENTS LIKELY TO RESULT IN A CLAIM	●	V.(B).(2).(a). & (b)., pages 9–10
10	**DEFENSE PROVISIONS**		
64	AFFIRMATIVE DUTY TO DEFEND	●	I.(B)., page 1
65	NO AFFIRMATIVE DUTY TO DEFEND	—	
66	AFFIRMATIVE ADVANCEMENT PROVISIONS	—	
67	INSURED MUST RETURN ADVANCED AMOUNTS IF NOT COVERED	—	
68	INSURED/INSURER CHOOSES COUNSEL	—	Insured choice available by endorsement
69	INSURED/INSURER APPROVES COUNSEL	—	
70	INSURED/INSURER CONSULTED IN COUNSEL SELECTION	—	
11	**SETTLEMENT PROVISIONS**		
71	HAMMER CLAUSE	●	V.(D).(1)., page 10
72	CONSULTATION PROVISION	—	
73	CONSENT PROVISION	●	Two-way	V.(D).(1)., page 10
12	**ALLOCATION OF LOSS PROVISIONS**		
74	STIPULATED PROVISIONS	—	
13	**COVERAGES**		
75	DISCRIMINATION	●	As employment practices wrongful act	II.(F).(2)., page 3
76	SPECIFIC ENUMERATED ACTIVITIES	●	II.(D)., page 2
77	PLUS BROAD OMNIBUS WORDING	●	II.(D)., page 2
78	SPECIFIC ENUMERATED CLASSES	●	II.(D)., page 2
79	PLUS BROAD OMNIBUS WORDING	●	II.(D)., page 2
80	AGAINST THIRD PARTIES	—	
81	DISCRIMINATION NOT DEFINED	—	
82	SEXUAL HARASSMENT	●	As employment practices wrongful act	II.(F).(3)., page 3
83	HOSTILE ENVIRONMENT	●	II.(G).(1)., page 3
84	QUID-PRO-QUO	●	II.(G).(1)., page 3
85	SEXUAL HARASSMENT NOT DEFINED	—	
86	WRONGFUL TERMINATION	●	As employment practices wrongful act	II.(F).(1)., page 3
87	BREACH OF IMPLIED CONTRACT	●	II.(R)., page 5
88	BREACH OF EXPRESS CONTRACT	—	
89	VIOLATION OF PUBLIC POLICY	●	II.(R)., page 5
90	VIOLATION OF GOOD FAITH & FAIR DEALING	—	
91	OBLIGATIONS TO MAKE PAYMENTS	—	
92	CONSTRUCTIVE DISCHARGE	●	As employment practices wrongful act	II.(R)., page 5
93	WRONGFUL TERMINATION NOT DEFINED	—	
94	OTHER EMPLOYMENT VIOLATIONS/OFFENSES	—	
95	WRONGFUL HIRING	—	
96	WRONGFUL PROMOTION/DEMOTION	●	II.(R)., page 5
97	WRONGFUL EVALUATION/DISCIPLINE	●	As workplace tort	II.(F).(5)., page 3 and II.(Q)., page 5

EXECUTIVE RISK SPECIALTY INSURANCE COMPANY B22170 [2/97]

#	Comparison Query		Comment	Policy Reference
98	FAMILY AND MEDICAL LEAVE ACT	—		
99	DEFAMATION	—		
100	MISREPRESENTATION	●	As workplace tort	II.(F).(5)., page 3 and II.(Q)., page 5
101	RETALIATION	●	As employment practices wrongful act	II.(F).(4)., page 3
102	MENTAL ANGUISH	—		
103	INVASION OF PRIVACY	—		
104	HUMILIATION	—		
105	EMOTIONAL DISTRESS	—		
106	OTHER PERSONAL INJURY OFFENSES	—		
107	POLICY SILENT	—		
	14 EXCLUSIONS			
108	**ADA ACCOMMODATION EXPENSES**	●		II.(I)., page 4
109	**ASSAULT & BATTERY**	—		
110	**BACK PAY**	—		
111	**BODILY INJURY**	—		
112	BODILY INJURY	—		
113	DEATH	—		
114	DISEASE	—		
115	SICKNESS	—		
116	**BREACH OF EMPLOYMENT CONTRACT**	●		II.(I)., page 4
117	EXPRESS CONTRACT	●		II.(I)., page 4
118	*WRITTEN CONTRACT*	●		II.(I)., page 4
119	*ORAL CONTRACT*	—		
120	IMPLIED CONTRACT	—		
121	**CLASS ACTION LAWSUITS**	—		
122	**CONSEQUENTIAL LOSS**	—		
123	APPLIES TO BODILY INJURY	—		
124	APPLIES TO INSURED EVENT	—		
125	BROTHER/SISTER	—		
126	CHILD	—		
127	DOMESTIC PARTNER	—		
128	PARENT	—		
129	SPOUSE	—		
130	**COST OF ARBITRATION HEARINGS SUBJECT TO**	●		II.(I)., page 4
131	EMPLOYMENT HANDBOOK	—		
132	LABOR GRIEVANCE	●		II.(I)., page 4
133	OTHER EMPLOYMENT POLICY OR PROCEDURE	—		
134	**COVERAGE ELSEWHERE**	—		
135	OTHER AVAILABLE INSURANCE	—		
136	OTHER INDEMNIFICATION	—		
137	SHARING PROVISION	—		
138	**FAILURE TO EXERCISE CARE WHEN TERMINATING**	—		
139	**FINES/PENALTIES**	●		II.(I)., page 4
140	CIVIL	●		II.(I)., page 4
141	CRIMINAL	●		II.(I)., page 4
142	EXEMPLARY DAMAGES	—		
143	PUNITIVE DAMAGES	—	Excludable by endorsement	
144	MULTIPLIED DAMAGES	●	Exception applies	II.(I)., page 4
145	**FRONT PAY**	—		
146	EXCLUSION APPLIES ONLY IF EMPLOYER HAD OPPORTUNITY TO REINSTATE EMPLOYEE BUT DID NOT DO SO	—		
147	**INTENTIONAL ACTS**	—		
148	CRIMINAL ACTS	—		
149	CRIMINAL PROCEEDING	—		
150	DISHONEST PURPOSE	—		
151	FRAUDULENT ACTS	—		
152	FRAUDULENT CLAIMS	—		
153	INTENTIONAL VIOLATIONS OF LAW	—		
154	WILLFUL FAILURE TO COMPLY WITH LAW	—		
155	MALICIOUS PURPOSE	—		
156	**LIABILITY OF OTHERS**	●		III.(G)., page 6
157	**LIQUIDATED DAMAGES**	●		II.(I)., page 4
158	**LOSS ARISING OUT OF CHANGES IN OPERATIONS**	—		
159	ACQUISITION	—		
160	CHANGE IN CONTROL	—		
161	DOWNSIZING OR REDUCTION IN FORCE	—		
162	*% OF WORKFORCE*	—		
163	*WITHIN X DAYS*	—		

	Comparison Query		Comment	Policy Reference
164	FINANCIAL IMPAIRMENT	—		
165	BANKRUPTCY	—		
166	INSOLVENCY	—		
167	LIQUIDATION	—		
168	RECEIVERSHIP	—		
169	FINANCIAL INABILITY TO PAY	—		
170	MERGER	—		
171	PLANT OR FACILITY CLOSING	—		
172	REORGANIZATION	—		
173	TEMPORARY SHUTDOWN	—		
174	**MATTERS DEEMED UNINSURABLE**	●		II.(I)., page 4
175	**NON-MONETARY RELIEF**	—		
176	DECLATORY RELIEF	—		
177	DISGORGEMENT	—		
178	INJUNCTIVE RELIEF	●	See also III.(E)., page 6	II.(I)., page 4
179	JOB REINSTATEMENT	—		
180	NON-MONETARY DAMAGES/RELIEF	●	See also III.(E)., page 6	II.(I)., page 4
181	OTHER EQUITABLE REMEDIES	—		
182	**OBLIGATION TO PROVIDE BENEFITS**	—		
183	COBRA	●		III.(C)., page 6
184	DISABILITY	—		
185	ERISA	●		III.(A)., page 5
186	SOCIAL SECURITY	●		III.(C)., page 6
187	OTHER RETIREMENT BENEFITS	—		
188	UNEMPLOYMENT	●		III.(C)., page 6
189	WORKERS' COMPENSATION	●		III.(C)., page 6
190	**PERSONAL INJURY OFFENSES**	—		
191	DEFAMATION	—		
192	EMOTIONAL DISTRESS/UPSET	—		
193	HUMILIATION	—		
194	LIBEL	—		
195	MENTAL ANGUISH	—		
196	PERSONAL INJURY	—		
197	SLANDER	—		
198	**PRIOR ACTS**	—		
199	PRIOR ACTS	●		I.(A)., page 1
200	PRIOR KNOWLEDGE	●	Severability applies	III.(F).(1)., page 6
201	PRIOR/PENDING LITIGATION	—		
202	**PROPERTY DAMAGE**	—		
203	INTANGIBLE PROPERTY	—		
204	LOSS OF USE	—		
205	TANGIBLE PROPERTY	—		
206	**RETALIATORY ACTIONS OF EMPLOYER**	—		
207	FOR FAILING TO PERFORM ACTS AGAINST PUBLIC POLICY	—		
208	FOR FILING A COMPLAINT OR BENEFIT CLAIM	—		
209	**STRIKES/LOCKOUTS**	●		III.(H)., page 6
210	**VIOLATION OF LAWS**	—		
211	ANY LAW	—		
212	FMLA	—		
213	OSHA	—		
214	POLLUTION LAWS	—		
215	RICO	—		
216	SEC	—		
217	WARN	●		III.(B)., page 5

15 CONDITIONS

	Comparison Query		Comment	Policy Reference
218	**ARBITRATION**	●		V.(K)., page 14
219	MANDATORY	●		V.(K)., page 14
220	BINDING	●		V.(K)., page 14
221	CHOICE OF LAW PROVISION	—		
222	SITUS	●	New York, NY	V.(K)., page 14
223	**TERRITORY**	●		V.(A)., page 9
224	LIMITED	—		
225	WORLDWIDE	●		V.(A)., page 9
226	**NEWLY FORMED/ACQUIRED ENTITIES**	—		
227	AUTOMATIC COVERAGE (X DAYS)	90	> 10% company assets involved	IV.(B).(1)., pages 7–8
228	NOTIFY INSURER WITHIN X DAYS	90		IV.(B).(1)., pages 7–8

EXECUTIVE RISK SPECIALTY INSURANCE COMPANY B22170 [2/97]

Policy Comparison Worksheet

Executive Risk Specialty Insurance Company

Policy Form No.: B24775
Edition Date: 8/97

Risks Considered: Private companies
Limits Available: $10 million
Minimum Retention: $2,500

Contact: Executive Risk Communications
82 Hopmeadow Street
Simsbury, CT 06070-7683
800/432-8168
860/408-2288 (fax)
info@execrisk.com

KEY TO SYMBOLS
● = Specifically contains queried provision of feature
○ = Unable to determine
— = Silent

#	Comparison Query		Comment	Policy Reference
	1 APPLICATION			
1	ATTACHES TO AND FORMS A PART OF THE POLICY	●		II.(A)., page 2
2	CONTAINS WARRANTY STATEMENTS	○		
3	CONTAINS SEVERABILITY PROVISIONS	●		IV.(K)., page 15
	2 POLICY TYPE			
4	UNITARY STAND ALONE POLICY	—		
	ENDORSEMENT OR PART OF	—		
5	DIRECTORS AND OFFICERS POLICY	●		
6	PACKAGE POLICY	—		
7	UMBRELLA POLICY	—		
8	ERRORS AND OMISSIONS POLICY	—		
9	OTHER	—		
10	CLAIMS-MADE	●		
11	OCCURRENCE	—		
	3 WHO IS INSURED			
12	BUSINESS ENTITY	●		II.(H)., page 3
13	AUTOMATIC COVERAGE FOR SUBSIDIARIES	●	See also II.(C)., page 2	II.(H)., page 3
14	DIRECTORS & OFFICERS	●		II.(I).(1)., page 4
15	EMPLOYEES	●		II.(I).(2)., page 4
16	PART-TIME	●		II.(F)., page 2
17	SEASONAL	●		II.(F)., page 2
18	TEMPORARY	●		II.(F)., page 2
19	SUPERVISORS & MANAGERS	●		II.(F)., page 2
20	FORMER EMPLOYEES	●		II.(I).(2)., page 4
21	VOLUNTEERS	—		
22	INDEPENDENT CONTRACTORS	—		
23	EXCLUDED	●		II.(F)., page 2
24	SILENT	—		
25	SHAREHOLDERS	—		
	4 LIMIT OF LIABILITY			
26	AGGREGATE	●		IV.(A).(1).(c)., page 9
27	INCLUDES PUNITIVE DAMAGES WHERE NOT UNINSURABLE	●	Also by endorsement	II.(J)., page 4
28	DEFENSE COSTS INCLUDED WITHIN LIMIT OF LIABILITY	●	See also IV.(A).(3)., page 10	IV.(A).(1).(a)., page 9
29	DEFENSE COSTS PAID IN ADDITION TO LIMIT OF LIABILITY	—		
	5 DEDUCTIBLE			
30	APPLIES TO EACH INDIVIDUAL CLAIM	○		II.(O)., page 4
31	APPLIES TO EACH OCCURRENCE OR WRONGFUL PRACTICE	—		
32	INCLUDES ALL CLAIMS FROM ONE ACT	●		II.(O)., page 4
33	SUBJECT TO ANNUAL AGGREGATE	—		
34	CO-PAYMENT APPLIES	—		
35	LIMIT OF LIABILITY NOT REDUCED	—		
36	INCLUDES DEFENSE COSTS	●		IV.(B).(1)., page 10
37	REDUCED UNDER SPECIFIED CIRCUMSTANCES (SEE POLICY)	—		

#	Comparison Query	Comment	Policy Reference
	6 WHAT IS A CLAIM		
38	ORAL COMPLAINT TO INSURED	—	
39	WRITTEN COMPLAINT TO INSURED	●	II.(B)., page 2
40	COMPLAINT MUST CONTAIN A DEMAND FOR DAMAGES	—	
41	COMPLAINT FILED WITH EEOC	—	
42	OR SIMILAR STATE AUTHORITY	—	
43	AGENCY MUST HAVE POWER TO ADJUDICATE	—	
44	ADMINISTRATIVE PROCEEDING	—	
45	ARBITRATION PROCEEDING	—	
46	ANY INCIDENT REPORTED TO INSURER	—	
47	SUIT	—	
48	CLAIM DOES NOT INCLUDE ARBITRATION SUBJECT TO	—	
49	COLLECTIVE BARGAINING AGREEMENT	—	
50	EMPLOYEE POLICY OR MANUAL	—	
51	CLAIM NOT DEFINED	—	
	7 CLAIM REPORTING PROVISIONS TO INSURER		
52	IMMEDIATELY	—	
53	AS SOON AS POSSIBLE	—	
54	AS SOON AS PRACTICABLE	●	IV.(G).(1)., page 8
55	WITHIN POLICY PERIOD	—	
56	WITHIN X DAYS OF EXPIRATION	—	
57	WITHIN X DAYS	—	
	8 EXTENDED REPORTING FEATURES		
58	ELECTION PERIOD (DAYS)	30	IV.(F)., page 12
59	ADDITIONAL PREMIUM (% OF ANNUAL PREMIUM)	○	Specified by underwriter—See Item 7 of Declarations	IV.(F)., page 12
60	ADDITIONAL REPORTING PERIOD (MONTHS)	○	Specified by underwriter—See Item 6 of Declarations	IV.(F)., page 12
61	NO REINSTATEMENT OF LIMITS	—	
	9 POTENTIAL CLAIM REPORTING PROVISIONS		
62	NONE (SEE ALSO "CLAIM" ABOVE)	—	
63	INCIDENTS LIKELY TO RESULT IN A CLAIM	●	IV.(G).(2)., page 12
	10 DEFENSE PROVISIONS		
64	AFFIRMATIVE DUTY TO DEFEND	●	I.(C)., page 1
65	NO AFFIRMATIVE DUTY TO DEFEND	—	
66	AFFIRMATIVE ADVANCEMENT PROVISIONS	—	
67	INSURED MUST RETURN ADVANCED AMOUNTS IF NOT COVERED	—	
68	INSURED/INSURER CHOOSES COUNSEL	—	
69	INSURED/INSURER APPROVES COUNSEL	—	
70	INSURED/INSURER CONSULTED IN COUNSEL SELECTION	—	
	11 SETTLEMENT PROVISIONS		
71	HAMMER CLAUSE	●	IV.(C).(1).(a). & (b)., page 11
72	CONSULTATION PROVISION	—	
73	CONSENT PROVISION	●	Two-way	IV.(C).(1)., page 11
	12 ALLOCATION OF LOSS PROVISIONS		
74	STIPULATED PROVISIONS	—	
	13 COVERAGES		
75	DISCRIMINATION	●	II.(G).(1)., page 3
76	SPECIFIC ENUMERATED ACTIVITIES	●	II.(G).(1)., page 3
77	*PLUS BROAD OMNIBUS WORDING*	●	II.(G).(1)., page 3
78	SPECIFIC ENUMERATED CLASSES	●	II.(G).(1)., page 3
79	*PLUS BROAD OMNIBUS WORDING*	●	II.(G).(1)., page 3
80	AGAINST THIRD PARTIES	—	Coverage available by endorsement	
81	DISCRIMINATION NOT DEFINED	●	II.(G).(1)., page 3
82	SEXUAL HARASSMENT	●	II.(G).(2)., page 3
83	HOSTILE ENVIRONMENT	●	II.(G).(2)., page 3
84	QUID-PRO-QUO	●	II.(G).(2)., page 3
85	SEXUAL HARASSMENT NOT DEFINED	●	II.(G).(2)., page 3
86	WRONGFUL TERMINATION	●	II.(G).(6)., page 3
87	BREACH OF IMPLIED CONTRACT	●	See also II.(G).(7)., page 3	II.(G).(6)., page 3
88	BREACH OF EXPRESS CONTRACT	—	
89	VIOLATION OF PUBLIC POLICY	●	II.(G).(6)., page 3
90	VIOLATION OF GOOD FAITH & FAIR DEALING	—	
91	OBLIGATIONS TO MAKE PAYMENTS	—	
92	CONSTRUCTIVE DISCHARGE	●	II.(G).(6)., page 3
93	WRONGFUL TERMINATION NOT DEFINED	●	
94	OTHER EMPLOYMENT VIOLATIONS/OFFENSES	●	II.(G).(1)., page 3
95	WRONGFUL HIRING	●	II.(G).(1)., page 3
96	WRONGFUL PROMOTION/DEMOTION	●	II.(G).(1)., page 3
97	WRONGFUL EVALUATION/DISCIPLINE	●	II.(G).(5)., page 3

EXECUTIVE RISK SPECIALTY INSURANCE COMPANY B24775 [8/97]

#	Comparison Query		Comment	Policy Reference
98	FAMILY AND MEDICAL LEAVE ACT	—		
99	DEFAMATION	●		III.(B).(2).(a)., page 6
100	MISREPRESENTATION	●		II.(G).(5), page 3
101	RETALIATION	●		II.(G).(4), page 3
102	MENTAL ANGUISH	●		III.(B).(2).(a)., page 6
103	INVASION OF PRIVACY	—		
104	HUMILIATION	—		
105	EMOTIONAL DISTRESS	●		III.(B).(2).(a)., page 6
106	OTHER PERSONAL INJURY OFFENSES	●		III.(B).(2).(a)., page 6
107	POLICY SILENT	—		

14 EXCLUSIONS

#	Comparison Query		Comment	Policy Reference
108	**ADA ACCOMMODATION EXPENSES**	—		
109	**ASSAULT & BATTERY**	●		III.(B).(2).(a)., page 6
110	**BACK PAY**	—		
111	**BODILY INJURY**	●		III.(B).(2).(a)., page 6
112	BODILY INJURY	●		III.(B).(2).(a)., page 6
113	DEATH	●		III.(B).(2).(a)., page 6
114	DISEASE	●		III.(B).(2).(a)., page 6
115	SICKNESS	●		III.(B).(2).(a)., page 6
116	**BREACH OF EMPLOYMENT CONTRACT**	—		
117	EXPRESS CONTRACT	—		
118	WRITTEN CONTRACT	—		
119	ORAL CONTRACT	—		
120	IMPLIED CONTRACT	—		
121	**CLASS ACTION LAWSUITS**	—		
122	**CONSEQUENTIAL LOSS**	—		
123	APPLIES TO BODILY INJURY	●	Loss of consortium	III.(B).(2).(a)., page 6
124	APPLIES TO INSURED EVENT	—		
125	BROTHER/SISTER	—		
126	CHILD	—		
127	DOMESTIC PARTNER	—		
128	PARENT	—		
129	SPOUSE	—		
130	**COST OF ARBITRATION HEARINGS SUBJECT TO**	—		
131	EMPLOYMENT HANDBOOK	—		
132	LABOR GRIEVANCE	—		
133	OTHER EMPLOYMENT POLICY OR PROCEDURE	—		
134	**COVERAGE ELSEWHERE**	—		
135	OTHER AVAILABLE INSURANCE	●		IV.(D).(1)., page 11
136	OTHER INDEMNIFICATION	—		
137	SHARING PROVISION	—		
138	**FAILURE TO EXERCISE CARE WHEN TERMINATING**	—		
139	**FINES/PENALTIES**	●		III.(B).(1)., page 6
140	CIVIL	—		
141	CRIMINAL	—		
142	EXEMPLARY DAMAGES	—		
143	PUNITIVE DAMAGES	—		
144	MULTIPLIED DAMAGES	●		III.(B).(1)., page 6
145	**FRONT PAY**	—		
146	EXCLUSION APPLIES ONLY IF EMPLOYER HAD OPPORTUNITY TO REINSTATE EMPLOYEE BUT DID NOT DO SO	—		
147	**INTENTIONAL ACTS**	●		III.(A).(1)., page 5
148	CRIMINAL ACTS	—		
149	CRIMINAL PROCEEDING	—		
150	DISHONEST PURPOSE	●	If established	III.(A).(1)., page 5
151	FRAUDULENT ACTS	●	If established	III.(A).(1)., page 5
152	FRAUDULENT CLAIMS	—		
153	INTENTIONAL VIOLATIONS OF LAW	●	If established	III.(A).(1)., page 5
154	WILLFUL FAILURE TO COMPLY WITH LAW	○	If established	III.(A).(1)., page 5
155	MALICIOUS PURPOSE	—		
156	**LIABILITY OF OTHERS**	●	As respects company only	III.(B).(6)., page 7
157	**LIQUIDATED DAMAGES**	—		
158	**LOSS ARISING OUT OF CHANGES IN OPERATIONS**	—		
159	ACQUISITION	—		
160	CHANGE IN CONTROL	—		
161	DOWNSIZING OR REDUCTION IN FORCE	—		
162	% OF WORKFORCE	—		
163	WITHIN X DAYS	—		

EXECUTIVE RISK SPECIALTY INSURANCE COMPANY B24775 [8/97]

#	Comparison Query		Comment	Policy Reference
164	FINANCIAL IMPAIRMENT	—		
165	*BANKRUPTCY*	—		
166	*INSOLVENCY*	—		
167	*LIQUIDATION*	—		
168	*RECEIVERSHIP*	—		
169	FINANCIAL INABILITY TO PAY	—		
170	MERGER	—		
171	PLANT OR FACILITY CLOSING	—		
172	REORGANIZATION	—		
173	TEMPORARY SHUTDOWN	—		
174	**MATTERS DEEMED UNINSURABLE**	●		III.(B).(1)., page 6
175	**NON-MONETARY RELIEF**	●		III.(A).(2)., page 5
176	DECLATORY RELIEF	—		
177	DISGORGEMENT	—		
178	INJUNCTIVE RELIEF	—		
179	JOB REINSTATEMENT	—		
180	NON-MONETARY DAMAGES/RELIEF	●		III.(A).(2)., page 5
181	OTHER EQUITABLE REMEDIES	—		
182	**OBLIGATION TO PROVIDE BENEFITS**	—		
183	COBRA	●		III.(A).(3)., page 5
184	DISABILITY	●		III.(A).(3)., page 5
185	ERISA	●		III.(B).(4)., page 7
186	SOCIAL SECURITY	●		III.(A).(3)., page 5
187	OTHER RETIREMENT BENEFITS	—		
188	UNEMPLOYMENT	●		III.(A).(3)., page 5
189	WORKERS' COMPENSATION	●		III.(A).(3)., page 5
190	**PERSONAL INJURY OFFENSES**	●		III.(B).(2).(a)., page 6
191	DEFAMATION	—		
192	EMOTIONAL DISTRESS/UPSET	—		
193	HUMILIATION	—		
194	LIBEL	—		
195	MENTAL ANGUISH	—		
196	PERSONAL INJURY	—		
197	SLANDER	—		
198	**PRIOR ACTS**	—		
199	PRIOR ACTS	—		
200	PRIOR KNOWLEDGE	—		
201	PRIOR/PENDING LITIGATION	●		III.(B).(2).(c).(i)., page 6
202	**PROPERTY DAMAGE**	●		III.(B).(2).(a)., page 6
203	INTANGIBLE PROPERTY	—		
204	LOSS OF USE	●		III.(B).(2).(a)., page 6
205	TANGIBLE PROPERTY	●		III.(B).(2).(a)., page 6
206	**RETALIATORY ACTIONS OF EMPLOYER**	—		
207	FOR FAILING TO PERFORM ACTS AGAINST PUBLIC POLICY	—		
208	FOR FILING A COMPLAINT OR BENEFIT CLAIM	—		
209	**STRIKES/LOCKOUTS**	—		
210	**VIOLATION OF LAWS**	—		
211	ANY LAW	—		
212	FMLA	—		
213	OSHA	●		III.(A).(3)., page 5
214	POLLUTION LAWS	●		III.(B).(2).(b)., page 5
215	RICO	—		
216	SEC	—		
217	WARN	●		III.(A).(3)., page 5

15 CONDITIONS

#	Comparison Query		Comment	Policy Reference
218	**ARBITRATION**	—		
219	MANDATORY	—		
220	BINDING	—		
221	CHOICE OF LAW PROVISION	—		
222	SITUS	—		
223	**TERRITORY**	—		
224	LIMITED	—		
225	WORLDWIDE	—		
226	**NEWLY FORMED/ACQUIRED ENTITIES**	●		IV.(H)., page 13
227	AUTOMATIC COVERAGE (X DAYS)	90	> 25% company assets involved	IV.(H)., page 13
228	NOTIFY INSURER WITHIN X DAYS	90	> 25% company assets involved	IV.(H)., page 13

EXECUTIVE RISK SPECIALTY INSURANCE COMPANY B24775 [8/97]

Policy Comparison Worksheet

Fireman's Fund Insurance Company

Policy Form No.: 5240-12-94
Edition Date: 12/94

Risks Considered: Non-Profit Organizations (except hospitals)
Limits Available: $15,000,000
Minimum Retention: None

Contact: Mary Anne Tankersley
ALTRU, Inc.
3975 Erie Avenue
Cincinnati, OH 45208
800/529-8850
513/271-8899 (fax)

KEY TO SYMBOLS
● = Specifically contains queried provision of feature
○ = Unable to determine
— = Silent

#	Comparison Query		Comment	Policy Reference
	1 APPLICATION			
1	ATTACHES TO AND FORMS A PART OF THE POLICY	●		Preamble 1., page 1
2	CONTAINS WARRANTY STATEMENTS	—		
3	CONTAINS SEVERABILITY PROVISIONS	●		Preamble 1., page 1
	2 POLICY TYPE			
4	UNITARY STAND ALONE POLICY	●		
	ENDORSEMENT OR PART OF			
5	DIRECTORS AND OFFICERS POLICY	—		
6	PACKAGE POLICY	—		
7	UMBRELLA POLICY	—		
8	ERRORS AND OMISSIONS POLICY	—		
9	OTHER	●	Organization Liability Policy	
10	CLAIMS-MADE	●		
11	OCCURRENCE	—		
	3 WHO IS INSURED			
12	BUSINESS ENTITY	●		I.B. & C., page 2
13	AUTOMATIC COVERAGE FOR SUBSIDIARIES	●	See also VII.E., page 7	I.B. & C., page 2
14	DIRECTORS & OFFICERS	●		VII.B.1., page 7
15	EMPLOYEES	●		VII.B.1., page 7
16	PART-TIME	—		
17	SEASONAL	—		
18	TEMPORARY	—		
19	SUPERVISORS & MANAGERS	—		
20	FORMER EMPLOYEES	●		VII.B.1., page 7
21	VOLUNTEERS	●		VII.B.1., page 7
22	INDEPENDENT CONTRACTORS	—		
23	EXCLUDED	—		
24	SILENT	●		
25	SHAREHOLDERS	—		
	4 LIMIT OF LIABILITY			
26	AGGREGATE	●		III.B., page 4
27	INCLUDES PUNITIVE DAMAGES WHERE NOT UNINSURABLE	—		
28	DEFENSE COSTS INCLUDED WITHIN LIMIT OF LIABILITY	●		VII.F., page 7
29	DEFENSE COSTS PAID IN ADDITION TO LIMIT OF LIABILITY	—		
	5 DEDUCTIBLE			
30	APPLIES TO EACH INDIVIDUAL CLAIM	●	Conditions apply	III.A., page 4
31	APPLIES TO EACH OCCURRENCE OR WRONGFUL PRACTICE	●	Conditions apply	I.D., page 2
32	INCLUDES ALL CLAIMS FROM ONE ACT	●	Conditions apply	I.D., page 2
33	SUBJECT TO ANNUAL AGGREGATE	—		
34	CO-PAYMENT APPLIES	—		
35	LIMIT OF LIABILITY NOT REDUCED	—		
36	INCLUDES DEFENSE COSTS	●	See also VII.F., page 7	Preamble, page 1
37	REDUCED UNDER SPECIFIED CIRCUMSTANCES (SEE POLICY)	—		

	Comparison Query		Comment	Policy Reference
	6 WHAT IS A CLAIM			
38	ORAL COMPLAINT TO INSURED	—		
39	WRITTEN COMPLAINT TO INSURED	●	See also I.D., page 2	VII.A., page 7
40	COMPLAINT MUST CONTAIN A DEMAND FOR DAMAGES	—		
41	COMPLAINT FILED WITH EEOC	—		
42	OR SIMILAR STATE AUTHORITY	—		
43	AGENCY MUST HAVE POWER TO ADJUDICATE	—		
44	ADMINISTRATIVE PROCEEDING	●		VII.A., page 7
45	ARBITRATION PROCEEDING	—		
46	ANY INCIDENT REPORTED TO INSURER	—		
47	SUIT	●		VII.A., page 7
48	CLAIM DOES NOT INCLUDE ARBITRATION SUBJECT TO	—		
49	COLLECTIVE BARGAINING AGREEMENT	—		
50	EMPLOYEE POLICY OR MANUAL	—		
51	CLAIM NOT DEFINED	—		
	7 CLAIM REPORTING PROVISIONS TO INSURER			
52	IMMEDIATELY	—		
53	AS SOON AS POSSIBLE	—		
54	AS SOON AS PRACTICABLE	●		IV.A.2., page 4
55	WITHIN POLICY PERIOD	—		
56	WITHIN X DAYS OF EXPIRATION	—		
57	WITHIN X DAYS	—		
	8 EXTENDED REPORTING FEATURES			
58	ELECTION PERIOD (DAYS)	30		V., page 5
59	ADDITIONAL PREMIUM (% OF ANNUAL PREMIUM)	40		V., page 5
60	ADDITIONAL REPORTING PERIOD (MONTHS)	12		V., page 5
61	NO REINSTATEMENT OF LIMITS	●		V., page 5
	9 POTENTIAL CLAIM REPORTING PROVISIONS			
62	NONE (SEE ALSO "CLAIM" ABOVE)	—		
63	INCIDENTS LIKELY TO RESULT IN A CLAIM	●		I.D., page 2
	10 DEFENSE PROVISIONS			
64	AFFIRMATIVE DUTY TO DEFEND	—		
65	NO AFFIRMATIVE DUTY TO DEFEND	●	See also I.E., page 2	Preamble, page 1
66	AFFIRMATIVE ADVANCEMENT PROVISIONS	●	Pay on current basis	I.E.2., page 2
67	INSURED MUST RETURN ADVANCED AMOUNTS IF NOT COVERED	—		
68	INSURED/INSURER CHOOSES COUNSEL	—		
69	INSURED/INSURER APPROVES COUNSEL	—		
70	INSURED/INSURER CONSULTED IN COUNSEL SELECTION	—		
	11 SETTLEMENT PROVISIONS			
71	HAMMER CLAUSE	●		I.E.3., page 2
72	CONSULTATION PROVISION	—		
73	CONSENT PROVISION	●	Insurer must consent	I.E.1., page 2
	12 ALLOCATION OF LOSS PROVISIONS			
74	STIPULATED PROVISIONS	—		
	13 COVERAGES			
75	DISCRIMINATION	●	As wrongful act	VII.J., following 2., page 8
76	SPECIFIC ENUMERATED ACTIVITIES	—		
77	PLUS BROAD OMNIBUS WORDING	—		
78	SPECIFIC ENUMERATED CLASSES	●		VII.J., following 2., page 8
79	PLUS BROAD OMNIBUS WORDING	—		
80	AGAINST THIRD PARTIES	—		
81	DISCRIMINATION NOT DEFINED	●		
82	SEXUAL HARASSMENT	●	As wrongful act	VII.J., following 2., page 8
83	HOSTILE ENVIRONMENT	—		
84	QUID-PRO-QUO	—		
85	SEXUAL HARASSMENT NOT DEFINED	●		
86	WRONGFUL TERMINATION			
87	BREACH OF IMPLIED CONTRACT	●	As wrongful act	VII.J., following 2., page 8
88	BREACH OF EXPRESS CONTRACT	●	As wrongful act	VII.J., following 2., page 8
89	VIOLATION OF PUBLIC POLICY	—		
90	VIOLATION OF GOOD FAITH & FAIR DEALING	—		
91	OBLIGATIONS TO MAKE PAYMENTS	—		
92	CONSTRUCTIVE DISCHARGE	—		
93	WRONGFUL TERMINATION NOT DEFINED	●		
94	OTHER EMPLOYMENT VIOLATIONS/OFFENSES	●		VII.J., following 2., page 8
95	WRONGFUL HIRING	—		
96	WRONGFUL PROMOTION/DEMOTION	—		
97	WRONGFUL EVALUATION/DISCIPLINE	—		

	Comparison Query		Comment	Policy Reference
98	FAMILY AND MEDICAL LEAVE ACT	—		
99	DEFAMATION	●	As wrongful act	VII.J., following 2., page 8
100	MISREPRESENTATION	—		
101	RETALIATION	—		
102	MENTAL ANGUISH	—		
103	INVASION OF PRIVACY	●	As wrongful act	VII.J., following 2., page 8
104	HUMILIATION	—		
105	EMOTIONAL DISTRESS	—		
106	OTHER PERSONAL INJURY OFFENSES	●	As wrongful act	VII.J., following 2., page 8
107	POLICY SILENT	—		

14 EXCLUSIONS

			Comment	Policy Reference
108	**ADA ACCOMMODATION EXPENSES**	—		
109	**ASSAULT & BATTERY**	—		
110	**BACK PAY**	—		
111	**BODILY INJURY**	●		II.C., page 3
112	BODILY INJURY	●		II.C., page 3
113	DEATH	●		II.C., page 3
114	DISEASE	●		II.C., page 3
115	SICKNESS	●		II.C., page 3
116	**BREACH OF EMPLOYMENT CONTRACT**	—		
117	EXPRESS CONTRACT	—		
118	*WRITTEN CONTRACT*	—		
119	*ORAL CONTRACT*	—		
120	IMPLIED CONTRACT	—		
121	**CLASS ACTION LAWSUITS**	—		
122	**CONSEQUENTIAL LOSS**	—		
123	APPLIES TO BODILY INJURY	—		
124	APPLIES TO INSURED EVENT	—		
125	BROTHER/SISTER	—		
126	CHILD	—		
127	DOMESTIC PARTNER	—		
128	PARENT	—		
129	SPOUSE	—		
130	**COST OF ARBITRATION HEARINGS SUBJECT TO**	—		
131	EMPLOYMENT HANDBOOK	—		
132	LABOR GRIEVANCE	—		
133	OTHER EMPLOYMENT POLICY OR PROCEDURE	—		
134	**COVERAGE ELSEWHERE**	●		VI.E.2., page 6
135	OTHER AVAILABLE INSURANCE	●	Exception applies	VI.E.2., page 6
136	OTHER INDEMNIFICATION	●		VI.E.3., page 6
137	SHARING PROVISION	—		
138	**FAILURE TO EXERCISE CARE WHEN TERMINATING**	—		
139	**FINES/PENALTIES**	●		VII.F.3., page 7
140	CIVIL	—		
141	CRIMINAL	—		
142	EXEMPLARY DAMAGES	●		VII.F.1., page 7
143	PUNITIVE DAMAGES	●		VII.F.1., page 7
144	MULTIPLIED DAMAGES	●		VII.F.2., page 7
145	**FRONT PAY**	—		
146	EXCLUSION APPLIES ONLY IF EMPLOYER HAD OPPORTUNITY TO REINSTATE EMPLOYEE BUT DID NOT DO SO	—		
147	**INTENTIONAL ACTS**	●		II.A.1., page 3
148	CRIMINAL ACTS	—		
149	CRIMINAL PROCEEDING	—		
150	DISHONEST PURPOSE	●	In-fact provision	II.A.1., page 3
151	FRAUDULENT ACTS	●	In-fact provision	II.A.1., page 3
152	FRAUDULENT CLAIMS	—		
153	INTENTIONAL VIOLATIONS OF LAW	●	In-fact provision	II.A.2., page 3
154	WILLFUL FAILURE TO COMPLY WITH LAW	●	In-fact provision	II.A.2., page 3
155	MALICIOUS PURPOSE	—		
156	**LIABILITY OF OTHERS**	—		
157	**LIQUIDATED DAMAGES**	—		
158	**LOSS ARISING OUT OF CHANGES IN OPERATIONS**	—		
159	ACQUISITION	—		
160	CHANGE IN CONTROL	—		
161	DOWNSIZING OR REDUCTION IN FORCE	—		
162	*% OF WORKFORCE*	—		
163	*WITHIN X DAYS*	—		

FIREMAN'S FUND INSURANCE COMPANY 5240-12-94 [12/94]

#	Comparison Query		Comment	Policy Reference
164	FINANCIAL IMPAIRMENT	—		
165	*BANKRUPTCY*	—		
166	*INSOLVENCY*	—		
167	*LIQUIDATION*	—		
168	*RECEIVERSHIP*	—		
169	FINANCIAL INABILITY TO PAY	—		
170	MERGER	—		
171	PLANT OR FACILITY CLOSING	—		
172	REORGANIZATION	—		
173	TEMPORARY SHUTDOWN	—		
174	**MATTERS DEEMED UNINSURABLE**	●		VII.F.4., page 7
175	**NON-MONETARY RELIEF**	—		
176	DECLATORY RELIEF	—		
177	DISGORGEMENT	—		
178	INJUNCTIVE RELIEF	—		
179	JOB REINSTATEMENT	—		
180	NON-MONETARY DAMAGES/RELIEF	—		
181	OTHER EQUITABLE REMEDIES	—		
182	**OBLIGATION TO PROVIDE BENEFITS**	—		
183	COBRA	—		
184	DISABILITY	—		
185	ERISA	●		II.H., page 3
186	SOCIAL SECURITY	—		
187	OTHER RETIREMENT BENEFITS	—		
188	UNEMPLOYMENT	—		
189	WORKERS' COMPENSATION	—		
190	**PERSONAL INJURY OFFENSES**	—		
191	DEFAMATION	—		
192	EMOTIONAL DISTRESS/UPSET	—		
193	HUMILIATION	—		
194	LIBEL	—		
195	MENTAL ANGUISH	—		
196	PERSONAL INJURY	—		
197	SLANDER	—		
198	**PRIOR ACTS**			
199	PRIOR ACTS	●	Claim reported under prior policy	II.G.1., page 3
200	PRIOR KNOWLEDGE	●	Claim reported under prior policy	II.G.1., page 3
201	PRIOR/PENDING LITIGATION	●		II.G.2., page 3
202	**PROPERTY DAMAGE**	●		II.D., page 3
203	INTANGIBLE PROPERTY	—		
204	LOSS OF USE	●		II.D., page 3
205	TANGIBLE PROPERTY	●		II.D., page 3
206	**RETALIATORY ACTIONS OF EMPLOYER**	—		
207	FOR FAILING TO PERFORM ACTS AGAINST PUBLIC POLICY	—		
208	FOR FILING A COMPLAINT OR BENEFIT CLAIM	—		
209	**STRIKES/LOCKOUTS**	—		
210	**VIOLATION OF LAWS**	—		
211	ANY LAW	—		
212	FMLA	—		
213	OSHA	—		
214	POLLUTION LAWS	●		II.E., page 3
215	RICO	—		
216	SEC	—		
217	WARN	—		

15 CONDITIONS

#	Comparison Query		Comment	Policy Reference
218	**ARBITRATION**	—		
219	MANDATORY	—		
220	BINDING	—		
221	CHOICE OF LAW PROVISION	—		
222	SITUS	—		
223	**TERRITORY**	—		
224	LIMITED	—		
225	WORLDWIDE	—		
226	**NEWLY FORMED/ACQUIRED ENTITIES**	●		VI.F.1. & 2., page 6
227	AUTOMATIC COVERAGE (X DAYS)	60		VI.F.1. & 2., page 6
228	NOTIFY INSURER WITHIN X DAYS	60		VI.F.1. & 2., page 6

FIREMAN'S FUND INSURANCE COMPANY 5240-12-94 [12/94]

Policy Comparison Worksheet

Fireman's Fund Insurance Company

Policy Form No.: 5241-6-96
Edition Date: 6/96

Risks Considered: Non-Profit Organizations (except hospitals)
Limits Available: $15,000,000
Minimum Retention: None

Contact: Mary Anne Tankersley
ALTRU, Inc.
3975 Erie Avenue
Cincinnati, OH 45208
800/529-8850
513/271-8899 (fax)

KEY TO SYMBOLS
● = Specifically contains queried provision of feature
○ = Unable to determine
— = Silent

#	Comparison Query		Comment	Policy Reference
	1 APPLICATION			
1	ATTACHES TO AND FORMS A PART OF THE POLICY	●		Preamble, 1., page 1
2	CONTAINS WARRANTY STATEMENTS	—		
3	CONTAINS SEVERABILITY PROVISIONS	●		Preamble, following 3., page 1
	2 POLICY TYPE			
4	UNITARY STAND ALONE POLICY	—		
	ENDORSEMENT OR PART OF	—		
5	DIRECTORS AND OFFICERS POLICY	—		
6	PACKAGE POLICY	—		
7	UMBRELLA POLICY	—		
8	ERRORS AND OMISSIONS POLICY	—		
9	OTHER	●	Organization Liability Policy	
10	CLAIMS-MADE	●		
11	OCCURRENCE	—		
	3 WHO IS INSURED			
12	BUSINESS ENTITY	●		VII.E., page 8
13	AUTOMATIC COVERAGE FOR SUBSIDIARIES	●		VII.C., page 7
14	DIRECTORS & OFFICERS	●		VII.B.1., page 7
15	EMPLOYEES	●		VII.B.1., page 7
16	PART-TIME	—		
17	SEASONAL	—		
18	TEMPORARY	—		
19	SUPERVISORS & MANAGERS	—		
20	FORMER EMPLOYEES	●		VII.B.1., page 7
21	VOLUNTEERS	●		VII.B.1., page 7
22	INDEPENDENT CONTRACTORS	—		
23	EXCLUDED	—		
24	SILENT	●		
25	SHAREHOLDERS	—		
	4 LIMIT OF LIABILITY			
26	AGGREGATE	●		III.B., page 4
27	INCLUDES PUNITIVE DAMAGES WHERE NOT UNINSURABLE	—		
28	DEFENSE COSTS INCLUDED WITHIN LIMIT OF LIABILITY	—		
29	DEFENSE COSTS PAID IN ADDITION TO LIMIT OF LIABILITY	—		
	5 DEDUCTIBLE			
30	APPLIES TO EACH INDIVIDUAL CLAIM	—		
31	APPLIES TO EACH OCCURRENCE OR WRONGFUL PRACTICE	●	See also III.A., page 4	I.B., page 2
32	INCLUDES ALL CLAIMS FROM ONE ACT	●	See also III.A., page 4	I.B., page 2
33	SUBJECT TO ANNUAL AGGREGATE	—		
34	CO-PAYMENT APPLIES	—		
35	LIMIT OF LIABILITY NOT REDUCED	—		
36	INCLUDES DEFENSE COSTS	—		
37	REDUCED UNDER SPECIFIED CIRCUMSTANCES (SEE POLICY)	—		

FIREMAN'S FUND INSURANCE COMPANY 5241-6-96 (6/96)

#	Comparison Query	Comment		Policy Reference
6	**WHAT IS A CLAIM**			
38	ORAL COMPLAINT TO INSURED	—		
39	WRITTEN COMPLAINT TO INSURED	●		I.B., page 2
40	COMPLAINT MUST CONTAIN A DEMAND FOR DAMAGES	●		VII.A., page 7
41	COMPLAINT FILED WITH EEOC	—		
42	OR SIMILAR STATE AUTHORITY	—		
43	AGENCY MUST HAVE POWER TO ADJUDICATE	—		
44	ADMINISTRATIVE PROCEEDING	●		VII.A., page 7
45	ARBITRATION PROCEEDING	—		
46	ANY INCIDENT REPORTED TO INSURER	●		I.B., page 2
47	SUIT	●		VII.A., page 7
48	CLAIM DOES NOT INCLUDE ARBITRATION SUBJECT TO	—		
49	COLLECTIVE BARGAINING AGREEMENT	—		
50	EMPLOYEE POLICY OR MANUAL	—		
51	CLAIM NOT DEFINED	—		
7	**CLAIM REPORTING PROVISIONS TO INSURER**			
52	IMMEDIATELY	—		
53	AS SOON AS POSSIBLE	—		
54	AS SOON AS PRACTICABLE	●	See also IV.A.2., page 5	I.A.2., page 2
55	WITHIN POLICY PERIOD	—		
56	WITHIN X DAYS OF EXPIRATION	—		
57	WITHIN X DAYS	—		
8	**EXTENDED REPORTING FEATURES**			
58	ELECTION PERIOD (DAYS)	30		V., page 5
59	ADDITIONAL PREMIUM (% OF ANNUAL PREMIUM)	40		V., page 5
60	ADDITIONAL REPORTING PERIOD (MONTHS)	12		V., page 5
61	NO REINSTATEMENT OF LIMITS	●		V., page 5
9	**POTENTIAL CLAIM REPORTING PROVISIONS**			
62	NONE (SEE ALSO "CLAIM" ABOVE)	—		
63	INCIDENTS LIKELY TO RESULT IN A CLAIM	●		I.B., page 2
10	**DEFENSE PROVISIONS**			
64	AFFIRMATIVE DUTY TO DEFEND	●		I.C., page 2
65	NO AFFIRMATIVE DUTY TO DEFEND	—		
66	AFFIRMATIVE ADVANCEMENT PROVISIONS	—		
67	INSURED MUST RETURN ADVANCED AMOUNTS IF NOT COVERED	—		
68	INSURED/INSURER CHOOSES COUNSEL	—		
69	INSURED/INSURER APPROVES COUNSEL	—		
70	INSURED/INSURER CONSULTED IN COUNSEL SELECTION	—		
11	**SETTLEMENT PROVISIONS**			
71	HAMMER CLAUSE	—		
72	CONSULTATION PROVISION	—		
73	CONSENT PROVISION	●	Insured must consent	I.C.2., page 2
12	**ALLOCATION OF LOSS PROVISIONS**			
74	STIPULATED PROVISIONS	—		
13	**COVERAGES**			
75	DISCRIMINATION	●	As "Wrongful Act"	VII.I., following 2., page 8
76	SPECIFIC ENUMERATED ACTIVITIES	—		
77	*PLUS BROAD OMNIBUS WORDING*	—		
78	SPECIFIC ENUMERATED CLASSES	●		VII.I., following 2., page 8
79	*PLUS BROAD OMNIBUS WORDING*	—		
80	AGAINST THIRD PARTIES	—		
81	DISCRIMINATION NOT DEFINED	●		
82	SEXUAL HARASSMENT	●	As "Wrongful Act"	VII.I., following 2., page 8
83	HOSTILE ENVIRONMENT	—		
84	QUID-PRO-QUO	—		
85	SEXUAL HARASSMENT NOT DEFINED	●		
86	WRONGFUL TERMINATION	—		
87	BREACH OF IMPLIED CONTRACT	●	See also VII.I., following 2., page 8	II.B., page 3
88	BREACH OF EXPRESS CONTRACT	●	See also VII.I., following 2., page 8	II.B., page 3
89	VIOLATION OF PUBLIC POLICY	—		
90	VIOLATION OF GOOD FAITH & FAIR DEALING	—		
91	OBLIGATIONS TO MAKE PAYMENTS	—		
92	CONSTRUCTIVE DISCHARGE	—		
93	WRONGFUL TERMINATION NOT DEFINED	—		
94	OTHER EMPLOYMENT VIOLATIONS/OFFENSES	●		VII.I., following 2., page 8
95	WRONGFUL HIRING	—		
96	WRONGFUL PROMOTION/DEMOTION	—		
97	WRONGFUL EVALUATION/DISCIPLINE	—		

FIREMAN'S FUND INSURANCE COMPANY 5241-6-96 [6/96]

#	Comparison Query		Comment	Policy Reference
98	FAMILY AND MEDICAL LEAVE ACT	—		
99	DEFAMATION	●	As wrongful act	VII.I., following 2., page 8
100	MISREPRESENTATION	—		
101	RETALIATION	—		
102	MENTAL ANGUISH	—		
103	INVASION OF PRIVACY	●	As wrongful act	VII.I., following 2., page 8
104	HUMILIATION	—		
105	EMOTIONAL DISTRESS	—		
106	OTHER PERSONAL INJURY OFFENSES	●	As wrongful act	VII.I., following 2., page 8
107	POLICY SILENT	—		

14 EXCLUSIONS

#	Comparison Query		Comment	Policy Reference
108	**ADA ACCOMMODATION EXPENSES**	—		
109	**ASSAULT & BATTERY**	—		
110	**BACK PAY**	—		
111	**BODILY INJURY**	●		II.C., page 3
112	BODILY INJURY	●		II.C., page 3
113	DEATH	●		II.C., page 3
114	DISEASE	●		II.C., page 3
115	SICKNESS	●		II.C., page 3
116	**BREACH OF EMPLOYMENT CONTRACT**	—		
117	EXPRESS CONTRACT	—		
118	*WRITTEN CONTRACT*	—		
119	*ORAL CONTRACT*	—		
120	IMPLIED CONTRACT	—		
121	**CLASS ACTION LAWSUITS**	—		
122	**CONSEQUENTIAL LOSS**	—		
123	APPLIES TO BODILY INJURY	—		
124	APPLIES TO INSURED EVENT	—		
125	BROTHER/SISTER	—		
126	CHILD	—		
127	DOMESTIC PARTNER	—		
128	PARENT	—		
129	SPOUSE	—		
130	**COST OF ARBITRATION HEARINGS SUBJECT TO**	—		
131	EMPLOYMENT HANDBOOK	—		
132	LABOR GRIEVANCE	—		
133	OTHER EMPLOYMENT POLICY OR PROCEDURE	—		
134	**COVERAGE ELSEWHERE**			
135	OTHER AVAILABLE INSURANCE	●	Exception applies	VI.E.2., page 6
136	OTHER INDEMNIFICATION	—		
137	SHARING PROVISION	—		
138	**FAILURE TO EXERCISE CARE WHEN TERMINATING**	—		
139	**FINES/PENALTIES**	●		VII.D.3., page 8
140	CIVIL	—		
141	CRIMINAL	—		
142	EXEMPLARY DAMAGES	●		VII.D.1., page 8
143	PUNITIVE DAMAGES	●		VII.D.1., page 8
144	MULTIPLIED DAMAGES	●		VII.D.2., page 8
145	**FRONT PAY**	—		
146	EXCLUSION APPLIES ONLY IF EMPLOYER HAD OPPORTUNITY TO REINSTATE EMPLOYEE BUT DID NOT DO SO	—		
147	**INTENTIONAL ACTS**	●		II.A.1. & 2., page 3
148	CRIMINAL ACTS	—		
149	CRIMINAL PROCEEDING	—		
150	DISHONEST PURPOSE	●	"In fact" provision	II.A.1., page 3
151	FRAUDULENT ACTS	●	"In fact" provision	II.A.1., page 3
152	FRAUDULENT CLAIMS	—		
153	INTENTIONAL VIOLATIONS OF LAW	●	"In fact" provision	II.A.2., page 3
154	WILLFUL FAILURE TO COMPLY WITH LAW	●	"In fact" provision	II.A.2., page 3
155	MALICIOUS PURPOSE	—		
156	**LIABILITY OF OTHERS**	—		
157	**LIQUIDATED DAMAGES**	—		
158	**LOSS ARISING OUT OF CHANGES IN OPERATIONS**			
159	ACQUISITION	—		
160	CHANGE IN CONTROL	—		
161	DOWNSIZING OR REDUCTION IN FORCE	—		
162	*% OF WORKFORCE*	—		
163	*WITHIN X DAYS*	—		

FIREMAN'S FUND INSURANCE COMPANY 5241-6-96 [6/96]

#	Comparison Query		Comment	Policy Reference
164	FINANCIAL IMPAIRMENT	—		
165	BANKRUPTCY	—		
166	INSOLVENCY	—		
167	LIQUIDATION	—		
168	RECEIVERSHIP	—		
169	FINANCIAL INABILITY TO PAY	—		
170	MERGER	—		
171	PLANT OR FACILITY CLOSING	—		
172	REORGANIZATION	—		
173	TEMPORARY SHUTDOWN	—		
174	**MATTERS DEEMED UNINSURABLE**	●		VII.D.4., page 8
175	**NON-MONETARY RELIEF**	—		
176	DECLATORY RELIEF	—		
177	DISGORGEMENT	—		
178	INJUNCTIVE RELIEF	—		
179	JOB REINSTATEMENT	—		
180	NON-MONETARY DAMAGES/RELIEF	—		
181	OTHER EQUITABLE REMEDIES	—		
182	**OBLIGATION TO PROVIDE BENEFITS**	—		
183	COBRA	—		
184	DISABILITY	—		
185	ERISA	●	Exceptions apply	II.H.1. page 4
186	SOCIAL SECURITY	—		
187	OTHER RETIREMENT BENEFITS	—		
188	UNEMPLOYMENT	—		
189	WORKERS' COMPENSATION	—		
190	**PERSONAL INJURY OFFENSES**	—		
191	DEFAMATION	—		
192	EMOTIONAL DISTRESS/UPSET	—		
193	HUMILIATION	—		
194	LIBEL	—		
195	MENTAL ANGUISH	—		
196	PERSONAL INJURY	—		
197	SLANDER	—		
198	**PRIOR ACTS**	●		II.G.1., page 4
199	PRIOR ACTS	●	Reported under prior policy	II.G.1., page 4
200	PRIOR KNOWLEDGE	○	Reported under prior policy	II.G.1., page 4
201	PRIOR/PENDING LITIGATION	●		II.G.2., page 4
202	**PROPERTY DAMAGE**	●		II.D., page 3
203	INTANGIBLE PROPERTY	—		
204	LOSS OF USE	●		II.D., page 3
205	TANGIBLE PROPERTY	●		II.D., page 3
206	**RETALIATORY ACTIONS OF EMPLOYER**	—		
207	FOR FAILING TO PERFORM ACTS AGAINST PUBLIC POLICY	—		
208	FOR FILING A COMPLAINT OR BENEFIT CLAIM	—		
209	**STRIKES/LOCKOUTS**	—		
210	**VIOLATION OF LAWS**	—		
211	ANY LAW	—		
212	FMLA	—		
213	OSHA	—		
214	POLLUTION LAWS	—		
215	RICO	—		
216	SEC	—		
217	WARN	—		

15 CONDITIONS

#	Comparison Query		Comment	Policy Reference
218	**ARBITRATION**	—		
219	MANDATORY	—		
220	BINDING	—		
221	CHOICE OF LAW PROVISION	—		
222	SITUS	—		
223	**TERRITORY**	—		
224	LIMITED	—		
225	WORLDWIDE	—		
226	**NEWLY FORMED/ACQUIRED ENTITIES**	●		VI.F.1. & 2., pages 6–7
227	AUTOMATIC COVERAGE (X DAYS)	60		VI.F.1. & 2., pages 6–7
228	NOTIFY INSURER WITHIN X DAYS	60		VI.F.1. & 2., pages 6–7

FIREMAN'S FUND INSURANCE COMPANY 5241-6-96 [6/96]

Policy Comparison Worksheet

Fireman's Fund Insurance Company

Policy Form No.: 7006-10-96
Edition Date: 10/96

Risks Considered: All except employee leasing companies, law firms and municipalities
Limits Available: $5,000,000
Minimum Retention: $2,500

Contact: James R. Grieser
Professional Risk Co.
600 University Street, Suite 2501
Seattle, WA 98101-1129
206/621-8808
206/682-9176 (fax)
jrg@wexfordgroup.com

KEY TO SYMBOLS
● = Specifically contains queried provision of feature
○ = Unable to determine
— = Silent

#	Comparison Query		Comment	Policy Reference
	1 APPLICATION			
1	ATTACHES TO AND FORMS A PART OF THE POLICY	●		Preamble, page 1
2	CONTAINS WARRANTY STATEMENTS	—		
3	CONTAINS SEVERABILITY PROVISIONS	—		
	2 POLICY TYPE			
4	UNITARY STAND ALONE POLICY	●		
	ENDORSEMENT OR PART OF	—		
5	DIRECTORS AND OFFICERS POLICY	—		
6	PACKAGE POLICY	—		
7	UMBRELLA POLICY	—		
8	ERRORS AND OMISSIONS POLICY	—		
9	OTHER	—		
10	CLAIMS-MADE	●		
11	OCCURRENCE	—		
	3 WHO IS INSURED			
12	BUSINESS ENTITY	●		III., page 3
13	AUTOMATIC COVERAGE FOR SUBSIDIARIES	—		
14	DIRECTORS & OFFICERS	●		III., page 3
15	EMPLOYEES	●		III., page 3
16	PART-TIME	—		
17	SEASONAL	—		
18	TEMPORARY	—		
19	SUPERVISORS & MANAGERS	—		
20	FORMER EMPLOYEES	—		
21	VOLUNTEERS	—		
22	INDEPENDENT CONTRACTORS	—		
23	EXCLUDED	—		
24	SILENT	●		
25	SHAREHOLDERS	●		III., page 3
	4 LIMIT OF LIABILITY			
26	AGGREGATE	●		IV.B., page 3
27	INCLUDES PUNITIVE DAMAGES WHERE NOT UNINSURABLE	—		
28	DEFENSE COSTS INCLUDED WITHIN LIMIT OF LIABILITY	●	See also IV.B., page 3	I.B., page 1
29	DEFENSE COSTS PAID IN ADDITION TO LIMIT OF LIABILITY	—		
	5 DEDUCTIBLE			
30	APPLIES TO EACH INDIVIDUAL CLAIM	—		
31	APPLIES TO EACH OCCURRENCE OR WRONGFUL PRACTICE	●		IV.E., page 4
32	INCLUDES ALL CLAIMS FROM ONE ACT	●		IV.E., page 4
33	SUBJECT TO ANNUAL AGGREGATE	—		
34	CO-PAYMENT APPLIES	—		
35	LIMIT OF LIABILITY NOT REDUCED	—		
36	INCLUDES DEFENSE COSTS	●		IV.E., page 4
37	REDUCED UNDER SPECIFIED CIRCUMSTANCES (SEE POLICY)	—		

FIREMAN'S FUND INSURANCE COMPANY 7006-10-96 [10/96]

#	Comparison Query		Comment	Policy Reference
	6 WHAT IS A CLAIM			
38	ORAL COMPLAINT TO INSURED	—		
39	WRITTEN COMPLAINT TO INSURED	●	See also VIII.A., page 6	I.D., page 2
40	COMPLAINT MUST CONTAIN A DEMAND FOR DAMAGES	●	See also VIII.A., page 6	VIII.A., page 6
41	COMPLAINT FILED WITH EEOC	—		
42	OR SIMILAR STATE AUTHORITY	—		
43	AGENCY MUST HAVE POWER TO ADJUDICATE	—		
44	ADMINISTRATIVE PROCEEDING	●		VIII.A., page 6
45	ARBITRATION PROCEEDING	—		
46	ANY INCIDENT REPORTED TO INSURER			
47	SUIT	●		VIII.A., page 6
48	CLAIM DOES NOT INCLUDE ARBITRATION SUBJECT TO	●		VIII.A., page 6
49	COLLECTIVE BARGAINING AGREEMENT	●		VIII.A., page 6
50	EMPLOYEE POLICY OR MANUAL	●		VIII.A., page 6
51	CLAIM NOT DEFINED	●		
	7 CLAIM REPORTING PROVISIONS TO INSURER			
52	IMMEDIATELY	—		
53	AS SOON AS POSSIBLE	—		
54	AS SOON AS PRACTICABLE	●	See also V.A., page 4	I.C., page 1
55	WITHIN POLICY PERIOD	—		
56	WITHIN X DAYS OF EXPIRATION	60		I.C., page 1
57	WITHIN X DAYS	—		
	8 EXTENDED REPORTING FEATURES			
58	ELECTION PERIOD (DAYS)	60		VI., page 4
59	ADDITIONAL PREMIUM (% OF ANNUAL PREMIUM)	200		VI., page 4
60	ADDITIONAL REPORTING PERIOD (MONTHS)	○	Specified by underwriter—see ERP Endorsement	VI., page 4
61	NO REINSTATEMENT OF LIMITS	●		VI., page 4
	9 POTENTIAL CLAIM REPORTING PROVISIONS			
62	NONE (SEE ALSO "CLAIM" ABOVE)	—		
63	INCIDENTS LIKELY TO RESULT IN A CLAIM	●		I.D., page 2
	10 DEFENSE PROVISIONS			
64	AFFIRMATIVE DUTY TO DEFEND	●		I.B., page 1
65	NO AFFIRMATIVE DUTY TO DEFEND	—		
66	AFFIRMATIVE ADVANCEMENT PROVISIONS	—		
67	INSURED MUST RETURN ADVANCED AMOUNTS IF NOT COVERED	—		
68	INSURED/INSURER CHOOSES COUNSEL	—		
69	INSURED/INSURER APPROVES COUNSEL	—		
70	INSURED/INSURER CONSULTED IN COUNSEL SELECTION	—		
	11 SETTLEMENT PROVISIONS			
71	HAMMER CLAUSE	—		
72	CONSULTATION PROVISION	—		
73	CONSENT PROVISION	—		
	12 ALLOCATION OF LOSS PROVISIONS			
74	STIPULATED PROVISIONS	—		
	13 COVERAGES			
75	DISCRIMINATION	●		I.A., page 1
76	SPECIFIC ENUMERATED ACTIVITIES	—		
77	PLUS BROAD OMNIBUS WORDING	●	Unlawful treatment	VIIIC., page 6
78	SPECIFIC ENUMERATED CLASSES	●		VIIIC., page 6
79	PLUS BROAD OMNIBUS WORDING	●		VIIIC., page 6
80	AGAINST THIRD PARTIES	—		
81	DISCRIMINATION NOT DEFINED	—		
82	SEXUAL HARASSMENT	●		I.A., page 1
83	HOSTILE ENVIRONMENT	●		VIII.F., page 6
84	QUID-PRO-QUO	●		VIII.F., page 6
85	SEXUAL HARASSMENT NOT DEFINED	—		
86	WRONGFUL TERMINATION	●		I.A., page 1
87	BREACH OF IMPLIED CONTRACT	●		VIII.G., page 6
88	BREACH OF EXPRESS CONTRACT	—		
89	VIOLATION OF PUBLIC POLICY	—		
90	VIOLATION OF GOOD FAITH & FAIR DEALING	—		
91	OBLIGATIONS TO MAKE PAYMENTS	—		
92	CONSTRUCTIVE DISCHARGE	—		
93	WRONGFUL TERMINATION NOT DEFINED	—		
94	OTHER EMPLOYMENT VIOLATIONS/OFFENSES	●		VII.H., page 7
95	WRONGFUL HIRING	●		VII.H., page 7
96	WRONGFUL PROMOTION/DEMOTION	●		VII.H., page 7
97	WRONGFUL EVALUATION/DISCIPLINE	●		VII.H., page 7

FIREMAN'S FUND INSURANCE COMPANY 7006-10-96 [10/96]

	Comparison Query		Comment	Policy Reference
98	FAMILY AND MEDICAL LEAVE ACT	—		
99	DEFAMATION	●		VIII.G., page 6
100	MISREPRESENTATION	—		
101	RETALIATION	—		
102	MENTAL ANGUISH	●		II.B., page 2
103	INVASION OF PRIVACY	●		VIII.G., page 6
104	HUMILIATION	●		II.B., page 2
105	EMOTIONAL DISTRESS	●	See also VIII.G., page 6	II.B., page 2
106	OTHER PERSONAL INJURY OFFENSES	—		
107	POLICY SILENT	—		
14 EXCLUSIONS				
108	**ADA ACCOMMODATION EXPENSES**	●		II.G., pages 2–3
109	**ASSAULT & BATTERY**	—		
110	**BACK PAY**	—		
111	**BODILY INJURY**	—		
112	BODILY INJURY	●		II.B., page 2
113	DEATH	●		II.B., page 2
114	DISEASE	●		II.B., page 2
115	SICKNESS	●		II.B., page 2
116	**BREACH OF EMPLOYMENT CONTRACT**	●		VIII.G., page 6
117	EXPRESS CONTRACT	●		VIII.G., page 6
118	*WRITTEN CONTRACT*	●		VIII.G., page 6
119	*ORAL CONTRACT*	—		
120	IMPLIED CONTRACT	—		
121	**CLASS ACTION LAWSUITS**	—		
122	**CONSEQUENTIAL LOSS**			
123	APPLIES TO BODILY INJURY	●		II.B., page 2
124	APPLIES TO INSURED EVENT	—		
125	BROTHER/SISTER	●		II.B., page 2
126	CHILD	●		II.B., page 2
127	DOMESTIC PARTNER	●		II.B., page 2
128	PARENT	●		II.B., page 2
129	SPOUSE	●		II.B., page 2
130	**COST OF ARBITRATION HEARINGS SUBJECT TO**	—		
131	EMPLOYMENT HANDBOOK	—		
132	LABOR GRIEVANCE	—		
133	OTHER EMPLOYMENT POLICY OR PROCEDURE	—		
134	**COVERAGE ELSEWHERE**			
135	OTHER AVAILABLE INSURANCE	●		IV.E.2., page 5
136	OTHER INDEMNIFICATION	—		
137	SHARING PROVISION	●	See also IV.F., page 5	IV.E.3., page 5
138	**FAILURE TO EXERCISE CARE WHEN TERMINATING**	—		
139	**FINES/PENALTIES**	●		II.E., page 2
140	CIVIL	—		
141	CRIMINAL	—		
142	EXEMPLARY DAMAGES	—		
143	PUNITIVE DAMAGES	—		
144	MULTIPLIED DAMAGES	●		II.E., page 2
145	**FRONT PAY**	—		
146	EXCLUSION APPLIES ONLY IF EMPLOYER HAD OPPORTUNITY TO REINSTATE EMPLOYEE BUT DID NOT DO SO	—		
147	**INTENTIONAL ACTS**	●		II.A., page 2
148	CRIMINAL ACTS	—		
149	CRIMINAL PROCEEDING	—		
150	DISHONEST PURPOSE	—		
151	FRAUDULENT ACTS	—		
152	FRAUDULENT CLAIMS	—		
153	INTENTIONAL VIOLATIONS OF LAW	●	Employment practice law	II.D., page 2
154	WILLFUL FAILURE TO COMPLY WITH LAW	—		
155	MALICIOUS PURPOSE	—		
156	**LIABILITY OF OTHERS**	●		II.J., page 3
157	**LIQUIDATED DAMAGES**	●		II.E., page 2
158	**LOSS ARISING OUT OF CHANGES IN OPERATIONS**	—		
159	ACQUISITION	—		
160	CHANGE IN CONTROL	—		
161	DOWNSIZING OR REDUCTION IN FORCE	—		
162	*% OF WORKFORCE*	—		
163	*WITHIN X DAYS*	—		

FIREMAN'S FUND INSURANCE COMPANY 7006-10-96 [10/96]

	Comparison Query		Comment	Policy Reference
164	FINANCIAL IMPAIRMENT	—		
165	*BANKRUPTCY*	—		
166	*INSOLVENCY*	—		
167	*LIQUIDATION*	—		
168	*RECEIVERSHIP*	—		
169	FINANCIAL INABILITY TO PAY	—		
170	MERGER	—		
171	PLANT OR FACILITY CLOSING	—		
172	REORGANIZATION	—		
173	TEMPORARY SHUTDOWN	—		
174	**MATTERS DEEMED UNINSURABLE**	●		II.E., page 2
175	**NON-MONETARY RELIEF**	●		II.E., page 2
176	DECLATORY RELIEF	—		
177	DISGORGEMENT	—		
178	INJUNCTIVE RELIEF	—		
179	JOB REINSTATEMENT	—		
180	NON-MONETARY DAMAGES/RELIEF	●		II.E., page 2
181	OTHER EQUITABLE REMEDIES	—		
182	**OBLIGATION TO PROVIDE BENEFITS**	—		
183	COBRA	●		III.F., page 2
184	DISABILITY	●		II.I., page 3
185	ERISA	●		II.F., page 2
186	SOCIAL SECURITY	—		
187	OTHER RETIREMENT BENEFITS	—		
188	UNEMPLOYMENT	●		II.I., page 3
189	WORKERS' COMPENSATION	●		II.I., page 3
190	**PERSONAL INJURY OFFENSES**	—		
191	DEFAMATION	—		
192	EMOTIONAL DISTRESS/UPSET	—		
193	HUMILIATION	—		
194	LIBEL	—		
195	MENTAL ANGUISH	—		
196	PERSONAL INJURY	—		
197	SLANDER	—		
198	**PRIOR ACTS**	●		I.C., page 1
199	PRIOR ACTS	●		I.C., page 1
200	PRIOR KNOWLEDGE	●		I.C., page 1
201	PRIOR/PENDING LITIGATION	—		
202	**PROPERTY DAMAGE**	●		
203	INTANGIBLE PROPERTY	—		
204	LOSS OF USE	●		II.C., page 2
205	TANGIBLE PROPERTY	●		II.C., page 2
206	**RETALIATORY ACTIONS OF EMPLOYER**	—		
207	FOR FAILING TO PERFORM ACTS AGAINST PUBLIC POLICY	—		
208	FOR FILING A COMPLAINT OR BENEFIT CLAIM	—		
209	**STRIKES/LOCKOUTS**	●		II.H., page 2
210	**VIOLATION OF LAWS**	—		
211	ANY LAW	—		
212	FMLA	—		
213	OSHA	—		
214	POLLUTION LAWS	—		
215	RICO	—		
216	SEC	—		
217	WARN	●		II.F., page 2
	15 CONDITIONS			
218	**ARBITRATION**	—		
219	MANDATORY	—		
220	BINDING	—		
221	CHOICE OF LAW PROVISION	—		
222	SITUS	—		
223	**TERRITORY**	●		I.C., page 1
224	LIMITED	●		I.C., page 1
225	WORLDWIDE	—		
226	**NEWLY FORMED/ACQUIRED ENTITIES**	●		III., page 3
227	AUTOMATIC COVERAGE (X DAYS)	90		III., page 3
228	NOTIFY INSURER WITHIN X DAYS	—		

FIREMAN'S FUND INSURANCE COMPANY 7006-10-96 [10/96]

Policy Comparison Worksheet

Fireman's Fund Insurance Company

Policy Form No.: 7006-1-98
Edition Date: 1/98

Risks Considered: All except public entities, law firms and employee leasing companies

Limits Available: $5,000,000
Minimum Retention: $2,500

Contact: James R. Grieser
Professional Risk Co.
600 University Street, Suite 2501
Seattle, WA 98101-1129
206/621-8808
206/682-9176 (fax)
jrg@wexfordgroup.com

KEY TO SYMBOLS
● = Specifically contains queried provision of feature
○ = Unable to determine
— = Silent

#	Comparison Query		Comment	Policy Reference
	1 APPLICATION			
1	ATTACHES TO AND FORMS A PART OF THE POLICY	●		Preamble, page 1
2	CONTAINS WARRANTY STATEMENTS	—		
3	CONTAINS SEVERABILITY PROVISIONS	—		
	2 POLICY TYPE			
4	UNITARY STAND ALONE POLICY	●		
	ENDORSEMENT OR PART OF	—		
5	DIRECTORS AND OFFICERS POLICY	—		
6	PACKAGE POLICY	—		
7	UMBRELLA POLICY	—		
8	ERRORS AND OMISSIONS POLICY	—		
9	OTHER	—		
10	CLAIMS-MADE	●		
11	OCCURRENCE	—		
	3 WHO IS INSURED			
12	BUSINESS ENTITY	●		III., page 3
13	AUTOMATIC COVERAGE FOR SUBSIDIARIES	—		
14	DIRECTORS & OFFICERS	●		III., page 3
15	EMPLOYEES	●		III., page 3
16	PART-TIME	●		III., page 3
17	SEASONAL	●		III., page 3
18	TEMPORARY	●		III., page 3
19	SUPERVISORS & MANAGERS	—		
20	FORMER EMPLOYEES	●		III., page 3
21	VOLUNTEERS	—		
22	INDEPENDENT CONTRACTORS			
23	EXCLUDED	—		
24	SILENT	●	Coverage available by endorsement	
25	SHAREHOLDERS	●		III., page 3
	4 LIMIT OF LIABILITY			
26	AGGREGATE	●		IV.B., pages 3–4
27	INCLUDES PUNITIVE DAMAGES WHERE NOT UNINSURABLE	—		
28	DEFENSE COSTS INCLUDED WITHIN LIMIT OF LIABILITY	●		I.B., page 1
29	DEFENSE COSTS PAID IN ADDITION TO LIMIT OF LIABILITY	—		
	5 DEDUCTIBLE			
30	APPLIES TO EACH INDIVIDUAL CLAIM	—		
31	APPLIES TO EACH OCCURRENCE OR WRONGFUL PRACTICE	●		IV.E., page 4
32	INCLUDES ALL CLAIMS FROM ONE ACT	●		IV.E., page 4
33	SUBJECT TO ANNUAL AGGREGATE	—		
34	CO-PAYMENT APPLIES	—		
35	LIMIT OF LIABILITY NOT REDUCED	—		
36	INCLUDES DEFENSE COSTS	●		IV.E., page 4
37	REDUCED UNDER SPECIFIED CIRCUMSTANCES (SEE POLICY)	—		

FIREMAN'S FUND INSURANCE COMPANY 7006-1-98 [1/98]

Comparison Query		Comment	Policy Reference
6 WHAT IS A CLAIM			
38 ORAL COMPLAINT TO INSURED	●	See also VIII.A., page 6	I.D., page 2
39 WRITTEN COMPLAINT TO INSURED	●		I.D., page 2
40 COMPLAINT MUST CONTAIN A DEMAND FOR DAMAGES	—		
41 COMPLAINT FILED WITH EEOC	—		
42 OR SIMILAR STATE AUTHORITY	—		
43 AGENCY MUST HAVE POWER TO ADJUDICATE	—		
44 ADMINISTRATIVE PROCEEDING	●		VIII.A., page 6
45 ARBITRATION PROCEEDING	—		
46 ANY INCIDENT REPORTED TO INSURER	●	Reported by insured	I.D., page 2
47 SUIT	●		VIII.A., page 6
48 CLAIM DOES NOT INCLUDE ARBITRATION SUBJECT TO	●		VIII.A., page 6
49 COLLECTIVE BARGAINING AGREEMENT	●		VIII.A., page 6
50 EMPLOYEE POLICY OR MANUAL	●		VIII.A., page 6
51 CLAIM NOT DEFINED	—		
7 CLAIM REPORTING PROVISIONS TO INSURER			
52 IMMEDIATELY	—		
53 AS SOON AS POSSIBLE	—		
54 AS SOON AS PRACTICABLE	●	See also V.A., page 4	I.C., page 2
55 WITHIN POLICY PERIOD	—		
56 WITHIN X DAYS OF EXPIRATION	60		I.C., page 2
57 WITHIN X DAYS	—		
8 EXTENDED REPORTING FEATURES			
58 ELECTION PERIOD (DAYS)	60		VI., page 4
59 ADDITIONAL PREMIUM (% OF ANNUAL PREMIUM)	○	Specified by underwriter	VI., page 4
60 ADDITIONAL REPORTING PERIOD (MONTHS)	○	Specified by underwriter	VI., page 4
61 NO REINSTATEMENT OF LIMITS	●		VI., page 4
9 POTENTIAL CLAIM REPORTING PROVISIONS			
62 NONE (SEE ALSO "CLAIM" ABOVE)	—		
63 INCIDENTS LIKELY TO RESULT IN A CLAIM	●		I.D., page 2
10 DEFENSE PROVISIONS			
64 AFFIRMATIVE DUTY TO DEFEND	●		I.B., page 1
65 NO AFFIRMATIVE DUTY TO DEFEND	—		
66 AFFIRMATIVE ADVANCEMENT PROVISIONS	—		
67 INSURED MUST RETURN ADVANCED AMOUNTS IF NOT COVERED	—		
68 INSURED/INSURER CHOOSES COUNSEL	—		
69 INSURED/INSURER APPROVES COUNSEL	—		
70 INSURED/INSURER CONSULTED IN COUNSEL SELECTION	—		
11 SETTLEMENT PROVISIONS			
71 HAMMER CLAUSE	—		
72 CONSULTATION PROVISION	—		
73 CONSENT PROVISION	—		
12 ALLOCATION OF LOSS PROVISIONS			
74 STIPULATED PROVISIONS	—		
13 COVERAGES			
75 DISCRIMINATION	●		VIII.J., page 7
76 SPECIFIC ENUMERATED ACTIVITIES	—		
77 PLUS BROAD OMNIBUS WORDING	●	Unlawful treatment	VIIIC., page 6
78 SPECIFIC ENUMERATED CLASSES	●		VIIIC., page 6
79 PLUS BROAD OMNIBUS WORDING	●		VIIIC., page 6
80 AGAINST THIRD PARTIES	—		
81 DISCRIMINATION NOT DEFINED	—		
82 SEXUAL HARASSMENT	●	See also VIII.J., page 7	VIII.F., page 6
83 HOSTILE ENVIRONMENT	●		VIII.F., page 6
84 QUID-PRO-QUO	●		VIII.F., page 6
85 SEXUAL HARASSMENT NOT DEFINED	—		
86 WRONGFUL TERMINATION	●	See also VIII.J., page 7	VIII.G., page 6
87 BREACH OF IMPLIED CONTRACT	●		VIII.G., page 6
88 BREACH OF EXPRESS CONTRACT	—		
89 VIOLATION OF PUBLIC POLICY	●		VIII.G., page 6
90 VIOLATION OF GOOD FAITH & FAIR DEALING	—		
91 OBLIGATIONS TO MAKE PAYMENTS	—		
92 CONSTRUCTIVE DISCHARGE	●		VIII.G., page 6
93 WRONGFUL TERMINATION NOT DEFINED	—		
94 OTHER EMPLOYMENT VIOLATIONS/OFFENSES	—		
95 WRONGFUL HIRING	●		VIII.I., page 7
96 WRONGFUL PROMOTION/DEMOTION	●		VIII.J., page 7
97 WRONGFUL EVALUATION/DISCIPLINE	●		VIII.J., page 7

FIREMAN'S FUND INSURANCE COMPANY 7006-1-98 [1/98]

	Comparison Query		Comment	Policy Reference
98	FAMILY AND MEDICAL LEAVE ACT	—		
99	DEFAMATION	●		VIII.I., page 7
100	MISREPRESENTATION	●		VIII.I., page 7
101	RETALIATION	●		VIII.J., page 7
102	MENTAL ANGUISH	—		
103	INVASION OF PRIVACY	●		VIII.I., page 7
104	HUMILIATION	—		
105	EMOTIONAL DISTRESS	●		VIII.I., page 7
106	OTHER PERSONAL INJURY OFFENSES	—		
107	POLICY SILENT	—		

14 EXCLUSIONS

	Comparison Query		Comment	Policy Reference
108	**ADA ACCOMMODATION EXPENSES**	●		II.E., page 3
109	**ASSAULT & BATTERY**	—		
110	**BACK PAY**	—		
111	**BODILY INJURY**	●	Exceptions apply	II.A., page 2
112	BODILY INJURY	●	Exceptions apply	II.A., page 2
113	DEATH	●	Exceptions apply	II.A., page 2
114	DISEASE	●	Exceptions apply	II.A., page 2
115	SICKNESS	●	Exceptions apply	II.A., page 2
116	**BREACH OF EMPLOYMENT CONTRACT**	—		
117	EXPRESS CONTRACT	●		VIII.G., pages 6–7
118	WRITTEN CONTRACT	●		VIII.G., pages 6–7
119	ORAL CONTRACT	—		
120	IMPLIED CONTRACT	—		
121	**CLASS ACTION LAWSUITS**	—		
122	**CONSEQUENTIAL LOSS**	●		II.A., page 2
123	APPLIES TO BODILY INJURY	●		II.A., page 2
124	APPLIES TO INSURED EVENT	—		
125	BROTHER/SISTER	●		II.A., page 2
126	CHILD	●		II.A., page 2
127	DOMESTIC PARTNER	●		II.A., page 2
128	PARENT	●		II.A., page 2
129	SPOUSE	●		II.A., page 2
130	**COST OF ARBITRATION HEARINGS SUBJECT TO**	—		
131	EMPLOYMENT HANDBOOK	—		
132	LABOR GRIEVANCE	—		
133	OTHER EMPLOYMENT POLICY OR PROCEDURE	—		
134	**COVERAGE ELSEWHERE**			
135	OTHER AVAILABLE INSURANCE	—		
136	OTHER INDEMNIFICATION	—		
137	SHARING PROVISION	●	Exception applies	VII.E., page 5
138	**FAILURE TO EXERCISE CARE WHEN TERMINATING**	—		
139	**FINES/PENALTIES**	●		II.D., page 2
140	CIVIL	—		
141	CRIMINAL	—		
142	EXEMPLARY DAMAGES	—		
143	PUNITIVE DAMAGES	—		
144	MULTIPLIED DAMAGES	●		II.D., page 2
145	**FRONT PAY**	—		
146	EXCLUSION APPLIES ONLY IF EMPLOYER HAD OPPORTUNITY TO REINSTATE EMPLOYEE BUT DID NOT DO SO	—		
147	**INTENTIONAL ACTS**	—		
148	CRIMINAL ACTS	—		
149	CRIMINAL PROCEEDING	—		
150	DISHONEST PURPOSE	—		
151	FRAUDULENT ACTS	—		
152	FRAUDULENT CLAIMS	—		
153	INTENTIONAL VIOLATIONS OF LAW	●		II.C., page 2
154	WILLFUL FAILURE TO COMPLY WITH LAW	●		II.C., page 2
155	MALICIOUS PURPOSE	—		
156	**LIABILITY OF OTHERS**	●		II.I., page 3
157	**LIQUIDATED DAMAGES**	●		II.D., page 2
158	**LOSS ARISING OUT OF CHANGES IN OPERATIONS**	—		
159	ACQUISITION	—		
160	CHANGE IN CONTROL	—		
161	DOWNSIZING OR REDUCTION IN FORCE	—		
162	% OF WORKFORCE	—		
163	WITHIN X DAYS	—		

	Comparison Query		Comment	Policy Reference
164	FINANCIAL IMPAIRMENT	—		
165	BANKRUPTCY	—		
166	INSOLVENCY	—		
167	LIQUIDATION	—		
168	RECEIVERSHIP	—		
169	FINANCIAL INABILITY TO PAY	—		
170	MERGER	—		
171	PLANT OR FACILITY CLOSING	—		
172	REORGANIZATION	—		
173	TEMPORARY SHUTDOWN	—		
174	**MATTERS DEEMED UNINSURABLE**	●		II.D., page 2
175	**NON-MONETARY RELIEF**	—		
176	DECLATORY RELIEF	—		
177	DISGORGEMENT	—		
178	INJUNCTIVE RELIEF	—		
179	JOB REINSTATEMENT	—		
180	NON-MONETARY DAMAGES/RELIEF	●		II.D., page 2
181	OTHER EQUITABLE REMEDIES	—		
182	**OBLIGATION TO PROVIDE BENEFITS**	—		
183	COBRA	●		II.E., page 3
184	DISABILITY	●	Retaliation/discrimination exception	II.H., page 3
185	ERISA	●		II.E., page 2
186	SOCIAL SECURITY	—		
187	OTHER RETIREMENT BENEFITS	—		
188	UNEMPLOYMENT	●		II.H., page 3
189	WORKERS' COMPENSATION	●	Retaliation/discrimination exception	II.H., page 3
190	**PERSONAL INJURY OFFENSES**	—		
191	DEFAMATION	—		
192	EMOTIONAL DISTRESS/UPSET	—		
193	HUMILIATION	—		
194	LIBEL	—		
195	MENTAL ANGUISH	—		
196	PERSONAL INJURY	—		
197	SLANDER	—		
198	**PRIOR ACTS**	—		
199	PRIOR ACTS	●	Coverage available by endorsement	I.C., page 1
200	PRIOR KNOWLEDGE	●		I.C., page 1
201	PRIOR/PENDING LITIGATION	—		
202	**PROPERTY DAMAGE**	●		II.B., page 2
203	INTANGIBLE PROPERTY	—		
204	LOSS OF USE	●		II.B., page 2
205	TANGIBLE PROPERTY	●		II.B., page 2
206	**RETALIATORY ACTIONS OF EMPLOYER**	—		
207	FOR FAILING TO PERFORM ACTS AGAINST PUBLIC POLICY	—		
208	FOR FILING A COMPLAINT OR BENEFIT CLAIM	—		
209	**STRIKES/LOCKOUTS**	●		III.G., page 3
210	**VIOLATION OF LAWS**	—		
211	ANY LAW	—		
212	FMLA	—		
213	OSHA	—		
214	POLLUTION LAWS	—		
215	RICO	—		
216	SEC	—		
217	WARN	●		II.E., page 3
	15 CONDITIONS			
218	**ARBITRATION**	—		
219	MANDATORY	—		
220	BINDING	—		
221	CHOICE OF LAW PROVISION	—		
222	SITUS	—		
223	**TERRITORY**	●		I.C., page 1
224	LIMITED	—		
225	WORLDWIDE	●		I.C., page 1
226	**NEWLY FORMED/ACQUIRED ENTITIES**	●		III., page 3
227	AUTOMATIC COVERAGE (X DAYS)	90	If > 51% ownership	III., page 3
228	NOTIFY INSURER WITHIN X DAYS	—		

FIREMAN'S FUND INSURANCE COMPANY 7006-1-98 [1/98]

Policy Comparison Worksheet

First Specialty Insurance Corporation
(Employers Reinsurance Group)

Policy Form No.: FSIC-1491A
Edition Date: 01/96

Risks Considered: All except law firms and employee leasing companies
Limits Available: $1,000,000
Minimum Retention: $5,000

Contact: Ron Kettner
First Specialty Insurance Corporation
5200 Metcalf
Overland Park, KS 66201
913/676-5339
913/676-5359 (fax)

KEY TO SYMBOLS
● = Specifically contains queried provision of feature
○ = Unable to determine
— = Silent

#	Comparison Query		Comment	Policy Reference
	1 APPLICATION			
1	ATTACHES TO AND FORMS A PART OF THE POLICY	●		Section XVIII., page 7
2	CONTAINS WARRANTY STATEMENTS	—		
3	CONTAINS SEVERABILITY PROVISIONS	—		
	2 POLICY TYPE			
4	UNITARY STAND ALONE POLICY	●		
	ENDORSEMENT OR PART OF	—		
5	DIRECTORS AND OFFICERS POLICY	—		
6	PACKAGE POLICY	—		
7	UMBRELLA POLICY	—		
8	ERRORS AND OMISSIONS POLICY	—		
9	OTHER	—		
10	CLAIMS-MADE	●		
11	OCCURRENCE	—		
	3 WHO IS INSURED			
12	BUSINESS ENTITY	●		Section V.(a), page 3
13	AUTOMATIC COVERAGE FOR SUBSIDIARIES	—		
14	DIRECTORS & OFFICERS	●		Section V.(a), page 3
15	EMPLOYEES	●		Section V.(a), page 3
16	PART-TIME	—		
17	SEASONAL	—		
18	TEMPORARY	—		
19	SUPERVISORS & MANAGERS	—		
20	FORMER EMPLOYEES	—		
21	VOLUNTEERS	—		
22	INDEPENDENT CONTRACTORS	—		
23	EXCLUDED	—		
24	SILENT	●		
25	SHAREHOLDERS	●		Section V.(a), page 3
	4 LIMIT OF LIABILITY			
26	AGGREGATE	●		Section IV., page 2
27	INCLUDES PUNITIVE DAMAGES WHERE NOT UNINSURABLE	—		
28	DEFENSE COSTS INCLUDED WITHIN LIMIT OF LIABILITY	●		Section V.(b).(2)., page 3
29	DEFENSE COSTS PAID IN ADDITION TO LIMIT OF LIABILITY	—		
	5 DEDUCTIBLE			
30	APPLIES TO EACH INDIVIDUAL CLAIM	—		
31	APPLIES TO EACH OCCURRENCE OR WRONGFUL PRACTICE	●		Section IV., page 2
32	INCLUDES ALL CLAIMS FROM ONE ACT	●		Section IV., page 2
33	SUBJECT TO ANNUAL AGGREGATE	—		
34	CO-PAYMENT APPLIES	—		
35	LIMIT OF LIABILITY NOT REDUCED	—		
36	INCLUDES DEFENSE COSTS	●		Section IV., page 2
37	REDUCED UNDER SPECIFIED CIRCUMSTANCES (SEE POLICY)	—		

	Comparison Query		Comment	Policy Reference
	6 WHAT IS A CLAIM			
38	**ORAL COMPLAINT TO INSURED**	—		
39	**WRITTEN COMPLAINT TO INSURED**	—		
40	**COMPLAINT MUST CONTAIN A DEMAND FOR DAMAGES**	●		Section V.(c), page 3
41	**COMPLAINT FILED WITH EEOC**	●		Section V.(c), page 3
42	OR SIMILAR STATE AUTHORITY	●		Section V.(c), page 3
43	AGENCY MUST HAVE POWER TO ADJUDICATE	—		
44	**ADMINISTRATIVE PROCEEDING**	—		
45	**ARBITRATION PROCEEDING**	—		
46	**ANY INCIDENT REPORTED TO INSURER**	—		
47	**SUIT**	●	Notice of legal process	Section V.(c), page 3
48	**CLAIM DOES NOT INCLUDE ARBITRATION SUBJECT TO**	—		
49	COLLECTIVE BARGAINING AGREEMENT	—		
50	EMPLOYEE POLICY OR MANUAL	—		
51	**CLAIM NOT DEFINED**	●		
	7 CLAIM REPORTING PROVISIONS TO INSURER			
52	**IMMEDIATELY**	○	Prompt notice	Section X., page 5
53	**AS SOON AS POSSIBLE**	—		
54	**AS SOON AS PRACTICABLE**	—		
55	**WITHIN POLICY PERIOD**	●		Section V.(c), page 3
56	**WITHIN X DAYS OF EXPIRATION**	—		
57	**WITHIN X DAYS**	—		
	8 EXTENDED REPORTING FEATURES			
58	**ELECTION PERIOD (DAYS)**	60		Section VIII., page 4
59	**ADDITIONAL PREMIUM (% OF ANNUAL PREMIUM)**	100		Section VIII., page 4
60	**ADDITIONAL REPORTING PERIOD (MONTHS)**	12		Section VIII., page 4
61	**NO REINSTATEMENT OF LIMITS**	—		
	9 POTENTIAL CLAIM REPORTING PROVISIONS			
62	**NONE (SEE ALSO "CLAIM" ABOVE)**	—		
63	**INCIDENTS LIKELY TO RESULT IN A CLAIM**	●	See also Section X.(b), page 5	Section V.(c), page 3
	10 DEFENSE PROVISIONS			
64	**AFFIRMATIVE DUTY TO DEFEND**	●		Section II., page 1
65	**NO AFFIRMATIVE DUTY TO DEFEND**	—		
66	AFFIRMATIVE ADVANCEMENT PROVISIONS	—		
67	INSURED MUST RETURN ADVANCED AMOUNTS IF NOT COVERED	—		
68	**INSURED/INSURER CHOOSES COUNSEL**	—		
69	**INSURED/INSURER APPROVES COUNSEL**	—		
70	**INSURED/INSURER CONSULTED IN COUNSEL SELECTION**	—		
	11 SETTLEMENT PROVISIONS			
71	**HAMMER CLAUSE**	●		Section II., page 1
72	**CONSULTATION PROVISION**	—		
73	**CONSENT PROVISION**	●	Two-way	Section II., page 1
	12 ALLOCATION OF LOSS PROVISIONS			
74	**STIPULATED PROVISIONS**	—		
	13 COVERAGES			
75	**DISCRIMINATION**	●		Section V.(d), page 3
76	SPECIFIC ENUMERATED ACTIVITIES	—		
77	*PLUS BROAD OMNIBUS WORDING*	—		
78	SPECIFIC ENUMERATED CLASSES	●		Section V.(e), page 3
79	*PLUS BROAD OMNIBUS WORDING*	—		
80	AGAINST THIRD PARTIES	○		Section IV.(e), page 2
81	DISCRIMINATION NOT DEFINED	—		
82	**SEXUAL HARASSMENT**	●		Section V.(d), page 3
83	HOSTILE ENVIRONMENT	—		
84	QUID-PRO-QUO	—		
85	SEXUAL HARASSMENT NOT DEFINED	●		
86	**WRONGFUL TERMINATION**	●		Section V.(d), page 3
87	BREACH OF IMPLIED CONTRACT	—		
88	BREACH OF EXPRESS CONTRACT	●		Section V.(d), page 3
89	VIOLATION OF PUBLIC POLICY	—		
90	VIOLATION OF GOOD FAITH & FAIR DEALING	—		
91	OBLIGATIONS TO MAKE PAYMENTS	—		
92	CONSTRUCTIVE DISCHARGE	—		
93	WRONGFUL TERMINATION NOT DEFINED	●		
94	**OTHER EMPLOYMENT VIOLATIONS/OFFENSES**			
95	WRONGFUL HIRING	●		Section V.(d), page 3
96	WRONGFUL PROMOTION/DEMOTION	●		Section V.(d), page 3
97	WRONGFUL EVALUATION/DISCIPLINE	●		Section V.(d), page 3

FIRST SPECIALTY INSURANCE CORPORATION (EMPLOYERS REINSURANCE GROUP) FSIC-1491A [01/96]

	Comparison Query		Comment	Policy Reference
98	FAMILY AND MEDICAL LEAVE ACT	—		
99	DEFAMATION	●		Section V.(d), page 3
100	MISREPRESENTATION	●		Section V.(d), page 3
101	RETALIATION	●		Section V.(d), page 3
102	MENTAL ANGUISH	●		Section VI.(b), page 3
103	INVASION OF PRIVACY	●		Section V.(d), page 3
104	HUMILIATION	●		Section VI.(b), page 3
105	EMOTIONAL DISTRESS	●		Section V.(d), page 3
106	OTHER PERSONAL INJURY OFFENSES	—		
107	POLICY SILENT	—		
	14 EXCLUSIONS			
108	**ADA ACCOMMODATION EXPENSES**	●		Section VI.(j), page 4
109	**ASSAULT & BATTERY**	●		Section VI.(g), page 4
110	**BACK PAY**	—		
111	**BODILY INJURY**	●		Section VI.(b), page 3
112	BODILY INJURY	●		Section VI.(b), page 3
113	DEATH	●		Section VI.(b), page 3
114	DISEASE	●		Section VI.(b), page 3
115	SICKNESS	●		Section VI.(b), page 3
116	**BREACH OF EMPLOYMENT CONTRACT**	—		
117	EXPRESS CONTRACT	—		
118	WRITTEN CONTRACT	—		
119	ORAL CONTRACT	—		
120	IMPLIED CONTRACT	—		
121	**CLASS ACTION LAWSUITS**	—		
122	**CONSEQUENTIAL LOSS**	—		
123	APPLIES TO BODILY INJURY	—		
124	APPLIES TO INSURED EVENT	—		
125	BROTHER/SISTER	—		
126	CHILD	—		
127	DOMESTIC PARTNER	—		
128	PARENT	—		
129	SPOUSE	—		
130	**COST OF ARBITRATION HEARINGS SUBJECT TO**	—		
131	EMPLOYMENT HANDBOOK	—		
132	LABOR GRIEVANCE	—		
133	OTHER EMPLOYMENT POLICY OR PROCEDURE	—		
134	**COVERAGE ELSEWHERE**	●		Section XII., page 5
135	OTHER AVAILABLE INSURANCE	●		Section XII., page 5
136	OTHER INDEMNIFICATION	—		
137	SHARING PROVISION	—		
138	**FAILURE TO EXERCISE CARE WHEN TERMINATING**	—		
139	**FINES/PENALTIES**	●		Section VI.(e), page 4
140	CIVIL	—		
141	CRIMINAL	—		
142	EXEMPLARY DAMAGES	●		Section VI.(e), page 4
143	PUNITIVE DAMAGES	●		Section VI.(e), page 4
144	MULTIPLIED DAMAGES	●		Section VI.(e), page 4
145	**FRONT PAY**	—		
146	EXCLUSION APPLIES ONLY IF EMPLOYER HAD OPPORTUNITY TO REINSTATE EMPLOYEE BUT DID NOT DO SO	—		
147	**INTENTIONAL ACTS**	●		Section VI.(a), page 3
148	CRIMINAL ACTS	●		Section VI.(a), page 3
149	CRIMINAL PROCEEDING	—		
150	DISHONEST PURPOSE	●		Section VI.(a), page 3
151	FRAUDULENT ACTS	●		Section VI.(a), page 3
152	FRAUDULENT CLAIMS	●		Section VI.(a), page 3
153	INTENTIONAL VIOLATIONS OF LAW	—		
154	WILLFUL FAILURE TO COMPLY WITH LAW	—		
155	MALICIOUS PURPOSE	●		Section VI.(a), page 3
156	**LIABILITY OF OTHERS**	●		Section VI.(d), page 4
157	**LIQUIDATED DAMAGES**	—		
158	**LOSS ARISING OUT OF CHANGES IN OPERATIONS**	—		
159	ACQUISITION	—		
160	CHANGE IN CONTROL	—		
161	DOWNSIZING OR REDUCTION IN FORCE	—		
162	% OF WORKFORCE	—		
163	WITHIN X DAYS	—		

FIRST SPECIALTY INSURANCE CORPORATION (EMPLOYERS REINSURANCE GROUP) FSIC-1491A [01/96]

	Comparison Query		Comment	Policy Reference
164	FINANCIAL IMPAIRMENT	—		
165	BANKRUPTCY	—		
166	INSOLVENCY	—		
167	LIQUIDATION	—		
168	RECEIVERSHIP	—		
169	FINANCIAL INABILITY TO PAY	—		
170	MERGER	—		
171	PLANT OR FACILITY CLOSING	—		
172	REORGANIZATION	—		
173	TEMPORARY SHUTDOWN	—		
174	**MATTERS DEEMED UNINSURABLE**			
175	**NON-MONETARY RELIEF**	—		
176	DECLATORY RELIEF	—		
177	DISGORGEMENT	—		
178	INJUNCTIVE RELIEF	—		
179	JOB REINSTATEMENT	—		
180	NON-MONETARY DAMAGES/RELIEF	—		
181	OTHER EQUITABLE REMEDIES	—		
182	**OBLIGATION TO PROVIDE BENEFITS**			
183	COBRA	●		Section VI.(i)., page 4
184	DISABILITY	●		Section VI.(h)., page 4
185	ERISA	●		Section VI.(i)., page 4
186	SOCIAL SECURITY	●		Section VI.(i)., page 4
187	OTHER RETIREMENT BENEFITS	●		Section VI.(f)., page 4
188	UNEMPLOYMENT	●		Section VI.(i)., page 4
189	WORKERS' COMPENSATION	●		Section VI.(i)., page 4
190	**PERSONAL INJURY OFFENSES**	—		
191	DEFAMATION	—		
192	EMOTIONAL DISTRESS/UPSET	—		
193	HUMILIATION	—		
194	LIBEL	—		
195	MENTAL ANGUISH	—		
196	PERSONAL INJURY	—		
197	SLANDER	—		
198	**PRIOR ACTS**			
199	PRIOR ACTS	●	By endorsement	
200	PRIOR KNOWLEDGE	●	If prior notice given	Section VI.(k)., page 4
201	PRIOR/PENDING LITIGATION	—		
202	**PROPERTY DAMAGE**	●		Section VI.(c)., page 4
203	INTANGIBLE PROPERTY	—		
204	LOSS OF USE	●		Section VI.(c)., page 4
205	TANGIBLE PROPERTY	—		
206	**RETALIATORY ACTIONS OF EMPLOYER**	—		
207	FOR FAILING TO PERFORM ACTS AGAINST PUBLIC POLICY	—		
208	FOR FILING A COMPLAINT OR BENEFIT CLAIM	—		
209	**STRIKES/LOCKOUTS**	—		
210	**VIOLATION OF LAWS**	●		Section VI.(i)., page 4
211	ANY LAW	●		Section VI.(i)., page 4
212	FMLA	—		
213	OSHA	—		
214	POLLUTION LAWS	—		
215	RICO	●		Section VI.(i)., page 4
216	SEC	—		
217	WARN	●		Section VI.(i)., page 4

15 CONDITIONS

218	**ARBITRATION**	—		
219	MANDATORY	—		
220	BINDING	—		
221	CHOICE OF LAW PROVISION	—		
222	SITUS	—		
223	**TERRITORY**			
224	LIMITED	—		
225	WORLDWIDE	—		
226	**NEWLY FORMED/ACQUIRED ENTITIES**	—		
227	AUTOMATIC COVERAGE (X DAYS)	—		
228	NOTIFY INSURER WITHIN X DAYS	○	Prior to change	Section XI., page 5

FIRST SPECIALTY INSURANCE CORPORATION (EMPLOYERS REINSURANCE GROUP) FSIC-1491A [01/96]

Policy Comparison Worksheet

Genesis Indemnity Insurance Company

Policy Form No.: GIIC 8001
Edition Date: 06/97

Risks Considered: All but employee leasing and law firms
Limits Available: $25,000,000
Minimum Retention: $5,000

Contact: Richard M. Gibson
Genesis Professional Liability Underwriters
25550 Chagrin Boulevard, Suite 300
Beachwood, OH 44122
216/766-5093
216/591-0906 (fax)
rgibson@genre.com

KEY TO SYMBOLS
● = Specifically contains queried provision of feature
○ = Unable to determine
— = Silent

#	Comparison Query		Comment	Policy Reference
	1 APPLICATION			
1	ATTACHES TO AND FORMS A PART OF THE POLICY	●	See also policy I., page 1	Application, page 5
2	CONTAINS WARRANTY STATEMENTS	●		Policy VIII.C.(1)., page 9
3	CONTAINS SEVERABILITY PROVISIONS	●	Non-imputation	Policy, VIII.C.(2). and (3)., page 9
	2 POLICY TYPE			
4	UNITARY STAND ALONE POLICY	●		
	ENDORSEMENT OR PART OF	—		
5	DIRECTORS AND OFFICERS POLICY	—		
6	PACKAGE POLICY	—		
7	UMBRELLA POLICY	—		
8	ERRORS AND OMISSIONS POLICY	—		
9	OTHER	—		
10	CLAIMS-MADE	●		
11	OCCURRENCE	—		
	3 WHO IS INSURED			
12	BUSINESS ENTITY	●		II.H., page 2
13	AUTOMATIC COVERAGE FOR SUBSIDIARIES	●		II.C., page 1
14	DIRECTORS & OFFICERS	●		II.H., page 2
15	EMPLOYEES	●		II.H., page 2
16	PART-TIME	●		II.E., page 1
17	SEASONAL	●		II.E., page 1
18	TEMPORARY	●		II.E., page 1
19	SUPERVISORS & MANAGERS	●		II.H., page 2
20	FORMER EMPLOYEES	—		
21	VOLUNTEERS	—		
22	INDEPENDENT CONTRACTORS	—		
23	EXCLUDED	●		II.E., page 1
24	SILENT	—		
25	SHAREHOLDERS	—		
	4 LIMIT OF LIABILITY			
26	AGGREGATE	●		V.F., page 6
27	INCLUDES PUNITIVE DAMAGES WHERE NOT UNINSURABLE	—		
28	DEFENSE COSTS INCLUDED WITHIN LIMIT OF LIABILITY	●		V.D., page 5
29	DEFENSE COSTS PAID IN ADDITION TO LIMIT OF LIABILITY	—		
	5 DEDUCTIBLE			
30	APPLIES TO EACH INDIVIDUAL CLAIM	●		V.C., page 5
31	APPLIES TO EACH OCCURRENCE OR WRONGFUL PRACTICE	—		
32	INCLUDES ALL CLAIMS FROM ONE ACT	●		V.B., page 5
33	SUBJECT TO ANNUAL AGGREGATE	—		
34	CO-PAYMENT APPLIES	—		
35	LIMIT OF LIABILITY NOT REDUCED	—		
36	INCLUDES DEFENSE COSTS	●		V.D., page 5
37	REDUCED UNDER SPECIFIED CIRCUMSTANCES (SEE POLICY)	—		

GENESIS INDEMNITY INSURANCE COMPANY GIIC-8001 [06/97]

Comparison Query	Comment	Policy Reference
6 WHAT IS A CLAIM		
38 ORAL COMPLAINT TO INSURED	●	II.B., page 1
39 WRITTEN COMPLAINT TO INSURED	●	II.B., page 1
40 COMPLAINT MUST CONTAIN A DEMAND FOR DAMAGES	○	II.B., page 1
41 COMPLAINT FILED WITH EEOC	●	II.B., page 1
42 OR SIMILAR STATE AUTHORITY	—	
43 AGENCY MUST HAVE POWER TO ADJUDICATE	—	
44 ADMINISTRATIVE PROCEEDING	●	II.B., page 1
45 ARBITRATION PROCEEDING	●	II.B., page 1
46 ANY INCIDENT REPORTED TO INSURER	—	
47 SUIT	●	II.B., page 1
48 CLAIM DOES NOT INCLUDE ARBITRATION SUBJECT TO	●	II.B., page 1
49 COLLECTIVE BARGAINING AGREEMENT	●	II.B., page 1
50 EMPLOYEE POLICY OR MANUAL	—	
51 CLAIM NOT DEFINED	—	
7 CLAIM REPORTING PROVISIONS TO INSURER		
52 IMMEDIATELY	—	
53 AS SOON AS POSSIBLE	—	
54 AS SOON AS PRACTICABLE	●	VII.A., pages 6–7
55 WITHIN POLICY PERIOD	—	
56 WITHIN X DAYS OF EXPIRATION	—	
57 WITHIN X DAYS	60	VII.A., pages 6–7
8 EXTENDED REPORTING FEATURES		
58 ELECTION PERIOD (DAYS)	30	III.D., pages 3–4
59 ADDITIONAL PREMIUM (% OF ANNUAL PREMIUM)	○ Specified by underwriter—see Item 7 of Declarations	III.D., pages 3–4
60 ADDITIONAL REPORTING PERIOD (MONTHS)	36	III.B., page 3
61 NO REINSTATEMENT OF LIMITS	●	III.E., page 4
9 POTENTIAL CLAIM REPORTING PROVISIONS		
62 NONE (SEE ALSO "CLAIM" ABOVE)	—	
63 INCIDENTS LIKELY TO RESULT IN A CLAIM	●	VII.B., page 7
10 DEFENSE PROVISIONS		
64 AFFIRMATIVE DUTY TO DEFEND	● Per mandatory endorsement	
65 NO AFFIRMATIVE DUTY TO DEFEND	—	
66 AFFIRMATIVE ADVANCEMENT PROVISIONS	—	
67 INSURED MUST RETURN ADVANCED AMOUNTS IF NOT COVERED	—	
68 INSURED/INSURER CHOOSES COUNSEL	—	
69 INSURED/INSURER APPROVES COUNSEL		
70 INSURED/INSURER CONSULTED IN COUNSEL SELECTION		
11 SETTLEMENT PROVISIONS		
71 HAMMER CLAUSE	●	VII.D., page 7
72 CONSULTATION PROVISION	—	
73 CONSENT PROVISION	● Two-way	VI.A., page 6 and VII.D., page 7
12 ALLOCATION OF LOSS PROVISIONS		
74 STIPULATED PROVISIONS	●	V.E., page 5
13 COVERAGES		
75 DISCRIMINATION	● As wrongful employment act	II.O.(2)., page 3
76 SPECIFIC ENUMERATED ACTIVITIES	●	II.F., page 2
77 PLUS BROAD OMNIBUS WORDING	—	
78 SPECIFIC ENUMERATED CLASSES	●	II.F., page 2
79 PLUS BROAD OMNIBUS WORDING	●	II.F., page 2
80 AGAINST THIRD PARTIES	— Coverage available by endorsement	
81 DISCRIMINATION NOT DEFINED	—	
82 SEXUAL HARASSMENT	● Coverage available by endorsement	II.O.(3)., page 3
83 HOSTILE ENVIRONMENT	●	II.G.(1)., page 2
84 QUID-PRO-QUO	●	II.G.(1)., page 2
85 SEXUAL HARASSMENT NOT DEFINED	—	
86 WRONGFUL TERMINATION	● Coverage available by endorsement	II.O.(1)., page 3
87 BREACH OF IMPLIED CONTRACT	●	II.P., page 3
88 BREACH OF EXPRESS CONTRACT	—	
89 VIOLATION OF PUBLIC POLICY	—	
90 VIOLATION OF GOOD FAITH & FAIR DEALING	—	
91 OBLIGATIONS TO MAKE PAYMENTS	—	
92 CONSTRUCTIVE DISCHARGE	●	II.P., page 3
93 WRONGFUL TERMINATION NOT DEFINED	—	
94 OTHER EMPLOYMENT VIOLATIONS/OFFENSES	—	
95 WRONGFUL HIRING	● If discrimination	II.F., page 2
96 WRONGFUL PROMOTION/DEMOTION	● If discrimination	II.F., page 2
97 WRONGFUL EVALUATION/DISCIPLINE	—	

GENESIS INDEMNITY INSURANCE COMPANY GIIC-8001 [06/97]

	Comparison Query		Comment	Policy Reference
98	FAMILY AND MEDICAL LEAVE ACT	—		
99	DEFAMATION	●	If discrimination	II.F., page 2
100	MISREPRESENTATION	—		
101	RETALIATION	●	As wrongful employment act	II.O.(4)., page 3
102	MENTAL ANGUISH	—		
103	INVASION OF PRIVACY	—		
104	HUMILIATION	—		
105	EMOTIONAL DISTRESS	—		
106	OTHER PERSONAL INJURY OFFENSES	—		
107	POLICY SILENT	—		
	14 EXCLUSIONS			
108	**ADA ACCOMMODATION EXPENSES**	●		II.J. (4), page 2
109	**ASSAULT & BATTERY**	—		
110	**BACK PAY**	—		
111	**BODILY INJURY**	●		IV.A., page 4
112	BODILY INJURY	●		IV.A., page 4
113	DEATH	●		IV.A., page 4
114	DISEASE	●		IV.A., page 4
115	SICKNESS	●		IV.A., page 4
116	**BREACH OF EMPLOYMENT CONTRACT**	—		
117	EXPRESS CONTRACT	—		
118	WRITTEN CONTRACT	—		
119	ORAL CONTRACT	—		
120	IMPLIED CONTRACT	—		
121	**CLASS ACTION LAWSUITS**	—		
122	**CONSEQUENTIAL LOSS**	—		
123	APPLIES TO BODILY INJURY	—		
124	APPLIES TO INSURED EVENT	—		
125	BROTHER/SISTER	—		
126	CHILD	—		
127	DOMESTIC PARTNER	—		
128	PARENT	—		
129	SPOUSE	—		
130	**COST OF ARBITRATION HEARINGS SUBJECT TO**	—		
131	EMPLOYMENT HANDBOOK	—		
132	LABOR GRIEVANCE	—		
133	OTHER EMPLOYMENT POLICY OR PROCEDURE	—		
134	**COVERAGE ELSEWHERE**	●		VIII.M., page 10
135	OTHER AVAILABLE INSURANCE	●		VIII.M., page 10
136	OTHER INDEMNIFICATION	—		
137	SHARING PROVISION	●		VIII.M., page 10
138	**FAILURE TO EXERCISE CARE WHEN TERMINATING**	—		
139	**FINES/PENALTIES**	●		II.J., page 2
140	CIVIL	●		II.J., page 2
141	CRIMINAL	●		II.J., page 2
142	EXEMPLARY DAMAGES	●		Per mandatory endorsement
143	PUNITIVE DAMAGES	●		Per mandatory endorsement
144	MULTIPLIED DAMAGES	●		Per mandatory endorsement
145	**FRONT PAY**	—		
146	EXCLUSION APPLIES ONLY IF EMPLOYER HAD OPPORTUNITY TO REINSTATE EMPLOYEE BUT DID NOT DO SO	—		
147	**INTENTIONAL ACTS**	—		
148	CRIMINAL ACTS	—		
149	CRIMINAL PROCEEDING	—		
150	DISHONEST PURPOSE	—		
151	FRAUDULENT ACTS	—		
152	FRAUDULENT CLAIMS	—		
153	INTENTIONAL VIOLATIONS OF LAW	—		
154	WILLFUL FAILURE TO COMPLY WITH LAW	—		
155	MALICIOUS PURPOSE	—		
156	**LIABILITY OF OTHERS**	●		IV.C., page 5
157	**LIQUIDATED DAMAGES**	—		
158	**LOSS ARISING OUT OF CHANGES IN OPERATIONS**	—		
159	ACQUISITION	—		
160	CHANGE IN CONTROL	—		
161	DOWNSIZING OR REDUCTION IN FORCE	—		
162	% OF WORKFORCE	—		
163	WITHIN X DAYS	—		

GENESIS INDEMNITY INSURANCE COMPANY GIIC-8001 [06/97]

	Comparison Query	Comment		Policy Reference
164	FINANCIAL IMPAIRMENT	—		
165	BANKRUPTCY	—		
166	INSOLVENCY	—		
167	LIQUIDATION	—		
168	RECEIVERSHIP	—		
169	FINANCIAL INABILITY TO PAY	—		
170	MERGER	—		
171	PLANT OR FACILITY CLOSING	—		
172	REORGANIZATION	—		
173	TEMPORARY SHUTDOWN	—		
174	**MATTERS DEEMED UNINSURABLE**	●		II.J.(5)., page 2
175	**NON-MONETARY RELIEF**	—		
176	DECLATORY RELIEF	—		
177	DISGORGEMENT	—		
178	INJUNCTIVE RELIEF	—		
179	JOB REINSTATEMENT	—		
180	NON-MONETARY DAMAGES/RELIEF	●		II.J., page 2
181	OTHER EQUITABLE REMEDIES	—		
182	**OBLIGATION TO PROVIDE BENEFITS**	—		
183	COBRA	●	Exception applies	IV.B., pages 4–5
184	DISABILITY	—		IV.B., pages 4–5
185	ERISA	●	Exception applies	IV.B., pages 4–5
186	SOCIAL SECURITY	—		
187	OTHER RETIREMENT BENEFITS	—		
188	UNEMPLOYMENT	—		
189	WORKERS' COMPENSATION	●	Exception applies	IV.B., pages 4–5
190	**PERSONAL INJURY OFFENSES**	—		
191	DEFAMATION	●	Exception applies	IV.A., page 4
192	EMOTIONAL DISTRESS/UPSET	—		
193	HUMILIATION	—		
194	LIBEL	●	Exception applies	IV.A., page 4
195	MENTAL ANGUISH	—		
196	PERSONAL INJURY	—		
197	SLANDER	●	Exception applies	IV.A., page 4
198	**PRIOR ACTS**	○		Declarations, Item 5
199	PRIOR ACTS	○		Declarations, Item 5
200	PRIOR KNOWLEDGE	—		
201	PRIOR/PENDING LITIGATION	—		
202	**PROPERTY DAMAGE**	●		III.A., page 4
203	INTANGIBLE PROPERTY	—		
204	LOSS OF USE	●		III.A., page 4
205	TANGIBLE PROPERTY	●		III.A., page 4
206	**RETALIATORY ACTIONS OF EMPLOYER**	—		
207	FOR FAILING TO PERFORM ACTS AGAINST PUBLIC POLICY	—		
208	FOR FILING A COMPLAINT OR BENEFIT CLAIM	—		
209	**STRIKES/LOCKOUTS**	●		IV.F., page 5
210	**VIOLATION OF LAWS**	—		
211	ANY LAW	—		
212	FMLA	—		
213	OSHA	●	Exception applies	IV.B., pages 4–5
214	POLLUTION LAWS	—		
215	RICO	—		
216	SEC	—		
217	WARN	●	Exception applies	IV.B., pages 4–5
	15 CONDITIONS			
218	**ARBITRATION**	—		
219	MANDATORY	—		
220	BINDING	—		
221	CHOICE OF LAW PROVISION	—		
222	SITUS	—		
223	**TERRITORY**	●		VIII.L., page 10
224	LIMITED	—		
225	WORLDWIDE	●		VIII.L., page 10
226	**NEWLY FORMED/ACQUIRED ENTITIES**	●		VIII.D., page 9
227	AUTOMATIC COVERAGE (X DAYS)			VIII.D., page 9
228	NOTIFY INSURER WITHIN X DAYS	60		VIII.D., page 9

GENESIS INDEMNITY INSURANCE COMPANY GIIC-8001 [06/97]

Policy Comparison Worksheet

Genesis Insurance Company

Policy Form No.: Frontline 8000
Edition Date: 6/97

Risks Considered: General accounts with less than 1,500 employees
Limits Available: $20,000,000
Minimum Retention: $5,000

Contact: Richard M. Gibson
Product Manager
Genesis Insurance Company
25550 Chagrin Boulevard
Beachwood, OH 44122
216/766-5093
216/591-0906 (fax)
rgibson@prms.com

KEY TO SYMBOLS
● = Specifically contains queried provision of feature
○ = Unable to determine
— = Silent

#	Comparison Query		Comment	Policy Reference
	1 APPLICATION			
1	ATTACHES TO AND FORMS A PART OF THE POLICY	●	See also II.A., page 1	VIII.C., page 8
2	CONTAINS WARRANTY STATEMENTS	—		
3	CONTAINS SEVERABILITY PROVISIONS	—		
	2 POLICY TYPE			
4	UNITARY STAND ALONE POLICY	●		
	ENDORSEMENT OR PART OF			
5	DIRECTORS AND OFFICERS POLICY	—		
6	PACKAGE POLICY	—		
7	UMBRELLA POLICY	—		
8	ERRORS AND OMISSIONS POLICY	—		
9	OTHER	—		
10	CLAIMS-MADE	●		
11	OCCURRENCE	—		
	3 WHO IS INSURED			
12	BUSINESS ENTITY	●		II.C., page 1
13	AUTOMATIC COVERAGE FOR SUBSIDIARIES	●		II.C., page 1
14	DIRECTORS & OFFICERS	●		II.H., page 2
15	EMPLOYEES	●		II.E., page 1
16	PART-TIME	●		II.E., page 1
17	SEASONAL	●		II.E., page 1
18	TEMPORARY	●		II.E., page 1
19	SUPERVISORS & MANAGERS	—		
20	FORMER EMPLOYEES	—		
21	VOLUNTEERS	—		
22	INDEPENDENT CONTRACTORS	—		
23	EXCLUDED	●		II.E., page 1
24	SILENT	—		
25	SHAREHOLDERS			
	4 LIMIT OF LIABILITY			
26	AGGREGATE	●		V.F., page 6
27	INCLUDES PUNITIVE DAMAGES WHERE NOT UNINSURABLE	●		II.J., page 2
28	DEFENSE COSTS INCLUDED WITHIN LIMIT OF LIABILITY	●		V.D., page 5
29	DEFENSE COSTS PAID IN ADDITION TO LIMIT OF LIABILITY	—		
	5 DEDUCTIBLE			
30	APPLIES TO EACH INDIVIDUAL CLAIM	●		V.C., page 5
31	APPLIES TO EACH OCCURRENCE OR WRONGFUL PRACTICE	●		V.B., page 5
32	INCLUDES ALL CLAIMS FROM ONE ACT	●		V.B., page 5
33	SUBJECT TO ANNUAL AGGREGATE	—		
34	CO-PAYMENT APPLIES	—		
35	LIMIT OF LIABILITY NOT REDUCED	—		
36	INCLUDES DEFENSE COSTS	●		V.D., page 5
37	REDUCED UNDER SPECIFIED CIRCUMSTANCES (SEE POLICY)	—		

GENESIS INSURANCE COMPANY Frontline 8000 [6/97]

#	Comparison Query	Comment	Policy Reference
	6 WHAT IS A CLAIM		
38	ORAL COMPLAINT TO INSURED	●	II.B., page 1
39	WRITTEN COMPLAINT TO INSURED	●	II.B., page 1
40	COMPLAINT MUST CONTAIN A DEMAND FOR DAMAGES	—	
41	COMPLAINT FILED WITH EEOC	●	II.B., page 1
42	OR SIMILAR STATE AUTHORITY	●	II.B., page 1
43	AGENCY MUST HAVE POWER TO ADJUDICATE	—	
44	ADMINISTRATIVE PROCEEDING	●	II.B., page 1
45	ARBITRATION PROCEEDING	●	II.B., page 1
46	ANY INCIDENT REPORTED TO INSURER	—	
47	SUIT	●	II.B., page 1
48	CLAIM DOES NOT INCLUDE ARBITRATION SUBJECT TO	●	II.B., page 1
49	COLLECTIVE BARGAINING AGREEMENT	●	II.B., page 1
50	EMPLOYEE POLICY OR MANUAL		
51	CLAIM NOT DEFINED	—	
	7 CLAIM REPORTING PROVISIONS TO INSURER		
52	IMMEDIATELY	—	
53	AS SOON AS POSSIBLE	—	
54	AS SOON AS PRACTICABLE	●	VII.A., pages 6–7
55	WITHIN POLICY PERIOD	—	
56	WITHIN X DAYS OF EXPIRATION	—	
57	WITHIN X DAYS	60	VII.A., pages 6–7
	8 EXTENDED REPORTING FEATURES		
58	ELECTION PERIOD (DAYS)	30	III.D., page 3
59	ADDITIONAL PREMIUM (% OF ANNUAL PREMIUM)	○	Specified by underwriter—see Item 7 of Declarations	III.D., page 3
60	ADDITIONAL REPORTING PERIOD (MONTHS)	36	III.B., page 3
61	NO REINSTATEMENT OF LIMITS	●	III.E., page 4
	9 POTENTIAL CLAIM REPORTING PROVISIONS		
62	NONE (SEE ALSO "CLAIM" ABOVE)	—	
63	INCIDENTS LIKELY TO RESULT IN A CLAIM	●	VII.B., page 7
	10 DEFENSE PROVISIONS		
64	AFFIRMATIVE DUTY TO DEFEND	●	By mandatory endorsement	
65	NO AFFIRMATIVE DUTY TO DEFEND	—	
66	AFFIRMATIVE ADVANCEMENT PROVISIONS	—	
67	INSURED MUST RETURN ADVANCED AMOUNTS IF NOT COVERED	—	
68	INSURED/INSURER CHOOSES COUNSEL	—	
69	INSURED/INSURER APPROVES COUNSEL	—	
70	INSURED/INSURER CONSULTED IN COUNSEL SELECTION	—	
	11 SETTLEMENT PROVISIONS		
71	HAMMER CLAUSE	—	
72	CONSULTATION PROVISION	—	
73	CONSENT PROVISION	●	Insurer must consent	VI.A., page 6
	12 ALLOCATION OF LOSS PROVISIONS		
74	STIPULATED PROVISIONS	●	V.B. and E., page 5
	13 COVERAGES		
75	DISCRIMINATION	●	II.O.,(2)., page 3
76	SPECIFIC ENUMERATED ACTIVITIES	●	II.F., page 2
77	PLUS BROAD OMNIBUS WORDING	—	
78	SPECIFIC ENUMERATED CLASSES	●	II.F., page 2
79	PLUS BROAD OMNIBUS WORDING	●	II.F., page 2
80	AGAINST THIRD PARTIES	—	
81	DISCRIMINATION NOT DEFINED	—	
82	SEXUAL HARASSMENT	●	II.O.(3)., page 3
83	HOSTILE ENVIRONMENT	●	II.G.(1). & (2)., page 2
84	QUID-PRO-QUO	●	II.G.(1). & (2)., page 2
85	SEXUAL HARASSMENT NOT DEFINED	—	
86	WRONGFUL TERMINATION	●	II.O.(1)., page 3
87	BREACH OF IMPLIED CONTRACT	●	II.P., page 3
88	BREACH OF EXPRESS CONTRACT	—	
89	VIOLATION OF PUBLIC POLICY	—	
90	VIOLATION OF GOOD FAITH & FAIR DEALING	—	
91	OBLIGATIONS TO MAKE PAYMENTS	—	
92	CONSTRUCTIVE DISCHARGE	●	II.P., page 3
93	WRONGFUL TERMINATION NOT DEFINED	—	
94	OTHER EMPLOYMENT VIOLATIONS/OFFENSES	—	
95	WRONGFUL HIRING	—	
96	WRONGFUL PROMOTION/DEMOTION	—	
97	WRONGFUL EVALUATION/DISCIPLINE	—	

GENESIS INSURANCE COMPANY Frontline 8000 [6/97]

	Comparison Query		Comment	Policy Reference
98	FAMILY AND MEDICAL LEAVE ACT	—		
99	DEFAMATION	—		
100	MISREPRESENTATION	—		
101	RETALIATION	●	See also II.O.(4)., page 3	II.P., page 3
102	MENTAL ANGUISH	●		II.J., page 2
103	INVASION OF PRIVACY	—		
104	HUMILIATION	—		
105	EMOTIONAL DISTRESS	●		II.J., page 2
106	OTHER PERSONAL INJURY OFFENSES	—		
107	POLICY SILENT	—		
	14 EXCLUSIONS			
108	**ADA ACCOMMODATION EXPENSES**	●		II.J., page 2
109	**ASSAULT & BATTERY**	—		
110	**BACK PAY**	—		
111	**BODILY INJURY**	●		IV.A., page 4
112	BODILY INJURY	●		IV.A., page 4
113	DEATH	●		IV.A., page 4
114	DISEASE	●		IV.A., page 4
115	SICKNESS	●		IV.A., page 4
116	**BREACH OF EMPLOYMENT CONTRACT**	●		II.J., page 2
117	EXPRESS CONTRACT	●		II.J., page 2
118	*WRITTEN CONTRACT*	—		
119	*ORAL CONTRACT*	—		
120	IMPLIED CONTRACT	—		
121	**CLASS ACTION LAWSUITS**	—		
122	**CONSEQUENTIAL LOSS**	—		
123	APPLIES TO BODILY INJURY	—		
124	APPLIES TO INSURED EVENT	—		
125	BROTHER/SISTER	—		
126	CHILD	—		
127	DOMESTIC PARTNER	—		
128	PARENT	—		
129	SPOUSE	—		
130	**COST OF ARBITRATION HEARINGS SUBJECT TO**	—		
131	EMPLOYMENT HANDBOOK	—		
132	LABOR GRIEVANCE	—		
133	OTHER EMPLOYMENT POLICY OR PROCEDURE	—		
134	**COVERAGE ELSEWHERE**	●		VIII.M., page 10
135	OTHER AVAILABLE INSURANCE	—		
136	OTHER INDEMNIFICATION	—		
137	SHARING PROVISION	●	If other insurance also primary	VIII.M., page 10
138	**FAILURE TO EXERCISE CARE WHEN TERMINATING**	—		
139	**FINES/PENALTIES**	●		II.J., page 2
140	CIVIL	●		II.J., page 2
141	CRIMINAL	●		II.J., page 2
142	EXEMPLARY DAMAGES	—		
143	PUNITIVE DAMAGES	—		
144	MULTIPLIED DAMAGES	—		
145	**FRONT PAY**	—		
146	EXCLUSION APPLIES ONLY IF EMPLOYER HAD OPPORTUNITY TO REINSTATE EMPLOYEE BUT DID NOT DO SO	—		
147	**INTENTIONAL ACTS**			
148	CRIMINAL ACTS	—		
149	CRIMINAL PROCEEDING	—		
150	DISHONEST PURPOSE	—		
151	FRAUDULENT ACTS	—		
152	FRAUDULENT CLAIMS	—		
153	INTENTIONAL VIOLATIONS OF LAW	—		
154	WILLFUL FAILURE TO COMPLY WITH LAW	—		
155	MALICIOUS PURPOSE	—		
156	**LIABILITY OF OTHERS**	●		II.C., page 5
157	**LIQUIDATED DAMAGES**	—		
158	**LOSS ARISING OUT OF CHANGES IN OPERATIONS**	—		
159	ACQUISITION	—		
160	CHANGE IN CONTROL	—		
161	DOWNSIZING OR REDUCTION IN FORCE	—		
162	*% OF WORKFORCE*	—		
163	*WITHIN X DAYS*	—		

GENESIS INSURANCE COMPANY Frontline 8000 [6/97]

#	Comparison Query	Comment		Policy Reference
164	FINANCIAL IMPAIRMENT	—		
165	BANKRUPTCY	—		
166	INSOLVENCY	—		
167	LIQUIDATION	—		
168	RECEIVERSHIP	—		
169	FINANCIAL INABILITY TO PAY	—		
170	MERGER	—		
171	PLANT OR FACILITY CLOSING	—		
172	REORGANIZATION	—		
173	TEMPORARY SHUTDOWN	—		
174	**MATTERS DEEMED UNINSURABLE**	●		II.J., page 2
175	**NON-MONETARY RELIEF**	●		II.J., page 2
176	DECLATORY RELIEF	—		
177	DISGORGEMENT	—		
178	INJUNCTIVE RELIEF	—		
179	JOB REINSTATEMENT	—		
180	NON-MONETARY DAMAGES/RELIEF	●		II.J., page 2
181	OTHER EQUITABLE REMEDIES	—		
182	**OBLIGATION TO PROVIDE BENEFITS**	—		
183	COBRA	●	Exceptions apply	II.B., pages 4–5
184	DISABILITY	—		
185	ERISA	●		IV.B., page 4
186	SOCIAL SECURITY	—		
187	OTHER RETIREMENT BENEFITS	—		
188	UNEMPLOYMENT	—		
189	WORKERS' COMPENSATION	●	Exceptions apply	II.B., pages 4–5
190	**PERSONAL INJURY OFFENSES**	●		II.A., page 4
191	DEFAMATION	●	Unless employment-related	II.A., page 4
192	EMOTIONAL DISTRESS/UPSET	—		
193	HUMILIATION	—		
194	LIBEL	●	Unless employment-related	II.A., page 4
195	MENTAL ANGUISH	—		
196	PERSONAL INJURY	—		
197	SLANDER	●	Unless employment-related	II.A., page 4
198	**PRIOR ACTS**	—		
199	PRIOR ACTS	—		
200	PRIOR KNOWLEDGE	●	Prior notice to insurer	II.E., page 4
201	PRIOR/PENDING LITIGATION	—		
202	**PROPERTY DAMAGE**	●		II.A., page 4
203	INTANGIBLE PROPERTY	—		
204	LOSS OF USE	●		IV.A., page 4
205	TANGIBLE PROPERTY	●		IV.A., page 4
206	**RETALIATORY ACTIONS OF EMPLOYER**	—		
207	FOR FAILING TO PERFORM ACTS AGAINST PUBLIC POLICY	—		
208	FOR FILING A COMPLAINT OR BENEFIT CLAIM	—		
209	**STRIKES/LOCKOUTS**	●		II.F., page 5
210	**VIOLATION OF LAWS**	—		
211	ANY LAW	—		
212	FMLA	—		
213	OSHA	●	Exceptions apply	II.B., pages 4–5
214	POLLUTION LAWS	—		
215	RICO	—		
216	SEC	—		
217	WARN	●	Exceptions apply	II.B., page 4–5

15 CONDITIONS

#	Comparison Query	Comment		Policy Reference
218	**ARBITRATION**	—		
219	MANDATORY	—		
220	BINDING	—		
221	CHOICE OF LAW PROVISION	—		
222	SITUS	—		
223	**TERRITORY**	●		VIII.L., page 10
224	LIMITED	—		
225	WORLDWIDE	●		VIII.L., page 10
226	**NEWLY FORMED/ACQUIRED ENTITIES**	●		VIII.D., page 10
227	AUTOMATIC COVERAGE (X DAYS)	—		
228	NOTIFY INSURER WITHIN X DAYS	60		VIII.D., page 10

GENESIS INSURANCE COMPANY Frontline 8000 [6/97]

Policy Comparison Worksheet

Great American Insurance Companies

Policy Form No.: D.710-35
Edition Date: 11/85

Risks Considered: General accounts
Limits Available: $5,000,000
Minimum Retention: $10,000

Contact: Jeffrey Gauthier
Great American Insurance Companies
1515 Woodfield Road, Suite 850
Schaumberg, IL 60173
847/330-6750
847/330-6890 (fax)
gaiceld@megsinet.net

KEY TO SYMBOLS
● = Specifically contains queried provision of feature
○ = Unable to determine
— = Silent

#	Comparison Query		Comment	Policy Reference
1	**APPLICATION**			
1	ATTACHES TO AND FORMS A PART OF THE POLICY	●		Policy, VIII.B., page 4
2	CONTAINS WARRANTY STATEMENTS	—		
3	CONTAINS SEVERABILITY PROVISIONS	—		
2	**POLICY TYPE**			
4	UNITARY STAND ALONE POLICY	—		
	ENDORSEMENT OR PART OF			
5	DIRECTORS AND OFFICERS POLICY	●	Policy form D.100A (2/90)	
6	PACKAGE POLICY	—		
7	UMBRELLA POLICY	—		
8	ERRORS AND OMISSIONS POLICY	—		
9	OTHER	—		
10	CLAIMS-MADE	●		
11	OCCURRENCE	—		
3	**WHO IS INSURED**			
12	BUSINESS ENTITY	●		Endorsement, I.B., page 1
13	AUTOMATIC COVERAGE FOR SUBSIDIARIES	●		Policy, III.A., page 2
14	DIRECTORS & OFFICERS	●		Endorsement, I.A., page 1
15	EMPLOYEES	●		Endorsement, 3.A., page 2
16	PART-TIME	—		
17	SEASONAL	—		
18	TEMPORARY	—		
19	SUPERVISORS & MANAGERS	—		
20	FORMER EMPLOYEES	—		
21	VOLUNTEERS	—		
22	INDEPENDENT CONTRACTORS			
23	EXCLUDED	—		
24	SILENT	●		
25	SHAREHOLDERS	—		
4	**LIMIT OF LIABILITY**			
26	AGGREGATE	●		Endorsement, 2.E., page 2
27	INCLUDES PUNITIVE DAMAGES WHERE NOT UNINSURABLE	—		
28	DEFENSE COSTS INCLUDED WITHIN LIMIT OF LIABILITY	●		Endorsement, 2.E., page 2
29	DEFENSE COSTS PAID IN ADDITION TO LIMIT OF LIABILITY	—		
5	**DEDUCTIBLE**			
30	APPLIES TO EACH INDIVIDUAL CLAIM	●		Policy, V.C., page 3
31	APPLIES TO EACH OCCURRENCE OR WRONGFUL PRACTICE	—		
32	INCLUDES ALL CLAIMS FROM ONE ACT	●		Policy, V.B., page 3
33	SUBJECT TO ANNUAL AGGREGATE	—		
34	CO-PAYMENT APPLIES	—		
35	LIMIT OF LIABILITY NOT REDUCED	—		
36	INCLUDES DEFENSE COSTS	●		Policy, V.D., page 3
37	REDUCED UNDER SPECIFIED CIRCUMSTANCES (SEE POLICY)	—		

GREAT AMERICAN INSURANCE COMPANIES D.710-35 [11/85]

#	Comparison Query	Comment	Policy Reference
6	**WHAT IS A CLAIM**		
38	ORAL COMPLAINT TO INSURED	—	
39	WRITTEN COMPLAINT TO INSURED	●	Endorsement, 2.B., page 2
40	COMPLAINT MUST CONTAIN A DEMAND FOR DAMAGES	●	Endorsement, 2.B., page 2
41	COMPLAINT FILED WITH EEOC	●	Endorsement, 2.B., page 2
42	OR SIMILAR STATE AUTHORITY	●	Endorsement, 2.B., page 2
43	AGENCY MUST HAVE POWER TO ADJUDICATE	—	
44	ADMINISTRATIVE PROCEEDING	●	Any proceeding	Endorsement, 2.B., page 2
45	ARBITRATION PROCEEDING	○	Endorsement, 2.B., page 2
46	ANY INCIDENT REPORTED TO INSURER	●	Endorsement, 2.B., page 2
47	SUIT	●	Any proceeding	Endorsement, 2.B., page 2
48	CLAIM DOES NOT INCLUDE ARBITRATION SUBJECT TO	—	
49	COLLECTIVE BARGAINING AGREEMENT	—	
50	EMPLOYEE POLICY OR MANUAL	—	
51	CLAIM NOT DEFINED	—	
7	**CLAIM REPORTING PROVISIONS TO INSURER**		
52	IMMEDIATELY	—	
53	AS SOON AS POSSIBLE	—	
54	AS SOON AS PRACTICABLE	●	Policy, VII.A., page 4
55	WITHIN POLICY PERIOD	●	Policy, VII.A., page 4
56	WITHIN X DAYS OF EXPIRATION		
57	WITHIN X DAYS	90	Policy, VII.A., page 4
8	**EXTENDED REPORTING FEATURES**		
58	ELECTION PERIOD (DAYS)	10	Policy, II.C., page 2
59	ADDITIONAL PREMIUM (% OF ANNUAL PREMIUM)	50	Policy, II.A., page 2
60	ADDITIONAL REPORTING PERIOD (MONTHS)	3	Policy, II.A., page 2
61	NO REINSTATEMENT OF LIMITS	—	
9	**POTENTIAL CLAIM REPORTING PROVISIONS**		
62	NONE (SEE ALSO "CLAIM" ABOVE)	—	
63	INCIDENTS LIKELY TO RESULT IN A CLAIM	●	Policy, VII.B., page 4
10	**DEFENSE PROVISIONS**		
64	AFFIRMATIVE DUTY TO DEFEND	—	
65	NO AFFIRMATIVE DUTY TO DEFEND	●	Policy, VI.B., page 3
66	AFFIRMATIVE ADVANCEMENT PROVISIONS	●	Policy, VI.D., page 3
67	INSURED MUST RETURN ADVANCED AMOUNTS IF NOT COVERED	●	Policy, VI.D., page 3
68	INSURED/INSURER CHOOSES COUNSEL	—	
69	INSURED/INSURER APPROVES COUNSEL	●	Policy, VI.B., page 3
70	INSURED/INSURER CONSULTED IN COUNSEL SELECTION	●	Policy, VI.B., page 3
11	**SETTLEMENT PROVISIONS**		
71	HAMMER CLAUSE	—	
72	CONSULTATION PROVISION	—	
73	CONSENT PROVISION	●	Insurer must consent	Policy, VI.A, page 4
12	**ALLOCATION OF LOSS PROVISIONS**		
74	STIPULATED PROVISIONS	—	
13	**COVERAGES**		
75	DISCRIMINATION	●	Endorsement, 2.A., page 1
76	SPECIFIC ENUMERATED ACTIVITIES	—	
77	PLUS BROAD OMNIBUS WORDING	—	
78	SPECIFIC ENUMERATED CLASSES	—	
79	PLUS BROAD OMNIBUS WORDING	—	
80	AGAINST THIRD PARTIES	—	
81	DISCRIMINATION NOT DEFINED	●	
82	SEXUAL HARASSMENT	●	Endorsement, 2.A., page 1
83	HOSTILE ENVIRONMENT	●	Endorsement, 2.A., page 1
84	QUID-PRO-QUO	●	Endorsement, 2.A., page 1
85	SEXUAL HARASSMENT NOT DEFINED	●	
86	WRONGFUL TERMINATION	●	Endorsement, 2.A., page 1
87	BREACH OF IMPLIED CONTRACT	—	
88	BREACH OF EXPRESS CONTRACT	—	
89	VIOLATION OF PUBLIC POLICY	—	
90	VIOLATION OF GOOD FAITH & FAIR DEALING	—	
91	OBLIGATIONS TO MAKE PAYMENTS	—	
92	CONSTRUCTIVE DISCHARGE	●	Endorsement, 2.A., page 1
93	WRONGFUL TERMINATION NOT DEFINED	●	
94	**OTHER EMPLOYMENT VIOLATIONS/OFFENSES**		
95	WRONGFUL HIRING	●	Endorsement, 2.A., page 1
96	WRONGFUL PROMOTION/DEMOTION	●	Endorsement, 2.A., page 1
97	WRONGFUL EVALUATION/DISCIPLINE	●	Endorsement, 2.A., page 1

GREAT AMERICAN INSURANCE COMPANIES D.710-35 [11/85]

#	Comparison Query	Comment		Policy Reference
98	FAMILY AND MEDICAL LEAVE ACT	—		
99	DEFAMATION	—		
100	MISREPRESENTATION	●		Endorsement, 2.A., page 1
101	RETALIATION	●		Endorsement, 2.A., page 1
102	MENTAL ANGUISH	—		
103	INVASION OF PRIVACY	—		
104	HUMILIATION	—		
105	EMOTIONAL DISTRESS	—		
106	OTHER PERSONAL INJURY OFFENSES	—		
107	POLICY SILENT	—		
	14 EXCLUSIONS			
108	**ADA ACCOMMODATION EXPENSES**	●		Endorsement, 4.B.2., page 3
109	**ASSAULT & BATTERY**	—		
110	**BACK PAY**	—		
111	**BODILY INJURY**			
112	BODILY INJURY	●		Endorsement, 2.C., page 2
113	DEATH	●		Endorsement, 2.C., page 2
114	DISEASE	●		Endorsement, 2.C., page 2
115	SICKNESS	●		Endorsement, 2.C., page 2
116	**BREACH OF EMPLOYMENT CONTRACT**			
117	EXPRESS CONTRACT	—		
118	*WRITTEN CONTRACT*	●	Obligation to pay	Endorsement, 4.B.3., page 3
119	*ORAL CONTRACT*	—		
120	IMPLIED CONTRACT	—		
121	**CLASS ACTION LAWSUITS**	—		
122	**CONSEQUENTIAL LOSS**			
123	APPLIES TO BODILY INJURY	—		
124	APPLIES TO INSURED EVENT	—		
125	BROTHER/SISTER	—		
126	CHILD	—		
127	DOMESTIC PARTNER	—		
128	PARENT	—		
129	SPOUSE	—		
130	**COST OF ARBITRATION HEARINGS SUBJECT TO**			
131	EMPLOYMENT HANDBOOK	—		
132	LABOR GRIEVANCE	—		
133	OTHER EMPLOYMENT POLICY OR PROCEDURE	—		
134	**COVERAGE ELSEWHERE**			
135	OTHER AVAILABLE INSURANCE	●		Policy, IV.E., page 3
136	OTHER INDEMNIFICATION	—		
137	SHARING PROVISION	—		
138	**FAILURE TO EXERCISE CARE WHEN TERMINATING**			
139	**FINES/PENALTIES**	●		Policy, III.E., page 2
140	CIVIL	●		Policy, III.E., page 2
141	CRIMINAL	●		Policy, III.E., page 2
142	EXEMPLARY DAMAGES	●		Policy, III.E., page 2
143	PUNITIVE DAMAGES	●		Policy, III.E., page 2
144	MULTIPLIED DAMAGES	●		Policy, III.E., page 2
145	**FRONT PAY**	—		
146	EXCLUSION APPLIES ONLY IF EMPLOYER HAD OPPORTUNITY TO REINSTATE EMPLOYEE BUT DID NOT DO SO	—		
147	**INTENTIONAL ACTS**			
148	CRIMINAL ACTS	●	If established in fact	Policy, IV.D., page 4
149	CRIMINAL PROCEEDING	—		
150	DISHONEST PURPOSE	●	If established in fact	Policy, IV.D., page 4
151	FRAUDULENT ACTS	●	If established in fact	Policy, IV.D., page 4
152	FRAUDULENT CLAIMS	—		
153	INTENTIONAL VIOLATIONS OF LAW	—		
154	WILLFUL FAILURE TO COMPLY WITH LAW	—		
155	MALICIOUS PURPOSE	—		
156	**LIABILITY OF OTHERS**	—		
157	**LIQUIDATED DAMAGES**	—		
158	**LOSS ARISING OUT OF CHANGES IN OPERATIONS**			
159	ACQUISITION	—		
160	CHANGE IN CONTROL	—		
161	DOWNSIZING OR REDUCTION IN FORCE			
162	*% OF WORKFORCE*	—		
163	*WITHIN X DAYS*	—		

#	Comparison Query	Comment		Policy Reference
164	FINANCIAL IMPAIRMENT	—		
165	*BANKRUPTCY*	—		
166	*INSOLVENCY*	—		
167	*LIQUIDATION*	—		
168	*RECEIVERSHIP*	—		
169	FINANCIAL INABILITY TO PAY	—		
170	MERGER	—		
171	PLANT OR FACILITY CLOSING	—		
172	REORGANIZATION	—		
173	TEMPORARY SHUTDOWN	—		
174	**MATTERS DEEMED UNINSURABLE**	●		Policy, III.E., page 2
175	**NON-MONETARY RELIEF**			
176	DECLATORY RELIEF	—		
177	DISGORGEMENT	—		
178	INJUNCTIVE RELIEF	—		
179	JOB REINSTATEMENT	—		
180	NON-MONETARY DAMAGES/RELIEF	●		Endorsement, 4.B.1., page 3
181	OTHER EQUITABLE REMEDIES	—		
182	**OBLIGATION TO PROVIDE BENEFITS**			
183	COBRA	●		Endorsement, 4.B.1., page 3
184	DISABILITY	—		
185	ERISA	●		Endorsement, 4.B., following 3., page 3
186	SOCIAL SECURITY	—		
187	OTHER RETIREMENT BENEFITS	—		
188	UNEMPLOYMENT	—		
189	WORKERS' COMPENSATION	—		
190	**PERSONAL INJURY OFFENSES**			
191	DEFAMATION	—		
192	EMOTIONAL DISTRESS/UPSET	—		
193	HUMILIATION	—		
194	LIBEL	—		
195	MENTAL ANGUISH	—		
196	PERSONAL INJURY	—		
197	SLANDER	—		
198	**PRIOR ACTS**			
199	PRIOR ACTS	—		
200	PRIOR KNOWLEDGE	—		
201	PRIOR/PENDING LITIGATION	—		
202	**PROPERTY DAMAGE**			
203	INTANGIBLE PROPERTY	—		
204	LOSS OF USE	●		Endorsement, 2.C., page 2
205	TANGIBLE PROPERTY	●		Endorsement, 2.C., page 2
206	**RETALIATORY ACTIONS OF EMPLOYER**	—		
207	FOR FAILING TO PERFORM ACTS AGAINST PUBLIC POLICY	—		
208	FOR FILING A COMPLAINT OR BENEFIT CLAIM	—		
209	**STRIKES/LOCKOUTS**	—		
210	**VIOLATION OF LAWS**			
211	ANY LAW	—		
212	FMLA	—		
213	OSHA	●		Endorsement, 4.B.1., page 3
214	POLLUTION LAWS	●		Policy, IV.J., page 3
215	RICO	—		
216	SEC	—		
217	WARN	●		Endorsement, 4.B.1., page 3
	15 CONDITIONS			
218	**ARBITRATION**			
219	MANDATORY	—		
220	BINDING	—		
221	CHOICE OF LAW PROVISION	—		
222	SITUS			
223	**TERRITORY**			
224	LIMITED	—		
225	WORLDWIDE	—		
226	**NEWLY FORMED/ACQUIRED ENTITIES**			
227	AUTOMATIC COVERAGE (X DAYS)	●	No time limit—subsidiaries	Policy, III.C., page 2
228	NOTIFY INSURER WITHIN X DAYS	90	Subsidiaries	Policy, III.C., page 2

GREAT AMERICAN INSURANCE COMPANIES D.710-35 [11/85]

Policy Comparison Worksheet

Great American Insurance Companies

Policy Form No.: D.9100
Edition Date: 6/97

Risks Considered: Non-profit organizations/associations
Limits Available: $5,000,000
Minimum Retention: $500

Contact: Todd Weber
Great American Insurance Companies
1515 Woodfield Road, Suite 850
Schaumberg, IL 60173
847/330-6750
847/330-6890 (fax)
gaiceld@megsinet.net

KEY TO SYMBOLS
● = Specifically contains queried provision of feature
○ = Unable to determine
— = Silent

#	Comparison Query		Comment	Policy Reference
	1 APPLICATION			
1	ATTACHES TO AND FORMS A PART OF THE POLICY	●		VIII.B., page 4
2	CONTAINS WARRANTY STATEMENTS	—		
3	CONTAINS SEVERABILITY PROVISIONS	—		
	2 POLICY TYPE			
4	UNITARY STAND ALONE POLICY	●		
	ENDORSEMENT OR PART OF			
5	DIRECTORS AND OFFICERS POLICY	—		
6	PACKAGE POLICY	—		
7	UMBRELLA POLICY	—		
8	ERRORS AND OMISSIONS POLICY	—		
9	OTHER	—		
10	CLAIMS-MADE	●		
11	OCCURRENCE	—		
	3 WHO IS INSURED			
12	BUSINESS ENTITY	●		III.B., page 2
13	AUTOMATIC COVERAGE FOR SUBSIDIARIES	●		III.B., page 2
14	DIRECTORS & OFFICERS	●		IIII.C., page 2
15	EMPLOYEES	●		IIII.C., page 2
16	PART-TIME	—		
17	SEASONAL	—		
18	TEMPORARY	—		
19	SUPERVISORS & MANAGERS	—		
20	FORMER EMPLOYEES	●		IIII.C., page 2
21	VOLUNTEERS	●		IIII.C., page 2
22	INDEPENDENT CONTRACTORS			
23	EXCLUDED	—		
24	SILENT	●		IIII.C., page 2
25	SHAREHOLDERS			
	4 LIMIT OF LIABILITY			
26	AGGREGATE	●		V.A., page 3
27	INCLUDES PUNITIVE DAMAGES WHERE NOT UNINSURABLE	—		
28	DEFENSE COSTS INCLUDED WITHIN LIMIT OF LIABILITY	●	If incurred by insured	V.C., page 3
29	DEFENSE COSTS PAID IN ADDITION TO LIMIT OF LIABILITY	●	If incurred by insurer	V.C., page 3
	5 DEDUCTIBLE			
30	APPLIES TO EACH INDIVIDUAL CLAIM	●		V.B., page 3
31	APPLIES TO EACH OCCURRENCE OR WRONGFUL PRACTICE	●		V.B., page 3
32	INCLUDES ALL CLAIMS FROM ONE ACT	●		V.B., page 3
33	SUBJECT TO ANNUAL AGGREGATE	—		
34	CO-PAYMENT APPLIES	—		
35	LIMIT OF LIABILITY NOT REDUCED			
36	INCLUDES DEFENSE COSTS	●	If incurred by insured	V.C., page 3
37	REDUCED UNDER SPECIFIED CIRCUMSTANCES (SEE POLICY)	—		

GREAT AMERICAN INSURANCE COMPANIES D.9100 [6/97]

#	Comparison Query	Comment	Policy Reference
	6 WHAT IS A CLAIM		
38	ORAL COMPLAINT TO INSURED	—	
39	WRITTEN COMPLAINT TO INSURED	●	II.K., page 2
40	COMPLAINT MUST CONTAIN A DEMAND FOR DAMAGES	●	Money damages	II.K., page 2
41	COMPLAINT FILED WITH EEOC	●		II.K., page 2
42	OR SIMILAR STATE AUTHORITY	●		II.K., page 2
43	AGENCY MUST HAVE POWER TO ADJUDICATE	—	
44	ADMINISTRATIVE PROCEEDING	●	Any proceeding	II.K., page 2
45	ARBITRATION PROCEEDING	○	Any proceeding	
46	ANY INCIDENT REPORTED TO INSURER	—	
47	SUIT	●	Any proceeding	
48	CLAIM DOES NOT INCLUDE ARBITRATION SUBJECT TO		
49	COLLECTIVE BARGAINING AGREEMENT	—	
50	EMPLOYEE POLICY OR MANUAL	—	
51	CLAIM NOT DEFINED	—	
	7 CLAIM REPORTING PROVISIONS TO INSURER		
52	IMMEDIATELY	—	
53	AS SOON AS POSSIBLE	—	
54	AS SOON AS PRACTICABLE	●		VII.A., page 3
55	WITHIN POLICY PERIOD	—	
56	WITHIN X DAYS OF EXPIRATION	—	
57	WITHIN X DAYS	—	
	8 EXTENDED REPORTING FEATURES		
58	ELECTION PERIOD (DAYS)	90		II.B., page 2
59	ADDITIONAL PREMIUM (% OF ANNUAL PREMIUM)	40		II.B., page 2
60	ADDITIONAL REPORTING PERIOD (MONTHS)	12		II.B., page 2
61	NO REINSTATEMENT OF LIMITS	●		II.E., page 2
	9 POTENTIAL CLAIM REPORTING PROVISIONS		
62	NONE (SEE ALSO "CLAIM" ABOVE)	—	
63	INCIDENTS LIKELY TO RESULT IN A CLAIM	●		VII.B., page 3
	10 DEFENSE PROVISIONS		
64	AFFIRMATIVE DUTY TO DEFEND	●		I., page 2
65	NO AFFIRMATIVE DUTY TO DEFEND	—	
66	AFFIRMATIVE ADVANCEMENT PROVISIONS	—	
67	INSURED MUST RETURN ADVANCED AMOUNTS IF NOT COVERED	—	
68	INSURED/INSURER CHOOSES COUNSEL	—	
69	INSURED/INSURER APPROVES COUNSEL	—	
70	INSURED/INSURER CONSULTED IN COUNSEL SELECTION	—	
	11 SETTLEMENT PROVISIONS		
71	HAMMER CLAUSE	●		VI.B., page 3
72	CONSULTATION PROVISION	—	
73	CONSENT PROVISION	●	Insurer must consent	VI.A., page 3
	12 ALLOCATION OF LOSS PROVISIONS		
74	STIPULATED PROVISIONS	—	
	13 COVERAGES		
75	DISCRIMINATION	●		III.F., page 2
76	SPECIFIC ENUMERATED ACTIVITIES	—	
77	*PLUS BROAD OMNIBUS WORDING*	—	
78	SPECIFIC ENUMERATED CLASSES	—	
79	*PLUS BROAD OMNIBUS WORDING*	—	
80	AGAINST THIRD PARTIES	—	
81	DISCRIMINATION NOT DEFINED	●	
82	SEXUAL HARASSMENT	●		III.F., page 2
83	HOSTILE ENVIRONMENT	●	Any kind	III.F., page 2
84	QUID-PRO-QUO	●	Any kind	III.F., page 2
85	SEXUAL HARASSMENT NOT DEFINED	●	
86	WRONGFUL TERMINATION	●		III.F., page 2
87	BREACH OF IMPLIED CONTRACT	—	
88	BREACH OF EXPRESS CONTRACT	—	
89	VIOLATION OF PUBLIC POLICY	—	
90	VIOLATION OF GOOD FAITH & FAIR DEALING	—	
91	OBLIGATIONS TO MAKE PAYMENTS	—	
92	CONSTRUCTIVE DISCHARGE	●		III.F., page 2
93	WRONGFUL TERMINATION NOT DEFINED	●	
94	OTHER EMPLOYMENT VIOLATIONS/OFFENSES		
95	WRONGFUL HIRING	●		III.F., page 2
96	WRONGFUL PROMOTION/DEMOTION	●		III.F., page 2
97	WRONGFUL EVALUATION/DISCIPLINE	●		III.F., page 2

GREAT AMERICAN INSURANCE COMPANIES D.9100 [6/97]

#	Comparison Query	Comment		Policy Reference
98	FAMILY AND MEDICAL LEAVE ACT	—		
99	DEFAMATION	—		
100	MISREPRESENTATION	●		III.F., page 2
101	RETALIATION	●		III.F., page 2
102	MENTAL ANGUISH	●		IV.D., page 3
103	INVASION OF PRIVACY	●	Wrongful entry	IV.D., page 3
104	HUMILIATION	—		
105	EMOTIONAL DISTRESS	●		IV.D., page 3
106	OTHER PERSONAL INJURY OFFENSES	●		IV.D., page 3
107	POLICY SILENT			

14 EXCLUSIONS

#	Comparison Query	Comment		Policy Reference
108	**ADA ACCOMMODATION EXPENSES**	●		IV.J., page 3
109	**ASSAULT & BATTERY**	●		IV.D., page 3
110	**BACK PAY**	—		
111	**BODILY INJURY**	●		IV.D., page 3
112	BODILY INJURY	●		IV.D., page 3
113	DEATH	●		IV.D., page 3
114	DISEASE	●		IV.D., page 3
115	SICKNESS	●		IV.D., page 3
116	**BREACH OF EMPLOYMENT CONTRACT**			
117	EXPRESS CONTRACT	—		
118	WRITTEN CONTRACT	—		
119	ORAL CONTRACT	—		
120	IMPLIED CONTRACT	—		
121	**CLASS ACTION LAWSUITS**	—		
122	**CONSEQUENTIAL LOSS**			
123	APPLIES TO BODILY INJURY	—		
124	APPLIES TO INSURED EVENT	—		
125	BROTHER/SISTER	—		
126	CHILD	—		
127	DOMESTIC PARTNER	—		
128	PARENT	—		
129	SPOUSE	—		
130	**COST OF ARBITRATION HEARINGS SUBJECT TO**			
131	EMPLOYMENT HANDBOOK	—		
132	LABOR GRIEVANCE	—		
133	OTHER EMPLOYMENT POLICY OR PROCEDURE	—		
134	**COVERAGE ELSEWHERE**			
135	OTHER AVAILABLE INSURANCE	●		IV.B., page 3
136	OTHER INDEMNIFICATION	—		
137	SHARING PROVISION	—		
138	**FAILURE TO EXERCISE CARE WHEN TERMINATING**	—		
139	**FINES/PENALTIES**	●		II.G., page 2
140	CIVIL	●		II.G., page 2
141	CRIMINAL	●		II.G., page 2
142	EXEMPLARY DAMAGES	●		II.G., page 2
143	PUNITIVE DAMAGES	●		II.G., page 2
144	MULTIPLIED DAMAGES	●		II.G., page 2
145	**FRONT PAY**	—		
146	EXCLUSION APPLIES ONLY IF EMPLOYER HAD OPPORTUNITY TO REINSTATE EMPLOYEE BUT DID NOT DO SO	—		
147	**INTENTIONAL ACTS**			
148	CRIMINAL ACTS	●	Non-imputation	IV.A., page 3
149	CRIMINAL PROCEEDING	—		
150	DISHONEST PURPOSE	●	Non-imputation	IV.A., page 3
151	FRAUDULENT ACTS	●	Non-imputation	IV.A., page 3
152	FRAUDULENT CLAIMS	—		
153	INTENTIONAL VIOLATIONS OF LAW	—		
154	WILLFUL FAILURE TO COMPLY WITH LAW	—		
155	MALICIOUS PURPOSE	—		
156	**LIABILITY OF OTHERS**	●		IV.I., page 3
157	**LIQUIDATED DAMAGES**	—		
158	**LOSS ARISING OUT OF CHANGES IN OPERATIONS**			
159	ACQUISITION	—		
160	CHANGE IN CONTROL	—		
161	DOWNSIZING OR REDUCTION IN FORCE	—		
162	% OF WORKFORCE	—		
163	WITHIN X DAYS	—		

#	Comparison Query	Comment	Policy Reference
164	FINANCIAL IMPAIRMENT	—	
165	*BANKRUPTCY*	—	
166	*INSOLVENCY*	—	
167	*LIQUIDATION*	—	
168	*RECEIVERSHIP*	—	
169	FINANCIAL INABILITY TO PAY	—	
170	MERGER	—	
171	PLANT OR FACILITY CLOSING	—	
172	REORGANIZATION	—	
173	TEMPORARY SHUTDOWN	—	
174	**MATTERS DEEMED UNINSURABLE**	●	II.G., page 2
175	**NON-MONETARY RELIEF**		
176	DECLATORY RELIEF	—	
177	DISGORGEMENT	—	
178	INJUNCTIVE RELIEF	—	
179	JOB REINSTATEMENT	—	
180	NON-MONETARY DAMAGES/RELIEF	—	
181	OTHER EQUITABLE REMEDIES	—	
182	**OBLIGATION TO PROVIDE BENEFITS**		
183	COBRA	—	
184	DISABILITY	—	
185	ERISA	●	IV.E., page 3
186	SOCIAL SECURITY	—	
187	OTHER RETIREMENT BENEFITS	—	
188	UNEMPLOYMENT	—	
189	WORKERS' COMPENSATION	—	
190	**PERSONAL INJURY OFFENSES**		
191	DEFAMATION	—	
192	EMOTIONAL DISTRESS/UPSET	—	
193	HUMILIATION	—	
194	LIBEL	—	
195	MENTAL ANGUISH	—	
196	PERSONAL INJURY	—	
197	SLANDER	—	
198	**PRIOR ACTS**		
199	PRIOR ACTS	—	
200	PRIOR KNOWLEDGE	—	
201	PRIOR/PENDING LITIGATION	●	IV.C.(2)., page 3
202	**PROPERTY DAMAGE**		
203	INTANGIBLE PROPERTY	—	
204	LOSS OF USE	●	IV.D., page 3
205	TANGIBLE PROPERTY	●	
206	**RETALIATORY ACTIONS OF EMPLOYER**	—	
207	FOR FAILING TO PERFORM ACTS AGAINST PUBLIC POLICY	—	
208	FOR FILING A COMPLAINT OR BENEFIT CLAIM	—	
209	**STRIKES/LOCKOUTS**	—	
210	**VIOLATION OF LAWS**		
211	ANY LAW	—	
212	FMLA	—	
213	OSHA	—	
214	POLLUTION LAWS	●	IV.G., page 3
215	RICO	—	
216	SEC	—	
217	WARN	—	

15 CONDITIONS

#	Comparison Query	Comment	Policy Reference
218	**ARBITRATION**		
219	MANDATORY	—	
220	BINDING	—	
221	CHOICE OF LAW PROVISION	—	
222	SITUS	—	
223	**TERRITORY**		
224	LIMITED	—	
225	WORLDWIDE	—	
226	**NEWLY FORMED/ACQUIRED ENTITIES**		
227	AUTOMATIC COVERAGE (X DAYS)	—	
228	NOTIFY INSURER WITHIN X DAYS	30	VIII.D.(1)., page 4

GREAT AMERICAN INSURANCE COMPANIES D.9100 [6/97]

Policy Comparison Worksheet

Gulf Insurance Group
(Rockwood Programs)

Policy Form No.: RP 8002g
Edition Date: 11/97

Risks Considered: All except employee leasing firms and financial institutions
Limits Available: $5,000,000
Minimum Retention: $2,500

Contact: Darryl McCallin
Rockwood Programs, Inc.
228 Philadelphia Pike
Wilmington, DE 19809
800/558-8808
darryl_mccallin@blanca.com (e-mail)

KEY TO SYMBOLS
● = Specifically contains queried provision of feature
○ = Unable to determine
— = Silent

#	Comparison Query	Symbol	Comment	Policy Reference
	1 APPLICATION			
1	ATTACHES TO AND FORMS A PART OF THE POLICY	●		Application, V., page 2
2	CONTAINS WARRANTY STATEMENTS	●		VI.L.1., page 7
3	CONTAINS SEVERABILITY PROVISIONS	—		
	2 POLICY TYPE			
4	UNITARY STAND ALONE POLICY	●		
	ENDORSEMENT OR PART OF	—		
5	DIRECTORS AND OFFICERS POLICY	—		
6	PACKAGE POLICY	—		
7	UMBRELLA POLICY	—		
8	ERRORS AND OMISSIONS POLICY	—		
9	OTHER	—		
10	CLAIMS-MADE	●		
11	OCCURRENCE	—		
	3 WHO IS INSURED			
12	BUSINESS ENTITY	●		III.B., page 3
13	AUTOMATIC COVERAGE FOR SUBSIDIARIES	●		III.D., page 3
14	DIRECTORS & OFFICERS	●	Directors only	III.F., page 4
15	EMPLOYEES	●		III.F., page 4
16	PART-TIME	●		VIII.D., page 9
17	SEASONAL	●		VIII.D., page 9
18	TEMPORARY	●		VIII.D., page 9
19	SUPERVISORS & MANAGERS	—		
20	FORMER EMPLOYEES	—		
21	VOLUNTEERS	—		
22	INDEPENDENT CONTRACTORS	—		
23	EXCLUDED	●		VIII.D., page 9
24	SILENT	—		
25	SHAREHOLDERS	●		III.B., page 3
	4 LIMIT OF LIABILITY			
26	AGGREGATE	●		IV.B., page 4
27	INCLUDES PUNITIVE DAMAGES WHERE NOT UNINSURABLE	—		
28	DEFENSE COSTS INCLUDED WITHIN LIMIT OF LIABILITY	●		I.A.2.e)., page 2
29	DEFENSE COSTS PAID IN ADDITION TO LIMIT OF LIABILITY	—		
	5 DEDUCTIBLE			
30	APPLIES TO EACH INDIVIDUAL CLAIM	—		
31	APPLIES TO EACH OCCURRENCE OR WRONGFUL PRACTICE	●		V., page 4
32	INCLUDES ALL CLAIMS FROM ONE ACT	●		IV.D., page 4
33	SUBJECT TO ANNUAL AGGREGATE	—		
34	CO-PAYMENT APPLIES	—	Available by endorsement	
35	LIMIT OF LIABILITY NOT REDUCED	—		
36	INCLUDES DEFENSE COSTS	●	See also V., page 4	Preamble, page 1
37	REDUCED UNDER SPECIFIED CIRCUMSTANCES (SEE POLICY)	—		

GULF INSURANCE GROUP (ROCKWOOD PROGRAMS, INC.) RP 8002g [11/97]

#	Comparison Query	Comment	Policy Reference
	6 WHAT IS A CLAIM		
38	ORAL COMPLAINT TO INSURED	—	
39	WRITTEN COMPLAINT TO INSURED	●	VIII.B.1., page 8
40	COMPLAINT MUST CONTAIN A DEMAND FOR DAMAGES	●	Demand for monetary loss	VIII.B.1., page 8
41	COMPLAINT FILED WITH EEOC	—	
42	OR SIMILAR STATE AUTHORITY	—	
43	AGENCY MUST HAVE POWER TO ADJUDICATE	—	
44	ADMINISTRATIVE PROCEEDING	●	VIII.B.2., page 8
45	ARBITRATION PROCEEDING	●	VIII.B.4., page 8
46	ANY INCIDENT REPORTED TO INSURER	—	
47	SUIT	●	As civil proceeding	VIII.B.2., page 8
48	CLAIM DOES NOT INCLUDE ARBITRATION SUBJECT TO	—	
49	COLLECTIVE BARGAINING AGREEMENT	—	
50	EMPLOYEE POLICY OR MANUAL	—	
51	CLAIM NOT DEFINED	—	
	7 CLAIM REPORTING PROVISIONS TO INSURER		
52	IMMEDIATELY	—	
53	AS SOON AS POSSIBLE	—	
54	AS SOON AS PRACTICABLE	●	VI.D.3., page 5
55	WITHIN POLICY PERIOD	—	
56	WITHIN X DAYS OF EXPIRATION	—	
57	WITHIN X DAYS	—	
	8 EXTENDED REPORTING FEATURES		
58	ELECTION PERIOD (DAYS)	60	VI.G.3., page 6
59	ADDITIONAL PREMIUM (% OF ANNUAL PREMIUM)	200	VI.G.2., page 6
60	ADDITIONAL REPORTING PERIOD (MONTHS)	36	VI.G.1., page 6
61	NO REINSTATEMENT OF LIMITS	●	VI.G.4., page 6
	9 POTENTIAL CLAIM REPORTING PROVISIONS		
62	NONE (SEE ALSO "CLAIM" ABOVE)	—	
63	INCIDENTS LIKELY TO RESULT IN A CLAIM	●	VI.D.1., page 5
	10 DEFENSE PROVISIONS		
64	AFFIRMATIVE DUTY TO DEFEND	●	I.A.2.a)., page 1
65	NO AFFIRMATIVE DUTY TO DEFEND	—	
66	AFFIRMATIVE ADVANCEMENT PROVISIONS	—	
67	INSURED MUST RETURN ADVANCED AMOUNTS IF NOT COVERED	—	
68	INSURED/INSURER CHOOSES COUNSEL	●	Insurer chooses	I.A.2.a)., page 1
69	INSURED/INSURER APPROVES COUNSEL	—	
70	INSURED/INSURER CONSULTED IN COUNSEL SELECTION	—	
	11 SETTLEMENT PROVISIONS		
71	HAMMER CLAUSE	—	
72	CONSULTATION PROVISION	—	
73	CONSENT PROVISION	—	
	12 ALLOCATION OF LOSS PROVISIONS		
74	STIPULATED PROVISIONS	—	
	13 COVERAGES		
75	DISCRIMINATION	●	VIII.L.1., page 9
76	SPECIFIC ENUMERATED ACTIVITIES	●	VIII.C., pages 8–9
77	*PLUS BROAD OMNIBUS WORDING*	●	VIII.C., pages 8–9
78	SPECIFIC ENUMERATED CLASSES	●	VIII.C., pages 8–9
79	*PLUS BROAD OMNIBUS WORDING*	●	VIII.C., pages 8–9
80	AGAINST THIRD PARTIES	—	
81	DISCRIMINATION NOT DEFINED	—	
82	SEXUAL HARASSMENT	●	VIII.L.2., page 9
83	HOSTILE ENVIRONMENT	●	VIII.E., page 9
84	QUID-PRO-QUO	●	VIII.E., page 9
85	SEXUAL HARASSMENT NOT DEFINED	—	
86	WRONGFUL TERMINATION	●	VIII.L.3., page 9
87	BREACH OF IMPLIED CONTRACT	●	VIII.M., page 9
88	BREACH OF EXPRESS CONTRACT	—	
89	VIOLATION OF PUBLIC POLICY	—	
90	VIOLATION OF GOOD FAITH & FAIR DEALING	—	
91	OBLIGATIONS TO MAKE PAYMENTS	—	
92	CONSTRUCTIVE DISCHARGE	●	III.M., page 9
93	WRONGFUL TERMINATION NOT DEFINED	—	
94	OTHER EMPLOYMENT VIOLATIONS/OFFENSES	—	
95	WRONGFUL HIRING	—	
96	WRONGFUL PROMOTION/DEMOTION	—	
97	WRONGFUL EVALUATION/DISCIPLINE	●	As wrongful employment act	VIII.L, page 9

GULF INSURANCE GROUP (ROCKWOOD PROGRAMS, INC.) RP 8002g [11/97]

	Comparison Query		Comment	Policy Reference
98	FAMILY AND MEDICAL LEAVE ACT	—		
99	DEFAMATION	●	As wrongful employment act	VIII.L., page 9
100	MISREPRESENTATION	●	As wrongful employment act	VIII.L., page 9
101	RETALIATION	—		
102	MENTAL ANGUISH	●		II.B., page 2
103	INVASION OF PRIVACY	●	As wrongful employment act	VIII.L., page 9
104	HUMILIATION	●		II.B., page 2
105	EMOTIONAL DISTRESS	●		II.B., page 2
106	OTHER PERSONAL INJURY OFFENSES	—		
107	POLICY SILENT	—		
14 EXCLUSIONS				
108	**ADA ACCOMMODATION EXPENSES**	●		II.G., page 3
109	**ASSAULT & BATTERY**	—		
110	**BACK PAY**	—		
111	**BODILY INJURY**	●		II.B., page 2
112	BODILY INJURY	●		II.B., page 2
113	DEATH	●		VIII.A., page 8
114	DISEASE	●		VIII.A., page 8
115	SICKNESS	●		VIII.A., page 8
116	**BREACH OF EMPLOYMENT CONTRACT**	●		II.M., page 3
117	EXPRESS CONTRACT	—		
118	*WRITTEN CONTRACT*	●		II.M., page 3
119	*ORAL CONTRACT*	—		
120	IMPLIED CONTRACT	—		
121	**CLASS ACTION LAWSUITS**	—		
122	**CONSEQUENTIAL LOSS**	—		
123	APPLIES TO BODILY INJURY	—		
124	APPLIES TO INSURED EVENT	—		
125	BROTHER/SISTER	—		
126	CHILD	—		
127	DOMESTIC PARTNER	—		
128	PARENT	—		
129	SPOUSE	—		
130	**COST OF ARBITRATION HEARINGS SUBJECT TO**	—		
131	EMPLOYMENT HANDBOOK	—		
132	LABOR GRIEVANCE	—		
133	OTHER EMPLOYMENT POLICY OR PROCEDURE	—		
134	**COVERAGE ELSEWHERE**	—		
135	OTHER AVAILABLE INSURANCE	—		
136	OTHER INDEMNIFICATION	—		
137	SHARING PROVISION	●		VI.I. & J., page 7
138	**FAILURE TO EXERCISE CARE WHEN TERMINATING**	—		
139	**FINES/PENALTIES**	●		II.K., page 3
140	CIVIL	—		
141	CRIMINAL	—		
142	EXEMPLARY DAMAGES	●	Coverage available by endorsement	II.K., page 3
143	PUNITIVE DAMAGES	●	Coverage available by endorsement	II.K., page 3
144	MULTIPLIED DAMAGES	●		II.K., page 3
145	**FRONT PAY**	—		
146	EXCLUSION APPLIES ONLY IF EMPLOYER HAD OPPORTUNITY TO REINSTATE EMPLOYEE BUT DID NOT DO SO	—		
147	**INTENTIONAL ACTS**	●	Non-imputation of liability	II.I., page 3
148	CRIMINAL ACTS	●	Non-imputation of liability	II.I., page 3
149	CRIMINAL PROCEEDING	—		
150	DISHONEST PURPOSE	●	Non-imputation of liability	II.I., page 3
151	FRAUDULENT ACTS	●	Non-imputation of liability	II.I., page 3
152	FRAUDULENT CLAIMS	—		
153	INTENTIONAL VIOLATIONS OF LAW	—		
154	WILLFUL FAILURE TO COMPLY WITH LAW	●	Defense cost exception	II.D., page 2
155	MALICIOUS PURPOSE	●	Non-imputation of liability	II.I., page 3
156	**LIABILITY OF OTHERS**	●		II.E., page 2
157	**LIQUIDATED DAMAGES**	—		
158	**LOSS ARISING OUT OF CHANGES IN OPERATIONS**	—		
159	ACQUISITION	—		
160	CHANGE IN CONTROL	—		
161	DOWNSIZING OR REDUCTION IN FORCE	—	Excludable by endorsement	
162	*% OF WORKFORCE*	—	Excludable by endorsement	
163	*WITHIN X DAYS*	—	Excludable by endorsement	

GULF INSURANCE GROUP (ROCKWOOD PROGRAMS, INC.) RP 8002g [11/97]

	Comparison Query	Comment		Policy Reference
164	FINANCIAL IMPAIRMENT	—		
165	BANKRUPTCY	—		
166	INSOLVENCY	—		
167	LIQUIDATION	—		
168	RECEIVERSHIP	—		
169	FINANCIAL INABILITY TO PAY	—		
170	MERGER	—		
171	PLANT OR FACILITY CLOSING	—	Excludable by endorsement	
172	REORGANIZATION	—		
173	TEMPORARY SHUTDOWN	—		
174	**MATTERS DEEMED UNINSURABLE**	—		
175	**NON-MONETARY RELIEF**	●		II.J., page 3
176	DECLATORY RELIEF	●		II.J., page 3
177	DISGORGEMENT	●		II.J., page 3
178	INJUNCTIVE RELIEF	●		II.J., page 3
179	JOB REINSTATEMENT	●		II.J., page 3
180	NON-MONETARY DAMAGES/RELIEF	●		II.J., page 3
181	OTHER EQUITABLE REMEDIES	●		II.J., page 3
182	**OBLIGATION TO PROVIDE BENEFITS**	—		
183	COBRA	●		II.F., page 3
184	DISABILITY	●		II.C., page 2
185	ERISA	●		II.F., page 3
186	SOCIAL SECURITY	●		II.C., page 2
187	OTHER RETIREMENT BENEFITS	—		
188	UNEMPLOYMENT	●		II.C., page 2
189	WORKERS' COMPENSATION	●		II.C., page 2
190	**PERSONAL INJURY OFFENSES**	—		
191	DEFAMATION	—		
192	EMOTIONAL DISTRESS/UPSET	—		
193	HUMILIATION	—		
194	LIBEL	—		
195	MENTAL ANGUISH	—		
196	PERSONAL INJURY	—		
197	SLANDER	—		
198	**PRIOR ACTS**	—		
199	PRIOR ACTS	●		I.A.1., page 1
200	PRIOR KNOWLEDGE	●		II.L., page 3
201	PRIOR/PENDING LITIGATION	—		
202	**PROPERTY DAMAGE**	●		II.A., page 2
203	INTANGIBLE PROPERTY	—		
204	LOSS OF USE	●		VIII.I., page 9
205	TANGIBLE PROPERTY	●		VIII.I., page 9
206	**RETALIATORY ACTIONS OF EMPLOYER**	—		
207	FOR FAILING TO PERFORM ACTS AGAINST PUBLIC POLICY	—		
208	FOR FILING A COMPLAINT OR BENEFIT CLAIM	—		
209	**STRIKES/LOCKOUTS**	●		II.H., page 3
210	**VIOLATION OF LAWS**	—		
211	ANY LAW	—		
212	FMLA	—		
213	OSHA	—		
214	POLLUTION LAWS	—		
215	RICO	—		
216	SEC	—		
217	WARN	●		II.F., page 3
	15 CONDITIONS			
218	**ARBITRATION**	●		VI.A., pages 4–5
219	MANDATORY	●		VI.A., pages 4–5
220	BINDING	●		VI.A., pages 4–5
221	CHOICE OF LAW PROVISION	—		
222	SITUS	—		
223	**TERRITORY**	●		I.A.3., page 2
224	LIMITED	—		
225	WORLDWIDE	●		I.A.3., page 2
226	**NEWLY FORMED/ACQUIRED ENTITIES**	●		III.E., page 4
227	AUTOMATIC COVERAGE (X DAYS)	90		III.E., page 4
228	NOTIFY INSURER WITHIN X DAYS	—		

Policy Comparison Worksheet

Hartford Insurance Companies

Policy Form No.: HC 00 55 03 96
Edition Date: 3/96

Contact: Hartford Insurance Co.
Regional Underwriters

Risks Considered: Small and medium-size businesses
Limits Available: $250,000 each claim
$500,000 aggregate
Minimum Retention: $3,000 each claim

KEY TO SYMBOLS
● = Specifically contains queried provision of feature
○ = Unable to determine
— = Silent

#	Comparison Query		Comment	Policy Reference
	1 APPLICATION			
1	ATTACHES TO AND FORMS A PART OF THE POLICY	—		
2	CONTAINS WARRANTY STATEMENTS	—		
3	CONTAINS SEVERABILITY PROVISIONS	●		IV.8., page 6
	2 POLICY TYPE			
4	UNITARY STAND ALONE POLICY	—		
	ENDORSEMENT OR PART OF	●		
5	DIRECTORS AND OFFICERS POLICY	—		
6	PACKAGE POLICY	●		
7	UMBRELLA POLICY	—		
8	ERRORS AND OMISSIONS POLICY	—		
9	OTHER	—		
10	CLAIMS-MADE	●		
11	OCCURRENCE	—		
	3 WHO IS INSURED			
12	BUSINESS ENTITY	●		II.1.d., page 3
13	AUTOMATIC COVERAGE FOR SUBSIDIARIES	—		
14	DIRECTORS & OFFICERS	●		II.1.d., page 3
15	EMPLOYEES	●		II.2.a., page 3
16	PART-TIME	—		
17	SEASONAL	—		
18	TEMPORARY	—		
19	SUPERVISORS & MANAGERS	●	As employees	II.2.a., page 3
20	FORMER EMPLOYEES	—		
21	VOLUNTEERS	—		
22	INDEPENDENT CONTRACTORS	—		
23	EXCLUDED	●		VI.7., page 8
24	SILENT	—		
25	SHAREHOLDERS	●		II.1.d., page 3
	4 LIMIT OF LIABILITY			
26	AGGREGATE	●		III.1.b., page 4
27	INCLUDES PUNITIVE DAMAGES WHERE NOT UNINSURABLE	—		
28	DEFENSE COSTS INCLUDED WITHIN LIMIT OF LIABILITY	●	See also III.1.c., page 4	I.1.a., page 1
29	DEFENSE COSTS PAID IN ADDITION TO LIMIT OF LIABILITY	—		
	5 DEDUCTIBLE			
30	APPLIES TO EACH INDIVIDUAL CLAIM	●		III.2.b., page 4
31	APPLIES TO EACH OCCURRENCE OR WRONGFUL PRACTICE	●		I.1.d., page 2
32	INCLUDES ALL CLAIMS FROM ONE ACT	●		I.1.d., page 2
33	SUBJECT TO ANNUAL AGGREGATE	—		
34	CO-PAYMENT APPLIES	—		
35	LIMIT OF LIABILITY NOT REDUCED	●		III.1.c., page 4
36	INCLUDES DEFENSE COSTS	●		III.2.b., page 4
37	REDUCED UNDER SPECIFIED CIRCUMSTANCES (SEE POLICY)	—		

HARTFORD INSURANCE COMPANIES HC 00 55 03 96 [3/96]

#	Comparison Query	Comment		Policy Reference
6	**WHAT IS A CLAIM**			
38	**ORAL COMPLAINT TO INSURED**	●		VI.3., page 8
39	**WRITTEN COMPLAINT TO INSURED**	●		VI.3., page 8
40	**COMPLAINT MUST CONTAIN A DEMAND FOR DAMAGES**	●		VI.3., page 8
41	**COMPLAINT FILED WITH EEOC**	●		VI.3.b., page 8
42	OR SIMILAR STATE AUTHORITY	●		VI.3.b., page 8
43	AGENCY MUST HAVE POWER TO ADJUDICATE			
44	**ADMINISTRATIVE PROCEEDING**	●		VI.3.(iii), page 8
45	**ARBITRATION PROCEEDING**	●		VI.3.(i), page 8
46	**ANY INCIDENT REPORTED TO INSURER**	—		
47	**SUIT**	●	Civil proceeding	VI.3., page 8
48	**CLAIM DOES NOT INCLUDE ARBITRATION SUBJECT TO**	—		
49	COLLECTIVE BARGAINING AGREEMENT	—		
50	EMPLOYEE POLICY OR MANUAL	—		
51	**CLAIM NOT DEFINED**			
7	**CLAIM REPORTING PROVISIONS TO INSURER**			
52	**IMMEDIATELY**	—		
53	**AS SOON AS POSSIBLE**	—		
54	**AS SOON AS PRACTICABLE**	●	Written notice	IV.3., page 5
55	**WITHIN POLICY PERIOD**	—		
56	**WITHIN X DAYS OF EXPIRATION**	—		
57	**WITHIN X DAYS**	30		IV.3.b.(2), page 5
8	**EXTENDED REPORTING FEATURES**			
58	**ELECTION PERIOD (DAYS)**	60		V.3., page 7
59	**ADDITIONAL PREMIUM (% OF ANNUAL PREMIUM)**	200		V.3., page 7
60	**ADDITIONAL REPORTING PERIOD (MONTHS)**	36		V.3., page 7
61	**NO REINSTATEMENT OF LIMITS**	●		V.5., page 7
9	**POTENTIAL CLAIM REPORTING PROVISIONS**			
62	**NONE (SEE ALSO "CLAIM" ABOVE)**	—		
63	**INCIDENTS LIKELY TO RESULT IN A CLAIM**	●		IV.3.a., page 5
10	**DEFENSE PROVISIONS**			
64	**AFFIRMATIVE DUTY TO DEFEND**	●		I.1., page 1
65	**NO AFFIRMATIVE DUTY TO DEFEND**	—		
66	AFFIRMATIVE ADVANCEMENT PROVISIONS	—		
67	INSURED MUST RETURN ADVANCED AMOUNTS IF NOT COVERED	—		
68	**INSURED/INSURER CHOOSES COUNSEL**	—		
69	**INSURED/INSURER APPROVES COUNSEL**	—		
70	**INSURED/INSURER CONSULTED IN COUNSEL SELECTION**	—		
11	**SETTLEMENT PROVISIONS**			
71	**HAMMER CLAUSE**	—		
72	**CONSULTATION PROVISION**	—		
73	**CONSENT PROVISION**	—		
12	**ALLOCATION OF LOSS PROVISIONS**			
74	**STIPULATED PROVISIONS**	—		
13	**COVERAGES**			
75	**DISCRIMINATION**	●	As wrongful employment practice	VI.14.e., page 9
76	SPECIFIC ENUMERATED ACTIVITIES	●		VI.14.e., page 9
77	*PLUS BROAD OMNIBUS WORDING*	—		
78	SPECIFIC ENUMERATED CLASSES	●		VI.14.e., page 9
79	*PLUS BROAD OMNIBUS WORDING*	—		
80	AGAINST THIRD PARTIES	—		
81	DISCRIMINATION NOT DEFINED	●		
82	**SEXUAL HARASSMENT**	—		
83	HOSTILE ENVIRONMENT	—		
84	QUID-PRO-QUO	—		
85	SEXUAL HARASSMENT NOT DEFINED	—		
86	**WRONGFUL TERMINATION**	●	As wrongful employment practice	VI.14.d., page 9
87	BREACH OF IMPLIED CONTRACT	—		
88	BREACH OF EXPRESS CONTRACT	—		
89	VIOLATION OF PUBLIC POLICY	—		
90	VIOLATION OF GOOD FAITH & FAIR DEALING	—		
91	OBLIGATIONS TO MAKE PAYMENTS	—		
92	CONSTRUCTIVE DISCHARGE	●		VI.14.d., page 9
93	WRONGFUL TERMINATION NOT DEFINED	●		
94	**OTHER EMPLOYMENT VIOLATIONS/OFFENSES**	●		VI.14., page 9
95	WRONGFUL HIRING	●		VI.14.a., page 9
96	WRONGFUL PROMOTION/DEMOTION	●		VI.14.b. and c., page 9
97	WRONGFUL EVALUATION/DISCIPLINE	●		VI.14.b. and c., page 9

HARTFORD INSURANCE COMPANIES HC 00 55 03 96 [3/96]

	Comparison Query	Comment		Policy Reference
98	FAMILY AND MEDICAL LEAVE ACT	—		
99	DEFAMATION	●		VI.14.f., page 9
100	MISREPRESENTATION	—		
101	RETALIATION	—		
102	MENTAL ANGUISH	—		
103	INVASION OF PRIVACY	●		VI.14.g., page 9
104	HUMILIATION	—		
105	EMOTIONAL DISTRESS	—		
106	OTHER PERSONAL INJURY OFFENSES	—		
107	POLICY SILENT	—		
	14 EXCLUSIONS			
108	**ADA ACCOMMODATION EXPENSES**	●		I.2.h., page 2
109	**ASSAULT & BATTERY**	—		
110	**BACK PAY**	—		
111	**BODILY INJURY**	●		I.2.a., page 2
112	BODILY INJURY	●		VI.2., page 8
113	DEATH	●		VI.2., page 8
114	DISEASE	●		VI.2., page 8
115	SICKNESS	●		VI.2., page 8
116	**BREACH OF EMPLOYMENT CONTRACT**	●		I.2.b., page 2
117	EXPRESS CONTRACT	●		I.2.b., page 2
118	WRITTEN CONTRACT	—		
119	ORAL CONTRACT	—		
120	IMPLIED CONTRACT	—		
121	**CLASS ACTION LAWSUITS**	—		
122	**CONSEQUENTIAL LOSS**	—		
123	APPLIES TO BODILY INJURY	—		
124	APPLIES TO INSURED EVENT	—		
125	BROTHER/SISTER	—		
126	CHILD	—		
127	DOMESTIC PARTNER	—		
128	PARENT	—		
129	SPOUSE	—		
130	**COST OF ARBITRATION HEARINGS SUBJECT TO**	—		
131	EMPLOYMENT HANDBOOK	—		
132	LABOR GRIEVANCE	—		
133	OTHER EMPLOYMENT POLICY OR PROCEDURE	—		
134	**COVERAGE ELSEWHERE**	●		IV.5., page 5
135	OTHER AVAILABLE INSURANCE	●		IV.5., page 5
136	OTHER INDEMNIFICATION	—		
137	SHARING PROVISION	●		IV.5.b., page 5
138	**FAILURE TO EXERCISE CARE WHEN TERMINATING**	—		
139	**FINES/PENALTIES**	●		I.2.f., page 2
140	CIVIL	●		I.2.f., page 2
141	CRIMINAL	●		I.2.f., page 2
142	EXEMPLARY DAMAGES	●		VI.5., page 8
143	PUNITIVE DAMAGES	●		VI.5., page 8
144	MULTIPLIED DAMAGES	●		VI.5., page 8
145	**FRONT PAY**	●		I.2.g., page 2
146	EXCLUSION APPLIES ONLY IF EMPLOYER HAD OPPORTUNITY TO REINSTATE EMPLOYEE BUT DID NOT DO SO	—		
147	**INTENTIONAL ACTS**	●	Intentional acts	I.2.e., page 2
148	CRIMINAL ACTS	—		
149	CRIMINAL PROCEEDING	—		
150	DISHONEST PURPOSE	—		
151	FRAUDULENT ACTS	—		
152	FRAUDULENT CLAIMS	—		
153	INTENTIONAL VIOLATIONS OF LAW	—		
154	WILLFUL FAILURE TO COMPLY WITH LAW	●		I.2.o., page 3
155	MALICIOUS PURPOSE	—		
156	**LIABILITY OF OTHERS**	●		I.2.d., page 2
157	**LIQUIDATED DAMAGES**	—		
158	**LOSS ARISING OUT OF CHANGES IN OPERATIONS**	—		
159	ACQUISITION	—		
160	CHANGE IN CONTROL	—		
161	DOWNSIZING OR REDUCTION IN FORCE	—		
162	% OF WORKFORCE	—		
163	WITHIN X DAYS	—		

HARTFORD INSURANCE COMPANIES HC 00 55 03 96 [3/96]

#	Comparison Query	Comment	Policy Reference
164	**FINANCIAL IMPAIRMENT**	●	I.2.m., page 2
165	*BANKRUPTCY*	● Termination of employment	I.2.m., page 2
166	*INSOLVENCY*	—	
167	*LIQUIDATION*	● Termination of employment	I.2.m., page 2
168	*RECEIVERSHIP*	● Termination of employment	I.2.m., page 2
169	FINANCIAL INABILITY TO PAY	—	
170	MERGER	—	
171	PLANT OR FACILITY CLOSING	—	
172	REORGANIZATION	● *Termination of employment*	I.2.m., page 2
173	TEMPORARY SHUTDOWN	—	
174	**MATTERS DEEMED UNINSURABLE**	●	I.2.n., page 3
175	**NON-MONETARY RELIEF**	—	
176	DECLATORY RELIEF	—	
177	DISGORGEMENT	—	
178	INJUNCTIVE RELIEF	—	
179	JOB REINSTATEMENT	—	
180	NON-MONETARY DAMAGES/RELIEF	—	
181	OTHER EQUITABLE REMEDIES	—	
182	**OBLIGATION TO PROVIDE BENEFITS**	●	I.2.c., page 2
183	COBRA	●	I.2.c.(2), page 2
184	DISABILITY	●	I.2.c.(1), page 2
185	ERISA	●	I.2.c.(2), page 2
186	SOCIAL SECURITY	—	
187	OTHER RETIREMENT BENEFITS	—	
188	UNEMPLOYMENT	●	I.2.c.(1), page 2
189	WORKERS' COMPENSATION	●	I.2.c.(1), page 2
190	**PERSONAL INJURY OFFENSES**	●	I.2.a., page 2
191	DEFAMATION	—	
192	EMOTIONAL DISTRESS/UPSET	—	
193	HUMILIATION	—	
194	LIBEL	● Written publication of material	I.2.j., page 2
195	MENTAL ANGUISH	—	
196	PERSONAL INJURY	—	
197	SLANDER	● Oral publication of material	I.2.j., page 2
198	**PRIOR ACTS**	●	I.1.(b), pages 1–2
199	PRIOR ACTS	● Prior to retroactive date	I.1.(b), pages 1–2
200	PRIOR KNOWLEDGE	—	
201	PRIOR/PENDING LITIGATION	—	
202	**PROPERTY DAMAGE**	●	I.2.a., page 2
203	INTANGIBLE PROPERTY	—	
204	LOSS OF USE	●	VI.12.a., page 9
205	TANGIBLE PROPERTY	●	VI. 2.a., page 9
206	**RETALIATORY ACTIONS OF EMPLOYER**	●	I.2.K., page 3
207	FOR FAILING TO PERFORM ACTS AGAINST PUBLIC POLICY	●	I.2.K., page 3
208	FOR FILING A COMPLAINT OR BENEFIT CLAIM	●	I.2.K., page 3
209	**STRIKES/LOCKOUTS**	●	I.2.l., page 3
210	**VIOLATION OF LAWS**	—	
211	ANY LAW	—	
212	FMLA	—	
213	OSHA	●	I.2.c.(2), page 2
214	POLLUTION LAWS	●	I.2.i., page 3
215	RICO	—	
216	SEC	—	
217	WARN	●	I.2.c.(2), page 2

15 CONDITIONS

#	Comparison Query	Comment	Policy Reference
218	**ARBITRATION**	●	IV.1., pages 4–5
219	MANDATORY	●	IV.1., pages 4–5
220	BINDING	●	IV.1., pages 4–5
221	CHOICE OF LAW PROVISION	—	
222	SITUS	—	
223	**TERRITORY**	●	VI.4., page 8
224	LIMITED	—	
225	WORLDWIDE	●	VI.4., page 8
226	**NEWLY FORMED/ACQUIRED ENTITIES**	●	II.4., page 3
227	AUTOMATIC COVERAGE (X DAYS)	90	II.4.b., page 3
228	NOTIFY INSURER WITHIN X DAYS	60	II.4.a., page 3

HARTFORD INSURANCE COMPANIES HC 00 55 03 96 [3/96]

Policy Comparison Worksheet

Insurance Services Office (ISO)

Policy Form No.: EP 00 01 04 98
Edition Date: 04 98

Contact: Available through insurers only

Risks Considered: Varies by insurer
Limits Available: Varies by insurer
Minimum Retention: Varies by insurer

KEY TO SYMBOLS
● = Specifically contains queried provision feature
○ = Unable to determine
— = Does not specifically contain queried provision/feature

#	Comparison Query		Comment	Policy Reference
	1 APPLICATION			
1	ATTACHES TO AND FORMS A PART OF THE POLICY	—		
2	CONTAINS WARRANTY STATEMENTS	—	Varies by insurer	
3	CONTAINS SEVERABILITY PROVISIONS	—	Varies by insurer	
	2 POLICY TYPE			
4	UNITARY STAND ALONE POLICY	●		
	ENDORSEMENT OR PART OF	●		
5	DIRECTORS AND OFFICERS POLICY	—		
6	PACKAGE POLICY	●	ISO Commercial Package Policy	
7	UMBRELLA POLICY	—		
8	ERRORS AND OMISSIONS POLICY	—		
9	OTHER	—		
10	CLAIMS-MADE	●		
11	OCCURRENCE	—		
	3 WHO IS INSURED			
12	BUSINESS ENTITY	●		II.A.1.–4., page 3
13	AUTOMATIC COVERAGE FOR SUBSIDIARIES	—		
14	DIRECTORS & OFFICERS	●		II.A.4., page 3
15	EMPLOYEES	●	Coverage available by endorsement	EP 01 02 04 98
16	PART-TIME	—		
17	SEASONAL	—		
18	TEMPORARY	●	Included when covered by above endorsement	
19	SUPERVISORS & MANAGERS	●		II.B., page 3
20	FORMER EMPLOYEES	—		
21	VOLUNTEERS	—		
22	INDEPENDENT CONTRACTORS	—		
23	EXCLUDED	—		
24	SILENT	—		
25	SHAREHOLDERS	—		
	4 LIMIT OF LIABILITY			
26	AGGREGATE	●		III.B.1. & 2., page 3
27	INCLUDES PUNITIVE DAMAGES WHERE NOT UNINSURABLE	—		
28	DEFENSE COSTS INCLUDED WITHIN LIMIT OF LIABILITY	●		III.B.1. & 2., page 3
29	DEFENSE COSTS PAID IN ADDITION TO LIMIT OF LIABILITY	—		
	5 DEDUCTIBLE			
30	APPLIES TO EACH INDIVIDUAL CLAIM	—		
31	APPLIES TO EACH OCCURRENCE OR WRONGFUL PRACTICE	—		
32	INCLUDES ALL CLAIMS FROM ONE ACT	—		
33	SUBJECT TO ANNUAL AGGREGATE	—		
34	CO-PAYMENT APPLIES	●	Specified by underwriter—see Declarations	IV., page 3
35	LIMIT OF LIABILITY NOT REDUCED	●		IV., page 3
36	INCLUDES DEFENSE COSTS	●		IV., page 3
37	REDUCED UNDER SPECIFIED CIRCUMSTANCES (SEE POLICY)	—		

INSURANCE SERVICES OFFICE (ISO) EP 00 01 04 98 [04 98]

#	Comparison Query	Comment		Policy Reference
	6 WHAT IS A CLAIM			
38	ORAL COMPLAINT TO INSURED	—		
39	WRITTEN COMPLAINT TO INSURED	—		
40	COMPLAINT MUST CONTAIN A DEMAND FOR DAMAGES	●		VII.A., page 6
41	COMPLAINT FILED WITH EEOC	—		
42	OR SIMILAR STATE AUTHORITY	—		
43	AGENCY MUST HAVE POWER TO ADJUDICATE	—		
44	ADMINISTRATIVE PROCEEDING	●		VII.J.3., page 7
45	ARBITRATION PROCEEDING	●		VII.J.1., page 7
46	ANY INCIDENT REPORTED TO INSURER	●		I.A.3.b., page 1
47	SUIT	●		VII.A., page 6
48	CLAIM DOES NOT INCLUDE ARBITRATION SUBJECT TO	—		
49	COLLECTIVE BARGAINING AGREEMENT	—		
50	EMPLOYEE POLICY OR MANUAL	—		
51	CLAIM NOT DEFINED	—		
	7 CLAIM REPORTING PROVISIONS TO INSURER			
52	IMMEDIATELY	—		
53	AS SOON AS POSSIBLE	—		
54	AS SOON AS PRACTICABLE	●		V.C.1.b., page 3
55	WITHIN POLICY PERIOD	—		
56	WITHIN X DAYS OF EXPIRATION	—		
57	WITHIN X DAYS	—		
	8 EXTENDED REPORTING FEATURES			
58	ELECTION PERIOD (DAYS)	30		VI.D., page 6
59	ADDITIONAL PREMIUM (% OF ANNUAL PREMIUM)	200		VI.B., following 4., page 6
60	ADDITIONAL REPORTING PERIOD (MONTHS)	36		VI.B., page 6
61	NO REINSTATEMENT OF LIMITS	—		
	9 POTENTIAL CLAIM REPORTING PROVISIONS			
62	NONE (SEE ALSO "CLAIM" ABOVE)	—		
63	INCIDENTS LIKELY TO RESULT IN A CLAIM	●		V.C.4., page 4
	10 DEFENSE PROVISIONS			
64	AFFIRMATIVE DUTY TO DEFEND	●		I.A.1., page 1
65	NO AFFIRMATIVE DUTY TO DEFEND	—		
66	AFFIRMATIVE ADVANCEMENT PROVISIONS	—		
67	INSURED MUST RETURN ADVANCED AMOUNTS IF NOT COVERED	—		
68	INSURED/INSURER CHOOSES COUNSEL	●	Insurer—exceptions apply	V.J., page 4
69	INSURED/INSURER APPROVES COUNSEL	—		
70	INSURED/INSURER CONSULTED IN COUNSEL SELECTION	—		
	11 SETTLEMENT PROVISIONS			
71	HAMMER CLAUSE	●		V.B., page 3
72	CONSULTATION PROVISION	—		
73	CONSENT PROVISION	●	Insured must consent	I.A.1., page 1
	12 ALLOCATION OF LOSS PROVISIONS			
74	STIPULATED PROVISIONS	●	Defense expenses	V.J.3., page 5
	13 COVERAGES			
75	DISCRIMINATION	●	Included in definition of "injury"	VII.G.1., page 7
76	SPECIFIC ENUMERATED ACTIVITIES	●	Included in definition of "injury"	VII.G.1., page 7
77	PLUS BROAD OMNIBUS WORDING	—		
78	SPECIFIC ENUMERATED CLASSES	●		VII.D., page 6
79	PLUS BROAD OMNIBUS WORDING	●		VII.D., page 6
80	AGAINST THIRD PARTIES	—		
81	DISCRIMINATION NOT DEFINED	—		
82	SEXUAL HARASSMENT	●		VII.G.3., page 7
83	HOSTILE ENVIRONMENT	●		VII.I., page 7
84	QUID-PRO-QUO	●		VII.I., page 7
85	SEXUAL HARASSMENT NOT DEFINED	—		
86	WRONGFUL TERMINATION	●	Discrimination-related	VII.G.1., page 7
87	BREACH OF IMPLIED CONTRACT	—		
88	BREACH OF EXPRESS CONTRACT	—		
89	VIOLATION OF PUBLIC POLICY	—		
90	VIOLATION OF GOOD FAITH & FAIR DEALING	—		
91	OBLIGATIONS TO MAKE PAYMENTS	—		
92	CONSTRUCTIVE DISCHARGE	—		
93	WRONGFUL TERMINATION NOT DEFINED	●		
94	OTHER EMPLOYMENT VIOLATIONS/OFFENSES	●		VII.G.1., page 7
95	WRONGFUL HIRING	●	Discrimination-related	VII.G.1., page 7
96	WRONGFUL PROMOTION/DEMOTION	●		VII.G.1., page 7
97	WRONGFUL EVALUATION/DISCIPLINE	●		VII.G.1., page 7

INSURANCE SERVICES OFFICE (ISO) EP 00 01 04 98 [04 98]

	Comparison Query		Comment	Policy Reference
98	FAMILY AND MEDICAL LEAVE ACT	—		
99	DEFAMATION	●		VII.G.1., page 7
100	MISREPRESENTATION	—		
101	RETALIATION	●		I.B.10., page 2
102	MENTAL ANGUISH	○		VII.G.4., page 7
103	INVASION OF PRIVACY	—		
104	HUMILIATION	●	Discrimination-related	VII.G.1., page 7
105	EMOTIONAL DISTRESS	○		VII.G.4., page 7
106	OTHER PERSONAL INJURY OFFENSES	—		
107	POLICY SILENT	—		
14	**EXCLUSIONS**			
108	**ADA ACCOMMODATION EXPENSES**	●		I.B.4., page 2
109	**ASSAULT & BATTERY**	—		
110	**BACK PAY**	—		
111	**BODILY INJURY**			
112	BODILY INJURY	—		
113	DEATH	—		
114	DISEASE	—		
115	SICKNESS	—		
116	**BREACH OF EMPLOYMENT CONTRACT**	—		
117	EXPRESS CONTRACT	—		
118	WRITTEN CONTRACT	—		
119	ORAL CONTRACT	—		
120	IMPLIED CONTRACT	—		
121	**CLASS ACTION LAWSUITS**	—		
122	**CONSEQUENTIAL LOSS**	—		
123	APPLIES TO BODILY INJURY	—		
124	APPLIES TO INSURED EVENT	—		
125	BROTHER/SISTER	—		
126	CHILD	—		
127	DOMESTIC PARTNER	—		
128	PARENT	—		
129	SPOUSE	—		
130	**COST OF ARBITRATION HEARINGS SUBJECT TO**	—		
131	EMPLOYMENT HANDBOOK	—		
132	LABOR GRIEVANCE	—		
133	OTHER EMPLOYMENT POLICY OR PROCEDURE	—		
134	**COVERAGE ELSEWHERE**	●		V.E.1., page 4
135	OTHER AVAILABLE INSURANCE	—		
136	OTHER INDEMNIFICATION	—		
137	SHARING PROVISION	●	If other insurance applies	V.E.1., page 4
138	**FAILURE TO EXERCISE CARE WHEN TERMINATING**	—		
139	**FINES/PENALTIES**	●		I.A.1.B., page 1
140	CIVIL	●	See Insuring Agreement	I.A.1.B., page 1
141	CRIMINAL	●	See Insuring Agreement	I.A.1.B., page 1
142	EXEMPLARY DAMAGES	—		
143	PUNITIVE DAMAGES	—		
144	MULTIPLIED DAMAGES	—		
145	**FRONT PAY**	—		
146	EXCLUSION APPLIES ONLY IF EMPLOYER HAD OPPORTUNITY TO REINSTATE EMPLOYEE BUT DID NOT DO SO	—		
147	**INTENTIONAL ACTS**	●		I.B.1., page 1
148	CRIMINAL ACTS	●	Covers defense	I.B.1., page 1
149	CRIMINAL PROCEEDING	—		
150	DISHONEST PURPOSE	—		
151	FRAUDULENT ACTS	●	Covers defense	I.B.1., page 1
152	FRAUDULENT CLAIMS	—		
153	INTENTIONAL VIOLATIONS OF LAW	●	Covers defense	I.B.9., page 2
154	WILLFUL FAILURE TO COMPLY WITH LAW	—		
155	MALICIOUS PURPOSE	●	Covers defense	I.B.1., page 1
156	**LIABILITY OF OTHERS**	●		I.B.2., page 2
157	**LIQUIDATED DAMAGES**	—		
158	**LOSS ARISING OUT OF CHANGES IN OPERATIONS**	●		I.B.8., page 2
159	ACQUISITION	●		I.B.8., page 2
160	CHANGE IN CONTROL	●		I.B.8., page 2
161	DOWNSIZING OR REDUCTION IN FORCE	●		I.B.8., page 2
162	% OF WORKFORCE	—		
163	WITHIN X DAYS	—		

INSURANCE SERVICES OFFICE (ISO) EP 00 01 04 98 [04 98]

#	Comparison Query		Comment	Policy Reference
164	**FINANCIAL IMPAIRMENT**	●		I.B.8.a., page 2
165	*BANKRUPTCY*	●		I.B.8.a., page 2
166	*INSOLVENCY*	—		
167	*LIQUIDATION*	●		I.B.8.a., page 2
168	*RECEIVERSHIP*	●		I.B.8.a., page 2
169	FINANCIAL INABILITY TO PAY	—		
170	MERGER	●		I.B.8.a., page 2
171	PLANT OR FACILITY CLOSING	●		I.B.8.c., page 2
172	REORGANIZATION	—		
173	TEMPORARY SHUTDOWN	●	Conditional	I.B.8.d., page 2
174	**MATTERS DEEMED UNINSURABLE**	—		
175	**NON-MONETARY RELIEF**	●	See Insuring Agreement	I.A., page 1
176	DECLATORY RELIEF	—		
177	DISGORGEMENT	—		
178	INJUNCTIVE RELIEF	—		
179	JOB REINSTATEMENT	—		
180	NON-MONETARY DAMAGES/RELIEF	—		
181	OTHER EQUITABLE REMEDIES	—		
182	**OBLIGATION TO PROVIDE BENEFITS**			
183	COBRA	—		
184	DISABILITY	●		I.B.3., page 2
185	ERISA	—		
186	SOCIAL SECURITY	—		
187	OTHER RETIREMENT BENEFITS	—		
188	UNEMPLOYMENT	●		I.B.3., page 2
189	WORKERS' COMPENSATION	●		I.B.3., page 2
190	**PERSONAL INJURY OFFENSES**			
191	DEFAMATION	—		
192	EMOTIONAL DISTRESS/UPSET	—		
193	HUMILIATION	—		
194	LIBEL	—		
195	MENTAL ANGUISH	—		
196	PERSONAL INJURY	—		
197	SLANDER	—		
198	**PRIOR ACTS**	●		I.A.2.b., page 1
199	PRIOR ACTS	●		I.A.2.b., page 1
200	PRIOR KNOWLEDGE	—		
201	PRIOR/PENDING LITIGATION	—		
202	**PROPERTY DAMAGE**	—		
203	INTANGIBLE PROPERTY	—		
204	LOSS OF USE	—		
205	TANGIBLE PROPERTY	—		
206	**RETALIATORY ACTIONS OF EMPLOYER**	●		I.B.10., page 2
207	FOR FAILING TO PERFORM ACTS AGAINST PUBLIC POLICY	●		I.B.10., page 2
208	FOR FILING A COMPLAINT OR BENEFIT CLAIM	●		I.B.10., page 2
209	**STRIKES/LOCKOUTS**	●		I.B.6., page 2
210	**VIOLATION OF LAWS**	●	Important exceptions apply	I.B.5., page 2
211	ANY LAW	—		
212	FMLA	●		I.B.5., page 2
213	OSHA	—		
214	POLLUTION LAWS	—		
215	RICO	—		
216	SEC	—		
217	WARN	—		
	15 CONDITIONS			
218	**ARBITRATION**	—		
219	MANDATORY	—		
220	BINDING	—		
221	CHOICE OF LAW PROVISION	—		
222	SITUS	—		
223	**TERRITORY**	●		VII.B., page 6
224	LIMITED	—		
225	WORLDWIDE	●	Conditions apply	VII.B., page 6
226	**NEWLY FORMED/ACQUIRED ENTITIES**	—		
227	AUTOMATIC COVERAGE (X DAYS)	90	Coverage available by endorsement	
228	NOTIFY INSURER WITHIN X DAYS	—		

INSURANCE SERVICES OFFICE (ISO) EP 00 01 04 98 [04 98]

Policy Comparison Worksheet

Legion Insurance Companies

Policy Form No.: ERP-1
Edition Date: 7/98

Risks Considered: Members of associations
Limits Available: $5,000,000
Minimum Retention: $2,500

Contact: Richard V. Rupp, CPCU
AmTech E&S
P.O. Box M
San Mateo, CA 94402-0080
650/572-4665
650/572-4622 (fax)
rupprisk@aol.com
www.ccmc.com/calco

KEY TO SYMBOLS
● = Specifically contains queried provision of feature
○ = Unable to determine
— = Silent

#	Comparison Query		Comment	Policy Reference
	1 APPLICATION			
1	ATTACHES TO AND FORMS A PART OF THE POLICY	●		Application, page 7
2	CONTAINS WARRANTY STATEMENTS	●		Application, page 7
3	CONTAINS SEVERABILITY PROVISIONS	—		
	2 POLICY TYPE			
4	UNITARY STAND ALONE POLICY	●		
	ENDORSEMENT OR PART OF	—		
5	DIRECTORS AND OFFICERS POLICY	—		
6	PACKAGE POLICY	—		
7	UMBRELLA POLICY	—		
8	ERRORS AND OMISSIONS POLICY	—		
9	OTHER	—		
10	CLAIMS-MADE	●		
11	OCCURRENCE	—		
	3 WHO IS INSURED			
12	BUSINESS ENTITY	●		III.1.d., page 5
13	AUTOMATIC COVERAGE FOR SUBSIDIARIES	—		
14	DIRECTORS & OFFICERS	●		X.13., page 17
15	EMPLOYEES	●	At time of insured event	III.2.b., page 5
16	PART-TIME	●		X.6.a., page 15
17	SEASONAL	●		X.6.a., page 15
18	TEMPORARY	●		X.6.a., page 15
19	SUPERVISORS & MANAGERS	●		III.2.b., page 5
20	FORMER EMPLOYEES	—		
21	VOLUNTEERS	●		X.6.a., page 15
22	INDEPENDENT CONTRACTORS	●	If endorsed onto policy	X.6.c., page 15
23	EXCLUDED	—		
24	SILENT	—		
25	SHAREHOLDERS	●	See also X.13., page 17	III.1.d., page 5
	4 LIMIT OF LIABILITY			
26	AGGREGATE	●		IV.3., page 6
27	INCLUDES PUNITIVE DAMAGES WHERE NOT UNINSURABLE	●		X.12.d., page 17
28	DEFENSE COSTS INCLUDED WITHIN LIMIT OF LIABILITY	●		I.5.b., page 2
29	DEFENSE COSTS PAID IN ADDITION TO LIMIT OF LIABILITY	—		
	5 DEDUCTIBLE			
30	APPLIES TO EACH INDIVIDUAL CLAIM	●		V.4., page 7
31	APPLIES TO EACH OCCURRENCE OR WRONGFUL PRACTICE	—		
32	INCLUDES ALL CLAIMS FROM ONE ACT	●		V.4., page 7
33	SUBJECT TO ANNUAL AGGREGATE	—		
34	CO-PAYMENT APPLIES	—	Available by endorsement	
35	LIMIT OF LIABILITY NOT REDUCED	●		V.1., page 6
36	INCLUDES DEFENSE COSTS	●		V.2., page 6
37	REDUCED UNDER SPECIFIED CIRCUMSTANCES (SEE POLICY)	●		VI.1. and 2., page 7

#	Comparison Query	Comment	Policy Reference
	6 WHAT IS A CLAIM		
38	ORAL COMPLAINT TO INSURED	●	X.2., page 14
39	WRITTEN COMPLAINT TO INSURED	●	X.2., page 14
40	COMPLAINT MUST CONTAIN A DEMAND FOR DAMAGES	●	X.2., page 14
41	COMPLAINT FILED WITH EEOC	●	X.2., page 14
42	OR SIMILAR STATE AUTHORITY	●	X.2., page 14
43	AGENCY MUST HAVE POWER TO ADJUDICATE	—	
44	ADMINISTRATIVE PROCEEDING	●	X.2., page 14
45	ARBITRATION PROCEEDING	●	X.20., page 17
46	ANY INCIDENT REPORTED TO INSURER	—	
47	SUIT	●	X.2., page 14
48	CLAIM DOES NOT INCLUDE ARBITRATION SUBJECT TO	—	
49	COLLECTIVE BARGAINING AGREEMENT	●	X.2., page 14
50	EMPLOYEE POLICY OR MANUAL	—	
51	CLAIM NOT DEFINED	—	
	7 CLAIM REPORTING PROVISIONS TO INSURER		
52	IMMEDIATELY	—	
53	AS SOON AS POSSIBLE	●	VII.1.a., page 7
54	AS SOON AS PRACTICABLE	—	
55	WITHIN POLICY PERIOD	—	
56	WITHIN X DAYS OF EXPIRATION	—	
57	WITHIN X DAYS	30	VII.1.a., page 7
	8 EXTENDED REPORTING FEATURES		
58	ELECTION PERIOD (DAYS)	30	VIII.4., page 13
59	ADDITIONAL PREMIUM (% OF ANNUAL PREMIUM)	100	VIII.4., page 13
60	ADDITIONAL REPORTING PERIOD (MONTHS)	24	VIII.4., page 13
61	NO REINSTATEMENT OF LIMITS	● See also VIII.5., page 13	IV.4., page 6
	9 POTENTIAL CLAIM REPORTING PROVISIONS		
62	NONE (SEE ALSO "CLAIM" ABOVE)	—	
63	INCIDENTS LIKELY TO RESULT IN A CLAIM	●	VIII.6., pages 13–14
	10 DEFENSE PROVISIONS		
64	AFFIRMATIVE DUTY TO DEFEND	● Optional duty regarding criminal proceedings	I.2., page 2 and I.3., page 3
65	NO AFFIRMATIVE DUTY TO DEFEND	—	
66	AFFIRMATIVE ADVANCEMENT PROVISIONS	—	
67	INSURED MUST RETURN ADVANCED AMOUNTS IF NOT COVERED	—	
68	INSURED/INSURER CHOOSES COUNSEL	● Insurer	I.4.a., page 3
69	INSURED/INSURER APPROVES COUNSEL	—	
70	INSURED/INSURER CONSULTED IN COUNSEL SELECTION	●	I.4.a., page 3
	11 SETTLEMENT PROVISIONS		
71	HAMMER CLAUSE	●	I.6., page 4
72	CONSULTATION PROVISION	—	
73	CONSENT PROVISION	● Insured must consent	I.6., page 4
	12 ALLOCATION OF LOSS PROVISIONS		
74	STIPULATED PROVISIONS	—	
	13 COVERAGES		
75	DISCRIMINATION	●	I.1.a., page 2
76	SPECIFIC ENUMERATED ACTIVITIES	●	X.5., page 14
77	PLUS BROAD OMNIBUS WORDING	●	X.5., page 14
78	SPECIFIC ENUMERATED CLASSES	●	X.5., page 14
79	PLUS BROAD OMNIBUS WORDING	●	X.5., page 14
80	AGAINST THIRD PARTIES	—	
81	DISCRIMINATION NOT DEFINED	—	
82	SEXUAL HARASSMENT	● Any harassment	I.1.a., page 2
83	HOSTILE ENVIRONMENT	●	X.7.a., page 15
84	QUID-PRO-QUO	●	X.7.a., page 15
85	SEXUAL HARASSMENT NOT DEFINED	—	
86	WRONGFUL TERMINATION	● As inappropriate employment conduct	I.1.a., page 2
87	BREACH OF IMPLIED CONTRACT	●	X.8., page 15
88	BREACH OF EXPRESS CONTRACT	—	
89	VIOLATION OF PUBLIC POLICY	—	
90	VIOLATION OF GOOD FAITH & FAIR DEALING	●	X.8., page 15
91	OBLIGATIONS TO MAKE PAYMENTS	—	
92	CONSTRUCTIVE DISCHARGE	●	X.8., page 15
93	WRONGFUL TERMINATION NOT DEFINED	●	
94	OTHER EMPLOYMENT VIOLATIONS/OFFENSES	●	X.5., page 14 and X.8., pages 14–15
95	WRONGFUL HIRING	●	X.5., page 14
96	WRONGFUL PROMOTION/DEMOTION	● See also X.8.a., page 15	X.5., page 14
97	WRONGFUL EVALUATION/DISCIPLINE	● See also X.8.d., page 15	X.8.b., page 15

LEGION INSURANCE COMPANIES ERP-1 [7/98]

#	Comparison Query	Comment	Policy Reference
98	FAMILY AND MEDICAL LEAVE ACT	●	X.8., page 16
99	DEFAMATION	●	X.8.f., page 15
100	MISREPRESENTATION	●	X.8.f., page 15
101	RETALIATION	●	X.8.e., page 15
102	MENTAL ANGUISH	●	X.8.g., page 16
103	INVASION OF PRIVACY	●	X.8.i., page 16
104	HUMILIATION	—	
105	EMOTIONAL DISTRESS	●	X.8.g., page 16
106	OTHER PERSONAL INJURY OFFENSES	●	X.8.h. and i., page 16
107	POLICY SILENT	—	

14 EXCLUSIONS

#	Comparison Query	Comment	Policy Reference
108	**ADA ACCOMMODATION EXPENSES**	●	X.f., page 16
109	**ASSAULT & BATTERY**	—	
110	**BACK PAY**	—	
111	**BODILY INJURY**	—	
112	BODILY INJURY	—	
113	DEATH	—	
114	DISEASE	—	
115	SICKNESS	—	
116	**BREACH OF EMPLOYMENT CONTRACT**	—	
117	EXPRESS CONTRACT	●	X.8., page 16
118	WRITTEN CONTRACT	—	
119	ORAL CONTRACT	—	
120	IMPLIED CONTRACT	—	
121	**CLASS ACTION LAWSUITS**	—	
122	**CONSEQUENTIAL LOSS**	—	
123	APPLIES TO BODILY INJURY	—	
124	APPLIES TO INSURED EVENT	●	II.5., page 4
125	BROTHER/SISTER	●	II.5., page 4
126	CHILD	●	II.5., page 4
127	DOMESTIC PARTNER	●	II.5., page 4
128	PARENT	●	II.5., page 4
129	SPOUSE	●	II.5., page 4
130	**COST OF ARBITRATION HEARINGS SUBJECT TO**	—	
131	EMPLOYMENT HANDBOOK	—	
132	LABOR GRIEVANCE	—	
133	OTHER EMPLOYMENT POLICY OR PROCEDURE	—	
134	**COVERAGE ELSEWHERE**	—	
135	OTHER AVAILABLE INSURANCE	● Under specified conditions	VII.3.b., page 9
136	OTHER INDEMNIFICATION	—	
137	SHARING PROVISION	● See also VII.3.c., page 10	VII.3.a., page 9
138	**FAILURE TO EXERCISE CARE WHEN TERMINATING**	—	
139	**FINES/PENALTIES**	●	X.12., page 16
140	CIVIL	●	X.12., page 16
141	CRIMINAL	●	X.12., page 16
142	EXEMPLARY DAMAGES	—	
143	PUNITIVE DAMAGES	—	
144	MULTIPLIED DAMAGES	—	
145	**FRONT PAY**	—	
146	EXCLUSION APPLIES ONLY IF EMPLOYER HAD OPPORTUNITY TO REINSTATE EMPLOYEE BUT DID NOT DO SO	—	
147	**INTENTIONAL ACTS**	—	
148	CRIMINAL ACTS	—	
149	CRIMINAL PROCEEDING	—	
150	DISHONEST PURPOSE	—	
151	FRAUDULENT ACTS	—	
152	FRAUDULENT CLAIMS	●	VII.12., page 12
153	INTENTIONAL VIOLATIONS OF LAW	—	
154	WILLFUL FAILURE TO COMPLY WITH LAW	—	
155	MALICIOUS PURPOSE	—	
156	**LIABILITY OF OTHERS**	●	II.2., page 4
157	**LIQUIDATED DAMAGES**	●	X.12., page 16
158	**LOSS ARISING OUT OF CHANGES IN OPERATIONS**	—	
159	ACQUISITION	—	
160	CHANGE IN CONTROL	—	
161	DOWNSIZING OR REDUCTION IN FORCE	—	
162	% OF WORKFORCE	—	
163	WITHIN X DAYS	—	

LEGION INSURANCE COMPANIES ERP-1 [7/98]

#	Comparison Query	Comment		Policy Reference
164	FINANCIAL IMPAIRMENT	—		
165	BANKRUPTCY	—		
166	INSOLVENCY	—		
167	LIQUIDATION	—		
168	RECEIVERSHIP	—		
169	FINANCIAL INABILITY TO PAY	—		
170	MERGER	—		
171	PLANT OR FACILITY CLOSING	—		
172	REORGANIZATION	—		
173	TEMPORARY SHUTDOWN	—		
174	**MATTERS DEEMED UNINSURABLE**	●		X.12.g., page 17
175	**NON-MONETARY RELIEF**	—		
176	DECLATORY RELIEF	—		
177	DISGORGEMENT	—		
178	INJUNCTIVE RELIEF	—		
179	JOB REINSTATEMENT	—		
180	NON-MONETARY DAMAGES/RELIEF	●		X.12., page 16
181	OTHER EQUITABLE REMEDIES	—		
182	**OBLIGATION TO PROVIDE BENEFITS**	—		
183	COBRA	—		
184	DISABILITY	●	Exceptions apply	II.1., page 4
185	ERISA	●		II.3., page 4
186	SOCIAL SECURITY	—		
187	OTHER RETIREMENT BENEFITS	—		
188	UNEMPLOYMENT	●		II.1., page 4
189	WORKERS' COMPENSATION	●	Exceptions apply	II.1., page 4
190	**PERSONAL INJURY OFFENSES**	—		
191	DEFAMATION	—		
192	EMOTIONAL DISTRESS/UPSET	—		
193	HUMILIATION	—		
194	LIBEL	—		
195	MENTAL ANGUISH	—		
196	PERSONAL INJURY	—		
197	SLANDER	—		
198	**PRIOR ACTS**	●		By endorsement
199	PRIOR ACTS	●	Prior to retroactive date—by endorsement	
200	PRIOR KNOWLEDGE	●		I.1.c.(4)., page 2
201	PRIOR/PENDING LITIGATION	—		
202	**PROPERTY DAMAGE**	—		
203	INTANGIBLE PROPERTY	—		
204	LOSS OF USE	—		
205	TANGIBLE PROPERTY	—		
206	**RETALIATORY ACTIONS OF EMPLOYER**	—		
207	FOR FAILING TO PERFORM ACTS AGAINST PUBLIC POLICY	—		
208	FOR FILING A COMPLAINT OR BENEFIT CLAIM	—		
209	**STRIKES/LOCKOUTS**	●		II.4., page 4
210	**VIOLATION OF LAWS**	—		
211	ANY LAW	—		
212	FMLA	—		
213	OSHA	—		
214	POLLUTION LAWS	—		
215	RICO	—		
216	SEC	—		
217	WARN	●		II.6., page 5
	15 CONDITIONS			
218	**ARBITRATION**	—		
219	MANDATORY	—		
220	BINDING	—		
221	CHOICE OF LAW PROVISION	—		
222	SITUS	—		
223	**TERRITORY**	—		
224	LIMITED	—		
225	WORLDWIDE	●		IX., page 14
226	**NEWLY FORMED/ACQUIRED ENTITIES**	●		III.2.a., page 5
227	AUTOMATIC COVERAGE (X DAYS)	60	If own > 51%	III.2.a., page 5
228	NOTIFY INSURER WITHIN X DAYS	60		III.2.a., page 5

LEGION INSURANCE COMPANIES ERP-1 [7/98]

Policy Comparison Worksheet

Lexington Insurance Company

Policy Form No.: 65200
Edition Date: 12/95

Risks Considered: All except temporary help and employee leasing agencies
Limits Available: $5,000,000/$5,000,000
Minimum Retention: $2,500

Contact: Morefar Marketing, Inc.
501 Carr Road, Suite 101
Wilmington, DE 19809
302/761-5600
302/761-5659 (fax)

KEY TO SYMBOLS
● = Specifically contains queried provision of feature
○ = Unable to determine
— = Silent

#	Comparison Query		Comment	Policy Reference
	1 APPLICATION			
1	ATTACHES TO AND FORMS A PART OF THE POLICY	●		Preamble, page 1
2	CONTAINS WARRANTY STATEMENTS	—		
3	CONTAINS SEVERABILITY PROVISIONS	—		
	2 POLICY TYPE			
4	UNITARY STAND ALONE POLICY	●		
	ENDORSEMENT OR PART OF	—		
5	DIRECTORS AND OFFICERS POLICY	—		
6	PACKAGE POLICY	—		
7	UMBRELLA POLICY	—		
8	ERRORS AND OMISSIONS POLICY	—		
9	OTHER	—		
10	CLAIMS-MADE	●		
11	OCCURRENCE	—		
	3 WHO IS INSURED			
12	BUSINESS ENTITY	●		II.B., page 3
13	AUTOMATIC COVERAGE FOR SUBSIDIARIES	—		
14	DIRECTORS & OFFICERS	●		II.E., page 4
15	EMPLOYEES	●		II.E., page 4
16	PART-TIME	●		VIII.D., page 9
17	SEASONAL	●		VIII.D., page 9
18	TEMPORARY	●		VIII.D., page 9
19	SUPERVISORS & MANAGERS	●		VIII.D., page 9
20	FORMER EMPLOYEES	—		
21	VOLUNTEERS	—		
22	INDEPENDENT CONTRACTORS	—		
23	EXCLUDED	●		VIII.D., page 9
24	SILENT	—		
25	SHAREHOLDERS	●		II.B., page 3
	4 LIMIT OF LIABILITY			
26	AGGREGATE	●		III.B., page 4
27	INCLUDES PUNITIVE DAMAGES WHERE NOT UNINSURABLE	—		
28	DEFENSE COSTS INCLUDED WITHIN LIMIT OF LIABILITY	●	See also I.A.2.f., page 2	Preamble, page 1
29	DEFENSE COSTS PAID IN ADDITION TO LIMIT OF LIABILITY	—		
	5 DEDUCTIBLE			
30	APPLIES TO EACH INDIVIDUAL CLAIM	—		
31	APPLIES TO EACH OCCURRENCE OR WRONGFUL PRACTICE	●		V., page 4
32	INCLUDES ALL CLAIMS FROM ONE ACT	●		III.D., page 4
33	SUBJECT TO ANNUAL AGGREGATE	—		
34	CO-PAYMENT APPLIES	●	5%	IV., page 4
35	LIMIT OF LIABILITY NOT REDUCED	●		V., page 4
36	INCLUDES DEFENSE COSTS	●	See also V., page 4	Preamble, page 1
37	REDUCED UNDER SPECIFIED CIRCUMSTANCES (SEE POLICY)	—		

#	Comparison Query	Comment	Policy Reference
6	**WHAT IS A CLAIM**		
38	ORAL COMPLAINT TO INSURED	—	
39	WRITTEN COMPLAINT TO INSURED	●	Not in definition of "claim," but included in awareness provision
40	COMPLAINT MUST CONTAIN A DEMAND FOR DAMAGES	●	VIII.J., page 9
41	COMPLAINT FILED WITH EEOC	—	
42	OR SIMILAR STATE AUTHORITY	—	
43	AGENCY MUST HAVE POWER TO ADJUDICATE	—	
44	ADMINISTRATIVE PROCEEDING	●	VIII.J., page 9
45	ARBITRATION PROCEEDING	●	VIII.J., page 9
46	ANY INCIDENT REPORTED TO INSURER	●	Not in definition of "claim," but included in awareness provision	VI.F.1., page 5
47	SUIT	●	Not in definition of "claim," but included in awareness provision
48	CLAIM DOES NOT INCLUDE ARBITRATION SUBJECT TO	●	As an administrative proceeding	VIII.J., page 9
49	COLLECTIVE BARGAINING AGREEMENT	●		VIII.J., page 9
50	EMPLOYEE POLICY OR MANUAL	—	
51	CLAIM NOT DEFINED	—	
7	**CLAIM REPORTING PROVISIONS TO INSURER**		
52	IMMEDIATELY	—	
53	AS SOON AS POSSIBLE	—	
54	AS SOON AS PRACTICABLE	●	VI.F.2.b., page 5
55	WITHIN POLICY PERIOD	—	
56	WITHIN X DAYS OF EXPIRATION	60	VI.H.1., page 6
57	WITHIN X DAYS	—	
8	**EXTENDED REPORTING FEATURES**		
58	ELECTION PERIOD (DAYS)	60	VI.I.3., page 6
59	ADDITIONAL PREMIUM (% OF ANNUAL PREMIUM)	—	
60	ADDITIONAL REPORTING PERIOD (MONTHS)	36	VI.I.1., page 6
61	NO REINSTATEMENT OF LIMITS	—	
9	**POTENTIAL CLAIM REPORTING PROVISIONS**		
62	NONE (SEE ALSO "CLAIM" ABOVE)	—	
63	INCIDENTS LIKELY TO RESULT IN A CLAIM	●	VI.F., page 5
10	**DEFENSE PROVISIONS**		
64	AFFIRMATIVE DUTY TO DEFEND	●	I.A.2.a., page 1
65	NO AFFIRMATIVE DUTY TO DEFEND	—	
66	AFFIRMATIVE ADVANCEMENT PROVISIONS	—	
67	INSURED MUST RETURN ADVANCED AMOUNTS IF NOT COVERED	—	
68	INSURED/INSURER CHOOSES COUNSEL	●	Insurer	I.A.2.a., page 1
69	INSURED/INSURER APPROVES COUNSEL	—	
70	INSURED/INSURER CONSULTED IN COUNSEL SELECTION	—	
11	**SETTLEMENT PROVISIONS**		
71	HAMMER CLAUSE	—	
72	CONSULTATION PROVISION	—	
73	CONSENT PROVISION	—	
12	**ALLOCATION OF LOSS PROVISIONS**		
74	STIPULATED PROVISIONS	—	
13	**COVERAGES**		
75	DISCRIMINATION	●	See also VIII.M., page 9	I.A.1., page 1
76	SPECIFIC ENUMERATED ACTIVITIES	●	VIII.C., page 9
77	PLUS BROAD OMNIBUS WORDING	●	VIII.C., page 9
78	SPECIFIC ENUMERATED CLASSES	●	VIII.C., page 9
79	PLUS BROAD OMNIBUS WORDING	—	
80	AGAINST THIRD PARTIES	—	
81	DISCRIMINATION NOT DEFINED	—	
82	SEXUAL HARASSMENT	●	See also VIII.M., page 9	I.A.1., page 1
83	HOSTILE ENVIRONMENT	●	VIII.I., page 9
84	QUID-PRO-QUO	●	VIII.I., page 9
85	SEXUAL HARASSMENT NOT DEFINED	—	
86	WRONGFUL TERMINATION	●	See also VIII.M., page 9	I.A.1., page 1
87	BREACH OF IMPLIED CONTRACT	—	
88	BREACH OF EXPRESS CONTRACT	—	
89	VIOLATION OF PUBLIC POLICY	—	
90	VIOLATION OF GOOD FAITH & FAIR DEALING	—	
91	OBLIGATIONS TO MAKE PAYMENTS	—	
92	CONSTRUCTIVE DISCHARGE	—	
93	WRONGFUL TERMINATION NOT DEFINED	—	
94	OTHER EMPLOYMENT VIOLATIONS/OFFENSES	—	
95	WRONGFUL HIRING	●	If discrimination	VIII.C., page 9
96	WRONGFUL PROMOTION/DEMOTION	●	VIII.C., page 9
97	WRONGFUL EVALUATION/DISCIPLINE	—	

LEXINGTON INSURANCE COMPANY 65200 [12/95]

#	Comparison Query		Comment	Policy Reference
98	FAMILY AND MEDICAL LEAVE ACT	—		
99	DEFAMATION	—		
100	MISREPRESENTATION	—		
101	RETALIATION	—		
102	MENTAL ANGUISH	—		
103	INVASION OF PRIVACY	—		
104	HUMILIATION	—		
105	EMOTIONAL DISTRESS	—		
106	OTHER PERSONAL INJURY OFFENSES	—		
107	POLICY SILENT	●		
14 EXCLUSIONS				
108	**ADA ACCOMMODATION EXPENSES**	●		I.B.10., page 2
109	**ASSAULT & BATTERY**	●		I.B.18., page 3
110	**BACK PAY**	—		
111	**BODILY INJURY**	●		I.B.2., page 2
112	BODILY INJURY	●	Physical injury	VIII.A., page 9
113	DEATH	●		VIII.A., page 9
114	DISEASE	●		VIII.A., page 9
115	SICKNESS	●		VIII.A., page 9
116	**BREACH OF EMPLOYMENT CONTRACT**	●		VIII.N., pages 9–10
117	EXPRESS CONTRACT	●		VIII.N., pages 9–10
118	WRITTEN CONTRACT	●		VIII.N., pages 9–10
119	ORAL CONTRACT	●		VIII.N., pages 9–10
120	IMPLIED CONTRACT	—		
121	**CLASS ACTION LAWSUITS**	—		
122	**CONSEQUENTIAL LOSS**	●		I.B.15., page 3
123	APPLIES TO BODILY INJURY	—		
124	APPLIES TO INSURED EVENT	●	Wrongful act	I.B.15., page 3
125	BROTHER/SISTER	●		I.B.15., page 3
126	CHILD	●		I.B.15., page 3
127	DOMESTIC PARTNER	●		I.B.15., page 3
128	PARENT	●		I.B.15., page 3
129	SPOUSE	●		I.B.15., page 3
130	**COST OF ARBITRATION HEARINGS SUBJECT TO**	—		
131	EMPLOYMENT HANDBOOK	—		
132	LABOR GRIEVANCE	—		
133	OTHER EMPLOYMENT POLICY OR PROCEDURE	—		
134	**COVERAGE ELSEWHERE**	●		VI.L., page 7
135	OTHER AVAILABLE INSURANCE	●		VI.L.2., page 7
136	OTHER INDEMNIFICATION	—		
137	SHARING PROVISION	●		VI.L., page 7
138	**FAILURE TO EXERCISE CARE WHEN TERMINATING**	●		VIII.N., page 10
139	**FINES/PENALTIES**	●		I.B.20., page 3
140	CIVIL	—		
141	CRIMINAL	—		
142	EXEMPLARY DAMAGES	●		I.B.20., page 3
143	PUNITIVE DAMAGES	●		I.B.20., page 3
144	MULTIPLIED DAMAGES	●		I.B.20., page 3
145	**FRONT PAY**	—		
146	EXCLUSION APPLIES ONLY IF EMPLOYER HAD OPPORTUNITY TO REINSTATE EMPLOYEE BUT DID NOT DO SO	—		
147	**INTENTIONAL ACTS**	—		
148	CRIMINAL ACTS	●		I.B.17., page 3
149	CRIMINAL PROCEEDING	—		
150	DISHONEST PURPOSE	●		I.B.17., page 3
151	FRAUDULENT ACTS	●		I.B.17., page 3
152	FRAUDULENT CLAIMS	—		
153	INTENTIONAL VIOLATIONS OF LAW	—		
154	WILLFUL FAILURE TO COMPLY WITH LAW	●		I.B.4., page 2
155	MALICIOUS PURPOSE	●		I.B.17., page 3
156	**LIABILITY OF OTHERS**	●		I.B.5., page 2
157	**LIQUIDATED DAMAGES**	—		
158	**LOSS ARISING OUT OF CHANGES IN OPERATIONS**	●		I.B.16., page 3
159	ACQUISITION	—		
160	CHANGE IN CONTROL	—		
161	DOWNSIZING OR REDUCTION IN FORCE	●		I.B.16., page 3
162	% OF WORKFORCE	20		I.B.16., page 3
163	WITHIN X DAYS	60		I.B.16., page 3

LEXINGTON INSURANCE COMPANY 65200 [12/95]

#	Comparison Query	Comment	Policy Reference
164	FINANCIAL IMPAIRMENT	—	
165	BANKRUPTCY	—	
166	INSOLVENCY	—	
167	LIQUIDATION	—	
168	RECEIVERSHIP	—	
169	FINANCIAL INABILITY TO PAY	—	
170	MERGER	—	
171	PLANT OR FACILITY CLOSING	●	I.B.16., page 3
172	REORGANIZATION	●	I.B.16., page 3
173	TEMPORARY SHUTDOWN	—	
174	**MATTERS DEEMED UNINSURABLE**	●	I.B.21., page 3
175	**NON-MONETARY RELIEF**	●	I.B.19., page 3
176	DECLATORY RELIEF	●	IB.19., page 3
177	DISGORGEMENT	●	IB.19., page 3
178	INJUNCTIVE RELIEF	●	IB.19., page 3
179	JOB REINSTATEMENT	●	IB.19., page 3
180	NON-MONETARY DAMAGES/RELIEF	●	IB.19., page 3
181	OTHER EQUITABLE REMEDIES	●	IB.19., page 3
182	**OBLIGATION TO PROVIDE BENEFITS**	—	
183	COBRA	●	I.B.9., page 2
184	DISABILITY	●	I.B.3., page 2
185	ERISA	●	I.B.6., page 2
186	SOCIAL SECURITY	●	I.B.12., page 3
187	OTHER RETIREMENT BENEFITS	●	
188	UNEMPLOYMENT	●	I.B.3., page 2
189	WORKERS' COMPENSATION	●	I.B.3., page 2
190	**PERSONAL INJURY OFFENSES**	—	
191	DEFAMATION	—	
192	EMOTIONAL DISTRESS/UPSET	—	
193	HUMILIATION	—	
194	LIBEL	—	
195	MENTAL ANGUISH	—	
196	PERSONAL INJURY	—	
197	SLANDER	—	
198	**PRIOR ACTS**	●	I.A.1.a., page 1
199	PRIOR ACTS	●	I.A.1.a., page 1
200	PRIOR KNOWLEDGE	●	I.B.22., page 3
201	PRIOR/PENDING LITIGATION	—	
202	**PROPERTY DAMAGE**	●	I.B.1., page 2
203	INTANGIBLE PROPERTY	—	
204	LOSS OF USE	●	VIII.G., page 9
205	TANGIBLE PROPERTY	●	VIII.G., page 9
206	**RETALIATORY ACTIONS OF EMPLOYER**	●	I.B.13., page 3
207	FOR FAILING TO PERFORM ACTS AGAINST PUBLIC POLICY	●	I.B.13., page 3
208	FOR FILING A COMPLAINT OR BENEFIT CLAIM	●	I.B.13., page 3
209	**STRIKES/LOCKOUTS**	●	I.B.14., page 3
210	**VIOLATION OF LAWS**	—	
211	ANY LAW	—	
212	FMLA	—	
213	OSHA	●	I.B.11., page 2
214	POLLUTION LAWS	—	
215	RICO	—	
216	SEC	—	
217	WARN	●	I.B.7., page 2

15 CONDITIONS

#	Comparison Query	Comment	Policy Reference
218	**ARBITRATION**	●	VI.A., page 4
219	MANDATORY	●	VI.A., page 4
220	BINDING	●	VI.A., page 4
221	CHOICE OF LAW PROVISION	—	
222	SITUS	●	New York, NY	VI.A., page 4
223	**TERRITORY**	●	VI.E., page 5
224	LIMITED	●	VI.E., page 5
225	WORLDWIDE	—	
226	**NEWLY FORMED/ACQUIRED ENTITIES**	●	II.D., page 4
227	AUTOMATIC COVERAGE (X DAYS)	90	II.D., page 4
228	NOTIFY INSURER WITHIN X DAYS	—	

LEXINGTON INSURANCE COMPANY 65200 [12/95]

Policy Comparison Worksheet

Lexington Insurance Company

Policy Form No.: LEX-CM-EPLIT
Edition Date: 9/97

Risks Considered: General accounts
Limits Available: $100,000,000
Minimum Retention: $10,000

Contact: Rob Jurgel/Paul Cunningham
Lexington Insurance Company
200 State Street, Fourth Floor
Boston, MA 02109
617/330-8445
617/439-9794 (fax)

KEY TO SYMBOLS
● = Specifically contains queried provision of feature
○ = Unable to determine
— = Silent

#	Comparison Query		Comment	Policy Reference
	1 APPLICATION			
1	ATTACHES TO AND FORMS A PART OF THE POLICY	●		I., page 1
2	CONTAINS WARRANTY STATEMENTS	●		Application, page 5
3	CONTAINS SEVERABILITY PROVISIONS	—		
	2 POLICY TYPE			
4	UNITARY STAND ALONE POLICY	●		
	ENDORSEMENT OR PART OF	—		
5	DIRECTORS AND OFFICERS POLICY	—		
6	PACKAGE POLICY	—		
7	UMBRELLA POLICY	—		
8	ERRORS AND OMISSIONS POLICY	—		
9	OTHER	—		
10	CLAIMS-MADE	●		
11	OCCURRENCE	—		
	3 WHO IS INSURED			
12	BUSINESS ENTITY	●		III.B., page 3
13	AUTOMATIC COVERAGE FOR SUBSIDIARIES	●		III.B., page 3
14	DIRECTORS & OFFICERS	●	See also VII.D., page 5	III.B., page 3
15	EMPLOYEES	●		III.E., page 4
16	PART-TIME	●		VII.D., page 5
17	SEASONAL	●		VII.D., page 5
18	TEMPORARY	●		VII.D., page 5
19	SUPERVISORS & MANAGERS	●		VII.D., page 5
20	FORMER EMPLOYEES	●		
21	VOLUNTEERS	—		
22	INDEPENDENT CONTRACTORS	—	Coverage available by endorsement	
23	EXCLUDED	—		
24	SILENT	—		
25	SHAREHOLDERS	—		
	4 LIMIT OF LIABILITY			
26	AGGREGATE	●		V.B., page 4
27	INCLUDES PUNITIVE DAMAGES WHERE NOT UNINSURABLE	●		VII.F., page 6
28	DEFENSE COSTS INCLUDED WITHIN LIMIT OF LIABILITY	●		II.B.2.e., page 2
29	DEFENSE COSTS PAID IN ADDITION TO LIMIT OF LIABILITY	—		
	5 DEDUCTIBLE			
30	APPLIES TO EACH INDIVIDUAL CLAIM	●		VIII.A., page 7
31	APPLIES TO EACH OCCURRENCE OR WRONGFUL PRACTICE	—		
32	INCLUDES ALL CLAIMS FROM ONE ACT	●		VI.C., page 5
33	SUBJECT TO ANNUAL AGGREGATE	—		
34	CO-PAYMENT APPLIES	—		
35	LIMIT OF LIABILITY NOT REDUCED	—		
36	INCLUDES DEFENSE COSTS	●	See also VII.F., page 6	VIII.A., page 7
37	REDUCED UNDER SPECIFIED CIRCUMSTANCES (SEE POLICY)	—		

LEXINGTON INSURANCE COMPANY LEX-CM-EPLIT [9/97]

#	Comparison Query	Comment	Policy Reference
	6 WHAT IS A CLAIM		
38	ORAL COMPLAINT TO INSURED	●	VII.D., page 6
39	WRITTEN COMPLAINT TO INSURED	●	VII.A., page 5
40	COMPLAINT MUST CONTAIN A DEMAND FOR DAMAGES	●	VII.A., page 5
41	COMPLAINT FILED WITH EEOC	—	
42	OR SIMILAR STATE AUTHORITY	—	
43	AGENCY MUST HAVE POWER TO ADJUDICATE	—	
44	ADMINISTRATIVE PROCEEDING	●	VII.A., page 5
45	ARBITRATION PROCEEDING	●	As alternative dispute resolution proceeding	VII.A., page 5
46	ANY INCIDENT REPORTED TO INSURER	—	
47	SUIT	●	VII.A., page 5
48	CLAIM DOES NOT INCLUDE ARBITRATION SUBJECT TO	●	VII.A., page 5
49	COLLECTIVE BARGAINING AGREEMENT	●	VII.A., page 5
50	EMPLOYEE POLICY OR MANUAL	—	
51	CLAIM NOT DEFINED	—	
	7 CLAIM REPORTING PROVISIONS TO INSURER		
52	IMMEDIATELY	—	
53	AS SOON AS POSSIBLE	—	
54	AS SOON AS PRACTICABLE	●	X.A.2., page 8
55	WITHIN POLICY PERIOD	—	
56	WITHIN X DAYS OF EXPIRATION	—	
57	WITHIN X DAYS	—	
	8 EXTENDED REPORTING FEATURES		
58	ELECTION PERIOD (DAYS)	60	IX.C., page 7
59	ADDITIONAL PREMIUM (% OF ANNUAL PREMIUM)	200	IX.C., page 7
60	ADDITIONAL REPORTING PERIOD (MONTHS)	36	IX.C., page 7
61	NO REINSTATEMENT OF LIMITS	●	IX.D., pages 7–8
	9 POTENTIAL CLAIM REPORTING PROVISIONS		
62	NONE (SEE ALSO "CLAIM" ABOVE)	—	
63	INCIDENTS LIKELY TO RESULT IN A CLAIM	●	X.A.1., page 8
	10 DEFENSE PROVISIONS		
64	AFFIRMATIVE DUTY TO DEFEND	●	II.B.1., page 2
65	NO AFFIRMATIVE DUTY TO DEFEND	—	
66	AFFIRMATIVE ADVANCEMENT PROVISIONS	—	
67	INSURED MUST RETURN ADVANCED AMOUNTS IF NOT COVERED	—	
68	INSURED/INSURER CHOOSES COUNSEL	●	Insurer chooses	II.B.1., page 2
69	INSURED/INSURER APPROVES COUNSEL	●	Insured must consent	II.B.1., page 2
70	INSURED/INSURER CONSULTED IN COUNSEL SELECTION	●	II.B.1., page 2
	11 SETTLEMENT PROVISIONS		
71	HAMMER CLAUSE	●	II.B.2.d., page 2
72	CONSULTATION PROVISION	—	
73	CONSENT PROVISION	—	
	12 ALLOCATION OF LOSS PROVISIONS		
74	STIPULATED PROVISIONS	—	
	13 COVERAGES		
75	DISCRIMINATION	●	See also VII.(D).(1)., page 6	I., page 1
76	SPECIFIC ENUMERATED ACTIVITIES	●	VII.C., page 5
77	PLUS BROAD OMNIBUS WORDING	●	VII.C., page 5
78	SPECIFIC ENUMERATED CLASSES	●	VII.C., page 5
79	PLUS BROAD OMNIBUS WORDING	●	VII.C., page 5
80	AGAINST THIRD PARTIES	—	Coverage available by endorsement	
81	DISCRIMINATION NOT DEFINED	—	
82	SEXUAL HARASSMENT	●	See also VII.(D).(2)., page 6	I., page 1
83	HOSTILE ENVIRONMENT	●	VII.H., page 6
84	QUID-PRO-QUO	●	VII.H., page 6
85	SEXUAL HARASSMENT NOT DEFINED	—	
86	WRONGFUL TERMINATION	●	See also VII.(D).(3)., page 6	I., page 1
87	BREACH OF IMPLIED CONTRACT	●	VII.J., page 6
88	BREACH OF EXPRESS CONTRACT	—	
89	VIOLATION OF PUBLIC POLICY	—	
90	VIOLATION OF GOOD FAITH & FAIR DEALING	—	
91	OBLIGATIONS TO MAKE PAYMENTS	—	
92	CONSTRUCTIVE DISCHARGE	—	
93	WRONGFUL TERMINATION NOT DEFINED	—	
94	OTHER EMPLOYMENT VIOLATIONS/OFFENSES	●	VII.I., page 6
95	WRONGFUL HIRING	●	As workplace tort	VII.I., page 6
96	WRONGFUL PROMOTION/DEMOTION	●	As workplace tort	VII.I., page 6
97	WRONGFUL EVALUATION/DISCIPLINE	●	As workplace tort	VII.I., page 6

LEXINGTON INSURANCE COMPANY LEX-CM-EPLIT [9/97

	Comparison Query		Comment	Policy Reference
98	FAMILY AND MEDICAL LEAVE ACT	—		
99	DEFAMATION	●	As workplace tort	VII.I., page 6
100	MISREPRESENTATION	●	As workplace tort	VII.I., page 6
101	RETALIATION	●	As workplace tort	VII.I., page 6
102	MENTAL ANGUISH	—		
103	INVASION OF PRIVACY	●	As workplace tort	VII.I., page 6
104	HUMILIATION	—		
105	EMOTIONAL DISTRESS	●	As workplace tort	VII.I., page 6
106	OTHER PERSONAL INJURY OFFENSES	●	As workplace tort	VII.I., page 6
107	POLICY SILENT	—		
14 EXCLUSIONS				
108	**ADA ACCOMMODATION EXPENSES**	●		IV.F., page 4
109	**ASSAULT & BATTERY**	—		
110	**BACK PAY**	—		
111	**BODILY INJURY**			
112	BODILY INJURY	—		
113	DEATH	—		
114	DISEASE	—		
115	SICKNESS	—		
116	**BREACH OF EMPLOYMENT CONTRACT**	●		VII.J., page 6
117	EXPRESS CONTRACT	●		VII.J., page 6
118	WRITTEN CONTRACT	—		
119	ORAL CONTRACT	—		
120	IMPLIED CONTRACT	—		
121	**CLASS ACTION LAWSUITS**	—		
122	**CONSEQUENTIAL LOSS**	—		
123	APPLIES TO BODILY INJURY	—		
124	APPLIES TO INSURED EVENT	—		
125	BROTHER/SISTER	—		
126	CHILD	—		
127	DOMESTIC PARTNER	—		
128	PARENT	—		
129	SPOUSE	—		
130	**COST OF ARBITRATION HEARINGS SUBJECT TO**	—		
131	EMPLOYMENT HANDBOOK	—		
132	LABOR GRIEVANCE	—		
133	OTHER EMPLOYMENT POLICY OR PROCEDURE	—		
134	**COVERAGE ELSEWHERE**	●		X.B.2., page 9
135	OTHER AVAILABLE INSURANCE	●	If policy written as excess	X.B.2., page 9
136	OTHER INDEMNIFICATION	—		
137	SHARING PROVISION	—		
138	**FAILURE TO EXERCISE CARE WHEN TERMINATING**	—		
139	**FINES/PENALTIES**	●		VII.F., page 6
140	CIVIL	—		
141	CRIMINAL	●		VII.F., page 6
142	EXEMPLARY DAMAGES	—		
143	PUNITIVE DAMAGES	—		
144	MULTIPLIED DAMAGES	—		
145	**FRONT PAY**	—		
146	EXCLUSION APPLIES ONLY IF EMPLOYER HAD OPPORTUNITY TO REINSTATE EMPLOYEE BUT DID NOT DO SO	—		
147	**INTENTIONAL ACTS**	—		
148	CRIMINAL ACTS	—		
149	CRIMINAL PROCEEDING	—		
150	DISHONEST PURPOSE	—		
151	FRAUDULENT ACTS	—		
152	FRAUDULENT CLAIMS	—		
153	INTENTIONAL VIOLATIONS OF LAW	—		
154	WILLFUL FAILURE TO COMPLY WITH LAW	—		
155	MALICIOUS PURPOSE	—		
156	**LIABILITY OF OTHERS**	●		IV.B., page 4
157	**LIQUIDATED DAMAGES**	—		
158	**LOSS ARISING OUT OF CHANGES IN OPERATIONS**	—		
159	ACQUISITION	—		
160	CHANGE IN CONTROL	—		
161	DOWNSIZING OR REDUCTION IN FORCE	—		
162	% OF WORKFORCE	—		
163	WITHIN X DAYS	—		

LEXINGTON INSURANCE COMPANY LEX-CM-EPLIT [9/97]

	Comparison Query		Comment	Policy Reference
164	**FINANCIAL IMPAIRMENT**	—		
165	*BANKRUPTCY*	—		
166	*INSOLVENCY*	—		
167	*LIQUIDATION*	—		
168	*RECEIVERSHIP*	—		
169	FINANCIAL INABILITY TO PAY	—		
170	MERGER	—		
171	PLANT OR FACILITY CLOSING	—		
172	REORGANIZATION	—		
173	TEMPORARY SHUTDOWN	—		
174	**MATTERS DEEMED UNINSURABLE**	—		
175	**NON-MONETARY RELIEF**	—		
176	DECLATORY RELIEF	—		
177	DISGORGEMENT	—		
178	INJUNCTIVE RELIEF	—		
179	JOB REINSTATEMENT	—		
180	NON-MONETARY DAMAGES/RELIEF	—		
181	OTHER EQUITABLE REMEDIES	—		
182	**OBLIGATION TO PROVIDE BENEFITS**	—		
183	COBRA	—		
184	DISABILITY	●		IV.A., page 3
185	ERISA	●		IV.C., page 4
186	SOCIAL SECURITY	—		
187	OTHER RETIREMENT BENEFITS	—		
188	UNEMPLOYMENT	●		IV.A., page 3
189	WORKERS' COMPENSATION	●		IV.A., page 3
190	**PERSONAL INJURY OFFENSES**	—		
191	DEFAMATION	—		
192	EMOTIONAL DISTRESS/UPSET	—		
193	HUMILIATION	—		
194	LIBEL	—		
195	MENTAL ANGUISH	—		
196	PERSONAL INJURY	—		
197	SLANDER	—		
198	**PRIOR ACTS**	—		
199	PRIOR ACTS	—		
200	PRIOR KNOWLEDGE	—		
201	PRIOR/PENDING LITIGATION	—		
202	**PROPERTY DAMAGE**	—		
203	INTANGIBLE PROPERTY	—		
204	LOSS OF USE	—		
205	TANGIBLE PROPERTY	—		
206	**RETALIATORY ACTIONS OF EMPLOYER**	—		
207	FOR FAILING TO PERFORM ACTS AGAINST PUBLIC POLICY	—		
208	FOR FILING A COMPLAINT OR BENEFIT CLAIM	—		
209	**STRIKES/LOCKOUTS**	●	Wrongful termination/retaliation exception	IV.D., page 4
210	**VIOLATION OF LAWS**	—		
211	ANY LAW	—		
212	FMLA	—		
213	OSHA	—		
214	POLLUTION LAWS	—		
215	RICO	—		
216	SEC	—		
217	WARN	●		IV.E., page 4

15 CONDITIONS

218	**ARBITRATION**	●		X.L., pages 11–12
219	MANDATORY	●		X.L., pages 11–12
220	BINDING	●		X.L., pages 11–12
221	CHOICE OF LAW PROVISION	—		
222	SITUS	●	Boston, MA	X.L., pages 11–12
223	**TERRITORY**	—		
224	LIMITED	—		
225	WORLDWIDE	—		
226	**NEWLY FORMED/ACQUIRED ENTITIES**	●		III.D., page 3
227	AUTOMATIC COVERAGE (X DAYS)	●	< 20% employees involved—no time limit	III.D., page 3
228	NOTIFY INSURER WITHIN X DAYS	90	> 20% employees involved—no time limit	III.D., page 3

LEXINGTON INSURANCE COMPANY LEX-CM-EPLIT [9/97]

Policy Comparison Worksheet

London Market
(American Technology Excess and Surplus Insurance Services)

Policy Form No.: AmTech Form ERP-1
Edition Date: 11/96

Risks Considered: Professional associations
Limits Available: $2,000,000/$2,000,000
Minimum Retention: $5,000

Contact: Richard V. Rupp, CPCU
Managing Director
AmTech E&S
P.O. Box M
San Mateo, CA 94402-0080
415/572-4665
415/572-4662 (fax)
rupprisk@aol.com

KEY TO SYMBOLS
- ● = Specifically contains queried provision of feature
- ○ = Unable to determine
- — = Silent

#	Comparison Query		Comment	Policy Reference
	1 APPLICATION			
1	ATTACHES TO AND FORMS A PART OF THE POLICY	●		XI.I., page 12
2	CONTAINS WARRANTY STATEMENTS	●		
3	CONTAINS SEVERABILITY PROVISIONS	—		
	2 POLICY TYPE			
4	UNITARY STAND ALONE POLICY	●		
	ENDORSEMENT OR PART OF	—		
5	DIRECTORS AND OFFICERS POLICY	—		
6	PACKAGE POLICY	—		
7	UMBRELLA POLICY	—		
8	ERRORS AND OMISSIONS POLICY	—		
9	OTHER	—		
10	CLAIMS-MADE	●		
11	OCCURRENCE	—		
	3 WHO IS INSURED			
12	BUSINESS ENTITY	●		III.1.d., page 4
13	AUTOMATIC COVERAGE FOR SUBSIDIARIES	—		
14	DIRECTORS & OFFICERS	●		III.2.b., page 5
15	EMPLOYEES	●	See also XI.7., page 13	III.2.b., page 5
16	PART-TIME	●	See also XI.7., page 13	III.2.b., page 5
17	SEASONAL	●	See also XI.7., page 13	III.2.b., page 5
18	TEMPORARY	●	See also XI.7., page 13	III.2.b., page 5
19	SUPERVISORS & MANAGERS	●	See also XI.7., page 13	III.2.b., page 5
20	FORMER EMPLOYEES	—		
21	VOLUNTEERS	—		
22	INDEPENDENT CONTRACTORS	—		
23	EXCLUDED	●	Unless representing insured	XI.7., page 13
24	SILENT	—		
25	SHAREHOLDERS	●		III.1.d., page 4
	4 LIMIT OF LIABILITY			
26	AGGREGATE	●		IV.4., page 6
27	INCLUDES PUNITIVE DAMAGES WHERE NOT UNINSURABLE	●	Limitation applies	XI.12.d., page 14
28	DEFENSE COSTS INCLUDED WITHIN LIMIT OF LIABILITY	●		Preamble, 1., page 1
29	DEFENSE COSTS PAID IN ADDITION TO LIMIT OF LIABILITY	—		
	5 DEDUCTIBLE			
30	APPLIES TO EACH INDIVIDUAL CLAIM	●		V.4., page 6
31	APPLIES TO EACH OCCURRENCE OR WRONGFUL PRACTICE	●		V.4., page 6
32	INCLUDES ALL CLAIMS FROM ONE ACT	●		V.4., page 6
33	SUBJECT TO ANNUAL AGGREGATE	—		
34	CO-PAYMENT APPLIES	○	See defense provisions	VI., page 7
35	LIMIT OF LIABILITY NOT REDUCED	●		V.1., page 6
36	INCLUDES DEFENSE COSTS	●		V.2., page 6
37	REDUCED UNDER SPECIFIED CIRCUMSTANCES (SEE POLICY)	●		IX., page 12

#	Comparison Query	Comment		Policy Reference
	6 WHAT IS A CLAIM			
38	ORAL COMPLAINT TO INSURED	●		XI.3., page 13
39	WRITTEN COMPLAINT TO INSURED	●		XI.3., page 13
40	COMPLAINT MUST CONTAIN A DEMAND FOR DAMAGES	●		XI.3., page 13
41	COMPLAINT FILED WITH EEOC	—		
42	OR SIMILAR STATE AUTHORITY	—		
43	AGENCY MUST HAVE POWER TO ADJUDICATE	—		
44	ADMINISTRATIVE PROCEEDING	—		
45	ARBITRATION PROCEEDING	●		XI.3., page 13
46	ANY INCIDENT REPORTED TO INSURER	—		
47	SUIT	●	See also XI.18.a., page 15	XI.3., page 13
48	CLAIM DOES NOT INCLUDE ARBITRATION SUBJECT TO	●		XI.3., page 13
49	COLLECTIVE BARGAINING AGREEMENT	●		XI.3., page 13
50	EMPLOYEE POLICY OR MANUAL	—		
51	CLAIM NOT DEFINED	—		
	7 CLAIM REPORTING PROVISIONS TO INSURER			
52	IMMEDIATELY	—		
53	AS SOON AS POSSIBLE	●		VII.1.a., page 7
54	AS SOON AS PRACTICABLE	—		
55	WITHIN POLICY PERIOD	—		
56	WITHIN X DAYS OF EXPIRATION	—		
57	WITHIN X DAYS	30		VII.1.a., page 7
	8 EXTENDED REPORTING FEATURES			
58	ELECTION PERIOD (DAYS)	30		VIII.4., page 12
59	ADDITIONAL PREMIUM (% OF ANNUAL PREMIUM)	100		VIII.4., page 12
60	ADDITIONAL REPORTING PERIOD (MONTHS)	24		VIII.4., page 12
61	NO REINSTATEMENT OF LIMITS	●		VIII.5., page 12
	9 POTENTIAL CLAIM REPORTING PROVISIONS			
62	NONE (SEE ALSO "CLAIM" ABOVE)	—		
63	INCIDENTS LIKELY TO RESULT IN A CLAIM	●	See also XI.2., page 12	VII.1.d., page 8
	10 DEFENSE PROVISIONS			
64	AFFIRMATIVE DUTY TO DEFEND	○	Duty to pay "defense costs"	I.2., page 2
65	NO AFFIRMATIVE DUTY TO DEFEND	—		
66	AFFIRMATIVE ADVANCEMENT PROVISIONS	—		
67	INSURED MUST RETURN ADVANCED AMOUNTS IF NOT COVERED	—		
68	INSURED/INSURER CHOOSES COUNSEL	●	Insurer chooses	I.3.a., page 2
69	INSURED/INSURER APPROVES COUNSEL	●	Insurer approves if insured chooses	I.3.b., page 2
70	INSURED/INSURER CONSULTED IN COUNSEL SELECTION	○		I.3.b., page 2
	11 SETTLEMENT PROVISIONS			
71	HAMMER CLAUSE	●		I.5., page 3
72	CONSULTATION PROVISION	—		
73	CONSENT PROVISION	●		I.5., page 3
	12 ALLOCATION OF LOSS PROVISIONS			
74	STIPULATED PROVISIONS	—		
	13 COVERAGES			
75	DISCRIMINATION	—		
76	SPECIFIC ENUMERATED ACTIVITIES	●		XI.6., page 13
77	*PLUS BROAD OMNIBUS WORDING*	●		XI.6., page 13
78	SPECIFIC ENUMERATED CLASSES	●		XI.6., page 13
79	*PLUS BROAD OMNIBUS WORDING*	●		XI.6., page 13
80	AGAINST THIRD PARTIES	—		
81	DISCRIMINATION NOT DEFINED	—		
82	SEXUAL HARASSMENT	—		
83	HOSTILE ENVIRONMENT	●		XI.17., page 15
84	QUID-PRO-QUO	●		
85	SEXUAL HARASSMENT NOT DEFINED	—		
86	WRONGFUL TERMINATION	—	As ("Inapprorpiate Employment Conduct")	XI.9., pages 13–14
87	BREACH OF IMPLIED CONTRACT	●		XI.9., pages 13–14
88	BREACH OF EXPRESS CONTRACT	—		
89	VIOLATION OF PUBLIC POLICY	—		
90	VIOLATION OF GOOD FAITH & FAIR DEALING	—		
91	OBLIGATIONS TO MAKE PAYMENTS	—		
92	CONSTRUCTIVE DISCHARGE	●		XI.9., pages 13–14
93	WRONGFUL TERMINATION NOT DEFINED	●		
94	OTHER EMPLOYMENT VIOLATIONS/OFFENSES	—		
95	WRONGFUL HIRING	—		
96	WRONGFUL PROMOTION/DEMOTION	●		XI.9.a., page 14
97	WRONGFUL EVALUATION/DISCIPLINE	—		

LONDON MARKET/AMERICAN TECHNOLOGY EXCESS AND SURPLUS INSURANCE SERVICES AmTech Form ERP-1 [11/96]

#	Comparison Query	Comment	Policy Reference
98	FAMILY AND MEDICAL LEAVE ACT	—	
99	DEFAMATION	●	XI.9.c., page 14
100	MISREPRESENTATION	●	XI.9.c., page 14
101	RETALIATION	●	XI.9.b., page 14
102	MENTAL ANGUISH	●	XI.9.d., page 14
103	INVASION OF PRIVACY	●	XI.9.f., page 14
104	HUMILIATION		
105	EMOTIONAL DISTRESS	●	XI.9.d., page 14
106	OTHER PERSONAL INJURY OFFENSES	●	XI.9.e., page 14
107	POLICY SILENT	—	
14	**EXCLUSIONS**		
108	**ADA ACCOMMODATION EXPENSES**	●	XI.12.f., page 14
109	**ASSAULT & BATTERY**	—	
110	**BACK PAY**	—	
111	**BODILY INJURY**	—	
112	BODILY INJURY	—	
113	DEATH	—	
114	DISEASE	—	
115	SICKNESS	—	
116	**BREACH OF EMPLOYMENT CONTRACT**	—	
117	EXPRESS CONTRACT	—	
118	*WRITTEN CONTRACT*	—	
119	*ORAL CONTRACT*	—	
120	IMPLIED CONTRACT	—	
121	**CLASS ACTION LAWSUITS**	—	
122	**CONSEQUENTIAL LOSS**	●	II.5., page 4
123	APPLIES TO BODILY INJURY	—	
124	APPLIES TO INSURED EVENT	—	
125	BROTHER/SISTER	●	II.5., page 4
126	CHILD	●	II.5., page 4
127	DOMESTIC PARTNER	●	II.5., page 4
128	PARENT	●	II.5., page 4
129	SPOUSE	●	II.5., page 4
130	**COST OF ARBITRATION HEARINGS SUBJECT TO**	—	
131	EMPLOYMENT HANDBOOK	—	
132	LABOR GRIEVANCE	—	
133	OTHER EMPLOYMENT POLICY OR PROCEDURE	—	
134	**COVERAGE ELSEWHERE**	●	I.3.b.(1).&(2)., page 9
135	OTHER AVAILABLE INSURANCE	—	
136	OTHER INDEMNIFICATION	—	
137	SHARING PROVISION	●	I.3.b.(1).&(2)., page 9
138	**FAILURE TO EXERCISE CARE WHEN TERMINATING**	—	
139	**FINES/PENALTIES**	●	XI.12.a., page 14
140	CIVIL	●	XI.12.a., page 14
141	CRIMINAL	●	XI.12.a., page 14
142	EXEMPLARY DAMAGES	●	XI.12.b., page 14
143	PUNITIVE DAMAGES	●	XI.12.b., page 14
144	MULTIPLIED DAMAGES	—	
145	**FRONT PAY**	—	
146	EXCLUSION APPLIES ONLY IF EMPLOYER HAD OPPORTUNITY TO REINSTATE EMPLOYEE BUT DID NOT DO SO	—	
147	**INTENTIONAL ACTS**	—	
148	CRIMINAL ACTS	—	
149	CRIMINAL PROCEEDING	—	
150	DISHONEST PURPOSE	—	
151	FRAUDULENT ACTS	—	
152	FRAUDULENT CLAIMS	—	
153	INTENTIONAL VIOLATIONS OF LAW	—	
154	WILLFUL FAILURE TO COMPLY WITH LAW	—	
155	MALICIOUS PURPOSE	—	
156	**LIABILITY OF OTHERS**	●	II.2., page 3
157	**LIQUIDATED DAMAGES**	●	XI.C., page 14
158	**LOSS ARISING OUT OF CHANGES IN OPERATIONS**	—	
159	ACQUISITION	—	
160	CHANGE IN CONTROL	—	
161	DOWNSIZING OR REDUCTION IN FORCE	●	II.7., page 4
162	*% OF WORKFORCE*	20	II.7., page 4
163	*WITHIN X DAYS*	60	II.7., page 4

#	Comparison Query		Comment	Policy Reference
164	FINANCIAL IMPAIRMENT	—		
165	*BANKRUPTCY*	—		
166	*INSOLVENCY*	—		
167	*LIQUIDATION*	—		
168	*RECEIVERSHIP*	—		
169	FINANCIAL INABILITY TO PAY	—		
170	MERGER	—		
171	PLANT OR FACILITY CLOSING	●		II.7., page 4
172	REORGANIZATION	●		II.7., page 4
173	TEMPORARY SHUTDOWN	—		
174	**MATTERS DEEMED UNINSURABLE**	●		XI.12.g., page 14
175	**NON-MONETARY RELIEF**			
176	DECLATORY RELIEF	—		
177	DISGORGEMENT	—		
178	INJUNCTIVE RELIEF	—		
179	JOB REINSTATEMENT	—		
180	NON-MONETARY DAMAGES/RELIEF	●		XI.b., page 14
181	OTHER EQUITABLE REMEDIES	—		
182	**OBLIGATION TO PROVIDE BENEFITS**			
183	COBRA	—		
184	DISABILITY	●		II.1., page 3
185	ERISA	●		II.3., page 3
186	SOCIAL SECURITY	—		
187	OTHER RETIREMENT BENEFITS	—		
188	UNEMPLOYMENT	●		II.1., page 3
189	WORKERS' COMPENSATION	●		II.3., page 3
190	**PERSONAL INJURY OFFENSES**			
191	DEFAMATION	—		
192	EMOTIONAL DISTRESS/UPSET	—		
193	HUMILIATION	—		
194	LIBEL	—		
195	MENTAL ANGUISH	—		
196	PERSONAL INJURY	—		
197	SLANDER	—		
198	**PRIOR ACTS**			
199	PRIOR ACTS	—		
200	PRIOR KNOWLEDGE	●		I.1.b.(2)., page 2
201	PRIOR/PENDING LITIGATION	—		
202	**PROPERTY DAMAGE**			
203	INTANGIBLE PROPERTY	—		
204	LOSS OF USE	—		
205	TANGIBLE PROPERTY	—		
206	**RETALIATORY ACTIONS OF EMPLOYER**	—		
207	FOR FAILING TO PERFORM ACTS AGAINST PUBLIC POLICY	—		
208	FOR FILING A COMPLAINT OR BENEFIT CLAIM	—		
209	**STRIKES/LOCKOUTS**	●		II.4., page 4
210	**VIOLATION OF LAWS**			
211	ANY LAW	—		
212	FMLA	—		
213	OSHA	—		
214	POLLUTION LAWS	—		
215	RICO	—		
216	SEC	—		
217	WARN	●		II.6., page 4
15	**CONDITIONS**			
218	**ARBITRATION**	—		
219	MANDATORY	—		
220	BINDING	—		
221	CHOICE OF LAW PROVISION	—		
222	SITUS	—		
223	**TERRITORY**	—		
224	LIMITED	—		
225	WORLDWIDE	●	Restrictions apply	XI.4., page 13
226	**NEWLY FORMED/ACQUIRED ENTITIES**	—		
227	AUTOMATIC COVERAGE (X DAYS)	30		II.2.a., page 5
228	NOTIFY INSURER WITHIN X DAYS	30		II.2.a., page 5

LONDON MARKET/AMERICAN TECHNOLOGY EXCESS AND SURPLUS INSURANCE SERVICES AmTech Form ERP-1 [11/96]

Policy Comparison Worksheet

London Market
(CNA Re/St. Paul Re)

Policy Form No.: EPL (11/97A Broad)
Edition Date: 11/97

Risks Considered: General accounts
Limits Available: $10,000,000
Minimum Retention: $5,000

Contact: Viviane Krief Woodcock
IFIS, Inc.
600 Wilshire Boulevard, #1500
Los Angeles, CA 90017
213/833-0288
213/833-0277 (fax)
vkrief@ecom.net

KEY TO SYMBOLS
● = Specifically contains queried provision of feature
○ = Unable to determine
— = Silent

#	Comparison Query		Comment	Policy Reference
	1 APPLICATION			
1	ATTACHES TO AND FORMS A PART OF THE POLICY	●		Preamble, page 1
2	CONTAINS WARRANTY STATEMENTS	●		Application, page 4
3	CONTAINS SEVERABILITY PROVISIONS	—		
	2 POLICY TYPE			
4	UNITARY STAND ALONE POLICY	●		
	ENDORSEMENT OR PART OF	—		
5	DIRECTORS AND OFFICERS POLICY	—		
6	PACKAGE POLICY	—		
7	UMBRELLA POLICY	—		
8	ERRORS AND OMISSIONS POLICY	—		
9	OTHER	—		
10	CLAIMS-MADE	●		
11	OCCURRENCE	—		
	3 WHO IS INSURED			
12	BUSINESS ENTITY	●		II.1.B., page 3
13	AUTOMATIC COVERAGE FOR SUBSIDIARIES	—		
14	DIRECTORS & OFFICERS	●		II.7., page 4
15	EMPLOYEES	●		II.1.E., page 3
16	PART-TIME	●		II.7., page 4
17	SEASONAL	●		II.7., page 4
18	TEMPORARY	●		II.7., page 4
19	SUPERVISORS & MANAGERS	●		II.7., page 4
20	FORMER EMPLOYEES	—		
21	VOLUNTEERS	—		
22	INDEPENDENT CONTRACTORS	●	If dedicated agents of insured	II.7., page 4
23	EXCLUDED	●	If not dedicated agents	II.7., page 4
24	SILENT	—		
25	SHAREHOLDERS	●		II.I.B., page 3
	4 LIMIT OF LIABILITY			
26	AGGREGATE	●		VII.2., page 6
27	INCLUDES PUNITIVE DAMAGES WHERE NOT UNINSURABLE	●		I. Coverage A.2.E., page 1
28	DEFENSE COSTS INCLUDED WITHIN LIMIT OF LIABILITY	●	See also IV.4., page 5	I. Coverage A.2.E., page 1
29	DEFENSE COSTS PAID IN ADDITION TO LIMIT OF LIABILITY	—		
	5 DEDUCTIBLE			
30	APPLIES TO EACH INDIVIDUAL CLAIM	●		VIII., page 6
31	APPLIES TO EACH OCCURRENCE OR WRONGFUL PRACTICE	—		
32	INCLUDES ALL CLAIMS FROM ONE ACT	●		VIII., page 6
33	SUBJECT TO ANNUAL AGGREGATE	—		
34	CO-PAYMENT APPLIES	●	Specified by underwriter—see Item 4 of Declarations	IX., page 6
35	LIMIT OF LIABILITY NOT REDUCED	●		VIII., page 6
36	INCLUDES DEFENSE COSTS	●		VIII., page 6
37	REDUCED UNDER SPECIFIED CIRCUMSTANCES (SEE POLICY)	●		VIII., page 6

#	Comparison Query	Comment	Policy Reference
6	**WHAT IS A CLAIM**		
38	ORAL COMPLAINT TO INSURED	○	II.5., page 4
39	WRITTEN COMPLAINT TO INSURED	●	II.5., page 4
40	COMPLAINT MUST CONTAIN A DEMAND FOR DAMAGES	●	II.5., page 4
41	COMPLAINT FILED WITH EEOC	—	
42	OR SIMILAR STATE AUTHORITY	—	
43	AGENCY MUST HAVE POWER TO ADJUDICATE	—	
44	ADMINISTRATIVE PROCEEDING	●	II.5., page 4
45	ARBITRATION PROCEEDING	●	II.5., page 4
46	ANY INCIDENT REPORTED TO INSURER	—	
47	SUIT	●	II.5., page 4
48	CLAIM DOES NOT INCLUDE ARBITRATION SUBJECT TO	●	II.5., page 4
49	COLLECTIVE BARGAINING AGREEMENT	●	II.5., page 4
50	EMPLOYEE POLICY OR MANUAL	—	
51	CLAIM NOT DEFINED	—	
7	**CLAIM REPORTING PROVISIONS TO INSURER**		
52	IMMEDIATELY	—	
53	AS SOON AS POSSIBLE	—	
54	AS SOON AS PRACTICABLE	—	
55	WITHIN POLICY PERIOD	—	
56	WITHIN X DAYS OF EXPIRATION	—	
57	WITHIN X DAYS	30	X.2.A., page 6
8	**EXTENDED REPORTING FEATURES**		
58	ELECTION PERIOD (DAYS)	30	V.4., following C., page 5
59	ADDITIONAL PREMIUM (% OF ANNUAL PREMIUM)	100/145/165	V.4.A, B. & C., page 5
60	ADDITIONAL REPORTING PERIOD (MONTHS)	12/24/36	V.4.A, B. & C., page 5
61	NO REINSTATEMENT OF LIMITS	●	V.5., page 5
9	**POTENTIAL CLAIM REPORTING PROVISIONS**		
62	NONE (SEE ALSO "CLAIM" ABOVE)	—	
63	INCIDENTS LIKELY TO RESULT IN A CLAIM	● See also III.6., page 4	X.2.D., page 7
10	**DEFENSE PROVISIONS**		
64	AFFIRMATIVE DUTY TO DEFEND	●	IV.2., page 4
65	NO AFFIRMATIVE DUTY TO DEFEND	—	
66	AFFIRMATIVE ADVANCEMENT PROVISIONS	—	
67	INSURED MUST RETURN ADVANCED AMOUNTS IF NOT COVERED	—	
68	INSURED/INSURER CHOOSES COUNSEL	—	
69	INSURED/INSURER APPROVES COUNSEL	—	
70	INSURED/INSURER CONSULTED IN COUNSEL SELECTION	—	
11	**SETTLEMENT PROVISIONS**		
71	HAMMER CLAUSE	●	IV.5., page 5
72	CONSULTATION PROVISION	—	
73	CONSENT PROVISION	●	IV.5., page 5
12	**ALLOCATION OF LOSS PROVISIONS**		
74	STIPULATED PROVISIONS	—	
13	**COVERAGES**		
75	DISCRIMINATION	●	Preamble, page 1
76	SPECIFIC ENUMERATED ACTIVITIES	●	I. Coverage A.2.B., page 1
77	*PLUS BROAD OMNIBUS WORDING*	●	I. Coverage A.2.B., page 1
78	SPECIFIC ENUMERATED CLASSES	●	I. Coverage A.2.B., page 1
79	*PLUS BROAD OMNIBUS WORDING*	●	I. Coverage A.2.B., page 1
80	AGAINST THIRD PARTIES	●	I. Coverage B.1., page 2
81	DISCRIMINATION NOT DEFINED	—	
82	SEXUAL HARASSMENT	●	Preamble, page 1
83	HOSTILE ENVIRONMENT	●	I. Coverage A.2.C., page 1
84	QUID-PRO-QUO	●	
85	SEXUAL HARASSMENT NOT DEFINED	—	
86	WRONGFUL TERMINATION	● As inappropriate employment conduct	Preamble, page 1
87	BREACH OF IMPLIED CONTRACT	●	I. Coverage A.2.D.(i)., page 1
88	BREACH OF EXPRESS CONTRACT	—	
89	VIOLATION OF PUBLIC POLICY	—	
90	VIOLATION OF GOOD FAITH & FAIR DEALING	—	
91	OBLIGATIONS TO MAKE PAYMENTS	—	
92	CONSTRUCTIVE DISCHARGE	●	I. Coverage A.2.D.(i)., page 1
93	WRONGFUL TERMINATION NOT DEFINED	—	
94	OTHER EMPLOYMENT VIOLATIONS/OFFENSES	●	I. Coverage A.2.D., page 1
95	WRONGFUL HIRING	—	
96	WRONGFUL PROMOTION/DEMOTION	●	I. Coverage A.2.D.(ii)., page 1
97	WRONGFUL EVALUATION/DISCIPLINE	●	I. Coverage A.2.D.(ii)., page 1

LONDON MARKET/CNA RE/ST. PAUL RE EPL (11/97A Broad) [11/97]

	Comparison Query	Comment	Policy Reference
98	FAMILY AND MEDICAL LEAVE ACT	—	
99	DEFAMATION	●	I. Coverage A.2.D.(vi), page 1
100	MISREPRESENTATION	●	I. Coverage A.2.D.(iii), page 1
101	RETALIATION	●	I. Coverage A.2.D.(vii), page 1
102	MENTAL ANGUISH	●	I. Coverage A.2.D.(iv), page 1
103	INVASION OF PRIVACY	●	I. Coverage A.2.D.(vi), page 1
104	HUMILIATION	—	
105	EMOTIONAL DISTRESS	●	I. Coverage A.2.D.(iv), page 1
106	OTHER PERSONAL INJURY OFFENSES	●	I. Coverage A.2.D.(iv), (v), and (vi), page 1
107	POLICY SILENT	—	
14 EXCLUSIONS			
108	**ADA ACCOMMODATION EXPENSES**	●	I. Coverage A.2.E.(iv), page 2
109	**ASSAULT & BATTERY**	—	
110	**BACK PAY**	—	
111	**BODILY INJURY**	—	
112	BODILY INJURY	—	
113	DEATH	—	
114	DISEASE	—	
115	SICKNESS	—	
116	**BREACH OF EMPLOYMENT CONTRACT**	—	
117	EXPRESS CONTRACT	●	I. Coverage A.2.E.(v), page 2
118	WRITTEN CONTRACT	—	
119	ORAL CONTRACT	—	
120	IMPLIED CONTRACT	—	
121	**CLASS ACTION LAWSUITS**	—	
122	**CONSEQUENTIAL LOSS**	●	III.2., page 4
123	APPLIES TO BODILY INJURY	—	
124	APPLIES TO INSURED EVENT	●	III.2., page 4
125	BROTHER/SISTER	●	III.2., page 4
126	CHILD	●	III.2., page 4
127	DOMESTIC PARTNER	●	III.2., page 4
128	PARENT	●	III.2., page 4
129	SPOUSE	●	III.2., page 4
130	**COST OF ARBITRATION HEARINGS SUBJECT TO**	—	
131	EMPLOYMENT HANDBOOK	—	
132	LABOR GRIEVANCE	—	
133	OTHER EMPLOYMENT POLICY OR PROCEDURE	—	
134	**COVERAGE ELSEWHERE**	—	
135	OTHER AVAILABLE INSURANCE	—	
136	OTHER INDEMNIFICATION	—	
137	SHARING PROVISION	●	X.5., page 7
138	**FAILURE TO EXERCISE CARE WHEN TERMINATING**	—	
139	**FINES/PENALTIES**	●	I. Coverage A.2.E.(i), page 1
140	CIVIL	●	I. Coverage A.2.E.(i), page 1
141	CRIMINAL	●	I. Coverage A.2.E.(i), page 1
142	EXEMPLARY DAMAGES	—	
143	PUNITIVE DAMAGES	—	
144	MULTIPLIED DAMAGES	—	
145	**FRONT PAY**	—	
146	EXCLUSION APPLIES ONLY IF EMPLOYER HAD OPPORTUNITY TO REINSTATE EMPLOYEE BUT DID NOT DO SO	—	
147	**INTENTIONAL ACTS**	—	
148	CRIMINAL ACTS	—	
149	CRIMINAL PROCEEDING	—	
150	DISHONEST PURPOSE	—	
151	FRAUDULENT ACTS	—	
152	FRAUDULENT CLAIMS	●	X.12., page 8
153	INTENTIONAL VIOLATIONS OF LAW	—	
154	WILLFUL FAILURE TO COMPLY WITH LAW	—	
155	MALICIOUS PURPOSE	—	
156	**LIABILITY OF OTHERS**	●	As respects loss of income or extra expense	III.1., page 4
157	**LIQUIDATED DAMAGES**	—	
158	**LOSS ARISING OUT OF CHANGES IN OPERATIONS**	—	
159	ACQUISITION	—	
160	CHANGE IN CONTROL	—	
161	DOWNSIZING OR REDUCTION IN FORCE	—	
162	% OF WORKFORCE	—	
163	WITHIN X DAYS	—	

LONDON MARKET/CNA RE/ST. PAUL RE EPL (11/97A Broad) [11/97]

	Comparison Query	Comment		Policy Reference
164	FINANCIAL IMPAIRMENT	—		
165	BANKRUPTCY	—		
166	INSOLVENCY	—		
167	LIQUIDATION	—		
168	RECEIVERSHIP	—		
169	FINANCIAL INABILITY TO PAY	—		
170	MERGER	—		
171	PLANT OR FACILITY CLOSING	—		
172	REORGANIZATION	—		
173	TEMPORARY SHUTDOWN	—		
174	**MATTERS DEEMED UNINSURABLE**	●		I. Coverage A.2.E.(vi), page 2
175	**NON-MONETARY RELIEF**	—		
176	DECLATORY RELIEF	—		
177	DISGORGEMENT	—		
178	INJUNCTIVE RELIEF	—		
179	JOB REINSTATEMENT	—		
180	NON-MONETARY DAMAGES/RELIEF	●		I. Coverage A.2.E.(ii), page 1
181	OTHER EQUITABLE REMEDIES	—		
182	**OBLIGATION TO PROVIDE BENEFITS**	—		
183	COBRA	—		
184	DISABILITY	●	Exceptions apply	I. Coverage A.3.A., page 2
185	ERISA	●		I. Coverage A.3.B., page 2
186	SOCIAL SECURITY	—		
187	OTHER RETIREMENT BENEFITS	—		
188	UNEMPLOYMENT	●		I. Coverage A.3.A., page 2
189	WORKERS' COMPENSATION	●	Exceptions apply	I. Coverage A.3.A., page 2
190	**PERSONAL INJURY OFFENSES**	—		
191	DEFAMATION	—		
192	EMOTIONAL DISTRESS/UPSET	—		
193	HUMILIATION	—		
194	LIBEL	—		
195	MENTAL ANGUISH	—		
196	PERSONAL INJURY	—		
197	SLANDER	—		
198	**PRIOR ACTS**	—		
199	PRIOR ACTS	—		
200	PRIOR KNOWLEDGE	●		IV.1.C., page 4
201	PRIOR/PENDING LITIGATION	—		
202	**PROPERTY DAMAGE**	—		
203	INTANGIBLE PROPERTY	—		
204	LOSS OF USE	—		
205	TANGIBLE PROPERTY	—		
206	**RETALIATORY ACTIONS OF EMPLOYER**	—		
207	FOR FAILING TO PERFORM ACTS AGAINST PUBLIC POLICY	—		
208	FOR FILING A COMPLAINT OR BENEFIT CLAIM	—		
209	**STRIKES/LOCKOUTS**	●		I. Coverage A.3.C., page 2
210	**VIOLATION OF LAWS**	—		
211	ANY LAW	—		
212	FMLA	—		
213	OSHA	—		
214	POLLUTION LAWS	—		
215	RICO	—		
216	SEC	—		
217	WARN	●		I. Coverage A.3.D., page 2
	15 CONDITIONS			
218	**ARBITRATION**	—		
219	MANDATORY	—		
220	BINDING	—		
221	CHOICE OF LAW PROVISION	—		
222	SITUS	—		
223	**TERRITORY**	●		VI., page 5
224	LIMITED	—		
225	WORLDWIDE	●		VI., page 5
226	**NEWLY FORMED/ACQUIRED ENTITIES**	●		II.1.D., page 3
227	AUTOMATIC COVERAGE (X DAYS)	30		II.1.D., page 3
228	NOTIFY INSURER WITHIN X DAYS	—		

LONDON MARKET/CNA RE/ST. PAUL RE EPL (11/97A Broad) [11/97]

Policy Comparison Worksheet

London Market
(NAS Insurance Services, Inc.)

Policy Form No.: AIF 835/95
Edition Date: 2/97

Risks Considered: General accounts
Limits Available: $1 million
Minimum Retention: $2,500

Contact: Richard J. Robin, Vice President
NAS Insurance Services, Inc.
16633 Ventura Boulevard, Suite 500
Encino, CA 91436
818/382-2030
818/382-2040 (fax)
general@nasinsurance.com

KEY TO SYMBOLS
● = Specifically contains queried provision of feature
○ = Unable to determine
— = Silent

#	Comparison Query		Comment	Policy Reference
	1 APPLICATION			
1	ATTACHES TO AND FORMS A PART OF THE POLICY	●		II.5)., page 1
2	CONTAINS WARRANTY STATEMENTS	●		Application, page 2
3	CONTAINS SEVERABILITY PROVISIONS	—		
	2 POLICY TYPE			
4	UNITARY STAND ALONE POLICY	●		
	ENDORSEMENT OR PART OF	—		
5	DIRECTORS AND OFFICERS POLICY	—		
6	PACKAGE POLICY	—		
7	UMBRELLA POLICY	—		
8	ERRORS AND OMISSIONS POLICY	—		
9	OTHER	—		
10	CLAIMS-MADE	●		
11	OCCURRENCE	—		
	3 WHO IS INSURED			
12	BUSINESS ENTITY	●		III., Assured, page 1
13	AUTOMATIC COVERAGE FOR SUBSIDIARIES	—		
14	DIRECTORS & OFFICERS	●		III., Assured, page 1
15	EMPLOYEES	—		
16	PART-TIME	—		
17	SEASONAL	—		
18	TEMPORARY	—		
19	SUPERVISORS & MANAGERS	●		III., Assured, page 1
20	FORMER EMPLOYEES	—		
21	VOLUNTEERS	—		
22	INDEPENDENT CONTRACTORS	—		
23	EXCLUDED	—		
24	SILENT	—		
25	SHAREHOLDERS	—		
	4 LIMIT OF LIABILITY			
26	AGGREGATE	—		
27	INCLUDES PUNITIVE DAMAGES WHERE NOT UNINSURABLE	—		
28	DEFENSE COSTS INCLUDED WITHIN LIMIT OF LIABILITY	—		
29	DEFENSE COSTS PAID IN ADDITION TO LIMIT OF LIABILITY	—		
	5 DEDUCTIBLE			
30	APPLIES TO EACH INDIVIDUAL CLAIM	—		
31	APPLIES TO EACH OCCURRENCE OR WRONGFUL PRACTICE	●	Insured event	Declarations Page—Item 5
32	INCLUDES ALL CLAIMS FROM ONE ACT	—		
33	SUBJECT TO ANNUAL AGGREGATE	—		
34	CO-PAYMENT APPLIES	●		Declarations Page—Item 5
35	LIMIT OF LIABILITY NOT REDUCED	—		
36	INCLUDES DEFENSE COSTS	—		
37	REDUCED UNDER SPECIFIED CIRCUMSTANCES (SEE POLICY)	—		

LONDON MARKET/NAS INSURANCE SERVICES, INC. AIF 835/95 [2/97]

#	Comparison Query	Comment		Policy Reference
	6 WHAT IS A CLAIM			
38	ORAL COMPLAINT TO INSURED	—		
39	WRITTEN COMPLAINT TO INSURED	—		
40	COMPLAINT MUST CONTAIN A DEMAND FOR DAMAGES	—		
41	COMPLAINT FILED WITH EEOC	●		III., Insured Event, page 1
42	OR SIMILAR STATE AUTHORITY	●		III., Insured Event, page 1
43	AGENCY MUST HAVE POWER TO ADJUDICATE	—		
44	ADMINISTRATIVE PROCEEDING	—		
45	ARBITRATION PROCEEDING	●		III., Insured Event, page 1
46	ANY INCIDENT REPORTED TO INSURER	—		
47	SUIT	●		III., Insured Event, page 1
48	CLAIM DOES NOT INCLUDE ARBITRATION SUBJECT TO	—		
49	COLLECTIVE BARGAINING AGREEMENT	—		
50	EMPLOYEE POLICY OR MANUAL	—		
51	CLAIM NOT DEFINED	—		
	7 CLAIM REPORTING PROVISIONS TO INSURER			
52	IMMEDIATELY	—		
53	AS SOON AS POSSIBLE	—		
54	AS SOON AS PRACTICABLE	—		
55	WITHIN POLICY PERIOD	—		
56	WITHIN X DAYS OF EXPIRATION	—		
57	WITHIN X DAYS	—		
	8 EXTENDED REPORTING FEATURES			
58	ELECTION PERIOD (DAYS)	—		
59	ADDITIONAL PREMIUM (% OF ANNUAL PREMIUM)	—		
60	ADDITIONAL REPORTING PERIOD (MONTHS)	—		
61	NO REINSTATEMENT OF LIMITS	—		
	9 POTENTIAL CLAIM REPORTING PROVISIONS			
62	NONE (SEE ALSO "CLAIM" ABOVE)	—		
63	INCIDENTS LIKELY TO RESULT IN A CLAIM	—		
	10 DEFENSE PROVISIONS			
64	AFFIRMATIVE DUTY TO DEFEND	—		
65	NO AFFIRMATIVE DUTY TO DEFEND	—		
66	AFFIRMATIVE ADVANCEMENT PROVISIONS	—		
67	INSURED MUST RETURN ADVANCED AMOUNTS IF NOT COVERED	—		
68	INSURED/INSURER CHOOSES COUNSEL	●	Insured	VII., page 2
69	INSURED/INSURER APPROVES COUNSEL	—		
70	INSURED/INSURER CONSULTED IN COUNSEL SELECTION	—		
	11 SETTLEMENT PROVISIONS			
71	HAMMER CLAUSE	—		
72	CONSULTATION PROVISION	—		
73	CONSENT PROVISION	—		
	12 ALLOCATION OF LOSS PROVISIONS			
74	STIPULATED PROVISIONS	—		
	13 COVERAGES			
75	DISCRIMINATION	●		III., Insured Event, page 1
76	SPECIFIC ENUMERATED ACTIVITIES	—		
77	PLUS BROAD OMNIBUS WORDING	—		
78	SPECIFIC ENUMERATED CLASSES	●		III., Insured Event, page 1
79	PLUS BROAD OMNIBUS WORDING	—		
80	AGAINST THIRD PARTIES	—		
81	DISCRIMINATION NOT DEFINED	—		
82	SEXUAL HARASSMENT	●		III., Insured Event, page 1
83	HOSTILE ENVIRONMENT	—		
84	QUID-PRO-QUO	—		
85	SEXUAL HARASSMENT NOT DEFINED	—		
86	WRONGFUL TERMINATION	●		III., Insured Event, page 1
87	BREACH OF IMPLIED CONTRACT	—		
88	BREACH OF EXPRESS CONTRACT	—		
89	VIOLATION OF PUBLIC POLICY	—		
90	VIOLATION OF GOOD FAITH & FAIR DEALING	—		
91	OBLIGATIONS TO MAKE PAYMENTS	—		
92	CONSTRUCTIVE DISCHARGE	—		
93	WRONGFUL TERMINATION NOT DEFINED	—		
94	OTHER EMPLOYMENT VIOLATIONS/OFFENSES	—		
95	WRONGFUL HIRING	—		
96	WRONGFUL PROMOTION/DEMOTION	—		
97	WRONGFUL EVALUATION/DISCIPLINE	—		

	Comparison Query	Comment	Policy Reference
98	FAMILY AND MEDICAL LEAVE ACT	—	
99	DEFAMATION	—	
100	MISREPRESENTATION	—	
101	RETALIATION	—	
102	MENTAL ANGUISH	—	
103	INVASION OF PRIVACY	—	
104	HUMILIATION	—	
105	EMOTIONAL DISTRESS	—	
106	OTHER PERSONAL INJURY OFFENSES	—	
107	POLICY SILENT	—	
14 EXCLUSIONS			
108	**ADA ACCOMMODATION EXPENSES**	—	
109	**ASSAULT & BATTERY**	—	
110	**BACK PAY**	—	
111	**BODILY INJURY**	—	
112	BODILY INJURY	—	
113	DEATH	—	
114	DISEASE	—	
115	SICKNESS	—	
116	**BREACH OF EMPLOYMENT CONTRACT**	—	
117	EXPRESS CONTRACT	—	
118	*WRITTEN CONTRACT*	—	
119	*ORAL CONTRACT*	—	
120	IMPLIED CONTRACT	—	
121	**CLASS ACTION LAWSUITS**	—	
122	**CONSEQUENTIAL LOSS**	—	
123	APPLIES TO BODILY INJURY	—	
124	APPLIES TO INSURED EVENT	—	
125	BROTHER/SISTER	—	
126	CHILD	—	
127	DOMESTIC PARTNER	—	
128	PARENT	—	
129	SPOUSE	—	
130	**COST OF ARBITRATION HEARINGS SUBJECT TO**	—	
131	EMPLOYMENT HANDBOOK	—	
132	LABOR GRIEVANCE	—	
133	OTHER EMPLOYMENT POLICY OR PROCEDURE	—	
134	**COVERAGE ELSEWHERE**	—	
135	OTHER AVAILABLE INSURANCE	●	IV.1), page 2
136	OTHER INDEMNIFICATION	●	IV.1), page 2
137	SHARING PROVISION	—	
138	**FAILURE TO EXERCISE CARE WHEN TERMINATING**	—	
139	**FINES/PENALTIES**	—	
140	CIVIL	—	
141	CRIMINAL	—	
142	EXEMPLARY DAMAGES	—	
143	PUNITIVE DAMAGES	—	
144	MULTIPLIED DAMAGES	—	
145	**FRONT PAY**	—	
146	EXCLUSION APPLIES ONLY IF EMPLOYER HAD OPPORTUNITY TO REINSTATE EMPLOYEE BUT DID NOT DO SO	—	
147	**INTENTIONAL ACTS**	—	
148	CRIMINAL ACTS	—	
149	CRIMINAL PROCEEDING	—	
150	DISHONEST PURPOSE	—	
151	FRAUDULENT ACTS	—	
152	FRAUDULENT CLAIMS	—	
153	INTENTIONAL VIOLATIONS OF LAW	—	
154	WILLFUL FAILURE TO COMPLY WITH LAW	—	
155	MALICIOUS PURPOSE	—	
156	**LIABILITY OF OTHERS**	—	
157	**LIQUIDATED DAMAGES**	—	
158	**LOSS ARISING OUT OF CHANGES IN OPERATIONS**	—	
159	ACQUISITION	—	
160	CHANGE IN CONTROL	—	
161	DOWNSIZING OR REDUCTION IN FORCE	—	
162	*% OF WORKFORCE*	—	
163	*WITHIN X DAYS*	—	

LONDON MARKET/NAS INSURANCE SERVICES, INC. AIF 835/95 [2/97]

#	Comparison Query	Comment		Policy Reference
164	FINANCIAL IMPAIRMENT	—		
165	*BANKRUPTCY*	—		
166	*INSOLVENCY*	—		
167	*LIQUIDATION*	—		
168	*RECEIVERSHIP*	—		
169	FINANCIAL INABILITY TO PAY	—		
170	MERGER	—		
171	PLANT OR FACILITY CLOSING	—		
172	REORGANIZATION	—		
173	TEMPORARY SHUTDOWN	—		
174	**MATTERS DEEMED UNINSURABLE**	—		
175	**NON-MONETARY RELIEF**	—		
176	DECLATORY RELIEF	—		
177	DISGORGEMENT	—		
178	INJUNCTIVE RELIEF	—		
179	JOB REINSTATEMENT	—		
180	NON-MONETARY DAMAGES/RELIEF	—		
181	OTHER EQUITABLE REMEDIES	—		
182	**OBLIGATION TO PROVIDE BENEFITS**	—		
183	COBRA	—		
184	DISABILITY	—		
185	ERISA	—		
186	SOCIAL SECURITY	—		
187	OTHER RETIREMENT BENEFITS	—		
188	UNEMPLOYMENT	—		
189	WORKERS' COMPENSATION	●		IV.8)., page 2
190	**PERSONAL INJURY OFFENSES**	—		
191	DEFAMATION	—		
192	EMOTIONAL DISTRESS/UPSET	—		
193	HUMILIATION	—		
194	LIBEL	—		
195	MENTAL ANGUISH	—		
196	PERSONAL INJURY	—		
197	SLANDER	—		
198	**PRIOR ACTS**	—		
199	PRIOR ACTS	—		
200	PRIOR KNOWLEDGE	●	See also IV.5), page 2	II.3), page 1
201	PRIOR/PENDING LITIGATION	—		
202	**PROPERTY DAMAGE**	—		
203	INTANGIBLE PROPERTY	—		
204	LOSS OF USE	—		
205	TANGIBLE PROPERTY	—		
206	**RETALIATORY ACTIONS OF EMPLOYER**	—		
207	FOR FAILING TO PERFORM ACTS AGAINST PUBLIC POLICY	—		
208	FOR FILING A COMPLAINT OR BENEFIT CLAIM	—		
209	**STRIKES/LOCKOUTS**	—		
210	**VIOLATION OF LAWS**	—		
211	ANY LAW	—		
212	FMLA	—		
213	OSHA	—		
214	POLLUTION LAWS	●		IV.3), page 2
215	RICO	—		
216	SEC	—		
217	WARN	—		

15 CONDITIONS

#	Comparison Query	Comment		Policy Reference
218	**ARBITRATION**	●		VIII., page 2
219	MANDATORY	—		
220	BINDING	—		
221	CHOICE OF LAW PROVISION	—		
222	SITUS	—		
223	**TERRITORY**	—		
224	LIMITED	—		
225	WORLDWIDE	—		
226	**NEWLY FORMED/ACQUIRED ENTITIES**	—		
227	AUTOMATIC COVERAGE (X DAYS)	—		
228	NOTIFY INSURER WITHIN X DAYS	—		

LONDON MARKET/NAS INSURANCE SERVICES, INC. AIF 835/95 [2/97]

Policy Comparison Worksheet

London Market
(NAS Insurance Services, Inc.)

Policy Form No.: AIF 1653/95A
Edition Date: 2/97

Risks Considered:
Limits Available: $1 million per section
Minimum Retention: $5,000

Contact: Richard J. Robin, Vice President
NAS Insurance Services, Inc.
16633 Ventura Boulevard, Suite 500
Encino, CA 91436
818/382-2030
818/382-2040 (fax)
general@nasinsurance.com

KEY TO SYMBOLS
● = Specifically contains queried provision of feature
○ = Unable to determine
— = Silent

#	Comparison Query		Comment	Policy Reference
	1 APPLICATION			
1	ATTACHES TO AND FORMS A PART OF THE POLICY	●		Conditions 6., page 2
2	CONTAINS WARRANTY STATEMENTS	—		
3	CONTAINS SEVERABILITY PROVISIONS	—		
	2 POLICY TYPE			
4	UNITARY STAND ALONE POLICY	●		
	ENDORSEMENT OR PART OF	—		
5	DIRECTORS AND OFFICERS POLICY	—		
6	PACKAGE POLICY	—		
7	UMBRELLA POLICY	—		
8	ERRORS AND OMISSIONS POLICY	—		
9	OTHER	—		
10	CLAIMS-MADE	●		
11	OCCURRENCE	—		
	3 WHO IS INSURED			
12	BUSINESS ENTITY	●		Definitions, Assured, page 3
13	AUTOMATIC COVERAGE FOR SUBSIDIARIES	—		
14	DIRECTORS & OFFICERS	●		Definitions, Assured, page 3
15	EMPLOYEES	●		Definitions, Assured, page 3
16	PART-TIME	—		
17	SEASONAL	—		
18	TEMPORARY	—		
19	SUPERVISORS & MANAGERS	—		
20	FORMER EMPLOYEES	—		
21	VOLUNTEERS	—		
22	INDEPENDENT CONTRACTORS	—		
23	EXCLUDED	—		
24	SILENT	—		
25	SHAREHOLDERS	—		
	4 LIMIT OF LIABILITY			
26	AGGREGATE	●	Aggregate only	II., Section I., page 1
27	INCLUDES PUNITIVE DAMAGES WHERE NOT UNINSURABLE	—		
28	DEFENSE COSTS INCLUDED WITHIN LIMIT OF LIABILITY	—		
29	DEFENSE COSTS PAID IN ADDITION TO LIMIT OF LIABILITY	—		
	5 DEDUCTIBLE			
30	APPLIES TO EACH INDIVIDUAL CLAIM	●		III., page 1
31	APPLIES TO EACH OCCURRENCE OR WRONGFUL PRACTICE	—		
32	INCLUDES ALL CLAIMS FROM ONE ACT	—		
33	SUBJECT TO ANNUAL AGGREGATE	—		
34	CO-PAYMENT APPLIES	●	Specified by underwriter—see Declarations Page	IV., page 1
35	LIMIT OF LIABILITY NOT REDUCED	—		
36	INCLUDES DEFENSE COSTS	—		
37	REDUCED UNDER SPECIFIED CIRCUMSTANCES (SEE POLICY)	—		

Comparison Query	Comment		Policy Reference
6 WHAT IS A CLAIM			
38 ORAL COMPLAINT TO INSURED	—		
39 WRITTEN COMPLAINT TO INSURED	●		Definitions, Claim, page 3
40 COMPLAINT MUST CONTAIN A DEMAND FOR DAMAGES	●		Definitions, Claim, page 3
41 COMPLAINT FILED WITH EEOC	●		Definitions, Claim, page 3
42 OR SIMILAR STATE AUTHORITY	●		Definitions, Claim, page 3
43 AGENCY MUST HAVE POWER TO ADJUDICATE	—		
44 ADMINISTRATIVE PROCEEDING	—		
45 ARBITRATION PROCEEDING	●		Definitions, Claim, page 3
46 ANY INCIDENT REPORTED TO INSURER	—		
47 SUIT	●		Definitions, Claim, page 3
48 CLAIM DOES NOT INCLUDE ARBITRATION SUBJECT TO	—		
49 COLLECTIVE BARGAINING AGREEMENT	—		
50 EMPLOYEE POLICY OR MANUAL	—		
51 CLAIM NOT DEFINED	—		
7 CLAIM REPORTING PROVISIONS TO INSURER			
52 IMMEDIATELY	●		Conditions 2., page 2
53 AS SOON AS POSSIBLE	—		
54 AS SOON AS PRACTICABLE	—		
55 WITHIN POLICY PERIOD	—		
56 WITHIN X DAYS OF EXPIRATION	—		
57 WITHIN X DAYS	—		
8 EXTENDED REPORTING FEATURES			
58 ELECTION PERIOD (DAYS)	30		Definitions, Extended Reporting Period, B., page 3
59 ADDITIONAL PREMIUM (% OF ANNUAL PREMIUM)	200		Definitions, Extended Reporting Period, A., page 3
60 ADDITIONAL REPORTING PERIOD (MONTHS)	12		Definitions, Extended Reporting Period, A., page 3
61 NO REINSTATEMENT OF LIMITS	●		Definitions, Extended Reporting Period, D., page 3
9 POTENTIAL CLAIM REPORTING PROVISIONS			
62 NONE (SEE ALSO "CLAIM" ABOVE)	—		
63 INCIDENTS LIKELY TO RESULT IN A CLAIM	—		
10 DEFENSE PROVISIONS			
64 AFFIRMATIVE DUTY TO DEFEND	—		
65 NO AFFIRMATIVE DUTY TO DEFEND	●	Legal expense reimbursement	Section II., page 7
66 AFFIRMATIVE ADVANCEMENT PROVISIONS	—		
67 INSURED MUST RETURN ADVANCED AMOUNTS IF NOT COVERED	—		
68 INSURED/INSURER CHOOSES COUNSEL	●	Insurer chooses	I. Section II., page 1 and V.A., page 1
69 INSURED/INSURER APPROVES COUNSEL	—		
70 INSURED/INSURER CONSULTED IN COUNSEL SELECTION	—		
11 SETTLEMENT PROVISIONS			
71 HAMMER CLAUSE	●		V.C., page 1
72 CONSULTATION PROVISION	—		
73 CONSENT PROVISION	●	Two-way	V.A. and C., page 1
12 ALLOCATION OF LOSS PROVISIONS			
74 STIPULATED PROVISIONS	—		
13 COVERAGES			
75 DISCRIMINATION	●		Definitions, Claim 1), page 3
76 SPECIFIC ENUMERATED ACTIVITIES	—		
77 PLUS BROAD OMNIBUS WORDING	—		
78 SPECIFIC ENUMERATED CLASSES	●		Definitions Claim 1), page 3
79 PLUS BROAD OMNIBUS WORDING	●		Definitions Claim 1), page 3
80 AGAINST THIRD PARTIES	—		
81 DISCRIMINATION NOT DEFINED	●		
82 SEXUAL HARASSMENT	●		Definitions Claim 2), page 3
83 HOSTILE ENVIRONMENT	—		
84 QUID-PRO-QUO	—		
85 SEXUAL HARASSMENT NOT DEFINED	●		
86 WRONGFUL TERMINATION	●		Definitions Claim 3), page 3
87 BREACH OF IMPLIED CONTRACT	—		
88 BREACH OF EXPRESS CONTRACT	—		
89 VIOLATION OF PUBLIC POLICY	—		
90 VIOLATION OF GOOD FAITH & FAIR DEALING	—		
91 OBLIGATIONS TO MAKE PAYMENTS	—		
92 CONSTRUCTIVE DISCHARGE	—		
93 WRONGFUL TERMINATION NOT DEFINED	—		
94 OTHER EMPLOYMENT VIOLATIONS/OFFENSES	—		
95 WRONGFUL HIRING	—		
96 WRONGFUL PROMOTION/DEMOTION	—		
97 WRONGFUL EVALUATION/DISCIPLINE	—		

LONDON MARKET/NAS INSURANCE SERVICES, INC. AIF 1653/95A [2/97]

	Comparison Query	Comment	Policy Reference
98	FAMILY AND MEDICAL LEAVE ACT	—	
99	DEFAMATION	—	
100	MISREPRESENTATION	—	
101	RETALIATION	—	
102	MENTAL ANGUISH	—	
103	INVASION OF PRIVACY	—	
104	HUMILIATION	—	
105	EMOTIONAL DISTRESS	—	
106	OTHER PERSONAL INJURY OFFENSES	—	
107	POLICY SILENT	—	
	14 EXCLUSIONS		
108	**ADA ACCOMMODATION EXPENSES**	—	
109	**ASSAULT & BATTERY**	—	
110	**BACK PAY**	—	
111	**BODILY INJURY**	●	Exclusions 12), page 4
112	BODILY INJURY	●	Exclusions 12), page 4
113	DEATH	●	Exclusions 12), page 4
114	DISEASE	●	Exclusions 12), page 4
115	SICKNESS	●	Exclusions 12), page 4
116	**BREACH OF EMPLOYMENT CONTRACT**	—	
117	EXPRESS CONTRACT	—	
118	*WRITTEN CONTRACT*	—	
119	*ORAL CONTRACT*	—	
120	IMPLIED CONTRACT	—	
121	**CLASS ACTION LAWSUITS**	—	
122	**CONSEQUENTIAL LOSS**	—	
123	APPLIES TO BODILY INJURY	—	
124	APPLIES TO INSURED EVENT	—	
125	BROTHER/SISTER	—	
126	CHILD	—	
127	DOMESTIC PARTNER	—	
128	PARENT	—	
129	SPOUSE	—	
130	**COST OF ARBITRATION HEARINGS SUBJECT TO**	—	
131	EMPLOYMENT HANDBOOK	—	
132	LABOR GRIEVANCE	—	
133	OTHER EMPLOYMENT POLICY OR PROCEDURE	—	
134	**COVERAGE ELSEWHERE**	●	Conditions 11, page 2
135	OTHER AVAILABLE INSURANCE	●	Conditions 11, page 2
136	OTHER INDEMNIFICATION	●	Exclusions 1.a.), page 4
137	SHARING PROVISION	—	
138	**FAILURE TO EXERCISE CARE WHEN TERMINATING**	—	
139	**FINES/PENALTIES**	●	Definitions, Damages, page 3
140	CIVIL	—	
141	CRIMINAL	—	
142	EXEMPLARY DAMAGES	●	Definitions, Damages, page 3
143	PUNITIVE DAMAGES	●	Definitions, Damages, page 3
144	MULTIPLIED DAMAGES	●	Definitions, Damages, page 3
145	**FRONT PAY**	—	
146	EXCLUSION APPLIES ONLY IF EMPLOYER HAD OPPORTUNITY TO REINSTATE EMPLOYEE BUT DID NOT DO SO	—	
147	**INTENTIONAL ACTS**	—	
148	CRIMINAL ACTS	●	Exclusions 13), page 4
149	CRIMINAL PROCEEDING	—	
150	DISHONEST PURPOSE	—	
151	FRAUDULENT ACTS	—	
152	FRAUDULENT CLAIMS	●	Conditions 5, page 2
153	INTENTIONAL VIOLATIONS OF LAW	—	
154	WILLFUL FAILURE TO COMPLY WITH LAW	—	
155	MALICIOUS PURPOSE	—	
156	**LIABILITY OF OTHERS**	—	
157	**LIQUIDATED DAMAGES**	—	
158	**LOSS ARISING OUT OF CHANGES IN OPERATIONS**	—	
159	ACQUISITION	—	
160	CHANGE IN CONTROL	—	
161	DOWNSIZING OR REDUCTION IN FORCE	—	
162	*% OF WORKFORCE*	—	
163	*WITHIN X DAYS*	—	

LONDON MARKET/NAS INSURANCE SERVICES, INC. AIF 1653/95A [2/97]

	Comparison Query	Comment	Policy Reference
164	FINANCIAL IMPAIRMENT	—	
165	BANKRUPTCY	—	
166	INSOLVENCY	—	
167	LIQUIDATION	—	
168	RECEIVERSHIP	—	
169	FINANCIAL INABILITY TO PAY	—	
170	MERGER	—	
171	PLANT OR FACILITY CLOSING	—	
172	REORGANIZATION	—	
173	TEMPORARY SHUTDOWN	—	
174	**MATTERS DEEMED UNINSURABLE**	●	Definitions, Damages, page 3
175	**NON-MONETARY RELIEF**	—	
176	DECLATORY RELIEF	—	
177	DISGORGEMENT	—	
178	INJUNCTIVE RELIEF	—	
179	JOB REINSTATEMENT	—	
180	NON-MONETARY DAMAGES/RELIEF	—	
181	OTHER EQUITABLE REMEDIES	—	
182	**OBLIGATION TO PROVIDE BENEFITS**	—	
183	COBRA	—	
184	DISABILITY	●	Exclusions 12), page 4
185	ERISA	●	Exclusions 10), page 4
186	SOCIAL SECURITY	—	
187	OTHER RETIREMENT BENEFITS	—	
188	UNEMPLOYMENT	—	
189	WORKERS' COMPENSATION	●	Exclusions 12), page 4
190	**PERSONAL INJURY OFFENSES**	—	
191	DEFAMATION	—	
192	EMOTIONAL DISTRESS/UPSET	—	
193	HUMILIATION	—	
194	LIBEL	—	
195	MENTAL ANGUISH	—	
196	PERSONAL INJURY	—	
197	SLANDER	—	
198	**PRIOR ACTS**		
199	PRIOR ACTS	—	
200	PRIOR KNOWLEDGE	● See also Exclusions 6), page 4	Conditions 3, page 2
201	PRIOR/PENDING LITIGATION	—	
202	**PROPERTY DAMAGE**	●	Exclusions 12), page 4
203	INTANGIBLE PROPERTY	—	
204	LOSS OF USE	●	Exclusions 12), page 4
205	TANGIBLE PROPERTY	●	Exclusions 12), page 4
206	**RETALIATORY ACTIONS OF EMPLOYER**	—	
207	FOR FAILING TO PERFORM ACTS AGAINST PUBLIC POLICY	—	
208	FOR FILING A COMPLAINT OR BENEFIT CLAIM	—	
209	**STRIKES/LOCKOUTS**	—	
210	**VIOLATION OF LAWS**	—	
211	ANY LAW	—	
212	FMLA	—	
213	OSHA	—	
214	POLLUTION LAWS	●	Exclusions 4), page 4
215	RICO	●	Exclusions 11, page 4
216	SEC	—	
217	WARN	—	
	15 CONDITIONS		
218	**ARBITRATION**	● Exception applies	Conditions 8, page 2
219	MANDATORY	—	
220	BINDING	—	
221	CHOICE OF LAW PROVISION	—	
222	SITUS	—	
223	**TERRITORY**	—	
224	LIMITED	—	
225	WORLDWIDE	—	
226	**NEWLY FORMED/ACQUIRED ENTITIES**	—	
227	AUTOMATIC COVERAGE (X DAYS)	—	
228	NOTIFY INSURER WITHIN X DAYS	—	

LONDON MARKET/NAS INSURANCE SERVICES, INC. AIF 1653/95A [2/97]

Policy Comparison Worksheet

London Market
(NAS Insurance Services, Inc.)

Policy Form No.: AIF 2314
Edition Date: 4/98

Risks Considered: All except law firms
Limits Available: $2 million
Minimum Retention: $5,000

Contact: Richard J. Robin, Vice President
NAS Insurance Services, Inc.
16633 Ventura Boulevard, Suite 500
Encino, CA 91436
818/382-2030
818/382-2040 (fax)
general@nasinsurance.com

KEY TO SYMBOLS
● = Specifically contains queried provision of feature
○ = Unable to determine
— = Silent

#	Comparison Query	Symbol	Comment	Policy Reference
	1 APPLICATION			
1	ATTACHES TO AND FORMS A PART OF THE POLICY	●		Conditions 5., page 2
2	CONTAINS WARRANTY STATEMENTS	●		Application, page 2
3	CONTAINS SEVERABILITY PROVISIONS	—		
	2 POLICY TYPE			
4	UNITARY STAND ALONE POLICY	●		
	ENDORSEMENT OR PART OF	—		
5	DIRECTORS AND OFFICERS POLICY	—		
6	PACKAGE POLICY	—		
7	UMBRELLA POLICY	—		
8	ERRORS AND OMISSIONS POLICY	—		
9	OTHER	—		
10	CLAIMS-MADE	●		
11	OCCURRENCE	—		
	3 WHO IS INSURED			
12	BUSINESS ENTITY	●		Definitions, Insured, page 2
13	AUTOMATIC COVERAGE FOR SUBSIDIARIES	—		
14	DIRECTORS & OFFICERS	●		Definitions, Insured, page 2
15	EMPLOYEES	●		Definitions, Insured, page 2
16	PART-TIME	—		
17	SEASONAL	—		
18	TEMPORARY	—		
19	SUPERVISORS & MANAGERS	—		
20	FORMER EMPLOYEES	—		
21	VOLUNTEERS	—		
22	INDEPENDENT CONTRACTORS	—		
23	EXCLUDED	—		
24	SILENT	●		
25	SHAREHOLDERS	—		
	4 LIMIT OF LIABILITY			
26	AGGREGATE	●		II., page 1
27	INCLUDES PUNITIVE DAMAGES WHERE NOT UNINSURABLE	—		
28	DEFENSE COSTS INCLUDED WITHIN LIMIT OF LIABILITY	●		II., page 1
29	DEFENSE COSTS PAID IN ADDITION TO LIMIT OF LIABILITY	—		
	5 DEDUCTIBLE			
30	APPLIES TO EACH INDIVIDUAL CLAIM	●		III., page 1
31	APPLIES TO EACH OCCURRENCE OR WRONGFUL PRACTICE	—		
32	INCLUDES ALL CLAIMS FROM ONE ACT	—		
33	SUBJECT TO ANNUAL AGGREGATE	—		
34	CO-PAYMENT APPLIES	●	Specified by underwriter	IV., page 1
35	LIMIT OF LIABILITY NOT REDUCED	—		
36	INCLUDES DEFENSE COSTS	●		II., page 1
37	REDUCED UNDER SPECIFIED CIRCUMSTANCES (SEE POLICY)	—		

#	Comparison Query	Comment		Policy Reference
	6 WHAT IS A CLAIM			
38	ORAL COMPLAINT TO INSURED	—		
39	WRITTEN COMPLAINT TO INSURED	●		Definitions, Claim (c), page 2
40	COMPLAINT MUST CONTAIN A DEMAND FOR DAMAGES	●	Demand for payment	Definitions, Claim (c), page 2
41	COMPLAINT FILED WITH EEOC	●		Definitions, Claim (d), page 3
42	OR SIMILAR STATE AUTHORITY	●		Definitions, Claim (d), page 3
43	AGENCY MUST HAVE POWER TO ADJUDICATE	—		
44	ADMINISTRATIVE PROCEEDING	—		
45	ARBITRATION PROCEEDING	●		Definitions, Claim (b), page 2
46	ANY INCIDENT REPORTED TO INSURER	—		
47	SUIT	●		Definitions, Claim (a), page 2
48	CLAIM DOES NOT INCLUDE ARBITRATION SUBJECT TO	—		
49	COLLECTIVE BARGAINING AGREEMENT	●		Exclusions, 9), page 4
50	EMPLOYEE POLICY OR MANUAL	—		
51	CLAIM NOT DEFINED	—		
	7 CLAIM REPORTING PROVISIONS TO INSURER			
52	IMMEDIATELY	—		
53	AS SOON AS POSSIBLE	—		
54	AS SOON AS PRACTICABLE	●		Conditions 1., page 1
55	WITHIN POLICY PERIOD	—		
56	WITHIN X DAYS OF EXPIRATION	—		
57	WITHIN X DAYS	—		
	8 EXTENDED REPORTING FEATURES			
58	ELECTION PERIOD (DAYS)	30		Definitions, Extended Reporting Period, B., page 3
59	ADDITIONAL PREMIUM (% OF ANNUAL PREMIUM)	150		Definitions, Extended Reporting Period, A., page 3
60	ADDITIONAL REPORTING PERIOD (MONTHS)	12		Definitions, Extended Reporting Period, A., page 3
61	NO REINSTATEMENT OF LIMITS	●		Definitions, Extended Reporting Period, D., page 3
	9 POTENTIAL CLAIM REPORTING PROVISIONS			
62	NONE (SEE ALSO "CLAIM" ABOVE)	—		
63	INCIDENTS LIKELY TO RESULT IN A CLAIM	—		
	10 DEFENSE PROVISIONS			
64	AFFIRMATIVE DUTY TO DEFEND	●		V.A., page 1
65	NO AFFIRMATIVE DUTY TO DEFEND	—		
66	AFFIRMATIVE ADVANCEMENT PROVISIONS	—		
67	INSURED MUST RETURN ADVANCED AMOUNTS IF NOT COVERED	—		
68	INSURED/INSURER CHOOSES COUNSEL	●	Insurer	V.A., page 1
69	INSURED/INSURER APPROVES COUNSEL	—		
70	INSURED/INSURER CONSULTED IN COUNSEL SELECTION	—		
	11 SETTLEMENT PROVISIONS			
71	HAMMER CLAUSE	●		V.C., page 1
72	CONSULTATION PROVISION	—		
73	CONSENT PROVISION	●	2-way	V.A. & C., page 1
	12 ALLOCATION OF LOSS PROVISIONS			
74	STIPULATED PROVISIONS	—		
	13 COVERAGES			
75	DISCRIMINATION	●		Definitions, Claim 1), page 3
76	SPECIFIC ENUMERATED ACTIVITIES	●		Definitions, Claim 1), page 3
77	PLUS BROAD OMNIBUS WORDING	—		
78	SPECIFIC ENUMERATED CLASSES	●		Definitions, Claim 1), page 3
79	PLUS BROAD OMNIBUS WORDING	●		Definitions, Claim 1), page 3
80	AGAINST THIRD PARTIES	—	Coverage available by endorsement	
81	DISCRIMINATION NOT DEFINED	●		
82	SEXUAL HARASSMENT	●		Definitions, Claim 2), page 3
83	HOSTILE ENVIRONMENT	—		
84	QUID-PRO-QUO	—		
85	SEXUAL HARASSMENT NOT DEFINED	●		
86	WRONGFUL TERMINATION	●		Definitions, Claim 3), page 3
87	BREACH OF IMPLIED CONTRACT	—		
88	BREACH OF EXPRESS CONTRACT	—		
89	VIOLATION OF PUBLIC POLICY	—		
90	VIOLATION OF GOOD FAITH & FAIR DEALING	—		
91	OBLIGATIONS TO MAKE PAYMENTS	—		
92	CONSTRUCTIVE DISCHARGE	—		
93	WRONGFUL TERMINATION NOT DEFINED	●		
94	OTHER EMPLOYMENT VIOLATIONS/OFFENSES	●		Definitions, Claim 3), page 3
95	WRONGFUL HIRING	●		Definitions, Claim 3), page 3
96	WRONGFUL PROMOTION/DEMOTION	●		Definitions, Claim 3), page 3
97	WRONGFUL EVALUATION/DISCIPLINE	●		Definitions, Claim 3), page 3

LONDON MARKET/NAS INSURANCE SERVICES, INC. AIF 2314 [4/98]

	Comparison Query	Comment		Policy Reference
98	FAMILY AND MEDICAL LEAVE ACT	—		
99	DEFAMATION	—		
100	MISREPRESENTATION	—		
101	RETALIATION	●		Definitions, Claim 3), page 3
102	MENTAL ANGUISH	●		Definitions, Claim 3), page 3
103	INVASION OF PRIVACY	●		Definitions, Claim 3), page 3
104	HUMILIATION	—		
105	EMOTIONAL DISTRESS	●		Definitions, Claim 3), page 3
106	OTHER PERSONAL INJURY OFFENSES	●		Definitions, Claim 3), page 3
107	POLICY SILENT	—		
	14 EXCLUSIONS			
108	**ADA ACCOMMODATION EXPENSES**	●		Exclusions 10), page 4
109	**ASSAULT & BATTERY**	—		
110	**BACK PAY**	—		
111	**BODILY INJURY**	●		Exclusions 12), page 4
112	BODILY INJURY	●		Exclusions 12), page 4
113	DEATH	●		Exclusions 12), page 4
114	DISEASE	●		Exclusions 12), page 4
115	SICKNESS	●		Exclusions 12), page 4
116	**BREACH OF EMPLOYMENT CONTRACT**	—		
117	EXPRESS CONTRACT	—		
118	WRITTEN CONTRACT	—		
119	ORAL CONTRACT	—		
120	IMPLIED CONTRACT	—		
121	**CLASS ACTION LAWSUITS**	—		
122	**CONSEQUENTIAL LOSS**	—		
123	APPLIES TO BODILY INJURY	—		
124	APPLIES TO INSURED EVENT	—		
125	BROTHER/SISTER	—		
126	CHILD	—		
127	DOMESTIC PARTNER	—		
128	PARENT	—		
129	SPOUSE	—		
130	**COST OF ARBITRATION HEARINGS SUBJECT TO**	—		
131	EMPLOYMENT HANDBOOK	—		
132	LABOR GRIEVANCE	—		
133	OTHER EMPLOYMENT POLICY OR PROCEDURE	—		
134	**COVERAGE ELSEWHERE**	—		
135	OTHER AVAILABLE INSURANCE	●		Conditions 10., page 2
136	OTHER INDEMNIFICATION	●		Exclusions, 1a), page 3
137	SHARING PROVISION	—		
138	**FAILURE TO EXERCISE CARE WHEN TERMINATING**	—		
139	**FINES/PENALTIES**	●	See also Exclusions 7), page 4	Definitions, Damages, page 3
140	CIVIL	—		
141	CRIMINAL	—		
142	EXEMPLARY DAMAGES	●	See also Exclusions 7), page 4	Definitions, Damages, page 3
143	PUNITIVE DAMAGES	●	See also Exclusions 7), page 4	Definitions, Damages, page 3
144	MULTIPLIED DAMAGES	●	See also Exclusions 7), page 4	Definitions, Damages, page 3
145	**FRONT PAY**	—		
146	EXCLUSION APPLIES ONLY IF EMPLOYER HAD OPPORTUNITY TO REINSTATE EMPLOYEE BUT DID NOT DO SO	—		
147	**INTENTIONAL ACTS**	—		
148	CRIMINAL ACTS	●	Non-imputation	Exclusions 8), page 4
149	CRIMINAL PROCEEDING	—		
150	DISHONEST PURPOSE	—		
151	FRAUDULENT ACTS	—		
152	FRAUDULENT CLAIMS	●		Conditions 4., page 2
153	INTENTIONAL VIOLATIONS OF LAW	—		
154	WILLFUL FAILURE TO COMPLY WITH LAW	—		
155	MALICIOUS PURPOSE	—		
156	**LIABILITY OF OTHERS**	●		Exclusions 11), page 4
157	**LIQUIDATED DAMAGES**	—		
158	**LOSS ARISING OUT OF CHANGES IN OPERATIONS**	—		
159	ACQUISITION	—		
160	CHANGE IN CONTROL	—		
161	DOWNSIZING OR REDUCTION IN FORCE	—		
162	% OF WORKFORCE	—		
163	WITHIN X DAYS	—		

LONDON MARKET/NAS INSURANCE SERVICES, INC. AIF 2314 [4/98]

#	Comparison Query		Comment	Policy Reference
164	FINANCIAL IMPAIRMENT	—		
165	*BANKRUPTCY*	—		
166	*INSOLVENCY*	—		
167	*LIQUIDATION*	—		
168	*RECEIVERSHIP*	—		
169	FINANCIAL INABILITY TO PAY	—		
170	MERGER	—		
171	PLANT OR FACILITY CLOSING	—		
172	REORGANIZATION	—		
173	TEMPORARY SHUTDOWN	—		
174	**MATTERS DEEMED UNINSURABLE**	●		Definitions, Damages, page 3
175	**NON-MONETARY RELIEF**	—		
176	DECLATORY RELIEF	—		
177	DISGORGEMENT	—		
178	INJUNCTIVE RELIEF	—		
179	JOB REINSTATEMENT	—		
180	NON-MONETARY DAMAGES/RELIEF	—		
181	OTHER EQUITABLE REMEDIES	—		
182	**OBLIGATION TO PROVIDE BENEFITS**	—		
183	COBRA	—		
184	DISABILITY	●		Exclusions 12), page 4
185	ERISA	●		Exclusions 17), page 4
186	SOCIAL SECURITY	—		
187	OTHER RETIREMENT BENEFITS	—		
188	UNEMPLOYMENT	—		
189	WORKERS' COMPENSATION	●	See also Exclusions 13), page 4	Exclusions 12), page 4
190	**PERSONAL INJURY OFFENSES**	—		
191	DEFAMATION	—		
192	EMOTIONAL DISTRESS/UPSET	—		
193	HUMILIATION	—		
194	LIBEL	—		
195	MENTAL ANGUISH	—		
196	PERSONAL INJURY	—		
197	SLANDER	—		
198	**PRIOR ACTS**	—		
199	PRIOR ACTS	—		
200	PRIOR KNOWLEDGE	●	See also Exclusions 4), page 4	Conditions 2., page 1
201	PRIOR/PENDING LITIGATION	—		
202	**PROPERTY DAMAGE**	●		Exclusions 12), page 4
203	INTANGIBLE PROPERTY	—		
204	LOSS OF USE	●		Exclusions 12), page 4
205	TANGIBLE PROPERTY	●		Exclusions 12), page 4
206	**RETALIATORY ACTIONS OF EMPLOYER**	—		
207	FOR FAILING TO PERFORM ACTS AGAINST PUBLIC POLICY	—		
208	FOR FILING A COMPLAINT OR BENEFIT CLAIM	—		
209	**STRIKES/LOCKOUTS**	●		Exclusions 15), page 4
210	**VIOLATION OF LAWS**	—		
211	ANY LAW	—		
212	FMLA	—		
213	OSHA	●		Exclusions 19), page 4
214	POLLUTION LAWS	—		
215	RICO	●		Exclusions 14), page 4
216	SEC	—		
217	WARN	●		Exclusions 18), page 4
	15 CONDITIONS			
218	**ARBITRATION**	●	Exception applies	Conditions 7., page 2
219	MANDATORY	—		
220	BINDING	—		
221	CHOICE OF LAW PROVISION	—		
222	SITUS	—		
223	**TERRITORY**	●		Conditions 11., page 2
224	LIMITED	●		Conditions 11., page 2
225	WORLDWIDE	—		
226	**NEWLY FORMED/ACQUIRED ENTITIES**	—		
227	AUTOMATIC COVERAGE (X DAYS)	—		
228	NOTIFY INSURER WITHIN X DAYS	—		

LONDON MARKET/NAS INSURANCE SERVICES, INC. AIF 2314 [4/98]

Policy Comparison Worksheet

London Market
(NAS Insurance Services, Inc.)

Policy Form No.: CBPLI98
Edition Date: 4/98

Risks Considered: General accounts
Limits Available: $5 million
Minimum Retention: $5,000

Contact: Richard J. Robin, Vice President
NAS Insurance Services, Inc.
16633 Ventura Boulevard, Suite 500
Encino, CA 91436
818/382-2030
818/382-2040 (fax)
general@nasinsurance.com

KEY TO SYMBOLS
● = Specifically contains queried provision of feature
○ = Unable to determine
— = Silent

#	Comparison Query		Comment	Policy Reference
	1 APPLICATION			
1	ATTACHES TO AND FORMS A PART OF THE POLICY	●		X.A., page 6
2	CONTAINS WARRANTY STATEMENTS	●		Application, page 3
3	CONTAINS SEVERABILITY PROVISIONS	●	Exception applies	X.B., page 6
	2 POLICY TYPE			
4	UNITARY STAND ALONE POLICY	●	Business practices liability	
	ENDORSEMENT OR PART OF	—		
5	DIRECTORS AND OFFICERS POLICY	—		
6	PACKAGE POLICY	—		
7	UMBRELLA POLICY	—		
8	ERRORS AND OMISSIONS POLICY	—		
9	OTHER	—		
10	CLAIMS-MADE	●		
11	OCCURRENCE	—		
	3 WHO IS INSURED			
12	BUSINESS ENTITY	●		II.I., page 1
13	AUTOMATIC COVERAGE FOR SUBSIDIARIES	●		II.I., page 1
14	DIRECTORS & OFFICERS	●		II.J.1)., page 2
15	EMPLOYEES	●		II.J.1)., page 2
16	PART-TIME	—		
17	SEASONAL	—		
18	TEMPORARY	—		
19	SUPERVISORS & MANAGERS	—		
20	FORMER EMPLOYEES	●		II.J.2)., page 2
21	VOLUNTEERS	—		
22	INDEPENDENT CONTRACTORS	—		
23	EXCLUDED	—		
24	SILENT	●		
25	SHAREHOLDERS	—		
	4 LIMIT OF LIABILITY			
26	AGGREGATE	●		IV.B., page 5
27	INCLUDES PUNITIVE DAMAGES WHERE NOT UNINSURABLE	—		
28	DEFENSE COSTS INCLUDED WITHIN LIMIT OF LIABILITY	●	See also V.B., page 5	II.L. page 2
29	DEFENSE COSTS PAID IN ADDITION TO LIMIT OF LIABILITY	—		
	5 DEDUCTIBLE			
30	APPLIES TO EACH INDIVIDUAL CLAIM	●		IV.C., page 5
31	APPLIES TO EACH OCCURRENCE OR WRONGFUL PRACTICE	—		
32	INCLUDES ALL CLAIMS FROM ONE ACT	●		IV.A., page 4
33	SUBJECT TO ANNUAL AGGREGATE	—		
34	CO-PAYMENT APPLIES	—		
35	LIMIT OF LIABILITY NOT REDUCED	—		
36	INCLUDES DEFENSE COSTS	●		IV.C., page 5
37	REDUCED UNDER SPECIFIED CIRCUMSTANCES (SEE POLICY)	—		

#	Comparison Query	Comment	Policy Reference
	6 WHAT IS A CLAIM		
38	ORAL COMPLAINT TO INSURED	—	
39	WRITTEN COMPLAINT TO INSURED	●	II.D., page 1
40	COMPLAINT MUST CONTAIN A DEMAND FOR DAMAGES	●	II.D., page 1
41	COMPLAINT FILED WITH EEOC	—	
42	OR SIMILAR STATE AUTHORITY	—	
43	AGENCY MUST HAVE POWER TO ADJUDICATE	—	
44	ADMINISTRATIVE PROCEEDING	●	Administrative or regulatory	II.D., page 1
45	ARBITRATION PROCEEDING	—	
46	ANY INCIDENT REPORTED TO INSURER	—	
47	SUIT	●	II.D., page 1
48	CLAIM DOES NOT INCLUDE ARBITRATION SUBJECT TO	—	
49	COLLECTIVE BARGAINING AGREEMENT	—	
50	EMPLOYEE POLICY OR MANUAL	—	
51	CLAIM NOT DEFINED	—	
	7 CLAIM REPORTING PROVISIONS TO INSURER		
52	IMMEDIATELY	—	
53	AS SOON AS POSSIBLE	—	
54	AS SOON AS PRACTICABLE	●	VI.A., page 5
55	WITHIN POLICY PERIOD	—	
56	WITHIN X DAYS OF EXPIRATION	60	VI.A., page 5
57	WITHIN X DAYS	—	
	8 EXTENDED REPORTING FEATURES		
58	ELECTION PERIOD (DAYS)	30	XIII.B., page 8
59	ADDITIONAL PREMIUM (% OF ANNUAL PREMIUM)	100	XIII.A., page 8
60	ADDITIONAL REPORTING PERIOD (MONTHS)	12	XIII.A., page 8
61	NO REINSTATEMENT OF LIMITS	●	XIII.C., page 8
	9 POTENTIAL CLAIM REPORTING PROVISIONS		
62	NONE (SEE ALSO "CLAIM" ABOVE)	—	
63	INCIDENTS LIKELY TO RESULT IN A CLAIM	●	VI.B., page 5
	10 DEFENSE PROVISIONS		
64	AFFIRMATIVE DUTY TO DEFEND	●	V.A., page 5
65	NO AFFIRMATIVE DUTY TO DEFEND	—	
66	AFFIRMATIVE ADVANCEMENT PROVISIONS	—	
67	INSURED MUST RETURN ADVANCED AMOUNTS IF NOT COVERED	—	
68	INSURED/INSURER CHOOSES COUNSEL	—	
69	INSURED/INSURER APPROVES COUNSEL	—	
70	INSURED/INSURER CONSULTED IN COUNSEL SELECTION	—	
	11 SETTLEMENT PROVISIONS		
71	HAMMER CLAUSE	●	V.C., page 5
72	CONSULTATION PROVISION	—	
73	CONSENT PROVISION	●	Two-way	V.C. and D., page 5
	12 ALLOCATION OF LOSS PROVISIONS		
74	STIPULATED PROVISIONS	●	VI.A., and B., page 6
	13 COVERAGES		
75	DISCRIMINATION	●	II.P., page 2
76	SPECIFIC ENUMERATED ACTIVITIES	—	
77	*PLUS BROAD OMNIBUS WORDING*	—	
78	SPECIFIC ENUMERATED CLASSES	—	
79	*PLUS BROAD OMNIBUS WORDING*	—	
80	AGAINST THIRD PARTIES	—	
81	DISCRIMINATION NOT DEFINED	—	
82	SEXUAL HARASSMENT	●	II.P., page 2
83	HOSTILE ENVIRONMENT	—	
84	QUID-PRO-QUO	—	
85	SEXUAL HARASSMENT NOT DEFINED	●	
86	WRONGFUL TERMINATION	●	II.P., page 2
87	BREACH OF IMPLIED CONTRACT	—	
88	BREACH OF EXPRESS CONTRACT	—	
89	VIOLATION OF PUBLIC POLICY	—	
90	VIOLATION OF GOOD FAITH & FAIR DEALING	—	
91	OBLIGATIONS TO MAKE PAYMENTS	—	
92	CONSTRUCTIVE DISCHARGE	—	
93	WRONGFUL TERMINATION NOT DEFINED	●	
94	OTHER EMPLOYMENT VIOLATIONS/OFFENSES	●	II.P., page 2
95	WRONGFUL HIRING	●	II.P., page 2
96	WRONGFUL PROMOTION/DEMOTION	●	II.P., page 2
97	WRONGFUL EVALUATION/DISCIPLINE	●	II.P., page 2

LONDON MARKET/NAS INSURANCE SERVICES, INC. CBPLI98 [4/98]

	Comparison Query	Comment		Policy Reference
98	FAMILY AND MEDICAL LEAVE ACT	—		
99	DEFAMATION	●		II.P., page 2
100	MISREPRESENTATION	●		II.P., page 2
101	RETALIATION	●		II.P., page 2
102	MENTAL ANGUISH			
103	INVASION OF PRIVACY	●		II.P., page 2
104	HUMILIATION	—		
105	EMOTIONAL DISTRESS	●		II.P., page 2
106	OTHER PERSONAL INJURY OFFENSES	—		
107	POLICY SILENT	—		
	14 EXCLUSIONS			
108	**ADA ACCOMMODATION EXPENSES**	●	Defense cost exception	III.G., page 3
109	**ASSAULT & BATTERY**	—		
110	**BACK PAY**	—		
111	**BODILY INJURY**	●		III.K., page 4
112	BODILY INJURY	●		III.K., page 4
113	DEATH	●		III.K., page 4
114	DISEASE	●		III.K., page 4
115	SICKNESS	●		III.K., page 4
116	**BREACH OF EMPLOYMENT CONTRACT**	—		
117	EXPRESS CONTRACT	—		
118	WRITTEN CONTRACT	—		
119	ORAL CONTRACT	—		
120	IMPLIED CONTRACT	—		
121	**CLASS ACTION LAWSUITS**	—		
122	**CONSEQUENTIAL LOSS**	—		
123	APPLIES TO BODILY INJURY	—		
124	APPLIES TO INSURED EVENT	—		
125	BROTHER/SISTER	—		
126	CHILD	—		
127	DOMESTIC PARTNER	—		
128	PARENT	—		
129	SPOUSE	—		
130	**COST OF ARBITRATION HEARINGS SUBJECT TO**	—		
131	EMPLOYMENT HANDBOOK	—		
132	LABOR GRIEVANCE	—		
133	OTHER EMPLOYMENT POLICY OR PROCEDURE	—		
134	**COVERAGE ELSEWHERE**	●	Exception applies	IX., page 6
135	OTHER AVAILABLE INSURANCE	●		IX., page 6
136	OTHER INDEMNIFICATION	—		
137	SHARING PROVISION	—		
138	**FAILURE TO EXERCISE CARE WHEN TERMINATING**	—		
139	**FINES/PENALTIES**	●		II.L., page 2
140	CIVIL	—		
141	CRIMINAL	—		
142	EXEMPLARY DAMAGES	—		
143	PUNITIVE DAMAGES	●		II.L., page 2
144	MULTIPLIED DAMAGES	●		II.L., page 2
145	**FRONT PAY**	—		
146	EXCLUSION APPLIES ONLY IF EMPLOYER HAD OPPORTUNITY TO REINSTATE EMPLOYEE BUT DID NOT DO SO	—		
147	**INTENTIONAL ACTS**	—		
148	CRIMINAL ACTS	—		
149	CRIMINAL PROCEEDING	—		
150	DISHONEST PURPOSE	—		
151	FRAUDULENT ACTS	●	If established—Non-imputation	III.B., page 3
152	FRAUDULENT CLAIMS	—		
153	INTENTIONAL VIOLATIONS OF LAW	●	If established—Non-imputation	III.D., page 3
154	WILLFUL FAILURE TO COMPLY WITH LAW	—		
155	MALICIOUS PURPOSE	—		
156	**LIABILITY OF OTHERS**	—		
157	**LIQUIDATED DAMAGES**	—		
158	**LOSS ARISING OUT OF CHANGES IN OPERATIONS**	—		
159	ACQUISITION	—		
160	CHANGE IN CONTROL	—		
161	DOWNSIZING OR REDUCTION IN FORCE	—		
162	% OF WORKFORCE	—		
163	WITHIN X DAYS	—		

#	Comparison Query		Comment	Policy Reference
164	FINANCIAL IMPAIRMENT	—		
165	*BANKRUPTCY*	—		
166	*INSOLVENCY*	—		
167	*LIQUIDATION*	—		
168	*RECEIVERSHIP*	—		
169	FINANCIAL INABILITY TO PAY	—		
170	MERGER	—		
171	PLANT OR FACILITY CLOSING	—		
172	REORGANIZATION	—		
173	TEMPORARY SHUTDOWN	—		
174	**MATTERS DEEMED UNINSURABLE**	●		II.L., page 2
175	**NON-MONETARY RELIEF**	—		
176	DECLATORY RELIEF	—		
177	DISGORGEMENT	—		
178	INJUNCTIVE RELIEF	—		
179	JOB REINSTATEMENT	—		
180	NON-MONETARY DAMAGES/RELIEF	—		
181	OTHER EQUITABLE REMEDIES	—		
182	**OBLIGATION TO PROVIDE BENEFITS**	—		
183	COBRA	—		
184	DISABILITY	—		
185	ERISA	—		
186	SOCIAL SECURITY	—		
187	OTHER RETIREMENT BENEFITS	—		
188	UNEMPLOYMENT	—		
189	WORKERS' COMPENSATION	—		
190	**PERSONAL INJURY OFFENSES**	—		
191	DEFAMATION	●	Exceptions apply	III.L., page 4
192	EMOTIONAL DISTRESS/UPSET	—		
193	HUMILIATION	—		
194	LIBEL	●	Exceptions apply	III.L., page 4
195	MENTAL ANGUISH	—		
196	PERSONAL INJURY	—		
197	SLANDER	●	Exceptions apply	III.L., page 4
198	**PRIOR ACTS**	—		
199	PRIOR ACTS	—		
200	PRIOR KNOWLEDGE	●		III.A.4), page 3
201	PRIOR/PENDING LITIGATION	●		III.A.1), page 3
202	**PROPERTY DAMAGE**	●		III.K., page 4
203	INTANGIBLE PROPERTY	—		
204	LOSS OF USE	●		III.K., page 4
205	TANGIBLE PROPERTY	●		III.K., page 4
206	**RETALIATORY ACTIONS OF EMPLOYER**	—		
207	FOR FAILING TO PERFORM ACTS AGAINST PUBLIC POLICY	—		
208	FOR FILING A COMPLAINT OR BENEFIT CLAIM	—		
209	**STRIKES/LOCKOUTS**	—		
210	**VIOLATION OF LAWS**	—		
211	ANY LAW	—		
212	FMLA	—		
213	OSHA	●		III.J., page 4
214	POLLUTION LAWS	—		
215	RICO	—		
216	SEC	—		
217	WARN	●		III.J., page 4

15 CONDITIONS

#	Comparison Query		Comment	Policy Reference
218	**ARBITRATION**	●		VIII., page 6
219	MANDATORY	●		VIII., page 6
220	BINDING	●		VIII., page 6
221	CHOICE OF LAW PROVISION	—		
222	SITUS	—		
223	**TERRITORY**	—		
224	LIMITED	—		
225	WORLDWIDE	—		
226	**NEWLY FORMED/ACQUIRED ENTITIES**	●		XI.A., page 7
227	AUTOMATIC COVERAGE (X DAYS)	○	Conditions apply—see policy	XI.A., page 7
228	NOTIFY INSURER WITHIN X DAYS	○	Conditions apply—see policy	XI.A., page 7

LONDON MARKET/NAS INSURANCE SERVICES, INC. CBPLI98 [4/98]

Policy Comparison Worksheet

London Market
(U.S. Risk Underwriters, Inc.)

Policy Form No.: DISC3/98/CO
Edition Date: 3/98

Risks Considered: All except employee leasing companies
Limits Available: $5,000,000
Minimum Retention: $2,500

Contact: Caren Patton, Jay Alston or Keli Eddings
U.S. Risk Underwriters, Inc.
10210 N. Central Expressway, #500
Dallas, TX 75231
214/265-2448
214/739-1421 (fax)
caren@usrisk.com

KEY TO SYMBOLS
● = Specifically contains queried provision of feature
○ = Unable to determine
— = Silent

#	Comparison Query		Comment	Policy Reference
	1 APPLICATION			
1	ATTACHES TO AND FORMS A PART OF THE POLICY	●		VIII.1., page 8
2	CONTAINS WARRANTY STATEMENTS	○		VIII.3., pages 8–9
3	CONTAINS SEVERABILITY PROVISIONS	●		VIII.1., page 8
	2 POLICY TYPE			
4	UNITARY STAND ALONE POLICY	●		
	ENDORSEMENT OR PART OF			
5	DIRECTORS AND OFFICERS POLICY	—		
6	PACKAGE POLICY	—		
7	UMBRELLA POLICY	—		
8	ERRORS AND OMISSIONS POLICY	—		
9	OTHER	—		
10	CLAIMS-MADE	●		
11	OCCURRENCE	—		
	3 WHO IS INSURED			
12	BUSINESS ENTITY	●		III.A.1., page 2
13	AUTOMATIC COVERAGE FOR SUBSIDIARIES	—		
14	DIRECTORS & OFFICERS	●		III.A.2., page 2
15	EMPLOYEES	●		III.A.2., page 2
16	PART-TIME	—	Coverage available by endorsement	
17	SEASONAL	—	Coverage available by endorsement	
18	TEMPORARY	—	Coverage available by endorsement	
19	SUPERVISORS & MANAGERS	—	Coverage available by endorsement	
20	FORMER EMPLOYEES	●		III.A.2., page 2
21	VOLUNTEERS	—		
22	INDEPENDENT CONTRACTORS	—		
23	EXCLUDED	—	Excludable by endorsement	
24	SILENT	●		
25	SHAREHOLDERS	—		
	4 LIMIT OF LIABILITY			
26	AGGREGATE	●		V.4., page 7
27	INCLUDES PUNITIVE DAMAGES WHERE NOT UNINSURABLE	●	Limited coverage	V.3., page 6
28	DEFENSE COSTS INCLUDED WITHIN LIMIT OF LIABILITY	●		III.D., page 3
29	DEFENSE COSTS PAID IN ADDITION TO LIMIT OF LIABILITY	—		
	5 DEDUCTIBLE			
30	APPLIES TO EACH INDIVIDUAL CLAIM	●		Item D. of Declarations
31	APPLIES TO EACH OCCURRENCE OR WRONGFUL PRACTICE	—		
32	INCLUDES ALL CLAIMS FROM ONE ACT	●		V.2., page 6
33	SUBJECT TO ANNUAL AGGREGATE	—		
34	CO-PAYMENT APPLIES	—	Coverage available by endorsement	
35	LIMIT OF LIABILITY NOT REDUCED	—		
36	INCLUDES DEFENSE COSTS	●		V.1., page 6
37	REDUCED UNDER SPECIFIED CIRCUMSTANCES (SEE POLICY)	—		

LONDON MARKET/U.S. RISK UNDERWRITERS, INC. DISC3/98/CO [3/98]

	Comparison Query	Comment		Policy Reference
	6 WHAT IS A CLAIM			
38	ORAL COMPLAINT TO INSURED	—		
39	WRITTEN COMPLAINT TO INSURED	●		III.G., page 5
40	COMPLAINT MUST CONTAIN A DEMAND FOR DAMAGES	●		III.G., page 5
41	COMPLAINT FILED WITH EEOC	●		III.G., page 5
42	OR SIMILAR STATE AUTHORITY	●	Government agency	III.G., page 5
43	AGENCY MUST HAVE POWER TO ADJUDICATE	—		
44	ADMINISTRATIVE PROCEEDING	—		
45	ARBITRATION PROCEEDING	●		III.G., page 5
46	ANY INCIDENT REPORTED TO INSURER	—		
47	SUIT	●		III.G., page 5
48	CLAIM DOES NOT INCLUDE ARBITRATION SUBJECT TO	—		
49	COLLECTIVE BARGAINING AGREEMENT	—		
50	EMPLOYEE POLICY OR MANUAL	—		
51	CLAIM NOT DEFINED	—		
	7 CLAIM REPORTING PROVISIONS TO INSURER			
52	IMMEDIATELY	—		
53	AS SOON AS POSSIBLE	—		
54	AS SOON AS PRACTICABLE	●		VI.1., page 7
55	WITHIN POLICY PERIOD	—		
56	WITHIN X DAYS OF EXPIRATION	30		VI.1., page 7
57	WITHIN X DAYS	—		
	8 EXTENDED REPORTING FEATURES			
58	ELECTION PERIOD (DAYS)	30		II., page 2
59	ADDITIONAL PREMIUM (% OF ANNUAL PREMIUM)	75	150% for 24-month period	II., page 2
60	ADDITIONAL REPORTING PERIOD (MONTHS)	12	24-month period available	II., page 2
61	NO REINSTATEMENT OF LIMITS	●		II., page 2
	9 POTENTIAL CLAIM REPORTING PROVISIONS			
62	NONE (SEE ALSO "CLAIM" ABOVE)	—		
63	INCIDENTS LIKELY TO RESULT IN A CLAIM	●		VIII.14.a) and b), page 11
	10 DEFENSE PROVISIONS			
64	AFFIRMATIVE DUTY TO DEFEND	●		I., page 1
65	NO AFFIRMATIVE DUTY TO DEFEND	—		
66	AFFIRMATIVE ADVANCEMENT PROVISIONS	—		
67	INSURED MUST RETURN ADVANCED AMOUNTS IF NOT COVERED	—		
68	INSURED/INSURER CHOOSES COUNSEL	—		
69	INSURED/INSURER APPROVES COUNSEL	—		
70	INSURED/INSURER CONSULTED IN COUNSEL SELECTION	—		
	11 SETTLEMENT PROVISIONS			
71	HAMMER CLAUSE	●		VII, page 8
72	CONSULTATION PROVISION	—		
73	CONSENT PROVISION	●	Two-way	VI.4., page 7 and VII., page 8
	12 ALLOCATION OF LOSS PROVISIONS			
74	STIPULATED PROVISIONS	—		
	13 COVERAGES			
75	DISCRIMINATION	●		I., page 1
76	SPECIFIC ENUMERATED ACTIVITIES	●		III.B., page 3
77	PLUS BROAD OMNIBUS WORDING	●		III.B., page 3
78	SPECIFIC ENUMERATED CLASSES	●		III.B., page 3
79	PLUS BROAD OMNIBUS WORDING	●		III.B., page 3
80	AGAINST THIRD PARTIES	—	Excludable by endorsement	
81	DISCRIMINATION NOT DEFINED	—		
82	SEXUAL HARASSMENT	—		
83	HOSTILE ENVIRONMENT	—		
84	QUID-PRO-QUO	—		
85	SEXUAL HARASSMENT NOT DEFINED	—		
86	WRONGFUL TERMINATION	●		I., page 1
87	BREACH OF IMPLIED CONTRACT	●		III.C., page 3
88	BREACH OF EXPRESS CONTRACT	—		
89	VIOLATION OF PUBLIC POLICY	—		
90	VIOLATION OF GOOD FAITH & FAIR DEALING	—		
91	OBLIGATIONS TO MAKE PAYMENTS	—		
92	CONSTRUCTIVE DISCHARGE	—		
93	WRONGFUL TERMINATION NOT DEFINED	—		
94	OTHER EMPLOYMENT VIOLATIONS/OFFENSES	—		
95	WRONGFUL HIRING	—		
96	WRONGFUL PROMOTION/DEMOTION	—		
97	WRONGFUL EVALUATION/DISCIPLINE	—		

	Comparison Query		Comment	Policy Reference
98	FAMILY AND MEDICAL LEAVE ACT	—		
99	DEFAMATION	●		IV.C., page 5
100	MISREPRESENTATION	—		
101	RETALIATION	—		
102	MENTAL ANGUISH	—		
103	INVASION OF PRIVACY	●		IV.C., page 5
104	HUMILIATION	—		
105	EMOTIONAL DISTRESS	—		
106	OTHER PERSONAL INJURY OFFENSES	—		
107	POLICY SILENT	—		
14 EXCLUSIONS				
108	**ADA ACCOMMODATION EXPENSES**	●	See also IV.H., page 6	III.D.(5), page 4
109	**ASSAULT & BATTERY**	●		IV.B., page 5
110	**BACK PAY**	●		III.D.(8), page 4
111	**BODILY INJURY**	●		IV.A., page 5
112	BODILY INJURY	●		IV.A., page 5
113	DEATH	●		IV.A., page 5
114	DISEASE	●		IV.A., page 5
115	SICKNESS	●		IV.A., page 5
116	**BREACH OF EMPLOYMENT CONTRACT**	●		III.C., page 3
117	EXPRESS CONTRACT	●		III.C., page 3
118	WRITTEN CONTRACT	—		
119	ORAL CONTRACT	—		
120	IMPLIED CONTRACT	—		
121	**CLASS ACTION LAWSUITS**	—		
122	**CONSEQUENTIAL LOSS**	●		IV.A., page 5
123	APPLIES TO BODILY INJURY	●	Loss of consortium	IV.A., page 5
124	APPLIES TO INSURED EVENT	—		
125	BROTHER/SISTER	—		
126	CHILD	—		
127	DOMESTIC PARTNER	—		
128	PARENT	—		
129	SPOUSE	—		
130	**COST OF ARBITRATION HEARINGS SUBJECT TO**	—		
131	EMPLOYMENT HANDBOOK	—		
132	LABOR GRIEVANCE	—		
133	OTHER EMPLOYMENT POLICY OR PROCEDURE	—		
134	**COVERAGE ELSEWHERE**	●		VIII.6, page 10
135	OTHER AVAILABLE INSURANCE	●		VIII.6, page 10
136	OTHER INDEMNIFICATION	—		
137	SHARING PROVISION	—		
138	**FAILURE TO EXERCISE CARE WHEN TERMINATING**	—		
139	**FINES/PENALTIES**	●	If not uninsurable	III.D.(2), page 3
140	CIVIL	—		
141	CRIMINAL	—		
142	EXEMPLARY DAMAGES	●	If not uninsurable	III.D.(3), page 3
143	PUNITIVE DAMAGES	●	Coverage available by endorsement	III.D.(3), page 3
144	MULTIPLIED DAMAGES	●	If not uninsurable	V.3., page 6
145	**FRONT PAY**	—		
146	EXCLUSION APPLIES ONLY IF EMPLOYER HAD OPPORTUNITY TO REINSTATE EMPLOYEE BUT DID NOT DO SO	—		
147	**INTENTIONAL ACTS**	—		
148	CRIMINAL ACTS	—		
149	CRIMINAL PROCEEDING	—		
150	DISHONEST PURPOSE	—		
151	FRAUDULENT ACTS	—		
152	FRAUDULENT CLAIMS	●		VIII.12., page 11
153	INTENTIONAL VIOLATIONS OF LAW	—		
154	WILLFUL FAILURE TO COMPLY WITH LAW	—		
155	MALICIOUS PURPOSE	—		
156	**LIABILITY OF OTHERS**	—		
157	**LIQUIDATED DAMAGES**	●		III.D.(8), page 4
158	**LOSS ARISING OUT OF CHANGES IN OPERATIONS**	—		
159	ACQUISITION	—		
160	CHANGE IN CONTROL	—		
161	DOWNSIZING OR REDUCTION IN FORCE	—	Excludable by endorsement	
162	% OF WORKFORCE	—		
163	WITHIN X DAYS	—		

LONDON MARKET/U.S. RISK UNDERWRITERS, INC.   DISC3/98/CO [3/98]

#	Comparison Query	Comment	Policy Reference
164	**FINANCIAL IMPAIRMENT**	—	
165	*BANKRUPTCY*	—	
166	*INSOLVENCY*	—	
167	*LIQUIDATION*	—	
168	*RECEIVERSHIP*	—	
169	FINANCIAL INABILITY TO PAY	—	
170	MERGER	—	
171	PLANT OR FACILITY CLOSING	—	
172	REORGANIZATION	—	Excludable by endorsement
173	TEMPORARY SHUTDOWN	—	Excludable by endorsement
174	**MATTERS DEEMED UNINSURABLE**	●	III.D.(4)., page 3
175	**NON-MONETARY RELIEF**	●	III.D.(7)., page 3
176	DECLATORY RELIEF	—	
177	DISGORGEMENT	—	
178	INJUNCTIVE RELIEF	●	IV.G., page 6
179	JOB REINSTATEMENT	—	
180	NON-MONETARY DAMAGES/RELIEF	●	III.D.(7)., page 3
181	OTHER EQUITABLE REMEDIES	—	
182	**OBLIGATION TO PROVIDE BENEFITS**	—	
183	COBRA	—	
184	DISABILITY	—	
185	ERISA	●	IV.E., page 5
186	SOCIAL SECURITY	—	
187	OTHER RETIREMENT BENEFITS	—	
188	UNEMPLOYMENT	—	
189	WORKERS' COMPENSATION	—	
190	**PERSONAL INJURY OFFENSES**	●	IV.C., page 5
191	DEFAMATION	●	Unless result of "wrongful act"	IV.C., page 5
192	EMOTIONAL DISTRESS/UPSET	—	
193	HUMILIATION	—	
194	LIBEL	●	Unless result of "wrongful act"	IV.C., page 5
195	MENTAL ANGUISH	—	
196	PERSONAL INJURY	—	
197	SLANDER	●	Unless result of "wrongful act"	IV.C., page 5
198	**PRIOR ACTS**	—	
199	PRIOR ACTS	—	
200	PRIOR KNOWLEDGE	●	IV.F.(i)., page 6
201	PRIOR/PENDING LITIGATION	—	Excludable by endorsement
202	**PROPERTY DAMAGE**	●	IV.A., page 5
203	INTANGIBLE PROPERTY	—	
204	LOSS OF USE	●	IV.A., page 5
205	TANGIBLE PROPERTY	●	IV.A., page 5
206	**RETALIATORY ACTIONS OF EMPLOYER**	—	
207	FOR FAILING TO PERFORM ACTS AGAINST PUBLIC POLICY	—	
208	FOR FILING A COMPLAINT OR BENEFIT CLAIM	—	
209	**STRIKES/LOCKOUTS**	—	
210	**VIOLATION OF LAWS**	—	
211	ANY LAW	—	
212	FMLA	—	
213	OSHA	—	
214	POLLUTION LAWS	—	
215	RICO	●	IV.D., page 5
216	SEC	—	
217	WARN	—	
	15 CONDITIONS		
218	**ARBITRATION**	—	
219	MANDATORY	—	
220	BINDING	—	
221	CHOICE OF LAW PROVISION	—	
222	SITUS	—	
223	**TERRITORY**	●	VIII.13., page 11
224	LIMITED	—	
225	WORLDWIDE	●	VIII.13., page 11
226	**NEWLY FORMED/ACQUIRED ENTITIES**	●	III.A.4., page 3
227	AUTOMATIC COVERAGE (X DAYS)	30	If > 51% ownership	III.A.4., page 3
228	NOTIFY INSURER WITHIN X DAYS	—	

LONDON MARKET/U.S. RISK UNDERWRITERS, INC. DISC3/98/CO [3/98]

Policy Comparison Worksheet

National Union Fire Insurance Co.
(American International Companies)

Policy Form No.: 67548
Edition Date: 4/97

Risks Considered: General accounts
Limits Available: $50,000,000
Minimum Retention: $25,000 to $250,000

Contact: Paul J. Schiavone
Assistant Vice President/Divisional Counsel
National Union Fire Insurance Co.
175 Water Street, 5th Floor
New York, NY 10038
212/458-1418
212/458-1474 (fax)

KEY TO SYMBOLS
● = Specifically contains queried provision of feature
○ = Unable to determine
— = Silent

#	Comparison Query		Comment	Policy Reference
	1 APPLICATION			
1	ATTACHES TO AND FORMS A PART OF THE POLICY	●		Preamble, page 1
2	CONTAINS WARRANTY STATEMENTS	●		Application, page 5
3	CONTAINS SEVERABILITY PROVISIONS	—		
	2 POLICY TYPE			
4	UNITARY STAND ALONE POLICY	●		
	ENDORSEMENT OR PART OF	—		
5	DIRECTORS AND OFFICERS POLICY	—		
6	PACKAGE POLICY	—		
7	UMBRELLA POLICY	—		
8	ERRORS AND OMISSIONS POLICY	—		
9	OTHER	—		
10	CLAIMS-MADE	●		
11	OCCURRENCE	—		
	3 WHO IS INSURED			
12	BUSINESS ENTITY	●		2.(b).(2)., page 4
13	AUTOMATIC COVERAGE FOR SUBSIDIARIES	●		2.(c), page 2
14	DIRECTORS & OFFICERS	●		2.(i).(1)., page 4
15	EMPLOYEES	●		2.(g)., pages 2–3
16	PART-TIME	●		2.(g)., pages 2–3
17	SEASONAL	●		2.(g)., pages 2–3
18	TEMPORARY	●		2.(g)., pages 2–3
19	SUPERVISORS & MANAGERS	●		2.(g)., pages 2–3
20	FORMER EMPLOYEES	●		2.(g)., pages 2–3
21	VOLUNTEERS	—		
22	INDEPENDENT CONTRACTORS	●	Qualifications apply	2.(g)., pages 2–3
23	EXCLUDED	○	Coverage available by endorsement	2.(g)., pages 2–3
24	SILENT	—		
25	SHAREHOLDERS	—		
	4 LIMIT OF LIABILITY			
26	AGGREGATE	●		5., page 9
27	INCLUDES PUNITIVE DAMAGES WHERE NOT UNINSURABLE	—	Coverage available by endorsement	
28	DEFENSE COSTS INCLUDED WITHIN LIMIT OF LIABILITY	●		5., page 9
29	DEFENSE COSTS PAID IN ADDITION TO LIMIT OF LIABILITY	—		
	5 DEDUCTIBLE			
30	APPLIES TO EACH INDIVIDUAL CLAIM	●	Indemnifiable loss only (exceptions also apply)	6., page 9
31	APPLIES TO EACH OCCURRENCE OR WRONGFUL PRACTICE	●	Indemnifiable loss only (exceptions also apply)	6., page 9
32	INCLUDES ALL CLAIMS FROM ONE ACT	●	Indemnifiable loss only (exceptions also apply)	6., page 9
33	SUBJECT TO ANNUAL AGGREGATE	—		
34	CO-PAYMENT APPLIES	—		
35	LIMIT OF LIABILITY NOT REDUCED	—		
36	INCLUDES DEFENSE COSTS	●	See also II.(I)., page 4	6., page 9
37	REDUCED UNDER SPECIFIED CIRCUMSTANCES (SEE POLICY)	●		6., pages 9–10

#	Comparison Query	Comment	Policy Reference
	6 WHAT IS A CLAIM		
38	ORAL COMPLAINT TO INSURED	—	
39	WRITTEN COMPLAINT TO INSURED	●	2.(b).(1)., page 1
40	COMPLAINT MUST CONTAIN A DEMAND FOR DAMAGES	●	2.(b).(1)., page 1
41	COMPLAINT FILED WITH EEOC	●	2.(b)., pages 1–2
42	OR SIMILAR STATE AUTHORITY	●	2.(b)., pages 1–2
43	AGENCY MUST HAVE POWER TO ADJUDICATE	—	
44	ADMINISTRATIVE PROCEEDING	●	2.(b).(2)., page 1
45	ARBITRATION PROCEEDING	●	2.(b).(2)., page 1
46	ANY INCIDENT REPORTED TO INSURER	—	
47	SUIT	●	2.(b).(2)., page 1
48	CLAIM DOES NOT INCLUDE ARBITRATION SUBJECT TO	●	2.(b)., page 2
49	COLLECTIVE BARGAINING AGREEMENT	●	2.(b)., page 2
50	EMPLOYEE POLICY OR MANUAL	—	
51	CLAIM NOT DEFINED	—	
	7 CLAIM REPORTING PROVISIONS TO INSURER		
52	IMMEDIATELY	—	
53	AS SOON AS POSSIBLE	—	
54	AS SOON AS PRACTICABLE	●	7.(a)., page 10
55	WITHIN POLICY PERIOD	●	7.(a).(1)., page 10
56	WITHIN X DAYS OF EXPIRATION	30	7.(a).(2)., page 10
57	WITHIN X DAYS	—	
	8 EXTENDED REPORTING FEATURES		
58	ELECTION PERIOD (DAYS)	30	10., page 14
59	ADDITIONAL PREMIUM (% OF ANNUAL PREMIUM)	○	Specified by underwriter	10., page 14
60	ADDITIONAL REPORTING PERIOD (MONTHS)	12, 24, 36	10., page 14
61	NO REINSTATEMENT OF LIMITS	—	
	9 POTENTIAL CLAIM REPORTING PROVISIONS		
62	NONE (SEE ALSO "CLAIM" ABOVE)	—	
63	INCIDENTS LIKELY TO RESULT IN A CLAIM	●	7.(c)., page 11
	10 DEFENSE PROVISIONS		
64	AFFIRMATIVE DUTY TO DEFEND	●	Insured's option	1. Defense Provisions, page 1 and 8., page 11
65	NO AFFIRMATIVE DUTY TO DEFEND	●	Insured's option	1. Defense Provisions, page 1 and 8., page 11
66	AFFIRMATIVE ADVANCEMENT PROVISIONS	●	1. Defense Provisions, page 1 and 8., page 11
67	INSURED MUST RETURN ADVANCED AMOUNTS IF NOT COVERED	●	8., page 12
68	INSURED/INSURER CHOOSES COUNSEL	●	Insured's option; See 9., page 13	8., page 12
69	INSURED/INSURER APPROVES COUNSEL	●	Insured's option	9. page 13
70	INSURED/INSURER CONSULTED IN COUNSEL SELECTION	—	
	11 SETTLEMENT PROVISIONS		
71	HAMMER CLAUSE	●	Also applies to retention amount	8., page 12
72	CONSULTATION PROVISION	—	
73	CONSENT PROVISION	●	Insurer must consent	8., page 12
	12 ALLOCATION OF LOSS PROVISIONS		
74	STIPULATED PROVISIONS	—	
	13 COVERAGES		
75	DISCRIMINATION	●	2.(h).(3)., page 3
76	SPECIFIC ENUMERATED ACTIVITIES	—	
77	PLUS BROAD OMNIBUS WORDING	—	
78	SPECIFIC ENUMERATED CLASSES	●	2.(h).(3)., page 3
79	PLUS BROAD OMNIBUS WORDING	●	2.(h).(3)., page 3
80	AGAINST THIRD PARTIES	●	2.(h)., following (12)., page 3
81	DISCRIMINATION NOT DEFINED	—	
82	SEXUAL HARASSMENT	●	2.(h).(2)., page 3
83	HOSTILE ENVIRONMENT	●	2.(h).(2)., page 3
84	QUID-PRO-QUO	●	2.(h).(2)., page 3
85	SEXUAL HARASSMENT NOT DEFINED	—	
86	WRONGFUL TERMINATION	●	2.(h).(1)., page 3
87	BREACH OF IMPLIED CONTRACT	●	2.(h).(1)., page 3
88	BREACH OF EXPRESS CONTRACT	—	
89	VIOLATION OF PUBLIC POLICY	—	
90	VIOLATION OF GOOD FAITH & FAIR DEALING	—	
91	OBLIGATIONS TO MAKE PAYMENTS	—	
92	CONSTRUCTIVE DISCHARGE	●	2.(h).(1)., page 3
93	WRONGFUL TERMINATION NOT DEFINED	—	
94	**OTHER EMPLOYMENT VIOLATIONS/OFFENSES**		
95	WRONGFUL HIRING	●	2.(h).(7)., page 3
96	WRONGFUL PROMOTION/DEMOTION	●	2.(h).(7). & (8)., page 3
97	WRONGFUL EVALUATION/DISCIPLINE	●	2.(h).(8)., page 3 and 2.(h).(9)., page 3

NATIONAL UNION FIRE INSURANCE CO. (AMERICAN INTERNATIONAL COMPANIES) 67548 [4/97]

	Comparison Query		Comment	Policy Reference
98	FAMILY AND MEDICAL LEAVE ACT	—		
99	DEFAMATION	●		2.(h).(6)., page 3
100	MISREPRESENTATION	●		2.(h).(5)., page 3
101	RETALIATION	●		2.(h).(4)., page 3
102	MENTAL ANGUISH	—		
103	INVASION OF PRIVACY	●		2.(h).(6)., page 3
104	HUMILIATION	●		2.(h).(6)., page 3
105	EMOTIONAL DISTRESS	●		
106	OTHER PERSONAL INJURY OFFENSES	●		2.(h).(6)., page 3
107	POLICY SILENT	—		
	14 EXCLUSIONS			
108	**ADA ACCOMMODATION EXPENSES**	●		2.(k)., page 5
109	**ASSAULT & BATTERY**	—		
110	**BACK PAY**	—		
111	**BODILY INJURY**	●		4.(h)., page 8
112	BODILY INJURY	●		4.(h)., page 8
113	DEATH	●		4.(h)., page 8
114	DISEASE	●		4.(h)., page 8
115	SICKNESS	●		4.(h)., page 8
116	**BREACH OF EMPLOYMENT CONTRACT**			
117	EXPRESS CONTRACT	—		
118	WRITTEN CONTRACT	—		
119	ORAL CONTRACT	—		
120	IMPLIED CONTRACT	—		
121	**CLASS ACTION LAWSUITS**	—		
122	**CONSEQUENTIAL LOSS**			
123	APPLIES TO BODILY INJURY	—		
124	APPLIES TO INSURED EVENT	—		
125	BROTHER/SISTER	—		
126	CHILD	—		
127	DOMESTIC PARTNER	—		
128	PARENT	—		
129	SPOUSE	—		
130	**COST OF ARBITRATION HEARINGS SUBJECT TO**			
131	EMPLOYMENT HANDBOOK	—		
132	LABOR GRIEVANCE	—		
133	OTHER EMPLOYMENT POLICY OR PROCEDURE	—		
134	**COVERAGE ELSEWHERE**			
135	OTHER AVAILABLE INSURANCE	●		14., page 16
136	OTHER INDEMNIFICATION	—		
137	SHARING PROVISION	—		
138	**FAILURE TO EXERCISE CARE WHEN TERMINATING**	—		
139	**FINES/PENALTIES**	●		2.(l)., pages 4–5
140	CIVIL	●		2.(l)., pages 4–5
141	CRIMINAL	●		2.(l)., pages 4–5
142	EXEMPLARY DAMAGES	●	Coverage available by endorsement	2.(l)., pages 4–5
143	PUNITIVE DAMAGES	●	Coverage available by endorsement	2.(l)., pages 4–5
144	MULTIPLIED DAMAGES	●	Coverage available by endorsement	2.(l)., pages 4–5
145	**FRONT PAY**	—		
146	EXCLUSION APPLIES ONLY IF EMPLOYER HAD OPPORTUNITY TO REINSTATE EMPLOYEE BUT DID NOT DO SO	—		
147	**INTENTIONAL ACTS**	●		4.(b)., page 7
148	CRIMINAL ACTS	●		4.(b)., page 7
149	CRIMINAL PROCEEDING	—		
150	DISHONEST PURPOSE	—		
151	FRAUDULENT ACTS	●		4.(b)., page 7
152	FRAUDULENT CLAIMS	—		
153	INTENTIONAL VIOLATIONS OF LAW	—		
154	WILLFUL FAILURE TO COMPLY WITH LAW	—		
155	MALICIOUS PURPOSE	—		
156	**LIABILITY OF OTHERS**	●		4.(k)., page 9
157	**LIQUIDATED DAMAGES**	—		
158	**LOSS ARISING OUT OF CHANGES IN OPERATIONS**	—		
159	ACQUISITION	—		
160	CHANGE IN CONTROL	—		
161	DOWNSIZING OR REDUCTION IN FORCE	—		
162	% OF WORKFORCE	—		
163	WITHIN X DAYS	—		

NATIONAL UNION FIRE INSURANCE CO. (AMERICAN INTERNATIONAL COMPANIES) 67548 [4/97]

#	Comparison Query	Comment		Policy Reference
164	FINANCIAL IMPAIRMENT	—		
165	BANKRUPTCY	—		
166	INSOLVENCY	—		
167	LIQUIDATION	—		
168	RECEIVERSHIP	—		
169	FINANCIAL INABILITY TO PAY	—		
170	MERGER	—		
171	PLANT OR FACILITY CLOSING	—		
172	REORGANIZATION	—		
173	TEMPORARY SHUTDOWN	—		
174	**MATTERS DEEMED UNINSURABLE**	●		2.(k)., page 5
175	**NON-MONETARY RELIEF**	—		
176	DECLATORY RELIEF	—		
177	DISGORGEMENT	—		
178	INJUNCTIVE RELIEF	—		
179	JOB REINSTATEMENT	—		
180	NON-MONETARY DAMAGES/RELIEF	—		
181	OTHER EQUITABLE REMEDIES	—		
182	**OBLIGATION TO PROVIDE BENEFITS**	—		
183	COBRA	●		4.(j)., page 8
184	DISABILITY	●		2.(k)., page 5
185	ERISA	●		4.(j)., page 8
186	SOCIAL SECURITY	●		2.(k)., page 5
187	OTHER RETIREMENT BENEFITS	●		2.(k)., page 5
188	UNEMPLOYMENT	●		2.(k)., page 5
189	WORKERS' COMPENSATION	●		2.(k)., page 5
190	**PERSONAL INJURY OFFENSES**	—		
191	DEFAMATION	—		
192	EMOTIONAL DISTRESS/UPSET	—		
193	HUMILIATION	—		
194	LIBEL	—		
195	MENTAL ANGUISH	—		
196	PERSONAL INJURY	—		
197	SLANDER	—		
198	**PRIOR ACTS**	●		4.(c)., page 8
199	PRIOR ACTS	●	Prior to continuity date	4.(c)., page 8
200	PRIOR KNOWLEDGE	●		4.(c)., pages 7–8
201	PRIOR/PENDING LITIGATION	●		4.(d)., page 8
202	**PROPERTY DAMAGE**	●		4.(h)., page 8
203	INTANGIBLE PROPERTY	—		
204	LOSS OF USE	●		4.(h)., page 8
205	TANGIBLE PROPERTY	●		4.(h)., page 8
206	**RETALIATORY ACTIONS OF EMPLOYER**	—		
207	FOR FAILING TO PERFORM ACTS AGAINST PUBLIC POLICY	—		
208	FOR FILING A COMPLAINT OR BENEFIT CLAIM	—		
209	**STRIKES/LOCKOUTS**	—		
210	**VIOLATION OF LAWS**	—		
211	ANY LAW	—		
212	FMLA	—		
213	OSHA	●		4.(j)., page 8
214	POLLUTION LAWS	—		
215	RICO	—		
216	SEC	—		
217	WARN	●		4.(j)., page 8
	15 CONDITIONS			
218	**ARBITRATION**	●	ADR proceeding	17., page 17
219	MANDATORY	●	ADR proceeding	17., page 17
220	BINDING	●	Arbitration only	17., page 18
221	CHOICE OF LAW PROVISION	—		
222	SITUS	●	Multiple choices for insured	17., page 18
223	**TERRITORY**	—		
224	LIMITED	—		
225	WORLDWIDE	—		
226	**NEWLY FORMED/ACQUIRED ENTITIES**	—		
227	AUTOMATIC COVERAGE (X DAYS)	—		
228	NOTIFY INSURER WITHIN X DAYS	—		

NATIONAL UNION FIRE INSURANCE CO. (AMERICAN INTERNATIONAL COMPANIES) 67548 [4/97]

Policy Comparison Worksheet

Northland Insurance Companies

Policy Form No.: S1110-EP
Edition Date: 6/97

Risks Considered: Companies with three or more employees
Limits Available: $5,000,000
Minimum Retention: $2,500

Contact: Gwen L. Holler, CPCU
Northland Insurance Companies
1295 Northland Drive
St. Paul, MN 55120-1146
612/688-4510
612/688-4280 (fax)
gwen.holler@northlandins.com

KEY TO SYMBOLS
● = Specifically contains queried provision of feature
○ = Unable to determine
— = Silent

#	Comparison Query		Comment	Policy Reference
	1 APPLICATION			
1	ATTACHES TO AND FORMS A PART OF THE POLICY	●		VIII.F., page 5
2	CONTAINS WARRANTY STATEMENTS	●		VIII.F., page 5
3	CONTAINS SEVERABILITY PROVISIONS	●		VIII.G., page 5
	2 POLICY TYPE			
4	UNITARY STAND ALONE POLICY	●		
	ENDORSEMENT OR PART OF	—		
5	DIRECTORS AND OFFICERS POLICY	—		
6	PACKAGE POLICY	—		
7	UMBRELLA POLICY	—		
8	ERRORS AND OMISSIONS POLICY	—		
9	OTHER	—		
10	CLAIMS-MADE	●		
11	OCCURRENCE	—		
	3 WHO IS INSURED			
12	BUSINESS ENTITY	●		II.A.4., page 2
13	AUTOMATIC COVERAGE FOR SUBSIDIARIES	●	90 days	VIII.H., page 5
14	DIRECTORS & OFFICERS	●		II.A.4., page 2
15	EMPLOYEES	●	At time of wrongful employment practice	II.B.1., page 2
16	PART-TIME	●		III.D., page 2
17	SEASONAL	●		III.D., page 2
18	TEMPORARY	●		III.D., page 2
19	SUPERVISORS & MANAGERS	—		
20	FORMER EMPLOYEES	—		
21	VOLUNTEERS	—	Coverage available by endorsement	
22	INDEPENDENT CONTRACTORS			
23	EXCLUDED	●	Coverage available by endorsement	III.D., page 2
24	SILENT	—		
25	SHAREHOLDERS	●		II.A.4., page 2
	4 LIMIT OF LIABILITY			
26	AGGREGATE	●		V.B., page 3
27	INCLUDES PUNITIVE DAMAGES WHERE NOT UNINSURABLE	—		
28	DEFENSE COSTS INCLUDED WITHIN LIMIT OF LIABILITY	●		V.C., page 3
29	DEFENSE COSTS PAID IN ADDITION TO LIMIT OF LIABILITY	—		
	5 DEDUCTIBLE			
30	APPLIES TO EACH INDIVIDUAL CLAIM	●		VI., page 3
31	APPLIES TO EACH OCCURRENCE OR WRONGFUL PRACTICE	—		
32	INCLUDES ALL CLAIMS FROM ONE ACT	●		VI., page 3
33	SUBJECT TO ANNUAL AGGREGATE	—		
34	CO-PAYMENT APPLIES	—		
35	LIMIT OF LIABILITY NOT REDUCED	●		VI., page 3
36	INCLUDES DEFENSE COSTS	●	Legal fees only	VI., page 3
37	REDUCED UNDER SPECIFIED CIRCUMSTANCES (SEE POLICY)	—		

NORTHLAND INSURANCE COMPANIES S1110-EP [6/97]

#	Comparison Query	Comment	Policy Reference
6	**WHAT IS A CLAIM**		
38	ORAL COMPLAINT TO INSURED	—	
39	WRITTEN COMPLAINT TO INSURED	●	III.A.1., page 2
40	COMPLAINT MUST CONTAIN A DEMAND FOR DAMAGES	●	
41	COMPLAINT FILED WITH EEOC	—	
42	OR SIMILAR STATE AUTHORITY	—	
43	AGENCY MUST HAVE POWER TO ADJUDICATE	—	
44	ADMINISTRATIVE PROCEEDING	—	
45	ARBITRATION PROCEEDING	●	If insurer agrees	III.A.3., page 2
46	ANY INCIDENT REPORTED TO INSURER	—	
47	SUIT	●	Civil proceeding	III.A.4., page 2
48	CLAIM DOES NOT INCLUDE ARBITRATION SUBJECT TO	●		III.A., page 2
49	COLLECTIVE BARGAINING AGREEMENT	●		III.A., page 2
50	EMPLOYEE POLICY OR MANUAL	—	
51	CLAIM NOT DEFINED	—	
7	**CLAIM REPORTING PROVISIONS TO INSURER**		
52	IMMEDIATELY	—	
53	AS SOON AS POSSIBLE	—	
54	AS SOON AS PRACTICABLE	●		I.A.1.a., page 1
55	WITHIN POLICY PERIOD	—	
56	WITHIN X DAYS OF EXPIRATION	60		I.A.1.a., page 1
57	WITHIN X DAYS	—	
8	**EXTENDED REPORTING FEATURES**		
58	ELECTION PERIOD (DAYS)	30		VII.A., page 3
59	ADDITIONAL PREMIUM (% OF ANNUAL PREMIUM)	100		VII.B., page 4
60	ADDITIONAL REPORTING PERIOD (MONTHS)	12		VII.B., page 3
61	NO REINSTATEMENT OF LIMITS	●		VII.B., page 4
9	**POTENTIAL CLAIM REPORTING PROVISIONS**		
62	NONE (SEE ALSO "CLAIM" ABOVE)	—	
63	INCIDENTS LIKELY TO RESULT IN A CLAIM	●		I.A.1., following d., page 1
10	**DEFENSE PROVISIONS**		
64	AFFIRMATIVE DUTY TO DEFEND	●		I.A.2., page 1
65	NO AFFIRMATIVE DUTY TO DEFEND	—	
66	AFFIRMATIVE ADVANCEMENT PROVISIONS	—	
67	INSURED MUST RETURN ADVANCED AMOUNTS IF NOT COVERED	—	
68	INSURED/INSURER CHOOSES COUNSEL	●		I.A.2., page 1
69	INSURED/INSURER APPROVES COUNSEL	—	
70	INSURED/INSURER CONSULTED IN COUNSEL SELECTION	●	Insured consulted	I.A.2., page 1
11	**SETTLEMENT PROVISIONS**		
71	HAMMER CLAUSE	—	
72	CONSULTATION PROVISION	—	
73	CONSENT PROVISION	●	Insured must consent	I.A.2., page 1
12	**ALLOCATION OF LOSS PROVISIONS**		
74	STIPULATED PROVISIONS	—	
13	**COVERAGES**		
75	DISCRIMINATION	●		III.E.1., page 2
76	SPECIFIC ENUMERATED ACTIVITIES	●		III.E.1., page 2
77	PLUS BROAD OMNIBUS WORDING	●		III.E.1., page 2
78	SPECIFIC ENUMERATED CLASSES	●		III.E.1., page 2
79	PLUS BROAD OMNIBUS WORDING	—	
80	AGAINST THIRD PARTIES	—	
81	DISCRIMINATION NOT DEFINED	●	
82	SEXUAL HARASSMENT	●		III.E.2., page 2
83	HOSTILE ENVIRONMENT	●		III.E.2., page 2
84	QUID-PRO-QUO	●		III.E.2., page 2
85	SEXUAL HARASSMENT NOT DEFINED	●	
86	WRONGFUL TERMINATION	●		III.E.2., page 2
87	BREACH OF IMPLIED CONTRACT	●		I.B.3., page 1
88	BREACH OF EXPRESS CONTRACT	—	
89	VIOLATION OF PUBLIC POLICY	—	
90	VIOLATION OF GOOD FAITH & FAIR DEALING	—	
91	OBLIGATIONS TO MAKE PAYMENTS	—	
92	CONSTRUCTIVE DISCHARGE	—	
93	WRONGFUL TERMINATION NOT DEFINED	●	
94	OTHER EMPLOYMENT VIOLATIONS/OFFENSES	●		III.E., pages 2–3
95	WRONGFUL HIRING	●	See also III.E.3., page 2	III.E.1., page 2
96	WRONGFUL PROMOTION/DEMOTION	●	See also III.E.3., page 2	III.E.1., page 2
97	WRONGFUL EVALUATION/DISCIPLINE	●	See also III.E.3., page 3	III.E.1., page 2

NORTHLAND INSURANCE COMPANIES S1110-EP [6/97]

	Comparison Query	Comment	Policy Reference
98	FAMILY AND MEDICAL LEAVE ACT	—	
99	DEFAMATION	●	III.E.3., page 3
100	MISREPRESENTATION	●	III.E.3., page 3
101	RETALIATION	●	III.E.3., page 3
102	MENTAL ANGUISH	●	I.B.1., page 1
103	INVASION OF PRIVACY	●	III.E.3., page 3
104	HUMILIATION	●	I.B.1., page 1
105	EMOTIONAL DISTRESS	●	I.B.1., page 1
106	OTHER PERSONAL INJURY OFFENSES	—	
107	POLICY SILENT	—	

14 EXCLUSIONS

	Comparison Query	Comment	Policy Reference
108	**ADA ACCOMMODATION EXPENSES**	—	
109	**ASSAULT & BATTERY**	—	
110	**BACK PAY**	—	
111	**BODILY INJURY**	●	I.B.1., page 1
112	BODILY INJURY	●	I.B.1., page 1
113	DEATH	●	I.B.1., page 1
114	DISEASE	●	I.B.1., page 1
115	SICKNESS	●	I.B.1., page 1
116	**BREACH OF EMPLOYMENT CONTRACT**	—	
117	EXPRESS CONTRACT	—	
118	WRITTEN CONTRACT	—	
119	ORAL CONTRACT	—	
120	IMPLIED CONTRACT	—	
121	**CLASS ACTION LAWSUITS**	—	
122	**CONSEQUENTIAL LOSS**	—	
123	APPLIES TO BODILY INJURY	—	
124	APPLIES TO INSURED EVENT	—	
125	BROTHER/SISTER	—	
126	CHILD	—	
127	DOMESTIC PARTNER	—	
128	PARENT	—	
129	SPOUSE	—	
130	**COST OF ARBITRATION HEARINGS SUBJECT TO**	—	
131	EMPLOYMENT HANDBOOK	—	
132	LABOR GRIEVANCE	—	
133	OTHER EMPLOYMENT POLICY OR PROCEDURE	—	
134	**COVERAGE ELSEWHERE**	●	VIII.D.1.a. & b., page 4
135	OTHER AVAILABLE INSURANCE	●	Conditions apply	VIII.D.1.a. & b., page 4
136	OTHER INDEMNIFICATION	—	
137	SHARING PROVISION	●	VIII.D. 2. & 3., page 5
138	**FAILURE TO EXERCISE CARE WHEN TERMINATING**	—	
139	**FINES/PENALTIES**	—	
140	CIVIL	—	
141	CRIMINAL	—	
142	EXEMPLARY DAMAGES	—	
143	PUNITIVE DAMAGES	—	
144	MULTIPLIED DAMAGES	—	
145	**FRONT PAY**	—	
146	EXCLUSION APPLIES ONLY IF EMPLOYER HAD OPPORTUNITY TO REINSTATE EMPLOYEE BUT DID NOT DO SO	—	
147	**INTENTIONAL ACTS**	●	I.B.5., page 2
148	CRIMINAL ACTS	●	I.B.5., page 2
149	CRIMINAL PROCEEDING	●	I.B.5., page 2
150	DISHONEST PURPOSE	—	
151	FRAUDULENT ACTS	●	I.B.5., page 2
152	FRAUDULENT CLAIMS	—	
153	INTENTIONAL VIOLATIONS OF LAW	—	
154	WILLFUL FAILURE TO COMPLY WITH LAW	●	I.B.5., page 2
155	MALICIOUS PURPOSE	●	I.B.5., page 2
156	**LIABILITY OF OTHERS**	●	I.B.3., page 1
157	**LIQUIDATED DAMAGES**	—	
158	**LOSS ARISING OUT OF CHANGES IN OPERATIONS**	—	
159	ACQUISITION	—	
160	CHANGE IN CONTROL	—	
161	DOWNSIZING OR REDUCTION IN FORCE	—	
162	% OF WORKFORCE	—	
163	WITHIN X DAYS	—	

NORTHLAND INSURANCE COMPANIES S1110-EP [6/97]

#	Comparison Query	Comment		Policy Reference
164	FINANCIAL IMPAIRMENT	—		
165	BANKRUPTCY	—		
166	INSOLVENCY	—		
167	LIQUIDATION	—		
168	RECEIVERSHIP	—		
169	FINANCIAL INABILITY TO PAY	—		
170	MERGER	—		
171	PLANT OR FACILITY CLOSING	—		
172	REORGANIZATION	—		
173	TEMPORARY SHUTDOWN	—		
174	**MATTERS DEEMED UNINSURABLE**	—		
175	**NON-MONETARY RELIEF**	—		
176	DECLATORY RELIEF	—		
177	DISGORGEMENT	—		
178	INJUNCTIVE RELIEF	—		
179	JOB REINSTATEMENT	—		
180	NON-MONETARY DAMAGES/RELIEF	—		
181	OTHER EQUITABLE REMEDIES	—		
182	**OBLIGATION TO PROVIDE BENEFITS**	—		
183	COBRA	●		I.B.6., page 2
184	DISABILITY	●		I.B.4., page 2
185	ERISA	●		I.B.6., page 2
186	SOCIAL SECURITY	●		I.B.6., page 2
187	OTHER RETIREMENT BENEFITS	—		
188	UNEMPLOYMENT	●		I.B.4., page 2
189	WORKERS' COMPENSATION	●		I.B.4., page 2
190	**PERSONAL INJURY OFFENSES**			
191	DEFAMATION	—		
192	EMOTIONAL DISTRESS/UPSET	—		
193	HUMILIATION	—		
194	LIBEL	—		
195	MENTAL ANGUISH	—		
196	PERSONAL INJURY	—		
197	SLANDER	—		
198	**PRIOR ACTS**	●		I.A.1.c., page 1
199	PRIOR ACTS	●	Coverage available by endorsement	I.A.1.c., page 1
200	PRIOR KNOWLEDGE	●		I.A.1.d., page 1
201	PRIOR/PENDING LITIGATION	—		
202	**PROPERTY DAMAGE**	●		I.B.2., page 1
203	INTANGIBLE PROPERTY	—		
204	LOSS OF USE	●		I.B.2., page 1
205	TANGIBLE PROPERTY	●		I.B.2., page 1
206	**RETALIATORY ACTIONS OF EMPLOYER**	—		
207	FOR FAILING TO PERFORM ACTS AGAINST PUBLIC POLICY	—		
208	FOR FILING A COMPLAINT OR BENEFIT CLAIM	—		
209	**STRIKES/LOCKOUTS**	●		I.B.4., page 2
210	**VIOLATION OF LAWS**	—		
211	ANY LAW	—		
212	FMLA	—		
213	OSHA	●		I.B.6., page 2
214	POLLUTION LAWS	—		
215	RICO	—		
216	SEC	—		
217	WARN	●		I.B.6., page 2

15 CONDITIONS

#	Comparison Query	Comment		Policy Reference
218	**ARBITRATION**	—		
219	MANDATORY	—		
220	BINDING	—		
221	CHOICE OF LAW PROVISION	—		
222	SITUS	—		
223	**TERRITORY**	●		III.B., page 2
224	LIMITED	—		
225	WORLDWIDE	●		III.B., page 2
226	**NEWLY FORMED/ACQUIRED ENTITIES**	●		VIII.H., page 5
227	AUTOMATIC COVERAGE (X DAYS)	90		VIII.H., page 5
228	NOTIFY INSURER WITHIN X DAYS	90		VIII.H., page 5

NORTHLAND INSURANCE COMPANIES S1110-EP [6/97]

Policy Comparison Worksheet

Pacific Insurance Company, Ltd.
(First State Management Group, Inc.)

Policy Form No.: PL-364
Edition Date: 5/98

Risks Considered: All except temporary help agencies, law firms, municipalities
Limits Available: $10,000,000
Minimum Retention: $5,000

Contact: Jim Seward
First State Management Group, Inc.
150 Federal Street
Boston, MA 02110-1753
617/526-7792
617/526-0612 (fax)

KEY TO SYMBOLS
● = Specifically contains queried provision of feature
○ = Unable to determine
— = Silent

#	Comparison Query		Comment	Policy Reference
	1 APPLICATION			
1	ATTACHES TO AND FORMS A PART OF THE POLICY	●		II.A., page 2
2	CONTAINS WARRANTY STATEMENTS	●		Application, page 4
3	CONTAINS SEVERABILITY PROVISIONS	—		
	2 POLICY TYPE			
4	UNITARY STAND ALONE POLICY	●		
	ENDORSEMENT OR PART OF	—		
5	DIRECTORS AND OFFICERS POLICY	—		
6	PACKAGE POLICY	—		
7	UMBRELLA POLICY	—		
8	ERRORS AND OMISSIONS POLICY	—		
9	OTHER	—		
10	CLAIMS-MADE	●		
11	OCCURRENCE	—		
	3 WHO IS INSURED			
12	BUSINESS ENTITY	●		III.F.(1)., page 3
13	AUTOMATIC COVERAGE FOR SUBSIDIARIES	●		II.F.(2)., page 3
14	DIRECTORS & OFFICERS	●		II.F.(3)., page 3
15	EMPLOYEES	●		II.F.(5)., pages 3–4
16	PART-TIME	●		II.F.(5)., pages 3–4
17	SEASONAL	●		II.F.(5)., pages 3–4
18	TEMPORARY	●		II.F.(5)., pages 3–4
19	SUPERVISORS & MANAGERS	●		II.F.(5)., pages 3–4
20	FORMER EMPLOYEES	●		II.F.(5)., pages 3–4
21	VOLUNTEERS	—		
22	INDEPENDENT CONTRACTORS	—		
23	EXCLUDED	●	Coverage available by endorsement	II.F.(5)., page 4
24	SILENT	—		
25	SHAREHOLDERS	—		
	4 LIMIT OF LIABILITY			
26	AGGREGATE	●		VIII.C., page 9
27	INCLUDES PUNITIVE DAMAGES WHERE NOT UNINSURABLE	—	Coverage available by endorsement	
28	DEFENSE COSTS INCLUDED WITHIN LIMIT OF LIABILITY	●	See also VIII.D., page 9	VIII.A., page 9
29	DEFENSE COSTS PAID IN ADDITION TO LIMIT OF LIABILITY	—		
	5 DEDUCTIBLE			
30	APPLIES TO EACH INDIVIDUAL CLAIM	●		VIII.F.(1)., page 10
31	APPLIES TO EACH OCCURRENCE OR WRONGFUL PRACTICE	—		
32	INCLUDES ALL CLAIMS FROM ONE ACT	●		VIII.G.(1)., page 10
33	SUBJECT TO ANNUAL AGGREGATE	—		
34	CO-PAYMENT APPLIES	—		
35	LIMIT OF LIABILITY NOT REDUCED	—		
36	INCLUDES DEFENSE COSTS	●		VIII.F.(2)., page 10
37	REDUCED UNDER SPECIFIED CIRCUMSTANCES (SEE POLICY)	—		

PACIFIC INSURANCE COMPANY, LTD. PL-364 [5/98]

	Comparison Query	Comment	Policy Reference
	6 WHAT IS A CLAIM		
38	ORAL COMPLAINT TO INSURED	—	
39	WRITTEN COMPLAINT TO INSURED	●	II.B.(1)., page 2
40	COMPLAINT MUST CONTAIN A DEMAND FOR DAMAGES	●	Monetary relief	II.B.(1)., page 2
41	COMPLAINT FILED WITH EEOC	●		II.B.(3)., page 2
42	OR SIMILAR STATE AUTHORITY	●		II.B.(3)., page 2
43	AGENCY MUST HAVE POWER TO ADJUDICATE	—	
44	ADMINISTRATIVE PROCEEDING	●		II.B.(3)., page 2
45	ARBITRATION PROCEEDING	●		II.B.(4)., page 2
46	ANY INCIDENT REPORTED TO INSURER	—	
47	SUIT	●		II.B.(2)., page 2
48	CLAIM DOES NOT INCLUDE ARBITRATION SUBJECT TO	●		II.B. following (4)., page 2
49	COLLECTIVE BARGAINING AGREEMENT	●		II.B. following (4)., page 2
50	EMPLOYEE POLICY OR MANUAL	—	
51	CLAIM NOT DEFINED	—	
	7 CLAIM REPORTING PROVISIONS TO INSURER		
52	IMMEDIATELY	—	
53	AS SOON AS POSSIBLE	—	
54	AS SOON AS PRACTICABLE	●		IX.A.(1)., page 10
55	WITHIN POLICY PERIOD	—	
56	WITHIN X DAYS OF EXPIRATION	60		IX.A.(1)., page 10
57	WITHIN X DAYS	—	
	8 EXTENDED REPORTING FEATURES		
58	ELECTION PERIOD (DAYS)	30		VI.D., page 9
59	ADDITIONAL PREMIUM (% OF ANNUAL PREMIUM)	○	Specified by underwriter–See Item 6.(b). of Declarations	VI., page 8
60	ADDITIONAL REPORTING PERIOD (MONTHS)	○	Specified by underwriter–See Item 6.(a). of Declarations	VI., page 8
61	NO REINSTATEMENT OF LIMITS	●		VI.E., page 9
	9 POTENTIAL CLAIM REPORTING PROVISIONS		
62	NONE (SEE ALSO "CLAIM" ABOVE)	—	
63	INCIDENTS LIKELY TO RESULT IN A CLAIM	●		V., pages 7–8
	10 DEFENSE PROVISIONS		
64	AFFIRMATIVE DUTY TO DEFEND	●	See also III.A., page 6	I.B., page 1
65	NO AFFIRMATIVE DUTY TO DEFEND	—	
66	AFFIRMATIVE ADVANCEMENT PROVISIONS	●	Claims within deductible	VIII.F.(2)., page 10
67	INSURED MUST RETURN ADVANCED AMOUNTS IF NOT COVERED	—	
68	INSURED/INSURER CHOOSES COUNSEL	●	Insurer selects	III.A., page 6
69	INSURED/INSURER APPROVES COUNSEL	●	Insured consents	III.A., page 6
70	INSURED/INSURER CONSULTED IN COUNSEL SELECTION	●	Insured consulted	III.A., page 6
	11 SETTLEMENT PROVISIONS		
71	HAMMER CLAUSE	●		III.B., page 6
72	CONSULTATION PROVISION	—	
73	CONSENT PROVISION	●	Two-way	II.B. page 6 and IX.B.(2)., page 11
	12 ALLOCATION OF LOSS PROVISIONS		
74	STIPULATED PROVISIONS	—	
	13 COVERAGES		
75	DISCRIMINATION	●		II.K.(10)., page 5
76	SPECIFIC ENUMERATED ACTIVITIES	—	
77	*PLUS BROAD OMNIBUS WORDING*	●		II.K.(10)., page 5
78	SPECIFIC ENUMERATED CLASSES	●		II.K.(10)., page 5
79	*PLUS BROAD OMNIBUS WORDING*	●		II.K.(10)., page 5
80	AGAINST THIRD PARTIES	—	Coverage available by endorsement	
81	DISCRIMINATION NOT DEFINED	●	
82	SEXUAL HARASSMENT	●		II.K.(11)., page 5
83	HOSTILE ENVIRONMENT	●		II.K.(11)., page 5
84	QUID-PRO-QUO	●		II.K.(11)., page 5
85	SEXUAL HARASSMENT NOT DEFINED	●	
86	WRONGFUL TERMINATION	●		II.K.(1)., page 4
87	BREACH OF IMPLIED CONTRACT	●		II.K.(6)., page 5
88	BREACH OF EXPRESS CONTRACT	○	Written or oral contract	II.K.(6)., page 5
89	VIOLATION OF PUBLIC POLICY	—	
90	VIOLATION OF GOOD FAITH & FAIR DEALING	—	
91	OBLIGATIONS TO MAKE PAYMENTS	—	
92	CONSTRUCTIVE DISCHARGE	●		II.K.(1)., page 4
93	WRONGFUL TERMINATION NOT DEFINED	●	
94	OTHER EMPLOYMENT VIOLATIONS/OFFENSES	●		II.K., pages 4–5
95	WRONGFUL HIRING	●	See also II.K.(14)., page 5	II.K.(2)., page 4
96	WRONGFUL PROMOTION/DEMOTION	●		II.K.(2)., page 4
97	WRONGFUL EVALUATION/DISCIPLINE	●	See also II.K.(14)., page 5	II.K.(2)., page 4

PACIFIC INSURANCE COMPANY, LTD. PL-364 [5/98]

#	Comparison Query	Comment		Policy Reference
98	FAMILY AND MEDICAL LEAVE ACT	●		II.K.(13)., page 5
99	DEFAMATION	●		II.K.(7)., page 5
100	MISREPRESENTATION	●		II.K.(7)., page 5
101	RETALIATION	●		II.K.(12)., page 5
102	MENTAL ANGUISH	—		
103	INVASION OF PRIVACY	●		II.K.(8)., page 5
104	HUMILIATION	—		
105	EMOTIONAL DISTRESS	●		II.K.(9)., page 5
106	OTHER PERSONAL INJURY OFFENSES	—		
107	POLICY SILENT	—		

14 EXCLUSIONS

#	Comparison Query	Comment		Policy Reference
108	**ADA ACCOMMODATION EXPENSES**	●		VI.H., page 7
109	**ASSAULT & BATTERY**	●		IV.E., page 7
110	**BACK PAY**	—		
111	**BODILY INJURY**	●		IV.E., page 7
112	BODILY INJURY	●		IV.E., page 7
113	DEATH	●		IV.E., page 7
114	DISEASE	●		IV.E., page 7
115	SICKNESS	●		IV.E., page 7
116	**BREACH OF EMPLOYMENT CONTRACT**	—		
117	EXPRESS CONTRACT	—		
118	*WRITTEN CONTRACT*	—		
119	*ORAL CONTRACT*	—		
120	IMPLIED CONTRACT	—		
121	**CLASS ACTION LAWSUITS**	—		
122	**CONSEQUENTIAL LOSS**	—		
123	APPLIES TO BODILY INJURY	—		
124	APPLIES TO INSURED EVENT	—		
125	BROTHER/SISTER	—		
126	CHILD	—		
127	DOMESTIC PARTNER	—		
128	PARENT	—		
129	SPOUSE	—		
130	**COST OF ARBITRATION HEARINGS SUBJECT TO**	—		
131	EMPLOYMENT HANDBOOK	—		
132	LABOR GRIEVANCE	—		
133	OTHER EMPLOYMENT POLICY OR PROCEDURE	—		
134	**COVERAGE ELSEWHERE**	●		X.C., page 12
135	OTHER AVAILABLE INSURANCE	●		X.C., page 12
136	OTHER INDEMNIFICATION	—		
137	SHARING PROVISION	—		
138	**FAILURE TO EXERCISE CARE WHEN TERMINATING**	—		
139	**FINES/PENALTIES**	●		II.E.(2)., page 3
140	CIVIL	●		
141	CRIMINAL	●		
142	EXEMPLARY DAMAGES	●	Coverage available by endorsement	II.E.(3)., page 3
143	PUNITIVE DAMAGES	●	Coverage available by endorsement	II.E.(3)., page 3
144	MULTIPLIED DAMAGES	●	Coverage available by endorsement	II.E.(3)., page 3
145	**FRONT PAY**	—		
146	EXCLUSION APPLIES ONLY IF EMPLOYER HAD OPPORTUNITY TO REINSTATE EMPLOYEE BUT DID NOT DO SO	—		
147	**INTENTIONAL ACTS**	—		
148	CRIMINAL ACTS	●	Non-imputation applies	IV.A., page 6
149	CRIMINAL PROCEEDING	—		
150	DISHONEST PURPOSE	●	Non-imputation applies	IV.A., page 6
151	FRAUDULENT ACTS	●	Non-imputation applies	IV.A., page 6
152	FRAUDULENT CLAIMS	●		IX.D., page 11
153	INTENTIONAL VIOLATIONS OF LAW	—		
154	WILLFUL FAILURE TO COMPLY WITH LAW	—		
155	MALICIOUS PURPOSE	●	Non-imputation applies	IV.A., page 6
156	**LIABILITY OF OTHERS**	—		
157	**LIQUIDATED DAMAGES**	●	Coverage available by endorsement	II.E.(3)., page 3
158	**LOSS ARISING OUT OF CHANGES IN OPERATIONS**	—		
159	ACQUISITION	—		
160	CHANGE IN CONTROL	—		
161	DOWNSIZING OR REDUCTION IN FORCE	—		
162	*% OF WORKFORCE*	—		
163	*WITHIN X DAYS*	—		

PACIFIC INSURANCE COMPANY, LTD. PL-364 [5/98]

	Comparison Query	Comment		Policy Reference
164	FINANCIAL IMPAIRMENT	—		
165	BANKRUPTCY	—		
166	INSOLVENCY	—		
167	LIQUIDATION	—		
168	RECEIVERSHIP	—		
169	FINANCIAL INABILITY TO PAY	—		
170	MERGER	—		
171	PLANT OR FACILITY CLOSING	—		
172	REORGANIZATION	—		
173	TEMPORARY SHUTDOWN	—		
174	**MATTERS DEEMED UNINSURABLE**	●		II.E.(1)., page 3
175	**NON-MONETARY RELIEF**	—		
176	DECLATORY RELIEF	—		
177	DISGORGEMENT	—		
178	INJUNCTIVE RELIEF	—		
179	JOB REINSTATEMENT	—		
180	NON-MONETARY DAMAGES/RELIEF	●		II.E.(4)., page 3
181	OTHER EQUITABLE REMEDIES	—		
182	**OBLIGATION TO PROVIDE BENEFITS**	—		
183	COBRA	●		IV.C., page 6
184	DISABILITY	●		IV.F., page 7
185	ERISA	●		IV.D.(3)., page 7
186	SOCIAL SECURITY	●		IV.F., page 7
187	OTHER RETIREMENT BENEFITS	—		
188	UNEMPLOYMENT	●		IV.F., page 7
189	WORKERS' COMPENSATION	●		IV.F., page 7
190	**PERSONAL INJURY OFFENSES**	—		
191	DEFAMATION	—		
192	EMOTIONAL DISTRESS/UPSET	—		
193	HUMILIATION	—		
194	LIBEL	—		
195	MENTAL ANGUISH	—		
196	PERSONAL INJURY	—		
197	SLANDER	—		
198	**PRIOR ACTS**	—		
199	PRIOR ACTS			
200	PRIOR KNOWLEDGE	●		II.K.(1)., following (14)., page 5
201	PRIOR/PENDING LITIGATION	●		IV.B.(2)., page 6
202	**PROPERTY DAMAGE**	●		IV.E., page 7
203	INTANGIBLE PROPERTY	—		
204	LOSS OF USE	●		IV.E., page 7
205	TANGIBLE PROPERTY	●		IV.E., page 7
206	**RETALIATORY ACTIONS OF EMPLOYER**	—		
207	FOR FAILING TO PERFORM ACTS AGAINST PUBLIC POLICY	—		
208	FOR FILING A COMPLAINT OR BENEFIT CLAIM	—		
209	**STRIKES/LOCKOUTS**	●		IV.G., page 7
210	**VIOLATION OF LAWS**	—		
211	ANY LAW	—		
212	FMLA	—		
213	OSHA	●		IV.C., page 6
214	POLLUTION LAWS	—	Excluded by endorsement	
215	RICO	—		
216	SEC	—		
217	WARN	●		IV.C., page 6
	15 CONDITIONS			
218	**ARBITRATION**	—		
219	MANDATORY	—		
220	BINDING	—		
221	CHOICE OF LAW PROVISION	—		
222	SITUS	—		
223	**TERRITORY**	●		VII., page 9
224	LIMITED	—		
225	WORLDWIDE	●		VII., page 9
226	**NEWLY FORMED/ACQUIRED ENTITIES**	●		X.F.(2).(a)., page 14
227	AUTOMATIC COVERAGE (X DAYS)	—		
228	NOTIFY INSURER WITHIN X DAYS	30		X.F.(2).(a)., page 14

PACIFIC INSURANCE COMPANY, LTD. PL-364 [5/98]

Policy Comparison Worksheet

Philadelphia Indemnity Insurance Company

Policy Form No.: PI-DF-1
Edition Date: 9/95
Risks Considered: Non-profit organizations (except hospitals)
Limits Available: $10,000,000
Minimum Retention: None

Contact: James J. Maguire, Jr., ARM
Philadelphia Indemnity Insurance Company
One Bala Plaza, Suite 100
Bala Cynwyd, PA 19004
610/617-7762
610/617-7940 (fax)
phlyjjmjr@aol.com

KEY TO SYMBOLS
● = Specifically contains queried provision of feature
○ = Unable to determine
— = Silent

#	Comparison Query		Comment	Policy Reference
	1 APPLICATION			
1	ATTACHES TO AND FORMS A PART OF THE POLICY	●		IX.A., page 4
2	CONTAINS WARRANTY STATEMENTS	—		
3	CONTAINS SEVERABILITY PROVISIONS	●		IX.B., page 4
	2 POLICY TYPE			
4	UNITARY STAND ALONE POLICY	—		
	ENDORSEMENT OR PART OF	—		
5	DIRECTORS AND OFFICERS POLICY	●		
6	PACKAGE POLICY	—		
7	UMBRELLA POLICY	—		
8	ERRORS AND OMISSIONS POLICY	—		
9	OTHER	—		
10	CLAIMS-MADE	●		
11	OCCURRENCE	—		
	3 WHO IS INSURED			
12	BUSINESS ENTITY	●	See also II.H.2., page 2	II.F., page 2
13	AUTOMATIC COVERAGE FOR SUBSIDIARIES	●		II.F., page 2
14	DIRECTORS & OFFICERS	●		II.E., page 1
15	EMPLOYEES	●		II.E., page 1
16	PART-TIME	—		
17	SEASONAL	—		
18	TEMPORARY	—		
19	SUPERVISORS & MANAGERS	—		
20	FORMER EMPLOYEES	—		
21	VOLUNTEERS	●		II.E., page 1
22	INDEPENDENT CONTRACTORS	—		
23	EXCLUDED	—		
24	SILENT	—		
25	SHAREHOLDERS	—		
	4 LIMIT OF LIABILITY			
26	AGGREGATE	●		IV.A., page 3
27	INCLUDES PUNITIVE DAMAGES WHERE NOT UNINSURABLE	—		
28	DEFENSE COSTS INCLUDED WITHIN LIMIT OF LIABILITY	●		IV.A., page 3
29	DEFENSE COSTS PAID IN ADDITION TO LIMIT OF LIABILITY	—		
	5 DEDUCTIBLE			
30	APPLIES TO EACH INDIVIDUAL CLAIM	●		IV.B., page 3
31	APPLIES TO EACH OCCURRENCE OR WRONGFUL PRACTICE	—		
32	INCLUDES ALL CLAIMS FROM ONE ACT	●		IV.E.1., page 3
33	SUBJECT TO ANNUAL AGGREGATE	—		
34	CO-PAYMENT APPLIES	—		
35	LIMIT OF LIABILITY NOT REDUCED	—		
36	INCLUDES DEFENSE COSTS	●		IV.B., page 3
37	REDUCED UNDER SPECIFIED CIRCUMSTANCES (SEE POLICY)	—		

Comparison Query	Comment	Policy Reference
6 WHAT IS A CLAIM		
38 ORAL COMPLAINT TO INSURED	—	
39 WRITTEN COMPLAINT TO INSURED	●	II.B.3., page 1
40 COMPLAINT MUST CONTAIN A DEMAND FOR DAMAGES	—	
41 COMPLAINT FILED WITH EEOC	—	
42 OR SIMILAR STATE AUTHORITY	—	
43 AGENCY MUST HAVE POWER TO ADJUDICATE	—	
44 ADMINISTRATIVE PROCEEDING	●	II.B.2., page 1
45 ARBITRATION PROCEEDING	—	
46 ANY INCIDENT REPORTED TO INSURER	●	II.B.3., page 1
47 SUIT	●	II.B.1., page 1
48 CLAIM DOES NOT INCLUDE ARBITRATION SUBJECT TO	—	
49 COLLECTIVE BARGAINING AGREEMENT	—	
50 EMPLOYEE POLICY OR MANUAL	—	
51 CLAIM NOT DEFINED	—	
7 CLAIM REPORTING PROVISIONS TO INSURER		
52 IMMEDIATELY	—	
53 AS SOON AS POSSIBLE	—	
54 AS SOON AS PRACTICABLE	●	VII.A., page 4
55 WITHIN POLICY PERIOD	●	VII.A., page 4
56 WITHIN X DAYS OF EXPIRATION	60	VII.A., page 4
57 WITHIN X DAYS	—	
8 EXTENDED REPORTING FEATURES		
58 ELECTION PERIOD (DAYS)	30	XI.A. & B., pages 4–5
59 ADDITIONAL PREMIUM (% OF ANNUAL PREMIUM)	35	XI.A. & B., pages 4–5
60 ADDITIONAL REPORTING PERIOD (MONTHS)	12	XI.A. & B., pages 4–5
61 NO REINSTATEMENT OF LIMITS	—	
9 POTENTIAL CLAIM REPORTING PROVISIONS		
62 NONE (SEE ALSO "CLAIM" ABOVE)	—	
63 INCIDENTS LIKELY TO RESULT IN A CLAIM	●	VII.B., page 4
10 DEFENSE PROVISIONS		
64 AFFIRMATIVE DUTY TO DEFEND	● Upon request of insured	V.F., page 3
65 NO AFFIRMATIVE DUTY TO DEFEND	●	I.C., page 1
66 AFFIRMATIVE ADVANCEMENT PROVISIONS	●	VI., page 4
67 INSURED MUST RETURN ADVANCED AMOUNTS IF NOT COVERED	●	VI., page 4
68 INSURED/INSURER CHOOSES COUNSEL	● Insured	V.E., page 3
69 INSURED/INSURER APPROVES COUNSEL	—	
70 INSURED/INSURER CONSULTED IN COUNSEL SELECTION	—	
11 SETTLEMENT PROVISIONS		
71 HAMMER CLAUSE	●	V.I., page 3
72 CONSULTATION PROVISION	—	
73 CONSENT PROVISION	● Two-way	V.A., page 3 and V.H., page 4
12 ALLOCATION OF LOSS PROVISIONS		
74 STIPULATED PROVISIONS	—	
13 COVERAGES		
75 DISCRIMINATION	●	II.D.2., page 1
76 SPECIFIC ENUMERATED ACTIVITIES	●	II.D.2., page 1
77 PLUS BROAD OMNIBUS WORDING	—	
78 SPECIFIC ENUMERATED CLASSES	●	II.D.2., page 1
79 PLUS BROAD OMNIBUS WORDING	●	II.D.2., page 1
80 AGAINST THIRD PARTIES	—	
81 DISCRIMINATION NOT DEFINED	●	II.D.2., page 1
82 SEXUAL HARASSMENT	●	II.D.3., page 1
83 HOSTILE ENVIRONMENT	●	II.D.3., page 1
84 QUID-PRO-QUO	●	II.D.3., page 1
85 SEXUAL HARASSMENT NOT DEFINED	●	II.D.3., page 1
86 WRONGFUL TERMINATION	●	II.D.1., page 1
87 BREACH OF IMPLIED CONTRACT	●	II.D.1., page 1
88 BREACH OF EXPRESS CONTRACT	● Written consent	II.D.1., page 1
89 VIOLATION OF PUBLIC POLICY	—	
90 VIOLATION OF GOOD FAITH & FAIR DEALING	—	
91 OBLIGATIONS TO MAKE PAYMENTS	—	
92 CONSTRUCTIVE DISCHARGE	—	
93 WRONGFUL TERMINATION NOT DEFINED	●	II.D.1., page 1
94 OTHER EMPLOYMENT VIOLATIONS/OFFENSES	—	
95 WRONGFUL HIRING	—	
96 WRONGFUL PROMOTION/DEMOTION	—	
97 WRONGFUL EVALUATION/DISCIPLINE	—	

PHILADELPHIA INDEMNITY INSURANCE COMPANY PI-DF-1 [9/95]

#	Comparison Query		Comment	Policy Reference
98	FAMILY AND MEDICAL LEAVE ACT	—		
99	DEFAMATION	—		
100	MISREPRESENTATION	—		
101	RETALIATION	—		
102	MENTAL ANGUISH	●	Exclusion deleted by endorsement	
103	INVASION OF PRIVACY	—		
104	HUMILIATION	—		
105	EMOTIONAL DISTRESS	●	Exclusion deleted by endorsement	
106	OTHER PERSONAL INJURY OFFENSES	—		
107	POLICY SILENT	—		
	14 EXCLUSIONS			
108	**ADA ACCOMMODATION EXPENSES**			
109	**ASSAULT & BATTERY**	—		
110	**BACK PAY**	—		
111	**BODILY INJURY**	●		III.B., page 2
112	BODILY INJURY	●		III.B., page 2
113	DEATH	●		III.B., page 2
114	DISEASE	●		III.B., page 2
115	SICKNESS	●		III.B., page 2
116	**BREACH OF EMPLOYMENT CONTRACT**	○		III.L.2., page 3
117	EXPRESS CONTRACT	○		III.L.2., page 3
118	WRITTEN CONTRACT	—		
119	ORAL CONTRACT	—		
120	IMPLIED CONTRACT	—		
121	**CLASS ACTION LAWSUITS**	—		
122	**CONSEQUENTIAL LOSS**	●		III.B., page 2
123	APPLIES TO BODILY INJURY	●	Loss of consortium	III.B., page 2
124	APPLIES TO INSURED EVENT	—		
125	BROTHER/SISTER	—		
126	CHILD	—		
127	DOMESTIC PARTNER	—		
128	PARENT	—		
129	SPOUSE	—		
130	**COST OF ARBITRATION HEARINGS SUBJECT TO**	—		
131	EMPLOYMENT HANDBOOK	—		
132	LABOR GRIEVANCE	—		
133	OTHER EMPLOYMENT POLICY OR PROCEDURE	—		
134	**COVERAGE ELSEWHERE**	●		XV., page 5
135	OTHER AVAILABLE INSURANCE	●		XV., page 5
136	OTHER INDEMNIFICATION	—		
137	SHARING PROVISION	—		
138	**FAILURE TO EXERCISE CARE WHEN TERMINATING**	—		
139	**FINES/PENALTIES**	●		II.G.1., page 2
140	CIVIL	●		II.G.1., page 2
141	CRIMINAL	●		II.G.1., page 2
142	EXEMPLARY DAMAGES	●		II.G.4., page 2
143	PUNITIVE DAMAGES	●		II.G.4., page 2
144	MULTIPLIED DAMAGES	●		II.G.4., page 2
145	**FRONT PAY**	—		
146	EXCLUSION APPLIES ONLY IF EMPLOYER HAD OPPORTUNITY TO REINSTATE EMPLOYEE BUT DID NOT DO SO	—		
147	**INTENTIONAL ACTS**	○		III.J., page 3
148	CRIMINAL ACTS	—		
149	CRIMINAL PROCEEDING	—		
150	DISHONEST PURPOSE	—		
151	FRAUDULENT ACTS	—		
152	FRAUDULENT CLAIMS	—		
153	INTENTIONAL VIOLATIONS OF LAW	○		III.J., page 3
154	WILLFUL FAILURE TO COMPLY WITH LAW	○		III.J., page 3
155	MALICIOUS PURPOSE	—		
156	**LIABILITY OF OTHERS**	●		III.L.1., page 3
157	**LIQUIDATED DAMAGES**	—		
158	**LOSS ARISING OUT OF CHANGES IN OPERATIONS**	—		
159	ACQUISITION	—		
160	CHANGE IN CONTROL	—		
161	DOWNSIZING OR REDUCTION IN FORCE	—		
162	% OF WORKFORCE	—		
163	WITHIN X DAYS	—		

PHILADELPHIA INDEMNITY INSURANCE COMPANY PI-DF-1 [9/95]

	Comparison Query	Comment	Policy Reference
164	**FINANCIAL IMPAIRMENT**	—	
165	*BANKRUPTCY*	—	
166	*INSOLVENCY*	—	
167	*LIQUIDATION*	—	
168	*RECEIVERSHIP*	—	
169	FINANCIAL INABILITY TO PAY	—	
170	MERGER	—	
171	PLANT OR FACILITY CLOSING	—	
172	REORGANIZATION	—	
173	TEMPORARY SHUTDOWN	—	
174	**MATTERS DEEMED UNINSURABLE**	●	II.G.3., page 2
175	**NON-MONETARY RELIEF**	—	
176	DECLATORY RELIEF	—	
177	DISGORGEMENT	—	
178	INJUNCTIVE RELIEF	—	
179	JOB REINSTATEMENT	—	
180	NON-MONETARY DAMAGES/RELIEF	—	
181	OTHER EQUITABLE REMEDIES	—	
182	**OBLIGATION TO PROVIDE BENEFITS**	—	
183	COBRA	—	
184	DISABILITY	—	
185	ERISA	●	III.F., page 3
186	SOCIAL SECURITY	—	
187	OTHER RETIREMENT BENEFITS	—	
188	UNEMPLOYMENT	—	
189	WORKERS' COMPENSATION	—	
190	**PERSONAL INJURY OFFENSES**	—	
191	DEFAMATION	—	
192	EMOTIONAL DISTRESS/UPSET	—	
193	HUMILIATION	—	
194	LIBEL	—	
195	MENTAL ANGUISH	—	
196	PERSONAL INJURY	—	
197	SLANDER	—	
198	**PRIOR ACTS**	—	
199	PRIOR ACTS	—	
200	PRIOR KNOWLEDGE	—	
201	PRIOR/PENDING LITIGATION	●	III.G., page 3
202	**PROPERTY DAMAGE**	●	III.B., page 2
203	INTANGIBLE PROPERTY	—	
204	LOSS OF USE	●	III.B., page 2
205	TANGIBLE PROPERTY	●	III.B., page 2
206	**RETALIATORY ACTIONS OF EMPLOYER**	—	
207	FOR FAILING TO PERFORM ACTS AGAINST PUBLIC POLICY	—	
208	FOR FILING A COMPLAINT OR BENEFIT CLAIM	—	
209	**STRIKES/LOCKOUTS**	—	
210	**VIOLATION OF LAWS**	—	
211	ANY LAW	—	
212	FMLA	—	
213	OSHA	—	
214	POLLUTION LAWS	●	III.D., page 2
215	RICO	—	
216	SEC	—	
217	WARN	—	

15 CONDITIONS

	Comparison Query	Comment	Policy Reference
218	**ARBITRATION**	—	
219	MANDATORY	—	
220	BINDING	—	
221	CHOICE OF LAW PROVISION	—	
222	SITUS	—	
223	**TERRITORY**	—	
224	LIMITED	—	
225	WORLDWIDE	—	
226	**NEWLY FORMED/ACQUIRED ENTITIES**	●	II.K., page 2
227	AUTOMATIC COVERAGE (X DAYS)	30	II.K., page 2
228	NOTIFY INSURER WITHIN X DAYS	30	II.K., page 2

PHILADELPHIA INDEMNITY INSURANCE COMPANY PI-DF-1 [9/95]

Policy Comparison Worksheet

Philadelphia Insurance Companies

Policy Form No.: PI-ES-1560
Edition Date: 12/96

Risks Considered: Small to mid-size private and public companies
Limits Available: $10,000,000
Minimum Retention: $10,000

Contact: James J. Maguire, Jr., ARM
Philadelphia Insurance Companies
One Bala Plaza, Suite 100
Bala Cynwyd, PA 19004
610/617-7900
610/617-7940 (fax)
phlyjjmjr@aol.com

KEY TO SYMBOLS
- ● = Specifically contains queried provision of feature
- ○ = Unable to determine
- — = Silent

#	Comparison Query		Comment	Policy Reference
	1 APPLICATION			
1	ATTACHES TO AND FORMS A PART OF THE POLICY	●		Part 5.A., page 7
2	CONTAINS WARRANTY STATEMENTS	—		
3	CONTAINS SEVERABILITY PROVISIONS	●		Part 6.E., page 9
	2 POLICY TYPE			
4	UNITARY STAND ALONE POLICY	—		
	ENDORSEMENT OR PART OF			
5	DIRECTORS AND OFFICERS POLICY	—		
6	PACKAGE POLICY	—		
7	UMBRELLA POLICY	—		
8	ERRORS AND OMISSIONS POLICY	—		
9	OTHER	●	Executive Safeguard	
10	CLAIMS-MADE	●		
11	OCCURRENCE	—		
	3 WHO IS INSURED			
12	BUSINESS ENTITY	●		Part 2.II.C.1., page 3
13	AUTOMATIC COVERAGE FOR SUBSIDIARIES	●		Part 5.B., page 7
14	DIRECTORS & OFFICERS	●		Part 2.II.C.1., page 3
15	EMPLOYEES	●		Part 2.II.C.1., page 3
16	PART-TIME	●		Part 2.II.C.1., page 3
17	SEASONAL	●		Part 2.II.C.1., page 3
18	TEMPORARY	—		
19	SUPERVISORS & MANAGERS	—		
20	FORMER EMPLOYEES	—		
21	VOLUNTEERS	—		
22	INDEPENDENT CONTRACTORS			
23	EXCLUDED	●		Part 2.II.C.1, page 3
24	SILENT	—		
25	SHAREHOLDERS	—		
	4 LIMIT OF LIABILITY			
26	AGGREGATE	●		Part 6.A., page 8
27	INCLUDES PUNITIVE DAMAGES WHERE NOT UNINSURABLE	—		
28	DEFENSE COSTS INCLUDED WITHIN LIMIT OF LIABILITY	●	See also II.D., page 3	Part 6.A., page 8
29	DEFENSE COSTS PAID IN ADDITION TO LIMIT OF LIABILITY	—		
	5 DEDUCTIBLE			
30	APPLIES TO EACH INDIVIDUAL CLAIM	●		Part 6.A., page 8
31	APPLIES TO EACH OCCURRENCE OR WrONGFUL PRACTICE	—		
32	INCLUDES ALL CLAIMS FROM ONE ACT	—		
33	SUBJECT TO ANNUAL AGGREGATE	—		
34	CO-PAYMENT APPLIES	—		
35	LIMIT OF LIABILITY NOT REDUCED	—		
36	INCLUDES DEFENSE COSTS	●	See also Part 6.A., page 8	Part 2.II.D., page 3
37	REDUCED UNDER SPECIFIED CIRCUMSTANCES (SEE POLICY)	—		

#	Comparison Query	Comment	Policy Reference
	6 WHAT IS A CLAIM		
38	ORAL COMPLAINT TO INSURED	—	Part 2.II.A.1., page 3
39	WRITTEN COMPLAINT TO INSURED	●	
40	COMPLAINT MUST CONTAIN A DEMAND FOR DAMAGES	●	Relief	Part 2.II.A.1., page 3
41	COMPLAINT FILED WITH EEOC	○		Part 2.II.A.2., page 3
42	OR SIMILAR STATE AUTHORITY	○		Part 2.II.A.2., page 3
43	AGENCY MUST HAVE POWER TO ADJUDICATE	○		Part 2.II.A.2., page 3
44	ADMINISTRATIVE PROCEEDING	●		Part 2.II.A.2., page 3
45	ARBITRATION PROCEEDING	●		Part 2.II.A.2., page 3
46	ANY INCIDENT REPORTED TO INSURER	—		
47	SUIT	●		Part 2.II.A.2., page 3
48	CLAIM DOES NOT INCLUDE ARBITRATION SUBJECT TO	●		Part 2.II.A.2., page 3
49	COLLECTIVE BARGAINING AGREEMENT	●		Part 2.II.A.2., page 3
50	EMPLOYEE POLICY OR MANUAL	—		
51	CLAIM NOT DEFINED	—		
	7 CLAIM REPORTING PROVISIONS TO INSURER		
52	IMMEDIATELY	—		
53	AS SOON AS POSSIBLE	—		
54	AS SOON AS PRACTICABLE	●		Part 6.C.1., page 9
55	WITHIN POLICY PERIOD	—		
56	WITHIN X DAYS OF EXPIRATION	90		Part 6.C.1., page 9
57	WITHIN X DAYS	—		
	8 EXTENDED REPORTING FEATURES		
58	ELECTION PERIOD (DAYS)	30		Part 6.J., page 10
59	ADDITIONAL PREMIUM (% OF ANNUAL PREMIUM)	50		Part 6.J., page 10
60	ADDITIONAL REPORTING PERIOD (MONTHS)	12		Part 6.J., page 10
61	NO REINSTATEMENT OF LIMITS	—		
	9 POTENTIAL CLAIM REPORTING PROVISIONS		
62	NONE (SEE ALSO "CLAIM" ABOVE)	—		
63	INCIDENTS LIKELY TO RESULT IN A CLAIM	●		Part 6.C.2., page 9
	10 DEFENSE PROVISIONS		
64	AFFIRMATIVE DUTY TO DEFEND	—	Coverage available by endorsement	
65	NO AFFIRMATIVE DUTY TO DEFEND	●		Part 6.B.1., page 8
66	AFFIRMATIVE ADVANCEMENT PROVISIONS	●		Part 6.B.2., page 9
67	INSURED MUST RETURN ADVANCED AMOUNTS IF NOT COVERED	—		
68	INSURED/INSURER CHOOSES COUNSEL	●	Either	Part 6.B.2., page 9
69	INSURED/INSURER APPROVES COUNSEL	●	Insurer	Part 6.B.2., page 9
70	INSURED/INSURER CONSULTED IN COUNSEL SELECTION	●	2-way	Part 6.B.2., page 9
	11 SETTLEMENT PROVISIONS		
71	HAMMER CLAUSE	●		Part 6.B.6., page 9
72	CONSULTATION PROVISION	—		
73	CONSENT PROVISION	●	2-way	Part 6.B.3., page 9
	12 ALLOCATION OF LOSS PROVISIONS		
74	STIPULATED PROVISIONS	—		
	13 COVERAGES		
75	DISCRIMINATION	●	As "Wrongful Act"	Part 2.II.E.5., page 3
76	SPECIFIC ENUMERATED ACTIVITIES	—		
77	PLUS BROAD OMNIBUS WORDING	—		
78	SPECIFIC ENUMERATED CLASSES	—		
79	PLUS BROAD OMNIBUS WORDING	—		
80	AGAINST THIRD PARTIES	—		
81	DISCRIMINATION NOT DEFINED	●		
82	SEXUAL HARASSMENT	●	As "Wrongful Act"	Part 2.II.E.11., page 3
83	HOSTILE ENVIRONMENT	—		
84	QUID-PRO-QUO	—		
85	SEXUAL HARASSMENT NOT DEFINED	●		
86	WRONGFUL TERMINATION	—	As "Wrongful Act"	Part 2.II.E.1., page 3
87	BREACH OF IMPLIED CONTRACT	—		
88	BREACH OF EXPRESS CONTRACT	●	Written or oral	Part 2.II.E.2., page 3
89	VIOLATION OF PUBLIC POLICY	—		
90	VIOLATION OF GOOD FAITH & FAIR DEALING	—		
91	OBLIGATIONS TO MAKE PAYMENTS	—		
92	CONSTRUCTIVE DISCHARGE	—		
93	WRONGFUL TERMINATION NOT DEFINED	—		
94	OTHER EMPLOYMENT VIOLATIONS/OFFENSES	●		Part 2.E., page 3
95	WRONGFUL HIRING	●		Part 2.II.E.4., page 3
96	WRONGFUL PROMOTION/DEMOTION	●		Part 2.II.E.4., page 3
97	WRONGFUL EVALUATION/DISCIPLINE	●	See also II.E.8., page 3	Part 2.II.E.7., page 3

PHILADELPHIA INSURANCE COMPANIES PI-ES-1560 (12/96)

#	Comparison Query	Comment		Policy Reference
98	FAMILY AND MEDICAL LEAVE ACT	—		
99	DEFAMATION	●	See also III.f., page 4	II.E.10., page 3
100	MISREPRESENTATION	●		II.E.3., page 2
101	RETALIATION	—		
102	MENTAL ANGUISH	●		III.f., page 4
103	INVASION OF PRIVACY	●		II.E.9., page 3
104	HUMILIATION	—		
105	EMOTIONAL DISTRESS	●		III.f., page 4
106	OTHER PERSONAL INJURY OFFENSES	—		
107	POLICY SILENT	—		
	14 EXCLUSIONS			
108	**ADA ACCOMMODATION EXPENSES**	—		
109	**ASSAULT & BATTERY**	—		
110	**BACK PAY**	—		
111	**BODILY INJURY**	●		III.f., page 4
112	BODILY INJURY	●		III.f., page 4
113	DEATH	●		III.f., page 4
114	DISEASE	●		III.f., page 4
115	SICKNESS	●		III.f., page 4
116	**BREACH OF EMPLOYMENT CONTRACT**	●	non-imputation applies	III.b., page 3
117	EXPRESS CONTRACT	●	non-imputation applies	III.b., page 3
118	*WRITTEN CONTRACT*	●	non-imputation applies	III.b., page 3
119	*ORAL CONTRACT*	●	non-imputation applies	III.b., page 3
120	IMPLIED CONTRACT	—		
121	**CLASS ACTION LAWSUITS**	—		
122	**CONSEQUENTIAL LOSS**	—		
123	APPLIES TO BODILY INJURY	—		
124	APPLIES TO INSURED EVENT	—		
125	BROTHER/SISTER	—		
126	CHILD	—		
127	DOMESTIC PARTNER	—		
128	PARENT	—		
129	SPOUSE	—		
130	**COST OF ARBITRATION HEARINGS SUBJECT TO**	—		
131	EMPLOYMENT HANDBOOK	—		
132	LABOR GRIEVANCE	—		
133	OTHER EMPLOYMENT POLICY OR PROCEDURE	—		
134	**COVERAGE ELSEWHERE**	—		
135	OTHER AVAILABLE INSURANCE	—		
136	OTHER INDEMNIFICATION	—		
137	SHARING PROVISION	—		
138	**FAILURE TO EXERCISE CARE WHEN TERMINATING**	—		
139	**FINES/PENALTIES**	●		II.D.1., page 3
140	CIVIL	●		II.D.1., page 3
141	CRIMINAL	●		II.D.1., page 3
142	EXEMPLARY DAMAGES	●		II.D.3., page 3
143	PUNITIVE DAMAGES	●		II.D.3., page 3
144	MULTIPLIED DAMAGES	●		II.D.3., page 3
145	**FRONT PAY**	—		
146	EXCLUSION APPLIES ONLY IF EMPLOYER HAD OPPORTUNITY TO REINSTATE EMPLOYEE BUT DID NOT DO SO	—		
147	**INTENTIONAL ACTS**	—		
148	CRIMINAL ACTS	●	Non-imputation	III.a., page 3
149	CRIMINAL PROCEEDING	—		
150	DISHONEST PURPOSE	●	Non-imputation	III.a., page 3
151	FRAUDULENT ACTS	●	Non-imputation	III.a., page 3
152	FRAUDULENT CLAIMS	●		Part 6.P., page 11
153	INTENTIONAL VIOLATIONS OF LAW	●	Non-imputation	III.a., page 3
154	WILLFUL FAILURE TO COMPLY WITH LAW	—		
155	MALICIOUS PURPOSE	—		
156	**LIABILITY OF OTHERS**	●	Non-imputation	III.b., pages 3–4
157	**LIQUIDATED DAMAGES**	—		
158	**LOSS ARISING OUT OF CHANGES IN OPERATIONS**	—		
159	ACQUISITION	—		
160	CHANGE IN CONTROL	—		
161	DOWNSIZING OR REDUCTION IN FORCE	—		
162	*% OF WORKFORCE*	—		
163	*WITHIN X DAYS*	—		

#	Comparison Query	Comment	Policy Reference
164	FINANCIAL IMPAIRMENT	—	
165	*BANKRUPTCY*	—	
166	*INSOLVENCY*	—	
167	*LIQUIDATION*	—	
168	*RECEIVERSHIP*	—	
169	FINANCIAL INABILITY TO PAY	—	
170	MERGER	—	
171	PLANT OR FACILITY CLOSING	—	
172	REORGANIZATION	—	
173	TEMPORARY SHUTDOWN	—	
174	**MATTERS DEEMED UNINSURABLE**	●	II.D.2., page 3
175	**NON-MONETARY RELIEF**	●	III.j., page 4
176	DECLATORY RELIEF	—	
177	DISGORGEMENT	—	
178	INJUNCTIVE RELIEF	—	
179	JOB REINSTATEMENT	—	
180	NON-MONETARY DAMAGES/RELIEF	●	III.j., page 4
181	OTHER EQUITABLE REMEDIES	—	
182	**OBLIGATION TO PROVIDE BENEFITS**		
183	COBRA	●	III.e., page 4
184	DISABILITY	●	Retaliation exception	III.c., page 4
185	ERISA	●	III.e., page 4
186	SOCIAL SECURITY	●	Retaliation exception	III.c., page 4
187	OTHER RETIREMENT BENEFITS	—	
188	UNEMPLOYMENT	●	Retaliation exception	III.c., page 4
189	WORKERS' COMPENSATION	●	Retaliation exception	III.c., page 4
190	**PERSONAL INJURY OFFENSES**		
191	DEFAMATION	—	
192	EMOTIONAL DISTRESS/UPSET	—	
193	HUMILIATION	—	
194	LIBEL	—	
195	MENTAL ANGUISH	—	
196	PERSONAL INJURY	—	
197	SLANDER	—	
198	**PRIOR ACTS**	—	
199	PRIOR ACTS	—	
200	PRIOR KNOWLEDGE	—	
201	PRIOR/PENDING LITIGATION	●	III.i., page 4
202	**PROPERTY DAMAGE**	●	III.f., page 4
203	INTANGIBLE PROPERTY	—	
204	LOSS OF USE	●	III.f., page 4
205	TANGIBLE PROPERTY	●	III.f., page 4
206	**RETALIATORY ACTIONS OF EMPLOYER**	—	
207	FOR FAILING TO PERFORM ACTS AGAINST PUBLIC POLICY	—	
208	FOR FILING A COMPLAINT OR BENEFIT CLAIM	—	
209	**STRIKES/LOCKOUTS**	●	III.d., page 4
210	**VIOLATION OF LAWS**		
211	ANY LAW	—	
212	FMLA	—	
213	OSHA	●	Retaliation exception	III.e., page 4
214	POLLUTION LAWS	—	
215	RICO	—	
216	SEC	—	
217	WARN	●	III.e., page 4
	15 CONDITIONS		
218	**ARBITRATION**	●	Part 6.M., page 10
219	MANDATORY	●	Part 6.M., page 10
220	BINDING	●	Part 6.M., page 10
221	CHOICE OF LAW PROVISION	—	
222	SITUS	—	
223	**TERRITORY**	●	Part 6.G., page 10
224	LIMITED	—	
225	WORLDWIDE	●	Part 6.G., page 10
226	**NEWLY FORMED/ACQUIRED ENTITIES**	—	
227	AUTOMATIC COVERAGE (X DAYS)	—	
228	NOTIFY INSURER WITHIN X DAYS	—	

PHILADELPHIA INSURANCE COMPANIES PI-ES-1560 [12/96]

Policy Comparison Worksheet

Reliance Insurance Company of Illinois
(Reliance National Risk Specialists)

Policy Form No.: GL 00 R424 00 0498
Edition Date: 4/98

Risks Considered: All except California law firms and temporary help agencies
Limits Available: $25,000,000
Minimum Retention: $25,000

Contact: Lisa DeSimone
77 Water Street, 25th Floor
New York, NY 10005
212/858-6379
212/858-9810 (fax)
lisa.desimone@reliancenational.com

KEY TO SYMBOLS
● = Specifically contains queried provision of feature
○ = Unable to determine
— = Silent

#	Comparison Query		Comment	Policy Reference
	1 APPLICATION			
1	ATTACHES TO AND FORMS A PART OF THE POLICY	—		
2	CONTAINS WARRANTY STATEMENTS	●		Application, page 5
3	CONTAINS SEVERABILITY PROVISIONS	●		VIII.(I)., page 12
	2 POLICY TYPE			
4	UNITARY STAND ALONE POLICY	●		
	ENDORSEMENT OR PART OF	—		
5	DIRECTORS AND OFFICERS POLICY	—		
6	PACKAGE POLICY	—		
7	UMBRELLA POLICY	—		
8	ERRORS AND OMISSIONS POLICY	—		
9	OTHER	—		
10	CLAIMS-MADE	●		
11	OCCURRENCE	—		
	3 WHO IS INSURED			
12	BUSINESS ENTITY	●		IV.(G)., page 4
13	AUTOMATIC COVERAGE FOR SUBSIDIARIES	●		IV.(C)., page 3
14	DIRECTORS & OFFICERS	●		IV.(H).(1)., page 4
15	EMPLOYEES	●		IV.(H).(2)., page 4
16	PART-TIME	●		IV.(E).(1)., pages 3–4
17	SEASONAL	●		IV.(E).(1)., pages 3–4
18	TEMPORARY	●		IV.(E).(1)., pages 3–4
19	SUPERVISORS & MANAGERS	●		IV.(E).(1)., pages 3–4
20	FORMER EMPLOYEES	●		IV.(E).(1)., pages 3–4
21	VOLUNTEERS	—		
22	INDEPENDENT CONTRACTORS	●	If scheduled on policy	IV.(E).(3)., page 4
23	EXCLUDED	—		
24	SILENT	—		
25	SHAREHOLDERS	—		
	4 LIMIT OF LIABILITY			
26	AGGREGATE	●		VI.(A)., page 7
27	INCLUDES PUNITIVE DAMAGES WHERE NOT UNINSURABLE	—	Coverage available	
28	DEFENSE COSTS INCLUDED WITHIN LIMIT OF LIABILITY	●		IV.(J)., page 4 and VI.(E)., page 8
29	DEFENSE COSTS PAID IN ADDITION TO LIMIT OF LIABILITY	—		
	5 DEDUCTIBLE			
30	APPLIES TO EACH INDIVIDUAL CLAIM	●		VI.(B)., page 7
31	APPLIES TO EACH OCCURRENCE OR WRONGFUL PRACTICE	—		
32	INCLUDES ALL CLAIMS FROM ONE ACT	●		VI.(D)., page 8
33	SUBJECT TO ANNUAL AGGREGATE	—		
34	CO-PAYMENT APPLIES	—		
35	LIMIT OF LIABILITY NOT REDUCED	—		
36	INCLUDES DEFENSE COSTS	●		Declarations page
37	REDUCED UNDER SPECIFIED CIRCUMSTANCES (SEE POLICY)	●		VI.(C)., page 8

#	Comparison Query	Comment	Policy Reference
	6 WHAT IS A CLAIM		
38	ORAL COMPLAINT TO INSURED	—	
39	WRITTEN COMPLAINT TO INSURED	●	IV.(A).(1)., page 3
40	COMPLAINT MUST CONTAIN A DEMAND FOR DAMAGES	●	Demand for relief	IV.(A).(1)., page 3
41	COMPLAINT FILED WITH EEOC	●		IV.(A).(3)., page 3
42	OR SIMILAR STATE AUTHORITY	●		IV.(A).(3)., page 3
43	AGENCY MUST HAVE POWER TO ADJUDICATE	—		
44	ADMINISTRATIVE PROCEEDING	●		IV.(A).(3)., page 3
45	ARBITRATION PROCEEDING	●		IV.(A).(3)., page 3
46	ANY INCIDENT REPORTED TO INSURER	—		
47	SUIT	●		IV.(A).(2)., page 3
48	CLAIM DOES NOT INCLUDE ARBITRATION SUBJECT TO	—		
49	COLLECTIVE BARGAINING AGREEMENT	—		
50	EMPLOYEE POLICY OR MANUAL	—		
51	CLAIM NOT DEFINED	—		
	7 CLAIM REPORTING PROVISIONS TO INSURER		
52	IMMEDIATELY	—		
53	AS SOON AS POSSIBLE	—		
54	AS SOON AS PRACTICABLE	●		I., page 1
55	WITHIN POLICY PERIOD	—		
56	WITHIN X DAYS OF EXPIRATION	60		I., page 1
57	WITHIN X DAYS	—		
	8 EXTENDED REPORTING FEATURES		
58	ELECTION PERIOD (DAYS)	30		II.(A)., page 1
59	ADDITIONAL PREMIUM (% OF ANNUAL PREMIUM)	○	Specified by endorsement—See Item E of Declarations	II.(A)., page 1
60	ADDITIONAL REPORTING PERIOD (MONTHS)	○	Specified by endorsement—See Item E of Declarations	II.(A)., page 1
61	NO REINSTATEMENT OF LIMITS	●		VI.(A)., page 7
	9 POTENTIAL CLAIM REPORTING PROVISIONS		
62	NONE (SEE ALSO "CLAIM" ABOVE)	—		
63	INCIDENTS LIKELY TO RESULT IN A CLAIM	●		VII.(A)., page 8
	10 DEFENSE PROVISIONS		
64	AFFIRMATIVE DUTY TO DEFEND	●	If insured requests	III.(A)., page 2
65	NO AFFIRMATIVE DUTY TO DEFEND	●		III.(A)., page 2
66	AFFIRMATIVE ADVANCEMENT PROVISIONS	●	If insured defends	III.(C)., page 2
67	INSURED MUST RETURN ADVANCED AMOUNTS IF NOT COVERED	●		III.(C)., page 2
68	INSURED/INSURER CHOOSES COUNSEL	—		
69	INSURED/INSURER APPROVES COUNSEL	—		
70	INSURED/INSURER CONSULTED IN COUNSEL SELECTION	—		
	11 SETTLEMENT PROVISIONS		
71	HAMMER CLAUSE	●	If policy limits > $10,000,000	
72	CONSULTATION PROVISION	—		
73	CONSENT PROVISION	●	Insurer must consent	III.(B)., page 2
	12 ALLOCATION OF LOSS PROVISIONS		
74	STIPULATED PROVISIONS	—		
	13 COVERAGES		
75	DISCRIMINATION	●	As wrongful act	IV.(N).(3)., page 6
76	SPECIFIC ENUMERATED ACTIVITIES	—		
77	*PLUS BROAD OMNIBUS WORDING*	—		
78	SPECIFIC ENUMERATED CLASSES	●		IV.(N).(3)., page 6
79	*PLUS BROAD OMNIBUS WORDING*	●		IV.(N).(3)., page 6
80	AGAINST THIRD PARTIES	—		
81	DISCRIMINATION NOT DEFINED	●		
82	SEXUAL HARASSMENT	●	As wrongful act	IV.(N).(2)., page 5
83	HOSTILE ENVIRONMENT	●		IV.(N).(2)., page 5
84	QUID-PRO-QUO	●		IV.(N).(2)., page 5
85	SEXUAL HARASSMENT NOT DEFINED	●		
86	WRONGFUL TERMINATION	●	As wrongful act	IV.(N).(1)., page 5
87	BREACH OF IMPLIED CONTRACT	—		
88	BREACH OF EXPRESS CONTRACT	—		
89	VIOLATION OF PUBLIC POLICY	—		
90	VIOLATION OF GOOD FAITH & FAIR DEALING	—		
91	OBLIGATIONS TO MAKE PAYMENTS	—		
92	CONSTRUCTIVE DISCHARGE	●		IV.(N).(1)., page 5
93	WRONGFUL TERMINATION NOT DEFINED	●		
94	OTHER EMPLOYMENT VIOLATIONS/OFFENSES	●		IV.(N)., pages 5–6
95	WRONGFUL HIRING	●		IV.(N).(1)., page 5
96	WRONGFUL PROMOTION/DEMOTION	●		IV.(N).(1)., page 5
97	WRONGFUL EVALUATION/DISCIPLINE	●		IV.(N).(1)., page 5

RELIANCE INSURANCE COMPANY OF ILLINOIS GL 00 R424 00 0498 [4/98]

#	Comparison Query		Comment	Policy Reference
98	FAMILY AND MEDICAL LEAVE ACT	●		IV.(N).(8)., page 6
99	DEFAMATION	●		IV.(N).(4)., page 6
100	MISREPRESENTATION	●		IV.(N).(4)., page 6
101	RETALIATION	●		IV.(N).(6)., page 6
102	MENTAL ANGUISH	—		
103	INVASION OF PRIVACY	●		IV.(N).(4)., page 6
104	HUMILIATION	●		
105	EMOTIONAL DISTRESS	●		IV.(N).(4)., page 6
106	OTHER PERSONAL INJURY OFFENSES	—		
107	POLICY SILENT	—		
14 EXCLUSIONS				
108	**ADA ACCOMMODATION EXPENSES**	●		IV.(J)., page 5
109	**ASSAULT & BATTERY**	—		
110	**BACK PAY**	—		
111	**BODILY INJURY**	●		V.(A)., page 6
112	BODILY INJURY	●		V.(A)., page 6
113	DEATH	●		V.(A)., page 6
114	DISEASE	●		V.(A)., page 6
115	SICKNESS	●		V.(A)., page 6
116	**BREACH OF EMPLOYMENT CONTRACT**	●		IV.(J)., page 5
117	EXPRESS CONTRACT	●		IV.(J)., page 5
118	WRITTEN CONTRACT	●		IV.(J)., page 5
119	ORAL CONTRACT	—		
120	IMPLIED CONTRACT	—		
121	**CLASS ACTION LAWSUITS**	—		
122	**CONSEQUENTIAL LOSS**	—		
123	APPLIES TO BODILY INJURY	—		
124	APPLIES TO INSURED EVENT	—		
125	BROTHER/SISTER	—		
126	CHILD	—		
127	DOMESTIC PARTNER	—		
128	PARENT	—		
129	SPOUSE	—		
130	**COST OF ARBITRATION HEARINGS SUBJECT TO**	—		
131	EMPLOYMENT HANDBOOK	—		
132	LABOR GRIEVANCE	—		
133	OTHER EMPLOYMENT POLICY OR PROCEDURE	—		
134	**COVERAGE ELSEWHERE**	●		VIII.(E)., page 10
135	OTHER AVAILABLE INSURANCE	●	Exception applies	VIII.(E)., page 10
136	OTHER INDEMNIFICATION	—		
137	SHARING PROVISION	—		
138	**FAILURE TO EXERCISE CARE WHEN TERMINATING**	—		
139	**FINES/PENALTIES**	●		IV.(J)., page 5
140	CIVIL	—		
141	CRIMINAL	—		
142	EXEMPLARY DAMAGES	●	Coverage available if insurable	IV.(J)., pages 4–5
143	PUNITIVE DAMAGES	●	Coverage available if insurable	IV.(J)., pages 4–5
144	MULTIPLIED DAMAGES	●	Coverage available if insurable	IV.(J)., pages 4–5
145	**FRONT PAY**	—		
146	EXCLUSION APPLIES ONLY IF EMPLOYER HAD OPPORTUNITY TO REINSTATE EMPLOYEE BUT DID NOT DO SO	—		
147	**INTENTIONAL ACTS**	●		V.(F)., page 7
148	CRIMINAL ACTS	—		
149	CRIMINAL PROCEEDING	—		
150	DISHONEST PURPOSE	●	If established by adjudication	IV.(F)., page 7
151	FRAUDULENT ACTS	●	If established by adjudication	IV.(F)., page 7
152	FRAUDULENT CLAIMS	—		
153	INTENTIONAL VIOLATIONS OF LAW	●	If established by adjudication	IV.(J)., page 5
154	WILLFUL FAILURE TO COMPLY WITH LAW	—		
155	MALICIOUS PURPOSE	●	If established by adjudication	IV.(J)., page 5
156	**LIABILITY OF OTHERS**	—		
157	**LIQUIDATED DAMAGES**	●	Coverage available if insurable	IV.(J)., pages 4–5
158	**LOSS ARISING OUT OF CHANGES IN OPERATIONS**	—		
159	ACQUISITION	—		
160	CHANGE IN CONTROL	—		
161	DOWNSIZING OR REDUCTION IN FORCE	—		
162	% OF WORKFORCE	—		
163	WITHIN X DAYS	—		

RELIANCE INSURANCE COMPANY OF ILLINOIS GL 00 R424 00 0498 [4/98]

#	Comparison Query	Comment		Policy Reference
164	FINANCIAL IMPAIRMENT	—		
165	*BANKRUPTCY*	—		
166	*INSOLVENCY*	—		
167	*LIQUIDATION*	—		
168	*RECEIVERSHIP*	—		
169	FINANCIAL INABILITY TO PAY	—		
170	MERGER	—		
171	PLANT OR FACILITY CLOSING	—		
172	REORGANIZATION	—		
173	TEMPORARY SHUTDOWN	—		
174	**MATTERS DEEMED UNINSURABLE**	—		
175	**NON-MONETARY RELIEF**	—		
176	DECLATORY RELIEF	●	Claim expense exception	V.(H)., page 7
177	DISGORGEMENT	●	Claim expense exception	V.(H)., page 7
178	INJUNCTIVE RELIEF	●	Claim expense exception	V.(H)., page 7
179	JOB REINSTATEMENT	●	Claim expense exception	V.(H)., page 7
180	NON-MONETARY DAMAGES/RELIEF	—		
181	OTHER EQUITABLE REMEDIES	●	Claim expense exception	V.(H)., page 7
182	**OBLIGATION TO PROVIDE BENEFITS**	—		
183	COBRA	●	Retaliation exception	V.(D)., page 7
184	DISABILITY	●	Retaliation exception	V.(C)., page 6
185	ERISA	●	Retaliation exception	V.(D)., page 7
186	SOCIAL SECURITY	—		
187	OTHER RETIREMENT BENEFITS	●	Retaliation exception	V.(C)., page 6
188	UNEMPLOYMENT	●	Retaliation exception	V.(C)., page 6
189	WORKERS' COMPENSATION	●	Retaliation exception	V.(C)., page 6
190	**PERSONAL INJURY OFFENSES**	—		
191	DEFAMATION	—		
192	EMOTIONAL DISTRESS/UPSET	—		
193	HUMILIATION	—		
194	LIBEL	—		
195	MENTAL ANGUISH	—		
196	PERSONAL INJURY	—		
197	SLANDER	—		
198	**PRIOR ACTS**	—		
199	PRIOR ACTS	—		
200	PRIOR KNOWLEDGE	—		
201	PRIOR/PENDING LITIGATION	●		V.(G)., page 7
202	**PROPERTY DAMAGE**	●		V.(A)., page 6
203	INTANGIBLE PROPERTY	—		
204	LOSS OF USE	●		V.(A)., page 6
205	TANGIBLE PROPERTY	●		V.(A)., page 6
206	**RETALIATORY ACTIONS OF EMPLOYER**	—		
207	FOR FAILING TO PERFORM ACTS AGAINST PUBLIC POLICY	—		
208	FOR FILING A COMPLAINT OR BENEFIT CLAIM	—		
209	**STRIKES/LOCKOUTS**	—		
210	**VIOLATION OF LAWS**	—		
211	ANY LAW	—		
212	FMLA	—		
213	OSHA	●	Retaliation exception	V.(D)., pages 6–7
214	POLLUTION LAWS	—		
215	RICO	—		
216	SEC	—		
217	WARN	●	Retaliation exception	V.(D)., pages 6–7
	15 CONDITIONS			
218	**ARBITRATION**	—		
219	MANDATORY	—		
220	BINDING	—		
221	CHOICE OF LAW PROVISION	—		
222	SITUS	—		
223	**TERRITORY**	●		VIII.(A)., page 9
224	LIMITED	—		
225	WORLDWIDE	●		VIII.(A)., page 9
226	**NEWLY FORMED/ACQUIRED ENTITIES**	●		VIII.(H).(1)., pages 10–11
227	AUTOMATIC COVERAGE (X DAYS)	—	If < 20% of insured's employees—No time limit	VIII.(H).(1)., pages 10–11
228	NOTIFY INSURER WITHIN X DAYS	90	If > 20% of insured's employees—No time limit	VIII.(H).(1)., page 11

RELIANCE INSURANCE COMPANY OF ILLINOIS GL 00 R424 00 0498 [4/98]

Policy Comparison Worksheet

Reliance Insurance Company of Illinois
(Reliance National Risk Specialists)

Policy Form No.: GL 00 R430 00 0498
Edition Date: 4/98

Risks Considered: All except high-tech companies and financial institutions
Limits Available: $5,000,000
Minimum Retention: $25,000

Contact: Lisa DeSimone
77 Water Street, 25th Floor
New York, NY 10005
212/858-6379
212/858-9810 (fax)
lisa.desimone@reliancenational.com

KEY TO SYMBOLS
● = Specifically contains queried provision of feature
○ = Unable to determine
— = Silent

#	Comparison Query	Comment	Policy Reference
	1 APPLICATION		
1	ATTACHES TO AND FORMS A PART OF THE POLICY	—	
2	CONTAINS WARRANTY STATEMENTS	—	
3	CONTAINS SEVERABILITY PROVISIONS	●	IX.(I)., pages 16–17
	2 POLICY TYPE		
4	UNITARY STAND ALONE POLICY	●	
	ENDORSEMENT OR PART OF	—	
5	DIRECTORS AND OFFICERS POLICY	—	
6	PACKAGE POLICY	—	
7	UMBRELLA POLICY	—	
8	ERRORS AND OMISSIONS POLICY	—	
9	OTHER	—	
10	CLAIMS-MADE	●	
11	OCCURRENCE	—	
	3 WHO IS INSURED		
12	BUSINESS ENTITY	●	IV.(C)., page 4
13	AUTOMATIC COVERAGE FOR SUBSIDIARIES	●	IV.(C)., page 4
14	DIRECTORS & OFFICERS	●	IV.(J).(1)., page 6
15	EMPLOYEES	●	IV.(J).(2)., page 6
16	PART-TIME	●	IV.(E).(1)., page 4
17	SEASONAL	●	IV.(E).(1)., page 4
18	TEMPORARY	●	IV.(E).(1)., page 4
19	SUPERVISORS & MANAGERS	●	IV.(E).(1)., page 4
20	FORMER EMPLOYEES	●	IV.(E).(1)., page 4
21	VOLUNTEERS	—	
22	INDEPENDENT CONTRACTORS	● If scheduled on policy	IV.(E).(3)., page 4
23	EXCLUDED	—	
24	SILENT	—	
25	SHAREHOLDERS	—	
	4 LIMIT OF LIABILITY		
26	AGGREGATE	●	VI.(A)., page 11
27	INCLUDES PUNITIVE DAMAGES WHERE NOT UNINSURABLE	● Coverage availalbe	IV.(L)., page 6
28	DEFENSE COSTS INCLUDED WITHIN LIMIT OF LIABILITY	●	VI.(G)., page 12
29	DEFENSE COSTS PAID IN ADDITION TO LIMIT OF LIABILITY	—	
	5 DEDUCTIBLE		
30	APPLIES TO EACH INDIVIDUAL CLAIM	●	VI.(B)., page 11
31	APPLIES TO EACH OCCURRENCE OR WRONGFUL PRACTICE	—	
32	INCLUDES ALL CLAIMS FROM ONE ACT	●	VI.(D)., page 11
33	SUBJECT TO ANNUAL AGGREGATE	—	
34	CO-PAYMENT APPLIES	—	
35	LIMIT OF LIABILITY NOT REDUCED	—	
36	INCLUDES DEFENSE COSTS	●	Declarations Page
37	REDUCED UNDER SPECIFIED CIRCUMSTANCES (SEE POLICY)	●	VI.(C)., page 11

RELIANCE INSURANCE COMPANY OF ILLINOIS GL 00 R430 00 0498 [4/98]

#	Comparison Query	Comment	Policy Reference
	6 WHAT IS A CLAIM		
38	ORAL COMPLAINT TO INSURED	—	
39	WRITTEN COMPLAINT TO INSURED	●	IV.(A).(1)., page 4
40	COMPLAINT MUST CONTAIN A DEMAND FOR DAMAGES	●	Demand for relief	IV.(A).(1)., page 4
41	COMPLAINT FILED WITH EEOC	●		IV.(A).(3)., page 4
42	OR SIMILAR STATE AUTHORITY	●		IV.(A).(3)., page 4
43	AGENCY MUST HAVE POWER TO ADJUDICATE	—		
44	ADMINISTRATIVE PROCEEDING	●		IV.(A).(3)., page 4
45	ARBITRATION PROCEEDING	●		IV.(A).(3)., page 4
46	ANY INCIDENT REPORTED TO INSURER	—		
47	SUIT	●		IV.(A).(2)., page 4
48	CLAIM DOES NOT INCLUDE ARBITRATION SUBJECT TO	—		
49	COLLECTIVE BARGAINING AGREEMENT	—		
50	EMPLOYEE POLICY OR MANUAL	—		
51	CLAIM NOT DEFINED	—		
	7 CLAIM REPORTING PROVISIONS TO INSURER		
52	IMMEDIATELY	—		
53	AS SOON AS POSSIBLE	—		
54	AS SOON AS PRACTICABLE	●		I., following (C)., page 1
55	WITHIN POLICY PERIOD	—		
56	WITHIN X DAYS OF EXPIRATION	60		I., following (C)., page 1
57	WITHIN X DAYS	—		
	8 EXTENDED REPORTING FEATURES		
58	ELECTION PERIOD (DAYS)	30		II.(A)., pages 1–2
59	ADDITIONAL PREMIUM (% OF ANNUAL PREMIUM)	○	Specified by underwriter—See Item E of Declarations	II.(A)., pages 1–2
60	ADDITIONAL REPORTING PERIOD (MONTHS)	○	Specified by underwriter—See Item E of Declarations	II.(A)., pages 1–2
61	NO REINSTATEMENT OF LIMITS	●		VI.(A)., page 11
	9 POTENTIAL CLAIM REPORTING PROVISIONS		
62	NONE (SEE ALSO "CLAIM" ABOVE)	—		
63	INCIDENTS LIKELY TO RESULT IN A CLAIM	●		VIII.(A)., page 12
	10 DEFENSE PROVISIONS		
64	AFFIRMATIVE DUTY TO DEFEND	●	If insured requests	III.(A)., page 3
65	NO AFFIRMATIVE DUTY TO DEFEND	●		III.(A)., page 3
66	AFFIRMATIVE ADVANCEMENT PROVISIONS	●	If insured defends	III.(C)., page 3
67	INSURED MUST RETURN ADVANCED AMOUNTS IF NOT COVERED	●		III.(C)., page 3
68	INSURED/INSURER CHOOSES COUNSEL	—		
69	INSURED/INSURER APPROVES COUNSEL	—		
70	INSURED/INSURER CONSULTED IN COUNSEL SELECTION	—		
	11 SETTLEMENT PROVISIONS		
71	HAMMER CLAUSE	—		
72	CONSULTATION PROVISION	—		
73	CONSENT PROVISION	●	Insurer must consent	III.(B)., page 3
	12 ALLOCATION OF LOSS PROVISIONS		
74	STIPULATED PROVISIONS	●		VII., page 12
	13 COVERAGES		
75	DISCRIMINATION	●	As Employment Practices Claim	IV.(F).(3)., page 5
76	SPECIFIC ENUMERATED ACTIVITIES	—		
77	*PLUS BROAD OMNIBUS WORDING*	—		
78	SPECIFIC ENUMERATED CLASSES	●		IV.(F).(3)., page 5
79	*PLUS BROAD OMNIBUS WORDING*	●		IV.(F).(3)., page 5
80	AGAINST THIRD PARTIES	—		
81	DISCRIMINATION NOT DEFINED	●		
82	SEXUAL HARASSMENT	●	As Employment Practices Claim	IV.(F).(2)., page 5
83	HOSTILE ENVIRONMENT	●		IV.(F).(2)., page 5
84	QUID-PRO-QUO	●		IV.(F).(2)., page 5
85	SEXUAL HARASSMENT NOT DEFINED	●		
86	WRONGFUL TERMINATION	●	As Employment Practices Claim	IV.(F).(1)., page 5
87	BREACH OF IMPLIED CONTRACT	—		
88	BREACH OF EXPRESS CONTRACT	—		
89	VIOLATION OF PUBLIC POLICY	—		
90	VIOLATION OF GOOD FAITH & FAIR DEALING	—		
91	OBLIGATIONS TO MAKE PAYMENTS	—		
92	CONSTRUCTIVE DISCHARGE	●		IV.(F).(1)., page 5
93	WRONGFUL TERMINATION NOT DEFINED	●		
94	OTHER EMPLOYMENT VIOLATIONS/OFFENSES	●		IV.(F)., page 5
95	WRONGFUL HIRING	●		IV.(F).(1)., page 5
96	WRONGFUL PROMOTION/DEMOTION	●		IV.(F).(1)., page 5
97	WRONGFUL EVALUATION/DISCIPLINE	●		IV.(F).(1)., page 5

RELIANCE INSURANCE COMPANY OF ILLINOIS GL 00 R430 00 0498 [4/98]

#	Comparison Query	Comment	Policy Reference
98	FAMILY AND MEDICAL LEAVE ACT	●	IV.(F).(8)., page 6
99	DEFAMATION	●	IV.(F).(4)., page 5
100	MISREPRESENTATION	●	IV.(F).(4)., page 5
101	RETALIATION	●	IV.(F).(6)., page 5
102	MENTAL ANGUISH	—	
103	INVASION OF PRIVACY	●	IV.(F).(4)., page 5
104	HUMILIATION	●	
105	EMOTIONAL DISTRESS	●	IV.(F).(4)., page 5
106	OTHER PERSONAL INJURY OFFENSES	—	
107	POLICY SILENT	—	
	14 EXCLUSIONS		
108	**ADA ACCOMMODATION EXPENSES**	●	IV.(I), page 7
109	**ASSAULT & BATTERY**	—	
110	**BACK PAY**	—	
111	**BODILY INJURY**	●	V.(A).(1)., page 8
112	BODILY INJURY	●	V.(A).(1)., page 8
113	DEATH	●	V.(A).(1)., page 8
114	DISEASE	●	V.(A).(1)., page 8
115	SICKNESS	●	V.(A).(1)., page 8
116	**BREACH OF EMPLOYMENT CONTRACT**	—	
117	EXPRESS CONTRACT	—	
118	WRITTEN CONTRACT	—	
119	ORAL CONTRACT	—	
120	IMPLIED CONTRACT	—	
121	**CLASS ACTION LAWSUITS**	—	
122	**CONSEQUENTIAL LOSS**	—	
123	APPLIES TO BODILY INJURY	—	
124	APPLIES TO INSURED EVENT	—	
125	BROTHER/SISTER	—	
126	CHILD	—	
127	DOMESTIC PARTNER	—	
128	PARENT	—	
129	SPOUSE	—	
130	**COST OF ARBITRATION HEARINGS SUBJECT TO**	—	
131	EMPLOYMENT HANDBOOK	—	
132	LABOR GRIEVANCE	—	
133	OTHER EMPLOYMENT POLICY OR PROCEDURE	—	
134	**COVERAGE ELSEWHERE**	●	IX.(E), page 14
135	OTHER AVAILABLE INSURANCE	●	IX.(E), page 14
136	OTHER INDEMNIFICATION	—	
137	SHARING PROVISION	—	
138	**FAILURE TO EXERCISE CARE WHEN TERMINATING**	—	
139	**FINES/PENALTIES**	●	IV.(L)., page 7
140	CIVIL	●	IV.(L)., page 7
141	CRIMINAL	●	IV.(L)., page 7
142	EXEMPLARY DAMAGES	—	
143	PUNITIVE DAMAGES	—	
144	MULTIPLIED DAMAGES	—	
145	**FRONT PAY**	—	
146	EXCLUSION APPLIES ONLY IF EMPLOYER HAD OPPORTUNITY TO REINSTATE EMPLOYEE BUT DID NOT DO SO	●	V.(A).(10), page 10
147	**INTENTIONAL ACTS**	—	
148	CRIMINAL ACTS	—	
149	CRIMINAL PROCEEDING	—	
150	DISHONEST PURPOSE	● If established in fact	V.(A).(10), page 10
151	FRAUDULENT ACTS	● If established in fact	V.(A).(10), page 10
152	FRAUDULENT CLAIMS	—	
153	INTENTIONAL VIOLATIONS OF LAW	● If established in fact	V.(A).(10), page 10
154	WILLFUL FAILURE TO COMPLY WITH LAW	—	
155	MALICIOUS PURPOSE	● If established in fact	V.(A).(10), page 10
156	**LIABILITY OF OTHERS**	—	
157	**LIQUIDATED DAMAGES**	—	
158	**LOSS ARISING OUT OF CHANGES IN OPERATIONS**	—	
159	ACQUISITION	—	
160	CHANGE IN CONTROL	—	
161	DOWNSIZING OR REDUCTION IN FORCE	—	
162	% OF WORKFORCE	—	
163	WITHIN X DAYS	—	

RELIANCE INSURANCE COMPANY OF ILLINOIS GL 00 R430 00 0498 [4/98]

#	Comparison Query	Comment		Policy Reference
164	**FINANCIAL IMPAIRMENT**	—		
165	*BANKRUPTCY*	—		
166	*INSOLVENCY*	—		
167	*LIQUIDATION*	—		
168	*RECEIVERSHIP*	—		
169	FINANCIAL INABILITY TO PAY	—		
170	MERGER	—		
171	PLANT OR FACILITY CLOSING	—		
172	REORGANIZATION	—		
173	TEMPORARY SHUTDOWN	—		
174	**MATTERS DEEMED UNINSURABLE**	●		IV.(L)., page 7
175	**NON-MONETARY RELIEF**	—		
176	DECLATORY RELIEF	●	Claim expense exception	V.(B).(1)., page 10
177	DISGORGEMENT	●	Claim expense exception	V.(B).(1)., page 10
178	INJUNCTIVE RELIEF	●	Claim expense exception	V.(B).(1)., page 10
179	JOB REINSTATEMENT	●	Claim expense exception	V.(B).(1)., page 10
180	NON-MONETARY DAMAGES/RELIEF	—		
181	OTHER EQUITABLE REMEDIES	●	Claim expense exception	V.(B).(1)., page 10
182	**OBLIGATION TO PROVIDE BENEFITS**			
183	COBRA	●	Retaliation exception	V.(A).(8)., page 9
184	DISABILITY	●	Retaliation exception	V.(A).(7)., page 9
185	ERISA	●	Retaliation exception	V.(A).(8)., page 9
186	SOCIAL SECURITY	—		
187	OTHER RETIREMENT BENEFITS	●	Retaliation exception	V.(A).(7)., page 9
188	UNEMPLOYMENT	●	Retaliation exception	V.(A).(7)., page 9
189	WORKERS' COMPENSATION	●	Retaliation exception	V.(A).(7)., page 9
190	**PERSONAL INJURY OFFENSES**	—		
191	DEFAMATION	—		
192	EMOTIONAL DISTRESS/UPSET	—		
193	HUMILIATION	—		
194	LIBEL	—		
195	MENTAL ANGUISH	—		
196	PERSONAL INJURY	—		
197	SLANDER	—		
198	**PRIOR ACTS**	—		
199	PRIOR ACTS	—		
200	PRIOR KNOWLEDGE	—		
201	PRIOR/PENDING LITIGATION	●		V.(A).(9)., page 10
202	**PROPERTY DAMAGE**	●		V.(A).(1)., page 8
203	INTANGIBLE PROPERTY	—		
204	LOSS OF USE	●		V.(A).(1)., page 8
205	TANGIBLE PROPERTY	●		V.(A).(1)., page 8
206	**RETALIATORY ACTIONS OF EMPLOYER**	—		
207	FOR FAILING TO PERFORM ACTS AGAINST PUBLIC POLICY	—		
208	FOR FILING A COMPLAINT OR BENEFIT CLAIM	—		
209	**STRIKES/LOCKOUTS**	—		
210	**VIOLATION OF LAWS**	—		
211	ANY LAW	—		
212	FMLA	—		
213	OSHA	●	Retaliation exception	V.(A).(8)., page 9
214	POLLUTION LAWS	—		
215	RICO	—		
216	SEC	—		
217	WARN	●	Retaliation exception	V.(A).(8)., page 9
	15 CONDITIONS			
218	**ARBITRATION**	—		
219	MANDATORY	—		
220	BINDING	—		
221	CHOICE OF LAW PROVISION	—		
222	SITUS	—		
223	**TERRITORY**	●		IX.(A)., page 13
224	LIMITED	—		
225	WORLDWIDE	●		IX.(A)., page 13
226	**NEWLY FORMED/ACQUIRED ENTITIES**	●		IX.(H).(1).
227	AUTOMATIC COVERAGE (X DAYS)	●	If < 20% assets involved, no time limit	IX.(H).(1).
228	NOTIFY INSURER WITHIN X DAYS	90	If > 20% assets involved, no time limit	

RELIANCE INSURANCE COMPANY OF ILLINOIS GL 00 R430 00 0498 [4/98]

Policy Comparison Worksheet

Reliance National

Policy Form No.: DO 00 R324 00 0696
Edition Date: 06/96

Risks Considered: General accounts
Limits Available: $25,000,000
Minimum Retention: $25,000

Contact: Gary N. Dubois
Reliance National
77 Water Street
New York, NY 10005
212/858-3618
212/858-6686 (fax)
gary.dubois@reliancenational.com

KEY TO SYMBOLS
● = Specifically contains queried provision of feature
○ = Unable to determine
— = Silent

#	Comparison Query	Symbol	Comment	Policy Reference
	1 APPLICATION			
1	ATTACHES TO AND FORMS A PART OF THE POLICY	●		Policy, Preamble, page 1
2	CONTAINS WARRANTY STATEMENTS	—		
3	CONTAINS SEVERABILITY PROVISIONS	—		
	2 POLICY TYPE			
4	UNITARY STAND ALONE POLICY	—		
	ENDORSEMENT OR PART OF			
5	DIRECTORS AND OFFICERS POLICY	●	Policy form DO 00 R292 00 0696	
6	PACKAGE POLICY	—		
7	UMBRELLA POLICY	—		
8	ERRORS AND OMISSIONS POLICY	—		
9	OTHER	—		
10	CLAIMS-MADE	●		
11	OCCURRENCE	—		
	3 WHO IS INSURED			
12	BUSINESS ENTITY	—		
13	AUTOMATIC COVERAGE FOR SUBSIDIARIES	—		
14	DIRECTORS & OFFICERS	●		Endorsement (3), page 1
15	EMPLOYEES	●		Endorsement (3), page 1
16	PART-TIME	—		Endorsement (3), page 1
17	SEASONAL	—		
18	TEMPORARY	—		
19	SUPERVISORS & MANAGERS	●		
20	FORMER EMPLOYEES	—		
21	VOLUNTEERS	—		
22	INDEPENDENT CONTRACTORS	—		
23	EXCLUDED	—		
24	SILENT	●		
25	SHAREHOLDERS	—		
	4 LIMIT OF LIABILITY			
26	AGGREGATE	●		Policy VI.(A)., page 9
27	INCLUDES PUNITIVE DAMAGES WHERE NOT UNINSURABLE	●		Policy IV.(J)., page 5
28	DEFENSE COSTS INCLUDED WITHIN LIMIT OF LIABILITY	●		Policy IV.(G)., page 9
29	DEFENSE COSTS PAID IN ADDITION TO LIMIT OF LIABILITY	—		
	5 DEDUCTIBLE			
30	APPLIES TO EACH INDIVIDUAL CLAIM	●		Policy VI.(B)., page 9
31	APPLIES TO EACH OCCURRENCE OR WRONGFUL PRACTICE	●		Policy VI.(D)., page 9
32	INCLUDES ALL CLAIMS FROM ONE ACT	●		Policy VI.(D)., page 9
33	SUBJECT TO ANNUAL AGGREGATE	—		
34	CO-PAYMENT APPLIES	—		
35	LIMIT OF LIABILITY NOT REDUCED	—		
36	INCLUDES DEFENSE COSTS	●		Policy VI.(D)., page 9
37	REDUCED UNDER SPECIFIED CIRCUMSTANCES (SEE POLICY)	—		

RELIANCE NATIONAL DO 00 R324 00 0696 [0696]

#	Comparison Query		Comment	Policy Reference
	6 WHAT IS A CLAIM			
38	ORAL COMPLAINT TO INSURED	—		
39	WRITTEN COMPLAINT TO INSURED	●		Policy IV.(A).(1)., page 4
40	COMPLAINT MUST CONTAIN A DEMAND FOR DAMAGES	●		Policy IV.(A).(1)., page 4
41	COMPLAINT FILED WITH EEOC	—		
42	OR SIMILAR STATE AUTHORITY	—		
43	AGENCY MUST HAVE POWER TO ADJUDICATE	—		
44	ADMINISTRATIVE PROCEEDING	●		Policy IV.(A).(3)., page 4
45	ARBITRATION PROCEEDING	—		
46	ANY INCIDENT REPORTED TO INSURER			
47	SUIT	●	Civil proceeding	Policy IV.(A).(2)., page 4
48	CLAIM DOES NOT INCLUDE ARBITRATION SUBJECT TO			
49	COLLECTIVE BARGAINING AGREEMENT	—		
50	EMPLOYEE POLICY OR MANUAL	—		
51	CLAIM NOT DEFINED	—		
	7 CLAIM REPORTING PROVISIONS TO INSURER			
52	IMMEDIATELY	—		
53	AS SOON AS POSSIBLE	—		
54	AS SOON AS PRACTICABLE	●		Policy I., following (C)., page 1
55	WITHIN POLICY PERIOD	●		Policy I., following (C)., page 1
56	WITHIN X DAYS OF EXPIRATION	60		Policy I., following (C)., page 1
57	WITHIN X DAYS	—		
	8 EXTENDED REPORTING FEATURES			
58	ELECTION PERIOD (DAYS)	30		Policy II.(B)., page 2
59	ADDITIONAL PREMIUM (% OF ANNUAL PREMIUM)	○	Specified by underwriter—see Item G. of Declarations	Policy II.(B)., page 2
60	ADDITIONAL REPORTING PERIOD (MONTHS)	○	Specified by underwriter—see Item G. of Declarations	Policy II.(B)., page 2
61	NO REINSTATEMENT OF LIMITS	—		
	9 POTENTIAL CLAIM REPORTING PROVISIONS			
62	NONE (SEE ALSO "CLAIM" ABOVE)	—		
63	INCIDENTS LIKELY TO RESULT IN A CLAIM	●		Policy VIII.(A)., pages 10–11
	10 DEFENSE PROVISIONS			
64	AFFIRMATIVE DUTY TO DEFEND	—		
65	NO AFFIRMATIVE DUTY TO DEFEND	●		Policy III.(B)., page 3
66	AFFIRMATIVE ADVANCEMENT PROVISIONS	●		Policy III.(C)., page 3
67	INSURED MUST RETURN ADVANCED AMOUNTS IF NOT COVERED	●		Policy III.(C)., pages 3–4
68	INSURED/INSURER CHOOSES COUNSEL	—		
69	INSURED/INSURER APPROVES COUNSEL	—		
70	INSURED/INSURER CONSULTED IN COUNSEL SELECTION	—		
	11 SETTLEMENT PROVISIONS			
71	HAMMER CLAUSE	—		
72	CONSULTATION PROVISION	—		
73	CONSENT PROVISION	●	Insurer must consent	Policy III.(A)., page 3
	12 ALLOCATION OF LOSS PROVISIONS			
74	STIPULATED PROVISIONS	●		Policy VII., page 10
	13 COVERAGES			
75	DISCRIMINATION	●	Employment-related	Endorsement (2)., page 1
76	SPECIFIC ENUMERATED ACTIVITIES	—		
77	PLUS BROAD OMNIBUS WORDING	—		
78	SPECIFIC ENUMERATED CLASSES	—		
79	PLUS BROAD OMNIBUS WORDING	—		
80	AGAINST THIRD PARTIES	—		
81	DISCRIMINATION NOT DEFINED	●		
82	SEXUAL HARASSMENT	●		Endorsement (2)., page 1
83	HOSTILE ENVIRONMENT	—		
84	QUID-PRO-QUO	—		
85	SEXUAL HARASSMENT NOT DEFINED	●		
86	WRONGFUL TERMINATION	●		Endorsement (2)., page 1
87	BREACH OF IMPLIED CONTRACT	—		
88	BREACH OF EXPRESS CONTRACT	—		
89	VIOLATION OF PUBLIC POLICY	—		
90	VIOLATION OF GOOD FAITH & FAIR DEALING	—		
91	OBLIGATIONS TO MAKE PAYMENTS	—		
92	CONSTRUCTIVE DISCHARGE	●		Endorsement (2)., page 1
93	WRONGFUL TERMINATION NOT DEFINED	●		
94	**OTHER EMPLOYMENT VIOLATIONS/OFFENSES**			
95	WRONGFUL HIRING	●		Endorsement (2)., page 1
96	WRONGFUL PROMOTION/DEMOTION	●		Endorsement (2)., page 1
97	WRONGFUL EVALUATION/DISCIPLINE			

RELIANCE NATIONAL DO 00 R324 00 0696 [0696]

#	Comparison Query		Comment	Policy Reference
98	FAMILY AND MEDICAL LEAVE ACT	—		
99	DEFAMATION	—		
100	MISREPRESENTATION	—		
101	RETALIATION	—		
102	MENTAL ANGUISH	—		
103	INVASION OF PRIVACY	—		
104	HUMILIATION	—		
105	EMOTIONAL DISTRESS	—		
106	OTHER PERSONAL INJURY OFFENSES	—		
107	POLICY SILENT	●		
	14 EXCLUSIONS			
108	**ADA ACCOMMODATION EXPENSES**	—		
109	**ASSAULT & BATTERY**	—		
110	**BACK PAY**	—		
111	**BODILY INJURY**			
112	BODILY INJURY	●		Endorsement (3)., page 2
113	DEATH	●		Endorsement (3)., page 2
114	DISEASE	●		Endorsement (3)., page 2
115	SICKNESS	●		Endorsement (3)., page 2
116	**BREACH OF EMPLOYMENT CONTRACT**			
117	EXPRESS CONTRACT	—		
118	*WRITTEN CONTRACT*	—		
119	*ORAL CONTRACT*	—		
120	IMPLIED CONTRACT	—		
121	**CLASS ACTION LAWSUITS**	—		
122	**CONSEQUENTIAL LOSS**			
123	APPLIES TO BODILY INJURY	—		
124	APPLIES TO INSURED EVENT	—		
125	BROTHER/SISTER	—		
126	CHILD	—		
127	DOMESTIC PARTNER	—		
128	PARENT	—		
129	SPOUSE	—		
130	**COST OF ARBITRATION HEARINGS SUBJECT TO**			
131	EMPLOYMENT HANDBOOK	—		
132	LABOR GRIEVANCE	—		
133	OTHER EMPLOYMENT POLICY OR PROCEDURE	—		
134	**COVERAGE ELSEWHERE**			
135	OTHER AVAILABLE INSURANCE	●		Policy IX.(E)., page 12
136	OTHER INDEMNIFICATION	—		
137	SHARING PROVISION	—		
138	**FAILURE TO EXERCISE CARE WHEN TERMINATING**	—		
139	**FINES/PENALTIES**	●		Policy IV.(J)., page 5
140	CIVIL	—		
141	CRIMINAL	—		
142	EXEMPLARY DAMAGES	●	If uninsurable by law	Policy IV.(J)., page 5
143	PUNITIVE DAMAGES	●	If uninsurable by law	Policy IV.(J)., page 5
144	MULTIPLIED DAMAGES	●	If uninsurable by law	Policy IV.(J)., page 5
145	**FRONT PAY**	—		
146	EXCLUSION APPLIES ONLY IF EMPLOYER HAD OPPORTUNITY TO REINSTATE EMPLOYEE BUT DID NOT DO SO	—		
147	**INTENTIONAL ACTS**			
148	CRIMINAL ACTS			
149	CRIMINAL PROCEEDING			
150	DISHONEST PURPOSE	●	If established	Policy V.(J)., page 8
151	FRAUDULENT ACTS	●	If established	Policy V.(J)., page 8
152	FRAUDULENT CLAIMS	—		
153	INTENTIONAL VIOLATIONS OF LAW	●	If established	Policy V.(J)., page 8
154	WILLFUL FAILURE TO COMPLY WITH LAW	○	If established	Policy V.(J)., page 8
155	MALICIOUS PURPOSE	—		
156	**LIABILITY OF OTHERS**	—		
157	**LIQUIDATED DAMAGES**	—		
158	**LOSS ARISING OUT OF CHANGES IN OPERATIONS**			
159	ACQUISITION	—		
160	CHANGE IN CONTROL	—		
161	DOWNSIZING OR REDUCTION IN FORCE	—		
162	*% OF WORKFORCE*	—		
163	*WITHIN X DAYS*	—		

#	Comparison Query	Comment	Policy Reference
164	FINANCIAL IMPAIRMENT	—	
165	BANKRUPTCY	—	
166	INSOLVENCY	—	
167	LIQUIDATION	—	
168	RECEIVERSHIP	—	
169	FINANCIAL INABILITY TO PAY	—	
170	MERGER	—	
171	PLANT OR FACILITY CLOSING	—	
172	REORGANIZATION	—	
173	TEMPORARY SHUTDOWN	—	
174	**MATTERS DEEMED UNINSURABLE**	●	Policy IV.(J)., page 5
175	**NON-MONETARY RELIEF**		
176	DECLATORY RELIEF	—	
177	DISGORGEMENT	—	
178	INJUNCTIVE RELIEF	—	
179	JOB REINSTATEMENT	—	
180	NON-MONETARY DAMAGES/RELIEF	—	
181	OTHER EQUITABLE REMEDIES	—	
182	**OBLIGATION TO PROVIDE BENEFITS**		
183	COBRA	—	
184	DISABILITY	—	
185	ERISA	●	Policy V.(G)., page 8
186	SOCIAL SECURITY	—	
187	OTHER RETIREMENT BENEFITS	—	
188	UNEMPLOYMENT	—	
189	WORKERS' COMPENSATION	—	
190	**PERSONAL INJURY OFFENSES**		
191	DEFAMATION	●	Policy V.(A)., page 6
192	EMOTIONAL DISTRESS/UPSET	●	Policy V.(A)., page 6
193	HUMILIATION	●	Policy V.(A)., page 6
194	LIBEL	—	
195	MENTAL ANGUISH	●	Policy V.(A)., page 6
196	PERSONAL INJURY	—	
197	SLANDER		
198	**PRIOR ACTS**		
199	PRIOR ACTS	—	
200	PRIOR KNOWLEDGE	●	Endorsement (1)., page 2
201	PRIOR/PENDING LITIGATION	●	Endorsement (2)., page 2
202	**PROPERTY DAMAGE**		
203	INTANGIBLE PROPERTY	—	
204	LOSS OF USE	●	Endorsement (3)., page 2
205	TANGIBLE PROPERTY	●	Endorsement (3)., page 2
206	**RETALIATORY ACTIONS OF EMPLOYER**		
207	FOR FAILING TO PERFORM ACTS AGAINST PUBLIC POLICY	—	
208	FOR FILING A COMPLAINT OR BENEFIT CLAIM	—	
209	**STRIKES/LOCKOUTS**	—	
210	**VIOLATION OF LAWS**		
211	ANY LAW	—	
212	FMLA	—	
213	OSHA	—	
214	POLLUTION LAWS	●	Policy V.(E)., page 7
215	RICO	—	
216	SEC	—	
217	WARN	—	

15 CONDITIONS

#	Comparison Query	Comment	Policy Reference
218	**ARBITRATION**		
219	MANDATORY	—	
220	BINDING	—	
221	CHOICE OF LAW PROVISION		
222	SITUS	—	
223	**TERRITORY**		
224	LIMITED	—	
225	WORLDWIDE	●	Policy IX.(A)., page 11
226	**NEWLY FORMED/ACQUIRED ENTITIES**		
227	AUTOMATIC COVERAGE (X DAYS)	○	No time limit specified	Policy IX.(H).(2)., page 14
228	NOTIFY INSURER WITHIN X DAYS	○	No time limit specified	Policy IX.(H).(2)., page 14

RELIANCE NATIONAL DO 00 R324 00 0696 [0696]

Policy Comparison Worksheet

Steadfast Insurance Company

Policy Form No.: STF-PL-100-B CW
Edition Date: 4/97

Risks Considered: General accounts
Limits Available: $50,000,000
Minimum Retention: $25,000

Contact: Lisa L. Reynolds
Steadfast Insurance Company
One Liberty Plaza, 30th Floor
New York, NY 10006
212/748-2375
212/513-1239 (fax)

KEY TO SYMBOLS
● = Specifically contains queried provision of feature
○ = Unable to determine
— = Silent

#	Comparison Query		Comment	Policy Reference
	1 APPLICATION			
1	ATTACHES TO AND FORMS A PART OF THE POLICY	●	See also VIII.C., page 11	I., Preamble, page 3
2	CONTAINS WARRANTY STATEMENTS	—		
3	CONTAINS SEVERABILITY PROVISIONS	—		
	2 POLICY TYPE			
4	UNITARY STAND ALONE POLICY	●		
	ENDORSEMENT OR PART OF	—		
5	DIRECTORS AND OFFICERS POLICY	—		
6	PACKAGE POLICY	—		
7	UMBRELLA POLICY	—		
8	ERRORS AND OMISSIONS POLICY	—		
9	OTHER	—		
10	CLAIMS-MADE	●		
11	OCCURRENCE	—		
	3 WHO IS INSURED			
12	BUSINESS ENTITY	●		III.F., page 6
13	AUTOMATIC COVERAGE FOR SUBSIDIARIES	—		
14	DIRECTORS & OFFICERS	●		III.F., page 6
15	EMPLOYEES	●		III.F., page 6
16	PART-TIME	●		III.E., page 6
17	SEASONAL	●		III.E., page 6
18	TEMPORARY	●		III.E., page 6
19	SUPERVISORS & MANAGERS	—		
20	FORMER EMPLOYEES	●		III.E., page 6
21	VOLUNTEERS	●		III.E., page 6
22	INDEPENDENT CONTRACTORS	—		
23	EXCLUDED	●		III.E., page 6
24	SILENT	—		
25	SHAREHOLDERS	●		III.F., page 6
	4 LIMIT OF LIABILITY			
26	AGGREGATE	●		V.B., pages 8–9
27	INCLUDES PUNITIVE DAMAGES WHERE NOT UNINSURABLE	—	Coverage available by endorsement	
28	DEFENSE COSTS INCLUDED WITHIN LIMIT OF LIABILITY	●		III.C., page 5
29	DEFENSE COSTS PAID IN ADDITION TO LIMIT OF LIABILITY	—		
	5 DEDUCTIBLE			
30	APPLIES TO EACH INDIVIDUAL CLAIM	●		VI.A. page 9
31	APPLIES TO EACH OCCURRENCE OR WRONGFUL PRACTICE	—		
32	INCLUDES ALL CLAIMS FROM ONE ACT	●		III.A., page 5
33	SUBJECT TO ANNUAL AGGREGATE	●		V.B., pages 8–9
34	CO-PAYMENT APPLIES	○	Specified by underwriter—see item 6. of Declarations	VI.B., page 9
35	LIMIT OF LIABILITY NOT REDUCED	—		
36	INCLUDES DEFENSE COSTS	●	See also III.I., page 6	VI.A., page 9
37	REDUCED UNDER SPECIFIED CIRCUMSTANCES (SEE POLICY)	—		

STEADFAST INSURANCE COMPANY STF-PL-100-B CW (4/97)

	Comparison Query	Comment	Policy Reference
	6 WHAT IS A CLAIM		
38	ORAL COMPLAINT TO INSURED	—	
39	WRITTEN COMPLAINT TO INSURED	●	III.A., page 5
40	COMPLAINT MUST CONTAIN A DEMAND FOR DAMAGES	●	
41	COMPLAINT FILED WITH EEOC	●	Any governmental body	III.A., page 5
42	OR SIMILAR STATE AUTHORITY	●	Any governmental body	III.A., page 5
43	AGENCY MUST HAVE POWER TO ADJUDICATE	—	
44	ADMINISTRATIVE PROCEEDING	●		III.A., page 5
45	ARBITRATION PROCEEDING	●	Alternative Dispute Resolution	III.A., page 5
46	ANY INCIDENT REPORTED TO INSURER	—	
47	SUIT	●	Civil action	III.A., page 5
48	CLAIM DOES NOT INCLUDE ARBITRATION SUBJECT TO	—	
49	COLLECTIVE BARGAINING AGREEMENT	—	
50	EMPLOYEE POLICY OR MANUAL	—	
51	CLAIM NOT DEFINED	—	
	7 CLAIM REPORTING PROVISIONS TO INSURER		
52	IMMEDIATELY	—	
53	AS SOON AS POSSIBLE	—	
54	AS SOON AS PRACTICABLE	●	VIII.A.1., page 10
55	WITHIN POLICY PERIOD	—	
56	WITHIN X DAYS OF EXPIRATION	—	
57	WITHIN X DAYS	—	
	8 EXTENDED REPORTING FEATURES		
58	ELECTION PERIOD (DAYS)	30	VII.E., page 9
59	ADDITIONAL PREMIUM (% OF ANNUAL PREMIUM)	○	Specified by underwriter—see Item 9. of Declarations	VII.D., page 9
60	ADDITIONAL REPORTING PERIOD (MONTHS)	12	VII.B., page 9
61	NO REINSTATEMENT OF LIMITS	●	VII., following E., page 9
	9 POTENTIAL CLAIM REPORTING PROVISIONS		
62	NONE (SEE ALSO "CLAIM" ABOVE)	—	
63	INCIDENTS LIKELY TO RESULT IN A CLAIM	●	VIII.A.1., page 10
	10 DEFENSE PROVISIONS		
64	AFFIRMATIVE DUTY TO DEFEND	●	II.B.1., page 4
65	NO AFFIRMATIVE DUTY TO DEFEND	—	
66	AFFIRMATIVE ADVANCEMENT PROVISIONS	—	
67	INSURED MUST RETURN ADVANCED AMOUNTS IF NOT COVERED	—	
68	INSURED/INSURER CHOOSES COUNSEL	●	Insurer	II.B.1., page 4
69	INSURED/INSURER APPROVES COUNSEL	●	Insured	II.B.1., page 4
70	INSURED/INSURER CONSULTED IN COUNSEL SELECTION	—	
	11 SETTLEMENT PROVISIONS		
71	HAMMER CLAUSE	●	II.B.6., page 4
72	CONSULTATION PROVISION	—	
73	CONSENT PROVISION	●	Insured must consent	II.B.4., page 4
	12 ALLOCATION OF LOSS PROVISIONS		
74	STIPULATED PROVISIONS	—	
	13 COVERAGES		
75	DISCRIMINATION	●	I. Preamble, page 3
76	SPECIFIC ENUMERATED ACTIVITIES	●	III.D., page 5
77	PLUS BROAD OMNIBUS WORDING	●	III.D., page 5
78	SPECIFIC ENUMERATED CLASSES	●	III.D., page 5
79	PLUS BROAD OMNIBUS WORDING	●	III.D., page 5
80	AGAINST THIRD PARTIES	—	
81	DISCRIMINATION NOT DEFINED	—	
82	SEXUAL HARASSMENT	●	Any harassment	I. Preamble, page 3
83	HOSTILE ENVIRONMENT	●	III.K., page 7
84	QUID-PRO-QUO	●	III.K., page 7
85	SEXUAL HARASSMENT NOT DEFINED	—	
86	WRONGFUL TERMINATION	●	Or treatment	I. Preamble, page 3
87	BREACH OF IMPLIED CONTRACT	●	III.L., page 7
88	BREACH OF EXPRESS CONTRACT	—	
89	VIOLATION OF PUBLIC POLICY	—	
90	VIOLATION OF GOOD FAITH & FAIR DEALING	—	
91	OBLIGATIONS TO MAKE PAYMENTS	—	
92	CONSTRUCTIVE DISCHARGE	—	
93	WRONGFUL TERMINATION NOT DEFINED	—	
94	OTHER EMPLOYMENT VIOLATIONS/OFFENSES	●	III.B., page 5 and III.L., page 7
95	WRONGFUL HIRING	●	III.B., page 5
96	WRONGFUL PROMOTION/DEMOTION	●	III.L., page 7
97	WRONGFUL EVALUATION/DISCIPLINE	—	

STEADFAST INSURANCE COMPANY STF-PL-100-B CW [4/97]

#	Comparison Query	Comment	Policy Reference
98	FAMILY AND MEDICAL LEAVE ACT	—	
99	DEFAMATION	●	III.B., page 5
100	MISREPRESENTATION	—	
101	RETALIATION	●	III.L., page 7
102	MENTAL ANGUISH	—	
103	INVASION OF PRIVACY	●	III.B., page 5
104	HUMILIATION	—	
105	EMOTIONAL DISTRESS	●	III.B., page 5
106	OTHER PERSONAL INJURY OFFENSES	●	III.B., page 5
107	POLICY SILENT	—	

14 EXCLUSIONS

#	Comparison Query	Comment	Policy Reference
108	**ADA ACCOMMODATION EXPENSES**	●	IV.G., page 8
109	**ASSAULT & BATTERY**	—	
110	**BACK PAY**	—	
111	**BODILY INJURY**		
112	BODILY INJURY	—	
113	DEATH	—	
114	DISEASE	—	
115	SICKNESS	—	
116	**BREACH OF EMPLOYMENT CONTRACT**	●	IV.I., page 8
117	EXPRESS CONTRACT	●	IV.I., page 8
118	*WRITTEN CONTRACT*	●	IV.I., page 8
119	*ORAL CONTRACT*	—	
120	IMPLIED CONTRACT	—	
121	**CLASS ACTION LAWSUITS**	—	
122	**CONSEQUENTIAL LOSS**	—	
123	APPLIES TO BODILY INJURY	—	
124	APPLIES TO INSURED EVENT	—	
125	BROTHER/SISTER	—	
126	CHILD	—	
127	DOMESTIC PARTNER	—	
128	PARENT	—	
129	SPOUSE	—	
130	**COST OF ARBITRATION HEARINGS SUBJECT TO**	—	
131	EMPLOYMENT HANDBOOK	—	
132	LABOR GRIEVANCE	—	
133	OTHER EMPLOYMENT POLICY OR PROCEDURE	—	
134	**COVERAGE ELSEWHERE**	—	
135	OTHER AVAILABLE INSURANCE	—	
136	OTHER INDEMNIFICATION	—	
137	SHARING PROVISION	●	VIII.B.2., page 11
138	**FAILURE TO EXERCISE CARE WHEN TERMINATING**	—	
139	**FINES/PENALTIES**	●	See also IV.F., page 8	III.I.c., page 6
140	CIVIL	●	See also IV.F., page 8	III.I.c., page 6
141	CRIMINAL	●	See also IV.F., page 8	III.I.c., page 6
142	EXEMPLARY DAMAGES	●	See also IV.F., page 8	III.I.c., page 6
143	PUNITIVE DAMAGES	●	Coverage available by endorsement	III.I.e., page 6
144	MULTIPLIED DAMAGES	●	See also IV.F., page 8	III.I.d., page 6
145	**FRONT PAY**	—	
146	EXCLUSION APPLIES ONLY IF EMPLOYER HAD OPPORTUNITY TO REINSTATE EMPLOYEE BUT DID NOT DO SO	—	
147	**INTENTIONAL ACTS**	●	If proven—severability applies	IV.H., page 8
148	CRIMINAL ACTS	—	
149	CRIMINAL PROCEEDING	—	
150	DISHONEST PURPOSE	—	
151	FRAUDULENT ACTS	—	
152	FRAUDULENT CLAIMS	—	
153	INTENTIONAL VIOLATIONS OF LAW	—	
154	WILLFUL FAILURE TO COMPLY WITH LAW	—	
155	MALICIOUS PURPOSE	—	
156	**LIABILITY OF OTHERS**	●	IV.B., page 7
157	**LIQUIDATED DAMAGES**	—	
158	**LOSS ARISING OUT OF CHANGES IN OPERATIONS**	—	
159	ACQUISITION	—	
160	CHANGE IN CONTROL	—	
161	DOWNSIZING OR REDUCTION IN FORCE	—	
162	*% OF WORKFORCE*	—	
163	*WITHIN X DAYS*	—	

STEADFAST INSURANCE COMPANY STF-PL-100-B CW [4/97]

#	Comparison Query	Comment		Policy Reference
164	FINANCIAL IMPAIRMENT	—		
165	BANKRUPTCY	—		
166	INSOLVENCY	—		
167	LIQUIDATION	—		
168	RECEIVERSHIP	—		
169	FINANCIAL INABILITY TO PAY	—		
170	MERGER	—		
171	PLANT OR FACILITY CLOSING	—		
172	REORGANIZATION	—		
173	TEMPORARY SHUTDOWN	—		
174	**MATTERS DEEMED UNINSURABLE**	●	See also III.I.g., page 7	III.B., page 5
175	**NON-MONETARY RELIEF**	●		III.I.h., page 7
176	DECLATORY RELIEF	—		
177	DISGORGEMENT	—		
178	INJUNCTIVE RELIEF	●		IV.G., page 8
179	JOB REINSTATEMENT	—		
180	NON-MONETARY DAMAGES/RELIEF	●	See also IV.G., page 8	III.I.h., page 7
181	OTHER EQUITABLE REMEDIES	—		
182	**OBLIGATION TO PROVIDE BENEFITS**	—		
183	COBRA	●		IV.A., page 7
184	DISABILITY	●		IV.A., page 7
185	ERISA	●		IV.A., page 7
186	SOCIAL SECURITY	—		
187	OTHER RETIREMENT BENEFITS	—		
188	UNEMPLOYMENT	●		IV.A., page 7
189	WORKERS' COMPENSATION	●		IV.A., page 7
190	**PERSONAL INJURY OFFENSES**	—		
191	DEFAMATION	—		
192	EMOTIONAL DISTRESS/UPSET	—		
193	HUMILIATION	—		
194	LIBEL	—		
195	MENTAL ANGUISH	—		
196	PERSONAL INJURY	—		
197	SLANDER	—		
198	**PRIOR ACTS**	●		II.A.2.c., page 4
199	PRIOR ACTS	●	Prior to "Insured Event Date"	II.A.2.c., page 4
200	PRIOR KNOWLEDGE	—		
201	PRIOR/PENDING LITIGATION	—		
202	**PROPERTY DAMAGE**	—		
203	INTANGIBLE PROPERTY	—		
204	LOSS OF USE	—		
205	TANGIBLE PROPERTY	—		
206	**RETALIATORY ACTIONS OF EMPLOYER**	—		
207	FOR FAILING TO PERFORM ACTS AGAINST PUBLIC POLICY	—		
208	FOR FILING A COMPLAINT OR BENEFIT CLAIM	—		
209	**STRIKES/LOCKOUTS**	●		IV.C., page 8
210	**VIOLATION OF LAWS**	—		
211	ANY LAW	—		
212	FMLA	—		
213	OSHA	●		IV.A., page 7
214	POLLUTION LAWS	—		
215	RICO	—		
216	SEC	—		
217	WARN	●		IV.D., page 8
	15 CONDITIONS			
218	**ARBITRATION**	●		VIII.N., page 14
219	MANDATORY	●		VIII.N.1., page 14
220	BINDING	—		
221	CHOICE OF LAW PROVISION	—		
222	SITUS	●	New York, NY	VIII.N.2., page 14
223	**TERRITORY**	●		VIII.M., page 13
224	LIMITED	—		
225	WORLDWIDE	●		VIII.M., page 13
226	**NEWLY FORMED/ACQUIRED ENTITIES**	●		VIII.H.1.a. & b., page 12
227	AUTOMATIC COVERAGE (X DAYS)	30		VIII.H.1.a. & b., page 12
228	NOTIFY INSURER WITHIN X DAYS	○	No time limit specified	VIII.H.b.(1)., page 12

STEADFAST INSURANCE COMPANY STF-PL-100-B CW [4/97]

Policy Comparison Worksheet

Steadfast Insurance Company

Policy Form No.: U-DO-457-A (CW)
Edition Date: 4/97

Risks Considered: New/difficult to place companies
Limits Available: $50,000,000
Minimum Retention: None

Contact: Jay M. Dipasupil
Steadfast Insurance Company
One Liberty Plaza, 30th Floor
New York, NY 10006
212/748-2372
212/513-1239 (fax)

KEY TO SYMBOLS
● = Specifically contains queried provision of feature
○ = Unable to determine
— = Silent

#	Comparison Query		Comment	Policy Reference
	1 APPLICATION			
1	ATTACHES TO AND FORMS A PART OF THE POLICY	●		Policy V.B., page 6
2	CONTAINS WARRANTY STATEMENTS	—		
3	CONTAINS SEVERABILITY PROVISIONS	—		
	2 POLICY TYPE			
4	UNITARY STAND ALONE POLICY	—		
	ENDORSEMENT OR PART OF			
5	DIRECTORS AND OFFICERS POLICY	●	Policy form STF-DO-109-A (CW) (12/95)	
6	PACKAGE POLICY	—		
7	UMBRELLA POLICY	—		
8	ERRORS AND OMISSIONS POLICY	—		
9	OTHER	—		
10	CLAIMS-MADE	●		
11	OCCURRENCE	—		
	3 WHO IS INSURED			
12	BUSINESS ENTITY	●		Policy III.B., page 4
13	AUTOMATIC COVERAGE FOR SUBSIDIARIES	●		Policy III.B., page 4
14	DIRECTORS & OFFICERS	●		Policy, Item 6, Declarations
15	EMPLOYEES	—		
16	PART-TIME	—		
17	SEASONAL	—		
18	TEMPORARY	—		
19	SUPERVISORS & MANAGERS	—		
20	FORMER EMPLOYEES	—		
21	VOLUNTEERS	—		
22	INDEPENDENT CONTRACTORS			
23	EXCLUDED	—		
24	SILENT	●		
25	SHAREHOLDERS			
	4 LIMIT OF LIABILITY			
26	AGGREGATE	●	Per Item 2 (B) of Declarations	Endorsement 9., page 2
27	INCLUDES PUNITIVE DAMAGES WHERE NOT UNINSURABLE	—		
28	DEFENSE COSTS INCLUDED WITHIN LIMIT OF LIABILITY	●		Endorsement 9., page 3
29	DEFENSE COSTS PAID IN ADDITION TO LIMIT OF LIABILITY	—		
	5 DEDUCTIBLE			
30	APPLIES TO EACH INDIVIDUAL CLAIM	●		Endorsement 9., page 2
31	APPLIES TO EACH OCCURRENCE OR WRONGFUL PRACTICE	●	See Endorsement 9., page 3	Endorsement 9., page 2
32	INCLUDES ALL CLAIMS FROM ONE ACT	●	See Endorsement 9., page 3	Endorsement 9., page 3
33	SUBJECT TO ANNUAL AGGREGATE	—		
34	CO-PAYMENT APPLIES	●	Specified by underwriter—see Item 5 of Declarations	Endorsement 9., page 3
35	LIMIT OF LIABILITY NOT REDUCED			
36	INCLUDES DEFENSE COSTS	●	See also Policy III.H., page 4	Endorsement 9., page 3
37	REDUCED UNDER SPECIFIED CIRCUMSTANCES (SEE POLICY)	—		

#	Comparison Query	Comment	Policy Reference
6	**WHAT IS A CLAIM**		
38	ORAL COMPLAINT TO INSURED	—	
39	WRITTEN COMPLAINT TO INSURED	●	Policy III.A.1., page 4
40	COMPLAINT MUST CONTAIN A DEMAND FOR DAMAGES	●	Policy III.A.1., page 4
41	COMPLAINT FILED WITH EEOC	—	
42	OR SIMILAR STATE AUTHORITY	—	
43	AGENCY MUST HAVE POWER TO ADJUDICATE	—	
44	ADMINISTRATIVE PROCEEDING	—	
45	ARBITRATION PROCEEDING	—	
46	ANY INCIDENT REPORTED TO INSURER	—	
47	SUIT	●	Policy III.A.2., page 4
48	CLAIM DOES NOT INCLUDE ARBITRATION SUBJECT TO		
49	COLLECTIVE BARGAINING AGREEMENT	—	
50	EMPLOYEE POLICY OR MANUAL	—	
51	CLAIM NOT DEFINED	—	
7	**CLAIM REPORTING PROVISIONS TO INSURER**		
52	IMMEDIATELY	—	
53	AS SOON AS POSSIBLE	—	
54	AS SOON AS PRACTICABLE	●	Policy V.H., page 9
55	WITHIN POLICY PERIOD	—	
56	WITHIN X DAYS OF EXPIRATION	30	Policy V.H., page 9
57	WITHIN X DAYS	—	
8	**EXTENDED REPORTING FEATURES**		
58	ELECTION PERIOD (DAYS)	15	Policy II.B., page 3
59	ADDITIONAL PREMIUM (% OF ANNUAL PREMIUM)	○ Specified by underwriter—see Item 7(A) of Declarations	Policy II.B., page 3
60	ADDITIONAL REPORTING PERIOD (MONTHS)	○ Specified by underwriter—see Item 7(B) of Declarations	Policy II.B., page 3
61	NO REINSTATEMENT OF LIMITS	—	
9	**POTENTIAL CLAIM REPORTING PROVISIONS**		
62	NONE (SEE ALSO "CLAIM" ABOVE)	—	
63	INCIDENTS LIKELY TO RESULT IN A CLAIM	—	
10	**DEFENSE PROVISIONS**		
64	AFFIRMATIVE DUTY TO DEFEND	—	
65	NO AFFIRMATIVE DUTY TO DEFEND	●	Policy V.F., page 8
66	AFFIRMATIVE ADVANCEMENT PROVISIONS	● Regarding covered loss only	Policy V.D., page 7
67	INSURED MUST RETURN ADVANCED AMOUNTS IF NOT COVERED	●	Policy V.D., page 7
68	INSURED/INSURER CHOOSES COUNSEL	—	
69	INSURED/INSURER APPROVES COUNSEL	—	
70	INSURED/INSURER CONSULTED IN COUNSEL SELECTION	—	
11	**SETTLEMENT PROVISIONS**		
71	HAMMER CLAUSE	●	Policy V.F., page 8
72	CONSULTATION PROVISION	—	
73	CONSENT PROVISION	● Two-way	Policy V.F., page 8
12	**ALLOCATION OF LOSS PROVISIONS**		
74	STIPULATED PROVISIONS	●	Policy V.D., page 7
13	**COVERAGES**		
75	DISCRIMINATION	●	Endorsement 2.(a)., page 1
76	SPECIFIC ENUMERATED ACTIVITIES	—	
77	*PLUS BROAD OMNIBUS WORDING*	—	
78	SPECIFIC ENUMERATED CLASSES	—	
79	*PLUS BROAD OMNIBUS WORDING*	—	
80	AGAINST THIRD PARTIES	—	
81	DISCRIMINATION NOT DEFINED	●	
82	SEXUAL HARASSMENT	●	Endorsement 2.(a)., page 1
83	HOSTILE ENVIRONMENT	—	
84	QUID-PRO-QUO	—	
85	SEXUAL HARASSMENT NOT DEFINED	●	
86	WRONGFUL TERMINATION	●	Endorsement a.(a)., page 1
87	BREACH OF IMPLIED CONTRACT	—	
88	BREACH OF EXPRESS CONTRACT	● Oral or written	Endorsement a.(a)., page 1
89	VIOLATION OF PUBLIC POLICY	—	
90	VIOLATION OF GOOD FAITH & FAIR DEALING	—	
91	OBLIGATIONS TO MAKE PAYMENTS	—	
92	CONSTRUCTIVE DISCHARGE	—	
93	WRONGFUL TERMINATION NOT DEFINED	—	
94	OTHER EMPLOYMENT VIOLATIONS/OFFENSES		
95	WRONGFUL HIRING	●	Endorsement a.(a)., page 1
96	WRONGFUL PROMOTION/DEMOTION	●	Endorsement a.(a)., page 1
97	WRONGFUL EVALUATION/DISCIPLINE	●	Endorsement a.(a)., page 1

STEADFAST INSURANCE COMPANY U-DO-457-A (CW) [4/97]

#	Comparison Query	Mark	Comment	Policy Reference
98	FAMILY AND MEDICAL LEAVE ACT	—		
99	DEFAMATION	●		Endorsement 2.(a), page 1
100	MISREPRESENTATION	●		Endorsement 2.(a), page 1
101	RETALIATION	—		
102	MENTAL ANGUISH	—		
103	INVASION OF PRIVACY	—		
104	HUMILIATION	—		
105	EMOTIONAL DISTRESS	●		Endorsement 2.(a), page 1
106	OTHER PERSONAL INJURY OFFENSES	●		Endorsement 2.(a), page 1
107	POLICY SILENT	—		
14 EXCLUSIONS				
108	**ADA ACCOMMODATION EXPENSES**	●	Defense cost exception	Endorsement 7.G., page 2
109	**ASSAULT & BATTERY**	—		
110	**BACK PAY**	—		
111	**BODILY INJURY**			
112	BODILY INJURY	●		Endorsement 6.(b), page 2
113	DEATH	●		Endorsement 6.(b), page 2
114	DISEASE	●		Endorsement 6.(b), page 2
115	SICKNESS	●		Endorsement 6.(b), page 2
116	**BREACH OF EMPLOYMENT CONTRACT**	●		
117	EXPRESS CONTRACT	○	Any contract—defense exception	Endorsement 7.F., page 2
118	WRITTEN CONTRACT	○	Any contract—defense exception	Endorsement 7.F., page 2
119	ORAL CONTRACT	○	Any contract—defense exception	Endorsement 7.F., page 2
120	IMPLIED CONTRACT	○	Any contract—defense exception	Endorsement 7.F., page 2
121	**CLASS ACTION LAWSUITS**	—		
122	**CONSEQUENTIAL LOSS**			
123	APPLIES TO BODILY INJURY	—		
124	APPLIES TO INSURED EVENT	—		
125	BROTHER/SISTER	—		
126	CHILD	—		
127	DOMESTIC PARTNER	—		
128	PARENT	—		
129	SPOUSE	—		
130	**COST OF ARBITRATION HEARINGS SUBJECT TO**			
131	EMPLOYMENT HANDBOOK	—		
132	LABOR GRIEVANCE	—		
133	OTHER EMPLOYMENT POLICY OR PROCEDURE	—		
134	**COVERAGE ELSEWHERE**			
135	OTHER AVAILABLE INSURANCE	●		Policy II.I., page 9
136	OTHER INDEMNIFICATION	—		
137	SHARING PROVISION	—		
138	**FAILURE TO EXERCISE CARE WHEN TERMINATING**	—		
139	**FINES/PENALTIES**	●		Policy III.H., page 4
140	CIVIL	—		
141	CRIMINAL	—		
142	EXEMPLARY DAMAGES	●		Policy III.H., page 4
143	PUNITIVE DAMAGES	●		Policy III.H., page 4
144	MULTIPLIED DAMAGES	●		Policy III.H., page 4
145	**FRONT PAY**	●	Defense cost exception	Endorsement 7.D., page 2
146	EXCLUSION APPLIES ONLY IF EMPLOYER HAD OPPORTUNITY TO REINSTATE EMPLOYEE BUT DID NOT DO SO	●	Defense cost exception	Endorsement 7.D., page 2
147	**INTENTIONAL ACTS**			
148	CRIMINAL ACTS	—		
149	CRIMINAL PROCEEDING	—		
150	DISHONEST PURPOSE	—		
151	FRAUDULENT ACTS	●	If established	Endorsement 8.C., page 2
152	FRAUDULENT CLAIMS	—		
153	INTENTIONAL VIOLATIONS OF LAW	●	If established	Endorsement 8.C., page 2
154	WILLFUL FAILURE TO COMPLY WITH LAW	●	If established	Endorsement 8.C., page 2
155	MALICIOUS PURPOSE	—		
156	**LIABILITY OF OTHERS**	—		
157	**LIQUIDATED DAMAGES**	—		
158	**LOSS ARISING OUT OF CHANGES IN OPERATIONS**			
159	ACQUISITION	—		
160	CHANGE IN CONTROL	—		
161	DOWNSIZING OR REDUCTION IN FORCE	—		
162	% OF WORKFORCE	—		
163	WITHIN X DAYS	—		

	Comparison Query		Comment	Policy Reference
164	FINANCIAL IMPAIRMENT	—		
165	*BANKRUPTCY*	—		
166	*INSOLVENCY*	—		
167	*LIQUIDATION*	—		
168	*RECEIVERSHIP*	—		
169	FINANCIAL INABILITY TO PAY	—		
170	MERGER	—		
171	PLANT OR FACILITY CLOSING	—		
172	REORGANIZATION	—		
173	TEMPORARY SHUTDOWN	—		
174	**MATTERS DEEMED UNINSURABLE**	●		Policy III.H., page 4
175	**NON-MONETARY RELIEF**			
176	DECLATORY RELIEF	—		
177	DISGORGEMENT	—		
178	INJUNCTIVE RELIEF	—		
179	JOB REINSTATEMENT	●	Defense cost exception	Endorsement 7.C., page 2
180	NON-MONETARY DAMAGES/RELIEF	●	Defense cost exception	Endorsement 7.E., page 2
181	OTHER EQUITABLE REMEDIES	—		
182	**OBLIGATION TO PROVIDE BENEFITS**			
183	COBRA	●		Endorsement 8.A., page 2
184	DISABILITY	●	Retaliation exception	Endorsement 7.A., page 2
185	ERISA	●		Policy IV.A.4., page 5
186	SOCIAL SECURITY	—		
187	OTHER RETIREMENT BENEFITS	—		
188	UNEMPLOYMENT	●	Retaliation exception	Endorsement 7.A., page 2
189	WORKERS' COMPENSATION	●	Retaliation exception	Endorsement 7.A., page 2
190	**PERSONAL INJURY OFFENSES**			
191	DEFAMATION	—		
192	EMOTIONAL DISTRESS/UPSET	—		
193	HUMILIATION	—		
194	LIBEL	—		
195	MENTAL ANGUISH	—		
196	PERSONAL INJURY	—		
197	SLANDER	—		
198	**PRIOR ACTS**			
199	PRIOR ACTS	—		
200	PRIOR KNOWLEDGE	—		
201	PRIOR/PENDING LITIGATION	●		Policy IV.A.2., page 5
202	**PROPERTY DAMAGE**			
203	INTANGIBLE PROPERTY	—		
204	LOSS OF USE	●		Endorsement 6.(b), page 2
205	TANGIBLE PROPERTY	●		Endorsement 6.(b), page 2
206	**RETALIATORY ACTIONS OF EMPLOYER**			
207	FOR FAILING TO PERFORM ACTS AGAINST PUBLIC POLICY	—		
208	FOR FILING A COMPLAINT OR BENEFIT CLAIM	—		
209	**STRIKES/LOCKOUTS**	●		Endorsement 8.B., page 2
210	**VIOLATION OF LAWS**			
211	ANY LAW	—		
212	FMLA	—		
213	OSHA	●		Endorsement 8.A., page 2
214	POLLUTION LAWS	●		Policy IV.A.6., page 5
215	RICO	—		
216	SEC	—		
217	WARN	●		Endorsment 8.A., page 2

15 CONDITIONS

218	**ARBITRATION**			
219	MANDATORY	—		
220	BINDING	—		
221	CHOICE OF LAW PROVISION	—		
222	SITUS	—		
223	**TERRITORY**			
224	LIMITED	—		
225	WORLDWIDE	●		Policy V.G., page 8
226	**NEWLY FORMED/ACQUIRED ENTITIES**			
227	AUTOMATIC COVERAGE (X DAYS)	●	No time limit	Policy V.E.1., page 7
228	NOTIFY INSURER WITHIN X DAYS	○	As soon as practicable	Policy V.E.1., page 7

STEADFAST INSURANCE COMPANY U-DO-457-A (CW) [4/97]

Policy Comparison Worksheet

Swett & Crawford
(insured may choose CNA Reinsurance Co., Limited or Lloyds of London)

Policy Form No.: EPLX-987
Edition Date: 7/1/98

Risks Considered: No country clubs/public entities
Limits Available: $25,000,000
Minimum Retention: $5,350/$5,000

Contact: Rachel McKinney
Underwriting Manager
Swett & Crawford
515 S. Figueroa Street, Suite 600
Los Angeles, CA 90071
213/439-3415
213/439-3454 (fax)
Sherrie Beckham, Lead Underwriter
213/439-3416

KEY TO SYMBOLS
● = Specifically contains queried provision of feature
○ = Unable to determine
— = Silent

#	Comparison Query		Comment	Policy Reference
	1 APPLICATION			
1	ATTACHES TO AND FORMS A PART OF THE POLICY	●		VIII.G., page 12
2	CONTAINS WARRANTY STATEMENTS	●		
3	CONTAINS SEVERABILITY PROVISIONS	●	Applies to top management only	II.K., page 5
	2 POLICY TYPE			
4	UNITARY STAND ALONE POLICY	●		
	ENDORSEMENT OR PART OF	—		
5	DIRECTORS AND OFFICERS POLICY	—		
6	PACKAGE POLICY	—		
7	UMBRELLA POLICY	—		
8	ERRORS AND OMISSIONS POLICY	—		
9	OTHER	—		
10	CLAIMS-MADE	●		
11	OCCURRENCE			
	3 WHO IS INSURED			
12	BUSINESS ENTITY	●		II.H., page 4
13	AUTOMATIC COVERAGE FOR SUBSIDIARIES	●		II.H., page 4
14	DIRECTORS & OFFICERS	●		II.H., page 4
15	EMPLOYEES	●		II.F., page 4
16	PART-TIME	●		II.F., page 4
17	SEASONAL	●		II.F., page 4
18	TEMPORARY	●		II.F., page 4
19	SUPERVISORS & MANAGERS	●		II.F., page 4
20	FORMER EMPLOYEES	●		II.H., page 4
21	VOLUNTEERS	●		II.F., page 4
22	INDEPENDENT CONTRACTORS	●	If they claim to be employees	II.F., page 4
23	EXCLUDED			
24	SILENT			
25	SHAREHOLDERS	●		II.H., page 4
	4 LIMIT OF LIABILITY			
26	AGGREGATE	●		V.B., page 8
27	INCLUDES PUNITIVE DAMAGES WHERE NOT UNINSURABLE	●		II.J., page 4
28	DEFENSE COSTS INCLUDED WITHIN LIMIT OF LIABILITY	●		I.B., page 1
29	DEFENSE COSTS PAID IN ADDITION TO LIMIT OF LIABILITY			
	5 DEDUCTIBLE			
30	APPLIES TO EACH INDIVIDUAL CLAIM	●		VI., page 9
31	APPLIES TO EACH OCCURRENCE OR WRONGFUL PRACTICE			
32	INCLUDES ALL CLAIMS FROM ONE ACT	●		VI., page 9
33	SUBJECT TO ANNUAL AGGREGATE			
34	CO-PAYMENT APPLIES			
35	LIMIT OF LIABILITY NOT REDUCED	●		VI., page 9
36	INCLUDES DEFENSE COSTS	●		VI., page 9
37	REDUCED UNDER SPECIFIED CIRCUMSTANCES (SEE POLICY)			

#	Comparison Query	Comment		Policy Reference
	6 WHAT IS A CLAIM			
38	ORAL COMPLAINT TO INSURED	●		II.A., page 3
39	WRITTEN COMPLAINT TO INSURED	●		II.A., page 3
40	COMPLAINT MUST CONTAIN A DEMAND FOR DAMAGES	—		
41	COMPLAINT FILED WITH EEOC	—		
42	OR SIMILAR STATE AUTHORITY	—		
43	AGENCY MUST HAVE POWER TO ADJUDICATE	—		
44	ADMINISTRATIVE PROCEEDING	●		II.A., page 3
45	ARBITRATION PROCEEDING	●		II.A., page 3
46	ANY INCIDENT REPORTED TO INSURER	●		VIII.B., page 10
47	SUIT	●		II.A., page 3
48	CLAIM DOES NOT INCLUDE ARBITRATION SUBJECT TO	●		II.A., page 3
49	COLLECTIVE BARGAINING AGREEMENT	●		II.A., page 3
50	EMPLOYEE POLICY OR MANUAL	—		
51	CLAIM NOT DEFINED	●		
	7 CLAIM REPORTING PROVISIONS TO INSURER			
52	IMMEDIATELY	—		
53	AS SOON AS POSSIBLE	—		
54	AS SOON AS PRACTICABLE	—		
55	WITHIN POLICY PERIOD	—		
56	WITHIN X DAYS OF EXPIRATION	—		
57	WITHIN X DAYS	10	10 days of notice to top management	VIII.A.1., page 9
	8 EXTENDED REPORTING FEATURES			
58	ELECTION PERIOD (DAYS)	15		IV.C., page 8
59	ADDITIONAL PREMIUM (% OF ANNUAL PREMIUM)	100/150/175		IV.C., page 8
60	ADDITIONAL REPORTING PERIOD (MONTHS)	12/24/36		IV.C., page 8
61	NO REINSTATEMENT OF LIMITS	—		
	9 POTENTIAL CLAIM REPORTING PROVISIONS			
62	NONE (SEE ALSO "CLAIM" ABOVE)	—		
63	INCIDENTS LIKELY TO RESULT IN A CLAIM	●		VIII.B., page 10
	10 DEFENSE PROVISIONS			
64	AFFIRMATIVE DUTY TO DEFEND	●		I.B., page 1
65	NO AFFIRMATIVE DUTY TO DEFEND	—		
66	AFFIRMATIVE ADVANCEMENT PROVISIONS	—		
67	INSURED MUST RETURN ADVANCED AMOUNTS IF NOT COVERED	—		
68	INSURED/INSURER CHOOSES COUNSEL	●	Insurer chooses	I.B., page 1
69	INSURED/INSURER APPROVES COUNSEL	—		
70	INSURED/INSURER CONSULTED IN COUNSEL SELECTION	●	Insured consulted by underwriters	I.B., page 1
	11 SETTLEMENT PROVISIONS			
71	HAMMER CLAUSE	●		I.C., page 2
72	CONSULTATION PROVISION	●		I.C., page 2
73	CONSENT PROVISION	●		
	12 ALLOCATION OF LOSS PROVISIONS			
74	STIPULATED PROVISIONS	—		
	13 COVERAGES			
75	DISCRIMINATION	●		II.E., page 3
76	SPECIFIC ENUMERATED ACTIVITIES	●		II.E., page 3
77	PLUS BROAD OMNIBUS WORDING	●		II.E., page 3
78	SPECIFIC ENUMERATED CLASSES	●		II.E., page 3
79	PLUS BROAD OMNIBUS WORDING	●		II.E., page 3
80	AGAINST THIRD PARTIES	●		II.P., page 5
81	DISCRIMINATION NOT DEFINED	—		
82	SEXUAL HARASSMENT	●		II.G., page 4
83	HOSTILE ENVIRONMENT	●		II.G., page 4
84	QUID-PRO-QUO	●		II.G., page 4
85	SEXUAL HARASSMENT NOT DEFINED	—		
86	WRONGFUL TERMINATION	●		II.Q.(1)., page 6
87	BREACH OF IMPLIED CONTRACT	●		II.Q.(4)., page 6
88	BREACH OF EXPRESS CONTRACT	●	Defense costs only	II.J., page 5
89	VIOLATION OF PUBLIC POLICY	●		II.Q.(5)., page 5
90	VIOLATION OF GOOD FAITH & FAIR DEALING	●		II.Q.(4)., page 6
91	OBLIGATIONS TO MAKE PAYMENTS	●	If not part of a written employment contract	II.J., page 5
92	CONSTRUCTIVE DISCHARGE	●		II.Q.(1)., page 6
93	WRONGFUL TERMINATION NOT DEFINED	—		
94	OTHER EMPLOYMENT VIOLATIONS/OFFENSES	●		II.I., page 4 and II.Q., page 6
95	WRONGFUL HIRING	●		II.I., page 4
96	WRONGFUL PROMOTION/DEMOTION	●		II.Q., page 6
97	WRONGFUL EVALUATION/DISCIPLINE	●		II.Q., page 6

SWETT & CRAWFORD (CNA REINSURANCE CO., LIMITED OR LLOYD'S OF LONDON) EPLX-987 [7/1/98]

	Comparison Query	Comment		Policy Reference
98	FAMILY AND MEDICAL LEAVE ACT	●		II.Q., page 6
99	DEFAMATION	●		II.Q., page 6
100	MISREPRESENTATION	●		II.Q., page 6
101	RETALIATION	●		II.Q., page 6
102	MENTAL ANGUISH	●		II.Q., page 6
103	INVASION OF PRIVACY	●		II.Q., page 6
104	HUMILIATION	●		II.Q., page 6
105	EMOTIONAL DISTRESS	●		II.Q., page 6
106	OTHER PERSONAL INJURY OFFENSES	●		II.Q., page 6
107	POLICY SILENT	—		
	14 EXCLUSIONS			
108	**ADA ACCOMMODATION EXPENSES**	●		II.J., page 5
109	**ASSAULT & BATTERY**	—		
110	**BACK PAY**	—		
111	**BODILY INJURY**	—		
112	BODILY INJURY	—		
113	DEATH	—		
114	DISEASE	—		
115	SICKNESS	—		
116	**BREACH OF EMPLOYMENT CONTRACT**	●		II.J., page 4
117	EXPRESS CONTRACT	●	Defense provided	II.J., page 4
118	WRITTEN CONTRACT	●	Defense provided	II.J., page 4
119	ORAL CONTRACT	—		
120	IMPLIED CONTRACT	—		
121	**CLASS ACTION LAWSUITS**	—		
122	**CONSEQUENTIAL LOSS**	—		
123	APPLIES TO BODILY INJURY	—		
124	APPLIES TO INSURED EVENT	—		
125	BROTHER/SISTER	—		
126	CHILD	—		
127	DOMESTIC PARTNER	—		
128	PARENT	—		
129	SPOUSE	—		
130	**COST OF ARBITRATION HEARINGS SUBJECT TO**	●		II.A., page 3
131	EMPLOYMENT HANDBOOK	—		
132	LABOR GRIEVANCE	●		II.A., page 3
133	OTHER EMPLOYMENT POLICY OR PROCEDURE	—		
134	**COVERAGE ELSEWHERE**	●		VIII.D., page 11
135	OTHER AVAILABLE INSURANCE	●		VIII.D., page 11
136	OTHER INDEMNIFICATION	—		
137	SHARING PROVISION	—		
138	**FAILURE TO EXERCISE CARE WHEN TERMINATING**	—		
139	**FINES/PENALTIES**	●		II.J., page 4
140	CIVIL	●		II.J., page 4
141	CRIMINAL	●		II.J., page 4
142	EXEMPLARY DAMAGES	—		
143	PUNITIVE DAMAGES	—		
144	MULTIPLIED DAMAGES	—		
145	**FRONT PAY**	—		
146	EXCLUSION APPLIES ONLY IF EMPLOYER HAD OPPORTUNITY TO REINSTATE EMPLOYEE BUT DID NOT DO SO	—		
147	**INTENTIONAL ACTS**	—		
148	CRIMINAL ACTS	●		I.D., page 2
149	CRIMINAL PROCEEDING	●		I.D., page 2
150	DISHONEST PURPOSE	—		
151	FRAUDULENT ACTS	—		
152	FRAUDULENT CLAIMS	—		
153	INTENTIONAL VIOLATIONS OF LAW	—		
154	WILLFUL FAILURE TO COMPLY WITH LAW	—		
155	MALICIOUS PURPOSE	—		
156	**LIABILITY OF OTHERS**	●		III.B., page 6
157	**LIQUIDATED DAMAGES**	—		
158	**LOSS ARISING OUT OF CHANGES IN OPERATIONS**			
159	ACQUISITION	—		
160	CHANGE IN CONTROL			
161	DOWNSIZING OR REDUCTION IN FORCE			
162	% OF WORKFORCE			
163	WITHIN X DAYS			

#	Comparison Query	Comment	Policy Reference
164	**FINANCIAL IMPAIRMENT**	—	
165	*BANKRUPTCY*	—	
166	*INSOLVENCY*	—	
167	*LIQUIDATION*	—	
168	*RECEIVERSHIP*	—	
169	FINANCIAL INABILITY TO PAY	—	
170	MERGER	—	
171	PLANT OR FACILITY CLOSING	—	
172	REORGANIZATION	—	
173	TEMPORARY SHUTDOWN	—	
174	**MATTERS DEEMED UNINSURABLE**	—	
175	**NON-MONETARY RELIEF**	—	
176	DECLATORY RELIEF	—	
177	DISGORGEMENT	—	
178	INJUNCTIVE RELIEF	—	
179	JOB REINSTATEMENT	—	
180	NON-MONETARY DAMAGES/RELIEF	—	
181	OTHER EQUITABLE REMEDIES	—	
182	**OBLIGATION TO PROVIDE BENEFITS**	—	
183	COBRA	—	
184	DISABILITY	● Retaliation/discrimination exception	III.A., page 6
185	ERISA	● Retaliation/discrimination exception	III.C., page 6
186	SOCIAL SECURITY	● Included if a part of damages	II.J., page 5
187	OTHER RETIREMENT BENEFITS	● Included if a part of damages	II.J., page 5
188	UNEMPLOYMENT	● Retaliation/discrimination exception	II.J., page 6 & III.A, page 6
189	WORKERS' COMPENSATION	● Retaliation/discrimination exception	III.A., page 6
190	**PERSONAL INJURY OFFENSES**	—	
191	DEFAMATION	—	
192	EMOTIONAL DISTRESS/UPSET	—	
193	HUMILIATION	—	
194	LIBEL	—	
195	MENTAL ANGUISH	—	
196	PERSONAL INJURY	—	
197	SLANDER	—	
198	**PRIOR ACTS**	—	
199	PRIOR ACTS	—	
200	PRIOR KNOWLEDGE	● By endorsement/applies to top management only	
201	PRIOR/PENDING LITIGATION	● By endorsement	
202	**PROPERTY DAMAGE**	—	
203	INTANGIBLE PROPERTY	—	
204	LOSS OF USE	—	
205	TANGIBLE PROPERTY	—	
206	**RETALIATORY ACTIONS OF EMPLOYER**	—	
207	FOR FAILING TO PERFORM ACTS AGAINST PUBLIC POLICY	—	
208	FOR FILING A COMPLAINT OR BENEFIT CLAIM	—	
209	**STRIKES/LOCKOUTS**	● Retaliation/discrimination exception	III.D., page 7
210	**VIOLATION OF LAWS**	—	
211	ANY LAW	—	
212	FMLA	—	II.Q.5., page 7
213	OSHA	—	
214	POLLUTION LAWS	—	
215	RICO	—	
216	SEC	—	
217	WARN	● Exception applies	III.E., page 7
	15 CONDITIONS		
218	**ARBITRATION**	—	
219	MANDATORY	—	
220	BINDING	—	
221	CHOICE OF LAW PROVISION	—	
222	SITUS	—	
223	**TERRITORY**	●	VIII.K., page 12
224	LIMITED	—	
225	WORLDWIDE	● Worldwide with suits brought anywhere	VIII.K., page 12
226	**NEWLY FORMED/ACQUIRED ENTITIES**	●	I.E., page 2
227	AUTOMATIC COVERAGE (X DAYS)	60 Less than 25% increase in emp.	I.E., page 2
228	NOTIFY INSURER WITHIN X DAYS	60	I.E., page 2

SWETT & CRAWFORD (CNA REINSURANCE CO., LIMITED OR LLOYD'S OF LONDON) EPLX-987 [7/1/98]

Policy Comparison Worksheet

Travelers Property Casualty
(G. J. Sullivan Company)

Policy Form No.: DHN 1001
Edition Date: 4/98

Risks Considered: Private healthcare
Limits Available: $25,000,000
Minimum Retention: $5,000

Contact: Paul Bubnis
135 N. Los Robles, #290
Pasadena, CA 91101
626/584-7461
626/564-9911 (fax)
bubnispees.gjs.com

KEY TO SYMBOLS
● = Specifically contains queried provision of feature
○ = Unable to determine
— = Silent

#	Comparison Query		Comment	Policy Reference
	1 APPLICATION			
1	ATTACHES TO AND FORMS A PART OF THE POLICY	●		VIII.H., pages 8–9
2	CONTAINS WARRANTY STATEMENTS	—		
3	CONTAINS SEVERABILITY PROVISIONS	—		
	2 POLICY TYPE			
4	UNITARY STAND ALONE POLICY	—		
	ENDORSEMENT OR PART OF	—		
5	DIRECTORS AND OFFICERS POLICY	●		
6	PACKAGE POLICY	—		
7	UMBRELLA POLICY	—		
8	ERRORS AND OMISSIONS POLICY	—		
9	OTHER	—		
10	CLAIMS-MADE	●		
11	OCCURRENCE	—		
	3 WHO IS INSURED			
12	BUSINESS ENTITY	●		II.I. & J., page 2
13	AUTOMATIC COVERAGE FOR SUBSIDIARIES	●		II.J., page 2
14	DIRECTORS & OFFICERS	●		II.K.1., page 2
15	EMPLOYEES	●		II.K.1., page 2
16	PART-TIME	●		II.F., page 2
17	SEASONAL	●		II.F., page 2
18	TEMPORARY	●		II.F., page 2
19	SUPERVISORS & MANAGERS	—		
20	FORMER EMPLOYEES	●		II.F., page 2
21	VOLUNTEERS	●		II.F., page 2
22	INDEPENDENT CONTRACTORS	—		
23	EXCLUDED	●		II.F., page 2
24	SILENT	—		
25	SHAREHOLDERS	—		
	4 LIMIT OF LIABILITY			
26	AGGREGATE	●		VII.A., page 5
27	INCLUDES PUNITIVE DAMAGES WHERE NOT UNINSURABLE	—	Coverage available by endorsement	
28	DEFENSE COSTS INCLUDED WITHIN LIMIT OF LIABILITY	●	See also VII.B., page 5	II.L.2., page 2
29	DEFENSE COSTS PAID IN ADDITION TO LIMIT OF LIABILITY	—		
	5 DEDUCTIBLE			
30	APPLIES TO EACH INDIVIDUAL CLAIM	●		V., page 5
31	APPLIES TO EACH OCCURRENCE OR WRONGFUL PRACTICE	—		
32	INCLUDES ALL CLAIMS FROM ONE ACT	●		II.B., following 4., page 1
33	SUBJECT TO ANNUAL AGGREGATE	—		
34	CO-PAYMENT APPLIES	—		
35	LIMIT OF LIABILITY NOT REDUCED	—		
36	INCLUDES DEFENSE COSTS	●		V.A., page 5
37	REDUCED UNDER SPECIFIED CIRCUMSTANCES (SEE POLICY)	—		

#	Comparison Query	Comment	Policy Reference
6	**WHAT IS A CLAIM**		
38	ORAL COMPLAINT TO INSURED	—	
39	WRITTEN COMPLAINT TO INSURED	●	II.B.1., page 9
40	COMPLAINT MUST CONTAIN A DEMAND FOR DAMAGES	●	II.B.1., page 9
41	COMPLAINT FILED WITH EEOC	●	II.B.4., page 9
42	OR SIMILAR STATE AUTHORITY	●	II.B.4., page 9
43	AGENCY MUST HAVE POWER TO ADJUDICATE	—	
44	ADMINISTRATIVE PROCEEDING	●	II.B.4., page 9
45	ARBITRATION PROCEEDING	—	
46	ANY INCIDENT REPORTED TO INSURER		
47	SUIT	●	II.B.2., page 9
48	CLAIM DOES NOT INCLUDE ARBITRATION SUBJECT TO	—	
49	COLLECTIVE BARGAINING AGREEMENT	—	
50	EMPLOYEE POLICY OR MANUAL	—	
51	CLAIM NOT DEFINED	—	
7	**CLAIM REPORTING PROVISIONS TO INSURER**		
52	IMMEDIATELY	—	
53	AS SOON AS POSSIBLE	—	
54	AS SOON AS PRACTICABLE	●	XIII.A.1., page 8
55	WITHIN POLICY PERIOD	—	
56	WITHIN X DAYS OF EXPIRATION	60	XIII.A.1., page 8
57	WITHIN X DAYS	—	
8	**EXTENDED REPORTING FEATURES**		
58	ELECTION PERIOD (DAYS)	30	XII.B.4., page 8
59	ADDITIONAL PREMIUM (% OF ANNUAL PREMIUM)	○	Per schedule in policy	XII.B., page 7
60	ADDITIONAL REPORTING PERIOD (MONTHS)	○	Per schedule in policy	XII.B., page 7
61	NO REINSTATEMENT OF LIMITS	●	XII.B.1., page 7
9	**POTENTIAL CLAIM REPORTING PROVISIONS**		
62	NONE (SEE ALSO "CLAIM" ABOVE)	—	
63	INCIDENTS LIKELY TO RESULT IN A CLAIM	●	IX., page 6
10	**DEFENSE PROVISIONS**		
64	AFFIRMATIVE DUTY TO DEFEND	—	
65	NO AFFIRMATIVE DUTY TO DEFEND	●	VIII.A., pages 5–6
66	AFFIRMATIVE ADVANCEMENT PROVISIONS	●	VIII.C., page 6
67	INSURED MUST RETURN ADVANCED AMOUNTS IF NOT COVERED	●	VIII.C., page 6
68	INSURED/INSURER CHOOSES COUNSEL	—	
69	INSURED/INSURER APPROVES COUNSEL	—	
70	INSURED/INSURER CONSULTED IN COUNSEL SELECTION	—	
11	**SETTLEMENT PROVISIONS**		
71	HAMMER CLAUSE	●	VIII.B., page 6
72	CONSULTATION PROVISION	●	VIII.A., pages 5–6
73	CONSENT PROVISION	●	Insured must consent	VIII.B., page 6
12	**ALLOCATION OF LOSS PROVISIONS**		
74	STIPULATED PROVISIONS	—	
13	**COVERAGES**		
75	DISCRIMINATION	●	As wrongful employment practice	I.A. & I.B., page 1
76	SPECIFIC ENUMERATED ACTIVITIES	●	II.D., pages 1–2
77	*PLUS BROAD OMNIBUS WORDING*	●	II.D., pages 1–2
78	SPECIFIC ENUMERATED CLASSES	●	II.D., pages 1–2
79	*PLUS BROAD OMNIBUS WORDING*	●	II.D., pages 1–2
80	AGAINST THIRD PARTIES	—	
81	DISCRIMINATION NOT DEFINED	—	
82	SEXUAL HARASSMENT	●	As wrongful employment practice	I.A. & I.B., page 1
83	HOSTILE ENVIRONMENT	●	II.U.3., page 3
84	QUID-PRO-QUO	●	II.U.1., page 3
85	SEXUAL HARASSMENT NOT DEFINED	—	
86	WRONGFUL TERMINATION	●	As wrongful employment practice	I.A. & I.B., page 1
87	BREACH OF IMPLIED CONTRACT	●	See also II.Z., page 3	II.Y.(6)., page 3
88	BREACH OF EXPRESS CONTRACT	—	
89	VIOLATION OF PUBLIC POLICY	—	
90	VIOLATION OF GOOD FAITH & FAIR DEALING		
91	OBLIGATIONS TO MAKE PAYMENTS	—	
92	CONSTRUCTIVE DISCHARGE	●	II.Z., page 3
93	WRONGFUL TERMINATION NOT DEFINED	—	
94	OTHER EMPLOYMENT VIOLATIONS/OFFENSES	●	II.Y., page 3
95	WRONGFUL HIRING	—	
96	WRONGFUL PROMOTION/DEMOTION	●	II.Y.(14)., page 3
97	WRONGFUL EVALUATION/DISCIPLINE	●	See also II.Y.(12)., page 3	II.Y.(7). & (8)., page 3

TRAVELERS PROPERTY CASUALTY DHN 1001 [4/98]

#	Comparison Query	Comment	Policy Reference
98	FAMILY AND MEDICAL LEAVE ACT	—	
99	DEFAMATION	●	II.Y.(17)., page 3
100	MISREPRESENTATION	●	II.Y.(16)., page 3
101	RETALIATION	●	As wrongful employment practice	II.Y.(4)., page 3
102	MENTAL ANGUISH	—	
103	INVASION OF PRIVACY	●	YY.Y.(15)., page 3
104	HUMILIATION	—	
105	EMOTIONAL DISTRESS	●	II.Y.(18)., page 3
106	OTHER PERSONAL INJURY OFFENSES	—	
107	POLICY SILENT	—	

14 EXCLUSIONS

#	Comparison Query	Comment	Policy Reference
108	**ADA ACCOMMODATION EXPENSES**	●	III.B.4., pages 4–5
109	**ASSAULT & BATTERY**	—	
110	**BACK PAY**	—	
111	**BODILY INJURY**	●	III.A.1., page 3
112	BODILY INJURY	●	III.A.1., page 3
113	DEATH	●	III.A.1., page 3
114	DISEASE	●	III.A.1., page 3
115	SICKNESS	●	III.A.1., page 3
116	**BREACH OF EMPLOYMENT CONTRACT**	—	
117	EXPRESS CONTRACT	—	
118	*WRITTEN CONTRACT*	—	
119	*ORAL CONTRACT*	—	
120	IMPLIED CONTRACT	—	
121	**CLASS ACTION LAWSUITS**	—	
122	**CONSEQUENTIAL LOSS**	—	
123	APPLIES TO BODILY INJURY	—	
124	APPLIES TO INSURED EVENT	—	
125	BROTHER/SISTER	—	
126	CHILD	—	
127	DOMESTIC PARTNER	—	
128	PARENT	—	
129	SPOUSE	—	
130	**COST OF ARBITRATION HEARINGS SUBJECT TO**	—	
131	EMPLOYMENT HANDBOOK	—	
132	LABOR GRIEVANCE	—	
133	OTHER EMPLOYMENT POLICY OR PROCEDURE	—	
134	**COVERAGE ELSEWHERE**	●	III.A.6., page 4
135	OTHER AVAILABLE INSURANCE	●	See also XIII.C., page 8	III.A.6., page 4
136	OTHER INDEMNIFICATION	●	XIII.C., page 8
137	SHARING PROVISION	—	
138	**FAILURE TO EXERCISE CARE WHEN TERMINATING**	—	
139	**FINES/PENALTIES**	●	Exceptions apply	II.L.1., following II.L.3., page 2
140	CIVIL	●	Exceptions apply	II.L.1., following II.L.3., page 2
141	CRIMINAL	●	Exceptions apply	II.L.1., following II.L.3., page 2
142	EXEMPLARY DAMAGES	●	Exceptions apply	II.L.1., following II.L.3., page 2
143	PUNITIVE DAMAGES	●	Exceptions apply	II.L.1., following II.L.3., page 2
144	MULTIPLIED DAMAGES	●	Exceptions apply	II.L.1., following II.L.3., page 2
145	**FRONT PAY**	●	III.B.6., page 5
146	EXCLUSION APPLIES ONLY IF EMPLOYER HAD OPPORTUNITY TO REINSTATE EMPLOYEE BUT DID NOT DO SO	●	III.B.6., page 5
147	**INTENTIONAL ACTS**	●	III.B.2., page 4
148	CRIMINAL ACTS	—	
149	CRIMINAL PROCEEDING	—	
150	DISHONEST PURPOSE	●	III.B.2., page 4
151	FRAUDULENT ACTS	●	III.B.2., page 4
152	FRAUDULENT CLAIMS	—	
153	INTENTIONAL VIOLATIONS OF LAW	●	III.B.2., page 4
154	WILLFUL FAILURE TO COMPLY WITH LAW	—	
155	MALICIOUS PURPOSE	—	
156	**LIABILITY OF OTHERS**	●	III.A.10., page 4
157	**LIQUIDATED DAMAGES**	●	Exceptions apply	II.L.1. following II.L.3., page 2
158	**LOSS ARISING OUT OF CHANGES IN OPERATIONS**	—	
159	ACQUISITION	—	
160	CHANGE IN CONTROL	—	
161	DOWNSIZING OR REDUCTION IN FORCE	—	
162	*% OF WORKFORCE*	—	
163	*WITHIN X DAYS*	—	

#	Comparison Query	Comment		Policy Reference
164	FINANCIAL IMPAIRMENT	—		
165	BANKRUPTCY	—		
166	INSOLVENCY	—		
167	LIQUIDATION	—		
168	RECEIVERSHIP	—		
169	FINANCIAL INABILITY TO PAY	—		
170	MERGER	—		
171	PLANT OR FACILITY CLOSING	—		
172	REORGANIZATION	—		
173	TEMPORARY SHUTDOWN	—		
174	**MATTERS DEEMED UNINSURABLE**	●	Uninsurable relief	II.L.1. following II.L.3., page 2
175	**NON-MONETARY RELIEF**	—		
176	DECLATORY RELIEF	—		
177	DISGORGEMENT	—		
178	INJUNCTIVE RELIEF	●		III.B.4., pages 4–5
179	JOB REINSTATEMENT	—		
180	NON-MONETARY DAMAGES/RELIEF	—		
181	OTHER EQUITABLE REMEDIES	●		III.B.4., pages 4–5
182	**OBLIGATION TO PROVIDE BENEFITS**	—		
183	COBRA	●	Retaliation exception	III.B.3., page 4
184	DISABILITY	●	Retaliation exception	III.B.3., page 4
185	ERISA	●		III.A.4., page 4
186	SOCIAL SECURITY	●	Retaliation exception	III.B.3., page 4
187	OTHER RETIREMENT BENEFITS	—		
188	UNEMPLOYMENT	●	Retaliation exception	III.B.3., page 4
189	WORKERS' COMPENSATION	●	Retaliation exception	III.B.3., page 4
190	**PERSONAL INJURY OFFENSES**	—		
191	DEFAMATION	—		
192	EMOTIONAL DISTRESS/UPSET	—		
193	HUMILIATION	—		
194	LIBEL	—		
195	MENTAL ANGUISH	—		
196	PERSONAL INJURY	—		
197	SLANDER	—		
198	**PRIOR ACTS**	●		III.A.3., page 4
199	PRIOR ACTS	●	Coverage available by endorsement	III.A.3., page 4
200	PRIOR KNOWLEDGE	○		III.A.3., page 4
201	PRIOR/PENDING LITIGATION	○		III.A.3., page 4
202	**PROPERTY DAMAGE**	●		III.A.1., page 3
203	INTANGIBLE PROPERTY	—		
204	LOSS OF USE	●		III.A.1., page 3
205	TANGIBLE PROPERTY	●		III.A.1., page 3
206	**RETALIATORY ACTIONS OF EMPLOYER**	—		
207	FOR FAILING TO PERFORM ACTS AGAINST PUBLIC POLICY	—		
208	FOR FILING A COMPLAINT OR BENEFIT CLAIM	—		
209	**STRIKES/LOCKOUTS**	—		
210	**VIOLATION OF LAWS**	—		
211	ANY LAW	—		
212	FMLA	—		
213	OSHA	●	Retaliation exception	III.B.3., page 4
214	POLLUTION LAWS	●		III.A.2., page 4
215	RICO	—		
216	SEC	—		
217	WARN	●	Retaliation exception	III.B.3., page 4

15 CONDITIONS

#	Comparison Query		Comment	Policy Reference
218	**ARBITRATION**	—		
219	MANDATORY	—		
220	BINDING	—		
221	CHOICE OF LAW PROVISION	—		
222	SITUS	—		
223	**TERRITORY**	●		XIV., page 9
224	LIMITED	—		
225	WORLDWIDE	●		XIV., page 9
226	**NEWLY FORMED/ACQUIRED ENTITIES**	●		XI.B.3., page 7
227	AUTOMATIC COVERAGE (X DAYS)	●	No time limit– < 25% company assets involved	XI.B.3., page 7
228	NOTIFY INSURER WITHIN X DAYS	90	> 25% company assets involved	XI.B.3., page 7

TRAVELERS PROPERTY CASUALTY DHN 1001 [4/98]

Policy Comparison Worksheet

United Educators Risk Retention Group, Inc.

Policy Form No.: ELL
Edition Date: February 1997

Risks Considered: Educational institutions
Limits Available: $25,000,000
Minimum Retention: $10,000 independent schools
$5,000 colleges

Contact: Bruce P. Bernstein, CPCU
United Educators Risk Retention Group, Inc.
2 Wisconsin Circle, Suite 1040
Chevy Chase, MD 20895
301/215-6421
301/907-4908 (fax)
bbernstein@ue.org

KEY TO SYMBOLS
● = Specifically contains queried provision of feature
○ = Unable to determine
— = Silent

#	Comparison Query		Comment	Policy Reference
	1 APPLICATION			
1	ATTACHES TO AND FORMS A PART OF THE POLICY	●		12., page 7
2	CONTAINS WARRANTY STATEMENTS	●		12., page 7
3	CONTAINS SEVERABILITY PROVISIONS	—		
	2 POLICY TYPE			
4	UNITARY STAND ALONE POLICY	—		
	ENDORSEMENT OR PART OF	—		
5	DIRECTORS AND OFFICERS POLICY	—		
6	PACKAGE POLICY	—		
7	UMBRELLA POLICY	—		
8	ERRORS AND OMISSIONS POLICY	—		
9	OTHER	●	Educators Liability	
10	CLAIMS-MADE	●		
11	OCCURRENCE	—		
	3 WHO IS INSURED			
12	BUSINESS ENTITY	●		2. Included Entity, page 2
13	AUTOMATIC COVERAGE FOR SUBSIDIARIES	○		Included Entity, b., page 2
14	DIRECTORS & OFFICERS	●		2. Individual Insureds, a., page 2
15	EMPLOYEES	●		2. Individual Insureds, b., page 2
16	PART-TIME	—		
17	SEASONAL	—		
18	TEMPORARY	—		
19	SUPERVISORS & MANAGERS	—		
20	FORMER EMPLOYEES	—		
21	VOLUNTEERS	●		2. Individual Insureds, b., page 2
22	INDEPENDENT CONTRACTORS	—		
23	EXCLUDED	—		
24	SILENT	●		
25	SHAREHOLDERS	—		
	4 LIMIT OF LIABILITY			
26	AGGREGATE	●		3.h., page 4
27	INCLUDES PUNITIVE DAMAGES WHERE NOT UNINSURABLE	●		2. Damages C.(2)., page 2
28	DEFENSE COSTS INCLUDED WITHIN LIMIT OF LIABILITY	●		2. Loss, page 3
29	DEFENSE COSTS PAID IN ADDITION TO LIMIT OF LIABILITY	—		
	5 DEDUCTIBLE			
30	APPLIES TO EACH INDIVIDUAL CLAIM	●		2. Self-insured Retention, page 3
31	APPLIES TO EACH OCCURRENCE OR WRONGFUL PRACTICE	—		
32	INCLUDES ALL CLAIMS FROM ONE ACT	—		
33	SUBJECT TO ANNUAL AGGREGATE	—		
34	CO-PAYMENT APPLIES	—		
35	LIMIT OF LIABILITY NOT REDUCED	—		
36	INCLUDES DEFENSE COSTS	●		
37	REDUCED UNDER SPECIFIED CIRCUMSTANCES (SEE POLICY)	—		

#	Comparison Query	Comment	Policy Reference
	6 WHAT IS A CLAIM		
38	ORAL COMPLAINT TO INSURED	—	
39	WRITTEN COMPLAINT TO INSURED	●	2. Claim, page 1
40	COMPLAINT MUST CONTAIN A DEMAND FOR DAMAGES	—	
41	COMPLAINT FILED WITH EEOC	—	
42	OR SIMILAR STATE AUTHORITY	—	
43	AGENCY MUST HAVE POWER TO ADJUDICATE	—	
44	ADMINISTRATIVE PROCEEDING	—	
45	ARBITRATION PROCEEDING	—	
46	ANY INCIDENT REPORTED TO INSURER	—	
47	SUIT	—	
48	CLAIM DOES NOT INCLUDE ARBITRATION SUBJECT TO	—	
49	COLLECTIVE BARGAINING AGREEMENT	—	
50	EMPLOYEE POLICY OR MANUAL	—	
51	CLAIM NOT DEFINED	—	
	7 CLAIM REPORTING PROVISIONS TO INSURER		
52	IMMEDIATELY	—	
53	AS SOON AS POSSIBLE	—	
54	AS SOON AS PRACTICABLE	●	13., page 7
55	WITHIN POLICY PERIOD	—	
56	WITHIN X DAYS OF EXPIRATION	60	13., page 7
57	WITHIN X DAYS	—	
	8 EXTENDED REPORTING FEATURES		
58	ELECTION PERIOD (DAYS)	10	20.a., page 8
59	ADDITIONAL PREMIUM (% OF ANNUAL PREMIUM)	100	20., page 8
60	ADDITIONAL REPORTING PERIOD (MONTHS)	12	20., page 8
61	NO REINSTATEMENT OF LIMITS	●	20.b., page 8
	9 POTENTIAL CLAIM REPORTING PROVISIONS		
62	NONE (SEE ALSO "CLAIM" ABOVE)	—	
63	INCIDENTS LIKELY TO RESULT IN A CLAIM	●	14., page 7
	10 DEFENSE PROVISIONS		
64	AFFIRMATIVE DUTY TO DEFEND	●	Optional Defense Provision A	4., page 4
65	NO AFFIRMATIVE DUTY TO DEFEND	●	Defense Provision B	4., page 4
66	AFFIRMATIVE ADVANCEMENT PROVISIONS	—	
67	INSURED MUST RETURN ADVANCED AMOUNTS IF NOT COVERED	—	
68	INSURED/INSURER CHOOSES COUNSEL	○	Optional alternatives	4., page 4
69	INSURED/INSURER APPROVES COUNSEL	●	4., page 4
70	INSURED/INSURER CONSULTED IN COUNSEL SELECTION	●	4., page 4
	11 SETTLEMENT PROVISIONS		
71	HAMMER CLAUSE	—	
72	CONSULTATION PROVISION	—	
73	CONSENT PROVISION	●	2-way	7. & 8., page 5
	12 ALLOCATION OF LOSS PROVISIONS		
74	STIPULATED PROVISIONS	●	As respects liability of joint ventures	3.c., page 4
	13 COVERAGES		
75	DISCRIMINATION	●	2. Damages, page 1
76	SPECIFIC ENUMERATED ACTIVITIES	—	
77	PLUS BROAD OMNIBUS WORDING	—	
78	SPECIFIC ENUMERATED CLASSES	—	
79	PLUS BROAD OMNIBUS WORDING	—	
80	AGAINST THIRD PARTIES	—	
81	DISCRIMINATION NOT DEFINED	●	
82	SEXUAL HARASSMENT	—	Coverage available by endorsement	
83	HOSTILE ENVIRONMENT	—	
84	QUID-PRO-QUO	—	
85	SEXUAL HARASSMENT NOT DEFINED	—	
86	WRONGFUL TERMINATION	●	2. Damages, page 1
87	BREACH OF IMPLIED CONTRACT	○	2. Damages, page 1
88	BREACH OF EXPRESS CONTRACT	○	2. Damages, page 1
89	VIOLATION OF PUBLIC POLICY	—	
90	VIOLATION OF GOOD FAITH & FAIR DEALING	—	
91	OBLIGATIONS TO MAKE PAYMENTS	—	
92	CONSTRUCTIVE DISCHARGE	●	2. Damages, page 1
93	WRONGFUL TERMINATION NOT DEFINED	●	
94	**OTHER EMPLOYMENT VIOLATIONS/OFFENSES**		
95	WRONGFUL HIRING	●	2. Damages, page 1
96	WRONGFUL PROMOTION/DEMOTION	●	2. Damages, page 1
97	WRONGFUL EVALUATION/DISCIPLINE	●	2. Damages, page 1

UNITED EDUCATORS RISK RETENTION GROUP, INC. ELL (February 1997)

	Comparison Query	Comment	Policy Reference
98	FAMILY AND MEDICAL LEAVE ACT	—	
99	DEFAMATION	—	
100	MISREPRESENTATION	—	
101	RETALIATION	—	
102	MENTAL ANGUISH	—	
103	INVASION OF PRIVACY	●	2. Damages, page 1
104	HUMILIATION	●	2. Damages, page 1
105	EMOTIONAL DISTRESS	—	
106	OTHER PERSONAL INJURY OFFENSES	●	2. Damages, page 1
107	POLICY SILENT	—	
	14 EXCLUSIONS		
108	**ADA ACCOMMODATION EXPENSES**	—	
109	**ASSAULT & BATTERY**	●	See also 11.k., page 6	11.i., page 5
110	**BACK PAY**	—	
111	**BODILY INJURY**	●		11.i., page 5
112	BODILY INJURY	●		11.i., page 5
113	DEATH	●		11.i., page 5
114	DISEASE	●		11.i., page 5
115	SICKNESS	●		11.i., page 5
116	**BREACH OF EMPLOYMENT CONTRACT**		
117	EXPRESS CONTRACT	●		11.l., page 6
118	WRITTEN CONTRACT	●		11.l., page 6
119	ORAL CONTRACT	●		11.l., page 6
120	IMPLIED CONTRACT	●		11.l., page 6
121	**CLASS ACTION LAWSUITS**	—	
122	**CONSEQUENTIAL LOSS**		
123	APPLIES TO BODILY INJURY	—	
124	APPLIES TO INSURED EVENT	—	
125	BROTHER/SISTER	—	
126	CHILD	—	
127	DOMESTIC PARTNER	—	
128	PARENT	—	
129	SPOUSE	—	
130	**COST OF ARBITRATION HEARINGS SUBJECT TO**		
131	EMPLOYMENT HANDBOOK	—	
132	LABOR GRIEVANCE	—	
133	OTHER EMPLOYMENT POLICY OR PROCEDURE	—	
134	**COVERAGE ELSEWHERE**		
135	OTHER AVAILABLE INSURANCE	●		25., page 9
136	OTHER INDEMNIFICATION	—	
137	SHARING PROVISION	—	
138	**FAILURE TO EXERCISE CARE WHEN TERMINATING**	—	
139	**FINES/PENALTIES**	●	Fines	2.b. and c., pages 1 and 2
140	CIVIL	—	
141	CRIMINAL	—	
142	EXEMPLARY DAMAGES	—	
143	PUNITIVE DAMAGES	●	Unless insurable under law	2.c., page 2
144	MULTIPLIED DAMAGES	●	
145	**FRONT PAY**	—	
146	EXCLUSION APPLIES ONLY IF EMPLOYER HAD OPPORTUNITY TO REINSTATE EMPLOYEE BUT DID NOT DO SO	—	
147	**INTENTIONAL ACTS**		
148	CRIMINAL ACTS	—	
149	CRIMINAL PROCEEDING	—	
150	DISHONEST PURPOSE	—	
151	FRAUDULENT ACTS	—	
152	FRAUDULENT CLAIMS	—	
153	INTENTIONAL VIOLATIONS OF LAW	●		11.c., page 5
154	WILLFUL FAILURE TO COMPLY WITH LAW	—	
155	MALICIOUS PURPOSE	—	
156	**LIABILITY OF OTHERS**	—	
157	**LIQUIDATED DAMAGES**	—	
158	**LOSS ARISING OUT OF CHANGES IN OPERATIONS**		
159	ACQUISITION	—	
160	CHANGE IN CONTROL	—	
161	DOWNSIZING OR REDUCTION IN FORCE	—	
162	% OF WORKFORCE	—	
163	WITHIN X DAYS	—	

UNITED EDUCATORS RISK RETENTION GROUP, INC. ELL (February 1997)

	Comparison Query		Comment	Policy Reference
164	FINANCIAL IMPAIRMENT	—		
165	*BANKRUPTCY*	—		
166	*INSOLVENCY*	—		
167	*LIQUIDATION*	—		
168	*RECEIVERSHIP*	—		
169	FINANCIAL INABILITY TO PAY			
170	MERGER			
171	PLANT OR FACILITY CLOSING			
172	REORGANIZATION			
173	TEMPORARY SHUTDOWN			
174	**MATTERS DEEMED UNINSURABLE**	—		
175	**NON-MONETARY RELIEF**			
176	DECLATORY RELIEF	—		
177	DISGORGEMENT	—		
178	INJUNCTIVE RELIEF	●	Cost of compliance	2.d., page 2, 11.Q., page 6
179	JOB REINSTATEMENT	—		
180	NON-MONETARY DAMAGES/RELIEF	●		2.d., page 2, 11.Q., page 6
181	OTHER EQUITABLE REMEDIES	—		
182	**OBLIGATION TO PROVIDE BENEFITS**			
183	COBRA	—		
184	DISABILITY	—		
185	ERISA	●	Coverage available by endorsement	11.e., page 5
186	SOCIAL SECURITY	—		
187	OTHER RETIREMENT BENEFITS	—		
188	UNEMPLOYMENT	—		
189	WORKERS' COMPENSATION	—		
190	**PERSONAL INJURY OFFENSES**			
191	DEFAMATION	—		
192	EMOTIONAL DISTRESS/UPSET	●	Coverage available by endorsement	11.i., page 5
193	HUMILIATION	—		
194	LIBEL	—		
195	MENTAL ANGUISH	●	Mental injury—Coverage available by endorsement	11.i., page 5
196	PERSONAL INJURY	—		
197	SLANDER	—		
198	**PRIOR ACTS**			
199	PRIOR ACTS	●		11.b., page 5
200	PRIOR KNOWLEDGE	●	Prior claims/notice	11.a., page 5
201	PRIOR/PENDING LITIGATION	●		11.a., page 5
202	**PROPERTY DAMAGE**			
203	INTANGIBLE PROPERTY	—		
204	LOSS OF USE	●		11.j., page 6
205	TANGIBLE PROPERTY	●		11.j., page 6
206	**RETALIATORY ACTIONS OF EMPLOYER**	—		
207	FOR FAILING TO PERFORM ACTS AGAINST PUBLIC POLICY	—		
208	FOR FILING A COMPLAINT OR BENEFIT CLAIM	—		
209	**STRIKES/LOCKOUTS**	—		
210	**VIOLATION OF LAWS**			
211	ANY LAW	—		
212	FMLA	—		
213	OSHA	—		
214	POLLUTION LAWS	●		11.n., page 6
215	RICO	—		
216	SEC	—		
217	WARN	—		
	15 CONDITIONS			
218	**ARBITRATION**	●		22., page 8
219	MANDATORY	●		22., page 8
220	BINDING	●		22., page 8
221	CHOICE OF LAW PROVISION	●	State of New York	24., page 8
222	SITUS	●	State of New York	23., page 8
223	**TERRITORY**	—		
224	LIMITED	—		
225	WORLDWIDE	—		
226	**NEWLY FORMED/ACQUIRED ENTITIES**			
227	AUTOMATIC COVERAGE (X DAYS)	●	<1% assets involved	2. Included Entity d.(5)., page 2
228	NOTIFY INSURER WITHIN X DAYS	○		

UNITED EDUCATORS RISK RETENTION GROUP, INC. ELL (February 1997)

Policy Comparison Worksheet

United States Fidelity & Guaranty Company

Policy Form No.: FID 600
Edition Date: 11/95

Risks Considered: All except law firms and temporary employee leasing companies
Limits Available: $10,000,000
Minimum Retention: $5,000

Contact: William A. Chapdelaine
United States Fidelity & Guaranty Company
6225 Smith Avenue
Baltimore, MD 21209
800/664-8734
410/205-5372 (fax)

KEY TO SYMBOLS
● = Specifically contains queried provision of feature
○ = Unable to determine
— = Silent

#	Comparison Query		Comment	Policy Reference
	1 APPLICATION			
1	ATTACHES TO AND FORMS A PART OF THE POLICY	●		Declarations page
2	CONTAINS WARRANTY STATEMENTS	—		
3	CONTAINS SEVERABILITY PROVISIONS	●		V.C., pages 8–9
	2 POLICY TYPE			
4	UNITARY STAND ALONE POLICY	●		
	ENDORSEMENT OR PART OF	—		
5	DIRECTORS AND OFFICERS POLICY	—		
6	PACKAGE POLICY	—		
7	UMBRELLA POLICY	—		
8	ERRORS AND OMISSIONS POLICY	—		
9	OTHER	—		
10	CLAIMS-MADE	●		
11	OCCURRENCE	—		
	3 WHO IS INSURED			
12	BUSINESS ENTITY	●		II.F.1., page 2
13	AUTOMATIC COVERAGE FOR SUBSIDIARIES	●		II.C., page 1
14	DIRECTORS & OFFICERS	●	Directors	II.F.2., page 2
15	EMPLOYEES	●		II.F.3., page 2
16	PART-TIME	—		
17	SEASONAL	—		
18	TEMPORARY	—		
19	SUPERVISORS & MANAGERS	●	Any salaried employee	II.E., page 2
20	FORMER EMPLOYEES	●		II.F.3., page 2
21	VOLUNTEERS	—		
22	INDEPENDENT CONTRACTORS	—		
23	EXCLUDED	●		II.E., page 2
24	SILENT	—		
25	SHAREHOLDERS	—		
	4 LIMIT OF LIABILITY			
26	AGGREGATE	●		IV.C., page 5
27	INCLUDES PUNITIVE DAMAGES WHERE NOT UNINSURABLE	—		
28	DEFENSE COSTS INCLUDED WITHIN LIMIT OF LIABILITY	●	See also IV.C., page 5	IV.B.3., page 5
29	DEFENSE COSTS PAID IN ADDITION TO LIMIT OF LIABILITY	—		
	5 DEDUCTIBLE			
30	APPLIES TO EACH INDIVIDUAL CLAIM	●		IV.D., page 11
31	APPLIES TO EACH OCCURRENCE OR WRONGFUL PRACTICE	●		V.B., page 8
32	INCLUDES ALL CLAIMS FROM ONE ACT	●		V.B., page 8
33	SUBJECT TO ANNUAL AGGREGATE	—		
34	CO-PAYMENT APPLIES	●	Specified by underwriter—see Item 6 of Declarations	IV.D., page 6
35	LIMIT OF LIABILITY NOT REDUCED	●		
36	INCLUDES DEFENSE COSTS	●		IV.D., page 6
37	REDUCED UNDER SPECIFIED CIRCUMSTANCES (SEE POLICY)	—		

UNITED STATES FIDELITY & GUARANTY COMPANY   FID 600 [11/95]

#	Comparison Query	Comment		Policy Reference
	6 WHAT IS A CLAIM			
38	ORAL COMPLAINT TO INSURED	—		
39	WRITTEN COMPLAINT TO INSURED	●		II.B.1., page 1
40	COMPLAINT MUST CONTAIN A DEMAND FOR DAMAGES	●		II.B.1., page 1
41	COMPLAINT FILED WITH EEOC	○		IV.B.4., page 5
42	OR SIMILAR STATE AUTHORITY	○		IV.B.4., page 5
43	AGENCY MUST HAVE POWER TO ADJUDICATE	—		
44	ADMINISTRATIVE PROCEEDING	●		II.B.3., page 1
45	ARBITRATION PROCEEDING	●		II.B.2.b., page 1
46	ANY INCIDENT REPORTED TO INSURER	—		
47	SUIT	●	Civil proceeding	II.B.2.a., page 1
48	CLAIM DOES NOT INCLUDE ARBITRATION SUBJECT TO	—		
49	COLLECTIVE BARGAINING AGREEMENT	—		
50	EMPLOYEE POLICY OR MANUAL	—		
51	CLAIM NOT DEFINED	—		
	7 CLAIM REPORTING PROVISIONS TO INSURER			
52	IMMEDIATELY	—		
53	AS SOON AS POSSIBLE	—		
54	AS SOON AS PRACTICABLE	●		V.A.1.b., page 7
55	WITHIN POLICY PERIOD	—		
56	WITHIN X DAYS OF EXPIRATION	60		V.A.1.b., page 7
57	WITHIN X DAYS	—		
	8 EXTENDED REPORTING FEATURES			
58	ELECTION PERIOD (DAYS)	30		V.F., page 9
59	ADDITIONAL PREMIUM (% OF ANNUAL PREMIUM)	75		V.F., page 9
60	ADDITIONAL REPORTING PERIOD (MONTHS)	12		V.F., page 9
61	NO REINSTATEMENT OF LIMITS	●		IV.C., page 5
	9 POTENTIAL CLAIM REPORTING PROVISIONS			
62	NONE (SEE ALSO "CLAIM" ABOVE)	—		
63	INCIDENTS LIKELY TO RESULT IN A CLAIM	●		V.A.4., page 8
	10 DEFENSE PROVISIONS			
64	AFFIRMATIVE DUTY TO DEFEND	●		IV.B.1., page 5
65	NO AFFIRMATIVE DUTY TO DEFEND	—		
66	AFFIRMATIVE ADVANCEMENT PROVISIONS	—		
67	INSURED MUST RETURN ADVANCED AMOUNTS IF NOT COVERED	—		
68	INSURED/INSURER CHOOSES COUNSEL	—		
69	INSURED/INSURER APPROVES COUNSEL	—		
70	INSURED/INSURER CONSULTED IN COUNSEL SELECTION	—		
	11 SETTLEMENT PROVISIONS			
71	HAMMER CLAUSE	—		
72	CONSULTATION PROVISION	—		
73	CONSENT PROVISION	●	Insurer must consent; Exception applies	V.A.3., page 8
	12 ALLOCATION OF LOSS PROVISIONS			
74	STIPULATED PROVISIONS	—		
	13 COVERAGES			
75	DISCRIMINATION	●		II.O.e., page 3
76	SPECIFIC ENUMERATED ACTIVITIES	●		II.O.e., page 3
77	*PLUS BROAD OMNIBUS WORDING*	—		
78	SPECIFIC ENUMERATED CLASSES	●		II.O.e., page 3
79	*PLUS BROAD OMNIBUS WORDING*	—		
80	AGAINST THIRD PARTIES	—		
81	DISCRIMINATION NOT DEFINED	—		
82	SEXUAL HARASSMENT	●	Harassment	II.O.e., page 3
83	HOSTILE ENVIRONMENT	—		
84	QUID-PRO-QUO	—		
85	SEXUAL HARASSMENT NOT DEFINED	●		
86	WRONGFUL TERMINATION	●		II.O.d., page 3
87	BREACH OF IMPLIED CONTRACT	—		
88	BREACH OF EXPRESS CONTRACT	—		
89	VIOLATION OF PUBLIC POLICY	—		
90	VIOLATION OF GOOD FAITH & FAIR DEALING	—		
91	OBLIGATIONS TO MAKE PAYMENTS	—		
92	CONSTRUCTIVE DISCHARGE	●		II.O.d., page 3
93	WRONGFUL TERMINATION NOT DEFINED	●		
94	OTHER EMPLOYMENT VIOLATIONS/OFFENSES	●		II.O.a., page 3
95	WRONGFUL HIRING	●		II.O.a., page 3
96	WRONGFUL PROMOTION/DEMOTION	●		II.O.b. & c., page 3
97	WRONGFUL EVALUATION/DISCIPLINE	●		II.O.b. & c., page 3

UNITED STATES FIDELITY & GUARANTY COMPANY FID 600 [11/95]

#	Comparison Query		Comment	Policy Reference
98	FAMILY AND MEDICAL LEAVE ACT	—		
99	DEFAMATION	●		II.O.f., page 3
100	MISREPRESENTATION	—		
101	RETALIATION	●		II.O.d., page 3
102	MENTAL ANGUISH	—		
103	INVASION OF PRIVACY	●		II.O.g., page 3
104	HUMILIATION	●		II.O.e., page 3
105	EMOTIONAL DISTRESS	—		
106	OTHER PERSONAL INJURY OFFENSES	●		II.O.g., page 3
107	POLICY SILENT	—		
	14 EXCLUSIONS			
108	**ADA ACCOMMODATION EXPENSES**	●		III.I.6., page 2
109	**ASSAULT & BATTERY**	—		
110	**BACK PAY**	—		
111	**BODILY INJURY**	●		III.I., page 4
112	BODILY INJURY	●		III.I., page 4
113	DEATH	●		III.I., page 4
114	DISEASE	●		III.I., page 4
115	SICKNESS	●		III.I., page 4
116	**BREACH OF EMPLOYMENT CONTRACT**	—		
117	EXPRESS CONTRACT	—		
118	*WRITTEN CONTRACT*	—		
119	*ORAL CONTRACT*	—		
120	IMPLIED CONTRACT	—		
121	**CLASS ACTION LAWSUITS**	—		
122	**CONSEQUENTIAL LOSS**	—		
123	APPLIES TO BODILY INJURY	—		
124	APPLIES TO INSURED EVENT	—		
125	BROTHER/SISTER	—		
126	CHILD	—		
127	DOMESTIC PARTNER	—		
128	PARENT	—		
129	SPOUSE	—		
130	**COST OF ARBITRATION HEARINGS SUBJECT TO**	—		
131	EMPLOYMENT HANDBOOK	—		
132	LABOR GRIEVANCE	—		
133	OTHER EMPLOYMENT POLICY OR PROCEDURE	—		
134	**COVERAGE ELSEWHERE**	●		VI.B.1. & 2., page 10
135	OTHER AVAILABLE INSURANCE	—		
136	OTHER INDEMNIFICATION	—		
137	SHARING PROVISION	●		VI.B.1. & 2., page 10
138	**FAILURE TO EXERCISE CARE WHEN TERMINATING**	—		
139	**FINES/PENALTIES**	●		II.I.1., page 2
140	CIVIL	●		II.I.1., page 2
141	CRIMINAL	●		II.I.1., page 2
142	EXEMPLARY DAMAGES	●		II.I.3., page 2
143	PUNITIVE DAMAGES	●		II.I.3., page 2
144	MULTIPLIED DAMAGES	●		II.I.3., page 2
145	**FRONT PAY**	●		II.I.5., page 2
146	EXCLUSION APPLIES ONLY IF EMPLOYER HAD OPPORTUNITY TO REINSTATE EMPLOYEE BUT DID NOT DO SO	—		
147	**INTENTIONAL ACTS**	●	Vicarious liability exception	III.D., page 3
148	CRIMINAL ACTS	●		III.H., page 4
149	CRIMINAL PROCEEDING	—		
150	DISHONEST PURPOSE	●		III.H., page 4
151	FRAUDULENT ACTS	●		III.H., page 4
152	FRAUDULENT CLAIMS	—		
153	INTENTIONAL VIOLATIONS OF LAW	○	Vicarious liability exception	III.D., page 3
154	WILLFUL FAILURE TO COMPLY WITH LAW	○	Vicarious liability exception	III.D., page 3
155	MALICIOUS PURPOSE	—		
156	**LIABILITY OF OTHERS**	●		III.E., page 3
157	**LIQUIDATED DAMAGES**	●		II.I.3., page 2
158	**LOSS ARISING OUT OF CHANGES IN OPERATIONS**	—		
159	ACQUISITION	—		
160	CHANGE IN CONTROL	—		
161	DOWNSIZING OR REDUCTION IN FORCE	—		
162	*% OF WORKFORCE*	—		
163	*WITHIN X DAYS*	—		

UNITED STATES FIDELITY & GUARANTY COMPANY FID 600 [11/95]

	Comparison Query	Comment	Policy Reference
164	FINANCIAL IMPAIRMENT	—	
165	BANKRUPTCY	—	
166	INSOLVENCY	—	
167	LIQUIDATION	—	
168	RECEIVERSHIP	—	
169	FINANCIAL INABILITY TO PAY	—	
170	MERGER	—	
171	PLANT OR FACILITY CLOSING	—	
172	REORGANIZATION	—	
173	TEMPORARY SHUTDOWN	—	
174	**MATTERS DEEMED UNINSURABLE**	●	II.I.9., page 2
175	**NON-MONETARY RELIEF**	●	II.I.4., page 2
176	DECLATORY RELIEF	—	
177	DISGORGEMENT	—	
178	INJUNCTIVE RELIEF	●	II.I.4., page 2
179	JOB REINSTATEMENT	—	
180	NON-MONETARY DAMAGES/RELIEF	—	
181	OTHER EQUITABLE REMEDIES	●	II.I.4., page 2
182	**OBLIGATION TO PROVIDE BENEFITS**		
183	COBRA	●	III.F.3., page 4
184	DISABILITY	●	Exception applies	III.F.1., page 4
185	ERISA	●	III.F.2., page 4
186	SOCIAL SECURITY	—	
187	OTHER RETIREMENT BENEFITS	●	III.F.2., page 4
188	UNEMPLOYMENT	●	Exception applies	III.F.1., page 4
189	WORKERS' COMPENSATION	●	Exception applies	III.F.1., page 4
190	**PERSONAL INJURY OFFENSES**	—	
191	DEFAMATION	—	
192	EMOTIONAL DISTRESS/UPSET	—	
193	HUMILIATION	—	
194	LIBEL	—	
195	MENTAL ANGUISH	—	
196	PERSONAL INJURY	—	
197	SLANDER	—	
198	**PRIOR ACTS**	●	III.A., page 3
199	PRIOR ACTS	●	III.A., page 3
200	PRIOR KNOWLEDGE	●	If prior notice given	III.B., page 3
201	PRIOR/PENDING LITIGATION	—	
202	**PROPERTY DAMAGE**	●	III.I., page 4
203	INTANGIBLE PROPERTY	—	
204	LOSS OF USE	●	III.I., page 4
205	TANGIBLE PROPERTY	●	III.I., page 4
206	**RETALIATORY ACTIONS OF EMPLOYER**	—	
207	FOR FAILING TO PERFORM ACTS AGAINST PUBLIC POLICY	—	
208	FOR FILING A COMPLAINT OR BENEFIT CLAIM	—	
209	**STRIKES/LOCKOUTS**	—	
210	**VIOLATION OF LAWS**		
211	ANY LAW	—	
212	FMLA	—	
213	OSHA	●	III.F.3., page 4
214	POLLUTION LAWS	—	
215	RICO	—	
216	SEC	—	
217	WARN	●	III.F.3., page 4
	15 CONDITIONS		
218	**ARBITRATION**	—	
219	MANDATORY	—	
220	BINDING	—	
221	CHOICE OF LAW PROVISION	—	
222	SITUS	—	
223	**TERRITORY**	●	VI.A., page 10
224	LIMITED	●	VI.A., page 10
225	WORLDWIDE	—	
226	**NEWLY FORMED/ACQUIRED ENTITIES**	●	IV.A., page 5
227	AUTOMATIC COVERAGE (X DAYS)	90	IV.A., page 5
228	NOTIFY INSURER WITHIN X DAYS	90	IV.A.1., page 5

UNITED STATES FIDELITY & GUARANTY COMPANY FID 600 [11/95]

Policy Comparison Worksheet

United States Liability Insurance Group

Policy Form No.: EPLJ
Edition Date: 1/98

Risks Considered: General accounts (less than 200 employees)
Limits Available: $2,000,000
Minimum Retention: $2,500

Contact: Christopher Higgins, CPCU, RPLU
United States Liability Insurance Group
1030 Continental Drive
King of Prussia, PA 19406
800/523-5545
610/687-0080 (fax)

KEY TO SYMBOLS
- ● = Specifically contains queried provision of feature
- ○ = Unable to determine
- — = Silent

#	Comparison Query		Comment	Policy Reference
	1 APPLICATION			
1	ATTACHES TO AND FORMS A PART OF THE POLICY	●		II.A.(1)., page 1
2	CONTAINS WARRANTY STATEMENTS	●		IX.A., page 5
3	CONTAINS SEVERABILITY PROVISIONS	●		IX.B., page 5
	2 POLICY TYPE			
4	UNITARY STAND ALONE POLICY	●		
	ENDORSEMENT OR PART OF	—		
5	DIRECTORS AND OFFICERS POLICY	—		
6	PACKAGE POLICY	—		
7	UMBRELLA POLICY	—		
8	ERRORS AND OMISSIONS POLICY	—		
9	OTHER	—		
10	CLAIMS-MADE	●		
11	OCCURRENCE	—		
	3 WHO IS INSURED			
12	BUSINESS ENTITY	●		II.G., page 2
13	AUTOMATIC COVERAGE FOR SUBSIDIARIES	●		II.I., page 2
14	DIRECTORS & OFFICERS	●		II.F., page 2
15	EMPLOYEES	●		II.F., page 2
16	PART-TIME	—		
17	SEASONAL	—		
18	TEMPORARY	●	See also II.N., page 2	II.F., page 2
19	SUPERVISORS & MANAGERS	●	As employees	II.F., page 2
20	FORMER EMPLOYEES	●		II.F., page 2
21	VOLUNTEERS	●		II.N., page 2
22	INDEPENDENT CONTRACTORS	—		
23	EXCLUDED	—		
24	SILENT	●		
25	SHAREHOLDERS	—		
	4 LIMIT OF LIABILITY			
26	AGGREGATE	●		IV.A., page 3
27	INCLUDES PUNITIVE DAMAGES WHERE NOT UNINSURABLE	—		
28	DEFENSE COSTS INCLUDED WITHIN LIMIT OF LIABILITY	—		
29	DEFENSE COSTS PAID IN ADDITION TO LIMIT OF LIABILITY	●		IV.C., page 2
	5 DEDUCTIBLE			
30	APPLIES TO EACH INDIVIDUAL CLAIM	●		IV.D., page 3
31	APPLIES TO EACH OCCURRENCE OR WRONGFUL PRACTICE	●		IV.F., page 3
32	INCLUDES ALL CLAIMS FROM ONE ACT	●		IV.F., page 3
33	SUBJECT TO ANNUAL AGGREGATE	—		
34	CO-PAYMENT APPLIES	—		
35	LIMIT OF LIABILITY NOT REDUCED	—		
36	INCLUDES DEFENSE COSTS	●		IV.D., page 3
37	REDUCED UNDER SPECIFIED CIRCUMSTANCES (SEE POLICY)	—		

#	Comparison Query	Comment		Policy Reference
6	**WHAT IS A CLAIM**			
38	ORAL COMPLAINT TO INSURED	—		
39	WRITTEN COMPLAINT TO INSURED	●		II.B.1., page 1
40	COMPLAINT MUST CONTAIN A DEMAND FOR DAMAGES	—		
41	COMPLAINT FILED WITH EEOC	○		II.B.2., page 1
42	OR SIMILAR STATE AUTHORITY	—		
43	AGENCY MUST HAVE POWER TO ADJUDICATE	—		
44	**ADMINISTRATIVE PROCEEDING**	●		II.B.2., page 1
45	**ARBITRATION PROCEEDING**	—		
46	**ANY INCIDENT REPORTED TO INSURER**	—		
47	**SUIT**	●	Judicial proceeding	II.B.2., page 1
48	**CLAIM DOES NOT INCLUDE ARBITRATION SUBJECT TO**	—		
49	COLLECTIVE BARGAINING AGREEMENT	—		
50	EMPLOYEE POLICY OR MANUAL	—		
51	**CLAIM NOT DEFINED**	—		
7	**CLAIM REPORTING PROVISIONS TO INSURER**			
52	**IMMEDIATELY**	—		
53	**AS SOON AS POSSIBLE**	—		
54	**AS SOON AS PRACTICABLE**	●		VII.A., page 4
55	**WITHIN POLICY PERIOD**	—		
56	**WITHIN X DAYS OF EXPIRATION**	60	See also VII.A., page 4	I.B.3., page 1
57	**WITHIN X DAYS**	—		
8	**EXTENDED REPORTING FEATURES**			
58	**ELECTION PERIOD (DAYS)**	15		V.A., page 3
59	**ADDITIONAL PREMIUM (% OF ANNUAL PREMIUM)**	75/125/175		V.A., page 3
60	**ADDITIONAL REPORTING PERIOD (MONTHS)**	12/24/36		V.A., page 3
61	**NO REINSTATEMENT OF LIMITS**	●		V.C., page 4
9	**POTENTIAL CLAIM REPORTING PROVISIONS**			
62	**NONE (SEE ALSO "CLAIM" ABOVE)**	—		
63	**INCIDENTS LIKELY TO RESULT IN A CLAIM**	●		VII.C., page 4
10	**DEFENSE PROVISIONS**			
64	**AFFIRMATIVE DUTY TO DEFEND**	●		I.B., page 1
65	**NO AFFIRMATIVE DUTY TO DEFEND**	—		
66	AFFIRMATIVE ADVANCEMENT PROVISIONS	—		
67	INSURED MUST RETURN ADVANCED AMOUNTS IF NOT COVERED	—		
68	**INSURED/INSURER CHOOSES COUNSEL**	●	Insurer	II.D., page 1
69	**INSURED/INSURER APPROVES COUNSEL**	—		
70	**INSURED/INSURER CONSULTED IN COUNSEL SELECTION**	—		
11	**SETTLEMENT PROVISIONS**			
71	**HAMMER CLAUSE**	●		VI., page 4
72	**CONSULTATION PROVISION**	—		
73	**CONSENT PROVISION**	●	Two-way	VI., page 4
12	**ALLOCATION OF LOSS PROVISIONS**			
74	**STIPULATED PROVISIONS**	—		
13	**COVERAGES**			
75	**DISCRIMINATION**	●		II.N., page 2
76	SPECIFIC ENUMERATED ACTIVITIES	●		II.E., page 1
77	*PLUS BROAD OMNIBUS WORDING*	—		
78	SPECIFIC ENUMERATED CLASSES	●		II.E., page 1
79	*PLUS BROAD OMNIBUS WORDING*	—		
80	AGAINST THIRD PARTIES	—		
81	DISCRIMINATION NOT DEFINED	—		
82	**SEXUAL HARASSMENT**	●	Includes third-party harassment	II.N., page 2
83	HOSTILE ENVIRONMENT	●		II.L., page 2
84	QUID-PRO-QUO	●		II.L., page 2
85	SEXUAL HARASSMENT NOT DEFINED	—		
86	**WRONGFUL TERMINATION**	●		II.N., page 2
87	BREACH OF IMPLIED CONTRACT	●		II.O., page 2
88	BREACH OF EXPRESS CONTRACT	—		
89	VIOLATION OF PUBLIC POLICY	—		
90	VIOLATION OF GOOD FAITH & FAIR DEALING	—		
91	OBLIGATIONS TO MAKE PAYMENTS	—		
92	CONSTRUCTIVE DISCHARGE	—		
93	WRONGFUL TERMINATION NOT DEFINED	—		
94	**OTHER EMPLOYMENT VIOLATIONS/OFFENSES**	—		
95	WRONGFUL HIRING	●		II.E., page 1
96	WRONGFUL PROMOTION/DEMOTION	●		II.E., page 1
97	WRONGFUL EVALUATION/DISCIPLINE	—		

UNITED STATES LIABILITY INSURANCE GROUP EPLJ [1/98]

#	Comparison Query	Comment		Policy Reference
98	FAMILY AND MEDICAL LEAVE ACT	●		II.N., page 2
99	DEFAMATION	●		III.A., page 2
100	MISREPRESENTATION	—		
101	RETALIATION	—		
102	MENTAL ANGUISH	●		III.A., page 2
103	INVASION OF PRIVACY	—		
104	HUMILIATION	●		III.A., page 2
105	EMOTIONAL DISTRESS	●		III.A., page 2
106	OTHER PERSONAL INJURY OFFENSES	●		III.A., page 2
107	POLICY SILENT	—		

14 EXCLUSIONS

#	Comparison Query	Comment		Policy Reference
108	**ADA ACCOMMODATION EXPENSES**	●		III.G., page 3
109	**ASSAULT & BATTERY**	—		
110	**BACK PAY**	—		
111	**BODILY INJURY**	●		III.A., page 2
112	BODILY INJURY	●		III.A., page 2
113	DEATH	●		III.A., page 2
114	DISEASE	●		III.A., page 2
115	SICKNESS	●		III.A., page 2
116	**BREACH OF EMPLOYMENT CONTRACT**	●		II.D., page 2
117	EXPRESS CONTRACT	●		II.D., page 2
118	*WRITTEN CONTRACT*	—		
119	*ORAL CONTRACT*	—		
120	IMPLIED CONTRACT	—		
121	**CLASS ACTION LAWSUITS**	—		
122	**CONSEQUENTIAL LOSS**	—		
123	APPLIES TO BODILY INJURY	—		
124	APPLIES TO INSURED EVENT	—		
125	BROTHER/SISTER	—		
126	CHILD	—		
127	DOMESTIC PARTNER	—		
128	PARENT	—		
129	SPOUSE	—		
130	**COST OF ARBITRATION HEARINGS SUBJECT TO**	—		
131	EMPLOYMENT HANDBOOK	—		
132	LABOR GRIEVANCE	—		
133	OTHER EMPLOYMENT POLICY OR PROCEDURE	—		
134	**COVERAGE ELSEWHERE**	●		XIV., page 5
135	OTHER AVAILABLE INSURANCE	●		XIV., page 5
136	OTHER INDEMNIFICATION	—		
137	SHARING PROVISION	—		
138	**FAILURE TO EXERCISE CARE WHEN TERMINATING**	—		
139	**FINES/PENALTIES**	●		II.H., page 2
140	CIVIL	●		II.H., page 2
141	CRIMINAL	●		II.H., page 2
142	EXEMPLARY DAMAGES	●		II.H., page 2
143	PUNITIVE DAMAGES	●		II.H., page 2
144	MULTIPLIED DAMAGES	●		II.H., page 2
145	**FRONT PAY**	—		
146	EXCLUSION APPLIES ONLY IF EMPLOYER HAD OPPORTUNITY TO REINSTATE EMPLOYEE BUT DID NOT DO SO	—		
147	**INTENTIONAL ACTS**	●	Severability applies	III.B., pages 2–3
148	CRIMINAL ACTS	○	Severability applies	III.B., pages 2–3
149	CRIMINAL PROCEEDING	—		
150	DISHONEST PURPOSE	○	Severability applies	III.B., pages 2–3
151	FRAUDULENT ACTS	—		
152	FRAUDULENT CLAIMS	—		
153	INTENTIONAL VIOLATIONS OF LAW	●	Severability applies	III.B., pages 2–3
154	WILLFUL FAILURE TO COMPLY WITH LAW	●	Severability applies	III.B., pages 2–3
155	MALICIOUS PURPOSE	●	Severability applies	III.B., pages 2–3
156	**LIABILITY OF OTHERS**	●		III.F., page 3
157	**LIQUIDATED DAMAGES**	—		
158	**LOSS ARISING OUT OF CHANGES IN OPERATIONS**	—		
159	ACQUISITION	—		
160	CHANGE IN CONTROL	—		
161	DOWNSIZING OR REDUCTION IN FORCE	—		
162	*% OF WORKFORCE*	—		
163	*WITHIN X DAYS*	—		

UNITED STATES LIABILITY INSURANCE GROUP EPLJ [1/98]

#	Comparison Query	Comment	Policy Reference
164	FINANCIAL IMPAIRMENT	—	
165	BANKRUPTCY	—	
166	INSOLVENCY	—	
167	LIQUIDATION	—	
168	RECEIVERSHIP	—	
169	FINANCIAL INABILITY TO PAY	—	
170	MERGER	—	
171	PLANT OR FACILITY CLOSING	—	
172	REORGANIZATION	—	
173	TEMPORARY SHUTDOWN	—	
174	**MATTERS DEEMED UNINSURABLE**	●	II.H., page 2
175	**NON-MONETARY RELIEF**	—	
176	DECLATORY RELIEF	—	
177	DISGORGEMENT	—	
178	INJUNCTIVE RELIEF	—	
179	JOB REINSTATEMENT	—	
180	NON-MONETARY DAMAGES/RELIEF	—	
181	OTHER EQUITABLE REMEDIES	—	
182	**OBLIGATION TO PROVIDE BENEFITS**	—	
183	COBRA	—	
184	DISABILITY	●	III.D., page 3
185	ERISA	●	III.C., page 3
186	SOCIAL SECURITY	—	
187	OTHER RETIREMENT BENEFITS	—	
188	UNEMPLOYMENT	●	II.D., page 3
189	WORKERS' COMPENSATION	●	II.D., page 3
190	**PERSONAL INJURY OFFENSES**	—	
191	DEFAMATION	—	
192	EMOTIONAL DISTRESS/UPSET	—	
193	HUMILIATION	—	
194	LIBEL	—	
195	MENTAL ANGUISH	—	
196	PERSONAL INJURY	—	
197	SLANDER	—	
198	**PRIOR ACTS**	●	I.B.1., page 1
199	PRIOR ACTS	●	Prior to retroactive date	I.B.1., page 1
200	PRIOR KNOWLEDGE	●	I.B.2., page 1
201	PRIOR/PENDING LITIGATION	●	III.E., page 3
202	**PROPERTY DAMAGE**	●	III.A., page 2
203	INTANGIBLE PROPERTY		
204	LOSS OF USE	●	III.A., page 2
205	TANGIBLE PROPERTY	●	III.A., page 2
206	**RETALIATORY ACTIONS OF EMPLOYER**	—	
207	FOR FAILING TO PERFORM ACTS AGAINST PUBLIC POLICY	—	
208	FOR FILING A COMPLAINT OR BENEFIT CLAIM	—	
209	**STRIKES/LOCKOUTS**	●	III.H., page 3
210	**VIOLATION OF LAWS**	—	
211	ANY LAW	—	
212	FMLA	—	
213	OSHA	—	
214	POLLUTION LAWS	—	
215	RICO	—	
216	SEC	—	
217	WARN	—	

15 CONDITIONS

#	Comparison Query	Comment	Policy Reference
218	**ARBITRATION**	—	
219	MANDATORY	—	
220	BINDING	—	
221	CHOICE OF LAW PROVISION	—	
222	SITUS	—	
223	**TERRITORY**	—	
224	LIMITED	—	
225	WORLDWIDE	—	
226	**NEWLY FORMED/ACQUIRED ENTITIES**	●	XVI.B., page 6
227	AUTOMATIC COVERAGE (X DAYS)	—	
228	NOTIFY INSURER WITHIN X DAYS	30	XVI.B., page 6

UNITED STATES LIABILITY INSURANCE GROUP EPLJ [1/98]

Policy Comparison Worksheet

X.L. Insurance Company, Ltd.

Policy Form No.: EPLI-005
Edition Date: 7/98

Risks Considered: General accounts
Limits Available: $100,000,000
Minimum Retention: $1,000,000

Contact: Paul Miller
X.L. Insurance Company, Ltd.
Cumberland House
One Victoria Street
Hamilton HM JX, Bermuda
441/292-8515
441/292-1566 (fax)

KEY TO SYMBOLS
● = Specifically contains queried provision of feature
○ = Unable to determine
— = Silent

#	Comparison Query	Symbol	Comment	Policy Reference
	1 APPLICATION			
1	ATTACHES TO AND FORMS A PART OF THE POLICY	●		I., page 3
2	CONTAINS WARRANTY STATEMENTS	—		
3	CONTAINS SEVERABILITY PROVISIONS	—		
	2 POLICY TYPE			
4	UNITARY STAND ALONE POLICY	●		
	ENDORSEMENT OR PART OF	—		
5	DIRECTORS AND OFFICERS POLICY	—		
6	PACKAGE POLICY	—		
7	UMBRELLA POLICY	—		
8	ERRORS AND OMISSIONS POLICY	—		
9	OTHER	—		
10	CLAIMS-MADE	●		
11	OCCURRENCE	—		
	3 WHO IS INSURED			
12	BUSINESS ENTITY	●		IV.G., page 7
13	AUTOMATIC COVERAGE FOR SUBSIDIARIES	●		IV.A.(1)., page 5
14	DIRECTORS & OFFICERS	●		IV.G., page 7
15	EMPLOYEES	●		IV.G., page 7
16	PART-TIME	●		IV.E., page 6
17	SEASONAL	●		IV.E., page 6
18	TEMPORARY	●		IV.E., page 6
19	SUPERVISORS & MANAGERS	—		
20	FORMER EMPLOYEES	●		IV.G., page 7
21	VOLUNTEERS	—		
22	INDEPENDENT CONTRACTORS	●	Exceptions apply	IV.E., page 6
23	EXCLUDED	—		
24	SILENT	—		
25	SHAREHOLDERS	●		IV.G., page 7
	4 LIMIT OF LIABILITY			
26	AGGREGATE	●		VI.B., page 10
27	INCLUDES PUNITIVE DAMAGES WHERE NOT UNINSURABLE	●		IV.J.(1), page 7
28	DEFENSE COSTS INCLUDED WITHIN LIMIT OF LIABILITY	●		III.F., page 4
29	DEFENSE COSTS PAID IN ADDITION TO LIMIT OF LIABILITY	—		
	5 DEDUCTIBLE			
30	APPLIES TO EACH INDIVIDUAL CLAIM	●	See also VI.B., page 10	Declarations—Item 5
31	APPLIES TO EACH OCCURRENCE OR WRONGFUL PRACTICE	—		
32	INCLUDES ALL CLAIMS FROM ONE ACT	●		IV.B, page 5
33	SUBJECT TO ANNUAL AGGREGATE	—		
34	CO-PAYMENT APPLIES	—		
35	LIMIT OF LIABILITY NOT REDUCED	—		
36	INCLUDES DEFENSE COSTS	●	See also IV.J.(3)., page 8	VI.C., page 11
37	REDUCED UNDER SPECIFIED CIRCUMSTANCES (SEE POLICY)	—		

X.L. INSURANCE COMPANY, LTD. EPLI-005 [7/98]

#	Comparison Query	Comment		Policy Reference
	6 WHAT IS A CLAIM			
38	ORAL COMPLAINT TO INSURED	—		
39	WRITTEN COMPLAINT TO INSURED	●		IV.B., page 5
40	COMPLAINT MUST CONTAIN A DEMAND FOR DAMAGES	●		IV.B., page 5
41	COMPLAINT FILED WITH EEOC	—		
42	OR SIMILAR STATE AUTHORITY	—		
43	AGENCY MUST HAVE POWER TO ADJUDICATE	—		
44	ADMINISTRATIVE PROCEEDING	●		IV.B., page 5
45	ARBITRATION PROCEEDING	●		IV.B., page 5
46	ANY INCIDENT REPORTED TO INSURER	—		
47	SUIT	●		IV.B., page 5
48	CLAIM DOES NOT INCLUDE ARBITRATION SUBJECT TO	—		
49	COLLECTIVE BARGAINING AGREEMENT	—		
50	EMPLOYEE POLICY OR MANUAL	—		
51	CLAIM NOT DEFINED	—		
	7 CLAIM REPORTING PROVISIONS TO INSURER			
52	IMMEDIATELY	—		
53	AS SOON AS POSSIBLE	—		
54	AS SOON AS PRACTICABLE	—		
55	WITHIN POLICY PERIOD	—		
56	WITHIN X DAYS OF EXPIRATION	30	Prior to expiration via Bordereaux	VII.A.2., page 12
57	WITHIN X DAYS	—		
	8 EXTENDED REPORTING FEATURES			
58	ELECTION PERIOD (DAYS)	30		VII.I.2.g., page 20
59	ADDITIONAL PREMIUM (% OF ANNUAL PREMIUM)	100		VII.I.2.e., page 19
60	ADDITIONAL REPORTING PERIOD (MONTHS)	12		VII.I.2.b., page 19
61	NO REINSTATEMENT OF LIMITS	●		VII.I.2.h., page 20
	9 POTENTIAL CLAIM REPORTING PROVISIONS			
62	NONE (SEE ALSO "CLAIM" ABOVE)	—		
63	INCIDENTS LIKELY TO RESULT IN A CLAIM	●		VII.A.4., page 13
	10 DEFENSE PROVISIONS			
64	AFFIRMATIVE DUTY TO DEFEND	—		
65	NO AFFIRMATIVE DUTY TO DEFEND	●		III.A., page 3
66	AFFIRMATIVE ADVANCEMENT PROVISIONS	●		III.D., page 4
67	INSURED MUST RETURN ADVANCED AMOUNTS IF NOT COVERED	●		II.D., page 4
68	INSURED/INSURER CHOOSES COUNSEL	●	Insured chooses	III.B., page 3
69	INSURED/INSURER APPROVES COUNSEL	●	Insurer approves if expenses > $100,000	III.B., page 3
70	INSURED/INSURER CONSULTED IN COUNSEL SELECTION	●		III.B., pages 3–4
	11 SETTLEMENT PROVISIONS			
71	HAMMER CLAUSE	●	Coinsurance provision	III.E., page 4
72	CONSULTATION PROVISION	—		
73	CONSENT PROVISION	●	Insurer must consent	III.C., page 4
	12 ALLOCATION OF LOSS PROVISIONS			
74	STIPULATED PROVISIONS	—		
	13 COVERAGES			
75	DISCRIMINATION	●	See also IV.F.(2)., page 6	IV.B., page 5
76	SPECIFIC ENUMERATED ACTIVITIES	—		
77	PLUS BROAD OMNIBUS WORDING	—		
78	SPECIFIC ENUMERATED CLASSES	—		
79	PLUS BROAD OMNIBUS WORDING	—		
80	AGAINST THIRD PARTIES	—	Coverage available by endorsement	
81	DISCRIMINATION NOT DEFINED	●		
82	SEXUAL HARASSMENT	●	See also IV.F.(3)., page 6	IV.B., page 5
83	HOSTILE ENVIRONMENT	●		IV.F.(3)., page 6
84	QUID-PRO-QUO	●		IV.F.(3)., page 6
85	SEXUAL HARASSMENT NOT DEFINED	—		
86	WRONGFUL TERMINATION	●	See also IV.F.(4)., page 6	IV.B., page 5
87	BREACH OF IMPLIED CONTRACT	○		IV.M., page 8
88	BREACH OF EXPRESS CONTRACT	—		
89	VIOLATION OF PUBLIC POLICY	—		
90	VIOLATION OF GOOD FAITH & FAIR DEALING	—		
91	OBLIGATIONS TO MAKE PAYMENTS	—		
92	CONSTRUCTIVE DISCHARGE	●		IV.M., page 5
93	WRONGFUL TERMINATION NOT DEFINED	—		
94	OTHER EMPLOYMENT VIOLATIONS/OFFENSES	—		
95	WRONGFUL HIRING	●	As common law violation	IV.C., pages 5–6
96	WRONGFUL PROMOTION/DEMOTION	●	As common law violation	IV.C., pages 5–6
97	WRONGFUL EVALUATION/DISCIPLINE	●	As common law violation	IV.C., pages 5–6

X.L. INSURANCE COMPANY, LTD.   EPLI-005 [7/98]

#	Comparison Query		Comment	Policy Reference
98	FAMILY AND MEDICAL LEAVE ACT	—		
99	DEFAMATION	●	As common law violation	IV.C., pages 5–6
100	MISREPRESENTATION	●	As common law violation	IV.C., pages 5–6
101	RETALIATION	●		IV.F.(5)., page 6
102	MENTAL ANGUISH	—		
103	INVASION OF PRIVACY	●		IV.F.(6)., page 6
104	HUMILIATION	●	As common law violation	IV.C., pages 5–6
105	EMOTIONAL DISTRESS	●	As common law violation	IV.C., pages 5–6
106	OTHER PERSONAL INJURY OFFENSES	●	As common law violation	IV.C., pages 5–6
107	POLICY SILENT	—		
14	**EXCLUSIONS**			
108	**ADA ACCOMMODATION EXPENSES**	●		IV.J.(3)., page 8
109	**ASSAULT & BATTERY**	—		
110	**BACK PAY**	—		
111	**BODILY INJURY**	—		
112	BODILY INJURY	—		
113	DEATH	—		
114	DISEASE	—		
115	SICKNESS	—		
116	**BREACH OF EMPLOYMENT CONTRACT**	●		IV.J.(3)., page 8
117	EXPRESS CONTRACT	—		
118	*WRITTEN CONTRACT*	●	Exception for defense costs	IV.J.(3)., page 8
119	*ORAL CONTRACT*	—		
120	IMPLIED CONTRACT	—		
121	**CLASS ACTION LAWSUITS**	—		
122	**CONSEQUENTIAL LOSS**	—		
123	APPLIES TO BODILY INJURY	—		
124	APPLIES TO INSURED EVENT	—		
125	BROTHER/SISTER	—		
126	CHILD	—		
127	DOMESTIC PARTNER	—		
128	PARENT	—		
129	SPOUSE	—		
130	**COST OF ARBITRATION HEARINGS SUBJECT TO**	—		
131	EMPLOYMENT HANDBOOK	—		
132	LABOR GRIEVANCE	—		
133	OTHER EMPLOYMENT POLICY OR PROCEDURE	—		
134	**COVERAGE ELSEWHERE**	—		
135	OTHER AVAILABLE INSURANCE	—		
136	OTHER INDEMNIFICATION	—		
137	SHARING PROVISION	—		
138	**FAILURE TO EXERCISE CARE WHEN TERMINATING**	—		
139	**FINES/PENALTIES**	●		IV.J.(1)., page 7
140	CIVIL	—		
141	CRIMINAL	●		IV.J.(1)., page 7
142	EXEMPLARY DAMAGES	—		
143	PUNITIVE DAMAGES	—		
144	MULTIPLIED DAMAGES	—		
145	**FRONT PAY**	—		
146	EXCLUSION APPLIES ONLY IF EMPLOYER HAD OPPORTUNITY TO REINSTATE EMPLOYEE BUT DID NOT DO SO	—		
147	**INTENTIONAL ACTS**	●	Defense costs exception severability applies	V.H., page 10
148	CRIMINAL ACTS	—		
149	CRIMINAL PROCEEDING	●	Defense costs exception severability applies	V.I., page 10
150	DISHONEST PURPOSE	—		
151	FRAUDULENT ACTS	—		
152	FRAUDULENT CLAIMS	—		
153	INTENTIONAL VIOLATIONS OF LAW	—		
154	WILLFUL FAILURE TO COMPLY WITH LAW	—		
155	MALICIOUS PURPOSE	—		
156	**LIABILITY OF OTHERS**	●		V.B., page 9
157	**LIQUIDATED DAMAGES**	—		
158	**LOSS ARISING OUT OF CHANGES IN OPERATIONS**	—		
159	ACQUISITION	—		
160	CHANGE IN CONTROL	—		
161	DOWNSIZING OR REDUCTION IN FORCE	—		
162	*% OF WORKFORCE*	—		
163	*WITHIN X DAYS*	—		

X.L. INSURANCE COMPANY, LTD. EPLI-005 [7/98]

	Comparison Query		Comment	Policy Reference
164	FINANCIAL IMPAIRMENT	—		
165	BANKRUPTCY	—		
166	INSOLVENCY	—		
167	LIQUIDATION	—		
168	RECEIVERSHIP	—		
169	FINANCIAL INABILITY TO PAY	—		
170	MERGER	—		
171	PLANT OR FACILITY CLOSING	●	See also Warn Act exclusion	V.G., page 10
172	REORGANIZATION	—		
173	TEMPORARY SHUTDOWN	—		
174	**MATTERS DEEMED UNINSURABLE**	—		
175	**NON-MONETARY RELIEF**	●		IV.J.(3)., page 8
176	DECLATORY RELIEF	—		
177	DISGORGEMENT	—		
178	INJUNCTIVE RELIEF	●		IV.J.(3)., page 8
179	JOB REINSTATEMENT	—		
180	NON-MONETARY DAMAGES/RELIEF	●		IV.J.(3)., page 8
181	OTHER EQUITABLE REMEDIES	—		
182	**OBLIGATION TO PROVIDE BENEFITS**	—		
183	COBRA	—		
184	DISABILITY	●		V.A., pages 8–9
185	ERISA	●	Exception applies	V.A., pages 8–9
186	SOCIAL SECURITY	—		
187	OTHER RETIREMENT BENEFITS	—		
188	UNEMPLOYMENT	●		V.A., pages 8–9
189	WORKERS' COMPENSATION	●		V.A., pages 8–9
190	**PERSONAL INJURY OFFENSES**	—		
191	DEFAMATION	—		
192	EMOTIONAL DISTRESS/UPSET	—		
193	HUMILIATION	—		
194	LIBEL	—		
195	MENTAL ANGUISH	—		
196	PERSONAL INJURY	—		
197	SLANDER	—		
198	**PRIOR ACTS**	—		
199	PRIOR ACTS	—		
200	PRIOR KNOWLEDGE	●	Non-imputation	V.C.(2)., page 9 and VII.J.1., page 20
201	PRIOR/PENDING LITIGATION	—		
202	**PROPERTY DAMAGE**	—		
203	INTANGIBLE PROPERTY	—		
204	LOSS OF USE	—		
205	TANGIBLE PROPERTY	—		
206	**RETALIATORY ACTIONS OF EMPLOYER**	—		
207	FOR FAILING TO PERFORM ACTS AGAINST PUBLIC POLICY	—		
208	FOR FILING A COMPLAINT OR BENEFIT CLAIM	—		
209	**STRIKES/LOCKOUTS**	●		V.F., pages 9–10
210	**VIOLATION OF LAWS**	—		
211	ANY LAW	—		
212	FMLA	—		
213	OSHA	●		V.E., page 9
214	POLLUTION LAWS	—		
215	RICO	—		
216	SEC	—		
217	WARN	●		V.G., page 10
15	**CONDITIONS**			
218	**ARBITRATION**	●		VII.E., page 14
219	MANDATORY	●		VII.E.(1)., page 14
220	BINDING	●		VII.E.(3)., page 15
221	CHOICE OF LAW PROVISION	●	New York—Exceptions apply	VII.F., pages 16–17
222	SITUS	●	London, England	VII.E.(1)., page 14
223	**TERRITORY**	●		VII.D., page 14
224	LIMITED	—		
225	WORLDWIDE	●		VII.D., page 14
226	**NEWLY FORMED/ACQUIRED ENTITIES**	●		VII.K.2., page 21
227	AUTOMATIC COVERAGE (X DAYS)	90	If > 1,000/5% of employees	VII.K.2., page 21
228	NOTIFY INSURER WITHIN X DAYS	30	If < 1,000/5% of employees	VII.K.2., page 21

X.L. INSURANCE COMPANY, LTD. EPLI-005 [7/98]

Policy Comparison Worksheet

Zurich American Insurance Company

Policy Form No.: STF-EPL-101-A
Edition Date: 3/98

Risks Considered: General accounts
Limits Available: $50,000,000
Minimum Retention: $25,000

Contact: Lisa R. McElroy
Assistant Vice President
Zurich American Insurance Group
One Liberty Plaza, 30th Floor
New York, NY 10006
212/748-2375
212/619-0790 (fax)
lisa.mcelroy@zurich.com

KEY TO SYMBOLS
● = Specifically contains queried provision of feature
○ = Unable to determine
— = Silent

#	Comparison Query		Comment	Policy Reference
	1 APPLICATION			
1	ATTACHES TO AND FORMS A PART OF THE POLICY	●	See also V.C., page 6	Application, page 7
2	CONTAINS WARRANTY STATEMENTS	●		Policy, V.C., page 6
3	CONTAINS SEVERABILITY PROVISIONS	●		Policy, V.C., page 6
	2 POLICY TYPE			
4	UNITARY STAND ALONE POLICY	●		
	ENDORSEMENT OR PART OF	—		
5	DIRECTORS AND OFFICERS POLICY	—		
6	PACKAGE POLICY	—		
7	UMBRELLA POLICY	—		
8	ERRORS AND OMISSIONS POLICY	—		
9	OTHER	—		
10	CLAIMS-MADE	●		
11	OCCURRENCE	—		
	3 WHO IS INSURED			
12	BUSINESS ENTITY	●		III.H., page 4
13	AUTOMATIC COVERAGE FOR SUBSIDIARIES	●		III.R., page 3
14	DIRECTORS & OFFICERS	●		III.G.1., page 3
15	EMPLOYEES	●		III.G.2., page 4
16	PART-TIME	●		III.E., page 3
17	SEASONAL	●		II.E., page 3
18	TEMPORARY	●		II.E., page 3
19	SUPERVISORS & MANAGERS	—		
20	FORMER EMPLOYEES	●		II.E., page 3
21	VOLUNTEERS	●		II.E., page 3
22	INDEPENDENT CONTRACTORS	●	If law treats as employee	II.E., page 3
23	EXCLUDED	—		
24	SILENT	—		
25	SHAREHOLDERS			
	4 LIMIT OF LIABILITY			
26	AGGREGATE	●		V.A., pages 5–6
27	INCLUDES PUNITIVE DAMAGES WHERE NOT UNINSURABLE	—	Coverage available by endorsement	
28	DEFENSE COSTS INCLUDED WITHIN LIMIT OF LIABILITY	●	See also III.J., page 4	V.A., pages 5–6
29	DEFENSE COSTS PAID IN ADDITION TO LIMIT OF LIABILITY	—		
	5 DEDUCTIBLE			
30	APPLIES TO EACH INDIVIDUAL CLAIM	●		V.A., pages 5–6
31	APPLIES TO EACH OCCURRENCE OR WRONGFUL PRACTICE	—		
32	INCLUDES ALL CLAIMS FROM ONE ACT	●		V.A., pages 5–6
33	SUBJECT TO ANNUAL AGGREGATE	—		
34	CO-PAYMENT APPLIES	●		V.A., pages 5–6
35	LIMIT OF LIABILITY NOT REDUCED	—		
36	INCLUDES DEFENSE COSTS	●		V.A., pages 5–6
37	REDUCED UNDER SPECIFIED CIRCUMSTANCES (SEE POLICY)	—		

#	Comparison Query	Comment	Policy Reference
6	**WHAT IS A CLAIM**		
38	ORAL COMPLAINT TO INSURED	—	
39	WRITTEN COMPLAINT TO INSURED	●	III.A.1., page 3
40	COMPLAINT MUST CONTAIN A DEMAND FOR DAMAGES	●	III.A.1., page 3
41	COMPLAINT FILED WITH EEOC	●	III.A.3., page 3
42	OR SIMILAR STATE AUTHORITY	●	III.D., page 3
43	AGENCY MUST HAVE POWER TO ADJUDICATE	●	III.D., page 3
44	ADMINISTRATIVE PROCEEDING	●	Administrative or regulatory	III.A.3., page 4
45	ARBITRATION PROCEEDING	●		III.A.5., page 3
46	ANY INCIDENT REPORTED TO INSURER	—	
47	SUIT	●		III.A.2., page 3
48	CLAIM DOES NOT INCLUDE ARBITRATION SUBJECT TO	—	
49	COLLECTIVE BARGAINING AGREEMENT	—	
50	EMPLOYEE POLICY OR MANUAL	—	
51	CLAIM NOT DEFINED	—	
7	**CLAIM REPORTING PROVISIONS TO INSURER**		
52	IMMEDIATELY	—	
53	AS SOON AS POSSIBLE	—	
54	AS SOON AS PRACTICABLE	●		V.B., page 6
55	WITHIN POLICY PERIOD	—	
56	WITHIN X DAYS OF EXPIRATION	90		V.B., page 6
57	WITHIN X DAYS	—	
8	**EXTENDED REPORTING FEATURES**		
58	ELECTION PERIOD (DAYS)	30		II.B., page 3
59	ADDITIONAL PREMIUM (% OF ANNUAL PREMIUM)	○	Specified by underwriter—See Item 7.(a). of Declarations	II.B., page 3
60	ADDITIONAL REPORTING PERIOD (MONTHS)	○	Specified by underwriter—See Item 7.(b). of Declarations	II.B., page 3
61	NO REINSTATEMENT OF LIMITS	—	
9	**POTENTIAL CLAIM REPORTING PROVISIONS**		
62	NONE (SEE ALSO "CLAIM" ABOVE)	—	
63	INCIDENTS LIKELY TO RESULT IN A CLAIM	●		V.B., page 6
10	**DEFENSE PROVISIONS**		
64	AFFIRMATIVE DUTY TO DEFEND	●		I.B., page 1
65	NO AFFIRMATIVE DUTY TO DEFEND	—	
66	AFFIRMATIVE ADVANCEMENT PROVISIONS	—	
67	INSURED MUST RETURN ADVANCED AMOUNTS IF NOT COVERED	—	
68	INSURED/INSURER CHOOSES COUNSEL	●	Insurer chooses	I.B., page 1
69	INSURED/INSURER APPROVES COUNSEL	●	Insured must consent	I.B., page 1
70	INSURED/INSURER CONSULTED IN COUNSEL SELECTION	—	
11	**SETTLEMENT PROVISIONS**		
71	HAMMER CLAUSE	●		I.B., page 1
72	CONSULTATION PROVISION	—	
73	CONSENT PROVISION	●	Two-way	I.B., page 1
12	**ALLOCATION OF LOSS PROVISIONS**		
74	STIPULATED PROVISIONS	—	
13	**COVERAGES**		
75	DISCRIMINATION	●	As wrongful employment act	III.O., page 4
76	SPECIFIC ENUMERATED ACTIVITIES	—	
77	*PLUS BROAD OMNIBUS WORDING*	●		III.O., page 4
78	SPECIFIC ENUMERATED CLASSES	—	
79	*PLUS BROAD OMNIBUS WORDING*	—	
80	AGAINST THIRD PARTIES	—	Coverage available by endorsement	
81	DISCRIMINATION NOT DEFINED	●	
82	SEXUAL HARASSMENT	●	As wrongful employment act	III.O., page 4
83	HOSTILE ENVIRONMENT	○		III.O., page 4
84	QUID-PRO-QUO	—	
85	SEXUAL HARASSMENT NOT DEFINED	●	
86	WRONGFUL TERMINATION	●	As wrongful employment act	III.O., page 4
87	BREACH OF IMPLIED CONTRACT	●		III.O., page 4
88	BREACH OF EXPRESS CONTRACT	●	Oral or written	III.O., page 4
89	VIOLATION OF PUBLIC POLICY	—	
90	VIOLATION OF GOOD FAITH & FAIR DEALING	—	
91	OBLIGATIONS TO MAKE PAYMENTS	—	
92	CONSTRUCTIVE DISCHARGE	●		III.O., page 4
93	WRONGFUL TERMINATION NOT DEFINED	●		III.O., page 4
94	OTHER EMPLOYMENT VIOLATIONS/OFFENSES	●	As wrongful employment act	III.O., page 4
95	WRONGFUL HIRING	●		III.O., page 4
96	WRONGFUL PROMOTION/DEMOTION	●		III.O., page 4
97	WRONGFUL EVALUATION/DISCIPLINE	●		III.O., page 4

ZURICH AMERICAN INSURANCE COMPANY STF-EPL-101-A [3/98]

#	Comparison Query		Comment	Policy Reference
98	FAMILY AND MEDICAL LEAVE ACT	—		
99	DEFAMATION	●	Employment-related	III.O., page 4
100	MISREPRESENTATION	●	Employment-related	III.O., page 4
101	RETALIATION	●		III.O., page 4
102	MENTAL ANGUISH	●		III.A.4., page 5
103	INVASION OF PRIVACY	●	Employment-related	III.O., page 4
104	HUMILIATION	—		
105	EMOTIONAL DISTRESS	●	Employment-related	III.O., page 4
106	OTHER PERSONAL INJURY OFFENSES	●		III.O., page 4
107	POLICY SILENT	—		

14 EXCLUSIONS

#	Comparison Query		Comment	Policy Reference
108	**ADA ACCOMMODATION EXPENSES**	—		
109	**ASSAULT & BATTERY**	—		
110	**BACK PAY**	—		
111	**BODILY INJURY**	●		III.A.4., page 5
112	BODILY INJURY	●		III.A.4., page 5
113	DEATH	●		III.A.4., page 5
114	DISEASE	●		III.A.4., page 5
115	SICKNESS	●		III.A.4., page 5
116	**BREACH OF EMPLOYMENT CONTRACT**	—		
117	EXPRESS CONTRACT	—		
118	WRITTEN CONTRACT	—		
119	ORAL CONTRACT	—		
120	IMPLIED CONTRACT	—		
121	**CLASS ACTION LAWSUITS**	—		
122	**CONSEQUENTIAL LOSS**	—		
123	APPLIES TO BODILY INJURY	—		
124	APPLIES TO INSURED EVENT	—		
125	BROTHER/SISTER	—		
126	CHILD	—		
127	DOMESTIC PARTNER	—		
128	PARENT	—		
129	SPOUSE	—		
130	**COST OF ARBITRATION HEARINGS SUBJECT TO**	—		
131	EMPLOYMENT HANDBOOK	—		
132	LABOR GRIEVANCE	—		
133	OTHER EMPLOYMENT POLICY OR PROCEDURE	—		
134	**COVERAGE ELSEWHERE**	●		V.G., page 8
135	OTHER AVAILABLE INSURANCE	—		
136	OTHER INDEMNIFICATION	—		
137	SHARING PROVISION	●		V.G., page 8
138	**FAILURE TO EXERCISE CARE WHEN TERMINATING**	—		
139	**FINES/PENALTIES**	●		III.J.(2)., page 4
140	CIVIL	—		
141	CRIMINAL	—		
142	EXEMPLARY DAMAGES	●	Coverage available by endorsement	III.J.(5)., page 4
143	PUNITIVE DAMAGES	●	Coverage available by endorsement	III.J.(5)., page 4
144	MULTIPLIED DAMAGES	●	Coverage available by endorsement	III.J.(5)., page 4
145	**FRONT PAY**	—		
146	EXCLUSION APPLIES ONLY IF EMPLOYER HAD OPPORTUNITY TO REINSTATE EMPLOYEE BUT DID NOT DO SO	—		
147	**INTENTIONAL ACTS**	—		
148	CRIMINAL ACTS	—		
149	CRIMINAL PROCEEDING	—		
150	DISHONEST PURPOSE	—		
151	FRAUDULENT ACTS	—		
152	FRAUDULENT CLAIMS	—		
153	INTENTIONAL VIOLATIONS OF LAW	—		
154	WILLFUL FAILURE TO COMPLY WITH LAW	—		
155	MALICIOUS PURPOSE	—		
156	**LIABILITY OF OTHERS**	—		
157	**LIQUIDATED DAMAGES**	—		
158	**LOSS ARISING OUT OF CHANGES IN OPERATIONS**	—		
159	ACQUISITION	—		
160	CHANGE IN CONTROL	—		
161	DOWNSIZING OR REDUCTION IN FORCE	—		
162	% OF WORKFORCE	—		
163	WITHIN X DAYS	—		

	Comparison Query	Comment		Policy Reference
164	FINANCIAL IMPAIRMENT	—		
165	BANKRUPTCY	—		
166	INSOLVENCY	—		
167	LIQUIDATION	—		
168	RECEIVERSHIP	—		
169	FINANCIAL INABILITY TO PAY	—		
170	MERGER	—		
171	PLANT OR FACILITY CLOSING	—		
172	REORGANIZATION	—		
173	TEMPORARY SHUTDOWN	—		
174	**MATTERS DEEMED UNINSURABLE**	●		III.J.(6)., page 4
175	**NON-MONETARY RELIEF**	—		
176	DECLATORY RELIEF	—		
177	DISGORGEMENT	—		
178	INJUNCTIVE RELIEF	●		III.J.(4)., page 4
179	JOB REINSTATEMENT	—		
180	NON-MONETARY DAMAGES/RELIEF	●		III.J.(4)., page 4
181	OTHER EQUITABLE REMEDIES	—		
182	**OBLIGATION TO PROVIDE BENEFITS**	—		
183	COBRA	●	Retaliation exception	IV.A.(3).(vi)., page 5
184	DISABILITY	●	Retaliation exception	IV.A.(3).(i)., page 5
185	ERISA	●	Retaliation exception	IV.A.(3).(ii)., page 5
186	SOCIAL SECURITY	●	Retaliation exception	IV.A.(3).(i)., page 5
187	OTHER RETIREMENT BENEFITS	—		
188	UNEMPLOYMENT	●	Retaliation exception	IV.A.(3).(i)., page 5
189	WORKERS' COMPENSATION	●	Retaliation exception	IV.A.(3).(i)., page 5
190	**PERSONAL INJURY OFFENSES**	—		
191	DEFAMATION	—		
192	EMOTIONAL DISTRESS/UPSET	—		
193	HUMILIATION	—		
194	LIBEL	—		
195	MENTAL ANGUISH	—		
196	PERSONAL INJURY	—		
197	SLANDER	—		
198	**PRIOR ACTS**	—		
199	PRIOR ACTS	—		
200	PRIOR KNOWLEDGE	—		
201	PRIOR/PENDING LITIGATION	●		IV.A.2., page 5
202	**PROPERTY DAMAGE**	●		III.A.4., page 5
203	INTANGIBLE PROPERTY	—		
204	LOSS OF USE	●		III.A.4., page 5
205	TANGIBLE PROPERTY	●		III.A.4., page 5
206	**RETALIATORY ACTIONS OF EMPLOYER**	—		
207	FOR FAILING TO PERFORM ACTS AGAINST PUBLIC POLICY	—		
208	FOR FILING A COMPLAINT OR BENEFIT CLAIM	—		
209	**STRIKES/LOCKOUTS**	—		
210	**VIOLATION OF LAWS**	—		
211	ANY LAW	—		
212	FMLA	—		
213	OSHA	●	Retaliation exception	IV.A.(3).(vii)., page 5
214	POLLUTION LAWS	—		
215	RICO	—		
216	SEC	—		
217	WARN	●	Retaliation exception	IV.A.(3).(v)., page 5
	15 CONDITIONS			
218	**ARBITRATION**	●		V.E., page 7
219	MANDATORY	●		V.E., page 7
220	BINDING	●		V.E., page 7
221	CHOICE OF LAW PROVISION	—		
222	SITUS	—		
223	**TERRITORY**	●		V.F., page 7
224	LIMITED	—		
225	WORLDWIDE	●		V.F., page 7
226	**NEWLY FORMED/ACQUIRED ENTITIES**	●		V.D.1., page 7
227	AUTOMATIC COVERAGE (X DAYS)	●	No time limit	IV.D.1., page 7
228	NOTIFY INSURER WITHIN X DAYS	90	Addition of employees—See policy	V.D.2.6., page 7

ZURICH AMERICAN INSURANCE COMPANY STF-EPL-101-A [3/98]

Policy Comparison Worksheet

Zurich Insurance Company

Policy Form No.: U-DO-111-A (CW) (2/97)
Edition Date: 2/97

Risks Considered: General accounts
Limits Available: $10,000,000
Minimum Retention: None

Contact: Jay M. Dipasupil
Zurich Insurance Company
One Liberty Plaza, 30th Floor
New York, NY 10006
212/748-2372
212/513-1239 (fax)

KEY TO SYMBOLS
- ● = Specifically contains queried provision of feature
- ○ = Unable to determine
- — = Silent

#	Comparison Query	Symbol	Comment	Policy Reference
	1 APPLICATION			
1	ATTACHES TO AND FORMS A PART OF THE POLICY	●		Preamble, page 3
2	CONTAINS WARRANTY STATEMENTS	—		
3	CONTAINS SEVERABILITY PROVISIONS	—		
	2 POLICY TYPE			
4	UNITARY STAND ALONE POLICY	●		
	ENDORSEMENT OR PART OF			
5	DIRECTORS AND OFFICERS POLICY	—		
6	PACKAGE POLICY	—		
7	UMBRELLA POLICY	—		
8	ERRORS AND OMISSIONS POLICY	—		
9	OTHER	—		
10	CLAIMS-MADE	●		
11	OCCURRENCE	—		
	3 WHO IS INSURED			
12	BUSINESS ENTITY	●	See also III.H., page 4	III.B., page 4
13	AUTOMATIC COVERAGE FOR SUBSIDIARIES	●		III.B., page 4
14	DIRECTORS & OFFICERS	●		III.I., page 4
15	EMPLOYEES	●		III.I., page 4
16	PART-TIME	—		
17	SEASONAL	—		
18	TEMPORARY	—		
19	SUPERVISORS & MANAGERS	●		III.I., page 4
20	FORMER EMPLOYEES	—		
21	VOLUNTEERS	—		
22	INDEPENDENT CONTRACTORS			
23	EXCLUDED	—		
24	SILENT	●		III.I., page 4
25	SHAREHOLDERS			
	4 LIMIT OF LIABILITY			
26	AGGREGATE	●		V.C., page 8
27	INCLUDES PUNITIVE DAMAGES WHERE NOT UNINSURABLE	●	To maximum of $100,000	III.K., page 4
28	DEFENSE COSTS INCLUDED WITHIN LIMIT OF LIABILITY	●		V.C., page 8
29	DEFENSE COSTS PAID IN ADDITION TO LIMIT OF LIABILITY	—		
	5 DEDUCTIBLE			
30	APPLIES TO EACH INDIVIDUAL CLAIM	●		V.C., page 9
31	APPLIES TO EACH OCCURRENCE OR WRONGFUL PRACTICE	—		
32	INCLUDES ALL CLAIMS FROM ONE ACT	●		V.C., page 9
33	SUBJECT TO ANNUAL AGGREGATE	—		
34	CO-PAYMENT APPLIES	—		
35	LIMIT OF LIABILITY NOT REDUCED	—		
36	INCLUDES DEFENSE COSTS	●	See also III.K., page 5	V.C., page 9
37	REDUCED UNDER SPECIFIED CIRCUMSTANCES (SEE POLICY)	—		

ZURICH INSURANCE COMPANY U-DO-111-A (CW) [2/97]

#	Comparison Query	Comment	Policy Reference
	6 WHAT IS A CLAIM		
38	ORAL COMPLAINT TO INSURED	—	
39	WRITTEN COMPLAINT TO INSURED	●	III.A.1., page 4
40	COMPLAINT MUST CONTAIN A DEMAND FOR DAMAGES	●	III.A.1., page 4
41	COMPLAINT FILED WITH EEOC	●	III.A.4., page 4
42	OR SIMILAR STATE AUTHORITY	●	III.A.4., page 4
43	AGENCY MUST HAVE POWER TO ADJUDICATE	—	
44	ADMINISTRATIVE PROCEEDING	●	III.A.4., page 4
45	ARBITRATION PROCEEDING	●	III.A.5., page 4
46	ANY INCIDENT REPORTED TO INSURER	—	
47	SUIT	●	Civil proceeding	III.A.2., page 4
48	CLAIM DOES NOT INCLUDE ARBITRATION SUBJECT TO		
49	COLLECTIVE BARGAINING AGREEMENT	—	
50	EMPLOYEE POLICY OR MANUAL	—	
51	CLAIM NOT DEFINED	—	
	7 CLAIM REPORTING PROVISIONS TO INSURER		
52	IMMEDIATELY	—	
53	AS SOON AS POSSIBLE	—	
54	AS SOON AS PRACTICABLE	●	V.H., pages 10–11
55	WITHIN POLICY PERIOD	—	
56	WITHIN X DAYS OF EXPIRATION	90	V.H., pages 10–11
57	WITHIN X DAYS	—	
	8 EXTENDED REPORTING FEATURES		
58	ELECTION PERIOD (DAYS)	30	II.B., page 3
59	ADDITIONAL PREMIUM (% OF ANNUAL PREMIUM)	○	Specified by underwriter—see Item 7(A) of Declarations	II.B., page 3
60	ADDITIONAL REPORTING PERIOD (MONTHS)	○	Specified by underwriter—see Item 7(B) of Declarations	II.B., page 3
61	NO REINSTATEMENT OF LIMITS		
	9 POTENTIAL CLAIM REPORTING PROVISIONS		
62	NONE (SEE ALSO "CLAIM" ABOVE)	—	
63	INCIDENTS LIKELY TO RESULT IN A CLAIM	●	V.H., pages 10–11
	10 DEFENSE PROVISIONS		
64	AFFIRMATIVE DUTY TO DEFEND	●	V.F., page 10
65	NO AFFIRMATIVE DUTY TO DEFEND	—	
66	AFFIRMATIVE ADVANCEMENT PROVISIONS	—	
67	INSURED MUST RETURN ADVANCED AMOUNTS IF NOT COVERED	—	
68	INSURED/INSURER CHOOSES COUNSEL	●	Insurer	V.F., page 10
69	INSURED/INSURER APPROVES COUNSEL	—	
70	INSURED/INSURER CONSULTED IN COUNSEL SELECTION	—	
	11 SETTLEMENT PROVISIONS		
71	HAMMER CLAUSE	●	V.F., page 10
72	CONSULTATION PROVISION	—	
73	CONSENT PROVISION	●	Two-way	V.F., page 10
	12 ALLOCATION OF LOSS PROVISIONS		
74	STIPULATED PROVISIONS	●	V.D., page 9
	13 COVERAGES		
75	DISCRIMINATION	●	III.E., page 4
76	SPECIFIC ENUMERATED ACTIVITIES	—	
77	PLUS BROAD OMNIBUS WORDING	—	
78	SPECIFIC ENUMERATED CLASSES	—	
79	PLUS BROAD OMNIBUS WORDING	—	
80	AGAINST THIRD PARTIES	—	
81	DISCRIMINATION NOT DEFINED	●	
82	SEXUAL HARASSMENT	●	III.E., page 4
83	HOSTILE ENVIRONMENT	—	
84	QUID-PRO-QUO	—	
85	SEXUAL HARASSMENT NOT DEFINED	●	
86	WRONGFUL TERMINATION	●	III.E., page 4
87	BREACH OF IMPLIED CONTRACT	—	
88	BREACH OF EXPRESS CONTRACT	●	III.E., page 4
89	VIOLATION OF PUBLIC POLICY	—	
90	VIOLATION OF GOOD FAITH & FAIR DEALING	—	
91	OBLIGATIONS TO MAKE PAYMENTS	—	
92	CONSTRUCTIVE DISCHARGE	—	
93	WRONGFUL TERMINATION NOT DEFINED	●	
94	**OTHER EMPLOYMENT VIOLATIONS/OFFENSES**		
95	WRONGFUL HIRING	●	III.E., page 4
96	WRONGFUL PROMOTION/DEMOTION	●	III.E., page 4
97	WRONGFUL EVALUATION/DISCIPLINE	●	III.E., page 4

ZURICH INSURANCE COMPANY U-DO-111-A (CW) [2/97]

	Comparison Query		Comment	Policy Reference
98	FAMILY AND MEDICAL LEAVE ACT	—		
99	DEFAMATION	●		III.E., page 4
100	MISREPRESENTATION	●		III.E., page 4
101	RETALIATION	—		
102	MENTAL ANGUISH	●	See also III.E., page 4	IV.A.5., page 6
103	INVASION OF PRIVACY	●		III.E., page 4
104	HUMILIATION	—		
105	EMOTIONAL DISTRESS	●	See also IV.A.5., page 6	III.E., page 4
106	OTHER PERSONAL INJURY OFFENSES	—		
107	POLICY SILENT	—		

14 EXCLUSIONS

	Comparison Query		Comment	Policy Reference
108	**ADA ACCOMMODATION EXPENSES**	●		IV.B.7., page 7
109	**ASSAULT & BATTERY**	—		
110	**BACK PAY**	—		
111	**BODILY INJURY**	●		IV.A.5., page 6
112	BODILY INJURY	●		IV.A.5., page 6
113	DEATH	●		IV.A.5., page 6
114	DISEASE	●		IV.A.5., page 6
115	SICKNESS	●		IV.A.5., page 6
116	**BREACH OF EMPLOYMENT CONTRACT**			
117	EXPRESS CONTRACT	—		
118	*WRITTEN CONTRACT*	●	Any contract or agreement	IV.B.6., page 7
119	*ORAL CONTRACT*	—		
120	IMPLIED CONTRACT	—		
121	**CLASS ACTION LAWSUITS**	—		
122	**CONSEQUENTIAL LOSS**			
123	APPLIES TO BODILY INJURY	—		
124	APPLIES TO INSURED EVENT	—		
125	BROTHER/SISTER	—		
126	CHILD	—		
127	DOMESTIC PARTNER	—		
128	PARENT	—		
129	SPOUSE	—		
130	**COST OF ARBITRATION HEARINGS SUBJECT TO**			
131	EMPLOYMENT HANDBOOK	—		
132	LABOR GRIEVANCE	—		
133	OTHER EMPLOYMENT POLICY OR PROCEDURE	—		
134	**COVERAGE ELSEWHERE**			
135	OTHER AVAILABLE INSURANCE	●		V.I., page 7
136	OTHER INDEMNIFICATION	—		
137	SHARING PROVISION	—		
138	**FAILURE TO EXERCISE CARE WHEN TERMINATING**			
139	**FINES/PENALTIES**	●		III.K.3., page 5
140	CIVIL	—		
141	CRIMINAL	—		
142	EXEMPLARY DAMAGES	●	If less than $100,000	III.I.4., page 5
143	PUNITIVE DAMAGES	●	If less than $100,000	III.I.4., page 5
144	MULTIPLIED DAMAGES	●	If less than $100,000	III.I.4., page 5
145	**FRONT PAY**	●		IV.B.4., page 7
146	EXCLUSION APPLIES ONLY IF EMPLOYER HAD OPPORTUNITY TO REINSTATE EMPLOYEE BUT DID NOT DO SO	●		IV.B.4., page 7
147	**INTENTIONAL ACTS**			
148	CRIMINAL ACTS	●		IV.A.12., page 7
149	CRIMINAL PROCEEDING	—		
150	DISHONEST PURPOSE	—		
151	FRAUDULENT ACTS	●		IV.A.12., page 7
152	FRAUDULENT CLAIMS	—		
153	INTENTIONAL VIOLATIONS OF LAW	○	Violation of statute	IV.A.12., page 7
154	WILLFUL FAILURE TO COMPLY WITH LAW	●	If established by adjudication	IV.A.12., page 7
155	MALICIOUS PURPOSE	—		
156	**LIABILITY OF OTHERS**	—		
157	**LIQUIDATED DAMAGES**	—		
158	**LOSS ARISING OUT OF CHANGES IN OPERATIONS**			
159	ACQUISITION	—		
160	CHANGE IN CONTROL	—		
161	DOWNSIZING OR REDUCTION IN FORCE	—		
162	*% OF WORKFORCE*	—		
163	*WITHIN X DAYS*	—		

ZURICH INSURANCE COMPANY U-DO-111-A (CW) [2/97]

#	Comparison Query	Comment	Policy Reference
164	**FINANCIAL IMPAIRMENT**	—	
165	BANKRUPTCY	—	
166	INSOLVENCY	—	
167	LIQUIDATION	—	
168	RECEIVERSHIP	—	
169	FINANCIAL INABILITY TO PAY	—	
170	MERGER	—	
171	PLANT OR FACILITY CLOSING	—	
172	REORGANIZATION	—	
173	TEMPORARY SHUTDOWN	—	
174	**MATTERS DEEMED UNINSURABLE**	●	III.K.5., page 5
175	**NON-MONETARY RELIEF**		
176	DECLATORY RELIEF	—	
177	DISGORGEMENT	—	
178	INJUNCTIVE RELIEF	—	
179	JOB REINSTATEMENT	●	IV.B.3., page 7
180	NON-MONETARY DAMAGES/RELIEF	●	IV.B.5., page 7
181	OTHER EQUITABLE REMEDIES	—	
182	**OBLIGATION TO PROVIDE BENEFITS**		
183	COBRA	●	IV.C.1., page 7
184	DISABILITY	●	Retaliation exception	IV.B.1., page 7
185	ERISA	●		IV.A.4., page 6
186	SOCIAL SECURITY	—	
187	OTHER RETIREMENT BENEFITS	—	
188	UNEMPLOYMENT	—	
189	WORKERS' COMPENSATION	●	Retaliation exception	IV.B.1., page 7
190	**PERSONAL INJURY OFFENSES**		
191	DEFAMATION	—	
192	EMOTIONAL DISTRESS/UPSET	—	
193	HUMILIATION	—	
194	LIBEL	—	
195	MENTAL ANGUISH	—	
196	PERSONAL INJURY	—	
197	SLANDER	—	
198	**PRIOR ACTS**		
199	PRIOR ACTS	—	
200	PRIOR KNOWLEDGE	—	
201	PRIOR/PENDING LITIGATION	●	IV.A.2., page 6
202	**PROPERTY DAMAGE**		
203	INTANGIBLE PROPERTY	—	
204	LOSS OF USE	●	IV.A.5., page 6
205	TANGIBLE PROPERTY	●	IV.A.5., page 6
206	**RETALIATORY ACTIONS OF EMPLOYER**		
207	FOR FAILING TO PERFORM ACTS AGAINST PUBLIC POLICY	—	
208	FOR FILING A COMPLAINT OR BENEFIT CLAIM	—	
209	**STRIKES/LOCKOUTS**	●	IV.C.2., page 7
210	**VIOLATION OF LAWS**		
211	ANY LAW	—	
212	FMLA	—	
213	OSHA	●	IV.C.1., page 7
214	POLLUTION LAWS	●	Retaliation exception	IV.A.6., page 6
215	RICO	—	
216	SEC	—	
217	WARN	●	IV.C.1., page 7
	15 CONDITIONS		
218	**ARBITRATION**		
219	MANDATORY	—	
220	BINDING	—	
221	CHOICE OF LAW PROVISION	—	
222	SITUS	—	
223	**TERRITORY**		
224	LIMITED	—	
225	WORLDWIDE	●	V.G., page 10
226	**NEWLY FORMED/ACQUIRED ENTITIES**		
227	AUTOMATIC COVERAGE (X DAYS)	●	No limit if <25% company assets involved	V.E., page 9
228	NOTIFY INSURER WITHIN X DAYS	○	As soon as practicable	V.E., pages 9–10

ZURICH INSURANCE COMPANY U-DO-111-A (CW) [2/97]

Policy Comparison Worksheet

Zurich Insurance Company

Policy Form No.: U-DO-457-A (CW)
Edition Date: 4/97

Risks Considered: Large companies (public and private)
Limits Available: $50,000,000
Minimum Retention: None

Contact: Jay M. Dipasupil
Zurich Insurance Company
One Liberty Plaza, 30th Floor
New York, NY 10006
212/748-2372
212/513-1239 (fax)

KEY TO SYMBOLS
● = Specifically contains queried provision of feature
○ = Unable to determine
— = Silent

#	Comparison Query	Comment	Policy Reference
	1 APPLICATION		
1	ATTACHES TO AND FORMS A PART OF THE POLICY	●	Policy C., page 7
2	CONTAINS WARRANTY STATEMENTS	—	
3	CONTAINS SEVERABILITY PROVISIONS	—	
	2 POLICY TYPE		
4	UNITARY STAND ALONE POLICY	—	
	ENDORSEMENT OR PART OF		
5	DIRECTORS AND OFFICERS POLICY	● Policy form U-DO-100-A (CW) (5/93)	
6	PACKAGE POLICY	—	
7	UMBRELLA POLICY	—	
8	ERRORS AND OMISSIONS POLICY	—	
9	OTHER	—	
10	CLAIMS-MADE	●	
11	OCCURRENCE	—	
	3 WHO IS INSURED		
12	BUSINESS ENTITY	●	Policy III.B., page 4
13	AUTOMATIC COVERAGE FOR SUBSIDIARIES	●	Policy III.B., page 4
14	DIRECTORS & OFFICERS	●	Policy III.F., page 4
15	EMPLOYEES	—	
16	PART-TIME	—	
17	SEASONAL	—	
18	TEMPORARY	—	
19	SUPERVISORS & MANAGERS	—	
20	FORMER EMPLOYEES	—	
21	VOLUNTEERS	—	
22	INDEPENDENT CONTRACTORS		
23	EXCLUDED	—	
24	SILENT	●	
25	SHAREHOLDERS	—	
	4 LIMIT OF LIABILITY		
26	AGGREGATE	●	Endorsement 9., page 2
27	INCLUDES PUNITIVE DAMAGES WHERE NOT UNINSURABLE	—	
28	DEFENSE COSTS INCLUDED WITHIN LIMIT OF LIABILITY	●	Endorsement 9., page 3
29	DEFENSE COSTS PAID IN ADDITION TO LIMIT OF LIABILITY	—	
	5 DEDUCTIBLE		
30	APPLIES TO EACH INDIVIDUAL CLAIM	●	Endorsement 9., page 2
31	APPLIES TO EACH OCCURRENCE OR WRONGFUL PRACTICE	● See also Endorsement 9., page 3	Endorsement 9., page 2
32	INCLUDES ALL CLAIMS FROM ONE ACT	●	Endorsement 9., page 3
33	SUBJECT TO ANNUAL AGGREGATE	—	
34	CO-PAYMENT APPLIES	● Specified by underwriter—see Item 5 of Declarations	Endorsement 9., page 3
35	LIMIT OF LIABILITY NOT REDUCED	—	
36	INCLUDES DEFENSE COSTS	● See also Policy III.H., page 4	Endorsement 9., page 3
37	REDUCED UNDER SPECIFIED CIRCUMSTANCES (SEE POLICY)	—	

ZURICH INSURANCE COMPANY U-DO-457-A (CW) [4/97]

#	Comparison Query	Comment	Policy Reference
	6 WHAT IS A CLAIM		
38	ORAL COMPLAINT TO INSURED	—	
39	WRITTEN COMPLAINT TO INSURED	●	Policy III.A.1., page 4
40	COMPLAINT MUST CONTAIN A DEMAND FOR DAMAGES	●	Policy III.A.1., page 4
41	COMPLAINT FILED WITH EEOC		
42	OR SIMILAR STATE AUTHORITY	—	
43	AGENCY MUST HAVE POWER TO ADJUDICATE	—	
44	ADMINISTRATIVE PROCEEDING	—	
45	ARBITRATION PROCEEDING	—	
46	ANY INCIDENT REPORTED TO INSURER	—	
47	SUIT	● Civil proceeding	Policy III.A.2., page 4
48	CLAIM DOES NOT INCLUDE ARBITRATION SUBJECT TO		
49	COLLECTIVE BARGAINING AGREEMENT	—	
50	EMPLOYEE POLICY OR MANUAL	—	
51	CLAIM NOT DEFINED	—	
	7 CLAIM REPORTING PROVISIONS TO INSURER		
52	IMMEDIATELY	—	
53	AS SOON AS POSSIBLE	—	
54	AS SOON AS PRACTICABLE	●	Policy V.H., page 9
55	WITHIN POLICY PERIOD	—	
56	WITHIN X DAYS OF EXPIRATION	90	Policy V.H., page 9
57	WITHIN X DAYS		
	8 EXTENDED REPORTING FEATURES		
58	ELECTION PERIOD (DAYS)	15	Policy II.B., page 3
59	ADDITIONAL PREMIUM (% OF ANNUAL PREMIUM)	○ Specified by underwriter—see Item 7(A) of Declarations	Policy II.B., page 3
60	ADDITIONAL REPORTING PERIOD (MONTHS)	○ Specified by underwriter—see Item 7(B) of Declarations	Policy II.B., page 3
61	NO REINSTATEMENT OF LIMITS	—	
	9 POTENTIAL CLAIM REPORTING PROVISIONS		
62	NONE (SEE ALSO "CLAIM" ABOVE)	—	
63	INCIDENTS LIKELY TO RESULT IN A CLAIM	●	Policy V.H., page 9
	10 DEFENSE PROVISIONS		
64	AFFIRMATIVE DUTY TO DEFEND	—	
65	NO AFFIRMATIVE DUTY TO DEFEND	●	Policy V.F., page 8
66	AFFIRMATIVE ADVANCEMENT PROVISIONS	● Regarding covered loss	Policy V.D., page 7
67	INSURED MUST RETURN ADVANCED AMOUNTS IF NOT COVERED	●	Policy V.D., page 7
68	INSURED/INSURER CHOOSES COUNSEL	—	
69	INSURED/INSURER APPROVES COUNSEL	—	
70	INSURED/INSURER CONSULTED IN COUNSEL SELECTION	—	
	11 SETTLEMENT PROVISIONS		
71	HAMMER CLAUSE	—	
72	CONSULTATION PROVISION	—	
73	CONSENT PROVISION	● Two-way	Policy V.F., page 7
	12 ALLOCATION OF LOSS PROVISIONS		
74	STIPULATED PROVISIONS	●	Policy V.D., page 7
	13 COVERAGES		
75	DISCRIMINATION	●	Endorsement 2.(a)., page 1
76	SPECIFIC ENUMERATED ACTIVITIES	—	
77	*PLUS BROAD OMNIBUS WORDING*	—	
78	SPECIFIC ENUMERATED CLASSES	—	
79	*PLUS BROAD OMNIBUS WORDING*	—	
80	AGAINST THIRD PARTIES	—	
81	DISCRIMINATION NOT DEFINED	●	Endorsement 2.(a)., page 1
82	SEXUAL HARASSMENT	●	Endorsement 2.(a)., page 1
83	HOSTILE ENVIRONMENT	—	
84	QUID-PRO-QUO	—	
85	SEXUAL HARASSMENT NOT DEFINED	●	Endorsement 2.(a)., page 1
86	WRONGFUL TERMINATION	●	Endorsement 2.(a)., page 1
87	BREACH OF IMPLIED CONTRACT	—	
88	BREACH OF EXPRESS CONTRACT	● Oral or written	Endorsement 2.(a)., page 1
89	VIOLATION OF PUBLIC POLICY	—	
90	VIOLATION OF GOOD FAITH & FAIR DEALING	—	
91	OBLIGATIONS TO MAKE PAYMENTS	—	
92	CONSTRUCTIVE DISCHARGE	—	
93	WRONGFUL TERMINATION NOT DEFINED	—	
94	OTHER EMPLOYMENT VIOLATIONS/OFFENSES		
95	WRONGFUL HIRING	●	Endorsement 2.(a)., page 1
96	WRONGFUL PROMOTION/DEMOTION	●	Endorsement 2.(a)., page 1
97	WRONGFUL EVALUATION/DISCIPLINE	●	Endorsement 2.(a)., page 1

ZURICH INSURANCE COMPANY U-DO-457-A (CW) [4/97]

	Comparison Query	Comment	Policy Reference
98	FAMILY AND MEDICAL LEAVE ACT	—	
99	DEFAMATION	●	Endorsement 2.(a)., page 1
100	MISREPRESENTATION	●	Endorsement 2.(a)., page 1
101	RETALIATION	—	
102	MENTAL ANGUISH	—	
103	INVASION OF PRIVACY	—	
104	HUMILIATION	—	
105	EMOTIONAL DISTRESS	●	Endorsement 2.(a)., page 1
106	OTHER PERSONAL INJURY OFFENSES	●	Endorsement 2.(a)., page 1
107	POLICY SILENT	—	
14 EXCLUSIONS			
108	**ADA ACCOMMODATION EXPENSES**	●	Defense cost exception	Endorsement 7.G., page 2
109	**ASSAULT & BATTERY**	—	
110	**BACK PAY**	—	
111	**BODILY INJURY**		
112	BODILY INJURY	●	Endorsement 6.(b)., page 2
113	DEATH	●	Endorsement 6.(b)., page 2
114	DISEASE	●	Endorsement 6.(b)., page 2
115	SICKNESS	●	Endorsement 6.(b)., page 2
116	**BREACH OF EMPLOYMENT CONTRACT**		
117	EXPRESS CONTRACT	○	Any contract—defense exception	Endorsement 7.F., page 2
118	WRITTEN CONTRACT	○	Any contract—defense exception	Endorsement 7.F., page 2
119	ORAL CONTRACT	○	Any contract—defense exception	Endorsement 7.F., page 2
120	IMPLIED CONTRACT	○	Any contract—defense exception	Endorsement 7.F., page 2
121	**CLASS ACTION LAWSUITS**	—	
122	**CONSEQUENTIAL LOSS**		
123	APPLIES TO BODILY INJURY	—	
124	APPLIES TO INSURED EVENT	—	
125	BROTHER/SISTER	—	
126	CHILD	—	
127	DOMESTIC PARTNER	—	
128	PARENT	—	
129	SPOUSE	—	
130	**COST OF ARBITRATION HEARINGS SUBJECT TO**		
131	EMPLOYMENT HANDBOOK	—	
132	LABOR GRIEVANCE	—	
133	OTHER EMPLOYMENT POLICY OR PROCEDURE	—	
134	**COVERAGE ELSEWHERE**		
135	OTHER AVAILABLE INSURANCE	●	Policy V.I., page 9
136	OTHER INDEMNIFICATION	—	
137	SHARING PROVISION	—	
138	**FAILURE TO EXERCISE CARE WHEN TERMINATING**	—	
139	**FINES/PENALTIES**	●	Policy III.H., page 4
140	CIVIL		
141	CRIMINAL		
142	EXEMPLARY DAMAGES	●	Policy III.H., page 4
143	PUNITIVE DAMAGES	●	Policy III.H., page 4
144	MULTIPLIED DAMAGES	●	Policy III.H., page 4
145	**FRONT PAY**	●	Defense cost exception	Endorsement 7.D., page 2
146	EXCLUSION APPLIES ONLY IF EMPLOYER HAD OPPORTUNITY TO REINSTATE EMPLOYEE BUT DID NOT DO SO	●	Defense cost exception	Endorsement 7.D., page 2
147	**INTENTIONAL ACTS**		
148	CRIMINAL ACTS	—	
149	CRIMINAL PROCEEDING	—	
150	DISHONEST PURPOSE	—	
151	FRAUDULENT ACTS	●	If established	Endorsement 8.C., page 2
152	FRAUDULENT CLAIMS	—	
153	INTENTIONAL VIOLATIONS OF LAW	●	If established	Endorsement 8.C., page 2
154	WILLFUL FAILURE TO COMPLY WITH LAW	●	If established	Endorsement 8.C., page 2
155	MALICIOUS PURPOSE	—	
156	**LIABILITY OF OTHERS**	—	
157	**LIQUIDATED DAMAGES**	—	
158	**LOSS ARISING OUT OF CHANGES IN OPERATIONS**		
159	ACQUISITION	—	
160	CHANGE IN CONTROL	—	
161	DOWNSIZING OR REDUCTION IN FORCE	—	
162	% OF WORKFORCE	—	
163	WITHIN X DAYS	—	

ZURICH INSURANCE COMPANY U-DO-457-A (CW) [4/97]

#	Comparison Query	Comment		Policy Reference
164	FINANCIAL IMPAIRMENT	—		
165	BANKRUPTCY	—		
166	INSOLVENCY	—		
167	LIQUIDATION	—		
168	RECEIVERSHIP	—		
169	FINANCIAL INABILITY TO PAY	—		
170	MERGER	—		
171	PLANT OR FACILITY CLOSING	—		
172	REORGANIZATION	—		
173	TEMPORARY SHUTDOWN	—		
174	**MATTERS DEEMED UNINSURABLE**	●		Policy III.H., page 4
175	**NON-MONETARY RELIEF**			
176	DECLATORY RELIEF	—		
177	DISGORGEMENT	—		
178	INJUNCTIVE RELIEF	—		
179	JOB REINSTATEMENT	●	Defense cost exception	Endorsement 7.C., page 2
180	NON-MONETARY DAMAGES/RELIEF	●		Endorsement 7.E., page 2
181	OTHER EQUITABLE REMEDIES	—		
182	**OBLIGATION TO PROVIDE BENEFITS**			
183	COBRA	●		Endorsement 8.A., page 2
184	DISABILITY	●	Retaliation exception	Endorsement 7.A., page 2
185	ERISA	●		Policy
186	SOCIAL SECURITY	—		
187	OTHER RETIREMENT BENEFITS	—		
188	UNEMPLOYMENT	●	Retaliation exception	Endorsement 7.A., page 2
189	WORKERS' COMPENSATION	●	Retaliation exception	Endorsement 7.A., page 2
190	**PERSONAL INJURY OFFENSES**			
191	DEFAMATION	—		
192	EMOTIONAL DISTRESS/UPSET	—		
193	HUMILIATION	—		
194	LIBEL	—		
195	MENTAL ANGUISH	—		
196	PERSONAL INJURY	—		
197	SLANDER	—		
198	**PRIOR ACTS**			
199	PRIOR ACTS	—		
200	PRIOR KNOWLEDGE	—		
201	PRIOR/PENDING LITIGATION	●		Policy IV.A.2., page 5
202	**PROPERTY DAMAGE**			
203	INTANGIBLE PROPERTY	—		
204	LOSS OF USE	●		Endorsement 6.(b)., page 2
205	TANGIBLE PROPERTY	●		Endorsement 6.(b)., page 2
206	**RETALIATORY ACTIONS OF EMPLOYER**	—		
207	FOR FAILING TO PERFORM ACTS AGAINST PUBLIC POLICY	—		
208	FOR FILING A COMPLAINT OR BENEFIT CLAIM	—		
209	**STRIKES/LOCKOUTS**	●		Endorsement 8.(b)., page 2
210	**VIOLATION OF LAWS**			
211	ANY LAW	—		
212	FMLA	—		
213	OSHA	●		Endorsement 8.A., page 2
214	POLLUTION LAWS	●		Policy VI.A.6., page 5
215	RICO	—		
216	SEC	—		
217	WARN	●		Endorsement 8.A., page 2
	15 CONDITIONS			
218	**ARBITRATION**			
219	MANDATORY	—		
220	BINDING	—		
221	CHOICE OF LAW PROVISION	—		
222	SITUS	—		
223	**TERRITORY**			
224	LIMITED	—		
225	WORLDWIDE	●		Policy V.G., page 9
226	**NEWLY FORMED/ACQUIRED ENTITIES**			
227	AUTOMATIC COVERAGE (X DAYS)	●	No time limit	Policy V.F.1., page 8
228	NOTIFY INSURER WITHIN X DAYS	○	As soon as practicable—conditions apply	Policy V.F.1., page 8

ZURICH INSURANCE COMPANY U-DO-457-A (CW) [4/97]

APPENDIX A

Specimen EPL Form

The following employment practices liability insurance application and policy form are examples of the content and structure of stand-alone EPL coverage. The specimen application and policy form do not constitute a recommendation by the authors or publisher of coverage or an endorsement of any particular policy form, policy wording, agent, broker, insurance company or other service provider.

Specimen

Employment Practices Liability Insurance

DECLARATIONS PAGE

These Declarations along with the completed, signed application, including attachments and the policy with endorsements shall constitute the contract between the Insured and the Underwriters.

Previous No: Authority Ref. No: Certificate No:

SECTION I.   Named Insured:
                    Principal Address:

                    State of Incorporation:

SECTION II.   Policy Period:
                                    to
                    at 12.01 a.m. Standard Time at the Principal Address stated in Section I.

SECTION III.   Premium:

SECTION IV.   Authorized Representative for Claim Notification:

SECTION V.   Limits of Liability: each Insured Event Limit
                                                     Total Aggregate Limit

SECTION VI.   Deductible:

                    Excess of: any One Insured Event

SECTION VII.   Program Administrator:

SECTION VIII.   Special Endorsements attached to this Policy.

Specimen

Employment Practices Liability Insurance

This policy covers Claims first made against the Insured during the Policy Period or an extension thereof arising from Insured Events within the terms, conditions, limitations and exclusions set forth below. It has been issued in reliance upon statements made to the Underwriters in the application and attachments forming a part of this policy.

This is a claims made policy which includes costs of defense within the coverage limits. Terms in bold print are defined terms and have a special meaning as set forth in Section II. Definitions.

I. COVERAGE.

A.1. The Underwriters agree to pay **Loss** amounts on behalf of the **Insured(s)** on account of a **Claim** by a **Claimant** because of an **Insured Event** to which this policy applies. Subject to its terms, conditions and exclusions, this policy applies if the **Claim** is first made against the **Insured** during the Policy Period or any extension thereof.

A.2. The Underwriters agree to pay **Loss** amounts on behalf of the **Insured(s)** on account of a **Claim** first made against the **Insured** during the Policy Period or any extension thereof by a **Third Party Claimant** because of **Third Party Insured Events**. Coverage for **Claims** by **Third Party Claimants** is not available for (a) class actions; (b) assault and battery, or (c) bodily injury.

B. Underwriters have the right and duty to defend any **Claim** for an **Insured Event** made or brought against any **Insured** to which this policy applies, even if the allegations are groundless, false or fraudulent. Underwriters will give consideration to the **Insured's** preference for defense counsel; however, the final decision rests with Underwriters. Underwriters have no duty to provide other services or take other actions. The duty to defend any **Claim** ends when the **Coverage Limits** that apply have been exhausted.

Underwriters have the duty to pay **Defense Costs** incurred for the defense of any **Claim controlled** by Underwriters. Payment of **Defense Costs** is included in the **Coverage Limits**. They are not in addition to the **Coverage Limits**. Underwriters will pay **Defense Costs** before paying any damages from an **Insured Event**. Once **Defense Costs** are paid by Underwriters, Underwriters will not seek to recover those **Defense Costs** from any **Insured**.

C. Underwriters have the right to investigate and settle any **Claim** in the manner and to the extent that they believe is proper. The **Insured** may take over control of any outstanding **Claim** previously reported only if Underwriters agree or if a court orders the take over of control. If the **Coverage Limits** are exhausted, Underwriters will notify the Named Insured of all outstanding **Claims** so that the **Insureds** can take over control of their defense. Underwriters will help transfer control. During the transfer of control, Underwriters agree to take whatever steps are necessary to continue the defense of any outstanding **Claim** and avoid a default judgment during the transfer of control. If Underwriters do so, the **Insureds** agree that Underwriters do not waive or give up any rights. The **Insureds** also agree to pay reasonable expenses Underwriters incur for taking such steps after the **Coverage Limits** are exhausted.

Underwriters will not settle any **Claim** before consulting with the Named Insured. If the **Insureds** refuse to consent to any settlement recommended by Underwriters or their representatives and the **Insureds** elect to contest or continue any legal proceedings, then Underwriters' liability shall not exceed the amount for which the **Claim** could have been settled including **Defense Costs** incurred with Underwriters' consent, up to the date of such refusal.

D. Optional Defense of Criminal Claims. At the request of the Named Insured, Underwriters shall have the option, but not the duty, to defend any criminal proceedings brought against any **Insured**. Should Underwriters in their sole discretion exercise the option to defend any criminal proceeding, any **Defense Costs** incurred therein shall reduce and may exhaust the **Coverage Limits**. The exercise of the option to defend any criminal proceeding shall not serve to render Underwriters liable for any other **Loss** incurred in connection with any criminal proceedings, and Underwriters shall retain the right to withdraw from the defense upon giving thirty (30) days notice. Whether or not Underwriters exercise the option to defend criminal proceedings, Underwriters shall defend, subject to the policy's terms and conditions, any civil proceeding brought against an **Insured** which alleges the same or similar **Insured Events** as a criminal proceeding.

E. <u>Newly Acquired or Formed Entities</u>. Any entity that the Named Insured acquires or forms while this policy is in effect is an **Insured**, if the Named Insured owns more than 50% of it. However, no newly acquired or formed entity is covered for more than sixty (60) days or the remainder of the Policy Period, whichever is less, from the date that it is acquired or formed unless Underwriters agree to cover such acquisition or newly formed entity within such sixty (60) day period in consideration of an additional premium to be set by Underwriters. If such acquisition or newly formed entity results in less than a 25% increase in the number of **Employees** measured at inception of this policy, no additional premium will be charged. However, in such case, notice must be provided to Underwriters within the sixty- (60) day period before coverage will apply to any **Claim** first made after the sixty- (60) day period. Notwithstanding any of the foregoing, any acquired or formed entity is not covered for **Loss** that results from an **Insured Event** that happened or first commenced before the Named Insured acquired or formed it; nor for **Loss** covered under any other insurance.

II. DEFINITIONS.

A. **Claim(s)** means:

1. an oral or written complaint where specific charges of **Discrimination, Harassment, Negligent Hiring** and/or **Wrongful Employment Decision** are made;

2. a written demand in which damages are alleged;

3. a civil action or an administrative proceeding; or

4. an arbitration proceeding, a mediation proceeding, or other alternative dispute resolution proceedings to which any **Insured** must submit or to which any **Insured** submits with Underwriters' consent.

Claim includes the defense of a civil action requesting an injunction or other non-monetary relief.

Notwithstanding the foregoing, **Claim** shall not include criminal proceedings or labor or grievance arbitration subject to a collective bargaining agreement. The date of Claim, for purposes of Section I. COVERAGE A. and Section IV. WHEN COVERAGE IS PROVIDED, **will** be the date a written **Claim** is made against the **Insured** or the date the **Insured** notifies Underwriters of an oral complaint, whichever comes first.

B. **Claimant** means a current or former **Employee**, an applicant for employment with an insured entity, or the Equal Employment Opportunity Commission or a similar state or federal agency acting on behalf of such current or former **Employee** or applicant for employment.

C. **Coverage Limits** means the amounts shown in section V. of the Declarations.

D. **Defense Costs** means those reasonable and necessary expenses that result from the investigation, settlement or defense of a specific **Claim**, including but not limited to attorney fees and expenses, the cost of legal proceedings, the cost of appeal bonds and the cost of bonds to release property being used to secure a legal obligation (but only for bond amounts within the **Coverage Limits** of this policy that apply; Underwriters have no obligation to furnish such bonds).

Defense Costs do not include salaries and expenses of any **Insureds** or any fees and expenses of Underwriters' attorneys.

E. **Discrimination** means termination of the employment relationship, a demotion or failure or refusal to hire or promote or denial of an employment benefit or the taking of any adverse or differential employment action including but not limited to retaliation because of race, color, religion, age, sex, sexual orientation, sexual preference, disability (including AIDS), pregnancy or national origin, or any other basis prohibited by federal, state or local law.

F. **Employee** means an individual whose labor or service is engaged by and directed by an insured entity. This includes but is not limited to part-time, seasonal, volunteer, temporary and leased **Employees** as well as any individual employed in a supervisory, managerial or confidential position. Independent contractors who claim to be an **Employee** of an insured entity will be **Claimants** but only with respect to the conduct of any insured entity's business. No coverage is available for **Claims** by independent contractors for overtime pay, vacation pay, or any employee benefits.

G. **Harassment** means unwelcome sexual or non-sexual advances, requests for sexual or non-sexual favors or other verbal or physical conduct of a sexual or non-sexual nature that:

1. explicitly or implicitly are made a condition of employment,

2. are used as a basis for employment decisions, or

3. create a work environment that interferes with performance.

Harassment includes allegations of assault and battery, but only if they are related to a charge of sexual harassment.

H. **Insured(s)** means the Named Insured shown in section I. of the Declarations, and any current or former director, officer, or **Employee** of the Named Insured in their respective capacities with the Named Insured. For non-U.S. entities, the equivalent positions are also insureds. If the Named Insured is a corporation, any entity more than 50% owned is an **Insured** along with such entity's current or former directors, officers and **Employees** in their respective capacities with the insured entity. Stockholders are also **Insureds** but only with respect to their liability as stockholders. If the Named Insured is a limited liability corporation, managers are also **Insureds**. If the Named Insured is a partnership or joint venture, partners or co-venturers and their spouses are also **Insureds** but only for the conduct of the Named Insured's business. However, no person or entity is covered for the conduct of any current or past partnership or joint venture not named in the Declarations.

I. **Insured Event** means actual or alleged acts of **Discrimination, Harassment, Negligent Hiring,** and/or a **Wrongful Employment Decision,** by an **Insured**; and **Third Party Insured Events**.

J. **Loss** means:

1. a. damages, including, but not limited to, **Punitive Damages**, liquidated damages, back pay, front pay and damages representing lost insurance benefits;

   b. judgments (including prejudgment and post judgment interest awarded against an **Insured** on that part of any judgment paid or to be paid by Underwriters);

   c. settlements;

   d. statutory attorney fees; and

   e. **Defense Costs**.

2. With respect to **Punitive Damages**, the applicable law for purposes of insurability will be the law most favorable to the **Insured** provided the most favorable law has a reasonable relationship to the **Claim**.

   Loss which will be deemed reasonably related includes the law:

   a. of the state where the **Insured** is incorporated or has a place of business;

   b. of the state where the **Claim** is pending;

   c. of the state where any **Insured Event** happened; or

   d. of the country where Underwriters have their place of business.

3. **Loss** shall not include:

   a. payment of insurance plan benefits claimed by or on behalf of retired **Employees**, or that a **Claimant** would have been entitled to as an **Employee** had the **Insured** provided the **Claimant** with a continuation of insurance, except as damages representing lost insurance benefits;

   b. costs incurred by any **Insured** to modify or adapt any building or property in order to make such building or property more accessible or accommodating to any disabled person;

   c. amounts owed under federal, state or local wage and hour laws, however, this shall not apply to any **Claim** under the federal Equal Pay Act or similar state laws;

d. commissions, bonuses, profit sharing or benefits pursuant to a contract of employment;

e. severance payments;

f. amounts owed under a written or express contract of employment for a definite period of time, however, **Defense Costs** for **Claims** of breach of a written or express contract of employment for a definite period of time are covered; and

g. civil or criminal fines or penalties imposed by law, or taxes.

K. **Management or Supervisory Employee** means directors, owners of a sole proprietorship, partners, chief executive officer, chief financial officer, chief operating officer, executive director, in-house attorneys, risk management personnel, the human resources manager or any **Employee** performing the human resources management function.

L. **Negligent Hiring** means an allegation by a **Claimant** that an insured entity is liable for **Discrimination** or **Harassment** because of negligence in the employment of any **Employee**.

M. **One Insured Event** means:

1. one or more covered allegations which are related by an unbroken chain of events;

2. related allegations made by or on behalf of the same person; or

3. class action or other multiple plaintiff suits arising out of any covered allegation(s).

N. **Punitive Damages** means punitive damages, exemplary damages, and additional damages resulting from the multiplication of compensatory damages.

O. **Third Party Claimant** means any natural person who is not an **Employee** who makes a **Claim**.

P. **Third Party Insured Events** shall mean actual or alleged acts of discrimination against or sexual harassment of a **Third Party Claimant** by an **Insured** which violate any federal, state or local statute which prohibits discrimination or sexual harassment.

Q. **Wrongful Employment Decision** means:

1. termination, actual or constructive, of an employment relationship in any manner which is against the law and wrongful;

2. allegations of wrongful demotion, retaliation, misrepresentation, promissory estoppel and, intentional interference with contract; which arise from an employment decision to employ, terminate, evaluate, discipline, promote or demote;

3. defamation, infliction of emotional distress or mental anguish, humiliation, false imprisonment, invasion of privacy and other personal injury allegations which arise from the terminating, disciplining, promoting or demoting of an **Employee**;

4. allegations of breach of an implied employment contract and breach of the covenant of good faith and fair dealing in the employment contract;

5. employment terminations, disciplinary actions, demotions or other employment decisions which violate public policy or the Family Medical Leave Act or similar state law;

6. violations of the Uniformed Services Employment and Reemployment Rights Act;

7. allegations of breach of an **Employees'** federal, state or local civil rights including but not limited to any violation of the Civil Rights Act of 1886 or 42 U.S.C. Section 1983;

8. allegations of retaliation against any **Insured** including but not limited to retaliation for filing claims under the Federal False Claims Act, retaliation in connection with whistle blowing, retaliation for union activities or in connection with strikes or lockouts; and

9. allegations of wrongful deprivation of career opportunity or failure to grant tenure.

III. EXCLUSIONS.

A. **Workers' Compensation**. This policy does not cover any **Loss** arising out of any obligation under any workers' compensation law, disability benefits or unemployment compensation law or any similar law. This exclusion shall not apply to any **Claim** for retaliation or **Discrimination** on account of filing a workers' compensation claim, an unemployment compensation claim, or a claim for disability benefits.

B. **Liability Assumed by Contract**. This policy does not cover any **Loss**, which any **Insured** is obligated to pay by reason of the assumption of another's liability for an **Insured Event** in a contract or agreement. This exclusion will not apply to liability for damages because of an **Insured Event** that any **Insured** would have without such contract or agreement.

C. **Employee Retirement Income Security Act**. This policy does not cover any **Loss** arising from the Employee Retirement Income Security Act of 1974, or any amendments thereto, or any similar federal, state or local law. This exclusion shall not apply to any **Claim** under section 510 of ERISA.

D. **Strikes and Lockouts**. This policy does not cover any **Loss** arising out of a lockout, strike, picket line, replacement or other similar actions resulting from labor disputes or labor negotiations or any protections contained within the National Labor Relations Act. This exclusion shall not apply to any **Claim** for retaliation in connection with a lockout, strike, picket line, replacement or similar labor disputes or negotiations or any protections contained within the National Labor Relations Act.

E. **W.A.R.N. Act**. This policy does not cover any **Loss** arising out of the Workers Adjustment and Retraining Notification Act, or any amendment thereto, or any similar federal, state or local law. This exclusion shall not apply if the Named Insured consulted with legal counsel and made a good faith attempt to comply with the law.

IV. WHEN COVERAGE IS PROVIDED.

A. This policy applies only to **Claims** arising out of an **Insured Event** which are first made during the Policy Period as shown in section II. of the Declarations or during the Limited Reporting Period if applicable or notice received in accordance with Section VIII.B. All **Claims** because of **One Insured Event** will be considered to have been made on the date that the first of those **Claims** was first made.

B. **Limited Reporting Period** means the thirty (30) day period starting with the end of the Policy Period as shown in section II. of the Declarations during which **Claims** because of **Insured Events** that happen or commence before the end of the Policy Period as shown in section II. of the Declarations may be first made.

The Limited Reporting Period does not extend the Policy Period or change the scope of coverage provided. Underwriters will consider any **Claim** first made during the Limited Reporting Period to have been made on the last date on which this policy is in effect.

The Limited Reporting Period will apply if this policy is canceled or not renewed for any reason other than non-payment of premium. Coverage under the Limited Reporting Period may not be canceled. However, the Limited Reporting Period will not apply to **Claims** if other insurance the **Insureds** buy covers them or would cover them if its limits of coverage had not been exhausted.

C. **Extended Reporting Period**. If this policy is canceled or non-renewed for any reason other than non-payment of premium, an Extended Reporting Period of 12 months from the end of the Policy Period shown in section II. of the Declarations can be added by means of the payment of the additional premium of 100% of the annual premium charged for the Policy Period, as shown in section III. of the Declarations. An Extended Reporting Period of 24 months can be added for an additional premium of 150%, and 36 months for an additional premium of 175%.

The Extended Reporting Period will not apply unless Underwriters receive a written request for it within fifteen (15) days after the end of the Policy Period shown in section II. of the Declarations or its prior cancellation date, if applicable, nor will it take effect unless the additional premium is paid within thirty (30) days after the end of the Policy Period shown in section II. of the Declarations, or the cancellation date if applicable. Once that premium is paid, the Extended Reporting Period may not be canceled and the premium will be fully earned.

Coverage under an Extended Reporting Period is limited to **Insured Events** that happen prior to the expiration or cancellation of the policy and are otherwise covered by the policy.

D. The limits of liability that apply as shown in section V. of the Declarations shall not be renewed nor increased by the addition of either Limited or Extended Reporting Periods.

V. COVERAGE LIMITS.

A. The limits shown in section V. of the Declarations are the most Underwriters will pay regardless of the number of **Insureds** or **Claims** made.

B. **Total Aggregate Limit**. This is the most Underwriters will pay for the combined total of all **Claims** first made during the Policy Period for **Loss** that results from all **Insured Events**.

C. **Each Insured Event Limit**. This is the most Underwriters will pay for **Claims** first made during the Policy Period for **Loss** that results from any **One Insured Event** regardless of the number of **Claims**.

D. If the Policy Period is extended, the limits shown in section V. of the Declarations shall not in any way increase. For purposes of the limits of liability any policy extension is considered to be part of and not in addition to the preceding Policy Period.

VI. DEDUCTIBLE.

Underwriters' obligation to pay under this policy applies only to the amount of **Loss** in excess of any deductible amount shown in section VI. of the Declarations, and the **Coverage Limits** will not be reduced by the amount of such deductible.

The deductible amount applies to all **Claims** arising out of any **One Insured Event** regardless of the number of **Claimants** or **Third Party Claimants** who allege damages. This means there will be one deductible for each **One Insured Event**.

VII. EXTENSION OF COVERAGE.

Coverage is extended to spouses of **Insureds** who are defendants and to estates, heirs, legal representatives or assigns of **Insureds**, upon the death, incapacity or bankruptcy of the **Insureds**; but only on account of **Insured Events**.

VIII. CONDITIONS.

Underwriters have no duty to provide coverage under this policy unless there has been full compliance with all the conditions contained in this policy.

A. Duties in the event of a Claim.

1. The Named Insured must see to it that Underwriters or their authorized representatives, as shown in section IV. of the Declarations, are notified within ten (10) days of the time that a **Management or Supervisory Employee** becomes aware of the making of a **Claim**.

    Notice should include:

    a. The identity of the person(s) alleging **Discrimination, Harassment, Negligent Hiring** or **Wrongful Employment Decision**;

    b. The identity of the **Insured(s)** who allegedly committed the **Discrimination, Harassment, Negligent Hiring** or **Wrongful Employment Decision**;

    c. The identity of any witnesses to the alleged **Discrimination, Harassment, Negligent Hiring** or **Wrongful Employment Decision**; and

    d. The dates the **Insured Event** took place.

2. The Named Insured and any other **Insured** must:

a. Immediately send Underwriters or their authorized representatives copies of any demands, notices, summonses or legal papers received in connection with the **Claim;**

b. Authorize Underwriters or their authorized representatives to obtain records and other information;

c. Cooperate with Underwriters or their authorized representatives in the investigation or defense of the **Claim**; and

d. Assist Underwriters or their authorized representatives, upon their request, in the enforcement of any right against any person or organization, which may be liable to the **Insured** because of injury or damage to which this policy may apply.

3. No **Insureds** will, except at their own cost, voluntarily make a payment, assume any obligation, make any settlement or incur any expense without Underwriters' consent. Subsequent payments which are deemed by Underwriters as having been prejudiced by any such voluntary payment will also be the sole responsibility of the **Insured**.

B. **Awareness Clause.**

If during the Policy Period any **Management or Supervisory Employee** becomes aware of an **Insured Event** which they reasonably believe may result in a future **Claim** and they or the Named Insured or any insured entity provide(s) notice in writing to Underwriters of such **Insured Event** prior to the end of the Policy Period, then any **Claim** subsequently arising from such **Insured Event** shall be deemed to have been made on the last day of the Policy Period. Such notice must describe the **Insured Event** in reasonable detail and provide the name or names of the potential **Claimant(s)**.

C. **Legal action against Underwriters.**

No person or organization has a right under this policy to 1) join Underwriters as a party or otherwise bring Underwriters into a suit asking for damages from an **Insured**, or 2) sue Underwriters on this policy unless all of its terms have been fully complied with.

A person or organization may sue Underwriters to recover on an agreed settlement or on a final judgment against an **Insured** obtained after an actual trial, but Underwriters will not be liable for damages that are not payable under the terms of this policy or that are in excess of the applicable **Coverage Limits**. An agreed settlement means a settlement and release of liability signed by Underwriters, the **Insured** and the **Claimant** or the **Claimant's** legal representative.

D. **Other Insurance.**

If other valid and collectable insurance is available to the **Insured** covering a **Loss** also covered by this policy, other than insurance that is specifically stated to be in excess of this policy, the insurance afforded by this policy shall be in excess of and shall not contribute with such other insurance. Nothing herein shall be construed to make this policy subject to the terms, conditions and limitations of any other insurance. Notwithstanding the foregoing, this policy shall assume control of the defense and seek contribution directly from such other insurance.

E. **Premium.**

Premium shown in section III. of the Declarations of this policy is for the Policy Period as shown in section II. of the Declarations.

F. **Cancellation.**

The Named Insured may cancel this policy by mailing to Underwriters or the Program Administrator shown in section VII. of the Declarations written notice stating when thereafter such cancellation shall be effective. Underwriters may cancel this policy for non-payment of premium only by mailing to the Named Insured at the address shown in section I. of the Declarations of this policy, written notice stating when not less than ten (10) days thereafter such cancellation shall be effective. This mailing of notice as aforesaid shall be sufficient proof of notice. The effective date and hour of cancellation as stated in the notice shall become the end of the Policy Period and section II. of the Declarations shall be deemed to be amended to reflect the cancellation date. Delivery of such written notice shall be equivalent to mailing.

If the Named Insured cancels, the earned premium shall be computed in accordance with the NMA45 short rate table and procedure. If Underwriters cancel, earned premium shall be computed pro rata. Premium adjustment may be made either at the time cancellation is effected or as soon as practicable after cancellation becomes effective, but payment or tender of unearned premium is not a condition of cancellation.

The policy is subject to a minimum earned premium of 25% of the total annual premium.

G. Statements in Application.

By accepting this policy, the **Insureds** agree that 1) the statements in the Application and any attachments are accurate, complete and material; 2) Underwriters have issued this policy in reliance upon the statements in the Application and attachments; and 3) the Application and any attachments thereto, whether the original or a copy, including a facsimile copy, are deemed part of this policy.

H. Non-Renewal.

If Underwriters decide not to renew this policy, Underwriters will mail or deliver to the Named Insured shown in section I. of the Declarations written notice of the non-renewal not less than thirty (30) days before the end of the Policy Period as shown in section II. of the Declarations. If notice is mailed, proof of mailing will be sufficient notice of non-renewal.

I. Subrogation.

If any **Insured** has rights to recover all or part of any payments Underwriters have made under this policy, those rights are transferred to Underwriters; the **Insureds** must do nothing after a **Loss** to impair them. At Underwriters' request, the **Insureds** will bring suit or transfer those rights to Underwriters and help enforce them. Underwriters will not seek to enforce any subrogation rights against any **Insureds.**

J. Bankruptcy.

Bankruptcy or insolvency of the **Insured** or of the **Insured's** estate will not relieve Underwriters of their obligations under this policy.

K. Coverage Territory.

Coverage Territory is worldwide.

Specimen

Application For A Claims-Made Policy

I. General Information

A. Name of applicant _____

   Address _____

   City _____ State _____ Zip _____

B. Contact person _____ Title _____

   Phone _____ FAX _____

   When was company established? _____

C. ☐ Sole Proprietorship   ☐ Corporation   ☐ LLC
   ☐ Partnership   ☐ Franchise   ☐ Other
                                          (specify) _____

D. What is the nature of your business? _____

E. Was net income positive in most recent fiscal year?   ☐ Yes   ☐ No

   If answer is No, please explain in attachment when you anticipate net income will be positive.

F. Total Payroll: $ _____ for 12 months ended _____ (MM/YY)
   Primary SIC Code Number: _____

G. Have you purchased EPL Insurance before, whether specifically or attached
   to other coverages?   ☐ Yes   ☐ No

Years	Renewal Date	Carrier	Limit	Deductible	Premium

H. Has your EPL Insurance ever been cancelled or non-renewed?   ☐ Yes   ☐ No

   If YES, please explain on separate sheet.

I. Have you acquired any companies or purchased over 50% of the assets of
   any company in the past year?   ☐ Yes   ☐ No

   If answer is YES, on a separate sheet give date of acquisition, name of entity acquired, and
   number of employees acquired.

   With respect to acquired companies/assets, were any employees or officers
   terminated or do you plan to do so in the next twelve (12) months?   ☐ Yes   ☐ No

   If so, How many?   Employees _____ Officers _____

APPENDIX A

J. Have you had any plant, facility, branch or office closings, consolidations, work force reduction or layoffs affecting 20% or more of the total number of employees within the past 12 months?   ☐ Yes   ☐ No

Do you anticipate any of the above in the next 12 months?   ☐ Yes   ☐ No

If YES to either of the above questions, please provide details on a separate sheet.

K. In the case of downsizing, would you consult employment law counsel prior to taking any action?   ☐ Yes   ☐ No

II. Training of Managers/Supervisors

A. Have your managers and/or supervisors attended any educational seminars on employer-employee relations in the past year including general hiring, firing, promoting, demoting?   ☐ Yes   ☐ No

Specifically on Sexual Harassment?   ☐ Yes   ☐ No

Sexual Harassment training for all employees?   ☐ Yes   ☐ No

Who conducted the training(s)? _____

III. Loss/Claim History

A. Furnish loss/claim history (5 years) for all wrongful termination, discrimination and harassment (sexual or non-sexual) claims or incidents (whether insured or not and whether or not any loss has been paid thus far), and including any EEOC or similar state administrative filing. If none, please state NONE. **N/A is not an acceptable answer.** Use a separate piece of paper if needed. Since this coverage is also for Third Party Claims, please disclose any Claims for Discrimination, Sexual Harassment or ADA violations from customers, clients, vendors or other natural persons who are non-employees.

Date claim first made	Legal Expenses including attorney fees	Damages/settlements	Total incurred
_____	_____	_____	_____
_____	_____	_____	_____

Please fill out a Supplemental Claim Form completely for each claim.

B. Is/Are any Management or Supervisory Employee(s) (as defined in the policy) aware of any facts, incidents, or circumstances which may result in claim(s) being made against you? For example, but not by way of limitation, we consider it reasonable for you to foresee that a claim may be brought against you if a current or former employee, applicant for employment, or a customer, client, vendor or other natural person who is a non-employee, has expressed dissatisfaction with the employment relationship or the employment application process or a Third Party relationship by:

- Making a formal complaint to a supervisory employee of discrimination, harassment or unfair employment practices;
- Threatening to hire an attorney;
- Asking for a severance package in excess of what is being offered;
- Complaining of discrimination, harassment or unfair treatment and threatening to do something about it;
- Frequent complaining of discrimination, harassment or unfair treatment; or
- Complaining of a failure to accommodate per ADA law.

If any Management or Supervisory Employee(s) is/are aware of any fact(s,) incident(s) or circumstance(s) as described above please answer "Yes" here and disclose each incident on a fully completed Supplemental Claim Form. Anything that is disclosed or should have been disclosed is excluded from coverage:
☐ Yes   ☐ No

If the answer is YES, please fill out a Supplemental Claim Form for each incident.

IV. Employees (including all owners, officers, shareholders on the payroll)

A. Number of employees one year ago:

   Full Time _____   Part Time _____   Temp/Agency _____

B. Hired during the past year:

   Full Time _____   Part Time _____   Temp/Agency _____

C. Left voluntarily during the past year:

   Full Time _____   Part Time _____   Temp/Agency _____

D. Terminated involuntarily during the past year (fired, laid off, etc.):

   Full Time _____   Part Time _____   Temp/Agency _____

   How many of these had salary and/or commission income of $75,000 or more? _____

E. **Current Number of Employees (A + B - C&D = E):**

   Full Time _____   **Part Time** _____   **Temp/Agency** _____   Annual **Seasonal** _____

F. Are all Temp/Agency on the Agency payroll?   ☐ Yes   ☐ No

G. How many months of the year do the seasonal employees average? _____

H. How many employees are leased per a Leasing Agreement? _____ Please attach Agreement.

I. How many of the total employees are members of a union? _____

J. How many supervisors/managers do you have? _____ How many are women? _____

   How many are non-Caucasian? _____

K. Salary/com ranges*   Full-time   Part-time   Temp/Agency   Seasonal

   Less than $25K   _____   _____   _____   _____

   $25K to $74,999   _____   _____   _____   _____

   $75K and over   _____   _____   _____   _____

   How many making $75 K and over are owners, partners, shareholders, etc.? _____

   NOTE: Ranges must add up to totals listed in "E." above. - * Include commissions/bonuses in salary ranges.

L. Does the Applicant have an at-will employment relationship with all employees other than those with written employment contracts?   ☐ Yes   ☐ No

APPENDIX A

V. Human Resource Policies and Procedures

A. Do you have a Human Resources or Personnel Dept./Manager? ☐ Yes ☐ No

If NO, who handles this function?

Name _____ Title _____

B. Do you require job applicants to use an employment application? ☐ Yes ☐ No
If YES, attach a copy.

Does it contain "at-will" wording? ☐ Yes ☐ No

C. Do you do the following pre-employment screening? (mark X if yes)

Check employment history _____ Check credentials/licensing testing _____ Credit check _____

Check references _____ Check for criminal record _____ Psychological tests _____

Post offer physical _____ Post offer drug/alcohol testing _____ In house? _____ Third party? _____

D. Do you publish an employee handbook? ☐ Yes ☐ No

If Yes, attach a copy and answer the following:

Do you distribute it to all employees? ☐ Yes ☐ No

Do they sign they received it? ☐ Yes ☐ No

Date current Handbook was last reviewed/updated? _____
Date of next review/update? _____

Is this review/update done by legal counsel experienced in employment Law? ☐ Yes ☐ No

If **NO**, who does the review/update? _____

E. Does Handbook contain the following policies?

1. Sexual Harassment? ☐ Yes ☐ No

    If Yes, is it distributed annually to all employees? ☐ Yes ☐ No

2. Equal Employment Opportunity? ☐ Yes ☐ No

    If yes, does it list protected classes? ☐ Yes ☐ No

    If yes, do you use omnibus wording: "including all classes protected by federal, state or local law"? ☐ Yes ☐ No

3. Americans with Disabilities Act? ☐ Yes ☐ No

4. Open Door for complaints? ☐ Yes ☐ No

5. "At-will" wording? ☐ Yes ☐ No

6. Family & Medical Leave Act? ☐ Yes ☐ No

7. Separate Pregnancy Leave? ☐ Yes ☐ No

	8.	Substance Abuse?	☐ Yes	☐ No
	9.	Arbitration Agreements?	☐ Yes	☐ No
		If yes, have at least 90% of employees signed?	☐ Yes	☐ No
F.	Do you provide regular, written performance evaluations for all or most employees?		☐ Yes	☐ No
G.	Do you have written job descriptions for all or most job classifications?		☐ Yes	☐ No
H.	Do you provide employees with a "Hot Line" phone number in order to register complaints?		☐ Yes	☐ No

If Answer is Yes, please attach information regarding the "Hot Line."

I. Which of the following must review terminations prior to any action being taken? Check which ones:

　　1. Owners/Upper Management/Managing Partners ____

　　2. HR Manager or person in charge of HR ____

　　3. Outside legal counsel experienced in employment law ____

　　If none are checked, who does the review? _____

J. Do you regularly consult with legal counsel that specializes in employment law to discuss employee-employer relations issues?　　☐ Yes　　☐ No

If YES to I.(c) or J., who is this employment law counsel?

Name _____

Firm _____

City _____　　State _____

Phone No. _____

The Applicant warrants on its behalf and on behalf of all Management and Supervisory Employees (as defined in the policy) that after full investigation and inquiry the statements set forth herein are true and include all material information.

The Applicant further warrants on its behalf and on behalf of all Management and Supervisory Employees (as defined in the policy) that if the information supplied on this application changes between the date of this application and the inception date of the policy, it will immediately notify Insurer through the producing broker of such change. Signing of this application does not bind Underwriters to offer nor the Applicant to accept insurance, but it is agreed that this application (facsimile or copy or original) shall be the basis of the insurance and will be attached to and made a part of the policy should a policy be issued. If a facsimile or copy is submitted for attachment to the policy, then the Applicant warrants that the facsimile or copy is a true and current duplicate of the original. It is also acknowledged that the information in this application has been verified by the individual in charge of Human Resources.

Date　　　　Applicant's Authorized Signature　　　Title
　　　　　　(Partner/Officer/Owner)

APPENDIX A

Supplemental Claim/Insured Event/Incident Form

This form is to be completed if any question in Section III. Loss History, A. or B. of the Application is answered "yes." Please complete a separate sheet for each claim or incident and answer all questions fully. Prior to attaching to the Application, a principal, partner or officer of the Applicant must sign and date this sheet and attach it to the signed application along with any explanations. No full Indication can be given without this complete information.

1. Name of Applicant:_____
2. Name of individual(s) employed by Applicant charged by employee in claim/incident:
   [Defendant(s)]: _____ Title: _____
   [Defendant(s)]: _____ Title: _____
   [Defendant(s)]: _____ Title: _____
3. Name of Employee making complaint/allegations in incident (Plaintiff): _____
4. Date of alleged Wrongful Employment Practice: _____
5. Date Applicant became aware of alleged Wrongful Employment Practice: _____
6. How did Applicant become aware?   a) Personally observed incident _____   b) Verbal complaint from employee _____   c) Written notice from employee or employee's attorney _____   d) Verbal/written notice from someone else other than involved employee _____   e) Filing with state agency _____   f) Filing with EEOC _____   g) Receipt of lawsuit _____   h) Other _____ (please detail) _____
   _____
7. Name of Insurer Claim Reported to (if any): _____
8. Are you represented by an attorney? _____   If yes, name of attorney and law firm: _____
   Does attorney specialize in Employment Practice Liability litigation? _____
9. Present status of Claim/Incident: _____ Pending   _____ Closed   _____ In Suit
10. **If Closed,** Total Damages Paid: _____   Total Expenses Paid: _____
11. **If EEOC/State Agency** filing:
    a. Has right to sue letter been issued? _____   Date: _____
       Date right to sue expires (or did expire)? _____
    b. Has determination of fault been decided? _____
       What was determination? _____
       If employee has a right to sue what date does (did) this expire? _____
12. **If pending,** is employee demanding a settlement amount? _____   How much? $ _____
    Has employer offered a settlement amount? _____   How much? $ _____
    Insurer's Loss Reserve (if Insurance Co. involved) $ _____
    Legal expenses to date: $ _____
13. Detailed description of employee's complaint and Applicant's response (put on separate sheet if not enough room here): _____
    _____
14. Explain what actions have been taken to prevent an incident like this happening again: _____
    _____
    _____

I understand information submitted herein becomes a part of my Application and is subject to the same warranty and conditions.

_____   _____
Applicant's Signature   Date

APPENDIX B

ISO's Employment-Related Practices Liability Coverage Form (EP 00 01 04 98)

EMPLOYMENT-RELATED PRACTICES LIABILITY
EP 00 01 04 98

EMPLOYMENT-RELATED PRACTICES LIABILITY COVERAGE FORM

Various provisions in this policy restrict coverage. Read the entire policy carefully to determine rights, duties and what is and is not covered.

Throughout this policy the words "you" and "your" refer to the Named Insured shown in the Declarations, and any other person or organization qualifying as a Named Insured under this policy. The words "we", "us" and "our" refer to the company providing this insurance.

The word "insured" means any person or organization qualifying as such under Section II – Who Is An Insured.

Other words and phrases that appear in quotation marks have special meaning. Refer to Section VII – Definitions.

SECTION I – EMPLOYMENT-RELATED PRACTICES LIABILITY COVERAGE

A. Insuring Agreement

1. We will pay those sums the insured becomes legally obligated to pay as damages resulting from an "injury" to which this insurance applies. We will have the right and duty to defend the insured against any "suit" seeking those damages. However, we will have no duty to defend the insured against any "suit" seeking damages because of an "injury" to which this insurance does not apply. We may, at our discretion, investigate any incident that may result in "injury". We may, with your written consent, settle any "claim" that may result. But:

   a. The amount we will pay for damages or "defense expenses" is limited as described in Section III – Limit Of Insurance and in Section IV – Co-payment;

   b. The coverage and duty to defend provided by this policy will end when we have used up the applicable limit of insurance for "defense expenses" or the payment of judgments or settlements.

   No other obligation or liability to pay sums, such as civil or criminal fines, imposed on you or any other insured, or to perform acts or services is covered unless explicitly provided for under Supplementary Payments.

2. This insurance applies to "injury" only if:

   a. The "injury" arises out of an offense that takes place in the "coverage territory";

   b. The offense out of which the "injury" arose did not commence before the Retroactive Date, if any, shown in the Declarations or after the end of the policy period; and

   c. A "claim" because of the "injury" is first made against any insured, in accordance with Paragraph 3. below, during the policy period or the Section VI – Extended Reporting Period, if provided.

3. A "claim" will be deemed to have been made at the earlier of the following times:

   a. When notice of such "claim" is received by any insured and reported to us in writing; or

   b. When a "claim" against an insured is made directly to us in writing.

   A "claim" received by the insured during the policy period and reported to us within 30 days after the end of the policy period will be considered to have been reported within the policy period. However, this 30 day grace period does not apply to "claims" that are covered under any subsequent insurance you purchase, or that would be covered but for exhaustion of the amount of insurance applicable to such "claims".

4. All "claims" arising out of an "injury" to the same person, including damages claimed by any person for care, loss of services or death resulting at any time from the "injury", will be deemed to have been made at the time the first of such "claims" is made, regardless of the number of "claims" subsequently made.

B. Exclusions

This insurance does not apply to:

1. **Criminal, Fraudulent Or Malicious Acts**

   An insured's liability arising out of criminal, fraudulent or malicious acts or omissions by that insured, or arising out of that insured's knowing acquiescence or failure to act, or instruction, direction, or approval given to another concerning such acts or omissions.

EP 00 01 04 98 Copyright, Insurance Services Office, Inc., 1997 Page 1 of 7

APPENDIX B

This exclusion does not affect our duty to defend, in accordance with Paragraph **A.1.** above, an insured prior to determining, through the appropriate legal processes, that that insured is responsible for a criminal, fraudulent or malicious act or omission or has instructed, directed or provided approval for another concerning such acts or omissions.

2. **Contractual Liability**

   "Injury" for which the insured is obligated to pay damages by reason of the assumption of liability in a contract or agreement. This exclusion does not apply to liability for damages that the insured would have in the absence of the contract or agreement.

3. **Workers Compensation And Similar Laws**

   Any obligation of the insured under a workers compensation, disability benefits or unemployment compensation law or any similar law.

4. **Americans With Disabilities Act**

   "Injury" arising out of your failure to comply with any of the accommodations for the disabled required of you by, or any expenses incurred as the result of modifications made to accommodate any person pursuant to, the Americans With Disabilities Act, or any amendments thereto, or any similar state or local statutes, rules or regulations to the extent that they prescribe responsibilities or duties concerning the same acts or omissions.

5. **Violation Of Laws Applicable To Employers**

   A violation of your responsibilities or duties required by any other federal, state or local statutes, rules or regulations, and any rules or regulations promulgated therefor or amendments thereto, except for the following: Title VII of the Civil Rights Act of 1964 and amendments thereto, the Age Discrimination in Employment Act, the Equal Pay Act, the Pregnancy Discrimination Act of 1978, the Immigration Reform Control Act of 1986 and the Family and Medical Leave Act of 1993 or any other similar state or local statutes, rules or regulations to the extent that they prescribe responsibilities or duties concerning the same acts or omissions.

6. **Strikes And Lockouts**

   "Injury" to any striking or locked-out "employee", or to an "employee" who has been temporarily or permanently replaced due to any labor dispute.

7. **Sexual Harassment**

   Liability of that insured who commits a "sexual harassment" offense.

   This exclusion does not affect our duty to defend that insured prior to determining, through the appropriate legal processes, that that insured has committed a "sexual harassment" offense, other than an assault or battery.

8. **Employment Termination Or Relocation Due To Business Decisions**

   "Injury" arising out of termination of employment, job relocation or reassignment, if the action is taken because:

   a. You have filed for bankruptcy protection, or you are placed in receivership or liquidation;

   b. You have merged with or been acquired by another business entity;

   c. You have closed an operation or a business location; or

   d. Your business location is partly closed or the size of an operation must be reduced because of fire or other disasters beyond your control.

9. **Intentional Injury**

   Liability of that insured who commits an act of intentional "discrimination" or coercion.

   This exclusion does not affect our duty to defend that insured prior to determining, through the appropriate legal processes, whether that insured committed such act.

10. **Retaliatory Actions**

    Liability arising out of an insured's retaliatory action against a person because the person has:

    a. Declined to perform an illegal or unethical act;

    b. Filed a complaint with a governmental authority or a "suit" against you or any other insured in which damages are claimed;

    c. Testified against you or any other insured at a legal proceeding; or

    d. Notified a proper authority of any aspect of your business operation which is illegal.

C. **Supplementary Payments**

   We will pay, with respect to any "claim" we investigate or settle, or any "suit" against an insured we defend:

   1. Prejudgment interest awarded against the insured on that part of the judgment we pay. If we make an offer to pay the applicable limit of insurance, we will not pay any prejudgment interest based on that period of time after the offer.

2. All interest on the full amount of any judgment that accrues after entry of the judgment and before we have paid, offered to pay, or deposited in court the part of the judgment that is within the applicable limit of insurance.

These payments will not reduce the limit of insurance nor be subject to Section IV – Co-payment.

SECTION II – WHO IS AN INSURED

A. If you are designated in the Declarations as:

1. An individual, you and your spouse are insureds.
2. A partnership or joint venture, you are an insured. Your partners or members are also insureds.
3. A limited liability company, you are an insured. Your members and managers are also insureds.
4. An organization other than a partnership, joint venture or limited liability company, you are an insured. Your "executive officers" and directors are also insureds.

B. Your "employees" who hold managerial or supervisory positions are also insureds.

No person or organization is an insured with respect to the conduct of any current or past partnership, joint venture or limited liability company that is not shown as a Named Insured in the Declarations.

SECTION III – LIMIT OF INSURANCE

A. The Limit of Insurance shown in the Declarations and the rules below fix the most we will pay regardless of the number of:

1. Insureds;
2. "Claims" made or "suits" brought; or
3. Persons, organizations or government agencies making "claims" or bringing "suits".

B. The Limit of Insurance is the most we will pay for the sum of:

1. All damages; and
2. All "defense expenses"

because of the total of all "claims" first made against an insured during the policy period.

The Limit of Insurance of this Coverage Part applies separately to each consecutive annual period and to any remaining period of less than 12 months, starting with the beginning of the policy period shown in the Declarations, unless the policy period is extended after issuance for an additional period of less than 12 months. In that case, the additional period will be deemed part of the last preceding period for purposes of determining the Limit of Insurance.

SECTION IV – CO-PAYMENT

This insurance does not cover that share of damages and "defense expenses" specified as the Co-payment in the Declarations of this policy for which you are responsible. Your share is based on the percentage of the actual incurred loss shown as the Co-payment in the Declarations of this policy, up to the maximum Co-payment amount shown in the Declarations of this policy. This percentage is continually applied to damages and "defense expenses", up to the maximum amount for the policy period.

You are required to pay your share of any damages and "defense expenses" when they are incurred. This Co-payment does not reduce the Section III – Limit of Insurance.

SECTION V – CONDITIONS

A. Bankruptcy

Bankruptcy or insolvency of the insured or of the insured's estate will not relieve us of our obligations under this policy.

B. Consent To Settle

If we recommend a settlement to you which is acceptable to the claimant, but to which you do not consent, the most we will pay as damages in the event of any later settlement or judgment is the amount for which the "claim" could have been settled, to which you did not give consent, less any co-payment.

C. Duties In The Event Of A "Claim" Or An Incident That May Result In "Injury"

1. If a "claim" is received by any insured, you must:
   a. Immediately record the specifics of the "claim" and the date received; and
   b. Notify us, in writing, as soon as practicable.
2. You and any other involved insured must:
   a. Immediately send us copies of any demands, notices, summonses or legal papers received in connection with the "claim";
   b. Authorize us to obtain records and other information; and
   c. Cooperate with us in the investigation or settlement of the "claim" or defense against the "suit".
   d. Assist us, upon our request, in the enforcement of any right against any person or organization which may be liable to the insured because of "injury" or damage to which this insurance may also apply.

3. No insured will, except at that insured's own cost, voluntarily make a payment, assume any obligation, or incur any expense without our written consent.

4. If you have knowledge of an incident which may result in "injury" and for which a "claim" has not yet been received, you must notify us, in writing, as soon as practicable.

D. Legal Action Against Us

No person or organization has a right under this policy:

1. To join us as a party or otherwise bring us into a "suit" asking for damages from an insured; or

2. To sue us on this policy unless all of its terms have been fully complied with.

A person or organization may sue us to recover on an agreed settlement or on a final judgment against an insured obtained after an actual trial; but we will not be liable for damages that are not payable under the terms of this policy or that are in excess of the applicable limit of insurance. An agreed settlement means a settlement and release of liability signed by us, the insured and the claimant or the claimant's legal representative.

We will also not be liable for the insured's share of loss or for any payment due because of a settlement or judgment for which the insured is responsible under Section IV – Co-payment.

E. Other Insurance

If other valid and collectible insurance is available to the insured for a loss we cover, our obligations are limited as follows:

1. **Primary Insurance**

    This insurance is primary. We will not seek contribution from any other insurance available to you or the involved insured unless the other insurance is specifically designed to cover your losses because of liability arising out of an "injury". Then we will share with that other insurance by the method described below.

2. **Method Of Sharing**

    If all of the other insurance permits contribution by equal shares, we will follow this method also. Under this approach each insurer contributes equal amounts until it has paid its applicable limit of insurance or none of the loss remains, whichever comes first.

    If any of the other insurance does not permit contribution by equal shares, we will contribute by limits. Under this method, each insurer's share is based on the ratio of its applicable limit of insurance to the total applicable limits of insurance of all insurers.

The method chosen for the handling of other valid insurance will not affect your responsibility to share in a loss with us as specified under Section IV – Co-payment.

F. Premium Audit

1. We will compute all premiums for this policy in accordance with our rules and rates.

2. Premium shown in this policy as advance premium is a deposit premium only. At the close of each audit period we will compute the earned premium for that period. Audit premiums are due and payable on notice to the first Named Insured. If the sum of the advance and audit premiums paid for the policy period is greater than the earned premium, we will return the excess to the first Named Insured.

3. The first Named Insured must keep records of the information we need for premium computation, and send us copies at such times as we may request.

G. Representations

By accepting this policy, you agree that:

1. The statements in the Declarations are accurate and complete;

2. Those statements are based upon representations you made to us; and

3. We have issued this policy in reliance upon your representations.

H. Separation Of Insureds

Except with respect to the Limit of Insurance, and any rights or duties specifically assigned in this policy to the first Named Insured, this insurance applies:

1. As if each Named Insured were the only Named Insured; and

2. Separately to each insured against whom "claim" is made.

I. Transfer Of Rights Of Recovery Against Others To Us

If the insured has rights to recover all or part of any payment we have made under this policy, those rights are transferred to us. The insured must do nothing after loss to impair them. At our request, the insured will bring "suit" or transfer those rights to us and help us enforce them.

J. If You Are Permitted To Retain Defense Counsel

If, by mutual agreement or court order, the insured is given the right to retain defense counsel and the Limit of Insurance has not been used up, the following provisions apply:

1. We retain the right, at our discretion, to:

    a. Settle, with the insured's consent, a "claim" handled by defense counsel retained by the insured or to approve or disapprove the settlement of such "claim". However, if your defense counsel recommends a settlement which is acceptable to the claimant and which we do not approve, the most you will pay for your share of loss based on the Section IV – Co-payment is the percentage of your share for which the "claim" could have been settled, to which we did not give consent, in the event of any later settlement or judgment; and

    b. Appeal any judgment, award or ruling at our expense.

2. You and any other involved insured must:

    a. Continue to comply with Section V – Paragraph C., Duties In The Event Of A "Claim" Or An Incident That May Result In "Injury" Condition as well as the other provisions of this policy; and

    b. Direct defense counsel of the insured to:

        (1) Furnish us with the information we may request to evaluate those "suits" for coverage under this policy; and

        (2) Cooperate with any counsel we may select to monitor or associate in the defense of those "suits".

3. If we defend you under a reservation of rights, both your and our counsel will be required to maintain records pertinent to your "defense expenses". These records will be used to determine the allocation of any "defense expenses" for which you may be solely responsible, including defense of an allegation not covered by this insurance.

K. Transfer Of Duties When Limit Of Insurance Is Used Up

1. If we conclude that, based on "claims" which have been reported to us and to which this insurance may apply, the limit of insurance is likely to be used up in the payment of judgments or settlements for damages or the payment of "defense expenses", we will notify the first Named Insured, in writing, to that effect.

2. When the limit of insurance has actually been used up in the payment of judgments or settlements for damages or the payment of "defense expenses", we will:

    a. Notify the first Named Insured in writing, as soon as practicable, that such a limit has actually been used up and that our duty to defend the insured against "suits" seeking damages subject to that limit has also ended;

    b. Initiate, and cooperate in, the transfer of control, to any appropriate insured, of all "suits" for which the duty to defend has ended for the reason described in Paragraph 2.a. above and which are reported to us before that duty to defend ended; and

    c. Take such steps, as we deem appropriate, to avoid a default in, or continue the defense of, such "suits" until such transfer is completed, provided the appropriate insured is cooperating in completing such transfer.

3. When 2.a. above has occurred, the first Named Insured, and any other insured involved in a "suit" seeking damages subject to that limit, must:

    a. Cooperate in the transfer of control of "suits"; and

    b. Arrange for the defense of such "suit" within such time period as agreed to between the appropriate insured and us. Absent any such agreement, arrangements for the defense of such "suit" must be made as soon as practicable.

4. We will take no action with respect to defense for any "claim" if such "claim" is reported to us after the applicable limit of insurance has been used up. It becomes the responsibility of the first Named Insured, and any other insured involved in such a "claim", to arrange defense for such "claim".

5. The first Named Insured will reimburse us as soon as practicable for expenses we incur in taking those steps we deem appropriate in accordance with Paragraph 2. above.

6. The exhaustion of the applicable limit of insurance and the resulting end of our duty to defend will not be affected by our failure to comply with any of the provisions of this Condition.

L. When We Do Not Renew

If we decide not to renew this policy, we will mail or deliver to the first Named Insured shown in the Declarations written notice of the nonrenewal at least 30 days before the end of the policy period, or earlier if required by the state law or regulation controlling the application of this Coverage Part.

If notice is mailed, proof of mailing will be sufficient proof of notice.

SECTION VI – EXTENDED REPORTING PERIOD

A. You will have the right to purchase an Extended Reporting Period from us if:
   1. This Coverage Part is cancelled or not renewed for any reason; or
   2. We renew or replace this Coverage Part with insurance that:
      a. Has a Retroactive Date later than the date shown in the Declarations of this Coverage Part; or
      b. Does not apply to "injury" on a claims-made basis.

B. An Extended Reporting Period, as specified in Paragraph A. above, lasts three years and is available only by endorsement and for an additional charge.

C. The Extended Reporting Period starts with the end of the policy period. It does not extend the policy period or change the scope of coverage provided. It applies only to "claims" to which the following applies:
   1. The "claim" is first made during the Extended Reporting Period;
   2. The "injury" occurs before the end of the policy period; and
   3. The offense out of which the "injury" arose did not commence before the Retroactive Date, if any.

D. You must give us a written request for the Extended Reporting Period Endorsement within thirty (30) days after the end of the policy period or the effective date of cancellation, whichever comes first.

E. The Extended Reporting Period will not go into effect unless you pay the additional premium promptly when due and any premium or co-payment you owe us for coverage provided under this policy. Once in effect, the Extended Reporting Period may not be cancelled.

F. We will determine the additional premium in accordance with our rules and rates. In doing so, we may take into account the following:
   1. The exposures insured;
   2. Previous types and amounts of insurance;
   3. Limit of Insurance available under this policy for future payment of damages; and
   4. Other related factors.

The additional premium will not exceed 200% of the annual premium for this policy.

G. When the Extended Reporting Period Endorsement is in effect, we will provide a Supplemental Limit of Insurance for any "claim" first made during the Extended Reporting Period.

The Supplemental Limit of Insurance will be equal to the dollar amount shown in the Declarations in effect at the end of the policy period.

Paragraph B. of Section III – Limit Of Insurance will be amended accordingly.

SECTION VII – DEFINITIONS

A. "Claim" means a "suit" or demand made by or for the injured person for damages because of alleged "injury".

B. "Coverage territory" means:
   1. The United States of America (including its territories or possessions) and Puerto Rico; or
   2. All parts of the world if the insured's responsibility to pay damages is determined in a "suit" on the merits brought in the territory described in Paragraph 1. above or in a settlement we agree to.

C. "Defense expenses" means payments allocated to a specific "claim" we investigate, settle or defend, for its investigation, settlement or defense, including:
   1. Fees and salaries of attorneys and paralegals we retain, including attorneys and paralegals who are our "employees".
   2. Fees of attorneys the insured retains when, by our mutual agreement or court order (or when required by administrative hearing or proceeding), the insured is given the right to retain defense counsel to defend against a "claim".
   3. All other litigation or administrative hearing expenses, including fees or expenses of expert witnesses hired either by us or by the defense attorney retained by an insured.
   4. Reasonable expenses incurred by the insured at our request to assist us in the investigation or defense of the "claim", including actual loss of earnings up to $250 a day because of time off from work.

5. Costs taxed against the insured in the "suit".

"Defense expenses" does not include salaries and expenses of our "employees" or the insured's "employees" (other than those described in Paragraphs 1. and 4. above).

D. "Discrimination" means violation of a person's civil rights with respect to such person's race, color, national origin, religion, gender, marital status, age, sexual orientation or preference, physical or mental condition, or any other protected class or characteristic established by any federal, state or local statutes, rules or regulations.

E. "Employee" includes a "leased worker" and a "temporary worker".

F. "Executive officer" means a person holding any of the officer positions created by your charter, constitution, by-laws or any other similar governing document.

G. "Injury" means injury to a person arising out of one or more of the following offenses:

1. Refusal to employ the person, termination of the person's employment, demotion or failure to promote, negative evaluation, reassignment, discipline, defamation or humiliation of the person, based on "discrimination" directed at that person;

2. Coercing that person to commit an unlawful act or omission within the scope of that person's employment;

3. Work-related "sexual harassment"; or

4. Other work-related verbal, physical, mental or emotional abuse directed at the person with respect to that person's race, color, national origin, religion, gender, marital status, age, sexual orientation or preference, physical or mental condition, or any other protected class or characteristic established by any federal, state or local statutes, rules or regulations.

H. "Leased worker" means a person leased to you by a labor leasing firm under an agreement between you and the labor leasing firm, to perform duties related to the conduct of your business. "Leased worker" does not include a "temporary worker".

I. "Sexual harassment" means unwelcome sexual advances, requests for sexual favors, or other verbal, visual or physical conduct of a sexual nature when such conduct:

1. Is linked with a decision affecting an individual's employment;

2. Interferes with an individual's job performance; or

3. Creates an intimidating, hostile or offensive working environment for an individual.

J. "Suit" means a civil proceeding in which damages because of "injury" to which this insurance applies are alleged, including:

1. An arbitration proceeding in which such damages are claimed and to which the insured must submit or does submit with our consent;

2. Any other alternative dispute resolution proceeding in which such damages are claimed and to which the insured submits with our consent; or

3. Any administrative proceeding or hearing conducted by a governmental agency (federal, state or local) having the proper legal authority over the matter in which such damages are claimed.

K. "Temporary worker" means a person who is furnished to you to substitute for a permanent "employee" on leave or to meet seasonal or short-term workload conditions.

POLICY NUMBER: EMPLOYMENT-RELATED PRACTICES LIABILITY
EP 28 01 04 98

THIS ENDORSEMENT CHANGES THE POLICY. PLEASE READ IT CAREFULLY.

EXTENDED REPORTING PERIOD ENDORSEMENT

This endorsement modifies insurance provided under the following:

EMPLOYMENT-RELATED PRACTICES LIABILITY COVERAGE PART

SCHEDULE

Premium $

(If no entry appears above, information required to complete this endorsement will be shown in the Declarations as applicable to this endorsement.)

A. An Extended Reporting Period is provided, as described in Section **VI** – Extended Reporting Period.

B. A Supplemental Limit of Insurance applies, as set forth in Paragraph **C.** below, to "claims" first received and recorded during the Extended Reporting Period. The limit is equal to the Limit of Insurance entered on the Declarations in effect at the end of the policy period.

C. Paragraph **B.** of **Section III – Limits Of Insurance** is replaced by the following:

    B. The Limit of Insurance is the most we will pay for the sum of:

        1. All damages; and

        2. All "defense expenses"

    because of the total of all "claims" first made against an insured, except "claims" first made and recorded during the Extended Reporting Period.

C. The Supplemental Limit of Insurance is the most we will pay for the sum of:

    1. All damages; and

    2. All "defense expenses"

for the total of all "claims" first received and recorded during the Extended Reporting Period.

D. Section III – Limits Of Insurance, as amended by Paragraph **C.** above, is otherwise unchanged and applies in its entirety.

E. This endorsement will not take effect unless the additional premium for it, as set forth in Section **VI,** is paid when due. If that premium is paid when due, this endorsement may not be cancelled.

EP 28 01 04 98   Copyright, Insurance Services Office, Inc., 1997

APPENDIX B

POLICY NUMBER: EMPLOYMENT-RELATED PRACTICES LIABILITY
EP 20 02 04 98

THIS ENDORSEMENT CHANGES THE POLICY. PLEASE READ IT CAREFULLY.

ADDITIONAL INSURED – CONTROLLING INTERESTS

This endorsement modifies insurance provided under the following:

EMPLOYMENT-RELATED PRACTICES LIABILITY COVERAGE PART

SCHEDULE

Name Of Person Or Organization:

(If no entry appears above, information required to complete this endorsement will be shown in the Declarations as applicable to this endorsement.)

Section II – Who Is An Insured is amended to include as an insured the person(s) or organization(s) shown in the Schedule, but only with respect to their liability arising out of:

1. Their financial control of you; and
2. Your employment-related practices.

EP 20 02 04 98 Copyright, Insurance Services Office, Inc., 1997 Page 1 of 1

APPENDIX B

POLICY NUMBER: EMPLOYMENT-RELATED PRACTICES LIABILITY
EP 20 01 04 98

THIS ENDORSEMENT CHANGES THE POLICY. PLEASE READ IT CAREFULLY.

ADDITIONAL INSURED – DESIGNATED PERSON OR ORGANIZATION

This endorsement modifies insurance provided under the following:

EMPLOYMENT-RELATED PRACTICES LIABILITY COVERAGE PART

SCHEDULE

Name Of Person Or Organization:

(If no entry appears above, information required to complete this endorsement will be shown in the Declarations as applicable to this endorsement.)

Section II – Who Is An Insured is amended to include as an insured the person(s) or organization(s) shown in the Schedule as an insured, but only with respect to liability arising out of your employment-related practices.

EP 20 01 04 98   Copyright, Insurance Services Office, Inc., 1997   Page 1 of 1

APPENDIX B

EMPLOYMENT-RELATED PRACTICES LIABILITY
EP 01 01 04 98

THIS ENDORSEMENT CHANGES THE POLICY. PLEASE READ IT CAREFULLY.

AMENDATORY ENDORSEMENT – NEWLY ACQUIRED ORGANIZATIONS

This endorsement modifies insurance provided under the following:

EMPLOYMENT-RELATED PRACTICES LIABILITY COVERAGE PART

The following paragraph is added to **Section II – Who Is An Insured:**

C. Any organization you newly acquire or form, other than a partnership, joint venture or limited liability company, and over which you maintain ownership or majority interest, will qualify as a Named Insured if there is no other similar insurance available to that organization. You must notify us of such acquisition or formation as soon as practicable. However, coverage under this provision:

1. Is afforded only until the 90th day after you acquire or form the organization, or the end of the policy period, whichever is earlier; and

2. Does not apply to an offense committed before you acquired or formed the organization.

EP 01 01 04 98   Copyright, Insurance Services Office, Inc., 1997   Page 1 of 1

APPENDIX B

APPENDIX C

Index Of Insurers

The following is a listing of facilities providing EPL insurance as of the edition date of this publication. As EPL insurance is one of the fastest growing areas of insurance, it is anticipated that additional facilities will be available in the near future.

Admiral Insurance Company
Derek M. Lucas
Monitor Liability Managers, Inc.
2850 W. Golf Road, Suite 800
Rolling Meadows, IL 60008
847/806-6590
847/806-6282 (fax)
dlucas@monitorgroup.com

Agricultural Excess & Surplus Insurance Company (AESIC)
Tom Siebers
1515 Woodfield Road, Suite 850
Schaumberg, IL 60130
847/330-6750
847/330-6890 (fax)
gaiceld@megsinet.net

American Equity Insurance Company
Ram Chandarana
Professional Underwriters Agency, Inc.
2907 Butterfield Road, Suite 320
Oak Brook, IL 60523
630/575-8111
630/575-0033 (fax)
www.puainc.comm

American International Specialty Lines Insurance Company
Morefar Marketing, Inc.
501 Carr Road, Suite 101
Wilmington, DE 19809
302/761-5600
302/761-5659 (fax)

Associated Electric & Gas Insurance Services, Limited (AEGIS)
Sandra A. Johnson
Vice President, Underwriting
Associated Electric & Gas Insurance Services, Limited
10 Exchange Place
Jersey City, NJ 07302
201/521-4658
201/521-4642 (fax)
johnsos%aegis@mcimail.com

Chubb Group
Michael J. Maloney
Chubb & Son, Inc.
15 Mountain View Road
Warren, NJ 07059
908/903-3494
908/903-3591 (fax)

Chubb Group
John A. Kuhn
Chubb Group
15 Mountain View Road
Warren, NJ 07059
908/903-2726
908/903-3591 (fax)

Chubb Group
A. Quentin Orza
Product Manager
Chubb Group
15 Mountain View Road
Warren, NJ 07059
908/903-2726
908/903-3591 (fax)

Chubb Group
Evan Rosenberg
Chubb Group of Insurance Companies
15 Mountain View Road
Warren, NJ 07059
908/903-3396
908/903-3246 (fax)
erosenberg@chubb.com

**CNA Reinsurance Company
(NAS Insurance Services, Inc.)**
Richard J. Robin, Vice President
NAS Insurance Services, Inc.
16333 Ventura Boulevard, #500
Encino, CA 91436
818/382-2030
818/382-2040 (fax)
general@nasinsurance.com

Colonia (AUSCO)
Available through excess and surplus lines brokers only

**Connecticut Indemnity Company
(Professional Risk Facilities, Inc.)**
Joseph S. Gravier, Jr.
Professional Risk Facilities, Inc.
300 Old Country Road
Mineola, NY 11501-4192
516/747-6060
516/747-6074 (fax)
prf@i-2000.com

Connecticut Specialty Insurance Company
Joseph S. Gravier, Jr.
Professional Risk Facilities, Inc.
300 Old Country Road
Mineola, NY 11501-4192
516/747-6060
516/747-6074 (fax)
prf@i-2000.com

Employers Reinsurance Corporation
Betty Weeks/ERC Specialty
Employers Reinsurance Corporation
5200 Metcalf
Overland Park, KS 66201
913/676-5327
913/676-5359 (fax)
betty.weeks@ercgroup.com

**Evanston Insurance Company
(Shand Morahan)**
Gerard Albanese
Evanston Insurance Company
1007 Church Street
Evanston, IL 60091
847/866-0874
847/866-0717 (fax)
albanese@markelcorp.com

Executive Risk Specialty Insurance Company
Heather Anderson
Executive Risk Communications
82 Hopmeadow Street
Simsbury, CT 06070-7683
800/432-8168
860/408-2288 (fax)
info@execrisk.com

Fireman's Fund Insurance Company
Mary Anne Tankersley
ALTRU, Inc.
3975 Erie Avenue
Cincinnati, OH 45208
800/529-8850
513/271-8899 (fax)

Fireman's Fund Insurance Company
James R. Grieser
Professional Risk Co.
600 University Street, Suite 2501
Seattle, WA 98101
206/621-8808
206/682-9176 (fax)
jrg@wexfordgroup.com

First Specialty Insurance Corporation (Employers Reinsurance Group)
Ron Kettner
First Specialty Insurance Corporation
5200 Metcalf
Overland Park, KS 66201
913/676-5339
913/676-5359 (fax)

Genesis Indemnity Insurance Company
Richard M. Gibson
Genesis Professional Liability Underwriters
25550 Chagrin Boulevard, Suite 300
Beachwood, OH 44122
216/766-5093
216/591-0906 (fax)
rgibson@genre.com

Genesis Insurance Company
Richard M. Gibson
Product Manager
Genesis Insurance Company
25550 Chagrin Boulevard
Beachwood, OH 44122
216/766-5093
216/591-0906 (fax)
rgibson@prms.com

Great American Insurance Companies
Jeffrey Gauthier
Great American Insurance Companies
1515 Woodfield Road, Suite 850
Schaumberg, IL 60173
847/330-6750
847/330-6890 (fax)
gaiceld@megsinet.net

Great American Insurance Companies
Todd Weber
Great American Insurance Companies
1515 Woodfield Road, Suite 850
Schaumberg, IL 60173
847/330-6750
847/330-6890 (fax)
gaiceld@megsinet.net

Gulf Insurance Group (Rockwood Programs)
Darryl McCallin
Rockwood Programs, Inc.
228 Philadelphia Pike
Wilmington, DE 19809
800/558-8808
darryl_mccallin@blanca.com (e-mail)

Hartford Insurance Companies
Hartford Insurance Co.
Regional Underwriters

Insurance Services Office (ISO)
Available through insurers only

Legion Insurance Companies
Richard V. Rupp, CPCU
AmTech E&S
P.O. Box M
San Mateo, CA 94402-0080
650/572-4665
650/572-4622 (fax)
rupprisk@aol.com
www.ccmc.com/calco

Lexington Insurance Company
Morefar Marketing, Inc.
501 Carr Road, Suite 101
Wilmington, DE 19809
302/761-5600
302/761-5659 (fax)

Lexington Insurance Company
Rob Jurgel/Paul Cunningham
Lexington Insurance Company
200 State Street, Fourth Floor
Boston, MA 02109
617/330-8445
617/439-9794 (fax)

London Market (American Technology Excess and Surplus Insurance Services)
Richard V. Rupp, CPCU
Managing Director
AmTech E&S
P.O. Box M
San Mateo, CA 94402-0080
415/572-4665
415/572-4662 (fax)
rupprisk@aol.com

London Market (CNA Re/St. Paul Re)
Viviane Krief Woodcock
IFIS, Inc.
600 Wilshire Boulevard, #1500
Los Angeles, CA 90017
213/833-0288
213/833-0277 (fax)
vkrief@ecom.net

London Market (NAS Insurance Services, Inc.)
Richard J. Robin, Vice President
NAS Insurance Services, Inc.
16633 Ventura Boulevard, Suite 500
Encino, CA 91436
818/382-2030
818/382-2040 (fax)
general@nasinsurance.com

London Market (U.S. Risk Underwriters, Inc.)
Caren Patton, Jay Alston or Keli Eddings
U.S. Risk Underwriters, Inc.
10210 N. Central Expressway, #500
Dallas, TX 75231
214/265-2448
214/739-1421 (fax)
caren@usrisk.com

National Union Fire Insurance Co. (American International Companies)
Paul J. Schiavone
Assistant Vice President/Divisional Counsel
National Union Fire Insurance Co.
175 Water Street, 5th Floor
New York, NY 10038
212/458-1418
212/458-1474 (fax)

Northland Insurance Companies
Gwen L. Holler, CPCU
Northland Insurance Companies
1295 Northland Drive
St. Paul, MN 55120-1146
612/688-4510
612/688-4280 (fax)
gwen.holler@northlandins.com

Pacific Insurance Company, Ltd. (First State Management Group, Inc.)
Jim Seward
First State Management Group, Inc.
150 Federal Street
Boston, MA 02110-1753
617/526-7792
617/526-0612 (fax)

Philadelphia Insurance Companies
James J. Maguire, Jr., ARM
Philadelphia Insurance Companies
One Bala Plaza, Suite 100
Bala Cynwyd, PA 19004
610/617-7900
610/617-7940 (fax)
phlyjjmjr@aol.com

Reliance Insurance Company of Illinois (Reliance National Risk Specialists)
Lisa DeSimone
77 Water Street, 25th Floor
New York, NY 10005
212/858-6379
212/858-9810 (fax)
lisa.desimone@reliancenational.com

Reliance National
Gary N. Dubois
Reliance National
77 Water Street
New York, NY 10005
212/858-3618
212/858-6686 (fax)
gary.dubois@reliancenational.com

Steadfast Insurance Company
Lisa L. Reynolds
Steadfast Insurance Company
One Liberty Plaza, 30th Floor
New York, NY 10006
212/748-2375
212/513-1239 (fax)

Steadfast Insurance Company
Jay M. Dipasupil
Steadfast Insurance Company
One Liberty Plaza, 30th Floor
New York, NY 10006
212/748-2372
212/513-1239 (fax)

Swett & Crawford (insured may choose CNA Reinsurance Co., Limited or Lloyds of London)
Rachel McKinney
Underwriting Manager
Swett & Crawford
515 S. Figueroa Street, Suite 600
Los Angeles, CA 90071
213/439-3415
213/439-3454 (fax)
Sherrie Beckham, Lead Underwriter
213/439-3416

Travelers Property Casualty (G. J. Sullivan Company)
Paul Bubnis
135 N. Los Robles, #290
Pasadena, CA 91101
626/584-7461
626/564-9911 (fax)
bubnispees.gjs.com

United Educators Risk Retention Group, Inc.
Bruce P. Bernstein, CPCU
United Educators Risk Retention Group, Inc.
2 Wisconsin Circle, Suite 1040
Chevy Chase, MD 20895
301/215-6421
301/907-4908 (fax)
bbernstein@ue.org

United States Fidelity & Guaranty Company
William A. Chapdelaine
United States Fidelity & Guaranty Company
6225 Smith Avenue
Baltimore, MD 21209
800/664-8734
410/205-5372 (fax)

United States Liability Insurance Group
Christopher Higgins, CPCU, RPLU
United States Liability Insurance Group
1030 Continental Drive
King of Prussia, PA 19406
800/523-5545
610/687-0080 (fax)

X.L. Insurance Company, Ltd.
Paul Miller
X.L. Insurance Company, Ltd.
Cumberland House
One Victoria Street
Hamilton HM JX, Bermuda
441/292-8515
441/292-1566 (fax)

Zurich American Insurance Company
Lisa R. McElroy
Assistant Vice President
Zurich-American Insurance Group
One Liberty Plaza, 30th Floor
New York, NY 10006
212/748-2375
212/619-0790 (fax)
lisa.mcelroy@zurich.com

Zurich Insurance Company
Jay M. Dipasupil
Zurich Insurance Company
One Liberty Plaza, 30th Floor
New York, NY 10006
212/748-2372
212/513-1239 (fax)

APPENDIX D

Quick Checklist Of Desirable EPLI Policy Features

The following are features generally associated with broad EPL insurance coverage. Use this checlist as a quick guide in conducting your own analysis of coverage.

- **Broad definition of Employment Practices Violations, including:**
  - Discrimination (not limited to specified types or classes and no requirement that harassment or wrongful termination be discrimination-based)
  - Harassment (sexual and otherwise)
  - Wrongful termination
  - Retaliation
  - Employment-related misrepresentation
  - Employment-related personal injury, including libel, slander, humiliation, defamation, invasion of privacy
  - Failure to employ, promote
  - Wrongful evaluation, discipline
  - Constructive discharge
  - Violation of federal, state and local employment practices laws (including Pregnancy Discrimination Act, Family and Medical Leave Act, Americans With Disabilities Act, Equal Pay Act)
  - Third-party discrimination
  - Provides defense even if coverage excluded for claims alleging violation of express/written contracts

- **Broad definition of Insured, including**
  - The entity/organization
  - Directors and officers
  - Former and current employees, whether supervisors, managers, part-time, temporary, seasonal or leased
  - Automatic coverage for newly acquired/formed entities (including subsidiaries)

- **Broad definition of Claim, including**
  - Lawsuits or other actions filed by EEOC or other state or federal agencies
  - Arbitration or other administrative proceedings
  - Oral and written complaints
  - No damage required

- ☐ **Broad definition of Loss, including**
    - ☐ Settlements, judgements and defense expenses
    - ☐ Compensatory damages
    - ☐ Punitive and exemplary damages (where insurable)
    - ☐ Pre-judgment and post-judgment interest

- ☐ **Appropriate defense provision**
    - ☐ Duty to defend
    - ☐ No duty to defend
    - ☐ Flexible

- ☐ **Insured has voice in selection of counsel**

- ☐ **Provides full "prior acts" coverage (i.e., no retroactive date)**

- ☐ **Limited exclusions, including**
    - ☐ No bodily injury exclusion
    - ☐ Intentional acts exclusion limited to situations where proven
    - ☐ No exclusion for mental anguish or emotional distress
    - ☐ Contains severability/non-imputation of liability provisions as respects knowledge of prior acts or other proven intentional acts
    - ☐ No pollution exclusion
    - ☐ No downsizing exclusion

- ☐ **Miscellaneous provisions:**
    - ☐ Single retention/deductible applies to all claims arising from one act
    - ☐ Waiver/reduction of deductible/retention in certain circumstances
    - ☐ Insured must consent to settlement by insurer
    - ☐ Policy noncancellable by insurer (except for non-payment of premium)
    - ☐ Worldwide coverage
    - ☐ Extended discovery period available if either insured/insurer cancels or nonrenews policy
    - ☐ Automatic runoff coverage in event of change of control
    - ☐ Reporting of potential claims triggers policy coverage, even if claim submitted after policy period or discovery period
    - ☐ Insured allowed minimum of 30 days to purchase extended reporting or discovery period

APPENDIX E

EPL Insurance Exclusions Usage

EPL Insurance Policy Exclusion	Percent of Policies Reviewed Containing Exclusion
ADA ACCOMMODATION EXPENSES	68
ASSAULT & BATTERY	21
BACK PAY	3
BODILY INJURY	
BODILY INJURY	77
DEATH	77
DISEASE	77
SICKNESS	77
BREACH OF EMPLOYMENT CONTRACT	25
EXPRESS CONTRACT	38
WRITTEN CONTRACT	28
ORAL CONTRACT	8
IMPLIED CONTRACT	2
CLASS ACTION LAWSUITS	0
CONSEQUENTIAL LOSS	13
APPLIES TO BODILY INJURY	13
APPLIES TO INSURED EVENT	7
BROTHER/SISTER	15
CHILD	15
DOMESTIC PARTNER	15
PARENT	15
SPOUSE	15
COST OF ARBITRATION HEARINGS SUBJECT TO	7
EMPLOYMENT HANDBOOK	0
LABOR GRIEVANCE	8
OTHER EMPLOYMENT POLICY OR PROCEDURE	0
COVERAGE ELSEWHERE	35
OTHER AVAILABLE INSURANCE	70
OTHER INDEMNIFICATION	8
SHARING PROVISION	28
FAILURE TO EXERCISE CARE WHEN TERMINATING	3
FINES/PENALTIES	88
CIVIL	46
CRIMINAL	50
EXEMPLARY DAMAGES	58
PUNITIVE DAMAGES	65
MULTIPLIED DAMAGES	75
FRONT PAY	16
EXCLUSION APPLIES ONLY IF EMPLOYER HAD OPPORTUNITY TO REINSTATE EMPLOYEE BUT DID NOT DO SO	13

EPL Insurance Policy Exclusion	Percent of Policies Reviewed Containing Exclusion
INTENTIONAL ACTS	23
CRIMINAL ACTS	38
CRIMINAL PROCEEDING	7
DISHONEST PURPOSE	40
FRAUDULENT ACTS	58
FRAUDULENT CLAIMS	18
INTENTIONAL VIOLATIONS OF LAW	35
WILLFUL FAILURE TO COMPLY WITH LAW	25
MALICIOUS PURPOSE	25
LIABILITY OF OTHERS	67
LIQUIDATED DAMAGES	20
LOSS ARISING OUT OF CHANGES IN OPERATIONS	
ACQUISITION	5
CHANGE IN CONTROL	2
DOWNSIZING OR REDUCTION IN FORCE	8
FINANCIAL IMPAIRMENT	2
BANKRUPTCY	5
INSOLVENCY	0
LIQUIDATION	5
RECEIVERSHIP	5
FINANCIAL INABILITY TO PAY	0
MERGER	3
PLANT OR FACILITY CLOSING	11
REORGANIZATION	10
TEMPORARY SHUTDOWN	2
MATTERS DEEMED UNINSURABLE	75
NON-MONETARY RELIEF	15
DECLATORY RELIEF	10
DISGORGEMENT	10
INJUNCTIVE RELIEF	26
JOB REINSTATEMENT	15
NON-MONETARY DAMAGES/RELIEF	52
OTHER EQUITABLE REMEDIES	13
OBLIGATION TO PROVIDE BENEFITS	
COBRA	60
DISABILITY	67
ERISA	93
SOCIAL SECURITY	35
OTHER RETIREMENT BENEFITS	13
UNEMPLOYMENT	67
WORKERS' COMPENSATION	78

EPL Insurance Policy Exclusion	Percent of Policies Reviewed Containing Exclusion
PERSONAL INJURY OFFENSES	
DEFAMATION	8
EMOTIONAL DISTRESS/UPSET	5
HUMILIATION	3
LIBEL	8
MENTAL ANGUISH	5
SLANDER	8
PRIOR ACTS	38
PRIOR KNOWLEDGE	57
PRIOR/PENDING LITIGATION	45
PROPERTY DAMAGE	53
INTANGIBLE PROPERTY	8
LOSS OF USE	77
TANGIBLE PROPERTY	73

EPL Insurance Policy Exclusion	Percent of Policies Reviewed Containing Exclusion
RETALIATORY ACTIONS OF EMPLOYER	5
FOR FAILING TO PERFORM ACTS AGAINST PUBLIC	7
FOR FILING A COMPLAINT OR BENEFIT CLAIM	7
STRIKES/LOCKOUTS	47
VIOLATION OF LAWS	
ANY LAW	5
FMLA	2
OSHA	52
POLLUTION LAWS	33
RICO	8
SEC	0
WARN	75

APPENDIX F

EPL Insurance Capacity— Maximum Per-Claim Limit Of Liability

Insurer Policy Form Number [Date]	Maximum Per-Claim Limit
Insurance Services Office (ISO) EP 00 01 04 98 [04 98]	varies by insurer
Hartford Insurance Companies HC 00 55 03 96 [3/96]	$250,000
Colonia (AUSCO) EPL 6000 (3/95) [3/95]	$1,000,000
First Specialty Insurance Corporation (Employers Reinsurance Group) FSIC-1491A [01/96]	$1,000,000
London Market (NAS Insurance Services, Inc.) AIF 835/95 [2/97]	$1,000,000
London Market (NAS Insurance Services, Inc.) AIF 1653/95A [2/97]	$1,000,000 per section
American Equity Insurance Company 11197 [11/97]	$2,000,000
London Market (NAS Insurance Services, Inc.) AIF 2314 [4/98]	$2,000,000
United States Liability Insurance Group EPLJ [1/98]	$2,000,000
London Market (American Technology Excess & Surplus Insurance Services) AmTech Form ERP-1 [11/96]	$2,000,000
CNA Reinsurance Company Ltd. (NAS Insurance Services, Inc.) C/NA/S [12/97]	$5,000,000
Admiral Insurance Company EPL 4000 [10/97]	$5,000,000
Agricultural Excess & Surplus Insurance Company (AESIC) D 5717-19 [6/93]	$5,000,000
Connecticut Indemnity Company (Professional Risk Facilities, Inc.) 40609-0 [2/94]	$5,000,000
Connecticut Specialty Insurance Company OL 001-0 [4/98]	$5,000,000
Employers Reinsurance Corporation ERC 1491A [1995]	$5,000,000
Evanston Insurance Company (Shand Morahan) EIC 3071-1 9/97 [9/97]	$5,000,000
Fireman's Fund Insurance Company 7006-10-96 [10/96]	$5,000,000
Fireman's Fund Insurance Company 7006-1-98 [1/98]	$5,000,000
Great American Insurance Companies D.710-35 [11/85]	$5,000,000
Great American Insurance Companies D.9100 [6/97]	$5,000,000

Insurer Policy Form Number [Date]	Maximum Per-Claim Limit
Gulf Insurance Group (Rockwood Programs, Inc.) RP 8002g [11/97]	$5,000,000
Legion Insurance Companies ERP-1 [7/98]	$5,000,000
London Market (NAS Insurance Services, Inc.) CBPLI98 [4/98]	$5,000,000
London Market (U.S. Risk Underwriters, Inc.) DISC3/98/CO [3/98]	$5,000,000
Northland Insurance Companies S1110-EP [6/97]	$5,000,000
Reliance Insurance Company of Illinois (Reliance National Risk Specialists) GL 00 R430 00 0498 [4/98]	$5,000,000
American International Specialty Lines Insurance Company 64198 (12/95) [12/95]	$5,000,000
Lexington Insurance Company 65200 [12/95]	$5,000,000
Chubb Group 14-02-1968 [5-96]	$10,000,000
Executive Risk Specialty Insurance Company B22130 [1/96]	$10,000,000
Executive Risk Specialty Insurance Company B24775 [8/97]	$10,000,000
London Market (CNA Re/St. Paul Re) EPL (11/97A Broad) [11/97]	$10,000,000
Pacific Insurance Company, Ltd. (First State Management Group, Inc.) PL-364 [5/98]	$10,000,000
Philadelphia Indemnity Insurance Company PI-DF-1 [9/95]	$10,000,000
Philadelphia Insurance Companies PI-ES-1560 [12/96]	$10,000,000
United States Fidelity & Guaranty Company FID 600 [11/95]	$10,000,000
Zurich Insurance Company U-DO-111-A (CW) [2/97]	$10,000,000
Fireman's Fund Insurance Company 5240-12-94 [12/94]	$15,000,000
Fireman's Fund Insurance Company 5241-6-96 [6/96]	$15,000,000
Genesis Insurance Company Frontline 8000 [6/97]	$20,000,000
Chubb Group 17-02-1345 [3-97]	$25,000,000
Executive Risk Specialty Insurance Company B22170 [2/97]	$25,000,000
Genesis Indemnity Insurance Company GIIC-8001 [06/97]	$25,000,000
Reliance Insurance Company of Illinois (Reliance National Risk Specialists) GL 00 R424 00 0498 [4/98]	$25,000,000
Reliance National DO 00 R324 00 0696 [0696]	$25,000,000
Swett & Crawford (CNA Reinsurance Co., Limited or Lloyd's of London) EPLX-987 [7/1/98]	$25,000,000
Travelers Property Casualty (G. J. Sullivan Company) DHN 1001 [4/98]	$25,000,000
United Educators Risk Retention Group, Inc. ELL [February 1997]	$25,000,000

Insurer Policy Form Number [Date]	Maximum Per-Claim Limit
Associated Electric & Gas Insurance Services, Limited (AEGIS) 8262 (1/98) [1/98]	$35,000,000
Executive Risk Specialty Insurance Company B22167 [2/97]	$40,000,000
Chubb Group 14-02-0953 [8/96]	$50,000,000
Chubb Group 14-02-2009 [5-96]	$50,000,000
National Union Fire Insurance Co. (American International Companies) 67548 [4/97]	$50,000,000
Steadfast Insurance Company STF-PL-100-B CW [4/97]	$50,000,000
Steadfast Insurance Company U-DO-457-A (CW) [4/97]	$50,000,000
Zurich American Insurance Company STF-EPL-101-A [3/98]	$50,000,000
Zurich Insurance Company U-DO-457-A (CW) [4/97]	$50,000,000
Lexington Insurance Company LEX-CM-EPLIT [9/97]	$100,000,000
X.L. Insurance Company, Ltd. EPLI-005 [7/98]	$100,000,000

APPENDIX F

APPENDIX G

EEOC District Offices

General Information: 800/669-4000 Nearest Office Referral
800/669-3362 Procedures and Regulations

ALABAMA
2121 Eighth Avenue North, Suite 823
Birmingham, AL 35203
205/731-0082
FTS 229-0082

ARIZONA
4520 N. Central Avenue, Suite 300
Phoenix, AZ 85012-1848
602/261-3882
FTS 261-3682

ARKANSAS
320 W. Capitol Avenue, Suite 621
Little Rock, AR 72201
501/324-5060

CALIFORNIA
1313 P Street, Suite 103
Fresno, CA 93721
209/487-5793

3660 Wilshire Boulevard, 5th Floor
Los Angeles, CA 90010
213/251-7278
FTS 983-7278

1333 Broadway, Room 430
Oakland, CA 94612
510/273-7588

401 B Street, Suite 1550
San Diego, CA 92101
619/557-7235

901 Market Street, Suite 500
San Francisco, CA 94103
415/995-5049
FTS 995-5049

96 N. 3rd Street
San Jose, CA 95113
408/291-7352

COLORADO
1845 Sherman Street, Second Floor
Denver, CO 80203
303/866-1300
FTS 564-1300

FLORIDA
Motto-Mall Building
1 NE. 1st Street, 6th Floor
Miami, FL 33132
305/536-4491
FTS 350-4491

501 E. Polk Street, 10th Floor
Tampa, FL 33602
813/228-2310

GEORGIA
10 Whitaker Street, Suite B
Savannah, GA 31401
912/944-4234

Citizens Trust Bank Building, 10th Floor
75 Piedmont Ave. NE, Suite 1100
Atlanta, GA 30335
404/331-6093
FTS 242-6093

HAWAII
677 Ala Moana Boulevard, Suite 404
Honolulu, HI 96813
808/541-3120

ILLINOIS
Federal Building, Room 930A
536 S. Clark Street, Room 930-A
Chicago, IL 60605
312/353-2713
FTS 353-2713

INDIANA
Federal Building, U.S. Courthouse
46 E. Ohio Street, Room 456
Indianapolis, IN 46204
317/226-7212
FTS 331-7212

KENTUCKY
600 Martin Luther King, Jr. Place, Suite 268
Louisville, KY 40202
502/582-6082

LOUISIANA
701 Loyola Avenue, Suite 60D
New Orleans, LA 70113
504/589-2329
FTS 682-2329

MARYLAND
109 Market Place, Suite 4000
Baltimore, MD 21202
301/962-3932
FTS 922-3932

MASSACHUSETTS
Room 100, 10th Floor
1 Congress Street
Boston, MA 02114
617/565-3200

MICHIGAN
McNamara Federal Building
477 Michigan Avenue, Room 1540
Detroit, MI 48226
313/226-7636
FTS 226-7636

MINNESOTA
220 2nd St. S., Room 108
Minneapolis, MN 55401
612/370-3330

MISSISSIPPI
207 W. Amite St.
Jackson, MS 39269
601/965-4537

MISSOURI
Central West Plaza Building, 4th Floor
625 N. Euclid Street
St. Louis, MO 63108
314/425-6585
FTS 279-6585

911 Walnut, 10th Floor
Kansas City, MO 64106
816/426-5773

NEW JERSEY
60 Park Place, Room 301
Newark, NJ 07102
201/645-6383

NEW MEXICO
505 Marquette NW, Suite 900
Albuquerque, NM 87102
505/766-2061

NEW YORK
28 Church Street, Room 301
Buffalo, NY 14202
716/846-4441

90 Church Street, Room 1505
New York, NY 10007
212/264-7161
FTS 264-7161

NORTH CAROLINA
5500 Central Avenue
Charlotte, NC 28212
704/567-7100
FTS 626-7100

324 W. Market Street, Room B-27
Greensboro, NC 27402
919/333-5174

1309 Annapolis Drive
Raleigh, NC 27601
919/856-4064

OHIO
525 Vine Street, Suite 810
Cincinnati, OH 45202
513/684-2851

One Playhouse Square
1375 Euclid Avenue, Room 600
Cleveland, OH 44115
216/522-2001
FTS 942-2001

OKLAHOMA
531 Couch Drive
Oklahoma City, OK 94612
405/231-4911

PENNSYLVANIA
1421 Cherry Street, 10th Floor
Philadelphia, PA 19102
215/656-7020

1000 Liberty Avenue, Room 2038-A
Pittsburgh, PA 15222
412/644-3444

SOUTH CAROLINA
15 S. Main Street, Suite 530
Greenville, SC 29601
803/241-4400

TENNESSEE
1407 Union Avenue, Suite 621
Memphis, TN 38104
901/521-2617
FTS 222-2617

50 Vantage Way, Suite 202
Nashville, TN 37228
615/736-5820

TEXAS
8303 Elmbrook Drive, 2nd Floor
Dallas, TX 75247
214/767-7015
FTS 729-7015

Suite 100, Building C, The Commons
El Paso, TX 79902
915/534-6550

405 Main Street, 6th Floor
Houston, TX 77002
713/653-3320
FTS 522-3320

5410 Fredericksburg Road, Suite 200
Mockingbird Plaza, Plaza II
San Antonio, TX 78229
512/229-4810
FTS 730-4810

VIRGINIA
1st Floor, SMA Building
252 Monticello Avenue
Norfolk, VA 23510
804/441-3470

3600 W. Broad Street, 2nd Floor
Richmond, VA 23230
804/771-2692

WASHINGTON
Arcade Plaza Building, 7th Floor
1321 2nd Avenue
Seattle, WA 98101
206/442-0968
FTS 399-0968

WISCONSIN
310 W. Wisconsin Avenue, Suite 800
Milwaukee, WI 53203
414/297-1111
FTS 362-1111

**WASHINGTON FIELD OFFICE
DIRECTOR EEOC**
1400 L Street, NW, Suite 200
Washington, DC 20005
202/275-7377
FTS 275-7377

APPENDIX G

APPENDIX H

State Agencies Regulating Employment Practices

ALABAMA
No State Agency
See EEOC Birmingham District Office
1900 Third Avenue N., Suite 101
Birmingham, AL 35203
205/731-0082

ALASKA
Alaska State Commission for Human Rights
800 A Street, Suite 204
Anchorage, AK 99501-3669
907/274-4692   800/478-4692

ARIZONA
Arizona Civil Rights Division
1275 W. Washington Street
Phoenix, AZ 85007
602/542-5263

ARKANSAS
No State Agency
See EEOC Little Rock Area Office
320 W. Capitol Ave, Suite 621
Little Rock, AR 72201
501/324-5060

CALIFORNIA
California Department of Fair Employment
 and Housing
2014 T Street, Suite 210
Sacramento, CA 95814
800/884-1684   916/227-2873

COLORADO
Colorado Civil Rights Division
1560 Broadway, Suite 1050
Denver, CO 80202
303/894-2997

CONNECTICUT
Connecticut Commission on Human Rights
 & Opportunities
90 Washington Street
Hartford, CT 06106
203/566-3350

DELAWARE
Delaware Department of Labor
State Office Building
820 North French Street, 6th Floor
Wilmington, DE 19801
302/577-2882

DISTRICT OF COLUMBIA
D.C. Commission on Human Rights
2000 14th Street NW, Third Floor
Washington, DC 20009
202/939-8740

FLORIDA
Florida Commission on Human Relations
325 John Knox Road, Bldg. F, Suite 240
Tallahassee, FL 32303-4149
904/488-7082   800/342-8170

GEORGIA
Georgia Commission on Equal Opportunity
710 Cain Tower, Peachtree Center
229 Peachtree Street, NE
Atlanta, GA 30303
404/656-7708

HAWAII
Hawaii Civil Rights Commission
888 Mililani Street, 2nd Floor
Honolulu, HI 96813
808/586-8636 (Oahu)
800/468-4644 ext 6-8636 (neighbor islands)

IDAHO
Idaho Human Rights Commission
450 W. State Street, First Floor
Boise, ID 83720
208/334-2873

ILLINOIS

Illinois Department of Human Rights
100 W. Randolph Street, Suite 10-100
Chicago, IL 60601
312/814-6200

INDIANA
Indiana Civil Rights Commission
100 N. Senate Avenue, Room N103
Indianapolis, IN 46204
317/232-2600   800/628-2909

IOWA
Iowa Civil Rights Commission
Grimes State Office Building
211 East Maple Street, 2nd Floor
Des Moines, IA 503109
515/281-4121

KANSAS
Kansas Commission on Civil Rights
Landon State Office Building, 8th Floor
900 SW Jackson Street, Suite 851 S.
Topeka, KS 66612-1258
913/296-3206

KENTUCKY
Kentucky Commission on Human Rights
The Heyburn Building, Suite 700
332 West Broadway
Louisville, KY 40202
502/595-4024   800/292-5566

LOUISIANA
No State Agency
See EEOC New Orleans District Office
701 Loyola Avenue, Suite 600
New Orleans, LA 70113
504/589-2329

MAINE
Maine Human Rights Commission
Statehouse Station 51
Augusta, ME 04333
207/624-6050

MARYLAND
Maryland Commission on Human Relations
20 E. Franklin Street
Baltimore, MD 21202
410/767-8600

MASSACHUSETTS
Massachusetts Commission Against
 Discrimination
1 Ashburton Place, Room 601
Boston, MA 02108
617/727-3990 (Boston)
413/739-2145 (Springfield)

MICHIGAN
Michigan Department of Civil Rights
333 South Capitol
Lansing, MI 48913
517/373-3590 (Lansing)
313/876-5544 (Detroit)
517/373-2884 (Women's Commission)

MINNESOTA
Minnesota Department of Human Rights
Bremer Tower
Seventh Place and Minnesota Street
St. Paul, MN 55101
612/296-5663

MISSISSIPPI
No State Agency
See EEOC Jackson Area Office
Cross Road Building Complex
207 W. Amite Street
Jackson, MI 39201

MISSOURI
Missouri Commission on Human rights
P.O. Box 1129
Jefferson City, MO 65102
314/751-3325   800/877-6247

MONTANA
Montana Human Rights Commission
616 Helena Avenue, Suite 302
P.O. Box 1728
Helena, MT 59624-1728
406/444-2884   800/542-0807

NEBRASKA
Nebraska Equal Employment Opportunity
  Commission
301 Centennial Mall South, 5th Floor
P.O. Box 94934
Lincoln, NE 68509
402/471-2024

NEVADA
Nevada Equal Rights Commission
1515 Tropicana Avenue, Suite 590
Las Vegas, NV 89158
702/486-7161 (Las Vegas)
702/688-1288 (Reno)

NEW HAMPSHIRE
New Hampshire Commission for
  Human Rights
163 Loudon Road
Concord, NH 03301-6053
603/271-2767
  Publishes the especially helpful *A Manual on Sexual Harassment*

NEW JERSEY
New Jersey Division on Civil Rights
383 W. State Street
Trenton, NJ 08618
609/292-4605

NEW MEXICO
New Mexico Human Rights Commission
Aspen Plaza
1596 Pacheco Street
Santa Fe, NM 87501

NEW YORK
New York State Division of Human Rights
Office of Sexual Harassment Issues
55 Hanson Place, Suite 346
Brooklyn, NY 11217
718/722-2060   800/427-2773

NORTH CAROLINA
State agency (for private employees):
North Carolina Human Relations
  Commission
121 W. Jones Street
Raleigh, NC 27603
919/733-7996   800/699-4000

State agency (for public employees):
North Carolina State Office of Administrative
  Hearings
424 North Blount Street
Raleigh, NC 27601
919/733-2691

NORTH DAKOTA
North Dakota Department of Labor
State Capitol Building
600 East Boulevard
Bismarck, ND 58505
701/328-2660

OHIO
Ohio Civil Rights Commission
220 Parsons Avenue
Columbus, OH 43215
216/379-3100 (Akron)
513/852-3344 (Cincinnati)
216/787-3150 (Cleveland)
614/466-5928 (Columbus)
513/285-6500 (Dayton)
419/245-2900 (Toledo)

OKLAHOMA
Oklahoma Human Rights Commission
2101 N. Lincoln Blvd, Room 480
Oklahoma City, OK 73105
405/521-3441 (Oklahoma City)
918/581-2733 (Tulsa)

OREGON
Oregon Bureau of Labor and Industry–
  Civil Rights Division
Suite 1070
800 NE Oregon St. #32
Portland, OR 97232
503/731-4075 ext.421 (Portland)
503/687-7460 (Eugene)

PENNSYLVANIA
Pennsylvania Human Relations Commission
101 S. Second Street, Suite 300
Harrisburg, PA 17105-3145
717/787-9784 (Harrisburg)
215/560-2496 (Philadelphia)
412/565-5395 (Pittsburgh)

RHODE ISLAND
Rhode Island Commission for Human Rights
10 Abbot Park Place
Providence, RI 02903
401/277-2661

SOUTH CAROLINA
South Carolina Human Affairs Commission
2611 Forest Drive
P.O. Box 4490
Columbia, SC 29240
803/253-6339   800/521-0725

SOUTH DAKOTA
South Dakota Division of Human Rights
222 E. Capitol, Suite 11
Pierre, SD 57501-5070
605/773-4493

TENNESSEE
Tennessee Human Rights Commission
530 Church Street, Suite 400
Nashville, TN 37243
615/741-5825

TEXAS
Texas Commission on Human Rights
8100 Cameron Road, Building B, Suite 525
Austin, TX 78754
512/837-8534

UTAH
Utah Industrial Commission–
  Anti-Discrimination Division
160 East 300 South
Salt Lake City, UT 84114
801/530-6801

VERMONT
Vermont Attorney General's Office
Civil Rights Division
109 State Street
Montpelier, VT 05609
802/828-3657

VIRGINIA
Council on Human rights
1100 Bank Street
Washington Building, 12th Floor
Richmond, VA 23219
804/225-2292

WASHINGTON
Washington State Human Rights
  Commission
711 S. Capitol Way, Suite 402
Olympia, WA 98504
360/753-6770 (Olympia)
206/464-6500 (Seattle)
509/456-4473 (Spokane)
509/575-2772 (Yakima)

WEST VIRGINIA
West Virginia Human Rights Commission
1321 Plaza East, Room 106
Charleston, WV 25301-1400
304/348-2616

WISCONSIN
Wisconsin Department of Industry,
  Labor and Human Relations
Equal Rights Division
P.O. Box 8928
201 East Washington Avenue
Madison, WI 53708
608/266-7552

APPENDIX I

Questions And Answers About Sexual Harassment

The following information is intended as a general overview of sexual harassment and does not carry the force of legal opinion.

Identifying Sexual Harassment

WHAT IS SEXUAL HARASSMENT? Sexual harassment is a form of sex discrimination that is a violation of Title VII of the Civil Rights Act of 1964. The EEOC's guidelines define two types of sexual harassment: "quid pro quo" and "hostile environment."

WHAT IS "QUID PRO QUO" SEXUAL HARASSMENT? Unwelcome sexual advances, requests for sexual favors and other verbal or physical conduct of a sexual nature constitute "quid pro quo" sexual harassment when (1) submission to such conduct is made either explicitly or implicitly a term or condition of an individual's employment, or (2) submission to or rejection of such conduct by an individual is used as the basis for employment decisions affecting such individual.

WHAT IS "HOSTILE ENVIRONMENT" SEXUAL HARASSMENT? Unwelcome sexual advances, requests for sexual favors, and other verbal or physical conduct of a sexual nature constitute "hostile environment" sexual harassment when such conduct has the purpose or effect of unreasonably interfering with an individual's work performance or creating an intimidating, hostile or offensive working environment.

WHAT FACTORS DETERMINE WHETER AN ENVIRONMENT IS "HOSTILE"? The central inquiry is whether the conduct "unreasonably interfered with an individual's work performance" or created "an intimidating, hostile, or offensive working environment." The EEOC will look at the following factors to determine whether an environment is hostile: (1) whether the conduct was verbal or physical or both; (2) how frequently it was repeated; (3) whether the conduct was hostile or patently offensive; (4) whether the alleged harasser was a co-worker or supervisor; (5) whether others joined in perpetrating the harassment; and (6) whether the harassment was directed at more than one individual. No one factor controls. An assessment is made based upon the totality of the circumstances.

WHAT IS UNWELCOME SEXUAL CONDUCT? Sexual conduct becomes unlawful only when it is unwelcome. The challenged conduct must be unwelcome in the sense that the employee did not solicit or incite it, and in the sense that the employee regarded the conduct as undesirable or offensive.

HOW WILL THE EEOC DETERMINE WHETHER CONDUCT IS UNWELCOME? When confronted with conflicting evidence as to whether conduct was welcome, the EEOC will look at the record as a whole and at the totality of the circumstances, evaluating each situation on a case-by-case basis. The investigation should determine whether the victim's conduct was consistent, or inconsistent, with his/her assertion that the sexual conduct was unwelcome.

WHO CAN BE A VICTIM OF SEXUAL HARASSMENT? The victim may be a woman or a man. The victim does not have to be of the opposite sex. The victim does not have to be the person harassed but could be anyone affected by the offensive conduct.

WHO CAN BE A SEXUAL HARASSER? The harasser may be a woman or a man. He or she can be the victim's supervisor, an agent of the employer, a supervisor in another area, a co-worker or a non-employee.

CAN ONE INCIDENT CONSTITUTE SEXUAL HARASSMENT? It depends. In "quid pro quo" cases, a single sexual advance may constitute harassment if it is linked to the granting or denial of employment or employment benefits. In contrast, unless the conduct is quite severe, a single incident or isolated incidents of offensive sexual conduct or remarks generally do not create a "hostile environment." A hostile environment claim usually requires a showing of a pattern of offensive conduct. However, a single, unusually severe incident of harassment may be sufficient to constitute a Title VII violation; the more severe the harassment, the less need to show a repetitive series of incidents. This is particularly true when the harassment is physical.

CAN VERBAL REMARKS CONSTITUTE SEXUAL HARASSMENI? Yes. The EEOC will evaluate the totality of the circumstances to ascertain the nature, frequency, context and intended target of the remarks. Relevant factors may include: (1) whether the remarks were hostile and derogatory; (2) whether the alleged harasser singled out the charging party; (3) whether the charging party participated in the exchange; and (4) the relationship between the charging party and the alleged harasser.

WHAT SHOULD A SEXUAL HARASSMENT VICTIM DO? The victim should directly inform the harasser that the conduct is unwelcome and must stop. It is important for the victim to communicate that the conduct is unwelcome, particularly when the alleged harasser may have some reason to believe that the advance may be welcomed. However, a victim of harassment need not always confront his/her harasser directly, so long as his/her conduct demonstrates that the harasser's behavior is unwelcome. The victim also should use any employer complaint mechanism or grievance system available. If these methods are ineffective, the victim should contact the EEOC as soon as possible (see *Filing a Charge,* below).

Preventing Sexual Harassment

WHAT SPECIFIC STEPS CAN AN EMPLOYER TAKE TO PREVENT SEXUAL HARASSMENT? Prevention is the best tool to eliminate sexual harassment in the workplace. Employers are encouraged to take all steps necessary to prevent sexual harassment from occurring. An effective preventive program should include an explicit policy against sexual harassment that is clearly and regularly communicated to employees and effectively implemented. The employer should affirmatively raise the subject with all supervisory and non-supervisory employees, express strong disapproval of such conduct and explain the sanctions for harassment.

SHOULD AN EMPLOYER HAVE A GRIEVANCE PROCEDURE? The employer should have a procedure for resolving sexual harassment complaints. The procedure should be designed to encourage victims of harassment to come forward and should not require a victim to complain first to an offending supervisor. They can do so by establishing an effective complaint or grievance process and taking immediate and appropriate action when an employee complains. It should ensure confidentiality as much as possible and provide effective remedies, including protection of victims and witnesses against retaliation.

WHAT IF AN EMPLOYER ASSERTS THAT IT HAS ELIMINATED THE HARASSMENT? When an employer asserts it has taken remedial action, the EEOC will investigate to determine whether the action was prompt, appropriate and effective. If the EEOC determines that the harassment has been eliminated, the victims made whole, and preventive measures instituted, the Commission normally will administratively close the charge because of the employer's prompt remedial action.

Filing A Charge

HOW DO I FILE A CHARGE OF DISCRIMINATION? Charges of sex discrimination may be filed at any field office of the U.S. Equal Employment Opportunity Commission. Field Offices are located in 50 cities throughout the United States and are listed in most local telephone directories under U.S. Government. To reach the nearest EEOC field office, dial toll free on 800/669-4000. More information on sexual harassment and information on all EEOC-enforced laws may be obtained by calling toll free on 800/669-EEOC. EEOC's toll-free TDD number is 800/800-3302.

WHAT ARE THE TIME LIMITS FOR FILING A CHARGE OF DISCRIMINATION? A charge of discrimination on the basis of sex must be filed with the EEOC within 180 days of the alleged discriminatory act, or within 300 days, if there is a state or local fair employment practices agency that enforces a *law prohibiting the same alleged discriminatory practice*. However, to protect legal rights, it is recommended that EEOC be contacted promptly when discrimination is believed to have occurred.

WHAT TYPES OF EVIDENCE WILL THE EEOC LOOK AT TO DETERMINE WHETHER SEXUAL HARASSMENT HAS OCCURRED? When investigating allegations of sexual harassment, EEOC will look at the whole record: the circumstances, such as the nature of the sexual advances and the context in which the alleged incidents occurred. The EEOC recognizes that sexual conduct may be private and unacknowledged, with no eyewitnesses. Corroborative evidence of any nature will be explored.

EEOC also will investigate whether any complaints or protests occurred. However, while a complaint or protest is helpful to a charging party's case, it is not a necessary element of the claim. Victims may fear repercussions from complaining about the harassment, and such fear may explain a delay in opposing the conduct. If the victim failed to complain or delayed in complaining, the investigation must ascertain why.

IF I FILE A DISCRIMINATION CHARGE, WHAT TYPES OF RELIEF ARE AVAILABLE? If you have been discriminated against on the basis of sex, you are entitled to a remedy that will place you in the position you would have been in if the discrimination had never occurred. You also may be entitled to hiring, promotion, reinstatement, back pay and other remuneration. You also may be entitled to damages to compensate you for future pecuniary losses, mental anguish and inconvenience. Punitive damages may be available, as well, if an employer acted with malice or reckless indifference. You also may be entitled to attorney's fees.

CAN MY EMPLOYER RETALIATE AGAINST ME FOR FILING A CHARGE WITH EEOC? It is unlawful for an employer or other covered entity to retaliate against someone who files a charge of discrimination, participates in an investigation or opposes discriminatory practices. Individuals who believe that they have been retaliated against should contact EEOC immediately. Even if an individual has already filed a charge of discrimination, he or she can file a new charge based on retaliation.

WHAT LAWS DOES EEOC ENFORCE? EEOC enforces Title VII of the Civil Rights Act of 1964, which prohibits employment discrimination based on race, color, religion, sex or national origin; the Age Discrimination in Employment Act; the Equal Pay Act; prohibitions against discrimination affecting individuals with disabilities in the federal government; sections of the Civil Rights Act of 1991; and Title I of the Americans with Disabilities Act, which prohibits discrimination against people with disabilities in the private sector and state and local governments.

SOURCE: U.S. Equal Employment Opportunity Commission EEOC-BK-SH

APPENDIX J

Facts About The Americans With Disabilities Act

Title I of the Americans with Disabilities Act of 1990, which took effect July 26, 1992, prohibits private employers, state and local governments, employment agencies and labor unions from discriminating against qualified individuals with disabilities in job application procedures, hiring, firing, advancement, compensation, job training and other terms, conditions and privileges of employment. An individual with a disability is a person who:

- Has a physical or mental impairment that substantially limits one or more major life activities;

- Has a record of such an impairment; or

- Is regarded as having such an impairment.

A qualified individual with a disability is an individual who, with or without reasonable accommodation, can perform the essential functions of the job in question. Reasonable accommodation may include, but is not limited to:

- Making existing facilities used by employees readily accessible to and usable by persons with disabilities;

- Job restructuring, modifying work schedules, reassignment to a vacant position;

- Acquiring or modifying equipment or devices; adjusting or modifying examinations, training materials or policies; and providing qualified readers or interpreters.

An employer is required to make an accommodation to the known disability of a qualified applicant or employee if it would not impose an undue hardship on the operation of the employer's business. Undue hardship is defined as an action requiring significant difficulty or expense when considered in light of factors such as an employer's size, financial resources and the nature and structure of its operation.

An employer is not required to lower quality or production standards to make an accommodation, nor is an employer obligated to provide personal use items such as glasses or hearing aids.

Medical Examinations And Inquiries

Employers may not ask job applicants about the existence, nature or severity of a disability. Applicants may be asked about their ability to perform specific job functions. A job offer may be conditioned on the results of a medical examination or inquiry, but only if the examination or inquiry is required for all entering employees in the job. Medical examinations or inquiries of employees must be job related and consistent with the employer's business needs.

Drug And Alcohol Abuse

Employees and applicants currently engaging in the illegal use of drugs are not covered by the ADA, when an employer acts on the basis of such use. Tests for illegal drugs are not subject to the ADA's restrictions on medical examinations. Employers may hold illegal drug users and alcoholics to the same performance standards as other employees.

EEOC Enforcement Of The ADA

The U.S. Equal Employment Opportunity Commission issued regulations to enforce the provisions of Title I of the ADA on July 26, 1991. The regulations took effect on July 26, 1992, and will cover employers with 25 or more employees. On July 26, 1994, employers with 15 or more employees were covered.

Filing A Charge

Charges of employment discrimination on the basis of disability, based on actions occurring on or after July 26, 1992, may be filed at any field office of the U.S. Equal Employment Opportunity Commission. Field offices are located in 50 cities throughout the United States and are listed in most telephone directories under U.S. Government. Information on all EEOC-enforced laws may be obtained by calling toll free 800/669-EEOC. EEOC's toll free TDD number is 800/800-3302.

SOURCE: U.S. Equal Employment Opportunity Commission EEOC-FS/E-5 (January 1992)

APPENDIX K

Facts About Disability-Related Tax Provisions

The Internal Revenue Code has three disability-related provisions of particular interest to businesses as well as people with disabilities.

Disabled Access Tax Credit (Title 26, Internal Revenue Code, Section 44)

This new tax credit is available to eligible small businesses in the amount of 50 percent of eligible access expenditures that exceed $250 but do not exceed $10,250 for a taxable year. A business may take the credit each year that it makes an eligible access expenditure.

Eligible small businesses are those businesses with either:

- $1 million or less in gross receipts for the preceding tax year; or
- 30 or fewer full-time employees during the preceding tax year.

Eligible access expenditures are amounts paid or incurred by an eligible small business for the purpose of enabling the business to comply with the applicable requirements of the Americans with Disabilities Act (ADA). These include amounts paid or incurred to:

- remove architectural, communication, physical or transportation barriers that prevent a business from being accessible to, or usable by, individuals with disabilities;
- provide qualified readers, taped texts and other effective methods of making materials accessible to people with visual impairments;
- provide qualified interpreters or other effective methods of making orally delivered materials available to individuals with hearing impairments;
- acquire or modify equipment or devices for individuals with disabilities; or
- provide other similar services, modifications, materials or equipment.

Expenditures that are not necessary to accomplish the above purposes are not eligible. Expenses in connection with new construction are not eligible. "Disability" has the same meaning as it does in the ADA. To be eligible for the tax credit, barrier removals or the provision of services, modifications, materials or equipment must meet technical standards of the ADA Accessibility Guidelines where applicable. These standards are incorporated in Department of Justice regulations implementing Title III of the ADA (28 CFR Part 36; 56 CFR 35544, July 26, 1991).

Example: Company A purchases equipment to meet its reasonable-accommodation obligation under the ADA for $8,000. The amount by which $8,000 exceeds S250 is $7,750. Fifty percent of S7,750 is S3,875. Company A may take a tax credit in the amount of $3,875 on its next tax return.

Example: Company B removes a physical barrier in accordance with its reasonable-accommodation obligation under the ADA. The barrier removal meets the ADA Accessibility Guidelines. The company spends $12,000 on this modification. The amount by which S12,000 exceeds $250 but not $10,250 is $10,000. Fifty percent of $10,000 is $5,000. Company B is eligible for a $5,000 tax credit on its next tax return.

Tax Deduction To Remove Architectural And Transportation Barriers To People With Disabilities And Elderly Individuals
(Title 26, Internal Revenue Code, Section 190)

The IRS allows a deduction up to $15,000 per year for "qualified architectural and transportation barrier removal expenses." Expenditures to make a facility or public transportation vehicle owned or leased in connection with a trade or business more accessible to, and usable by, individuals who are handicapped or elderly are eligible for the deduction. The definition of a "handicapped individual" is similar to the ADA definition of an "individual with a disability." To be eligible for this deduction, modifications must meet the requirements of standards established by IRS regulations implementing section 190.

Targeted Jobs Tax Credit
(Title 26, Internal Revenue Code, Section 51)

Employers are eligible to receive a tax credit up to 40 percent of the first $6,000 of first-year wages of a new employee with a disability who is referred by state or local vocational rehabilitation agencies, a State Commission on the Blind or the U.S. Department of Veterans Affairs, and certified by a State Employment Service. There is no credit after the first year of employment. For an employer to qualify for the credit, a worker must have been employed for at least 90 days or have completed at least 120 hours of work for the employer. The Tax Extension Act of 1991, Public Law 102-227, extended this tax credit through June 30, 1992.

IRS Publication No. 907, providing information on these provisions, may be obtained by calling 1-800/829-3676. For further information, contact the Internal Revenue Service, Office of the Chief Counsel, P.O. Box 7604, Ben Franklin Station, Washington, DC 20044, 202/566-3292 (voice only).

SOURCE: U.S. Equal Employment Opportunity Commission EEOC-FS/E-6

APPENDIX L

Other Labor- And Employment-Related Agencies

Each month federal and state agencies collect, analyze and publish data regarding a variety of employment-related issues. The following agencies are listed as sources of specialized information as described.

Labor Publications
Office of Insurance and Public Affairs
U.S. Department of Labor
200 Constitution Avenue, NW, Room S1032
Washington, DC 20210
202/219-7316

Free catalog of publications of the U.S. Department of Labor. Over 800 title listings, including ordering information.

Child Labor Laws
Child Labor Programs
Employment Standards Administration
200 Constitution Avenue, NW, Room S3510
Washington, DC 20210
202/219-7640

The Fair Labor Standards Act protects young workers from employment that might interfere with their educational opportunities or be hazardous to their health or well-being. There are different standards for work allowed, depending upon the age of the child. Contact the Child Labor Programs office for more information.

Government Contractors Employment Standards
Office of Federal Contract Compliance Program
Employment Standards Administration
U.S. Department of Labor
200 Constitution Avenue, NW, Room C3325
Washington, DC 20210
202/219-9475

This office ensures that federal contractors and subcontractors with federally assisted construction contracts do not discriminate against any employee or applicant for employment because of race, color, religion or national origin, and that these contractors take affirmative action to hire and promote qualified handicapped people, Vietnam-era veterans and disabled veterans of all wars. This office also investigates complaints to determine whether federal contractors are meeting these obligations.

Handicapped Persons Affirmative Action
Office of Federal Compliance Programs
Employment Standards Administration
U.S. Department of Labor
200 Constitution Avenue, NW, Room C3325
Washington, DC 20210
202/219-9475

The Rehabilitation Act of 1973 prohibits most employers doing business with the federal government from discriminating in employment against handicapped persons. Employers with contracts in excess of $2,500 must take affirmative action to hire and promote qualified handicapped persons.

Architectural and Transportation Barriers
United States Architectural and Transportation
Barriers Compliance Board
1331 F Street, NW, Suite 1000
Washington, DC 20004-1111
800/872-2253
info@access-board.gov
www.access-board.gov

The Board is the federal agency which develops minimum guidelines and requirements for standards issued under the Americans with Disabilities Act (ADA) and the Architectural Barriers Act (ABA), develops accessibility guidelines for telecommunications equipment and customer premises equipment under the Telecommunications Act, develops accessibility standards for electronic and information technology under section 508 of the Rehabilitation Act, provides technical assistance on those guidelines and standards, and enforces the Architectural Barriers Act.

Employment of People with Disabilities
President's Committee on Employment of
People with Disabilities
1331 F Street, NW., Suite 300
Washington, DC 20004
202/376-6200
202/376-6219 (fax)
202/376-6205 (TDD)
info@pcepd.gov
www.pcepd.gov

The President's Committee is a small federal agency whose Chairman and Vice Chairs are appointed by the President. The Chairman appoints the other Executive Board members and members of the six standing subcommittees. Directed by the Chairman and Executive Board, the Committee achieves its goals through the work of its subcommittee members and 37-member agency staff, in close cooperation with the Governor's Committees in the states, Puerto Rico and Guam and with Major's Committees through the United States.

History of Labor in the U.S.
Assistant Secretary for Policy
U.S. Department of Labor
200 Constitution Avenue, NW, Room S2109
Washington , DC 20210
202/219-6461

The Labor Historian can answer any historical inquiries regarding the Department. Questions usually come from Congressional offices, newspapers and students. As well as conducting their own research on various aspects of Department history, the Historian also assists those researching the Department of Labor. The Historian maintains a large photo collection which is open to the public.

Library on Labor Movement and Occupational Evolution
U.S. Department of Labor
200 Constitution Avenue, NW, Room N2439
Washington, DC 20210
202/219-6992

This library has a wealth of historical labor material, as well as collections of state labor department reports, documents, and trade union journals. The library is open to the public and staffed by reference librarians, who will assist you in locating materials. The library is open 8:15–4:45 Monday through Friday. Appointments are not necessary. The library also participates in the Inter-Library Loan system.

On-site Child Care
Women's Bureau
U.S. Department of Labor
200 Constitution Avenue, NW, Room S3309
Washington, DC 20210
202/219-6652

The free publication, Employers and Child Care: Benefiting Work and Family, is designed for employers and employees concerned with developing programs and policies to assist in quality and cost-efficient child care programs while parents are at work. Created to help in a vast array of situations, it provides guidance to those who wish to improve employee productivity and business' ability to recruit and retain the best workers. It is designed for people who are concerned about fulfilling two essential and often conflicting responsibilities—working and caring for their families. The Women's Bureau also can provide you with the fact-sheet entitled Child Care: An Overview, which can provide you with more general information on issues related to child care and the workplace.

Roadmap to All Labor Data
Superintendent of Documents
Government Printing Office
Washington, DC 29402
202/783-3238

The BLS Handbook of Methods provides comprehensive information for each major program of the Bureau of Labor Statistics on sources of data, statistical procedures, where the data are published, and their uses and limitations. It includes descriptions for labor force statistics, occupational pay surveys,

Employment Cost Index, productivity measures, Consumer Price Index, and much more. The cost is $11.

Veterans and Federal Contracts
Veterans Employment and Training
U.S. Department of Labor
200 Constitution Avenue, NW, Room S1313
Washington, DC 20210
202/219-9116

Federal government contractors and subcontractors (with government contracts of $10,000 or more) are required by law to take affirmative action to employ and to advance in employment qualified special disabled and Vietnam-era Veterans. All suitable employment opening must be given to the nearest local State Employment Office. A Veterans Employment and Training Representative is located in each office to provide employment advice and assistance to veterans. Contact the Office of Federal Contract Compliance Programs if it appears that a contractor has failed to comply. Complaints can be made to: Office of Federal Contract Compliance Programs, U.S. Department of Labor, 200 Constitution Avenue, NW, Room C3325, Washington, DC 20210 202/219-9475

Veterans Employment Program
Assistant Secretary for Veterans
Employment and Training
U.S. Department of Labor
200 Constitution Avenue, NW, Room S1313
Washington, DC 20210
202/219-9116

Employment-related services designed to aid veterans include counseling, testing, and skills training; unemployment compensation for newly separated ex-service members while they look for civilian employment; tax credits for private employers who hire certain target groups of veterans; placement in private and public sector jobs; and reemployment rights assistance. For more information, contact the Veterans' Employment and Training Office.

Wage and Hour Investigations
Employment Standards Administration
U.S. Department of Labor
200 Constitution Avenue, NW, Room S3028
Washington, DC 20210
202/219-8353

This division administers the Fair Labor Standards Act, which includes minimum wage, overtime pay, and child labor provisions. Its responsibilities also have grown to include other laws and regulations which protect workers' wages and working conditions. Wage and Hour Division compliance officers across the country conduct investigations of employers covered by the various laws which the division administers, to determine whether workers are being paid in compliance with the laws. They also are responsible for investigating complaints filed by employees who allege that their employers discriminated against them for actions they took to further the purposes of various environmental protection laws, and for improving conditions for migrant farm workers.

Work Stoppages and Strikes
Office of Compensation and Working Conditions
Bureau of Labor Statistics
U.S. Department of Labor
441 G Street, NW, Room 2032
Washington, DC 20212
202/606-6275

This office generates monthly and annual data on major strikes and lock outs. The coverage includes all strikes and lock outs involving 1,000 workers or more and lasting more than one shift. This information measures collective bargaining and economic effects of work stoppages.

SOURCE: *Lesko's Infopower II*, Gale Research, Inc. Reprinted with permission.

APPENDIX M

EEOC Task Force

"Best Practices" Applicable To Equal Employment Laws

Many organizations believe that it makes economic sense to draw talent and ideas from all segments of the population. For such companies, pursuing diversity and equal employment opportunity is as important a business concept as increasing market share or maximizing profits.

A recent task force commissioned by the EEOC[1] set out to look at noteworthy business practices by which employers are complying with their EEO obligations and diversity objectives, especially practices thought to be creative or innovative. The task force also set out to catalogue its findings in such a way that they would be useful to employers, especially smaller and medium-sized employers who are less likely to employ professional personnel and legal staffs.

The task force cited several "best practices" that, if implemented, would be reasonably likely to promote equal employment opportunity.

---

[1] Initially, the task force sent letters directly to all employers with 25,000 or more employees (a total of some 231 companies), informing the employers of the creation of the task force and its mission. These companies employ 30% of the employees covered by the Commission's EEO-1 reports, and were felt to represent a statistically significant slice of all American workplaces.

The task force also sent more than 100 letters informing a wide variety of associations representing employers, employees and civil rights groups about the task force and its mission. The hope was that the organizations would further spread word of the task force and its mission to their members.

Further, the task force prepared and sent a survey questionnaire to nine organizations (limited to nine in accordance with the requirements of the Paperwork Reduction Act) selected to represent a broad cross-section of our stakeholders. These included AFL-CIO, Equal Employment Advisory Council, Equal Employment Opportunity Committee of the Labor and Employment Law Section of the American Bar Association, Leadership Conference on Civil Rights, National Association of Minority Contractors, National Association of Manufacturers, National Federation of Independent Business, Society for Human Resource Management, United States Chamber of Commerce.

The task force sent letters to each member of the Senate Labor and Human Resources Committee and the House Committee on Education and the Workforce informing them of our mission. These letters stressed that we would welcome Congressional input on all matters under task force consideration. A subsequent letter to the chairmen and ranking members of these committees added a further specific inquiry as to whether National Labor Relations Act standards on employer-employee committees impede formulation of employer best practices in the area of EEO compliance or diversity efforts.

These best practices are described below, and may give employers valuable examples of what has worked for other employers. Be aware that individual tailoring of a given "best practice" to the requirements of the individual employer or worksite may be necessary.

What Is A Best Practice?

Simply put, a best practice is the best way to perform a process or function. In the view of the EEOC task force, a best practice must also conform with the requirements of the various employment laws.[2]

A best practice should promote equal employment opportunity and address one or more barriers that adversely impact equal employment opportunity. Not only must there be a serious commitment from management to comply with and promote EEO objectives, but additionally, management accountability for equal employment opportunity is a necessary component of any worthy program. There also must be effective communication between management and the intended beneficiaries of the practice. The practice must embrace fairness to all employees. Finally, the practice must be implemented conscientiously and should show noteworthy results.

Recruitment And Hiring

The focus of recruitment and hiring should be on affirmative recruitment programs and strategies designed to create a diverse workforce, such as internships, work/study, and other education and training programs used for hiring.

- Identify the applicable barriers to equal employment opportunity.

- Delineate goals.

- Make a plan for implementing goals.

- Establish a policy for recruitment and hiring, including criteria, procedures, responsible individuals, and applicability that seeks to promote diversity and affirmative action.

- Ensure that there is a communication network notifying interested persons of opportunities, including advertising within the organization and, where

---

[2] These include:
- Title VII of the Civil Rights Act of 1964, as amended;
- Age Discrimination in Employment Act of 1967, as amended;
- Americans with Disabilities Act of 1990;
- Equal Pay Act of 1963, as amended; and
- applicable sections of the Civil Rights Act of 1991.

applicable, with minority, persons with disabilities, older persons, and women-focused media.

- Communicate the competencies, skills, and abilities that are required for available positions.

- Communicate about family-friendly and work-friendly policies on programs.

- Participate in career and job fairs and open houses.

- Use employee recruiter, referral, and search firms with instructions to assemble a diverse candidate pool.

- Use internships, work/study, co-op, and scholarship programs to attract and develop interested and qualified candidates.

- Develop and support educational programs and become more involved with educational institutions that can refer a diverse talent pool.

- Ensure that personnel involved in the recruitment and hiring process are well trained in their equal employment opportunity responsibilities.

- Eliminate practices which exclude or present barriers to minorities, women, persons with disabilities, older persons, or any individual.

- Include progress in equal employment opportunity recruitment and hiring as factors in management evaluation.

Promotion And Advancement

The focus of promotion and career advancement should be on programs that eliminate barriers to the advancement of women, people from diverse ethnic and racial groups, persons with disabilities, and older workers. Programs such as mentoring, education and training for purposes of promotion, and career enhancement have proven effective for many organizations. These might include the following:

- Identify the applicable barriers to equal employment opportunity.

- Delineate goals.

- Make a plan for implementing goals.

- Establish a policy for recruitment and hiring, including criteria, procedures, responsible individuals, and applicability that seeks to promote diversity and affirmative action.

- Develop methods to identify high-potential persons.

- Establish a communication network notifying interested persons of opportunities, including advertising within the organization and the general media, as well as media that is focused on minorities, persons with disabilities, older persons and women.

- Communicate the competencies, skills, and abilities required.

- Provide for succession planning.

- Develop career plans and programs for high potential employees.

- Provide sufficient training and opportunities for continuing education.

- Ensure that tools for continuous learning and optimum job performance are available.

- Provide job transfer/rotation programs for career enhancing developmental experiences.

- Provide employee resource centers, so individuals may have more opportunities to develop career plans.

- Establish mentoring and networking programs and systems to help develop high potential individuals.

- Eliminate practices which exclude or present barriers to minorities, women, persons with disabilities, older persons, or any individuals.

- Ensure that personnel involved in the promotion and advancement process are well trained in their equal employment opportunity responsibilities.

- Include progress in equal employment opportunity in advancement and promotion as factors in management evaluation.

Terms And Conditions Of Employment

The focus of terms and conditions should include disability and religious accommodation programs, such as effective mechanisms for addressing reasonable accommodation requests. The focus also should include sexual harassment, pay equity, insurance, and employee benefits. Additionally, many companies cited work-life and family-friendly policies and practices as very supportive of their diversity and equal employment opportunity objectives. Employees and dependents with disabilities, as well as men also have benefited greatly from such programs. Most importantly, these programs have enabled many organizations to recruit and retain high quality employees, including minorities, women, and persons with disabilities. Some companies report that work-life and family-friendly programs are an integral part of their diversity, equal employment, and affirmative-action efforts.

- Identify the applicable barriers to equal employment opportunity.

- Delineate goals.

- Make a plan for implementing goals.

- Establish a policy for recruitment and hiring, including criteria, procedures, responsible individuals, and applicability that seeks to promote diversity and affirmative action.

- Monitor compensation practices and performance appraisal systems for discrimination.

- Ensure that employee compensation is linked to performance and skills.

- Support family-friendly policies, including day care, elder care and employee assistance programs.

- Support work-friendly policies, including flexible hours, alternate work schedules, work at home, job sharing, part-time job opportunities and liberal leave.

- Establish and enforce a zero tolerance sexual harassment policy.

- Establish and enforce an anti-discrimination policy.

- Provide guidance and training for managers and employees in support of anti-sexual harassment and discrimination policies.

- Proactively support reasonable accommodation in the workplace:
    - For persons with disabilities
    - For religion
    - For pregnancy and other family-life issues

- Eliminate practices which exclude or present barriers to minorities, women, persons with disabilities, older persons, or any individuals.

- Assist interested employees with retirement planning.

- Link management pay to the contribution they make to ensuring a "discrimination-free" work environment.

Termination And Downsizing

The focus of termination and downsizing is on such areas as retraining and placement programs for employees displaced by downsizing programs, and nondiscriminatory early retirement programs.

- Establish a staffing plan, including a needs assessment for the short and the long terms.

- Plan for the future—make adjustments now to limit future downsizing.

- Avoid or minimize laying off workers.

- Establish a communication plan for the employees.

- Formulate an outplacement plan.

- Consider an early retirement program to ameliorate the possible downsizing of other employees.

- Provide for training, placement, and/or redeployment programs within the company.

- Consider assistance to laid-off workers to find new jobs, including outplacement, severance pay, counseling, education, training, grants, and loans.

- Establish a rehire list for laid-off workers.

- Ensure that personnel involved in the termination and downsizing process is well trained in equal employment opportunity responsibilities.

- Link management pay to performance and progress in equal employment opportunity when undergoing termination and downsizing.

Alternative Dispute Resolution

Alternative dispute resolution focuses on early resolution of employment discrimination complaints, and voluntary and effective alternative dispute resolution programs.

- Establish a policy for alternative dispute resolution, including procedures and responsible individuals.

- Emphasize that retaliation against employees who pursue their legal rights is prohibited.

- Provide for and carry out disciplinary action against those who retaliate.

- Consider all program options.

    - Employee hotline
    - Ombudsman program
    - Peer review panel program
    - Senior management review program
    - Mediation program
    - Arbitration program

- Ensure that third-party facilitators (e.g., mediators) and decision makers (e.g., arbitrators) are well trained.

- Ensure that in any program the procedures are fair.

- Voluntary employee participation is the best.

- Link management pay to performance and progress.

Other Policies, Programs And Practices

- Conduct training programs in EEO rights and responsibilities including, but not limited to:

- Gender awareness
- Diversity
- Disability, pregnancy, and religious accommodation
- Harassment prevention
- Affirmative action

▶ Such training should be given to all employees.

▶ Encourage and support formation of employee groups along diversity lines (e.g., women, men, minorities, persons with disabilities, older persons, religious persons) to actively participate within the company in EEO matters.

▶ Form a Diversity Council with representatives of all interested organizations to discuss matters of equal employment opportunity.

▶ Encourage high-level management participation and interaction with employees and employee groups, and ensure employee access to management.

▶ Consider special emphasis programs and other events recognizing and highlighting the contributions of various cultural and/or social heritages.

▶ Publish a pamphlet or handbook detailing EEO rights and responsibilities, as well as diversity and affirmative action programs.

▶ Conduct assessments and surveys of employees, asking for their views as to what is right and what needs improvement in the company's conduct of its equal employment opportunity programs.

- Suggestions for improvements should be encouraged
- Be prepared to act on worthy suggestions

▶ Develop business relationships with minority-, disability-, and women-owned businesses.

▶ Participate in the community and show that the company is a good corporate citizen.

- This may facilitate additional good will with the company's employees, enhancing pride in their employer
- It may also encourage residents of the community to be more interested in working for the company

- Partner with other organizations (e.g., educational institutions, professional associations, civic associations, other companies, government agencies, interest/advocacy groups) to facilitate equal employment initiatives generally.

    - Such partnerships do not have to be narrowly focused on the specific equal employment opportunity interests of the particular participating company, but may be for the good of equal employment opportunity generally

- Consider obtaining the assistance of expert consultants.

Management Commitment And Accountability

Management commitment and accountability are the driving forces behind a company's EEO policies, programs and practices. As such they should focus on what management can do to facilitate equal employment opportunities. Accountability refers to the mechanisms in evaluating management's performance involving equal employment opportunity programs. Tools such as performance appraisals, compensation incentives, and other evaluation measures can increase a manager's ability to set high standards and demonstrate progress.

- The CEO must be firmly behind the equal employment opportunity programs of the company. It may be desirable, or even necessary, that the CEO launch and monitor initiatives.

- The management commitment must be clearly and continually communicated throughout the organization and preferably outside as well.

    - A key element in that communication should be the concept that in a diverse nation and in a diverse world, having a diverse workforce is a necessary asset for continued success into the 21st century.

- Management must have continuing reviews and assessments of equal employment opportunity programs of the company.

- Goals that have been set must be reviewed for what has been accomplished and the results appropriately assessed.

- Equal employment opportunity, including diversity, affirmative action, and the ability to respect and work effectively with diverse people, must be a performance standard.

- Managers' compensation must be tied, in part, to their performance on EEO evaluations. Accountability should be incorporated into performance reviews at all levels of the organization.

APPENDIX N

EPL Policy Comparison Worksheet Request Form

If you are a current Policy Express subscriber and do not find a policy comparison worksheet of the EPL policy you need in *The EPL Book* or at our Policy Express archive, complete and mail the request form to:

> Policy Express Library
> Griffin Communications, Inc.
> 1420 Bristol Street North, Suite 220
> Newport Beach, CA 92660

A completed policy comparison worksheet will be faxed to you and posted to the Policy Express archive.[1]

---

[1] Please allow four to six weeks.

PolicyAnalysis Plus

PolicyExpress
EMPLOYMENT PRACTICES LIABILITY

Policy Comparison Worksheet Request Form

Complete and mail this form to:
Policy Express Library
Griffin Communications, Inc.
1420 Bristol Street North, Suite 220
Newport Beach, CA 92660

Name _____

Company _____

Address _____

City _____ State _____ Zip _____

Phone _____ Fax _____

E-mail _____

Profession _____

Policy Form Requested _____

Insurance Company _____

Policy Form Name _____

Policy Form Number _____

Policy Form Edition Date _____

Insurance Company Contact Name (if known) _____

PLEASE INCLUDE A COPY OF THE POLICY FORM IF AVAILABLE.

DR   DRQ   PR   AC   FC   ☐☐

1420 Bristol Street North, Suite 220, Newport Beach, CA 92660
Telephone 949.752.1058   Fax 949.955.1929
griffcom@ix.netcom.com   www.griffincom.com

About The Authors

ANDREW KAPLAN

Andrew Kaplan is a management labor consultant with the Century City, California law firm of Silver & Freedman. He is a 1973 graduate of the Boalt Law School at the University of California at Berkeley.

Mr. Kaplan is a frequent speaker to business and professional groups on the topics of wrongful discharge, personnel policies, sexual harassment and discrimination, workers' compensation and other labor relations matters. His articles on these and other employment matters have appeared in numerous national magazines.

RACHEL McKINNEY

Rachel McKinney is a Senior Underwriter with the wholesale brokerage firm of Swett & Crawford, Inc., where she specializes in the placement of directors and officers, errors and omissions and employment practices liability insurance. She is a graduate of Bradley University in Economics and Journalism. Ms. McKinney recently developed, and now manages, the firm's national employment practices liability insurance product line. In addition to being a frequent and popular lecturer to agent and broker groups, industry associations and employers, she also teaches Continuing Education courses dealing with directors and officers, professional errors and omissions and employment practices liability insurance issues.

Ms. McKinney is active in insurance industry organizations, helping found the southern California regional chapter for the National Association of Insurance Women. She is recipient of the 1995 Professional Liability Underwriting Society Founders Award.

BETH A. SCHROEDER

Beth Schroeder is a partner in the employment law department of Silver & Freedman. She represents employers in all phases of employer-employee relations including state and federal wage and hour claims and litigation, OSHA matters, immigration control, unemployment and workers' compensation claims, union-organizing activities and unfair labor practices charges before the National Labor Relations Board. Ms. Schroeder specializes in Title VII, ADA and other federal and state anti-discrimination laws.

Ms. Schroeder received her Juris Doctorate in 1985 from the University of California at Los Angeles. She is a regular speaker to business and professionals on a wide variety of employment issues.

LEONARD SURDYK

Leonard Surdyk is a partner in the Chicago law firm of Davidson Mandell & Menkes. He is admitted to practice law in Illinois, before the United States District Court for the Northern District of Illinois and the United States Courts of Appeals for the Ninth and Tenth Circuits. His practice focuses on professional indemnity and employment practices insurance issues. Mr. Surdyk is a frequent lecturer on insurance matters and has co-edited textbooks for the Professional Liability Underwriting Society dealing with directors and officers liability insurance and medical and non-medical professional liability.

Mr. Surdyk graduated with high distinction in Political Science and Psychology from Loyola University and received his Juris Doctorate, also with high distinction, from the University of Illinois, where he was an associate editor of the *University of Illinois Law Review*.

GARY W. GRIFFIN, ARM

Gary Griffin has more than 17 years' experience in broker operations, risk management consulting, and publishing of risk and insurance references. His expertise includes employment practices insurance issues, directors and officers liability, professional liability, pollution liability, and umbrella liability insurance.

Mr. Griffin is senior editor for *The EPL Book, The Umbrella Book, The D&O Book* and *The Risk Management Letter*. He also developed, designed and manages Griffin Communications, Inc.'s annual Employment Practices Liability and Insurance National Forum, a two-day seminar covering a broad range of employment practices liability and insurance issues. Mr. Griffin has been a frequent lecturer on employment practices and was the EPL session leader at the 1996 RIMS convention in Atlanta. Gary also has written numerous articles for national periodicals, including *The Compleate Lawyer* and *Fleet Financial Magazine*.

■ ■ ■

In addition to the dogged efforts of the authors and editors of *The EPL Book*, many individuals provided valuable insight and assistance, without which this book would not be possible. By mention below, we recognize their important contributions.

Gerard Albanese
Evanston Insurance Company

Jay Alston
U.S. Risk Underwriters, Inc.

Heather Anderson
Executive Risk Specialty Insurance
 Company

Sherrie Beckham
Swett & Crawford

Bruce P. Bernstein, CPCU
United Educators Risk Retention Group,
 Inc.

Karen Brown
Orthodyne

Paul Bubnis
Travelers Property Casualty (G. J. Sullivan
 Company)

James Bukowski, Ph.D.
Warren, McVeigh & Griffin, Inc.

Ram Chandarana
Professional Underwriters Agency, Inc.

William A. Chapdelaine
United States Fidelity & Guaranty
 Company

Colonia (AUSCO)

Paul Cunningham
Lexington Insurance Company

Lisa DeSimone
Reliance Insurance Company of Illinois
 (Reliance National Risk Specialists)

Jay M. Dipasupil
Steadfast Insurance Company

Joan Dolinsky
Cotkin & Collins

Gary N. Dubois
Reliance National

Keli Eddings
U.S. Risk Underwriters, Inc.

Jeffrey Gauthier
Great American Insurance Companies

Richard M. Gibson
Genesis Insurance Company

Richard M. Gibson
Genesis Professional Liability
   Underwriters

Joseph S. Gravier, Jr.
Professional Risk Facilities, Inc.

James R. Grieser
Professional Risk Co.

Hartford Insurance Companies

Christopher Higgins, CPCU, RPLU
United States Liability Insurance Group

Gwen L. Holler, CPCU
Northland Insurance Companies

Insurance Services Office (ISO)

Sandra A. Johnson
Associated Electric & Gas Insurance
   Services, Limited

Rob Jurgel
Lexington Insurance Company

Ron Kettner
First Specialty Insurance Corporation

John A. Kuhn
Chubb Group

Derek M. Lucas
Monitor Liability Managers, Inc.

James J. Maguire, Jr., ARM
Philadelphia Indemnity Insurance
   Company

Michael J. Maloney
Chubb & Son, Inc.

Darryl McCallin
Rockwood Programs, Inc.

Lisa R. McElroy
Zurich American Insurance Group

Rachel McKinney
Swett & Crawford

Paul Miller
X.L. Insurance Company, Ltd.

Morefar Marketing, Inc.

A. Quentin Orza
Chubb Group

Caren Patton
U.S. Risk Underwriters, Inc.

Lisa L. Reynolds
Steadfast Insurance Company

Gail M. Richman
Jury Verdict Research

Richard J. Robin
NAS Insurance Services, Inc.

Walt L. Robinson
Pinkerton Security & Investigation
   Services

Evan Rosenberg
Chubb Group of Insurance Companies

Richard V. Rupp, CPCU
AmTech E&S

Paul J. Schiavone
National Union Fire Insurance Co.

Alan P. Schreibman
Integrated Risk Management

Jim Seward
First State Management Group, Inc.

Tom Siebers
Agricultural Excess & Surplus
   Insurance Company (AESIC)

Mary Anne Tankersley
ALTRU, Inc.

Todd Weber
Great American Insurance Companies

Betty Weeks/ERC Specialty
Employers Reinsurance Corporation

Viviane Krief Woodcock
IFIS, Inc.

Index

A

Acquisitions, 169, 173, 212, 237
   exclusions for, 212
ADA, 10–11, 38–40, 42–44, 49–52, 58–59, 62, 78, 81, 204, 223, 229, 258, 557, 576–578, 582
ADA accommodation expenses, 202
ADEA, 8–10, 38, 40, 45–46, 51–52, 62–63, 78, 98, 204, 208, 223, 229
   exclusion for liquidated damages, 208
Adjudication
   binding, 225
Administrative complaints
   responding to, 112
Administrative law judge, 14–15
Administrative proceedings, 225
Advancement of defense expense payments, 183
Advertising injury, 120–121, 189
Affirmative action, 12, 581, 583, 586, 588–589, 592–593
Age Discrimination In Employment Act Of 1967. *See* ADEA.
Alcohol testing, 79
Aliens, 13
Allocation of defense expense payments, 183
Alternative dispute resolution, 591. *See also* Arbitration and mediation.
Americans With Disabilities Act Of 1990. *See* ADA.
Anti-stacking-deductible provisions, 175
Application
   completing the, 147
   employment, 78
Application considerations, 137
Arbitration, 75, 83, 98–103, 105, 208, 224, 239–241, 555, 557, 591
   advantages of, 98
   disadvantages of, 99
   mandated, 101
Assault, 35, 114, 120, 122, 132, 165, 188, 191–192, 216, 233, 260
Assault and battery, 191
Assessment of liability, 28

At-will employment doctrine
   demise of the, 30

B

Back pay, 207
Background checks, 78
Battery, 35, 114, 122, 132, 165, 188, 191–192, 216, 233, 260
Best practices, 585–586
BFOQ. *See* Bona fide occupational qualification.
Binding adjudication, 225
Bodily injury, 120–124, 126, 128–130, 165, 184, 188–192, 196–197, 556
   exclusions, 189
Bona fide occupational qualification (BFOQ), 9
Breach
   of employment contract, 192
   of express contract, 33
   of implied contract, 33
Broker, 114, 124, 143, 147–148, 150–152, 172, 186, 235, 249, 515

C

California Insurance Code Section 533, 213
Capacity
   EPL insurance, 252, 559
CGL. *See* Commercial general liability.
Change of control, 237
   exclusions for, 212
Charge data
   EEOC, 37
Choice of counsel, 181
Civil Rights Act Of 1866, 1, 7
Civil Rights Act Of 1964, 1, 30, 38, 259, 571, 574, 586
Claim
   definition of, 150, 154–156, 161, 164–166, 179–182, 185, 188, 194, 197, 199–201, 208–210, 212–213, 216, 218–221, 223, 225–226, 555
   potential, 156
Claim information, 150

Claim releases, 75
Claimant, 108, 111, 122, 157, 165, 192, 194, 196, 198–200, 202, 207, 216–217, 219, 222–225, 227
Claim-reporting requirements to the insurer, 155
Claims
    exclusions regarding financial impairment, 209
    release of, 97
Class action
    cases, 5
    claims, 107
    exclusions for, 254
    filing, 220
    suits, 72, 110, 165, 212, 220
COBRA, 195–196, 557
Coinsurance, 173, 177
Collective-bargaining agreements, 29
Combined-coverage format, 167
Commerce
    industry or activity affecting, 3–4, 8, 10–11, 14
Commercial general liability (CGL), 107, 119–125, 133, 189
Comparable worth, 8
Complaints
    filing with state agency/EEOC, 222
    oral, 222, 224
    verbal, 111
Composition of workforce (EEO-1), 141
Conciliation, 5, 11, 13
Conciliatory powers, 225
Conditional coverage provision, 238
Conditions, 214, 237–238, 241, 583, 589
Conduct
    intentional, 120, 125, 204–205, 213–214
    off-duty, 18
Consequential loss, 194, 557
Constructive discharge, 53–55
Contractual relations
    interference with, 35
Conversion, 35
Covenant of fair dealing, 34
Covenant of good faith, 34
Coverage grant, 164
Coverage terminates provision, 239
Coverage territory, 165, 241
Criminal acts, 215, 258
Criminal proceedings, 215

D

Damages, 3, 5–6, 8, 10–11, 22, 28, 34, 39, 50, 52, 55, 61, 63, 70, 75, 103, 105, 108–109, 113, 123–128, 138, 141, 157, 164, 166, 171–172, 180–181, 188–189, 193, 195–197, 199, 201–209, 217, 219–220, 223–227, 235–236, 256–258, 261, 556–557, 574
    potential, 28

Deductible reduction clauses, 176
Deductibles, 105, 130, 174–177, 183, 245, 556
Defamation, 31, 35, 79, 97, 124–126, 128, 130, 190–191, 234–236, 256–257, 555
Defense
    right of association, 185
    right to assume defense, 185
Defense counsel, 115–117, 181, 183, 186, 227, 258
Defense expense payments, 183
Defense issues, 108, 114, 181, 185
Defense provisions, 164
Department of Labor, 12
Directors and officers, 130–131, 169–170, 221
    insurance for, 129
Disability, 16, 83, 195, 223, 229–231, 557, 578, 592
Discharge, 31, 43, 53, 96, 197
    constructive, 53–55
Discipline, 43, 83, 113, 114
    employee, 95
Discriminating acts, 229–231
Discrimination, 1–2, 8–9, 16, 38, 40, 53–55, 58–59, 97–98, 102, 127, 206, 208, 213, 223, 228, 230, 259, 555, 568, 574, 586
    intentional, 7–8, 261
    sexual orientation, 3
Distribution of policy limits, 251
Diversity management, 75, 90–93
Double damages, 10
Downsizing, 211
Drug testing, 79
Duty to defend, 126, 129–130, 167, 179–181, 183–186, 201–203, 216, 221, 224, 243, 245, 258, 260–261, 556

E

EEO-1, 141
EEOC, 4–5, 8–9, 11, 14, 21–22, 28, 37–52, 62–63, 82, 98–100, 102, 112, 117, 139, 222–223, 225–226, 555, 563, 565, 567–568, 571–574, 576, 585–586
    charge data, 37
    filing complaints with, 222
    limitations of mandated arbitration, 101
    task force, 585–586
Emotional distress, 6, 28, 34, 52, 111, 120, 122, 127, 130, 189–191, 197, 203, 556
    infliction of, 21, 31, 79, 132, 234–236, 257
Employee, 15, 53, 81–88, 95, 143–144, 165, 196, 217, 233–234, 591
Employee handbook, 31, 70, 81–88, 94, 98, 105, 209, 224
Employee Retirement Income Security Act. *See* ERISA.
Employer size, 139
Employers liability, 121, 123–124, 126–129
    exclusion for, 123

Employment application, 78
Employment at-will doctrine, 29–30
Employment contract
    breach of, 192
Employment documentation, 140
Employment litigation survey, 37, 59–61
Employment policies, 67–68, 73, 75, 86, 89, 137, 142, 209, 225, 234
Employment practices
    insurance coverage for, 119
Employment Practices National Survey, 37, 57
Endorsements, 256, 262
Entity, 4, 72, 129–130, 157, 168–170, 173, 204–205, 210, 212, 217, 237–239, 260, 555, 574
EPL claims
    insurability of, 132
EPL endorsement, 130–131
EPL exclusion endorsement, 124
EPL exclusions, 557
EPL insurance, 63, 69, 73, 105, 111, 114, 116, 119, 123, 126, 131–132, 134, 137–139, 142–144, 147, 153–157, 160–161, 164–177, 179–181, 183–190, 192–196, 198–199, 201–204, 206–218, 220–226, 228, 232, 234–235, 237–245, 249–250, 252–255, 257–260, 262, 265–266, 549, 555, 557, 559
    arbitration and, 105
    capacity, 252, 559
    checklist of desirable features, 555
    effect of employers' buying habits, 250
    evolution of, 249
    market, 126, 249–250, 255
    market profile, 250
    pricing, 253
EPL policy, 266–267, 595
Equal Employment Opportunity Commission. See EEOC.
Equal Pay Act (EPA) Of 1963, 7, 38, 40, 47–48, 51–52, 63
ERISA, 15, 195–196, 557
ERP. See Extended reporting period.
Escape/non-liability clauses, 243
Excess other insurance provisions, 242
Exclusions, 124, 187, 193, 195, 198–199, 201, 207–208, 210, 214, 237–238, 246–247, 258
    ADA-accommodation expenses, 202
    assault and battery, 191
    bodily injury, 189
    change of control, 212
    claims arising from financial impairment, 209
    class action, 254
    class-action suit, 220
    criminal acts/proceedings, 215
    downsizing/reorganization, 211
    employers liability, 123
    EPL, 124, 557
    expected or intended injury, 123

    financial impairment, 209
    general rules, 187, 195
    intentional acts, 213
    liquidated damages under ADEA, 208
    mergers and acquisitions, 212
    non-monetary relief, 201
    other indemnification, 214
    other insurance, 214
    personal injury, 189
    plant or facility closings, 210
    prior and pending litigation, 219
    prior knowledge, 218
    retroactive date, 218
    usage of EPL, 557
    violation of public policy, 197
Expected-or-intended-injury exclusion, 123
Express contract
    breach of, 33
Extended-reporting-period (ERP) provisions, 160

F
Facility closings
    exclusions for, 210
Failure to provide benefits, 195
Fair dealing
    covenant of, 34
Fair Employment Practices Agencies (FEPAs), 38
Fair Labor Standards Act (FLSA), 7, 8
False arrest, 130
False imprisonment, 31, 35, 191, 234
Family and Medical Leave Act of 1993 (FMLA), 11, 58–59, 62, 83, 223, 558
Federal protected classes, 229
Financial impairment
    exclusion for claims, 209
Financial statements, 141
Fines, 203
Fraud, 31, 35, 206, 235, 257
Fraudulent acts, 258
Front pay, 10, 193, 203, 207–208, 557
Future pay, 207
Future turnover, 140

G
Good faith
    covenant of, 34
Governmental agencies, 14
Governmental entities, 8, 138
Grant of coverage, 164

H
Hammer clauses, 182
Harassment
    quid pro quo, 22, 232
Harassment policies, 89

Health benefits, 195
Hill, Anita, 2, 21
Hiring
   negligent, 1, 31, 257
Homosexual employees, 18
Hostile environment, 22–23, 28, 232, 571–572

I

Immigration, 13
Immigration Reform And Control Act Of 1986. *See* IRCA.
Implied contract
   breach of, 33
Indemnify coverage, 166
Independent contractors, 172
Industry or activity affecting commerce, 3–4, 8, 10–11, 14
Infliction of emotional distress, 21, 31, 79, 132, 234–236, 257
Injury
   intentional, 261
Innocent insureds, 146–147, 182
Insurability of punitive damages, 204
Insurance, 67–69, 72, 83, 114, 119, 125–126, 132–133, 135, 143, 146, 148, 155, 163–164, 166–167, 176, 179–182, 185, 189–190, 193–195, 197–202, 206, 208–209, 211–219, 225, 232, 236, 241–247, 249, 251, 258–261, 265, 581, 597
Insurance broker, 151
Insurance Services Office. *See* ISO.
Insured event, 157, 160, 166, 174
Insuring agreement, 164, 194, 256
Intentional acts
   exclusions for, 213
Intentional conduct, 120, 125, 204–205, 213–214
Intentional discrimination, 7–8, 261
Intentional injury, 261
Intentional torts, 213
Intentional wrongdoing, 213–214
Interference with contractual relations, 35
Interference with prospective business advantage, 35
Internet services, 267
Intervention, 107
Introductory language, 188
Invasion of privacy, 31, 130, 189, 191, 234–236, 257, 555
Investigation, 5–6, 14, 26, 70, 73, 82, 107–114, 117, 186, 225, 572, 574
   post-litigation, 110
   pre-litigation, 108
IRCA, 13
ISO, 119, 121, 123–125, 189, 212, 249, 255, 257–262, 531
ISO-CGL, 120–121, 123–125, 189

J

Job descriptions, 80–82, 143
Job offers, 80

L

Lawful activities, 18
Lawsuit, 223
Lawsuits
   legitimacy of, 60
   responding to, 112
Lawsuits experienced in the past five years, 62
Libel, 35, 130, 190–191, 555
Limit of liability, 168, 179, 182, 243
Limited automatic coverage provision, 238
Limits, 173
Liquidated damages, 8, 10–11, 202, 206–208
   exclusion under ADEA, 208
Litigation
   activity, 56
   costs, 61
Lockouts, 234, 259
Long-form application, 142
Loss
   consequential, 194, 557
Loss history, 139
Loss of consortium, 31, 188–190, 194
Loss prevention, 70, 75
Loss reduction, 70

M

Malicious acts, 258
Managers, 6–7, 23, 27, 31, 57, 60, 81, 85, 93, 147, 150–152, 169–170, 189, 256, 555, 589
Material misrepresentations and coverage implications, 145
Mediation, 38, 49, 75, 98, 104–105, 112, 116–117, 155, 176, 241, 591
Mental anguish, 120, 122, 130, 189, 190–191, 194, 197, 234, 556, 574
Mergers
   exclusions for, 212
Misrepresentation
   negligent, 31, 35

N

National Labor Relations Act. *See* NLRA.
National Labor Relations Board. *See* NLRB.
Negligent hiring, 1, 31, 257
Negligent misrepresentation, 31, 35
Negligent supervision, 31, 133
NLRA, 14
NLRB, 14–15, 62
Non-duty-to-defend policies, 181, 184, 216
Non-fraternization policies, 89
Non-imputation of liability, 245

Non-imputation provisions, 146
Non-monetary relief, 201
Not-for-profit organization liability insurance, 129

O

Occupational Safety And Health Act Of 1970. *See* OSHA.
Occurence-based policies, 125
Occurrence, 72, 92, 120–122, 126, 139, 153, 163, 215
Off-duty conduct, 18
Office of Veterans Reemployment Rights, 12
Oral complaints, 222
Oral notice, 222
OSHA, 199–200, 558
Other indemnification, 214
Other insurance, 214, 242

P

Past and future turnover, 140
Pay distribution, 141
Pay on behalf coverage, 166
Penalties, 203
Personal injury
    equirements, 120
    exclusions, 189
Policy Comparison Worksheet, 263, 265–514, 595, 597
    Request Form, 267, 595
Policy Express, 267, 595, 597
Policy limits distribution, 251
Pollution laws, 199, 558
Post-litigation investigation, 110
Potential claim, 156
Potential damages, 28
Pre-employment screening, 76
Pregnancy Discrimination Act Of 1978, 3, 259
Pre-litigation investigation, 108
Presidential Executive Order 11141, 9
Presidential Executive Order 11246, 3
Prior and pending litigation
    exclusion for, 219
Prior knowledge
    exclusion for, 218
Privacy
    invasion of, 31, 130, 189, 191, 234–236, 257, 555
Property damage, 196
Prospective business advantage
    interference with, 35
Protected activity, 14–15
Protected classes, 2–3, 229–231
Protected-class status, 18, 223
Provisions
    anti-stacking deductible, 175
    conditional coverage, 238
    coverage terminates, 239
    defense provisions, 164
    excess other insurance, 242
    extended-reporting period (ERP), 160
    limited automatic coverage, 238
    non-imputation, 146
Public policy, 31–33, 120, 125, 129, 132, 192, 197–199, 203, 213, 234, 261
Public policy exclusions
    violation of, 197
Public policy prohibitions, 125
Punitive damages, 6–7, 28, 34, 41, 50, 55, 64, 110, 113, 141, 171, 191, 197, 203–208, 254, 258
    effect on settlement, 203
    insurability of, 204

Q

Quasi contract claims, 35
Quid pro quo harassment, 22, 232

R

Racketeer Influenced Corruption Act. *See* RICO.
Reasonable woman, 23
Reference checks, 78
References, 78–80, 83, 86, 97, 119, 137, 153, 179, 187, 221, 237
Refusal of employment, 53
Reorganization, 211
Representations, 246
Responding
    to administrative complaints, 112
    to lawsuits, 112
    to verbal complaints, 110
    to written complaints, 111
Retaliatory action, 197, 261
Retirement, 15, 195, 196, 557
Retroactive date
    advancement of, 158
    exclusions, 218
RICO, 199–201, 558
Right of association, 185
Right to assume defense, 185
Right-to-sue letter, 5
Risk
    identification of, 69
Risk management, 65, 67–70, 124, 253
Risk management process, 68
Risk retention, 71
    amount of, 72

S

Screening
    pre-employment, 76
Section 1981, 7
Securities laws, 199–200
Security clearance, 13

Self-insured retention (SIR), 175, 180, 243
Settlement
   consent to, 181
   effect of punitive damages on, 203
Settlement agreements, 75, 97
Severability, 245
   provisions, 146
Sexual harassment, 2, 6–7, 17, 19–28, 35, 53–55, 57–58, 62, 70–71, 86, 88–93, 108–111, 116, 120–122, 125, 127–130, 132–134, 140, 143, 164–165, 171–172, 184, 188, 191–192, 204, 223, 227, 232–233, 235, 257, 260, 569, 571, 573–574, 589
   recognizing, 23
Sexual orientation, 2–3, 16, 18, 24, 53, 141
Sexual-orientation discrimination, 3
Short-form application, 143
Slander, 35, 130, 190–191, 555
Social Security, 83, 195
Stand-alone coverage format, 167
State agency
   filing complaint with, 222
State employment discrimination laws, 16
State issues, 141
Strikes, 234, 259, 583
Supervision
   negligent, 31, 133
Supervisor(s), 4, 6, 21, 24–25, 27, 76, 89, 133, 169–170, 235, 258, 571–573

T

Testing, 71, 76, 83
Third-party harasser, 28
Third-party liability, 19, 165, 254
   coverage for, 165
Thomas, Clarence, 21
Title VII Of The 1964 Civil Rights Act, 2–3, 6, 15, 25
Torts
   intentional, 213
   workplace, 233
Training, 70, 88, 583
Trigger, 114, 154, 156–157, 161, 164, 216, 223–224, 226–227
Turnover
   future, 140
   past, 140

U

Underwriting considerations, 137
Unemployment, 16, 83, 195, 557
Unfair dismissal, 29
Unfair termination, 29
Uniformed Services Employment and Reemployment Rights Act of 1994 (Uniformed Services Act), 12

United States Department of Labor, 11
Unlawful discharge, 29, 43

V

Verbal complaints, 111
   responding to, 110
Veterans, 12, 581, 583

W

WARN Act, 199–201, 558
Warranties, 144
Whistle blowers, 33
Who is insured, 169, 238, 256
Willful act, 132, 213
Willful Act Rule, 132
Workers' Adjustment And Retraining Notification Act. *See* WARN Act.
Workplace torts, 233
Written complaints
   responding to, 111
Written notice, 222
Written procedures, 70, 75
Wrongdoing
   intentional, 213–214
Wrongful discharge, 29, 31–32, 34–35, 41, 44–45, 47, 62, 75, 87, 132, 164
   preventing, 94
   theories of, 31
Wrongful employment practice, 2, 37–38, 49, 52, 54–55, 62–63, 67, 70, 73, 107–110, 113–114, 117, 119, 125, 138, 154, 157, 160, 164, 170–171, 174–175, 189–190, 192, 194, 196–197, 199, 207, 215–216, 219, 222, 224
Wrongful termination, 29, 52–55, 57–59, 62–63, 78, 82, 120, 122, 125, 130, 132, 138, 140–141, 168, 176, 191–193, 195–198, 223, 231, 233, 235–236, 257, 555

GCI Library

If it's not by Griffin Communications, Inc., it's not The EPL Book!

www.griffincom.com

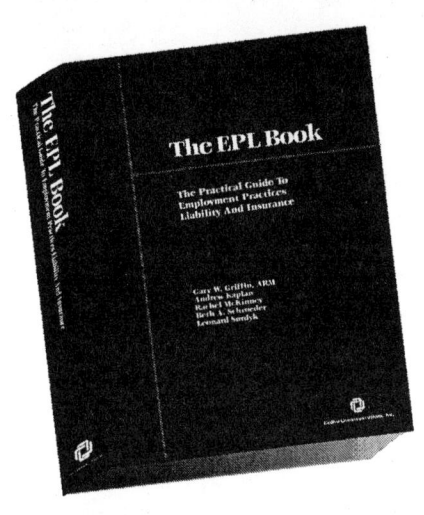

The EPL Book
A Practical Guide To Employment Practices Liability And Insurance

"The standard, a benchmark by which all other works in this area will be compared."
—BUSINESS INSURANCE

The EPL Book, second edition, is a stand-alone reference that puts an incredible amount of information at your fingertips. If you simply must have the latest information on employment practices liability and insurance, or if you just need a practical everyday reference on employment practices liability and insurance, you absolutely won't want to be without this updated edition.

The EPL Book is simply the best, most comprehensive resource on the subject of EPL insurance. Its easy-to-read format allows *The EPL Book* to be read cover to cover, or, using the detailed index, to be scanned for just those bits of information you need most. No theoretical or long-drawn-out dissertations, just to-the-point, unbiased information you can put to work immediately.

We've spent months revising and editing *The EPL Book*, adding the features and information our subscribers asked for. In all, we've added over 200 new and revised pages to *The EPL Book*, including:

- Expanded and updated discussions on the laws affecting the employment relationship
- A new chapter on the do's and don'ts of claims handling
- A new chapter on the EPL insurance market
- 60 time-saving EPL policy comparison charts
- An expanded and updated appendix and EPL resource guide
- A detailed analysis of the new ISO employment-related practices liability policy, including specimen policy form and endorsements

Plus Two Time-Saving Bonuses You Can't Get Anywhere Else!

PolicyExpress — Debuting in first quarter 1999, *EPL Book* subscribers will have access to Policy Express, our Internet policy archive service. You get around-the-clock access to policy form specimens, summary comparison worksheets and supplemental information.

PolicyAnalysis Plus — And, if you don't find the current policy form information you need in *The EPL Book*, let us know, and we will complete and send you a Policy Comparison Worksheet for that form. That's our exclusive PolicyAnalysis Plus guarantee!

More than 600 pages
ISBN 0-941360-13-X

© 1999 by Griffin Communications, Inc. All rights reserved.

Order Form

Send me _____ copies of "The EPL Book" at $135 + $12 shipping/handling each. (Foreign orders, call for shipping information.)

Send To:
Name _____
Title _____
Company _____
Address 1 _____
Address 2 _____
City _____ State _____ Zip _____
Telephone _____ Fax _____

Payment Method:
☐ Payment enclosed (California orders, add 7.75% sales tax per order)
☐ Bill me (add $10)
☐ American Express / MasterCard / VISA (circle one)

CARD NUMBER _____
EXPIRATION DATE _____
NAME AS IT APPEARS ON CARD _____
AUTHORIZED SIGNATURE _____

EPLE2

Ordering Is Easy!

BY MAIL
Send order form and payment to
Griffin Communications, Inc.
1420 Bristol Street North
Suite 220
Newport Beach, CA 92660

BY PHONE
Have all information ready and call
800.205.6218

BY FAX
Fax order form and payment information to
949.723.1817

GCI Library

www.griffincom.com

The D&O Book:
A Comparison Guide To Directors & Officers Liability Insurance Policies

> "This book is unique, providing discussions, chart comparisons, sample policy forms and graphic illustrations that are likely unavailable between covers in any other single source. It represents a handy tool kit for busy risk managers and insurance professionals trying to get a handle on this hard-to-fathom line of coverage."
>
> —BUSINESS INSURANCE

Attempting to understand directors and officers liability insurance may seem like an overwhelming endeavor at times. That's why we've created The D&O Book, a practical, easy-to-use comparison of directors & officers liability insurance policies.

The D&O Book was designed especially for insurance professionals, risk managers, attorneys and anyone who absolutely needs to understand directors & officers liability insurance. Using clear discussions, comparison charts, sample policy forms and graphic illustrations, *The D&O Book* lets busy risk managers and insurance professionals get a handle on the sometimes complex world of directors & officers liability insurance.

The D&O Book will help you save time comparing coverages and identifying improvements that may ensure superior coverage. Policy terms and provisions are made clear through concise discussion and focused analysis. Definitions and exclusions are explained in detail to help you understand the often subtle but significant differences in policy forms. Moreover, our comparison worksheets will allow you to compare important coverage features quickly and easily, helping you to identify and correct potential coverage problems and gaps.

© 1998 by Griffin Communications, Inc. All rights reserved.

Order Form

Send me ____ copies of "The D&O Book" (including one annual supplement service free) at $169 + $12 shipping/handling each. (Foreign orders, add $12.50.)

EPLE2

Send To:
Name _____
Title _____
Company _____
Address 1 _____
Address 2 _____
City _____ State _____ Zip _____
Telephone _____ Fax _____

Payment Method:
☐ Payment enclosed (California orders, add 7.75% sales tax per order)
☐ Bill me (add $10)
☐ American Express ☐ MasterCard ☐ VISA (circle one)   EXPIRATION DATE _____
CARD NUMBER _____
NAME AS IT APPEARS ON CARD _____
AUTHORIZED SIGNATURE _____

Ordering Is Easy!

BY MAIL
Send order form and payment to
Griffin Communications, Inc.
1420 Bristol Street North
Suite 220
Newport Beach, CA 92660

BY PHONE
Have all information ready and call
800.205.6218

BY FAX
Fax order form and payment information to
949.723.1817

What You'll Find In The D&O Book:

Policy Comparison Charts: Our charts summarize hundreds of hours of policy analysis, helping you identify coverage limitations and understand each policy's coverage limitations, terms, exclusion, coverage triggers and variations in the wording of insuring agreements.

Definitions: This section helps you wade through the world of D&O insurance by providing clear, concise definitions and discussions of major policy terms including *Claims, Potential Claims, Insured, Loss* and *Wrongful Act.*

Terms and Conditions: Major policy terms and conditions are discussed and explained in detail to help you answer tough D&O insurance questions. In-depth discussions of **Exclusions, Claims-Made Coverage Features, Duty to Defend, Policy Limits, Retentions and Deductibles,** as well as **specimen policy forms,** an **index of D&O insurers,** and much more.

More than 800 pages   Loose-leaf
ISBN 0-941360-11-3

GCI Library

If it's not by Griffin Communications, Inc., it's not The EPL Book!

www.griffincom.com

The EPL Book
A Practical Guide To Employment Practices Liability And Insurance

"The standard, a benchmark by which all other works in this area will be compared."
—BUSINESS INSURANCE

The EPL Book, second edition, is a stand-alone reference that puts an incredible amount of information at your fingertips. If you simply must have the latest information on employment practices liability and insurance, or if you just need a practical everyday reference on employment practices liability and insurance, you absolutely won't want to be without this updated edition.

The EPL Book is simply the best, most comprehensive resource on the subject of EPL insurance. Its easy-to-read format allows *The EPL Book* to be read cover to cover, or, using the detailed index, to be scanned for just those bits of information you need most. No theoretical or long-drawn-out dissertations, just to-the-point, unbiased information you can put to work immediately.

We've spent months revising and editing *The EPL Book*, adding the features and information our subscribers asked for. In all, we've added over 200 new and revised pages to *The EPL Book*, including:

- Expanded and updated discussions on the laws affecting the employment relationship
- A new chapter on the do's and don'ts of claims handling
- A new chapter on the EPL insurance market
- 60 time-saving EPL policy comparison charts
- An expanded and updated appendix and EPL resource guide
- A detailed analysis of the new ISO employment-related practices liability policy, including specimen policy form and endorsements

Plus Two Time-Saving Bonuses You Can't Get Anywhere Else!

PolicyExpress
Debuting in first quarter 1999, *EPL Book* subscribers will have access to Policy Express, our Internet policy archive service. You get around-the-clock access to policy form specimens, summary comparison worksheets and supplemental information.

PolicyAnalysis Plus
And, if you don't find the current policy form information you need in *The EPL Book*, let us know, and we wil complete and send you a Policy Comparison Worksheet for that form. That's our exclusive PolicyAnalysis Plus guarantee!

More than 600 pages
ISBN 0-941360-13-X

© 1999 by Griffin Communications, Inc. All rights reserved.

Order Form

Send me ____ copies of "The EPL Book" at $135 + $12 shipping/handling each. (Foreign orders, call for shipping information.)

EPLE2

Send To:
Name _____
Title _____
Company _____
Address 1 _____
Address 2 _____
City _____ State _____ Zip _____
Telephone _____ Fax _____

Payment Method:
☐ Payment enclosed (California orders, add 7.75% sales tax per order)
☐ Bill me (add $10)
☐ American Express / MasterCard / VISA (circle one)

EXPIRATION DATE ☐☐☐☐
CARD NUMBER ☐☐☐☐ ☐☐☐☐ ☐☐☐☐ ☐☐☐☐
NAME AS IT APPEARS ON CARD _____
AUTHORIZED SIGNATURE _____

Ordering Is Easy!

BY MAIL
Send order form and payment to
Griffin Communications, Inc.
1420 Bristol Street North
Suite 220
Newport Beach, CA 92660

BY PHONE
Have all information ready and call
800.205.6218

BY FAX
Fax order form and payment information to
949.723.1817

GCI Library

www.griffincom.com

The D&O Book:
A Comparison Guide To Directors & Officers Liability Insurance Policies

> "This book is unique, providing discussions, chart comparisons, sample policy forms and graphic illustrations that are likely unavailable between covers in any other single source. It represents a handy tool kit for busy risk managers and insurance professionals trying to get a handle on this hard-to-fathom line of coverage."
> —BUSINESS INSURANCE

Attempting to understand directors and officers liability insurance may seem like an overwhelming endeavor at times. That's why we've created The D&O Book, a practical, easy-to-use comparison of directors & officers liability insurance policies.

The D&O Book was designed especially for insurance professionals, risk managers, attorneys and anyone who absolutely needs to understand directors & officers liability insurance. Using clear discussions, comparison charts, sample policy forms and graphic illustrations, *The D&O Book* lets busy risk managers and insurance professionals get a handle on the sometimes complex world of directors & officers liability insurance.

The D&O Book will help you save time comparing coverages and identifying improvements that may ensure superior coverage. Policy terms and provisions are made clear through concise discussion and focused analysis. Definitions and exclusions are explained in detail to help you understand the often subtle but significant differences in policy forms. Moreover, our comparison worksheets will allow you to compare important coverage features quickly and easily, helping you to identify and correct potential coverage problems and gaps.

© 1998 by Griffin Communications, Inc. All rights reserved.

Order Form

Send me ____ copies of "The D&O Book" (including one annual supplement service free) at $169 + $12 shipping/handling each. (Foreign orders, add $12.50.)

EPLE2

Send To:
Name _____
Title _____
Company _____
Address 1 _____
Address 2 _____
City _____ State _____ Zip _____
Telephone _____ Fax _____

Payment Method:
☐ Payment enclosed (California orders, add 7.75% sales tax per order)
☐ Bill me (add $10)
☐ American Express MasterCard VISA (circle one)
EXPIRATION DATE
CARD NUMBER
NAME AS IT APPEARS ON CARD _____
AUTHORIZED SIGNATURE _____

Ordering Is Easy!

BY MAIL
Send order form and payment to
Griffin Communications, Inc.
1420 Bristol Street North
Suite 220
Newport Beach, CA 92660

BY PHONE
Have all information ready and call
800.205.6218

BY FAX
Fax order form and payment information to
949.723.1817

What You'll Find In The D&O Book:

Policy Comparison Charts: Our charts summarize hundreds of hours of policy analysis, helping you identify coverage limitations and understand each policy's coverage limitations, terms, exclusion, coverage triggers and variations in the wording of insuring agreements.

Definitions: This section helps you wade through the world of D&O insurance by providing clear, concise definitions and discussions of major policy terms including *Claims, Potential Claims, Insured, Loss* and *Wrongful Act.*

Terms and Conditions: Major policy terms and conditions are discussed and explained in detail to help you answer tough D&O insurance questions. In-depth discussions of **Exclusions, Claims-Made Coverage Features, Duty to Defend, Policy Limits, Retentions and Deductibles,** as well as **specimen policy forms,** an **index of D&O insurers,** and much more.

More than 800 pages   Loose-leaf
ISBN 0-941360-11-3

GCI Library

If it's not by Griffin Communications, Inc., it's not The EPL Book!

www.griffincom.com

The EPL Book
A Practical Guide To Employment Practices Liability And Insurance

"The standard, a benchmark by which all other works in this area will be compared."
—BUSINESS INSURANCE

The EPL Book, second edition, is a stand-alone reference that puts an incredible amount of information at your fingertips. If you simply must have the latest information on employment practices liability and insurance, or if you just need a practical everyday reference on employment practices liability and insurance, you absolutely won't want to be without this updated edition.

The EPL Book is simply the best, most comprehensive resource on the subject of EPL insurance. Its easy-to-read format allows *The EPL Book* to be read cover to cover, or, using the detailed index, to be scanned for just those bits of information you need most. No theoretical or long-drawn-out dissertations, just to-the-point, unbiased information you can put to work immediately.

We've spent months revising and editing *The EPL Book*, adding the features and information our subscribers asked for. In all, we've added over 200 new and revised pages to *The EPL Book*, including:

- Expanded and updated discussions on the laws affecting the employment relationship
- A new chapter on the do's and don'ts of claims handling
- A new chapter on the EPL insurance market
- 60 time-saving EPL policy comparison charts
- An expanded and updated appendix and EPL resource guide
- A detailed analysis of the new ISO employment-related practices liability policy, including specimen policy form and endorsements

Plus Two Time-Saving Bonuses You Can't Get Anywhere Else!

PolicyExpress — Debuting in first quarter 1999, *EPL Book* subscribers will have access to Policy Express, our Internet policy archive service. You get around-the-clock access to policy form specimens, summary comparison worksheets and supplemental information.

PolicyAnalysis Plus — And, if you don't find the current policy form information you need in *The EPL Book*, let us know, and we will complete and send you a Policy Comparison Worksheet for that form. That's our exclusive PolicyAnalysis Plus guarantee!

More than 600 pages
ISBN 0-941360-13-X

© 1999 by Griffin Communications, Inc. All rights reserved.

Order Form

Send me ____ copies of "The EPL Book" at $135 + $12 shipping/handling each. (Foreign orders, call for shipping information.)

EPLE2

Send To:
Name _____
Title _____
Company _____
Address 1 _____
Address 2 _____
City _____ State _____ Zip _____
Telephone _____ Fax _____

Payment Method:
☐ Payment enclosed (California orders, add 7.75% sales tax per order)
☐ Bill me (add $10)
☐ AMERICAN EXPRESS / MasterCard / VISA (circle one)

CARD NUMBER □□□□ □□□□ □□□□ □□□□
EXPIRATION DATE □□ □□

NAME AS IT APPEARS ON CARD _____
AUTHORIZED SIGNATURE _____

Ordering Is Easy!

BY MAIL
Send order form and payment to
Griffin Communications, Inc.
1420 Bristol Street North
Suite 220
Newport Beach, CA 92660

BY PHONE
Have all information ready and call
800.205.6218

BY FAX
Fax order form and payment information to
949.723.1817

GCI Library

www.griffincom.com

The D&O Book:
A Comparison Guide To Directors & Officers Liability Insurance Policies

> "This book is unique, providing discussions, chart comparisons, sample policy forms and graphic illustrations that are likely unavailable between covers in any other single source. It represents a handy tool kit for busy risk managers and insurance professionals trying to get a handle on this hard-to-fathom line of coverage."
> —BUSINESS INSURANCE

Attempting to understand directors and officers liability insurance may seem like an overwhelming endeavor at times. That's why we've created The D&O Book, a practical, easy-to-use comparison of directors & officers liability insurance policies.

The D&O Book was designed especially for insurance professionals, risk managers, attorneys and anyone who absolutely needs to understand directors & officers liability insurance. Using clear discussions, comparison charts, sample policy forms and graphic illustrations, *The D&O Book* lets busy risk managers and insurance professionals get a handle on the sometimes complex world of directors & officers liability insurance.

The D&O Book will help you save time comparing coverages and identifying improvements that may ensure superior coverage. Policy terms and provisions are made clear through concise discussion and focused analysis. Definitions and exclusions are explained in detail to help you understand the often subtle but significant differences in policy forms. Moreover, our comparison worksheets will allow you to compare important coverage features quickly and easily, helping you to identify and correct potential coverage problems and gaps.

© 1998 by Griffin Communications, Inc. All rights reserved.

Order Form

Send me ____ copies of "The D&O Book" (including one annual supplement service free) at $169 + $12 shipping/handling each. (Foreign orders, add $12.50.)

EPLE2

Send To:
Name _____
Title _____
Company _____
Address 1 _____
Address 2 _____
City _____ State _____ Zip _____
Telephone _____ Fax _____

Payment Method:
☐ Payment enclosed (California orders, add 7.75% sales tax per order)
☐ Bill me (add $10)
☐ AMERICAN EXPRESS MasterCard VISA (circle one)
Cards
CARD NUMBER ☐☐☐☐ ☐☐☐☐ ☐☐☐☐ ☐☐☐☐   EXPIRATION DATE ☐☐☐☐
NAME AS IT APPEARS ON CARD _____
AUTHORIZED SIGNATURE _____

Ordering Is Easy!

BY MAIL
Send order form and payment to
Griffin Communications, Inc.
1420 Bristol Street North
Suite 220
Newport Beach, CA 92660

BY PHONE
Have all information ready and call
800.205.6218

BY FAX
Fax order form and payment information to
949.723.1817

What You'll Find In The D&O Book:

Policy Comparison Charts: Our charts summarize hundreds of hours of policy analysis, helping you identify coverage limitations and understand each policy's coverage limitations, terms, exclusion, coverage triggers and variations in the wording of insuring agreements.

Definitions: This section helps you wade through the world of D&O insurance by providing clear, concise definitions and discussions of major policy terms including *Claims, Potential Claims, Insured, Loss* and *Wrongful Act.*

Terms and Conditions: Major policy terms and conditions are discussed and explained in detail to help you answer tough D&O insurance questions. In-depth discussions of **Exclusions, Claims-Made Coverage Features, Duty to Defend, Policy Limits, Retentions and Deductibles,** as well as **specimen policy forms,** an **index of D&O insurers,** and much more.

More than 800 pages   Loose-leaf
ISBN 0-941360-11-3